Congratulations!

As an instructor considering or adopting Parkin, *Economics, Microeconomics,* or *Macroeconomics,* 5e, you are entitled to a 12-month prepaid subscription to *The Economics Place*™, Addison Wesley Longman's premier online resource for students and instructors of economics.

To explore this valuable teaching and learning resource:

1. Launch your browser and go to www.economicsplace.com
2. Select the graphic for your book.
3. Enter your pre-assigned Activation ID and Password, exactly as they appear below, in the User ID and Password fields:

   Activation ID: ECPKEA12000941

   Password: protest

4. Select "Login"
5. Complete the online registration form to establish your personal User ID and Password.
6. Once your personal User ID and Password are confirmed, go to www.economicsplace.com/parkin5 to enter the site with your new User ID and Password.

This Activation ID and Password can be used only once to establish a subscription. This subscription to the *The Economics Place* is not transferable.

If you choose to adopt one of the Parkin texts, you will receive complimentary access to *The Economics Place* for the duration of the adoption. Additionally, all new student copies of the book will include access to *The Economics Place*.

Fifth Edition

Economics

MICHAEL PARKIN

The cover depicts dawn at Millennium Island (recently renamed from Caroline Island) in the South Pacific as viewed through the Parkin icon. This is the spot on our planet that many say will see the first dawn of the year 2000. You can look at this cover in many different ways. Here is what I see. ◆ First, this book together with its CD, Web site, and other supplements is the result of an extraordinary publishing effort to guide students into the new millennium and to face the challenges they will encounter armed with a clear and compelling account of the timeless principles of economics illuminated by the issues of our age. ◆ I also see a symbol of what economics (and all scientific endeavor) is about. The Parkin icon is like an economic model. We use models to understand reality. The model is abstract, like the diamond and its hole or aperture. The model distorts our view of the world by omitting some details. But at the same time, it permits us to see the focus of our interest in the brightest and clearest possible light.

Fifth Edition

Economics

MICHAEL PARKIN
University of Western Ontario

ADDISON-WESLEY

AN IMPRINT OF ADDISON WESLEY LONGMAN, INC.

**READING, MASSACHUSETTS • MENLO PARK, CALIFORNIA • NEW YORK • HARLOW, ENGLAND
DON MILLS, ONTARIO • SYDNEY • MEXICO CITY • MADRID • AMSTERDAM**

Executive Editor:	Denise J. Clinton
Senior Editor:	Andrea Shaw
Executive Development Manager:	Sylvia Mallory
Supplements Editor:	Deborah Kiernan
Development Assistant:	Judean Patten
Managing Editor:	James Rigney
Senior Production Supervisors:	Mary Sanger, Lou Bruno
Senior Design Supervisor	Gina Hagen
Technical Illustrator:	Richard Parkin
Photo Researcher:	Beth Anderson
Publishing Technology Manager	Sarah McCracken
Electronic Production Administrator:	Sally Simpson
Copyeditor:	Barbara Willette
Proofreaders:	Kathy Smith, Kris Smead
Indexer:	Robin Bade
Senior Manufacturing Manager:	Ralph Mattivello
Manufacturing Supervisor:	Tim McDonald
Marketing Manager:	Amy Cronin
Marketing Coordinator:	Jennifer Thalmann
Printer:	World Color

Library of Congress Cataloging-in-Publication Data

Parkin, Michael, 1939–
    Economics/Michael Parkin. — 5th ed.
        p.   cm.
    Includes bibliographical references and index.
    ISBN 0-201-45845-4
    1. Economics.   I. Title.
    HB171.5.P313   1999
    330—dc21   98–55285
                                          CIP

Printed in the United States of America.

1 2 3 4 5 6 7 8 9 – WCT – 0302010099

Text and photo credits appear on page C–1, which constitutes a continuation of the
copyright page.

To Robin

About Michael Parkin

Michael Parkin

received his training as an economist at the Universities of Leicester and Essex in England. Currently in the Department of Economics at the University of Western Ontario, Canada, Professor Parkin has held faculty appointments at Brown University, the University of Manchester, the University of Essex, and Bond University. He is a past president of the Canadian Economics Association and has served on the editorial boards of the *American Economic Review* and the *Journal of Monetary Economics* and as managing editor of the *Canadian Journal of Economics*. Professor Parkin's research on macroeconomics, monetary economics, and international economics has resulted in over 160 publications in journals and edited volumes, including the *American Economic Review*, the *Journal of Political Economy*, the *Review of Economic Studies*, the *Journal of Monetary Economics*, and the *Journal of Money, Credit and Banking*. He became most visible to the public with his work on inflation that discredited the use of wage and price controls. Michael Parkin also spearheaded the movement toward European monetary union. Professor Parkin is an experienced and dedicated teacher of introductory economics.

Preface

This book presents economics as a serious, lively, and evolving science. Its goal is to help the student to develop the "economic way of thinking" and to gain insights into how the economy works and how it might be made to work better. ◆ My goal is to make economics as accessible as possible yet to provide a thorough and complete coverage of the subject, not a slimmed-down or oversimplified selection. ◆ I am conscious that many students find economics hard, so I place the student at center stage and write for the student. I use a style and language that don't intimidate and that allow the student to concentrate on the substance. ◆ I open each chapter with a clear statement of learning objectives, a real-world student-friendly vignette to grab attention, and a brief preview. I illustrate principles with examples that are selected to hold the student's interest and to make the subject lively. And I put principles to work by using them to illuminate current real-world problems and issues. ◆ I present some new ideas, such as dynamic comparative advantage, game theory, the modern theory of the firm, public choice theory, rational expectations, new growth theory, and real business cycle theory. But I explain these topics with familiar core ideas and tools. ◆ Today's course springs from today's issues—the information revolution, the East Asian recession, and the expansion of global trade and investment. But the principles that we use to understand these issues remain the core principles of our science. ◆ Governments and international agencies place renewed emphasis on long-term fundamentals as they seek to sustain economic growth. This book reflects this emphasis. ◆ To enable students to access the latest information on the national and global economy, I have developed a companion Web site. And to provide active learning opportunities, I have developed the tutorials and quizzes on the accompanying *Economics in Action* CD.

The Fifth Edition Revision

Economics, FIFTH EDITION, RETAINS ALL THE improvements achieved in its predecessor with its emphasis on core principles, coverage of recent economic developments, brief yet accessible explanations, and strong pedagogy. New to this edition are:

- Revised and updated micro content
- Revised and updated macro content
- In-text review quizzes
- Parallel end-of-chapter problems
- Part wrap-ups

Revised and Updated Micro Content

The five major revisions in the micro chapters are:

1. Elasticity (Chapter 5): A revised predictions-oriented treatment of elasticity and a more extensive coverage of the elasticity of supply.
2. Efficiency and Equity (Chapter 6): A new discussion of the alternative views on equity and the fairness of market outcomes.
3. Organizing Production (Chapter 10): Entirely rewritten to provide an overview of all the issues in industrial and market organization. The sections on cost and profit have been simplified and thoroughly revised.
4. Monopolistic Competition (Chapter 14): A more extensive discussion of the role and effects of selling costs and advertising.
5. Regulation and Antitrust Law (Chapter 19): A thoroughly revised treatment of the antitrust laws and their application and an updated discussion of the Microsoft case and other recent cases.

Revised and Updated Macro Content

The four major revisions in the macro chapters are:

1. Measuring Employment and Unemployment (Chapter 24): A new chapter (based on Chapter 25 of the Fourth Edition) that covers the measurement issues in the labor market.
2. The Economy at Full Employment (Chapter 26): A new chapter that begins to build the story of the aggregate supply side of the economy and that explains how changes in population, capital,

and technology change potential GDP, employment, and the real wage rate. This chapter provides the foundation for the theory of aggregate supply and is the jumping-off point for two subsequent chapters on capital accumulation and economic growth.

3. Inflation (Chapter 33): An improved explanation and international illustration of the links between inflation and interest rates.
4. Thorough and extensive updating to reflect the U.S. economy and the global economy of 1998 and 1999, including events such as the evolution of the federal budget from deficit to surplus, the ongoing spectacular performance of the U.S. economy, recession in Asia, and turmoil in global financial markets.

In-Text Review Quizzes

I have replaced the in-text Reviews of the previous editions with Review Quizzes. These brief quizzes invite students to revisit the material they have just studied with a set of questions in mind. I hope that these quizzes will encourage a more critical and thoughtful rereading of any material that proves difficult for the student. The *Instructor's Manual* provides the answers.

Parallel End-of-Chapter Problems

I have reworked the end-of-chapter problems and created pairs of parallel problems. Robin Bade and I have provided the solutions to the odd-numbered problems at the end of the text, and these solutions together with those to the even-numbered problems provided by Melinda Nish appear in the *Instructor's Manual.* This arrangement provides help to students and flexibility to instructors who want to assign problems for credit.

Part Wrap-Ups

A new feature at the *end* of each part:

- Explains how the chapters relate to each other and fit into the larger picture.
- Provides a biographical sketch of the economist who developed the central idea of that part, and places the original contribution in its historical context.
- Presents an interview with a leading contemporary economist.

Features to Enhance Teaching and Learning

HERE I DESCRIBE THE CHAPTER FEATURES that are designed to enhance the learning process. Each chapter contains the following learning aids.

Chapter Objectives

A list of learning objectives enables students to see exactly where the chapter is going and to set their goals before they begin the chapter. I link these goals directly to the chapter's major headings.

After studying this chapter, you will be able to:

◾ **Explain the fundamental economic problem**

◾ **Define the production possibility frontier**

◾ **Define and calculate opportunity cost**

◾ **Explain the conditions in which resources are used efficiently**

◾ **Explain how economic growth expands production possibilities**

◾ **Explain how specialization and trade expand production possibilities**

Chapter Opener

A one-page student-friendly, attention-grabbing vignette raises questions that both motivate and focus the chapter.

Chapter 3

The Economic Problem

We live in a style that surprises our grandparents and would have astonished our great-grandparents. Most of us live in more spacious homes than they did. We eat more, grow taller, and are even born larger than they were. Video games, cellular phones, gene splices, and personal computers did not exist even 20 years ago. Economic growth has made us richer than our grandparents. And we are not alone in experiencing an expansion in the goods and services that we consume. Many nations around the world are not only sharing our experience: They are setting the pace. Before the recent Asia crisis, Hong Kong, Taiwan, Singapore, Korea, and China expanded at unheard-of rates. But economic growth does not liberate us from scarcity. Why not? Why, despite our immense wealth, must we still make choices and face costs? Why are there no "free lunches"? ◆ We see an incredible amount of specialization and trade in the world. Each one of us specializes in a particular job—as a lawyer, a car maker, a home maker. We have become so specialized that one farm worker can feed 100 people. Less than one sixth of the U.S. work force is employed in manufacturing. More than half of the work force is employed in wholesale and retail trade, banking and finance, government, and other services. Why do we specialize? How do we benefit from specialization and trade? ◆ Over many centuries, institutions and social arrangements have evolved that we take for granted. One of them is property rights and the political and legal system that protects them. Another is markets. Why have these social arrangements evolved? How do they increase production?

◇ These are the questions that we study in this chapter. We begin with the core economic problem: scarcity and choice and the concept of the production possibility frontier. We then learn about the central idea of economics—efficiency. We also discover how we can expand production by accumulating capital and by specializing and trading. ◆ What you will learn in this chapter is the foundation on which all economics is built. You will receive big dividends from a careful study of this material.

Making the Most of It

After studying this chapter, you will be able to:

◾ Explain the fundamental economic problem

◾ Define the production possibility frontier

◾ Define and calculate opportunity cost

◾ Explain the conditions in which resources are used efficiently

◾ Explain how economic growth expands production possibilities

◾ Explain how specialization and trade expand production possibilities

In-Text Review Quizzes

A review quiz at end of most major sections enables students to determine whether a topic needs further study before moving on.

R E V I E W   Q U I Z

- What is scarcity?
- What is the fundamental economic problem?
- Can you provide a definition of economics?
- What are the resources that can be used to produce goods and services?
- How do we cope with the fact that our wants cannot be satisfied with the available resources?

Key Terms

Highlighted terms within the text simplify the student's task of learning the vocabulary of economics. Each highlighted term appears in an end-of-chapter list with page numbers, an end-of-book glossary, boldfaced in the index, in the *Economics in Action* software, and on the Parkin Web site.

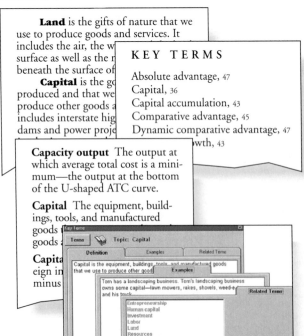

Land is the gifts of nature that we use to produce goods and services. It includes the air, the w surface as well as the r beneath the surface of

Capital is the g produced and that we produce other goods includes interstate hig dams and power proj

KEY TERMS

Absolute advantage, 47
Capital, 36
Capital accumulation, 43
Comparative advantage, 45
Dynamic comparative advantage, 47
wth, 43

Capacity output The output at which average total cost is a minimum—the output at the bottom of the U-shaped ATC curve.

Capital The equipment, buildings, tools, and manufactured goods
goods
Capita
eign in
minus

Key Figures and Tables

An icon ◆ identifies the most important figures and tables, and the end-of-chapter summary lists them. Instructor's overhead transparencies also contain enlarged and simplified images of most of these key figures.

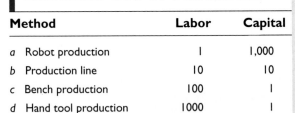

TABLE 10.3			◆
Efficient Use of Resources			

	Method	Labor	Capital
a	Robot production	1	1,000
b	Production line	10	10
c	Bench production	100	1
d	Hand tool production	1000	1

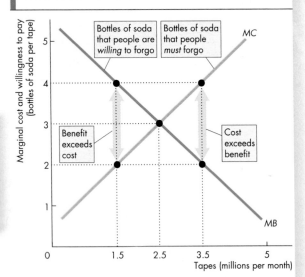

FIGURE 3.4 ◆
Efficient Use of Resources

The greater the quantity of tapes produced, the smaller is the marginal benefit (*MB*) from a tape—the fewer bottles of soda people are willing to give up to get an additional tape. But the greater the quantity of tapes produced, the greater is the marginal cost (*MC*) of a tape—the more bottles of soda people must give up to get an additional tape. When marginal benefit equals marginal cost, resources are being used efficiently.

Diagrams That Show the Action

This book has set new standards of clarity in its diagrams. My goal has always been to show "where the economic action is." The diagrams in this book continue to generate an enormously positive response, which confirms my view that graphical analysis is the most important tool available for teaching and learning economics. But many students find graphs hard to work with. For this reason, I have developed the entire art program with the study and review needs of the student in mind. The diagrams feature:

■ Shifted curves, equilibrium points, and other important features highlighted in red

■ Color-blended arrows to suggest movement

■ Graphs paired with data tables

■ Diagrams labeled with boxed notes

■ Extended captions that make each diagram and its caption a self-contained object for study and review.

Reading Between the Lines

Each chapter contains an economic analysis of a significant news article from the popular press together with a set of critical thinking questions that relate to the issues raised in the article.

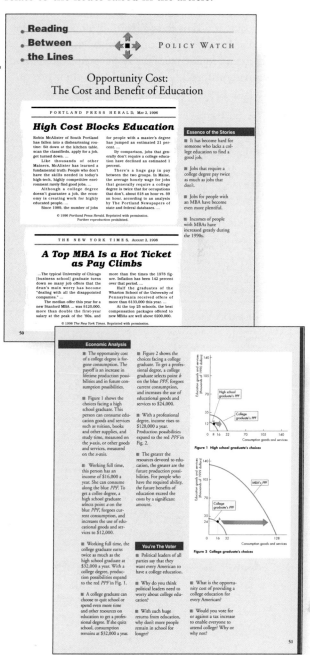

End-of-Chapter Study Material

Each chapter closes with a concise summary organized by major topics; lists of key terms, figures, and tables (all with page references); problems; and critical thinking questions. Items identified by the 🖥 icon link to the *Economics in Action* software CD included with the text. Items identified by the 🌐 icon link to the Parkin Web site at http://www.economicsplace.com. My hope is to encourage students to keep up to date and to become comfortable and efficient in their use of the Internet to access information.

SUMMARY

KEY POINTS

Resources and Wants (p. 36)

- Economic activity arises from scarcity—resources are insufficient to satisfy people's wants.
- Resources are labor, land, capital (including human capital), and entrepreneurship.
- We choose how to use our resources and try to get the most out of them.

Resources, Production Possibilities, and Opportunity Cost (pp. 37–39)

KEY FIGURES ◇

Figure 3.1   Production Possibility Frontier, 37
Figure 3.4   Efficient Use of Resources, 42
Figure 3.8   The Gains from Trade, 46
Figure 3.9   Circular Flows in the Market Economy, 49

KEY TERMS

Absolute advantage, 47
Capital, 36
Capital accumulation, 43
Comparative advantage, 45
Dynamic comparative advantage, 47
Economic growth, 43
Economics, 36
Efficient, 42
Entrepreneurship, 36

PROBLEMS

*1. Use the figure to calculate Wendell's opportunity cost of an hour of tennis when he increases the time he plays tennis from:
   a.   4 to 6 hours a week.
   b.   6 to 8 hours a week.

[graph: Grade in economics (percent) vs Tennis (hours per week), showing "Wendell's tradeoff" curve]

2. Use the figure to calculate Mary's opportunity cost of an hour of skating when she increases her time spent skating from:
   a.   2 to 4 hours a week.
   b.   4 to 6 hours a week.

CRITICAL THINKING

1. After you have studied *Reading Between the Lines* on pp. 50–51, answer the following questions:
   a.   Why does the *PPF* for education goods and services and consumption goods and services bow outward?
   b.   At what point on the blue *PPF* in Fig. 1 on p. 51 is the combination of education goods and services and consumption goods and services efficient? Explain your answer.
   c.   Students face rising tuition. Does higher tuition change the opportunity cost of education?
   d.   Who receives the benefits from education? Is the marginal cost of education equal to marginal benefit? Is resource use in the market for education efficient?

🌐 2. Use the links on the Parkin Web site and obtain data on the tuition and other costs of enrolling in the MBA program of a school that interests you. If an MBA graduate can earn as much as the amounts reported in the news article in *Reading Between the Lines* on pp. 50–51, does the marginal benefit of an MBA exceed its marginal cost? Why doesn't everyone study for an MBA?

For the Instructor

THIS BOOK ENABLES YOU TO ACHIEVE THREE objectives in your principles course:

- Focus on the core ideas.
- Explain the issues and problems of our time.
- Choose your own course structure.

Focus on the Core Ideas

You know how hard it is to encourage a student to think like an economist. But that is your goal. Consistent with this goal, the text focuses on and repeatedly uses the central ideas: choice; tradeoff; opportunity cost; the margin; incentives; the gains from voluntary exchange; the forces of demand, supply, and equilibrium; the pursuit of economic rent; and the effects of government actions on the economy.

Explain the Issues and Problems of Our Time

Students must *use* the core ideas and tools if they are to begin to understand them. There is no better way to motivate students than by using the tools of economics to explain the issues that confront students in today's world. These issues include the environment, immigration, widening income gaps, the productivity growth slowdown, budget deficits, restraining inflation, watching for the next recession, avoiding protectionism, and the long-term growth of output and incomes.

Choose Your Own Course Structure

You want to teach your own course. I have organized this book to enable you to do so. I demonstrate the book's flexibility in the flexibility chart and alternative sequences table that appear on pp. xxii–xxv. You can use this book to teach a traditional course that blends theory and policy or a current policy issues course. Your micro course can emphasize theory or policy. You can structure your macro course to emphasize long-term growth and supply-side fundamentals. Or you can follow a traditional macro sequence and emphasize short-term fluctuations. The choices are yours.

Instructor's Manual

The Instructor's Manual by Melinda Nish of Salt Lake Community College integrates the teaching and learning package and is a guide to all the supplements. An essay by Dennis Hoffman of Arizona State University explains how to use the *Economics in Action* software as a teaching tool.

Printed Test Banks

We now have three major test banks. Mark Rush of the University of Florida has thoroughly revised the earlier test banks and has coordinated the development of a new 3,000-question test bank written by fifteen outstanding and dedicated principles instructors. They are Sue Bartlett (University of South Florida), Kevin Carey (American University), Leo Chan (University of Kansas), Carol Dole (University of North Carolina, Charlotte), Donald Dutkowsky (Syracuse University), Andrew Foshee (McNeese State University), Jill H. Boylston Herndon (Hamline University), Veronica Kalich (Baldwin-Wallace College), Melinda Nish (Salt Lake Community College), Terry Olson (Truman State University), Rochelle Ruffer (Youngstown State University), Virginia Shingleton (Valparaiso University), Nora Underwood (University of California, Davis), Peter von Allmen (Moravian College), and Peter Zaleski (Villanova University).

Computerized Test Banks

The test banks are also available in Test Generator Software (TestGen-EQ with QuizMaster-EQ). Version 3.0 of the program, with a wealth of improved features, is now available. This software includes all the questions in the printed test banks. Fully networkable, it is available for Windows and Macintosh. TestGen-EQ's new graphical interface enables instructors easily to view, edit, and add questions; transfer questions to tests; and print different forms of tests. Tests can be formatted by varying fonts and styles, margins, and headers and footers, as in any word-processing document. Search and sort features let the instructor quickly locate questions and arrange them in a preferred order. QuizMaster-EQ, working with your school's computer network, automatically grades the exams, stores the results on disk, and allows the instructor to view or print a variety of reports.

Overhead Transparencies and Overlays

Full-color overhead transparencies (several with overlays) of enlarged and simplified key figures from the text will improve the clarity of your lectures. They are available to qualified adopters of the text (contact your Addison Wesley Longman sales representative).

PowerPoint Lecture Presentations

Charles Pflanz of Scottsdale Community College has developed a full-color Microsoft PowerPoint Lecture Presentation that breaks the chapters into lecture-size bites and includes key figures from the text, animated graphs, and speaking notes. The presentation can be used electronically in the classroom or can be printed to create hard-copy transparency masters. The lecture presentation is available for Macintosh and Windows to qualified adopters of the text (contact your Addison Wesley Longman sales representative).

Economics in Action Software

Instructors can use *Economics in Action* interactive software in the classroom. Its full-screen display option turns its many analytical graphs into "electronic transparencies" for live graph manipulation in lectures. Its real-world data sets and graphing utility bring animated time-series graphs and scatter diagrams to the classroom.

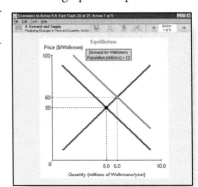

The Parkin Web Site

With the Fifth Edition of the textbook comes the debut of *The Economics Place* at www.economicsplace.com. This Internet-based learning environment contains tools for organizing students' grades from online quizzes, frequent updates of data in the text figures, and news you can use in the classroom. Use the Web site to motivate and organize lectures with electronic *Reading Between the Lines* and *Point-Counterpoint* or to create an online quiz for an in-class review.

For the Student

Study Guide

The Fifth Edition *Study Guide* by Mark Rush of the University of Florida is carefully coordinated with the main text and the test bank. Each chapter of the Study Guide contains:

- Key concepts
- Helpful hints
- True/false/uncertain questions that ask students to explain their answers
- Multiple-choice questions
- Short-answer questions
- Common questions or misconceptions that the student explains as if he or she were the teacher

Each part allows students to test their cumulative understanding with *Reading Between the Lines* exercises and sample midterm tests.

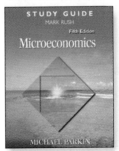

Economics in Action Interactive Software

With *Economics in Action* Release 5.0, which accompanies the Fifth Edition, students will have fun working the tutorials, answering questions that give instant explanations, and testing themselves ahead of their midterm tests. One of my students told me that using *EIA* is like having a private professor in your dorm room!

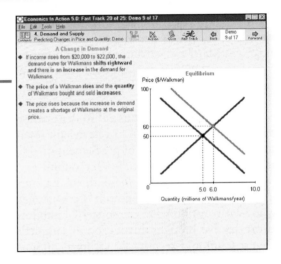

The Parkin Web Site

New for the Fifth Edition, *The Economics Place* Web site provides online quizzes, study tips, office hours, links, electronic *Reading Between the Lines*, a *Point-Counterpoint* feature that encourages students to participate in contemporary policy debates, and much more. You can reach the site at http://www.economicsplace.com.

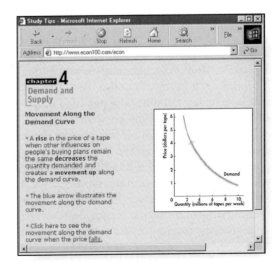

Acknowledgments

I THANK MY CURRENT AND FORMER COLLEAGUES and friends at the University of Western Ontario who have taught me so much. They are Jim Davies, Jeremy Greenwood, Ig Horstmann, Peter Howitt, Greg Huffman, David Laidler, Phil Reny, Chris Robinson, John Whalley, and Ron Wonnacott. I also thank Doug McTaggart and Christopher Findlay, co-authors of the Australian edition, and Melanie Powell and Kent Matthews, co-authors of the European edition. Suggestions arising from their adaptations of earlier editions have been helpful to me in preparing this edition.

I thank the several thousand students whom I have been privileged to teach. The instant response that comes from the look of puzzlement or enlightenment has taught me how to teach economics.

It is an especial joy to thank the many outstanding editors and others at Addison Wesley Longman who have contributed to the concerted publishing effort that has brought this edition to completion. Denise Clinton, Executive Editor for Economics and Finance, has been a constant source of inspiration and encouragement and has provided overall direction. Andrea Shaw, Senior Editor for Economics and my sponsoring editor, has ably coordinated the arrangements for this edition. Sylvia Mallory, Executive Development Manager, has brought her calm, creative, and professional direction to the development effort on this edition. Deborah Kiernan, Senior Supplements Editor, working with the most able team of authors, has managed the creation of a large and complex supplements package. Along with Mark Rush, Sylvia Mallory and Deb Kiernan have pulled together a "dream team" of questions authors and helped to create the best-ever principles of economics test bank. Judean Patten, Editorial Assistant, has cheerfully performed many helpful tasks at a moment's notice. Beth Anderson, Photo Researcher, has diligently persisted in her efforts until the required images were found. Melissa Honig, Senior Project Editor, has directed the development of *Economics in Action* and has been an appreciated and admired source of guidance on many matters relating to the electronic supplements. Amy Cronin, Marketing Manager, has provided inspired marketing direction. Regina Hagen, Senior Designer, has designed the cover, text, and package and surpassed the challenge of ensuring that we meet the highest design standards. Managing Editor James Rigney and Senior Production Supervisors Mary Sanger and Louis Bruno have worked miracles on a tight production schedule and coped calmly with late-changing content. I thank all of these wonderful people. It has been inspiring to work with them and to share in creating what I believe is a truly outstanding educational tool.

I thank the 17 supplements authors whose names appear on pp. xv and xvi. But I especially thank Mark Rush, who has yet again played a crucial role in creating another edition of this text and package. Mark has been a constant source of good advice and good humor. And I thank Art Woolf for his careful accuracy review of near-final pages.

I am most grateful to the thoughtful news clippers who have greatly helped in the task of writing the *Reading Between the Lines* features. They are Richard Fristensky (Bentley College), Susan Glanz (St. John's University), Jim Lee (Fort Hays State University), Kathryn Nantz (Fairfield University), and Paul Storer (Western Washington University).

I thank the people who work directly with me. Jeannie Gillmore has provided outstanding research assistance. Jane McAndrew has provided excellent library help. Richard Parkin has created the electronic art files and offered many ideas that have improved the figures in this book.

As with the previous editions, this one owes an enormous debt to Robin Bade. I dedicate this book to her and again thank her for her work. I could not have written this book without the unselfish help she has given me. My thanks to her are unbounded.

Classroom experience will test the value of this book. I would appreciate hearing from instructors and students about how I can continue to improve it in future editions.

Michael Parkin
London, Ontario, Canada
michael.parkin@ uwo.ca

Reviewers

Tajudeen Adenekan, Bronx Community College
Milton Alderfer, Miami-Dade Community College
William Aldridge, Shelton State Community College
Donald L. Alexander, Western Michigan University
Terence Alexander, Iowa State University
Stuart Allen, University of North Carolina, Greensboro
Sam Allgood, University of Nebraska, Lincoln
Neil Alper, Northeastern University
Alan Anderson, Fordham University
Lisa R. Anderson, College of William and Mary
Jeff Ankrom, Wittenberg University
Fatma Antar, Manchester Community Technical College
Kofi Apraku, University of North Carolina, Asheville
Moshen Bahmani-Oskooee, University of Wisconsin, Milwaukee
Donald Balch, University of South Carolina
Mehmet Balcilar, Wayne State University
A. Paul Ballantyne, University of Colorado
Sue Bartlett, University of South Florida
Valerie R. Bencivenga, University of Texas, Austin
Ben Bernanke, Princeton University
Margot Biery, Tarrant County Community College South
John Bittorowitz, Ball State University
Giacomo Bonanno, University of California, Davis
Sunne Brandmeyer, University of South Florida
Audie Brewton, Northeastern Illinois University
Baird Brock, Central Missouri State University
Byron Brown, Michigan State University
Jeffrey Buser, Columbus State Community College
Alison Butler, Florida International University
Tania Carbiener, Southern Methodist University
Kevin Carey, American University
Kathleen A. Carroll, University of Maryland, Baltimore County
Michael Carter, University of Massachusetts, Lowell
Adhip Chaudhuri, Georgetown University
Gopal Chengalath, Texas Tech University
Daniel Christiansen, Albion College
John J. Clark, Community College of Allegheny County, Allegheny Campus
Meredith Clement, Dartmouth College
Michael B. Cohn, U.S. Merchant Marine Academy
Robert Collinge, University of Texas, San Antonio

Doug Conway, Mesa Community College
Larry Cook, University of Toledo
Bobby Corcoran, Middle Tennessee State University
Kevin Cotter, Wayne State University
James Peery Cover, University of Alabama, Tuscaloosa
Eleanor D. Craig, University of Delaware
Jim Craven, Clark College
Stephen Cullenberg, University of California, Riverside
David Culp, Slippery Rock University
Norman V. Cure, Macomb Community College
Dan Dabney, University of Texas, Austin
Andrew Dane, Angelo State University
Joseph Daniels, Marquette University
David Denslow, University of Florida
Mark Dickie, University of Georgia
James Dietz, California State University, Fullerton
Carol Dole, University of North Carolina, Charlotte
Ronald Dorf, Inver Hills Community College
John Dorsey, University of Maryland, College Park
Amrik Singh Dua, Mt. San Antonio College
Thomas Duchesneau, University of Maine, Orono
Lucia Dunn, Ohio State University
Donald Dutkowsky, Syracuse University
John Edgren, Eastern Michigan University
David J. Eger, Alpena Community College
Harry Ellis, Jr., University of North Texas
Ibrahim Elsaify, State University of New York, Albany
Kenneth G. Elzinga, University of Virginia
M. Fazeli, Hofstra University
Philip Fincher, Louisiana Tech University
F. Firoozi, University of Texas, San Antonio
David Franck, University of North Carolina, Charlotte
Roger Frantz, San Diego State University
Alwyn Fraser, Atlantic Union College
Richard Fristensky, Bentley College
Eugene Gentzel, Pensacola Junior College
Andrew Gill, California State University, Fullerton
Robert Giller, Virginia Polytechnic Institute and State University
Robert Gillette, University of Kentucky
James N. Giordano, Villanova University
Maria Giuili, Diablo College
Susan Glanz, St. John's University
Richard Gosselin, Houston Community College
John Graham, Rutgers University
John Griffen, Worcester Polytechnic Institute
Robert Guell, Indiana State University
Jamie Haag, University of Oregon
Gail Heyne Hafer, Lindenwood University
Rik W. Hafer, Southern Illinois University

Daniel Hagen, Western Washington University
David R. Hakes, University of Northern Iowa
Craig Hakkio, Federal Reserve Bank, Kansas City
Ann Hansen, Westminster College
Jonathan Haughton, Northeastern University
Randall Haydon, Wichita State University
Jolien A. Helsel, Kent State University
Jill H. Boylston Herndon, Hamline University
John Herrmann, Rutgers University
John M. Hill, Delgado Community College
Lewis Hill, Texas Tech University
Steve Hoagland, University of Akron
Tom Hoerger, Vanderbilt University
Calvin Hoerneman, Delta College
George Hoffer, Virginia Commonwealth University
Dennis L. Hoffman, Arizona State University
Paul Hohenberg, Rensselaer Polytechnic Institute
Jim H. Holcomb, University of Texas, El Paso
Harry Holzer, Michigan State University
Djehane Hosni, University of Central Florida
Harold Hotelling, Jr., Lawrence Technical University
Calvin Hoy, County College of Morris
Julie Hunsaker, Wayne State University
Beth Ingram, University of Iowa
Michael Jacobs, Lehman College
Dennis Jansen, Texas A & M University
Frederick Jungman, Northwestern Oklahoma State University
Paul Junk, University of Minnesota, Duluth
Leo Kahane, California State University, Hayward
Veronica Kalich, Baldwin-Wallace College
John Kane, State University of New York, Oswego
E. Kang, St. Cloud State University
Arthur Kartman, San Diego State University
Manfred W. Keil, Claremont McKenna College
Rose Kilburn, Modesto Junior College
Robert Kirk, Indiana University–Purdue University, Indianapolis
Norman Kleinberg, City University of New York, Baruch College
Robert Kleinhenz, California State University, Fullerton
Joseph Kreitzer, University of St. Thomas
David Lages, Southwest Missouri State University
W. J. Lane, University of New Orleans
Leonard Lardaro, University of Rhode Island
Kathryn Larson, Elon College
Luther D. Lawson, University of North Carolina, Wilmington
Elroy M. Leach, Chicago State University
Jim Lee, Fort Hays State University

Jay Levin, Wayne State University
Arik Levinson, University of Wisconsin, Madison
Tony Lima, California State University, Hayward
William Lord, University of Maryland, Baltimore County
Nancy Lutz, Virginia Polytechnic Institute and State University
K.T. Magnusson, Salt Lake City Community College
Mark Maier, Glendale Community College
Beth Maloan, University of Tennessee, Martin
Jean Mangan, California State University, Sacramento
Michael Marlow, California Polytechnic State University
Akbar Marvasti, University of Houston
Wolfgang Mayer, University of Cincinnati
John McArthur, Wofford College
Amy McCormick, College of William and Mary
Russel McCullough, Iowa State University
Gerald McDougall, Wichita State University
Stephen McGary, Ricks College
Richard D. McGrath, College of William and Mary
Richard McIntyre, University of Rhode Island
John McLeod, Georgia Institute of Technology
Charles Meyer, Iowa State University
Peter Mieszkowski, Rice University
John Mijares, University of North Carolina, Asheville
Richard A. Miller, Wesleyan University
Judith W. Mills, Southern Connecticut State University
Glen Mitchell, Nassau Community College
Jeannette C. Mitchell, Rochester Institute of Technology
Khan Mohabbat, Northern Illinois University
W. Douglas Morgan, University of California, Santa Barbara
William Morgan, University of Wyoming
Joanne Moss, San Francisco State University
Edward Murphy, Southwest Texas State University
Kevin J. Murphy, Oakland University
Kathryn Nantz, Fairfield University
William S. Neilson, Texas A & M University
Bart C. Nemmers, University of Nebraska, Lincoln
Melinda Nish, Salt Lake Community College
Anthony O'Brien, Lehigh University
Mary Olson, Washington University
Terry Olson, Truman State University
James B. O'Niell, University of Delaware
Farley Ordovensky, University of the Pacific
Z. Edward O'Relley, North Dakota State University
Jan Palmer, Ohio University
Michael Palumbo, University of Houston

G. Hossein Parandvash, Western Oregon State
College
Randall Parker, East Carolina University
Robert Parks, Washington University
David Pate, St. John Fisher College
Donald Pearson, Eastern Michigan University
Mary Anne Pettit, Southern Illinois University,
Edwardsville
Kathy Phares, University of Missouri, St. Louis
William A. Phillips, University of Southern Maine
Dennis Placone, Clemson University
Charles Plot, California Institute of Technology,
Pasadena
Mannie Poen, Houston Community College
Kathleen Possai, Wayne State University
Ulrika Praski-Stahlgren, University College in
Gavle-Sandviken, Sweden
K.A. Quartey, Talladega College
Herman Quirmbach, Iowa State University
Jeffrey R. Racine, University of South Florida
Peter Rangazas, Indiana University–Purdue University,
Indianapolis
Vaman Rao, Western Illinois University
Laura Razzolini, University of Mississippi
J. David Reed, Bowling Green State University
Robert H. Renshaw, Northern Illinois University
W. Gregory Rhodus, Bentley College
John Robertson, Paducah Community College
Malcolm Robinson, University of North Carolina,
Greensboro
Richard Roehl, University of Michigan, Dearborn
Thomas Romans, State University of New York,
Buffalo
David R. Ross, Bryn Mawr College
Thomas Ross, St. Louis University
Robert J. Rossana, Wayne State University
Rochelle Ruffer, Youngstown State University
Mark Rush, University of Florida
Gary Santoni, Ball State University
John Saussy, Harrisburg Area Community College
David Schlow, Pennsylvania State University

Paul Schmitt, St. Clair County Community College
Martin Sefton, Indianapolis University
Rod Shadbegian, University of Massachusetts,
Dartmouth
Gerald Shilling, Eastfield College
Dorothy R. Siden, Salem State College
Scott Simkins, North Carolina Agricultural and
Technical State University
Chuck Skoro, Boise State University
Phil Smith, DeKalb College
William Doyle Smith, University of Texas, El Paso
Frank Steindl, Oklahoma State University
Jeffrey Stewart, New York University
Allan Stone, Southwest Missouri State University
Courtenay Stone, Ball State University
Paul Storer, Western Washington University
Mark Strazicich, Ohio State University, Newark
Robert Stuart, Rutgers University
Gilbert Suzawa, University of Rhode Island
David Swaine, Andrews University
Kay Unger, University of Montana
Anthony Uremovic, Joliet Junior College
David Vaughn, City University, Washington
Don Waldman, Colgate University
Francis Wambalaba, Portland State University
Rob Wassmer, Wayne State University
Paul A. Weinstein, University of Maryland,
College Park
Lee Weissert, St. Vincent College
Robert Whaples, Wake Forest University
Charles H. Whiteman, University of Iowa
Larry Wimmer, Brigham Young University
Mark Witte, Northwestern University
Willard E. Witte, Indiana University
Mark Wohar, University of Nebraska, Omaha
Cheonsik Woo, Clemson University
Douglas Wooley, Radford University
Arthur G. Woolf, University of Vermont
Ann Al Yasiri, University of Wisconsin, Platteville
John T. Young, Riverside Community College
Michael Youngblood, Rock Valley College.

Flexibility Chart

Core	Policy	Optional

1. What Is Economics?

3. The Economic Problem

4. Demand and Supply

5. Elasticity

6. Efficiency and Equity
A chapter that provides a non-technical explanation of efficiency and equity that unifies the micro coverage and permits early coverage of policy issues.

7. Markets in Action
A unique chapter that gives extensive applications of demand and supply.

2. Making and Using Graphs
A good chapter to assign to the student with a fear of graphs.

8. Utility and Demand
Although this chapter is optional, it may be covered if desired *before* demand in Chapter 4.

9. Possibilities, Preferences, and Choices
A full chapter on this strictly optional topic to ensure that it is covered clearly with intuitive explanations and illustrations. The standard short appendix treatment of this topic makes it indigestible.

10. Organizing Production
This chapter may be skipped or assigned as a reading.

11. Output and Costs

12. Perfect Competition

13. Monopoly

14. Monopolistic Competition and Oligopoly

15. Demand and Supply in Resource Markets
Enables you to cover all the resource market issues in a single chapter. Includes an explanation of present value.

16. Labor Markets

17. Inequality, Redistribution, and Health Care

Core	Policy	Optional

Four Alternative Micro Sequences

Traditional Theory and Policy Mix	Challenging Theory Emphasis	Public Choice Emphasis	Policy Emphasis (shorter)
3. The Economic Problem	3. The Economic Problem	1. What Is Economics?	1. What Is Economics?
4. Demand and Supply	4. Demand and Supply	3. The Economic Problem	2. Making and Using Graphs
5. Elasticity	5. Elasticity	4. Demand and Supply	3. The Economic Problem
6. Efficiency and Equity	6. Efficiency and Equity	5. Elasticity	
7. Markets in Action	7. Markets in Action	6. Efficiency and Equity	4. Demand and Supply
8. Utility and Demand or	9. Possibilities, Preferences, and Choices	7. Markets in Action	5. Elasticity
9. Possibilities, Preferences, and Choices		8. Utility and Demand	6. Efficiency and Equity
10. Organizing Production	10. Organizing Production	10. Organizing Production	7. Markets in Action
11. Output and Costs	11. Output and Costs	11. Output and Costs	15. Demand and Supply in Resource Markets
12. Perfect Competition	12. Perfect Competition	12. Perfect Competition	16. Labor Markets (optional)
13. Monopoly	13. Monopoly	13. Monopoly	
14. Monopolistic Competition and Oligopoly	14. Monopolistic Competition and Oligopoly	14. Monopolistic Competition and Oligopoly	17. Inequality, Redistribution, and Health Care
19. Regulation and Antitrust Law	15. Demand and Supply in Resource Markets	18. Market Failure and Public Choice	18. Market Failure and Public Choice
15. Demand and Supply in Resource Markets	21. Uncertainty and Information	19. Regulation and Antitrust Law	20. Externalities, the Environment, and Knowledge
17. Inequality, Redistribution, and Health Care	19. Regulation and Antitrust Law	20. Externalities, the Environment, and Knowledge	36. Trading with the World
36. Trading with the World	36. Trading with the World		

Four Alternative Macro Sequences

Brief Contents

Contents

Summary (Key Points, Key Figures and Tables, and Key Terms), Problems, and Critical Thinking appear at the end of each chapter.

💻   Chapters marked with this symbol are
included on the *Economics in Action* CD.

PART 9 AGGREGATE DEMAND AND INFLATION

Chapter 1

What Is Economics?

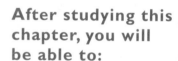

From the moment you wake up each morning to the moment you fall asleep again each night, your life is filled with *choices*. Your first choice is when to get up. Will you start running the moment the alarm goes off, or will you linger for a few minutes and listen to the radio? What will you wear today? You check the weather forecast and make that decision. Then, what will you have for breakfast? Will you drive to school or take the bus? Which classes will you attend? Which assignments will you complete? What will you do for lunch? Will you play tennis, swim, run, or skate today? How will you spend your evening? Will you study, relax at home with a video, or go to the movies? ◆ You face decisions like these every day. But on some days, you face choices that can change the entire direction of your life.

A Day in Your Life

What will you study? Will you major in economics, business, law, or film? ◆ While you are making your own decisions, other people are making theirs. And some of the decisions that other people make will have an impact on your own subsequent decisions. Your school decides its course offerings for next year. Stephen Spielberg decides what his next movie will be. A team of eye doctors decides on a new experiment that will lead them to a cure for nearsightedness. The U.S. Congress decides to reform Social Security. The Federal Reserve Board decides to cut interest rates. ◆ All these choices and decisions by you and everyone else are all examples of economics in your life.

◆ This chapter takes a first look at the subject you are about to study. It defines economics. Then it expands on that definition with five big questions that economists try to answer and eight big ideas that define the economic way of thinking. These questions and ideas are the foundation on which your course is built. The chapter concludes with a description of how economists go about their work, the scientific method they use, and the pitfalls they try to avoid. When you have completed your study of this chapter, you will have a good sense of what economics is about and you'll be ready to start learning economics and using it to gain a new view of the world.

After studying this chapter, you will be able to:

- ■ **Define economics**
- ■ **Explain the five big questions that economists seek to answer**
- ■ **Explain eight ideas that define the economic way of thinking**
- ■ **Describe how economists go about their work**

A Definition of Economics

ALL ECONOMIC QUESTIONS AND PROBLEMS ARISE from **scarcity**—they arise because our wants exceed the resources available to satisfy them.

We want good health and long life, material comfort, security, physical and mental recreation, and knowledge. None of these wants is completely satisfied for everyone, and everyone has some unsatisfied wants. While many people have all the material comfort they want, many others do not. And no one feels entirely satisfied with her or his state of health and expected length of life. No one feels entirely secure, even in the post–Cold War era, and no one has enough time for sport, travel, vacations, movies, theater, reading, and other leisure pursuits.

The poor and the rich alike, face scarcity. A child wants a 75¢ can of soft drink and a 50¢ pack of gum but has only $1.00 in her pocket. She experiences scarcity. A student wants to go to a party on Saturday night but also wants to spend that same night catching up on late assignments. He experiences scarcity. A millionaire wants to spend the weekend playing golf *and* attending a business strategy meeting and cannot do both. She experiences scarcity. Even parrots face scarcity—there just aren't enough crackers to go around!

Faced with scarcity, we must *choose* among the available alternatives.

Economics is the *science of choice*—the science that explains the choices that we make and how those choices change as we cope with scarcity.

Not only do I want a cracker—we all want a cracker!

Drawing by Modell; ©1985 *The New Yorker Magazine,* Inc.

Big Economic Questions

ALL ECONOMIC CHOICES CAN BE SUMMARIZED IN big questions about the goods and services we produce. These questions are: What? How? When? Where? Who?

1: What?

What goods and services are produced and in what quantities? **Goods and services** are all the things that we value and are willing to pay for. We produce a dazzling array of goods and services that range from necessities such as houses to leisure items such as camping vehicles and equipment. We build more than a million new homes every year. And these homes are more spacious and better equipped than they were twenty years ago. We make several million new leisure vehicles, tents, microwaves, refrigerators, telephones, television sets, and VCRs, all of which make outdoor living and vacations more attractive and more comfortable.

What determines whether we build more homes or make more camping gear and develop more campsites? How do these choices change over time? And how are they affected by the ongoing changes in technology that make an ever-wider array of goods and services available to us?

2: How?

How are goods and services produced? In a vineyard in France, basket-carrying workers pick the annual grape crop by hand. In a vineyard in California, a huge machine and a few workers do the same job that a hundred French grape harvesters do. Look around you and you will see many examples of this phenomenon—the same job being done in different ways. In some supermarkets, checkout clerks key in

prices. In others, they use a laser scanner. One farmer keeps track of his livestock feeding schedules and inventories by using paper and pencil records, while another uses a personal computer. GM hires workers to weld auto bodies in some of its plants and uses robots to do the job in others.

Why do we use machines in some cases and people in others? Does mechanization and technological change destroy more jobs than it creates? Does it make us better off or worse off?

3: When?

When are goods and services produced? On a building site, there is a surge of production activity and people must work overtime to keep production flowing fast enough. An auto factory closes for the summer, temporarily lays of its workers, and its production dries up.

Sometimes, economy-wide production slackens off and even shrinks in what is called a *recession*. At other times, economy-wide production expands rapidly. We call these ebbs and flows of production the *business cycle*. When production falls, jobs are lost and unemployment climbs. Once, during the Great Depression of the 1930s, production fell so much that one quarter of the workforce was jobless.

During the past few years, production has decreased in Russia and its Central and Eastern European neighbors as these countries try to change the way they organize their economies.

What makes production rise and fall? When will production fall again in the United States? Can the government prevent production from falling?

4: Where?

Where are goods and services produced? The Kellogg Company, of Battle Creek, Michigan, makes breakfast cereals in 20 countries and sells them in 160 countries. Kellogg's business in Japan is so huge that it has a Japanese language Website to promote its products! Honda, the Japanese auto producer, makes cars and motor cycles on most continents. "Globalization through localization" is its slogan. But it produces some cars in one country and ships them for sale in another.

In today's global economy, people who are separated by thousands of miles cooperate to produce many goods and services. Software engineers in Silicon Valley work via the Internet with programmers in India. American Express card charge slips are processed in Barbados. But there is a lot of local concentration of production as well. Most American carpets are made in Dalton, Georgia. And most of our movies are made in Los Angeles.

What determines where goods and services are produced? And how are changing patterns of production location changing the jobs we do and the wages we earn?

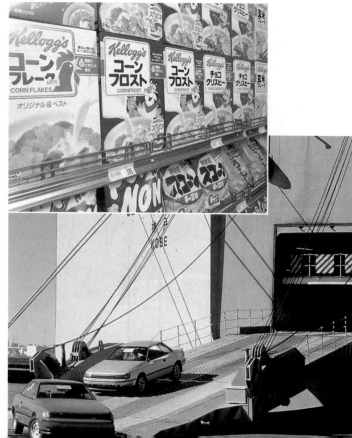

5: Who?

Who consumes the goods and services that are produced? Who consumes the goods and services produced depends on the incomes that people earn. Doctors earn much higher incomes than nurses and medical assistants. So doctors get more of the goods and services produced than nurses and medical assistants.

You probably know about many other persistent differences in incomes. Men, on the average, earn more than women. Whites, on the average, earn more than minorities. College graduates, on the average, earn more than high-school graduates do. Americans, on the average, earn more than Europeans, who in turn earn more on the average than Asians and Africans. But there are some significant exceptions. The people of Japan and Hong Kong now earn a similar amount to that of Americans. And there is a lot of income inequality throughout the world.

What determines the incomes we earn? Why do doctors earn larger incomes than nurses? Why do women and minorities earn less than white males?

R E V I E W   Q U I Z

- How would you define economics?
- What is scarcity? Give some examples of rich people and poor people facing scarcity.
- Give some examples, different from those in the chapter, of each of the five big economic questions.
- Why do you care about *what* goods and services are produced? Give some examples of goods that you value highly and goods on which you place a low value.
- Why do you care about *how* goods and services are produced? [Hint: Think about cost.]
- Why do you care about *when* or *where* goods and services are produced?
- Why do you care about *who* gets the goods and services that are produced?

These five big economic questions give you a sense of what economics is *about*. They tell you about the *scope of economics*. But they don't tell you what economics *is*. They don't tell you how economists *think* about these questions and seek answers to them. Let's find out how economists approach economic questions by looking at eight big ideas that define the *economic way of thinking*.

Big Ideas of Economics

WE CAN SUMMARIZE THE ECONOMIC WAY OF thinking in eight big ideas. Let's study them.

1: Choice, Tradeoff, and Opportunity Cost

A choice is a tradeoff—we give up something to get something else—and the highest-valued alternative we give up is the opportunity cost of the activity we choose.

Whatever we choose to do, we could have done something else instead. We tradeoff one thing for another. **Tradeoff** means giving up something to get something else. The highest-valued alternative we give up to get something is the **opportunity cost** of the activity chosen. "There's no such thing as a free lunch" is not just a clever throwaway line. It expresses the central idea of economics—that every choice involves a cost.

We use the term *opportunity cost* to emphasize that when we make a choice in the face of scarcity, we give up an opportunity to do something else. The opportunity cost of any action is the highest-valued alternative forgone. The action that you choose not to do—the highest-valued alternative forgone—is the cost of the action that you choose to do.

You can quit school right now or you can remain in school. If you quit and take a job at McDonalds, you might earn enough to buy some CDs, go to the movies, and spend lots of free time with your friends. If you remain in school, you can't afford these things. You will be able to buy these things later, and that is one of the payoffs from being in school. But for now, when you've bought your books, you have nothing left for CDs and movies. And doing assignments means that you've got less time for hanging around with your friends. The opportunity cost of being in school is the alternative things that you would have done if you had quit school.

Opportunity cost is the highest-valued alternative forgone. It is not *all* the possible alternatives forgone. For example, your economics lecture is at 8:30 on a Monday morning. You contemplate two alternatives to the lecture: staying in bed for an hour or jogging for an hour. You can't stay in bed and jog for that same hour. The opportunity cost of attending the lecture is the forgone hour in bed *or* the forgone hour of jogging. If these are the only alternatives you consider, then you have to decide which one you would do if you did not go to the lecture. The opportunity cost of attending a lecture for a jogger is a forgone hour of exercise; the opportunity cost of attending a lecture for a late sleeper is a forgone hour in bed.

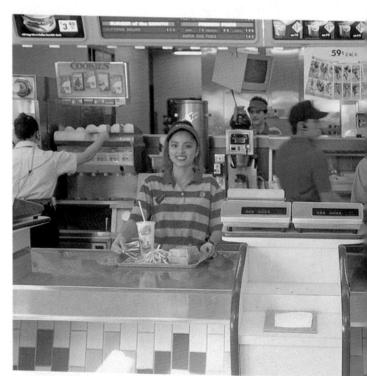

2: Margins and Incentives

We make choices in small steps, or at the margin, and choices are influenced by incentives. Everything that we do involves a decision to do a little bit more or a little bit less of an activity. You can allocate the next hour between studying and e-mailing your friends. But the choice is not "all-or-nothing." You must decide how many minutes to allocate to each activity. To make this decision, you compare the benefit of a little bit more study time with its cost—you make your choice at the **margin**.

The mother of a young child must decide how to allocate her time between being with her child and working for an income. Like your decision about study time, this decision too involves comparing the benefit of a little bit more income with the cost of a little bit less time with her child.

The benefit that arises from an increase in an activity is called **marginal benefit**. For example, suppose that a mother is working 2 days a week and is thinking about increasing her work to 3 days. Her marginal benefit is the benefit she will get from the additional day of work. It is *not* the benefit she gets from all 3 days. The reason is that she already has the benefit from 2 days work, so she doesn't count this benefit as resulting from the decision she is now making.

The cost of an increase in an activity is called **marginal cost**. For the mother of the young child, the marginal cost of increasing her work to 3 days a week is the cost of the additional day not spent with her child. It does not include the cost of the 2 days she is already working.

To make her decision, the mother compares the marginal benefit from an extra day of work with its marginal cost. If the marginal benefit exceeds the marginal cost, she works the extra day. If the marginal cost exceeds the marginal benefit, she does not work the extra day.

By evaluating marginal benefits and marginal costs and choosing only those actions that bring greater benefit than cost, we use our scarce resources in the way that makes us as well off as possible.

Our choices respond to incentives. An **incentive** is an inducement to take a particular action. The inducement can be a benefit—a carrot—or a cost—a stick. A change in opportunity cost—in marginal cost—and a change in marginal benefit changes the incentives that we face and leads to changes in our actions.

For example, suppose the daily wage rate rises and nothing else changes. With a higher daily wage rate, the marginal benefit of working increases. For the young mother, the opportunity cost of spending a day with her child has increased. She now has a bigger incentive to work an extra day a week. Whether or not she does so depends on how she evaluates the marginal benefit of the additional income and marginal cost of spending less time with her child.

Similarly, suppose the cost of day care rises and nothing else changes. The higher cost of day care increases the marginal cost of working. For the young mother, the opportunity cost of spending a day with her child has decreased. She now has a smaller incentive to work an extra day a week. Again, whether or not she changes her actions in response to a change in incentives depends on how she evaluates the marginal benefit and marginal cost.

The central idea of economics is that by looking for changes in marginal cost and marginal benefit, we can predict the way choices will change in response to changes in incentives.

3: Voluntary Exchange and Efficient Markets

Voluntary exchange makes both buyers and sellers better off, and markets are an efficient way to organize exchange.

When you shop for food, you give up some money in exchange for a basket of vegetables. But the food is worth the price you have to pay. You are better off having exchanged some of your money for the vegetables. The food store receives a payment that makes its operator happy too. Both you and the food store operator gain from your purchase.

Similarly, when you work at a summer job, you receive a wage that you've decided is sufficient to compensate you for the leisure time you must give up. But the value of your work to the firm that hires you is at least as great as the wage it pays you. So again, both you and your employer gain from a **voluntary exchange**.

You are better off when you buy your food. And you are better off when you sell your labor during the summer vacation. Whether you are a buyer or a seller, you gain from voluntary exchange with others. What is true for you is true for everyone. Everyone gains from voluntary exchange.

In our economy, exchanges take place in **markets** and for money. We sell our labor in exchange for an income in the labor market. And we buy the goods and services we've chosen to consume in a wide variety of markets—markets for vegetables, coffee, movies, videos, muffins, haircuts, and so on. At the other side of these transactions, firms buy our labor and sell us the hundreds of different consumer goods and services we buy.

Markets are **efficient** in the sense that they send resources to the place where they are valued most highly. For example, a frost kills Florida's orange crop and sends the price of orange juice through the roof. This increase in price, with all other prices remaining unchanged, increases the opportunity cost of drinking orange juice. The people who place the highest value on orange juice are the ones who keep drinking it. People who place a lower value on orange juice now have an incentive to substitute other fruit juices.

Markets are not the only way to organize the economy. An alternative is called a command system. In a **command system**, some people give orders (commands) and other people obey those orders. A command system is used in the military and in many firms. And it was used in the former Soviet Union to organize the entire economy. But the market is a superior method of organizing an entire economy.

4: Market Failure

The market does not always work efficiently and sometimes, government action is necessary to make the use of resources efficient.

Market failure is a state in which the market does not use resources efficiently. If you pay attention to the news media, you might get the impression that the market almost never does a good job. It makes credit card interest rates too high. It makes the wages of fast-food workers too low. It causes the price of coffee to go through the ceiling every time Brazil has a serious frost. It increases the world price of oil when political instability threatens the Middle East. These examples are not cases of market failure. They are examples of the market doing its job of helping us to allocate our scarce resources and ensure that they are used in the activities in which they are most highly valued.

Buyers never like it when prices rise. But sellers love it. And sellers never like it when prices fall. But buyers are happy. Rising and falling prices make news because they bring changes in fortunes. Some people win and some lose. Everyone gains from voluntary exchange, as you've just seen, but other things remaining the same, the higher the price, the more the seller gains and the less the buyer gains.

Because a high price brings a bigger gain to the seller, there is an incentive for sellers to try to control a market. When a single producer controls an entire market, the producer can restrict the quantity available and raise the price. This action brings market failure. The quantity of the good available is too small. Some people believe that Intel restricts the quantity of computer chips when it introduces a new design in order to get a high price for it. Eventually, the price falls, but at first, Intel sells its new design for a high price and makes a bigger profit.

Market failure can also arise when producers don't take into account the costs they impose on other people. For example, electric utilities create pollution, such as acid rain, that destroys plants and forests and lowers farm production. If these costs were taken into account, we would produce less electricity.

Market failure can also arise because some goods, such as national defense, must be consumed equally by everyone. None of us has an incentive voluntarily to pay our share of the cost of such a good. Instead, we try to free ride on everyone else. But if everyone tries to free ride, no one gets a ride!

To overcome market failure, governments regulate markets with antitrust laws and environmental protection laws; discourage the production and consumption of some goods and services (tobacco and alcohol for example) by taxing them; encourage the production and consumption of some goods and services (health care and schooling for example) by subsidizing them; and directly provide some goods and services (national defense, for example).

5: Expenditure, Income, and the Value of Production

For the economy as a whole, expenditure *equals* income and *equals* the value of production.

When you buy a coffee milk shake, you spend $2. But what happens to that money? The server gets some of it in wages, the owner of the building gets some of it as rent, and the owner of the milk bar gets some of it as profit. The suppliers of the milk, ice cream, and coffee also get some of your $2. But these suppliers spend part of what they receive on wages and rent. And they keep part of it as profit. Your $2 of **expenditure** creates exactly $2 of **income** for all the people who have contributed to making the milk shake, going all the way back to the farmer in Brazil who grew the coffee beans.

Your expenditure generates incomes of an equal amount. The same is true for everyone else's expenditure. So, for the economy as a whole, total expenditure on goods and services equals total income.

One way to value the things you buy is to use the prices you pay for them. So the value all of the goods and services bought equals total expenditure. Another way to value the items you buy is to use the cost of production. This cost is the total amount paid to the people who produced the items—the total income generated by your expenditure. But we've just seen that total expenditure and total income are equal, so they also equal the **value of production**.

6: Living Standards and Productivity Growth

Living standards improve when production per person increases.

By automating a car production line, one worker can produce a greater output. But if one worker can produce more cars, then more people can enjoy owning a car. The same is true for all goods and services. By increasing output per person, we enjoy a higher standard of living and buy more goods and services.

The dollar value of production can increase for any of three reasons: because prices rise, because production per person—**productivity**—increases, or because the population increases.

But only an increase in productivity brings an improvement in living standards. A rise in prices brings higher incomes, but only in dollars. The extra income is just enough to pay the higher prices, not enough to buy more goods and services. An increase in population brings an increase in *total* production, but not an increase in production per person.

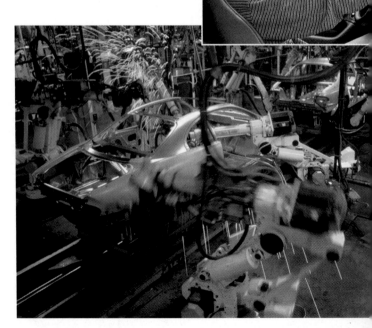

7: Inflation: A Monetary Problem

Prices rise in a process called **inflation** when the quantity of money increases faster than production. This process leads to a situation in which "too much money is chasing too few goods." As people bring more money to market, sellers see that they can raise their prices. But when these sellers go to buy their supplies, they find that the prices they face increase. With too much money around, money starts to lose value.

In some countries, inflation has been rapid. One such country is Poland. Since 1990, prices in Poland have risen more than seven-fold. In the United States, we have moderate inflation of less than 2 percent a year.

Some people say that by increasing the quantity of money, we can create jobs. The idea is that if more money is put into the economy, when it is spent, businesses sell more and so hire more labor to produce more goods and services.

Initially, an increase in money might increase production and create jobs. But eventually, it only increases prices and leaves production and jobs unchanged.

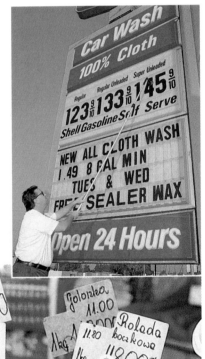

8: Unemployment: Productive and Wasteful

Unemployment can result from market failure and be wasteful. But some unemployment is productive.

Unemployment is ever present. Sometimes its rate is low and sometimes it is high. Also, unemployment fluctuates over the business cycle.

Some unemployment is normal and efficient. We choose to take our time finding a suitable job rather than rushing to accept the first one that comes along. Similarly, businesses take their time in filling vacancies. The unemployment that results from these careful searches for jobs and workers improves productivity because it helps to assign people to their most productive jobs.

Some unemployment results from fluctuations in expenditure and can be wasteful.

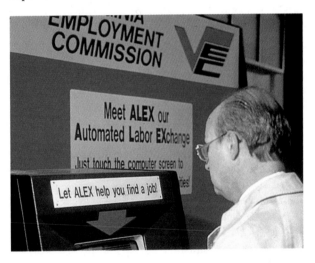

REVIEW QUIZ

- Give some examples of *tradeoffs* that you have made and the *opportunity costs* you've incurred today.
- Give some examples of *marginal* cost and *marginal* benefit.
- How do markets enable both buyers and sellers to gain from exchange and why do markets sometimes fail?
- Why for the economy as a whole, does expenditure equal income and the value of production?
- What makes living standards rise?
- What makes prices rise?
- Is unemployment always a problem?

What Economists Do

ECONOMISTS USE THE EIGHT BIG IDEAS THAT YOU have just studied to search for answers to the five big questions that you reviewed at the start of this chapter. But how do they go about their work? What special problems and pitfalls do they encounter? And do they always agree on the answers?

Microeconomics and Macroeconomics

Economists approach their work from either a micro or a macro perspective. These two perspectives define the two major branches of the subject:

■ Microeconomics
■ Macroeconomics

Microeconomics is the study of the decisions of individual people and businesses and the interaction of those decisions in markets.

Macroeconomics is the study of the national economy and the global economy. It seeks to explain *average* prices and *total* employment, income, and production.

You can take either a micro or a macro view of the spectacular display of national flags in a Korean sports stadium. The micro view is of a single participant and the actions he or she is taking. The macro view is the patterns formed by the joint actions of all the individuals participating in the entire display.

Microeconomics seeks to explain the prices and quantities of individual goods and services. It also

studies the effects of government regulation and taxes on the prices and quantities of individual goods and services. For example, microeconomics studies the forces that determine the prices of cars and the quantities of cars produced and sold. It also studies the effects of regulations and taxes on the prices and quantities of cars.

Macroeconomics studies the effects of taxes, government spending, and the government budget surplus or deficit on total jobs and incomes. It also studies the effects of money and interest rates.

Economic Science

Economics is a social science (along with political science, psychology, and sociology). A major task of economists is to discover how the economic world works. In pursuit of this goal, economists (like all scientists) distinguish between two types of statements:

■ What *is*
■ What *ought* to be

Statements about what *is* are called *positive* statements. They say what is currently believed about the way the world operates. A positive statement might be right or wrong. And we can test a positive statement by checking it against the facts. When a chemist does an experiment in her laboratory, she is attempting to check a positive statement against the facts.

Statements about what *ought* to be are called *normative* statements. These statements depend on values and cannot be tested. When Congress debates a motion, it is ultimately trying to decide what ought to be. It is making a normative statement.

To see the distinction between positive and normative statements, consider the controversy over global warming. Some scientists believe that centuries of the burning of coal and oil are increasing the carbon dioxide content of the earth's atmosphere and leading to higher temperatures that eventually will have devastating consequences for life on this planet. "Our planet is warming because of an increased carbon dioxide buildup in the atmosphere" is a positive statement. It can (in principle and with sufficient

data) be tested. "We ought to cut back on our use of carbon-based fuels such as coal and oil" is a normative statement. You may agree with or disagree with this statement, but you can't test it. It is based on values. Health-care reform provides an economic example of the distinction. "Universal health care will cut the amount of work time lost to illness" is a positive statement. "Every American should have equal access to health care" is a normative statement.

The task of economic science is to discover and catalog positive statements that are consistent with what we observe in the world and that enable us to understand how the economic world works. This task is a large one that can be broken into three steps:

- Observation and measurement
- Model building
- Testing models

Observation and Measurement First, economists keep track of the amounts and locations of natural and human resources, of wages and work hours, of the prices and quantities of the different goods and services produced, of taxes and government spending, and of the quantities of goods and services bought from and sold to other countries. This list gives a flavor of the array of things that economists can observe and measure.

Model Building The second step toward understanding how the economic world works is to build a model. An **economic model** is a description of some aspect of the economic world that includes only those features of the world that are needed for the purpose at hand. A model is simpler than the reality it describes. What a model includes and what it leaves out result from *assumptions* about what is essential and what are inessential details.

You can see how ignoring details is useful—even essential—to our understanding by thinking about a model that you see every day, the TV weather map. The weather map is a model that helps to predict the temperature, wind speed and direction, and precipitation over a future period. The weather map shows lines called isobars—lines of equal barometric pressure. It doesn't show the interstate highways. The reason is that our theory of the weather tells us that the pattern of air pressure, not the location of the highways, determines the weather.

An economic model is similar to a weather map. It tells us how a number of variables are determined by a number of other variables. For example, an economic model of the 1994 Los Angeles earthquake might tell us the effects of the earthquake and the government's relief efforts on the number of houses and apartments, rents and prices, jobs, and commuting times.

Testing The third step is testing the model. A model's predictions may correspond to or be in conflict with the facts. By comparing the model's predictions with the facts, we are able to test a model and develop an economic theory. An **economic theory** is a generalization that summarizes what we think we understand about the economic choices that people make and the performance of industries and entire economies. It is a bridge between an economic model and the real economy.

A theory is created by a process of building and testing models. For example, meteorologists have a theory that if the isobars form a particular pattern at a particular time of the year (a model), then it will snow (reality). They have developed this theory by repeated observation and by carefully recording the weather that follows specific pressure patterns.

Economics is a young science. It was born in 1776 with the publication of Adam Smith's *The Wealth of Nations* (see pp. 56–57). Over the past 225 years, economics has discovered many useful theories. But in many areas, economists are still looking for answers. The gradual accumulation of economic knowledge gives most economists some faith that their methods will, eventually, provide usable answers to the big economic questions.

But progress in economics comes slowly. Let's look at some of the obstacles to progress in economics.

Obstacles and Pitfalls in Economics

We cannot easily do economic experiments. And most economic behavior has many simultaneous causes. For these two reasons, it is difficult in economics to unscramble cause and effect.

Unscrambling Cause and Effect By changing one factor at a time and holding all the other relevant factors constant, we isolate the factor of interest and are able to investigate its effects in the clearest possible way. This logical device, that all scientists use to identify cause and effect, is called ***ceteris paribus***. *Ceteris paribus* is a Latin term that means "other things being equal" or "if all other relevant things remain the same." Ensuring that other things are equal is crucial in many activities, including athletic events, and all successful attempts to make scientific progress use this device.

Economic models (like the models in all other sciences) enable the influence of one factor at a time to be isolated in the imaginary world of the model. When we use a model, we are able to imagine what would happen if only one factor changed. But *ceteris paribus* can be a problem in economics when we try to test a model.

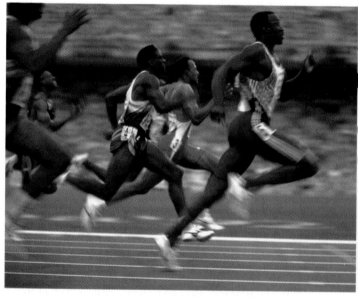

Laboratory scientists, such as chemists and physicists, perform experiments by actually holding all the relevant factors constant except for the one under investigation. In the non-experimental sciences such as economics (and astronomy), we usually observe the outcomes of the *simultaneous* operation of many factors. Consequently, it is hard to sort out the effects of each individual factor and to compare the effects with what a model predicts. To cope with this problem, economists take three complementary approaches.

First, they look for pairs of events in which other things were equal (or similar). An example might be to study the effects of unemployment insurance on the unemployment rate by comparing the United States with Canada on the presumption that the people in the two economies are sufficiently similar. Second, economists use statistical tools—called *econometrics*. And third, when they can, they perform experiments. This relatively new approach puts real subjects (usually students) in a decision-making situation and varies their incentives in some way to discover how they respond to one factor at a time.

Economists try to avoid *fallacies*—errors of reasoning that lead to a wrong conclusion. But two fallacies are common, and you need to be on your guard to avoid them. They are the

- Fallacy of composition
- *Post hoc* fallacy

Fallacy of Composition The fallacy of composition is the (false) statement that what is true of the parts is true of the whole or that what is true of the whole is true of the parts. Think of the true statement, "Speed kills," and its implication, going more slowly saves lives. If an entire freeway moves at a lower speed, everyone on the highway has a safer ride.

But suppose that one driver only slows down and all the other drivers try to maintain their original speed. In this situation, there will probably be more accidents because more cars will change lanes to overtake the slower vehicle. So, in this example, what is true for the whole is not true for a part.

The fallacy of composition arises mainly in macroeconomics, and it stems from the fact that the parts interact with each other to produce an outcome for the whole that might differ from the intent of the parts. For example, a firm lays off some workers to

cut costs and improve its profits. If all firms take similar actions, incomes fall and so does spending. The firm sells less, and its profits don't improve.

Post Hoc Fallacy Another Latin phrase—*post hoc ergo propter hoc*—means "after this, therefore because of this." The *post hoc* fallacy is the error of reasoning that a first event *causes* a second event because the first occurred before the second. Suppose you are a visitor from a far off world. You observe lots of people shopping in early December and then you see them opening gifts and partying on Christmas day. Does the shopping cause Christmas, you wonder. After a deeper study, you discover that Christmas causes the shopping. A later event causes an earlier event.

Unraveling cause and effect is difficult in economics. And just looking at the timing of events often doesn't help. For example, the stock market booms, and some months later the economy expands—jobs and incomes grow. Did the stock market boom cause the economy to expand? Possibly, but perhaps businesses started to plan the expansion of production because a new technology that lowered costs had become available. As knowledge of the plans spread, the stock market reacted to *anticipate* the economic expansion. To disentangle cause and effect, economists use economic models and data and, to the extent that they can, perform experiments.

Economics is a challenging science. Does the difficulty of getting answers in economics mean that anything goes and that economists disagree on most questions? Perhaps you've heard the joke: "If you laid all the economists in the world end to end, they still wouldn't reach agreement." Does the joke make a valid point?

Agreement and Disagreement

Economists agree on a remarkably wide range of questions. And surprisingly, the agreed view of economists often disagrees with the popular and sometimes politically correct view. When Fed Chairman Alan Greenspan testifies before the Senate Banking Committee, his words are rarely controversial among economists, even when they generate endless debate in the press and Congress.

Here are twelve propositions[1] with which at least 7 out of every 10 economists broadly agree:

- Tariffs and import restrictions make most people worse off.
- A large federal budget deficit has an adverse effect on the economy.
- Cash payments to welfare recipients make them better off than do transfers-in-kind of equal cash value.
- A minimum wage increases unemployment among young workers and low skilled workers.
- A tax cut can help to lower unemployment when the unemployment rate is high.
- The distribution of income in the United States should be more equal.
- Inflation is primarily caused by a rapid rate of money creation.
- The government should restructure welfare along the lines of a "negative income tax."
- Rent ceilings cut the availability of housing.
- Pollution taxes are more effective than pollution limits.
- The redistribution of income is a legitimate role for the U.S. government.
- The federal budget should be balanced on the average over the business cycle, but not every year.

Which are positive and which are normative? Notice that economists are willing to offer their opinions on normative issues as well as their professional views on positive questions. Be on the lookout for normative propositions dressed up as positive propositions.

---

[1] These are propositions generally supported or supported with provisos by more than 7 out of 10 economists according to a survey by Richard M. Alston, J.R. Kearl, and Michael B. Vaughan, "Is There a Consensus Among Economists," *American Economic Review*, 82 (May 1992), pp. 203–209. I have simplified the language in some cases, and you should check the original for the exact propositions and percentages agreeing.

R E V I E W   Q U I Z

- What is the distinction between microeconomics and macroeconomics? Provide an example (not in the chapter) of a micro issue and a macro issue.
- What is the distinction between a positive statement and a normative statement? Provide an example (different from those in the chapter) of each type of statement.
- What is a model? Can you think of a model that you might use (probably without thinking of it as a model) in your everyday life?
- What is a theory? Why is the statement, "It might work in theory but it doesn't work in practice" a silly statement? [Hint: Think about what a theory is and how it is used.]
- What is the *ceteris paribus* assumption and how is it used?
- Try to think of some everyday examples of fallacies.

You are now ready to start *doing* economics. As you get into the subject, you will see that we rely heavily on graphs. You must be comfortable with this method of reasoning. If you need some help with it, take your time in working carefully through Chapter 2. If you are already comfortable with graphs, then you are ready to jump right into Chapter 3 and begin to study the fundamental economic problem, scarcity.

SUMMARY

KEY POINTS

A Definition of Economics (p. 2)

- Economics is the *science of choice*—the science that explains the choices that we make to cope with scarcity.

Big Economic Questions (pp. 2–5)

- Economists try to answer five big questions about goods and services:

  1. What?
  2. How?
  3. When?
  4. Where?
  5. Who?

  What are the goods and services produced, *how*, *when*, and *where* are they produced, and *who* consumes them?

- These questions interact to determine the standards of living and the distribution of well-being in the United States and around the world.

Big Ideas of Economics (pp. 6–11)

- A choice is a tradeoff and the highest-valued alternative forgone is the opportunity cost of what is chosen.
- Choices are made at the margin and are influenced by incentives.
- Markets enable both buyers and sellers to gain from voluntary exchange.
- Sometimes government actions are needed to overcome market failure.
- For the economy as a whole, expenditure equals income and equals the value of production.
- Living standards rise when production per person increases.
- Prices rise when the quantity of money increases faster than production.
- Unemployment can result from market failure but can also be productive.

What Economists Do (pp. 12–16)

- Microeconomics is the study of individual decisions, and macroeconomics is the study of the economy as a whole.
- Positive statements are about what *is* and normative statements are about what *ought* to be.
- To explain the economic world, economists build and test economic models.
- Economists use the *ceteris paribus* assumption to try to disentangle cause and effect, and they are careful to avoid the fallacy of composition and the *post hoc* fallacy.
- Economists agree on a wide range of questions about how the economy works.

KEY TERMS

Ceteris paribus, 14
Command system, 8
Economics, 2
Economic model, 13
Economic theory, 13
Efficient, 8
Expenditure, 10
Goods and services, 2
Incentive, 7
Income, 10
Inflation, 11
Macroeconomics, 12
Margin, 7
Marginal benefit, 7
Marginal cost, 7
Market, 8
Market failure, 9
Microeconomics, 12
Opportunity cost, 6
Productivity, 10
Scarcity, 2
Tradeoff, 6
Unemployment, 11
Value of production, 10
Voluntary exchange, 8

PROBLEMS

*1. You plan to go to school this summer. If you do, you won't be able to take your usual job that pays $6,000 for the summer and you won't be able to live at home for free. The cost of your tuition will be $2,000, textbooks $200, and living expenses $1,400. What is the opportunity cost of going to summer school?

2. You plan a major adventure trip for the summer. You won't be able to take your usual summer job that pays $6,000 and you won't be able to live at home for free. The cost of your travel on the trip will be $3,000, film and video tape will cost you $200, and your food will cost $1,400. What is the opportunity cost of taking this trip?

*3. The local mall has free parking, but the mall is always very busy and it usually takes 30 minutes to find a parking space. Today when you found a vacant spot, Harry also wanted it. Is parking really free at this mall? If not, what did it cost you to park today? When you parked your car today, did you impose any costs on Harry? Explain your answers.

4. The university has built a new parking garage. There is always an available parking spot but it costs $1 a day. Before the new garage was built, it usually took 15 minutes of cruising to find a parking space. Compare the opportunity cost of parking in the new garage with that in the old parking lot. Which is less costly and by how much?

CRITICAL THINKING

1. Use the link on the Parkin Web site to visit *Resources For Economists on the Internet*. Scroll down the page and click on General Interest. Visit the "general interest" sites and become familiar with the types of information they contain.

2. Use the link on the Parkin Web site to visit *The Dismal Scientist* ®™—the best free lunch on the Web! In the "Economic Profile" box, enter your zip code and click "Get the profile."
   a. What is the number of people employed (nonfarm employment) in your area?

b. Has employment increased or decreased?
c. What is income per person (per capita income) in your area?

3. This man is homeless, and you can see all his possessions in the photograph.

Use the five big questions and the eight big ideas of economics to organize a short essay about the economic life of the man in the photograph. Does he face scarcity? Does he make choices? Can you interpret his choices as being in his own best interest? Can either his own choices or the choices of others make this man better off? If so, how?

4. Use the link on the Parkin Web site to visit *CNNfn*.
   a. What is the top economic news story today?
   b. With which of the five big questions does it deal? (Hint: It must deal with at least one of them and might deal with more than one.)
   c. Which of the eight big ideas seem to be relevant to understanding this news item?
   d. Write a brief summary of the news item in a few bulleted points, using as much as possible of the economic vocabulary that you have learned in this chapter and that is in the key terms list on p. 17.

Chapter 2

Making and Using Graphs

British Prime Minister Benjamin Disraeli is reputed to have said that "There are three kinds of lies: lies, damned lies, and statistics." One of the most powerful ways of conveying statistical information is in the form of a graph. And like statistics, graphs can lie. But the right graph does not lie. It reveals a relationship that would otherwise be obscure. ◆ Graphs are a modern invention. They first appeared in the late eighteenth century, long after the discovery of logarithms and calculus. But today, in the age of the personal computer and video display, graphs have become as important as words and numbers. How do economists use graphs? What types of graphs do they use? What do graphs reveal and what can they hide? ◆ The big questions that economics tries to answer—questions that you studied in

Three Kinds of Lies

Chapter 1—are difficult ones. They involve relationships among a large number of variables. Almost nothing in economics has a single cause. Instead, a large number of variables interact with each other. It is often said that in economics, everything depends on everything else. Changes in the quantity of ice cream consumed are caused by changes in the price of ice cream, the temperature, and many other factors. How can we make and interpret graphs of relationships among several variables?

◆ In this chapter, you are going to look at the kinds of graphs that economists use. You are going to learn how to make them and read them. You are also going to learn how to determine the magnitude of the influence of one variable on another by calculating the slope of a line and of a curve. ◆ There are no graphs or techniques used in this book that are more complicated than those described and explained in this chapter. If you are already familiar with graphs, you may want to skip (or skim) this chapter. Whether you study this chapter thoroughly or give it a quick pass, you can use it as a handy reference, returning to it whenever you need extra help in understanding the graphs that you encounter in your study of economics.

After studying this chapter, you will be able to:

- ■ Make and interpret a time-series graph, a scatter diagram, and a cross-section graph

- ■ Distinguish between linear and nonlinear relationships and between relationships that have a maximum and a minimum

- ■ Define and calculate the slope of a line

- ■ Graph relationships among more than two variables

Graphing Data

GRAPHS REPRESENT A QUANTITY AS A DISTANCE on a line. Figure 2.1 gives two examples. A distance on the horizontal line represents temperature, measured in degrees Fahrenheit. A movement from left to right shows an increase in temperature. A movement from right to left shows a decrease in temperature. The point marked 0 represents zero degrees Fahrenheit. To the right of 0, the temperatures are positive. To the left of 0, the temperatures are negative (as indicated by the minus sign in front of the numbers).

A distance on the vertical line represents altitude or height, measured in thousands of feet above sea level. The point marked 0 represents sea level. Points above 0 represent feet above sea level. Points below 0 (indicated by a minus sign) represent feet below sea level.

There are no rigid rules about the scale for a graph. The scale is determined by the range of the variables being graphed.

The main point of a graph is to enable us to visualize the relationship between two variables. And to accomplish this, we set two scales perpendicular to each other, like those in Fig. 2.1.

The two scale lines are called *axes*. The vertical line is called the *y*-axis, and the horizontal line is called the *x*-axis. The letters *x* and *y* appear on the axes of Fig. 2.1. Each axis has a zero point, which is shared by the two axes. This zero point, common to both axes, is called the *origin*.

To show something in a two-variable graph, we need two pieces of information. We need the value of the variable *x* and the value of the variable *y*. For example, off the coast of Alaska on a winter's day, the temperature is 32 degrees, which we will call the value of *x*. A fishing boat is located at 0 feet above sea level, which we'll call the value of *y*. These two bits of information appear as point *a* in Fig. 2.1. A climber at the top of Mount McKinley on a very cold day is 20,320 feet above sea level and the temperature is 0 degrees. These two pieces of information appear as point *b*. The position of the climber on a warmer day might be at the point marked *c*. This point represents the peak of Mt. McKinley when the temperature is 32 degrees.

Two lines, called coordinates, can be drawn from point *c* in the graph. One of these lines runs from *c* to the horizontal axis. This line is called the *y*-coordinate. Its length is the same as the value marked off on

FIGURE 2.1

Making a Graph

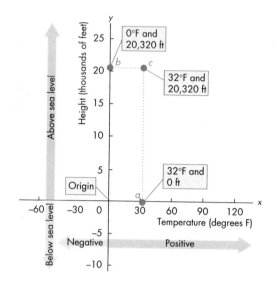

All graphs have axes that measure quantities as distances. Here, the horizontal axis (*x*-axis) measures temperature. A rightward movement shows an increase in temperature. The vertical axis (*y*-axis) measures height. An upward movement shows an increase in height. Point *a* represents a fishing boat at sea level (0 on the *y*-axis) on a day when the temperature is 32° (32° on the *x*-axis). Point *b* represents a climber at the top of Mt. McKinley (20,320 feet above sea level on the *y*-axis) on a day when the temperature on Mt. McKinley is 0° (0° on the *x*-axis). Point *c* represents a climber at the top of Mt. McKinley, 20,320 feet above sea level (on the *y*-axis) on a day when the temperature on Mt. McKinley is 32° (on the *x*-axis).

the *y*-axis. The other of these lines runs from *c* to the vertical axis. This line is called the *x*-coordinate. Its length is the same as the value marked off on the *x*-axis. To describe a point in a graph, we simply use the values of its *x*- and *y*-coordinates.

Graphs like that in Fig. 2.1 can be used to show any type of quantitative data about two variables. Economists use graphs similar to the one in Fig. 2.1 to reveal and describe the relationships among economic variables. To do so, they use three main types of graphs, which we'll now study. They are:

- Scatter diagrams
- Time-series graphs
- Cross-section graphs

Scatter Diagrams

A **scatter diagram** plots the value of one economic variable against the value of another variable. Such a graph is used to reveal whether a relationship exists between two economic variables. It is also used to describe a relationship.

Consumption and Income　Figure 2.2(a) shows a scatter diagram of the relationship between consumption and income. The *x*-axis measures average income, and the *y*-axis measures average consumption. Each point shows consumption per person and income per person (on the average) in the United States in a given year from 1990 to 1997. The points for the eight years are "scattered" within the graph. Each point is labeled with a two-digit number that shows us its year. For example, the point marked 96 shows us that in 1996, income per person was $19,200 and consumption per person was $17,750.

The dots in this graph form a pattern, which reveals that as income increases, consumption also increases.

Phone Calls and Price　Figure 2.2(b) shows a scatter diagram of the relationship between the number of international phone calls made from the United States and the average price per minute.

The dots in this graph reveal that as the price per minute falls, the number of calls increases.

Unemployment and Inflation　Figure 2.2(c) shows a scatter diagram of inflation and unemployment in the United States. The dots in this graph form a pattern that shows us there is no clear relationship between these two variables. By its lack of a distinct pattern, the graph shows us that there is no simple relationship between inflation and unemployment in the United States.

Correlation and Causation　A scatter diagram that shows a clear relationship between two variables, such as Fig. 2.2(a) or Fig. 2.2(b), tells us that the two variables have a high correlation. When a high correlation is present, we can predict the value of one variable from the value of the other variable. But correlation does not imply causation. Sometimes a high correlation is just a coincidence, but sometimes it does

FIGURE 2.2

Scatter Diagrams

(a) Consumption and income

(b) International phone calls and prices

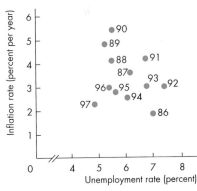

(c) Unemployment and inflation

A scatter diagram reveals the relationship between two variables. Part (a) shows the relationship between consumption and income between 1990 and 1997. Each point shows the values of the two variables in a specific year. For example, in 1996, average income was $19,200 and average consumption was $17,750. The pattern formed by the points shows that as income increases, so does consumption. Part (b) shows the relationship between the price of an international phone call and the number of phone calls made per year between 1970 and 1993. This graph shows that as the price of a phone call has fallen, the number of calls made has increased. Part (c) shows the inflation rate and unemployment rate in the United States between 1986 and 1997. This graph shows that inflation and unemployment are not closely related.

arise from a causal relationship. It is likely, for example, that increasing income causes increasing consumption (Fig. 2.2a) and that falling phone call prices cause more calls to be made (Fig. 2.2b).

Breaks in the Axes   Two of the graphs you've just looked at, Fig. 2.2(a) and Fig. 2.2(c), have breaks in their axes, as shown by the small gaps. The breaks indicate that there are jumps from the origin, 0, to the first values recorded.

In Fig. 2.2(a), the breaks are used because the lowest value of consumption exceeds $15,000 and the lowest value of income exceeds $16,500. With no breaks in the axes of this graph, there would be a lot of empty space, all the points would be crowded into the top right corner, and we would not be able to see whether a relationship exists between these two variables. By breaking the axes, we are able to bring the relationship into view.

Putting a break in the axes is like using a zoom lens to bring the relationship into the center of the graph and magnify it so that it fills the graph.

Misleading Graphs   Breaks can be used to highlight a relationship. But they can also be used to mislead and create a wrong impression—to make a graph that lies. The most common way of making a graph lie is to use axis breaks and to also either stretch or compress a scale. The most effective way to see the power of this kind of lie is to make some graphs that use this technique. For example, redraw Fig. 2.2(a) but make the *y*-axis that measures consumption run from zero to $45,000 and keep the *x*-axis the same as the one shown. The graph will now create the impression that despite huge income growth, consumption has barely changed.

To avoid being misled, it is a good idea to get into the habit of always looking closely at the values and the labels on the axes of a graph before you start to interpret it.

Time-Series Graphs

A **time-series graph** measures time (for example, months or years) on the *x*-axis and the variable or variables in which we are interested on the *y*-axis. Figure 2.3 shows an example of a time-series graph. In this graph, time (on the *x*-axis) is measured in years, which run from 1968 to 1998. The variable that we are interested in is the price of coffee, and it is measured on the *y*-axis.

A time-series graph conveys an enormous amount of information quickly and easily, as this example illustrates. It shows:

1. The *level* of the price of coffee—when it is *high* and *low*. When the line is a long way from the *x*-axis, the price is high. When the line is close to the *x*-axis, the price is low.

2. How the price *changes*—whether it *rises* or *falls*. When the line slopes upward, as in 1976, the price is rising. When the line slopes downward, as in 1978, the price is falling.

3. The *speed* with which the price changes—whether it rises or falls *quickly* or *slowly*. If the line is very steep, then the price rises or falls quickly. If the line is not steep, the price rises or falls slowly. For example, the price rose very quickly in 1976 and 1977. The price went up again in 1993 but slowly. Similarly, when the price was falling in 1978, it fell quickly, but during the early 1980s, it fell more slowly.

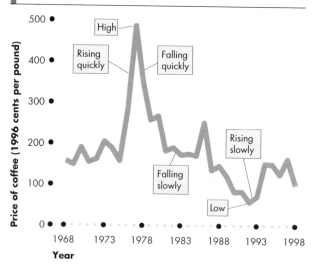

FIGURE 2.3

A Time-Series Graph

A time-series graph plots the level of a variable on the *y*-axis against time (day, week, month, or year) on the *x*-axis. This graph shows the price of coffee (in 1996 cents per pound) each year from 1968 to 1998. It shows us when the price of coffee was *high* and when it was *low*, when the price *increased* and when it *decreased*, and when it changed *quickly* and when it changed *slowly*.

A time-series graph also reveals whether there is a trend. A **trend** is a general tendency for a variable to rise or fall. You can see that the price of coffee had a general tendency to fall from the mid-1970s to the early 1990s. That is, although there were ups and downs in the price, there was a general tendency for it to fall.

A time-series graph also lets us compare different periods quickly. Figure 2.3 shows that the 1980s were different from the 1970s. The price of coffee fluctuated more violently in the 1970s than it did in the 1980s. This graph conveys a wealth of information, and it does so in much less space than we have used to describe only some of its features.

Comparing Two Time Series Sometimes we want to use a time-series graph to compare two different variables. For example, suppose you want to know whether the balance of the government's budget fluctuates with the unemployment rate. You can examine the government's budget balance and the unemployment rate by drawing a graph of each of them on the same time scale. But we can measure the government's budget balance either as a surplus or as a deficit. Figure 2.4(a) plots the budget surplus. The scale of the unemployment rate is on the left side of the figure, and the scale of the government's budget surplus is on the right. The orange line shows unemployment, and the blue line shows the budget surplus. This figure shows that the unemployment rate and the government's budget surplus move in opposite directions. For example, when the unemployment rate decreases, the budget surplus increases.

Figure 2.4(b) uses a scale for the government's budget balance measured as a deficit. That is, we flip the right-side scale over. This figure shows that the unemployment rate and the government's budget deficit move in the same direction. The budget deficit and the unemployment rate increase together and decrease together.

Scatter Diagram for Comparing Two Time Series We can compare two time series in a graph like Fig. 2.4 or in a scatter diagram like Fig. 2.2. Which is better? There is no right answer to this question. If the purpose of the graph is to show *both* the way two variables have changed over time and how they are related to each other, then the time-series graph does the better job. But if the purpose of the graph is to check the strength of the relationship between two variables, then a scatter diagram does a better job. A relationship that looks strong in a time-series graph often looks weak in a scatter diagram.

FIGURE 2.4

Time-Series Relationships

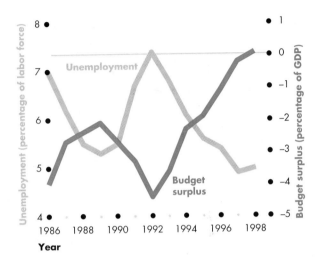

(a) Unemployment and budget surplus

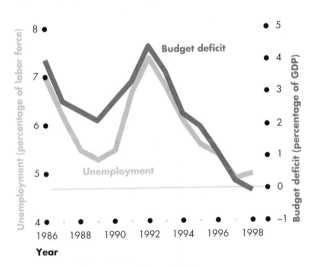

(b) Unemployment and budget deficit

These two graphs show the unemployment rate and the balance of the government's budget. The unemployment line is identical in the two parts. Part (a) shows the budget surplus—*taxes minus spending*—on the right scale. It is hard to see a relationship between the budget surplus and unemployment. Part (b) shows the budget as a deficit—*spending minus taxes*. It inverts the scale of part (a). With the scale for the budget balance inverted, the graph reveals a tendency for unemployment and the budget deficit to move together.

Cross-Section Graphs

A **cross-section graph** shows the values of an economic variable for different groups in a population at a point in time. Figure 2.5 is an example of a cross-section graph. It shows average income per person in the ten largest metropolitan areas in the United States in 1995. This graph uses bars rather than dots and lines, and the length of each bar indicates average income per person. Figure 2.5 enables you to compare the average incomes per person in these ten cities. And you can do so much more quickly and clearly than by looking at a list of numbers.

The cross-section graph in Fig. 2.5 is also an example of a *bar chart*. We often use bars rather than lines in cross-section graphs, but there are no fixed rules about whether to use lines, dots, or bars. It is a matter of taste.

You've now seen how we can use graphs in economics to show economic data and to reveal relationships between variables. Next, we're going to learn how to use graphs in a more abstract way. We'll learn how economists use graphs to construct and display economic models.

FIGURE 2.5

A Cross-Section Graph

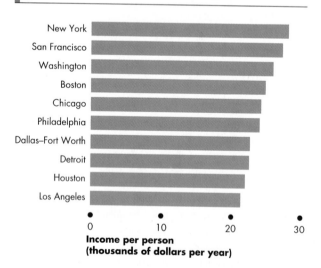

A cross-section graph shows the level of a variable across the members of a population. This graph shows the average income per person in each of the ten largest metropolitan areas in the United States in 1995.

Graphs Used in Economic Models

THE GRAPHS USED IN ECONOMICS ARE NOT always designed to show real-world data. Often they are used to show general relationships among the variables in an economic model.

An **economic model** is a stripped down, simplified description of an economy or of a component of an economy such as a business or a household. It consists of statements about economic behavior that can be expressed as equations or as curves in a graph. Economists use models to explore the effects of different policies or other influences on the economy in ways that are similar to the use of model airplanes in wind tunnels and models of the climate.

You will encounter many different kinds of graphs in economic models, but there are some repeating patterns. Once you've learned to recognize these patterns, you will instantly understand the meaning of a graph. Here, we'll look at the different types of curves that are used in economic models, and we'll see some everyday examples of each type of curve. The patterns to look for in graphs are the four cases in which:

■ Variables move in the same direction
■ Variables move in opposite directions
■ Variables have a maximum or a minimum
■ Variables are unrelated

Let's look at these four cases.

Variables That Move in the Same Direction

Figure 2.6 shows graphs of the relationships between two variables that move up and down together. A relationship between two variables that move in the same direction is called a **positive relationship** or a **direct relationship**. Such a relationship is shown by a line that slopes upward.

Figure 2.6 shows three types of relationships, one that has a straight line and two that have curved lines. But all the lines in these three graphs are called curves. Any line on a graph—no matter whether it is straight or curved—is called a *curve*.

A relationship shown by a straight line is called a **linear relationship**. Figure 2.6(a) shows a linear

FIGURE 2.6
Positive (Direct) Relationships

(a) Positive linear relationship

(b) Positive becoming steeper

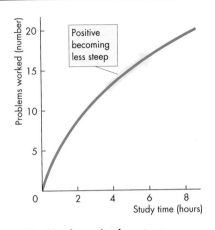

(c) Positive becoming less steep

Each part of this figure shows a positive (direct) relationship between two variables. That is, as the value of the variable measured on the *x*-axis increases, so does the value of the variable measured on the *y*-axis. Part (a) shows a linear relationship—as the two variables increase together, we move along a straight line. Part (b) shows a positive relationship such that as the two variables increase together, we move along a curve that becomes steeper. Part (c) shows a positive relationship such that as the two variables increase together, we move along a curve that becomes flatter.

relationship between the number of miles traveled in 5 hours and speed. For example, point *a* shows us that we will travel 200 miles in 5 hours if our speed is 40 miles an hour. If we double our speed to 80 miles an hour, we will travel 400 miles in 5 hours.

Part (b) shows the relationship between distance sprinted and recovery time (the time it takes the heart rate to return to its normal resting rate). This relationship is an upward-sloping one shown by a curved line that starts out fairly flat but then becomes steeper as we move along the curve away from the origin. The reason this curve slopes upward and becomes steeper is because the additional recovery time needed from sprinting an additional 100 yards increases. It takes less than 5 minutes to recover from 100 yards but more than 10 minutes to recover from the third 100 yards.

Part (c) shows the relationship between the number of problems worked by a student and the amount of study time. This relationship is shown by an upward-sloping curved line that starts out fairly steep and becomes flatter as we move away from the origin. Study time becomes less productive as you study for more hours and become more tired.

Variables That Move in Opposite Directions

Figure 2.7 shows relationships between things that move in opposite directions. A relationship between variables that move in opposite directions is called a **negative relationship** or an **inverse relationship**.

Part (a) shows the relationship between the number of hours available for playing squash and the number of hours for playing tennis. One extra hour spent playing tennis means one hour less playing squash and vice versa. This relationship is negative and linear.

Part (b) shows the relationship between the cost per mile traveled and the length of a journey. The longer the journey, the lower is the cost per mile. But as the journey length increases, the cost per mile decreases, and the fall in the cost is smaller, the longer the journey. This feature of the relationship is shown by the fact that the curve slopes downward, starting out steep at a short journey length and then becoming flatter as the journey length increases. This relationship arises because some of the costs are fixed,

FIGURE 2.7

Negative (Inverse) Relationships

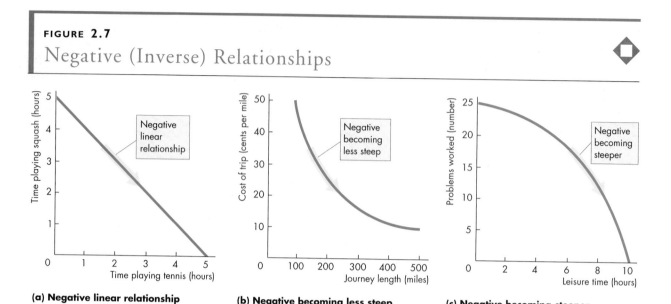

(a) Negative linear relationship

(b) Negative becoming less steep

(c) Negative becoming steeper

Each part of this figure shows a negative (inverse) relationship between two variables. Part (a) shows a linear relationship—as one variable increases and the other variable decreases, we move along a straight line. Part (b) shows a negative relationship such that as the journey length increases, the curve becomes less steep. Part (c) shows a negative relationship such that as leisure time increases, the curve becomes steeper.

---

such as auto insurance, and the fixed costs are spread over a longer journey.

Part (c) shows the relationship between the amount of leisure time and the number of problems worked by a student. Increasing leisure time produces an increasingly large reduction in the number of problems worked. This relationship is a negative one that starts out with a gentle slope at a small number of leisure hours and becomes steeper as the number of leisure hours increases. This relationship is a different view of the idea shown in Fig. 2.6(c).

Variables That Have a Maximum or a Minimum

Many relationships in economic models have a maximum or a minimum. For example, firms try to make the maximum possible profit and to produce at the lowest possible cost. Figure 2.8 shows relationships that have a maximum or a minimum.

Part (a) shows the relationship between rainfall and wheat yield. When there is no rainfall, wheat will

not grow, so the yield is zero. As the rainfall increases up to 10 days a month, the wheat yield also increases. With 10 rainy days each month, the wheat yield reaches its maximum at 40 bushels an acre (point *a*). Rain in excess of 10 days a month starts to lower the yield of wheat. If every day is rainy, the wheat suffers from a lack of sunshine and the yield falls back to zero. This relationship is one that starts out sloping upward, reaches a maximum, and then slopes downward.

Part (b) shows the reverse case—a relationship that begins sloping downward, falls to a minimum, and then slopes upward. An example of such a relationship is the gasoline cost per mile as the speed of travel increases. At low speeds, the car is creeping along in a traffic snarl-up. The number of miles per gallon is low, so the gasoline cost per mile is high. At very high speeds, the car is traveling faster than its most efficient speed, and again the number of miles per gallon is low and the gasoline cost per mile is high. At a speed of 55 miles an hour, the gasoline cost per mile traveled is at its minimum (point *b*). This relationship is one that starts out sloping downward, reaches a minimum, and then slopes upward.

FIGURE 2.8
Maximum and Minimum Points

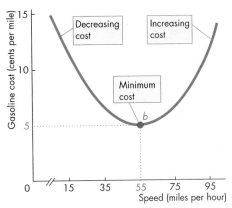

Part (a) shows a relationship that has a maximum point, *a*. The curve slopes upward as it rises to its maximum point, is flat at its maximum, and then slopes downward. Part (b) shows a relationship with a minimum point, *b*. The curve slopes downward as it falls to its minimum, is flat at its minimum, and then slopes upward.

(a) Relationship with a maximum

(b) Relationship with a minimum

Variables That Are Unrelated

There are many situations in which no matter what happens to the value of one variable, the other variable remains constant. Sometimes we want to show the independence between two variables in a graph, and Fig. 2.9 shows two ways of achieving this.

In describing the graphs in Fig. 2.6 through 2.9, we have talked about the slopes of curves. Let's look more closely at the concept of slope.

FIGURE 2.9
Variables That Are Unrelated

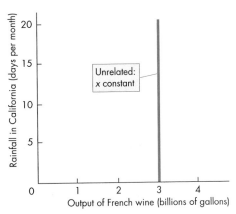

This figure shows how we can graph two variables that are unrelated to each other. In part (a), a student's grade in economics is plotted at 75 percent regardless of the price of bananas on the *x*-axis. The curve is horizontal. In part (b), the output of the vineyards of France does not vary with the rainfall in California. The curve is vertical.

(a) Unrelated: *y* constant

(b) Unrelated: *x* constant

The Slope of a Relationship

WE CAN MEASURE THE INFLUENCE OF ONE VARIABLE on another by the slope of the relationship. The **slope** of a relationship is the change in the value of the variable measured on the y-axis divided by the change in the value of the variable measured on the x-axis. We use the Greek letter Δ (*delta*) to represent "change in." Thus Δy means the change in the value of the variable measured on the y-axis, and Δx means the change in the value of the variable measured on the x-axis. Therefore the slope of the relationship is

$$\Delta y / \Delta x.$$

If a large change in the variable measured on the y-axis (Δy) is associated with a small change in the variable measured on the x-axis (Δx), the slope is large and the curve is steep. If a small change in the variable measured on the y-axis (Δy) is associated with a large change in the variable measured on the x-axis (Δx), the slope is small and the curve is flat.

We can make the idea of slope sharper by doing some calculations.

The Slope of a Straight Line

The slope of a straight line is the same regardless of where on the line you calculate it. Thus the slope of a straight line is constant. Let's calculate the slopes of the lines in Fig. 2.10. In part (a), when x increases from 2 to 6, y increases from 3 to 6. The change in x is +4—that is, Δx is 4. The change in y is +3—that

---

FIGURE 2.10

The Slope of a Straight Line

(a) Positive slope

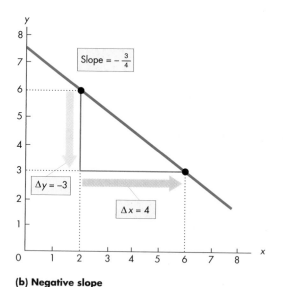

(b) Negative slope

To calculate the slope of a straight line, we divide the change in the value of the variable measured on the y-axis (Δy) by the change in the value of the variable measured on the x-axis (Δx) as we move along the curve. Part (a) shows the calculation of a positive slope. When x increases from 2 to 6, Δx equals 4.

That change in x brings about an increase in y from 3 to 6, so Δy equals 3. The slope ($\Delta y/\Delta x$) equals ¾. Part (b) shows the calculation of a negative slope. When x increases from 2 to 6, Δx equals 4. That increase in x brings about a decrease in y from 6 to 3, so Δy equals –3. The slope ($\Delta y/\Delta x$) equals –¾.

is, Δy is 3. The slope of that line is

$$\frac{\Delta y}{\Delta x} = \frac{3}{4}.$$

In part (b), when x increases from 2 to 6, y decreases from 6 to 3. The change in y is *minus* 3— that is, Δy is –3. The change in x is *plus* 4—that is, Δx is 4. The slope of the curve is

$$\frac{\Delta y}{\Delta x} = \frac{-3}{4}.$$

Notice that the two slopes have the same magnitude (3/4), but the slope of the line in part (a) is positive (+3/+4 = 3/4), while that in part (b) is negative (–3/+4 = –3/4). The slope of a positive relationship is positive; the slope of a negative relationship is negative.

The Slope of a Curved Line

The slope of a curved line is trickier. The slope of a curved line is not constant. Its slope depends on where on the line we calculate it. There are two ways to calculate the slope of a curved line: You can calculate the slope at a point, or you can calculate the slope across an arc of the line. Let's look at the two alternatives.

Slope at a Point   To calculate the slope at a point on a curve, you need to construct a straight line that has the same slope as the curve at the point in question. Figure 2.11 shows how this is done. Suppose you want to calculate the slope of the curve at point a. Place a ruler on the graph so that it touches point a and no other point on the curve, then draw a straight line along the edge of the ruler. The straight red line is this line, and it is the tangent to the curve at point a. If the ruler touches the curve only at point a, then the slope of the curve at point a must be the same as the slope of the edge of the ruler. If the curve and the ruler do not have the same slope, the line along the edge of the ruler will cut the curve instead of just touching it.

Now that you have found a straight line with the same slope as the curve at point a, you can calculate the slope of the curve at point a by calculating the slope of the straight line. Along the straight line, as x increases from 0 to 4 ($\Delta x = 4$), y increases from 2 to 5

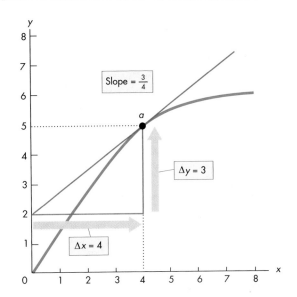

FIGURE 2.11

Slope at a Point

To calculate the slope of the curve at point a, draw the red line that just touches the curve at a—the tangent. The slope of this straight line is calculated by dividing the change in y by the change in x along the line. When x increases from 0 to 4, Δx equals 4. That change in x is associated with an increase in y from 2 to 5, so Δy equals 3. The slope of the red line is 3/4. So the slope of the curve at point a is 3/4.

($\Delta y = 3$). Therefore the slope of the line is

$$\frac{\Delta y}{\Delta x} = \frac{3}{4}.$$

Thus the slope of the curve at point a is 3/4.

Slope Across an Arc   An arc of a curve is a piece of a curve. In Fig. 2.12, you are looking at the same curve as in Fig. 2.11. But instead of calculating the slope at point a, we are going to calculate the slope across the arc from b to c. You can see that the slope at b is greater than the slope at c. When we calculate the slope across an arc, we are calculating the average slope between two points. As we move along the arc from b to c, x increases from 3 to 5 and y increases from 4 to 5.5. The change in x is 2 ($\Delta x = 2$), and the

FIGURE 2.12
Slope Across an Arc

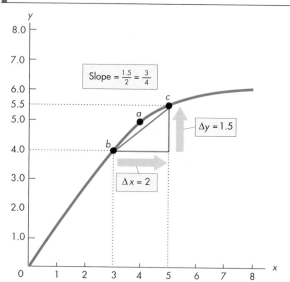

To calculate the average slope of the curve along the arc *bc*, draw a straight line from *b* to *c*. The slope of the line *bc* is calculated by dividing the change in *y* by the change in *x*. In moving from *b* to *c*, Δx equals 2 and Δy equals 1.5. The slope of the line *bc* is 1.5 divided by 2, or $\frac{3}{4}$. So the slope of the curve across the arc *bc* is $\frac{3}{4}$.

change in *y* is 1.5 ($\Delta y = 1.5$). Therefore the slope of the line is

$$\frac{\Delta y}{\Delta x} = \frac{15}{2} = \frac{3}{4}.$$

Thus the slope of the curve across the arc *bc* is 3/4.

This calculation gives us the slope of the curve between points *b* and *c*. The actual slope calculated is the slope of the straight line from *b* to *c*. This slope approximates the average slope of the curve along the arc *bc*. In this particular example, the slope across the arc *bc* is identical to the slope of the curve at point *a*. But the calculation of the slope of a curve does not always work out so neatly. You might have some fun constructing counterexamples.

You now know how to make and interpret a graph. But so far, we've limited our attention to graphs of two variables. We're now going to learn how to graph more than two variables.

Graphing Relationships Among More Than Two Variables

WE HAVE SEEN THAT WE CAN GRAPH THE RELA-tionship between two variables as a point formed by the *x*- and *y*-coordinates in a two-dimensional graph. You may be thinking that although a two-dimensional graph is informative, most of the things in which you are likely to be interested involve relationships among many variables, not just two. For example, the amount of ice cream consumed depends on the price of ice cream and the temperature. If ice cream is expensive and the temperature is low, people eat much less ice cream than when ice cream is inexpensive and the temperature is high. For any given price of ice cream, the quantity consumed varies with the temperature, and for any given temperature, the quantity of ice cream consumed varies with its price.

Figure 2.13 shows a relationship among three variables. The table shows the number of gallons of ice cream consumed each day at various temperatures and ice cream prices. How can we graph these numbers?

To graph a relationship that involves more than two variables, we use the *ceteris paribus* assumption.

Ceteris Paribus The Latin phrase **ceteris paribus**, means "other things remaining the same." Every laboratory experiment is an attempt to create *ceteris paribus* and isolate the relationship of interest. We use the same method to make a graph.

Figure 2.13(a) shows an example. There, you can see what happens to the quantity of ice cream consumed when the price of ice cream varies while the temperature is held constant. The line labeled 70°F shows the relationship between ice cream consumption and the price of ice cream if the temperature is 70°F. The numbers used to plot that line are those in the third column of the table in Fig. 2.13. For example, if the temperature is 70°F, 10 gallons are consumed when the price is 60¢ a scoop, and 18 gallons are consumed when the price is 30¢ a scoop. The curve labeled 90°F shows consumption as the price varies if the temperature is 90°F.

We can also show the relationship between ice cream consumption and temperature while the price of ice cream remains constant, as shown in Fig. 2.13(b). The curve labeled 60¢ shows how the consumption

FIGURE 2.13

Graphing a Relationship Among Three Variables

(a) Price and consumption at a given temperature

(b) Temperature and consumption at a given price

(c) Temperature and price at a given consumption

Price	Ice cream consumption			
(cents per scoop)	(gallons per day)			
	30°F	50°F	70°F	90°F
15	12	18	25	50
30	10	12	18	37
45	7	10	13	27
60	5	7	10	20
75	3	5	7	14
90	2	3	5	10
105	1	2	3	6

The quantity of ice cream consumed depends on its price and the temperature. The table gives some hypothetical numbers that tell us how many gallons of ice cream are consumed each day at different prices and different temperatures. For example, if the price is 60¢ a scoop and the temperature is 70°F, 10 gallons of ice cream are consumed. This set of values is highlighted in the table and each part of the figure. To graph a relationship among three variables, the value of one variable is held constant. Part (a) shows the relationship between price and consumption when temperature is held constant. One curve holds temperature at 90°F and the other at 70°F. Part (b) shows the relationship between temperature and consumption when the price is held constant. One curve holds the price at 60¢ a scoop and the other at 15¢ a scoop. Part (c) shows the relationship between temperature and price when consumption is held constant. One curve holds consumption at 10 gallons and the other at 7 gallons.

of ice cream varies with the temperature when ice cream costs 60¢ a scoop, and a second curve shows the relationship when ice cream costs 15¢ a scoop. For example, at 60¢ a scoop, 10 gallons are consumed when the temperature is 70°F and 20 gallons when the temperature is 90°F.

Figure 2.13(c) shows the combinations of temperature and price that result in a constant consumption of ice cream. One curve shows the combination that results in 10 gallons a day being consumed, and the other shows the combination that results

in 7 gallons a day being consumed. A high price and a high temperature lead to the same consumption as a lower price and a lower temperature. For example, 10 gallons of ice cream are consumed at 90°F and 90¢ a scoop, at 70°F and 60¢ a scoop, and at 50°F and 45¢ a scoop.

◆ With what you have learned about graphs, you can move forward with your study of economics. There are no graphs in this book that are more complicated than those that have been explained here.

SUMMARY

KEY POINTS

Graphing Data (pp. 20–24)

- Time-series graphs show trends, cycles, and other fluctuations in economic data.
- Scatter diagrams show the relationship between two variables. They show whether two variables are positively related, negatively related, or unrelated.
- Cross-section graphs show how variables change across the members of a population.

Graphs Used in Economic Models (pp. 24–27)

- Graphs are used to show relationships among variables in economic models.
- Relationships can be positive (an upward-sloping curve), negative (a downward-sloping curve), positive and then negative (have a maximum point), negative and then positive (have a minimum point), or unrelated (a horizontal or vertical curve).

The Slope of a Relationship (pp. 28–30)

- The slope of a relationship is calculated as the change in the value of the variable measured on the y-axis divided by the change in the value of the variable measured on the x-axis—that is, $\Delta y/\Delta x$.
- A straight line has a constant slope.
- A curved line has a varying slope. To calculate the slope of a curved line, we calculate the slope at a point or across an arc.

Graphing Relationships Among More Than Two Variables (pp. 30–31)

- To graph a relationship among more than two variables, we hold constant the values of all the variables except two.
- We then plot the value of one of the variables against the value of another.

KEY FIGURES

KEY TERMS

REVIEW QUIZ

- What are the three types of graphs used to show economic data?
- Give an example of a time-series graph.
- List three things that a time-series graph shows quickly and easily.
- Give three examples, different from those in the chapter, of scatter diagrams that show a positive relationship, a negative relationship, and no relationship.
- Draw some graphs to show the relationships between two variables:
  a. That move in the same direction.
  b. That move in opposite directions.
  c. That have a maximum.
  d. That have a minimum.
- Which of the relationships in the previous question is a positive relationship and which a negative relationship?
- What are the two ways of calculating the slope of a curved line?
- How do we graph a relationship among more than two variables?

PROBLEMS

The spreadsheet provides data on the U.S. economy: Column A is the year, column B is the inflation rate, column C is the interest rate, column D is the growth rate, and column E is the unemployment rate. Use this spreadsheet to answer problems 1, 2, 3, and 4.

	A	B	C	D	E
1	1980	13.5	11.9	–0.1	7.1
2	1981	10.3	14.2	0.8	7.6
3	1982	6.2	13.8	–1.1	9.7
4	1983	3.2	12.0	1.5	9.6
5	1984	4.3	12.7	2.8	7.5
6	1985	3.6	11.4	1.4	7.2
7	1986	1.9	9.0	1.2	7.0
8	1987	3.6	9.4	1.5	6.2
9	1988	4.1	9.7	1.9	5.5
10	1989	4.8	9.3	1.1	5.3
11	1990	5.4	9.3	1.2	5.5
12	1991	4.2	7.9	–0.9	6.7
13	1992	3.0	7.0	2.7	7.4
14	1993	3.0	5.8	2.3	6.8
15	1994	2.6	7.1	3.5	6.1
16	1995	2.8	6.6	2.0	5.6
17	1996	3.0	6.4	2.8	5.4
18	1997	2.3	6.4	3.8	4.9
19	1998	2.0	5.5	2.9	5.0

*1. a. Draw a time-series graph of the inflation rate.
   b. In which year(s) (i) was inflation highest, (ii) was inflation lowest, (iii) did it increase, (iv) did it decrease, (v) did it increase most, and (vi) did it decrease most?
   c. What was the main trend in inflation?

2. a. Draw a time-series graph of the interest rate.
   b. In which year(s) (i) was the interest rate highest, (ii) was it lowest, (iii) did it increase, (iv) did it decrease, (v) did it increase most, and (vi) did it decrease most?
   c. What was the main trend in the interest rate?

*3. Draw a scatter diagram to show the relationship between the inflation rate and the interest rate. Describe the relationship.

4. Draw a scatter diagram to show the relationship between the growth rate and the unemployment rate. Describe the relationship.

*5. Draw a graph to show the relationship between the two variables x and y:

x	0	1	2	3	4	5	6	7	8
y	0	1	4	9	16	25	36	49	64

   a. Is the relationship positive or negative?
   b. Does the slope of the relationship increase or decrease as the value of x increases?
   c. Think of some economic relationships that might be similar to this one.

6. Draw a graph that shows the relationship between two variables x and y:

x	0	1	2	3	4	5
y	50	48	44	32	16	0

   a. Is the relationship positive or negative?
   b. Does the slope of the relationship increase or decrease as the value of x increases?
   c. Think of some economic relationships that might be similar to this one.

*7. In problem 5, calculate the slope of the relationship between x and y when x equals 4.

8. In problem 6, calculate the slope of the relationship between x and y when x equals 3.

*9. In problem 5, calculate the slope of the relationship across the arc when x increases from 3 to 4.

10. In problem 6, calculate the slope of the relationship across the arc when x increases from 4 to 5.

*11. Calculate the slope of the relationship shown at point a in the following figure.

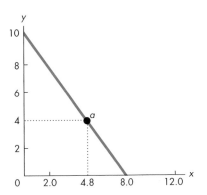

12. Calculate the slope of the relationship shown at point *a* in the following figure.

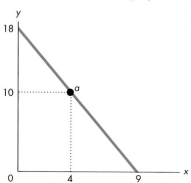

*13. Use the following figure to calculate the slope of the relationship:

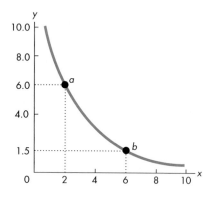

a.   At points *a* and *b*.
b.   Across the arc *ab*.

14. Use the following figure to calculate the slope of the relationship:

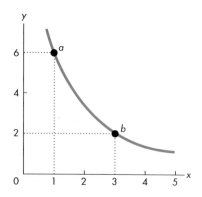

a.   At points *a* and *b*.
b.   Across the arc *ab*.

*15. The table gives the price of a balloon ride, the temperature, and the number of rides a day:

| Price | Balloon rides (number per day) | | |
(dollars per ride)	50°F	70°F	90°F
5.00	32	40	50
10.00	27	32	40
15.00	18	27	32
20.00	10	18	27

Draw graphs to show the relationship between
a.   The price and the number of rides, holding the temperature constant.
b.   The number of rides and temperature, holding the price constant.
c.   The temperature and price, holding the number of rides constant.

16. The table gives the price of an umbrella, rainfall, and the number of umbrellas purchased:

| Price | Umbrellas (number per day) | | |
(dollars per umbrella)	0 mm	2 mm	10 mm
10	7	8	12
20	4	7	8
30	2	4	7
40	1	2	4

Draw graphs to show the relationship between
a.   The price and the number of umbrellas purchased, holding rainfall constant.
b.   The number of umbrellas purchased and rainfall, holding the price constant.
c.   Rainfall and the price, holding the number of umbrellas purchased constant.

17. Use the link on the Parkin Web site and find Consumer Price Index (CPI) for the latest 12 months. Make a graph of the CPI. During the most recent month, is the CPI rising or falling? Is the rate of rise or fall increasing or decreasing?

18. Use the link on the Parkin Web site and find the unemployment rate for the latest 12 months. Graph the unemployment rate. During the most recent month, is it rising or falling? Is the rate of rise or fall increasing or decreasing?

Chapter 3

The Economic Problem

We live in a style that surprises our grandparents and would have astonished our great-grandparents. Most of us live in more spacious homes than they did. We eat more, grow taller, and are even born larger than they were. Video games, cellular phones, gene splices, and personal computers did not exist even 20 years ago. Economic growth has made us richer than our grandparents. And we are not alone in experiencing an expansion in the goods and services that we consume. Many nations around the world are not only sharing our experience: They are setting the pace. Before the recent Asia crisis, Hong Kong, Taiwan, Singapore, Korea, and China expanded at unheard-of rates. But economic growth does not liberate us from scarcity. Why not? Why, despite our immense wealth, must we still make choices and face costs? Why are there no "free lunches"? ◆ We see an incredible amount of specialization and trade in the world. Each one of us specializes in a particular job—as a lawyer, a car maker, a home maker. We have become so specialized that one farm worker can feed 100 people. Less than one sixth of the U.S. work force is employed in manufacturing. More than half of the work force is employed in wholesale and retail trade, banking and finance, government, and other services. Why do we specialize? How do we benefit from specialization and trade? ◆ Over many centuries, institutions and social arrangements have evolved that we take for granted. One of them is property rights and the political and legal system that protects them. Another is markets. Why have these social arrangements evolved? How do they increase production?

Making the Most of It

◆ These are the questions that we study in this chapter. We begin with the core economic problem: scarcity and choice and the concept of the production possibility frontier. We then learn about the central idea of economics—efficiency. We also discover how we can expand production by accumulating capital and by specializing and trading. ◆ What you will learn in this chapter is the foundation on which all economics is built. You will receive big dividends from a careful study of this material.

After studying this chapter, you will be able to:

■ Explain the fundamental economic problem

■ Define the production possibility frontier

■ Define and calculate opportunity cost

■ Explain the conditions in which resources are used efficiently

■ Explain how economic growth expands production possibilities

■ Explain how specialization and trade expand production possibilities

Resources and Wants

TWO FACTS DOMINATE OUR LIVES:

■ We have limited resources.
■ We have unlimited wants.

These two facts define **scarcity**, a condition in which the resources available are insufficient to satisfy people's wants.

Scarcity is a universal fact of life. It confronts each one of us individually, and it confronts our families, local communities, and nations.

The fundamental economic problem is to use our limited resources to produce the items that we value most highly. **Economics** is the study of the *choices* people make to cope with *scarcity*. It is the study of how we each individually try to get the most out of our own limited resources and of how in that endeavor, we interact with each other. Let's look a bit more closely at our limited resources and unlimited wants.

Limited Resources

The resources that can be used to produce goods and services are grouped into four categories:

1. Labor
2. Land
3. Capital
4. Entrepreneurship

Labor is the time and effort that we devote to producing goods and services. It includes the physical and mental work of people who make cars and cola, gum and glue, wallpaper and watering cans.

Land is the gifts of nature that we use to produce goods and services. It includes the air, the water, and the land surface as well as the minerals that lie beneath the surface of the earth.

Capital is the goods that we have produced and that we can now use to produce other goods and services. It includes interstate highways, buildings, dams and power projects, airports and jumbo jets, car production lines, shirt factories, and cookie shops.

Capital also includes **human capital**, which is the knowledge and skill that people obtain from education and on-the-job training. You are building human capital right now as you work on your economics course and other subjects. And your human capital will continue to grow when you get a full-time

job and become better at it. Human capital improves the *quality* of labor.

Entrepreneurship is the resource that organizes labor, land, and capital. Entrepreneurs make business decisions, bear the risks that arise from these decisions, and come up with new ideas about what, how, when, and where to produce.

Our limited resources are converted into goods and services by using the technologies available. These technologies are limited by our knowledge—our human capital—and by our other resources.

Unlimited Wants

Our wants are limited only by our imaginations and are effectively unlimited. We want food and drink, clothing, housing, education, and health care. We want some of these things so badly that we call them *necessities*. But we also want many other things. We want cars and airplanes, movie theaters and videos, popcorn and soda, Walkmans and tapes, books and magazines, restaurant meals, vacations at the beach and in the mountains, music and poetry, and instant telecommunication across the globe.

Some of these wants are less pressing than others, but they are all wants. We even want things that are technologically impossible today but about which we fantasize. We want to live longer and healthier lives. Some of us want to hitchhike the galaxy and be beamed around the universe.

Because our wants exceed our resources, we must make choices. We must rank our wants and decide which wants to satisfy and which to leave unsatisfied. We try to get the most out of our resources.

R E V I E W   Q U I Z

- What is scarcity?
- What is the fundamental economic problem?
- Can you provide a definition of economics?
- What are the resources that can be used to produce goods and services?
- How do we cope with the fact that our wants cannot be satisfied with the available resources?

We'll begin our study of the choices people make by looking at the limits to production and at a fundamental implication of choice—opportunity cost.

Resources, Production Possibilities, and Opportunity Cost

EVERY WORKING DAY, IN MINES, FACTORIES, shops, and offices and on farms and construction sites across the United States, 131 million people produce a vast variety of goods and services valued at around $30 billion. The quantities of goods and services that can be produced are limited by our available resources and by technology. That limit is described by the production possibility frontier.

The **production possibility frontier** (*PPF*) is the boundary between those combinations of goods and services that can be produced and those that cannot.

To illustrate the production possibility frontier in a graph, we focus our attention on two goods at a time. In focusing on two goods, we hold the quantities produced of all the other goods and services constant—a device called the *ceteris paribus* assumption. That is, we look at a *model* of the economy in which everything remains the same except for the production of the two goods we are currently considering.

Let's look at the production possibility frontier for two goods that most students buy: bottles of soda and blank audio tapes.

Production Possibility Frontier

The *production possibility frontier* for soda and tapes shows the limits to the production of these two goods, given the total resources available to produce them. Figure 3.1 shows this production possibility frontier. The table lists some combinations of the quantities of tapes and soda that can be produced given the resources available, and the figure graphs these combinations. The quantity of tapes produced is shown on the *x*-axis, and the quantity of soda produced is shown on the *y*-axis. (The numbers are hypothetical.)

Because the *PPF* shows the *limits* to production, we cannot attain the points outside the frontier. They are points that describe wants that cannot be satisfied. We can produce at all the points *inside* the *PPF* and *on* the *PPF*. They are attainable points.

Suppose that in a typical month, 4 million tapes and 5 million bottles of soda are produced. Figure 3.1 shows this combination as point *e* and as possibility *e* in the table. Figure 3.1 also shows other production possibilities. For example, we might stop

FIGURE 3.1
Production Possibility Frontier

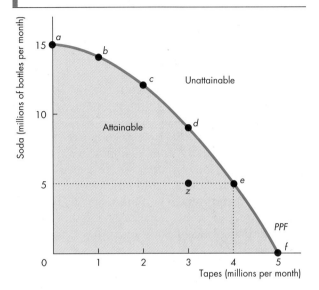

Possibility	Tapes (millions per month)		Soda (millions of bottles per month)
a	0	and	15
b	1	and	14
c	2	and	12
d	3	and	9
e	4	and	5
f	5	and	0

The table lists six points on the production possibility frontier for tapes and soda. Row *a* tells us that if we produce no tapes, the maximum quantity of soda we can produce is 15 million bottles a month. The rows of the table are graphed as points *a, b, c, d, e,* and *f* in the figure. The line passing through these points is the production possibility frontier (*PPF*). It separates the attainable from the unattainable. We can produce at any point inside the orange area or on the frontier. Points outside the frontier are unattainable. Points inside the frontier such as point z are inefficient because it is possible to use the available resources to produce more of either or both goods.

producing tapes and move all the people who produce them into bottling soda. This case is shown as point *a* in the figure and possibility *a* in the table.

The quantity of soda produced increases to 15 million bottles a month, and tape production dries up. Alternatively, we might close down the bottling plants and switch all the resources into producing tapes. In this situation, we produce 5 million tapes a month. This case is shown as point *f* in the figure and possibility *f* in the table.

Production Efficiency

We achieve **production efficiency** if we cannot produce more of one good without producing less of some other good. When production is efficient, we are at a point *on* the *PPF*. If we are at a point *inside* the *PPF*, such as point *z*, production is *inefficient* because we have some *unused* resources or we have some *misallocated* resources or both.

Resources are unused when they are idle but could be working. For example, we might leave some of the bottling plants idle or some workers might be unemployed.

Resources are *misallocated* when they are assigned to tasks for which they are not the best match. For example, we might assign skilled bottling machine operators to work in a tape factory and skilled tape makers to work in a bottling plant. We could get more tapes *and* more bottles of soda from these same workers if we reassigned them to the tasks that more closely match their skills.

If we produce at a point inside the *PPF* such as *z*, we can use our resources more efficiently to produce more tapes, more soda, or more of *both* tapes and soda. But if we produce at a point *on* the *PPF*, we are using our resources efficiently and we can produce more of one good only if we produce less of the other. We face a *tradeoff.*

Tradeoff

On the production possibility frontier, every choice involves a **tradeoff**—we must give up something to get something else. On the *PPF* in Fig. 3.1, we must give up some soda to get more tapes (or give up some tapes to get more soda).

Tradeoffs arise in every imaginable real-world situation. At any given point in time, we have a fixed amount of labor, land, capital, and entrepreneurship. By using our available technologies, we can employ these resources to produce goods and services. But we are limited in what we can produce. This limit defines a boundary between what we can attain and what we

cannot attain. This boundary is the real-world's production possibility frontier, and it defines the tradeoffs that we must make. On our real-world *PPF*, we can produce more of any one good or service only if we produce less of some other goods or services.

When doctors say we must spend more on AIDS and cancer research, they are suggesting a tradeoff: more medical research for less of some other things. When the President says he wants to spend more on education and health care, he is suggesting a tradeoff: more education and health care for less national defense or less private spending (because of higher taxes). When your parents say that you should study more, they are suggesting a tradeoff: more study time for less leisure or less sleep. When an environmental group argues for less logging, it is suggesting a tradeoff: greater conservation of endangered wildlife for less paper.

All tradeoffs involve a cost—an opportunity cost.

Opportunity Cost

The **opportunity cost** of an action is the highest-valued alternative forgone. We can make the concept of opportunity cost more precise by using the production possibility frontier. Along the frontier, there are only two goods, so there is only one alternative forgone—some quantity of the other good. Given our current resources and technology, we can produce more tapes only if we produce fewer bottles of soda. The opportunity cost of producing an additional tape is the number of bottles of soda we must forgo. Similarly, the opportunity cost of producing an additional bottle of soda is the quantity of tapes we must forgo.

For example, at point *c* in Fig. 3.1, we produce fewer tapes and more bottles of soda than we do at point *d*. If we choose point *d* over point *c*, the additional 1 million tapes *cost* 3 million bottles of soda. One tape costs 3 bottles of soda.

We can also work out the opportunity cost of choosing point *c* over point *d* in Fig. 3.1. If we move from point *d* to point *c*, the quantity of soda produced increases by 3 million bottles and the quantity of tapes produced decreases by 1 million. So if we choose point *c* over point *d*, the additional 3 million bottles of soda *cost* 1 million tapes. One bottle of soda costs 1/3 of a tape.

Opportunity Cost Is a Ratio   Opportunity cost is a ratio. It is the decrease in the quantity produced of one good divided by the increase in the quantity produced of another good as we move along the production possibility frontier.

Because opportunity cost is a ratio, the opportunity cost of producing soda is equal to the *inverse* of the opportunity cost of producing tapes. Check this proposition by returning to the calculations we've just worked through. When we move along the *PPF* from *c* to *d*, the opportunity cost of a tape is 3 bottles of soda. The inverse of 3 is 1/3, so if we decrease the production of tapes and increase the production of soda by moving from *d* to *c*, the opportunity cost of a bottle of soda must be 1/3 of a tape. You can check that this number is correct. If we move from *d* to *c*, we produce 3 million more bottles of soda and 1 million fewer tapes. Because 3 million bottles cost 1 million tapes, the opportunity cost of 1 bottle of soda is 1/3 of a tape.

Increasing Opportunity Cost The opportunity cost of a tape increases as the quantity of tapes produced increases. Also, the opportunity cost of soda increases as the quantity of soda produced increases. This phenomenon of increasing opportunity cost is reflected in the *shape* of the *PPF*—it is bowed outward.

When a large quantity of soda and a small quantity of tapes are produced—between points *a* and *b* in Fig. 3.1—the frontier has a gentle slope. A given increase in the quantity of tapes *costs* a small decrease in the quantity of soda, so the opportunity cost of a tape is a small amount of soda.

When a large quantity of tapes and a small quantity of soda are produced—between points *e* and *f* in Fig. 3.1—the frontier is steep. A given increase in the quantity of tapes *costs* a large decrease in the quantity of soda, so the opportunity cost of a tape is a large amount of soda.

The production possibility frontier is bowed outward because resources are not all equally productive in all activities. Production workers with many years of experience working for PepsiCo are very good at producing soda but not very good at making tapes. So if we move these people from PepsiCo to 3M, we get a small increase in the quantity of tapes but a large decrease in the quantity of soda.

Similarly, plastics engineers and production workers who have spent many years working for 3M are good at producing tapes but not so good at bottling soda. So if we move these people from 3M to PepsiCo, we get a small increase in the quantity of soda but a large decrease in the quantity of tapes. The more we try to produce of either good, the less productive are the additional resources we use to

produce that good and the larger is the opportunity cost of a unit of that good.

Increasing Opportunity Costs Are Everywhere Just about every activity that you can think of is one with an *increasing* opportunity cost. Two examples are the production of food and the production of health-care services. We allocate the most skillful farmers and the most fertile land to the production of food. And we allocate the best doctors and least fertile land to the production of health-care services. If we shift fertile land and tractors away from farming to hospitals and ambulances and ask farmers to become hospital porters, the production of food drops drastically and the increase in the production of health-care services is small. The opportunity cost of a unit of health-care services rises. Similarly, if we shift our resources away from health care toward farming, we must use more doctors and nurses as farmers and more hospitals as hydroponic tomato factories. The decrease in the production of health-care services is large, but the increase in food production is small. The opportunity cost of a unit of food rises.

This example is extreme and unlikely, but these same considerations apply to any pair of goods that you can imagine: housing and diamonds, wheelchairs and golf carts, pet food and breakfast cereals.

R E V I E W   Q U I Z

- How does the production possibility frontier illustrate scarcity?
- How does the production possibility frontier illustrate production efficiency?
- How does the production possibility frontier show that every choice involves a tradeoff?
- How does the production possibility frontier illustrate opportunity cost?
- Why is opportunity cost a ratio?
- Why does the *PPF* for most goods bow outward so that opportunity cost increases as the quantity produced of a good increases?

We've seen that production possibilities are limited by the production possibility frontier. And we've seen that production on the *PPF* is efficient. But there are many possible quantities we can produce on the *PPF*. How do we choose among them? How do we know which point on the frontier is the best one?

Using Resources Efficiently

How do we decide whether to spend more on AIDS and cancer research? Whether to vote for an education and health-care package or a tax cut? Whether to join an environmental group and press for a greater conservation of endangered wildlife?

These are big questions that have enormous consequences. But the essence of the answer can be seen by thinking about the simpler question: How do we decide how many tapes and how many bottles of soda to produce?

We decide by calculating and comparing two numbers:

- Marginal cost
- Marginal benefit

Marginal Cost

Marginal cost is the opportunity cost of producing *one more unit* of a good or service. You've seen how we can calculate opportunity cost as we move along the production possibility frontier. The marginal cost of a tape is the opportunity cost of *one* tape—the quantity of soda that must be given up to get one more tape—as we move along the *PPF*.

Figure 3.2 illustrates the marginal cost of a tape. If all the available resources are used to produce soda, 15 million bottles of soda and no tapes are produced. If we now decide to produce 1 million tapes, how much soda do we have to give up? You can see the answer in Fig. 3.2(a). To produce 1 million more tapes, we move from *a* to *b* and the quantity of soda decreases by 1 million bottles to 14 million a month. So the opportunity cost of the first 1 million tapes is 1 million bottles of soda.

If we decide to increase the production of tapes to 2 million, how much soda must we give up? This time, we move from *b* to *c* and the quantity of soda decreases by 2 million bottles. So the second million tapes cost 2 million bottles of soda.

You can repeat this calculation for an increase in the quantity of tapes produced from 2 million to 3 million, then to 4 million, and finally to 5 million. Figure 3.2(a) shows these opportunity costs as a series of steps. Each additional million tapes costs more bottles of soda than the preceding million did.

We've just calculated the opportunity cost of tapes in blocks of 1 million at a time and generated

Opportunity Cost and Marginal Cost

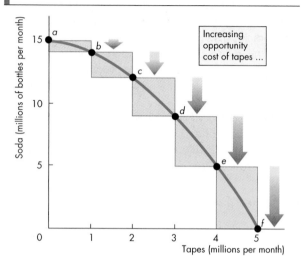

(a) *PPF* **and opportunity cost**

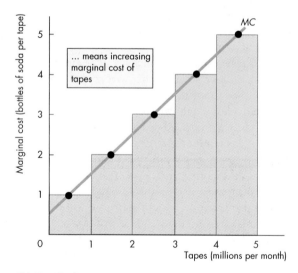

(b) Marginal cost

Opportunity cost is measured along the *PPF* in part (a). If the production of tapes increases from zero to 1 million, the opportunity cost of the first 1 million tapes is 1 million bottles of soda. If the production of tapes increases from 1 million to 2 million, the opportunity cost of the second 1 million tapes is 2 million bottles of soda. The opportunity cost of tapes increases as the production of tapes increases. Marginal cost is the opportunity cost of producing one more unit. Part (b) shows the marginal cost of a tape as the *MC* curve.

the steps in Fig. 3.2(a). If we now calculate the opportunity cost of tapes one at a time, we obtain the *marginal cost* of a tape. In Fig. 3.2(b), the line labeled *MC* shows the marginal cost of a tape. The marginal cost of each additional tape in terms of forgone soda increases, so the marginal cost curve slopes upward.

Marginal Benefit

To use our resources efficiently, we must compare the marginal cost of a tape with its marginal benefit. **Marginal benefit** is the benefit that a person receives from consuming one more unit of a good or service. The marginal benefit from a good or service is measured as the maximum amount that a person is willing to pay for one more unit of it. It is a general principle that the more we have of any good or service, the smaller is our marginal benefit from it—the principle of *decreasing marginal benefit*.

To understand the principle of decreasing marginal benefit, think about your own marginal benefit from tapes. If tapes are very hard to come by and you can buy only one or two a year, you might be willing to pay a high price to get one more tape. But if tapes are readily available and you have as many as you can use, you are willing to pay almost nothing for yet one more tape.

In everyday life, we think of prices as money—as dollars per tape. But you have just been thinking about cost as opportunity cost, which is not a dollar cost but a cost in terms of a forgone alternative. You can also think about prices in the same terms. The price you pay for something is not the number of dollars you give up, but the goods and services that you would have bought with those dollars.

To see this idea more clearly, let's continue with the example we used to study the *PPF* and opportunity cost: tapes and soda. The marginal benefit from a tape can be expressed as the number of bottles of soda that a person is willing to forgo to get a tape. Figure 3.3 illustrates the marginal benefit from tapes. Marginal benefit is the way people feel about different quantities of goods, and we can't derive it from the *PPF*. The numbers in Fig. 3.3 are *assumed*.

In row *a*, 0.5 million tapes a month are available and at that quantity, people are willing to pay 5 bottles of soda for a tape. As the quantity of tapes available increases, the amount that people are willing to pay for a tape falls. When 4.5 million tapes a month are available, people are willing to pay only 1 bottle of soda for a tape.

FIGURE **3.3**

Marginal Benefit

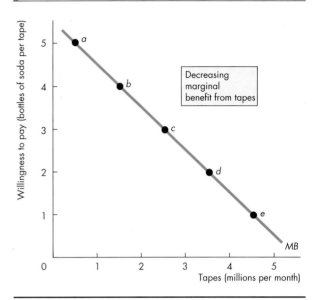

Possibility	Tapes (millions per month)	Willingness to pay (bottles per tape)
a	0.5	5
b	1.5	4
c	2.5	3
d	3.5	2
e	4.5	1

The fewer the number of tapes available, the more soda people are willing to give up to get an additional tape. If only 0.5 million tapes a month are available, people are willing to pay 5 bottles of soda for a tape. But if 4.5 million tapes a month are available, people will pay only 1 bottle of soda for a tape. Decreasing marginal benefit is a universal feature of people's preferences.

The marginal benefit from a tape and the opportunity cost of a tape are both measured in bottles of soda. But they are not the same concept. The *opportunity cost* of a tape is the amount of soda that people *must forgo* to get another tape. The *marginal benefit* from a tape is the amount of soda that people *are willing to forgo* to get another tape.

You now know how to calculate marginal cost and marginal benefit. Let's use these concepts to discover the efficient quantity of tapes to produce.

Efficient Use of Resources

Resource use is **efficient** when we produce the goods and services that we value most highly. That is, when we are using our resources efficiently, we cannot produce more of any good without giving up something that we value even more highly.

We always choose *at the margin*. We compare marginal cost and marginal benefit. If the marginal benefit from a good exceeds the marginal cost of the good, we increase production of that good. If marginal cost exceeds marginal benefit, we decrease production of the good. And if marginal benefit equals marginal cost, we stick with the current production.

This principle is just like the decisions you make when you go shopping. You have $10 to spend and are thinking about buying a CD or a box of floppy disks. You figure that you will get more value from the CD than from the floppy disks, so you spend your $10 on the CD. You have allocated scarce resources to their highest-valued use. The marginal benefit from a CD is greater than (or equal to) its marginal cost, the box of floppy disks. The marginal benefit from a box of floppy disks is less than its marginal cost. No matter what the good or service, if you can afford it and you think it is worth the price, you buy it. If you think it not worth its price, you pass it up.

We can illustrate an efficient use of resources by continuing to use the example of soda and tapes. Figure 3.4 shows the marginal cost and marginal benefit of tapes. Suppose we produce 1.5 million tapes a month. The marginal cost of a tape is 2 bottles of soda. But the marginal benefit from a tape is 4 bottles of soda. Because someone values an additional tape more highly than it costs to produce, we can get more value from our resources by moving some of them out of soda production and into tape production.

Now suppose we produce 3.5 million tapes a month. The marginal cost of a tape is now 4 bottles of soda. But the marginal benefit from a tape is only 2 bottles of soda. Because an additional tape costs more to produce than anyone thinks it is worth, we can get more value from our resources by moving some of them away from tape production and into soda production.

But suppose we produce 2.5 million tapes a month. Marginal cost and marginal benefit are now equal at 3 bottles of soda. This allocation of resources between tapes and soda is efficient. If more tapes are produced, the forgone soda is worth more than the additional tapes. If fewer tapes are produced, the forgone tapes are worth more than the additional soda.

FIGURE 3.4
Efficient Use of Resources

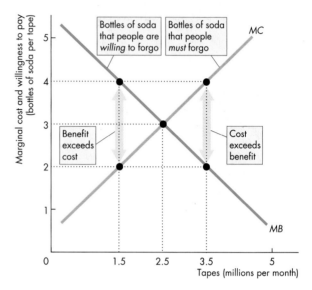

The greater the quantity of tapes produced, the smaller is the marginal benefit (*MB*) from a tape—the fewer bottles of soda people are willing to give up to get an additional tape. But the greater the quantity of tapes produced, the greater is the marginal cost (*MC*) of a tape—the more bottles of soda people must give up to get an additional tape. When marginal benefit equals marginal cost, resources are being used efficiently.

R E V I E W   Q U I Z

- What is marginal cost and how is it measured?
- What is the relationship between marginal cost and the production possibility frontier?
- What is marginal benefit and how is it measured?
- How does the marginal benefit from a good change as the quantity of that good increases? Why?
- What conditions must be satisfied if resources are used efficiently? Why?

You now understand the limits to production and the conditions under which resources are used efficiently. Your next task is to study the expansion of production possibilities.

Economic Growth

DURING THE PAST 30 YEARS, PRODUCTION IN THE United States has expanded by 80 percent. Such an expansion of production is called **economic growth**. Can economic growth enable us to overcome scarcity and avoid opportunity cost? You are going to see that economic growth does not overcome scarcity and avoid opportunity cost. You are also going to see that the faster we make production grow, the greater is the opportunity cost of economic growth.

The Cost of Economic Growth

Two key factors influence economic growth: technological change and capital accumulation. **Technological change** is the development of new goods and of better ways of producing goods and services. **Capital accumulation** is the growth of capital resources.

As a consequence of technological change and capital accumulation, we have an enormous quantity of cars that enable us to produce more transportation than when we had only horses and carriages; we have satellites that make global communications possible on a scale that is much larger than that produced by the earlier cable technology. But new technologies and new capital have an opportunity cost. To use resources in research and development and to produce new capital, we must decrease our production of consumption goods and services. Let's look at this opportunity cost.

Instead of studying the *PPF* of tapes and soda, we'll hold the quantity of soda produced constant and examine the *PPF* for tapes and tape-making machines. Figure 3.5 shows this *PPF* as the blue curve *abc*. If we devote no resources to producing tape-making machines, we produce at point *a*. If we produce 3 million tapes a month, we can produce 6 tape-making machines at point *b*. If we produce no tapes, we can produce 10 tape-making machines a month at point *c*.

The amount by which our production possibilities expand depends on the resources we devote to technological change and capital accumulation. If we devote no resources to this activity (point *a*), the frontier remains at *abc*—the blue curve in Fig. 3.5. If we cut the current production of tapes and produce 6 machines a month (point *b*), then in the future, we'll have more capital and our *PPF* rotates outward to the

FIGURE **3.5**

Economic Growth

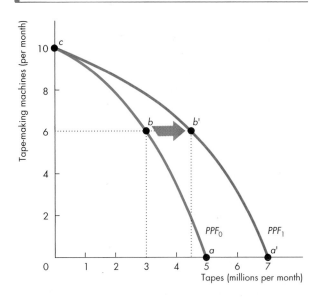

PPF_0 shows the limits to the production of tapes and tape-making equipment, with the production of all other goods and services remaining constant. If we devote no resources to producing tape-making machines and produce 5 million tapes a month, we remain stuck at point *a*. But if we decrease tape production to 3 million a month and produce 6 tape-making machines a month, at point *b*, our production possibilities will expand. After a year, the production possibility frontier shifts outward to PPF_1 and we can produce at point *b'*, a point outside the original *PPF*. We can shift the *PPF* outward, but we cannot avoid opportunity cost. The opportunity cost of producing more tapes in the future is fewer tapes today.

position shown by the red curve. The fewer resources we devote to producing tapes and the more resources we devote to producing machines, the greater is the expansion of our production possibilities.

Economic growth is not free. To make it happen, we devote resources to producing new machines and fewer resources to producing tapes. In Fig. 3.5, we move from *a* to *b*. There is no free lunch. The opportunity cost of more tapes in the future is fewer tapes today. Also, economic growth is no magic formula for abolishing scarcity. On the new production possibility frontier, we continue to face opportunity costs.

The ideas about economic growth that we have explored in the setting of the audio tape industry also apply to nations. Let's look at two examples.

Economic Growth in the United States and Hong Kong

If as a nation we devote all our resources to producing consumer goods and none to research and capital accumulation, our production possibilities in the future will be the same as they are today. To expand our production possibilities in the future, we must devote fewer resources to producing consumption goods and some resources to accumulating capital and developing technologies so we can produce more consumption goods in the future. The decrease in today's consumption is the opportunity cost of an increase in future consumption.

The experiences of the United States and Hong Kong make a striking example of the effects of our choices on the rate of economic growth. In 1960, the production possibilities per person in the United States were more than four times those in Hong Kong (see Fig. 3.6). The United States devoted one fifth of its resources to accumulating capital and the other four fifths to consumption. In 1960, the United States was at point *a* on its *PPF*. Hong Kong devoted one third of its resources to accumulating capital and two thirds to consumption. In 1960, Hong Kong was at point *a* on its *PPF*.

Since 1960, both countries have experienced economic growth, but growth in Hong Kong has been more rapid than in the United States. Because Hong Kong devoted a bigger fraction of its resources to accumulating capital, its production possibilities have expanded more quickly.

In 1998, the *PPF* per person in the United States and Hong Kong were similar. If Hong Kong continues to devote more resources to accumulating capital than we do (at point *b* on its 1998 *PPF*), it will continue to grow more rapidly than the United States and its frontier will move out beyond our own. But if Hong Kong increases consumption and decreases capital accumulation (moving to point *c* on its 1998 *PPF*), then its rate of economic growth will slow.

The United States is typical of the rich industrial countries, which include the United States, Western Europe, and Japan. Hong Kong is typical of the fast-growing Asian economies, which include Taiwan, Thailand, South Korea, and China. Growth in these countries has slowed during the past two years, but before the slowdown, these countries expanded production by between 5 percent and almost 10 percent a year. If these high growth rates are restored, these other countries will eventually close the gap on the United States as Hong Kong has done.

FIGURE 3.6

Economic Growth in the United States and Hong Kong

In 1960, the production possibilities per person in the United States were much larger than those in Hong Kong. But Hong Kong devoted more of its resources to accumulating capital than did the United States, so its production possibility frontier has shifted outward more quickly than has that of the United States. In 1998, the two production possibilities per person were similar.

- What are the two key factors that generate economic growth?
- How does economic growth influence the production possibility frontier?
- What is the opportunity cost of economic growth?
- Why has Hong Kong experienced faster economic growth than the United States has?

Next, we're going to study another way we expand our production possibilities—the amazing fact that buyers and sellers gain from specialization and trade.

Gains from Trade

PEOPLE CAN PRODUCE FOR THEMSELVES ALL THE goods that they consume, or they can concentrate on producing one good (or perhaps a few goods) and then trade with others—exchange some of their own goods for those of others. Concentrating on the production of only one good or a few goods is called *specialization*. We are going to discover how people gain by specializing in the production of the good in which they have a *comparative advantage* and trading with each other.

Comparative Advantage

A person has a **comparative advantage** in an activity if that person can perform the activity at a lower opportunity cost than anyone else. Differences in opportunity costs arise from differences in individual abilities and from differences in the characteristics of other resources.

No one excels at everything. One person is an outstanding pitcher but a poor catcher; another person is a brilliant lawyer but a poor teacher. In almost all human endeavors, what one person does easily, someone else finds difficult. The same applies to land and capital. One plot of land is fertile but has no mineral deposits; another plot of land has outstanding views but is infertile. One machine has great precision but is difficult to operate; another machine is fast but often breaks down.

Although no one excels at everything, some people excel and can outperform others in many activities. But such a person does not have a *comparative* advantage in every activity. For example, John Grisham is a better lawyer than most people. But he is an even better writer of fast-paced thrillers. His *comparative* advantage is in writing.

Because people's abilities and the quality of their resources differ, they have different opportunity costs of producing various goods. Such differences give rise to comparative advantage. Let's explore the idea of comparative advantage by looking at two audio cassette factories, one operated by Tom and the other operated by Nancy.

Tom's Factory   To simplify the story quite a lot, suppose that audio cassettes have just two components: a length of tape and a plastic case. Tom has two production lines, one for tape and one for cases.

FIGURE **3.7**

Production Possibilities in Tom's Factory

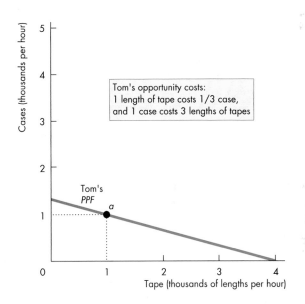

Tom can produce tape and cassette cases along the production possibility frontier *PPF*. For Tom, the opportunity cost of 1 length of tape is $1/3$ of a case and the opportunity cost of 1 case is 3 lengths of tape. If Tom produces at point *a*, he can produce 1,000 cassette cases and 1,000 lengths of tape an hour.

Figure 3.7 shows Tom's production possibility frontier for tape and cases. It tells us that if Tom uses all his resources to make tape, he can produce 4,000 lengths of tape an hour. The *PPF* in Fig. 3.7 also tells us that if Tom uses all his resources to make cases, he can produce 1,333 cases an hour. But to produce cases, Tom must decrease his production of tape. For each 1 case produced, he must decrease his production of tape by 3 lengths.

Tom's opportunity cost of producing 1 case is 3 lengths of tape.

Similarly, if Tom wants to increase his production of tape, he must decrease his production of cases. For each 1,000 lengths of tape produced, he must decrease his production of cases by 333. So

Tom's opportunity cost of producing 1 length of tape is 0.333 case.

Nancy's Factory The other factory, operated by Nancy, can also produce cases and tape. But Nancy's factory has machines that are custom made for case production, so they are more suitable for producing cases than tape. Also, Nancy's work force is more skilled in making cases.

This difference between the two factories means that Nancy's production possibility frontier—shown along with Tom's *PPF* in Fig. 3.8—is different from Tom's. If Nancy uses all her resources to make tape, she can produce 1,333 lengths an hour. If she uses all her resources to make cases, she can produce 4,000 an hour. To produce tape, Nancy must decrease her production of cases. For each 1,000 additional lengths of tape produced, she must decrease her production of cases by 3,000.

Nancy's opportunity cost of producing 1 length of tape is 3 cases.

Similarly, if Nancy wants to increase her production of cases, she must decrease her production of tape. For each 1,000 additional cases produced, she must decrease her production of tape by 333 lengths. So

Nancy's opportunity cost of producing 1 case is 0.333 length of tape.

Suppose that Tom and Nancy produce both tapes and cases and that each produces 1,000 lengths of tape and 1,000 cases—1,000 cassettes—an hour. That is, each produces at point *a* on their production possibility frontiers. Total production is 2,000 cassettes an hour.

In which of the two goods does Nancy have a comparative advantage? Recall that comparative advantage is a situation in which one person's opportunity cost of producing a good is lower than another person's opportunity cost of producing that same good. Nancy has a comparative advantage in producing cases. Nancy's opportunity cost of a case is 0.333 length of tape, whereas Tom's is 3 lengths of tape.

You can see her comparative advantage by looking at the production possibility frontiers for Nancy and Tom in Fig. 3.8. Nancy's production possibility frontier is steeper than Tom's. To produce one more case, Nancy gives up less tape than Tom. Hence Nancy's opportunity cost of a case is less than Tom's. This means that Nancy has a comparative advantage in producing cases.

FIGURE 3.8

The Gains from Trade

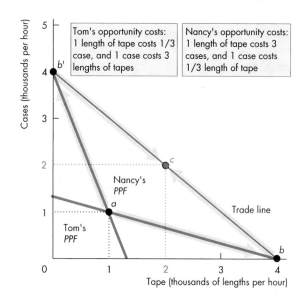

Tom and Nancy each produce at point *a* on their respective *PPFs*. Nancy has a comparative advantage in cases, and Tom has a comparative advantage in tape. If Nancy specializes in cases, she produces at point *b'* on her *PPF*. If Tom specializes in tape, he produces at point *b* on his *PPF*. They then exchange cases for tape along the red "Trade line." Nancy buys tape from Tom for less than her opportunity cost of producing it, and Tom buys cases from Nancy for less than his opportunity cost of producing them. Each goes to point *c*—a point outside his or her *PPF*—where each has 2,000 cassettes an hour. Tom and Nancy double their rate of production with no change in resources.

Tom's comparative advantage is in producing tape. His production possibility frontier is less steep than Nancy's. This means that Tom gives up fewer cases to produce one more length of tape than Nancy does. Tom's opportunity cost of producing a length of tape is 0.333 case, which is less than Nancy's 3 cases. So Tom has a comparative advantage in producing tape.

Because Nancy has a comparative advantage in cases and Tom in tape, they can both gain from specialization and exchange.

Achieving the Gains from Trade

If Tom, who has a comparative advantage in tape production, puts all his resources into that activity, he can produce 4,000 lengths of tape an hour—point *b* on his *PPF*. If Nancy, who has a comparative advantage in producing cases, puts all her resources into that activity, she can produce 4,000 cases an hour—point *b* on her *PPF*. By specializing, Tom and Nancy together can produce 4,000 cases and 4,000 lengths of tape an hour, double their total production without specialization. By specialization and exchange, Tom and Nancy can get *outside* their production possibility frontiers.

To achieve the gains from specialization, Tom and Nancy must trade with each other. Suppose they agree to the following deal: Each hour, Nancy produces 4,000 cases, Tom produces 4,000 lengths of tape, and Nancy supplies Tom with 2,000 cases in exchange for 2,000 lengths of tape. With this deal in place, Tom and Nancy move along the red "Trade line" to point *c*. At this point, each produces 2,000 cassettes an hour—double their previous production rate. These are the gains from specialization and trade.

Both parties to the trade share the gains. Nancy, who can produce tape at an opportunity cost of 3 cases per length of tape, can buy tape from Tom for a price of 1 case per length. Tom, who can produce cases at an opportunity cost of 3 lengths of tape per case, can buy cases from Nancy at a price of 1 length per case. Nancy gets her tape more cheaply, and Tom gets his cases more cheaply.

Absolute Advantage

Suppose that Nancy invents and patents a production process that makes her *four* times as productive as she was before in the production of both cases and tape. With her new technology, Nancy can produce 16,000 cases an hour (4 times the original 4,000) if she puts all her resources into that activity. Alternatively, she can produce 5,332 lengths of tape (4 times the original 1,333) if she puts all her resources into that activity. Nancy now has an **absolute advantage** in producing *both* goods—using the same quantity of resources as Tom, she can produce more of both goods than Tom can produce.

But Nancy does not have a *comparative* advantage in both goods. She can produce four times as much of *both* goods as before, but her *opportunity cost* of

1 length of tape is still 3 cases. And this opportunity cost is higher than Tom's. So Nancy can still get tape at a lower cost by exchanging cases for tape with Tom.

A key point to recognize is that it is *not* possible for *anyone* to have a comparative advantage in *everything*. So gains from specialization and trade are always available when opportunity costs diverge.

Dynamic Comparative Advantage

At any given point in time, the available resources and technologies determine the comparative advantages that individuals and nations have. But just by repeatedly producing a particular good or service, people become more productive in that activity, a phenomenon called **learning-by-doing**. Learning-by-doing is the basis of *dynamic* comparative advantage. **Dynamic comparative advantage** is a comparative advantage that a person (or country) possesses as a result of having specialized in a particular activity and, as a result of learning-by-doing, having become the producer with the lowest opportunity cost.

Hong Kong and Singapore are examples of countries that have pursued dynamic comparative advantage vigorously. They have developed industries in which initially they did not have a comparative advantage but, through learning-by-doing, became low opportunity cost producers in those industries. A specific example is the decision to develop a genetic engineering industry in Singapore. Singapore probably did not have a comparative advantage in genetic engineering initially. But it might develop one as its scientists and production workers become more skilled in this activity.

R E V I E W   Q U I Z

- What gives a person a comparative advantage in producing a good?
- Why is not possible for anyone to have a comparative advantage at everything?
- What are the gains from specialization and trade?
- Explain the source of the gains from specialization and trade.
- Distinguish between comparative advantage and absolute advantage.
- What is dynamic comparative advantage and how does it arise?

The Market Economy

INDIVIDUALS AND COUNTRIES GAIN BY SPECIALIZ-
ing in the production of those goods and services in
which they have a comparative advantage and trading
with each other. This source of economic wealth was
identified by Adam Smith in his *Wealth of Nations,*
published in 1776—see pp. 56–57.

To enable billions of people who specialize in
producing millions of different goods and services to
reap these gains, trade must be organized. But trade
need not be *planned* or *managed* by a central authority. In fact, when such an arrangement has been tried,
as it was for 60 years in Russia, the result has been
less than dazzling.

Trade is organized by using social institutions.
The two key ones are:

- Property rights
- Markets

Property Rights

Property rights are social arrangements that govern the ownership, use, and disposal of resources,
goods, and services. *Real property* includes land and
buildings—the things we call property in ordinary
speech—and durable goods such as plant and equipment. *Financial property* includes stocks and bonds
and money in the bank. *Intellectual property* is the
intangible product of creative effort. This type of
property includes books, music, computer programs,
and inventions of all kinds and is protected by copyrights and patents.

If property rights are not enforced, the incentive
to specialize and produce the goods in which each
person has a comparative advantage is weakened, and
some of the potential gains from specialization and
trade are lost. If people can easily steal the production
of others, then time, energy, and resources are devoted
not to production, but to protecting possessions.

Establishing property rights is one of the greatest
challenges facing Russia and other Eastern European
nations as they seek to develop market economies.
Even in countries where property rights are well
established, such as the United States, protecting
intellectual property is proving to be a challenge in
the face of modern technologies that make it relatively easy to copy audio and video material, computer programs, and books.

Markets

In ordinary speech, the word *market* means a place
where people buy and sell goods such as fish, meat,
fruits, and vegetables. In economics, a *market* has a
more general meaning. A **market** is any arrangement that enables buyers and sellers to get information and to do business with each other. An example
is the market in which oil is bought and sold—the
world oil market. The world oil market is not a place.
It is the network of oil producers, oil users, whole-
salers, and brokers who buy and sell. In the world oil
market, decision makers do not meet physically. They
make deals throughout the world by telephone, fax,
and direct computer link.

In the example we've just studied, Nancy and
Tom get together and do a deal. They agree to
exchange cassette cases for lengths of tape. But in a
market economy, Nancy sells cassette cases to a dealer
in plastic products and buys lengths of tape from a
dealer in electronic recording media. Similarly, Tom
buys cassette cases and sells lengths of tape in these
same two markets. Tom can use Nancy's cases and
Nancy can use Tom's lengths of tape and yet be
unaware of each other's existence.

Circular Flows in the Market Economy

Figure 3.9 identifies two types of markets: goods
markets and resource markets. *Goods markets* are
those in which goods and services are bought and
sold. *Resource markets* are those in which productive
resources are bought and sold.

Households decide how much of their labor,
land, capital, and entrepreneurship to sell or rent in
resource markets. They receive incomes in the form
of wages, rent, interest, and profit. Households also
decide how to spend their incomes on goods and services produced by firms. Firms decide the quantities
of resources to hire, how to use them to produce
goods and services, what goods and services to
produce, and in what quantities.

Figure 3.9 shows the flows that result from these
decisions by households and firms. The red flows
are the resources that go from households through
resource markets to firms and the goods and services
that go from firms through goods markets to households. The green flows in the opposite direction are
the payments made in exchange for these items.

How do markets coordinate all these decisions?

FIGURE 3.9

Circular Flows in the Market Economy

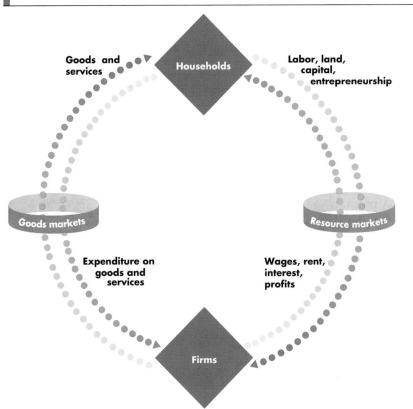

Households and firms make economic choices. Households choose the quantities of labor, land, capital, and entrepreneurship to sell or rent to firms in exchange for wages, rent, interest, and profits. Households also choose how to spend their incomes on the various types of goods and services available. Firms choose the quantities of resources to hire and the quantities of the various goods and services to produce. Goods markets and resource markets coordinate these choices of households and firms. Resources and goods flow clockwise (red), and money payments flow counterclockwise (green).

Coordinating Decisions

Markets coordinate individual decisions through price adjustments. To see how, think about your local market for hamburgers. Suppose that some people who want to buy hamburgers are not able to do so. To make the choices of buyers and sellers compatible, buyers must scale down their appetites or more hamburgers must be offered for sale (or both must happen). A rise in the price of hamburgers produces this outcome. A higher price encourages producers to offer more hamburgers for sale. It also curbs the appetite for hamburgers and changes some lunch plans. Fewer people buy hamburgers, and more buy hot dogs. More hamburgers (and more hot dogs) are offered for sale.

Alternatively, suppose that more hamburgers are available than people want to buy. In this case, to make the choices of buyers and sellers compatible, more hamburgers must be bought or fewer hamburgers must be offered for sale (or both). A fall in the price of hamburgers achieves this outcome. A lower price encour-

ages firms to produce a smaller quantity of hamburgers. It also encourages people to buy more hamburgers.

R E V I E W   Q U I Z

- Why are social arrangements such as markets and property rights necessary?
- What are the main functions of markets?

◆ You have now begun to see how economists approach economic questions. Scarcity, choice, and divergent opportunity cost explain why we specialize and trade and why property rights and markets have developed. You can see the lessons you've learned in this chapter all around you. *Reading Between the Lines* on pp. 50–51 gives an example. It explores the *PPF* of a student like you and the choices that students must make that influence their own economic growth—the growth of their incomes.

Opportunity Cost:
The Cost and Benefit of Education

P O R T L A N D   P R E S S   H E R A L D , May 2, 1996

High Cost Blocks Education

Robin McAlister of South Portland has fallen into a disheartening routine: Sit down at the kitchen table, scan the classifieds, apply for a job, get turned down. ...

Like thousands of other Mainers, McAlister has learned a fundamental truth: People who don't have the skills needed in today's high-tech, highly competitive environment rarely find good jobs. ...

Although a college degree doesn't guarantee a job, the economy is creating work for highly educated people. ...

Since 1989, the number of jobs for people with a master's degree has jumped an estimated 21 percent. ...

By comparison, jobs that generally don't require a college education have declined an estimated 1 percent.

There's a huge gap in pay between the two groups. In Maine, the average hourly wage for jobs that generally require a college degree is twice that for occupations that don't, about $18 an hour vs. $9 an hour, according to an analysis by The Portland Newspapers of state and federal databases. ...

Essence of the Stories

■ It has become hard for someone who lacks a college education to find a good job.

■ Jobs that require a college degree pay twice as much as jobs that don't.

■ Jobs for people with an MBA have become even more plentiful.

■ Incomes of people with MBAs have increased greatly during the 1990s.

T H E   N E W   Y O R K   T I M E S , August 2, 1998

A Top MBA Is a Hot Ticket as Pay Climbs

...The typical University of Chicago [business school] graduate turns down so many job offers that the dean's main worry has become "dealing with all the disappointed companies." ...

The median offer this year for a new Stanford MBA ... was $120,000, more than double the first-year salary at the peak of the '80s, and more than five times the 1978 figure. Inflation has been 142 percent over that period. ...

Half the graduates of the Wharton School of the University of Pennsylvania received offers of more than $133,000 this year. ...

At the top 25 schools, the best compensation packages offered to new MBAs are well above $200,000.

Economic Analysis

■ The opportunity cost of a college degree is forgone consumption. The payoff is an increase in lifetime production possibilities and in future consumption possibilities.

■ Figure 1 shows the choices facing a high school graduate. This person can consume education goods and services such as tuition, books and other supplies, and study time, measured on the *y*-axis, or other goods and services, measured on the *x*-axis.

■ Working full time, this person has an income of $16,000 a year. She can consume along the blue *PPF*. To get a college degree, a high school graduate selects point *a* on the blue *PPF*, forgoes current consumption, and increases the use of educational goods and services to $12,000.

■ Working full time, the college graduate earns twice as much as the high school graduate at $32,000 a year. With a college degree, production possibilities expand to the red *PPF* in Fig. 1.

■ A college graduate can choose to quit school or spend even more time and other resources on education to get a professional degree. If she quits school, consumption remains at $32,000 a year.

■ Figure 2 shows the choices facing a college graduate. To get a professional degree, a college graduate selects point *b* on the blue *PPF*, forgoes current consumption, and increases the use of educational goods and services to $24,000.

■ With a professional degree, income rises to $128,000 a year. Production possibilities expand to the red *PPF* in Fig. 2.

■ The greater the resources devoted to education, the greater are the future production possibilities. For people who have the required ability, the future benefits of education exceed the costs by a significant amount.

You're The Voter

■ Political leaders of all parties say that they want every American to have a college education.

■ Why do you think political leaders need to worry about college education?

■ With such huge returns from education, why don't more people remain in school for longer?

■ What is the opportunity cost of providing a college education for every American?

■ Would you vote for or against a tax increase to enable everyone to attend college? Why or why not?

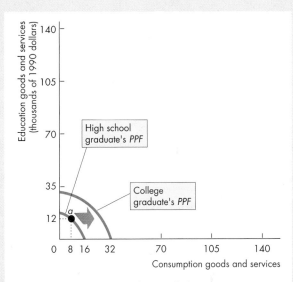

Figure 1 High school graduate's choices

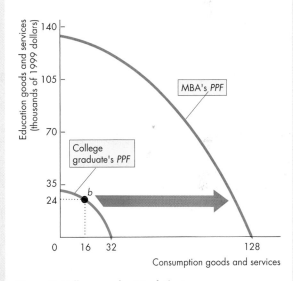

Figure 2 College graduate's choices

51

SUMMARY

KEY POINTS

Resources and Wants (p. 36)

■ Economic activity arises from scarcity—resources are insufficient to satisfy people's wants.

■ Resources are labor, land, capital (including human capital), and entrepreneurship.

■ We choose how to use our resources and try to get the most out of them.

Resources, Production Possibilities, and Opportunity Cost (pp. 37–39)

■ The production possibility frontier, *PPF*, is the boundary between production levels that are attainable and those that are not attainable when all the available resources are used to their limit.

■ Production efficiency occurs at points on the *PPF*.

■ Along the *PPF*, the opportunity cost of producing more of one good is the amount of the other good that must be given up.

■ The opportunity cost of a good increases as the production of the good increases.

Using Resources Efficiently (pp. 40–42)

■ The marginal cost of a good is the opportunity cost of producing one more unit.

■ The marginal benefit from a good is the maximum amount of another good that a person is willing to forgo to obtain more of the first good.

■ The marginal benefit of a good decreases as the amount available increases.

■ Resources are used efficiently when the marginal cost of each good is equal to its marginal benefit.

Economic Growth (pp. 43–44)

■ Economic growth, which is the expansion of production possibilities, results from capital accumulation and technological change.

■ The opportunity cost of economic growth is forgone current consumption.

Gains from Trade (pp. 45–47)

■ A person has a comparative advantage in producing a good if that person can produce the good at a lower opportunity cost than everyone else can.

■ It is *not* possible for *anyone* to have a comparative advantage at *everything*.

■ People gain by specializing in the activity in which they have a comparative advantage and trading with others.

The Market Economy (pp. 48–49)

■ Property rights and markets enable people to gain from specialization and trade.

■ Markets coordinate decisions and help to allocate resources to *higher*-valued uses.

KEY FIGURES

KEY TERMS

PROBLEMS

*1. Use the figure to calculate Wendell's opportunity cost of an hour of tennis when he increases the time he plays tennis from:
   a.   4 to 6 hours a week.
   b.   6 to 8 hours a week.

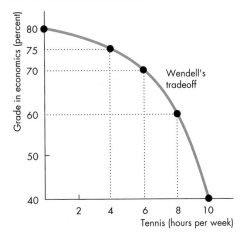

2. Use the figure to calculate Mary's opportunity cost of an hour of skating when she increases her time spent skating from:
   a.   2 to 4 hours a week.
   b.   4 to 6 hours a week.

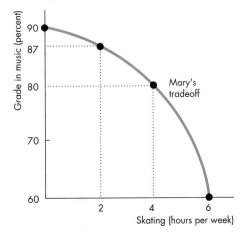

*3. In problem 1, describe the relationship between the time Wendell spends playing tennis and the opportunity cost of an hour of tennis.

4. In problem 2, describe the relationship between the time Mary spends skating and the opportunity cost of an hour of skating.

*5. Wendell, in problem 1, has the following marginal benefit curve:

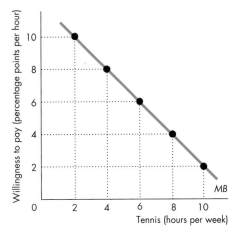

a.   If Wendell uses his time efficiently, what grade will he get?
b.   Why would Wendell be worse off getting a higher grade?

6. Mary, in problem 2, has the following marginal benefit curve:

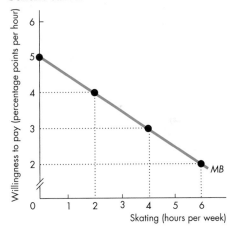

a.   If Mary uses her time efficiently, how much skating will she do?
b.   Why would Mary be worse off spending fewer hours skating?

*7. Leisureland's production possibilities are:

Food (pounds per month)		Sunscreen (gallons per month)
300	and	0
200	and	50
100	and	100
0	and	150

a.   Draw a graph of Leisureland's production possibility frontier.

b. What are Leisureland's opportunity costs of producing food and sunscreen at each output in the table?

8. Jane's Island's production possibilities are:

Corn (pounds per month)		Cloth (yards per month)
3.0	and	0
2.0	and	2
1.0	and	4
0	and	6

a. Draw a graph of the *PPF* on Jane's Island.
b. What are Jane's opportunity costs of producing corn and cloth at each output in the table?

*9. In problem 7, to get a gallon of sunscreen the people of Leisureland are willing to give up 5 pounds of food if they have 25 gallons of sunscreen; 2 pounds of food if they have 75 gallons of sunscreen; and 1 pound of food if they have 125 gallons of sunscreen.

a. Draw a graph of Leisureland's marginal benefit from sunscreen.
b. What is the efficient quantity of sunscreen?

10. In problem 8, to get a yard of cloth Jane is willing to give up 0.75 pound of corn if she has 2 yards of cloth; 0.50 pound of corn if she has 4 yards of cloth; and 0.25 pound of corn if she has 6 yards of cloth.

a. Draw a graph of Jane's marginal benefit from corn.
b. What is Jane's efficient quantity of corn?

*11. Busyland's production possibilities are:

Food (pounds per month)		Sunscreen (gallons per month)
150	and	0
100	and	100
50	and	200
0	and	300

Calculate Busyland's opportunity costs of food and sunscreen at each output in the table.

12. Joe's production possibilities are:

Corn (pounds per month)		Cloth (yards per month)
6	and	0.0
4	and	1.0
2	and	2.0
0	and	3.0

What are Joe's opportunity costs of producing corn and cloth at each output in the table?

*13. In problems 7 and 11, Leisureland and Busyland each produce and consume 100 pounds of food and 100 gallons of sunscreen per month; and they do not trade. Now the countries begin to trade with each other.

a. What good does Leisureland sell to Busyland and what good does it buy from Busyland?
b. If Leisureland and Busyland divide the total output of food and sunscreen equally, what are the gains from trade?

14. In problems 8 and 12, Jane's Island produces and consumes 1 pound of corn and 4 yards of cloth. Joe's Island produces and consumes 4 pounds of corn and 1 yard of cloth. Now the islands begin to trade.

a. What good does Jane sell to Joe and what good does Jane buy from Joe?
b. If Jane and Joe divide the total output of corn and cloth equally, what are the gains from trade?

CRITICAL THINKING

1. After you have studied *Reading Between the Lines* on pp. 50–51, answer the following questions:
a. Why does the *PPF* for education goods and services and consumption goods and services bow outward?
b. At what point on the blue *PPF* in Fig. 1 on p. 51 is the combination of education goods and services and consumption goods and services efficient? Explain your answer.
c. Students face rising tuition. Does higher tuition change the opportunity cost of education?
d. Who receives the benefits from education? Is the marginal cost of education equal to marginal benefit? Is resource use in the market for education efficient?

2. Use the links on the Parkin Web site and obtain data on the tuition and other costs of enrolling in the MBA program of a school that interests you. If an MBA graduate can earn as much as the amounts reported in the news article in *Reading Between the Lines* on pp. 50–51, does the marginal benefit of an MBA exceed its marginal cost? Why doesn't everyone study for an MBA?

Your Economic Revolution

You are making progress in your study of economics. You've already encountered the big questions and big ideas of economics. And you've learned about the key insight of Adam Smith, the founder of economics: specialization and exchange create economic wealth. ◆ You are studying economics at a time that future historians will call the *Information Revolution*. We reserve the word 'Revolution' for big events that influence all future generations. ◆ During the *Agricultural Revolution*, which occurred 10,000 years ago, people learned to domesticate animals and plant crops. They stopped roaming in search of food and settled in villages and eventually towns and cities, where they developed markets in which to exchange their products. ◆ During the *Industrial Revolution*, which began 240 years ago, people used science to create new technologies. This revolution brought extraordinary wealth for some but created conditions in which others were left behind. It brought social and political tensions that we still face today. ◆ During today's *Information Revolution*, people who have the ability and opportunity to embrace the new technologies are prospering on an unimagined scale. But the incomes and living standards of the less educated are falling behind, and social and political tensions are increasing. Today's revolution has a global dimension. Some of the winners live in previously poor countries in Asia, and some of the losers live here in the United States. ◆ So you are studying economics at an interesting time. Whatever *your* motivation is for studying economics, *my* objective is to help you do well in your course, to enjoy it, and to develop a deeper understanding of the economic world around you. ◆ There are three reasons why I hope that we both succeed: First, a decent understanding of economics will help you to become a full participant in the Information Revolution. Second, an understanding of economics will help you play a more effective role as a citizen and voter and enable you to add your voice to those who are looking for solutions to our social and political problems. Third, you will enjoy the sheer fun of *understanding* the forces at play and how they are shaping our world. ◆ If you are finding economics interesting, think seriously about majoring in the subject. A degree in economics gives the best training available in problem solving, offers lots of opportunities to develop conceptual skills, and opens doors to a wide range of graduate courses, including the MBA, and to a wide range of jobs. You can read more about the benefits of an economics degree in Robert Whaples's essay in your *Study Guide*. ◆ Economics was born during the Industrial Revolution. We'll look at its birth and meet its founder, Adam Smith. Then we'll talk about economic revolutions and other matters with one of today's leading economists, Nobel Laureate, Professor Douglass North of Washington University in St. Louis.

The Sources of Economic Wealth

The Father of Economics

Adam Smith *was a giant of a scholar who contributed to ethics and jurisprudence as well as economics. Born in 1723 in Kirkcaldy, a small fishing town near Edinburgh, Scotland, Smith was the only child of the town's customs officer (who died before Adam was born).*

His first academic appointment, at age 28, was as Professor of Logic at the University of Glasgow. He subsequently became tutor to a wealthy Scottish duke, whom he accompanied on a two-year grand European tour, following which he received a pension of £300 a year—ten times the average income at that time.

With the financial security of his pension, Smith devoted ten years to writing An Inquiry into the Nature and Causes of **The Wealth of Nations**, *which was published in 1776. Many people had written on economic issues before Adam Smith, but he made economics a science. Smith's account was so broad and authoritative that no subsequent writer on economics could advance ideas without tracing their connections to those of Adam Smith.*

"It is not from the benevolence of the butcher, the brewer, or the baker that we expect our dinner, but from their regard to their own interest."

ADAM SMITH
The Wealth of Nations

The Issues

Why are some nations wealthy while others are poor? This question lies at the heart of economics. And it leads directly to a second question: What can poor nations do to become wealthy?

Adam Smith, who is regarded by many scholars as the founder of economics, attempted to answer these questions in his book *The Wealth of Nations*, published in 1776. Smith was pondering these questions at the height of the Industrial Revolution. During these years, new technologies were invented and applied to the manufacture of cotton and wool cloth, iron, transportation, and agriculture.

Smith wanted to understand the sources of economic wealth, and he brought his acute powers of observation and abstraction to bear on the question. His answer:

- The division of labor
- Free markets

The division of labor—breaking tasks down into simple tasks and becoming skilled in those tasks—is the source of "the greatest improvement in the productive powers of labor," said Smith. The division of labor became even more productive when it was applied to creating new technologies. Scientists and engineers, trained in extremely narrow fields, became specialists at inventing. Their powerful skills accelerated the advance of technology, so by the 1820s, machines could make consumer goods faster and more accurately than any craftsman could. And by the 1850s, machines could make other machines that labor alone could never have made.

But, said Smith, the fruits of the division of labor are limited by the extent of the market. To make the market as large as possible, there must be no impediments to free trade both within a country and among countries. Smith argued that when each person makes the best possible economic choice, that choice leads as if by "an invisible hand" to the best outcome for society as a whole. The butcher, the brewer, and the baker each pursue their own interests but, in doing so, also serve the interests of everyone else.

Then

Adam Smith speculated that one person, working hard, using the hand tools available in the 1770s, might possibly make 20 pins a day. Yet, he observed, by using those same hand tools but breaking the process into a number of individually small operations in which people specialize—by the **division of labor**—ten people could make a staggering 48,000 pins a day. One draws out the wire, another straightens it, a third cuts it, a fourth points it, a fifth grinds it. Three specialists make the head, and a fourth attaches it. Finally, the pin is polished and packaged. But a large market is needed to support the division of labor: One factory employing ten workers would need to sell more than 15 million pins a year to stay in business.

Now

If Adam Smith were here today, the computer chip would fascinate him. He would see it as an extraordinary example of the productivity of the division of labor and of the use of machines to make machines that make other machines. From a design of a chip's intricate circuits, cameras transfer an image to glass plates that work like stencils. Workers prepare silicon wafers on which the circuits are printed. Some slice the wafers, others polish them, others bake them, and yet others coat them with a light-sensitive chemical. Machines transfer a copy of the circuit onto the wafer. Chemicals then etch the design onto the wafer. Further processes deposit atom-sized transistors and aluminum connectors. Finally, a laser separates the hundreds of chips on the wafer. Every stage in the process of creating a computer chip uses other computer chips. And like the pin of the 1770s, the computer chip of the 1990s benefits from a large market—a global market—to buy chips in the huge quantities in which they are produced efficiently.

Many economists have worked on the big themes that Adam Smith began. One of these economists is Douglass North, of Washington University, whom you can meet on the following pages.

Douglass North, *who teaches economics and economic history at Washington University in St. Louis, was born in Cambridge, Massachusetts, in 1920. He was an undergraduate and graduate student at the University of California, Berkeley, where he earned his Ph.D. in 1952. Professor North has pioneered the study of economic institutions such as stable government, the rule of law, and private property rights and the role these institutions play in fostering economic development and sustained income growth. He has used his ideas to explain why the United States and*

Douglass North

Western Europe have evolved from low-income agricultural societies 200 years ago into high-income complex societies today. In 1993, Professor North was awarded the Nobel Prize for Economic Science for this work. Michael Parkin talked with Professor North about his work and its relevance to today's—and tomorrow's—world.

Professor North, what attracted you to economics?

I grew up during the Great Depression, and when I was a student at the University of California at Berkeley, I became a Marxist. I thought that Marxists had the answers to the economic concerns that were so prevalent during the Depression. If the market economy of capitalism was replaced by the planned economy of socialism, the Depression and other economic ills could, I then believed, be cured.

At Berkeley, I looked for courses that would enable me to understand why some countries were rich and some poor. That is how I was drawn toward economic history.

After I graduated, World War II broke out, and I spent four years in the Merchant Marine. During those years, I read a whole slew of books. I decided that I wanted to save the world—like any good Marxist wanted to—and I decided that the way to save it was to understand what made economies work badly and work well. And I've been pursuing that utopian goal ever since.

How did you abandon your Marxist beginning? Was there a sudden revelation or was it a gradual process?

Converting from Marxism was a very slow process. My first teaching job was at the University of Washington in Seattle in 1950. I used to play chess every day with my colleague, Donald Gordon. He was a good economist, and over three years of playing chess every day and talking economics, I gradually evolved away from Marxism and became a mainstream economist.

What are the key economic principles that guide your work—the principles and perspectives the economist brings to a study of long-term historical processes?

There are two. The first is the importance of transactions costs—the costs that people incur in order to do business with each other.

Economics attempts to understand how societies cope with the problem of scarcity—with the fact that people's wants always outstrip their limited resources. Traditionally, economists have focused on how resources are allocated at a moment of time—what determines today's allocation of spending between high schools and hospitals, computers and cars. Economic history deals with how societies evolve over time and tries to discover why some societies become wealthy while others remain poor. I became convinced that the economic way of reasoning underlying the economic principles is the right way to understand how societies evolve over time. But this conviction led me on a long trail.

Back in the days when I was learning economics, economic theories were based on the *assumption* that people could specialize and exchange their products in markets that function efficiently. They ignored transaction costs—the costs that people incur when they do business with each other and the costs that governments and firms incur to make markets work. So the first problem was to think about how exchange takes place in the face of large transactions costs.

And the second principle?

The second principle is that transactions costs depend crucially on the way that human beings structure the economic order—on their institutions. And this fact gave me my second problem, to think about how institutions evolve to make markets work better over time.

When an economist talks about economic institutions, what exactly is he or she talking about? What are these institutions?

Institutions are rules of the society that structure the interaction among people. Institutions are made up of formal rules, like constitutions and statute law, and common rules and regulations. But they're also more than that. They are the informal ways by which people deal with each other every day, which you could think of as norms of behavior.

Institutions are the framework within which all of human interaction—political, social, and economic—takes place. And so, understanding how those work, why they work well in some circumstances, and why they work badly in others is the key, really, to the wealth of nations. Some examples of economic institutions include antitrust laws, patent laws, and bankruptcy laws.

Can economists explain the radically different institutional evolution of the United States and Russia?

This question is at the very heart of what economic history should be about. The United States inherited a set of institutions—among them common law and property rights—from Great Britain. These institutions had made Britain the world's leading nation by the end of the eighteenth century. The United States modified Britain's institutions and elaborated on them. The result has been two and a half centuries of economic growth. Much of the rest of the world, and Russia in particular,

evolved institutions that didn't work very well.

In Britain and the United States, the governments evolved a set of rules that provided a lot of freedom and latitude for people to make contracts and agreements among themselves. These rules produced economic efficiency on an unparalleled scale and led to sustained economic growth.

Russia, as well as some other Eastern European and Third World countries, chose a different economic path based on Communism, which turned out to be an institution that could not sustain economic growth.

The goal of research in economic development and economic history is to understand exactly what led to this very different process of change among countries such as the United States and Russia.

> To have efficient markets, a country needs rules and regulations that provide incentives for people to be creative and become increasingly productive.

How do you explain the economic success of China and economic failure of Russia?

China had political authoritarianism at the top, and those authorities have either deliberately or accidentally loosened control in the provinces. The result has made for a very lucrative combination of local Communist Party officials teaming up with entrepreneurs, who got their capital and sometimes their training from the

59

governments of Hong Kong and Taiwan, being let loose to pursue business ventures. And that's a unique situation. This certainly doesn't appear likely to happen in the former Soviet Union.

I think the biggest economic lessons are from successful Asian economies. Despite recent setbacks, countries such as South Korea and Taiwan show us that a proper dose of government can accelerate the process of creating efficient markets. To have efficient markets, a country needs rules and regulations that provide incentives for people to be creative and to become increasingly productive. We also learn from the Asian crisis and recession of 1998 that the conditions for efficient markets change over time as technologies and market conditions change. This ongoing change requires continual updating of the rules to maintain efficient conditions. It doesn't happen automatically. Asia has shown us that while governments can sometimes hasten the evolution of efficient markets, they can also sometimes thwart the continuation of efficient markets.

How would you characterize the changes that are taking place in today's global and national economy?

I look at economic revolutions as changes in knowledge that fundamentally changed the whole economic social organization of societies. The origin and development of agriculture were the first economic revolution. This economic revolution probably occurred in the eighth millennium

B.C. Agriculture completely altered the pace of economic and all other kinds of human change. Human beings settled down into villages and towns. This eventually led to the growth of exchange and to the whole basis for civilization. Agriculture enormously increased productivity potential and the potential for human progress.

The next real fundamental economic change was the application of science to technology. I would say there's never been a time in human history in which there's been as dramatic a setting of change as we're seeing in the world we live in today. I think it's extraordinary. It's a very exciting world to live in, particularly for an economic historian. I have argued that something happened in the nineteenth century, which I call the Second Economic Revolution: There was a systematic wedding of science to technology that led to the development of the disciplines of physics, chemistry, genetics, and biology. This revolution has completely changed the way in which all of modern economic activity takes place and the way that human beings live and interact.

The personal and social implications of that revolution are enormous. As a result of this revolution, we live packed together in huge cities, many of which are plagued by crime on a scale that frightens us, and we depend for our economic well-being on millions of people we do not know. Many people have benefited from the advances in technology and enjoy unimagined high living standards, while many others have

been left behind and are not sharing in the prosperity that the second economic revolution has created. So, combined with the prosperity of this economic revolution, we've created a set of social, political, and economic problems that we haven't figured out how to solve. And they may overwhelm us down the road.

> I think the most important thing in the world is to have a creative, stimulating, exciting life. . . . Find out what things excite you, and pursue them all your life.

What is your advice to a student who is just setting out to become an economist? How should the student approach his or her work? What are the things to study?

You should find excitement and challenge in the things you do and pursue them. At a university, this means that you ought to bug your professors. You should be continually trying to get a lot out of them. I think most university students don't get out of school what they could. Both in and out of class, you should ask questions and pursue the answers to those questions. I think that's terribly important.

I think the most important thing in the world is to have a creative, stimulating, exciting life. Everybody can do that in their own way, depending on their own curiosities, interests, and talents. Find out what things excite you, and pursue them all your life.

Chapter 4

Demand and Supply

Slide, rocket, and roller coaster—
Disneyland rides? No. Commonly
used descriptions of price changes. ◆ CD
players have taken a price slide from around
$1,100 (in today's money) in 1983 to less than
$100 today. And during these years, the quantity of
CD players bought has increased steadily. What caused
this price slide? Why didn't brisk buying keep the
price high? ◆ The price of health care has rocketed. Yet despite
rocketing prices, people buy more health services every year. Why?
◆ The prices of bananas, coffee, and other agricultural commodities
follow a roller coaster. Why does the price of bananas roller-coaster
even when people's tastes for bananas barely change? ◆ The prices of
many things we buy are remarkably steady. For example, the price of an
audio cassette tape has not changed much.
But despite its steady price, the number of
tapes people buy increases each year. Why do
people buy more tapes even though their
price is no lower than it was a decade ago?
And why do firms sell more tapes even
though they can't get higher prices for them?
◆ Economics is about the choices people
make to cope with scarcity. These choices are guided by costs and benefits and are coordinated through markets. ◆ The tool that explains how
markets work is demand and supply. It is central to the whole of economics. It is used to study issues as diverse as wages and jobs, rents and
housing, pollution, crime, consumer protection, education, welfare,
health care, the value of money, and interest rates.

Slide, Rocket, and Roller Coaster

◆ Your careful study of this topic will bring big rewards both in
your further study of economics and in your everyday life. Once you
understand demand and supply, you will view the world through new
eyes. When you have completed your study of demand and supply,
you will be able to explain how prices are determined and make predictions about price slides, rockets, and roller coasters. But first, we're
going to take a closer look at the idea of price. Just what is a price?

After studying this chapter, you will be able to:

■ Distinguish between a money price and a relative price

■ Explain the main influences on demand

■ Explain the main influences on supply

■ Explain how prices and quantities bought and sold are deter-mined by demand and supply

■ Explain why some prices fall, some rise, and some fluctuate

■ Use demand and supply to make pre-dictions about price changes

Price and Opportunity Cost

ECONOMIC ACTIONS ARISE FROM SCARCITY—WANTS exceed the resources available to satisfy them. Faced with *scarcity*, we must make choices. And to make choices, we compare *costs* and *benefits*. Choices are influenced by opportunity costs. Producers offer items for sale only if the price is high enough to cover their opportunity cost. And consumers respond to changing opportunity cost by seeking cheaper alternatives to expensive items.

We are going to study the way people respond to *prices* and the forces that determine prices. But to pursue these tasks, we need to understand the relationship between a price and an opportunity cost.

In everyday life, the *price* of an object is the number of dollars that must be given up in exchange for it. Economists refer to this price as the *money price*.

The *opportunity cost* of an action is the highest-valued alternative forgone. If, when you buy a cup of coffee, the highest-valued thing you forgo is some gum, then the opportunity cost of buying a coffee is the *quantity* of gum forgone. We can calculate this quantity from the money prices of coffee and gum.

If the money price of coffee is $1 a cup and the money price of gum is 50¢ a pack, then the opportunity cost of one cup of coffee is two packs of gum. To calculate this opportunity cost, we divide the price of a cup of coffee by the price of a pack of gum and find the *ratio* of one price to the other. The ratio of one price to another is called a **relative price**, and a *relative price is an opportunity cost.*

We can express the relative price of coffee in terms of gum or any other good. The normal way of expressing a relative price is in terms of a "basket" of all goods and services. To calculate this relative price, we divide the money price of a good by the money price of a "basket" of all goods (called a *price index*). The resulting relative price is expressed in the buying power of money in a particular year. It tells us the opportunity cost of an item in terms of how much of the "basket" we must give up to buy it.

Figure 4.1 shows the money price and the relative price of wheat. The money price (green) has fluctuated but has tended to rise. The relative price (red) peaked in 1974 and has tended to fall since that year.

The theory of demand and supply that we are about to study determines *relative prices,* and the word "price" means *relative* price. When we predict that a price will fall, we do not mean that its *money*

FIGURE 4.1

The Price of Wheat

The money price of wheat—the number of dollars that must be given up for a bushel of wheat—has fluctuated between $1.50 and $6.20. But the *relative* price or *opportunity cost* of wheat, expressed in 1998 dollars, has fluctuated between $4.10 and $16.25 and has tended to fall. The fall in the relative price of wheat is obscured by the behavior of the money price.

Sources: International Financial Statistics, International Monetary Fund, Washington, DC, 1999.

price will fall—although it might. We mean that its *relative* price will fall. That is, its price will fall *relative* to the average price of other goods and services.

R E V I E W   Q U I Z

- Explain the distinction between a money price and a relative price.
- Why is a relative price is an opportunity cost?
- Can you think of an example of a good whose money price and relative price have risen?
- Can you think of an example of a good whose money price and relative price have fallen?

Let's now begin our study of demand and supply, starting with demand.

Demand

IF YOU DEMAND SOMETHING, THEN YOU

1. Want it,
2. Can afford it, and
3. Have made a definite plan to buy it.

Wants are the unlimited desires or wishes that people have for goods and services. How many times have you thought that you would like something "if only you could afford it" or "if it weren't so expensive"? Scarcity guarantees that many—perhaps most—of our wants will never be satisfied. Demand reflects a decision about which wants to satisfy.

The **quantity demanded** of a good or service is the amount that consumers plan to buy during a given time period at a particular price. The quantity demanded is not necessarily the same amount as the quantity actually bought. Sometimes the quantity demanded is greater than the amount of goods available, so the quantity bought is less than the quantity demanded.

The quantity demanded is measured as an amount per unit of time. For example, suppose that you consume one cup of coffee a day. The quantity of coffee that you demand can be expressed as 1 cup a day or 7 cups a week or 365 cups a year. Without a time dimension, we cannot tell whether a particular quantity demanded is large or small.

What Determines Buying Plans?

The amount of any particular good or service that consumers plan to buy depends on many factors. The main ones are:

1. The price of the good
2. The prices of related goods
3. Expected future prices
4. Income
5. Population
6. Preferences

We first look at the relationship between the quantity demanded and the price of a good. To study this relationship, we hold constant all other influences on consumers' planned purchases and ask: How does the quantity demanded of the good vary as its price varies, other things remaining the same?

The Law of Demand

The law of demand states:

Other things remaining the same, the higher the price of a good, the smaller is the quantity demanded.

Why does a higher price reduce the quantity demanded? For two reasons:

1. Substitution effect
2. Income effect

Substitution Effect When the price of a good rises, other things remaining the same, its *relative* price—its opportunity cost—rises. Although each good is unique, it has *substitutes*—other goods that can be used in its place. As the opportunity cost of a good rises, people buy less of that good and more of its substitutes.

Income Effect When a price changes and all other influences on buying plans remain unchanged, the price rises *relative* to people's incomes. So faced with a higher price and an unchanged income, people cannot afford to buy all the things they previously bought. The quantities demanded of at least some goods and services must be decreased. Normally, the good whose price has increased is one of those bought in a smaller quantity.

To see the substitution effect and the income effect at work, think about the effects of changes in the price of blank audio cassette tapes. Many different goods provide a service similar to that provided by a tape. For example, a compact disc, a prerecorded tape, a radio or television broadcast, and a live concert all provide similar services to a tape. Suppose that tapes initially sell for $3 each and then the price doubles to $6. People now substitute compact discs and prerecorded tapes for blank tapes—the substitution effect. And faced with a tighter budget, they buy fewer tapes as well as less of other goods and services—the income effect. The quantity of tapes demanded decreases for these two reasons.

Now suppose the price of a tape falls to $1. People now substitute blank tapes for compact discs and prerecorded tapes—the substitution effect. And with a budget that now has some slack from the lower price of tapes, people buy more tapes as well as more of other goods and services—the income effect. The quantity of tapes demanded increases for these two reasons.

Demand Curve and Demand Schedule

You are now about to study one of the two most used curves in economics, the demand curve. And you are going to encounter one of the most critical distinctions: the distinction between *demand* and *quantity demanded.*

The term **demand** refers to the entire relationship between the quantity demanded and the price of a good, and it is illustrated by the demand curve and the demand schedule. The term *quantity demanded* refers to a point on a demand curve—the quantity demanded at a particular price.

Figure 4.2 shows the demand curve for tapes. A **demand curve** shows the relationship between the quantity demanded of a good and its price when all other influences on consumers' planned purchases remain the same.

The table in Fig. 4.2 is the demand schedule for tapes. A *demand schedule* lists the quantities demanded at each different price when all the other influences on consumers' planned purchases—such as income, population, preferences, and future prices—remain the same. For example, if the price of a tape is $1, the quantity demanded is 9 million tapes a week. If the price of a tape is $5, the quantity demanded is 2 million tapes a week. The other rows of the table show the quantities demanded at prices of $2, $3, and $4.

We graph the demand schedule as a demand curve with the quantity demanded on the horizontal axis and the price on the vertical axis. The points on the demand curve labeled *a* through *e* represent the rows of the demand schedule. For example, point *a* on the graph represents a quantity demanded of 9 million tapes a week at a price of $1 a tape.

Willingness and Ability to Pay   Another way of looking at the demand curve is as a willingness-and-ability-to-pay curve. And the willingness-and-ability-to-pay is a measure of *marginal benefit.*

If a small quantity is available, the highest price that someone is willing and able to pay for one more unit is high. But as the quantity available increases, the marginal benefit of each additional unit falls and the highest price that someone is willing and able to pay for it also falls along the demand curve.

In Fig. 4.2, if 2 million tapes are available each week, the highest price that someone is willing to pay for the 2 millionth tape is $5. But if 9 million tapes are available each week, someone is willing to pay only $1 for the last tape bought.

FIGURE 4.2
The Demand Curve

	Price (dollars per tape)	Quantity (millions of tapes per week)
a	1	9
b	2	6
c	3	4
d	4	3
e	5	2

The table shows a demand schedule listing the quantity of tapes demanded at each price if all other influences on buyers' plans remain the same. At a price of $1 a tape, 9 million tapes a week are demanded; at a price of $3 a tape, 4 million tapes a week are demanded. The demand curve shows the relationship between quantity demanded and price, everything else remaining the same.

The demand curve slopes downward: As price decreases, the quantity demanded increases. The demand curve can be read in two ways. For a given price, it tells us the quantity that people plan to buy. For example, at a price of $3 a tape, the quantity demanded is 4 million tapes a week. For a given quantity, the demand curve tells us the maximum price that consumers are willing and able to pay for the last tape available. For example, the maximum price that consumers will pay for the 6 millionth tape is $2.

A Change in Demand

When any factor that influences buying plans other than the price of the good changes, there is a **change in demand**. Figure 4.3 illustrates an increase in demand. When demand increases, the demand curve shifts rightward and the quantity demanded is greater at each and every price. For example, at a price of $5, on the original (blue) demand curve, the quantity demanded is 2 million tapes a week. On the new (red) demand curve, the quantity demanded is 6 million tapes a week. Look closely at the numbers in the table in Fig. 4.3 and check that the quantity demanded is higher at each price.

Let's look at the factors that bring a change in demand. There are five key factors to consider.

1. Prices of Related Goods The quantity of tapes that consumers plan to buy depends in part on the prices of substitutes for tapes. A **substitute** is a good that can be used in place of another good. For example, a bus ride is a substitute for a train ride; a hamburger is a substitute for a hot dog, and a compact disc is a substitute for a tape. If the price of a substitute for a tape increases, people buy less of the substitute and more tapes. For example, if the price of a CD rises, people buy fewer CDs and more tapes. The demand for tapes increases.

The quantity of tapes that people plan to buy also depends on the prices of complements of tapes. A **complement** is a good that is used in conjunction with another good. Hamburgers and fries are complements. So are spaghetti and meat sauce, and so are tapes and Walkmans. If the price of a Walkman falls, people buy more Walkmans *and more tapes*. It is a fall in the price of a Walkman that increases the demand for tapes in Fig. 4.3.

2. Expected Future Prices If the price of a good is expected to rise in the future and if the good can be stored, the opportunity cost of obtaining the good for future use is lower now than it will be when the price has increased. So people retime their purchase—they substitute over time. They buy more of the good now before its price is expected to rise (and less after), so the current demand for the good increases.

For example, suppose that Florida is hit by a severe frost that damages the season's orange crop. You expect the price of orange juice to soar. So, anticipating the higher price, you fill your freezer with enough frozen juice to get you through the next six months. Your current demand for frozen orange juice has increased (and your future demand has decreased).

FIGURE 4.3

An Increase in Demand

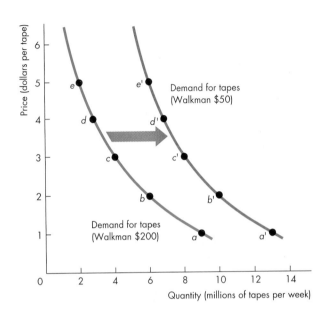

Original demand schedule Walkman $200			New demand schedule Walkman $50		
	Price (dollars per tape)	Quantity (millions of tapes per week)		Price (dollars per tape)	Quantity (millions of tapes per week)
a	1	9	a'	1	13
b	2	6	b'	2	10
c	3	4	c'	3	8
d	4	3	d'	4	7
e	5	2	e'	5	6

A change in any influence on buyers' plans other than the price of the good itself results in a new demand schedule and a shift of the demand curve. A change in the price of a Walkman changes the demand for tapes. At a price of $3 a tape (row c of the table), 4 million tapes a week are demanded when the Walkman costs $200 and 8 million tapes a week are demanded when the Walkman costs only $50. A *fall* in the price of a Walkman *increases* the demand for tapes because the Walkman is a complement of tapes. When demand *increases*, the demand curve shifts *rightward*, as shown by the shift arrow and the resulting red curve.

Similarly, if the price of a good is expected to fall in the future, the opportunity cost of buying the good in the present is high relative to what it is expected to be in the future. So again, people retime their purchases. They buy less of the good now before its price is expected to fall (and more after), so the current demand for the good decreases.

Computer prices are constantly falling, and this fact poses a dilemma. Will you buy a new computer now, in time for the start of the school year, or will you wait until the price has fallen some more? Because people expect computer prices to keep falling, the current demand for computers is less (the future demand is greater) than it otherwise would be.

3. Income   Another influence on demand is consumer income. When income increases, consumers buy more of most goods, and when income decreases, they buy less of most goods. Although an increase in income leads to an increase in the demand for *most* goods, it does not lead to an increase in the demand for *all* goods. A **normal good** is one for which demand increases as income increases. An **inferior good** is one for which demand decreases as income increases. Long-distance transportation has examples of both normal goods and inferior goods. As incomes increase, the demand for air travel (a normal good) increases and the demand for long-distance bus trips (an inferior good) decreases.

4. Population   Demand also depends on the size and the age structure of the population. The larger the population, the greater is the demand for all goods and services. And the smaller the population, the smaller is the demand for all goods and services.

For example, the demand for car parking spaces or movies or tapes or just about anything you can imagine is much greater in New York City (population 7.5 million) than it is in Boise, Idaho (population 150,000).

Also, the larger the proportion of the population in a given age group, the greater is the demand for the types of goods and services used by that age group.

For example, between 1988 and 1998, the number of 20–24 year olds in the United States decreased by 2 million. As a result, the demand for college places decreased during those years. During those same years, the number of Americans aged 85 years and over increased by more than 1 million. As a result, the demand for nursing home services increased.

TABLE 4.1
The Demand for Tapes

The Law of Demand

The quantity of tapes demanded

Decreases if:	*Increases if:*
■ The price of a tape rises	■ The price of a tape falls

Changes in Demand

The demand for tapes

Decreases if:	*Increases if:*
■ The price of a substitute falls	■ The price of a substitute rises
■ The price of a complement rises	■ The price of a complement falls
■ The price of a tape is expected to fall in the future	■ The price of a tape is expected to rise in the future
■ Income falls*	■ Income rises*
■ The population decreases	■ The population increases

*A tape is a normal good.

5. Preferences   Demand depends on preferences. *Preferences* are an individual's attitudes toward goods and services. For example, a rock music fanatic has a much greater taste for tapes than does a tone-deaf workaholic. As a consequence, even if they have the same incomes, their demands for tapes will be very different.

Table 4.1 summarizes the influences on demand and the direction of those influences.

A Change in the Quantity Demanded Versus a Change in Demand

Changes in the factors that influence buyers' plans cause either a change in the quantity demanded or a change in demand. Equivalently, they cause either a movement along the demand curve or a shift of the demand curve.

The distinction between a change in the quantity demanded and a change in demand is the same as that between a movement along the demand curve and a shift of the demand curve.

A point on the demand curve shows the quantity demanded at a given price. So a movement along the demand curve shows a **change in the quantity demanded**. The entire demand curve shows demand. So a shift of the demand curve shows a **change in demand**. Figure 4.4 illustrates and summarizes these distinctions.

Movement Along the Demand Curve If the price of a good changes but everything else remains the same, there is a movement along the demand curve. The negative slope of the demand curve reveals that a decrease in the price of a good or service increases the quantity demanded—the law of demand.

In Fig. 4.4, if the price of a good falls when everything else remains the same, the quantity demanded of that good increases and there is a movement down the demand curve D_0. If the price rises when everything else remains the same, the quantity demanded decreases and there is a movement up the demand curve D_0.

A Shift of the Demand Curve If the price of a good remains constant but some other influence on buyers' plans changes, there is a change in demand for that good. We illustrate a change in demand as a shift of the demand curve. For example, a fall in the price of the Walkman—a complement of tapes—increases the demand for tapes. We illustrate this increase in the demand for tapes with a new demand schedule and a new demand curve. If the price of the Walkman falls, consumers buy more tapes regardless of whether the price of a tape is high or low. That is what a rightward shift of the demand curve shows—that more tapes are bought at each and every price.

In Fig. 4.4, when any influence on buyers' planned purchases changes, other than the price of the good, the demand curve shifts and there is a *change* (an increase or a decrease) *in demand*. A rise in income (for a normal good), in population, in the price of a substitute, or in the expected future price of the good or a fall in the price of a complement shifts the demand curve rightward (to the red demand curve D_1). This represents an *increase in demand*. A fall in income (for a normal good), in population, in the price of a substitute, or in the expected future price of the good or a rise in the price of a complement shifts the demand curve leftward (to the red demand curve D_2). This represents a *decrease in demand*. (For an inferior good, the effects of changes in income are in the direction opposite to those described above.)

FIGURE 4.4

A Change in the Quantity Demanded Versus a Change in Demand

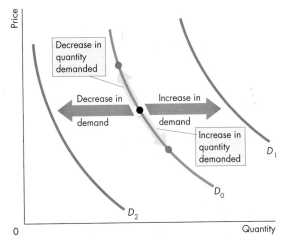

When the price of the good changes, there is a movement along the demand curve and a *change in the quantity demanded*, shown by the blue arrows on demand curve D_0. When any other influence on buying plans changes, there is a shift of the demand curve and a *change in demand*. An increase in demand shifts the demand curve rightward (from D_0 to D_1). A decrease in demand shifts the demand curve leftward (from D_0 to D_2).

REVIEW QUIZ

- Can you define the *quantity demanded* of a good or service?
- What is the *law of demand* and how do we illustrate it?
- If a fixed amount of a good is available, what does the demand curve tell us about the price that consumers are willing to pay for that fixed quantity?
- Can you list all the influences on buying plans that *change demand* and for each influence say whether it increases demand or decreases demand?
- What happens to the quantity of CDs demanded and the demand for CDs if the price of a CD falls and all other influences on buying plans remain the same?

Supply

IF A FIRM SUPPLIES A GOOD OR SERVICE, THE FIRM

1. Has the resources and technology to produce it,
2. Can profit from producing it, and
3. Has made a definite plan to produce it and sell it.

A supply is more that just having the *resources* and the *technology* to produce something. *Resources and technology* are the constraints that limit what is possible.

Many useful things can be produced, but they are not produced unless it is profitable to do so. Supply reflects a decision about which technologically feasible items to produce.

The **quantity supplied** of a good or service is the amount that producers plan to sell during a given time period at a particular price. The quantity supplied is not necessarily the same amount as the quantity actually sold. Sometimes the quantity supplied is greater than the quantity demanded, so the quantity bought is less than the quantity supplied.

Like the quantity demanded, the quantity supplied is measured as an amount per unit of time. For example, suppose that GM produces 1,000 cars a day. The quantity of cars supplied by GM can be expressed as 1,000 a day or 7,000 a week or 365,000 a year. Without the time dimension, we cannot tell whether a particular number is large or small.

What Determines Selling Plans?

The amount of any particular good or service that producers plan to sell depends on many factors. The main ones are:

1. The price of the good
2. The prices of resources used to produce the good
3. The prices of related goods produced
4. Expected future prices
5. The number of suppliers
6. Technology

Let's first look at the relationship between the price of a good and the quantity supplied. To study this relationship, we hold constant all the other influences on the quantity supplied. We ask: How does the quantity supplied of a good vary as its price varies?

The Law of Supply

The law of supply states:

> Other things remaining the same, the higher the price of a good, the greater is the quantity supplied.

Why does a higher price increase the quantity supplied? It is because of *increasing marginal cost*. As the quantity produced of any good increases, the marginal cost of producing the good increases. (You can refresh your memory of increasing marginal cost in Chapter 3, p. 40.)

It is never worth producing a good if the price received for it does not at least cover marginal cost. So when the price of a good rises, other things remaining the same, producers are willing to incur the higher marginal cost and increase production. The higher price brings forth an increase in the quantity supplied.

Let's now illustrate the law of supply with a supply curve and a supply schedule.

Supply Curve and Supply Schedule

You are now going to study the second of the two most used curves in economics, the supply curve. And you're going to learn about the critical distinction between *supply* and *quantity supplied*.

The term **supply** refers to the entire relationship between the quantity supplied and the price of a good, and it is illustrated by the supply curve and the supply schedule. The term *quantity supplied* refers to a point on a supply curve—the quantity supplied at a particular price.

Figure 4.5 shows the supply curve of tapes. A **supply curve** shows the relationship between the quantity supplied of a good and its price when all other influences on producers' planned sales remain the same. It is a graph of a supply schedule.

The table in Fig. 4.5 sets out the supply schedule for tapes. A *supply schedule* lists the quantities supplied at each different price when all the other influences on producers' planned sales remain the same. For example, if the price of a tape is $1, the quantity supplied is zero—on row *a* of the table. If the price of a tape is $2, the quantity supplied is 3 million tapes a week—on row *b*. The other rows of the table show the quantities supplied at prices of $3, $4, and $5.

FIGURE 4.5

The Supply Curve

The table shows the supply schedule of tapes. For example, at $2 a tape, 3 million tapes a week are supplied; at $5 a tape, 6 million tapes a week are supplied. The supply curve shows the relationship between the quantity supplied and price, everything else remaining the same. The supply curve usually slopes upward: As the price of a good increases, so does the quantity supplied.

A supply curve can be read in two ways. For a given price, its tells us the quantity that producers plan to sell. And for a given quantity, it tells us the minimum price that producers are willing to accept for that quantity.

	Price (dollars per tape)	Quantity (millions of tapes per week)
a	1	0
b	2	3
c	3	4
d	4	5
e	5	6

To make a supply curve, we graph the quantity supplied on the horizontal axis and the price on the vertical axis, just as in the case of the demand curve. The points on the supply curve labeled *a* through *e* represent the rows of the supply schedule. For example, point *a* on the graph represents a quantity supplied of zero at a price of $1 a tape.

Minimum Supply Price Just as the demand curve has two interpretations, so too does the supply curve. The demand curve can be interpreted as a willingness-and-ability-to-pay curve. The supply curve can be interpreted as a minimum-supply-price curve. It tells us the lowest price at which someone can profitably sell another unit.

If a small quantity is produced, the lowest price at which someone can profitably sell one more unit is low. But if a large quantity is produced, the lowest price at which someone can profitably sell one more unit is high.

In Fig. 4.5, if 6 million tapes are produced each week, the lowest price that a producer is willing to accept for the 6 millionth tape is $5. But if only 4 million tapes are produced each week, the lowest price that a producer is willing to accept for the 4 millionth tape is $3.

A Change in Supply

When any factor that influences selling plans other than the price of the good changes, there is a **change in supply**. Let's look at the five key factors that change supply.

1. Prices of Productive Resources The prices of productive resources influence supply. The easiest way to see this influence is to think about the supply curve as a minimum-supply-price curve. If the prices of productive resources rise, the lowest price a producer is willing to accept rises so supply decreases. For example, during 1996, the price of jet fuel increased and the supply of air transportation decreased. Similarly, a rise in the minimum wage decreased the supply of hamburgers. If the wages of tape producers rise, the supply of tapes decreases.

2. Prices of Related Goods Produced The prices of related goods and services that firms produce influence supply. For example, if the price of prerecorded tapes rises, the supply of blank tapes decreases. Blank tapes and prerecorded tapes are *substitutes in produc-*

tion—goods that can be produced by using the same resources. If the price of beef rises, the supply of cowhide increases. Beef and cowhide are *complements in production*—goods that must be produced together.

3. Expected Future Prices   If the price of a good is expected to rise, the return from selling the good in the future is higher than it is in the present. So the current supply decreases.

4. The Number of Suppliers   Supply also depends on the number of suppliers. The larger the number of firms that produce a good, the greater is the supply of the good. As firms enter an industry, the supply in that industry increases. As firms leave an industry, the supply in that industry decreases. For example, over the past two years, there has been a huge increase in the number of firms that produce and manage World Wide Web sites. As a result, the supply of Internet and World Wide Web services has increased enormously.

5. Technology   New technologies create new products and lower the costs of producing existing products. As a result they change supply. For example, the development of a new technology for tape production by Sony and Minnesota Mining and Manufacturing (3M) has lowered the cost of producing tapes and increased the supply of tapes.

Figure 4.6 illustrates an increase in supply. When supply increases, the supply curve shifts rightward and the quantity supplied is larger at each and every price. For example, at a price of $2, on the original (blue) supply curve, the quantity supplied is 3 million tapes a week. On the new (red) supply curve, the quantity supplied is 6 million tapes a week. Look closely at the numbers in the table in Fig. 4.6 and check that the quantity supplied is larger at each price.

Table 4.2 summarizes the influences on supply and the directions of those influences.

A Change in the Quantity Supplied Versus a Change in Supply

Changes in the factors that influence producers' planned sales cause either a change in the quantity supplied or a change in supply. Equivalently, they cause either a movement along the supply curve or a shift of the supply curve.

A point on the supply curve shows the quantity supplied at a given price. So a movement along the

FIGURE 4.6

An Increase in Supply

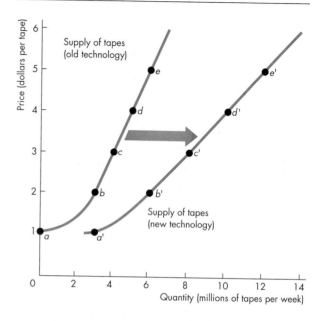

Original supply schedule			New supply schedule		
Old technology			New technology		
	Price (dollars per tape)	**Quantity** (millions of tapes per week)		**Price** (dollars per tape)	**Quantity** (millions of tapes per week)
a	1	0	a'	1	3
b	2	3	b'	2	6
c	3	4	c'	3	8
d	4	5	d'	4	10
e	5	6	e'	5	12

A change in any influence on sellers' plans other than the price of the good itself results in a new supply schedule and a shift of the supply curve. For example, if Sony and 3M invent a new, cost-saving technology for producing tapes, the supply of tapes changes.

At a price of $3 a tape, 4 million tapes a week are supplied when producers use the old technology (row *c* of the table) and 8 million tapes a week are supplied when producers use the new technology. An advance in technology *increases* the supply of tapes and shifts the supply curve *rightward*, as shown by the shift arrow and the resulting red curve.

supply curve shows a **change in the quantity supplied**. The entire supply curve shows supply. So a shift of the supply curve shows a **change in supply**.

Figure 4.7 illustrates and summarizes these distinctions. If the price of a good falls and everything else remains the same, the quantity supplied of that good decreases and there is a movement down the supply curve S_0. If the price of a good rises and everything else remains the same, the quantity supplied increases and there is a movement up the supply curve S_0. When any other influence on selling plans changes, the supply curve shifts and there is a change in supply. If the supply curve is S_0 and if production costs fall supply increases and the supply curve shifts to the red supply curve S_1. If production costs rise, supply decreases and the supply curve shifts to the red supply curve S_2.

FIGURE 4.7
A Change in the Quantity Supplied Versus a Change in Supply

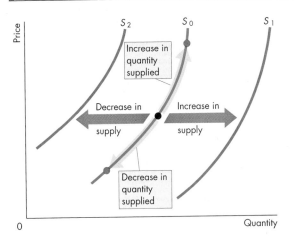

When the price of the good changes, there is a movement along the supply curve and a *change in the quantity supplied*, shown by the blue arrows on supply curve S_0. When any other influence on selling plans changes, there is a shift of the supply curve and a *change in supply*. An increase in supply shifts the supply curve rightward (from S_0 to S_1). A decrease in supply shifts the supply curve shifts leftward (from S_0 to S_2).

TABLE 4.2
The Supply of Tapes

The Law of Supply

The quantity of tapes supplied

Decreases if:
- The price of a tape falls

Increases if:
- The price of a tape rises

Changes in Supply

The supply of tapes

Decreases if:
- The price of a resource used to produce tapes rises
- The price of a substitute in production rises
- The price of a complement in production falls
- The price of a tape is expected to rise in the future
- The number of tape producers decreases

Increases if:
- The price of a resource used to produce tapes falls
- The price of a substitute in production falls
- The price of a complement in production rises
- The price of a tape is expected to fall in the future
- The number of tape producers increases
- More efficient technologies for producing tapes are discovered

REVIEW QUIZ

- Can you define the *quantity supplied* of a good or service?
- What is the *law of supply* and how do we illustrate it?
- If consumers are willing to buy only a given quantity, what does the supply curve tell us about the price at which firms will supply that quantity?
- Can you list all the influences on selling plans that *change supply* and for each influence say whether it increases supply or decreases supply?

Your next task is to use what you've learned about demand and supply and learn how prices and quantities are determined.

Market Equilibrium

WE HAVE SEEN THAT WHEN THE PRICE OF A GOOD rises, the quantity demanded decreases and the quantity supplied increases. We are now going to see how prices coordinate the plans of buyers and sellers and achieve an equilibrium.

An *equilibrium* is a situation in which opposing forces balance each other. Equilibrium in a market occurs when the price balances the plans of buyers and sellers. The **equilibrium price** is the price at which the quantity demanded equals the quantity supplied. The **equilibrium quantity** is the quantity bought and sold at the equilibrium price. A market moves toward its equilibrium because:

- Price regulates buying and selling plans
- Price adjusts when plans don't match

Price as a Regulator

The price of a good regulates the quantities demanded and supplied. If the price is too high, the quantity supplied exceeds the quantity demanded. If the price is too low, the quantity demanded exceeds the quantity supplied. There is one price at which the quantity demanded equals the quantity supplied. Let's work out what that price is.

Figure 4.8 shows the market for tapes. The table shows the demand schedule (from Fig. 4.2) and the supply schedule (from Fig. 4.5). If the price of a tape is $1, the quantity demanded is 9 million tapes a week, but no tapes are supplied. The quantity demanded exceeds the quantity supplied by 9 million tapes a week. In other words, at a price of $1 a tape, there is a shortage of 9 million tapes a week. This shortage is shown in the final column of the table. At a price of $2 a tape, there is still a shortage, but only of 3 million tapes a week. If the price of a tape is $5, the quantity supplied exceeds the quantity demanded. The quantity supplied is 6 million tapes a week, but the quantity demanded is only 2 million. There is a surplus of 4 million tapes a week. The one price at which there is neither a shortage nor a surplus is $3 a tape. At that price, the quantity demanded is equal to the quantity supplied: 4 million tapes a week. The equilibrium price is $3 a tape, and the equilibrium quantity is 4 million tapes a week.

Figure 4.8 shows that the demand curve and supply curve intersect at the equilibrium price of $3 a

FIGURE 4.8

Equilibrium

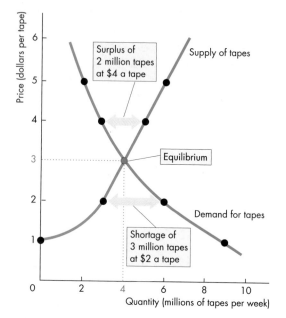

Price (dollars per tape)	Quantity demanded	Quantity supplied	Shortage (–) or surplus (+)
	(millions of tapes per week)		
1	9	0	–9
2	6	3	–3
3	4	4	0
4	3	5	+2
5	2	6	+4

The table lists the quantities demanded and quantities supplied as well as the shortage or surplus of tapes at each price. If the price is $2 a tape, 6 million tapes a week are demanded and 3 million are supplied. There is a shortage of 3 million tapes a week, and the price rises. If the price is $4 a tape, 3 million tapes a week are demanded and 5 million are supplied. There is a surplus of 2 million tapes a week, and the price falls. If the price is $3 a tape, 4 million tapes a week are demanded and 4 million are supplied. There is neither a shortage nor a surplus. Neither buyers nor sellers have any incentive to change the price. The price at which the quantity demanded equals the quantity supplied is the equilibrium price.

tape. At each price *above* $3 a tape, there is a surplus of tapes. For example, at $4 a tape, the surplus is 2 million tapes a week, as shown by the blue arrow. At each price *below* $3 a tape, there is a shortage of tapes. For example, at $2 a tape, the shortage is 3 million tapes a week, as shown by the red arrow.

Price Adjustments

You've seen that if the price is below equilibrium there is a shortage and if the price is above equilibrium there is a surplus. But can we count on the price to change and eliminate a shortage or surplus? We can, because such price changes are mutually beneficial to both buyers and sellers. Let's see why the price changes when there is a shortage or a surplus.

A Shortage Forces the Price Up   Suppose the price of a tape is $2. Consumers plan to buy 6 million tapes a week, and producers plan to sell 3 million tapes a week. Consumers can't force producers to sell more than they plan, so the quantity actually offered for sale is 3 million tapes a week. In this situation, powerful forces operate to increase the price and move it toward the equilibrium price. Some producers, noticing lines of unsatisfied consumers, move their prices up. Some producers increase their output. As producers push their prices up, the price rises toward its equilibrium. The rising price reduces the shortage because it decreases the quantity demanded and increases the quantity supplied. When the price has increased to the point at which there is no longer a shortage, the forces moving the price stop operating and the price comes to rest at its equilibrium.

A Surplus Forces the Price Down   Suppose the price of a tape is $4. Producers plan to sell 5 million tapes a week, and consumers plan to buy 3 million tapes a week. Producers cannot force consumers to buy more than they plan, so the quantity that is actually bought is 3 million tapes a week. In this situation, powerful forces operate to lower the price and move it toward the equilibrium price. Some producers, unable to sell the quantities of tapes they planned to sell, cut their prices. In addition, some producers scale back production. As producers cut prices, the price falls toward its equilibrium. The falling price decreases the surplus because it increases the quantity demanded and decreases the quantity supplied. When the price has fallen to the point at which there is no longer a surplus, the forces moving the price

stop operating, and the price comes to rest at its equilibrium.

The Best Deal Available for Buyers and Sellers

When the price is below equilibrium, it is forced upward toward the equilibrium. Why don't buyers resist the increase and refuse to buy at the higher price? Because they value the good more highly than the current price and they cannot satisfy all their demands at the current price. In some markets— an example is the market for rental accommodation in Atlanta during the 1996 Olympic Games—the buyers might even be the ones who force the price upward by offering higher prices to divert the limited quantities away from other buyers.

When the price is above equilibrium, it is bid downward toward the equilibrium. Why don't sellers resist this decrease and refuse to sell at the lower price? Because their minimum supply price is below the current price and they cannot sell all they would like to at the current price. Normally, it is the sellers who force the price downward by offering lower prices to gain market share from their competitors.

At the price at which the quantity demanded and the quantity supplied are equal, neither buyers nor sellers can do business at a better price. Buyers pay the highest price they are willing to pay for the last unit bought, and sellers receive the lowest price at which they are willing to supply the last unit sold.

When people freely make offers to buy and sell, and when demanders try to buy at the lowest possible price and suppliers try to sell at the highest possible price, the price at which trade takes place is the equilibrium price—the price at which the quantity demanded equals the quantity supplied. The price coordinates the plans of buyers and sellers.

R E V I E W   Q U I Z

- What is the *equilibrium price* of a good or service?
- Over what range of prices does a shortage arise?
- Over what range of prices does a surplus arise?
- What happens to the price when there is a shortage?
- What happens to the price when there is a surplus?
- Why is the price at which the quantity demanded equals the quantity supplied the equilibrium price?
- Why is the equilibrium price the best deal available for both buyers and seller?

Predicting Changes in Price and Quantity

THE DEMAND AND SUPPLY THEORY WE HAVE JUST studied provides us with a powerful way of analyzing influences on prices and the quantities bought and sold. According to the theory, a change in price stems from either a change in demand or a change in supply or a change in both. Let's look first at the effects of a change in demand.

A Change in Demand

What happens to the price and quantity of tapes if the demand for tapes increases? We can answer this question with a specific example. Suppose the price of a Walkman falls from $200 to $50. Because the Walkman and tapes are complements, the demand for tapes increases, as is shown in the table in Fig. 4.9. The original demand schedule and the new one are set out in the first three columns of the table. The table also shows the supply schedule for tapes.

The original equilibrium price is $3 a tape. At that price, 4 million tapes a week are demanded and supplied. When demand increases, the price that makes the quantity demanded equal the quantity supplied is $5 a tape. At this price, 6 million tapes are bought and sold each week. When demand increases, both the price and the quantity increase.

Figure 4.9 shows these changes. The figure shows the original demand for and supply of tapes. The original equilibrium price is $3 a tape, and the quantity is 4 million tapes a week. When demand increases, the demand curve shifts rightward. The equilibrium price rises to $5 a tape, and the quantity supplied increases to 6 million tapes a week, as highlighted in the figure. There is an *increase in the quantity supplied* but *no change in supply*—a movement along, but no shift of, the supply curve.

We can reverse the exercise that we've just conducted. We can work out what happens if we start at a price of $5 a tape with 6 million tapes a week being bought and sold and then demand decreases to its original level. Such a decrease in demand might arise from a fall in the price of CDs or CD players (both substitutes for tapes). The decrease in demand shifts the demand curve leftward. The equilibrium price falls to $3 a tape, and the equilibrium quantity decreases to 4 million tapes a week.

FIGURE 4.9

The Effects of a Change in Demand

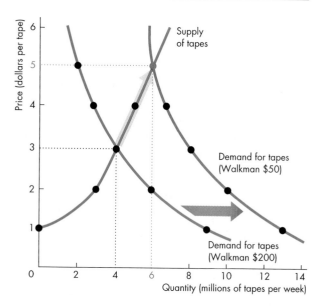

Price (dollars per tape)	Quantity demanded (millions of tapes per week)		Quantity supplied (millions of tapes per week)
	Walkman $200	Walkman $50	
1	9	13	0
2	6	10	3
3	4	8	4
4	3	7	5
5	2	6	6

With the price of a Walkman at $200, the demand for tapes is the blue curve. The equilibrium price is $3 a tape, and the equilibrium quantity is 4 million tapes a week. When the price of a Walkman falls from $200 to $50, the demand for tapes increases and the demand curve shifts rightward to become the red curve.

At $3 a tape, there is now a shortage of 4 million tapes a week. The price of a tape rises to a new equilibrium of $5 a tape. As the price rises to $5, the quantity supplied increases—shown by the blue arrow on the supply curve—to the new equilibrium quantity of 6 million tapes a week. Following an increase in demand, the quantity supplied increases but supply does not change—the supply curve does not shift.

We can now make our first two predictions:

1. When demand increases, both the price and the quantity increase.
2. When demand decreases, both the price and the quantity decrease.

A Change in Supply

Suppose that Sony and 3M introduce a new cost-saving technology in their tape production plants. The new technology increases the supply of tapes. The new supply schedule (the same one that was shown in Fig. 4.6) is presented in the table in Fig. 4.10. What are the new equilibrium price and quantity? The answer is highlighted in the table: The price falls to $2 a tape, and the quantity increases to 6 million a week. You can see why by looking at the quantities demanded and supplied at the old price of $3 a tape. The quantity supplied at that price is 8 million tapes a week, and there is a surplus of tapes. The price falls. Only when the price is $2 a tape does the quantity supplied equal the quantity demanded.

Figure 4.10 illustrates the effect of an increase in supply. It shows the demand curve for tapes and the original and new supply curves. The initial equilibrium price is $3 a tape and the quantity is 4 million tapes a week. When the supply increases, the supply curve shifts rightward. The equilibrium price falls to $2 a tape, and the quantity demanded increases to 6 million tapes a week, highlighted in the figure. There is an *increase in the quantity demanded* but *no change in demand*—a movement along, but no shift of, the demand curve.

The exercise that we've just conducted can be reversed. If we start out at a price of $2 a tape with 6 million tapes a week being bought and sold, we can work out what happens if supply decreases to its original level. Such a decrease in supply might arise from an increase in the cost of labor or raw materials. The decrease in supply shifts the supply curve leftward. The equilibrium price rises to $3 a tape, and the equilibrium quantity decreases to 4 million tapes a week.

We can now make two more predictions:

1. When supply increases, the quantity increases and the price falls.
2. When supply decreases, the quantity decreases and the price rises.

FIGURE 4.10
The Effects of a Change in Supply

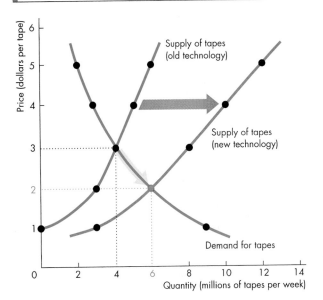

Price (dollars per tape)	Quantity demanded (millions of tapes per week)	Quantity supplied (millions of tapes per week)	
		old technology	new technology
1	9	0	3
2	6	3	6
3	4	4	8
4	3	5	10
5	2	6	12

With the old technology, the supply of tapes is shown by the blue supply curve. The equilibrium price is $3 a tape, and the equilibrium quantity is 4 million tapes a week. When the new technology is adopted, the supply of tapes increases and the supply curve shifts rightward to become the red curve.

At $3 a tape, there is now a surplus of 4 million tapes a week. The price of a tape falls to a new equilibrium of $2 a tape. As the price falls to $2, the quantity demanded increases—shown by the blue arrow on the demand curve—to the new equilibrium quantity of 6 million tapes a week. Following an increase in supply, the quantity demanded increases but demand does not change—the demand curve does not shift.

A Change in Both Demand and Supply

You can now predict the effects of a change in either demand or supply on the price and the quantity. But what happens if *both* demand and supply change together? To answer this question, we look first at the case in which demand and supply move in the same direction—either both increase or both decrease. Then we look at the case in which they move in opposite directions—demand decreases and supply increases or demand increases and supply decreases.

Demand and Supply Change in the Same Direction

We've seen that an increase in the demand for tapes increases the price of tapes and increases the quantity bought and sold. And we've seen that an increase in the supply of tapes lowers the price of tapes and increases the quantity bought and sold. Let's now examine what happens when both of these changes occur together.

The table in Fig. 4.11 brings together the numbers that describe the original quantities demanded and supplied and the new quantities demanded and supplied after the fall in the price of the Walkman and the improved tape production technology. These same numbers are illustrated in the graph. The original (blue) demand and supply curves intersect at a price of $3 a tape and a quantity of 4 million tapes a week. The new (red) supply and demand curves also intersect at a price of $3 a tape but at a quantity of 8 million tapes a week.

An increase in either demand or supply increases the quantity. So when both demand and supply increase, so does quantity.

An increase in demand raises the price, and an increase in supply lowers the price, so we can't say whether the price will rise or fall when demand and supply increase together. In this example, the price does not change. But notice that if demand increases by slightly more than the amount shown in the figure, the price will rise. And if supply increases by slightly more than the amount shown in the figure, the price will fall.

We can now make two more predictions:

1. When *both* demand and supply increase, the quantity increases and the price increases, decreases, or remains constant.
2. When *both* demand and supply decrease, the quantity decreases and the price increases, decreases, or remains constant.

FIGURE 4.11
The Effects of an Increase in Both Demand and Supply

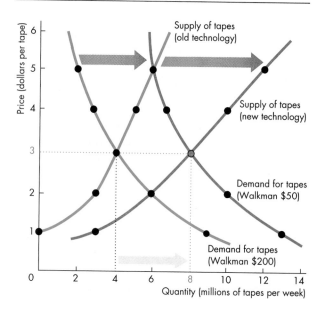

	Original quantities (millions of tapes per week)		New quantities (millions of tapes per week)	
Price (dollars per tape)	**Quantity demanded** Walkman $200	**Quantity supplied** old technology	**Quantity demanded** Walkman $50	**Quantity supplied** new technology
1	9	0	13	3
2	6	3	10	6
3	4	4	8	8
4	3	5	7	10
5	2	6	6	12

When a Walkman costs $200 and the old technology is used to produce tapes, the price of a tape is $3 and the quantity is 4 million tapes a week. A fall in the price of a Walkman increases the demand for tapes, and improved technology increases the supply of tapes. The new supply curve intersects the new demand curve at $3 a tape, the same price as before, but the quantity increases to 8 million tapes a week. These increases in demand and supply increase the quantity but leave the price unchanged.

Demand and Supply Change in Opposite Directions

Let's now see what happens when demand and supply change together but move in *opposite* directions. An improved production technology increases the supply of tapes as before. But now the price of CD players falls. A CD player is a *substitute* for tapes. With less costly CD players, more people buy them and switch from buying tapes to buying discs, and the demand for tapes decreases.

The table in Fig. 4.12 describes the original and new demand and supply schedules. These schedules are shown as the original (blue) and new (red) demand and supply curves in the graph. The original demand and supply curves intersect at a price of $5 a tape and a quantity of 6 million tapes a week. The new supply and demand curves intersect at a price of $2 a tape and at the original quantity of 6 million tapes a week.

A decrease in demand or an increase in supply lowers the price. So when a decrease in demand and an increase in supply occur together, the price falls.

A decrease in demand decreases the quantity, and an increase in supply increases the quantity, so we can't say for sure which way the quantity will change when demand decreases and supply increases at the same time. In this example, the decrease in demand and the increase in supply are such that the increase in quantity brought about by an increase in supply is offset by the decrease in quantity brought about by a decrease in demand—so the quantity does not change. But notice that if demand had decreased by slightly more, the quantity would have decreased. And if supply had increased by slightly more, the quantity would have increased.

We can now make two more predictions:

1. When demand decreases and supply increases, the price falls and the quantity increases, decreases, or remains constant.
2. When demand increases and supply decreases, the price rises and the quantity increases, decreases, or remains constant.

- What is the effect on the price of a tape and the quantity of tapes if (a) the price of a CD rises or (b) the price of a Walkman rises or (c) more firms start to produce tapes or (d) tape producers' wages rise or (e) any pair of these events occur at the same time? (Draw the diagrams!)

FIGURE 4.12

The Effects of a Decrease in Demand and an Increase in Supply

Price (dollars per tape)	Original quantities (millions of tapes per week)		New quantities (millions of tapes per week)	
	Quantity demanded CD player $400	Quantity supplied old technology	Quantity demanded CD player $200	Quantity supplied new technology
1	13	0	9	3
2	10	3	6	6
3	8	4	4	8
4	7	5	3	10
5	6	6	2	12

When a CD player costs $400 and the old technology is used to produce tapes, the price of a tape is $5 and the quantity is 6 million tapes a week. A fall in the price of a CD player decreases the demand for tapes, and improved technology increases the supply of tapes. The new supply curve intersects the new demand curve at $2 a tape, a lower price, but in this case the quantity remains constant at 6 million tapes a week. The decrease in demand and increase in supply lower the price but leave the quantity unchanged.

CD Players, Health Care, and Bananas

Earlier in this chapter, we looked at some facts about prices and quantities of CD players, health care, and bananas. Let's use the theory of demand and supply that we have just studied to explain the movements in the prices and quantities of those goods.

A Price Slide: CD Players   Figure 4.13(a) shows the market for CD players. In 1983, when CD players were first manufactured, very few producers made them and the supply was small. The supply curve was S_0. In 1983, there weren't many titles on CDs and the demand for CD players was small. The demand curve was D_0. The quantities supplied and demanded in 1983 were equal at Q_0, and the price was \$1,100 (1994 dollars). As the technology for making CD players improved and as more and more factories began to produce CD players, the supply increased by a large amount and the supply curve shifted rightward from S_0 to S_1. At the same time, increases in incomes, a decrease in the price of CDs, and an increase in the number of titles on CDs increased the demand for CD players. But the increase in demand was much smaller than the increase in supply. The demand curve shifted rightward from D_0 to D_1. With the new demand curve D_1 and the new supply curve S_1, the equilibrium price fell to \$170 in 1994 and the quantity increased to Q_1. The large increase in supply combined with a smaller increase in demand resulted in an increase in the quantity of CD players and a dramatic fall in the price. Figure 4.13(a) shows the CD player price slide.

A Price Rocket: Health Care   Figure 4.13(b) shows the market for health-care services. In 1980, the supply curve for health-care services was S_0. Advances in medical technology have greatly increased the range and complexity of conditions that can be treated and have increased the supply of health-care services. But large increases in doctors' compensation and costs have escalated the cost of providing health care and have decreased supply. The net change in supply resulting from these two opposing forces has been an increase. The supply curve has shifted rightward from S_0 to S_1. At the same time that supply increased by a relatively modest amount, the demand for health care increased enormously. Some of the increase resulted from higher incomes, some from an aging population, and some from a demand for newly available treatments. The combination of these influences on demand resulted in the demand curve shifting from D_0 to D_1. The combined effect of a large increase in demand and a small increase in supply was an increase in the quantity from Q_0 to Q_1 and an increase in price from 100 (an index number) in 1980 to 167 in 1998. Figure 4.13(b) shows the health-care price rocket.

A Price Roller Coaster: Bananas   Figure 4.13(c) shows the market for bananas. The demand for bananas—curve D—does not change much over the years. But the supply of bananas, which depends mainly on the weather, fluctuates between S_0 and S_1. With good growing conditions, the supply curve is S_1. With bad growing conditions, supply decreases and the supply curve is S_0. As a consequence of fluctuations in supply, the quantity fluctuates between Q_0 and Q_1. The price of bananas fluctuates between 33 cents per pound (1995 cents), the maximum price, and 20 cents per pound, the minimum price. Figure 4.13(c) shows the banana price roller coaster.

The Invisible Hand   Adam Smith said that each buyer and seller in a market "is led by an invisible hand to promote an end which was no part of his intention." What did he mean? He meant that when each one of us makes decisions to buy or sell to achieve the best outcome for ourselves and when our decisions are coordinated in free markets, we end up achieving the best outcome for everyone.

Although markets are amazing instruments, it turns out that they do not always work quite as perfectly as Adam Smith imagined. If you go on to study *micro*economics, you will discover the conditions under which markets are efficient and why they sometimes fail to achieve the best possible outcome for everyone. If you go on to study *macro*economics, you will discover the reasons why the market economy produces fluctuations in output and employment and sometimes creates persistent unemployment.

◆ You now know the basic theory of demand and supply. By using this theory, you can explain past price and quantity fluctuations and make predictions about future fluctuations. *Reading Between the Lines* on pp. 80–81 shows you the theory in action in the market for oranges. You will see many news articles that you can better understand by using your knowledge of demand and supply. Watch for stories about frosts, droughts, and floods and their effects on the prices of many crops and other items.

FIGURE 4.13

Price Slide, Rocket, and Roller Coaster

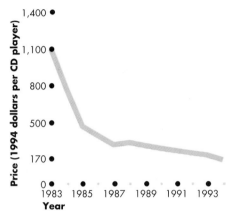

(a) Price slide: CD players

A large increase in the supply of CD players, from S_0 to S_1 combined with a small increase in demand, from D_0 to D_1, resulted in an increase in the quantity of CD players bought and sold from Q_0 to Q_1. The average price of CD players fell from \$1,100 in 1983 to \$170 in 1994—a price slide.

Source: U.S. Bureau of the Census, Statistical Abstract of the United States: 1994 (114th edition). Washington, D.C., 1994.

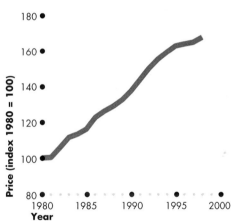

(b) Price rocket: health care

A large increase in demand for health care, from D_0 to D_1, combined with a small increase in the supply, from S_0 to S_1, has resulted in an increase in the quantity of health care, from Q_0 to Q_1 and a rise in the price of health care from 100 in 1980 to 167 in 1998—a price rocket.

Source: Economic Report of the President, 1999.

(c) Price roller coaster: bananas

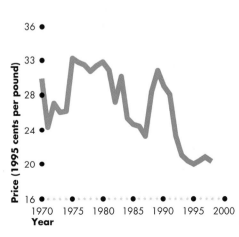

The demand for bananas remains constant at D. But supply fluctuates between S_0 and S_1. As a result, the price of bananas has fluctuated between 20 cents per pound and 33 cents per pound—a price roller coaster.

Source: International Financial Statistics, International Monetary Fund, Washington, D.C., February, 1999.

Demand and Supply:
The Price of Oranges

USA TODAY, JANUARY 4, 1999

Orange Prices Start to Rise after Calif. Freeze

LOS ANGELES—Consumers will pay dramatically more for fresh oranges, the result of a killer freeze in California that has already doubled whole-sale prices.

The coming price rise is the last in a string of calamities that struck agriculture in 1998.

California navel oranges "will be in very limited quantities," and "what is available will be higher in price," said Paul Bernish, spokesman for Kroger, the nation's largest supermarket chain.

"So far, at least, price increases for citrus products have not been passed along to consumers," Bernish said.

Food Lion, with 1,208 stores mostly in the Southeast, said store prices on fresh oranges will rise 20% to 30% this week, less than the 100% increase it's paying at wholesale. "We're trying to absorb as much of that (the price increase) as we can," spokeswoman Chris Ahearn said.

California supplies about 80% of the nation's eating oranges and lemons. Four days of freezing temperatures in the Central Valley last month caused about $530 million in damage. ...

For fresh oranges, the prices are already rising. A standard 37½-pound box of oranges is selling at wholesale for $20 to $24 depending on size and quality, double the price before the frost, the California Farm Bureau Federation reported. ...

Essence of the Story

■ In December 1998, four days of freezing temperatures destroyed a large part of the California crop of navel oranges.

■ During early January 1999, the wholesale price of navel oranges doubled.

■ At the same time, the store price of navel oranges increased by 20 percent to 30 percent.

■ Orange growers sell their production to major supermarket chains in a **wholesale market**.

■ Supermarket chains sell oranges to consumers in a **retail market**.

■ A serious 4-day freeze in California wiped out a large quantity of navel oranges and led to a rise in their price. The wholesale price increased by more than the retail price.

■ Why did the retail price rise? Why did the wholesale price rise by a larger percentage than the retail price?

■ Figure 1 shows the wholesale market for California navel oranges. The demand curve is *D*. Before the freeze, the supply curve was S_{98}. The price was $11 a box, and 2 million boxes a week were bought.

■ In December 1998, freezing temperatures destroyed a large quantity of oranges and the supply of oranges decreased. The supply curve shifted leftward to S_{99}.

■ The price increased to $22 a box (a 100 percent increase, as reported in the news article).

■ The increase in price did not change demand. The demand curve did not shift. But the increase in price brought a *decrease in the quantity*

demanded, which is shown by a *movement along the demand curve.*

■ Figure 2 shows the retail market for California navel oranges. The demand curve is *D*. Before the freeze, the supply curve was S_{98}. The price was 50 cents a pound, and 2 million boxes a week were bought.

■ The decrease in supply shifted the supply curve leftward to S_{99}.

■ The price increased to 65 cents a pound (a 30 percent increase, as reported in the news article).

■ The wholesale price increased by a larger percentage than the retail price, and the profits of supermarkets were squeezed.

■ The percentage rise in the wholesale price exceeded the percentage rise in the retail price because of the way the quantity demanded responds to a price change.

■ A supermarket must stock navel oranges if it is to attract customers who want to buy the oranges even at a higher-than-normal price.

■ A supermarket that does not stock navel oranges loses customers, and its sales of a wide range of items decrease.

Figure 1 The wholesale market

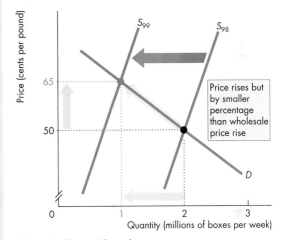

Figure 2 The retail market

■ So a relatively large price rise is needed to allocate the smaller quantity of oranges to the supermarkets.

■ Consumers have many alternatives to navel oranges. When the price of navel oranges rises, some consumers switch to grapefruit and other types of fruit and stop buying oranges. So the quantity of oranges demanded decreases sharply.

■ So a relatively small price rise is sufficient to allocate the smaller quantity of oranges to consumers.

■ In the news article, Chris Ahearn says that Food Lion is trying to absorb the price rise. But the forces of demand and supply prevent supermarkets from raising the retail price by as much as the rise in the wholesale price.

81

MATHEMATICAL NOTE
Demand, Supply, and Market Equilibrium

Demand Curve

The law of demand says that as the price of a good or service falls, the quantity demanded of it increases. We illustrate the law of demand by setting out a demand schedule, by drawing a graph of the demand curve, or by writing down an equation. When the demand curve is a straight line, a linear equation describes it. The equation that describes a downward-sloping demand curve is

$$P = a - bQ_D,$$

where P is the price and Q_D is the quantity demanded. The a and b are positive constants.

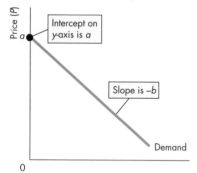

This equation tells us three things:
1. The price at which no one is willing to buy the good (Q_D is zero). That is, if the price is a, then the quantity demanded is zero. You can see the price a on the graph. It is the price at which the demand curve hits the y-axis—what we call the demand curve's "intercept on the y-axis."
2. That as the price falls, the quantity demanded increases. If Q_D is a positive number, then the price P must be less than a. And as Q_D gets larger, the price P becomes smaller. That is, as the quantity increases, the maximum price that buyers are willing to pay for the good falls.
3. The constant b tells us how fast the maximum price that someone is willing to pay for the good falls as the quantity increases. That is, the constant b tells us about the steepness of the demand curve. The equation tells us that the slope of the demand curve is $-b$.

Supply Curve

The law of supply says that as the price of a good or service rises, the quantity supplied of it increases. We illustrate the law of supply by setting out a supply schedule, by drawing a graph of the supply curve, or by writing down an equation. When the supply curve is a straight line, a linear equation describes the supply curve. The equation that describes an upward-sloping supply curve is

$$P = c + dQ_S,$$

where P is the price and Q_S the quantity supplied. The c and d are positive constants.

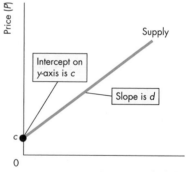

This equation tells us three things:
1. The price at which no one is willing to sell the good (Q_S is zero) That is, if the price is c, then the quantity supplied is zero. You can see the price c on the graph. It is the price at which the supply curve hits the y-axis—what we call the supply curve's "intercept on the y-axis."
2. That as the price rises, the quantity supplied increases. If Q_S is a positive number, then the price P must be greater than c. And as Q_S increases, the price P gets larger. That is, as the quantity increases, the minimum price that sellers are willing to accept rises.
3. The constant d tells us how fast the minimum price at which someone is willing to sell the good rises as the quantity increases. That is, the constant d tells us about the steepness of the supply curve. The equation tells us that the slope of the supply is d.

Market Equilibrium

Demand and supply determine market equilibrium. The figure shows the equilibrium price (P^*) and equilibrium quantity (Q^*) at the intersection of the demand curve and the supply curve.

We can use the equations to find the equilibrium price and equilibrium quantity. The price of a good will adjust until the quantity demanded equals the quantity supplied. That is,

$$Q_D = Q_S.$$

So at the equilibrium price (P^*) and equilibrium quantity (Q^*),

$$Q_D = Q_S = Q^*.$$

To find the equilibrium price and equilibrium quantity:

First substitute Q^* for Q_D in the demand equation and Q^* for Q_S in the supply equation. Then the price is the equilibrium price (P^*), which gives

$$P^* = a - bQ^*,$$
$$P^* = c + dQ^*.$$

Notice that,

$$a - bQ^* = c + dQ^*$$

Now, solve for Q^*

$$a - c = bQ^* + dQ^*$$
$$a - c = (b + d)Q^*$$
$$Q^* = \frac{a - c}{b + d}.$$

To find the equilibrium price (P^*), substitute for Q^* in either the demand equation or the supply equation.

Using the demand equation,

$$P^* = a - b\left(\frac{a - c}{b + d}\right)$$
$$P^* = \frac{a(b + d) - b(a - c)}{b + d}$$
$$P^* = \frac{ad + bc}{b + d}.$$

Alternatively, using the supply equation,

$$P^* = c + d\left(\frac{a - c}{b + d}\right)$$
$$P^* = \frac{c(b + d) + d(a - c)}{b + d}$$
$$P^* = \frac{cb + da}{b + d}$$
$$P^* = \frac{ad + bc}{b + d}.$$

An Example

The demand for ice cream cones is

$$P = 800 - 2Q_D.$$

The supply of ice cream cones is

$$P = 200 + 1Q_S.$$

The price of a cone is expressed in cents, and the quantities are expressed in cones per day.

To find the equilibrium price (P^*) and equilibrium quantity (Q^*), substitute Q^* for Q_D and Q_S and P^* for P.

That is,

$$P^* = 800 - 2Q^*$$
$$P^* = 200 + 1Q^*$$

Now solve for Q^*:

$$800 - 2Q^* = 200 + 1Q^*$$
$$600 = 3Q^*$$
$$Q^* = 200$$

And

$$P^* = 800 - 2Q^*$$
$$= 800 - 2(200)$$
$$= 400$$

The equilibrium price is $4 a cone, and the equilibrium quantity is 200 cones per day.

SUMMARY

KEY POINTS

Price and Opportunity Cost (p. 62)

- Opportunity cost is a relative price. We measure relative price by dividing the price of one good by the price (index) of a basket of all goods.
- Demand and supply determines relative prices.

Demand (pp. 63–67)

- Demand is the relationship between the quantity demanded of a good and its price when all other influences on buying plans remain the same.
- The higher the price of a good, other things remaining the same, the smaller is the quantity demanded.
- Demand depends on the prices of substitutes and complements, expected future prices, income, population, and preferences.

Supply (pp. 68–71)

- Supply is the relationship between the quantity supplied of a good and its price when all other influences on selling plans remain the same.
- The higher the price of a good, other things remaining the same, the greater is the quantity supplied.
- Supply depends on the prices of resources used to produce a good, the prices of related goods produced, expected future prices, the number of producers, and technology.

Market Equilibrium (pp. 72–73)

- At the equilibrium price, the quantity demanded equals the quantity supplied.
- At prices above equilibrium, there is a surplus and the price falls.
- At prices below equilibrium, there is a shortage and the price rises.

Predicting Changes in Price and Quantity (pp. 74–79)

- An increase in demand brings a rise in price and an increase in the quantity supplied. (A decrease in demand brings a fall in price and a decrease in the quantity supplied.)
- An increase in supply brings a fall in price and an increase in the quantity demanded. (A decrease in supply brings a rise in price and a decrease in the quantity demanded.)
- An increase in demand and an increase in supply bring an increased quantity but an ambiguous price change. An increase in demand and a decrease in supply raise the price and bring an ambiguous quantity change.

KEY FIGURES ◆

KEY TERMS

PROBLEMS

*1. What is the effect on the price of a tape and the quantity of tapes sold if:
   a. The price of a CD rises?
   b. The price of a Walkman rises?
   c. The supply of CD players increases?
   d. Consumers' incomes increase?
   e. Workers who make tapes get a pay raise?
   f. The price of a Walkman rises at the same time as the workers who make tapes get a pay raise?

2. What is the effect on the price of hotdogs and the quantity of hotdogs sold if:
   a. The price of a hamburger rises?
   b. The price of a hotdog bun rises?
   c. The supply of hotdog sausages increases?
   d. Consumers' incomes decrease?
   e. The wage rate of a hotdog seller increases?
   f. If the wage rate of the hotdog seller rises and at the same time prices of ketchup, mustard, and relish fall?

*3. Suppose that one of the following events occurs:
   a. The price of crude oil rises.
   b. The price of a car rises.
   c. All speed limits on highways are abolished.
   d. Robot technology cuts car production costs.
   Which of the above events increases or decreases (state which):
      (i) The demand for gasoline.
      (ii) The supply of gasoline.
      (iii) The quantity of gasoline demanded.
      (iv) The quantity of gasoline supplied.

4. Suppose that one of the following events occurs:
   a. The price of wool rises.
   b. The price of sweaters falls.
   c. A close substitute for wool is invented.
   d. A new high-speed loom is invented.
   Which of the above events increases or decreases (state which):
      (i) The demand for wool.
      (ii) The supply of wool.
      (iii) The quantity of wool demanded.
      (iv) The quantity of wool supplied.

*5. The figure illustrates the market for pizza.
   a. Label the curves in the figure.
   b. What are the equilibrium price of a pizza and the equilibrium quantity of pizza?

6. The figure illustrates market for bread.
   a. Label the curves in the figure.
   b. What are the equilibrium price of bread and the equilibrium quantity of bread?

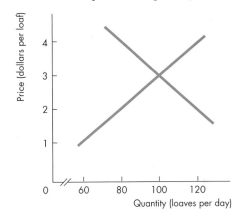

*7. The demand and supply schedules for gum are:

Price (cents per pack)	Quantity demanded (millions of packs a week)	Quantity supplied (millions of packs a week)
20	180	60
30	160	80
40	140	100
50	120	120
60	100	140
70	80	160
80	60	180

   a. What are the equilibrium price and equilibrium quantity of gum?
   b. If gum was 70 cents a pack, describe the situation in the gum market and explain what would happen to the price of gum.

8. The demand and supply schedules for potato chips are:

Price (cents per bag)	Quantity demanded	Quantity supplied
	(millions of bags per week)	
40	170	90
50	160	100
60	150	110
70	140	120
80	130	130
90	120	140
100	110	150
110	100	160

  a. What are the equilibrium price and equilibrium quantity of potato chips?
  b. If chips were 60 cents a bag, describe the situation in the market for potato chips and explain what would happen to the price of a bag of chips.

*9. In problem 7, suppose that a fire destroys some gum-producing factories and the supply of gum decreases by 40 million packs a week.
  a. Has there been a shift in or a movement along the supply curve of gum?
  b. Has there been a shift in or a movement along the demand curve for gum?
  c. What is the new equilibrium price and quantity of gum?

10. In problem 8, suppose a new snack food comes onto the market and as a result the demand for potato chips decreases by 40 million bags per week.
  a. Has there been a shift in or a movement along the supply curve of chips?
  b. Has there been a shift in or a movement along the demand curve for chips?
  c. What is the new equilibrium price and quantity of chips?

*11. In problem 9, suppose an increase in the teenage population increases the demand for gum by 40 million packs per week at the same time as the fire occurs. What is the new equilibrium price and quantity of gum?

12. In problem 10, suppose that a flood destroys several potato farms and as a result supply decreases by 20 million bags a week at the same time as the new snack food comes onto the market. What is the new equilibrium price and quantity of gum?

CRITICAL THINKING

1. After you have studied *Reading Between the Lines* on pp. 80–81, answer the following questions:
  a. Why does the supply of oranges decrease but the demand for oranges not change? How can the demand not change when the quantity available decreases?
  b. Explain to Chris Ahearn and Paul Bernish (the spokespeople for Food Lion and Kroger) why the retail price of oranges is out of their control. How would you explain the forces that determine the prices in both the wholesale market and the retail market?
  c. Gray Davis, the governor of California, wants your advice on what to do about the effects of the freeze on the orange market. In particular, he wants to know what can be done to keep the price of oranges down and the incomes of the orange growers up. Write a brief report to Mr. Davis outlining his options, if he has any, or explaining why there is nothing he can do, if that is your opinion.
  c. Use the links on the Parkin Web site and obtain the latest data on the quantities of oranges produced in the United States.

2. Use the links on the Parkin Web site and obtain data on the prices and quantities of wheat.
  a. Make a figure similar to Fig. 1 on page 81 to illustrate the market for wheat in 1998.
  b. Show the changes in demand and supply and the changes in the quantity demanded and the quantity supplied that are consistent with the price and quantity data.

3. Use the link on the Parkin Web site and read the story about the prices of millennium cruises.
  a. Describe how the millennium changes the price of a cruise.
  b. Use the demand and supply model to explain what happens to the price when there is an increase in demand and no change in supply.
  c. What do you predict would happen to the price of a cruise if air fares to Australia and the South Pacific decreased?
  d. What do you predict would happen to the price of a cruise if the price of oil increased?

Chapter 5

Elasticity

Your pizza business is earning you a good profit but you are worried. You've just learned that a major pizza franchise is planning a big expansion in your neighborhood. You know that the resulting increase in supply will lower the price of pizza and bring tough competition for you. But how big a price fall will you have to cope with? Will there be little change in pizza consumption and a large fall in price? Or will there be a huge increase in pizza consumption and little change in price? To answer these questions, you need a measure of the responsiveness of the quantity of pizza demanded to the price of pizza. ◆ Faced with tough competition from your pizzeria, the burger shop next door has cut its prices. How will the lower price of burgers affect the demand for your pizza? Will it wipe you out of business or make only a small dent in your sales? To answer this question, you need a measure of the responsiveness of the demand for your pizza to the price of burgers, a substitute for pizza. ◆ The economy is booming, and people's incomes are rising. You know that with more income to spend, people will buy more pizza. But how much more pizza will people buy? Will the higher incomes bring a large increase in your sales or will they make only a small difference? To answer this question, you need a measure of the responsiveness of the demand for pizza to consumers' incomes. ◆ As incomes increase, you expect the demand for pizza to increase. But will the increase in demand bring a rise in price with little change in the quantity bought? Or will it bring a huge increase in pizza consumption with little change in price? To answer this question, you need a measure of the responsiveness of the quantity of pizza supplied to a change in the price of pizza.

Predicting Prices

◆ In this chapter, you will learn how to answer questions like the ones just posed. You will learn about elasticity, a measure of the responsiveness of quantities bought and sold to changes in prices and other influences on buyers' and sellers' plans.

After studying this chapter, you will be able to:

■ Define and calculate the price elasticity of demand

■ Use a total revenue test and an expenditure test to estimate the price elasticity of demand

■ Explain the factors that influence the price elasticity of demand

■ Define and calculate the cross elasticity of demand

■ Define and calculate the income elasticity of demand

■ Define and calculate the elasticity of supply

The Price Elasticity of Demand

YOU KNOW THAT WHEN SUPPLY INCREASES, THE equilibrium price falls and the equilibrium quantity increases. But does the price fall by a large amount and the quantity increase by a little? Or does the price barely fall and the quantity increase by a large amount?

The answer depends on the responsiveness of the quantity demanded to a change in price. You can see why by studying Fig. 5.1, which shows two possible scenarios in a local pizza market. Fig. 5.1(a) shows one scenario, and Fig. 5.1(b) shows the other.

In both cases, supply is initially S_0. In part (a), the demand for pizza is shown by the demand curve D_a. In part (b), the demand for pizza is shown by the demand curve D_b. Initially, in both cases, the price is $20 a pizza and the quantity of pizza produced and consumed is 10 pizzas an hour.

Now a large pizza franchise opens up and the supply of pizza increases. The supply curve shifts rightward to S_1. In case (a), the price of a pizza falls by an enormous $15 to $5 and the quantity increases by only 3 to 13 pizzas an hour. In contrast, in case (b), the price falls by only $5 to $15 a pizza and the quantity increases by 7 to 17 pizzas an hour.

The different outcomes arise from differing degrees of responsiveness of the quantity demanded to a change in price. But what do we mean by responsiveness? One possible answer is slope. The slope of demand curve D_a is steeper than the slope of demand curve D_b.

In this example, we can compare the slopes of the two demand curves. But we can't always do so. The reason is that the slope of a demand curve depends on the units in which we measure the price and quantity. And we often must compare the demand curves for different goods and services that are measured in unrelated units. For example, a pizza producer might want to compare the demand for pizza with the demand for soda. Which quantity demanded is more responsive to a price change? This question can't be answered by comparing the slopes of two demand curves. The units of measurement of pizza and soda are unrelated. The question can be answered with a measure of responsiveness that is independent of units of measurement. Elasticity is such a measure.

The **price elasticity of demand** is a units-free measure of the responsiveness of the quantity demanded of a good to a change in its price when all other influences on buyers' plans remain the same.

FIGURE 5.1

How a Change in Supply Changes Price and Quantity

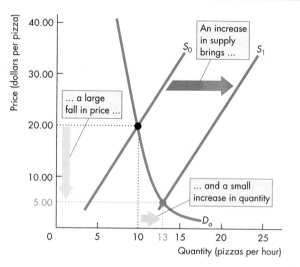

(a) Large price change and small quantity change

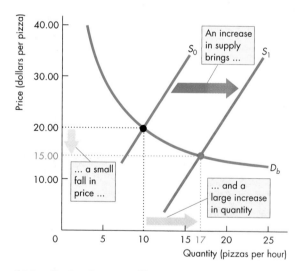

(b) Small price change and large quantity change

Initially, the price is $20 a pizza and the quantity sold is 10 pizzas an hour. Then supply increases from S_0 to S_1. In part (a), the price falls by $15 to $5 a pizza and the quantity increases by only 3 to 13 pizzas an hour. In part (b), the price falls by only $5 to $15 a pizza and the quantity increases by 7 to 17 pizzas an hour. This price change is smaller and quantity change is larger than in case (a). The quantity demanded is more responsive to price in case (b) than in case (a).

Calculating Elasticity

We calculate the *price elasticity of demand* by using the formula

$$\text{Price elasticity of demand} = \frac{\text{Percentage change in quantity demanded}}{\text{Percentage change in price}}.$$

To use this formula, we need to know the quantities demanded at different prices when all other influences on buyers' plans remain the same. Suppose we have the data on prices and quantities demanded of pizza and calculate the price elasticity of demand for pizza.

Figure 5.2 zooms in on the demand curve for pizza and shows how the quantity demanded responds to a small change in price. Initially, the price is $20.50 a pizza and 9 pizzas an hour are sold—the original point in the figure. The price then falls to $19.50 a pizza and the quantity demanded increases to 11 pizzas an hour—the new point in the figure. When the price falls by $1 a pizza, the quantity demanded increases by 2 pizzas an hour.

To calculate the price elasticity of demand, we express the changes in price and quantity demanded as percentages of the *average price* and the *average quantity*. By using the average price and average quantity, we calculate the elasticity at a point on the demand curve midway between the original point and the new point. The original price is $20.50 and the new price is $19.50, so the average price is $20. The $1 price decrease is 5 percent of the average price. That is,

$$\Delta P / P_{ave} = (\$1/\$20) \times 100 = 5\%.$$

The original quantity demanded is 9 pizzas and the new quantity demanded is 11 pizzas, so the average quantity demanded is 10 pizzas. The 2 pizza increase in the quantity demanded is 20 percent of the average quantity. That is,

$$\Delta Q / Q_{ave} = (2/10) \times 100 = 20\%.$$

So the price elasticity of demand, which is the percentage change in the quantity demanded (20 percent) divided by the percentage change in price (5 percent), is 4. That is,

$$\text{Price elasticity of demand} = \frac{\%\Delta Q}{\%\Delta P}$$
$$= \frac{20\%}{5\%} = 4.$$

FIGURE 5.2

Calculating the Elasticity of Demand ◆

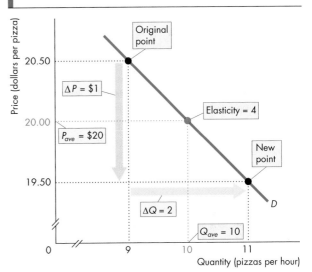

The elasticity of demand is calculated by using the formula*

$$\text{Price elasticity of demand} = \frac{\text{Percentage change in quantity demanded}}{\text{Percentage change in price}}$$
$$= \frac{\%\Delta Q}{\%\Delta P}$$
$$= \frac{\Delta Q / Q_{ave}}{\Delta P / P_{ave}}$$
$$= \frac{2/10}{1/20}$$
$$= 4.$$

This calculation measures the elasticity at an average price of $20 a pizza and an average quantity of 10 pizzas an hour.

*In the formula, the Greek letter delta (Δ) stands for "change in" and %Δ stands for "percentage change in."

Average Price and Quantity   Notice that we use the *average* price and *average* quantity. We do this because it gives the most precise measurement of elasticity—at the midpoint between the original price and the new price. If the price falls from $20.50 to $19.50, the $1 price change is 4.9 percent of $20.50. The 2 pizza change in quantity is 22.2 percent of 9, the original quantity. So if we use these numbers, the elasticity of demand is 22.2 divided by 4.9, which equals 4.5. If the price rises from $19.50 to $20.50, the $1 price change is 5.1 percent of $19.50. The 2 pizza change in quantity is 18.2 percent of 11, the original quantity. So if we use these numbers, the elasticity of demand is 18.2 divided by 5.1, which equals 3.6.

By using percentages of the *average* price and *average* quantity, we get the same value for the elasticity regardless of whether the price falls from $20.50 to $19.50 or rises from $19.50 to $20.50.

Percentages and Proportions Elasticity is the ratio of the *percentage* change in the quantity demanded to the percentage change in the price. It is also, equivalently, the proportionate change in the quantity demanded divided by the proportionate change in the price. The proportionate change in price is $\Delta P/P_{ave}$, and the proportionate change in quantity demanded is $\Delta Q/Q_{ave}$. The percentage changes are the proportionate changes multiplied by 100. So when we divide one percentage change by another, the 100s cancel and the result is the same as we get by using the proportionate changes.

A Units-Free Measure Now that you've calculated a price elasticity of demand, you can see why it is a *units-free measure*. Elasticity is a units-free measure because the percentage change in each variable is independent of the units in which the variable is measured. And the ratio of the two percentages is a number without units.

Minus Sign and Elasticity When the price of a good *rises*, the quantity demanded *decreases* along the demand curve. Because a *positive* change in price brings a *negative* change in the quantity demanded, the price elasticity of demand is a negative number. But it is the magnitude, or *absolute value*, of the price elasticity of demand that tells us how responsive— how elastic—demand is. To compare elasticities, we use the magnitude of the price elasticity of demand and ignore the minus sign.

Inelastic and Elastic Demand

Figure 5.3 shows three demand curves that cover the entire range of possible elasticities of demand. In Fig. 5.3(a), the quantity demanded is constant regardless of the price. If the quantity demanded remains constant when the price changes, then the price elasticity of demand is zero and the good is said to have **perfectly inelastic demand.** One good that has a very low price elasticity of demand (perhaps zero over some price range) is insulin. Insulin is of such

importance to some diabetics that if the price rises or falls, they do not change the quantity they buy.

If the percentage change in the quantity demanded equals the percentage change in price, then the price elasticity equals 1 and the good is said to have **unit elastic demand**. The demand in Fig. 5.3(b) is an example of unit elastic demand.

Between the cases shown in parts (a) and (b) of Fig. 5.3 is the general case in which the percentage change in the quantity demanded is less than the percentage change in price. In this case, the price elasticity of demand is between zero and 1, and the good is said to have **inelastic demand.** Food and housing are examples of goods with inelastic demand.

If the quantity demanded changes by an infinitely large percentage in response to a tiny price change, then the price elasticity of demand is infinity, and the good is said to have **perfectly elastic demand.** Fig. 5.3(c) shows perfectly elastic demand. An example of a good that has a very high elasticity of demand (almost infinite) is soda from two campus machines located side by side. If the two machines offer soda for the same price, some people buy from one and some from the other. But if one machine's price is higher than the other's price, even by a small amount, no one will buy from the machine with the higher price. Sodas from the two machines are perfect substitutes.

Between the cases in parts (b) and (c) of Fig. 5.3 is the general case in which the percentage change in the quantity demanded exceeds the percentage change in price. In this case, the price elasticity is greater than 1 and the good is said to have **elastic demand**. Automobiles and furniture are examples of goods that have elastic demand.

Elasticity Along a Straight-Line Demand Curve

Along a straight-line demand curve like the one shown in Fig. 5.4, the elasticity varies. At high prices and small quantities, the elasticity is large and at low prices and large quantities, the elasticity is small. To convince yourself of this fact, calculate the elasticity at three different average prices.

First, suppose the price falls from $25 to $15 a pizza. The quantity demanded increases from zero to 20 pizzas an hour. The average price is $20, so the percentage change in price is $10 divided by $20 multiplied by 100, which equals 50. The average quantity is 10 pizzas, so the percentage change in quantity is 20 pizzas divided by 10 pizzas multiplied

FIGURE 5.3

Inelastic and Elastic Demand

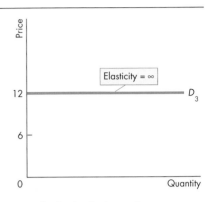

(a) Perfectly inelastic demand   **(b) Unit elastic demand**   **(c) Perfectly elastic demand**

Each demand illustrated here has a constant elasticity. The demand curve in part (a) illustrates the demand for a good that has a zero elasticity of demand. The demand curve in part (b) illustrates the demand for a good with a unit elasticity of demand. And the demand curve in part (c) illustrates the demand for a good with an infinite elasticity of demand.

by 100, which equals 200. So dividing the percentage change in the quantity demanded (200) by the percentage change in price (50), you see that the elasticity of demand at an average price of $20 is 4.

Next, suppose that the price falls from $15 to $10 a pizza. The quantity demanded increases from 20 to 30 pizzas an hour. The average price is now $12.50, so the percentage change in price is $5 divided by $12.50 multiplied by 100, which equals 40 percent. The average quantity is 25 pizzas an hour, so the percentage change in the quantity demanded is 10 pizzas divided by 25 pizzas multiplied by 100, which also equals 40 percent. So dividing the percentage change in the quantity demanded (40) by the percentage change in price (40), you see that the elasticity of demand at an average price of $12.50 is 1. The elasticity of demand is always equal to one at the midpoint of a straight-line demand curve.

Finally, suppose that the price falls from $10 to zero. The quantity demanded increases from 30 to 50 pizzas an hour. The average price is now $5, so the percentage change in price is $10 divided by $5 multiplied by 100, which is 200 percent. The average quantity is 40 pizzas, so the percentage change in the quantity demanded is 20 pizzas divided by 40 pizzas multiplied by 100, which is 50 percent. So dividing the percentage change in the quantity demanded (50) by the percentage change in price (200), the elasticity of demand at an average price of $5 is ¼.

FIGURE 5.4

Elasticity Along a Straight-Line Demand Curve

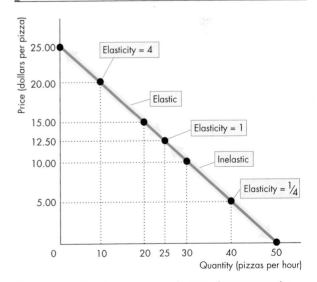

On a straight-line demand curve, elasticity decreases as the price falls and the quantity demanded increases. Demand is unit elastic at the midpoint of the demand curve (elasticity is 1). Above the midpoint, demand is elastic; and below the midpoint, demand is inelastic.

Total Revenue and Elasticity

The **total revenue** from the sale of a good equals the price of the good multiplied by the quantity sold. When a price changes, total revenue also changes. But a rise in price does not always increase total revenue. The change in total revenue depends on the elasticity of demand in the following way:

- If demand is elastic, a 1 percent price cut increases the quantity sold by more than 1 percent and total revenue increases.
- If demand is unit elastic, a 1 percent price cut increases the quantity sold by 1 percent and so total revenue does not change.
- If demand is inelastic, a 1 percent price cut increases the quantity sold by less than 1 percent and total revenue decreases.

We can use this relationship between elasticity and total revenue to estimate elasticity using the total revenue test. The **total revenue test** is a method of estimating the price elasticity of demand by observing the change in total revenue that results from a price change (with all other influences on the quantity sold remaining unchanged).

- If a price cut increases total revenue, demand is elastic.
- If a price cut decreases total revenue, demand is inelastic.
- If a price cut leaves total revenue unchanged, demand is unit elastic.

Figure 5.5 shows the connection between the elasticity of demand and total revenue. In part (a), over the price range from $25 to $12.50, demand is elastic. Over the price range from $12.50 to zero, demand is inelastic. At a price of $12.50, demand is unit elastic.

Figure 5.5(b) shows total revenue. At a price of $25, the quantity sold is zero, so total revenue is also zero. At a price of zero, the quantity demanded is 50 pizzas an hour but total revenue is again zero. A price cut in the elastic range brings an increase in total revenue—the percentage increase in the quantity demanded is greater than the percentage decrease in price. A price cut in the inelastic range brings a decrease in total revenue—the percentage increase in the quantity demanded is less than the percentage decrease in price. At a unit elasticity, total revenue is at a maximum.

FIGURE 5.5

Elasticity and Total Revenue

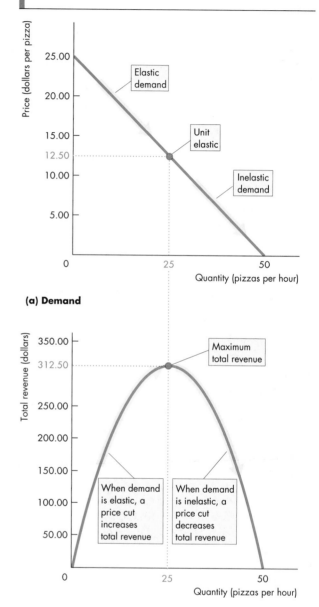

(a) Demand

(b) Total revenue

When demand is elastic, in the price range from $25 to $12.50, a decrease in price (part a) brings an increase in total revenue (part b). When demand is inelastic, in the price range from $12.50 to zero, a decrease in price (part a) brings a decrease in total revenue (part b). When demand is unit elastic, at a price of $12.50 (part a), total revenue is at a maximum (part b).

Your Expenditure and Your Elasticity

When a price changes, the change in your expenditure on the good depends on *your* elasticity of demand.

- If your demand is elastic, a 1 percent price cut increases the quantity you buy by more than 1 percent and your expenditure on the item increases.
- If your demand is unit elastic, a 1 percent price cut increases the quantity you buy by 1 percent and so your expenditure on the item does not change.
- If your demand is inelastic, a 1 percent price cut increases the quantity you buy by less than 1 percent and your expenditure on the item decreases.

So if when the price of an item falls, you spend more on it, your demand for that item is elastic; if you spend the same amount, your demand is unit elastic; and if you spend less, your demand is inelastic.

The Factors That Influence the Elasticity of Demand

Table 5.1 lists some estimates of actual elasticities in the United States. You can see that these real-world elasticities of demand range from 1.52 for metals, the good with the most elastic demand in the table, to 0.12 for food, the good with the most inelastic demand in the table. What makes the demand for some goods elastic and the demand for others inelastic?

Elasticity depends on three main factors:

- The closeness of substitutes
- The proportion of income spent on the good
- The time elapsed since a price change

Closeness of Substitutes The closer the substitutes for a good or service, the more elastic is the demand for it. For example, oil has substitutes but none that are very close (imagine a steam-driven, coal-fueled car or a nuclear-powered jetliner). So the demand for oil is inelastic. Metals have substitutes such as plastics, so the demand for metals is elastic.

The degree of substitutability between two goods also depends on how narrowly (or broadly) we define them. For example, the elasticity of demand for meat is low, but the elasticity of demand for beef, lamb, or chicken is high. The elasticity of demand for personal computers is low, but the elasticity of demand for a Compaq, Dell, or IBM is high.

TABLE 5.1

Some Real-World Price Elasticities of Demand

Good or Service	Elasticity
Elastic Demand	
Metals	1.52
Electrical engineering products	1.39
Mechanical engineering products	1.30
Furniture	1.26
Motor vehicles	1.14
Instrument engineering products	1.10
Professional services	1.09
Transportation services	1.03
Inelastic Demand	
Gas, electricity, and water	0.92
Oil	0.91
Chemicals	0.89
Beverages (all types)	0.78
Clothing	0.64
Tobacco	0.61
Banking and insurance services	0.56
Housing services	0.55
Agricultural and fish products	0.42
Books, magazines, and newspapers	0.34
Food	0.12

Sources: Ahsan Mansur and John Whalley, "Numerical Specification of Applied General Equilibrium Models: Estimation, Calibration, and Data," in *Applied General Equilibrium Analysis,* eds. Herbert E. Scarf and John B. Shoven (New York: Cambridge University Press, 1984), 109, and Henri Theil, Ching-Fan Chung, and James L. Seale, Jr., *Advances in Econometrics, Supplement 1, 1989, International Evidence on Consumption Patterns* (Greenwich, Conn: JAI Press, Inc., 1989). Reprinted with permission.

In everyday language, we call some goods, such as food and housing, *necessities* and other goods, such as exotic vacations, *luxuries.* A necessity is a good that has poor substitutes and that is crucial for our well-being. So generally, a necessity has an inelastic demand. A luxury is a good that usually has many substitutes, one of which is not buying it. So a luxury generally has an elastic demand.

Proportion of Income Spent on the Good Other things remaining the same, the greater the proportion of income spent on a good, the more elastic is the demand for it.

Think about your own elasticity of demand for chewing gum and housing. If the price of chewing gum doubles, you consume almost as much gum as before. Your demand for gum is inelastic. If apartment rents double, you shriek and look for more students to share accommodation with you. Your demand for housing is more elastic than your demand for gum. Why the difference? Housing takes a large proportion of your budget and gum takes only a tiny proportion. You don't like either price increase, but you hardly notice the higher price of gum, while the higher rent puts your budget under severe strain.

Figure 5.6 shows the proportion of income spent on food and the price elasticity of demand for food in 10 countries. This figure confirms the general tendency we have just described. The larger the proportion of income spent on food, the larger is the price elasticity of demand for food. For example, in Tanzania, a nation where average incomes are 3.3 percent of incomes in the United States and where 62 percent of income is spent on food, the price elasticity of demand for food is 0.77. In contrast, in the United States, where 12 percent of income is spent on food, the elasticity of demand for food is 0.12.

Time Elapsed Since a Price Change The longer the time that has elapsed since a price change, the more elastic is demand. When a price rises, consumers often continue to buy similar quantities of a good for a while. But given enough time, they find acceptable and less costly substitutes. As this process of substitution occurs, the quantity purchased of a good or service that has become more expensive gradually decreases. When a price falls, consumers buy more of the good. But as time passes, they find ever more creative ways of using inexpensive items and demand becomes more elastic. For example, some Japanese farmers have discovered that they can use an inexpensive pager to tell their cows when it is milking time!

FIGURE 5.6

Price Elasticities in 10 Countries

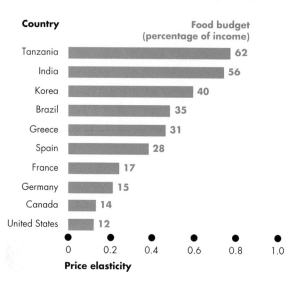

As income increases and the proportion of income spent on food decreases, the demand for food becomes less elastic.

Source: Henri Theil, Chung-Fan Chung, and James L. Seale, Jr., Advances in Econometrics, Supplement I, 1989, International Evidence on Consumption Patterns (Greenwich, Conn: JAI Press, Inc., 1989).

REVIEW QUIZ

- Why do we need a units-free measure of the responsiveness of the quantity demanded of a good or service to a change in its price?
- Can you define and calculate the price elasticity of demand?
- Why, when we calculate the price elasticity of demand, do we express the change in price as a percentage of the *average* price and the change in quantity as a percentage of the *average* quantity?
- What is the total revenue test and why does it work?
- What are the main influences on the elasticity of demand that make the demand for some goods elastic and the demand for other goods inelastic?

You've now completed your study of the *price* elasticity of demand. Two other elasticity concepts tell us the effects of other influences on demand. Let's look at these other elasticities of demand.

More Elasticities of Demand

BACK AT THE PIZZERIA, YOU ARE TRYING TO WORK out how a price cut by the burger shop next door will affect the demand for your pizza. You know that pizzas and burgers are substitutes. And you know that when the price of a substitute for pizza falls, the demand for pizza decreases. But by how much?

You also know that pizza and soda are complements. And you know that if the price of a complement of pizza falls, the demand for pizza increases. So you wonder whether you might keep your customers by cutting the price you charge for soda. But you want to know by how much you must cut the price of soda to hold onto your customers in the face of the cheaper burgers next door.

To answer these questions, you need to calculate the cross elasticity of demand. Let's examine this elasticity measure.

Cross Elasticity of Demand

We measure the influence of a change in the price of substitutes or complements by using the concept of the cross elasticity of demand. The **cross elasticity of demand** is a measure of the responsiveness of the demand for a good to a change in the price of a substitute or complement, other things remaining the same. It is calculated by using the formula

$$\text{Cross elasticity of demand} = \frac{\text{Percentage change in quantity demanded}}{\text{Percentage change in price of a substitute or complement}}.$$

The cross elasticity of demand can be positive or negative. It is positive for a substitute and negative for a complement.

Figure 5.7 illustrates the cross elasticity of demand. Pizza and burgers are substitutes. Because they are substitutes, when the price of a burger falls, the demand for pizza decreases. The demand curve for pizza shifts leftward from D_0 to D_1. Because a *fall* in the price of a burger brings a *decrease* in the demand for pizza, the cross elasticity of demand for pizza with respect to the price of a burger is *positive*. Both the price and the quantity change in the same direction.

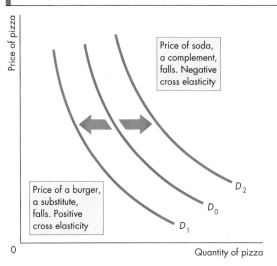

FIGURE 5.7

Cross Elasticity of Demand

A burger is a *substitute* for pizza. When the price of a burger falls, the demand for pizza decreases and the demand curve for pizza shifts leftward from D_0 to D_1. The cross elasticity of the demand for pizza with respect to the price of a burger is *positive*. Soda is a *complement* of pizza. When the price of soda falls, the demand for pizza increases and the demand curve for pizza shifts rightward from D_0 to D_2. The cross elasticity of the demand for pizza with respect to the price of soda is *negative*.

Pizza and soda are complements. Because they are complements, when the price of soda falls, the demand for pizza increases. The demand curve for pizza shifts rightward from D_0 to D_2. Because a *fall* in the price of soda brings an *increase* in the demand for pizza, the cross elasticity of demand for pizza with respect to the price of soda is *negative*. The price and quantity change in *opposite* directions.

The magnitude of the cross elasticity of demand determines how far the demand curve shifts. The larger the cross elasticity (absolute value), the greater is the change in demand and the larger is the shift in the demand curve.

If two items are very close substitutes, such as two brands of spring water, the cross elasticity is large. If two items are close complements, such as movies and popcorn, the cross elasticity is large.

If two items are somewhat unrelated to each other, such as newspapers and orange juice, the cross elasticity is small, and perhaps zero.

Income Elasticity of Demand

The economy is expanding and people are enjoying rising incomes. This prosperity is bringing an increase in the demand for all types of goods and services. But by how much will the demand for pizza increase?

The answer depends on the income elasticity of demand for the good. The **income elasticity of demand** is a measure of the responsiveness of the demand for a good or service to a change in income, other things remaining the same. It is calculated by using the formula

$$\text{Income elasticity of demand} = \frac{\text{Percentage change in quantity demanded}}{\text{Percentage change in income}}.$$

Income elasticities of demand can be positive or negative and fall into three interesting ranges:

1. Greater than 1 (*normal* good, income elastic)
2. Between zero and 1 (*normal* good, income inelastic)
3. Less than zero (*inferior* good)

Figure 5.8(a) shows an income elasticity of demand that is greater than 1. As income increases, the quantity demanded increases, but the quantity

demanded increases faster than income. Examples of goods in this category are ocean cruises, international travel, jewelry, and works of arts.

Figure 5.8(b) shows an income elasticity of demand that is between zero and 1. In this case, the quantity demanded increases as income increases, but income increases faster than the quantity demanded. Examples of goods in this category are food, clothing, newspapers, and magazines.

Figure 5.8(c) shows an income elasticity of demand that eventually becomes negative. In this case, the quantity demanded increases as income increases until it reaches a maximum at income *m*. As income continues to increase above *m*, the quantity demanded decreases. The elasticity of demand is positive but less than 1 up to income *m*. Beyond income *m*, the income elasticity of demand is negative. Examples of goods in this category are small motorcycles, potatoes, and rice. Low-income consumers buy most of these goods. At low income levels, the demand for such goods increases as income increases. But as income increases above *m*, consumers replace these goods with superior alternatives. For example, a small car replaces the motorcycle; fruit, vegetables, and meat begin to appear in a diet that was heavy in rice or potatoes.

FIGURE 5.8

Income Elasticity of Demand

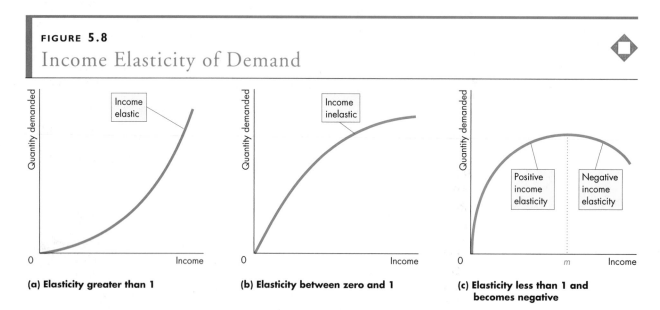

(a) Elasticity greater than 1

(b) Elasticity between zero and 1

(c) Elasticity less than 1 and becomes negative

Income elasticity of demand has three ranges of values. In part (a), income elasticity of demand is greater than 1. As income increases along the *x*-axis, the quantity demanded increases but by a bigger percentage than the increase in income. In part (b), income elasticity of demand is between zero and 1. As income increases, the quantity demanded increases but by a smaller percentage than the increase in income. In part (c), the income elasticity of demand is positive at low incomes but becomes negative as income increases above level *m*. Maximum consumption of this good occurs at the income *m*.

Real-World Income Elasticities of Demand

Table 5.2 shows estimates of some income elasticities in the United States. Necessities such as food and clothing are income inelastic, while luxuries such as airline and foreign travel are income elastic.

But what is a necessity and what is a luxury depend on the level of income. For people with a low income, food and clothing can be luxuries. So the *level* of income has a big effect on income elasticities of demand. Figure 5.9 shows this effect on the income elasticity of demand for food in 10 countries. In countries with low incomes, such as Tanzania and India, the income elasticity of demand for food is high. In countries with high incomes, such as the United States, it is low.

TABLE 5.2
Some Real-World Income Elasticities of Demand

Elastic Demand

Airline travel	5.82
Movies	3.41
Foreign travel	3.08
Electricity	1.94
Restaurant meals	1.61
Local buses and trains	1.38
Haircuts	1.36
Cars	1.07

Inelastic Demand

Tobacco	0.86
Alcoholic beverages	0.62
Furniture	0.53
Clothing	0.51
Newspapers and magazines	0.38
Telephone	0.32
Food	0.14

Sources: H.S. Houthakker and Lester D. Taylor, *Consumer Demand in the United States* (Cambridge, Mass.: Harvard University Press, 1970), and Henri Theil, Ching-Fan Chung, and James L. Seale, Jr., *Advances in Econometrics, Supplement 1, 1989, International Evidence on Consumption Patterns* (Greenwich, Conn.: JAI Press, Inc., 1989). Reprinted with permission.

FIGURE 5.9
Income Elasticities in 10 Countries

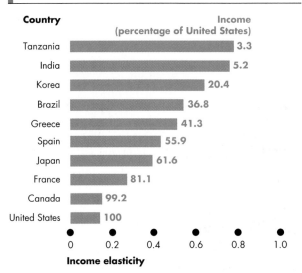

As income increases, the income elasticity of demand for food decreases. For low-income consumers, a larger percentage of any increase in income is spent on food than for high-income consumers.

Source: Henri Theil, Ching-Fan Chung, and James L. Seale, Jr., *Advances in Econometrics, Supplement 1, 1989, International Evidence on Consumption Patterns* (Greenwich, Conn.: JAI Press, Inc., 1989).

R E V I E W   Q U I Z

- What does the cross elasticity of demand measure?
- What does the sign (positive versus negative) of the cross elasticity of demand tell us about the relationship between two goods?
- What does the income elasticity of demand measure?
- What does the sign (positive versus negative) of the income elasticity of demand tell us about a good?
- Why does the level of income influence the magnitude of the income elasticity of demand?

You've now completed your study of the *cross elasticity* of demand and the *income elasticity* of demand. Let's look at the other side of a market and examine the elasticity of supply.

Elasticity of Supply

YOU KNOW THAT WHEN DEMAND INCREASES, THE equilibrium price rises and the equilibrium quantity increases. But does the price rise by a large amount and the quantity increase by a little? Or does the price barely rise and the quantity increase by a large amount?

The answer depends on the responsiveness of the quantity supplied to a change in price. You can see why by studying Fig. 5.10, which shows two possible scenarios in a local pizza market. Fig. 5.10(a) shows one scenario, and Fig. 5.10(b) shows the other.

In both cases, demand is initially D_0. In part (a), the supply of pizza is shown by the supply curve S_a. In part (b), the supply of pizza is shown by the supply curve S_b. Initially, in both cases, the price is $20 a pizza and the quantity produced and consumed is 10 pizzas an hour.

Now an increase in income and population increases the demand for pizza. The demand curve shifts rightward to D_1. In case (a), the price rises by $10 to $30 a pizza and the quantity increases by only 3 to 13 an hour. In contrast, in case (b), the price rises by only $1 to $21 a pizza and the quantity increases by 10 to 20 pizzas an hour.

The different outcomes arise from differing degrees of responsiveness of the quantity supplied to a change in price. We measure the degree of responsiveness by using the concept of the elasticity of supply.

Calculating the Elasticity of Supply

The **elasticity of supply** measures the responsiveness of the quantity supplied to a change in the price of a good when all other influences on selling plans remain the same. It is calculated by using the formula

$$\frac{\text{Elasticity}}{\text{of supply}} = \frac{\text{Percentage change in quantity supplied}}{\text{Percentage change in price}}.$$

We use the same method that you learned when you studied the elasticity of demand. Let's calculate the elasticity of supply for the supply curves in Fig. 5.10.

In Fig. 5.10(a), when the price rises from $20 to $30, the price rise is $10 and the average price is $25, so the price rises by 40 percent of the average price. The quantity increases from 10 to 13, so the increase

---

FIGURE **5.10**

How a Change in Demand Changes Price and Quantity

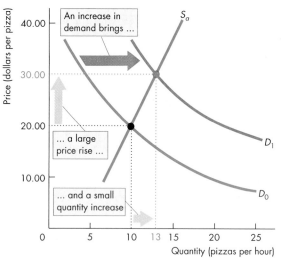

(a) Large price change and small quantity change

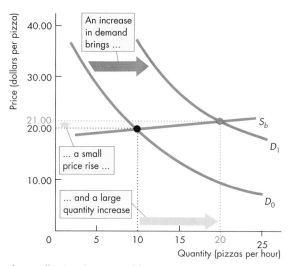

(b) Small price change and large quantity change

Initially, the price is $20 a pizza and the quantity sold is 10 pizzas an hour. Then incomes and population increase and demand increases from D_0 to D_1. In part (a), the price rises by $10 to $30 a pizza and the quantity increases by only 3 to 13 pizzas an hour. In part (b), the price rises by only $1 to $21 a pizza and the quantity increases by 10 to 20 pizzas an hour. The quantity supplied is more responsive to price in case (b) than in case (a).

is 3, the average quantity is 11.5, and the quantity increases by 26 percent. The elasticity of supply is equal to 26 percent divided by 40 percent, which equals 0.65.

In Fig. 5.10(b), when the price rises from $20 to $21, the price rise is $1 and the average price is $20.50, so the price rises by 4.9 percent of the average price. The quantity increases from 10 to 20, so the increase is 10, the average quantity is 15, and the quantity increases by 67 percent. The elasticity of supply is equal to 67 percent divided by 4.9 percent, which equals 13.67.

Figure 5.11 shows the range of supply elasticities. If the quantity supplied is fixed regardless of the price, the supply curve is vertical and the elasticity of supply is zero. Supply is perfectly inelastic. This case is shown in Fig. 5.11(a). A special intermediate case occurs when the percentage change in price equals the percentage change in quantity. Supply is then unit elastic. This case is shown in Fig. 5.11(b). No matter how steep the supply curve is, if it is linear and passes through the origin, supply is unit elastic. If there is a price at which sellers are willing to offer any quantity for sale, the supply curve is horizontal and the elasticity of supply is infinite. Supply is perfectly elastic. This case is shown in Fig. 5.11(c).

The Factors That Influence the Elasticity of Supply

The magnitude of the elasticity of supply depends on:

- Resource substitution possibilities
- Time frame for the supply decision

Resource Substitution Possibilities Some goods and services can be produced only by using unique or rare productive resources. These items have a low, and perhaps a zero, elasticity of supply. Other goods and services can be produced by using commonly available resources that could be allocated to a wide variety of alternative tasks. Such items have a high elasticity of supply.

A van Gogh painting is an example of a good with a vertical supply curve and an elasticity of supply of zero. At the other extreme, wheat can be grown on land that is almost equally good for growing corn. So it is just as easy to grow wheat as corn, and the opportunity cost of wheat in terms of forgone corn is almost constant. As a result, the supply curve of wheat is almost horizontal and its elasticity of supply is very large. Similarly, when a good is produced in many different countries (for example, sugar and beef), the supply of the good is highly elastic.

FIGURE 5.11
Inelastic and Elastic Supply

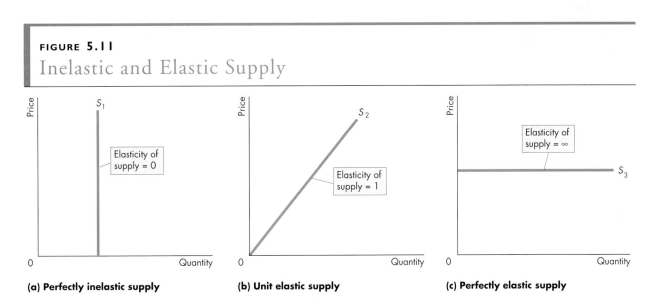

(a) Perfectly inelastic supply

(b) Unit elastic supply

(c) Perfectly elastic supply

Each supply illustrated here has a constant elasticity. The supply curve in part (a) illustrates the supply of a good that has a zero elasticity of supply. The supply curve in part (b) illustrates the supply for a good with a unit elasticity of supply. All linear supply curves that pass through the origin have a unit elasticity. The supply curve in part (c) illustrates the supply for a good with an infinite elasticity of supply.

The supply of most goods and services lies between the two extremes. The quantity produced can be increased but only by incurring higher cost. If a higher price is offered, the quantity supplied increases. Such goods and services have an elasticity of supply between zero and infinity.

Time Frame for the Supply Decision   To study the influence of the length of time elapsed since a price change, we distinguish three time frames of supply:

■ Momentary supply
■ Long-run supply
■ Short-run supply

When the price of a good rises or falls, the *momentary supply curve* shows the response of the quantity supplied immediately following a price change.

Some goods, such as fruits and vegetables, have a perfectly inelastic momentary supply—a vertical supply curve. The quantities supplied depend on crop-planting decisions made earlier. In the case of oranges, for example, planting decisions have to be made many years in advance of the crop being available. The momentary supply curve is vertical because, on a given day, no matter what the price of oranges, producers cannot change their output. They have picked, packed, and shipped their crop to market, and the quantity available for that day is fixed.

In contrast, some goods have a perfectly elastic momentary supply. Long-distance phone calls are an example. When many people simultaneously make a call, there is a big surge in the demand for telephone cables, computer switching, and satellite time, and the quantity supplied increases (up to the physical limits of the telephone system). But the price remains constant. Long-distance carriers monitor fluctuations in demand and reroute calls to ensure that the quantity supplied equals the quantity demanded without changing the price.

The *long-run supply curve* shows the response of the quantity supplied to a change in price after all the technologically possible ways of adjusting supply have been exploited. In the case of oranges, the long run is the time it takes new plantings to grow to full maturity—about 15 years. In some cases, the long-run adjustment occurs only after a completely new production plant has been built and workers have been trained to operate it—typically a process that might take several years.

The *short-run supply curve* shows how the quantity supplied responds to a price change when only *some* of the technologically possible adjustments to production have been made. The first adjustment that is usually made is in the amount of labor employed. To increase output in the short run, firms work their labor force overtime and perhaps hire additional workers. To decrease their output in the short run, firms lay off workers or reduce their hours of work. With the passage of time, firms can make additional adjustments, perhaps training additional workers or buying additional tools and other equipment. The short-run response to a price change, unlike the momentary and long-run responses, is not a unique response but a sequence of adjustments.

The short-run supply curve slopes upward because producers can take actions quite quickly to change the quantity supplied in response to a price change. For example, if the price of oranges falls, growers can stop picking and leave oranges to rot on the tree. Or if the price rises, they can use more fertilizer and improved irrigation to increase the yields of their existing trees. In the long run, they can plant more trees and increase the quantity supplied even more in response to a given price rise.

R E V I E W   Q U I Z

■ Why do we need to measure of the responsiveness of the quantity supplied of a good or service to a change in its price?
■ Can you define and calculate the elasticity of supply?
■ What are the main influences on the elasticity of supply that make the supply of some goods elastic and the supply of other goods inelastic?
■ Can you provide examples of goods or services whose elasticity of supply are (a) zero, (b) greater than zero but less than infinity, and (c) infinity?
■ How does the time frame over which a supply decision is made influence the elasticity of supply?

◆ You have now studied the theory of demand and supply, and you have learned how to measure the elasticities of demand and supply. Table 5.3 summarizes all the elasticities that you've met in this chapter. In the next chapter, we are going to study the efficiency of competitive markets. But before we do that, take a look at *Reading Between the Lines* on pp. 102–103 to see elasticity in action.

TABLE 5.3
A Compact Glossary of Elasticities

Price Elasticities of Demand

A relationship is described as	When its magnitude is	Which means that
Perfectly elastic or infinitely elastic	Infinity	The smallest possible increase in price causes an infinitely large decrease in the quantity demanded*
Elastic	Less than infinity but greater than 1	The percentage decrease in the quantity demanded exceeds the percentage increase in price
Unit elastic	1	The percentage decrease in the quantity demanded equals the percentage increase in price
Inelastic	Greater than zero but less than 1	The percentage decrease in the quantity demanded is less than the percentage increase in price
Perfectly inelastic or completely inelastic	Zero	The quantity demanded is the same at all prices

Cross Elasticities of Demand

A relationship is described as	When its value is	Which means that
Perfect substitutes	Infinity	The smallest possible increase in the price of one good causes an infinitely large increase in the quantity demanded of the other good
Substitutes	Positive, less than infinity	If the price of one good increases, the quantity demanded of the other good also increases
Independent	Zero	The quantity demanded of one good remains constant, regardless of the price of the other good
Complements	Less than zero	The quantity demanded of one good decreases when the price of the other good increases

Income Elasticities of Demand

A relationship is described as	When its value is	Which means that
Income elastic (normal good)	Greater than 1	The percentage increase in the quantity demanded is greater than the percentage increase in income
Income inelastic (normal good)	Less than 1 but greater than zero	The percentage increase in the quantity demanded is less than the percentage increase in income
Negative income elastic (inferior good)	Less than zero	When income increases, quantity demanded decreases

Elasticities of Supply

A relationship is described as	When its magnitude is	Which means that
Perfectly elastic	Infinity	The smallest possible increase in price causes an infinitely large increase in the quantity supplied
Elastic	Less than infinity but greater than 1	The percentage increase in the quantity supplied exceeds the percentage increase in the price
Inelastic	Greater than zero but less than 1	The percentage increase in the quantity supplied is less than the percentage increase in the price
Perfectly inelastic	Zero	The quantity supplied is the same at all prices

*In each description, the directions of change may be reversed. For example, in this case: The smallest possible *decrease* in price causes an infinitely large *increase* in the quantity demanded.

Elasticity in Action: The Market for Gas

USA TODAY, FEBRUARY 4, 1999

Gas Wars Send Prices Plummeting

Gas wars across the nation are driving already-low fuel costs to their cheapest levels in more than two decades.

Prices have plummeted into the 70-cents-a-gallon range at some warring stations from Hawaii to Pennsylvania.

Some stations in Virginia and New Jersey are selling fuel for 57 to 59 cents a gallon to lure motorists from rival dealers across the street. Not since the 1960s and '70s has competition between stations made gas such a bargain.

"Let the wars rage on," says Eric Pressman, who filled his Toyota MR2 for $7 in Dale City, Va.

The average national price of self-serve, unleaded gas dropped to 97.9 cents a gallon last month. That's the lowest since 1979 and 18 cents cheaper than the same time last year, according to AAA.

When adjusted for inflation, prices are the lowest in history. ...

A glut of crude oil and improvements in manufacturing have created a gas surplus. As a result, oil prices fell to an average of $12 a barrel last month, down from $15 in January 1998. That's the lowest level in a quarter century. ...

Motorists should enjoy cheap driving all year. Good summer driving weather probably will increase fuel demands and could bump prices 5 to 10 cents a gallon. But analysts don't expect dramatic price increases.

Essence of the Story

■ The national average price of self-serve unleaded gas was 97.9 cents a gallon in January 1999, down 18 cents a gallon from its January 1998 level.

■ Prices in some Virginia and New Jersey gas stations were 57 to 59 cents a gallon, and many gas stations across the nation had prices in the 70-cents-a-gallon range.

■ These gas prices are the lowest in 20 years; adjusted for inflation, they are the lowest ever.

■ The price of crude oil fell from $15 in January 1998 to $12 a barrel in January 1999, its lowest level in 25 years.

■ If good summer driving weather increases the demand for gasoline, the price could rise by 5 to 10 cents a gallon.

Economic Analysis

■ Figure 1 shows the price of gasoline since 1959. The green line is the money price, and the red line is the relative price (the price adjusted for inflation)—see Chapter 4, p. 62.

■ As the news article reports, adjusted for inflation, the price in January 1999 was the lowest ever.

■ The money price is the lowest since 1979 except for 1986-1989, when the price was also roughly the same as in 1999 (a slight error in the news article).

■ The price of gasoline has fallen because the supply of gasoline has increased. And the fall in price is relatively large because the *demand for gasoline is inelastic.*

■ Figure 2 illustrates the effects of an increase in supply. The demand for gasoline is *D*. Initially, the supply of gasoline is S_{98}, and the price is $1.26 (126 cents) a gallon.

■ The supply of gasoline increases to S_{99}. In Fig. 2, the elasticity of demand for gasoline is (approximately) 0.5. So the price falls to 98 cents a gallon, and the quantity increases from 7 million barrels a day to 8 million barrels a day.

■ If the demand for gasoline were elastic, the increase in supply would bring only a small fall in price. Its main effect would be to bring a relatively large increase in the equilibrium quantity.

■ Figure 3 illustrates the effect of an increase in the demand for gasoline during the summer. Demand increases from D_{Jan} to D_{Jul}. The price rise is the upper end of the range predicted in the news article. The elasticity of supply is (approximately) 0.9.

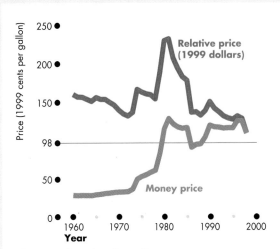

Figure 1 The price of gasoline

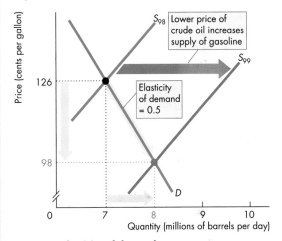

Figure 2 Elasticity of demand

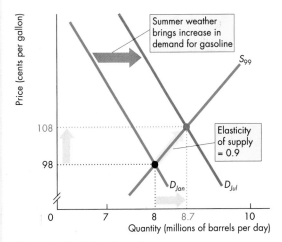

Figure 3 Elasticity of supply

103

SUMMARY

KEY POINTS

The Price Elasticity of Demand (pp. 88–94)

- Elasticity is a measure of the responsiveness of the quantity demanded of a good to a change in its price.
- Price elasticity of demand equals the percentage change in the quantity demanded divided by the percentage change in price.
- The larger the magnitude of the elasticity of demand, the greater is the responsiveness of the quantity demanded to a given change in price.
- Price elasticity of demand depends on how easily one good serves as a substitute for another, the proportion of income spent on the good, and the length of time elapsed since the price change.
- If demand is elastic, a decrease in price leads to an increase in total revenue. If demand is unit elastic, a decrease in price leaves total revenue unchanged. And if demand is inelastic, a decrease in price leads to a decrease in total revenue.

More Elasticities of Demand (pp. 95–97)

- Cross elasticity of demand measures the responsiveness of demand for one good to a change in the price of a substitute or a complement.
- The cross elasticity of demand with respect to the price of a substitute is positive. The cross elasticity of demand with respect to the price of a complement is negative.
- Income elasticity of demand measures the responsiveness of demand to a change in income. For a normal good, the income elasticity of demand is positive. For an inferior good, the income elasticity of demand is negative.
- When the income elasticity is greater than 1, as income increases, the percentage of income spent on the good increases.
- When the income elasticity is less than 1 but greater than zero, as income increases, the percentage of income spent on the good decreases.

Elasticity of Supply (pp. 98–100)

- Elasticity of supply measures the responsiveness of the quantity supplied of a good to a change in its price.
- Elasticities of supply range between zero (vertical supply curve) and infinity (horizontal supply curve).
- Supply decisions have three time frames: momentary, long run, and short run.
- Momentary supply refers to the response of sellers to a price change at the instant that the price changes.
- Long-run supply refers to the response of sellers to a price change when all the technologically feasible adjustments in production have been made.
- Short-run supply refers to the response of sellers to a price change after some adjustments in production have been made.

KEY FIGURES AND TABLE

KEY TERMS

PROBLEMS

*1. Rain spoils the strawberry crop. As a result, the price rises from $4 to $6 a box and the quantity demanded decreases from 1,000 to 600 boxes a week. Over this price range,
   a. What is the price elasticity of demand?
   b. Describe the demand for strawberries.

2. Good weather brings a bumper tomato crop. The price of tomatoes falls from $6 to $4 a basket and the quantity demanded increases from 200 to 400 baskets a day. Over this price range,
   a. What is the price elasticity of demand?
   b. Describe the demand for tomatoes.

*3. The figure shows the demand for videotape rentals.

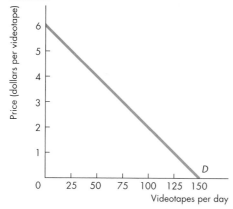

   a. Calculate the elasticity of demand for a rise in rental price from $3 to $5.
   b. At what price is the elasticity of demand equal to 1, infinity, and zero?

4. The figure shows the demand for pens.

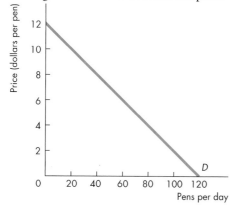

   a. Calculate the elasticity of demand for a rise in price from $2 to $4.

   b. At what prices is the elasticity of demand equal to 1, greater than 1, and less than 1?

*5. If the quantity of dental services demanded increases by 10 percent when the price of dental services falls by 10 percent, is the demand for dental service inelastic, elastic, or unit elastic?

6. If the quantity of fish demanded decreases by 5 percent when the price of fish rises by 10 percent, is the demand for fish elastic, inelastic, or unit elastic?

*7. The demand schedule for computer chips is:

Price (dollars per chip)	Quantity demanded (millions of chips per year)
200	50
250	45
300	40
350	35
400	30

   a. What happens to total revenue if the price of a chip falls from $400 to $350?
   b. What happens to total revenue if the price of a chip falls from $350 to $300?
   c. At what price is total revenue a maximum?
   d. What quantity of chips will be sold at the price that answers problem 7(c)?
   e. At an average price of $350, is the demand for chips elastic or inelastic? Use the total revenue test to answer this question.

8. The demand schedule for coffee is:

Price (dollars per pound)	Quantity demanded (millions of pounds per year)
10	30
15	25
20	20
25	15

   a. What happens to total revenue if the price of coffee rises from $10 to $20 per pound?
   b. What happens to total revenue if the price rises from $15 to $25 per pound?
   c. What price will maximize total revenue?
   d. What quantity of coffee will be sold at the price that answers problem 8(c)?
   e. At an average price of $15 a pound, is the demand for coffee elastic or inelastic? Use the total revenue test to answer this question.

*9. In problem 7, at $250 a chip, is the demand for chips elastic or inelastic? Use the total revenue test to answer this question.

10. In problem 8, at $15 a pound, is the demand for coffee elastic or inelastic? Use the total revenue test to answer this question.

*11. If a 12 percent rise in the price of orange juice decreases the quantity of orange juice demanded by 22 percent and increases the quantity of apple juice demanded by 14 percent, calculate the cross elasticity of demand between orange juice and apple juice.

12. If a 10 percent fall in the price of beef increases the quantity of beef demanded by 15 percent and decreases the quantity of chicken demanded by 20 percent, calculate the cross elasticity of demand between beef and chicken.

*13. Last year, Alex's income increased from $3,000 to $5,000. Alex increased his consumption of bagels from 4 to 8 a month and decreased his consumption of donuts from 12 to 6 a month. Calculate Alex's income elasticity of demand for i) bagels, and ii) donuts.

14. Last year Judy's income increased from $10,000 to $12,000. Judy increased her demand for concert tickets by 10 percent and decreased her demand for bus rides by 5 percent. Calculate Judy's income elasticity of demand for i) concert tickets and ii) bus rides.

💻*15. The table gives the supply schedule for long-distance phone calls:

Price (cents per minute)	Quantity supplied (millions of minutes per day)
10	200
20	400
30	600
40	800

Calculate the elasticity of supply when
a. The price falls from 40 cents to 30 cents a minute.
b. The price is 20 cents a minute.

16. The table gives the supply schedule for shoes.

Price (dollars per pair)	Quantity supplied (millions of pairs per year)
120	1200
125	1400
130	1600
135	1800

Calculate the elasticity of supply when
a. The price rises from $125 to $135 a pair.
b. The price is $125 a pair.

CRITICAL THINKING

1. According to the news article in *Reading Between the Lines* on pp. 102–103, a glut of crude oil caused the supply of gasoline to increase during 1998 and early 1999:
   a. What do you think the article means by "a glut of crude oil"? Answer this question by using the concepts of demand, supply, quantity demanded, and quantity supplied.
   b. Why do you think the reported glut of crude oil caused the price of crude oil to fall? Use the concept of elasticity in your answer to this question.
   c. Calculate the elasticity of demand implied by the data and curves in Fig. 2 on p. 103.
   d. Calculate by approximately how much the price of gasoline would have fallen if the elasticity of demand for gasoline was 2 and the quantity of gasoline increased from 7 million barrels a day to 8 million barrels a day.
   e. Calculate the elasticity of supply implied by the data and curves in Fig. 3 on p. 103.

2. Use the link on the Parkin Web site and:
   a. Find the price of gasoline in the summer of 1999. Did the predictions of the news article occur?
   b. Use the tools of demand and supply and the concept of elasticity to explain the recent changes in the price of gasoline.
   c. Find the latest price of crude oil.
   d. Use the tools of demand and supply and the concept of elasticity to explain the recent changes in the price of crude oil.

3. Use the link on the Parkin Web site and:
   a. Find the number of gallons in a barrel.
   b. What is the cost of the crude oil in one gallon of gasoline?
   c. What are the other costs that make up the total cost of a gallon of gasoline?
   d. If the price of crude oil falls by 10 percent, by what percentage would you expect the price of gasoline to change, other things remaining the same?
   e. In light of your answer to part (d), do you think the elasticity of demand for crude oil is greater than, less than, or equal to the elasticity of demand for gasoline?

Chapter 6

Efficiency and Equity

People constantly strive to get more for less. As consumers, we love a bargain. We enjoy telling our friends about the great deal we got on CDs or some other item we bought at a surprisingly low price. Every time we buy something or decide *not* to buy something, we express our view about how scarce resources should be used. We try to spend our incomes in ways that get the most out of our scarce resources. For example, we balance the pleasure we get from our expenditure on movies against that we get from our textbooks. ◆ Is the allocation of our resources between leisure and education, pizza and submarine sandwiches, roller blades and squash balls, and all the other things we buy the right one? Could we get more out of our resources if we spent

More for Less

more on some goods and services and less on others? ◆ Scientists and engineers devote enormous efforts to finding new technologies for producing goods and services. Workers in factories and on assembly lines make suggestions that increase productivity. Is our economy efficient at producing goods and services? Do we get the most out of our scarce resources in our factories, offices, and shops?

◆ Some firms make huge profits year after year. Microsoft, for example, has generated enough profit over the past ten years to rocket Bill Gates, one of its founders, into the position of being one of the richest people in the world. Is that kind of business success a sign of efficiency? ◆ And is it fair that Bill Gates is so incredibly rich while others live in miserable poverty?

◈ These are the kinds of questions you'll explore in this chapter. You will first learn some concepts that enable you to think about efficiency more broadly than the everyday use of that word. You will discover that competitive markets can be efficient. But you will also discover some sources of inefficiency that can be addressed with government action. And you will discover that firms that make huge profits, while efficient in one sense, might be inefficient in a broader sense.

After studying this chapter, you will be able to:

- ◼ **Define efficiency**
- ◼ **Distinguish between value and price and define consumer surplus**
- ◼ **Distinguish between cost and price and define producer surplus**
- ◼ **Explain the conditions in which competitive markets move resources to their highest-valued uses**
- ◼ **Explain the obstacles to efficiency in our economy**
- ◼ **Explain the main ideas about fairness and evaluate claims that competitive markets result in unfair outcomes**

Efficiency: A Refresher

IT IS HARD TO TALK ABOUT EFFICIENCY IN ORDI-
nary conversation without generating both disagreement and misunderstanding. Many people see efficiency as a clearly desirable goal. To an engineer, an
entrepreneur, a politician, a working mother, or
an economist, getting more for less seems like an
obviously sensible thing to aim for. But some people
think that the pursuit of efficiency conflicts with
other goals. And they believe the other goals are
more worthy of pursuit. Environmental protection
groups worry about contamination from "efficient"
nuclear power plants. And car producers worry about
competition from "efficient" foreign producers.

Economists use the idea of efficiency in a way
that avoids these conflicts. Resource use is **efficient**
when we produce the goods and services that people
value most highly (see Chapter 3, pp. 40-42). Equivalently, resource use is efficient when we cannot produce more of a good or service without giving up
some other good or service that we value more highly.

If people value a nuclear-free environment more
highly than they value cheap electric power, it is efficient to use higher-cost, nonnuclear technologies to
produce electricity. Efficiency is not a cold, mechanical concept. It is a concept based on value, and value
is based on people's feelings.

Think about the efficient quantity of pizza. To
produce more pizza, we must give up some other
goods and services. For example, we might give up
some submarine sandwiches. To get more pizzas, we
forgo submarine sandwiches. If we produce fewer
pizzas, we can produce more submarine sandwiches.
What is the efficient quantity of pizza to produce? The
answer depends on marginal benefit and marginal cost.

Marginal Benefit

If we consume one more pizza, we receive a marginal
benefit. **Marginal benefit** is the benefit that a person receives from consuming one more unit of a good
or service. The marginal benefit from a good or service
is measured as the maximum amount that a person is
willing to pay for one more unit of it. So the marginal
benefit from a pizza is the maximum amount of other
goods and services that people are willing to give up to
get one more pizza. The marginal benefit from pizza
decreases as the quantity of pizza consumed increases—
the principle of *decreasing marginal benefit*.

We can express the marginal benefit from a pizza
as the number of submarine sandwiches that people
are willing to forgo to get one more pizza. But we can
also express marginal benefit as the dollar value of
other goods and services that people are willing to
forgo. Figure 6.1 shows the marginal benefit from
pizza expressed in this way. As the quantity of pizza
increases, the value of other items that people are
willing to forgo to get yet one more pizza decreases.

Marginal Cost

If we produce one more pizza, we incur a marginal
cost. **Marginal cost** is the opportunity cost of producing *one more unit* of a good or service. The marginal cost of a good or service is measured as the

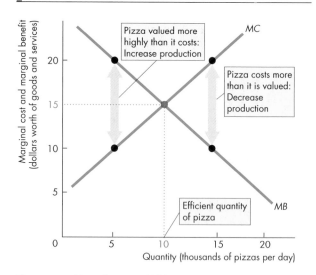

FIGURE 6.1

The Efficient Quantity of Pizza

The marginal benefit curve (MB) shows what people *are willing to* forgo to get one more pizza. The marginal cost curve (MC) shows what people *must* forgo to get one more pizza. If fewer than 10,000 pizzas a day are produced, marginal benefit exceeds marginal cost. Greater value can be obtained by producing more pizzas. If more than 10,000 pizzas a day are produced, marginal cost exceeds marginal benefit. Greater value can be obtained by producing fewer pizzas. If 10,000 pizzas a day are produced, marginal benefit equals marginal cost and the effi-cient quantity of pizza is available.

value of the best alternative forgone. So the marginal cost of a pizza is the value of the best alternative forgone to get one more pizza. The marginal cost of a pizza increases as the quantity of pizza produced increases—the principle of *increasing marginal cost*.

We can express marginal cost as the number of submarine sandwiches we must forgo to get one more pizza. But we can also express marginal cost as the dollar value of other goods and services we must forgo. Figure 6.1 shows the marginal cost of pizza expressed in this way. As the quantity of pizza produced increases, the value of other items we must forgo to get yet one more pizza increases.

Efficiency and Inefficiency

To determine the efficient quantity of pizza, we compare the marginal cost of a pizza with the marginal benefit from a pizza. There are three possible cases:

- Marginal benefit exceeds marginal cost.
- Marginal cost exceeds marginal benefit.
- Marginal benefit equals marginal cost.

Marginal Benefit Exceeds Marginal Cost Suppose the quantity of pizza produced is 5,000 a day. Figure 6.1 shows that at this quantity, the marginal benefit of a pizza is $20. That is, when the quantity of pizza available is 5,000 a day, people are willing to pay $20 for the 5,000th pizza.

Figure 6.1 also shows that the marginal cost of the 5,000th pizza is $10. That is, to produce one more pizza, the value of other goods and services that we must forgo is $10. If pizza production increases from 4,999 to 5,000, the value of the additional pizza is $20 and its marginal cost is $10. By producing this pizza, the value of the pizza produced exceeds the value of the goods and services forgone by $10. Resources are used more efficiently—they create more value—if we produce an extra pizza and fewer other goods and services. This same reasoning applies all the way up to the 9,999th pizza. Only when we get to the 10,000th pizza does marginal benefit not exceed marginal cost.

Marginal Cost Exceeds Marginal Benefit Suppose the quantity of pizza produced is 15,000 a day. Figure 6.1 shows that at this quantity, the marginal benefit of a pizza is $10. That is, when the quantity of pizza available is 15,000 a day, people are willing to pay $10 for the 15,000th pizza.

Figure 6.1 also shows that the marginal cost of the 15,000th pizza is $20. That is, to produce one

more pizza, the value of the other goods and services that we must forgo is $20.

If pizza production decreases from 15,000 to 14,999, the value of the one pizza forgone is $10 and its marginal cost is $20. So by not producing this pizza, the value of the other goods and services produced exceeds the value of the pizza forgone by $10. Resources are used more efficiently—they create more value—if we produce one fewer pizza and more other goods and services. This same reasoning applies all the way down to the 10,001st pizza. Only when we get to the 10,000th pizza does marginal cost not exceed marginal benefit.

Marginal Benefit Equals Marginal Cost Suppose the quantity of pizza produced is 10,000 a day. Figure 6.1 shows that at this quantity, the marginal benefit of a pizza is $15. That is, when the quantity of pizza available is 10,000 a day, people are willing to pay $15 for the 10,000th pizza.

Figure 6.1 also shows that the marginal cost of the 10,000th pizza is $15. That is, to produce one more pizza, the value of other goods and services that we must forgo is $15.

In this situation, we cannot increase the value of the goods and services produced by either increasing or decreasing the quantity of pizza. If we increase the quantity of pizza, the 10,001st pizza costs more to produce than it is worth. If we decrease the quantity of pizza produced, the 9,999th pizza is worth more than it costs to produce. So when marginal benefit equals marginal cost, resource use is efficient.

REVIEW QUIZ

- If the marginal benefit of pizza exceeds the marginal cost of pizza, are we producing too much pizza and too little of other goods, or are we producing too little pizza and too much of other goods?
- If the marginal cost of pizza exceeds the marginal benefit of pizza, are we producing too much pizza and too little of other goods, or are we producing too little pizza and too much of other goods?
- What is the relationship between the marginal benefit of pizza and the marginal cost of pizza when we are producing the efficient quantity of pizza?

Does a competitive pizza market produce the efficient quantity of pizza? Let's answer this question.

Value, Price, and Consumer Surplus

To investigate whether a competitive market is efficient, we need to learn about the connection between demand and marginal benefit and supply and marginal cost.

Value, Willingness to Pay, and Demand

In everyday life, we talk about "getting value for money." When we use this expression we are distinguishing between *value* and *price*. Value is what we get, and price is what we pay.

The **value** of one more unit of a good or service is its *marginal benefit*. Marginal benefit can be expressed as the maximum price that people are willing to pay for another unit of the good or service. The willingness to pay for a good or service determines the demand for it.

In Fig. 6.2(a), the demand curve shows the quantity demanded at each price. For example, when the price of a pizza is $15, the quantity demanded is 10,000 pizzas a day. In Fig. 6.2(b), the demand curve shows the maximum price that people are willing to pay when there is a given quantity. For example, when 10,000 pizzas a day are available, the most that people are willing to pay for a pizza is $15. This interpretation means that the marginal benefit from the 10,000th pizza is $15.

When we draw a demand curve, we use a *relative price*, not a *money price*. A relative price is expressed in dollar units, but it measures the number of dollars worth of other goods and services forgone to obtain one more unit of the good in question (see Chapter 4, p. 62). So a demand curve tells us the quantity of other goods and services that people are willing to forgo to get an additional unit of a good. But this is what a marginal benefit curve tells us, too. So:

A demand curve is a marginal benefit curve.

We don't always have to pay the maximum price that we are willing to pay. When we buy something, we often get a bargain. Let's see how.

FIGURE 6.2

Demand, Willingness to Pay, and Marginal Benefit

(a) Price determines quantity demanded

(b) Quantity determines willingness to pay

The demand curve for pizza, D, shows the quantity of pizza demanded at each price, other things remaining the same. It also shows the maximum price that consumers are willing to pay if a given quantity of pizza is available. At a price of $15,

the quantity demanded is 10,000 pizzas a day (part a). If 10,000 pizzas a day are available, the maximum price that consumers are willing to pay for the 10,000th pizza is $15 (part b).

Consumer Surplus

When people buy something for less than it is worth to them, they receive a consumer surplus. A **consumer surplus** is the value of a good minus the price paid for it.

To understand consumer surplus, let's look at Lisa's demand for pizza, which is shown in Fig. 6.3. Lisa likes pizza, but the marginal benefit she gets from it decreases quickly as her consumption increases.

To keep things simple, suppose Lisa can buy pizza by the slice and that there are 10 slices in a pizza. If a pizza costs $2.50 a slice (or $25 a pizza), Lisa spends her fast food budget on items that she values more highly than pizza. At $2 a slice (or $20 a pizza), she buys 10 slices (one pizza) a week. At $1.50 a slice, she buys 20 slices a week; at $1 a slice, she buys 30 slices a week; and at 50 cents a slice ($5 a pizza), she eats nothing but pizza and buys 40 slices a week.

Lisa's demand curve for pizza in Fig. 6.3 is also her *willingness-to-pay* or marginal benefit curve. It tells us that if Lisa can have only 10 slices a week, she is willing to pay $2 a slice. Her marginal benefit from the 10th slice is $2. If she can have 20 slices a week, she is willing to pay $1.50 for the 20th slice. Her marginal benefit from the 20th slice is $1.50.

Figure 6.3 also shows Lisa's consumer surplus from pizza when the price of pizza is $1.50 a slice. At this price, she buys 20 slices a week. A price of $1.50 a slice is the most she is willing to pay for the 20th slice, so its marginal benefit is exactly the price she pays for it.

But Lisa is willing to pay almost $2.50 for the first slice. So the marginal benefit from this slice is close to $1 more than she pays for it. She receives a *consumer surplus* of almost $1 from her first slice of pizza. At a quantity of 10 slices of pizza a week, Lisa's marginal benefit is $2 a slice. So on this slice, she receives a consumer surplus of 50 cents. To calculate Lisa's consumer surplus, we must find the consumer surplus on each slice and add these surpluses together. This sum is the area of the green triangle in Fig. 6.3. This area is equal to the base of the triangle (20 slices of pizza per week) multiplied by the height of the triangle ($1) divided by 2, or $10 a week.

The blue rectangle in Fig. 6.3 is the amount that Lisa pays for pizza, which is $30 a week—20 slices at $1.50 a slice.

All goods and services are like the pizza example you've just studied. Because of decreasing marginal benefit, people receive more benefit from their consumption than the amount they pay.

FIGURE 6.3
A Consumer's Demand and Consumer Surplus

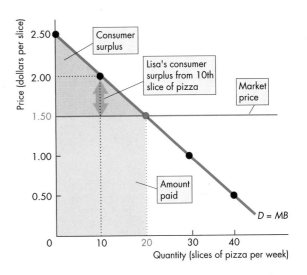

Lisa's demand curve for pizza tells us that at $2.50 a slice, she does not buy pizza. At $2 a slice, she buys 10 slices a week; at $1.50 a slice, she buys 20 slices a week. Lisa's demand curve also tells us that she is willing to pay $2 for the 10th slice and $1.50 for the 20th. She actually pays $1.50 a slice—the market price—and buys 20 slices a week. Her consumer surplus from pizza is $10—the area of the green triangle.

R E V I E W   Q U I Z

- How do we measure the value or marginal benefit of a good or service?
- Can you explain the relationship between marginal benefit and the demand curve?
- What is consumer surplus and how do we measure it?

You've seen how we distinguish between value—marginal benefit—and price. And you've seen that buyers receive a consumer surplus because marginal benefit exceeds price. Next, we're going to study the connection between supply and marginal cost and learn about producer surplus.

Cost, Price, and Producer Surplus

WHAT YOU ARE NOW GOING TO LEARN ABOUT cost, price, and producer surplus parallels the related ideas about value, price, and consumer surplus that you've just studied.

Firms are in business to make a profit. To do so, they must sell their output for a price that exceeds the cost of production. Let's look at the relationship between cost and price.

Cost, Minimum Supply-Price, and Supply

Firms undertake the most elaborate schemes to earn profits. Earning a profit means receiving more (or at least receiving no less) for the sale of a good or service than the cost of producing it. Just as consumers distinguish between *value* and *price*, so producers distinguish between *cost* and *price*. Cost is what a producer gives up, and price is what a producer receives.

The cost of producing one more unit of a good or service is its *marginal cost*. Marginal cost is the minimum price that producers must receive to induce them to produce another unit of the good or service. This minimum acceptable price determines supply.

In Fig. 6.4(a), the supply curve shows the quantity supplied at each price. For example, when the price of a pizza is $15, the quantity supplied is 10,000 pizzas a day. In Fig. 6.4(b), the supply curve shows the minimum price that producers must be offered to produce a given quantity of pizza. For example, if 10,000 pizzas a day are to be produced, the minimum price that producers must be offered is $15 a pizza. This second view of the supply curve means that the marginal cost of the 10,000th pizza is $15.

Because the price is a relative price, a supply curve tells us the quantity of other goods and services that *sellers must forgo* to produce one more unit of the good. But a marginal cost curve also tells us the quantity of other goods and services that we must

---

FIGURE 6.4

Supply, Minimum Supply-Price, and Marginal Cost

(a) Price determines quantity supplied

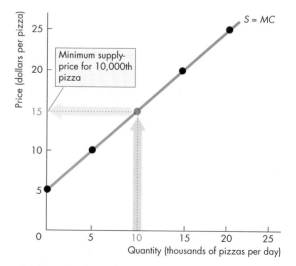

(b) Quantity determines minimum supply-price

The supply curve of pizza, S, shows the quantity of pizza supplied at each price, other things remaining the same. It also shows the minimum price that producers must be offered if a given quantity of pizza is to be produced. At a price of $15,

the quantity supplied is 10,000 pizzas a day (part a). If 10,000 pizzas a day are produced, the minimum price that producers must be offered for the 10,000th pizza is $15 (part b).

forgo to get one more unit of the good. So:

A supply curve is a marginal cost curve.

Producers don't always wind up receiving their minimum supply-price. If the price they receive exceeds the cost they incur, they earn a surplus. This surplus earned by producers is analogous to consumer surplus. Let's look at producer surplus.

Producer Surplus

When a firm sells something for more than it costs to produce, the firm obtains a producer surplus. A **producer surplus** is the price of a good minus the opportunity cost of producing it. To understand producer surplus, let's look at Max's supply of pizza in Fig. 6.5.

Max can produce pizza or bake bread that people like a lot. The more pizza he bakes, the less bread he can bake. His opportunity cost of pizza is the value of the bread he must forgo. This opportunity cost increases as Max increases his production of pizza. If a pizza sells for only $5, Max produces no pizza. He uses his kitchen to bake bread. Pizza just isn't worth producing. But at $10 a pizza, Max produces 50 pizzas a day, and at $15 a pizza, he produces 100 a day.

Max's supply curve is also his *minimum supply-price* curve. It tells us that if Max can sell only one pizza a day, the minimum that he must be paid for it is $5. If he can sell 50 pizzas a day, the minimum that he must be paid for the 50th pizza is $10, and so on.

Figure 6.5 also shows Max's producer surplus. If the price of pizza is $15, Max plans to sell 100 pizzas a day. The minimum that he must be paid for the 100th pizza is $15. So its opportunity cost is exactly the price he receives for it. But his opportunity cost of the first pizza is only $5. So this first pizza costs $10 less to produce than he receives for it. Max receives a *producer surplus* from his first pizza of $10. He receives a slightly smaller producer surplus on the second pizza, less on the third, and so on until he receives no producer surplus on the 100th pizza.

Figure 6.5 shows Max's producer surplus as the blue triangle formed by the area above the supply curve and beneath the price line. This area is equal to the base of the triangle ($10 a slice) multiplied by the height (100 pizzas a week) divided by 2, or $500 a week. Figure 6.5 also shows Max's opportunity costs of production as the red area beneath the supply curve.

FIGURE 6.5

A Producer's Supply and Producer Surplus

Max's supply curve of pizza tells us that at a price of $5, Max plans to sell no pizza. At a price of $10, he plans to sell 50 pizzas a day; and at a price of $15, he plans to sell 100 pizzas a day. Max's supply curve also tells us that the minimum he must be offered is $10 for the 50th pizza a day and $15 for the 100th pizza a day. If the market price is $15 a pizza, he sells 100 pizzas a day and receives $1,500. The red area shows Max's cost of producing pizza, which is $1,000 a day, and the blue area shows his producer surplus, which is $500 a day.

R E V I E W   Q U I Z

- What is the relationship between the marginal cost or opportunity cost of producing a good or service and the minimum supply-price—the minimum price that producers must be offered?
- Can you explain the relationship between marginal cost and the supply curve?
- What is producer surplus and how do we measure it?

Consumer surplus and producer surplus can be used to measure the efficiency of a market. Let's see how we can use these concepts to study the efficiency of a competitive market.

Is the Competitive Market Efficient?

FIGURE 6.6 SHOWS THE MARKET FOR PIZZA. THE demand for pizza is shown by the demand curve, *D*. The supply of pizza is shown by the supply curve *S*. The equilibrium price is $15 a pizza, and the equilibrium quantity is 10,000 pizzas a day.

The market forces that you studied in Chapter 4 (pp. 72–73) will pull the pizza market to this equilibrium. If the price is greater than $15, a surplus will force the price down. If the price is less than $15, a shortage will force the price up. Only if the price is $15 is there neither a surplus nor a shortage and no forces operating to change the price.

So the market price and quantity are pulled toward their competitive equilibrium values. But is a competitive market efficient? Does it produce the efficient quantity of pizza?

Efficiency of a Competitive Market

The equilibrium in Fig. 6.6 is efficient. Resources are being used to produce the quantity of pizza that people value most highly. It is not possible to produce more pizza without giving up some other good or service that is valued more highly. And if a smaller quantity of pizza is produced, resources are used to produce some other good that is not valued as highly as the pizza forgone.

To see why the equilibrium in Fig. 6.6 is efficient, think about the interpretation of the demand curve as a marginal benefit curve and the supply curve as a marginal cost curve. The demand curve tells us the marginal benefit from pizza. The supply curve tells us the marginal cost of pizza. So where the demand curve and the supply curve intersect, marginal benefit equals marginal cost.

But this condition—marginal benefit equals marginal cost—is the condition that delivers an efficient use of resources. It puts resources to work in the activities that create the greatest possible value. So a competitive market is efficient.

If production is less than 10,000 pizzas a day, the marginal pizza is valued more highly that its opportunity cost. If production exceeds 10,000 pizzas a day, the marginal pizza costs more to produce than the value that consumers place on it. Only when 10,000

FIGURE 6.6

An Efficient Market for Pizza

Resources are used efficiently when the sum of consumer surplus and producer surplus is maximized. Consumer surplus is the area below the demand curve and above the market price line—the green triangle. Producer surplus is the area below the price line and above the supply curve—the blue triangle. Here consumer surplus is $50,000, and producer surplus is also $50,000. The total surplus is $100,000. This surplus is maximized when the willingness to pay equals the opportunity cost. The efficient quantity of pizza is 10,000 pizzas per day.

pizzas a day are produced is the marginal pizza worth exactly what it costs. The competitive market pushes the quantity of pizza produced to its efficient level of 10,000 a day. If production is less than 10,000 a day, a shortage raises the price, which stimulates an increase in production. If production exceeds 10,000 a day, a surplus lowers the price, which decreases production.

When the market is using resources efficiently at a competitive equilibrium, the sum of consumer surplus and producer surplus is maximized. At this equilibrium, resources are used in the activities in which they are valued most highly.

Buyers and sellers each attempt to do the best they can for themselves, and no one plans for an efficient outcome for society as a whole. Buyers seek the lowest possible price, and sellers seek the highest possible price. And the market comes to an equilibrium in which the gains from trade are as large as possible.

The Invisible Hand

Writing in his *Wealth of Nations* in 1776, Adam Smith (see pp. 56–57) was the first to suggest that competitive markets send resources to the uses in which they have the highest value. Smith believed that each participant in a competitive market is "led by an invisible hand to promote an end [the efficient use of resources] which was no part of his intention."

You can see the invisible hand at work in the cartoon. The cold drinks vendor has both cold drinks and shade. He has an opportunity cost of each and a minimum supply-price of each. The park-bench reader has a marginal benefit from a cold drink and from shade. You can see that the marginal benefit from shade exceeds the marginal cost, but the marginal cost of a cold drink exceeds its marginal benefit. The transaction that occurs creates gains from trade. The vendor obtains a producer surplus from selling the shade for more than its opportunity cost, and the reader obtains a consumer surplus from buying the shade for less than its marginal benefit. In the third frame of the cartoon, both the consumer and the producer are better off than they were in the first frame. The umbrella has moved to its highest-valued use.

The Invisible Hand at Work Today

The market economy relentlessly performs the activity illustrated in the cartoon and in Fig. 6.6 to achieve an efficient use of resources. And rarely has the market been working as hard as it is today. Think about a few of the changes taking place in our economy that the market is guiding toward an efficient use of resources.

New technologies have cut the cost of producing computers. As these advances have occurred, supply has increased and the price has fallen. Lower prices have encouraged an increase in the quantity demanded of this now less costly tool. The marginal benefit from computers is brought to equality with their marginal cost.

A Florida frost cuts the supply of oranges. With fewer oranges available, the marginal benefit from an orange increases. A shortage of oranges raises their price to allocate the smaller quantity available to the people who value them most highly.

Market forces persistently bring marginal cost and marginal benefit to equality and maximize value.

Drawing by M. Twohy; © 1985 The New Yorker Magazine, Inc.

Obstacles to Efficiency

ALTHOUGH MARKETS GENERALLY DO A GOOD JOB at sending resources to where they are most highly valued, they do not always get the correct answer. Sometimes markets overproduce a good or service, and sometimes they underproduce. The most significant obstacles to achieving an efficient allocation of resources in the market economy are

- Price ceilings and floors
- Taxes, subsidies, and quotas
- Monopoly
- Public goods
- External costs and external benefits

Price Ceilings and Floors A price ceiling is a regulation that makes it illegal to charge a higher price than a specified level. An example is a ceiling on apartment rents, which some cities impose. A price floor is a regulation that makes it illegal to pay a lower price than a specified level. An example is the minimum wage. (We study both of these restrictions on buyers and sellers in Chapter 7.)

The presence of a price ceiling or a price floor blocks the forces of demand and supply, resulting in a level of production that might exceed or fall short of the quantity determined in an unregulated market.

Taxes, Subsidies, and Quotas Taxes increase the prices paid by buyers and lower the prices received by sellers. Taxes decrease the quantity produced (for reasons that are explained in Chapter 7, on p. 135). All kinds of goods and services are taxed, but the goods with the highest taxes are on gasoline, alcohol, and tobacco.

Subsidies, which are payments by the government to producers, decrease the prices paid by buyers and increase the prices received by sellers. Subsidies increase the quantity produced.

Quotas, which are limits to the quantity that a firm is permitted to produce, restrict output below the level that a competitive market produces. Farms are sometimes subject to quotas.

Monopoly A **monopoly** is a firm that has sole control of a market. For example, Microsoft has a near monopoly on operating systems for personal computers. Although monopolies earn large profits, they prevent markets from achieving an efficient use of resources. The goal of a monopoly is to maximize profit; to achieve this goal, it restricts production and raises price. (We study monopoly in Chapter 13.)

Public Goods A **public good** is a good or service that is consumed simultaneously by everyone, even if they don't pay for it. Examples are national defense and the enforcement of law and order. Competitive markets would produce too small a quantity of public goods because of a *free-rider problem*: It is not in each person's interest to buy her or his share of a public good. So a competitive market produces less than the efficient quantity. (We study public goods in Chapter 18.)

External Costs and External Benefits An **external cost** is a cost not borne by the producer but borne by other people. The cost of pollution is an example of an external cost. When an electric power utility burns coal to generate electricity, it puts sulfur dioxide into the atmosphere. This pollutant falls as acid rain and damages vegetation and crops. The utility does not consider the cost of pollution when it decides the quantity of electric power to supply. Its supply is based on its own costs, not on the costs that it inflicts on others. As a result, the utility produces more power than the efficient quantity.

An **external benefit** is a benefit that accrues to people other than the buyer of a good. An example is when someone in a neighborhood paints her home or landscapes her yard. The homeowner does not consider her neighbor's marginal benefit when she decides whether to do this type of work. So the demand curve for house painting and yard improvement does not include all the benefits that accrue. In this case, the quantity falls short of the efficient quantity. (We study externalities in Chapter 20.)

The impediments to efficiency that we've just reviewed and that you will study in greater detail in later chapters result in two possible outcomes:

- Underproduction
- Overproduction

Underproduction

Suppose that one firm owned all the pizza outlets in a city and that it restricted the quantity of pizzas produced to 5,000 a day. Figure 6.7(a) shows that at this quantity, consumers are willing to pay $20 for the marginal pizza—marginal benefit is $20. The marginal cost of a pizza is only $10. So there is a gap between what people are willing to pay and what producers must be offered—between marginal benefit and marginal cost.

The sum of consumer surplus and producer surplus is decreased by the amount of the gray triangle in Fig. 6.7(a). This triangle is called deadweight loss. **Deadweight loss** is the decrease in consumer surplus and producer surplus that results from an inefficient level of production.

The 5,000th pizza brings a benefit of $20 and costs only $10 to produce. If we don't produce this pizza, we are wasting almost $10. Similar reasoning applies all the way up to the 9,999th pizza. By producing more pizza and less of other goods and services, we get more value from our resources.

The deadweight loss is borne by the entire society. It is not a loss for the consumers and a gain for the producer. It is a *social* loss.

FIGURE 6.7

Underproduction and Overproduction

(a) Underproduction

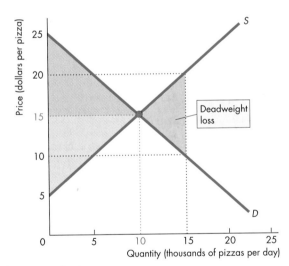

(b) Overproduction

If production is restricted to 5,000 a day, a deadweight loss (the gray triangle) arises. Consumer surplus and producer surplus are reduced to the green and blue areas. At 5,000 pizzas, the benefit of one more pizza exceeds its cost. The same is true for all levels of production up to 10,000 pizzas a day. If production increases to 15,000, a deadweight loss arises. At 15,000 pizzas a day, the cost of the 15,000th pizza exceeds its benefit. The cost of each pizza above 10,000 exceeds its benefit. Consumer surplus plus producer surplus equals the green and blue area minus the deadweight loss.

Overproduction

Suppose the pizza lobby gets the government to pay the pizza producers a fat subsidy and that production increases to 15,000 a day. Figure 6.7(b) shows that at this quantity, consumers are willing to pay only $10 for that marginal pizza but the opportunity cost of that pizza is $20. It now costs more to produce the marginal pizza than consumers are willing to pay for it. The gap gets smaller as production approaches 10,000 pizzas a day, but it is present at all quantities greater than 10,000 a day.

Again, deadweight loss is shown by the gray triangle. This loss must be subtracted from the producer and consumer surplus to calculate the gains from trade. The 15,000th pizza brings a benefit of only $10 but costs $20 to produce. If we produce this pizza, we are wasting almost $10. Similar reasoning applies all the way down to the 10,001st pizza. By producing less pizza and more of other goods and services, we get more value from our resources.

R E V I E W   Q U I Z

- Do competitive markets use resources efficiently? Explain why or why not.
- Do markets with a price ceiling or price floor, taxes, subsidies, quotas, monopoly power, public goods, or externalities result in the quantity produced being the efficient quantity?
- What is deadweight loss and in what conditions does it occur?
- Does a deadweight loss occur in a competitive market when the quantity produced equals the competitive equilibrium quantity and the resource allocation is efficient?

You now know the conditions under which the resource allocation is efficient. You've seen how a competitive market can be efficient, and you've seen some impediments to efficiency.

But is an efficient allocation of resources fair? Does the competitive market provide people with fair incomes for their work? And do people always pay a fair price for the things they buy? Don't we need the government to step into some competitive markets to prevent the price from rising too high or falling too low? Let's now study these questions.

Is the Competitive Market Fair?

WHEN A NATURAL DISASTER STRIKES, SUCH AS A severe winter storm or a hurricane, the prices of many essential items jump. The reason the prices jump is that some people have a greater demand and greater willingness to pay while the items are in limited supply. So the higher prices achieve an efficient allocation of scarce resources. News reports of these price hikes almost never talk about efficiency. Instead, they talk about fairness, or more particularly, unfairness. The claim is that it is unfair for profit-seeking dealers to cheat the victims of natural disaster.

Similarly, when low-skilled people work for a wage that is below what most would regard as a "living wage," the media and politicians talk of employers taking unfair advantage of their workers.

How do we decide if something is fair or unfair? You know when *you* think something is unfair. But how do you know? What are the *principles* of fairness?

Philosophers have tried for centuries to answer this question. Economists have offered their answers too. But before we look at the proposed answers, you should know that there is no universally agreed answer.

Economists agree about efficiency. That is, they agree that it makes sense to make the economic pie as large as possible and to bake it at the lowest possible cost. But they do not agree about fairness. That is, they do not agree about what are fair shares of the economic pie for all the people who make it. The reason is that ideas about fairness are not exclusively economic ideas. They touch on politics, ethics, and religion. Nevertheless, economists have thought about these issues and have a contribution to make. So let's examine the views of economists on this topic.

To think about fairness, think of economic life as a game—a serious game. All ideas about fairness can be divided into two broad groups. They are:

- It's not fair if the *result* isn't fair
- It's not fair if the *rules* aren't fair

It's Not Fair If the *Result* Isn't Fair

The earliest efforts to establish a principle of fairness were based on the view that the result is what matters. And the general idea was that it is unfair if people's incomes are too unequal. It is unfair that bank chairpersons earn millions of dollars a year while bank tellers earn only thousands of dollars a year. It is unfair that a storeowner enjoys a larger profit and her customers pay higher prices in the aftermath of a winter storm.

There was a lot of excitement during the nineteenth century when economists thought they had made the incredible discovery that efficiency requires equality of incomes. To make the economic pie as large as possible, it must be cut into equal pieces, one for each person. This idea turns out to be wrong, but there is a lesson in the reason that it is wrong. So this nineteenth century idea is worth a closer look.

Utilitarianism The nineteenth century idea that only equality brings efficiency is called utilitarianism. **Utilitarianism** is a principle that states that we should strive to achieve "the greatest happiness for the greatest number." The people who developed this idea were known as utilitarians. They included the most eminent minds, such as David Hume, Adam Smith, Jeremy Bentham, and John Stuart Mill.

Utilitarians argued that to achieve "the greatest happiness for the greatest number," income must be transferred from the rich to the poor up to the point of complete equality—to the point at which there are no rich and no poor.

They reasoned in the following way: First, everyone has the same basic wants and a similar capacity to enjoy life. Second, the greater a person's income, the smaller is the marginal benefit of a dollar. The millionth dollar spent by a rich person brings a smaller marginal benefit to that person than the marginal benefit of the thousandth dollar spent by a poorer person. So by transferring a dollar from the millionaire to the poorer person, more is gained than is lost and the two people added together are better off.

Figure 6.8 illustrates this utilitarian idea. Tom and Jerry each have the same marginal benefit curve, *MB*. (Marginal benefit is measured on the same scale of 1 to 3 for both Tom and Jerry.) Tom is at point *a*. He earns $5,000 a year, and his marginal benefit of a dollar of income is 3. Jerry is at point *b*. He earns $45,000 a year, and his marginal benefit of a dollar of income is 1. If a dollar is transferred from Jerry to Tom, Jerry loses 1 unit of marginal benefit and Tom gains 3 units. So together Tom and Jerry are better off. They are sharing the economic pie more efficiently. If a second dollar is transferred, the same thing happens: Tom gains more than Jerry loses. And the same is true for every dollar transferred until they each reach point *c*. At point *c*, Tom and Jerry each

FIGURE 6.8

Utilitarian Fairness

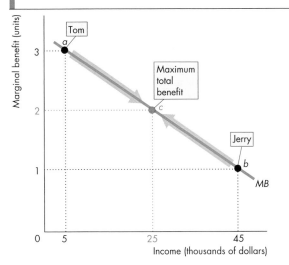

Tom earns $5,000 and has 3 units of marginal benefit at point *a*. Jerry earns $45,000 and has 1 unit of marginal benefit at point *b*. If income is transferred from Jerry to Tom, Jerry's loss is less than Tom's gain. Only when each of them has $25,000 and 2 units of marginal benefit (at point *c*) can the sum of their total benefit increase no further.

have $25,000 and each have a marginal benefit of 2 units. Now they are sharing the economic pie in the most efficient way. It is bringing the greatest attainable happiness to Tom and Jerry.

The Big Tradeoff One big problem with the utilitarian ideal of complete equality is that it ignores the costs of making income transfers. Recognizing the cost of making income transfers leads to what is called "the **big tradeoff**," which is a tradeoff between efficiency and fairness.

The big tradeoff is based on the following facts. Income can be transferred from people with high incomes to people with low incomes only by taxing incomes. Taxing people's income from employment makes them work less. It results in the quantity of labor being less than the efficient quantity. Taxing people's income from capital makes them save less. It results in the quantity of capital being less than the efficient quantity. With smaller quantities of both labor and capital, the quantity of goods and services produced is less than the efficient quantity. The economic pie shrinks.

The tradeoff is between the size of the economic pie and the degree of equality with which it is shared. The greater the amount of income redistribution through income taxes, the greater is the inefficiency—the smaller is the economic pie.

There is a second source of inefficiency. A dollar taken from a rich person does not end up as a dollar in the hands of a poorer person. Some of it is spent on administration of the tax and transfer system. The cost of tax-collecting agencies, such as the IRS, and welfare-administering agencies, such as Health Care Financing Administration that administers Medicaid and Medicare, must be paid with some of the taxes collected. Also, taxpayers hire accountants, auditors, and lawyers to help them ensure that they pay the correct amount of tax. These activities use skilled labor and capital resources that could otherwise be used to produce goods and services that people value.

You can see that when all these costs are taken into account, transferring a dollar from a rich person does not give a dollar to a poor person. It is even possible that with high taxes, those with low incomes end up being worse off. Suppose, for example, that highly taxed entrepreneurs decide to work less hard and shut down some of their businesses. Low-income workers get fired and must seek other, perhaps even lower-paid work.

Because of the big tradeoff, those who say that fairness is equality propose a modified version of utilitarianism.

Make the Poorest as Well Off as Possible A Harvard philosopher, John Rawls, proposed a modified version of utilitarianism in a classic book entitled *A Theory of Justice*, published in 1971. Rawls says that, after counting all the costs of income transfers, the fair distribution of the economic pie is the one that makes the poorest person as well off as possible. The incomes of rich people should be taxed and, after paying the costs of administering the tax and transfer system, what is left should be transferred to the poor. But the taxes must not be so high that they make the economic pie shrink to the point at which the poorest person ends up with a smaller piece. A bigger piece of a smaller pie can be less than a smaller piece of a bigger pie. The goal is to make the piece enjoyed by the poorest person as big as possible. Most likely, this piece will not be an equal share.

The "fair results" ideas require a change in the results after the game is over. Some economists say that these changes are themselves unfair and propose a different way of thinking about fairness.

It's Not Fair If the *Rules* Aren't Fair

The idea that it's not fair if the rules aren't fair is based on a fundamental principle that seems to be hard wired into the human brain. It is the symmetry principle. The **symmetry principle** is the requirement that people in similar situations be treated similarly. It is the moral principle that lies at the center of all the major religions and that says, in some form or other, "Behave toward other people in the way you expect them to behave toward you."

In economic life, this principle translates into *equality of opportunity*. But equality of opportunity to do what? This question is answered by another Harvard philosopher, Robert Nozick, in a book entitled *Anarchy, State, and Utopia,* published in 1974.

Nozick argues that the idea of fairness as an outcome or result cannot work and that fairness must be based on the fairness of the rules. He suggests that fairness obeys two rules:

1. The state must enforce laws that establish and protect private property.
2. Private property may be transferred from one person to another only by voluntary exchange.

The first rule says that everything that is valuable must be owned by individuals and that the state must ensure that theft is prevented. The second rule says that the only legitimate way a person can acquire property is to buy it in exchange for something else that the person owns. If these rules, which are the only fair rules, are followed, the result is fair. It doesn't matter how unequally the economic pie is shared provided that it is baked by people each one of whom voluntarily provides services in exchange for the share of the pie offered in compensation.

These rules satisfy the symmetry principle. And if these rules are not followed, the symmetry principle is broken. You can see these facts by imagining a world in which the laws are not followed.

First, suppose that some resources or goods are not owned. They are common property. Then everyone is free to participate in a grab to use these resources or goods. The strongest will prevail. But when the strongest prevails, the strongest effectively *owns* the resources or goods in question and prevents others from enjoying them.

Second, suppose that we do not insist on voluntary exchange for transferring ownership of resources from one person to another. The alternative is *involuntary* transfer. In simple language, the alternative is theft.

Both of these situations violate the symmetry principle. Only the strong get to acquire what they want. The weak end up with only the resources and goods that the strong don't want.

In contrast, if the two rules of fairness are followed, everyone, strong and weak, is treated in a similar way. All are free to use their resources and human skills to create things that are valued by themselves and others and to exchange the fruits of their efforts with each other. This is the only set of arrangements that obeys the symmetry principle.

Fairness and Efficiency If private property rights are enforced and if voluntary exchange takes place in a competitive market, resources will be allocated efficiently if there are no:

- Price ceilings and price floors
- Taxes, subsidies, and quotas
- Monopolies
- Public goods
- External costs and external benefits

And according to the Nozick rules, the resulting distribution of income and wealth will be fair. Let's study a concrete example to examine the claim that if resources are allocated efficiently, they are also allocated fairly.

A Price Hike in a Natural Disaster An earthquake has broken the pipes that deliver drinking water to a city. The price of bottled water jumps from $1 to $8 a bottle in the 30 or so shops that have water for sale.

First, let's agree that the water is being used *efficiently*. There is a fixed amount of bottled water in the city and, given the quantity available, some people are willing to pay $8 to get a bottle. The water goes to the people who value it most highly. Consumer surplus and producer surplus are maximized.

So the water resources are being used efficiently. But are they being used fairly? Shouldn't people who can't afford to pay $8 a bottle get some of the available water for a lower price that they can afford? Isn't the fair solution for the shops to sell water for a lower price that people can afford? Or perhaps it might be fairer if the government bought the water and then made it available to people through a government store at a "reasonable" price. Let's think about these alternative solutions to the water problem of this city.

The first answer that jumps into your mind is that the water should somehow be made available at a more reasonable price. But is this the correct answer?

Shop Offers Water for $5 Suppose that Chip, a shop owner, offers water at $5 a bottle. Who will buy it? There are two types of buyers. Chuck is an example of one type. He values water at $8—is willing to pay $8 a bottle. Recall that, given the quantity of water available, the equilibrium price is $8 a bottle. If Chuck buys the water, he consumes it. Chuck ends up with a consumer surplus of $3 on the bottle, and Chip receives $3 *less* of producer surplus.

Mitch is an example of the second type of buyer. Mitch would not pay $8 for a bottle. In fact, he wouldn't even pay $5 to consume a bottle of water. But he buys a bottle for $5. Why? Because he plans to sell the water to someone who is willing to pay $8 to consume it. When Mitch buys the water, Chip again receives a producer surplus of $3 *less* than he would receive if he charged the going market price. Mitch now becomes a water dealer. He sells the water for the going price of $8 and earns a producer surplus of $3.

So by being public spirited and offering water for less than the market price, Chip ends up $3 a bottle worse off, and the buyers end up $3 a bottle better off. The same people consume the water in both situations. They are the people who value the water at $8 a bottle. But the distribution of consumer surplus and producer surplus is different in the two cases. When Chip offers the water for $5 a bottle, he ends up with a smaller producer surplus and Chuck and Mitch end up with a larger consumer surplus and producer surplus.

So which is the fair arrangement? The one that favors Chip or the one that favors Chuck and Mitch? The fair-rules view is that both arrangements are fair. Chip voluntarily sells the water for $5, so in effect, he is helping the community to cope with its water problem. It is fair that he should help. But the choice is his. He owns the water. It is not fair that he should be compelled to help.

Government Buys Water Now suppose instead that the government buys all the water. The going price is $8 a bottle, so that's what the government pays. Now they offer the water for sale for $1 a bottle, its "normal" price.

The quantity of water supplied is exactly the same as before. But now, at $1 a bottle, the quantity demanded is much larger than the quantity supplied. There is a shortage of water.

Because there is a large water shortage, the government decides to ration the amount that anyone may buy. Everyone is allocated one bottle. So everyone lines up to collect his or her bottle. Two of these

people are Chuck and Mitch. Chuck, you'll recall, is willing to pay $8 a bottle. Mitch is willing to pay less than $5. But they both get a bargain. Chuck drinks his $1 bottle and enjoys a $7 consumer surplus. What does Mitch do? Does he drink his bottle? He does not. He sells it to another person who values the water at $8. And he enjoys a $7 producer surplus from his temporary water trading business.

So the people who value the water most highly consume it. But the consumer and producer surpluses are distributed in a different way from what the free market would have delivered. Again, the question arises, which arrangement is fair?

The main difference between the government scheme and Chip's private charitable contributions lies in the fact that to buy the water for $8 and sell it for $1, the government must tax someone $7 for each bottle sold. So whether this arrangement is fair depends on whether the taxes are fair.

Taxes are an involuntary transfer of private property, so according to the fair-rules view, they are unfair. But most economists, and most other people, think that there is such a thing as a fair tax. So it seems that the fair-rules view needs to be weakened a bit. Agreeing that there is such a thing as a fair tax is the easy part. Agreeing on what is a fair tax brings endless disagreement and debate.

REVIEW QUIZ

- What are the two big approaches to thinking about fairness?
- What is the utilitarian idea of fairness and what is wrong with it?
- What is the big tradeoff and what idea of fairness has been developed to deal with it?
- What is the main idea of fairness based on fair rules?

◆ You've now studied the two biggest issues that run right through the whole of economics: efficiency and equity, or fairness. In the next chapter, we study some sources of inefficiency and unfairness. And at many points throughout this book—and in your life—you will return to and use the ideas about efficiency and equity that you've learned in this chapter. *Reading Between the Lines* on pp. 122-123 looks at an example of an inefficiency—and, some would argue, an inequity—in our economy today.

Efficiency and Equity in Agriculture

THE NEW YORK TIMES, OCTOBER 16, 1998

Congress Disregards Free Market With Farm Bill

BY DIRK JOHNSON

CHICAGO—The agreement to spend $6 billion on the nation's farmers marks a departure, at least in spirit, from a landmark 1996 measure intended to move agriculture into a free market economy.

The aid, which comes in addition to the more than $5 billion that has already been appropriated for farmers this year, is intended to salve agricultural economy that has been hurt by weather disasters, crop disease and falling commodity prices.

The bid to rescue farmers is a contrast to the 1996 law, under which subsidies will be phased out by 2002.

"Congress is demonstrating an unwillingness to let the free market control the agricultural economy—at least in an election year," said Neil Harl, an agricultural economist at Iowa State University. "There is a big upside to the market approach. And there's a big downside. And that downside causes pain."

... In the view of some critics of the 1996 measure, including the more liberal National Farmers Union, the free market approach has led to overproduction of some crops, causing prices to fall.

"We've seen what happens when the market takes over—prices drop through the floor," said Marilyn Wentz, a spokeswoman for the National Farmers Union. ...

Critics of subsidies have long complained that farmers have no special right to a safety net. Unsuccessful farms should fail, just like unsuccessful drug stores and auto repair shops, critics say.

But Brent Kleinsasser, a grain farmer in Huron, South Dakota, said farmers were not the only ones who gained from aid to agriculture.

"The more farms there are, the longer food will stay cheap," he said. "When you get a handful of big corporations that control food production, the prices would go way up."

Essence of the Story

■ In 1996, Congress enacted a law to phase out farm subsidies by 2002.

■ Because of bad weather, crop diseases, and falling prices, Congress decided in 1998 to provide $6 billion for farmers in addition to $5 billion that it had provided earlier that year.

■ The National Farmers Union says that the free market approach to farming leads to overproduction of some crops and causes their prices to fall.

■ A South Dakota farmer says that everyone gains from aid to farmers because it prevents the control of food production from falling into the hands of big corporations that would raise prices.

■ Critics of farm subsidies say that unsuccessful farms, like unsuccessful drug stores and auto repair shops, should be allowed to fail.

Economic Analysis

■ Figure 1 shows the market for wheat. The demand curve, which is also the marginal benefit curve, is $D = MB$. The supply curve, which is also the marginal cost curve, is $S = MC$.

■ If the wheat market is competitive—what the news article calls a *free market*—equilibrium occurs at a price of $4 a bushel and 20 billion bushels a year—at the intersection of the demand curve and the supply curve. (The numbers are just an example.)

■ At the equilibrium, production is efficient—marginal benefit equals marginal cost. The green area is consumer surplus, and the blue area is producer surplus.

■ Figure 2 shows the outcome for an individual farmer when the price is $4 and the farmer's marginal cost is MC_0. The farmer produces 10,000 bushels, and the producer surplus is the sum of the blue triangles.

■ Figure 2 also shows what happens to an individual farmer when:
(i) Competition in the world economy lowers the price from $4 to $3 a bushel and
(ii) Bad weather lowers crop yields and increases marginal cost from MC_0 to MC_1.

■ The farmer cuts production to 2,000 bushels, where marginal cost equals price. Producer surplus shrinks to the small darker blue triangle. The farmer is in distress. But production is efficient.

■ Figure 3 shows what happens if Congress helps the farmer in distress by paying a subsidy on each unit of production. The subsidy lowers the farm's cost per unit, so marginal cost falls by the amount the subsidy.

■ In Fig. 3, the subsidy is $2 a bushel. It is equal to the vertical distance between the two MC curves. The farmer produces the quantity at which *marginal cost minus the subsidy* equals the price. So production increases to 10,000 bushels.

■ At this quantity, marginal cost is $5 a bushel and marginal benefit is $3 a bushel. Because marginal cost exceeds marginal benefit, overproduction of wheat occurs and a deadweight loss arises.

■ Subsidizing farmers helps farmers but is inefficient.

■ Because of global competition, there is little chance of markets for farm products being dominated by a small number of firms that could cut production and raise price.

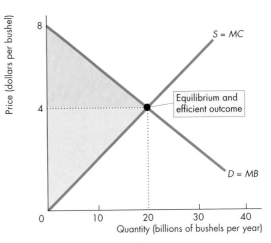

Figure 1 A free market in wheat

Figure 2 A farm in distress

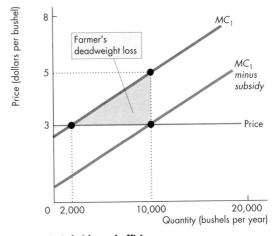

Figure 3 Subsidy and efficiency

123

SUMMARY

KEY POINTS

Efficiency: A Refresher (pp. 108–109)

- The marginal benefit received from a good or service—the benefit of consuming one additional unit—is the *value* of the good or service to its consumers.
- The marginal cost of a good or service—the cost of producing one additional unit—is the *opportunity* cost of one more unit to its producers.
- Resource allocation is efficient when marginal benefit equals marginal cost.
- If marginal benefit exceeds marginal cost, an increase in production uses resources more efficiently.
- If marginal cost exceeds marginal benefit, a decrease in production uses resources more efficiently.

Value, Price, and Consumer Surplus (pp. 110–111)

- Marginal benefit is measured by the maximum price that consumers are willing to pay for a good or service.
- Marginal benefit determines demand, and a demand curve is a marginal benefit curve.
- Value is what people are *willing to* pay; price is what people *must* pay.
- Consumer surplus equals value minus price, summed over the quantity consumed.

Cost, Price, and Producer Surplus (pp. 112–113)

- Marginal cost is measured by the minimum price producers must be offered to increase production by one unit.
- Marginal cost determines supply, and a supply curve is a marginal cost curve.
- Opportunity cost is what producers pay; price is what producers receive.
- Producer surplus equals price minus opportunity cost, summed over the quantity produced.

Is the Competitive Market Efficient? (pp. 114–115)

- In a competitive equilibrium, marginal benefit equals marginal cost and resource allocation is efficient.

Obstacles to Efficiency (pp. 114–117)

- Monopoly restricts production and creates deadweight loss.
- A competitive market provides too small a quantity of public goods because of the free-rider problem.
- A competitive market provides too large a quantity of goods and services that have external costs and too small a quantity of goods and services that have external benefits.

Is the Competitive Market Fair? (pp. 118–121)

- Ideas about fairness divide into two groups: fair *results* or fair *rules*.
- Fair-results ideas require income transfers from the rich to the poor.
- Fair-rules ideas require property rights and voluntary exchange.

KEY FIGURES

KEY TERMS

PROBLEMS

*1. The figure shows the demand for and supply of floppy disks.

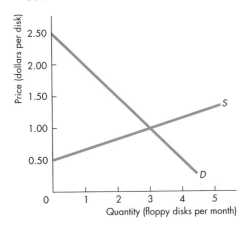

a. What are the equilibrium price and equilibrium quantity of floppy disks?
b. What is the consumer surplus?
c. What is the producer surplus?
d. What is the efficient quantity of floppy disks?

2. The figure shows the demand for and supply of cans of beans.

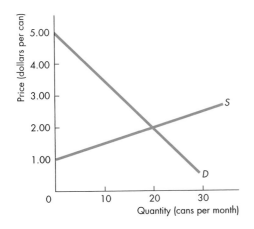

a. What are the equilibrium price and equilibrium quantity of cans of beans?
b. What is the consumer surplus?
c. What is the producer surplus?
d. What is the efficient quantity of beans?

*3. The table gives the demand and supply schedules for sandwiches:

Price (dollars per sandwich)	Quantity demanded (sandwiches per hour)	Quantity supplied (sandwiches per hour)
0	400	0
1	350	50
2	300	100
3	250	150
4	200	200
5	150	250
6	100	300
7	50	350
8	0	400

a. What is the maximum price that consumers are willing to pay for the 250th sandwich?
b. What is the minimum price that producers are willing to accept for the 250th sandwich?
c. Are 250 sandwiches an hour less than or greater than the efficient quantity?
d. What is the consumer surplus if the efficient quantity of sandwiches is produced?
e. What is the producer surplus if the efficient quantity of sandwiches is produced?
f. What is the deadweight loss if 250 sandwiches are produced?

4. The table gives the demand and supply schedules for spring water:

Price (dollars per bottle)	Quantity demanded (bottles per day)	Quantity supplied (bottles per day)
0	80	0
0.50	70	10
1.00	60	20
1.50	50	30
2.00	40	40
2.50	30	50
3.00	20	60
3.50	10	70
4.00	0	80

a. What is the maximum price that consumers are willing to pay for the 30th bottle?
b. What is the minimum price that producers are willing to accept for the 30th bottle?
c. Are 30 bottles a day less than or greater than the efficient quantity?
d. What is the consumer surplus if the efficient quantity of spring water is produced?

e. What is the producer surplus if the efficient quantity of spring water is produced?

f. What is the deadweight loss if 30 bottles are produced?

*5. The table gives the demand and supply schedules for train travel for Ben, Beth, and Bo:

Price (cents per passenger mile)	Quantity demanded (passenger miles)		
	Ben	Beth	Bo
10	500	300	60
20	450	250	50
30	400	200	40
40	350	150	30
50	300	100	20
60	250	50	10
70	200	0	0

a. If the price of train travel is 40 cents a passenger mile, what is the consumer surplus of each consumer?

b. Which consumer has the largest consumer surplus? Explain why.

c. If the price of train travel rises to 50 cents a passenger mile, what is the change in consumer surplus of each consumer?

6. The table gives the demand and supply schedules for bus travel for Joe, Jean, and Joy:

Price (cents per passenger mile)	Quantity demanded (passenger miles)		
	Joe	Jean	Joy
10	50	600	300
20	45	500	250
30	40	400	200
40	35	300	150
50	30	200	100
60	25	100	50
70	20	0	0

a. If the price of bus travel is 50 cents a passenger mile, what is the consumer surplus of each passenger?

b. Which passenger has the largest consumer surplus? Explain why.

c. If the price of bus travel falls to 30 cents a passenger mile, what is the change in consumer surplus of each passenger?

CRITICAL THINKING

1. Study *Reading Between the Lines* on pp. 122–123 on farm subsidies and then answer the following questions:

a. Is the quantity of farm output in the United States greater than, less than, or equal to the efficient quantity? Explain your answer by using the concepts of marginal benefit, marginal cost, price, consumer surplus, and producer surplus.

b. What, if anything, do you think Congress should do to make the farm sector efficient?

c. Explain what Professor Neil Harl means when he says, "There is a big upside to the market approach. And there's a big downside. And that downside causes pain."

d. Explain what Marilyn Wentz, spokeswoman for the National Farmers Union, means when she says, "We've seen what happens when the market takes over—prices drop through the floor." Do you agree with her? Why?

e. Do you agree or disagree with Brent Kleinsasser that everyone gains from aid to agriculture because it prevents a few big corporations from controlling production and raising prices? Why?

2. Use the link on the Parkin Web site to visit the U.S. Department of Agriculture and read the remarks President Clinton made when he signed the 1996 Farm Act. Do you agree or disagree with President Clinton? Why?

3. How would you set about determining whether the allocation of your time between studying different subjects is efficient? In what units would you measure marginal benefit and marginal cost? Explain your answer by using the concepts of marginal benefit, marginal cost, price, consumer surplus, and producer surplus.

Chapter 7

Markets in Action

In 1906, San Francisco suffered a devastating earthquake that destroyed more than half the city's homes but killed few people. How did San Francisco's housing market cope with this enormous shock? Did rents have to be controlled to keep housing affordable? Were scarce housing resources allocated to their highest-valued uses? ◆ Almost every day, a new machine is invented that saves labor and increases productivity. How do labor markets cope with labor-saving technological change? Do the wages of low-skilled workers fall? Do we need minimum wage laws to prevent wages from falling? Do minimum wages enable us to use labor efficiently? ◆ Almost everything we buy is taxed. How do taxes affect prices? Do they increase by the full amount of the tax so that we, the buyers, pay all the tax? Or does the seller pay part of the tax? Do

Turbulent Times

taxes help or hinder the market in its attempt to move resources to where they are valued most highly? ◆ Trade in items such as drugs, automatic firearms, and enriched uranium is illegal. What are the effects of laws that make trading in a good or service illegal on the amounts of such items consumed? And how do these laws affect the prices paid by those who trade illegally? ◆ In 1991, ideal conditions brought high grain yields. But in 1996, crops were devastated by drought and grain yields were low. How do farm prices and revenues react to such output fluctuations? And how do the actions of speculators and government agencies influence farm revenues?

◆ In this chapter, we study a variety of markets. We use the theory of demand and supply (Chapter 4) and the concepts of elasticity (Chapter 5) and efficiency (Chapter 6) to answer the questions just posed. We'll begin by studying two markets that have the biggest impacts on our lives: the housing market and the labor market. Governments often intervene in these markets to try to control prices. They impose rent ceilings and minimum wages. To set the scene for each, we're going to see how a market responds to turbulent events. We'll begin by seeing how a housing market copes with an extremely severe supply shock.

After studying this chapter, you will be able to:

- Explain how housing markets work and how price ceilings create housing shortages and inefficiency
- Explain how labor markets work and how minimum wage laws create unemployment and inefficiency
- Explain the effects of the sales tax
- Explain how markets for illegal goods work
- Explain why farm prices and revenues fluctuate
- Explain how speculation limits price fluctuations

Housing Markets and Rent Ceilings

To SEE HOW A MARKET COPES WITH A SUPPLY shock, let's transport ourselves to San Francisco in April 1906, as the city is suffering from a massive earthquake and fire. You can sense the enormity of San Francisco's problems by reading a headline from the *New York Times* on one of the first days of the crisis, April 19, 1906:

Over 500 Dead, $200,000,000 Lost in San Francisco Earthquake

Nearly Half the City Is in Ruins and 50,000 Are Homeless

The commander of federal troops in charge of the emergency described the magnitude of the problem:

> Not a hotel of note or importance was left standing. The great apartment houses had vanished . . . two hundred-and-twenty-five thousand people were . . . homeless.[1]

Almost overnight, more than half the people in a city of 400,000 had lost their homes. Temporary shelters and camps alleviated some of the problem, but it was also necessary to utilize the apartment buildings and houses left standing. As a consequence, they had to accommodate 40 percent more people than they had before the earthquake.

The *San Francisco Chronicle* was not published for more than a month after the earthquake. When the newspaper reappeared on May 24, 1906, the city's housing shortage—what would seem to be a major news item that would still be of grave importance—was not mentioned. Milton Friedman and George Stigler describe the situation:

> *There is not a single mention of a housing shortage*! The classified advertisements listed sixty-four offers of flats and houses for rent, and nineteen of houses for sale, against five advertisements of flats or houses wanted. Then and thereafter a considerable number of all types of accommodation except hotel rooms were offered for rent.[2]

How did San Francisco cope with such a devastating reduction in the supply of housing?

[1] Reported in Milton Friedman and George J. Stigler, "Roofs or Ceilings? The Current Housing Problem," in *Popular Essays on Current Problems*, vol. 1, no. 2 (New York: Foundation for Economic Education, 1946), 3–159.

[2] *Ibid.*, 3.

The Market Response to a Decrease in Supply

Figure 7.1 shows the market for housing in San Francisco. The demand curve for housing is *D*. There is a short-run supply curve, labeled *SS*, and a long-run supply curve, labeled *LS*.

The short-run supply curve shows the change in the quantity of housing supplied as the price (rent) changes while the number of houses and apartments remains constant. The short-run supply response arises from changes in the intensity with which existing buildings are used. The quantity of housing supplied increases if families rent out rooms that they previously used themselves, and it decreases if families use rooms that they previously rented out to others.

The long-run supply curve shows how the quantity of housing supplied responds to a change in price after enough time has elapsed for new apartments and houses to be erected or for existing ones to be destroyed. In Fig. 7.1, the long-run supply curve is *perfectly elastic*. We do not actually know that the long-run supply curve is perfectly elastic, but it is a reasonable assumption. It implies that the cost of building an apartment is much the same regardless of the numbers of apartments in existence.

The equilibrium price (rent) and quantity are determined at the point of intersection of the *short-run* supply curve and the demand curve. Before the earthquake, the equilibrium rent is $16 a month and the quantity is 100,000 units of housing.

Figure 7.1(a) shows the situation immediately after the earthquake. The destruction of buildings decreases the supply of housing and shifts the short-run supply curve *SS* leftward to *SS*$_A$. With no change in the population, the demand for housing is unchanged. If the rent remains at $16 a month, only 44,000 units of housing are available. But with only 44,000 units of housing available, the maximum rent that someone is willing to pay for the last available apartment is $24 a month. So rents rise. In Fig. 7.1(a), the rent rises to $20 a month.

As the rent rises, the quantity of housing demanded decreases and the quantity supplied increases to 72,000 units. These changes occur because people economize on their use of space and make spare rooms, attics, and basements available to others. The higher rent allocates the scarce housing to those people who value it most highly and are willing to pay most for it.

But the higher rent has other, long-run effects. Let's look at these long-run effects.

FIGURE **7.1**

The San Francisco
Housing Market in 1906

(a) After earthquake

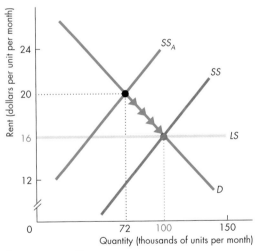

(b) Long-run adjustment

Part (a) shows that before the earthquake, 100,000 housing units
were rented at $16 a month. After the earthquake, the short-
run supply curve shifts from SS to SS_A. The rent rises to $20 a
month, and the quantity of housing decreases to 72,000 units.

With rent at $20 a month, there is profit in building new
apartments and houses. As the building program proceeds,
the short-run supply curve shifts rightward (part b). The rent
gradually falls to $16 a month, and the quantity of housing
increases to 100,000 units—as the arrowed line shows.

Long-Run Adjustments

With sufficient time for new apartments and houses
to be constructed, supply increases. The long-run
supply curve in Fig. 7.1(a) tells us that in the long
run, housing is supplied at a rent of $16 a month.
Because the rent of $20 a month exceeds the long-
run supply price, there is a building boom. More
apartments and houses are built, and the short-run
supply curve shifts gradually rightward.

Figure 7.1(b) shows the long-run adjustment.
As more housing is built, the short-run supply curve
shifts rightward and intersects the demand curve at
lower rents and larger quantities. The market equilibrium follows the arrows down the demand curve.
When the process ends, there is no further profit
in building. The rent is back at $16 a month, and
100,000 units of housing are available.

A Regulated Housing Market

We've just seen how a housing market responds to a
decrease in supply. And we've seen that a key part of
the adjustment process is a rise in the rent.

Suppose the government passes a law to stop the
rent from rising. Such a law is called a price ceiling.
A **price ceiling** is a regulation that makes it illegal
to charge a price higher than a specified level. When
a price ceiling is applied to housing markets, it is
called a **rent ceiling**. How does a rent ceiling affect
the housing market?

The effect of a price (rent) ceiling depends on
whether it is imposed at a level that is above or below
the equilibrium price (rent). A price ceiling set above
the equilibrium price has no effect. The reason is that
the price ceiling does not constrain the market forces.
The force of the law and the market forces are not in
conflict. But a price ceiling set below the equilibrium
price has powerful effects on a market. The reason is
that it attempts to prevent the price from regulating
the quantities demanded and supplied. The force of
the law and the market forces are in conflict, and one
(or both) of these forces must yield to some degree.
Let's study the effects of a price ceiling set below
the equilibrium price by returning to San Francisco.
What would have happened in San Francisco if a rent
ceiling of $16 a month—the rent before the earth-
quake—had been imposed after the earthquake?

This question and some answers are illustrated
in Fig. 7.2. At a rent of $16 a month, the quantity
of housing supplied is 44,000 units and the quantity

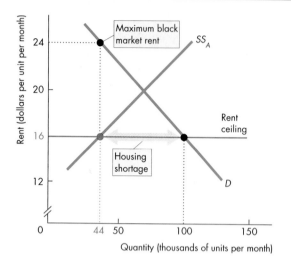

If there had been a rent ceiling of $16 a month, then the quantity of housing supplied after the earthquake would have been stuck at 44,000 units. People would willingly have paid $24 a month for the 44,000th unit. Because the last unit of housing available is worth more than the rent ceiling, frustrated renters will spend time searching for housing and frustrated renters and landlords will make deals in a black market.

demanded is 100,000 units. So there is a shortage of 56,000 units of housing.

But the story does not end here. Somehow, the 44,000 units of available housing must be allocated among people who demand 100,000 units. How is this allocation achieved? When a rent ceiling creates a housing shortage, two developments occur. They are:

- Search activity
- Black markets

Search Activity

The time spent looking for someone with whom to do business is called **search activity**. We spend some time in search activity almost every time we buy something. You want the latest hot CD, and you know 4 stores that stock it. But which store has the best deal? You need to spend a few minutes on the telephone finding out. In some markets, we spend

a lot of time searching. An example is the used car market. People spend a lot of time checking out alternative dealers and cars.

But when a price is regulated and there is a shortage, search activity increases. In rent-controlled housing markets, frustrated would-be renters scan the newspapers, not only for housing ads but also for death notices! Any information about newly available housing is useful. And they race to be first on the scene when news of a possible supplier breaks.

The *opportunity cost* of a good includes not only its price but also the value of the search time spent finding the good. So the opportunity cost of housing is equal to the rent (a regulated price) plus the time and other resources spent searching for the restricted quantity available. Search activity is costly. It uses time and other resources, such as telephones, cars, and gasoline, that could have been used in other productive ways. A rent ceiling controls the rent portion of the cost of housing, but it does not control the opportunity cost, which might even be *higher* than the rent would be if the market were unregulated.

Black Markets

A **black market** is an illegal market in which the price exceeds the legally imposed price ceiling. Black markets occur in rent-controlled housing, and scalpers run black markets in tickets for major sporting events and rock concerts.

When rent ceilings are in force, frustrated renters and landlords constantly seek ways to increase rents. One common way is for a new tenant to pay a high price for worthless fittings, such as $2,000 for threadbare drapes. Another is for the tenant to pay an exorbitant price for new locks and keys—called "key money."

The level of a black market rent depends on how tightly the rent ceiling is enforced. With loose enforcement, the black market rent is close to the unregulated rent. But with strict enforcement, the black market rent is equal to the maximum price that renters are willing to pay.

With strict enforcement of the rent ceiling in the San Francisco example shown in Fig. 7.2, the quantity of housing available remains at 44,000 units. A small number of people offer housing for rent at $24 a month—the highest rent that someone is willing to pay—and the government detects and punishes some of these black market traders.

Inefficiency of Rent Ceilings

In an unregulated market, the market determines the rent at which the quantity demanded equals the quantity supplied. In this situation, scarce housing resources are allocated efficiently. The sum of *consumer surplus* and *producer surplus*—the gains from trade—is maximized (see Chapter 6, pp. 110–111).

Figure 7.3 shows the inefficiency of a rent ceiling. If the rent is fixed at $16 per unit per month, 44,000 units are supplied. The producer surplus is shown by the blue triangle above the supply curve and below the rent line. Because the quantity of housing is less than the competitive quantity, there is a deadweight loss shown by the gray triangle. This loss is borne by the consumers who can't find housing and the producers who can't supply housing at the new lower price. Consumers who do find housing at the controlled rent gain. If no one incurs search cost, consumer surplus is shown by the sum of the green triangle and the red rectangle. But search costs might eat up part of the consumer surplus, possibly as much as the entire amount that consumers are willing to pay for the available housing, which is shown by the red rectangle.

So rent ceilings prevent scarce resources from flowing to their highest-valued use. But don't they ensure that scarce housing goes to the people whose need is greatest? The idea of need is complex. Who is to determine whether one person's "need" is greater than another person's? The unregulated market respects everyone's assessment of "need" by permitting each person's willingness to pay to allocate scarce resources.

When the law prevents rents from adjusting to bring the quantity demanded into equality with the quantity supplied, factors other than rent allocate the scarce housing. One of these factors is discrimination on the basis of race, ethnicity, or sex.

There are many modern examples of rent ceilings, but the best is New York City. One consequence of New York's rent ceilings is that families that have lived in the city for a long time—including some rich and famous ones—enjoy low rents, while newcomers pay high rents for hard-to-find apartments. At the same time, landlords in rent-controlled Harlem abandon entire city blocks to rats and drug dealers.

The effects of rent ceilings have led Assar Lindbeck, chairman of the economic science Nobel Prize committee, to suggest that rent ceilings are the most effective means yet for destroying cities, even more effective than the hydrogen bomb.

FIGURE 7.3
The Inefficiency of a Rent Ceiling

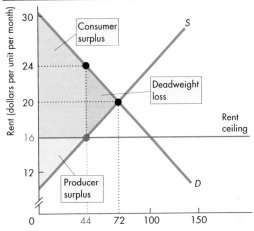

A rent ceiling of $16 a month decreases the quantity of housing supplied to 44,000 units. Producer surplus shrinks to the blue triangle and a deadweight loss (the gray triangle) arises. If people use no resources in search activity, consumer surplus is shown by the green triangle plus the red rectangle. But people might use resources in search activity equal to the amount they are willing to pay for the available housing, the red rectangle.

REVIEW QUIZ

- How does a decrease in the supply of housing change the equilibrium rent in the short run? Who gets to consume the scarce housing resources?
- What are the long-run effects of higher rents following a decrease in the supply of housing?
- What is a rent ceiling and what are the effects of a rent ceiling set above the equilibrium rent?
- What are the effects of a rent ceiling set below the equilibrium rent?
- How do scarce housing resources get allocated when a rent ceiling is in place?

You now know how a price ceiling (rent ceiling) works. Next, we'll learn about the effects of a price floor by studying minimum wages in the labor market.

The Labor Market and the Minimum Wage

FOR EACH ONE OF US, THE LABOR MARKET IS THE most important market in which we participate. It is the market that influences the jobs we get and the wages we earn. Firms decide how much labor to demand, and the lower the wage rate, the greater is the quantity of labor demanded. Households decide how much labor to supply, and the higher the wage rate, the greater is the quantity of labor supplied. The wage rate adjusts to make the quantity of labor demanded equal to the quantity supplied.

But the labor market is constantly hit by shocks, and wages and employment prospects constantly change. The most pervasive source of these shocks is the advance of technology.

New labor-saving technologies become available every year. As a result, the demand for some types of labor, usually the least skilled types, decreases. During the 1980s and 1990s, for example, the demand for telephone operators and television repair persons has decreased. Throughout the past 200 years, the demand for low-skilled farm laborers has steadily decreased.

How does the labor market cope with this continuous decrease in the demand for low-skilled labor? Doesn't it mean that the wages of low-skilled workers are constantly falling?

To answer these questions, we must study the market for low-skilled labor. And just as we did when we studied the housing market, we must look at both the short run and the long run.

In the short run, there is a given number of people who have a given skill, training, and experience. The short-run supply of labor describes how the number of hours of labor supplied by this given number of workers changes as the wage rate changes. To get workers to work more hours, they must be offered a higher wage rate.

In the long run, people can acquire new skills and find new types of jobs. The number of people in the low-skilled labor market depends on the wage rate in this market compared with other opportunities. If the wage rate of low-skilled labor is high enough, people will enter this market. If the wage rate is too low, people will leave it. Some will seek training to enter higher-skilled labor markets, and others will stop working and stay at home or retire.

The long-run supply of labor is the relationship between the quantity of labor supplied and the wage rate after enough time has passed for people to enter or leave the low-skilled labor market. If people can freely enter and leave the low-skilled labor market, the long-run supply of labor is *perfectly elastic*.

Figure 7.4 shows the market for low-skilled labor. Other things remaining the same, the lower the wage rate, the greater is the quantity of labor demanded by firms. The demand curve for labor, *D* in part (a), shows this relationship between the wage rate and the quantity of labor demanded. Other things remaining the same, the higher the wage rate, the greater is the quantity of labor supplied by households. But the longer the period of adjustment, the greater is the *elasticity of supply* of labor. The short-run supply curve is *SS*, and the long-run supply curve is *LS*. In the figure, long-run supply is assumed to be perfectly elastic (the *LS* curve is horizontal). This market is in equilibrium at a wage rate of $5 an hour and with 22 million hours of labor employed.

What happens if a labor-saving invention decreases the demand for low-skilled labor? Figure 7.4(a) shows the short-run effects of such a change. The demand curve before the new technology is introduced is the curve labeled *D*. After the introduction of the new technology, the demand curve shifts leftward to D_A. The wage rate falls to $4 an hour, and the quantity of labor employed decreases to 21 million hours. This short-run effect on the wage rate and employment is not the end of the story.

People who are now earning only $4 an hour look around for other opportunities. They see many other jobs (in markets for other types of skills) that pay more than $4 an hour. One by one, workers decide to go back to school or take jobs that pay less but offer on-the-job training. As a result, the short-run supply curve begins to shift leftward.

Figure 7.4(b) shows the long-run adjustment. As the short-run supply curve shifts leftward, it intersects the demand curve D_A at higher wage rates and lower levels of employment. The process ends when workers have no incentive to leave the market for low-skilled labor and the short-run supply curve has shifted all the way to SS_A. At this point, the wage rate has returned to $5 an hour and employment has decreased to 20 million hours a year.

Sometimes, the adjustment process that we've just described is rapid. At other times, it is slow and wages remain low for a long period. To boost the incomes of the lowest-paid workers, the government intervenes in the labor market and sets the minimum wage that employers are required to pay. Let's look at the effects of the minimum wage.

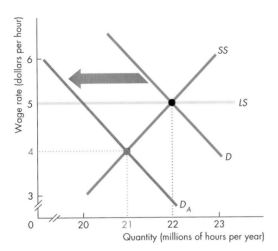

FIGURE 7.4

A Market for
Low-Skilled Labor

(a) After invention

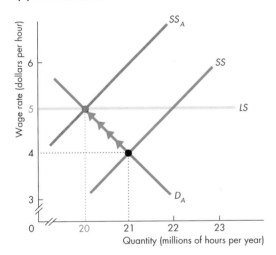

(b) Long-run adjustment

Part (a) shows the immediate effect of a labor-saving invention on the market for low-skilled labor. Initially, the wage rate is $5 an hour and 22 million hours of labor a year are employed. A labor-saving invention shifts the demand curve from D to D_A. The wage rate falls to $4 an hour, and employment decreases to 21 million hours a year. With the lower wage rate, some workers leave this market, and the short-run supply curve starts to shift gradually to SS_A (part b). The wage rate gradually increases, and the employment level decreases. In the long run, the wage rate returns to $5 an hour, and employment falls to 20 million hours a year.

The Minimum Wage

A **minimum wage law** is a regulation that makes hiring labor for less than a specified wage illegal. Figure 7.5 shows how a minimum wage law works. With no minimum wage, the equilibrium wage is $4 an hour. If the equilibrium wage *exceeds* the minimum wage, the law and market forces are not in conflict and the minimum wage has no effect. But if the equilibrium wage is *below* the minimum wage, the minimum wage is in conflict with the market forces and does have some effects on the labor market.

Suppose the government sets a minimum wage at $5 an hour. The horizontal red line in Fig. 7.5 shows this minimum wage. At $5 an hour, 20 million hours of labor are demanded (point *a*) and 22 million hours of labor are supplied (point *b*). There are 2 million hours of available labor that go unemployed.

With only 20 million hours demanded, some workers are willingly to supply that 20 millionth hour for $3. Frustrated unemployed workers spend time and other resources searching for a hard-to-find job.

FIGURE 7.5

Minimum Wage
and Unemployment

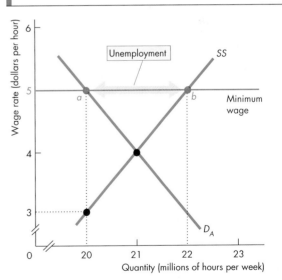

The demand curve for labor is D_A, and the supply curve is SS. In an unregulated market, the wage rate is $4 an hour and 21 million hours of labor a year are employed. If a minimum wage of $5 an hour is imposed, only 20 million hours are hired but 22 million hours are available. Unemployment—*ab*—of 2 million hours a year is created.

The Minimum Wage in Practice

The minimum wage in the United States is set by the federal government's Fair Labor Standards Act. Some state governments have passed state minimum wage laws that exceed the federal minimum. In 1998, the minimum wage is $5.15 an hour. The minimum has been increased from time to time and has fluctuated between 35 percent and more than 50 percent of the average wage of production workers.

You saw in Fig. 7.5 that the minimum wage brings unemployment. But how much unemployment does it bring? Economists do not agree on the answer to this question. Until recently, most economists believed that the minimum wage was a big contributor to high unemployment among low-skilled young workers. But recently this view has been challenged and the challenge rebutted.

David Card, a Canadian economist who works at the University of California at Berkeley, and Alan Krueger of Princeton University say that increases in the minimum wage have not decreased employment and created unemployment. Studying minimum wages in California, New Jersey, and Texas, they say that the employment rate of low-income workers increased following an increase in the minimum wage. They suggest three reasons why higher wages might increase employment. First, workers become more conscientious and productive. Second, workers are less likely to quit, so labor turnover, which is costly, is reduced. Third, managers make a firm's operations more efficient.

Most economists are skeptical about the suggestions by Card and Krueger. They ask two questions. First, if higher wages make workers more productive and reduce labor turnover, why don't firms freely pay the wage rates above the equilibrium wage to encourage more productive work habits? Second, are there other explanations for the employment responses that Card and Krueger have found?

Card and Krueger have got the timing wrong according to Daniel Hamermesh of the University of Texas at Austin. He says that firms cut employment *before* the minimum wage is increased in anticipation of the increase. If he is correct, looking for the effects of an increase *after* it has occurred misses its main effects. Finis Welch of Texas A&M University and Kevin Murphy of the University of Chicago say the employment effects that Card and Krueger found are caused by regional differences in economic growth, not changes in the minimum wage.

One effect of the minimum wage, according to Fig. 7.5, is an increase in the quantity of labor supplied. If this effect occurs, it might show up as an increase in the number of people who quit school before completing high school to look for work. Some economists say this response does occur.

Inefficiency of the Minimum Wage

An unregulated labor market allocates scarce labor resources to the jobs in which they are valued most highly. The minimum wage frustrates the market mechanism and results in unemployment—wasted labor resources—and an inefficient amount of job search.

In Fig. 7.5, with firms employing only 20 million hours of labor at the minimum wage, many people who are willing to supply labor are unable to get hired. You can see that the 20 millionth hour of labor is available for $3. That is, the lowest wage at which someone is willing to supply the 20 millionth hour—read off from the supply curve—is $3. Someone who manages to find a job earns $5 an hour—$2 an hour more than the lowest wage rate at which someone is willing to work. So it pays unemployed people to spend time and effort looking for work. Even though only 20 million hours of labor actually get employed, each person spends time and effort searching for one of the scarce jobs.

R E V I E W   Q U I Z

- How does a decrease in the demand for low-skilled labor change the wage rate in the short run?
- What are the long-run effects of a falling wage rate on the supply of low-skilled labor?
- What is a minimum wage law and what is the effect of a minimum wage that is set below the equilibrium wage?
- What is the effect of a minimum wage that is set above the equilibrium wage?

Next we're going to study a more widespread government intervention in markets: taxes, such as the state sales tax. We'll see how taxes change prices and quantities. We'll discover that the sales tax is not paid entirely by the consumer. And we'll see that usually, taxes create a deadweight loss.

Taxes

ALMOST EVERYTHING YOU BUY IS TAXED. BUT WHO really pays the tax? Because the sales tax is added to the price of a good or service when it is sold, isn't it obvious that *you*, the buyer, pay the tax? Isn't the price higher than it otherwise would be by an amount equal to the tax? It can be, but usually it isn't. And it is even possible that you actually pay none of the tax! Let's see how we can make sense of these apparently absurd statements.

Who Pays the Sales Tax?

Suppose the government puts a $10 sales tax on CD players. What are the effects of the sales tax on the price and quantity of CD players? To answer this question, we need to work out what happens to demand and supply in the market for CD players.

Figure 7.6 shows this market. The demand curve is *D*, and the supply curve is *S*. With no sales tax, the equilibrium price is $100 per CD player and 5,000 players are bought and sold each week.

When a good is taxed, it has two prices: a price that excludes the tax and a price that includes the tax. Buyers respond only to the price that includes the tax, because that is the price they pay. Sellers respond only to the price that excludes the tax, because that is the price they receive. The tax is like a wedge between these two prices.

Think of the price on the vertical axis of Fig. 7.6 as the price paid by buyers—the price that *includes* the tax. When a tax is imposed and the price changes, there is a change in the quantity demanded but no change in demand. That is, there is a movement along the demand curve and no shift of the demand curve.

But the supply changes and the supply curve shifts. The sales tax is like an increase in cost, so supply decreases and the supply curve shifts leftward to *S + tax*. To determine the position of this new supply curve, we add the tax to the minimum price that sellers are willing to accept for each quantity sold. For example, with no tax, sellers are willing to offer 5,000 players a week for $100 a player. So with a $10 tax, they will supply 5,000 players a week for $110—a price that includes the tax. The curve *S + tax* describes the terms on which sellers are willing to offer players for sale now that there is a $10 tax.

Equilibrium occurs where the new supply curve intersects the demand curve—at a price of $105 and

FIGURE 7.6

The Sales Tax

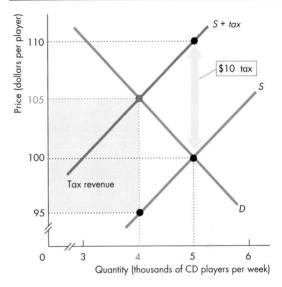

With no sales tax, 5,000 players a week are bought and sold at $100 each. A sales tax of $10 a player is imposed, and the supply curve shifts leftward to *S + tax*. In the new equilibrium, the price rises to $105 a player and the quantity decreases to 4,000 CD players a week. The sales tax raises the price by less than the tax, lowers the price received by the seller, and decreases the quantity. The sales tax brings in revenue to the government equal to the blue rectangle.

a quantity of 4,000 CD players a week. The $10 sales tax increases the price paid by the buyer by $5 a player. And it decreases the price received by the seller by $5 a player. So the buyer and the seller pay the $10 tax equally.

The tax brings in tax revenue to the government equal to the tax per item multiplied by the number of items sold. The blue area in Fig. 7.6 illustrates the tax revenue. The $10 tax on CD players brings in a tax revenue of $40,000 a week.

In this example, the buyer and the seller split the tax equally: The buyer pays $5 a player, and so does the seller. This equal sharing of the tax is a special case and does not usually occur. But some split of the tax between the buyer and seller is usual. Also, there are other special cases in which either the buyer or the seller pays the entire tax. The division of the tax between the buyer and the seller depends on the elasticities of demand and supply.

Tax Division and Elasticity of Demand

The division of the tax between the buyer and the seller depends, in part, on the elasticity of demand. There are two extreme cases:

- Perfectly inelastic demand—buyer pays.
- Perfectly elastic demand—seller pays.

Perfectly Inelastic Demand   Figure 7.7(a) shows the market for insulin, a vital daily medication of diabetics. Demand is perfectly inelastic at 100,000 doses a day, regardless of the price as shown by the vertical curve *D*. That is, a diabetic would sacrifice all other goods and services rather than not consume the insulin dose that provides good health. The supply curve of insulin is *S*. With no tax, the price is $2 a dose and the quantity is 100,000 doses a day.

If insulin is taxed at 20¢ a dose, we must add the tax to the minimum price at which drug companies are willing to sell insulin. The result is a new supply curve *S + tax*. The price rises to $2.20 a dose, but the quantity does not change. The buyer pays the entire sales tax of 20¢ a dose.

Perfectly Elastic Demand   Figure 7.7(b) shows the market for pink marker pens. Demand is perfectly elastic at $1 a pen as shown by the horizontal curve *D*. If pink pens are less expensive than the others, everyone uses pink. If pink pens are more expensive than the others, no one uses them. The supply curve is *S*. With no tax, the price of a pink marker is $1, and the quantity is 4,000 pens a week.

If a sales tax of 10¢ a pen is imposed on pink marker pens, we add the tax to the minimum price at which sellers are willing to offer them for sale and the new supply curve is *S + tax*. The price remains at $1 a pen, and the quantity decreases to 1,000 a week. The 10¢ sales tax leaves the price paid by the buyer unchanged but lowers the amount received by the seller by the full amount of the sales tax. As a result, sellers decrease the quantity offered for sale.

We've seen that when demand is perfectly inelastic, the buyer pays the entire tax, and when demand is perfectly elastic, the seller pays it. In the usual case, demand is neither perfectly inelastic nor perfectly elastic, and the tax is split between the buyer and the seller. But the division depends on the elasticity of demand. The more inelastic the demand, the larger is the amount of the tax paid by the buyer.

FIGURE **7.7**

Sales Tax and the Elasticity of Demand

(a) Inelastic demand

(b) Elastic demand

Part (a) shows the market for insulin. The demand for insulin is perfectly inelastic. With no tax, the price is $2 a dose and the quantity is 100,000 doses a day. A sales tax of 20¢ a dose shifts the supply curve to *S + tax*. The price rises to $2.20 a dose, but the quantity bought does not change. Buyers pay the entire tax. Part (b) shows the market for pink marker pens. The demand for pink pens is perfectly elastic. With no tax, the price is $1 a pen and the quantity is 4,000 pens a week. A sales tax of 10¢ a pink pen shifts the supply curve to *S + tax*. The price remains at $1 a pen, and the quantity of pink markers sold decreases to 1,000 a week. Sellers pay the entire tax.

Tax Division and Elasticity of Supply

The division of the tax between the buyer and the seller also depends, in part, on the elasticity of supply. Again, there are two extreme cases:

- Perfectly inelastic supply—seller pays.
- Perfectly elastic supply—buyer pays.

Perfectly Inelastic Supply Figure 7.8(a) shows the market for water from a mineral spring that flows at a constant rate that can't be controlled. Supply is perfectly inelastic at 100,000 bottles a week as shown by the supply curve S. The demand curve for the water from this spring is D. With no tax, the price is 50¢ a bottle and the 100,000 bottles that flow from the spring are bought.

Suppose this spring water is taxed at 5¢ a bottle. The supply curve does not change because the spring owners still produce 100,000 bottles a week even though the price they receive falls. But buyers are willing to buy the 100,000 bottles only if the price is 50¢ a bottle. So the price remains at 50¢ a bottle, and the seller pays the entire tax. The sales tax reduces the price received by sellers to 45¢ a bottle.

Perfectly Elastic Supply Figure 7.8(b) shows the market for sand from which computer-chip makers extract silicon. Supply of this sand is perfectly elastic at a price of 10¢ a pound as shown by the supply curve S. The demand curve for sand is D. With no tax, the price is 10¢ a pound and 5,000 pounds a week are bought.

If this sand is taxed at 1¢ a pound, we must add the tax to the minimum supply-price. Sellers are now willing to offer any quantity at 11¢ a pound along the curve S + tax. A new equilibrium is determined where the new supply curve intersects the demand curve—at a price of 11¢ a pound and a quantity of 3,000 pounds a week. The sales tax has increased the price paid by the buyer by the full amount of the tax—1¢ a pound—and has decreased the quantity sold.

We've seen that when supply is perfectly inelastic, the seller pays the entire tax, and when supply is perfectly elastic, the buyer pays it. In the usual case, supply is neither perfectly inelastic nor perfectly elastic, and the tax is split between the buyer and the seller. But the division between the buyer and the seller depends on the elasticity of supply. The more elastic the supply, the larger is the amount of the tax paid by the buyer.

FIGURE 7.8
Sales Tax and the Elasticity of Supply

(a) Inelastic supply

(b) Elastic supply

Part (a) shows the market for water from a mineral spring. Supply is perfectly inelastic. With no tax, the price is 50¢ a bottle. With a sales tax of 5¢ a bottle, the price remains at 50¢ a bottle. The number of bottles bought remains the same, but the price received by the seller decreases to 45¢ a bottle. The seller pays the entire tax. Part (b) shows the market for sand. Supply is perfectly elastic. With no tax, the price is 10¢ a pound and 5,000 pounds a week are bought. The sales tax of 1¢ a pound increases the minimum supply-price to 11¢ a pound. The supply curve shifts to S + tax. The price increases to 11¢ a pound. The buyer pays the entire tax.

Sales Taxes in Practice

Heavily taxed items such as alcohol, tobacco, and gasoline have a low elasticity of demand. So the buyer pays most of the tax. Also, because demand is inelastic, the quantity bought does not decrease much and the government collects a large tax revenue.

But sometimes, the government makes a mistake. In 1991, the federal government was scraping around for every dollar it could find to cut its deficit. It came up with a plan to put a 10 percent "luxury tax" on pleasure boats, private airplanes, high-priced cars, furs, and jewelry, which it estimated would bring in $300 million a year. But the government did not reckon on the high elasticity of demand for these items. The quantities of pleasure boats and other luxury items bought decreased by up to 90 percent, and the tax revenue collected was only one tenth the amount expected. The luxury tax was quickly abandoned.

This short-lived experiment with a luxury tax explains why the items that are taxed are those that have inelastic demands and why, in practice, buyers pay most of the taxes.

Taxes and Efficiency

You've seen that a sales tax places a wedge between the price paid by buyers and the price received by sellers. The price paid by buyers is also the buyers' willingness to pay, which measures marginal benefit. And the price received by sellers is the sellers' minimum supply-price, which equals marginal cost.

So, because a tax places a wedge between the buyers' price and the sellers' price, it also puts a wedge between marginal benefit and marginal cost and creates inefficiency. With a higher buying price and a lower selling price, the tax decreases the quantity produced and consumed and a deadweight loss arises. Figure 7.9 shows the inefficiency of taxes. Both the consumer surplus and producer surplus shrink. Part of each of these surpluses goes to the government in tax revenue—the light blue area in the figure. And part of the surpluses becomes a deadweight loss—the gray area.

In the extreme cases of perfectly inelastic demand and perfectly inelastic supply, the quantity does not change and there is no deadweight loss. The more inelastic is either demand or supply, the smaller is the decrease in quantity and the smaller is the deadweight loss. When demand or supply is perfectly inelastic, the quantity remains constant and there is no deadweight loss.

FIGURE 7.9

Taxes and Efficiency

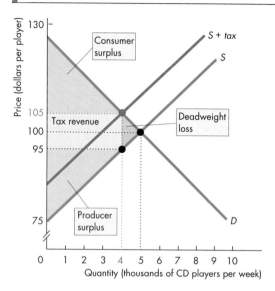

With no sales tax, 5,000 players a week are bought and sold at $100 each. With a sales tax of $10 a player, the buyers' price rises to $105 a player, the sellers' price falls to $95, and the quantity decreases to 4,000 CD players a week. Consumer surplus shrinks to the green area, and producer surplus shrinks to the dark blue area. Part of the loss of consumer surplus and producer surplus goes to the government as tax revenue, which is shown as the light blue area. A deadweight loss also arises, which is shown by the gray area.

REVIEW QUIZ

- How does the elasticity of demand influence the effect of a sales tax on the price paid by the buyer, the price received by the seller, the quantity, the tax revenue, and the deadweight loss?
- How does the elasticity of supply influence the effect of a sales tax on the price paid by the buyer, the price received by the seller, the quantity, the tax revenue, and the deadweight loss?
- Why do taxes create a deadweight loss?

Governments make the trading of some types of goods, such as drugs illegal. Let's see how the market works when trade in an illegal good takes place.

Markets for Illegal Goods

THE MARKETS FOR MANY GOODS AND SERVICES are regulated, and the buying and selling of some goods are illegal—the goods and services are illegal. The best-known examples of such goods are drugs, such as marijuana, cocaine, and heroin.

Despite the fact that these drugs are illegal, trade in them is a multibillion-dollar business. This trade can be understood by using the same economic model and principles that explain trade in legal goods. To study the market for illegal goods, we're first going to examine the prices and quantities that would prevail if these goods were not illegal. Next, we'll see how prohibition works. Then we'll see how a tax might limit consumption of these goods.

A Free Market for Drugs

Figure 7.10 shows the market for drugs. The demand curve, D, shows that, other things remaining the same, the lower the price of drugs, the larger is the quantity of drugs demanded. The supply curve, S, shows that, other things remaining the same, the lower the price of drugs, the smaller is the quantity supplied. If drugs were not illegal, the quantity bought and sold would be Q_c and the price would be P_c.

A Market for Illegal Drugs

When a good is illegal, the cost of trading in the good increases. By how much the cost increases and on whom the cost falls depend on the penalties for violating the law and the effectiveness with which the law is enforced. The larger the penalties and the more effective the policing, the higher are the costs. Penalties might be imposed on sellers, buyers, or both.

Penalties on Sellers Drug dealers in the United States face large penalties if their activities are detected. For example, a marijuana dealer could pay a $200,000 fine and serve a 15-year prison term. A heroin dealer could pay a $500,000 fine and serve a 20-year prison term. These penalties are part of the cost of supplying illegal drugs, and they bring a decrease in supply—a leftward shift in the supply curve. To determine the new supply curve, we add the cost of breaking the law to the minimum price

FIGURE 7.10

A Market for an Illegal Good

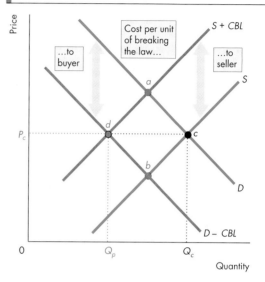

The demand curve for drugs is D, and the supply curve is S. If drugs are not illegal, the quantity bought and sold is Q_c at a price of P_c—point c. If selling drugs is illegal, the cost of breaking the law by selling drugs (CBL) is added to the minimum supply-price and supply decreases to $S + CBL$. The price rises, and the quantity bought decreases—point a. If buying drugs is illegal, the cost of breaking the law is subtracted from the maximum price that buyers are willing to pay, and demand decreases to $D - CBL$. The price falls, and the quantity bought decreases—point b. If both buying and selling are illegal, both the supply and demand curves shift, the quantity bought decreases even more, but (in this example) the price remains at its unregulated level—point d.

that drug dealers are willing to accept. In Fig. 7.10, the cost of breaking the law by selling drugs (CBL) is added to the minimum price that dealers will accept, and the supply curve shifts leftward to $S + CBL$. If penalties are imposed only on sellers, the market moves from point c to point a. The price increases, and the quantity bought decreases.

Penalties on Buyers In the United States, it is illegal to *possess* drugs such as marijuana, cocaine, and heroin. For example, possession of marijuana can bring a prison term of 1 year and possession of heroin can bring a prison term of 2 years. Penalties fall on buyers, and the cost of breaking the law must be subtracted from the value of the good to determine the maximum price buyers are willing to pay for the drugs. Demand decreases, and the demand curve shifts leftward. In Fig. 7.10, the demand curve shifts to $D - CBL$. With penalties imposed only on buyers, the market moves from point c to point b. The price and the quantity bought decrease.

Penalties on Both Sellers and Buyers

If penalties are imposed on sellers *and* buyers, both supply and demand decrease, and both the supply curve and the demand curve shift leftward. In Fig. 7.10, the costs of breaking the law are the same for both buyers and sellers, so both curves shift leftward by the same amount. The market moves to point d. The price remains at P_c, but the quantity bought decreases to Q_p.

The larger the penalties and the greater the degree of law enforcement, the larger is the decrease in demand and/or supply and the greater is the shift of the demand and/or supply curve. If the penalties are heavier on sellers, the supply curve shifts farther than the demand curve and the price rises above P_c. If the penalties are heavier on buyers, the demand curve shifts farther than the supply curve and the price falls below P_c. In the United States, the penalties on sellers are larger than those on buyers, so the quantity of drugs traded decreases and the price increases compared with an unregulated market.

With high enough penalties and effective law enforcement, it is possible to decrease demand and/or supply to the point at which the quantity bought is zero. But in reality, such an outcome is unusual. It does not happen in the case of illegal drugs. The key reason is the high cost of law enforcement and insufficient resources for the police to achieve effective enforcement. Because of this situation, some people suggest that drugs (and other illegal goods) should be legalized and sold openly but also be taxed at a high rate in the same way that legal drugs such as alcohol are taxed. How would such an arrangement work?

Legalizing and Taxing Drugs

From your study of the effects of taxes, it is easy to see that the quantity of drugs bought could be decreased if drugs were legalized and taxed. A sufficiently high tax could be imposed to decrease supply, raise the price, and achieve the same decrease in the quantity bought as with a prohibition on drugs. The government would collect a large tax revenue.

Illegal Trading to Evade the Tax   It is likely that an extremely high tax rate would be needed to cut the quantity of drugs bought to the level prevailing with a prohibition. It is also likely that many drug dealers and consumers would try to cover up their activities to evade the tax. If they did act in this way, they would face the cost of breaking the law—the tax law. If the penalty for tax law violation is as severe and as effectively policed as drug-dealing laws, the analysis we've already conducted applies also to this case. The quantity of drugs bought would depend on the penalties for law breaking and on the way in which the penalties are assigned to buyers and sellers.

Taxes Versus Prohibition: Some Pros and Cons
Which is more effective, prohibition or taxes? In favor of taxes and against prohibition is the fact that the tax revenue can be used to make law enforcement more effective. It can also be used to run a more effective education campaign against drugs. In favor of prohibition and against taxes is the fact that a prohibition sends a signal that might influence preferences, decreasing the demand for drugs. Also, some people intensely dislike the idea of the government profiting from trade in harmful substances.

R E V I E W   Q U I Z

- How does the imposition of a penalty for selling a drug influence demand, supply, price, and the quantity of the drug consumed?
- How does the imposition of a penalty for buying a drug influence demand, supply, price, and the quantity of the drug consumed?
- How does the imposition of a penalty for selling *or* buying a drug influence demand, supply, price, and the quantity of the drug consumed?
- Is there any case for legalizing drugs?

You've seen how government intervention in markets in the form of price ceilings, price floors, and taxes limits the quantity and creates inefficient resource use. You've also seen how in a market for an illegal good, the quantity can be decreased by imposing penalties on either buyers or sellers or by legalizing and taxing the good. In the next and final section of this chapter, we look at agricultural markets and see how governments try to stabilize farm revenues.

Stabilizing Farm Revenues

WHEN FLOODS COVERED VAST TRACTS OF THE
Midwest in the summer of 1993, many farmers saw
their crops wiped out. Farm output fluctuates a great
deal because of fluctuations in the weather. How do
changes in farm output affect farm prices and farm
revenues? And how might farm revenues be stabilized? Let's begin to answer these questions by looking at an agricultural market.

An Agricultural Market

Figure 7.11 shows the market for wheat. In both
parts, the demand curve for wheat is *D*. Once farmers have harvested their crop, they have no control
over the quantity supplied, and supply is inelastic
along a *momentary supply curve*. In normal climate
conditions, the momentary supply curve is MS_0 (in
both parts of the figure).

The price is determined at the point of intersection of the momentary supply curve and the demand
curve. In normal conditions, the price is $4 a bushel.
The quantity of wheat produced is 20 billion bushels,
and farm revenue is $80 billion. Suppose the oppor-
tunity cost to farmers of producing wheat is also $80
billion. Then in normal conditions, farmers just
cover their opportunity cost.

Poor Harvest Suppose there is a bad growing season,
resulting in a poor harvest. What happens to the
price of wheat and the revenue of farmers? These
questions are answered in Fig. 7.11(a). Supply
decreases, and the momentary supply curve shifts
leftward to MS_1, where 15 billion bushels of wheat
are produced. With a decrease in supply, the price
increases to $6 a bushel.

What happens to total farm revenue? It *increases*
to $90 billion. A decrease in supply has brought an
increase in price and an increase in farm revenue. It
does so because the demand for wheat is *inelastic*. The
percentage decrease in the quantity demanded is less
than the percentage increase in price. You can verify
this fact by noticing in Fig. 7.11(a) that the increase in
revenue from the higher price ($30 billion light blue
area) exceeds the decrease in revenue from the smaller
quantity ($20 billion red area). Farmers are now mak-
ing a revenue in excess of their opportunity cost.

Although total farm revenue increases when there
is a poor harvest, some farmers, whose entire crop is

FIGURE 7.11

Harvests, Farm Prices, and Farm Revenue

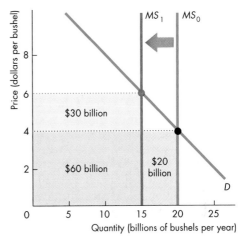

(a) Poor harvest: revenue increases

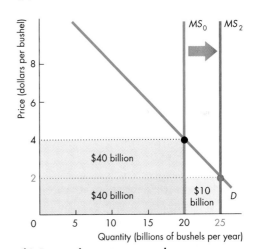

(b) Bumper harvest: revenue decreases

The demand curve for wheat is *D*. In normal times, the supply
curve is MS_0 and 20 million bushels are sold for $4 a bushel.
In part (a), a poor harvest decreases supply to MS_1. The price
rises to $6 a bushel, and farm revenue increases to $90 billion—the $30 billion increase from the higher price (light blue
area) exceeds the $20 billion decrease from the smaller quan-
tity (red area). In part (b), a bumper harvest increases supply
to MS_2. The price falls to $2 a bushel, and farm revenue
decreases to $50 billion—the $40 billion decrease from the
lower price (red area) exceeds the $10 billion increase from
the increase in the quantity sold (light blue area).

wiped out, suffer a decrease in revenue. Others, whose crop is unaffected, make an enormous gain.

Bumper Harvest   Figure 7.11(b) shows what happens in the opposite situation, when there is a bumper harvest. Now supply increases to 25 billion bushels, and the momentary supply curve shifts rightward to MS_2. With the increased quantity supplied, the price falls to $2 a bushel. Farm revenue decreases to $50 billion. It does so because the demand for wheat is inelastic. To see this fact, notice in Fig. 7.11(b) that the decrease in revenue from the lower price ($40 billion red area) exceeds the increase in revenue from the increase in the quantity sold ($10 billion light blue area).

Elasticity of Demand   In the example we've just worked through, demand is inelastic. If demand is elastic, the price fluctuations go in the same directions as those we've worked out, but revenue fluctuates in the opposite direction. Bumper harvests increase revenue, and poor harvests decrease it. But the demand for most agricultural products is inelastic, and the case we've studied is the relevant one.

Because farm prices fluctuate, institutions have evolved to stabilize them. There are two types of institutions:

- Speculative markets in inventories
- Farm price stabilization policy

Speculative Markets in Inventories

Many goods, including a wide variety of agricultural products, can be stored. These inventories provide a cushion between production and consumption. If production decreases, goods can be sold from inventory; if production increases, goods can be put into inventory.

In a market that has inventories, we must distinguish production from supply. The quantity produced is not the same as the quantity supplied. The quantity supplied exceeds the quantity produced when goods are sold from inventory. And the quantity supplied is less than the quantity produced when goods are put into inventory. Supply therefore depends on the behavior of inventory holders.

The Behavior of Inventory Holders   Inventory holders speculate. They hope to buy at a low price and sell at a high price. That is, they hope to buy goods and put them into inventory when the price is low and

sell them from inventory when the price is high. They make a profit or incur a loss equal to their selling price minus their buying price and minus the cost of storage.

But how do inventory holders know when to buy and when to sell? How do they know whether the price is high or low? To decide whether a price is high or low, inventory holders forecast future prices. If the current price is above the forecasted future price, inventory holders sell goods from inventory. If the current price is below the forecasted future price, inventory holders buy goods to put into inventory. This behavior by inventory holders makes the supply perfectly elastic at the price forecasted by inventory holders.

Let's work out what happens to price and quantity in a market in which inventories are held when production fluctuates. Let's look again at the wheat market.

Fluctuations in Production   In Fig. 7.12 the demand curve for wheat is D. Inventory holders expect the future price to be $4 a bushel. The supply curve is S—supply is perfectly elastic at the price expected by inventory holders. Production fluctuates between Q_1 and Q_2.

When production fluctuates and there are no inventories, the price and the quantity fluctuate. We saw this result in Fig. 7.11. But if there are inventories, the price does not fluctuate. When production decreases to Q_1, or 15 billion bushels, inventory holders sell 5 billion bushels from inventory and the quantity bought by consumers is 20 billion bushels. The price remains at $4 a bushel. When production increases to Q_2, or 25 billion bushels, inventory holders buy 5 billion bushels and consumers continue to buy 20 billion bushels. Again, the price remains at $4 a bushel. Inventories reduce price fluctuations. In Fig. 7.12, the price fluctuations are entirely eliminated. When there are costs of carrying inventories and when inventories become almost depleted, some price fluctuations do occur, but these fluctuations are smaller than those occurring in a market without inventories.

Farm Revenue   Even if inventory speculation succeeds in stabilizing prices, it does not stabilize farm revenue. With the price stabilized, farm revenue fluctuates as production fluctuates. But now bumper harvests always bring larger revenues than poor harvests do because the price is now constant and only the quantity fluctuates.

FIGURE 7.12
How Inventories Limit Price Changes

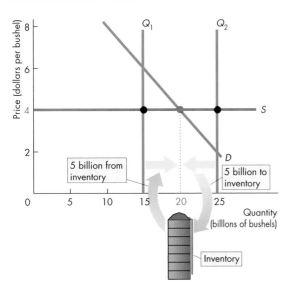

Inventory holders sell wheat from inventory if a poor harvest causes the price to rise above $4 a bushel and buy wheat to hold in inventory if a bumper harvest causes the price to fall below $4 a bushel, making supply (S) perfectly elastic. When production decreases to Q_1, 5 billion bushels are sold from inventory; when production increases to Q_2, 5 billion bushels are added to inventory. The price remains at $4 a bushel.

Farm Price Stabilization Policy

Most governments intervene in agricultural markets. The most extensive such intervention occurs in the European Union and Japan. Farm price intervention is not so extensive in the United States. But U.S. government regulations influence the prices of some items, examples of which are sugar and peanuts.

Governments intervene in agricultural markets in three ways. They:

1. Set production limits
2. Set price floors
3. Hold inventories

Production limits, which are called *quotas,* restrict the quantity produced and can result in the

price exceeding the price in an unregulated market. Farmers benefit from quotas because the price rises above the minimum supply-price. But consumers lose, and quotas create deadweight loss. Quotas exist mainly because of the power of the farm lobby.

Price floors, which are set above the equilibrium price, create surpluses. They work in a similar way to the minimum wage that we studied earlier. The minimum wage creates unemployment and price floors in agricultural markets create surpluses of food products. To make a price floor work, the government's price stabilization agency must buy the persistent surpluses. If the price is persistently greater than the equilibrium price, the government agency buys more than it sells and ends up with large inventory. Such has been the outcome in Europe, where they have "mountains" of butter and "lakes" of wine! The cost of buying and storing the inventory falls on taxpayers, and the main gainers are large, low-cost farms.

If the government price stabilization agency operates like a private inventory holder, it maintains the price close to the equilibrium price. It sells from inventory when price is above normal, and it buys for inventory when the price is below normal. But this type of intervention is not necessary because private trading can achieve the same outcome.

R E V I E W   Q U I Z

- Can you explain how poor harvests and bumper harvests influence farm prices and farm revenues?
- Can you explain how the existence of inventories and speculation influence farm prices and farm revenues?
- What are the main actions that governments take in farm markets and how do these actions influence farm prices and farm revenues?

◆ You now know how to use the demand and supply model to predict prices, to study government intervention in markets, and to study the sources and costs of inefficiency. Before you leave this topic, take a look at *Reading Between the Lines* on pp. 144–145 and see what is happening in the market for cigarettes in Michigan today.

Reading Between the Lines

Taxes and Illegal Activities

THE DETROIT NEWS, FEBRUARY 11, 1999

Cigarette Tax Revenue Soars

Tobacco tax revenue

The tax on cigarettes tripled in May 1994 to 75 cents a package. Here's what happened to state tobacco tax revenue. Fiscal years run from Oct. 1–Sept. 30.

Fiscal year	Tax collected	Percentage change from previous year
1992–93	$243.6 million	−1.0%
1993–94	$374.5 million	+53.7%
1994–95	$619.4 million	+65.4%
1995–96	$580.5 million	−6.3%
1996–97	$546.0 million	−5.9%
1997–98	$566.0 million	+3.7%

Source: Michigan Senate Fiscal Agency, *The Detroit News*.

BY B.G. GREGG AND CHARLIE CAIN / DETROIT NEWS LANSING BUREAU

LANSING—State tax receipts from cigarette sales jumped sharply in the five months since the state mandated each pack to carry a "Michigan" stamp designed to combat smuggling from low-tax states.

The additional $46 million in revenue amounted to a 20-percent boost over the previous year. ...

When Gov. John Engler first called for the cigarette stamp two years ago, he estimated that smuggling was a $17-million annual problem. ... "Now based on what we're seeing on the reports and the money coming in, we think it was $60 million and could be more," said Lyle Mather, administrator of the Motor Fuel and Tobacco Tax Division in the Treasury Department.

Smuggling became a problem in May 1994 when the cigarette tax was tripled from a quarter to 75-cents a pack as part of the Proposal A school refinance plan.

Before the stamp was required, it was difficult to determine, on its face, whether a pack or carton had paid Michigan taxes.

Michigan's 75-cent tax is the nation's seventh highest—more than double the national average. That invited smugglers to buy cigarettes in states with lower taxes, turn around and sell them here.

The cigarette tax is 3 cents in Kentucky, a nickel in North Carolina, and 7 cents in South Carolina. ...

"The new tax stamp has been effective in reducing the smuggling of cigarettes into Michigan," said state Atty. Gen. Jennifer Granholm. But she said criminals are still trying, with mixed success, to outsmart regulators. The latest problem is counterfeit tobacco stamps. ...

Essence of the Story

■ In 1994, Michigan increased its tax on cigarettes from 25 cents to 75 cents per package

■ The cigarette tax per package is 3 cents in Kentucky, 5 cents in North Carolina, and 7 cents in South Carolina.

■ The national average cigarette tax is less than half that in Michigan.

■ Michigan's cigarette tax revenue increased in the first year of the higher tax but then began to decrease.

■ The state tax administrator estimates that smuggling has cost the Michigan treasury $60 million or more each year.

■ In 1998, Michigan introduced a cigarette tax stamp that decreased smuggling and increased the state's tax revenue.

Economic Analysis

■ Figure 1 shows the market for cigarettes in Michigan before the 1994 tax increase.

■ The demand for cigarettes is *D*. This demand curve *assumes* an elasticity of demand equal to 0.61, which is the estimated price elasticity of demand for tobacco for the United States. (See Table 5.1, p. 93.)

■ The supply of cigarettes in Michigan is perfectly elastic. The reason is that the tobacco companies can sell their products anywhere in the world at the going before-tax price, so they are willing to sell any quantity in Michigan at that price.

■ With no cigarette tax, the equilibrium price is $2.75 per pack and 1,028 million packs a year are bought.

■ With a tax of 25 cents per pack, the supply curve shifts to $S + tax_0$. The price rises to $3.00 per pack, and the quantity bought decreases to 975 million packs per year. The state collects $244 million in tax, and there is a small deadweight loss.

■ Figure 2 shows the situation after the tax increased to 75 cents a pack but before the tax stamp law was introduced.

■ The supply curve shifts to $S + tax_1$. The price rises to $3.50 per pack, and the quantity bought decreases to 887 million packs per year. This decrease in the quantity bought is predicted by the assumed elasticity of demand of 0.61.

■ According to the news article, the state collected $562 million in tax revenue (average for 1995–1998). So at 75 cents a pack, the tax was paid on only 750 million packs.

■ If the elasticity of demand assumption is correct, 137 million packs of cigarettes per year are smuggled into Michigan. The smugglers collect $103 million a year that the state treasury loses.

■ The cost of smuggling calculated here is larger than the Michigan treasury's estimate of $60 million, which seems to be based on the belief that there was no smuggling before 1995 and that the elasticity of demand is greater than 1. Neither assumption is likely to be correct.

■ The tax stamp seems to have decreased smuggling but not eliminated it.

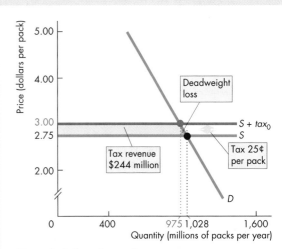

Figure 1 Before the tax increase

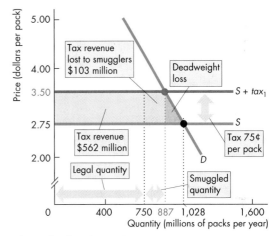

Figure 2 After the tax increase

You're The Voter

■ Would you vote for a law that taxes cigarettes in your state at a higher rate than the national average? Explain why.

■ Would you vote for a cigarette stamp tax law? Why or why not?

■ What other measures would you recommend the government take to deter smuggling? (Hint: Think about the analysis in this chapter of markets for illegal goods.)

145

SUMMARY

KEY POINTS

Housing Markets and Rent Ceilings (pp. 128–131)

- A decrease in the supply of housing decreases short-run supply and increases the equilibrium rent.
- The higher rent increases the quantity of housing supplied in the short run and stimulates building in the long run. The rent decreases, and the quantity of housing increases.
- If a rent ceiling prevents the rent from increasing, the quantity supplied remains constant and there is a housing shortage, which creates wasteful search and black markets.

The Labor Market and the Minimum Wage (pp. 132–134)

- A decrease in the demand for low-skilled labor lowers the wage rate and reduces employment.
- The lower wage rate encourages people with low skill to acquire more skill, which decreases the supply of low-skilled labor. The wage rises gradually to its original level, and employment decreases.
- Imposing a minimum wage above the equilibrium wage creates unemployment and an increase in the amount of time people spend searching for a job.
- Minimum wages hit young people who have the fewest skills hardest.

Taxes (pp. 135–138)

- When a good or service is taxed, usually the price increases and the quantity bought decreases but the price increases by less than the tax. The buyer pays part of the tax, and the seller pays part of the tax.
- The portion of the tax paid by the buyer and by the seller depends on the elasticity of demand and the elasticity of supply.
- The less elastic the demand and the more elastic the supply, the greater is the price increase, the smaller is the quantity decrease, and the larger is the portion of the tax paid by the buyer.

- If demand is perfectly elastic or supply is perfectly inelastic, the seller pays the entire tax. If demand is perfectly inelastic or supply is perfectly elastic, the buyer pays the entire tax.

Markets for Illegal Goods (pp. 139–140)

- Penalties on sellers of an illegal good increase the cost of selling the good and decrease its supply. Penalties on buyers decrease their willingness to pay and decrease the demand for the good.
- The higher the penalties and the more effective the law enforcement, the smaller is the quantity bought. The price is higher or lower than the unregulated price, depending on whether the penalties on sellers or buyers are higher.
- A tax set at a sufficiently high rate will decrease the quantity of a drug consumed, but there will be a tendency for the tax to be evaded.

Stabilizing Farm Revenues (pp. 141–143)

- Farm revenues fluctuate because supply fluctuates.
- The demand for most farm products is inelastic, so a decrease in supply increases the price and increases farm revenue, while an increase in supply decreases price and decreases farm revenue.
- Inventory holders and government agencies act to stabilize farm prices and revenues.

KEY FIGURES

KEY TERMS

PROBLEMS

*1. The figure shows the demand for and supply of rental housing in Village:

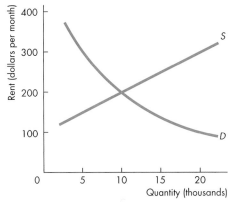

a. What are the equilibrium rent and equilibrium quantity of rented housing?

If a rent ceiling is set at $150 a month, what is:

b. The quantity of housing rented?
c. The shortage of housing?
d. The maximum price that someone is willing to pay for the last unit of housing available?

2. The figure shows the demand for and supply of rental housing in Township:

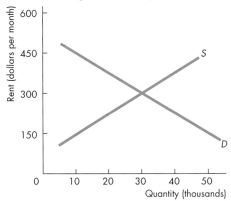

a. What are the equilibrium rent and equilibrium quantity of rented housing?

If a rent ceiling is set at $150 a month, what is:

b. The quantity of housing rented?
c. The shortage of housing?
d. The maximum price that someone is willing to pay for the last unit available?

*3. The table gives the demand for and supply of teenage labor:

Wage rate (dollars per hour)	Quantity demanded	Quantity supplied
	(hours per month)	
2	3,000	1,000
3	2,500	1,500
4	2,000	2,000
5	1,500	2,500
6	1,000	3,000

a. What are the equilibrium wage rate and level of employment?
b. What is the quantity of unemployment?
c. If a minimum wage of $3 an hour is set for teenagers, how many hours do they work?
d. If a minimum wage of $3 an hour is set for teenagers, how many hours of their labor is unemployed?
e. If a minimum wage is set at $5 an hour for teenagers, what are the quantities of employment and unemployment?
f. If a minimum wage is set at $5 an hour and demand increases by 500 hours a month, what is the wage rate paid to teenagers and how many hours of their labor is unemployed?

4. The table gives the demand for and supply of high school graduates:

Wage rate (dollars per hour)	Quantity demanded	Quantity supplied
	(hours per month)	
6	9,000	4,000
7	8,000	5,000
8	7,000	6,000
9	6,000	7,000
10	5,000	8,000

a. What are the equilibrium wage rate and level of employment?
b. What is the level of unemployment?
c. If a minimum wage is set at $7 an hour, how many hours do high school graduates work?
d. If a minimum wage is set at $7 an hour, how many hours of labor are unemployed?
e. If a minimum wage is set at $9 an hour, what are employment and unemployment?
f. If the minimum wage is $9 an hour and demand increases by 500 hours a month, what is the wage rate paid to high school graduates and how many hours of their labor are unemployed?

*5. The table gives the demand and supply schedules for chocolate brownies:

Price (cents per brownie)	Quantity demanded	Quantity supplied
	(millions per day)	
50	5	3
60	4	4
70	3	5
80	2	6
90	1	7

a. If brownies are not taxed, what is the price of a brownie and how many are consumed?
b. If brownies are taxed at 20¢ each, what is the price and how many brownies are consumed? Who pays the tax?

6. The demand and supply schedules for coffee are:

Price (dollars per cup)	Quantity demanded	Quantity supplied
	(cups per hour)	
1.50	90	30
1.75	70	40
2.00	50	50
2.25	30	60
2.75	10	70

a. If there is no tax on coffee, what is the price and how much coffee is consumed?
b. If a tax of 75¢ a cup is introduced, what is the price and how much coffee is consumed? Who pays the tax?

*7. The demand for and supply of rice is:

Price (dollars per box)	Quantity demanded	Quantity supplied
	(boxes per week)	
1.20	3,000	500
1.30	2,750	1,500
1.40	2,500	2,500
1.50	2,250	3,500
1.60	2,000	4,500

A storm destroys part of the crop and decreases supply by 500 boxes a week.
a. What do inventory holders do?
b. What is the price and what is farm revenue?

8. In problem 7 instead of a storm, perfect weather increases supply by 500 boxes a week.
a. What do inventory holders do?
b. What is the price and what is farm revenue?

CRITICAL THINKING

1. Study *Reading Between the Lines* on the market for cigarettes in Michigan on pp. 144–145 and answer the following questions.
   a. Suppose that the Michigan police steps up its rate of detecting smuggling. And suppose the demand and supply curves shown in Fig. 1 on p. 145 correctly describe the market for cigarettes in Michigan. Show in the figure the changes that result from the efforts of the Michigan police.
   b. Suppose that the price elasticity of demand is greater than the 0.61 that is used in the analysis on p. 145. In particular, suppose it is large enough to make the loss from smuggling the $60 million that the state treasury believes is the correct number. Draw new versions of Fig. 1 and Fig. 2 that are consistent with this view.
   c. Suppose that the people of Michigan want to decrease the amount of cigarette smoking. What level of tax per pack would be needed to achieve a 10 percent and a 20 percent decrease in smoking? What special problems would arise with taxes set at these levels?
   d. How other than by increasing the cigarette tax might we reduce the amount of cigarette smoking?

2. Use the links on the Parkin Web site to obtain information about cigarette tax rates, tax revenues, purchases, population, and income in the 50 states. Then answer the following questions about the relationship between the number of packs of cigarettes purchased and the price of a pack across the states.
   a. How would you describe the relationship?
   b. What does the relationship tell you about the demand for cigarettes?
   c. What does the relationship tell you about the amount of cigarette smuggling?

3. Use the links on the Parkin Web site to obtain information about farm programs in the United States. What are the main programs and what are their effects on the quantities of farm products, their prices, and economic efficiency?

Understanding How Markets Work

The four chapters that you've just studied explain how markets work. The market is an amazing instrument. It enables people who have never met and who know nothing about each other to interact and do business. It also enables us to allocate our scarce resources to the uses that we value most highly. Markets can be very simple or highly organized.

The Amazing Market

◆ A simple market is one that the American historian Daniel J. Boorstin describes in *The Discoverers* (p. 161). In the late fourteenth century,

> The Muslim caravans that went southward from Morocco across the Atlas Mountains arrived after twenty days at the shores of the Senegal River. There the Moroccan traders laid out separate piles of salt, of beads from Ceutan coral, and cheap manufactured goods. Then they retreated out of sight. The local tribesmen, who lived in the strip mines where they dug their gold, came to the shore and put a heap of gold beside each pile of Moroccan goods. Then they, in turn, went out of view, leaving the Moroccan traders either to take the gold offered for a particular pile or to reduce the pile of their merchandise to suit the offered price in gold. Once again the Moroccan traders withdrew, and the process went on. By this system of commercial etiquette, the Moroccans collected their gold.

An organized market is the New York Stock Exchange, which trades many millions of stocks each day. Another is an auction at which the U.S. government sells rights to broadcasters and cellular telephone companies for the use of the airwaves. ◆ All of these markets determine the prices at which exchanges take place and enable both buyers and sellers to benefit. ◆ Everything and anything that can be exchanged is traded in markets. There are markets for goods and services; for resources such as labor, capital, and raw materials; for dollars, pounds, and yen; for goods to be delivered now and for goods to be delivered in the future. Only the imagination places limits on what can be traded in markets. ◆ You began your study of markets in Chapter 4, by learning about the laws of demand and supply. There, you discovered the forces that make prices adjust to coordinate buying plans and selling plans. In Chapter 5, you learned how to calculate and use the concept of elasticity to predict the responsiveness of prices and quantities to changes in supply and demand. In Chapter 6, you studied efficiency and discovered the conditions under which a competitive market sends resources to uses in which they are valued most highly. And finally, in Chapter 7, you studied markets in action. There, you learned how markets cope with change and discovered how they operate when governments intervene to fix prices, impose taxes, or make some goods illegal. ◆ The laws of demand and supply that you've learned and used in these four chapters were discovered during the nineteenth century by some remarkable economists. We conclude our study of demand and supply and markets by looking at the lives and times of some of these economists and by talking to one of today's most influential economists who studies and creates sophisticated auction markets.

Discovering the Laws of Demand and Supply

The Economist

Alfred Marshall

(1842–1924) grew up in an England that was being transformed by the railroad and by the expansion of manufacturing. Mary Paley was one of Marshall's students at Cambridge, and when Alfred and Mary married, in 1877, celibacy rules barred Alfred from continuing to teach at Cambridge. By 1884, with more liberal rules, the Marshalls returned to Cambridge, where Alfred became Professor of Political Economy.

Many others had a hand in refining the theory of demand and supply, but the first thorough and complete statement of the theory as we know it today was set out by Alfred Marshall, with the acknowledged help of Mary Paley Marshall. Published in 1890, this monumental treatise, The Principles of Economics, *became the textbook on economics on both sides of the Atlantic for almost half a century. Marshall was an outstanding mathematician, but he kept mathematics and even diagrams in the background. His supply and demand diagram appears only in a footnote.*

"The forces to be dealt with are . . . so numerous, that it is best to take a few at a time. . . . Thus we begin by isolating the primary relations of supply, demand, and price"

ALFRED MARSHALL
The Principles of Economics

The Issues

The laws of demand and supply that you studied in Chapter 4 were discovered during the 1830s by Antoine-Augustin Cournot (1801–1877), a professor of mathematics at the University of Lyon, France. Although Cournot was the first to use demand and supply, it was the development

and expansion of the railroads during the 1850s that gave the newly emerging theory its first practical applications. Railroads then were at the cutting edge of technology just as airlines are today. And as in the airline industry today, competition among the railroads was fierce.

Dionysius Lardner (1793–1859), an Irish professor of philosophy at the University of London, used demand and supply to show railroad companies how they could increase their profits by cutting rates on long-distance business on which competition was fiercest and by raising rates on short-haul business on which they had less to fear from other transportation suppliers. Today, economists use the principles that Lardner worked out during the 1850s to calculate the freight rates and passenger fares that will give airlines the largest possible profit. And the rates calculated have a lot in common with the railroad rates of the nineteenth century. On local routes on which there is little competition, fares per mile are highest, and on long-distance routes on which the airlines compete fiercely, fares per mile are lowest.

Known satirically among scientists of the day as "Dionysius Diddler," Lardner worked on an amazing range of problems from astronomy to railway engineering to economics. A colorful character, he would have been a regular guest of David Letterman if late-night talk shows had been around in the 1850s. Lardner visited the École des Ponts et Chaussées (School of Bridges and Roads) in Paris and must have learned a great deal from Jules Dupuit.

In France, Jules Dupuit (1804–1866), a French engineer/economist, used demand to calculate the benefits from building a bridge and, once the bridge was built, for calculating the toll to charge for its use. His work was the forerunner of what is today called *cost-benefit analysis*. Working with the principles invented by Dupuit, economists today calculate the costs and benefits of highways and airports, dams, and power stations.

Then

Dupuit used the law of demand to determine whether a bridge or canal would be valued enough by its users to justify the cost of building it. Lardner first worked out the relationship between the cost of production and supply and used demand and supply theory to explain the costs, prices, and profits of railroad operations. He also used the theory to discover ways of increasing revenue by raising rates on short-haul business and lowering them on long-distance freight.

Now

Today, using the same principles that Dupuit devised, economists calculate whether the benefits of expanding airports and air-traffic control facilities are sufficient to cover their costs. Airline companies use the principles developed by Lardner to set their prices and to decide when to offer "seat sales." Like the railroads before them, the airlines charge a high price per mile on short flights, for which they face little competition, and a low price per mile on long flights, for which competition is fierce.

Markets do an amazing job. And the laws of demand and supply help us to understand how markets work. But in some situations, a market must be designed and institutions must be created to enable the market to operate. In recent years, economists have begun to use their tools to design and create markets. And one of the chief architects of new style markets is Paul Milgrom, whom you can meet on the following pages.

Paul R. Milgrom

is Professor of Economics at Stanford University and an Associate Editor of the American Economic Review, *the leading journal that publishes economic research. He is founder and president of Market Design, Inc., a young company that designs new auction and market rules for businesses and governments. Born in Detroit, Michigan, in 1948, Professor Milgrom was an undergraduate at the University of Michigan and a graduate student at Stanford University (Ph.D. 1979). He taught at Northwestern University and Yale University before returning to Stanford in 1987.*

Professor Milgrom is an economic theorist, which means that he uses mathematical techniques to study economic behavior. His work on auctions has been especially influential and has found practical applications in auctioning items ranging from radio spectrum (used in paging and cellular telephones) to mining rights.

Michael Parkin talked with Professor Milgrom about his work and how it connects with the theory of demand and supply developed by Cournot and Marshall.

Paul R. Milgrom

Professor Milgrom, how did you become an economist?
I came into the house of economics through an unmarked side door, not knowing where I was until I was well inside. The main entrance is through a graduate degree in economics, but I have no university degree in economics at any level. My undergraduate studies were in mathematics and statistics, and my graduate studies were in business. It was in graduate school that I stumbled across a brilliant study of auction theory by William Vickrey—work for which he was awarded the Nobel Prize 21 years later, in 1996. Vickrey's work surprised me and convinced me that mathematical analysis could help me to understand auctions and could even point the way to new, improved types of auctions.

Auctions, like all market arrangements, bring buyers and sellers together. Doesn't the supply and demand model explain how auctions work?
The supply and demand model is the economist's workhorse for day-to-day market analysis. It provides a wonderful way to summarize some of the main factors affecting prices and quantities and to explain how prices guide important choices.

But the model is silent about how the rules that govern trade are set or how they affect economic outcomes. Also, it is not very helpful for thinking about technology decisions that can have a huge impact on economic outcomes. For example, the way standards are set for cellular telephone systems determines whether the same phone will work on different systems in different parts of the nation and the world. In Europe, a single standard allows a consumer to go from country to country and still have a working telephone. In the United States, where no single standard exists, a consumer may find that her telephone fails to operate even with the system in the next town.

Obviously, that failure depresses the sales of cellular phone service, although it has nothing to do with the consumer preferences for communications or with the cost or availability of the cellular telephone technology.

So institutions influence prices and quantities and the kinds of plans that people make. And sometimes, institutions such as standards-setting bodies can solve problems that a market guided only by prices can't deal with effectively.

Let's return to auctions. What is auction theory? How does it relate to supply and demand?
Auctions are institutions that determine the prices and other terms at which buyers and sellers will trade. Auction theory explains how the rules of an auction affect its outcome.

Sellers want auctions that generate the highest price. Buyers want auctions that generate the lowest price. Auction houses want auctions that balance the interests of buyers and sellers and ensure a continuing flow of customers for future auctions.

In the U.S. auctions of radio spectrum, the government's main objective was to assign spectrum efficiently.

The supply and demand model does not include a place for auction rules. It supposes that buyers and sellers know all the relevant prices

when they make their decisions. In reality, that is not always true.

Often in an auction, bidders must make a choice without knowing all the relevant prices.

What are the main types of auctions and why are there so many different types? Why isn't one type best?
An auction may be either sealed or open. In a sealed auction, the bids are written and the best bids win. In open auctions, there is usually a sequence of bids with each bidder getting an opportunity to respond to the bids of others. Within these two auction types, there is great variety.

The sealed bid has two advantages over the open auction. First, the bidders don't have to be gathered together physically at one time to conduct the auction. In bidding at a used car warehouse, for example, the bidders (usually used car dealers) examine the cars at times that are convenient for themselves and leave behind a sealed envelope with their bids. There is a deadline for bids. When the deadline passes, the bids are opened and the bidders are notified of the results.

Second, it is harder for bidders to collude and depress the price received by the seller. With sealed bids, a member of a ring of buyers who agree to keep prices low might be tempted to submit a slightly higher bid and take advantage of the low bids by other ring members. The temptation to cheat in an open auction is much less, because the other ring members can punish the cheater by driving up the price when the member violates the agreement.

Open auctions have advantages, too. When a single item is being sold and price is the key factor, an open auction eliminates the guesswork of sealed bids. The bidder with the highest value can outbid the competitors. Also, when a large number of items are to be sold and the bidders are present for an open auction, the items can be sold quickly in sequence.

What advances have we made in auction theory?
Since Vickrey initiated auction theory some 35 years ago, we have improved our ability to predict how different types of auctions perform. And we've learned how to design auctions with particular objectives in mind. We even have developed mathematical descriptions of "optimal auctions," which are theoretically the best auction designs for achieving particular objectives.

We still haven't implemented an optimal auction in a real situation, but a small group of economists have used auction theory to design significant new auctions. Recently, I was among a group that proposed a brand-new auction design called a "simultaneous ascending auction." This type of auction is an open auction of many different items, all of which can be bid for simultaneously.

The U.S. Federal Communications Commission used such an auction to sell licenses to use radio spectrum for telecommunications services. The auction was the largest in history and generated gross revenues of $24 billion.

More important to me, the new auction design performed as predicted and led to much more

153

efficient license assignments than other kinds of auctions could have achieved.

The radio spectrum auctions have shaped competition in wireless communications and have determined which firms will operate businesses in which parts of the country.

Why did selling the frequency spectrum need a simultaneous ascending bid auction? And how does such an auction work?
Bidders want to acquire licenses to provide a wireless communications service covering certain geographic areas. A bidder might want to use one of two available bands of spectrum to provide services in, say, Los Angeles County. If either spectrum band will do and the bidder needs just one, then the licenses to use these bands are economic substitutes.

But a bidder might also be willing to pay more to acquire a license covering southern California if he or she could also acquire a license covering northern California. These licenses are complements. One reason why licenses might be complements is that the two areas can share some facilities and lower costs. Another reason is that an owner of both licenses might be able to provide a more valuable service to consumers and so charge a higher price for it.

The simultaneous ascending bid auction handles both situations well. In such an auction, the bid-ding for the northern and southern California licenses, and in fact *all* the licenses, goes on at the same time, and bidding remains open on all the individual licenses until bidding for all licenses is complete. In an auction like this, a bidder who is interested in the California licenses can bid for both and can cease bidding when the combination price gets too high. This is a far from perfect solution, but it is much better than any of the traditional alternatives and seems to have performed well in the sale of spectrum licenses in the United States.

What differences are today's information technologies making to the problems of auction design?
Without modern information technology, the simultaneous ascending auction of radio spectrum licenses couldn't have been conducted. In a large version of the auction, both the auctioneer and the bidders need to keep track of bids on hundreds or even thousands of licenses simultaneously. Software programs have been created to facilitate submitting bids and tracking the auction results.

> The best economists are technically able, curious about the world, concerned about human welfare, flexible in their perspectives, and dedicated to clear, analytical thinking.

How do you advise today's undergraduate to prepare for a career in economics? What besides economics should he or she study?
The best economists are technically able, curious about the world, concerned about human welfare, flexible in their perspectives, and dedicated to clear, analytical thinking. Courses can help with some of these things. Students can certainly learn mathematical and statistical concepts as undergraduates.

To enjoy a career as an economist, you have to go beyond the academic abstractions and incorporate elements that excite you. Many students study economics because of their specific social concerns, for example, wanting to understand the sources of poverty in their home countries and to discern the paths out of poverty. For those students, I recommend reading widely and studying other social sciences to learn about the culture and politics of poverty and the kinds of barriers they create to good economic policies. There are so many ways to incorporate one's pleasures in an economics career! I have friends and colleagues who've studied the economics of sports, of wine prices, of the performing arts, and of the Internet. By weaving their personal and professional interests together, they eliminate the sharp divide between their career and their leisure. These are the folks I hold up as role models.

Chapter 8

Utility and Demand

We need water to live. We don't need diamonds for much besides decoration. If the benefits of water far outweigh the benefits of diamonds, why, then, does water cost practically nothing while diamonds are terribly expensive? ◆ When the Organization of Petroleum Exporting Countries (OPEC) restricted its sale of oil in 1973, it created a dramatic rise in price, but people continued to use almost as much oil as they had before. Our demand for oil was price inelastic. But why? ◆ When the CD player was introduced in 1983, it cost more than $1,000, and consumers didn't buy very many. Since then, the price has decreased dramatically, and people are buying CD players in enormous quantities. Our demand for CD players is price elastic. What makes the demand for some things price elastic while the demand for others is price inelastic?

Water, Water, Everywhere

◆ Over the past 20 years, after the effects of inflation are removed, incomes in the United States have increased by 40 percent. Over that same period, expenditure on electricity has increased by more than 60 percent, while expenditure on transportation has increased by less than 20 percent. Thus the proportion of income spent on electricity has increased, and the proportion spent on transportation has decreased. Why, as incomes rise, does the proportion of income spent on some goods rise and that spent on others fall?

◆ In the preceding four chapters, we saw that demand has an important effect on the price of a good. But we did not analyze what exactly shapes a person's demand. This chapter examines household behavior and its influence on demand. It explains why demand for some goods is elastic and demand for other goods is inelastic. It also explains why the prices of some things, such as diamonds and water, are so out of proportion to their total benefits.

After studying this chapter, you will be able to:

- ■ Explain the household's budget constraint
- ■ Define total utility and marginal utility
- ■ Explain the marginal utility theory of consumer choice
- ■ Use marginal utility theory to predict the effects of changing prices and incomes
- ■ Explain the connection between individual demand and market demand
- ■ Explain the paradox of value

Household Consumption Choices

A HOUSEHOLD'S CONSUMPTION CHOICES ARE determined by many factors, but we can summarize all of these factors under two concepts:

■ Consumption possibilities
■ Preferences

Consumption Possibilities

A household's consumption choices are constrained by the household's income and by the prices of the goods and services it buys. The household has a given amount of income to spend and cannot influence the prices of the goods and services it buys.

The limits to a household's consumption choices are described by its *budget line.* Let's consider Lisa's household. Lisa has an income of $30 a month, and she plans to buy only two goods: movies and soda. Movies cost $6 each; soda costs $3 a six-pack. If Lisa spends all her income, she will reach the limits to her consumption of movies and soda.

Figure 8.1 illustrates Lisa's possible consumption of movies and soda. Rows *a* through *f* in the table show six possible ways of allocating $30 to these two goods. For example, Lisa can see 2 movies for $12 and buy 6 six-packs for $18 (row *c*). Points *a* through *f* in the figure illustrate the possibilities presented in the table. The line passing through these points is Lisa's budget line.

Lisa's budget line is a constraint on her choices. It marks the boundary between what she can afford and what she can not afford. She can afford all the points on the line and inside it. She cannot afford the points outside the line. The constraint on her consumption depends on prices of movies and soda and on her income. The constraint changes when the price of movies or soda changes or her income changes.

Preferences

How does Lisa divide her $30 between these two goods? The answer depends on her likes and dislikes—her *preferences.* Economists use the concept of utility to describe preferences. The benefit or satisfaction that a person gets from the consumption of a good or service is called **utility.** But what exactly is utility and in what units can we measure it? Utility is an abstract concept, and its units are arbitrary.

FIGURE 8.1

Consumption Possibilities

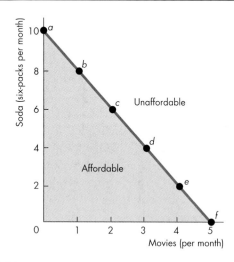

Possibility	Movies		Soda	
	Quantity	Expenditure (dollars)	Six-packs	Expenditure (dollars)
a	0	0	10	30
b	1	6	8	24
c	2	12	6	18
d	3	18	4	12
e	4	24	2	6
f	5	30	0	0

Rows *a* through *f* in the table show six possible ways that Lisa can allocate $30 to movies and soda. For example, Lisa can buy 2 movies and 6 six-packs (row *c*). The combination in each row costs $30. These possibilities are points *a* through *f* in the figure. The line through those points is a boundary between what Lisa can afford and what she cannot afford. Her choices must lie along the line *af* or inside the orange area.

Temperature—An Analogy Temperature is an abstract concept, and the units of temperature are arbitrary. You know when you feel hot, and you know when you feel cold. But you can't *observe* temperature. You can observe water turning to steam if it is hot enough or turning to ice if it is cold enough. And you can construct an instrument, called a thermometer, which can help you to predict when such changes will occur. The scale on the thermometer is what we call temperature. But the units in which we measure temperature are arbitrary. For example, we can accurately predict that when a Celsius thermometer shows a temperature of 0, water will turn to ice. But the units of measurement do not matter because this same event also occurs when a Fahrenheit thermometer shows a temperature of 32.

The concept of utility helps us to make predictions about consumption choices in much the same way that the concept of temperature helps us to make predictions about physical phenomena. Admittedly, marginal utility theory is not as precise as the theory that enables us to predict when water will turn to ice or steam.

Let's now see how we can use the concept of utility to describe preferences.

Total Utility

Total utility is the total benefit that a person gets from the consumption of goods and services. Total utility depends on the level of consumption—more consumption generally gives more total utility. Table 8.1 shows Lisa's total utility from movies and soda. If she sees no movies, she gets no utility from movies. If she sees 1 movie in a month, she gets 50 units of utility. As the number of movies she sees in a month increases, her total utility increases; if she sees 10 movies a month, she gets 250 units of total utility. The other part of the table shows Lisa's total utility from soda. If she drinks no soda, she gets no utility from soda. As the amount of soda she drinks increases, her total utility increases.

Marginal Utility

Marginal utility is the change in total utility that results from a one-unit increase in the quantity of a good consumed. The table in Fig. 8.2 shows the calculation of Lisa's marginal utility of movies. When the number of movies she sees increases from 4 to 5 a month, her total utility from movies increases from 150 units to 175 units. Thus for Lisa, the marginal utility of seeing a fifth movie each month is 25 units. Notice that marginal utility appears midway between the quantities of movies. It does so because it is the *change* in consumption from 4 to 5 movies that produces the *marginal* utility of 25 units. The table displays calculations of marginal utility for each number of movies seen.

TABLE 8.1

Lisa's Total Utility from Movies and Soda

Movies		Soda	
Quantity per month	Total utility	Six-packs per month	Total utility
0	0	0	0
1	50	1	75
2	88	2	117
3	121	3	153
4	150	4	181
5	175	5	206
6	196	6	225
7	214	7	243
8	229	8	260
9	241	9	276
10	250	10	291
11	256	11	305
12	259	12	318
13	261	13	330
14	262	14	341

Figure 8.2(a) illustrates the total utility that Lisa gets from movies. The more movies Lisa sees in a month, the more total utility she gets. Figure 8.2(b) illustrates her marginal utility. This graph tells us that as Lisa sees more movies, the marginal utility that she gets from watching movies decreases. For example, her marginal utility decreases from 50 units from the first movie to 38 units from the second and 33 units from the third. We call this decrease in marginal utility as the quantity of the good consumed increases the principle of **diminishing marginal utility**.

Marginal utility is positive but diminishes as the consumption of a good increases. Why does marginal utility have these two features? In Lisa's case, she likes movies, and the more she sees the better. That's why marginal utility is positive. The benefit that Lisa gets from the last movie seen is its marginal utility. To see why marginal utility diminishes, think about the following two situations: In one, you've

FIGURE 8.2

Total Utility and Marginal Utility

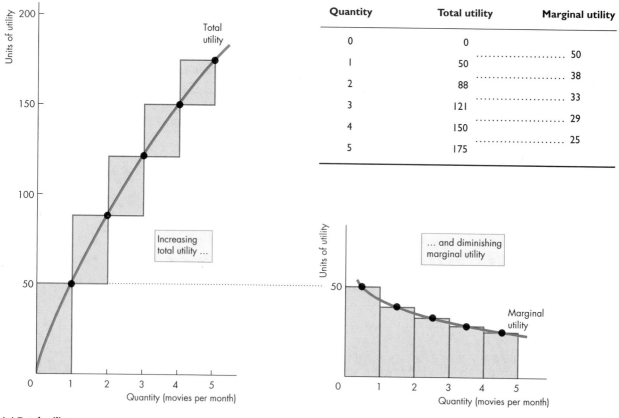

Quantity	Total utility	Marginal utility
0	0	
		50
I	50	
		38
2	88	
		33
3	121	
		29
4	150	
		25
5	175	

(a) Total utility

The table shows that as Lisa sees more movies her total utility from movies increases. The table also shows her marginal utility—the change in total utility resulting from seeing one additional movie. Marginal utility declines as consumption increases. The figure graphs Lisa's total utility and marginal

(b) Marginal utility

utility from movies. Part (a) shows her total utility. It also shows as a bar the extra total utility she gains from each additional movie—her marginal utility. Part (b) shows how Lisa's marginal utility from movies diminishes by placing the bars shown in part (a) side by side as a series of declining steps.

just been studying for 29 evenings. An opportunity arises to see a movie. The utility you get from seeing that movie is the marginal utility from seeing one movie in a month. In the second situation, you've been on a movie binge. For the past 29 nights, you have not even seen an assignment. You are up to your eyeballs in movies. You are happy enough to go to a movie once more. But the thrill that you get out of that thirtieth movie in 30 days is not very large. It is the marginal utility of the thirtieth movie in a month.

Maximizing Utility

A HOUSEHOLD'S INCOME AND THE PRICES THAT it faces limit the household's consumption choices, and the household's preferences determine the utility that it can obtain from each consumption possibility. Marginal utility theory assumes that the household chooses the consumption possibility that maximizes its total utility. This assumption of utility maximization is a way of expressing the fundamental economic problem—scarcity. People's wants exceed the resources available to satisfy those wants, so they must make hard choices. In making choices, they try to get the maximum attainable benefit—they try to maximize total utility.

Let's see how Lisa allocates $30 a month between movies and soda to maximize her total utility. We'll continue to assume that movies cost $6 each and soda costs $3 a six-pack.

The Utility-Maximizing Choice

The most direct way of calculating how Lisa spends her income to maximize her total utility is by making a table like Table 8.2. The rows of the table show the affordable combinations of movies and soda that lie along her budget line in Fig. 8.1. The table records three things: first, the number of movies seen and the total utility derived from them (the left side of the table); second, the number of six-packs consumed and the total utility derived from them (the right side of the table); and third, the total utility derived from both movies and soda (the center column).

The first row of Table 8.2 records the situation when Lisa watches no movies and buys 10 six-packs. In this case, Lisa gets no utility from movies and 291 units of total utility from soda. Her total utility from movies and soda (the center column) is 291 units. The rest of the table is constructed in the same way.

The consumption of movies and soda that maximizes Lisa's total utility is highlighted in the table. When Lisa sees 2 movies and buys 6 six-packs of soda, she gets 313 units of total utility. This is the best Lisa can do, given her preferences, given that she has only $30 to spend, and given the prices of movies and six-packs. If she buys 8 six-packs of soda, she can see only 1 movie. She gets 310 units of total utility, 3 less than the maximum attainable. If she sees 3 movies, she can drink only 4 six-packs. She gets 302 units of total utility, 11 less than the maximum attainable.

TABLE 8.2

Lisa's Affordable Combinations

| | Movies | | Total utility from movies and soda | Soda | |
	Quantity per month	Total utility		Total utility	Six-packs per month
a	0	0	291	291	10
b	1	50	310	260	8
c	2	88	313	225	6
d	3	121	302	181	4
e	4	150	267	117	2
f	5	175	175	0	0

We've just described Lisa's consumer equilibrium. A **consumer equilibrium** is a situation in which a consumer has allocated all his or her available income in the way that, given the prices of goods and services, maximizes his or her total utility. Lisa's consumer equilibrium is 2 movies and 6 six-packs.

In finding Lisa's consumer equilibrium, we measured her *total* utility from movies and soda. But there is a better way of determining a consumer equilibrium—one that does not involve measuring total utility at all. Let's look at this alternative.

Equalizing Marginal Utility per Dollar Spent

Another way to find out the allocation that maximizes a consumer's total utility is to make the marginal utility per dollar spent on each good equal for all goods. The **marginal utility per dollar spent** is the marginal utility obtained from the last unit of a good consumed divided by the price of the good. For example, Lisa's marginal utility from seeing the first movie is 50 units of utility. The price of a movie is $6, which means that when Lisa sees one movie the marginal utility per dollar spent on movies is 50 units divided by $6, or 8.33 units of utility per dollar.

Total utility is maximized when all the consumer's available income is spent and when the marginal utility per dollar spent is equal for all goods.

Lisa maximizes total utility when she spends all her income and consumes movies and soda such that

$$\frac{\text{Marginal utility from movies}}{\text{Price of a movie}} = \frac{\text{Marginal utility from soda}}{\text{Price of soda}}.$$

Call the marginal utility from movies MU_m, the marginal utility from soda MU_s, the price of a movie P_m, and the price of soda P_s. Then Lisa maximizes her utility when she spends all her income and when

$$\frac{MU_m}{P_m} = \frac{MU_s}{P_s}.$$

Let's use this formula to find Lisa's utility-maximizing consumption choice. In Table 8.3, each row exhausts Lisa's income of $30. The table sets out Lisa's marginal utilities (which are calculated from Table 8.1) and her marginal utility per dollar spent on each good. For example, in row b, Lisa's marginal utility from movies is 50 units, and since movies cost $6 each, her marginal utility per dollar spent on movies is 8.33 units per dollar (50 units divided by $6). You can see that Lisa's marginal utility per dollar spent on each good, like marginal utility itself, decreases as more of the good is consumed.

Lisa maximizes her total utility when the marginal utility per dollar spent on movies is equal to the marginal utility per dollar spent on soda—possibility c. Lisa consumes 2 movies and 6 six-packs.

TABLE 8.3

Equalizing Marginal Utilities per Dollar Spent

		Movies ($6 each)			Soda ($3 per six-pack)	
	Quantity	Marginal utility	Marginal utility per dollar spent	Six-packs	Marginal utility	Marginal utility per dollar spent
a	0			10	15	5.00
b	1	50	8.33	8	17	5.67
c	2	38	6.33	6	19	6.33
d	3	33	5.50	4	28	9.33
e	4	29	4.83	2	42	14.00
f	5	25	4.17	0		

Figure 8.3 shows why the rule "equalize marginal utility per dollar spent on all goods" works. Suppose that instead of 2 movies and 6 six-packs (possibility c), Lisa consumes 1 movie and 8 six-packs (possibility b). She then gets 8.33 units of utility per dollar spent on movies and 5.67 units per dollar spent on soda. Lisa can increase her total utility by buying less soda and seeing more movies. If she spends less on soda and more on movies, her total utility from soda decreases by 5.67 units per dollar and her total utility from movies increases by 8.33 units per dollar. Her total utility increases by 2.66 units per dollar.

FIGURE 8.3

Equalizing Marginal Utilities per Dollar Spent

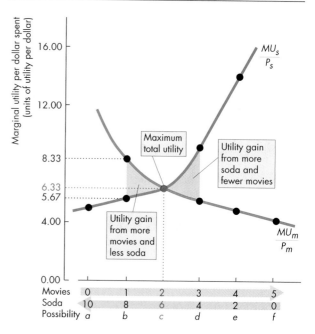

If Lisa consumes 1 movie and 8 six-packs (possibility b), she gets 8.33 units of utility from the last dollar spent on movies and 5.67 units of utility from the last dollar spent on soda. She can get more total utility by seeing one more movie. If she consumes 4 six-packs and 3 movies (possibility d), she gets 5.50 units of utility from the last dollar spent on movies and 9.33 units of utility from the last dollar spent on soda. She can increase her total utility by seeing one fewer movie. When Lisa's marginal utility per dollar spent on both goods is equal, her total utility is maximized.

Or suppose that Lisa consumes 3 movies and 4 six-packs (possibility *d*). In this situation, her marginal utility per dollar spent on movies (5.50) is less than her marginal utility per dollar spent on soda (9.33). Lisa can now increase her total utility by spending less on movies and more on soda.

The Power of Marginal Analysis   The method we've just used to find Lisa's utility-maximizing choice of movies and soda is an example of the power of marginal analysis. By comparing the marginal gain from having more of one good with the marginal loss from having less of another good, Lisa is able to ensure that she gets the maximum attainable utility.

In the example, Lisa chooses the combination in which the marginal utilities per dollar spent on movies and soda are equal. Because we buy goods and services in indivisible lumps, the numbers don't always work out so precisely. But the basic approach always works.

The rule to follow is very simple: If the marginal utility per dollar spent on movies exceeds the marginal utility per dollar spent on soda, see more movies and buy less soda; if the marginal utility per dollar spent on soda exceeds the marginal utility per dollar spent on movies, buy more soda and see fewer movies.

More generally, if the marginal gain from an action exceeds the marginal loss, take the action. You have met this principle before, and you will meet it time and again in your study of economics. And you will find yourself using it when you make your own economic choices, especially when you must make a big decision.

Units of Utility   In calculating Lisa's utility-maximizing choice in Table 8.3 and Fig. 8.3, we have not used the concept of total utility at all. All our calculations use marginal utility and price. By making the marginal utility per dollar spent equal for both goods, we know that Lisa maximizes her total utility.

This way of viewing maximum utility means that the units in which utility is measured do not matter. We could double or halve all the numbers measuring utility, or multiply them by any other positive number, or square them, or take their square roots. None of these transformations of the units used to measure utility makes any difference to the outcome. It is in this respect that utility is analogous to temperature. Our prediction about the freezing of water does not depend on the temperature scale; our prediction about the household's consumption choice does not depend on the units of utility.

R E V I E W   Q U I Z

- What is Lisa's goal when she chooses the quantities of movies and soda to consume?
- What two conditions are met if a consumer is maximizing utility?
- Explain why equalizing the marginal utility of each good does *not* maximize utility.
- Explain why equalizing the marginal utility per dollar spent on each good *does* maximize utility.

Predictions of Marginal Utility Theory

LET'S NOW USE MARGINAL UTILITY THEORY TO make some predictions. What happens to Lisa's consumption of movies and soda when their prices change and when her income changes?

To work out the effect of a change in price or income on the consumption choice: First, determine the combinations of movies and soda that just exhaust the new income at the new prices. Second, calculate the new marginal utilities per dollar spent. Third, determine the combination that makes the marginal utilities per dollar spent on movies and soda equal.

A Fall in the Price of Movies

Suppose that the price of a movie falls from $6 to $3. The rows of Table 8.4 show the combinations of movies and soda that exactly exhaust Lisa's $30 of income when movies cost $3 each and soda costs $3 a six-pack. Lisa's preferences do not change when prices change, so her marginal utility schedule remains the same as before. Now divide her marginal utility from movies by $3 to get the marginal utility per dollar spent on movies.

To find how Lisa responds to the fall in the price of a movie, compare her new utility-maximizing choice (Table 8.4) with her original choice (Table 8.3). Lisa sees more movies (up from 2 to 5 a month) and drinks less soda (down from 6 to 5 six-packs a month). That is, Lisa *substitutes* movies for soda. Figure 8.4 shows these effects. The fall in the price of a movie produces a movement along Lisa's demand curve for movies (part a) and shifts her demand curve for soda (part b).

<table>
<tr><th colspan="2">TABLE 8.4</th></tr>
</table>

TABLE 8.4
How a Change in Price of Movies Affects Lisa's Choices

FIGURE 8.4
A Fall in the Price of Movies

Movies ($3 each)		Soda ($3 per six-pack)	
Quantity	Marginal utility per dollar spent	Six-packs	Marginal utility per dollar spent
0		10	5.00
1	16.67	9	5.33
2	12.67	8	5.67
3	11.00	7	6.00
4	9.67	6	6.33
5	8.33	5	8.33
6	7.00	4	9.33
7	6.00	3	12.00
8	5.00	2	14.00
9	4.00	1	25.00
10	3.00	0	

(a) Movies

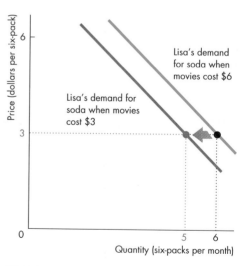

(b) Soda

A Rise in the Price of Soda

Now suppose that the price of soda rises from $3 to $6 a six-pack. The rows of Table 8.5 show the combinations of movies and soda that exactly exhaust Lisa's $30 of income when movies cost $3 each and soda costs $6 a six-pack. Lisa's preferences don't change when the price of soda changes. Now divide Lisa's marginal utility from soda by $6 to get her marginal utility per dollar spent on soda.

To find the effect of the rise in the price of soda on Lisa's utility-maximizing choice, compare her new choice (Table 8.5) with her previous choice (Table 8.4). When the price of soda increases, Lisa drinks less soda (down from 5 to 2 six-packs a month) and sees more movies (up from 5 to 6 a month). That is, Lisa *substitutes* movies for soda. Figure 8.5 shows these effects. The rise in the price of soda produces a movement along Lisa's demand curve for soda (part a) and shifts her demand curve for movies (part b).

When the price of a movie falls and the price of soda remains the same, the quantity of movies demanded by Lisa increases and, in part (a), Lisa moves along her demand curve for movies. Also, Lisa decreases her demand for soda and, in part (b), her demand curve for soda shifts leftward.

TABLE 8.5

How a Change in Price of Soda Affects Lisa's Choices

Movies ($3 each)		Soda ($6 per six-pack)	
Quantity	Marginal utility per dollar spent	Six-packs	Marginal utility per dollar spent
0		5	4.17
2	12.67	4	4.67
4	9.67	3	6.00
6	7.00	2	7.00
8	5.00	1	12.50
10	3.00	0	

Marginal utility theory predicts these two results:

1. When the price of a good rises, the quantity demanded of that good decreases.
2. If the price of one good rises, the demand for another good that can serve as a substitute increases.

Does this sound familiar? It should. These predictions of marginal utility theory correspond to the assumptions that we made about demand in Chapter 4. There we *assumed* that the demand curve for a good slopes downward, and we *assumed* that a rise in the price of a substitute increases demand.

We have now seen that marginal utility theory predicts how the quantities of goods and services that people demand respond to price changes. The theory helps us to understand both the shape and the position of the demand curve and how the demand curve for one good shifts when the price of another good changes. Marginal utility theory also helps us to understand one further thing about demand: how it changes when income changes. Let's study the effects of a change in income on consumption.

FIGURE 8.5

A Rise in the Price of Soda

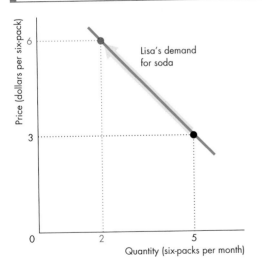

(a) Soda

When the price of soda rises and the price of movies remains the same, the quantity of soda demanded by Lisa decreases and, in part (a), Lisa moves along her demand curve for soda.

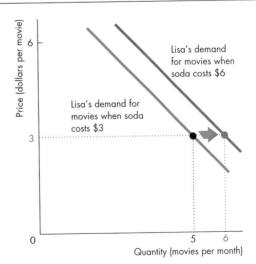

(b) Movies

Also, Lisa increases her demand for movies and, in part (b), her demand curve for movies shifts rightward.

A Rise in Income

Let's suppose that Lisa's income increases to $42 a month and that a movie costs $3 and a six-pack costs $3. We saw in Table 8.4 that with these prices and with an income of $30 a month, Lisa sees 5 movies and drinks 5 six-packs a month. We want to compare this choice of movies and soda with Lisa's choice when her income is $42. Table 8.6 shows the calculations needed to make the comparison. With $42, Lisa can see 14 movies a month and buy no soda or buy 14 six-packs a month and see no movies or choose any combination of the two goods in the rows of the table. We calculate the marginal utility per dollar spent in exactly the same way as we did

before and find the quantities at which the marginal utilities per dollar spent on movies and on soda are equal. With an income of $42, the marginal utility per dollar spent on each good is equal when Lisa sees 7 movies and drinks 7 six-packs of soda a month.

By comparing this situation with that in Table 8.4, we see that with an additional $12 a month, Lisa buys 2 more six-packs and sees 2 more movies a month. Lisa's response arises from her preferences, as described by her marginal utilities. Different preferences would produce different quantitative responses. With a larger income, the consumer always buys more of a *normal* good and less of an *inferior* good. For Lisa, soda and movies are normal goods. When her income increases, Lisa buys more of both goods.

You have now completed your study of the marginal utility theory of a household's consumption choices. Table 8.7 summarizes the key assumptions, implications, and predictions of the theory.

TABLE 8.6

Lisa's Choices with an Income of $42 a Month

Movies ($3 each)		Soda ($3 per six-pack)	
Quantity	Marginal utility per dollar spent	Six-packs	Marginal utility per dollar spent
0		14	3.67
1	16.67	13	4.00
2	12.67	12	4.33
3	11.00	11	4.67
4	9.67	10	5.00
5	**8.33**	9	5.33
6	7.00	8	5.67
7	6.00	7	6.00
8	5.00	6	6.33
9	4.00	**5**	**8.33**
10	3.00	4	9.33
11	2.00	3	12.00
12	1.00	2	14.00
13	0.67	1	25.00
14	0.33	0	

TABLE 8.7

Marginal Utility Theory

Assumptions

- A consumer derives utility from the goods consumed.

- Each additional unit of consumption yields additional total utility; marginal utility is positive.

- As the quantity of a good consumed increases, marginal utility decreases.

- A consumer's aim is to maximize total utility.

Implication

Total utility is maximized when all the available income is spent and when the marginal utility per dollar spent is equal for all goods.

Predictions

- Other things remaining the same, the higher the price of a good, the smaller is the quantity demanded of it (the law of demand).

- The higher the price of a good, the greater is the quantity demanded of substitutes for that good.

- The higher the consumer's income, the greater is the quantity demanded of normal goods.

Individual Demand and Market Demand

Marginal utility theory explains how an individual household spends its income and enables us to derive an individual household's demand curve. In earlier chapters, we used *market* demand curves. We can derive a *market* demand curve from individual demand curves. Let's see how.

The relationship between the total quantity demanded of a good and its price is called **market demand**. The market demand curve is what you studied in Chapter 4. The relationship between the quantity demanded of a good by a single individual and its price is called *individual demand.*

Figure 8.6 illustrates the relationship between individual demand and market demand. In this example, Lisa and Chuck are the only people. The market demand is the total demand of Lisa and Chuck. At $3 a movie, Lisa demands 5 movies a month and Chuck demands 2, so the total quantity demanded by the market is 7 movies a month. Lisa's demand curve for movies in part (a) and Chuck's in part (b) sum *horizontally* to give the market demand curve in part (c).

The market demand curve is the horizontal sum of the individual demand curves and is formed by adding the quantities demanded by each individual at each price.

Because marginal utility theory predicts that individual demand curves slope downward, it also predicts that market demand curves slope downward.

FIGURE 8.6
Individual and Market Demand Curves

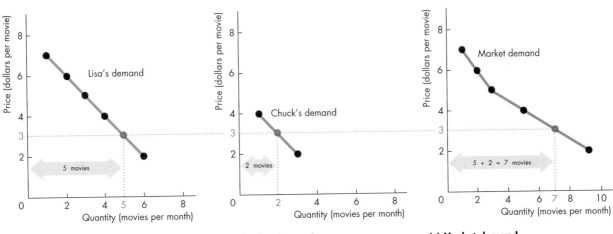

(a) Lisa's demand   **(b) Chuck's demand**   **(c) Market demand**

Price	Quantity of movies demanded		
(dollars per movie)	Lisa	Chuck	Market
7	1	0	1
6	2	0	2
5	3	0	3
4	4	1	5
3	5	2	7
2	6	3	9

The table and the figure illustrate how the quantity of movies demanded varies as the price of a movie varies. In the table, the market demand is the sum of the individual demands. For example, at a price of $3, Lisa demands 5 movies and Chuck demands 2 movies, so the total quantity demanded in the market is 7 movies. In the figure, the market demand curve is the horizontal sum of the individual demand curves. Thus when the price is $3, the market demand curve shows that the quantity demanded is 7 movies, the sum of the quantities demanded by Lisa and Chuck.

Marginal Utility and the Real World

Marginal utility theory can be used to answer a wide range of questions about the real world. The theory sheds light on why the demand for CD players is price elastic while the demand for oil is price inelastic and why the demand for electricity is income elastic while the demand for transportation is income inelastic. Elasticities are determined by preferences. The feature of our preferences that determines elasticity is the step size with which marginal utility declines—the steepness of the marginal utility steps in Fig. 8.2(b).

If marginal utility declines in big steps, a small change in the quantity bought brings a big change in the marginal utility per dollar spent. So it takes a big change in price or income to bring a small change in the quantity demanded—demand is inelastic. Conversely, if marginal utility diminishes slowly, even a large change in the quantity bought brings a small change in the marginal utility per dollar spent. So it takes only a small change in price or income to bring a large change in quantity—demand is elastic.

But marginal utility theory can do much more than explain households' *consumption* choices. It can be used to explain *all* the choices made by households. One of these choices, the allocation of time between work in the home, office, or factory and leisure is the theme of issues and ideas on pp. 192–193.

R E V I E W   Q U I Z

- When the price of a good falls and the prices of other goods and a consumer's income remain the same, what happens to the consumption of the good whose price has fallen and to the consumption of other goods?
- Elaborate on your answer to the previous question by using demand curves. For which good is there a change in demand and for which is there a change in the quantity demanded?
- If a consumer's income increases and if all goods are normal goods, how does the quantity bought of each good change?

We're going to end this chapter by returning to a recurring theme throughout your study of economics: the concept of efficiency and the distinction between price and value.

Efficiency, Price, and Value

MARGINAL UTILITY THEORY HELPS US TO DEEPEN our understanding of the concept of efficiency and also helps us to see more clearly the distinction between *value* and *price*. Let's see how.

Consumer Efficiency and Consumer Surplus

When Lisa allocates her limited budget to maximize utility, she is using her resources efficiently. Any other allocation of her budget wastes some resources.

But when Lisa has allocated her limited budget to maximize utility, she is *on* her demand curve for each good. A demand curve is a description of the quantity demanded at each price when utility is maximized. When we studied efficiency in Chapter 6, we learned that a demand curve is also a willingness-to-pay curve. It tells us a consumer's *marginal benefit*—the benefit from consuming an additional unit of a good. You can now give the idea of marginal benefit a deeper meaning:

Marginal benefit is the maximum price that a consumer is willing to pay for an extra unit of a good or service when utility is maximized.

The Paradox of Value

For centuries, philosophers have been puzzled by a paradox that we raised at the start of this chapter. Water, which is essential to life itself, costs little, but diamonds, which are useless compared to water, are expensive. Why? Adam Smith tried to solve this paradox. But not until the theory of marginal utility had been developed could anyone give a satisfactory answer.

You can solve this puzzle by distinguishing between *total* utility and *marginal* utility. The total utility that we get from water is enormous. But remember, the more we consume of something, the smaller is its marginal utility. We use so much water that its marginal utility—the benefit we get from one more glass of water—diminishes to a small value. Diamonds, on the other hand, have a small total utility relative to water, but because we buy few diamonds, they have a high marginal utility. When a household has maximized its total utility, it has allocated its

FIGURE 8.7

The Paradox of Value

(a) Water

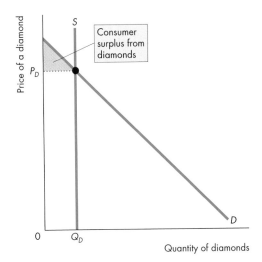

(b) Diamonds

Part (a) shows the demand for water, D, and the supply of water, S. The supply is (assumed to be) perfectly elastic at the price P_W. At this price, the quantity of water consumed is Q_W and the consumer surplus from water is the large green triangle. Part (b) shows the demand for diamonds, D, and the supply of diamonds, S. The supply is (assumed to be) perfectly inelastic at the quantity Q_D. At this quantity, the price of a diamond is P_D and the consumer surplus from diamonds is the small green triangle. Water is valuable—has a large consumer surplus—but is cheap. Diamonds are less valuable than water—have a smaller consumer surplus—but are expensive.

budget in the way that makes the marginal utility per dollar spent equal for all goods. That is, the marginal utility from a good divided by the price of the good is equal for all goods. This equality of marginal utilities per dollar spent holds true for diamonds and water: Diamonds have a high price and a high marginal utility. Water has a low price and a low marginal utility. When the high marginal utility of diamonds is divided by the high price of diamonds, the result is a number that equals the low marginal utility of water divided by the low price of water. The marginal utility per dollar spent is the same for diamonds as for water.

Another way to think about the paradox of value uses *consumer surplus*. Figure 8.7 explains the paradox of value by using this idea. The supply of water (part a) is assumed to be perfectly elastic at price P_W, so the quantity of water consumed is Q_W and the consumer surplus from water is the large green area. The supply of diamonds (part b) is perfectly inelastic at price Q_D, so the price of diamonds is P_D and the consumer surplus from diamonds is the small green area. Water is cheap but brings a large consumer surplus, while diamonds are expensive but bring a small consumer surplus.

R E V I E W Q U I Z

- Can you explain why, along a demand curve, a consumer's choices are efficient?
- Can you explain the paradox of value?
- Does water or diamonds have the greater marginal utility? Does water or diamonds have the greater total utility? Does water or diamonds have the greater consumer surplus?

◆ We've now completed our study of the marginal utility theory. And we've seen how the theory can be used to explain our real-world consumption choices. You can see the theory in action once again in *Reading Between the Lines* on pp. 168–169, where it is used to interpret some recent trends in the things that we drink.

The next chapter presents an alternative theory of household behavior. To help you see the connection between the two theories of consumer behavior, we'll continue with the same example. We'll meet Lisa again and discover another way of understanding how she gets the most out of her $30 a month.

Marginal Utility in Action

THE DETROIT NEWS, FEBRUARY 20, 1999

Coca-Cola Will Sell Bottled Water in U.S.

BY DAN SEWELL, AP BUSINESS WRITER

ATLANTA—Water. It's the real thing.

Coca-Cola Co. will begin selling bottled water in the United States this year.

It will be called Dasani (pronounced duh-SAW-nee), which doesn't mean anything in particular but is meant to convey "a clean, fresh taste."

"Suffice it to say, we think this is the right time for us to get into this market," said Coke spokesman Scott Jacobson. Bottled water is hot these days, outstripping soft drinks in sales growth.

Dasani is expected to be available nationwide and in Canada before this summer in a light blue plastic bottle.

"If it's a Coke brand, it's going to sell. Why they waited five or six years to get into it, I don't know," said Steve Tessereau, manager of a busy Texaco station in suburban Atlanta.

The maker of the world's most popular soft drink sells a brand of bottled water called BonAqua overseas but has been reluctant to get into the business in the United States, preferring instead to encourage people to drink Coke, Sprite and its other sodas.

To meet increased demand among health- and weight-conscious Americans, Coke in recent years has begun offering sports drinks and juices.

But as recently as last month, M. Douglas Ivester, chairman and chief executive, said Coke was leery of water: "There's an awful lot of water sold in the world. There's not an awful lot of money made selling water."

Bottled water sales have jumped from $2.65 billion in 1990 to $4.3 billion in 1998. Sales grew nearly 10 percent over 1997. The $56.3 billion carbonated soft drink market grew by only 3 percent last year.

Pepsi-Cola Co. started selling bottled water five years ago. Aquafina has since become the leading water brand in convenience stores.

Essence of the Story

- Bottled water sales grew from $2.65 billion in 1990 to $4.3 billion in 1998. They grew by almost 10 percent during 1998.

- Soda sales were $56.3 billion in 1998 but grew by only 3 percent during the year.

- Pepsi-Cola Co. started selling bottled water in 1993 and became the market leader.

- Coca-Cola Co. traditionally has tried to encourage people to drink Coke, Sprite, and its other sodas.

- But to meet the increased demand for non-soda beverages, Coke offers sports drinks and juices and began selling bottled water in the United States in 1999.

Economic Analysis

■ Consumption patterns change over time. Figure 1 shows some trends in the consumption of beverages in the United States during the 1990s.

■ The quantity of bottled water consumed and the quantity of soda consumed have increased.

■ The quantities of coffee and beer consumed have decreased.

■ You can understand these trends by using the marginal utility theory.

■ People receive utility from consuming bottled water, soda, coffee, and beer.

■ To maximize utility, people make the marginal utility per dollar spent equal for all goods. So people consume bottled water, soda, coffee, and beer in quantities that make the marginal utilities per dollar spent on each of them equal, as shown by the equation displayed below.

■ If the price of a good rises, other things remaining the same, the marginal utility of that good must increase to maintain maximum possible utility.

■ But marginal utility increases as the quantity consumed of the good decreases. So other things remaining the same, when the price of a good rises, the quantity consumed of that good decreases.

■ If prices explain the consumption trends in Fig. 1, then it must be that the prices of water and soda have fallen relative to the prices of beer and coffee.

■ The price of bottled water has fallen as high-cost spring water has been replaced with lower-cost water purified by reverse osmosis and carbon filtering.

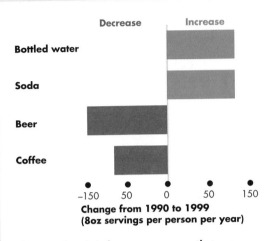

Figure 1 Trends in beverage consumption

■ The price of bottled water has also fallen as more firms have entered the water market, as Coca Cola is doing according to the news article.

■ Similarly, the price of soda has also fallen as more firms have entered the soda market and sales of generic sodas have taken off.

■ The price of coffee has increased through the 1990s because of low crop yields in some growing regions (Brazil experienced a very severe frost and drought in 1994) and because of export restrictions by major producers.

■ The true price, or opportunity cost, of beer has also increased. The money price of beer has not changed much. But improved policing and stiffer penalties for drunk driving have increased the opportunity cost of drinking beer.

■ You can see that the trends in drinking can be understood as the responses to changes in prices. The trends are not a mystery or a social phenomenon. They are the consequence of people trying to get the highest value from their scarce resources.

$$\frac{MU_{water}}{P_{water}} = \frac{MU_{soda}}{P_{soda}} = \frac{MU_{coffee}}{P_{coffee}} = \frac{MU_{beer}}{P_{beer}}$$

SUMMARY

KEY POINTS

Household Consumption Choices (pp. 156–158)

■ A household's choices are determined by its consumption possibilities and preferences.

■ A household's consumption possibilities are constrained by its income and by prices. Some combinations of goods are affordable, and some are not affordable.

■ A household's preferences can be described by marginal utility.

■ The key assumption of marginal utility theory is that the marginal utility of a good or service decreases as consumption of the good or service increases.

Maximizing Utility (pp. 159–161)

■ Marginal utility theory assumes that people buy the affordable combination of goods and services that maximizes total utility.

■ Total utility is maximized when all the available income is spent and when the marginal utility per dollar spent on each good is equal.

■ If the marginal utility per dollar spent on good *A* exceeds that on good *B*, the consumer can increase total utility by buying more of good *A* and less of good *B*.

Predictions of Marginal Utility Theory (pp. 161–166)

■ Marginal utility theory predicts the law of demand. That is, other things remaining the same, the higher the price of a good, the smaller is the quantity demanded of that good.

■ Marginal utility theory also predicts that other things remaining the same, the higher the income of a consumer, the larger is the quantity demanded of a normal good.

■ Market demand is the sum of all individual demands, and the market demand curve is found by summing horizontally all the individual demand curves.

Efficiency, Price, and Value (pp. 166–167)

■ When a consumer maximizes utility, he or she is using resources efficiently.

■ Marginal utility theory resolves the paradox of the relative value of water and diamonds.

■ When we talk loosely about value, we are thinking of *total* utility or consumer surplus. But price is related to *marginal* utility.

■ Water, which we consume in large amounts, has a high total utility and a large consumer surplus but has a low price and low marginal utility.

■ Diamonds, which we consume in small amounts, have a low total utility and a small consumer surplus but have a high price and a high marginal utility.

KEY FIGURES AND TABLE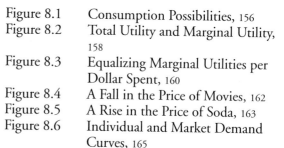

KEY TERMS

PROBLEMS

*1. Jason enjoys rock CDs and spy novels and spends $60 a month on them. The table shows the utility he gets from each good:

Quantity per month	Utility from rock CDs	Utility from spy novels
1	60	20
2	110	38
3	150	53
4	180	64
5	200	70
6	206	75

a. Draw graphs showing Jason's utility from rock CDs and from spy novels.

b. Compare the two utility graphs. Can you say anything about Jason's preferences?

c. Draw graphs that show Jason's marginal utility from rock CDs and from spy novels.

d. What do the two marginal utility graphs tell you about Jason's preferences?

e. If rock CDs and spy novels both cost $10 each, how does Jason spend the $60?

2. Mary enjoys classical CDs and travel books and spends $40 a month on them. The table shows the utility she gets from each good:

Quantity per month	Utility from classical CDs	Utility from travel books
1	30	30
2	40	38
3	48	44
4	54	46
5	58	47

a. Draw graphs showing Mary's utility from classical CDs and from travel books.

b. Compare the two utility graphs. Can you say anything about Mary's preferences?

c. Draw graphs that show Mary's marginal utility from classical CDs and from travel books.

d. What do the two marginal utility graphs tell you about Mary's preferences?

e. If a classical CD and a travel book cost $10 each, how does Mary spend the $40 a month?

*3. Max enjoys windsurfing and snorkeling. The table shows Max's utility from each sport:

Hours per day	Utility from windsurfing	Utility from snorkeling
1	120	40
2	220	76
3	300	106
4	360	128
5	400	140
6	412	150
7	422	158

Max has $35 to spend, and he can spend as much time as likes on his leisure pursuits. Windsurfing equipment rents for $10 an hour, and snorkeling equipment rents for $5 an hour.

a. Draw a graph that shows Max's budget line.

b. How long does he spend windsurfing and how long does he spend snorkeling?

4. Rob enjoys rock concerts and the opera. The table shows the utility he gets from each activity:

Concerts per month	Utility from rock concerts	Utility from operas
1	100	60
2	180	110
3	240	150
4	280	180
5	300	200
6	310	210

Rob has $100 a month to spend on concerts. A rock concert ticket is $20, and an opera ticket is $10.

a. Draw a graph that shows Rob's budget line.

b. How many rock concerts and how many operas does he attend?

*5. In problem 3, Max's sister gives him $20 to spend on his leisure pursuits, so he now has $55.

a. Draw a graph that shows Max's budget line.

b. How many hours does Max choose to windsurf and how many hours does he choose to snorkel now that he has $55 to spend?

6. In problem 4, Rob's uncle gives him $30 to spend on concert tickets, so he now has $130.

a. Draw a graph that shows Rob's budget line.

b. How many rock concerts and how many operas does he attend now that he has $130 to spend?

*7. In problem 5, if the rent on windsurfing equipment decreases to $5 an hour, how many hours does Max now windsurf and how many hours does he snorkel?

8. In problem 4, if the price of a rock concert decreases to $10, how many rock concerts and operas will Rob attend?

*9. Max takes a Club Med vacation, the cost of which includes unlimited sports activities. There is no extra charge for equipment. If Max windsurfs and snorkels for 6 hours a day, how many hours does he windsurf and how many hours does he snorkel?

10. Rob wins a lottery and has more than enough money to satisfy his desires for rock concerts and opera. He decides that he would like to see 5 concerts each month. How many rock concerts and how many operas does he now attend?

*11. Shirley's and Dan's demand schedules for popcorn are:

Price (cents per carton)	Quantity demanded by	
	Shirley	Dan
	(cartons per week)	
10	12	6
30	9	5
50	6	4
70	3	3
90	1	2

If Shirley and Dan are the only two individuals, what is the market demand for popcorn?

12. Ben's and Jerry's demand schedules for ice cream cones are:

Price (dollars per cone)	Quantity demanded by	
	Ben	Jerry
	(cones per week)	
1.00	8	10
1.30	7	8
1.50	6	6
1.70	5	4
1.90	4	2

If Ben and Jerry are the only two individuals, what is the market demand for ice cream cones?

CRITICAL THINKING

1. Study *Reading Between the Lines* on pp. 168–169 on beverage consumption in the United States during the 1990s and then answer the following questions:
   a. What facts about bottled water consumption are reported in the news article?
   b. How can we account for the increasing quantity of bottled water consumed using marginal utility theory?
   c. Use marginal utility theory to predict what will happen to bottled water consumption if its price rises sharply.
   d. Use marginal utility theory to predict what will happen to bottled water consumption as incomes rise.
   e. Do you think price changes and the marginal utility theory can explain all of the changes in beverage consumption in the United States during the 1990s, or do you think there are some other factors at work? If so, what are they?

2. Use the links on the Parkin Web site and read what Henry Schimberg, CEO of Coca-Cola Enterprises, says about the market for bottled water. Use the marginal utility theory you have learned in this chapter to interpret and explain Mr. Schimberg's remarks about the bottled water market.

3. Why do you think the percentage of income spent on food has decreased while the percentage of income spent on cars has increased during the past 50 years? Use the marginal utility theory to explain these trends.

4. Smoking is banned on all airline flights in the United States and on most international flights. Use marginal utility theory to explain your answers to the following questions:
   a. What effect does this ban have on the utility of (i) smokers and (ii) nonsmokers?
   b. How do you expect the ban to influence the decisions of (i) smokers and (ii) nonsmokers? In your answer to this question, consider decisions about smoking, flying, and the willingness to pay for a flight.

Chapter 9

Possibilities, Preferences, and Choices

Like the continents floating on the earth's mantle, our spending patterns change steadily over time. On such subterranean movements, business empires rise and fall. Goods such as home videos and microwave popcorn now appear on our shopping lists, while 78 rpm phonograph records and horse-drawn carriages have disappeared. Miniskirts appear, disappear, and reappear in cycles of fashion. ◆ But the glittering surface of our consumption obscures deeper and slower changes in how we spend. In the last few years, we've seen a proliferation of gourmet food shops and designer clothing boutiques. Yet we spend a smaller percentage of our income today on food and clothing than we did in 1950. At the same time, the percentage of our income spent on vacations and medical care has grown steadily. Why does consumer spending change over the years? How do people react to changes in income and changes in the prices of the things they buy? ◆ Similar subterranean movements govern the way we spend our time. For example, the average workweek has fallen steadily from 70 hours a week in the nineteenth century to 35 hours a week today. Although the average workweek is now much shorter than it once was, far more people now have jobs. This change has been especially dramatic for women, who are much more likely to work outside the home than they were in previous generations. Why has the average workweek declined? And why do more women work?

◆ In this chapter, we're going to study a model of choice that predicts the effects of changes in prices and incomes on what people buy and how much work they do.

Subterranean Movements

After studying this chapter, you will be able to:

- Calculate and graph a household's budget line
- Work out how the budget line changes when prices or income changes
- Make a map of preferences by using indifference curves
- Explain the choices that households make
- Predict the effects of price and income changes on consumption choices
- Predict the effects of wage changes on work-leisure choices

Consumption Possibilities

CONSUMPTION CHOICES ARE LIMITED BY INCOME and by prices. A household has a given amount of income to spend and cannot influence the prices of the goods and services it buys. The limits to a household's consumption choices are described by its **budget line**.

Let's look at Lisa's budget line.[1] Lisa has an income of $30 a month to spend. She buys two goods—movies and soda. Movies cost $6 each; soda costs $3 for a six-pack. Figure 9.1 shows alternative affordable ways for Lisa to consume movies and soda. Row *a* says that she can buy 10 six-packs of soda and see no movies, a combination of movies and soda that exhausts her monthly income of $30. Row *f* says that Lisa can watch 5 movies and drink no soda—another combination that exhausts the $30 available. Each of the other rows in the table also exhausts Lisa's income. (Check that each of the other rows costs exactly $30.) The numbers in the table define Lisa's consumption possibilities. We can graph Lisa's consumption possibilities as points *a* through *f* in Fig. 9.1.

Divisible and Indivisible Goods   Some goods—called divisible goods—can be bought in any quantity desired. Examples are gasoline and electricity. We can best understand household choice if we suppose that all goods and services are divisible. For example, Lisa can consume a half a movie a month *on the average* by seeing one movie every two months. When we think of goods as being divisible, the consumption possibilities are not just the points *a* through *f* shown in Fig. 9.1, but those points plus all the intermediate points that form the line running from *a* to *f*. Such a line is a budget line.

Lisa's budget line is a constraint on her choices. It marks the boundary between what is affordable and what is unaffordable. She can afford any point on the line and inside it. She cannot afford any point outside the line. The constraint on her consumption depends on prices and her income, and the constraint changes when prices or her income changes. Let's see how by studying the budget equation.

---

[1] If you have read the preceding chapter on marginal utility theory, you have already met Lisa. This tale of her thirst for soda and zeal for movies will sound familiar to you—up to a point. But in this chapter, we're going to use a different method for representing preferences—one that does not require us to resort to the idea of utility.

FIGURE 9.1
The Budget Line

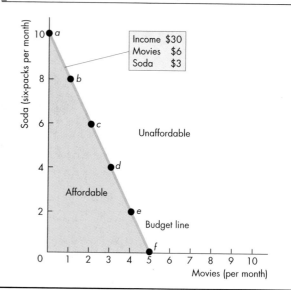

Consumption possibility	Movies (per month)	Soda (six-packs per month)
a	0	10
b	1	8
c	2	6
d	3	4
e	4	2
f	5	0

Lisa's budget line shows the boundary between what she can and cannot afford. The rows of the table list Lisa's affordable combinations of movies and soda when her income is $30, the price of soda is $3 a six-pack, and the price of a movie is $6. For example, row *a* tells us that Lisa exhausts her $30 income when she buys 10 six-packs and sees no movies. The figure graphs Lisa's budget line. Points *a* through *f* on the graph represent the rows of the table. For divisible goods, the budget line is the continuous line *af*. To calculate the equation for Lisa's budget line, start with expenditure equal to income:

$$\$3Q_s + \$6Q_m = \$30.$$

Divide by $3 to obtain

$$Q_s + 2Q_m = 10.$$

Subtract $2Q_m$ from both sides to obtain

$$Q_s = 10 - 2Q_m.$$

The Budget Equation

We can describe the budget line by using a *budget equation*. The budget equation starts with the fact that

$$\text{Expenditure} = \text{Income}.$$

Expenditure is equal to the sum of the price of each good multiplied by the quantity bought. For Lisa,

Expenditure = (Price of soda × Quantity of soda)
+ (Price of movie × Quantity of movies).

Call the price of soda P_s, the quantity of soda Q_s, the price of a movie P_m, the quantity of movies Q_m, and income y. Using these symbols, Lisa's budget equation is

$$P_s Q_s + P_m Q_m = y.$$

Or, using the prices Lisa faces, $3 for a six-pack and $6 for a movie, and Lisa's income, $30, we get

$$\$3\,Q_s + \$6\,Q_m = \$30.$$

Lisa can choose any quantities of soda (Q_s) and movies (Q_m) that satisfy this equation. To find the relationship between these quantities, first divide both sides of the equation by the price of soda (P_s) to get

$$Q_s + \frac{P_m}{P_s} \times Q_m = \frac{y}{P_s}.$$

Now subtract the term $(P_m/P_s) \times Q_m$ from both sides of this equation to give

$$Q_s = \frac{y}{P_s} - \frac{P_m}{P_s} \times Q_m.$$

For Lisa, income (y) is $30, the price of a movie (P_m) is $6, and the price of a six-pack (P_s) is $3. So Lisa must choose the quantities of movies and soda to satisfy the equation

$$Q_s = \frac{\$30}{\$3} - \frac{\$6}{\$3} \times Q_m$$

or

$$Q_s = 10 - 2\,Q_m.$$

To interpret the equation, go back to the budget line of Fig. 9.1 and check that the equation delivers that budget line. First set Q_m equal to zero. In this case, the budget equation tells us that Q_s, the quantity of soda, is y/P_s, which is 10 six-packs. This combination of Q_m and Q_s is the same as that shown in row *a* of the table in Fig. 9.1. Next set Q_m equal to 5.

Q_s is now equal to zero (row *f* of the table). Check that you can derive the other rows.

The budget equation contains two variables chosen by the household (Q_m and Q_s) and two variables (y/P_s and P_m/P_s) that the household takes as given. Let's look more closely at these variables.

Real Income A household's **real income** is the household's income expressed not as money but as a quantity of goods the household can afford to buy. Expressed in terms of soda, Lisa's real income is y/P_s. This quantity is the maximum number of six-packs that she can buy. It is equal to her money income divided by the price of soda. Lisa's income is $30 and the price of soda is $3 a six-pack, so her real income in terms of soda is 10 six-packs, which is shown in Fig. 9.1 as the point at which the budget line intersects the y-axis.

Relative Price A **relative price** is the price of one good divided by the price of another good. In Lisa's budget equation, the variable P_m/P_s is the relative price of a movie in terms of soda. For Lisa, P_m is $6 a movie and P_s is $3 a six-pack, so P_m/P_s is equal to 2 six-packs per movie. That is, to see one more movie, Lisa must give up 2 six-packs.

You've just calculated Lisa's opportunity cost of a movie. Recall that the opportunity cost of an action is the best alternative forgone. For Lisa to see 1 more movie a month, she must forgo 2 six-packs. You've also calculated Lisa's opportunity cost of soda. For Lisa to consume 2 more six-packs a month, she must give up seeing 1 movie. So her opportunity cost of 2 six-packs is 1 movie.

The relative price of a movie in terms of soda is the magnitude of the slope of Lisa's budget line. To calculate the slope of the budget line, recall the formula for slope (Chapter 2): Slope equals the change in the variable measured on the y-axis divided by the change in the variable measured on the x-axis as we move along the line. In Lisa's case (Fig. 9.1), the variable measured on the y-axis is the quantity of soda, and the variable measured on the x-axis is the quantity of movies. Along Lisa's budget line, as soda decreases from 10 to 0 six-packs, movies increase from 0 to 5. Therefore the magnitude of the slope of the budget line is 10 six-packs divided by 5 movies, or 2 six-packs per movie. The magnitude of this slope is exactly the same as the relative price we've just calculated. It is also the opportunity cost of a movie.

A Change in Prices When prices change, so does the budget line. The lower the price of the good

FIGURE 9.2

Changes in Prices and Income

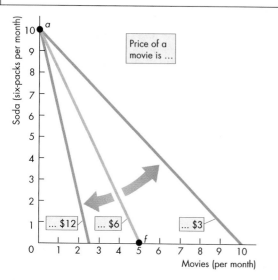

Price of a movie is ...

... $12   ... $6   ... $3

(a) A change in price

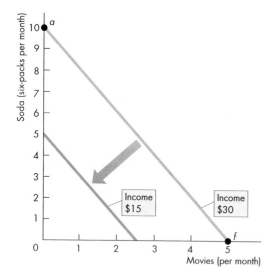

Income $15   Income $30

(b) A change in income

In part (a), the price of a movie changes. A fall in the price from $6 to $3 rotates the budget line outward and makes it flatter. A rise in the price from $6 to $12 rotates the budget line inward and makes it steeper.

In part (b), income falls from $30 to $15 while the prices of movies and soda remain constant. The budget line shifts leftward, but its slope does not change.

measured on the horizontal axis, other things remaining the same, the flatter is the budget line. For example, if the price of a movie falls from $6 to $3, real income in terms of soda does not change but the relative price of a movie falls. The budget line rotates outward and becomes flatter, as shown in Fig. 9.2(a). The higher the price of the good measured on the horizontal axis, other things remaining the same, the steeper is the budget line. For example, if the price of a movie rises from $6 to $12, the relative price of a movie increases. The budget line rotates inward and becomes steeper, as shown in Fig. 9.2(a).

A Change in Income   A change in *money income* changes real income but does not change the relative price. The budget line shifts, but its slope does not change. The bigger a household's money income, the bigger is real income and the farther to the right is the budget line. The smaller a household's money income, the smaller is real income and the farther to the left is the budget line. Figure 9.2(b) shows the effect of a change in money income on Lisa's budget line. The initial budget line is the same one that we began with in Fig. 9.1 when Lisa's income is $30. The new budget line shows the limits to Lisa's consumption if her income falls to $15 a month. The two budget lines have the same slope because they have the same relative price. The new budget line is closer to the origin than the initial one because Lisa's real income has decreased.

REVIEW QUIZ

- What does a household's budget line show?
- How do a household's real income and the relative price that it faces influence its budget line?
- If a household has an income of $40 and consumes only bus rides at $4 each and magazines at $2 each, what is the equation that describes its budget line?
- If the price of one good changes, what happens to the relative price and to the slope of the budget line?
- If a household's money income changes and no prices change, what happens to the household's real income and its budget line?

We've studied the limits to what a household can consume. Let's now learn how we can describe preferences and make a map that contains a lot of information about a household's preferences.

Preferences and Indifference Curves

Y̲O̲U̲ ̲A̲R̲E̲ ̲G̲O̲I̲N̲G̲ ̲T̲O̲ ̲D̲I̲S̲C̲O̲V̲E̲R̲ ̲A̲ ̲V̲E̲R̲Y̲ ̲N̲E̲A̲T̲ ̲I̲D̲E̲A̲—
that of drawing a map of a person's preferences. A preference map is based on the intuitively appealing assumption that people can sort all the possible combinations of goods into three groups: preferred, not preferred, and indifferent. To make this idea more concrete, let's ask Lisa to tell us how she ranks various combinations of movies and soda.

Figure 9.3(a) shows part of Lisa's answer. She tells us that she currently consumes 2 movies and 6 six-packs a month at point *c*. She then lists all the combinations of movies and soda that she says are equally acceptable to her as 2 movies and 6 six-packs a month are. When we plot these combinations of movies and soda, we get the green curve in Fig. 9.3(a). This curve is the key element in a map of preferences and is called an indifference curve.

An **indifference curve** is a line that shows combinations of goods among which a consumer is *indifferent*. The indifference curve in Fig. 9.3(a) tells us that Lisa is just as happy to consume 2 movies and 6 six-packs a month at point *c* as to consume the combination of movies and soda at point *g* or at any other point along the curve.

Lisa also says that she prefers any combination of movies and soda in the yellow area above the indifference curve in Fig. 9.3(a) to any combination on the indifference curve. And she prefers any combination on the indifference curve to any combination in the gray area below the indifference curve.

The indifference curve in Fig. 9.3(a) is just one of a whole family of such curves. This indifference curve appears again in Fig. 9.3(b) labeled I_1. The curves labeled I_0 and I_2 are two other indifference curves. Lisa prefers any point on indifference curve I_2 to any point on indifference curve I_1, and she prefers any point on I_1 to any point on I_0. We refer to I_2 as being a higher indifference curve than I_1 and I_1 as being higher than I_0.

A preference map is a series of indifference curves that resemble the contour lines on a map. By looking at the shape of the contour lines on a map, we can draw conclusions about the terrain. Similarly, by looking at the shape of indifference curves, we can draw conclusions about a person's preferences.

Let's learn how to "read" a preference map.

FIGURE 9.3

A Preference Map

(a) An indifference curve

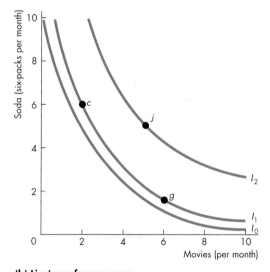

(b) Lisa's preference map

In part (a), Lisa consumes 6 six-packs of soda and 2 movies a month at point *c*. She is indifferent between all the points on the green indifference curve, such as *c* and *g*. She prefers any point above the indifference curve (yellow area) to any point on it, and she prefers any point on the indifference curve to any point below it (gray area). A preference map is a number of indifference curves. Part (b) shows three—I_0, I_1, and I_2— that are part of Lisa's preference map. She prefers point *j* to point *c* or *g*, so she prefers any point on I_2 to any point on I_1.

Marginal Rate of Substitution

The **marginal rate of substitution** (*MRS*) is the rate at which a person will give up good *y* (the good measured on the *y*-axis) to get more of good *x* (the good measured on the *x*-axis) and at the same time remain indifferent (remain on the same indifference curve). The marginal rate of substitution is measured by the magnitude of the slope of an indifference curve.

- If the indifference curve is *steep*, the marginal rate of substitution is *high*. The person is willing to give up a large quantity of good *y* to get a small quantity of good *x* while remaining indifferent.

- If the indifference curve is *flat*, the marginal rate of substitution is *low*. The person is willing to give up only a small amount of good *y* to get a large amount of good *x* to remain indifferent.

Figure 9.4 shows you how to calculate the marginal rate of substitution. Suppose that Lisa consumes 6 six-packs and 2 movies at point *c* on indifference curve I_1. Her marginal rate of substitution is calculated by measuring the magnitude of the slope of the indifference curve at point *c*. To measure this magnitude, place a straight line against, or tangent to, the indifference curve at point *c*. Along that line, as soda consumption decreases by 10 six-packs, movie consumption increases by 5. So at point *c*, Lisa is willing to give up soda for movies at the rate of 2 six-packs per movie. Her marginal rate of substitution is 2.

Now, suppose that Lisa consumes 6 movies and $1\frac{1}{2}$ six-packs at point *g* in Fig. 9.4. Her marginal rate of substitution is now measured by the slope of the indifference curve at point *g*. That slope is the same as the slope of the tangent to the indifference curve at point *g*. Here, as soda consumption decreases by 4.5 six-packs, movie consumption increases by 9. So at point *g*, Lisa is willing to give up soda for movies at the rate of $\frac{1}{2}$ six-pack per movie. Her marginal rate of substitution is $\frac{1}{2}$.

As Lisa's consumption of movies increases and her consumption of soda decreases, her marginal rate of substitution diminishes. Diminishing marginal rate of substitution is the key assumption of consumer theory. The assumption of **diminishing marginal rate of substitution** is a general tendency for the marginal rate of substitution to diminish as the consumer moves along an indifference curve, increasing consumption of the good measured on the *x*-axis and decreasing consumption of the good measured on the *y*-axis.

FIGURE 9.4

The Marginal Rate of Substitution

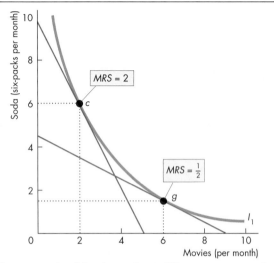

The magnitude of the slope of an indifference curve is called the marginal rate of substitution (*MRS*). The red line at point *c* tells us that Lisa is willing to give up 10 six-packs to see 5 movies. Her marginal rate of substitution at point *c* is 10 divided by 5, which equals 2. The red line at point *g* tells us that Lisa is willing to give up 4.5 six-packs to see 9 movies. Her marginal rate of substitution at point *g* is 4.5 divided by 9, which equals $\frac{1}{2}$.

Your Own Diminishing Marginal Rate of Substitution

You may be able to appreciate why we assume the principle of a diminishing marginal rate of substitution by thinking about your own preferences. Imagine that in a week, you consume 10 six-packs of soda and no movies. Most likely, you are willing to give up a lot of soda so that you can go to the movies just once. But now imagine that in a week, you consume 1 six-pack and 6 movies. Most likely you will now be willing to give up only a little soda to see a seventh movie. As a general rule, the greater the number of movies you see, the smaller is the quantity of soda you are willing to give up to see one additional movie.

The shape of a person's indifference curves incorporates the principle of the diminishing marginal rate of substitution because the curves are bowed toward the origin. The tightness of the bend of an indifference curve tells us how willing a person is to substitute one good for another while remaining indifferent. Let's look at some examples that make this point clear.

Degree of Substitutability

Most of us would not regard movies and soda as being close substitutes for each other. We probably have some fairly clear ideas about how many movies we want to see each month and how many cans of soda we want to drink. Nevertheless, to some degree, we are willing to substitute between these two goods. No matter how big a soda freak you are, there is surely some increase in the number of movies you can see that will compensate you for being deprived of a can of soda. Similarly, no matter how addicted you are to the movies, surely some number of cans of soda will compensate you for being deprived of seeing one movie. A person's indifference curves for movies and soda might look like those shown in Fig. 9.5(a).

Close Substitutes   Some goods substitute so easily for each other that most of us do not even notice which we are consuming. The different brands of personal computers are an example. As long as it has an "Intel inside" and runs Windows, most of us don't care

whether our PC is a Dell, a Compaq, a Toshiba, or any of a dozen other brands. The same holds true for marker pens. Most of us don't care whether we use a marker pen from the campus bookstore or the local supermarket. When two goods are perfect substitutes for each other, their indifference curves are straight lines that slope downward, as Fig. 9.5(b) illustrates. The marginal rate of substitution is constant.

Complements   Some goods cannot substitute for each other at all. Instead, they are complements. The complements in Fig. 9.5(c) are left and right running shoes. Indifference curves of perfect complements are L-shaped. One left running shoe and one right running shoe are as good as one left shoe and two right ones. Having two of each is preferred to having one of each, but having two of one and one of the other is no better than having one of each.

The extreme cases of perfect substitutes and perfect complements shown here don't often happen in reality. They do, however, illustrate that the shape of the indifference curve shows the degree of substitutability between two goods. The more perfectly substitutable

---

FIGURE 9.5
The Degree of Substitutability

(a) **Ordinary goods**   (b) **Perfect substitutes**   (c) **Perfect complements**

The shape of the indifference curves reveals the degree of substitutability between two goods. Part (a) shows the indifference curves for two ordinary goods: movies and soda. To consume less soda and remain indifferent, one must see more movies. The number of movies that compensates for a reduction in soda increases as less soda is consumed. Part (b) shows the indifference curves for two perfect substitutes. For

the consumer to remain indifferent, one fewer marker pen from the local supermarket must be replaced by one extra marker pen from the campus bookstore. Part (c) shows two perfect complements—goods that cannot be substituted for each other at all. Having two left running shoes with one right running shoe is no better than having one of each. But having two of each is preferred to having one of each.

"With the pork I'd recommend an Alsatian white or a Coke."

Drawing by Weber; © 1988 *The New Yorker Magazine*, Inc.

the two goods, the more nearly are their indifference curves straight lines and the less quickly does the marginal rate of substitution fall. Poor substitutes for each other have tightly curved indifference curves, approaching the shape of those shown in Fig. 9.5(c)

As you can see in the cartoon, according to the waiter's preferences, Coke and Alsatian white wine are perfect substitutes and each is a complement with pork. We hope the customers agree with him.

R E V I E W   Q U I Z

■ What is an indifference curve and how does an indifference map show preferences?

■ Why does an indifference curve slope downward and why is it bowed toward the origin?

■ What do we call the magnitude of the slope of an indifference curve?

■ What is the key assumption about a consumer's marginal rate of substitution?

The two components of the model of household choice are now in place: the budget line and the preference map. We will now use these components to work out the household's choice and to predict how choices change when prices and income change.

Predicting Consumer Behavior

WE ARE NOW GOING TO PREDICT THE QUANTITIES of movies and soda that Lisa *chooses* to buy. Figure 9.6 shows Lisa's budget line from Fig. 9.1 and her indifference curves from Fig. 9.3(b). We assume that Lisa consumes at her best affordable point, which is 2 movies and 6 six-packs—at point *c*. Here, Lisa:

■ Is on her budget line

■ Is on her highest attainable indifference curve

■ Has a marginal rate of substitution between movies and soda equal to the relative price of movies and soda.

For every point inside the budget line, such as point *i*, there are points *on* the budget line that Lisa

---

FIGURE 9.6

The Best Affordable Point

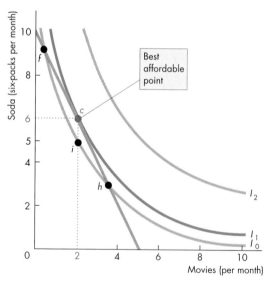

Lisa's best affordable point is *c*. At that point, she is on her budget line and also on the highest attainable indifference curve. At a point such as *h*, Lisa is willing to give up more movies in exchange for soda than she has to. She can move to point *i*, which is just as good as point *h*, and have some unspent income. She can spend that income and move to *c*, a point that she prefers to point *i*.

prefers. For example, she prefers all the points on the budget line between *f* and *h* to point *i*. So she chooses a point on the budget line.

Every point on the budget line lies on an indifference curve. For example, point *h* lies on the indifference curve I_0. At point *h*, Lisa's marginal rate of substitution is less than the relative price. Lisa is willing to give up more movies in exchange for soda than the budget line says she must give up. So she moves along her budget line from *h* toward *c*. As she does so, she passes through a number of indifference curves (not shown in the figure) located between indifference curves I_0 and I_1. All of these indifference curves are higher than I_0, and therefore Lisa prefers any point on them to point *h*. But when Lisa gets to point *c*, she is on the highest attainable indifference curve. If she keeps moving along the budget line, she starts to encounter indifference curves that are lower than I_1. So Lisa chooses point *c*.

At the chosen point, the marginal rate of substitution (the magnitude of the slope of the indifference curve) equals the relative price (the magnitude of the slope of the budget line).

Let's use this model of household choice to predict the effects on consumption of changes in prices and income. We'll begin by studying the effect of a change in price.

A Change in Price

The effect of a change in price on the quantity of a good consumed is called the **price effect**. We will use Fig. 9.7(a) to work out the price effect of a fall in the price of a movie. We start with movies costing $6 each, soda costing $3 a six-pack, and Lisa's income at $30 a month. In this situation, she consumes 6 six-packs and 2 movies a month at point *c*.

Now suppose that the price of a movie falls to $3. With a lower price of a movie, the budget line rotates outward and becomes flatter. (Check back to Fig. 9.2(a) for a refresher on how a price change affects the budget line.) The new budget line is the dark orange one in Fig. 9.7(a).

Lisa's best affordable point is now point *j*, where she consumes 5 movies and 5 six-packs of soda. Lisa drinks less soda and watches more movies now that movies cost less. She cuts her soda consumption from 6 to 5 six-packs and increases the number of movies she sees from 2 to 5 a month. Lisa substitutes movies for soda when the price of a movie falls and the price of soda and her income remain constant.

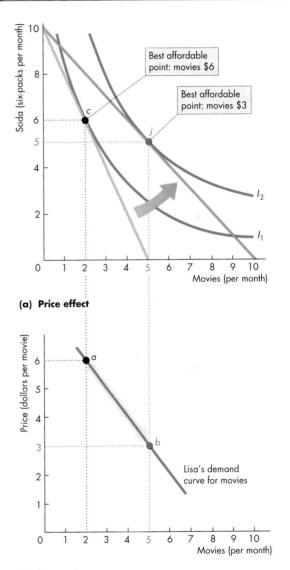

FIGURE 9.7

Price Effect and Demand Curve

(a) Price effect

(b) Demand curve

Initially, Lisa consumes at point *c* (part a). If the price of a movie falls from $6 to $3, she consumes at point *j*. The move from *c* to *j* is the price effect.

At a price of $6 a movie, Lisa sees 2 movies a month, at point *a* (part b). At a price of $3 a movie, she sees 5 movies a month, at point *b*. Lisa's demand curve traces out her best affordable quantity of movies as the price of a movie varies.

The Demand Curve   In Chapter 4, we asserted that the demand curve slopes downward. We can now derive a demand curve from a consumer's budget line and indifference curves. By doing so, we can see that the law of demand and the downward-sloping demand curve are consequences of the consumer's choosing his or her best affordable combination of goods.

To derive Lisa's demand curve for movies, lower the price of a movie and find her best affordable point at different prices. We've just done this for two movie prices in Fig. 9.7(a). Figure 9.7(b) highlights these two prices and two points that lie on Lisa's demand curve for movies. When the price of a movie is $6, Lisa sees 2 movies a month at point *a*. When the price falls to $3, she increases the number of movies she sees to 5 a month at point *b*. The demand curve is made up of these two points plus all the other points that tell us Lisa's best affordable consumption of movies at each movie price, given the price of soda and Lisa's income. As you can see, Lisa's demand curve for movies slopes downward. The lower the price of a movie, the more movies she watches each month. This is the law of demand.

Next, let's examine how Lisa changes her consumption of movies and soda when her income changes.

A Change in Income

The effect of a change in income on consumption is called the **income effect**. Let's work out the income effect by examining how consumption changes when income changes and prices remain constant. Figure 9.8(a) shows the income effect when Lisa's income falls. With an income of $30 and with a movie costing $3 and soda $3 a six-pack, she consumes at point *j*—5 movies and 5 six-packs. If her income falls to $21, she consumes at point *k*—consuming 4 movies and 3 six-packs. When Lisa's income falls, she consumes less of both goods. Movies and soda are normal goods.

The Demand Curve and the Income Effect   A change in income leads to a shift in the demand curve, as shown in Fig. 9.8(b). With an income of $30 and a movie costing $3, Lisa is at point *b* on demand curve D_0, the same curve as in Fig. 9.7. But when her income falls to $21, Lisa sees only 4 movies at point *c*. With less income, she plans to see fewer movies at each price, so her demand curve shifts leftward to D_1.

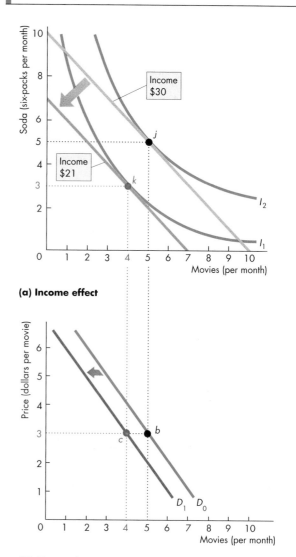

FIGURE 9.8

Income Effect and Change in Demand

(a) Income effect

(b) Demand curve

A change in income shifts the budget line and changes the best affordable point and changes consumption. In part (a), when Lisa's income decreases from $30 to $21, she consumes less of both movies and soda. In part (b), Lisa's demand curve for movies when her income is $30 is D_0. When Lisa's income decreases to $21, her demand curve for movies shifts leftward to D_1. Lisa's demand for movies decreases because she now sees fewer movies at each price.

Substitution Effect and Income Effect

For a normal good, a fall in price *always* increases the quantity bought. We can prove this assertion by dividing the price effect into two parts:

- Substitution effect
- Income effect

Figure 9.9(a) shows the price effect, and Fig. 9.9(b) divides that price effect into its two parts.

Substitution Effect   The **substitution effect** is the effect of a change in price on the quantity bought when the consumer (hypothetically) remains indifferent between the original and the new situation. To work out Lisa's substitution effect, we imagine that when the price of a movie falls, we cut Lisa's income by enough to keep her on the same indifference curve as before.

When the price of a movie falls from $6 to $3, suppose (hypothetically) that we cut Lisa's income to $21. What's special about $21? It is the income that is just enough, at the new price of a movie, to keep Lisa's best affordable point on the same indifference curve as her original consumption point *c*. Lisa's budget line is now the light orange line shown in Fig. 9.9(b). With the lower price of a movie and the smaller income, Lisa's best affordable point is *k* on indifference curve I_1. The move from *c* to *k* isolates the substitution effect of the price change. The substitution effect of the fall in the price of a movie is an increase in the consumption of movies from 2 to 4. The direction of the substitution effect never varies: When the relative price of a good falls, the consumer substitutes more of that good for the other good.

Income Effect   To calculate the substitution effect, we gave Lisa a $9 pay cut. Now let's give Lisa her $9 back. The $9 increase in income shifts Lisa's budget line outward, as shown in Fig. 9.9(b). The slope of the budget line does not change because both prices remain constant. This change in Lisa's budget line is similar to the one illustrated in Fig. 9.8. As Lisa's budget line shifts outward, her best affordable point becomes *j* on indifference curve I_2. The move from *k* to *j* isolates the income effect of the price change. The income effect of the fall of the price of movies is the increase in the quantity of movies consumed from 4 to 5. As Lisa's income increases, she increases her consumption of movies. For Lisa, movies are a normal good. For a normal good, the income effect reinforces the substitution effect.

FIGURE 9.9

Substitution Effect and Income Effect

(a) Price effect

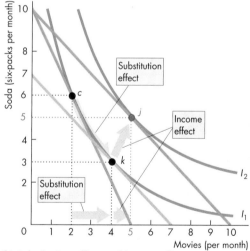

(b) Substitution effect and income effect

The price effect in part (a) can be separated into a substitution effect and an income effect in part (b). To isolate the substitution effect, we confront Lisa with the new price but keep her on her original indifference curve, I_1. The substitution effect is the move from *c* to *k*. To isolate the income effect, we confront Lisa with the new price of movies but increase her income so that she can move from the original indifference curve, I_1, to the new one, I_2. The income effect is the move from *k* to *j*.

Inferior Goods The example that we have just studied is that of a change in the price of a normal good. The effect of a change in the price of an inferior good is different. Recall that an inferior good is one whose consumption decreases as income increases. For an inferior good, the income effect is negative. Thus for an inferior good, a lower price does not always lead to an increase in the quantity demanded. The lower price has a substitution effect that increases the quantity demanded. But the lower price also has a negative income effect that reduces the demand for the inferior good. Thus the income effect offsets the substitution effect to some degree. If the negative income effect exceeded the positive substitution effect, the demand curve would slope upward. This case does not appear to occur in the real world.

Back to the Facts

We started this chapter by observing how consumer spending has changed over the years. The indifference curve model explains those changes. Spending patterns are determined by best affordable choices. Changes in prices and incomes change the best affordable choice and change consumption patterns.

R E V I E W   Q U I Z

■ When a consumer chooses the combination of goods and services to buy, what is she or he trying to achieve?

■ Explain the conditions that are met when a consumer has found the best affordable combination of goods to buy. (Use the terms "budget line," "marginal rate of substitution," and "relative price" in your explanation.)

■ If the price of a normal good falls, what happens to the quantity demanded of that good?

■ Into what two effects can we divide the effect of a price change?

■ For a normal good, does the income effect reinforce the substitution effect or does it partly offset the substitution effect?

The model of household choice can explain many other household choices. Let's look at one of them.

Work-Leisure Choices

HOUSEHOLDS MAKE MANY CHOICES OTHER THAN those about how to spend their income on the various goods and services available. We can use the model of consumer choice to understand many other household choices. Some of these are discussed on pp. 192–196. Here we'll study a key choice: how much labor to supply.

Labor Supply

Every week, we allocate our 168 hours between working—called *labor*—and all other activities—called *leisure.* How do we decide how to allocate our time between labor and leisure? We can answer this question by using the theory of household choice.

The more hours we spend on *leisure,* the smaller is our income. The relationship between leisure and income is described by an *income-time budget line.* Figure 9.10(a) shows Lisa's income-time budget line. If Lisa devotes the entire week to leisure—168 hours—she has no income and is at point *z.* By supplying labor in exchange for a wage, she can convert hours into income along the income-time budget line. The slope of that line is determined by the hourly wage rate. If the wage rate is $5 an hour, Lisa faces the flattest budget line. If the wage rate is $10 an hour, she faces the middle budget line. And if the wage rate is $15 an hour, she faces the steepest budget line.

Lisa buys leisure by not supplying labor and by forgoing income. The opportunity cost of an hour of leisure is the hourly wage rate forgone.

Figure 9.10(a) also shows Lisa's indifference curves for income and leisure. Lisa chooses her best attainable point. This choice of income and time allocation is just like her choice of movies and soda. She gets onto the highest possible indifference curve by making her marginal rate of substitution between income and leisure equal to her wage rate. Lisa's choice depends on the wage rate she can earn. At a wage rate of $5 an hour, Lisa chooses point *a* and works 20 hours a week (168 minus 148) for an income of $100 a week. At a wage rate of $10 an hour, she chooses point *b* and works 35 hours a week (168 minus 133) for an income of $350 a week. And at a wage rate of $15 an hour, she chooses point *c* and works 30 hours a week (168 minus 138) for an income of $450 a week.

FIGURE 9.10

The Supply of Labor

(a) Time allocation decision

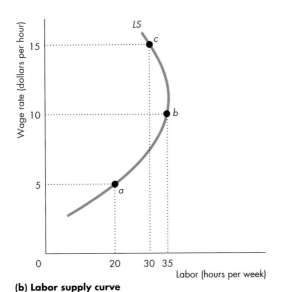

(b) Labor supply curve

In part (a), at a wage rate of $5 an hour, Lisa takes 148 hours of leisure and works 20 hours a week at point *a*. If the wage rate increases from $5 to $10, she decreases her leisure to 133 hours and increases her work to 35 hours a week at point *b*. But if the wage rate increases from $10 to $15, Lisa *increases* her leisure to 138 hours and *decreases* her work to 30 hours a week at point *c*. Part (b) shows Lisa's labor supply curve. Points *a*, *b*, and *c* on the supply curve correspond to Lisa's choices on her income-time budget lines in part (a).

The Labor Supply Curve

Figure 9.10(b) shows Lisa's labor supply curve. This curve shows that as the wage rate increases from $5 an hour to $10 an hour, Lisa increases the quantity of labor supplied from 20 hours a week to 35 hours a week. But when the wage rate increases to $15 an hour, she decreases her quantity of labor supplied to 30 hours a week.

Lisa's supply of labor is similar to that described for the economy as a whole at the beginning of this chapter. As wage rates have increased, work hours have decreased. At first, this pattern seems puzzling. We've seen that the hourly wage rate is the opportunity cost of leisure. So a higher wage rate means a higher opportunity cost of leisure. This fact on its own leads to a decrease in leisure and an increase in work hours. But instead, we've cut our work hours. Why? Because our incomes have increased. As the wage rate increases, incomes increase, so people demand more of all normal goods. Leisure is a normal good, so as incomes increase, people demand more leisure.

The higher wage rate has both a *substitution effect* and an *income effect*. The higher wage rate increases the opportunity cost of leisure and so leads to a substitution effect away from leisure. And the higher wage rate increases income and so leads to an income effect toward more leisure.

This theory of household choice can explain the facts about work patterns described at the beginning of this chapter. First, it can explain why the average workweek has fallen steadily from 70 hours in the nineteenth century to 35 hours today. The reason is that as wage rates have increased, although people have substituted work for leisure, they have also decided to use their higher incomes in part to consume more leisure. Second, the theory can explain why more women now have jobs in the labor market. The reason is that increases in their wage rates and improvements in their job opportunities have led to a substitution effect away from working at home and toward working in the labor market.

◆ This theory of household choice can also explain trends in vacation services, as you can see in *Reading Between the Lines* on pp. 186–187. In the chapters that follow, we're going to study the choices made by firms. We'll see how, in the pursuit of profit, firms make choices that determine the supply of goods and services and the demand for productive resources.

Indifference Curves in Action

THE LOS ANGELES TIMES, NOVEMBER 23, 1998

Pushing High End at Sea Level

BY E. SCOTT RECKARD, TIMES STAFF WRITER

Breakers toss salt into the breeze as a beachcomber eyes a tide pool. A skim-boarder shoots skyward, then plunges into the foam. On this warm fall day, in a Laguna Beach cove with surf-sculpted rock arches and bougainvillea-draped bluffs, just two sunbathers share the sand with the darting seabirds.

In the past, the few visitors here mostly scrambled down from Treasure Island, a bluff-top trailer park looking out to Santa Catalina Island. Retirees and middle-class families shared paradise with part-time residents such as John Wayne's widow, Pilar, and weekend fugitives from inland heat and smog. In the future, far more visitors will stroll down from the trailer park's replacement: a 275-room resort hotel, 18 estate homes and 19 condos for the wealthy, with beach trails, scenic overlooks and 70 parking slots for everyone else.

Here and at choice coastal sites from San Diego County to Santa Barbara, four- and five-star resorts will proliferate in the coming decades, along with upgrades of older hotels. At least 14 such projects are in various stages of development in Southern California, motivated by a web of economic, demographic and political factors. ...

Underlying these factors are prosperous times and the powerful demographics of an aging population. Analysts say millions of baby boomers in their peak earning years are demanding high-end recreation, often several short getaways a year instead of the long summer vacations of their childhoods.

As always, standing in between developers and the coastline are powerful and vocal environmental interests such as the Sierra Club, which has been adept at delaying big coastal projects for years. ...

Essence of the Story

■ Aging baby boomers in their peak earning years are demanding high-quality recreation facilities for several short vacations a year instead of a single long summer vacation.

■ To meet this demand, at least 14 projects to replace trailer parks with luxury resorts are in various stages of development on Southern California's choice coastal sites.

■ Environmental interests oppose and delay these big coastal projects.

Economic Analysis

■ A luxury resort is a normal good. A trailer park is an inferior good. (The quantity consumed of a normal good increases as income increases. The quantity consumed of an inferior good *decreases* as income *increases*.)

■ Figure 1 shows the *income effect* on the quantities consumed of trailer parks and luxury resorts. (Think of this consumer as the "average" consumer.)

■ At today's income and prices, we can consume either 30 trailer parks or 30 luxury resorts or any combination of the two along the budget line *ab*.

■ The best affordable point is where 20 trailer parks and 10 luxury resorts are consumed.

■ Suppose that in the future, incomes double. We can now consume either 60 trailer parks or 60 luxury resorts or any combination of the two along the budget line *cd*.

■ Now the best affordable point is where 10 trailer parks and 50 luxury resorts are consumed. Because a trailer park is an inferior good, when income increases, the quantity of trailer parks consumed decreases *if prices do not change*.

■ But prices are likely to change.

■ As more luxury resorts are built, environmental interests begin to block further development. This action increases the cost of building luxury resorts, which limits their supply and increases the prices that people must pay to use them.

■ At the same time, technological advances lower the relative price of trailers, so the cost of using trailer parks falls.

■ Instead of shifting outward to *cd*, the budget line shifts outward *and becomes less steep*. It shifts to *ef* in Figure 2.

■ Along the budget line *ef*, the relative price of trailer parks in terms of luxury resorts is lower than along budget lines *ab* and *cd*.

■ In this example, the consumer can just reach indifference curve I_1 on budget line *cd* and budget line *ef*.

■ With the prices and income that generate the budget line *ef*, the best affordable point is where 50 trailer parks and 20 luxury resorts are consumed.

Figure 1 An income effect

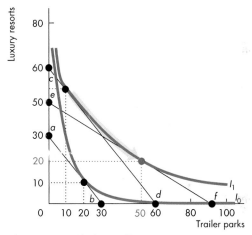

Figure 2 An substitute effect

■ The increase in trailer parks from 10 to 50 and the decrease in luxury resorts from 50 to 20 along I_1 is a *substitution effect*.

■ This analysis shows how changes in prices allocate scarce resources and prevent the over-development of ocean-side sites when they have a high environmental value.

SUMMARY

KEY POINTS

Consumption Possibilities (pp. 174–176)

- The budget line is the boundary between what the household can and cannot afford given its income and the prices of goods.
- The point at which the budget line intersects the *y*-axis is the household's real income in terms of the good measured on that axis.
- The magnitude of the slope of the budget line is the relative price of the good measured on the *x*-axis in terms of the good measured on the *y*-axis.
- A change in price changes the slope of the budget line. A change in income shifts the budget line but does not change its slope.

Preferences and Indifference Curves (pp. 177–180)

- A consumer's preferences can be represented by indifference curves. An indifference curve joins all the combinations of goods among which the consumer is indifferent.
- A consumer prefers any point above an indifference curve to any point on it and any point on an indifference curve to any point below it.
- The magnitude of the slope of an indifference curve is called the marginal rate of substitution.
- The marginal rate of substitution diminishes as consumption of the good measured on the *y*-axis decreases and consumption of the good measured on the *x*-axis increases.

Predicting Consumer Behavior (pp. 180-184)

- A household consumes at its best affordable point. This point is on the budget line and on the highest attainable indifference curve and has a marginal rate of substitution equal to relative price.
- The effect of a price change (the price effect) can be divided into a substitution effect and an income effect.
- The substitution effect is the effect of a change in price on the quantity bought when the consumer (hypothetically) remains indifferent between the original and the new situation.

- The substitution effect always results in an increase in consumption of the good whose relative price has fallen.
- The income effect is the effect of a change in income on consumption.
- For a normal good, the income effect reinforces the substitution effect. For an inferior good, the income effect works in the opposite direction to the substitution effect.

Work-Leisure Choices (pp. 184–185)

- The indifference curve model of household choice enables us to understand how a household allocates its time between work and leisure.
- Work hours have decreased and leisure hours have increased because the income effect on the demand for leisure has been greater than the substitution effect.

KEY FIGURES ◆

KEY TERMS

PROBLEMS

*1. Sara has an income of $12 a week. Popcorn costs $3 a bag, and cola costs $3 a can.
   a. What is Sara's real income in terms of cola?
   b. What is her real income in terms of popcorn?
   c. What is the relative price of cola in terms of popcorn?
   d. What is the opportunity cost of a can of cola?
   e. Calculate the equation for Sara's budget line (placing bags of popcorn on the left side).
   f. Draw a graph of Sara's budget line with cola on the x-axis.
   g. In part (f), what is the slope of Sara's budget line? What is it equal to?

2. Marc has an income of $20 per week. CDs cost $8 each, and root beer costs $4 a can.
   a. What is Marc's real income in terms of root beer?
   b. What is his real income in terms of CDs?
   c. What is the relative price of root beer in terms of CDs?
   d. What is the opportunity cost of a can of root beer?
   e. Calculate the equation for Marc's budget line (placing cans of root beer on the left side).
   f. Draw a graph of Marc's budget line with CDs on the x-axis.
   g. In part (f), what is the slope of Marc's budget line? What is it equal to?

*3. Sara's income and the prices she faces are the same as in problem 1. The figure illustrates Sara's preferences.

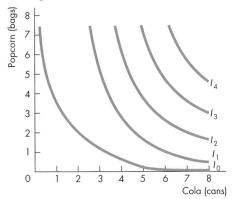

   a. What are the quantities of popcorn and cola that Sara buys?
   b. What is Sara's marginal rate of substitution of popcorn for cola at the point at which she consumes?

4. Marc's income and the prices he faces are the same as in problem 2. The figure illustrates his preferences.

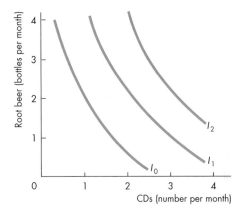

   a. What are the quantities of root beer and CDs that Marc buys?
   b. What is Marc's marginal rate of substitution of CDs for root beer at the point at which he consumes?

*5. Now suppose that in problem 3, the price of cola falls to $1.50 per can and the price of popcorn and Sara's income remain constant.
   a. Find the new quantities of cola and popcorn that Sara buys.
   b. Find two points on Sara's demand curve for cola.
   c. Find the substitution effect of the price change.
   d. Find the income effect of the price change.
   e. Is cola a normal good or an inferior good for Sara?
   f. Is popcorn a normal good or an inferior good for Sara?

6. Now suppose that in problem 4, the price of a CD falls to $4, the price of root beer and income remain constant.
   a. Find the new quantities of root beer and CDs that Marc buys.
   b. Find two points on Marc's demand curve for CDs.
   c. Find the substitution effect of the price change.

d. Find the income effect of the price change.
e. Are CDs a normal good or an inferior good for Marc?
f. Is root beer a normal good or an inferior good for Marc?

*7. Pam buys cookies and comic books. The price of a cookie is $1, and the price of a comic book is $2. Each month, Pam spends all of her income and buys 30 cookies and 5 comic books. Next month, the price of a cookie will fall to 50¢ and the price of a comic book will rise to $5. Assume that Pam's preference map is similar to that in Fig. 9.3(b).
a. Will Pam be able to buy 30 cookies and 5 comic books next month?
b. Will Pam want to buy 30 cookies and 5 comic books?
c. Which situation does Pam prefer: cookies at $1 and comic books at $2 or cookies at 50¢ and comic books at $3?
d. If Pam changes the quantities that she buys, which good will she buy more of and which will she buy less of?
e. When the prices change next month, will there be an income effect and a substitution effect at work or just one of them?

8. Pete buys tuna and golf balls. The price of tuna is $2.00 a can, and the price of golf balls is $1.00 each. Each month, Pete spends all of his income and buys 20 cans of tuna and 40 golf balls. Next month, the price of tuna will rise to $3.00 a can and the price of golf balls will fall to 50¢ each. Assume that Pete's preference map is similar to that in Fig. 9.3(b)
a. Will Pete be able to buy 20 cans of tuna and 40 golf balls next month?
b. Will Pete want to buy 20 cans of tuna and 40 golf balls?
c. Which situation does Pete prefer: tuna at $2 a can and golf balls at $1 each or tuna at $3 a can and golf balls at 50¢ each?
d. If Pete changes the quantities that he buys, which good will he buy more of and which will he buy less of?
e. When the prices change next month, will there be an income effect and a substitution effect at work or just one of them?

CRITICAL THINKING

1. Study *Reading Between the Lines* about trailer parks and luxury resorts on pp. 186–187, and then:
   a. Provide a demographic and economic profile of the people who buy the services of luxury resorts based on the information given in the news article.
   b. Discuss the alternative uses of the sites on which luxury resorts might be developed.
   c. Use the indifference curve model to explain the changes in buying patterns that the news article predicts will occur in the markets for trailer parks and luxury resorts.

2. Use the links on the Parkin Web site to obtain prices for luxury condominiums and trailer park accommodation. Draw a diagram that shows the budget line of a family that has $2,000 a month to spend.

3. Some people say that increasing the tobacco tax can help to limit smoking. Suppose the tobacco tax currently is 75 cents a pack and that a pack of cigarettes costs $3.50. If the tobacco tax doubled to $1.50:
   a. What would happen to the relative price of cigarettes and other goods and services?
   b. What would happen to the budget line showing the quantities of cigarettes and other goods and services that a person could afford to buy?
   c. How would a typical person change her or his purchases of cigarettes? Use a figure to show your answer to this question and separately identify the substitution effect and the income effect.

4. Jim spends his income on apartment rent, food, clothing, and vacations. He gets a pay raise from $3,000 a month to $4,000 a month. At the same time, airfares and other vacation-related costs increase by 50 percent while other prices remain unchanged.
   a. How do you think Jim will change his spending pattern as a result of the changes in his income and prices?
   b. Is Jim better off or worse off in his new situation? Why or why not?
   c. If *all* prices rise by 50 percent, how does Jim change his purchases? Is he now better off or worse off? Why?

Understanding Households' Choices

Making the Most of Life

The powerful forces of demand and supply shape the fortunes of families, businesses, nations, and empires in the same unrelenting way that the tides and winds shape rocks and coastlines. You saw in Chapters 4 through 7 how these forces raise and lower prices, increase and decrease quantities bought and sold, cause revenues to fluctuate, and send resources to their most valuable uses. ◆ These powerful forces begin quietly and privately with the choices that each one of us makes. Chapters 8 and 9 probe these individual choices. Chapter 8 explores the marginal utility theory of human decisions. This theory explains people's consumption plans. It also explains people's consumption of leisure time and its flip side, the supply of work time. Marginal utility theory can even be used to explain "non-economic" choices, such as whether to marry and how many children to have. In a sense, there are no non-economic choices. If there is scarcity, there must be choice. And economics studies all such choices. Chapter 9 describes a tool that enables us to make a map of people's likes and dislikes, a tool called an *indifference curve*. Indifference curves are considered an advanced topic, so this chapter is *strictly optional*. But the presentation of indifference curves in Chapter 9 is the clearest and most straightforward available, so if you want to learn about this tool, this chapter is the place to do so. ◆ The earliest economists (Adam Smith and his contemporaries) did not have a very deep understanding of households' choices. It was not until the nineteenth century that progress was made in this area. On the following pages, you can spend some time with Jeremy Bentham, the person who pioneered the use of the concept of utility to study of human choices, and with Gary Becker of the University of Chicago, who is one of today's most influential students of human behavior.

The Economist

Jeremy Bentham

(1748–1832), who lived in London, was the son and grandson of a lawyer and was himself trained as a barrister. But he rejected the opportunity to maintain the family tradition and, instead, spent his life as a writer, activist, and Member of Parliament in the pursuit of rational laws that would bring the greatest happiness to the greatest number of people.

Bentham, whose embalmed body is preserved to this day in a glass cabinet in the University of London, was the first person to use the concept of utility to explain human choices. But in Bentham's day, the distinction between explaining and prescribing was not a sharp one, and Bentham was ready to use his ideas to tell people how they ought to behave. He was one of the first to propose pensions for the retired, guaranteed employment, minimum wages, and social benefits such as free education and free medical care.

"... It is the greatest happiness of the greatest number that is the measure of right and wrong."

JEREMY BENTHAM
Fragment on Government

The Issues

The economic analysis of human behavior in the family, the workplace, the markets for goods and services, the markets for labor services, and financial markets is based on the idea that our behavior can be understood as a response to scarcity. Everything we do can be understood as a choice that maximizes total benefit subject to the constraints imposed by our limited resources and technology. If people's preferences are stable in the face of changing constraints, then we have a chance of predicting how they will respond to an evolving environment.

The economic approach explains the incredible change that has occurred during the past 100 years in the way women allocate their time as the consequence of changing constraints, not of changing attitudes. Technological advances have equipped the nation's farms and factories with machines that have increased the productivity of both women and men, thereby raising the wages they can earn. The increasingly technological world has increased the return to education for both women and men and has led to a large increase in high school and college graduates of both sexes. And equipped with an ever-widening array of gadgets and appliances that cut the time taken to do household jobs, an increasing proportion of women have joined the labor force.

The economic explanation might not be correct, but it is a powerful one. And if it is correct, the changing attitudes are a consequence, not a cause, of the economic advancement of women.

Now

By 1997, more than 60 percent of women were in the labor force, and although many had low-paying jobs, women were increasingly found in the professions and in executive positions. What brought about this dramatic change compared with 100 years earlier? Was it a change in preferences or a change in the constraints that women face?

Then

Economists explain people's actions as the consequences of choices that maximize total utility subject to constraints. In the 1890s, fewer than 20 percent of women chose market employment, and most of those who did had low-paying and unattractive jobs. The other 80 percent of women chose nonmarket work in the home. What constraints led to these choices?

Today, one economist who stands out above all others and who stands on the shoulders of Jeremy Bentham is Gary Becker of the University of Chicago. Professor Becker has transformed the way we think about human choices. You can meet him on the following pages.

Talking with

Gary S. Becker

*is Professor of Economics and Sociology
at the University of Chicago. Born in
1930 in Pottsville, Pennsylvania,
he was an undergraduate at
Princeton University and a
graduate student at the
University of Chicago. His
graduate supervisor was
Milton Friedman, and his
Ph.D. thesis became the book*
The Economics of
Discrimination, *a
work that profoundly
changed the way we
think about discrimi-
nation and economic
ways of reducing it.
Professor
Becker's other
major book,*
Human Capital,
*first published in
1964, has become a
classic and has influenced the thinking
of the Clinton Administration on education issues. In 1992 he was awarded
the Nobel Prize for Economic Science
for his work on human capital.*

*Professor Becker has revolutionized
the way we think about human decisions in all aspects of life. Michael
Parkin talked with Professor Becker
about his work and how it uses and
builds on the work of Jeremy Bentham.*

Why are you an economist?
When I went to Princeton, I was interested in mathematics, but I wanted to do
something for society. I took economics
in my freshman year by accident, and it
was a lucky accident. I found economics

Gary S. Becker

to be tremendously exciting intellectually because it could be used to understand the difference between capitalism
and socialism, what determined wages,
and how people are taxed. This was so
exciting to me that I didn't even worry
about job opportunities at the time.

Can we really hope to explain all
human choices by using models that
were invented initially to explain and
predict choices about the allocation of
income among alternative consumer
goods and services?
I think we can hope to explain all
human choices. All choices involve
making comparisons and assessing
how to allocate our time between work,
leisure, and taking care of children.
These are choices that are not in principle very different from the type of
choices involved in allocating income.
Whether economists succeed at the goal
of explaining everything, of course,
remains to be seen. We certainly haven't
done that yet, but I think we've made
considerable progress in expanding our
horizons with the theory of choice.

You are a professor of both economics
and sociology. Do you see these same
techniques that we've developed in
economics being used to address questions that are the traditional domain of
the sociologist? Or is sociology just a
totally different discipline?
Sociology is a discipline with many
different approaches. There is a small
but growing and vocal group of
sociologists who believe in what they
call *rational choice theory*, which is the
theory economists have used to explain
choices in markets. My late colleague,
James Coleman, was the leader of that
group. One of the issues they deal with

is the influence of peers on behavior. For example, imagine that I am a teenager facing choices of getting involved with drugs or heavy drinking or smoking because of peer pressure. How would rational choice theorists incorporate this peer pressure into an analysis of these choices? The simple approach they take is that my utility, or pleasure, depends not only on what I'm consuming but also on what my peers are doing. If they're doing something very different from what I'm doing, that reduces my utility partly because I receive less respect from them and feel less part of the group.

Therefore when I am trying to get as much utility as possible, I take into account what my peers are doing. But since we're all doing that, this leads to some equilibrium in this peer market. Instead of us all behaving independently, we are all behaving interdependently. I think economists have given social structures such as peer pressure far too little attention. One of the things I learned during my association with Coleman and other sociologists is a better appreciation of the importance of social factors in individual behavior.

Can you identify the historical figures that have been most influential to your thinking and your career?
Economics is a cumulative field in which we build on the giants who went earlier, and we try to add a little bit. And then other people build on our generation's contributions. The view I take of the broad scope of the economic approach has had a number of major practitioners,

including Jeremy Bentham, who stated and applied a very general view of utility-maximizing behavior to many problems, such as the factors that reduce crime.

Other nineteenth century people like Wicksteed and Marshall highlighted the rational choice aspect of economics. In the eighteenth century, Adam Smith already applied economic reasoning to political behavior. My work on human capital was very much influenced by Irving Fisher, Alfred Marshall, Milton Friedman, and Ted Schultz. Very few people's work, certainly not mine, spring out of nowhere. They have continuity with the past. What we do is try to build on the work of past economists and do a little more and a little better than what they did.

> Very few people's work, certainly not mine, spring out of nowhere. They have continuity with the past. What we do is try to build on the work of past economists and do a little more and a little better than what they did.

How would you characterize the major achievements of the economics of human behavior? What questions, for example, would have convincing answers?
The area of law and economics has been very successful in analyzing criminal behavior. Work by many lawyers and economists, particularly Judge Richard Posner and William Landes of the University of Chicago Law School, has produced

many successful applications. The question that economics of crime seeks to answer is: What determines the amount of crime that we have and how effective are various actions that governments can take in reducing the amount of crime? This analysis discusses apprehending and punishing criminals, giving better education to people who might commit crimes, reducing unemployment, and so on. They have basically said that fundamentally, the factors determining criminal behavior are not so different from the factors determining whether people become professors or not. People make choices, and these choices are conditional on their expected benefits and the cost. You can affect the number of people who decide to enter criminal activities by affecting the benefits and costs. To the extent that people make these calculations, they are more likely to enter crime when benefits are high relative to the cost.

One way to affect costs is to make it more likely that if somebody commits a crime they'll be captured, apprehended, convicted, and punished. That raises the cost and reduces crime. I think now that people accept this conclusion for most crimes.

But the economic approach is not simply a law and order approach. It also says that if you can increase the attractiveness to people of working at legal activities rather than illegal or criminal activities, you will also have less crime. One way to increase the attractiveness is to make it easier for people to find jobs and to earn more by improving their skills,

195

their education, and their training and also by improving the functioning of labor markets.

You've made a significant contribution to demographic economics. Nearly 40 years ago, you introduced the idea of children being durable goods. Can you talk about the evolution of this idea?
Demographers initially were extremely hostile to my point of view. However, I recently received the Irene Taeuber Award from the Population Association of America, their most prestigious demographic award. It was given to me in recognition of the value of the economic way of looking at demographic questions, including birth and marriage rates. Over time, the cumulative work of many economists working on population problems around the world made an impact.

The main payoffs from this work have been in our understanding of fertility. The conclusions from the economic approach are that the number of children people have is very much a function of two variables: costs and choices. Costs depend not only on how much food and shelter you give children, but also on the time of parents. In most societies, most of that time is the mother's time, which has a value. As we have become richer, and as women have become better educated and are working outside the home more, the cost to them of spending time on children has risen. As these costs have risen, families are deterred from having as many children as they had in the past. So one of the factors explaining the big decline in birth rates is the increasing costs of children.

The second variable that economists recognize is that families are making choices about the quality of children's lives in terms of their education, training, and health. In modern economies, this quality component has become very important because the emphasis in modern economies is on knowledge, technology, and skills. But there is a tradeoff. If you spend more on each child's skills, education, and training, you make children more costly and you are likely to have fewer children. Over the past 30 years, birth rates have been decreasing in most countries of the world, including India, China, parts of Asia, Latin America, some parts of Africa, Europe, and the United States.

> There are about 15 countries of the world that now have birth rates well below replacement levels. If families continue with these rates, the populations will eventually decline—and decline rapidly.

How do you respond to people who feel that explaining choices such as how many children to raise is deeply personal and that it is therefore immoral to think of children in these terms?
I think morality is misplaced in this area. We are trying to understand very major changes in the world. There are about 15 countries of the world that now have birth rates well below replacement levels. If families continue with these rates, these populations will eventually decline—and decline rapidly. This includes Germany, Italy, Spain,

Portugal, France, and Japan. It is important to understand why birth rates are going down. If this way of looking at it is a powerful tool for understanding why families have made these choices, then it would be immoral, I believe, to neglect this approach. If we are concerned about low birth rates, how can we go about raising them? Or if we want to understand what to expect in other countries that are experiencing significant economic development, we will miss out if we neglect an important set of considerations that help us to understand what's going on.

Is economics a subject that a young person can happily enter today? What are the major incentives for pursuing economics as an undergraduate?
I would certainly encourage a young person to enter economics for several reasons. There are many employment opportunities in economics, and it is also valuable if you decide to go into other areas such as the law, business, or even medicine. Economic issues, including the budget deficit, entitlement programs, minimum wages, and how to subsidize the elderly, are extremely important public policy issues.

I want also to stress that economics is a wonderful intellectual activity. To be able to take this very mysterious world we live in and to illuminate parts of it, important parts of it, through the use of economics is enormously intellectually satisfying and challenging for an undergraduate or for anybody else. So I would say it's both practical and satisfying. Who can ask for a better combination?

Chapter 10

Organizing Production

In the fall of 1990, a British scientist named Tim Berners-Lee invented the World Wide Web. This remarkable idea paved the way for the creation and growth of thousands of profitable businesses. One of these businesses is Netscape, which was founded by Marc Andreessen, the author of the now famous Navigator Web browser, and entrepreneur Jim Clark. ◆ How do Netscape and the other 20 million firms that operate in the United States make their business decisions? How do they operate efficiently? ◆ Businesses range from multinational giants, such as Microsoft, to small family restaurants and local Internet service providers. Three quarters of all firms are operated by their owners. But corporations (such as Netscape and Microsoft) account for 86 percent of all business sales. What are the different forms a firm can take? Why do some firms remain small while others become giants? Why are most firms owner-operated? ◆ Many businesses operate in a highly competitive environment and struggle to make a profit. Others, such as Microsoft, seem to have cornered the market on their products and make a large profit. What are the different types of market in which firms operate, and why is it harder to make a profit in some markets than others? ◆ Most of the components of an IBM personal computer are made by other firms. Microsoft created its Windows operating system, and Intel makes its processor chip. Other firms make hard drives and modems, and yet others make CD drives, sound cards, and so on. Why doesn't IBM make all its own computer components? Why does it leave these activities to other firms and buy from them in markets? How do firms decide what to make themselves and what to buy in the marketplace from other firms?

◆ In this chapter, we are going to learn about firms and the choices they make to cope with scarcity. We begin by studying the economic problems and choices that *all* firms face.

Spinning a Web

After studying this chapter, you will be able to:

■ Explain what a firm is and describe the economic problems that *all* firms face

■ Distinguish between technological efficiency and economic efficiency

■ Define and explain the principal-agent problem

■ Describe and distinguish between different types of business organization

■ Describe and distinguish between different types of markets in which firms operate

■ Explain why firms coordinate some economic activities and markets coordinate others

The Firm and Its Economic Problem

THE 20 MILLION FIRMS IN THE UNITED STATES differ in size and in the scope of what they do. But they all perform the same basic economic functions. Each **firm** is an institution that hires productive resources and that organizes those resources to produce and sell goods and services.

Our goal is to predict firm behavior. To do so, we need to know a firm's goals and the constraints it faces. We begin with the goals.

The Firm's Goal

If you asked a group of entrepreneurs what they are trying to achieve, you would get many different answers. Some would talk about making a quality product, others about business growth, others about market share, and others about job satisfaction of their work force. All of these goals might be pursued, but they are not the fundamental goal. They are means to a deeper goal.

A firm's goal is to *maximize profit*. A firm that does not seek to maximize profit is either eliminated or bought out by firms that do seek to maximize profit.

What exactly is the profit that a firm seeks to maximize? To answer this question, let's look at Sidney's Sweaters.

Measuring a Firm's Profit

Sidney runs a successful business that makes sweaters. Sidney's Sweaters receives $400,000 a year for the sweaters it sells. Its expenses are $80,000 a year for wool, $20,000 for utilities, $120,000 for labor, and $10,000 in interest on a bank loan. With receipts of $400,000 and expenses of $230,000, Sidney's Sweaters' annual surplus is $170,000.

Sidney's accountant lowers this number by $20,000, which he says is the depreciation (fall in value) of the firm's buildings and knitting machines during the year. (Accountants use Internal Revenue Service rules based on standards established by the Financial Accounting Standards Board to calculate the depreciation.) So the accountant reports that the profit of Sidney's Sweaters is $150,000 a year.

Sidney's accountant measures cost and profit to ensure that the firm pays the correct amount of income tax and to show the bank how its loan has been used. But we want to predict the decisions that a firm makes. These decisions respond to *opportunity cost* and *economic profit*.

Opportunity Cost

The **opportunity cost** of any action is the highest-valued alternative forgone. The action that you choose not to take—the highest-valued alternative forgone—is the cost of the action that you choose to take. For a firm, the opportunity cost of production is the value of the firm's best alternative use of its resources.

Opportunity cost is a real alternative forgone. But so that we can compare the cost of one action with that of another action, we express opportunity cost in money units. A firm's opportunity costs are:

- Explicit costs
- Implicit costs

Explicit Costs Explicit costs are paid in money. The amount paid for a resource could have been spent on something else, so it is the opportunity cost of using the resource. For Sidney, his expenditures on wool, utilities, wages, and bank interest are explicit costs.

Implicit Costs A firm incurs implicit costs when it forgoes an alternative action but does not make a payment. A firm incurs implicit costs when it:

1. Uses its own capital
2. Uses its owner's time or financial resources.

The cost of using its own capital is an implicit cost —and an opportunity cost—because the firm could rent the capital to another firm. The rental income forgone is the firm's opportunity cost of using its own capital. This opportunity cost is called the **implicit rental rate** of capital.

People rent houses, apartments, cars, telephones, and videotapes. And firms rent photocopiers, earth-moving equipment, satellite-launching services, and so on. If a firm rents capital, it incurs an *explicit* cost. If a firm buys the capital it uses, it incurs an *implicit* cost. The implicit rental rate of capital is made up of:

1. Economic depreciation
2. Interest forgone

Economic depreciation is change in the *market* value of capital over a given period. It is calculated as the market price of the capital at the beginning of the period minus its market price at the end of the period. For example, suppose that Sidney could have sold his buildings and knitting machines on December 31, 1998, for $400,000. If he can sell the same capital on December 31, 1999, for $375,000, his economic depreciation during 1999 is $25,000—the fall in the market value of the machines. This $25,000 is an implicit cost of using the capital during 1999.

The funds used to buy capital could have been used for some other purpose. And in their next best use, they would have yielded a return—an interest income. This forgone interest is part of the opportunity cost of using the capital. For example, Sidney's Sweaters could have bought government bonds instead of a knitting factory. The interest forgone on the government bonds is an implicit cost of operating the knitting factory.

Cost of Owner's Resources   A firm's owner often supplies *entrepreneurial ability*—the resource that organizes the business, makes business decisions, innovates, and bears the risk of running the business. The return to entrepreneurship is profit, and the *average* return for supplying entrepreneurial ability is called **normal profit**. Normal profit is part of a firm's opportunity cost, because it is the cost of a forgone alternative—running another firm. If normal profit in the textile business is $50,000 a year, this amount must be added to Sidney's costs to determine his opportunity cost.

The owner of a firm also can supply labor (in addition to entrepreneurship). The return to labor is a wage. And the opportunity cost of the owner's time spent working for the firm is the wage income forgone by not working in the best alternative job. Suppose that Sidney could take another job that pays $40,000 a year. By working for his knitting business and forgoing this income, Sidney incurs an opportunity cost of $40,000 a year.

Economic Profit

What is the bottom line—the profit or loss of the firm? A firm's **economic profit** is equal to its total revenue minus its opportunity cost. The firm's opportunity cost is the sum of its explicit costs and implicit costs. And the implicit costs, remember, include *normal profit*. The return to entrepreneurial ability is greater than normal

in a firm that makes a positive economic profit. And the return to entrepreneurial ability is less than normal in a firm that makes a negative economic profit—a firm that incurs an economic loss.

Economic Accounting: A Summary

Table 10.1 summarizes the economic accounting concepts that you've just studied. Sidney's Sweaters' total revenue is $400,000. Its opportunity cost is $365,000. And its economic profit is $35,000.

To achieve the objective of maximum profit—maximum economic profit—a firm must make five basic decisions:

1. What goods and services to produce and in what quantities
2. How to produce—the technology to use
3. How to organize and compensate its managers and workers
4. How to market and price its products
5. What to produce itself and what to buy from other firms

In all these decisions, a firm's actions are limited by the constraints that it faces. Our next task is to learn about these constraints.

TABLE 10.1

Economic Accounting

Item		Amount
Total revenue		**$400,000**
Opportunity Costs		
Wool	$80,000	
Utilities	20,000	
Wages paid	120,000	
Bank interest paid	10,000	
Total Explicit Costs		$230,000
Sidney's wages forgone	40,000	
Sidney's interest forgone	20,000	
Economic depreciation	25,000	
Normal profit	50,000	
Total Implicit Costs		$135,000
Total Cost		**$365,000**
Economic Profit		**$35,000**

The Firm's Constraints

Three features of its environment limit the maximum profit a firm can make. They are:

- Technology constraints
- Information constraints
- Market constraints

Technology Constraints Economists define technology broadly. A **technology** is any method of producing a good or service. Technology includes the detailed designs of machines. It also includes the layout of the workplace. And it includes the organization of the firm. For example, the shopping mall is a technology for producing retail services. It is a different technology from the catalog store, which in turn is different from the downtown store.

It might seem surprising that a firm's profits are limited by technology because technological advances are constantly increasing profit opportunities. Almost every day, we learn about some new technological advance that amazes us. With computers that speak and recognize our own speech and cars that can find the address we need in a city we've never visited before, we are able to accomplish ever more.

Technology is advancing. But at each point in time, to produce more output and gain more revenue, a firm must hire more resources and incur greater costs. The increase in profit that the firm can achieve is limited by the technology available for transforming resources into output. For example, using its current plant and work force, Ford can produce some maximum number of cars per day. To produce more cars per day, Ford must hire more resources and incur greater costs, which limits the increase in profit that Ford can make by selling the additional cars.

Information Constraints We never possess all the information we would like to have to make decisions. We lack information about both the future and the present. For example, suppose you plan to buy a new computer. When should you buy it? The answer depends on how the price is going to change in the future. Where should you buy it? The answer depends on the prices at hundreds of different computer shops. To get the best deal, you must compare the quality and prices in every shop. But the opportunity cost of this comparison exceeds the cost of the computer!

Similarly, a firm is constrained by limited information about the quality and effort of its work force,

the current and future buying plans of its customers, and the plans of its competitors. Workers slacken off when managers believe they are working hard. Customers switch to competing suppliers. Firms must compete against competition from a new firm.

Firms try to create incentive systems for workers to ensure that they work hard even when no one is monitoring their efforts. And firms spend millions of dollars on market research. But none of these efforts and expenditures eliminates the problems of incomplete information and uncertainty. And the cost of coping with limited information itself limits profit.

Market Constraints What each firm can sell and the price it can obtain are constrained by the willingness to pay of its customers and by the prices and marketing efforts of other firms. Similarly, the resources that each firm can buy and the prices it must pay are limited by the willingness of people to work for and invest in the firm. Firms spend billions of dollars a year marketing and selling their products. Some of the most creative minds strive to find the right message that will produce a knockout television advertisement. Market constraints and the expenditures firms make to overcome them limit the profit a firm can make.

R E V I E W   Q U I Z

- Why do firms seek to maximize profit? What happens to firms that don't pursue this goal?
- Why do accountants and economists calculate a firm's cost and profit in different ways?
- What are the items that make opportunity cost depart from the accountant's measure of cost?
- Why is normal profit an opportunity cost?
- What are the three types of constraint that firms face? How does each constraint limit the profit that a firm can make?

In the rest of this chapter and in Chapters 11 through 14, we study the decisions that firms make. We're going to learn how we can predict a firm's behavior as the response to the constraints that it faces and to changes in those constraints. We begin by taking a closer look at the technology constraints, information constraints, and market constraints that firms face.

Technology and Economic Efficiency

MICROSOFT EMPLOYS A LARGE WORK FORCE. AND most Microsoft workers possess a large amount of human capital, but the firm uses a small amount of physical capital. In contrast, a coal-mining company employs a huge amount of mining equipment (physical capital) and almost no labor. Why? The answer lies in the concept of efficiency. There are two concepts of production efficiency: technological efficiency and economic efficiency. **Technological efficiency** occurs when the firm produces a given output by using the least inputs. **Economic efficiency** occurs when the firm produces a given output at least cost. Let's explore the two concepts of efficiency by studying an example.

Suppose that there are four alternative techniques for making TV sets:

a. *Robot production.* One person monitors the entire computer-driven process.

b. *Production line.* Workers specialize in a small part of the job as the emerging TV set passes them on a production line.

c. *Bench production.* Workers specialize in a small part of the job but walk from bench to bench to perform their tasks.

d. *Hand-tool production.* A single worker uses a few hand tools to make a TV set.

Table 10.2 sets out the amounts of labor and capital that each of these four methods require to make 10 TV sets a day. Which of these alternative methods are technologically efficient?

Technological Efficiency

Recall that technological efficiency occurs when the firm produces a given output by using the least inputs. Inspect the numbers in the table and notice that method *a* uses the most capital but the least labor. Method *d* uses the most labor but the least capital. Methods *b* and *c* lie between the two extremes. They use less capital but more labor than method *a* and less labor but more capital than method *d*. Compare methods *b* and *c*. Method *c* requires 100 workers and 10 units of capital to produce 10 TV sets. Those same 10 TV sets can be produced by method *b* with 10 workers and the same 10 units of capital. Because method *c* uses the same amount of capital and more labor than method *b*, method *c* is not technologically efficient.

Are any of the other methods not technologically efficient? The answer is no. Each of the other methods is technologically efficient. Method *a* uses more capital but less labor than method *b*, and method *d* uses more labor but less capital than method *b*.

Which of the methods are economically efficient?

Economic Efficiency

Recall that economic efficiency occurs when the firm produces a given output at least cost. Suppose that labor costs $75 per person-day and that capital costs $250 per machine-day. Table 10.3(a) calculates the costs of using the different methods. By inspecting the table, you can see that method *b* has the lowest cost. Although method *a* uses less labor, it uses too much expensive capital. And although method *d* uses less capital, it uses too much expensive labor.

Method *c*, which is technologically inefficient, is also economically inefficient. It uses the same amount of capital as method *b* but 10 times as much labor, so it costs more. A technologically inefficient method is never economically efficient.

Although *b* is the economically efficient method in this example, method *a* or *d* could be economically efficient with different input prices.

First, suppose that labor costs $150 a person-day and capital costs only $1 a machine-day. Table 10.3(b)

TABLE 10.2

Four Ways of Making 10 TV Sets a Day

		Quantities of inputs	
	Method	Labor	Capital
a	Robot production	1	1,000
b	Production line	10	10
c	Bench production	100	10
d	Hand-tool production	1,000	1

TABLE 10.3
The Costs of Different Ways of Making 10 TV Sets a Day

(a) Four ways of making TVs

Method	Labor cost ($75 per day)		Capital cost ($250 per day)		Total cost	Cost per TV set
a	$75	+	$250,000	=	$250,075	$25,007.50
b	750	+	2,500	=	3,250	325.00
c	7,500	+	2,500	=	10,000	1,000.00
d	75,000	+	250	=	75,250	7,525.00

(b) Three ways of making TVs: High labor costs

Method	Labor cost ($150 per day)		Capital cost ($1,000 per day)		Total cost	Cost per TV set
a	$150	+	$1,000	=	$1,150	$115.00
b	1,500	+	10	=	1,510	151.00
d	150,000	+	1	=	150,001	15,000.10

(c) Three ways of making TVs: High capital costs

Method	Labor cost ($1 per day)		Capital cost ($1,000 per day)		Total cost	Cost per TV set
a	$1	+	$1,000,000	=	$1,000,001	$100,000.10
b	10	+	10,000	=	10,010	1,001.00
d	1,000	+	1,000	=	2,000	200.00

now shows the costs of making a TV set. In this case, method *a* is economically efficient. Capital is now so cheap relative to labor that the method that uses the most capital is the economically efficient method.

Second, suppose that labor costs only $1 a person-day while capital costs $1,000 a machine-day. Table 10.3(c) shows the costs in this case. Method *d*, which uses a lot of labor and little capital, is now the least-cost method and economically efficient method.

From these examples, you can see that while technological efficiency depends only on what is feasible, economic efficiency depends on the relative costs of resources. The economically efficient method is the one that uses the smaller amount of a more expensive resource and a larger amount of a less expensive resource.

A firm that is economically efficient maximizes profit. Natural selection favors efficient firms and opposes inefficient firms. Inefficient firms go out of business or are taken over by firms that lower costs. Profit-maximizing firms are better able to survive temporary adversity than are inefficient ones.

REVIEW QUIZ

- How do we define technological efficiency? Is a firm technologically efficient if it uses the latest technology? Why?
- How do we define economic efficiency? Is a firm economically inefficient if it can cut costs by producing less? Why?
- Explain the key distinction between technological efficiency and economic efficiency.
- Why do some firms use large amounts of capital and small amounts of labor while others use small amounts of capital and large amounts of labor?

You've now seen how the technology constraints that a firm faces influence the amounts of capital and labor that it employs. Next we study information constraints and the diversity of organization structures they generate.

Information and Organization

EACH FIRM ORGANIZES THE PRODUCTION OF goods and services by combining and coordinating the productive resources it hires. But there is variety across firms in how they organize production. Firms use a mixture of two systems:

- Command systems
- Incentive systems

Command Systems

A **command system** is a method of organizing production that uses a managerial hierarchy. Commands pass downward through the managerial hierarchy, and information passes upward. Managers spend most of their time collecting and processing information about the performance of the people under their control and making decisions about commands to issue and how best to get those commands implemented.

The military uses the purest form of command system. A commander-in-chief (in the United States, the President) makes the big decisions about strategic objectives. Beneath this highest level, generals organize their military resources. Beneath the generals, successively lower ranks organize smaller and smaller units but pay attention to ever increasing degrees of detail. At the bottom of the managerial hierarchy are the people who operate weapons systems.

Command systems in firms are not as rigid as they are in the military. But they share some similar features. A chief executive officer (CEO) sits at the top of a firm's command system. Senior executives who report to and receive commands from the CEO specialize in managing production, marketing, finance, personnel, and perhaps other aspects of the firm's operations. Beneath these senior managers might be several tiers of middle management ranks that stretch downward to the managers who supervise the day-to-day operations of the business. Beneath these managers are the people who operate the firm's machines and who make and sell goods and services.

Small firms have one or two layers of managers, while large firms have several layers. As production processes have become ever more complex, management ranks have swollen. Today, more people have management jobs than ever before. But the information revolution of the 1990s slowed the growth of management, and in some industries, it decreased the number of layers of managers and brought a shakeout of middle managers.

Managers make enormous efforts to be well informed. And they try hard to make good decisions and to issue commands that end up using resources efficiently. But managers always have incomplete information about what is happening in the divisions of the firm for which they are responsible. It is for this reason that firms use incentive systems as well as command systems to organize production.

Incentive Systems

An **incentive system** is a method of organizing production that uses a market-like mechanism inside the firm. Instead of issuing commands, senior managers create compensation schemes that will induce workers to perform in ways that maximize the firm's profit.

Selling organizations use incentive systems most extensively. Sales representatives who spend most of their working time alone and unsupervised are induced to work hard by being paid a small salary and a large performance-related bonus.

But incentive systems operate at all levels in a firm. A CEO's compensation plan includes a share in the firm's profit, and factory floor workers sometimes receive compensation based on the quantity they produce.

Mixing the Systems

Firms use a mixture of commands and incentives, and they choose the mixture to maximize profit. They use commands when it is easy to monitor performance or when a small deviation from an ideal performance is very costly. They use incentives when monitoring performance is either not possible or too costly to be worth doing.

For example, it is easy and not very costly to monitor the performance of workers on a production line. And if one person works too slowly, the entire line slows. So a production line is organized with a command system.

In contrast, it is costly to monitor a CEO. What, for example, did John Sculley (a former president of Apple Computer) contribute to the success and subsequent problems faced by Apple? This question cannot be answered with certainty, yet Apple must put someone in charge of operations and provide this person the *incentive* to be efficient. Incentives and the contracts that create them are an attempt to cope with a general problem called the principal-agent problem.

The Principal-Agent Problem

The **principal-agent problem** is the problem of devising compensation rules that induce an *agent* to act in the best interest of a *principal*. For example, the stockholders of Chase Manhattan Bank are *principals*, and the bank's managers are *agents*. The stockholders (the principals) must induce the managers (agents) to act in the stockholders' best interest. Similarly, Bill Gates (a principal) must induce the programmers developing Windows 2000 (agents) to work efficiently.

Agents, whether they are managers or workers, pursue their own goals and often impose costs on a principal. For example, the goal of a stockholder of the Chase Manhattan (a principal) is to maximize the bank's profit. But the bank's profit depends on the actions of its managers (agents) who have their own goals. Perhaps a manager takes a customer to a ball game on the pretense that she is building customer loyalty, when in fact she is simply taking on-the-job leisure. This same manager is also a principal, and her tellers are agents. The manager wants the tellers to work hard and attract new customers so that she can meet her operating targets. But the tellers enjoy conversations with each other and keep customers waiting in line. Nonetheless, the bank constantly strives to find ways of improving performance and increasing profits.

Coping with the Principal-Agent Problem

Issuing commands does not address the principal-agent problem. In most firms, the shareholders can't monitor the managers and often the managers can't monitor the workers. Each principal must create incentives that induce each agent to work in the interests of the principal. Three ways of attempting to cope with the principal-agent problem are:

- Ownership
- Incentive pay
- Long-term contracts

Ownership By assigning ownership (or part-ownership) of a business to the manager or workers, the principal can sometimes induce a job performance that increases the firm's profits. Part-ownership schemes for senior managers are quite common, but they are less common for workers. When United Airlines ran into problems a few years ago, it made all its employees owners of the company.

Incentive Pay Incentive pay schemes—pay related to performance—are very common. They are based on a variety of performance criteria such as profits or production or sales targets. Promoting an employee for good performance is another example of an incentive pay scheme.

Long-term Contracts Long-term contracts tie the long-term fortunes of managers and workers (agents) to the success of the principal(s)—the owner(s) of the firm. For example, a multiyear employment contract for a CEO encourages that person to take a long-term view and devise strategies that achieve maximum profit over a sustained period.

These three ways of coping with the principal-agent problem give rise to different types of business organization. Each type of business organization is a different response to the principal-agent problem. Each uses ownership, incentives, and long-term contracts in different ways. Let's look at the main types of business organization.

Types of Business Organization

The three main types of business organization are:

- Proprietorship
- Partnership
- Corporation

Proprietorship A *proprietorship* is a firm with a single owner—a proprietor—who has unlimited liability. *Unlimited liability* is the legal responsibility for all the debts of a firm up to an amount equal to the entire wealth of the owner. If a proprietorship cannot pay its debts, those to whom the firm owes money can claim the personal property of the owner. Corner stores, computer programmers, and artists are all examples of proprietorships.

The proprietor makes management decisions, receives the firm's profits, and is responsible for its losses. Profits from a proprietorship are taxed at the same rate as other sources of the proprietor's personal income.

Partnership A *partnership* is a firm with two or more owners who have unlimited liability. Partners must agree on an appropriate management structure and on how to divide the firm's profits among themselves. The profits of a partnership are taxed as the personal income of the owners. But each partner is legally liable for all the debts of the partnership (limited only by the wealth of an individual partner). Liability for the full debts of the partnership is called *joint unlimited liability*. Most law firms are partnerships.

Corporation A *corporation* is a firm owned by one or more limited liability stockholders. *Limited liability* means that the owners have legal liability only for the value of their initial investment. This limitation of liability means that if the corporation becomes bankrupt, its owners are not required to use their personal wealth to pay the corporation's debts.

Corporation profits are taxed independently of stockholders' incomes. Because stockholders pay taxes on the income they receive as dividends on stocks,

corporate profits are taxed twice. The stockholders also pay capital gains tax on the profit they earn by selling a stock for a higher price than they paid for it. Corporate stocks generate capital gains when a corporation retains some of its profit and reinvests it in profitable activities. So even retained earnings are taxed twice because the capital gains they generate are taxed.

Pros and Cons of Different Types of Firms

The different types of business organization arise as different ways of trying to cope with the principal-agent problem. Each has advantages in particular situations. And because of its special advantages, each type continues to exist. Each type also has its disadvantages, which explain why it has not driven out the other two.

Table 10.4 summarizes these pros and cons of the different types of firm.

TABLE 10.4

Pros and Cons of Different Types of Firms

Proprietorship	■ Easy to set up	■ Bad decisions not checked by need for consensus
	■ Simple decision making	■ Owner's entire wealth at risk
	■ Profits taxed only once as owner's income	■ Firm dies with owner
		■ Capital is expensive
		■ Labor is expensive
Partnership	■ Easy to set up	■ Achieving consensus may be slow and expensive
	■ Diversified decision making	■ Owners' entire wealth at risk
	■ Can survive withdrawal of partner	■ Withdrawal of partner may create capital shortage
	■ Profits taxed only once as owners' incomes	■ Capital is expensive
Corporation	■ Owners have limited liability	■ Complex management structure can make decisions slow and expensive
	■ Large-scale, low-cost capital available	■ Profits taxed twice as company profit and as stockholders' income
	■ Professional management not restricted by ability of owners	
	■ Perpetual life	
	■ Long-term labor contracts cut labor costs	

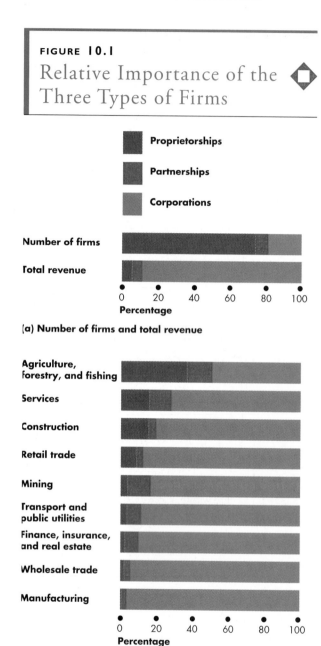

FIGURE 10.1

Relative Importance of the Three Types of Firms

(a) Number of firms and total revenue

(b) Total revenue in various industries

Three quarters of all firms are proprietorships, almost one fifth are corporations, and only one twentieth are partnerships. Corporations account for 89 percent of business revenue (part a). But proprietorships and partnerships account for a significant percentage of business revenue in some industries (part b).

Source: U.S. Bureau of the Census *Statistical Abstract of the United States: 1998*, 118th ed. (Washington, DC: 1998): Tables 855, 856, and 1103.

Relative Importance of Different Types of Firms

Figure 10.1(a) shows the relative importance of the three main types of firms in the U.S. economy. The figure also shows that the revenue of corporations is much larger than that of the other types of firms. Although only 19 percent of all firms are corporations, they generate 89 percent of revenue.

Figure 10.1(b) shows the percentage of revenue generated by the different types of firms in various industries. Proprietorships in agriculture, forestry, and fishing generate about 36 percent of the total revenue in those sectors. Proprietorships in the service sector, construction, and retail trades also generate a large percentage of total revenue. Partnerships in agriculture, forestry, and fishing generate about 14 percent of total revenue. Partnerships are more prominent in services; mining; and finance, insurance, and real estate than in other sectors. Corporations are important in all sectors, and in manufacturing, corporations have the field almost to themselves.

Why do corporations dominate the business scene? Why do the other types of business survive? And why are proprietorships and partnerships more prominent in some sectors? The answers to these questions lie in the pros and cons of the different types of business organization that are summarized in Table 10.4. Corporations dominate where a large amount of capital is used. But proprietorships dominate where flexibility in decision making is critical.

REVIEW QUIZ

- Explain the distinction between a command system and an incentive system.
- What is the principal-agent problem and what are the three ways in which firms try to cope with it?
- What are the three types of firm? Explain the major advantages and disadvantages of each type.
- Why do all three types of firm survive and in which sectors are the three types most prominent?

You've now seen how technology constraints influence a firm's use of capital and labor and how information constraints influence a firm's organization. We'll now look at market constraints and see how they influence the environment in which firms compete for business.

Markets and the Competitive Environment

THE MARKETS IN WHICH FIRMS OPERATE VARY A great deal. Some are highly competitive, with profits hard to come by. Some appear to be almost free from competition and have firms that earn large profits. Some markets are dominated by fierce advertising campaigns in which each firm seeks to persuade buyers that it has the best products. And some markets display a warlike character.

Economists identify four market types:

1. Perfect competition
2. Monopolistic competition
3. Oligopoly
4. Monopoly

Perfect competition arises when there are many firms, each selling an identical product; many buyers; and no restrictions on the entry of new firms into the industry. The many firms and buyers are all well informed about the prices of the products of each firm in the industry. The worldwide markets for corn, rice, and other grain crops are examples of perfect competition.

Monopolistic competition is a market structure in which a large number of firms compete by making similar but slightly different products. Making a product slightly different from the product of a competing firm is called **product differentiation**. Product differentiation gives a monopolistically competitive firm an element of monopoly power. The firm is the sole producer of the particular version of the good in question. For example, in the market for running shoes, Nike, Reebok, Fila, and Asics all make their own version of the perfect shoe. Each of these firms has a monopoly on a particular brand of shoe. Differentiated products are not necessarily different products. What matters is that consumers *perceive* them to be different. For example, various brands of aspirin are chemically identical (salicylic acid) and differ only in their packaging.

Oligopoly is a market structure in which a small number of firms compete. Computer software, airplane manufacture, and international air transportation are examples of oligopolistic industries. Oligopolies might produce almost identical products, such as the colas produced by Coke and Pepsi. Or they might produce differentiated products such as Chevrolet's Lumina and Ford's Taurus.

A **monopoly** is an industry that produces a good or service for which no close substitute exists and in which there is one supplier that is protected from competition by a barrier preventing the entry of new firms. In some places, the phone, gas, electricity, and water suppliers are local monopolies—monopolies that are restricted to a given location. Microsoft Corporation, the software developer that created Windows, the operating system used by PCs, is an example of a global monopoly.

Perfect competition is the most extreme form of competition. Monopoly is the most extreme absence of competition. The other two market types fall between these extremes.

Many factors must be taken into account to determine which market structure describes a particular real-world market. One of these factors is the extent to which the market is dominated by a small number of firms. To measure this feature of a market, economists use indexes called measures of concentration. Let's look at these measures.

Measures of Concentration

Economists use two measures of concentration:

1. The four-firm concentration ratio
2. The Herfindahl-Hirschman Index

The Four-Firm Concentration Ratio The **four-firm concentration ratio** is the percentage of the value of sales accounted for by the four largest firms in an industry. The range of the concentration ratio is from almost zero for perfect competition to 100 percent for monopoly. This ratio is the main measure used to assess market structure.

Table 10.5 shows two calculations of the four-firm concentration ratio, one for tires and one for printing. In this example, 14 firms produce tires. The largest four have 80 percent of the sales, so the four-firm concentration ratio is 80 percent. In the printing industry, with 1,004 firms, the largest four firms have only 0.5 percent of the sales, so the four-firm concentration ratio is 0.5 percent.

A low concentration ratio indicates a high degree of competition, and a high concentration ratio indicates an absence of competition. A monopoly has a concentration ratio of 100 percent—the largest (and only) firm has 100 percent of the sales. A four-firm concentration ratio that exceeds 60 percent is regarded as an indication of a market that is highly concentrated and dominated by a few firms in an oligopoly. A ratio of less than 40 percent is regarded as an indication of a competitive market.

The Herfindahl-Hirschman Index The **Herfindahl-Hirschman Index**—also called the HHI—is the square of the percentage market share of each firm summed over the largest 50 firms (or summed over all the firms if there are fewer than 50) in a market. For example, if there are four firms in a market and the market shares of the firms are 50 percent, 25 percent, 15 percent, and 10 percent, the Herfindahl-Hirschman Index is

$$\text{HHI} = 50^2 + 25^2 + 15^2 + 10^2 = 3{,}450.$$

In perfect competition, the HHI is small. For example, if each of the largest 50 firms in an industry

TABLE 10.5

Concentration Ratio Calculations

Tiremakers		Printers	
Firm	**Sales** (millions of dollars)	**Firm**	**Sales** (millions of dollars)
Top, Inc.	200	Fran's	2.5
ABC, Inc.	250	Ned's	2.0
Big, Inc.	150	Tom's	1.8
XYZ, Inc.	100	Jill's	1.7
Largest 4 firms	700	Largest 4 firms	8.0
Other 10 firms	175	Other 1,000 firms	1,592.0
Industry	875	Industry	1,600.0

Four-firm concentration ratios:

Tiremakers: $\dfrac{700}{875} \times 100 = 80\%$

Printers: $\dfrac{8}{1{,}600} \times 100 = 0.5\%$

has a market share of 0.1 percent, the HHI is $0.1^2 \times 50 = 0.5$. In a monopoly, the HHI is 10,000—the firm has 100 percent of the market: $100^2 = 10,000$.

The HHI became a popular measure of the degree of competition during the 1980s, when the Federal Trade Commission (FTC) used it to classify markets. A market in which the HHI is less than 1,000 is regarded as being competitive. A market in which the HHI lies between 1,000 and 1,800 is regarded as being moderately competitive. But a market in which the HHI exceeds 1,800 is regarded as being uncompetitive. The FTC scrutinizes any merger of firms in a market in which the HHI exceeds 1,000 and is likely to challenge a merger if the HHI exceeds 1,800.

Concentration Measures for the U.S. Economy

Figure 10.2 shows a selection of concentration ratios and HHIs for the United States calculated by the Department of Commerce.

Industries that produce chewing gum, household laundry equipment, light bulbs, breakfast cereals, and motor vehicles have a high degree of concentration and are oligopolies. The milk, ice cream, and commercial printing industries have low concentration measures and are highly competitive. Industries that produce pet food and cookies and crackers are moderately concentrated. These industries are examples of monopolistic competition.

Concentration measures are a useful indicator of the degree of competition in a market. But they must be supplemented by other information to determine a market's structure. Table 10.6 summarizes the range of other information along with the measures of concentration that determine which market structure describes a particular real-world market.

Limitations of Concentration Measures

The three main limitations of concentration measures alone as determinants of market structure are their failure to take proper account of:

■ The geographical scope of the market

■ Barriers to entry and firm turnover

■ The correspondence between a market and an industry

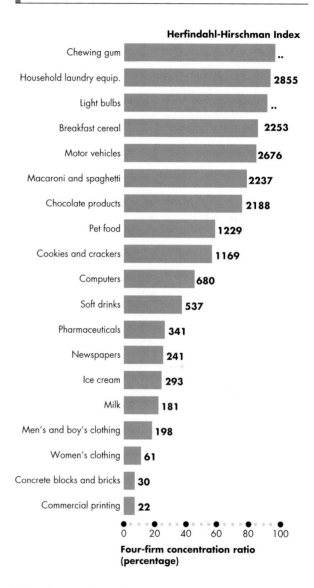

FIGURE 10.2

Concentration Measures in the United States

The industries that produce chewing gum, household laundry equipment, light bulbs, and motor vehicles are highly concentrated, while those that produce milk, ice cream, and commercial printing are highly competitive. The industries that produce pet foods and cookies and crackers have an intermediate degree of concentration.

Source: U.S. Department of Commerce, *Concentration Ratios in Manufacturing,* Washington D.C., 1996.

TABLE 10.6

Market Structure

Characteristics	Perfect competition	Monopolistic competition	Oligopoly	Monopoly
Number of firms in industry	Many	Many	Few	One
Product	Identical	Differentiated	Either identical or differentiated	No close substitutes
Barriers to entry	None	None	Moderate	High
Firm's control over price	None	Some	Considerable	Considerable or regulated
Concentration ratio	0	Low	High	100
HHI (approx. ranges)	Less than 100	101 to 999	More than 1,000	10,000
Examples	Wheat, corn	Food, clothing	Automobiles, cereals	Local water supply

---

Geographical Scope of Market Concentration measures take a national view of the market. Many goods are sold in a *national* market, but some are sold in a *regional* market and some in a *global* one. The newspaper industry consists of local markets. The concentration measures for newspapers are low, but there is a high degree of concentration in the newspaper industry in most cities. The auto industry has a global market. The biggest three U.S. car producers account for 92 percent of cars sold by U.S. producers, but they account for a smaller percentage of the total U.S. car market (including imports) and a smaller percentage of the global market for cars.

Barriers to Entry and Turnover Concentration measures don't measure barriers to entry. Some industries are highly concentrated but have easy entry and an enormous amount of turnover of firms. For example, many small towns have few restaurants but there are no restrictions on opening a restaurant and many firms attempt to do so.

Also, an industry might be competitive because of *potential entry*—because a few firms in a market face competition from many firms that can easily enter the market and will do so if economic profits are available.

Market and Industry To calculate concentration ratios, the Department of Commerce classifies each firm as being in a particular industry. But markets do not always correspond closely to industries for three reasons: First, markets are often narrower than industries. For example, the pharmaceutical industry, which has a low concentration ratio, operates in many separate markets for individual products—for example, measles vaccine and AIDS fighting drugs. These drugs do not compete with each other, so this industry, which looks competitive, includes firms that are monopolies (or near monopolies) in markets for individual drugs.

Second, most firms make several products. For example, Westinghouse makes electrical equipment and, among other things, gas-fired incinerators and plywood. So this one firm operates in at least three separate markets. But the Department of Commerce classifies Westinghouse as being in the electrical goods and equipment industry. The fact that Westinghouse competes with other producers of plywood does not show up in the concentration numbers for the plywood market.

Third, firms switch from one market to another depending on profit opportunities. For example, Motorola, which today produces cellular telephones and other communications products, has diversified from being a TV and computer chip maker. Motorola produces no TVs today. Publishers of newspapers, magazines, and textbooks are today rapidly diversifying into Internet and multimedia products. These switches among industries show that there is much scope for entering and exiting an industry and so measures of concentration have limited usefulness.

Despite their limitations, concentration measures do provide a basis for determining the degree of competition in an industry when they are combined with information about the geographical scope of the market, barriers to entry, and the extent to which large, multiproduct firms straddle a variety of markets.

FIGURE 10.3
The Market Structure of the U.S. Economy

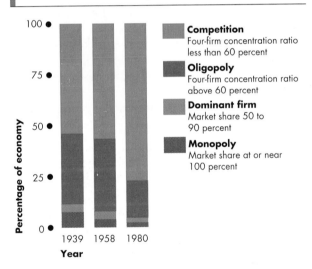

Three quarters of the U.S. economy is effectively competitive (perfect competition or monopolistic competition), one fifth is oligopoly, and the rest is monopoly. The economy became more competitive between 1939 and 1980. (Professor Shepherd, whose 1982 study remains the latest word on this topic, suspects that although some industries have become more concentrated, others have become less concentrated, so the net picture has probably not changed much since 1980.)

Source: William G. Shepherd, "Causes of Increased Competition in the U.S. Economy, 1939–1980," *Review of Economics and Statistics,* November 1982, pp. 613–626.

Market Structures in the U.S. Economy

How competitive are the markets of the United States? Do most U.S. firms operate in competitive markets or in markets with monopoly elements?

Figure 10.3 provides part of the answer to these questions. It shows the market structure of the U.S. economy and the trends in market structure between 1939 and 1980. (Unfortunately, comparable data for the 1980s and 1990s are not available.)

In 1980, three quarters of the value of goods and services bought and sold in the United States was traded in markets that are essentially competitive—markets that have almost perfect competition or monopolistic competition. Monopoly and the dominance of a single firm accounted for about 5 percent of sales. Oligopoly, which is found mainly in manufacturing, accounted for about 18 percent of sales.

Over the period covered by the data in Fig. 10.3, the U.S. economy became increasingly competitive. You can see that the competitive markets have expanded most (the blue areas) and the oligopoly markets have shrunk most (the red areas).

But also, during the past decade, the U.S. economy has become much more exposed to competition from the rest of the world. Figure 10.3 does not capture this international competition.

R E V I E W   Q U I Z

- What are the four market types? Explain the distinguishing characteristics of each.
- What are the two measures of concentration? Explain how each measure is calculated.
- Under what conditions do the measures of concentration give a good indication of the degree of competition in a market?
- Is our economy competitive? Is it becoming more competitive or less competitive?

You now know the variety of market structures in our economy and you know how we classify different types of firms and industries into these market types. Our final question in this chapter is what determines the things that firms decide to buy from other firms rather than produce for themselves?

Firms and Markets

AT THE BEGINNING OF THIS CHAPTER, WE DEFINED a firm as an institution that hires productive resources and organizes them to produce and sell goods and services. To organize production, firms coordinate the economic decisions and activities of many individuals. But firms are not the only coordinators of economic decisions. You learned in Chapter 4 that markets also coordinate decisions. By adjusting prices, markets make the decisions of buyers and sellers consistent—make the quantities demanded equal to the quantities supplied for different goods and services.

Markets can coordinate production. An example of market coordination versus firm coordination is the production of a rock concert. A promoter hires a stadium, some stage equipment, audio and video recording engineers and technicians, some rock groups, a superstar, a publicity agent, and a ticket agent—all market transactions—and sells tickets to thousands of rock fans, audio rights to a recording company, and video and broadcasting rights to a television network—another set of market transactions. If rock concerts were produced like corn flakes, the firm producing them would own all the capital used (stadiums, stage, sound and video equipment) and would employ all the labor needed (singers, engineers, salespeople, and so on).

Another example of market coordination versus firm coordination is *outsourcing*. A firm uses outsourcing when it buys parts or products from another firm rather than making them itself. The major automakers use outsourcing for windshields and windows, gearboxes, tires, and many other car parts.

What determines whether a firm or markets coordinate a particular set of activities? How does a firm decide whether to buy from another firm or to make an item itself? The answer is cost. Taking account of the opportunity cost of time as well as the costs of the other inputs, people use the method that costs least. In other words, they use the economically efficient method.

Firms coordinate economic activity when they can perform a task more efficiently than markets can. In such a situation, it is profitable to set up a firm. If markets can perform a task more efficiently than a firm can, people will use markets and any attempt to set up a firm to replace such market coordination will be doomed to failure.

Why Firms?

There are four key reasons why, in many instances, firms are more efficient than markets as coordinators of economic activity. Firms can achieve:

- Lower transactions costs
- Economies of scale
- Economies of scope
- Economies of team production

Transactions Costs The idea that firms exist because there are activities in which they are more efficient than markets was first suggested by University of Chicago economist and Nobel Laureate Ronald Coase. Coase focused on the firm's ability to reduce or eliminate transactions costs. **Transactions costs** are the costs arising from finding someone with whom to do business, of reaching an agreement about the price and other aspects of the exchange, and of ensuring that the terms of the agreement are fulfilled. *Market* transactions require buyers and sellers to get together and to negotiate the terms and conditions of their trading. Sometimes, lawyers have to be hired to draw up contracts. A broken contract leads to still more expenses. A *firm* can lower such transactions costs by reducing the number of individual transactions undertaken.

Consider, for example, two ways of getting your creaking car fixed.

Firm coordination: You take the car to the garage. The garage owner coordinates parts and tools as well as the mechanic's time, and your car gets fixed. You pay one bill for the entire job.

Market coordination: You hire a mechanic who diagnoses the problems and makes a list of the parts and tools needed to fix them. You buy the parts from the local wrecker's yard and rent the tools from ABC Rentals. You hire the mechanic again to fix the problems. You return the tools and pay your bills—wages to the mechanic, rental to ABC, and the cost of the parts used to the wrecker.

What determines the method that you use? The answer is cost. Taking account of the opportunity cost of your own time as well as the costs of the other inputs that you would have to buy, you will use the method that costs least. In other words, you will use the economically efficient method.

The first method requires that you undertake only one transaction with one firm. It's true that the firm has to undertake several transactions—hiring the labor and buying the parts and tools required to do the job. But the firm doesn't have to undertake those transactions simply to fix your car. One set of such transactions enables the firm to fix hundreds of cars. Thus there is an enormous reduction in the number of individual transactions that take place if people get their cars fixed at the garage rather than going through an elaborate sequence of market transactions.

Economies of Scale When the cost of producing a unit of a good falls as its output rate increases, economies of scale exist. Car makers, for example, experience economies of scale because as the scale of production increases, the firm can use cost-saving equipment and highly specialized labor. A car maker that produces only a few cars a year must use costly hand-tool methods. Economies of scale arise from specialization and the division of labor that can be reaped more effectively by firm coordination rather than market coordination.

Economies of Scope A firm experiences **economies of scope** when it uses specialized (and often expensive) resources to produce a *range of goods and services*. For example, Microsoft hires specialist programmers, designers, and marketing experts and uses their skills across a range of software products. As a result, Microsoft coordinates the resources that produce software at a lower cost than an individual can who buys all these services in markets.

Economies of Team Production A production process in which the individuals in a group specialize in mutually supportive tasks is *team production*. Sport provides the best example of team activity. Some team members specialize in pitching and some in batting, some in defense and some in offense. The production of goods and services offers many examples of team activity. For example, production lines in car and TV-manufacturing plants work most efficiently when individual activity is organized in teams, each specializing in a small task. You can also think of an entire firm as being a team. The team has buyers of raw material and other inputs, production workers, and salespeople. There are even specialists within these various groups. Each individual member of the team specializes, but the value of the output of the team and the profit that it earns depend on the coordinated activities of all the team's members. The idea that firms arise as a consequence of the economies of team production was first suggested by Armen Alchian and Harold Demsetz of the University of California at Los Angeles.

Because firms can economize on transactions costs, reap economies of scale, and organize efficient team production, it is firms rather than markets that coordinate most economic activity. But there are limits to the economic efficiency of firms. If a firm becomes too big or too diversified in the things that it seeks to do, the cost of management and monitoring per unit of output begins to rise, and at some point, the market becomes more efficient at coordinating the use of resources. IBM is an example of a firm that became too big to be efficient. In an attempt to restore efficient operations, IBM split up its large organization into a number of "Baby Blues," each of which specializes in a segment of the computer market.

Sometimes, firms enter into long-term relationships with each other that effectively cut out ordinary market transactions and make it difficult to see where one firm ends and another begins. For example, GM has long-term relationships with suppliers of windows, tires, and other parts. Wal-Mart has long-term relationships with suppliers of the goods it sells in its stores. Such relationships make transactions costs lower than they would be if GM or Wal-Mart went shopping on the open market each time it wanted new supplies.

R E V I E W   Q U I Z

- What are the two ways in which economic activity can be coordinated?
- What determines whether a firm or markets coordinate production?
- What are the main reasons why firms can often coordinate production at a lower cost than markets?

Reading Between the Lines on pp. 214–215 explores the economic problem faced by Levi Strauss, the firm that produces denim jeans. We continue to study firms and their decisions in the next four chapters. In Chapter 11, we learn about the relationships between cost and output at different output levels. These cost-output relationships are common to all types of firms in all types of markets. We then turn to problems that are special to firms in different types of markets—perfect competition in Chapter 12, monopoly in Chapter 13, and monopolistic competition and oligopoly in Chapter 14.

Levi Strauss's Economic Problem

THE WALL STREET JOURNAL, FEBRUARY 23, 1999

Levi Strauss to Close One-Half of Plants in North America, Cut Staff in Area

BY REBECCA QUICK

Taking the ax to its operations for the second time in just over a year, Levi Strauss and Co. said it will close half of its 22 manufacturing plants in North America, laying off about 5,900 employees, or 30% of its total in the U.S. and Canada. ...

The ... denim empire has seen sales of its pioneering jeans shrink, caught in a market squeeze between trendy, expensive jeans from designers like Ralph Lauren, and cheaper brands from department stores like J.C. Penney. Since 1990, Levi's market share of men's jeans dropped to 25% from 48%, according to Tactical Retail Solutions, a market-research firm in New York. And last week, Levi Strauss said its sales slumped 13% in 1998, to $6 billion from $6.9 billion a year earlier. ...

But the company said the latest round of closings wouldn't lower its production because it intends to shift much of the work to independent contractors in other countries. Many of Levi Strauss's competitors, including Guess and Tommy Hilfiger, have most if not all of their jeans produced overseas. There, labor costs are frequently much lower than the $10.12 an hour in wages and benefits paid to the average U.S. garment worker.

Aside from chopping its labor bills, Levi Strauss said it will also be able to reduce the time it takes to get apparel into stores. "The drawback to owning your own plant is that changing the line a plant produces is very time- and cost-consuming," said Clarence Grebey, a spokesman for Levi Strauss. "If we go to contractors to do that, we can get our consumers into the product more quickly." ...

Essence of the Story

■ Since 1990, Levi Strauss and Company's share of the market for men's jeans has shrunk from 48 percent to 25 percent as the market shares of designer and department store brands have expanded.

■ Most of Levi's competitors produce their jeans overseas, where labor costs are lower than those in the United States.

■ Levi plans to cut production in North America and transfer the work to independent contractors in other countries.

■ Beside cutting labor costs, Levi says that it can get its products into stores more quickly from contractors than from its own plants.

■ Figure 1 shows how Levi Strauss's market share has shrunk from 48 percent to 25 percent, squeezed by designer brands (such as Calvin Klein, Tommy Hilfiger, Mossimo, Ralph Lauren, and Donna Karan) and other brands (such as Lee, Wrangler, and The Gap) and store brands (such as J.C. Penney and Sears).

■ The predicament faced by Levi Strauss illustrates all the aspects of the firm and its economic problem as described in this chapter.

■ Levi Strauss and Company is in business to maximize profit. The firm might engage in philanthropic acts, but to do so, it must first maximize profit.

■ During the 1990s, the market for jeans became more competitive and the company's profit was squeezed.

■ Most large suppliers of jeans are publicly owned companies with many stockholders. Levi Strauss is a privately owned company that remains under the control of the descendants of Levi Strauss, who created the firm more than 100 years ago.

■ Jeans can be supplied to the consumer at the lowest possible cost if some firms specialize in *designing* jeans, some in *manufacturing* jeans, some in *marketing*, and some in *information* services.

■ The technology for *designing* and *marketing* jeans is sophisticated and uses the latest information systems. Firms link computers to retailers to manage inventories and use the Internet to obtain customers' measurements.

■ The technology for *manufacturing* jeans involves a small number of operations and basic parts. It uses simple machines and relatively low-skilled labor.

■ Because of the technology for manufacturing jeans, they can be made at least cost in countries that have low labor costs and by achieving economies from long production runs of one particular type of jeans.

■ By closing some of its factories in North America and buying jeans from specialist manufacturers, Levi Strauss is capturing these cost savings and economies.

Figure 1 Levi Strauss's share shrinks

S U M M A R Y

KEY POINTS

The Firm and Its Economic Problem (pp. 198–200)

- Firms hire and organize resources to produce and sell goods and services.
- Firms seek to maximize economic profit, which is total revenue minus opportunity cost.
- Technology, information, and markets limit a firm's profit.

Technology and Economic Efficiency (pp. 201–202)

- A method of production is technologically efficient when it is not possible to increase output without using more inputs.
- A method of production is economically efficient when the cost of producing a given output is as low as possible.

Information and Organization (pp. 203–206)

- Firms use a combination of command systems and incentive systems to organize production.
- Faced with incomplete information and uncertainty, firms induce managers and workers to perform in ways consistent with the firm's goals.
- Proprietorships, partnerships, and corporations use ownership, incentives, and long-term contracts to cope with the principal-agent problem.

Markets and the Competitive Environment (pp. 207–211)

- Perfect competition occurs when there are many buyers and sellers of an identical product and when new firms can easily enter a market.
- Monopolistic competition occurs when a large number of firms compete with each other by making slightly different products.
- Oligopoly is a situation in which a small number of firms compete with each other.
- Monopoly is a firm that produces a good or service for which there are no close substitutes and that is protected by a barrier that prevents the entry of competitors.

Firms and Markets (pp. 212–213)

- Firms coordinate economic activities when they can perform a task more efficiently—at lower cost—than markets can.
- Firms economize on transactions costs and achieve the benefits of economies of scale, economies of scope, and economies of team production.

KEY FIGURE AND TABLES ◆

KEY TERMS

PROBLEMS

*1. One year ago, Jack and Jill set up a vinegar bottling firm (called JJVB). Use the following information to calculate JJVB's explicit costs and implicit costs during its first year of operation:
   a. Jack and Jill put $50,000 of their own money into the firm.
   b. They bought equipment for $30,000.
   c. They hired one employee to help them for an annual wage of $20,000.
   d. Jack gave up his previous job, at which he earned $30,000, and spent all his time working for JJVB.
   e. Jill kept her old job, which paid $30 an hour, but gave up 10 hours of leisure each week (for 50 weeks) to work for JJVB.
   f. JJVB bought $10,000 of goods and services from other firms.
   g. The market value of the equipment at the end of the year was $28,000.

2. One year ago, Ms Moffat and Mr. Spieder opened a cheese firm (called MSCF). Use the following information to calculate MSCF's explicit costs and implicit costs during its first year of operation:
   a. Moffat and Spieder put $70,000 of their own money into the firm.
   b. They bought equipment for $40,000.
   c. They hired one employee to help them for an annual wage of $18,000.
   d. Moffat gave up her previous job, at which she earned $22,000, and spent all her time working for MSCF.
   e. Spieder kept his old job, which paid $20 an hour, but gave up 20 hours of leisure each week (for 50 weeks) to work for MSCF.
   f. MSCF bought $5,000 of goods from other firms.
   g. The market value of the equipment at the end of the year was $37,000.

*3. Four methods for doing a tax return are: personal computer, pocket calculator, pocket calculator with pencil and paper, pencil and paper. With a PC, the job takes an hour; with a pocket calculator, it takes 12 hours; with a pocket calculator and pencil and paper, it takes 12 hours; and with a pencil and paper, it takes 16 hours. The PC and its software cost $1,000, the pocket calculator costs $10, and the pencil and paper cost $1.
   a. Which, if any, of the methods is technologically efficient?
   b. Which method is economically efficient if the wage rate is
      (i) $5 an hour?
      (ii) $50 an hour?
      (iii) $500 an hour?

4. Sue can do her accounting assignment by using: a personal computer; a pocket calculator; a pocket calculator and a pencil and paper; or a pencil and paper. With a PC, Sue completes the job in half an hour; with a pocket calculator, it takes 4 hours; with a pocket calculator and with a pencil and paper, it takes 5 hours; and with a pencil and paper, it takes 14 hours. The PC and its software cost $2,000, the pocket calculator costs $15, and the pencil and paper cost $3.
   a. Which, if any, of the methods is technologically efficient?
   b. Which method is economically efficient if Sue's wage rate is
      (i) $10 an hour?
      (ii) $20 an hour?
      (iii) $50 an hour?

*5. Alternative ways of laundering 100 shirts are:

Method	Labor (hours)	Capital (machines)
a	1	10
b	5	8
c	20	4
d	50	1

   a. Which methods are technologically efficient?
   b. Which method is economically efficient if:
      (i) The wage rate is $1 an hour and the rental cost of a machine is $100 an hour?
      (ii) The wage rate is $5 an hour and the rental cost of a machine is $50 an hour?
      (iii) The wage rate is $50 an hour and the rental cost of a machine is $5 an hour?

6. Alternative ways of making 100 shirts a day are:

Method	Labor (hours)	Capital (machines)
a	10	50
b	20	40
c	50	20
d	100	10

a. Which methods are technologically efficient?
b. Which method is economically efficient if the hourly wage rate and rental rate are:
   (i) Wage rate $1, rental rate $100
   (ii) Wage rate $5, rental rate $50
   (iii) Wage rate $50, rental rate $5

*7. Sales of the firms in the tattoo industry are:

Firm	Sales (dollars)
Bright Spots	450
Freckles	325
Love Galore	250
Native Birds	200
Other 15 firms	800

a. Calculate the four firm concentration ratio.
b. What is the structure of the tattoo industry?

8. Sales of the firms in the pet food industry are:

Firm	Sales (thousands of dollars)
Big Collar, Inc.	50
Shiny Coat, Inc.	75
Friendly Pet, Inc.	60
Nature's Way, Inc.	65
Other 8 firms	400

a. Calculate the four firm concentration ratio.
b. What is the structure of the industry?

*9. Market shares of chocolate makers are:

Firm	Market share (percent)
Mayfair, Inc.	15
Bond, Inc.	10
Magic, Inc.	20
All Natural, Inc.	15
Truffles, Inc.	25
Gold, Inc.	15

a. Calculate the Herfindahl-Hirschman Index.
b. What is the structure of the industry?

10. Market shares of mat makers are:

Firm	Market share (percent)
Made-to-Last, Inc.	20
Big Wheel, Inc.	17
Magic Carpet, Inc.	22
Supreme, Inc.	17
Copra, Inc.	24

a. Calculate the Herfindahl-Hirschman Index.
b. What is the structure of the industry?

CRITICAL THINKING

 1. Study the news article about Levi Strauss and Company in *Reading Between the Lines* on pp. 214–215 and then:
a. Describe the economic problem that the firm faced in 1998.
b. Use the links on the Parkin Web site to find information about some of Levi Strauss's main competitors. What do you think the economic problems of these competitors are?
c. Do you think the market for blue jeans is an example of monopoly, oligopoly, monopolistic competition, or perfect competition? Explain your answer.
d. Use the links on the Parkin Web site to find information about *where* Levi Strauss and Company is closing factories. For the factory nearest to you, what special problems do you think will arise?
e. Compare and contrast how Levi Strauss achieves technological efficiency and economic efficiency.
f. If more and more manufacturing leaves the United States and goes to other countries, what do you think the effect will be on the U.S. economy? (Hint: Think about the *PPF* and efficiency.)

2. Use the links on the Parkin Web site to obtain information about the auto industry.
a. What are the main economic problems faced by auto producers?
b. Why are auto producers merging?

3. Use the links on the Parkin Web site to obtain information about the steel industry. Then describe the main economic problems faced by steel producers and explain why they are seeking protection from international competition.

Output and Costs

Size does not guarantee survival in business. Of the 100 largest companies in the United States in 1917, only 22 still remained in that league in 1997. But remaining small does not guarantee survival either. Every year, millions of small businesses close down. Call a random selection of restaurants and fashion boutiques from *last* year's yellow pages and see how many have vanished. What does a firm have to do to be one of the survivors? ◆ Firms differ in lots of ways—from Mom and Pop's convenience store to multinational giants producing hi-tech goods. But regardless of their size or what they produce, all firms must decide how much to produce and how to produce it. How do firms make these decisions? ◆ Most car makers in the United States can produce more cars than they can sell. Why do car makers have expensive equipment lying around that isn't fully used? Many electric utilities in the United States don't have enough production equipment on hand to meet demand on the coldest and hottest days and must buy power from other producers. Why don't these firms install more equipment so that they can supply the market themselves?

◇ In this chapter we are going to answer these questions. To do so, we will study the economic decisions of a small, imaginary firm—Sidney's Sweaters, Inc., a producer of knitted sweaters. The firm is owned and operated by Sidney. By studying the economic problems of Sidney's Sweaters and the way in which Sidney copes with them, we will get a clear view of the problems that face *all* firms—small ones like Sidney's Sweaters as well as the giants. We're going to begin by setting the scene and describing the time frames in which Sidney makes his business decisions.

Survival of the Fittest

After studying this chapter, you will be able to:

■ Distinguish between the short run and the long run

■ Explain the relationship between a firm's output and labor employed in the short run

■ Explain the relationship between a firm's output and costs in the short run

■ Derive and explain a firm's short-run cost curves

■ Explain the relationship between a firm's output and costs in the long run

■ Derive and explain a firm's long-run average cost curve

Decision Time Frames

PEOPLE WHO OPERATE FIRMS MAKE MANY DECIsions. All of the decisions are aimed at one overriding objective: maximum attainable profit. But the decisions are not all equally critical. Some of the decisions are big ones. Once made, they are costly (or impossible) to reverse. If such a decision turns out to be incorrect, it might lead to the failure of the firm. Some of the decisions are small ones. They are easily changed. If one of these decisions turns out to be incorrect, the firm can change its actions and survive.

The biggest decision that any firm makes is what industry to enter. For most entrepreneurs, their background knowledge and interests drive this decision. But the decision also depends on profit prospects. No one sets up a firm without believing that it will be profitable. And profit depends on total revenue and opportunity cost (see Chapter 10, pp. 198–199).

The firm that we study has already chosen the industry in which to operate. It has also chosen its most effective method of organization. But it has not decided the quantity to produce, the quantities of resources to hire, or the price at which to sell its output.

Decisions about the quantity to produce and the price to charge depend on the type of market in which the firm operates. Perfect competition, monopolistic competition, oligopoly, and monopoly all confront the firm with their own special problems.

But decisions about how to produce a given output do not depend on the type of market in which the firm operates. These decisions are similar for *all* types of firms in *all* types of markets.

The actions that a firm can take to influence the relationship between output and cost depend on how soon the firm wants to act. A firm that plans to change its output rate tomorrow has fewer options than one that plans to change its output rate six months from now.

To study the relationship between a firm's output decision and its costs, we distinguish two decision time frames:

- The short run
- The long run

The Short Run

The **short run** is a time frame in which the quantities of some resources are fixed. For most firms, the fixed resources are the firm's buildings and capital. The management organization and the technology it uses are also fixed in the short run. We call the collection of fixed resources the firm's *plant*. So in the short run, a firm's plant is fixed.

For Sidney's Sweaters, the fixed plant is its factory building and its knitting machines. For an electric power utility, the fixed plant is its buildings, generators, computers, and control systems. For an airport, the fixed plant is the runways, terminal buildings, and traffic control facilities.

To increase output in the short run, a firm must increase the quantity of variable inputs it uses. Labor is usually the variable input. So to produce more output, Sidney's Sweaters must hire more labor and operate its knitting machines for more hours per day. Similarly, an electric power utility must hire more labor and operate its generators for more hours per day. And an airport must hire more labor and operate its runways, terminals, and traffic control facilities for more hours per day.

Short-run decisions are easily reversed. The firm can increase or decrease output in the short run by increasing or decreasing the labor hours it hires.

The Long Run

The **long run** is a time frame in which the quantities of *all* resources can be varied. That is, the long run is a period in which the firm can change its *plant*.

To increase output in the long run, a firm is able to choose whether to change its plant as well as whether to increase the quantity of labor it hires. Sidney's Sweaters can decide whether to install some additional knitting machines, use a new type of machine, reorganize its management, or hire more labor. An electric power utility can decide whether to install more generators. And an airport can decide whether to build more runways, terminals, and traffic control facilities.

Long-run decisions are *not* easily reversed. Once a plant decision is made, the firm must live with it for some time. To emphasize this fact, we call the *past* cost of buying a new plant a **sunk cost**. A sunk cost is irrelevant to the firm's decisions. The only costs that influence its decisions are the short-run cost of changing its labor inputs and the long-run cost of changing its plant in the future.

We're going to study costs in the short run and the long run. We begin with the short run and describe the technology constraint the firm faces.

Short-Run Technology Constraint

To increase output in the short run, a firm must increase the quantity of labor employed. We describe the relationship between output and the quantity of labor employed by using three related concepts:

- Total product
- Marginal product
- Average product

These product concepts can be illustrated either by product schedules or product curves. Let's look first at the product schedules.

TABLE 11.1
Total Product, Marginal Product, and Average Product

	Labor (workers per day)	Total product (sweaters per day)	Marginal product (sweaters per additional worker)	Average product (sweaters per worker)
a	0	0		
			 4	
b	1	4		4.00
			 6	
c	2	10		5.00
			 3	
d	3	13		4.33
			 2	
e	4	15		3.75
			 1	
f	5	16		3.20

Total product is the total amount produced. Marginal product is the change in total product that results from a one-unit increase in labor. For example, when labor increases from 2 to 3 workers a day (row c to row d), total product increases from 10 to 13 sweaters. (Marginal product is shown between the rows to emphasize that it is the result of changing labor.) The marginal product of going from 2 to 3 workers is 3 sweaters. Average product is total product divided by the quantity of labor employed. For example, the average product of 3 workers is 4.33 sweaters per worker (13 sweaters a day divided by 3 workers).

Product Schedules

Table 11.1 shows some data that describe Sidney's Sweaters' total product, marginal product, and average product. The numbers tell us how Sidney's Sweaters' production increases as more workers are employed. They also tell us about the productivity of Sidney's Sweaters' labor force.

Focus first on the columns headed "Labor" and "Total product." **Total product** is the total quantity Sidney produced. You can see from the numbers in these columns that as Sidney employs more labor, total product increases. For example, when Sidney employs 1 worker, total product is 4 sweaters a day and when it employs 2 workers, total product is 10 sweaters a day. Each increase in the workers employed brings an increase in total product.

Marginal product tells us by how much total product increases when employment increases. The **marginal product** of labor is the increase in total product that results from a one-unit increase in the quantity of labor employed. For example, in Table 11.1, when Sidney increases employment from 2 to 3 workers, marginal product is 3 sweaters—total product goes from 10 to 13 sweaters.

Average product tells how productive workers are on the average. The **average product** of labor is equal to total product divided by the quantity of labor employed. For example, in Table 11.1, the average product of 3 workers is 4.33 sweaters per worker—13 sweaters a day divided by 3 workers.

If you look closely at the numbers in Table 11.1, you can see some patterns. For example, as labor increases, marginal product at first increases and then begins to decrease. For example, marginal product increases from 4 sweaters to 6 sweaters a day when the second worker is hired and then decreases to 3 sweaters a day when the third worker is hired. Average product also at first increases and then decreases. The relationships between employment and the three product concepts can be seen more clearly by looking at the product curves.

Product Curves

The product curves are graphs of the relationships between employment and the three product concepts you've just studied. They show how total product, marginal product, and average product change as employment changes. They also show the relationships among the three concepts. Let's look at the product curves.

Total Product Curve

Figure 11.1 shows Sidney's Sweaters' total product curve, *TP*. As employment increases, so does the number of sweaters knitted. Points *a* through *f* on the curve correspond to the same rows in Table 11.1.

The total product curve is similar to the *production possibility frontier* (explained in Chapter 3). It separates the attainable output levels from those that are unattainable. All the points that lie above the curve are unattainable. Points that lie below the curve, in the orange area, are attainable. But they are inefficient—they use more labor than is necessary to produce a given output. Only the points *on* the total product curve are technologically efficient.

Notice especially the shape of the total product curve. As employment increases from zero to 1 worker per day, the curve becomes steeper. Then, as employment continues to increase to 3, 4, and 5 workers a day, the curve becomes less steep. The steeper the slope of the total product curve, the greater is marginal product, as you are about to see.

FIGURE 11.1

Total Product Curve

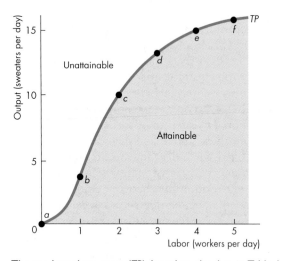

The total product curve (*TP*), based on the data in Table 11.1, shows how the quantity of sweaters produced changes as the quantity of labor employed changes. For example, 2 workers can produce 10 sweaters a day (point *c*). Points *a* through *f* on the curve correspond to the rows of Table 11.1. The total product curve separates attainable outputs from unattainable outputs. Points below the *TP* curve are inefficient.

Marginal Product Curve

Figure 11.2 shows Sidney's Sweaters' marginal product of labor. Part (a) reproduces the total product curve, which is the same as the total product curve in Fig. 11.1. Part (b) shows the marginal product curve, *MP*.

In part (a), the orange bars illustrate the marginal product of labor. The height of each bar measures marginal product. Marginal product is also measured by the slope of the total product curve. Recall that the slope of a curve is the change in the value of the variable measured on the *y*-axis—output—divided by the change in the variable measured on the *x*-axis—labor input—as we move along the curve. A one-unit increase in labor input, from 2 to 3 workers, increases output from 10 to 13 sweaters, so the slope from point *c* to point *d* is 3, the same as the marginal product that we've just calculated.

We've calculated the marginal product of labor for a series of unit increases in the quantity of labor. But labor is divisible into smaller units than one person. It is divisible into hours and even minutes. By varying the amount of labor in the smallest imaginable units, we can draw the marginal product curve shown in Fig. 11.2(b). The *height* of this curve measures the *slope* of the total product curve at a point. Part (a) shows that an increase in employment from 2 to 3 workers increases output from 10 to 13 sweaters (an increase of 3). The increase in output of 3 sweaters appears on the vertical axis of part (b) as the marginal product of going from 2 to 3 workers. We plot that marginal product at the midpoint between 2 and 3 workers. Notice that marginal product shown in Fig. 11.2(b) reaches a peak at 1.5 units of labor, and at that point, marginal product is 6 sweaters. The peak occurs at 1.5 units of labor because the total product curve is steepest when employment increases from 1 to 2 workers.

The total product and marginal product curves are different for different firms and different types of goods. Ford Motor Company's product curves are different from those of Jim's Burger Stand, which in turn are different from those of Sidney's sweater factory. But the shapes of the product curves are similar, because almost every production process has two features:

- Increasing marginal returns initially
- Diminishing marginal returns eventually

Increasing Marginal Returns Increasing marginal returns occur when the marginal product of an additional worker exceeds the marginal product of the

FIGURE 11.2
Marginal Product

(a) Total product

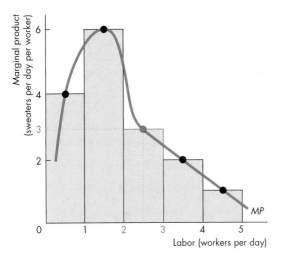

(b) Marginal product

Marginal product is illustrated by the orange bars. For example, when labor increases from 2 to 3, marginal product is the orange bar whose height is 3 sweaters. (Marginal product is shown midway between the labor inputs to emphasize that it is the result of *changing* inputs.) The steeper the slope of the total product curve (*TP*) in part (a), the larger is marginal product (*MP*) in part (b). Marginal product increases to a maximum (in this example, when the second worker is employed) and then declines—diminishing marginal returns.

previous worker. Increasing marginal returns arise from increased specialization and division of labor in the production process.

For example, if Sidney employs just one worker, that person must learn all the aspects of sweater production: running the knitting machines, fixing breakdowns, packaging and mailing sweaters, buying and checking the type and color of the wool. All these tasks must be performed by that one person.

If Sidney hires a second person, the two workers can specialize in different parts of the production process. As a result, two workers produce more than twice as much as one. The marginal product of the second worker is greater than the marginal product of the first worker. Marginal returns are increasing.

Diminishing Marginal Returns   Most production processes experience increasing marginal returns initially. But all production processes eventually reach a point of *diminishing* marginal returns. **Diminishing marginal returns** occur when the marginal product of an additional worker is less than the marginal product of the previous worker.

Diminishing marginal returns arise from the fact that more and more workers are using the same capital and working in the same space. As more workers are added, there is less and less for the additional workers to do that is productive. For example, if Sidney hires a third worker, output increases but not by as much as it did when he hired the second worker. In this case, after two workers are hired, all gains from specialization and the division of labor have been exhausted. By hiring a third worker, the factory produces more sweaters but the equipment is being operated closer to its limits. There are even times when the third worker has nothing to do because the machines are running without the need for further attention. Adding yet more and more workers continues to increase output but by successively smaller amounts. Marginal returns are diminishing. This phenomenon is such a pervasive one that it is called a "law"—"the law of diminishing returns." The **law of diminishing returns** states that

As a firm uses more of a variable input, with a given quantity of fixed inputs, the marginal product of the variable input eventually diminishes.

We are going to return to the law of diminishing returns when we study a firm's costs. But before we do that, let's look at the average product of labor and the average product curve.

Average Product Curve

Figure 11.3 illustrates Sidney's Sweaters' average product of labor, *AP*. It also shows the relationship between average product and marginal product. Points *b* through *f* on the average product curve correspond to those same rows in Table 11.1. Average product increases from 1 to 2 workers (its maximum value at point *c*) but then decreases as yet more workers are employed. Notice also that average product is largest when average product and marginal product are equal. That is, the marginal product curve cuts the average product curve at the point of maximum average product. For employment levels at which marginal product exceeds average product, average product is increasing. For employment levels at which marginal product is less than average product, average product is decreasing.

The relationship between the average and marginal product curves is a general feature of the relationship between the average and marginal values of any variable. Let's look at a familiar example.

FIGURE 11.3
Average Product

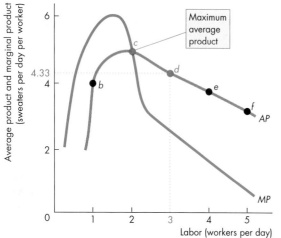

The figure shows the average product and the connection between the average product and marginal product. With 1 worker, marginal product exceeds average product, so average product is increasing. With 2 workers, marginal product equals average product, so average product is at its maximum. With more than 2 workers, marginal product is less than average product, so average product is decreasing.

Marginal Grade and Grade Point Average

To see the relationship between average product and marginal product, think about the similar relationship between Sidney's average grade and marginal grade over five semesters. (Suppose that Sidney is a part-time student who takes just one course each semester.) In the first semester, Sidney takes calculus and his grade is a 2. This grade is his marginal grade. It is also his average grade—his GPA. In the next semester, Sidney takes French and gets a 3. French is Sidney's marginal course, and his marginal grade is 3. His GPA rises to 2.5. Because his marginal grade exceeds his average grade, it pulls his average up. In the third semester, Sidney takes economics and gets a 4—his new marginal grade. Because his marginal grade exceeds his GPA, it again pulls his average up. Sidney's GPA is now 3, the average of 2, 3, and 4. The fourth semester, he takes history and gets a 3. Because his marginal grade is equal to his average, his GPA does not change. In the fifth semester, Sidney takes English and gets a 2. Because his marginal grade, a 2, is below his GPA of 3, his GPA falls.

This everyday relationship between marginal and average values agrees with that between marginal and average product. Sidney's GPA increases when his marginal grade exceeds his GPA. His GPA falls when his marginal grade is below his GPA. And his GPA is constant when his marginal grade equals his GPA. The relationship between marginal product and average product is exactly the same as that between Sidney's marginal and average grades.

REVIEW QUIZ

- Explain how the marginal product of labor and the average product of labor change as the quantity of labor employed increases (a) initially and (b) eventually.
- What is the law of diminishing returns? Why does marginal product eventually diminish?
- Explain the relationship between marginal product and average product. How does average product change when marginal product exceeds average product? How does average product change when average product exceeds marginal product? Why?

Sidney cares about his product curves because they influence his costs. Let's look at Sidney's costs.

Short-Run Cost

To produce more output in the short run, a firm must employ more labor, which means it must increase its costs. We describe the relationship between output and cost by using three cost concepts:

- Total cost
- Marginal cost
- Average cost

Total Cost

A firm's **total cost** (TC) is the cost of all the productive resources it uses. Total cost includes the cost of land, capital, and labor. It also includes the cost of entrepreneurship, which is *normal profit* (see Chapter 10, p. 199). We divide total cost into total fixed cost and total variable cost.

Total fixed cost (TFC) is the cost of all the firm's fixed inputs. Because the quantity of a fixed input does not change as output changes, fixed cost does not change as output changes.

Total variable cost (TVC) is the cost of all the firm's variable inputs. Because a firm must change the quantity of variable inputs to change its output, total variable cost changes as output changes.

Total cost is the sum of total fixed cost and total variable cost. That is,

$$TC = TFC + TVC.$$

The table in Fig. 11.4 shows Sidney's total costs. With one knitting machine that costs $25 a day, TFC is $25. To produce more sweaters, Sidney hires more labor, which costs $25 a day. TVC, which increases as output increases, is the number of workers multiplied by $25. For example, to produce 13 sweaters a day, Sidney hires 3 workers and TVC is $75. TC is the sum of TFC and TVC, so to produce 13 sweaters a day, Sidney's total cost, TC, is $100. Check the calculation in each row of the table.

Figure 11.4 graphs Sidney's total cost curves. These curves graph total cost against output. The green total fixed cost curve (TFC) is horizontal because total fixed cost does not change when output changes. It is a constant at $25. The purple total variable cost curve (TVC) and the blue total cost curve (TC) both increase with output. The vertical distance between the TVC and TC curve is total fixed cost as shown by the arrows.

Let's now look at Sidney's Sweaters' marginal cost.

FIGURE 11.4
Total Cost Curves

$$TC = TFC + TVC$$

	Labor (workers per day)	Output (sweaters per day)	Total fixed cost (*TFC*)	Total variable cost (*TVC*)	Total cost (*TC*)
			(dollars per day)		
a	0	0	25	0	25
b	1	4	25	25	50
c	2	10	25	50	75
d	3	13	25	75	100
e	4	15	25	100	125
f	5	16	25	125	150

Sidney rents a knitting machine for $25 a day. This amount is Sidney's Sweaters' total fixed cost. Sidney hires workers at a wage rate of $25 a day, and this cost is Sidney's Sweaters' total variable cost. For example, if Sidney employs 3 workers, total variable cost is (3 × $25), which equals $75. Total cost is the sum of total fixed cost and total variable cost. For example, when Sidney employs 3 workers, total cost is $100—total fixed cost of $25 plus total variable cost of $75. The graph shows Sidney's Sweaters' total cost curves. Total fixed cost (*TFC*) is constant—it graphs as a horizontal line—and total variable cost (*TVC*) increases as output increases. Total cost (*TC*) also increases as output increases. The vertical distance between the total cost curve and the total variable cost curve is total fixed cost, as illustrated by the two arrows.

Marginal Cost

In Fig. 11.4, total variable cost and total cost increase at a decreasing rate at small levels of output and then begin to increase at an increasing rate as output increases. To understand these patterns in the changes in total cost, we need to use the concept of *marginal cost.*

A firm's **marginal cost** is the increase in total cost that results from a one-unit increase in output. We calculate marginal cost as the increase in total cost divided by the increase in output. The table in Fig. 11.5 shows this calculation. When, for example, output increases from 10 sweaters to 13 sweaters, total cost increases from $75 to $100. The change in output is 3 sweaters, and the change in total cost is $25. The marginal cost of one of those 3 sweaters is ($25 ÷ 3), which equals $8.33.

Figure 11.5 graphs the marginal cost data in the table as the red marginal cost curve, *MC.* This curve is U-shaped because, when Sidney hires a second worker, marginal cost decreases, but when he hires a third, a fourth, and a fifth worker, marginal cost successively increases.

Marginal cost decreases at small outputs because of economies from greater specialization. It eventually increases because of *the law of diminishing returns.* The law of diminishing returns means that each additional worker produces a successively smaller addition to output. So to get an additional unit of output, ever more workers are required. Because more workers are required to produce one additional unit of output, the cost of the additional output—marginal cost—must eventually increase.

Marginal cost tells us how total cost changes as output changes. The final cost concept tells us what it costs, on the average, to produce a unit of output. Let's now look at Sidney's Sweaters' average costs.

Average Cost

There are three average costs:

1. Average fixed cost
2. Average variable cost
3. Average total cost

Average fixed cost (*AFC*) is total fixed cost per unit of output. **Average variable cost** (*AVC*) is total variable cost per unit of output. **Average total cost** (*ATC*) is total cost per unit output. The average cost concepts are calculated from the total cost concepts as follows:

$$TC = TFC + TVC.$$

Divide each total cost term by the quantity produced, *Q,* to give

$$\frac{TC}{Q} = \frac{TFC}{Q} + \frac{TVC}{Q}$$

or

$$ATC = AFC + AVC.$$

The table in Fig. 11.5 shows the calculation of average total cost. For example, when output is 10 sweaters, average fixed cost is ($25 ÷ 10), which equals $2.50, average variable cost is ($50 ÷ 10), which equals $5.00, and average total cost is ($75 ÷ 10), which equals $7.50. Note that average total cost is equal to average fixed cost ($2.50) plus average variable cost ($5.00).

Figure 11.5 shows the average cost curves. The green average fixed cost curve (*AFC*) slopes downward. As output increases, the same constant fixed cost is spread over a larger output. The blue average total cost curve (*ATC*) and the purple average variable cost curve (*AVC*) are U-shaped. The vertical distance between the average total cost and average variable cost curves is equal to average fixed cost—as indicated by the two arrows. That distance shrinks as output increases because average fixed cost declines with increasing output.

The marginal cost curve intersects the average variable cost curve and the average total cost curve at their minimum points. That is, when marginal cost is less than average cost, average cost is decreasing, and when marginal cost exceeds average cost, average cost is increasing. This relationship holds for both the *ATC* curve and the *AVC* curve and is another example of the relationship you saw in Figure 11.3 for average product and marginal product and in Sidney's course grades.

Why the Average Total Cost Curve Is U-Shaped

Average total cost, *ATC,* is the sum of average fixed cost, *AFC,* and average variable cost, *AVC.* So the shape of the *ATC* curve combines the shapes of the *AFC* and *AVC* curves. The U-shape of the average

FIGURE 11.5

Marginal Cost and Average Costs

Marginal cost is calculated as the change in total cost divided by the change in output. When output increases from 4 to 10 sweaters, an increase of 6, total cost increases by $25 and marginal cost is $25 ÷ 6, which equals $4.17. Each average cost concept is calculated by dividing the related total cost by output. When 10 sweaters are produced, AFC is $2.50 ($25 ÷ 10), AVC is $5 ($50 ÷ 10), and ATC is $7.50 ($75 ÷ 10).

The figure shows the marginal cost curve and the average cost curves. The marginal cost curve (MC) is U-shaped and intersects the average variable cost curve and the average total cost curve at their minimum points. Average fixed cost (AFC) decreases as output increases. The average total cost curve (ATC) and average variable cost curve (AVC) are U-shaped. The vertical distance between these two curves is equal to average fixed cost, as illustrated by the two arrows.

	Labor (workers per day)	Output (sweaters per day)	Total fixed cost (TFC)	Total variable cost (TVC)	Total cost (TC)	Marginal cost (MC) (dollars per additional sweater)	Average fixed cost (AFC)	Average variable cost (AVC)	Average total cost (ATC)
			(dollars per day)				(dollars per sweater)		
a	0	0	25	0	25		—	—	—
						6.25			
b	1	4	25	25	50		6.25	6.25	12.50
						4.17			
c	2	10	25	50	75		2.50	5.00	7.50
						8.33			
d	3	13	25	75	100		1.92	5.77	7.69
						12.50			
e	4	15	25	100	125		1.67	6.67	8.33
						25.00			
f	5	16	25	125	150		1.56	7.81	9.38

total cost curve arises from the influence of two opposing forces:

- Spreading fixed cost over a larger output
- Eventually diminishing returns

When output increases, the firm spreads its fixed costs over a larger output and its average fixed cost decreases—its average fixed cost curve slopes downward.

Diminishing returns means that as output increases, ever-larger amounts of labor are needed to produce an additional unit of output. So average

variable cost eventually increases, and the AVC curve eventually slopes upward.

The shape of the average total cost curve combines these two effects. Initially, as output increases, both average fixed cost and average variable cost decrease, so average total cost decreases and the ATC curve slopes downward. But as output increases further and diminishing returns set in, average variable cost begins to increase. Eventually, average variable cost increases more quickly than average fixed cost decreases, so average total cost increases and the ATC curve slopes upward.

Cost Curves and Product Curves

The technology that a firm uses determines its costs. Figure 11.6 shows the links between the firm's technology constraint (its product curves) and its cost curves. The upper part of the figure shows the average product curve and the marginal product curve—like those in Fig. 11.3. The lower part of the figure shows the average variable cost curve and the marginal cost curve—like those in Fig. 11.5.

The figure highlights the links between technology and costs. As labor increases initially, marginal product and average product rise and marginal cost and average variable cost fall. Then, at the point of maximum marginal product, marginal cost is a minimum. As labor increases further, marginal product diminishes and marginal cost increases. But average product continues to rise and average variable cost continues to fall. Then, at the point of maximum average product, average variable cost is a minimum. As labor increases further, average product diminishes and average variable cost increases.

Shifts in the Cost Curves

The position of a firm's short-run cost curves depends on two factors:

- Technology
- Prices of productive resources

Technology A technological change that increases productivity shifts the total product curve upward. It also shifts the marginal product curve and the average product curve upward. Because with a better technology, the same inputs can produce more output, technological change lowers costs and shifts the cost curves downward.

For example, advances in robot production techniques have increased productivity in the car industry. As a result, the product curves of Chrysler, Ford, and GM have shifted upward, and their cost curves have shifted downward. But the relationships between their product curves and cost curves have not changed. The curves are still linked in the way shown in Fig. 11.6.

Often, when technology advances, a firm uses more capital (a fixed input) and less labor (a variable input). For example, today telephone companies use computers to connect long-distance calls in place of

FIGURE 11.6

Product Curves and Cost Curves

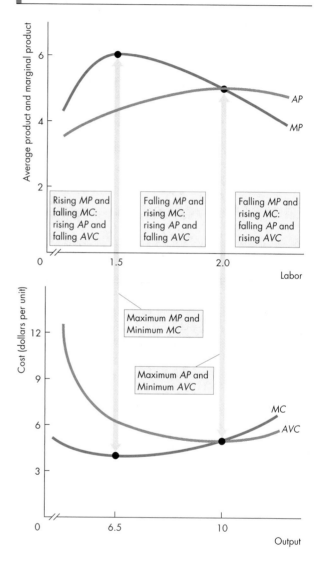

A firm's marginal product curve is linked to its marginal cost curve. If marginal product rises, marginal cost falls. If marginal product is a maximum, marginal cost is a minimum. If marginal product diminishes, marginal cost rises. A firm's average product curve is linked to its average variable cost curve. If average product rises, average variable cost falls. If average product is a maximum, average variable cost is a minimum. If average product diminishes, average variable cost rises.

TABLE 11.2

A Compact Glossary of Costs

Term	Symbol	Definition	Equation
Fixed cost		Cost that is independent of the output level; cost of a fixed input	
Variable cost		Cost that varies with the output level; cost of a variable input	
Total fixed cost	TFC	Cost of the fixed inputs	
Total variable cost	TVC	Cost of the variable inputs	
Total cost	TC	Cost of all inputs	$TC = TFC + TVC$
Total product	TP	Total quantity produced (output Q)	
Marginal cost	MC	Change in total cost resulting from a one-unit increase in output	$MC = \Delta TC \div \Delta Q$
Average fixed cost	AFC	Total fixed cost per unit of output	$AFC = TFC \div Q$
Average variable cost	AVC	Total variable cost per unit of output	$AVC = TVC \div Q$
Average total cost	ATC	Total cost per unit of output	$ATC = AFC + AVC$

the human operators they employed in the 1980s. When such a technological change occurs, fixed costs increase and variable costs decrease. This change in the mix of fixed cost and variable cost means that at small output levels, average total cost might increase, while at large output levels, average total cost decreases.

Prices of Resources An increase in the price of a productive resource increases costs and shifts the cost curves. But how the curves shift depends on which resource price changes. An increase in rent or some other component of *fixed* cost shifts the fixed cost curves (*TFC* and *AFC*) upward and shifts the total cost curve (*TC*) upward but leaves the variable cost curves (*AVC* and *TVC*) and the marginal cost curve (*MC*) unchanged. An increase in the wage rate or some other component of *variable* cost shifts the variable curves (*TVC* and *AVC*) upward and shifts the (*MC*) upward but leaves the fixed cost curves (*AFC* and *TFC*) unchanged. So, for example, if truck drivers' wage rate increases, the variable cost and marginal cost of transportation services increase. If the

interest expense paid by a trucking company increases, the fixed cost of transportation services increases.

You've now completed your study of short-run costs. All the concepts that you've met are summarized in a compact glossary in Table 11.2.

R E V I E W   Q U I Z

- What relationships do a firm's short-run cost curves show?
- How does marginal cost change as output increases (a) initially and (b) eventually?
- What does the law of *diminishing returns* imply for the shape of the marginal cost curve?
- What is the shape of the average fixed cost curve and why?
- What are the shapes of the average variable cost curve and the average total cost curve and why?

Long-Run Cost

IN THE SHORT RUN, A FIRM CAN VARY THE QUANtity of labor but the quantity of capital is fixed. In the long run, a firm can vary both the quantity of labor and the quantity of capital. We are now going to see how costs vary when the quantities of labor and capital vary. That is, we are going to study a firm's long-run costs. *Long-run cost* is the cost of production when a firm uses the economically efficient quantities of labor and capital. There are no *fixed* costs in the long run.

The behavior of long-run cost depends on the firm's *production function*, which is the relationship between the maximum output attainable and the quantities of both labor and capital.

The Production Function

Table 11.3 shows Sidney's Sweaters' production function. The table lists total product schedules for four different quantities of capital. We identify the quantity of capital by the plant size. The numbers for Plant 1 are for a factory with one knitting machine—the case we've just studied. The other three plants have 2, 3, and 4 machines. If Sidney's Sweaters doubles its capital to 2 knitting machines, the various amounts of labor can produce the outputs shown in the second column of the table. The last two columns show the outputs of yet larger quantities of capital.

Diminishing Returns Diminishing returns occur at all four quantities of capital as the quantity of labor increases. You can check that fact by calculating the marginal product of labor in plants with 2, 3, and 4 machines. At each plant size, as the quantity of labor increases, its marginal product (eventually) diminishes.

Diminishing Marginal Product of Capital Diminishing returns also occur as the quantity of capital increases. You can check that fact by calculating the marginal product of capital at a given quantity of labor. The *marginal product of capital* is the change in total product divided by the change in capital when the quantity of labor is constant—equivalently, the change in output resulting from a one-unit increase in the quantity of capital. For example, if Sidney's Sweaters has 3 workers and increases its capital from 1 machine to 2 machines, output increases from 13 to 18 sweaters a day. The marginal product of capital is 5 sweaters per day. If Sidney's Sweaters increases the

TABLE 11.3

The Production Function

Labor (workers per day)	Output (sweaters per day)			
	Plant 1	Plant 2	Plant 3	Plant 4
1	4	10	13	15
2	10	15	18	21
3	13	18	22	24
4	15	20	24	26
5	16	21	25	27
Knitting machines (number)	1	2	3	4

The table shows the total product data for four quantities of capital. The greater the plant size, the larger is the total product for any given quantity of labor. But for a given plant size, the marginal product of labor diminishes. And for a given quantity of labor, the marginal product of capital diminishes.

number of machines from 2 to 3, output increases from 18 to 22 sweaters per day. The marginal product of capital is 4 sweaters per day, down from 5 sweaters per day when 2 machines were used.

Let's now see what the production function implies for long-run costs.

Short-Run Cost and Long-Run Cost

Continue to assume that labor costs $25 per worker per day and capital costs $25 per machine per day. Using these input prices and the data in Table 11.3, we can calculate and graph the average total cost curves for factories with 1, 2, 3, and 4 knitting machines. We've already studied the costs of a factory with 1 machine in Figs. 11.4 and 11.5. In Fig. 11.7, the average total cost curve for that case is ATC_1. Figure 11.7 also shows the average total cost curve for a factory with 2 machines, ATC_2, with 3 machines, ATC_3, and with 4 machines, ATC_4.

You can see, in Fig. 11.7, that plant size has a big effect on the firm's average total cost. Two things stand out:

FIGURE 11.7

Short-Run Costs of Four Different Plants

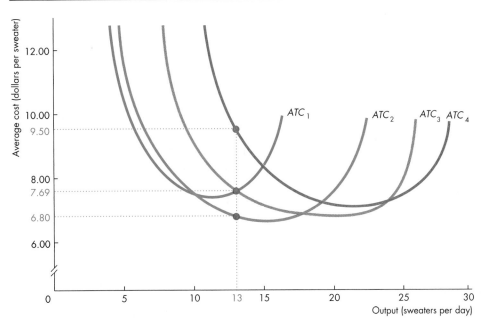

The figure shows short-run average total cost curves for four different quantities of capital. Sidney's Sweaters can produce 13 sweaters a day with 1 machine on ATC_1 or with 3 machines on ATC_3 for an average cost of $7.69 per sweater. Sydney's Sweaters can also produce 13 sweaters by using 2 knitting machines on ATC_2 for $6.80 per sweater or 4 machines on ATC_4 for $9.50 per sweater. If Sidney's Sweaters produces 13 sweaters a day, the least-cost method of production—the long-run method—is with 2 machines on ATC_2.

- Each short-run average total cost curve is U-shaped.
- For each short-run average total cost curve, the larger the plant, the greater is the output at which average total cost is a minimum.

Each short-run average total cost curve is U-shaped because, as the quantity of labor increases, its marginal product at first increases and then diminishes. And these patterns in the marginal product of labor, which we examined in some detail for the plant with 1 knitting machine on pp. 222–223, occur at all plant sizes.

The minimum average total cost for a larger plant occurs at a greater output than it does for a smaller plant because the larger plant has a higher fixed cost and therefore, for any given output level, a higher average fixed cost.

Which one of the short-run average cost curves Sidney's Sweaters operates on depends on its plant size. But in the long run, Sidney chooses the plant size. And which plant size he chooses depends on the output he plans to produce. The reason is that the average total cost of producing a given output depends on the plant size.

To see why, suppose that Sidney plans to produce 13 sweaters a day. With 1 machine, the average total

cost curve is ATC_1 (in Fig. 11.7) and the average total cost of 13 sweaters a day is $7.69 per sweater. With 2 machines, on ATC_2, average total cost is $6.80 per sweater. With 3 machines on ATC_3, average total cost is $7.69 per sweater, the same as with 1 machine. Finally, with 4 machines, on ATC_4, average total cost is $9.50 per sweater.

The economically efficient plant size for producing a given output is the one that has the lowest average total cost. For Sidney, the economically efficient plant to use to produce 13 sweaters a day is the one with 2 machines.

In the long run, Sidney chooses the plant size that minimizes average total cost. When a firm is producing a given output at the least possible cost, it is operating on its *long-run average cost curve*.

The **long-run average cost curve** is the relationship between the lowest attainable average total cost and output when both the plant size and labor are varied. The long-run average cost curve is a planning curve. It tells the firm the plant size and the quantity of labor to use at each output to minimize cost. Once the plant size is chosen, the firm operates on the short-run cost curves that apply to that plant size.

The Long-Run Average Cost Curve

Figure 11.8 shows Sidney's Sweaters' long-run average cost curve *LRAC*. This long-run average cost curve is derived from the short-run average total cost curves in Fig. 11.7. For output rates up to 10 sweaters a day, average total cost is the lowest on ATC_1. For output rates between 10 and 18 sweaters a day, average total cost is the lowest on ATC_2. For output rates between 18 and 24 sweaters a day, average total cost is the lowest on ATC_3. And for output rates in excess of 24 sweaters a day, average total cost is the lowest on ATC_4. The segment of each of the four average total cost curves along which the average total cost is lowest is highlighted in dark blue in Fig. 11.8. The scallop-shaped curve made up of these four segments is the long-run average cost curve.

Economies and Diseconomies of Scale

Economies of scale are features of a firm's technology that lead to falling long-run average cost as output increases. When economies of scale are present, the *LRAC* curve slopes downward. The *LRAC* curve in Fig. 11.8 shows that Sidney's Sweaters experiences economies of scale for outputs up to 15 sweaters a day.

With given input prices, economies of scale occur if the percentage increase in output exceeds the percentage increase in all inputs. For example, if, when a firm increases its labor and capital by 10 percent, output increases by more than 10 percent, its average total cost falls. Economies of scale are present.

The main source of economies of scale is greater specialization of both labor and capital. For example, if GM produces 100 cars a week, each worker must perform many different tasks and the capital must be general-purpose machines and tools. But if GM produces 10,000 cars a week, each worker specializes and becomes highly proficient in a small number of tasks. Also, the capital is specialized and productive.

Diseconomies of scale are features of a firm's technology that lead to rising long-run average cost as output increases. When diseconomies of scale are present, the *LRAC* curve slopes upward. In Fig. 11.8, Sidney's Sweaters experiences diseconomies of scale at outputs greater than 15 sweaters a day.

With given input prices, diseconomies of scale occur if the percentage increase in output is less than

---

FIGURE 11.8

Long-Run Average Cost Curve

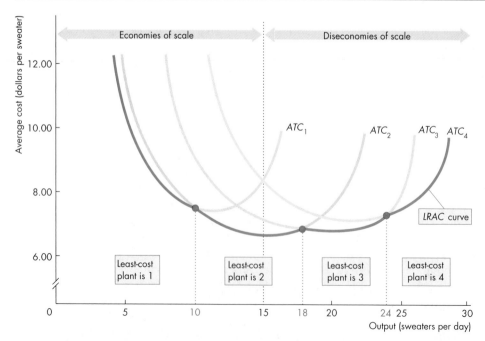

In the long run, Sidney's Sweaters can vary both capital and labor inputs. The long-run average cost curve traces the lowest attainable average total cost of production. Sidney's produces on its long-run average cost curve, if it uses 1 machine to produce up to 10 sweaters a day, 2 machines to produce between 10 and 18 sweaters a day, 3 machines to produce between 18 and 24 sweaters a day, and 4 machines to produce more than 24 sweaters a day. Within each range, Sidney's varies its output by varying the labor input.

the percentage increase in inputs. For example, if, when a firm increases its labor and capital by 10 percent, output increases by less than 10 percent, its average total cost rises. Diseconomies of scale are present.

The main source of diseconomies of scale is the difficulty of managing a very large enterprise. The larger the firm, the greater is the challenge of organizing it and the greater is the cost of communicating both up and down the management hierarchy and among managers. Eventually, management complexity brings rising average cost. Diseconomies of scale occur in all production processes but perhaps only at a very large output rate.

Constant returns to scale are features of a firm's technology that lead to constant long-run average cost as output increases. When constant returns to scale are present, the *LRAC* curve is horizontal.

With given input prices, constant returns to scale occur if the percentage increase in output equals the percentage increase in inputs. For example, if, when a firm increases its labor and capital by 10 percent, output increases by 10 percent, its average total cost is constant. Constant returns to scale are present.

For example, General Motors can double its production of Chevy Cavaliers by doubling its production facility for those cars. It can build an identical production line and hire an identical number of workers. With the two identical production lines, GM produces exactly twice as many cars.

Minimum Efficient Scale A firm experiences economies of scale up to some output level. Beyond that level, it moves into constant returns to scale or diseconomies of scale. A firm's **minimum efficient scale** is the smallest quantity of output at which long-run average cost reaches its lowest level.

The minimum efficient scale plays a role in determining market structure, as you will learn in the next three chapters. The minimum efficient scale also helps to answer some questions about real businesses.

Economies of Scale at Sidney's Sweaters Sidney's production function, shown in Table 11.3, illustrates economies of scale and diseconomies of scale. If Sidney's inputs increase from 1 machine and 1 worker to 2 of each, a 100 percent increase in all inputs, output increases by more than 100 percent, from 4 sweaters to 15 sweaters a day. Sidney's experiences economies of scale, and its long-run average cost decreases. But if Sidney's inputs increase to 3 machines and 3 workers, a 50 percent increase, output increases by less than 50 percent, from 15

sweaters to 22 sweaters a day. Now Sidney's experiences diseconomies of scale, and its long-run average cost increases. Sidney's minimum efficient scale is at 15 sweaters a day.

Producing Cars and Generating Electric Power At the beginning of this chapter, we posed the question: Why do car makers have expensive equipment lying around that isn't fully used? You can now answer this question. A car maker uses the plant that minimizes the average total cost of producing the output that it can sell. But it operates below the efficient minimum scale. Its short-run average total cost curve looks like ATC_1. If it could sell more cars, it would produce more cars and its average total cost would fall.

We also noted that many electric utilities don't have enough production equipment to meet demand on the coldest and hottest days and have to buy power from other producers. You can now see why. A power producer uses the plant size that minimizes the average total cost of producing the output that it can sell on a normal day. But it produces above the minimum efficient scale and experiences diseconomies of scale. Its short-run average total cost curve looks like ATC_3. With a larger plant size, its average total costs of producing its normal output would be higher.

REVIEW QUIZ

- What does a firm's production function show and how is it related to a total product curve?
- Does the law of diminishing returns apply to capital as well as labor? Explain why.
- What does a firm's long-run average cost curve show? How is it related to the firm's short-run average cost curves?
- What are economies of scale and diseconomies of scale? How do they arise? And what do they imply for the shape of the long-run average cost curve?
- How is a firm's minimum efficient scale determined?

◆ *Reading Between the Lines* on pp. 234–235 applies what you've learned about a firm's product curves and cost curves. It looks at the total product curves and cost curves of Exxon and Mobil before and after a proposed merger of these two oil producing giants.

Lowering the Cost of Oil

THE NEW YORK TIMES, DECEMBER 2, 1998

Exxon and Mobil Announce $80 Billion Deal to Create World's Largest Company

BY ALLEN R. MYERSON AND AGIS SALPUKAS

Exxon, the United States' largest oil company, formally agreed on Tuesday to buy Mobil, the next-largest, for $80 billion in stock, to form the world's biggest corporation. ...

The agreement would reunite the two largest pieces of John D. Rockefeller's Standard Oil Trust, which was broken up in 1911 in the nation's most celebrated antitrust case.

The companies contended Tuesday that they now confront global competitors and plunging energy prices, making their recombination and the resulting savings a necessity. But while the companies said they could save $2.8 billion annually, the greatest costs would be paid by employees. The companies said 9,000 workers out of 123,000 worldwide were likely to find themselves without jobs.

Lee Raymond, the chairman and chief executive of Exxon, who would add the title of president in the combined company, said repeatedly that further efficiency, not brute size, was his goal. "This is the case of the whole being greater than the sum of the parts," he said at a news conference, later adding: "I have always had the view that the objective is to be best. If in being best you also have to be biggest, that's fine."

Essence of the Story

■ Exxon and Mobil plan to merge.

■ The goal of the merger is to achieve cost savings, and the companies say that with the merger, costs can be cut by $2.8 billion a year.

■ The labor force of the merged company would be 9,000 workers fewer than the existing combined labor forces of the two companies.

■ Exxon and Mobil are huge firms that:
- Explore to find new oil and natural gas deposits
- Extract raw materials
- Transport raw materials to refineries
- Refine and process raw materials
- Transport and sell refined products

■ These firms are large because there are economies of scale in many of their production activities and especially in exploration.

■ Figure 1 shows the technology these firms face in the form of a total product curve. Exxon and Mobil operate on total product curve TP_0. Mobil employs 43,000 people and produces 1.46 billion barrels of oil a year, and Exxon employs 80,000 people and produces 3 billion barrels of oil a year.*

■ If Exxon and Mobil merge into a single very large firm, they will be able to operate on a new total product curve. The new curve is TP_1 in Fig. 1.

*The numbers of employees are data from Exxon and Mobil. The numbers of barrels produced are the author's calculation of the barrels of oil equivalent of Exxon's and Mobil's total sales. The firms actually sell several different products.

■ You can interpret Lee Raymond's statement, "This is the case of the whole being greater than the sum of the parts," as meaning that the combined firm does not move along the existing total product curve TP_0 but jumps to a new, higher total product curve TP_1 and increases productivity.

■ Figure 2 shows the effect of the merger on average total cost.

■ The average total cost curve on which the two firms operate before the merger is ATC_0. Both firms have a similar level of average total cost, but given the assumed total product curve in Fig. 1, Mobil operates in the region of falling average total cost and Exxon operates in the region of rising average total cost.

■ After the merger, the average total cost curve shifts to ATC_1. The bigger merged firm has greater fixed costs than the two separate firms, so at small output rates, average total cost is higher in the new firm than in the existing firms.

■ But at the large output rate at which the combined firm will operate, average total cost is lower for the merged firm.

Figure 1 Total product

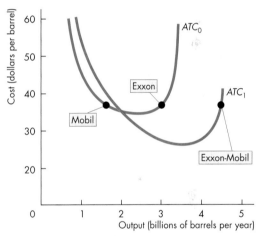

Figure 2 Average total cost

■ Notice that the new combined firm might operate on the upward-sloping portion of its new ATC curve, as in this example, even though it has benefited from economies of scale.

SUMMARY

KEY POINTS

Decision Time Frames (p. 220)

- In the short run, the quantity of one resource is fixed, and the quantities of the other resources can be varied.
- In the long run, the quantities of all resources can be varied.

Short-Run Technology Constraint (pp. 221–224)

- A total product curve shows the quantity a firm can produce with a given quantity of capital and different quantities of labor.
- Initially, the marginal product of labor increases as the quantity of labor increases but eventually, marginal product diminishes—the law of diminishing returns.
- Average product also increases initially and eventually diminishes.

Short-Run Cost (pp. 225–229)

- As output increases, total fixed cost is constant and total variable cost and total cost increase.
- As output increases, average fixed cost decreases; average variable cost, average total cost, and marginal cost decrease at small outputs and increase at large outputs. These cost curves are U-shaped.

Long-Run Cost (pp. 230–233)

- Long-run cost is the cost of production when all inputs—labor and capital—have been adjusted to their economically efficient levels.
- There is a set of short-run cost curves for each different plant size. There is one least-cost plant size for each output. The larger the output, the larger is the plant size that will minimize average total cost.
- The long-run average cost curve traces out the lowest attainable average total cost at each output when both capital and labor inputs can be varied.
- With economies of scale, the long-run average cost curve slopes downward. With diseconomies of scale, the long-run average cost curve slopes upward.

KEY FIGURES AND TABLE

KEY TERMS

PROBLEMS

*1. Rubber Duckies total product schedule is:

Labor (workers per week)	Output (boats per week)
1	1
2	3
3	6
4	10
5	15
6	21
7	26
8	30
9	33
10	35

a. Draw the total product curve.
b. Calculate the average product of labor and draw the average product curve.
c. Calculate the marginal product of labor and draw the marginal product curve.
d. What is the relationship between average product and marginal product when Rubber Duckies produces (i) fewer than 30 boats a week and (ii) more than 30 boats a week?

2. Charlie's Chocolates' total product schedule is:

Labor (workers per day)	Output (boxes per day)
1	12
2	24
3	48
4	84
5	132
6	192
7	240
8	276
9	300
10	312

a. Draw the total product curve.
b. Calculate the average product of labor and draw the average product curve.
c. Calculate the marginal product of labor and draw the marginal product curve.
d. What is the relationship between the average product and marginal product when Charlie's Chocolates produces (i) fewer than 276 boxes a day and (ii) more than 276 boxes a day?

*3. In problem 1, suppose that the price of labor is $400 a week and total fixed cost is $1,000 a week.
a. Calculate total cost, total variable cost, and total fixed cost for each output and draw the short-run total cost curves.
b. Calculate average total cost, average fixed cost, average variable cost, and marginal cost at each output and draw the short-run average and marginal cost curves.

4. In problem 2, the price of labor is $50 per day and total fixed costs are $50 per day.
a. Calculate total cost, total variable cost, and total fixed costs for each level of output and draw the short-run total cost curves.
b. Calculate average total cost, average fixed cost, average variable cost, and marginal cost at each level of output and draw the short-run average and marginal cost curves.

*5. In problem 3, suppose that Rubber Duckies' total fixed cost increases to $1,100 a week. Explain what changes occur to the short-run average and marginal cost curves.

6. In problem 4, suppose that the price of labor increases to $70 per day. Explain what changes occur to the short-run average and marginal cost curves.

*7. In problem 3, Rubber Duckies buys a second plant and now the total product of each quantity of labor doubles. The total fixed cost of operating each plant is $1,000 a week. The wage rate is $400 a week.
a. Set out the average total cost schedule when Rubber Duckies operates two plants.
b. Draw the long-run average cost curve.
c. Over what output range is it efficient to operate one plant and two plants?

8. In problem 4, Charlie's Chocolates buys a second plant and now the total product of each quantity of labor doubles. The total fixed cost of operating each plant is $50 a day. The wage rate is $50 a day.
a. Set out the average total cost curve when Charlie's operates two plants.
b. Draw the long-run average cost curve.
c. Over what output range is it efficient to operate one plant and two plants?

*9. The table shows the production function of Bonnie's Balloon Rides:

Labor (workers per day)	Output (rides per day)			
	Plant I	Plant 2	Plant 3	Plant 4
1	4	10	13	15
2	10	15	18	21
3	13	18	22	24
4	15	20	24	26
5	16	21	25	27
Balloons (number)	1	2	3	4

Bonnie must pay $500 a day for each balloon she rents and $250 a day for each balloon operator she hires.

a.   Find and graph the average total cost curve for each plant size.
b.   Draw Bonnie's long-run average cost curve.
c.   What is Bonnie's minimum efficient scale?
d.   Explain how Bonnie uses her long-run average cost curve to decide how many balloons to rent.

10. The table shows the production function of Mario's Pizza-to-Go.

Labor (workers per day)	Output (pizzas per day)			
	Plant I	Plant 2	Plant 3	Plant 4
1	4	8	11	13
2	8	12	15	17
3	11	15	18	20
4	13	17	20	22
Ovens (number)	1	2	3	4

Mario must pay $100 a day for each oven he rents and $75 a day for each kitchen hand he hires.

a.   Find and graph the average total cost curve for each plant size.
b.   Draw Mario's long-run average cost curve.
c.   Over what output range does Mario experience economies of scale?
d.   Explain how Mario uses his long-run average cost curve to decide how many ovens to rent.

CRITICAL THINKING

 1. Study *Reading Between the Lines* on pp. 234–235 and then:

a.   Sketch the average product curve and the marginal product curve that correspond to the total product curve TP_0.
b.   Sketch the average product curve and the marginal product curve that correspond to the total product curve TP_1.
c.   Why does Fig. 2 show Mobil operating on the downward-sloping portion of the *ATC* curve and Exxon operating on the upward-sloping portion?
d.   Use the links on the Parkin Web site to obtain information about the labor force, revenue, and cost of other big oil companies.
e.   Using the size of the labor force and total cost data, how does the merged Exxon-Mobil compare with the other big oil companies?
f.   Which of the big oil companies do you think is the most efficient and why?

 2. A telecommunication company is considering replacing human telephone operators with computers. This change will increase total fixed cost and decrease total variable cost. Either use the spreadsheet on the Parkin Web site or create your own example and sketch:

a.   The total cost curves for the original technology that uses human operators.
b.   The average cost curves for the original technology that uses human operators.
c.   The marginal cost curves for the original technology that uses human operators.
d.   The total cost curves for the new technology that uses computers.
e.   The average cost curves for the new technology that uses computers.
f.   The marginal cost curves for the new technology that uses computers.

 3. A spreadsheet on the Parkin Web site provides information about the cost of operating an ATM. Use the data to work out the average cost curves for an ATM. Under what conditions might a bank *not* install an ATM but use a human teller instead?

Chapter 12

Perfect Competition

In 1998, Americans spent more than $10 billion on ice cream. Competition in ice cream is fierce. National names such as Baskin-Robbins, Häagen-Dazs, and Ben and Jerry's compete with Bart's, Annabel's, and hundreds of private label store brands for a place in a crowded market. New firms enter and try their luck while other firms are squeezed out of the business. How does competition affect prices and profits? What causes some firms to enter an industry and others to leave it? What are the effects on profits and prices of new firms entering and old firms leaving an industry? ◆ On a typical day in 1998, a million people were unemployed because they had been laid off by employers seeking to trim their costs and avoid bankruptcy. Ice cream producers, computer makers, and firms in almost every sector of the economy laid off workers in 1995, even though the economy was expanding and the total number of jobs was growing. Why do firms lay off workers? When will a firm temporarily shut down, laying off its workers? ◆ Over the past few years, there has been a dramatic fall in the prices of personal computers. For example, a slow computer cost almost $4,000 a few years ago, and a fast one costs only $1,000 today. What goes on in an industry when the price of its output falls sharply? What happens to the profits of the firms producing such goods?

Hot Rivalry in Ice Cream

◆ Ice cream, computers, and most other goods are produced by more than one firm, and these firms compete with each other for sales. To study competitive markets, we are going to build a model of a market in which competition is as fierce and extreme as possible—more extreme than in the examples we've just considered. We call this situation "perfect competition."

After studying this chapter, you will be able to:

- Define perfect competition
- Explain how price and output are determined in a competitive industry
- Explain why firms sometimes shut down temporarily and lay off workers
- Explain why firms enter and leave an industry
- Predict the effects of a change in demand and of a technological advance
- Explain why perfect competition is efficient

Competition

THE FIRMS THAT YOU STUDY IN THIS CHAPTER face the force of raw competition. We call this extreme form of competition perfect competition. **Perfect competition** is an industry in which

- Many firms sell identical products to many buyers.
- There are no restrictions on entry into the industry.
- Established firms have no advantage over new ones.
- Sellers and buyers are well informed about prices.

Farming, fishing, wood pulping and paper milling, the manufacture of paper cups and plastic shopping bags, grocery retailing, photo finishing, lawn service, plumbing, painting, dry cleaning, and the provision of laundry services are all examples of highly competitive industries.

How Perfect Competition Arises

Perfect competition arises if the minimum efficient scale of a single producer is small relative to the demand for the good or service (see Chapter 11, pp. 233). A firm's **minimum efficient scale** is the smallest quantity of output at which long-run average cost reaches its lowest level. Where the minimum efficient scale of a firm is small relative to the demand, there is room for many firms in an industry.

Second, perfect competition arises if each firm is perceived to produce a good or service that has no unique characteristics so that consumers don't care which firm they buy from.

Price Takers

Firms in perfect competition must make many decisions. But one thing they do *not* decide is the price at which to sell their output. Firms in perfect competition are said to be price takers. A **price taker** is a firm that cannot influence the price of a good or service.

The key reason why a perfectly competitive firm is a price taker is that it produces a tiny proportion of the total output of a particular good and buyers are well informed about the prices of other firms.

Imagine that you are a wheat farmer in Kansas. You have a thousand acres under cultivation—which sounds like a lot. But then you go on a drive through Colorado, Oklahoma, Texas, and back up to Nebraska and the Dakotas. You find unbroken stretches of wheat covering millions of acres. And you know there are similar vistas in Canada, Argentina, Australia, and Ukraine. Your thousand acres is a drop in the ocean. Nothing makes your wheat any better than any other farmer's, and all the buyers of wheat know the price at which they can do business.

If everybody else sells their wheat for $4 a bushel and you want $4.10, why would people buy from you? They can simply go to the next farmer, and the one after that, and the next and buy all they need for $4. This price is determined in the market for wheat, and you are a *price taker*.

The *market* demand for wheat is not perfectly elastic. The market demand curve is downward sloping, and its elasticity depends on the substitutability of other grains such as barley, rye, corn, and rice for wheat. But the demand for wheat from farm *A* is perfectly elastic because wheat from farm *B* is a *perfect substitute* for wheat from farm *A*. A price taker faces a perfectly elastic demand curve.

Economic Profit and Revenue

A firm's goal is to maximize **economic profit**, which is equal to total revenue minus total cost. Total cost is the *opportunity cost* of production, which includes the firm's **normal profit**, the return that the firm's entrepreneur can obtain in the best alternative business.

A firm's **total revenue** equals the price of its output multiplied by the number of units of output sold (price × quantity). **Marginal revenue** is the change in total revenue that results from a one-unit increase in the quantity sold. Marginal revenue is calculated by dividing the change in total revenue by the change in the quantity sold.

Figure 12.1 illustrates these revenue concepts. Sidney's Sweaters is one of a thousand similar small firms. In Fig. 12.1(a), demand and supply in the sweater market determine the price, which is $25 a sweater. Sidney must take this price. He cannot influence it by changing the quantity of sweaters he produces.

The table shows three different quantities of sweaters produced. As the quantity varies, the price remains constant—in this example at $25 a sweater. Total revenue is equal to the price multiplied by the quantity sold. For example, if Sidney sells 8 sweaters, his total revenue is 8 × $25, which equals $200.

FIGURE 12.1
Demand, Price, and Revenue in Perfect Competition

(a) Sweater market

(b) Sidney's demand and marginal revenue

(c) Sidney's total revenue

Quantity sold (Q) (sweaters per day)	Price (P) (dollars per sweater)	Total revenue (TR = P × Q) (dollars)	Marginal revenue (MR = ΔTR/ΔQ) (dollars per additional sweater)
8	25	200	
			 25
9	25	225	
			 25
10	25	250	

Market demand and supply determine the market price. In part (a), the market price is $25 a sweater and 9,000 sweaters are bought and sold. Sidney faces a perfectly elastic demand at the market price of $25 a sweater, part (b). The table calculates Sidney's total revenue and marginal revenue. Part (b) of the figure shows Sidney's demand curve, which is also its marginal revenue curve (MR). Part (c) shows Sidney's total revenue curve (TR). Point *a* corresponds to the second row of the table.

Marginal revenue is the change in total revenue that results from a one-unit change in quantity. For example, when the quantity sold increases from 8 to 9, total revenue increases from $200 to $225, so marginal revenue is $25 a sweater. (Notice that in the table, marginal revenue appears *between* the lines for the quantities sold to remind you that marginal revenue results from the *change* in the quantity sold.)

Because the price remains constant when the quantity sold changes, the change in total revenue that results from a one-unit increase in the quantity sold equals price. Therefore in perfect competition, marginal revenue equals price.

Figure 12.1(b) shows Sidney's marginal revenue curve (MR). This curve tells us the change in total revenue that results from selling one more sweater. This curve is also the firm's demand curve. The firm, being a price taker, can sell any quantity it chooses at this price. The firm faces a perfectly elastic demand for its output.

The total revenue curve (TR) in part (c) shows the total revenue at each quantity sold. For example, if Sidney sells 9 sweaters, total revenue is $225 (point *a*). Because each additional sweater sold brings in a constant amount—$25—the total revenue curve is an upward-sloping straight line.

R E V I E W   Q U I Z

- Explain why a firm in perfect competition is a price taker.
- In perfect competition, what is the relationship between a firm's demand curve and the market demand curve?
- In perfect competition, why is a firm's demand curve also its marginal revenue curve?
- In perfect competition, why is the total revenue curve an upward-sloping straight line?

The Firm's Decisions in Perfect Competition

FIRMS IN A PERFECTLY COMPETITIVE INDUSTRY face a given market price and have the revenue curves that you've studied. These revenue curves summarize the market constraint faced by a perfectly competitive firm.

Firms also have a technology constraint, which is described by the product curves (total product, average product, and marginal product) that you studied in Chapter 11. The technology available to the firm determines its costs, which are described by the cost curves (total cost, average cost, and marginal cost) that you also studied in Chapter 11.

The task of the competitive firm is to make the maximum economic profit possible, given the constraints it faces. To achieve this objective, a firm must make four key decisions: two in the short run and two in the long run.

Short-Run Decisions The short run is a time frame in which each firm has a given plant and the number of firms in the industry is fixed. But many things can change in the short run, and the firm must react to these changes. For example, the price for which the firm can sell its output might have a seasonal fluctuation, or it might fluctuate with general business fluctuations. The firm must react to such short-run price fluctuations and decide:

1. Whether to produce or to shut down
2. If the decision is to produce, what quantity to produce

Long-Run Decisions The long run is a time frame in which each firm can change the size of its plant and decide whether to leave the industry. Other firms can decide to enter the industry. So in the long run, both the plant size of each firm and the number of firms in the industry can change. Also in the long run, the constraints facing firms can change. For example, the demand for the good can permanently fall, or technological advance can change the industry's costs. The firm must react to such long-run changes and decide:

1. Whether to increase or decrease its plant size
2. Whether to stay in the industry or leave it

The Firm and the Industry in the Short Run and the Long Run To study a competitive industry, we begin by looking at an individual firm's short-run decisions. We then see how the short-run decisions of all firms in a competitive industry combine to determine the industry price, output, and economic profit. Then we turn to the long run and study the effects of long-run decisions on the industry price, output, and economic profit. All the decisions we study are driven by a single objective: to maximize economic profit.

Profit-Maximizing Output

A perfectly competitive firm maximizes economic profit by choosing its output level. One way of finding the profit-maximizing output is to study a firm's total revenue and total cost and to find the output level at which total revenue exceeds total cost by the largest amount. Figure 12.2 shows how to do this for Sidney's Sweaters. The table lists Sidney's total revenue and total cost at different outputs, and part (a) of the figure shows Sidney's total revenue and total cost curves. These curves are graphs of the numbers shown in the first three columns of the table. The total revenue curve (*TR*) is the same as that in Fig. 12.1(c). The total cost curve (*TC*) is similar to the one that you met in Chapter 11. As output increases, so does total cost.

Economic profit equals total revenue minus total cost. The fourth column of the table in Fig. 12.2 shows Sidney's economic profit, and part (b) of the figure illustrates these numbers as Sidney's profit curve. This curve shows that Sidney makes an economic profit at outputs between 4 and 12 sweaters a day. At outputs less than 4 sweaters a day, Sidney incurs an economic loss. Sidney also incurs an economic loss if output exceeds 12 sweaters a day. At outputs of 4 sweaters and 12 sweaters a day, total cost equals total revenue and Sidney's economic profit is zero. An output at which total cost equals total revenue is called a *break-even point*. The firm's economic profit is zero but because normal profit is part of total cost, the firm makes normal profit at a break-even point. That is, at the break-even point, the entrepreneur makes an income equal to the best alternative return forgone.

Notice the relationship between the total revenue, total cost, and profit curves. Economic profit is measured by the vertical distance between the total revenue and total cost curves. When the total revenue

FIGURE 12.2
Total Revenue, Total Cost, and Economic Profit

(a) Revenue and cost

(b) Economic profit and loss

Quantity (Q) (sweaters per day)	Total revenue (TR) (dollars)	Total cost (TC) (dollars)	Economic profit (TR – TC) (dollars)
0	0	22	−22
1	25	45	−20
2	50	66	−16
3	75	85	−10
4	100	100	0
5	125	114	11
6	150	126	24
7	175	141	34
8	200	160	40
9	225	183	42
10	250	210	40
11	275	245	30
12	300	300	0
13	325	360	−35

The table lists Sidney's total revenue, total cost, and economic profit. Part (a) graphs the total revenue and total cost curves. Economic profit, in part (a), is the height of the blue area between the total cost and total revenue curves. Sidney's makes maximum economic profit, $42 a day ($225 − $183), when it produces 9 sweaters—the output at which the vertical distance between the total revenue and total cost curves is at its largest. At outputs of 4 sweaters a day and 12 sweaters a day, Sidney's makes zero economic profit—these are break-even points. At outputs less than 4 and greater than 12 sweaters a day, Sidney's incurs an economic loss. Part (b) shows Sidney's profit curve. The profit curve is at its highest when economic profit is at a maximum. The profit curve cuts the horizontal axis at the break-even points.

curve in part (a) is above the total cost curve, between 4 and 12 sweaters, the firm is making an economic profit, and the profit curve in part (b) is above the horizontal axis. At the break-even point, where the total cost and total revenue curves intersect, the profit curve intersects the horizontal axis. The profit curve is at a maximum when TR exceeds TC by the largest amount. In this example, profit maximization occurs at an output of 9 sweaters a day. At this output, Sidney's economic profit is $42 a day.

Marginal Analysis

Another way of finding the profit-maximizing output is to use *marginal analysis* and compare marginal revenue, *MR*, with marginal cost, *MC*. As output increases, marginal revenue remains constant but marginal cost changes. At low output levels, marginal cost decreases, but it eventually increases. So where the marginal cost curve intersects the marginal revenue curve, marginal cost is rising.

If marginal revenue exceeds marginal cost (if *MR > MC*), then the extra revenue from selling one more unit exceeds the extra cost incurred to produce it. The firm makes an economic profit on the marginal unit, so its economic profit increases if output increases.

If marginal revenue is less than marginal cost (if *MR < MC*), then the extra revenue from selling one more unit is less than the extra cost incurred to produce it. The firm incurs an economic loss on the marginal unit, so its economic profit decreases if output increases and its economic profit increases if output *decreases.*

If marginal revenue equals marginal cost (if *MR = MC*), economic profit is maximized. The rule *MR = MC* is a prime example of marginal analysis. Let's check that this rule works to find the profit-maximizing output by returning to Sidney's sweater factory.

Look at Fig. 12.3. The table records Sidney's marginal revenue and marginal cost. Marginal revenue is a constant $25 a sweater. Over the range of outputs shown in the table, marginal cost increases from $19 a sweater to $35 a sweater.

Focus on the highlighted rows of the table. If Sidney increases output from 8 sweaters to 9 sweaters, marginal revenue is $25 and marginal cost is $23. Because marginal revenue exceeds marginal cost, economic profit increases. The last column of the table shows that economic profit increases from $40 to $42, an increase of $2. The blue area in the figure shows this economic profit from the ninth sweater.

If Sidney increases output from 9 sweaters to 10 sweaters, marginal revenue is still $25, but marginal cost is $27. Because marginal revenue is less than marginal cost, economic profit decreases. The last column of the table shows that economic profit decreases from $42 to $40. The red area in the figure shows this loss from the tenth sweater.

Sidney maximizes economic profit by producing 9 sweaters a day, the quantity at which marginal revenue equals marginal cost.

FIGURE 12.3
Profit-Maximizing Output

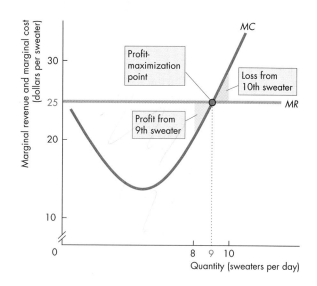

Quantity (Q) (sweaters per day)	Total revenue (TR) (dollars)	Marginal revenue (MR) (dollars per additional sweater)	Total cost (TC) (dollars)	Marginal cost (MC) (dollars per additional sweater)	Economic profit (TR − TC) (dollars)
7	175		141		34
		25		19	
8	200		160		40
		25		23	
9	225		183		42
		25		27	
10	250		210		40
		25		35	
11	275		245		30

Another way of finding the profit-maximizing output is to determine the output at which marginal revenue equals marginal cost. The table shows that if output increases from 8 to 9 sweaters, marginal cost is $23, which is less than the marginal revenue of $25. If output increases from 9 to 10 sweaters, marginal cost is $27, which exceeds the marginal revenue of $25. The figure shows that marginal cost and marginal revenue are equal when Sidney produces 9 sweaters a day. If marginal revenue exceeds marginal cost, an increase in output increases economic profit. If marginal revenue is less than marginal cost, an increase in output decreases economic profit. If marginal revenue equals marginal cost, economic profit is maximized.

The Firm's Short-Run Supply Curve

A perfectly competitive firm's short-run supply curve shows how the firm's profit-maximizing output varies as the market price varies, other things remaining the same. Figure 12.4 shows how to derive Sidney's supply curve. Part (a) shows Sidney's marginal cost and average variable cost curves, and part (b) shows Sidney's supply curve. There is a direct link between the marginal cost and average variable cost curves and the supply curve. Let's see what that link is.

Temporary Plant Shutdown In the short run, a firm cannot avoid incurring its fixed cost. But the firm can avoid variable costs by temporarily laying off its workers and shutting down. If a firm shuts down it produces no output and it incurs a loss equal to total fixed cost. This loss is the largest that a firm need incur. A firm shuts down if the price falls below the minimum of average variable cost. The **shutdown point** is the output and price at which the firm just covers its total variable cost—point s in Fig. 12.4(a). If the price is $17, the marginal revenue curve is MR_0 and the profit-maximizing output is 7 sweaters a day at point s. But both price and average variable cost equal $17, so Sidney makes no economic profit on these 7 sweaters. His economic loss equals total fixed cost. At a price below $17, no matter what quantity Sidney produces, average *variable* cost exceeds price and the economic loss exceeds total fixed cost. At a price below $17, Sidney shuts down.

The Short-Run Supply Curve If the price is above minimum average variable cost, Sidney maximizes profit by producing the output at which marginal cost equals price. We can determine the quantity produced at each price from the marginal cost curve. At a price of $25, the marginal revenue curve is MR_1 and Sidney maximizes profit by producing 9 sweaters. At a price of $31, the marginal revenue curve is MR_2 and Sidney produces 10 sweaters.

Sidney's short-run supply curve, shown in Fig. 12.4(b), has two separate parts: First, at prices that exceed minimum average variable cost, the supply curve is the same as the marginal cost curve above the shutdown point (s). Second, at prices below minimum average variable cost, Sidney shuts down and produces nothing. Its supply curve runs along the vertical axis. At a price of $17, Sidney is indifferent between shutting down and producing 7 sweaters a day. Either way, Sidney incurs a loss of $22 a day.

FIGURE 12.4
A Firm's Supply Curve

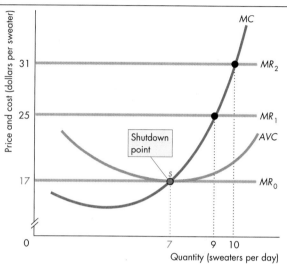

(a) Marginal cost and average variable cost

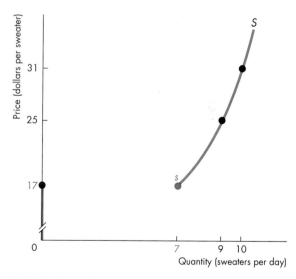

(b) Sidney's supply curve

Part (a) shows Sidney's profit-maximizing output at various market prices. At $25 a sweater, Sidney produces 9 sweaters. At $17 a sweater, Sidney produces 7 sweaters. At any price below $17 a sweater, Sidney produces nothing. Sidney's shutdown point is s. Part (b) shows Sidney's supply curve—the number of sweaters Sidney will produce at each price. It is made up of the marginal cost curve (part a) at all points above the average variable cost curve and the vertical axis at all prices below minimum average variable cost.

Short-Run Industry Supply Curve

The **short-run industry supply curve** shows the quantity supplied by the industry at each price when the plant size of each firm and the number of firms remain constant. The quantity supplied by the industry at a given price is the sum of the quantities supplied by all firms in the industry at that price.

Figure 12.5 shows the supply curve for the competitive sweater industry. In this example, the industry consists of 1,000 firms exactly like Sidney's Sweaters. At each price, the quantity supplied by the industry is 1,000 times the quantity supplied by a single firm.

The table in Fig. 12.5 shows the firm's and the industry's supply schedule and how the industry supply curve is constructed. At prices below $17, every firm in the industry shuts down; the quantity supplied by the industry is zero. At a price of $17, each firm is indifferent between shutting down and producing nothing or operating and producing 7 sweaters a day. Some firms will shut down and others will supply 7 sweaters a day. The quantity supplied by each firm is *either* 0 or 7 sweaters, but the quantity supplied by the industry is *between* 0 (all firms shut down) and 7,000 (all firms produce 7 sweaters a day each).

To construct the industry supply curve, we sum the quantities supplied by the individual firms. Each of the 1,000 firms in the industry has a supply schedule like Sidney's. At prices below $17, the industry supply curve runs along the price axis. At a price of $17, the industry supply curve is horizontal—supply is perfectly elastic. As the price rises above $17, each firm increases its quantity supplied, and the quantity supplied by the industry increases by 1,000 times that of each firm.

R E V I E W   Q U I Z

- Why does a firm in perfect competition produce the quantity at which marginal cost equals price?
- What is the lowest price at which a firm will produce an output? Explain why.
- What is the largest economic loss that a firm incurs in the short run and why?
- What is the relation among a firm's supply curve, its marginal cost curve, and its average variable cost curve?
- How do we derive an industry supply curve?

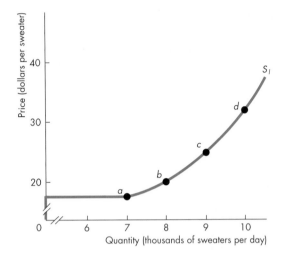

FIGURE 12.5

Industry Supply Curve

	Price (dollars) per sweater)	Quantity supplied by Sidney's Sweaters (sweaters per day)	Quantity supplied by industry (sweaters per day)
a	17	0 or 7	0 to 7,000
b	20	8	8,000
c	25	9	9,000
d	31	10	10,000

The industry supply schedule is the sum of the supply schedules of all individual firms. An industry that consists of 1,000 identical firms has a supply schedule similar to that of the individual firm, but the quantity supplied by the industry is 1,000 times as large as that of the individual firm (see table). The industry supply curve is S_I. Points $a, b, c,$ and d correspond to the rows of the table. At the shutdown price of $17, each firm produces either 0 or 7 sweaters per day, so the industry supply curve is perfectly elastic at the shutdown price.

So far, we have studied a single firm in isolation. We have seen that the firm's profit-maximizing actions depend on the market price, which the firm takes as given. But how is the market price determined? Let's find out.

Output, Price, and Profit in Perfect Competition

└─ TO DETERMINE THE MARKET PRICE AND THE quantity bought and sold in a perfectly competitive market, we need to study how market demand and market supply interact. We begin this process by studying a perfectly competitive market in the short run when the number of firms is fixed and each firm has a given plant size.

Short-Run Equilibrium

Industry demand and industry supply determine the market price and industry output. Figure 12.6(a) shows a short-run equilibrium. The supply curve S is the same as S_I in Fig. 12.5.

If demand is at the level shown by the demand curve D_1, the equilibrium price is $20. Although industry demand and supply determine this price, each firm takes the price as given and produces its

profit-maximizing output, which is 8 sweaters a day. Because the industry has 1,000 firms, industry output is 8,000 sweaters a day.

A Change in Demand

Changes in demand bring changes to short-run industry equilibrium. Figure 12.6(b) shows these changes.

If demand increases, the demand curve shifts rightward to D_2. The price rises to $25. At this price, each firm maximizes profit by increasing its output. The new output level is 9 sweaters a day for each firm and 9,000 sweaters a day for the industry.

If demand decreases, the demand curve shifts leftward to D_3. The price now falls to $17. At this price, each firm maximizes profit by decreasing its output. The new output level is 7 sweaters a day for each firm and 7,000 sweaters a day for the industry.

If the demand curve shifts farther leftward than D_3, the price remains constant at $17 because the industry supply curve is horizontal at that price. Some firms continue to produce 7 sweaters a day,

---

FIGURE 12.6

Short-Run Equilibrium

(a) Equilibrium

(b) Change in equilibrium

In part (a), the industry's supply curve is S. Demand is D_1, and the price is $20. At this price, each firm produces 8 sweaters a day and the industry produces 8,000 sweaters a day. In part (b), when demand increases to D_2, the price rises to $25 and

each firm increases its output to 9 sweaters a day. Industry output is 9,000 sweaters a day. When demand decreases to D_3, the price falls to $17 and each firm decreases its output to 7 sweaters a day. Industry output is 7,000 sweaters a day.

and others temporarily shut down. Firms are indifferent between these two activities, and whichever they choose, they incur an economic loss equal to total fixed cost. The number of firms that continue to produce is just enough to satisfy the market demand at a price of $17.

Let's now look at the profits that firms make and the losses they can incur in a short-run equilibrium.

Profits and Losses in the Short Run

In short-run equilibrium, although the firm produces the profit-maximizing output, it does not necessarily end up making an economic profit. It might do so, but it might alternatively break even (makes a normal profit) or incur an economic loss. To determine which of these outcomes occurs, we compare the firm's total revenue and total cost, or equivalently, we compare price with average total cost. If price equals average total cost, a firm breaks even—makes normal profit. If price exceeds average total cost, a firm makes an economic profit. If price is less than average total cost, a firm incurs an economic loss. Figure 12.7 shows these three possible short-run profit outcomes.

Three Possible Profit Outcomes In part (a), the price of a sweater is $20. Sidney produces 8 sweaters a day. Average total cost is also $20 a sweater, so Sidney makes normal profit and zero economic profit.

In part (b), the price of a sweater is $25. Profit is maximized when output is 9 sweaters a day. Here, price exceeds average total cost (*ATC*), so Sidney makes an economic profit. This economic profit is $42 a day. It is made up of $4.67 per sweater ($25.00 – $20.33) multiplied by the number of sweaters ($4.67 × 9 = $42). The blue rectangle shows this economic profit. The height of that rectangle is profit per sweater, $4.67, and the length is the quantity of sweaters produced, 9 a day, so the area of the rectangle measures Sidney's economic profit of $42 a day.

In part (c), the price of a sweater is $17. Here, price is less than average total cost and Sidney incurs an economic loss. Price and marginal revenue are $17 a sweater, and the profit-maximizing (in this case, loss-minimizing) output is 7 sweaters a day. Sidney's total revenue is $119 a day (7 × $17). Average total cost is $20.14 a sweater, so the economic loss is $3.14 per sweater ($20.14 – $17.00). This loss per sweater multiplied by the number of sweaters is $22 ($3.14 × 7 = $22). The red rectangle shows this

FIGURE 12.7
Three Possible Profit Outcomes in the Short Run

(a) Normal profit

(b) Economic profit

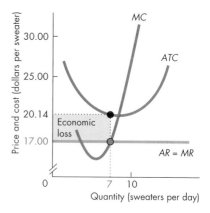

(c) Economic loss

In the short run, firms might break even (making a normal profit), make an economic profit, or incur an economic loss. If the price equals minimum average total cost, the firm breaks even and makes a normal profit (part a). If the price exceeds the average total cost of producing the profit-maximizing output, the firm makes an economic profit (the blue rectangle in part b). If the price is below minimum average total cost, the firm incurs an economic loss (the red rectangle in part c).

economic loss. The height of that rectangle is economic loss per sweater, $3.14, and the length is the quantity of sweaters produced, 7 a day, so the area of the rectangle measures Sidney's economic loss of $22 a day.

Long-Run Adjustments

In short-run equilibrium, a firm might make an economic profit, incur an economic loss, or break even (make normal profit). Although each of these three situations is a short-run equilibrium, only one of them is a long-run equilibrium. To see why, we need to examine the forces at work in a competitive industry in the long run.

In the long run, an industry adjusts in two ways:

- Entry and exit
- Changes in plant size

Let's look first at entry and exit.

Entry and Exit

In the long run, firms respond to economic profit and economic loss by either entering or exiting an industry. Firms enter an industry in which firms are making an economic profit, and they exit an industry in which firms are incurring an economic loss. Temporary economic profit or temporary economic loss, like the win or loss at a casino, do not trigger entry or exit. But the prospect of persistent economic profit or loss does.

Entry and exit influence price, the quantity produced, and economic profit. The immediate effect of these decisions is to shift the industry supply curve. If more firms enter an industry, supply increases and the industry supply curve shifts rightward. If firms exit an industry, supply decreases and the industry supply curve shifts leftward.

Let's see what happens when new firms enter an industry.

The Effects of Entry Figure 12.8 shows the effects of entry. Suppose that all the firms in the sweater industry have cost curves like Sidney's in Fig. 12.7. At any price greater than $20, firms make an economic profit. At any price less than $20, firms incur an economic loss. And at a price of $20, firms make zero economic profit. Also suppose that the demand curve for sweaters is D. If the industry supply curve is S_1, sweaters sell for $23 and 7,000 sweaters a day are produced. Firms in the industry

make an economic profit. This economic profit is a signal for new firms to enter the industry. As these events unfold, supply increases and the industry supply curve shifts rightward to S_0. With the greater supply and unchanged demand, the market price falls from $23 to $20 a sweater and the quantity produced by the industry increases from 7,000 to 8,000 sweaters a day.

Industry output increases, but Sidney's Sweaters and the other firms in the industry *decrease* output! As the price falls, each firm moves down along its supply curve and produces less. But because the number of firms in the industry increases, the industry as a whole produces more.

Because the price falls, each firm's economic profit decreases. When the price falls to $20, economic profit disappears and each firm makes a normal profit.

You have just discovered a key proposition:

As new firms enter an industry, the price falls and the economic profit of each existing firm decreases.

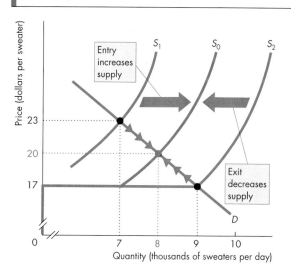

FIGURE 12.8

Entry and Exit

When new firms enter the sweater industry, the industry supply curve shifts rightward, from S_1 to S_0. The equilibrium price falls from $23 to $20, and the quantity produced increases from 7,000 to 8,000 sweaters. When firms exit the sweater industry, the industry supply curve shifts leftward, from S_2 to S_0. The equilibrium price rises from $17 to $20, and the quantity produced decreases from 9,000 to 8,000 sweaters.

An example of this process occurred during the 1980s in the personal computer industry. When IBM introduced its first PC, there was little competition and the price of a PC gave IBM a big profit. But new firms such as Compaq, NEC, Dell, and a host of others entered the industry with machines that were technologically identical to IBM's. In fact, they were so similar that they came to be called "clones." The massive wave of entry into the personal computer industry shifted the supply curve rightward and lowered the price and the economic profit for all firms.

Let's now look at the effects of exit.

The Effects of Exit Figure 12.8 shows the effects of exit. Suppose that firms' costs and market demand are the same as before. But now suppose the supply curve is S_2. The market price is $17, and 9,000 sweaters a day are produced. Firms now incur an economic loss. This economic loss is a signal for some firms to exit the industry. As firms exit, the supply curve shifts leftward to S_0. With the decrease in supply, industry output decreases from 9,000 to 8,000 sweaters and the price rises from $17 to $20.

As the price rises, Sidney's Sweaters, like each other firm in the industry, moves up along its supply curve and increases output. That is, for each firm that remains in the industry, the profit-maximizing output increases. Because the price rises and each firm sells more, economic loss decreases. When the price rises to $20, each firm makes normal profit.

You have just discovered a second key proposition:

As firms leave an industry, the price rises and the economic loss of each remaining firm decreases.

An example of a firm leaving an industry is International Harvester, a manufacturer of farm equipment. For decades, people associated the name "International Harvester" with tractors, combines, and other farm machines. But International Harvester wasn't the only maker of farm equipment. The industry became intensely competitive, and the firm began losing money.

International Harvester exited because it was incurring an economic loss. Its exit decreased supply and made it possible for the remaining firms in the industry to break even.

You've now seen how economic profits induce entry, which in turn lowers profits, and you've seen how economic losses induce exit, which in turn eliminates losses. Let's now look at changes in plant size.

Changes in Plant Size

A firm changes its plant size if, by doing so, it can lower its costs and increase its economic profit. You can probably think of lots of examples of firms changing their plant size.

One example that has almost certainly happened near your campus in recent years is a change in the plant size of Kinko's or similar copy shops. Another is the number of FedEx vans that you see on the streets and highways. Another is the number of square feet of retail space devoted to selling computers and video games. These are examples of firms increasing their plant size to seek larger profits.

There are also many examples of firms decreasing their plant size to avoid economic losses. One of these is Schwinn, the Chicago-based maker of bicycles. As competition from Asian bicycle makers became tougher, Schwinn cut back. Many firms have scaled back their operations—a process called *downsizing*—in recent years.

Figure 12.9 shows a situation in which Sidney can increase his profit by increasing the plant size. With its current plant, Sidney's marginal cost curve is MC_0 and its short-run average total cost curve is $SRAC_0$. The market price is $25 a sweater, so Sidney's marginal revenue curve is MR_0 and Sidney maximizes profit by producing 6 sweaters a day.

Sidney's Sweaters' long-run average cost curve is $LRAC$. By increasing its plant size—installing more knitting machines—it can move along its long-run average cost curve. As Sidney increases the plant size, the short-run marginal cost curve shifts rightward.

Recall that a firm's short-run supply curve is linked to its marginal cost curve. As Sidney's marginal cost curve shifts rightward, so does its supply curve. If Sidney's Sweaters and the other firms in the industry increase their plants, the short-run industry supply curve shifts rightward and the market price falls. The fall in the market price limits the extent to which Sidney can profit from increasing the plant size.

Figure 12.9 also shows Sidney's Sweaters in a long-run competitive equilibrium. This situation arises when the market price has fallen to $20 a sweater. Marginal revenue is MR_1, and Sidney maximizes profit by producing 8 sweaters a day. In this situation, Sidney cannot increase his profit by changing the plant size. Sidney is producing at minimum long-run average cost (point m on $LRAC$).

Because Sidney is producing at minimum long-run average cost, it has no incentive to change the plant size.

FIGURE 12.9
Plant Size and Long-Run Equilibrium

Initially, Sidney's plant has marginal cost curve MC_0 and short-run average total cost curve $SRAC_0$. The market price is $25 a sweater, and Sidney's marginal revenue is MR_0. The short-run profit-maximizing quantity is 6 sweaters a day. Sidney can increase his profit by increasing the plant size. If all firms in the sweater industry increase their plant sizes, the short-run industry supply increases and the market price falls. In long-run equilibrium, a firm operates with the plant size that minimizes its average cost. Here, Sidney operates the plant with short-run marginal cost MC_1 and short-run average cost $SRAC_1$. Sidney is also on the long-run average cost curve $LRAC$ and produces at point m. Output is 8 sweaters a day, and average total cost equals the price of a sweater—$20.

Either a bigger plant or a smaller plant has a higher long-run average cost. If Fig. 12.9 describes the situation of all firms in the sweater industry, the industry is in long-run equilibrium. No firm has an incentive to change its plant size. Also, because each firm is making zero economic profit (normal profit), no firm has an incentive to enter the industry or to leave it.

Long-Run Equilibrium

Long-run equilibrium occurs in a competitive industry when economic profit is zero (when firms earn normal profit). If the firms in a competitive industry are making economic profit, new firms enter the industry. If firms can lower their costs by increasing

their plant size, they expand. Each of these actions increases industry supply, shifts the industry supply curve rightward, lowers the price, and decreases economic profit.

Firms continue to enter and economic profit continues to decrease as long as firms in the industry are earning positive economic profits. When economic profit has been eliminated, firms stop entering the industry. And when firms are operating with the least-cost plant size, they stop expanding.

If the firms in a competitive industry are incurring an economic loss, some firms exit the industry. If firms can lower their costs by decreasing their plant size, they downsize. Each of these actions decreases industry supply, shifts the industry supply curve leftward, raises the price, and increases economic profit (shrinks economic loss).

Firms continue to exit and economic loss continues to shrink as long as firms in the industry are incurring economic losses. When economic loss has been eliminated, firms stop exiting the industry. And when firms are operating with the least-cost plant size, they stop downsizing.

So in long-run equilibrium in a competitive industry, firms neither enter nor exit the industry and neither expand nor downsize. Each firm earns normal profit.

REVIEW QUIZ

- When a firm in perfect competition produces the quantity that maximizes profit, what is the relationship among the firm's marginal cost, marginal revenue, and price?
- If firms in a competitive industry make economic profits, what happens to supply, price, output, and economic profit?
- If firms in a competitive industry incur economic losses, what happens to supply, price, output, and economic profit?

You've seen how a competitive industry adjusts toward its long-run equilibrium. But a competitive industry is rarely *in* a state of long-run equilibrium. It is constantly and restlessly evolving toward such an equilibrium. The constraints that firms face are constantly changing. The two most persistent sources of change are in tastes and technology. Let's see how a competitive industry reacts to such changes.

Changing Tastes and Advancing Technology

INCREASED AWARENESS OF THE HEALTH HAZARDS of smoking has caused a decrease in the demand for tobacco and cigarettes. The development of inexpensive car and air transportation has caused a huge decrease in the demand for long-distance trains and buses. Solid-state electronics have caused a large decrease in the demand for TV and radio repair. The development of good-quality inexpensive clothing has decreased the demand for sewing machines. What happens in a competitive industry when there is a permanent decrease in the demand for its products?

The development of the microwave oven has produced an enormous increase in demand for paper, glass, and plastic cooking utensils and for plastic wrap. The widespread use of the personal computer has brought a huge increase in the demand for floppy disks. What happens in a competitive industry when the demand for its product increases?

Advances in technology are constantly lowering the costs of production. New biotechnologies have dramatically lowered the costs of producing many food and pharmaceutical products. New electronic technologies have lowered the cost of producing just about every good and service. What happens in a competitive industry when technological change lowers its production costs?

Let's use the theory of perfect competition to answer these questions.

A Permanent Change in Demand

Figure 12.10(a) shows a competitive industry that initially is in long-run equilibrium. The demand curve is D_0, the supply curve is S_0, the market price is P_0, and industry output is Q_0. Figure 12.10(b) shows a single firm in this initial long-run equilibrium. The firm produces q_0 and makes a normal profit and zero economic profit.

Now suppose that demand decreases and the demand curve shifts leftward to D_1, as shown in part (a). The price falls to P_1, and the quantity supplied by the industry decreases from Q_0 to Q_1 as the industry slides down its short-run supply curve S_0. Part (b) shows the situation facing a firm. Price is now below the firm's minimum average total cost, so the firm incurs an economic loss. But to keep its loss to a minimum, the firm adjusts its output to keep marginal cost equal to price. At a price of P_1, each firm produces an output of q_1.

The industry is now in short-run equilibrium but not long-run equilibrium. It is in short-run equilibrium because each firm is maximizing profit. But it is not in long-run equilibrium because each firm is incurring an economic loss—its average total cost exceeds the price.

The economic loss is a signal for some firms to leave the industry. As they do so, short-run industry supply gradually decreases and the supply curve gradually shifts leftward. As industry supply decreases, the price rises. At each higher price, a firm's profit-maximizing output is greater, so the firms remaining in the industry increase their output as the price rises. Each firm slides up its marginal cost or supply curve (part b). That is, as firms exit the industry, industry output decreases but the output of the firms that remain in the industry increases. Eventually, enough firms leave the industry for the industry supply curve to have shifted to S_1 (part a). At this time, the price has returned to its original level, P_0. At this price, the firms remaining in the industry produce q_0, the same quantity that they produced before the decrease in demand. Because firms are now making normal profits and zero economic profit, no firm wants to enter or exit the industry. The industry supply curve remains at S_1, and industry output is Q_2. The industry is again in long-run equilibrium.

The difference between the initial long-run equilibrium and the final long-run equilibrium is the number of firms in the industry. A permanent decrease in demand has decreased the number of firms. Each remaining firm produces the same output in the new long-run equilibrium as it did initially and earns a normal profit. In the process of moving from the initial equilibrium to the new one, firms incur economic losses.

We've just worked out how a competitive industry responds to a permanent *decrease* in demand. A permanent increase in demand triggers a similar response, except in the opposite direction. The increase in demand brings a higher price, economic profit, and entry. Entry increases industry supply and eventually lowers the price to its original level.

The demand for airline travel in the United States has increased permanently in recent years, and the deregulation of the airlines has freed up firms to seek profit opportunities in this industry. The result has been a massive rate of entry of new airlines. The

FIGURE 12.10

A Decrease in Demand

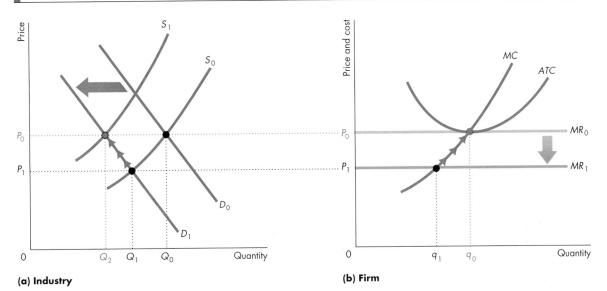

(a) Industry

(b) Firm

An industry starts out in long-run competitive equilibrium. Part (a) shows the industry demand curve D_0, the industry supply curve S_0, the equilibrium quantity Q_0, and the market price P_0. Each firm sells its output at price P_0, so its marginal revenue curve is MR_0 in part (b). Each firm produces q_0 and makes a normal profit. Demand decreases permanently from D_0 to D_1 (part a). The equilibrium price falls to P_1, each firm decreases its output to q_1 (part b), and industry output decreases to Q_1 (part a).

In this new situation, firms incur economic losses and some firms leave the industry. As they do so, the industry supply curve gradually shifts leftward, from S_0 to S_1. This shift gradually raises the market price from P_1 back to P_0. While the price is below P_0, firms incur economic losses and some firms leave the industry. Once the price has returned to P_0, each firm makes a normal profit. Firms have no further incentive to leave the industry. Each firm produces q_0, and industry output is Q_2.

process of competition and change in the airline industry is similar to what we have just studied (but with an increase in demand rather than a decrease in demand).

We've now studied the effects of a permanent change in demand for a good. To study these effects, we began and ended in a long-run equilibrium and examined the process that takes a market from one equilibrium to another. It is this process, not the equilibrium points, that describes the real world.

One feature of the predictions that we have just generated seems odd: In the long run, regardless of whether demand increases or decreases, the price returns to its original level. Is this outcome inevitable? In fact, it is not. It is possible for the long-run equilibrium price to remain the same, rise, or fall.

External Economies and Diseconomies

The change in the long-run equilibrium price depends on external economies and external diseconomies. **External economies** are factors beyond the control of an individual firm that lower its costs as the *industry* output increases. **External diseconomies** are factors outside the control of a firm that raise the firm's costs as industry output increases. With no external economies or external diseconomies, a firm's costs remain constant as the industry output changes.

Figure 12.11 illustrates these three cases and introduces a new supply concept: the long-run industry supply curve.

A **long-run industry supply curve** shows how the quantity supplied by an industry varies as the market price varies after all the possible adjustments have been made, including changes in plant size and the number of firms in the industry.

Part (a) shows the case we have just studied—no external economies or diseconomies. The long-run industry supply curve (LS_A) is perfectly elastic. In this case, a permanent increase in demand from D_0 to D_1 has no effect on the price in the long run. The increase in demand brings a temporary increase in price to P_S and a short-run quantity increase from Q_0 to Q_S. Entry increases short-run supply from S_0 to S_1, which lowers the price to its original level, P_0, and increases the quantity to Q_1.

Part (b) shows the case of external diseconomies. The long-run supply industry curve (LS_B) slopes upward. A permanent increase in demand from D_0 to D_1 increases the price in both the short run and the long run. As in the previous case, the increase in demand brings a temporary increase in price to P_S and a short-run quantity increase from Q_0 to Q_S. Entry increases short-run supply from S_0 to S_2, which lowers the price to P_2 and increases the quantity to Q_2.

One source of external diseconomies is congestion. The airline industry provides a good example. With bigger airline industry output, there is more congestion of airports and airspace, which results in longer delays and extra waiting time for passengers and airplanes. These external diseconomies mean that as the output of air transportation services increases (in the absence of technological advances), average cost increases. As a result, the long-run supply curve is upward sloping. So a permanent increase in demand brings an increase in quantity and a rise in the price. (Industries with external diseconomies might nonetheless have a falling price because technological advances shift the long-run supply curve downward.)

Part (c) shows the case of external economies. In this case, the long-run industry supply curve (LS_C) slopes downward. A permanent increase in demand from D_0 to D_1 increases the price in the short run and lowers it in the long run. Again, the increase in demand brings a temporary increase in price to P_S and a short-run quantity increase from Q_0 to Q_S. Entry increases short-run supply from S_0 to S_3, which lowers the price to P_3 and increases the quantity to Q_3.

FIGURE 12.11

Long-Run Changes in Price and Quantity

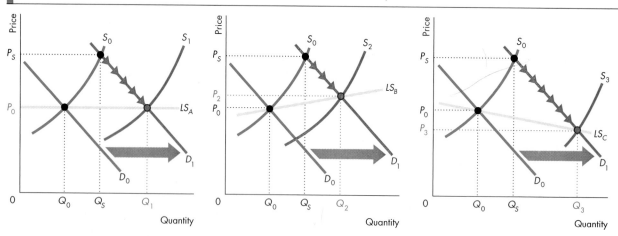

(a) Constant-cost industry

(b) Increasing-cost industry

(c) Decreasing-cost industry

Three possible changes in price and quantity occur in the long run. When demand increases from D_0 to D_1, entry occurs and the industry supply curve shifts from S_0 to S_1. In part (a), the long-run supply curve, LS_A, is horizontal. The quantity increases from Q_0 to Q_1, and the price remains constant at P_0. In part

(b), the long-run supply curve is LS_B; the price rises to P_2, and the quantity increases to Q_2. This case occurs in industries with external diseconomies. In part (c), the long-run supply curve is LS_C; the price falls to P_3, and the quantity increases to Q_3. This case occurs in an industry with external economies.

One of the best examples of external economies is the growth of specialist support services for an industry as it expands. As farm output increased in the nineteenth and early twentieth centuries, the services available to farmers expanded and average farm costs fell. For example, new firms specialized in the development and marketing of farm machinery and fertilizers. As a result, average farm costs decreased. Farms enjoyed the benefits of external economies. As a consequence, as the demand for farm products increased, the output increased but the price fell.

Over the long term, the prices of many goods and services have fallen, not because of external economies but because of technological change. Let's now study this influence on a competitive market.

Technological Change

Industries are constantly discovering lower-cost techniques of production. Most cost-saving production techniques cannot be implemented, however, without investing in new plant and equipment. As a consequence, it takes time for a technological advance to spread through an industry. Some firms whose plants are on the verge of being replaced will be quick to adopt the new technology, while other firms whose plants have recently been replaced will continue to operate with an old technology until they can no longer cover their average variable cost. Once average variable cost cannot be covered, a firm will scrap even a relatively new plant (embodying an old technology) in favor of a plant with a new technology.

New technology allows firms to produce at a lower cost. As a result, as firms adopt a new technology, their cost curves shift downward. With lower costs, firms are willing to supply a given quantity at a lower price, or, equivalently, they are willing to supply a larger quantity at a given price. In other words, industry supply increases, and the industry supply curve shifts rightward. With a given demand, the quantity produced increases and the price falls.

Two forces are at work in an industry undergoing technological change. Firms that adopt the new technology make an economic profit. So there is entry by new-technology firms. Firms that stick with the old technology incur economic losses. They either exit the industry or switch to the new technology.

As old-technology firms disappear and new-technology firms enter, the price falls and the quantity produced increases. Eventually, the industry arrives at a long-run equilibrium in which all the firms use the new technology and make a zero economic profit (a normal profit). Because in the long run competition eliminates economic profit, technological change brings only temporary gains to producers. But the lower prices and better products that technological advances bring are permanent gains for consumers.

The process that we've just described is one in which some firms experience economic profits and others experience economic losses. It is a period of dynamic change for an industry. Some firms do well, and others do badly. Often, the process has a geographical dimension—the expanding new-technology firms bring prosperity to what was once the boondocks, and traditional industrial regions decline. Sometimes, the new-technology firms are in a foreign country, while the old-technology firms are in the domestic economy. The information revolution of the 1990s has produced many examples of changes like these. Commercial banking, traditionally concentrated in New York, San Francisco, and other large cities, now flourishes in Charlotte, North Carolina, which has become the nation's number three commercial banking city. Television shows and movies, traditionally made in Los Angeles and New York, are now made in large numbers in Orlando, Florida. Technological advances are not confined to the information and entertainment industry. Even milk production is undergoing a major technological change because of genetic engineering.

REVIEW QUIZ

- Describe the course of events in a competitive industry that follow a decrease in demand. What happens to output, price, and economic profit in the short run and in the long run?
- Describe the course of events in a competitive industry that follow an increase in demand. What happens to output, price, and economic profit in the short run and in the long run?
- Describe the course of events in a competitive industry that follow the adoption of a new technology. What happens to output, price, and economic profit in the short run and in the long run?

Competition and Efficiency

A COMPETITIVE INDUSTRY CAN ACHIEVE AN EFFIcient use of resources. You studied efficiency in Chapter 6 using only the concepts of demand, supply, consumer surplus and producer surplus. But now that you have learned what lies behind the demand and supply curves of a competitive market, you can gain a deeper understanding of how the competitive market achieves efficiency.

Efficient Use of Resources

Recall that resource use is efficient when we produce the goods and services that people value most highly (see Chapter 6, pp. 108–109). If someone can become better off without anyone else becoming worse off, resources are not being used efficiently. For example, suppose we produce a computer that no one uses and that no one will ever use. Suppose also that some people are clamoring for more video games. If we produce one less computer and reallocate the unused resources to produce more video games, some people will become better off and no one will be worse off.

In the more technical language that you have learned, resource use is efficient when marginal benefit equals marginal cost. In the computer and video games example, the marginal benefit of video games exceeds the marginal cost. And the marginal cost of a computer exceeds its marginal benefit. So by producing fewer computers and more video games, we move resources toward a higher-value use.

Choices, Equilibrium, and Efficiency

We can use what you have learned about the decisions made by consumers and competitive firms and market equilibrium to describe an efficient use of resources.

Choices Consumers allocate their budgets to get the most value possible out of them. And we derive a consumer's demand curve by finding how the best budget allocation changes as the price of a good changes. So consumers get the most value out of their resources at all points along their demand curves, which are also their marginal benefit curves.

Competitive firms produce the quantity that maximizes profit. And we derive the firm's supply curve by finding the profit-maximizing quantity at each price. So firms get the most value out of their resources at all points along their supply curves, which are also their marginal cost curves. (On their supply curves, firms are *technologically efficient*—they get the maximum possible output from given inputs—and *economically efficient*—they combine resources to minimize cost. See Chapter 10, pp. 201–202.)

Equilibrium In competitive equilibrium, the quantity demanded equals the quantity supplied. So the price equals the consumers' marginal benefit and the producers' marginal cost. In this situation, the gains from trade between consumers and producers are maximized. These gains from trade are the consumer surplus plus the producer surplus.

The gains from trade for consumers are measured by *consumer surplus*, which is the area between the demand curve and the price paid. (See Chapter 6, p. 111.) The gains from trade for producers are measured by *producer surplus*, which is the area between the marginal cost curve and the price received. The total gains from trade are the sum of consumer surplus and producer surplus.

Efficiency If the people who consume and produce a good or service are the only ones affected by it, and if the market for it is in equilibrium, then resources are being used efficiently. They cannot be reallocated to increase their value.

In such a situation, there are no *external benefits* or *external costs*. **External benefits** are benefits that accrue to people other than the buyer of a good. For example, you might get a benefit from your neighbor's expenditure on her garden. Your neighbor buys the quantities of garden plants that make her as well off as possible, not her plus you.

In the absence of external benefits, the market demand curve measures marginal *social* benefit—the value that *everyone* places on one more unit of a good or service.

External costs are costs not borne by the producer of a good or service but by someone else. For example, a firm might lower its costs by polluting. The cost of pollution is an external cost. Firms produce the output level that maximizes their own profit and they do not count the cost of pollution as a charge against their profit.

In the absence of external costs, the market supply curve measures marginal *social* cost—the entire marginal cost that *anyone* bears to produce one more unit of a good or service.

An Efficient Allocation Figure 12.12 shows an efficient allocation. Consumers are efficient at all points on the demand curve, D (which is also the marginal benefit curve MB). Producers are efficient at all points on the supply curve, S (which is also the marginal cost curve MC). Resources are used efficiently at the quantity Q^* and price P^*. Marginal benefit equals marginal cost, and the sum of producer surplus (blue area) and consumer surplus (green area) is maximized.

If output is Q_0, marginal cost is C_0 and marginal benefit is B_0. Producers can supply more of the good for a cost lower than the price consumers are willing to pay and everyone gains by increasing the quantity produced. If output is greater than Q^*, marginal cost exceeds marginal benefit. It costs producers more to supply the good than the price consumers are willing to pay and everyone gains by decreasing the quantity produced.

Efficiency of Perfect Competition

Perfect competition achieves efficiency if there are no external benefits and external costs. In such a case, the benefits accrue to the buyers of the good and the costs are borne by its producer. In Fig. 12.12, the equilibrium quantity Q^* at the price P^* is efficient.

There are three main obstacles to efficiency:

1. Monopoly
2. Public goods
3. External costs and external benefits

Monopoly Monopoly (Chapter 13) restricts output below its competitive level to raise price and increase profit. Government policies (Chapter 19) arise to limit such use of monopoly power.

Public goods Goods such as national defense, the enforcement of law and order, the provision of clean drinking water, and the disposal of sewage and garbage are examples of public goods. Left to competitive markets, too small a quantity of them would be produced. Government institutions and policies (Chapter 18) help to overcome the problem of providing an efficient quantity of public goods.

External Costs and External Benefits The production of steel and chemicals can generate air and water pollution and perfect competition might produce too large a quantity of these goods. Government policies (Chapter 20) attempt to cope with external costs and benefits.

◆ You've now completed your study of perfect competition. And *Reading Between the Lines* on pp. 258–259 gives you an opportunity to use what you have learned to understand recent events in the highly competitive market for personal computers.

Although many markets approximate the model of perfect competition, many do not. Your next task is to study markets at the opposite extreme of market power—monopoly. Then, in Chapter 14, we'll study markets that lie between perfect competition and monopoly—monopolistic competition (competition with monopoly elements) and oligopoly (competition among a few producers). When you have completed this study, you'll have a toolkit that enables you to understand the variety of real-world markets.

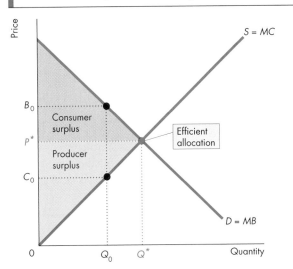

FIGURE 12.12

Efficiency of Competition

The efficient use of resources requires: consumers to be efficient, which occurs when they are on their demand curves; firms to be efficient, which occurs when they are on their supply curves; and the market to be in equilibrium with no external benefits or external costs. Resources are used efficiently at the quantity Q^* and the price P^*. With no external benefits or external costs, perfect competition achieves an efficient use of resources. If output is Q_0, the cost of producing one more unit, C_0, is less than its marginal benefit, B_0, and resources are not used efficiently.

Competition in the PC Industry

THE NEW YORK TIMES, NOVEMBER 13, 1998

Dell Reports Record Earnings and Revenues in 3rd Quarter

BY LAWRENCE M. FISHER

Dell Computer Corp. reported record third-quarter revenue and earnings Thursday as it continued to grow at several times the rate of the personal computer industry as a whole.

As always, Dell officials credited the strength of their direct sales model, in which the company bypasses distributors and dealers and builds each computer to order. Because the company holds very little inventory, it takes advantage of lower component costs, and is always selling a fresher product, which can command a higher profit margin. Dell said sales from its World Wide Web site exceeded $10 million a day for the first time during the quarter, three times the level in the quarter a year earlier.

Competitors have attempted to emulate the Dell model but with modest success so far. ...

For the quarter ended Nov. 1, Dell reported earnings of $384 million, ... up 55 percent from $248 million, in the [same] period a year earlier. Sales rose 51 percent, to $4.82 billion from $3.19 billion. ...

Dell has been gaining market share both internationally and in high-growth sectors like servers and laptop computers. ...

... while Compaq, IBM and Hewlett-Packard have all announced plans to emulate portions of Dell's business model, with various build-to-order plans, all have had difficulty in making the transition. Most are moving to a target inventory level of four weeks, while Dell maintains just eight days of inventory, allowing it to turn over inventory 46 times a year.

Essence of the Story

- Dell Computer Corporation is an efficient, low-cost, and profitable maker of PCs and servers.

- Dell sells directly to the customer and builds each computer to order. The firm maintains 8 days of inventory. An increasing volume of Dell's business is done on the Internet.

- Attempts to copy Dell's business model by Compaq, IBM, and Hewlett-Packard have been only modestly successful. These firms hold more than 4 weeks of inventories.

■ The PC industry is highly competitive. We'll assume that it is perfectly competitive because one supplier's PC is a very close substitute for another supplier's PC.

■ The industry is in short-run equilibrium but not in long-run equilibrium. Many firms are earning economic profit. And economic profit is encouraging the entry of new firms and the expansion of existing firms.

■ Figure 1 shows the market for PCs 5 years ago and the effects of entry on the price and quantity of PCs.

■ The industry demand curve is D. Five years ago, the industry supply curve was S_0. The price was \$5,000 per PC (think of this as an average PC), and the quantity produced by the industry was 25 million a year.

■ Supply then increases because of entry. The supply curve shifts rightward to S_1. (We'll assume that demand didn't change. In fact, demand did increase but by much less than the increase in supply.)

■ The price fell to \$3,000 per PC, and the quantity produced by the industry increased to 35 million a year.

■ Figure 2 shows the situation facing one PC producer that has not adopted the latest and least-cost technology for making PCs.

■ The marginal cost curve is MC_0, and the average total cost curve is ATC_0. At \$5,000 per PC, the marginal revenue curve is MR_0. The firm maximizes profit by producing 1 million PCs a year. Economic profit is \$500 million a year.

■ When the price falls to \$3,000 per PC, the marginal revenue curve is MR_1. If the firm sticks with its existing technology, it incurs an economic loss.

■ Figure 3 shows how the successful firm adopts a new technology to cut costs. Dell's build-to-order technology is an example because it lowers the cost of holding inventory.

■ When costs fall, the average total cost curve shifts downward to ATC_1 and the marginal cost curve shifts downward to MC_1. The firm expands output—in this example, to 3 million PCs a year. Economic profit is restored and, in this example, increases to \$1.5 billion a year.

Figure 1 PC industry

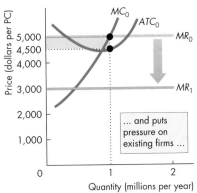

Figure 2 One PC firm

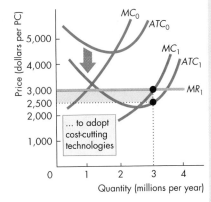

Figure 3 Cost-cutting technology

259

SUMMARY

KEY POINTS

Competition (pp. 240–241)

- Perfect competition arises when demand is large relative to the minimum efficient scale of production and when firms produce identical products.
- A perfectly competitive firm is a price taker.

The Firm's Decisions in Perfect Competition (pp. 242–246)

- The firm produces the output at which marginal revenue (price) equals marginal cost.
- If price is less than minimum average variable cost, the firm temporarily shuts down.
- A firm's supply curve is the upward-sloping part of its marginal cost curve above minimum average variable cost.
- An industry supply curve shows the sum of the quantities supplied by each firm at each price.

Output, Price, and Profit in Perfect Competition (pp. 247–251)

- Market demand and supply determine price.
- The firm produces the output at which price equals marginal cost.
- In the short run, a firm can make an economic profit, incur an economic loss, or break even.
- Economic profit induces entry. Economic loss induces exit.
- Entry and plant expansion increase supply and lower price and profit. Exit and plant contraction decrease supply and raise price and profit.
- In long-run equilibrium, economic profit is zero. There is no entry, exit, or change in plant size.

Changing Tastes and Advancing Technology (pp. 252–255)

- A permanent decrease in demand leads to a smaller industry output and a smaller number of firms.
- A permanent increase in demand leads to a larger industry output and a larger number of firms.

- The long-run effect of a change in demand on price depends on whether there are external economies (price falls) or external diseconomies (price rises) or neither (price remains constant).
- New technologies increase supply and in the long run lower the price and increase the quantity.

Competition and Efficiency (pp. 256–257)

- Resources are used efficiently when we produce goods and services in the quantities that people value most highly.
- When there are no external benefits and external costs, perfect competition achieves an efficient allocation. Marginal benefit equals marginal cost and the sum of consumer surplus and producer surplus is maximized.
- The existence of monopoly, public goods, and external costs and external benefits are obstacles to efficiency.

KEY FIGURES ◇

KEY TERMS

PROBLEMS

*1. Quick Copy is one of the many copy shops near the campus. The figure shows Quick Copy's cost curves.

a. If the market price of copying one page is 10 cents, what is Quick Copy's profit-maximizing output?

b. Calculate Quick Copy's profit.

c. With no change in demand or technology, how will the price change in the long run?

2. Bob's is one of many burger stands along the beach. The figure shows Bob's cost curves.

a. If the market price of a burger is $4, what is Bob's profit-maximizing output?

b. Calculate the profit that Bob's makes.

c. With no change in demand or technology, how will the price change in the long run?

*3. Pat's Pizza Kitchen is a price taker. Pat's cost of producing pizzas is:

Output (pizzas per hour)	Total cost (dollars per hour)
0	10
1	21
2	30
3	41
4	54
5	69

a. If a pizza sells for $14, what is Pat's profit-maximizing output per hour? How much economic profit does Pat make?

b. What is Pat's shutdown point?

c. Derive Pat's supply curve.

d. Over what price range will Pat leave the pizza industry?

e. Over what price range will other firms with costs identical to Pat's enter the industry?

f. What is the price of a pizza in the long run?

4. Lucy's Lasagna is a price taker. Lucy's cost of producing lasagna is:

Output (pizzas per hour)	Total cost (dollars per hour)
0	5
1	20
2	26
3	35
4	46
5	59

a. If lasagna sells for $7.50 a plate, what is Lucy's profit-maximizing output?

b. What is Lucy's shutdown point?

c. Over what price range will Lucy leave the lasagna industry?

d. Over what price range will other firms with costs identical to Lucy's enter the industry?

e. What is the price of lasagna in the long run?

*5. The market demand schedule for cassettes is:

Price (dollars per cassettes)	Quantity demanded (thousands of cassettes per week)
3.65	500
5.20	450
6.80	400
8.40	350
10.00	300
11.60	250
13.20	200
14.80	150

The market is perfectly competitive, and each firm has the following cost structure:

Output (cassettes per week)	Marginal cost (dollars per additional cassette)	Average variable cost (dollars per cassette)	Average total cost (dollars per cassette)
150	6.00	8.80	15.47
200	6.40	7.80	12.80
250	7.00	7.00	11.00
300	7.65	7.10	10.43
350	8.40	7.20	10.06
400	10.00	7.50	10.00
450	12.40	8.00	10.22
500	12.70	9.00	11.00

There are 1,000 firms in the industry.
a. What is the market price?
b. What is the industry's output?
c. What is the output produced by each firm?
d. What is the economic profit made by each firm?
e. Do firms enter or exit the industry?
f. What is the number of firms in the long run?

6. The same demand conditions as those in problem 5 prevail, and there are 1,000 firms in the industry, but total fixed costs increase by $980. What now are your answers to the questions in problem 5?

*7. In problem 5, a fall in the price of a compact disc decreases the demand for cassettes and the demand schedule becomes:

Price (dollars per cassette)	Quantity demanded (thousands of cassettes per week)
2.95	500
4.13	450
5.30	400
6.48	350
7.65	300
8.83	250
10.00	200
11.18	150

What now are your answers to the questions in problem 5?

8. In problem 6, a fall in the price of a compact disc decreases the demand for cassettes and the demand schedule becomes that given in problem 7. What now are your answers to the questions in problem 6?

CRITICAL THINKING

1. After you have studied *Reading Between the Lines* on pp. 258–259, answer the following questions.
   a. What is the main difference between the technology used by Dell Computer Corporation and that used by other PC makers?
   b. How does Dell get information about what its customers want to buy? (Hint: Visit http://www.dell.com)
   c. How do other firms get information about what their customers want to buy? (Hint: To whom do the other producers sell?)
   d. Why do you think Dell has a smaller inventory than most other PC producers?
   e. Is it always better to have a small inventory? If it is, why doesn't Dell cut its inventory to 2 days or 1 day?
   f. Suppose that PC technology stops advancing and the industry settles down into a long-run equilibrium. Describe that equilibrium and illustrate it in a graph.
   g. Suppose that PC technology does not stop advancing. Describe the evolution of the industry.

2. Why have the prices of pocket calculators and VCRs fallen? What do you expect has happened to the costs and economic profits of the firms that make these products? Explain your answer.

3. What has been the effect of an increase in world population on the wheat market and the individual wheat farmer? Explain your answer.

4. Visit the Parkin Web site and study the *Web Reading Between the Lines*, "Dumping Steel." Then answer the following questions:
   a. What is the argument in the news article about limiting steel imports?
   b. Do you agree with the argument? Why or why not?
   c. Why does the United States claim that foreign steel is being dumped here? (Use the links in the *Web Reading Between the Lines* to answer this question.)

Chapter 1

Monopoly

You have been reading a lot in this book about firms that want to maximize profit. But perhaps you've been looking around at some of the places where you do business and wondering whether they are really so intent on profit. After all, don't you get a student's discount when you get a haircut? Don't museums and movie theaters give discounts to students, too? And what about the airline that gives a discount for buying a ticket in advance? Are your barber and movie theater owner, as well as the museum and airline operators, simply generous folks to whom the model of profit-maximizing firms does not apply? Aren't they simply throwing profit away by cutting ticket prices and offering discounts? ◆ When you buy electric power, you don't shop around. You buy from your electric power utility, which is your only available supplier. If you live in New York City and want cable TV service, you have only one option: buy from Manhattan Cable. These are examples of a single producer of a good or service controlling its supply. Such firms are obviously not like firms in perfectly competitive industries.

The Profits of Generosity

They don't face a market-determined price. They can choose their own price. How do such firms behave? How do they choose the quantity to produce and the price at which to sell it? How does their behavior compare with firms in perfectly competitive industries? Do such firms charge prices that are too high and that damage the interests of consumers? Do such firms bring any benefits?

◆ In this chapter, we study markets in which an individual firm can influence the quantity of goods supplied and exert an influence on price. We also compare the performance of a firm in such markets with that of a competitive market and examine whether monopoly is as efficient as competition.

After studying this chapter, you will be able to:

- ■ Explain how monopoly arises and distinguish between single-price monopoly and price-discriminating monopoly
- ■ Explain how a single-price monopoly determines its output and price
- ■ Compare the performance and efficiency of single-price monopoly and competition
- ■ Define rent seeking and explain why it arises
- ■ Explain how price discrimination increases profit
- ■ Explain how monopoly regulation influences output, price, economic profit, and efficiency

Market Power

MARKET POWER AND COMPETITION ARE THE TWO forces that operate in most markets. **Market power** is the ability to influence the market, and in particular the market price, by influencing the total quantity offered for sale.

The firms in perfect competition that you studied in Chapter 12 have no market power. They face the force of raw competition and are price takers. The firms that we study in this chapter operate at the opposite extreme. They face no competition and exercise raw market power. We call this extreme *monopoly*. A **monopoly** is an industry that produces a good or service for which no close substitute exists and in which there is one supplier that is protected from competition by a barrier preventing the entry of new firms.

Examples of monopoly include your local phone, gas, electricity, and water suppliers as well as DeBeers, the South African diamond producer, and Microsoft Corporation, the software developer that created your computer's operating system.

How Monopoly Arises

Monopoly has two key features:

■ No close substitute
■ Barriers to entry

No Close Substitute Even if only one firm produces a good that has a close substitute, that firm effectively faces competition from the producers of the substitute. Water supplied by a local public utility is an example of a good that does not have close substitutes. While it does have a close substitute for drinking—bottled spring water—it has no effective substitutes for showering or washing a car.

Monopolies are constantly under attack from new products and ideas that substitute for products produced by monopolies. For example, Federal Express, UPS, the fax machine, and e-mail have weakened the monopoly of the U.S. Postal Service. Similarly, the satellite dish has weakened the monopoly of cable television companies.

But new products also are constantly creating monopolies. An example is Microsoft's monopoly in DOS during the 1980s and in the Windows operating system today.

Barriers to Entry Legal or natural constraints that protect a firm from potential competitors are **barriers to entry**. A firm can sometimes create its own barrier to entry by acquiring a significant portion of a key resource. DeBeers, for example, controls more than 80 percent of the world's supply of natural diamonds. But most monopolies arise from two other types of barrier: legal barriers and natural barriers.

Legal Barriers to Entry Legal barriers to entry create legal monopoly. A **legal monopoly** is a market in which competition and entry are restricted by the granting of a public franchise, government license, patent, or copyright,

A *public franchise* is an exclusive right granted to a firm to supply a good or service. An example is the U.S. Postal Service, which has the exclusive right to carry first-class mail. A *government license* controls entry into particular occupations, professions, and industries. Examples of this type of barrier to entry are medicine, law, dentistry, schoolteaching, architecture, and many other professional services. Licensing does not always create monopoly, but it does restrict competition.

A *patent* is an exclusive right granted to the inventor of a product or service. A *copyright* is an exclusive right granted to the author or composer of a literary, musical, dramatic, or artistic work. Patents and copyrights are valid for a limited time period that varies from country to country. In the United States, a patent is valid for 20 years. Patents encourage the *invention* of new products and production methods. They also stimulate *innovation*—the use of new inventions—by encouraging inventors to publicize their discoveries and offer them for use under license. Patents have stimulated innovations in areas as diverse as soybean seeds, pharmaceuticals, memory chips, and video games.

Natural Barriers to Entry Natural barriers to entry create a **natural monopoly**, which is an industry in which one firm can supply the entire market at a lower price than two or more firms can.

Figure 13.1 shows a natural monopoly in the distribution of electric power. Here, the demand curve for electric power is *D* and the average total cost curve is *ATC*. Because average total cost decreases as output increases, economies of scale prevail over the entire length of the *ATC* curve. One firm can produce 4 million kilowatt-hours at 5 cents a kilowatt-hour. At this price, the quantity demanded is 4 million kilowatt-hours. So if the price were 5 cents, one firm could supply the entire market. If two firms shared the market, it would cost each of them 10 cents a kilowatt-hour to produce a total of 4 million kilowatt-hours. If four firms shared the market, it would cost each of them 15 cents a kilowatt-hour to produce a total of 4 million kilowatt-hours. So in conditions like those shown in Fig. 13.1, one firm can supply the entire market at a lower cost than two or more firms can. The distribution of electric power is an example of natural monopoly. So is the distribution of water and gas.

Most monopolies are regulated in some way by government agencies. We will study such regulation at the end of this chapter. But for two reasons, we'll first study unregulated monopoly. First, we can better understand why governments regulate monopolies and the effects of regulation if we also know how an unregulated monopoly behaves. Second, even in industries with more than one producer, firms often have a degree of monopoly power, and the theory of monopoly sheds light on the behavior of such firms and industries.

A major difference between monopoly and competition is that a monopoly sets its own price. But in doing so, it faces a market constraint. Let's see how the market limits a monopoly's pricing choices.

Monopoly Price-Setting Strategies

All monopolies face a tradeoff between price and the quantity sold. To sell a larger quantity, the monopolist must charge a lower price. But there are two broad monopoly situations that create different tradeoffs. They are:

■ Price discrimination
■ Single price

Price Discrimination Many firms price discriminate, and most are *not* monopolies. Airlines offer a dizzying array of different prices for the same trip. Pizza producers charge one price for a single pizza and almost give away a second pizza. These are examples of *price discrimination*. **Price discrimination** is the practice of selling different units of a good or service for different prices. Different customers might pay different prices (like airline passengers), or one customer might pay different prices for different quantities bought (like the bargain price for a second pizza).

When a firm price discriminates, it looks as if it is doing its customers a favor. In fact, it is charging the highest possible price for each unit sold and making the largest possible profit.

Not all monopolies can price discriminate. The main obstacle to price discrimination is resale by customers who buy for a low price. Because of resale possibilities, price discrimination is limited to monopolies that sell services that cannot be resold.

FIGURE 13.1
Natural Monopoly

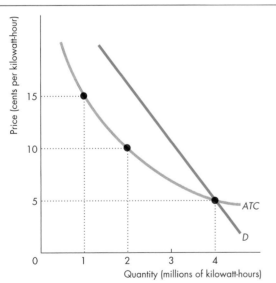

The demand curve for electric power is *D*, and the average total cost curve is *ATC*. Economies of scale exist over the entire *ATC* curve. One firm can distribute 4 million kilowatt-hours at a cost of 5 cents a kilowatt-hour. This same total output costs 10 cents a kilowatt-hour with two firms and 15 cents a kilowatt-hour with four firms. So one firm can meet the market demand at a lower cost than two or more firms can, and the market is a natural monopoly.

Single Price DeBeers sells diamonds (of a given size and quality) for the same price to all its customers. If it tried to sell at a low price to some customers and at a higher price to others, only the low-price customers would buy from DeBeers. Others would buy from DeBeers' low-price customers.

DeBeers is a *single-price* monopoly. A **single-price monopoly** is a firm that must sell each unit of its output for the same price to all its customers.

We'll look first at single-price monopoly.

A Single-Price Monopoly's Output and Price Decision

To UNDERSTAND HOW A SINGLE-PRICE MONOPOLY makes its output and price decision, we must first study the link between price and marginal revenue.

Price and Marginal Revenue

Because in a monopoly there is only one firm, the firm's demand curve is the market demand curve. Let's look at Bobbie's Barbershop, the sole supplier of haircuts in Cairo, Nebraska. The table in Fig. 13.2 shows Bobbie's demand schedule. At a price of $20, she sells no haircuts. The lower the price, the more haircuts per hour Bobbie can sell. For example, at $12, consumers demand 4 haircuts per hour (row *e*).

Total revenue (*TR*) is the price (*P*) multiplied by the quantity sold (*Q*). For example, in row *d*, Bobbie sells 3 haircuts at $14 each, so total revenue is $42. *Marginal revenue* (*MR*) is the change in total revenue (Δ*TR*) resulting from a one-unit increase in the quantity sold. For example, if the price falls from $16 (row *c*) to $14 (row *d*), the quantity sold increases from 2 to 3 haircuts. Total revenue rises from $32 to $42, so the change in total revenue is $10. Because the quantity sold increases by 1 haircut, marginal revenue equals the change in total revenue and is $10. Marginal revenue is placed between the two rows to emphasize that marginal revenue relates to the *change* in the quantity sold.

Figure 13.2 shows Bobbie's demand curve (*D*) and marginal revenue curve (*MR*) and also illustrates the calculation we've just made. Notice that at each level of output, marginal revenue is less than price—the marginal revenue curve lies below the demand curve. Why is marginal revenue less than price? The reason is that when the price is lowered to sell one more unit, two opposing forces affect total revenue. The lower price results in a revenue loss, and the increased quantity sold results in a revenue gain. For example, at a price of $16, Bobbie sells 2 haircuts (point *c*). If she lowers the price to $14, she sells 3 haircuts and has a revenue gain of $14 on the third haircut. But she now receives only $14 on the first two—$2 less than before. As a result, she loses $4 of revenue on the first 2 haircuts. To calculate marginal revenue, she must deduct this amount from the revenue gain of $14. So her marginal revenue is $10, which is less than the price.

FIGURE 13.2

Demand and Marginal Revenue

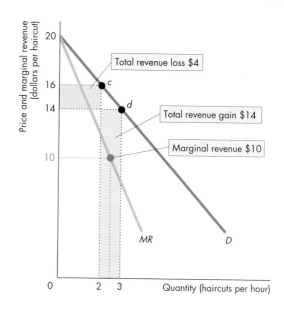

	Price (P) (dollars per haircut)	Quantity demanded (Q) (haircuts per hour)	Total revenue (TR = P × Q) (dollars)	Marginal revenue (MR = ΔTR/ΔQ) (dollars per additional haircut)
a	20	0	0	
				18
b	18	1	18	
				14
c	16	2	32	
				10
d	14	3	42	
				6
e	12	4	48	
				2
f	10	5	50	

The table shows Bobbie's demand schedule. Total revenue (*TR*) is price multiplied by quantity sold. For example, in row *c* the price is $16 a haircut, 2 haircuts are sold, and total revenue is $32. Marginal revenue (*MR*) is the change in total revenue that results from a one-unit increase in the quantity sold. For example, when the price falls from $16 to $14 a haircut, the quantity sold increases by 1 haircut and total revenue increases by $10. Marginal revenue is $10. The demand curve, *D*, and the marginal revenue curve, *MR*, are based on the numbers in the table and illustrate the calculation of marginal revenue when the price falls from $16 to $14.

Marginal Revenue and Elasticity

A single-price monopoly's marginal revenue is related to the *elasticity of demand* for its good. The demand for a good can be *elastic* (the elasticity of demand is greater than 1), *inelastic* (the elasticity of demand is less than 1), or *unit elastic* (the elasticity of demand is equal to 1). Demand is *elastic* if a 1 percent fall in price brings a greater than 1 percent increase in the quantity demanded. Demand is *inelastic* if a 1 percent fall in price brings a less than 1 percent increase in the quantity demanded. And demand is *unit elastic* if a 1 percent fall in price brings a 1 percent increase in the quantity demanded.

If demand is elastic, a fall in price brings an increase in total revenue—the increase in revenue from the increase in quantity sold outweighs the decrease in revenue from the lower price—and marginal revenue is positive. If demand is inelastic, a fall in price brings a decrease in total revenue—the increase in revenue from the increase in quantity sold is outweighed by the decrease in revenue from the lower price—and marginal revenue is negative. If demand is unit elastic, total revenue does not change—the increase in revenue from the increase in quantity sold offsets the decrease in revenue from the lower price—and marginal revenue is zero. (Chapter 5, pp. 92–93, explains the relationship between total revenue and elasticity more fully.)

Figure 13.3 illustrates the relationship between marginal revenue, total revenue, and elasticity. As the price of a haircut gradually falls from $20 to $10, the quantity of haircuts demanded increases from 0 to 5 an hour. Over this output range, marginal revenue is positive (part a), total revenue increases (part b), and the demand for haircuts is elastic. As the price falls from $10 to $0 a haircut, the quantity of haircuts demanded increases from 5 to 10 an hour. Over this output range, marginal revenue is negative (part a), total revenue decreases (part b), and the demand for haircuts is inelastic. When the price is $10 a haircut, marginal revenue is zero, total revenue is a maximum, and the demand for haircuts is unit elastic.

Monopoly Demand Is Always Elastic

The relationship between marginal revenue and elasticity that you've just discovered implies that a profit-maximizing monopoly never produces an output in the inelastic range of its demand curve. If it did so, it could charge a higher price, produce a smaller quantity, and increase its profit. Let's now look more closely at a monopoly's price and output decision.

FIGURE 13.3

Marginal Revenue and Elasticity

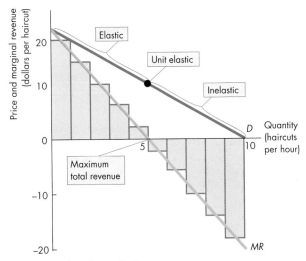

(a) Demand and marginal revenue curves

(b) Total revenue curve

Bobbie's demand curve (*D*) and marginal revenue curve (*MR*) are shown in part (a), and total revenue curve (*TR*) is shown in part (b). Over the range from 0 to 5 haircuts an hour, a price cut increases total revenue, so marginal revenue is positive, as shown by the blue bars. Demand is elastic. Over the range 5 to 10 haircuts an hour, a price cut decreases total revenue, so marginal revenue is negative, as shown by the red bars. Demand is inelastic. At 5 haircuts an hour, total revenue is maximized, and marginal revenue is zero. Demand is unit elastic.

Output and Price Decision

To determine the output level and price that maximize a monopoly's profit, we need to study the behavior of both revenue and costs as output varies. A monopoly and a competitive firm face the same types of technology and cost constraints. But they face different market constraints. The competitive firm is a price taker, whereas the monopoly's production decision influences the price it receives. Let's see how.

Bobbie's revenue, which we studied in Fig. 13.2, is shown again in Table 13.1. The table also contains information on Bobbie's costs and economic profit. Total cost (TC) rises as output increases, and so does total revenue (TR). Economic profit equals total revenue minus total cost. As you can see in the table, the maximum profit ($12) occurs when Bobbie sells 3 haircuts for $14 each. If she sells 2 haircuts for $16 each or 4 haircuts for $12 each, her economic profit will be only $8.

You can see why 3 haircuts is Bobbie's profit-maximizing output by looking at the marginal revenue and marginal cost columns. When Bobbie increases output from 2 to 3 haircuts, her marginal revenue is $10 and her marginal cost is $6. Profit increases by the difference—$4 an hour. If Bobbie increases output yet further, from 3 to 4 haircuts, her marginal revenue is $6 and her marginal cost is $10. In this case, marginal cost exceeds marginal revenue by $4, so profit decreases by $4 an hour. When marginal revenue exceeds marginal cost, profit increases if output increases. When marginal cost exceeds marginal revenue, profit increases if output decreases. When marginal cost and marginal revenue are equal, profit is maximized.

The information set out in Table 13.1 is shown graphically in Fig. 13.4. Part (a) shows Bobbie's total revenue curve (TR) and total cost curve (TC). Economic profit is the vertical distance between TR and TC. Bobbie maximizes her profit at 3 haircuts an hour—economic profit is $42 minus $30, or $12.

A monopoly, like a competitive firm, maximizes profit by producing the output at which marginal cost equals marginal revenue. Figure 13.4(b) shows Bobbie's demand curve (D) and marginal revenue curve (MR) along with her marginal cost curve (MC) and average total cost curve (ATC). Bobbie maximizes her profit by doing 3 haircuts an hour. But what price does she charge for a haircut? To set the price, the monopolist uses the demand curve and finds the highest price at which it can sell the profit-maximizing output. In Bobbie's case, the highest price at which she can sell 3 haircuts an hour is $14.

TABLE 13.1

A Monopoly's Output and Price Decision

Price (P) (dollars per haircut)	Quantity demanded (Q) (haircuts per hour)	Total revenue (TR = P × Q) (dollars)	Marginal revenue (MR = ΔTR/ΔQ) (dollars per additional haircut)	Total cost (TC) (dollars)	Marginal cost (MC = ΔTC/ΔQ) (dollars per additional haircut)	Profit (TR – TC) (dollars)
20	0	0		20		−20
			18		1	
18	1	18		21		−3
			14		3	
16	2	32		24		+8
			10		6	
14	3	42		30		+12
			6		10	
12	4	48		40		+8
			2		15	
10	5	50		55		−5

This table gives the information needed to find the profit-maximizing output and price. Total revenue (TR) equals price multiplied by the quantity sold. Profit equals total revenue minus total cost (TC). Profit is maximized when the price is $14 and 3 haircuts are sold. Total revenue is $42, total cost is $30, and economic profit is $12 ($42 – $30).

FIGURE 13.4

FIGURE 13.4

A Monopoly's Output and Price

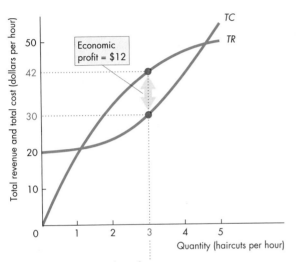

(a) **Total revenue and total cost curves**

(b) **Demand and marginal revenue and cost curves**

In part (a), economic profit equals total revenue (*TR*) minus total cost (*TC*) and is maximized at 3 haircuts an hour. In part (b), economic profit is maximized when marginal cost (*MC*) equals marginal revenue (*MR*). The price is determined by the demand curve (*D*) and is $14. Economic profit, the blue rectangle, is $12—the profit per haircut ($4) multiplied by 3 haircuts.

All firms maximize profit by producing the output at which marginal revenue equals marginal cost. For a competitive firm, price equals marginal revenue, so price also equals marginal cost. For a monopoly, price exceeds marginal revenue, so price also exceeds marginal cost.

A monopoly charges a price that exceeds marginal cost, but does it always make an economic profit? In Bobbie's case, when she produces 3 haircuts an hour, her average total cost is $10 (read from the *ATC* curve) and her price is $14 (read from the *D* curve). Her profit per haircut is $4 ($14 minus $10). Bobbie's economic profit is shown by the blue rectangle, which equals the profit per haircut ($4) multiplied by the number of haircuts (3), for a total of $12.

If firms in a perfectly competitive industry make a positive economic profit, new firms enter. That does not happen in a monopolistic industry. Barriers to entry prevent new firms from entering. So in a monopolistic industry, a firm can make a positive economic profit and continue to do so indefinitely. Sometimes that profit is large, as in the international diamond business.

Bobbie makes a positive economic profit. But suppose that the owner of the shop that Bobbie rents increases Bobbie's rent. If Bobbie pays an additional $12 an hour, her fixed cost increases by $12 an hour. Her marginal cost and marginal revenue don't change, so her profit-maximizing output remains at 3 haircuts an hour. Her profit decreases by $12 an hour to zero. If Bobbie pays more than an additional $12 an hour for her shop rent, she incurs an economic loss. If this situation were permanent, Bobbie would go out of business. But entrepreneurs are a hardy lot, and Bobbie might find another shop where the rent is less.

REVIEW QUIZ

- What is the relationship between marginal cost and marginal revenue when a single-price monopoly maximizes profit?
- How does a single-price monopoly determine the price it will charge its customers?
- What is the relationship among price, marginal revenue, and marginal cost when a single-price monopoly is maximizing profit?
- Why can a monopoly make a positive economic profit even in the long run?

Single-Price Monopoly and Competition Compared

IMAGINE AN INDUSTRY THAT IS MADE UP OF MANY small firms operating in perfect competition. Then imagine that a single firm buys out all these small firms and creates a monopoly.

What will happen in this industry? Will the price rise or fall? Will the quantity produced increase or decrease? Will economic profit increase or decrease? Will either the original competitive situation or the new monopoly situation be efficient?

These are the questions we're now going to answer. First, we look at the effects of monopoly on the price and quantity produced. Then we turn to the questions about efficiency.

Comparing Output and Price

Figure 13.5 shows the market we'll study. The market demand curve is D. The demand curve is the same, regardless of how the industry is organized. But the supply side and the equilibrium are different in monopoly and competition. First, let's look at the case of perfect competition.

Perfect Competition Initially, with many small perfectly competitive firms in the market, the market supply curve is S. This supply curve is obtained by summing the supply curves of all the individual firms in the market.

In perfect competition, equilibrium occurs where the supply curve and the demand curve intersect. The quantity produced by the industry is Q_C, and the price is P_C. Each firm takes the price P_C and maximizes its profit by producing the output at which its own marginal cost equals the price. Because each firm is a small part of the total industry, there is no incentive for any firm to try to manipulate the price by varying its output.

Monopoly Now suppose that this industry is taken over by a single firm. Consumers do not change, so the demand curve remains the same as in the case of perfect competition. But now the monopoly recognizes this demand curve as a constraint on its sales. And the monopoly is confronted with the marginal revenue curve, MR.

The monopoly maximizes profit by producing the quantity at which marginal revenue equals marginal

cost. To find the monopoly's marginal cost curve, first recall that in perfect competition, the industry supply curve is the sum of the supply curves of the firms in the industry. Also recall that each firm's supply curve is its marginal cost curve (see Chapter 12, p. 245). So when the industry is taken over by a single firm, competitive industry's supply curve becomes the monopoly's marginal cost curve. To remind you of this fact, the supply curve is also labeled MC.

The output at which marginal revenue equals marginal cost is Q_M. This output is smaller than the competitive output Q_C. And the monopoly charges the price P_M, which is higher than P_C. We have established that:

Compared to a perfectly competitive industry, a single-price monopoly restricts its output and charges a higher price.

We've seen how the output and price of a monopoly compare with those in a competitive industry. Let's now compare the efficiency of the two types of market.

FIGURE 13.5

Monopoly's Smaller Output and Higher Price

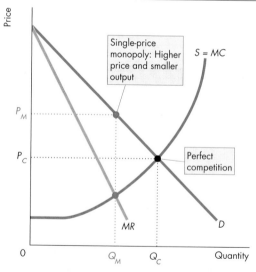

A competitive industry produces the quantity Q_C at price P_C. A single-price monopoly produces the quantity Q_M at which marginal revenue equals marginal cost and sells that quantity for the price P_M. Compared to perfect competition, a single-price monopoly restricts output and raises the price.

Efficiency Comparison

When we studied efficiency in perfect competition, (see Chapter 12, pp. 256-257), we discovered that if there are no external costs and benefits, perfect competition results in an efficient use of resources. Along the demand curve, consumers are efficient. Along the supply curve, producers are efficient. And where the curves intersect—the competitive equilibrium—both consumers and producers are efficient. Price equals marginal cost, and the sum of consumer surplus and producer surplus is maximized.

Monopoly restricts output below the competitive level and is inefficient. If a monopoly increases its output by one unit, marginal benefit exceeds marginal cost and resources are used more efficiently.

Figure 13.6 illustrates the inefficiency of monopoly and shows the loss of consumer and producer surpluses in a monopoly. In perfect competition (part a), consumers pay P_C for each unit. The marginal benefit to consumers is shown by the demand curve ($D = MB$). This price measures the value of the good to the consumer. Value minus price equals *consumer surplus* (see Chapter 6, p. 111). In Fig. 13.6(a), consumer surplus is shown by the green triangle.

The marginal cost of production (opportunity cost) in perfect competition is shown by the supply curve ($S = MC$). The amount received by the producer in excess of this marginal cost is *producer surplus*. In Fig. 13.6(a), the blue area shows producer surplus.

At the competitive equilibrium, marginal benefit equals marginal cost and the sum of consumer surplus and producer surplus is maximized. Resource use is efficient.

A monopoly (part b) restricts output to Q_M and sells that output for P_M. Consumer surplus decreases to the smaller green triangle. Consumers lose partly by having to pay more for the good and partly by getting less of it. Part of the original producer surplus is also lost. The total loss resulting from the smaller monopoly output (Q_M) is the gray triangle in Fig. 13.6(b). The part of the gray triangle above P_C is the loss of consumer surplus, and the part of the triangle below P_C is a loss of producer surplus. The entire gray triangle measures the loss of consumer surplus plus producer surplus. This loss is called the *deadweight loss*. The smaller output and higher price drive a wedge between marginal benefit and marginal cost and eliminates the producer surplus and the consumer surplus on the output that a competitive industry would have produced but that the monopoly does not.

FIGURE 13.6
Inefficiency of Monopoly

(a) Perfect competition

(b) Monopoly

In perfect competition (part a), the quantity Q_C is sold at the price P_C. Consumer surplus is shown by the green triangle. In long-run equilibrium, firms' economic profits are zero and consumer surplus is maximized. A single-price monopoly (part b) restricts output to Q_M and increases the price to P_M. Consumer surplus is the smaller green triangle. The monopoly takes the blue rectangle and creates a deadweight loss (the gray triangle).

Redistribution of Surpluses

You've seen that monopoly is inefficient. The sum of consumer surplus and producer surplus is smaller with monopoly than with competition. There is a social loss. But monopoly also brings a *redistribution* of surpluses.

Some of the loss in consumer surplus goes to the monopoly. In Fig. 13.6, the monopoly gets the difference between the higher price, P_M, and the competitive price, P_C, on the quantity sold, Q_M. So the monopoly takes the part of the consumer surplus shown by the blue rectangle. This portion of the loss of consumer surplus is not a loss to society. It is redistribution from consumers to the monopoly.

Rent Seeking

You've seen that monopoly creates a deadweight loss and so is inefficient. But the social cost of monopoly exceeds the deadweight loss because of an activity called rent seeking. **Rent seeking** is the attempt to capture a consumer surplus, a producer surplus, or an economic profit. The activity is not confined to monopoly. But attempting to capture the economic profit of a monopoly is a major form of rent seeking.

You've seen that a monopoly makes its economic profit by diverting part of consumer surplus to itself. Thus the pursuit of an economic profit by a monopoly is rent seeking. It is the attempt to capture consumer surplus.

Rent seekers pursue their goals in two main ways. They might

- Buy a monopoly
- Create a monopoly

Buy a Monopoly To rent seek by buying a monopoly, a person searches for a monopoly that is for sale at a lower price than the monopoly's economic profit. Trading taxicab licenses is an example of this type of rent seeking. In some cities, taxicabs are regulated. The city restricts both the fares and the number of taxis that can operate, so operating a taxi results in economic profit or rent. A person who wants to operate a taxi must buy a license from someone who already has one. This type of rent seeking transfers rents from the buyer to the seller of the monopoly. The only person who ends up with rent is the one who created the monopoly in the first place. Even so, people rationally devote their time and effort to seeking out profitable

monopoly businesses to buy. In the process, they use up scarce resources that could otherwise have been employed in producing goods and services.

Create a Monopoly Rent seeking by creating monopoly is mainly a political activity. It takes the form of lobbying and trying to influence the political process. Such influence might be sought by making campaign contributions in exchange for legislative support or by indirectly seeking to influence political outcomes through publicity in the media or more direct contacts with politicians and bureaucrats. An example of a monopoly right that was created in this way is the government-imposed restrictions on the quantities of textiles that may be imported into the United States. Another is a regulation that limits the number of oranges that may be sold in the United States. These are regulations that restrict output and increase price.

This type of rent seeking is a costly activity that uses up scarce resources. Taken together, firms spend billions of dollars lobbying Congress, state legislators, and local officials in the pursuit of licenses and laws that create barriers to entry and establish a monopoly right. Everyone has an incentive to rent seek, and because there are no barriers to entry into the rent-seeking activity, there is a great deal of competition for new monopoly rights.

Rent-Seeking Equilibrium

Barriers to entry create monopoly. But there is no barrier to entry into rent seeking. Rent seeking is like perfect competition. If an economic profit is available, a new rent seeker will try to get some of it. And competition among rent seekers pushes up the price that must be paid for a monopoly right to the point at which only a normal profit can be made by operating the monopoly. For example, competition for the right to operate a taxi in New York City leads to a price of more than $100,000 for a taxi license, which is sufficiently high to eliminate economic profit for taxi operators and leave them with normal profit.

Figure 13.7 shows a rent-seeking equilibrium. The cost of rent seeking is a fixed cost that must be added to a monopoly's other costs. Rent seeking and rent-seeking costs increase to the point at which no economic profit is made. The average total cost curve, which includes the fixed cost of rent seeking, shifts upward until it just touches the demand curve. Economic profit is zero. It has been lost in rent

FIGURE 13.7
Rent-Seeking Equilibrium

With competitive rent seeking, a monopoly uses all its economic profit to prevent another firm from taking its economic rent. The firm's rent-seeking costs are fixed costs. They add to total fixed cost and to average total cost. The *ATC* curve shifts upward until, at the profit-maximizing price, the firm breaks even.

seeking. Consumer surplus is unaffected. But the deadweight loss of monopoly now includes the original deadweight loss triangle plus the lost economic profit, shown by the enlarged gray area in the figure.

R E V I E W   Q U I Z

- Why does a single-price monopoly produce a smaller output and charge a higher price than what would prevail if the industry were perfectly competitive?
- Why is a single-price monopoly inefficient?
- What is rent seeking and how does it influence the inefficiency of monopoly?

So far, we've considered only a single-price monopoly. But many monopolies do not operate with a single price. Instead, they price discriminate. Let's now see how price-discriminating monopoly works.

Price Discrimination

PRICE DISCRIMINATION—SELLING A GOOD OR service at a number of different prices—is widespread. You encounter it when you travel, go to the movies, get your hair cut, buy pizza, or visit an art museum. Most price discriminators are *not* monopolies, but monopolies price discriminate when they can do so.

To be able to price discriminate, a monopoly must:

1. Identify and separate different buyer types
2. Sell a product that cannot be resold

Price discrimination is charging different prices for a single good or service because of differences in buyers' willingness to pay and not because of differences in production costs. So not all price *differences* are price *discrimination*. Some goods that are similar but not identical have different prices because they have different production costs. For example, the cost of producing electricity depends on time of day. If an electric power company charges a higher price for consumption between 7:00 and 9:00 in the morning and between 4:00 and 7:00 in the evening than it does at other times of the day, it is not price discriminating.

At first sight, it appears that price discrimination contradicts the assumption of profit maximization. Why would a movie operator allow children to see movies at half price? Why would a hairdresser charge students and senior citizens less? Aren't these firms losing profit by being nice to their customers?

Deeper investigation shows that far from losing profit, price discriminators make a bigger profit than they would otherwise. So a monopoly has an incentive to find ways of discriminating and charging each buyer the highest possible price. Some people pay less with price discrimination, but others pay more.

Price Discrimination and Consumer Surplus

The key idea behind price discrimination is to convert consumer surplus into economic profit. Demand curves slope downward because the value that people place on any good decreases as the quantity consumed of that good increases. When all the units consumed are sold for a single price, consumers benefit. The benefit is the value the consumers get from each unit of the good minus the price actually paid for it. We call this benefit *consumer surplus.* (If you need to refresh your understanding of consumer surplus, flip back to Chapter 6, page 111.) Price discrimination is an attempt by a monopoly to capture as much of the consumer surplus as possible for itself.

To extract every dollar of consumer surplus from every buyer, the monopoly would have to offer each individual customer a separate price schedule based on that customer's own willingness to pay. Clearly, such price discrimination cannot be carried out in practice because a firm does not have enough information about each consumer's demand curve.

But firms try to extract as much consumer surplus as possible, and to do so, they discriminate in two broad ways:

■ Among units of a good
■ Among groups of buyers

Discriminating Among Units of a Good One method of price discrimination charges each buyer a different price on each unit of a good bought. A discount for bulk buying is an example of this type of discrimination. The larger the order, the larger is the discount—and the lower is the price. (Note that some discounts for bulk arise from lower costs of production for greater bulk. In these cases, such discounts are not price discrimination.)

Discriminating Among Groups of Buyers Price discrimination often takes the form of discriminating between different groups of consumers on the basis of age, employment status, or some other easily distinguished characteristic. This type of price discrimination works when each group has a different average willingness to pay for the good or service.

For example, a face-to-face sales meeting with a customer might bring a large and profitable order. For salespeople and other business travelers, the marginal benefit from a trip is large and the price that such a traveler will pay for a trip is high. In contrast, for a vacation traveler, any of several different trips or even no vacation trip are options. So for vacation travelers, the marginal benefit of a trip is small and the price that such a traveler will pay for a trip is low. Because business travelers are willing to pay more than vacation travelers are, it is possible for an airline to profit by price discriminating between these two groups. Similarly, because students have a lower willingness to pay for a haircut than a working person does, it is possible for a hairdresser to profit by price discriminating between these two groups.

Let's see how an airline exploits the differences in demand by business and vacation travelers and increases its profit by price discriminating.

Profiting by Price Discriminating

Global Air has a monopoly on an exotic route. Figure 13.8 shows the demand curve (*D*) and the marginal revenue curve (*MR*) for travel on this route. It also shows Global Air's marginal cost curve (*MC*) and average total cost curve (*ATC*).

Initially, Global is a single-price monopoly and maximizes its profit by producing 8,000 trips a year (the quantity at which *MR* equals *MC*). The price is $1,200 per trip. The average total cost of a trip is $600, so economic profit is $600 a trip. On 8,000 trips, Global's economic profit is $4.8 million a year, shown by the blue rectangle. Global's customers enjoy a consumer surplus shown by the green triangle.

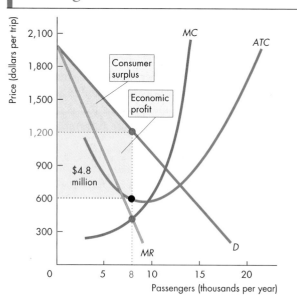

FIGURE 13.8

A Single Price of Air Travel

Global Airlines has a monopoly on an air route. The firm faces demand curve (*D*) and marginal revenue curve (*MR*). It has marginal cost curve (*MC*) and average total cost curve (*ATC*). As a single-price monopoly, Global maximizes profit by selling 8,000 trips a year at $1,200 a trip. Its profit is $4.8 million a year, which is shown by the blue rectangle. Global's customers enjoy a consumer surplus shown by the green triangle.

Global is struck by the fact that many of its customers are business travelers, and Global suspects that they are willing to pay more than $1,200 a trip. So Global does some market research, which tells Global that some business travelers are willing to pay as much as $1,800 a trip. Also, these customers almost always change their travel plans at the last moment. Another group of business travelers is willing to pay $1,600. These customers know a week ahead when they will travel, and they never want to stay over a weekend. Yet another group would pay up to $1,400, and these travelers know two weeks ahead when they will travel and they don't want to stay away over a weekend.

So Global announces a new fare schedule. No restrictions, $1,800; 7-days advance purchase, no cancellation, $1,600; 14-days advance purchase, no cancellation, $1,400; 14-days advance purchase, must stay over weekend, $1,200.

Figure 13.9 shows the outcome with this new fare structure and also shows why Global is pleased

with its new fares. It sells 2,000 seats at each of its four prices. Global's economic profit increases by the blue steps in Fig. 13.9. Its economic profit is now its original $4.8 million a year plus an additional $2.4 million from its new higher fares. Consumer surplus has shrunk to the smaller green area.

Perfect Price Discrimination

But Global reckons it can do even better. It plans to achieve **perfect price discrimination,** which is price discrimination that extracts the entire consumer surplus. To do so, Global must get creative and come up with a host of additional business fares ranging between $2,000 and $1,200, each of which appeals to a small segment of the business market and that together they extract the entire consumer surplus from the business travelers.

Once Global is discriminating finely between different customers and getting from each the maximum they are willing to pay, something special happens to marginal revenue. Recall that for the single-price monopoly, marginal revenue is less than price. The reason is that when the price is cut to sell a larger quantity, the price is lower on all units sold. But with perfect price discrimination, Global sells only the marginal seat at the lower price. All the other customers continue to buy for the highest price they are willing to pay. So for the perfect price discriminator, marginal revenue equals price and the demand curve becomes the marginal revenue curve.

With marginal revenue equal to price, Global can obtain yet greater profit by increasing output up to the point at which price (and marginal revenue) is equal to marginal cost.

So Global now seeks additional travelers who will not pay as much as $1,200 a trip but who will pay more than marginal cost. More creative pricing comes up with vacation specials and other fares that have combinations of advance reservation, minimum-stay, and other restrictions that make these fares unattractive to its existing customers but attractive to a further group of travelers. With all these fares and specials, Global increases sales, extracts the entire consumer surplus, and maximizes economic profit.

Figure 13.10 shows the outcome with perfect price discrimination. The dozens of fares paid by the original travelers who are willing to pay between $1,200 and $2,000 has extracted the entire consumer surplus from this group and converted it into economic profit for Global.

FIGURE 13.9
Price Discrimination

Global revises its fare structure. No restrictions at $1,800; 7-day advance purchase at $1,600; 14-day advance purchase at $1,400; and must stay over weekend at $1,200. Global sells 2,000 units at each of its four new fares. It economic profit increases by $2.4 million a year to $7.2 million a year, which is shown by the original blue rectangle plus the blue steps. Global's customers' consumer surplus shrinks.

FIGURE 13.10
Perfect Price Discrimination

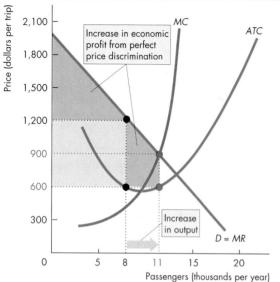

Dozens of fares discriminate among many different types of business traveler, and many new low fares with restrictions appeal to vacation travelers. With perfect price discrimination, Global's demand curve becomes its marginal revenue curve. Economic profit is maximized when the lowest price equals marginal cost. Global sells 11,000 tickets at between $2,000 and $900 each and makes an economic profit of $9.35 million a year.

The new fares between $900 and $1,200 have attracted 3,000 additional travelers, but Global has taken their entire consumer surplus also. Global is earning an economic profit of more than $9 million.

Real-world airlines are just as creative as Global, as you can see in the cartoon!

Would it bother you to hear how little I paid for this flight?

From William Hamilton, "Voodoo Economics," ©1992 by The Chronicle Publishing Company, p.3. Reprinted with permission of Chronicle Books.

Efficiency and Rent Seeking with Price Discrimination

With perfect price discrimination, output increases to the point at which price equals marginal cost—where the marginal cost curve intersects the demand curve. This output is identical to that of perfect competition. Perfect price discrimination pushes consumer surplus to zero but increases producer surplus to equal the sum of consumer surplus and producer surplus in perfect competition. Deadweight loss with perfect price discrimination is zero. So perfect price discrimination achieves efficiency.

The more perfectly the monopoly can price discriminate, the closer its output gets to the competitive output and the more efficient is the outcome.

But there are two differences between perfect competition and perfect price discrimination. First, the distribution of the surplus is different. It is shared by consumers and producers in perfect competition while the producer gets it all with perfect price discrimination. Second, because the producer grabs the surplus, rent seeking becomes profitable.

People use resources in pursuit of rents, and the bigger the rents, the more resources get used in pursuing them. With free entry into rent seeking, the long-run equilibrium outcome is that rent seekers use up the entire producer surplus.

REVIEW QUIZ

- What is price discrimination and how is it used to increase a monopoly's profit?
- What happens to consumer surplus when a monopoly price discriminates?
- What happens to consumer surplus, economic profit, and output if a monopoly perfectly price discriminates?
- What are some of the ways that real-world airlines use to price discriminate?

You've seen that monopoly is profitable for the monopolist but costly for other people. It results in inefficiency. Because of these features of monopoly, it is subject to policy debate and regulation. We'll now study the key monopoly policy issues.

Monopoly Policy Issues

THE COMPARISON OF MONOPOLY AND COMPETI-
tion makes monopoly look bad. Monopoly is inefficient, and it captures consumer surplus and converts
it into producer surplus or pure waste in the form of
rent-seeking costs. If monopoly is so bad, why do we
put up with it? Why don't we have laws that crack
down on monopoly so hard that it never rears its
head? We do indeed have laws that limit monopoly
power and regulate the prices that monopolies are
permitted to charge. But monopoly also brings some
benefits. We begin this review of monopoly policy
issues by looking at the benefits of monopoly. We
then look at monopoly regulation.

Gains from Monopoly

The main reasons why monopoly exists is that it has
potential advantages over a competitive alternative.
These advantages arise from:

- Incentives to innovation
- Economies of scale and economies of scope

Incentives to Innovation Invention leads to a wave of
innovation as new knowledge is applied to the production process. Innovation may take the form of
developing a new product or a lower-cost way of
making an existing product. Controversy has raged
over whether large firms with monopoly power or
small competitive firms lacking such monopoly
power are the most innovative. It is clear that some
temporary monopoly power arises from innovation.
A firm that develops a new product or process and
patents it obtains an exclusive right to that product
or process for the term of the patent.

But does the granting of a monopoly, even a
temporary one, to an innovator increase the pace of
innovation? One line of reasoning suggests that it
does. Without protection, an innovator is not able to
enjoy the profits from innovation for very long. Thus
the incentive to innovate is weakened. A contrary
argument is that monopolies can afford to be lazy
while competitive firms cannot. Competitive firms
must strive to innovate and cut costs even though
they know that they cannot hang on to the benefits
of their innovation for long. But that knowledge
spurs them on to greater and faster innovation.

The evidence on whether monopoly leads to
greater innovation than competition is mixed. Large
firms do more research and development than do
small firms. But measuring research and development
is measuring the volume of inputs into the process of
innovation. What matters is not input but output.
Two measures of the output of research and development are the number of patents and the rate of productivity growth. On these measures, there is no clear
evidence that big is better. But there is a clear pattern
in the process of diffusion of technological knowledge. After innovation, a new process or product
spreads gradually through the industry, with large
firms jumping on the bandwagon more quickly than
the remaining small firms. Thus large firms speed the
process of diffusion of technological advances.

Economies of Scale and Scope Economies of scale
and scope can lead to natural monopoly. And as you
saw at the beginning of this chapter, in a *natural
monopoly*, a single firm can produce at a lower average cost than a larger number of smaller firms can.

A firm experiences *economies of scale* when an
increase in its output of a good or service brings a
decrease in the average total cost of producing it—see
Chapter 11, pp. 232. A firm experiences *economies of
scope* when an increase in the *range of goods produced*
brings a decrease in average total cost—see Chapter 10,
p. 213. Economies of scope occur when different goods
can share specialized (and usually costly) capital
resources. For example, McDonald's can produce both
hamburgers and french fries at a lower average total cost
than can two separate firms—a burger firm and a
french fries firm—because at McDonald's hamburgers
and french fries share the use of specialized food storage
and preparation facilities. A firm that produces a wide
range of products can hire specialist computer programmers, designers, and marketing experts whose
skills can be used across the product range, thereby
spreading their costs and lowering the average total cost
of production of each of the goods.

There are many examples in which a combination
of economies of scale and economies of scope arise,
but not all of them lead to monopoly. Some examples
are the brewing of beer, the manufacture of refrigerators and other household appliances, the manufacture
of pharmaceuticals, and the refining of petroleum.

Examples of industries in which economies of
scale are so significant that they lead to a natural
monopoly are becoming more rare. Public utilities
such as gas, electric power, local telephone service,
and garbage collection once were natural monopolies.

But technological advances now enable us to separate the *production* of electric power or natural gas from its *distribution*. The provision of water, though, remains a natural monopoly.

Large-scale firms that have control over supply and can influence price—and that therefore behave like the monopoly firm that you've studied in this chapter—can reap economies of scale and scope. Small, competitive firms cannot. Consequently, there are situations in which the comparison of monopoly and competition that we made earlier in this chapter is not valid. Recall that we imagined the takeover of a large number of competitive firms by a monopoly firm. But we also assumed that the monopoly would use exactly the same technology as the small firms and have the same costs. If one large firm can reap economies of scale and scope, its marginal cost curve will lie below the supply curve of a competitive industry made up of many small firms. It is possible for such economies of scale and scope to be so large as to result in a larger output and lower price under monopoly than a competitive industry would achieve.

Where significant economies of scale and scope exist, it is usually worth putting up with monopoly and regulating its prices.

Regulating Natural Monopoly

Where demand and cost conditions create a natural monopoly, a federal, state, or local government agency usually steps in to regulate the prices of the monopoly. By regulating a monopoly, some of the worst aspects of monopoly can be avoided or at least made more moderate. Let's look at monopoly price regulation.

Figure 13.11 shows the demand curve *D*, the marginal revenue curve, *MR*, the long-run average cost curve *ATC*, and the marginal cost curve *MC* for a gas distribution company that is a natural monopoly.

The firm's marginal cost is constant at 10 cents per cubic foot. But average total cost decreases as output increases. The reason is that the natural gas company has a large investment in pipelines and so has high fixed costs. These fixed costs are part of the company's average total cost and so appear in the *ATC* curve. The average total cost curve slopes downward because as the number of cubic feet sold increases, the fixed cost is spread over a larger number units. (If you need to refresh your memory on how the average total cost curve is calculated, take a quick look back at Chapter 11, pp. 226–227.)

This one firm can supply the entire market at a lower cost than two firms can because average total cost is falling even when the entire market is supplied. (Refer back to pp. 264–265 if you need a quick refresher on natural monopoly.)

Profit Maximization First, suppose the natural gas company is not regulated and instead maximizes profit. Figure 13.11 shows the outcome in this case. The company produces 2 million cubic feet a day, the quantity at which marginal cost equals marginal revenue. It prices this gas at 20 cents a cubic foot and makes an economic profit of 2 cents a cubic foot, or $40,000 a day.

This outcome is fine for the gas company, but it is inefficient. Price or marginal benefit is 20 cents a cubic foot when marginal cost is only 10 cents a cubic foot. Also, the gas company is making a big profit. What can regulation do to improve this outcome?

The Efficient Regulation If the monopoly regulator wants to achieve an efficient use of resources, it must require the gas monopoly to produce the quantity of gas that brings marginal benefit into equality with marginal cost. Marginal benefit is what the consumer is willing to pay and is shown by the demand curve. Marginal cost is shown by the firm's marginal cost curve. You can see in Fig. 13.11 that this outcome occurs if the price is regulated at 10 cents per cubic foot and if 4 million cubic feet per day are produced. The regulation that produces this outcome is called a marginal cost pricing rule. A **marginal cost pricing rule** sets price equal to marginal cost. It maximizes total surplus in the regulated industry. In this example, that surplus is all consumer surplus and it equals the area of the triangle beneath the demand curve and above the marginal cost curve.

The marginal cost pricing rule is efficient. But it leaves the natural monopoly incurring an economic loss. Because average total cost falls as output increases, marginal cost is below average total cost. And because price equals marginal cost, price is below average total cost. Average total cost minus price is the loss per unit produced. It's pretty obvious that a natural gas company that is required to use a marginal cost pricing rule will not stay in business for long. How can a company cover its costs and, at the same time, obey a marginal cost pricing rule?

One possibility is price discrimination. The company might charge a higher price to some customers but marginal cost to the customers who pay least.

FIGURE 13.11

Regulating a Natural Monopoly

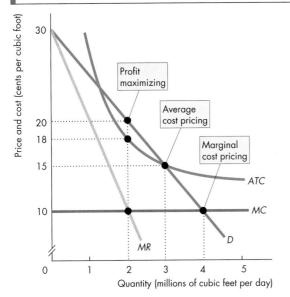

A natural monopoly is an industry in which average total cost is falling even when the entire market demand is satisfied. A natural gas producer faces the demand curve D. The firm's marginal cost is constant at 10 cents per cubic foot, as shown by the curve labeled MC. Fixed costs are large, and the average total cost curve, which includes average fixed cost, is shown as ATC. A marginal cost pricing rule sets the price at 10 cents per cubic foot and produces 4 million cubic feet per day. The firm incurs an economic loss. An average cost pricing rule sets the price at 15 cents per cubic foot and produces 3 million cubic feet per day. The firm makes a normal profit.

Another possibility is to use a two-part price (called a two-part tariff). For example, the gas company might charge a monthly fixed fee that covers its fixed cost and then charge for gas consumed at marginal cost.

But a natural monopoly cannot always cover its costs in these ways. If a natural monopoly cannot cover its total cost from its customers, and if the government wants it to follow a marginal cost pricing rule, the government must give the firm a subsidy. In such a case, the government raises the revenue for the subsidy by taxing some other activity. But as we saw in Chapter 7, taxes themselves generate deadweight loss. Thus the deadweight loss resulting from additional taxes must be subtracted from the efficiency

gained by forcing the natural monopoly to adopt a marginal cost pricing rule.

Average Cost Pricing Regulators almost never impose efficient pricing because of its consequences for the firm's profit. Instead, they compromise by permitting the firm to cover all its costs and to earn a normal profit. Normal profit, recall, is a cost of production and we include it along with the firm's other fixed costs in the average total cost curve. So pricing to cover cost and normal profit means setting price equal to average total cost—called an **average cost pricing rule**.

Figure 13.11 shows the average cost pricing outcome. The natural gas company charges 15 cents a cubic foot and sells 3 million cubic feet per day. This outcome is better for consumers than the unregulated profit-maximizing outcome. The price is 5 cents a cubic foot lower, and the quantity consumed is 1 million cubic feet per day more. And the outcome is better for the producer than the marginal cost pricing rule outcome. The firm earns normal profit. The outcome is inefficient, but less so than the unregulated profit-maximizing outcome.

R E V I E W   Q U I Z

- What are the two main reasons why monopoly is worth tolerating?
- Can you provide some examples of economies of scale and economies of scope?
- Why might the incentive to innovate be greater for a monopoly than for a small competitive firm?
- What is the price that achieves an efficient outcome for a regulated monopoly? And what is the problem with this price?
- Compare the consumer surplus, producer surplus, and deadweight loss that arises from average cost pricing with those of profit-maximization pricing and marginal cost pricing.

◆ You've now studied perfect competition and monopoly, and you've seen how price discrimination can increase a firm's profit. *Reading Between the Lines* on pp. 280–281 looks at price discrimination in action in the airline industry. In the next chapter, we study markets that lie between the extremes of competition and monopoly and that blend elements of the two.

Price Discrimination in Action

USA TODAY, FEBRUARY 23, 1999

Flights at a Premium

BY GARY STOLLER, USA TODAY

The cost of flying at the last minute has outraged large corporations, become a small-business owner's nightmare, and discouraged other spur-of-the-moment weekday travelers.

But are the complaints legitimate and the prices really restrictive if you need to get up and go immediately? USA TODAY analyzed roundtrip fares on nine randomly selected routes and found that on most routes the ticket price for a next-day flight was at least double the cheapest fare, which often required an advance purchase and a Saturday-night stay. And on some routes, the next-day fare was more than six times greater.

On the New York–San Francisco route, American and United telephone reservations agents quoted a $1,902 coach price, and a TWA agent provided a $1,909 fare. That's about $1,600 more than each airline's cheapest advance-purchase tickets. ...

Of the nine routes USA TODAY

analyzed, American's next-day $1,220 Dallas-Denver ticket cost more per mile—94 cents—than any other last-minute coach fare. The same coach seat on American could be had for $194, or 15 cents a mile with a ticket bought at least 21 days out. ...

"Unquestionably, the last-minute traveler pays a heavy penalty," says Norman Sherlock, executive director of the 2,000-member National Business Travel Association, which consists primarily of corporate travel managers. Airline pricing strategies "are designed to take advantage of that fact of life."

High last-minute prices are simply "the way airline pricing works," says David Fuscus, a spokesman for the Air Transport Association, which represents the airlines. "If a traveler books in advance, we know we're getting an economic benefit. But we also hold open seats for the last-minute traveler and take a chance that we're going to lose that economic benefit. So a person booking at the last minute pays a premium."

Essence of the Story

■ The cheapest airfares require a 21-day advance purchase and a Saturday-night stay.

■ The price for a next-day flight is more than double the cheapest fare, and on some routes it is more than six times greater.

■ On the New York–San Francisco route, American, United, and TWA charge about $1,900 for a next-day ticket and about $300 for the cheapest advance-purchase ticket.

■ Norman Sherlock, who represents business travelers, says, "the last-minute traveler pays a heavy penalty."

■ David Fuscus, who represents the airlines, says that the last-minute traveler pays a premium because the airlines hold seats open and run the risk of not filling them.

Economic Analysis

- The willingness to pay for a flight by someone who must travel to close a business deal is usually greater than the willingness to pay by someone who plans to travel to enjoy a relaxing weekend.

- Figure 1 shows the willingness to pay of 260 people who might take one American Airlines flight between New York and San Francisco.

- At one extreme are 20 people who are willing to pay $1,900 or even more for a seat. At the other extreme are 20 people who are willing to pay only $125 or less.

- Assume that American Airlines flies an airplane with 240 seats.

- Suppose that the airline offers all the seats for $269. Smart "seat traders" know that many people, especially last-minute travelers, are willing to pay much more than the $269 at which the airline is selling tickets. So they buy all the seats and resell them just before the flight.

- Envision the scene at the airport. Seat traders auction tickets, getting the highest prices possible from anxious travelers.

- Travelers pay the amount they are willing to pay. Seat traders capture the consumer surplus, and the airline scrapes by with a normal profit.

- We don't observe the scene just described. Instead, the airline sets prices to capture as much consumer surplus as possible by offering seats based on conditions such as Saturday-night stays and a 21-day advance purchase.

- Figure 2 shows the outcome when the airline offers six different fares ranging from $1,900 to $269. The consumer retains a small amount of consumer surplus (the green triangles), but the airline grabs most of it and converts it into producer surplus (the blue area).

- Norman Sherlock is not correct. Business travelers do not pay a penalty. They pay what they are willing to pay.

- David Fuscus is not correct. The airlines don't hold seats open and run the risk of not filling them. They sell each seat for the most the consumer is willing to pay for it.

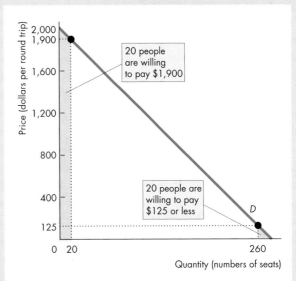

Figure 1 Willingness to pay

Figure 2 Capturing consumer surplus

You're The Voter

- Does airline price discrimination need government attention? Why or why not?

- Can the free market be relied upon to deliver the efficient quantity of air travel? Why or why not?

- How would you vote on a bill that requires the airlines to sell every seat for the same price? Why?

281

SUMMARY

KEY POINTS

Market Power (pp. 264–265)

- A monopoly is an industry with a single supplier of a good or service that has no close substitutes and in which barriers to entry prevent competition.
- Barriers to the entry may be legal (public franchise, license, patent, copyright, firm owns control of a resource) or natural (created by economies of scale).
- A monopoly might be able to price discriminate when there is no resale possibility.
- Where resale is possible, a firm charges one price.

A Single-Price Monopoly's Output and Price Decision (pp. 266–269)

- A monopoly's demand curve is the market demand curve, and a single-price monopoly's marginal revenue is less than price.
- A monopoly maximizes profit by producing the output at which marginal revenue equals marginal cost and by charging the maximum price that consumers are willing to pay for that output.

Single-Price Monopoly and Competition Compared (pp. 270–273)

- A single-price monopoly charges a higher price and produces a smaller quantity than a perfectly competitive industry.
- A single-price monopoly restricts output and creates a deadweight loss.
- Monopoly imposes costs that equal its deadweight loss plus the cost of the resources devoted to rent seeking.

Price Discrimination (pp. 273–276)

- Price discrimination is an attempt by the monopoly to convert consumer surplus into economic profit.
- Perfect price discrimination extracts all the consumer surplus. Such a monopoly charges a different price for each unit sold and obtains the maximum price that each consumer is willing to pay for each unit bought.

- With perfect price discrimination, the monopoly produces the same output as would a perfectly competitive industry.
- Rent seeking with perfect price discrimination might eliminate the entire consumer surplus and producer surplus.

Monopoly Policy Issues (pp. 277–279)

- Monopolies with large economies of scale and scope can produce a larger quantity at a lower price than a competitive industry can achieve, and monopoly might be more innovative than competition.
- Efficient regulation requires a monopoly to charge a price equal to marginal cost, but for a natural monopoly, such a price is less than average total cost.
- Average cost pricing is a compromise pricing rule that covers a firm's costs and provides a normal profit but is not efficient. It is more efficient than unregulated profit maximization.

KEY FIGURES AND TABLE

KEY TERMS

PROBLEMS

*1. Minnie's Mineral Springs, a single-price monopoly, faces the demand schedule:

Price (dollars per bottle)	Quantity demanded (bottles)
10	0
8	1
6	2
4	3
2	4
0	5

  a. Calculate Minnie's total revenue schedule.
  b. Calculate its marginal revenue schedule.

2 Dolly's Diamond Mines, a single-price monopoly, faces the demand schedule:

Price (dollars per pound)	Quantity demanded (pounds per day)
2,200	5
2,000	6
1,800	7
1,600	8
1,400	9
1,200	10

  a. Calculate Dolly's total revenue schedule.
  b. Calculate its marginal revenue schedule.

*3. Minnie's Mineral Springs in problem 1 has the following total cost:

Quantity produced (bottles)	Total cost (dollars)
0	1
1	3
2	7
3	13
4	21
5	31

Calculate the profit-maximizing levels of
  a. Output
  b. Price
  c. Marginal cost
  d. Marginal revenue
  e. Economic profit
  f. Does Minnie's use resources efficiently? Explain your answer.

4. Dolly's Diamond Mines in problem 2 has the following total cost:

Quantity produced (pounds per day)	Total cost (dollars)
5	8,000
6	9,000
7	10,200
8	11,600
9	13,200
10	15,000

Calculate the profit-maximizing levels of
  a. Output
  b. Price
  c. Marginal cost
  d. Marginal revenue
  e. Economic profit
  f. Does Dolly's Mines use resources efficiently? Explain your answer.

*5. The figure illustrates the situation facing the publisher of the only newspaper containing local news in an isolated community.

  a. What quantity of newspapers will maximize the publisher's profit?
  b. What price will the publisher charge?
  c. What is the publisher's daily total revenue?
  d. At the price charged for a newspaper, is the demand elastic or inelastic? Why?

6. In problem 5, the publisher installs a new printing press that makes the marginal cost constant at 20 cents per copy.
  a. What quantity of newspapers will maximize the publisher's profit?

b. What price will the publisher charge?
c. What is the publisher's daily total revenue?
d. At the price charged, is the demand for newspapers elastic or inelastic? Why?

*7. In problem 5, what is:
   a. The efficient quantity of newspapers to print each day? Explain your answer.
   b. The consumer surplus?
   c. The deadweight loss created by the monopoly newspaper publisher?

8. In problem 6, what is:
   a. The efficient quantity of newspapers to print each day? Explain your answer.
   b. The consumer surplus?
   c. The deadweight loss created by the monopoly newspaper publisher?

*9. What is the maximum value of resources that will be used in rent seeking to acquire Minnie's monopoly? Considering this loss, what is the total social cost of Minnie's monopoly?

10. What is the maximum value of resources that will be used in rent seeking to acquire Dolly's monopoly? Considering this loss, what is the total social cost of Minnie's monopoly?

*11. The figure shows the situation facing a natural monopoly.

What quantity will be produced and what will be the deadweight loss if the firm is:
   a. An unregulated profit maximizer?
   b. Regulated to earn only normal profit?
   c. Regulated to be efficient?

12. If in problem 11 marginal cost falls by 50 percent, what are the answers to the three questions posed in problem 11?

CRITICAL THINKING

 1. Study *Reading Between the Lines* on pp. 280–281 and then answer the following questions:
   a. Why can airlines price discriminate?
   b. Who benefits from and who pays for price discrimination?
   c. If price discrimination by the airlines were illegal, how would last-minute travelers get the seats they are willing to pay for?
   d. Does the ability to price discriminate guarantee the airlines a profitable business? Why or why not? Explain your answer.
   e. Why do you think the cost per mile between Dallas and Denver is higher than the cost per mile on other routes in the United States? (Hint: Think about competition on that route.)
   f. Use the links on the Parkin Web site and make some phone calls to obtain the alternative fares being offered today on an air route that appeals to you. Examine the criteria for the different fares and explain how the different fares capture consumer surplus.

 2. Use the links on the Parkin Web site to study the market for computer chips.
   a. Is it correct to call Intel a monopoly? Why or why not?
   b. How does Intel try to raise barriers to entry in this market?

 3. Use the links on the Parkin Web site to obtain information about Microsoft. Then answer the following questions.
   a. Is it correct to call Microsoft a monopoly? Why or why not?
   b. How do you think that Microsoft sets the price of Windows 98 and decides how many copies of the program to sell?
   c. How would the arrival of a viable alternative operating system to Windows affect Microsoft?
   d. How would you regulate the software industry to ensure that resources are used efficiently?
   e. "Anyone is free to buy stock in Microsoft, so everyone is free to share in Microsoft's economic profit, and the bigger that economic profit, the better for all." Evaluate this statement.

Chapter 14

Monopolistic Competition and Oligopoly

Every week, we receive a newspaper stuffed with supermarket fliers describing this week's "specials," providing coupons and other enticements, all designed to grab our attention and persuade us that A&P, Kroger, Safeway, Alpha Beta, Winn Dixie, Stop & Shop, Shop 'n' Save, and H.E.B.'s have the best deals in town. One claims the lowest price, another the best brands, yet another the best value for money even if its prices are not the lowest. How do firms locked in fierce competition with other firms set their prices, pick their products, and choose the quantities to produce? How are the profits of such firms affected by the actions of other firms? ◆ Before 1994, only one firm made the chips that drive IBM and compatible PCs: Intel Corporation. During 1994, the prices of powerful personal computers based on Intel's fast Pentium chips collapsed. The reason: Intel suddenly faced competition from new chip producers such as Advanced Micro Devices Inc. and Cyrix Corp. The price of Intel's Pentium processor, set at more than $1,000 when it was launched in 1993, fell to less than $200 by spring 1996, and today you can buy a Pentium-class computer for less than $600. How did competition among a small number of chip makers bring such rapid falls in the prices of chips and computers?

Fliers and War Games

◇ The theories of monopoly and perfect competition do not predict the kind of behavior that we've just described. There are no fliers and coupons, best brands, or price wars in perfect competition because each firm produces an identical product and is a price taker. And there are none in monopoly because each monopoly firm has the entire market to itself. To understand coupons, fliers, and price wars, we need the richer models explained in this chapter.

After studying this chapter, you will be able to:

- ■ Explain how price and output are determined in a monopolistically competitive industry
- ■ Explain why advertising costs are high in a monopolistically competitive industry
- ■ Explain why the price might be sticky in an oligopoly industry
- ■ Explain how price and output are determined when an industry has one dominant firm and several small firms
- ■ Use game theory to make predictions about price wars and competition among a small number of firms

Monopolistic Competition

YOU HAVE STUDIED TWO TYPES OF MARKET STRUCTURE: perfect competition and monopoly. In perfect competition, a large number of firms produce identical goods, there are no barriers to entry, and each firm is a price taker. In the long run, there is no economic profit. In monopoly, a single firm is protected from competition by barriers to entry and can make an economic profit, even in the long run.

Many real-world markets are competitive, but not as fiercely so as perfect competition. Firms in these markets possess some power to set their prices as monopolies do. We call this type of market *monopolistic competition.*

Monopolistic competition is a market structure in which:

■ A large number of firms compete
■ Each firm produces a differentiated product
■ Firms compete on product quality, price, and marketing
■ Firms are free to enter and exit.

Large Number of Firms

In monopolistic competition, as in perfect competition, the industry consists of a large number of firms. The presence of a large number of firms has three implications for the firms in the industry.

Small Market Share In monopolistic competition, each firm supplies a small part of the total industry output. Consequently, each firm has only limited power to influence the price of its product. Each firm's price can deviate from the average price of other firms by a relatively small amount.

Ignore Other Firms A firm in monopolistic competition must be sensitive to the average market price of the product. But it does not pay attention to any one individual competitor. Because all the firms are relatively small, no one firm can dictate market conditions, so no one firm's actions directly affect the actions of the other firms.

Collusion Impossible Firms in monopolistic competition would like to make agreements with each other to fix a higher price—called collusion. But because there are many firms, collusion is not possible.

Product Differentiation

A firm practices **product differentiation** if it makes a product that is slightly different from the products of competing firms. A differentiated product is one that is a close substitute but not a perfect substitute for the products of the other firms. Some people will pay more for one variety of the product, so when its price rises, the quantity demanded falls but it does not (necessarily) fall to zero. For example, Adidas, Asics, Diadora, Etonic, Fila, New Balance, Nike, Puma, and Reebok all make differentiated running shoes. Other things remaining the same, if the price of Adidas running shoes rises and the prices of the other shoes remain constant, Adidas sells fewer shoes and the other producers sell more. But Adidas shoes don't disappear unless the price rises by a large enough amount.

Competing on Quality, Price, and Marketing

Product differentiation enables a firm to compete with other firms in three areas: product quality, price, and marketing.

Quality The quality of a product is the physical attributes that make it different from the products of other firms. Quality includes design, reliability, the service provided to the buyer, and the buyer's ease of access to the product. Quality lies on a spectrum that runs from high to low. Some firms—Dell Computers is an example—offer high-quality products. They are well designed and reliable, and the customer receives quick and efficient service. Other firms offer lower-quality products. They are less well designed, might not work perfectly, or the buyer must travel some distance to obtain them.

Price Because of product differentiation, a firm in monopolistic competition faces a downward-sloping demand curve. So, like a monopoly, the firm can set both its price and its output. But there is a tradeoff between the product's quality and price. A firm that makes a high-quality product can charge a higher price than a firm that makes a low-quality product.

Marketing Because of product differentiation, a firm in monopolistic competition must market its product. Marketing takes two main forms: advertising and packaging. A firm that produces a high-quality product wants to sell it for a suitably high price. To be able to do so, the firm must advertise and package its product in a way that convinces buyers that they are getting the higher quality for which they are paying a higher price. For example, drug companies advertise and package their brand-name drugs to persuade buyers that these items are superior to the lower-priced generic alternatives. Similarly, a low-quality producer uses advertising and packaging to persuade buyers that although the quality is low, the low price more than compensates for this fact.

Entry and Exit

In monopolistic competition, there is free entry and free exit. Consequently, a firm cannot make an economic profit in the long run. When firms make an economic profit, new firms enter the industry. This entry lowers prices and eventually eliminates economic profit. When economic losses are incurred, some firms leave the industry. This exit increases prices and profits and eventually eliminates the economic loss. In long-run equilibrium, firms neither enter nor leave the industry and the firms in the industry make zero economic profit.

Examples of Monopolistic Competition

Figure 14.1 shows ten industries that are good examples of monopolistic competition. These industries have a large number of firms (shown in parentheses after the name of the industry). In the most concentrated of these industries, canned foods, the largest four firms produce only 25 percent of total sales and the largest twenty firms produce only 60 percent of total sales. Gas stations, food stores, dry cleaners, and haircutters also all operate in monopolistic competition.

R E V I E W   Q U I Z

- What are the distinguishing characteristics of monopolistic competition?
- How do firms in monopolistic competition compete?
- In addition to the examples shown in Fig. 14.1, provide some examples of industries around your school that operate in monopolistic competition.

FIGURE 14.1

Examples of Monopolistic Competition

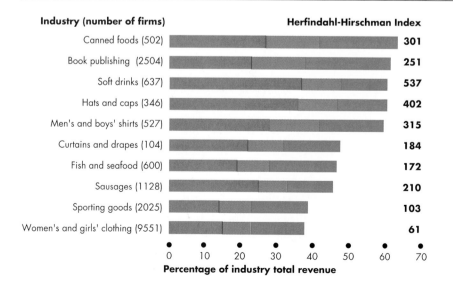

These industries operate in monopolistic competition. The number of firms in the industry is shown after the name of the industry. The red bars show the percentage of industry sales by the largest 4 firms. The green bars show the percentage of industry sales by the next 4 largest firms, and the blue bars show the percentage of industry sales by the next 12 largest firms. So the entire bar shows the percentage of industry sales by the largest 20 firms. The Herfindahl-Hirschman Index is shown on the right.

Output and Price in Monopolistic Competition

WE ARE NOW GOING TO LEARN HOW OUTPUT and price are determined in monopolistic competition. First, we will suppose that the firm has already decided on the quality of its product and on its marketing program. For a given product and a given amount of marketing activity, the firm faces given costs and market conditions.

Figure 14.2 shows how a firm in monopolistic competition determines its price and output. Part (a) deals with the short run, and part (b) deals with the long run. We'll concentrate first on the short run.

Short Run: Economic Profit

The demand curve *D* shows the demand for the firm's product. It is the demand curve for Nautica jackets, not jackets in general. The curve labeled *MR* is the marginal revenue curve associated with the demand curve. It is derived just like the marginal revenue curve of a single-price monopoly that you studied in Chapter 13, p. 266. The figure also shows the firm's average total cost (*ATC*) and marginal cost (*MC*). These curves are similar to the cost curves that you first encountered in Chapter 11.

Nautica maximizes profit by producing the output at which marginal revenue equals marginal cost. In Fig. 14.2, this output is 150 jackets a day. Nautica charges the maximum price that buyers are willing to pay for this quantity, which is determined by the demand curve. This price is $190 a jacket. When Nautica produces 150 jackets a day, its average total cost is $140 a jacket, so it makes a short-run economic profit of $7,500 a day ($50 a jacket multiplied by 150 jackets a day). The blue rectangle shows this economic profit.

So far, the firm in monopolistic competition looks just like a single-price monopoly. It produces

---

FIGURE 14.2

Output and Price in Monopolistic Competition

(a) Short run

(b) Long run

Part (a) shows the short-run outcome. Profit is maximized by producing 150 jackets per day and selling them for $190 per jacket. Average total cost is $140 per jacket, and the firm makes an economic profit (the blue rectangle) of $7,500 a day.

Economic profit encourages new entrants in the long run, and part (b) shows the long-run outcome. The entry of new firms

decreases each firm's demand and shifts the demand curve and marginal revenue curve leftward. When the demand curve has shifted to *D'*, the marginal revenue curve is *MR'* and the firm is in long-run equilibrium. The output that maximizes profit is 50 jackets a day, and the price is $145 per jacket. Average total cost is also $145 per jacket, so economic profit is zero.

the quantity at which marginal revenue equals marginal cost and then charges the highest price that buyers are willing to pay for that quantity, determined by the demand curve. The key difference between monopoly and monopolistic competition lies in what happens next.

Long Run: Zero Economic Profit

There is no restriction on entry in monopolistic competition, so economic profit attracts new entrants. As new firms enter the industry, the firm's demand curve and marginal revenue curve start to shift leftward. At each point in time, the firm maximizes its short-run profit by producing the quantity at which marginal revenue equals marginal cost and by charging the highest price that buyers are willing to pay for this quantity. But as the demand curve shifts leftward, the profit-maximizing quantity and price fall.

Figure 14.2(b) shows the long-run equilibrium. Nautica's demand curve has shifted leftward to D', and its marginal revenue curve has shifted leftward to MR'. Nautica produces 50 jackets a day and sells them at a price of $145 each. At this output level, average total cost is also $145 a jacket, so Nautica is making zero economic profit.

When all the firms are making zero economic profit, there is no incentive for new firms to enter the industry.

If demand is so low relative to costs that firms are incurring economic losses, exit will occur. As firms leave an industry, the demand facing the remaining firms increases and their demand curves shift rightward. The exit process ends when all firms in the industry are making zero economic profit.

Monopolistic Competition and Efficiency

When we studied a perfectly competitive industry, we discovered that in some circumstances, such an industry allocates resources efficiently. A key feature of efficiency is that marginal benefit equals marginal cost. Price measures marginal benefit, so efficiency requires price to equal marginal cost. When we studied monopoly, we discovered that such a firm creates an inefficient use of resources because it restricts output to a level at which price exceeds marginal cost. In such a situation, the marginal benefit exceeds marginal cost and production is less than its efficient level.

Monopolistic competition shares this feature of monopoly. Even though firms make zero economic profit in long-run equilibrium, the monopolistically competitive industry produces an output at which price equals average total cost but exceeds marginal cost. This outcome means that firms in monopolistic competition always have excess capacity in long-run equilibrium.

Excess Capacity   A firm's **capacity output** is the output at which average total cost is a minimum—the output at the bottom of the U-shaped *ATC* curve. This output is 100 jackets a day in Fig. 14.3. Firms in monopolistic competition always have *excess capacity* in the long run. In Fig. 14.3, the firm produces 50 jackets a day and has excess capacity of 50 jackets a day. That is, the firm produces a smaller output than that which minimizes average total cost. Consequently, the consumer pays a price that exceeds

FIGURE 14.3
Excess Capacity

In the long run, entry decreases demand to the point at which the firm makes zero economic profit. Here, the firm produces 50 jackets a day. The firm's capacity output is the output at which average total cost is a minimum. Here, capacity output is 100 jackets a day. Because the demand curve in monopolistic competition slopes downward, the output that maximizes profit is always less than capacity output in long-run equilibrium. The firm operates with excess capacity in long-run equilibrium.

minimum average total cost. This result arises from the fact that the firm faces a downward-sloping demand curve. The demand curve slopes down because of product differentiation, so product differentiation creates excess capacity.

You can see the excess capacity in monopolistic competition all around you. Family restaurants (except for the truly outstanding ones) almost always have some empty tables. You can always get a pizza delivered in less than 30 minutes. It is rare that every pump at a gas station is in use with customers waiting in line. There is always an abundance of realtors ready to help find or sell a home.

These industries are all examples of monopolistic competition. The firms have excess capacity. They could sell more by cutting their prices. But they would then incur losses.

Because in monopolistic competition, price exceeds marginal cost, this market structure, like monopoly, is inefficient. The marginal cost of producing one more unit of output is less than the marginal benefit to the consumer, determined by the price the consumer is willing to pay. But the inefficiency of monopolistic competition arises from product differentiation—from product variety. Consumers value variety, but it is achievable only if firms make differentiated products. So the loss in efficiency that occurs in monopolistic competition must be weighed against the gain of greater product variety.

REVIEW QUIZ

- How does a firm in monopolistic competition decide how much to produce and at what price to offer its product for sale?
- Why can a firm in monopolistic competition earn an economic profit only in the short run?
- Is monopolistic competition efficient?
- Why do firms in monopolistic competition operate with excess capacity?

You've seen how the firm in monopolistic competition determines its output and price in the short run and the long run when it produces a given product and undertakes a *given* marketing effort. But how does the firm choose its product quality and marketing effort? We'll now study these decisions.

Product Development and Marketing

WHEN WE STUDIED A FIRM'S OUTPUT AND PRICE decision, we supposed that it had already made its product and marketing decisions. We're now going to study these decisions and their impact on the firm's output, price, and economic profit.

Innovation and Product Development

To enjoy economic profits, firms in monopolistic competition must be in a state of continuous product development. The reason is that wherever economic profits are earned, imitators emerge and set up business. So to maintain its economic profit, a firm must seek out new products that will provide it with a competitive edge, even if only temporarily. A firm that manages to introduce a new and differentiated variety will temporarily increase the demand for its product and will be able to temporarily increase its price. It will make an economic profit. Eventually, new firms that make close substitutes for the new product will enter and compete away the economic profit arising from this initial advantage. So to restore economic profit, the firm must again innovate.

The decision to innovate is based on the same type of profit-maximizing calculation that you've already studied. Innovation and product development are costly activities, but they also bring in additional revenues. The firm must balance the cost and benefit at the margin. At a low level of product development, the marginal revenue from a better product exceeds the marginal cost. When the marginal dollar spent on product development brings in a dollar of revenue, the firm is spending the profit-maximizing amount on product development.

For example, when Eidos Interactive released Tomb Raider III, it was probably not the best game that Eidos could have created. Rather, it was the game that balanced the marginal benefit and willingness of the consumer to pay for further game enhancements against the marginal cost of these enhancements.

Efficiency and Product Innovation Is product innovation an efficient activity? Does it benefit the consumer? There are two views about these questions. One view is that monopolistic competition brings to market many improved products that bring great benefits to the consumer. Clothing, kitchen and other household appliances, computers, computer programs, cars, and many other products keep getting better every year, and the consumer benefits from these improved products.

But many so-called improvements amount to little more than changing the appearance of a product. And sometimes, the improvement is restricted to a different look in the packaging. In these cases, there is little objective benefit to the consumer.

But regardless of whether a product improvement is real or imagined, its value to the consumer is its marginal benefit, which equals the amount the consumer is willing to pay. In other words, the value of a product improvement is the increase in price that the consumer is willing to pay. The marginal benefit to the producer is marginal revenue, which equals marginal cost. Because price exceeds marginal cost in monopolistic competition, product development is not pushed to its efficient level.

Marketing

Some product differentiation is achieved by designing and developing products that are actually different from those of the other firms. But firms also attempt to create a consumer perception of product differentiation even when actual differences are small. Advertising and packaging are the principal means that firms use to achieve this end. An American Express card is a different product from a Visa card. But the actual differences are not the main ones that American Express emphasizes in its marketing. The deeper message is that if you use an American Express card, you can be like Tiger Woods (or some other high-profile successful person).

Marketing Expenditures Firms in monopolistic competition incur huge costs to persuade buyers to appreciate and value the differences between their own products and those of their competitors. So a large proportion of the prices that we pay cover the cost of selling a good. And this proportion is increasing. Advertising in newspapers and magazines and on radio and television is the main selling cost. But it is not the only one. Selling costs include the cost of shopping malls that look like movie sets; glossy catalogs and brochures; and the salaries, airfares, and hotel bills of salespeople.

The total scale of selling costs is hard to estimate, but some components can be measured. A survey conducted by a commercial agency suggests that for cleaning supplies and toys, around 15 percent of the price of an item is spent on advertising. Figure 14.4 shows some estimates for other industries.

For the U.S. economy as a whole, there are some 20,000 advertising agencies that employ more than 200,000 people and have total revenue of $45 billion. But these numbers are only part of the total cost of advertising because firms have their own internal advertising departments, the cost of which can only be guessed.

Advertising expenditures and other selling costs affect the profits of firms in two ways. They increase costs, and they change demand. Let's look at these effects.

Selling Costs and Total Costs Selling costs such as advertising expenditures increase the costs of a monopolistically competitive firm above those of a competitive firm or a monopoly. Advertising costs and other selling costs are fixed costs. They do not vary as total output varies. So, just like fixed production

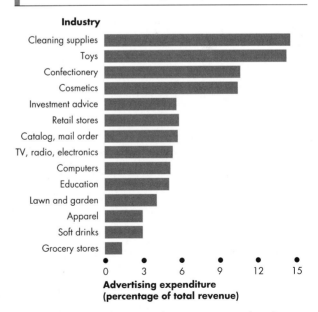

FIGURE 14.4
Advertising Expenditures

Advertising expenditures are a large percentage of total revenue for producers of cleaning supplies, toys, confectionery, and cosmetics.

Source: Schoenfeld & Associates, Lincolnwood, Illinois, reported at http://www.toolkit.cch.com/text/p03_7006.stm

costs, advertising costs per unit decrease as production increases.

Figure 14.5 shows how selling costs and advertising expenditures change a firm's average total cost. The blue curve shows the average total cost of production. The red curve shows the firm's average total cost of production plus advertising. The height of the red area between the two curves shows the average fixed cost of advertising. The *total* cost of advertising is fixed. But the *average* cost of advertising decreases as output increases.

The figure shows that if advertising increases the quantity sold by a large enough amount, it can lower average total cost. For example, if the quantity sold increases from 25 jackets a day with no advertising to 130 jackets a day with advertising, average total cost falls from $170 a jacket to $160 a jacket. The reason is that although the *total* fixed cost has increased, the greater fixed cost is spread over a greater output, so average total cost decreases.

FIGURE 14.5

Selling Costs and Total Cost

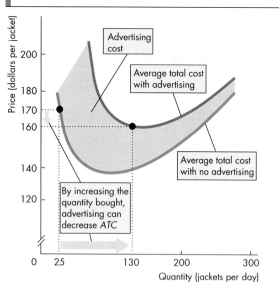

Selling costs such as the cost of advertising are fixed costs. When added to the average total cost of production, these costs increase average total cost (*ATC*) by a greater amount at small outputs than at large outputs. If advertising enables the quantity sold to increase from 25 jackets to 130 jackets a day, it *lowers* average total cost from $170 to $160 a jacket.

Selling Costs and Demand Advertising and other selling efforts change the demand for a firm's products. But how? Does demand increase or does it decrease? The most natural answer is that advertising increases demand. By informing people about the quality of its products or by persuading people to switch from the products of other firms, a firm might expect to increase the demand for its own products.

But all firms in monopolistic competition advertise. And all seek to persuade customers that they have the best deal around. If advertising enables a firm to survive, it might increase the number of firms. And to the extent that it increases the number of firms, it *decreases* the demand faced by any one firm.

Efficiency: The Bottom Line To the extent that selling costs provide consumers with services that they value and with information about the precise nature of the differentiation of products, they serve a useful purpose to the consumer and enable a better product choice to be made. But the opportunity cost of the additional service and information must be weighed against the gain to the consumer.

The bottom line on the question of efficiency of monopolistic competition is ambiguous. In some cases, the gains from extra product variety unquestionably offset the selling costs and the extra cost arising from excess capacity. The tremendous varieties of books and magazines, clothing, food, and drinks are examples of such gains. It is less easy to see the gains from being able to buy brand-name drugs that have a chemical composition identical to that of a generic alternative. But some people do willingly pay more for the brand-name alternative.

R E V I E W   Q U I Z

- What are the two main ways other than by adjusting price in which a firm in monopolistic competition competes with other firms?
- Why might product innovation and development be efficient and why might it be inefficient?
- How do advertising expenditures influence a firm's cost curves? Do they increase or decrease average total cost?
- How do advertising expenditures influence a firm's demand curve? Do they increase or decrease demand?
- Why is it difficult to determine whether monopolistic competition is efficient or inefficient? What is your opinion about the bottom line and why?

Oligopoly

ANOTHER TYPE OF MARKET THAT STANDS BETWEEN the extremes of perfect competition and monopoly is oligopoly. **Oligopoly** is a market structure in which a small number of firms compete.

In oligopoly, the quantity sold by any one firm depends on that firm's price *and* on the other firms' prices and quantities sold. To see why, suppose you run one of the three gas stations in a small town. If you cut your price and your two competitors don't cut theirs, your sales increase and the sales of the other two firms decrease. With lower sales, the other firms most likely cut their prices too. If they do cut their prices, your sales and profits take a tumble. So before deciding to cut your price, you must predict how the other firms will react and attempt to calculate the effects of those reactions on your own profit.

Several models have been developed to explain the prices and quantities in oligopoly markets. But no one theory has been found that can explain all the different types of behavior that we observe in such markets. The models fall into two broad groups: traditional models and game theory models. We'll look at examples of both types, starting with two traditional models.

The Kinked Demand Curve Model

The kinked demand curve model of oligopoly is based on the assumption that each firm believes that:

1. If it raises its price, others will not follow.
2. If it cuts its price, so will the other firms.

Figure 14.6 shows the demand curve (*D*) that a firm believes it faces. The demand curve has a kink at the current price, *P*, and quantity, *Q*. A small price rise above *P* brings a big decrease in the quantity sold. The other firms hold their current price and the firm has the highest price for the good, so it loses its market share. Even a large price cut below *P* brings only a small increase in the quantity demanded. In this case, other firms match the price cut, so the firm gets no price advantage over its competitors.

The kink in the demand curve creates a break in the marginal revenue curve (*MR*). To maximize profit, the firm produces the quantity at which marginal cost equals marginal revenue. That quantity, *Q*, is where the marginal cost curve passes through the gap *ab* in the marginal revenue curve. If marginal cost fluctuates

FIGURE 14.6

The Kinked Demand Curve Model

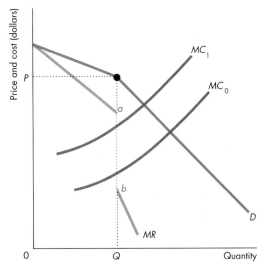

The price in an oligopoly market is *P*. Each firm believes it faces the demand curve *D*. A small price rise above *P* brings a big decrease in the quantity sold because other firms do not raise their prices. Even a big price cut below *P* brings only a small increase in the quantity sold because other firms also cut their prices. Because the demand curve is kinked, the marginal revenue curve, *MR*, has a break *ab*. Profit is maximized by producing *Q*. The marginal cost curve passes through the break in the marginal revenue curve. Marginal cost changes inside the range *ab* leave the price and quantity unchanged.

between *a* and *b*, like the marginal cost curves MC_0 and MC_1, the firm does not change its price or its output. Only if marginal cost fluctuates outside the range *ab* does the firm change its price and output. So the kinked demand curve model predicts that price and quantity are insensitive to small cost changes.

A problem with the kinked demand curve model is that the firms' beliefs about the demand curve are not always correct and firms can figure out that they are not correct. If marginal cost increases by enough to cause the firm to increase its price and if all firms experience the same increase in marginal cost, they all increase their prices together. The firm's belief that others will not join it in a price rise is incorrect. A firm that bases its actions on beliefs that are wrong does not maximize profit and might even end up incurring an economic loss.

Dominant Firm Oligopoly

A second traditional model explains a dominant firm oligopoly, which arises when one firm—the dominant firm—has a big cost advantage over the other firms and produces a large part of the industry output. The dominant firm sets the market price, and the other firms are price takers. Examples of dominant firm oligopoly are a large gasoline retailer or a big video rental store that dominates its local market.

To see how a dominant firm oligopoly works, suppose that 11 firms operate gas stations in a city. Big-G is the dominant firm. Figure 14.7 shows the market for gas in this city. In part (a), the demand curve D tells us the total quantity of gas demanded in the city at each price. The supply curve S_{10} is the supply curve of the 10 small suppliers.

Part (b) shows the situation facing Big-G. Its marginal cost curve is MC. Big-G's demand curve is XD,

and its marginal revenue curve is MR. Big-G's demand curve shows the excess demand not met by the 10 small firms. For example, at a price of $1 a gallon, the quantity demanded is 20,000 gallons, the quantity supplied by the 10 small firms is 10,000 gallons, and the excess quantity demanded is 10,000, measured by the distance ab in both parts of the figure.

To maximize profit, Big-G operates like a monopoly. It sells 10,000 gallons a week for a price of $1 a gallon. The 10 small firms take the price of $1 a gallon. They behave just like firms in perfect competition. The quantity of gas demanded in the entire city at $1 a gallon is 20,000 gallons, as shown in part (a). Of this amount, Big-G sells 10,000 gallons and the 10 small firms each sell 1,000 gallons.

The traditional theories of oligopoly do not enable us to understand all oligopoly markets, and in recent years, economists have developed new models based on game theory. Let's now learn about game theory.

FIGURE 14.7

A Dominant Firm Oligopoly

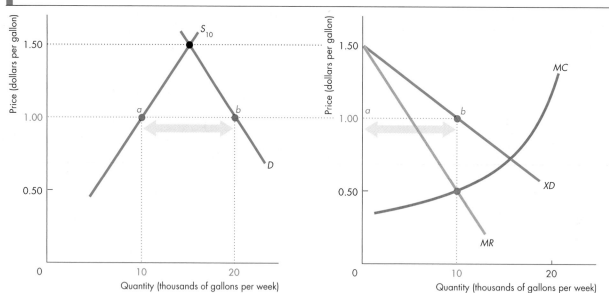

(a) Ten small firms and market demand

The demand curve for gas in a city is D in part (a). There are 10 small competitive firms that together have a supply curve of S_{10}. In addition, there is 1 large firm, Big-G, shown in part (b). Big-G faces the demand curve XD, determined as market demand D minus the supply of the other 10 firms S_{10}—the demand that is not satisfied by the small firms. Big-G's mar-

(b) Big-G's price and output decision

ginal revenue is MR, and its marginal cost is MC. Big-G sets its output to maximize profit by equating marginal cost, MC, and marginal revenue, MR. This output is 10,000 gallons per week. The price at which Big-G can sell this quantity is $1 a gallon. The other 10 firms take this price, and each firm sells 1,000 gallons per week.

Game Theory

The main tool that economists use to analyze *strategic behavior*—behavior that takes into account the expected behavior of others and the mutual recognition of interdependence—is called **game theory**. Game theory was invented by John von Neumann in 1937 and extended by von Neumann and Oskar Morgenstern in 1944. Today, it is one of the major research fields in economics.

Game theory seeks to understand oligopoly as well as other forms of economic, political, social, and even biological rivalries by using a method of analysis specifically designed to understand games of all types, including the familiar games of everyday life. We will begin our study of game theory, and its application to the behavior of firms, by thinking about familiar games.

What Is a Game?

What is a game? At first thought, the question seems silly. After all, there are many different games. There are ball games and parlor games, games of chance and games of skill. But what is it about all these different activities that make them games? What do all these games have in common? All games share three features:

- Rules
- Strategies
- Payoffs

Let's see how these common features of games apply to a game called "the prisoners' dilemma." This game, it turns out, captures some of the essential features of oligopoly, and it gives a good illustration of how game theory works and how it generates predictions.

The Prisoners' Dilemma

Art and Bob have been caught red-handed, stealing a car. Facing airtight cases, each will receive a sentence of 2 years for the crime. During his interviews with the two prisoners, the district attorney begins to suspect that he has stumbled on the two people who were responsible for a multimillion-dollar bank robbery some months earlier. But this is just a suspicion. The district attorney has no evidence on which he can convict them of the greater crime unless he can get them to confess. The district attorney decides to make the prisoners play a game with the following rules.

Rules Each prisoner (player) is placed in a separate room and cannot communicate with the other player. Each is told that he is suspected of having carried out the bank robbery and that:

If both of them confess to the larger crime, each will receive a sentence of 3 years for both crimes.

If he alone confesses and his accomplice does not, he will receive an even shorter sentence of 1 year while his accomplice will receive a 10-year sentence.

Strategies In game theory, **strategies** are all the possible actions of each player. Art and Bob each have two possible actions:

- Confess to the bank robbery
- Deny having committed the bank robbery

Payoffs Because there are two players, each with two strategies, there are four possible outcomes:

1. Both confess.
2. Both deny.
3. Art confesses and Bob denies.
4. Bob confesses and Art denies.

Each prisoner can work out exactly what happens to him—his *payoff*—in each of these four situations. We can tabulate the four possible payoffs for each of the prisoners in what is called a payoff matrix for the game. A **payoff matrix** is a table that shows the payoffs for every possible action by each player for every possible action by each other player.

Table 14.1 shows a payoff matrix for Art and Bob. The squares show the payoffs for each prisoner—the red triangle in each square shows Art's, and the blue triangle shows Bob's. If both prisoners confess (top left), each gets a prison term of 3 years. If Bob confesses but Art denies (top right), Art gets a 10-year sentence and Bob gets a 1-year sentence. If Art confesses and Bob denies (bottom left), Art gets a 1-year sentence and Bob gets a 10-year sentence. Finally, if both of them deny (bottom right), neither can be convicted of the bank robbery charge, but both are sentenced for the car theft—a 2-year sentence.

Equilibrium The equilibrium of a game occurs when player *A* takes the best possible action given the action of player *B* and player *B* takes the best possible action given the action of player *A*. In the case of the prisoners' dilemma, the equilibrium occurs when Art makes his best choice given Bob's choice and when Bob makes his best choice given Art's choice. Let's find the equilibrium of the prisoners' dilemma game.

First, look at the situation from Art's point of view. If Bob confesses, it pays Art to confess because in that case, he is sentenced to 3 years rather than 10 years. If Bob does not confess, it still pays Art to confess because in that case he receives 1 year rather than 2 years. So Art's best action is to confess.

Second, look at the situation from Bob's point of view. If Art confesses, it pays Bob to confess because in that case, he is sentenced to 3 years rather than 10 years. If Art does not confess, it still pays Bob to confess because in that case, he receives 1 year rather than 2 years. So Bob's best action is to confess.

Because each player's best action is to confess, each does confess, each gets a 3-year prison term, and the district attorney has solved the bank robbery. This is the equilibrium of the game.

Nash Equilibrium The equilibrium concept that we have used is called a **Nash equilibrium**; it is so named because it was first proposed by John Nash of Princeton University, who received the Nobel Prize for Economic Science in 1994.

The prisoners' dilemma has a special kind of Nash equilibrium called a dominant strategy equilibrium. A *dominant strategy* is a strategy that is the same regardless of the action taken by the other player. In other words, each player has a unique best action regardless of what the other player does. A **dominant strategy equilibrium** occurs when there is a dominant strategy for each player.

The Dilemma Now that you have found the solution to the prisoners' dilemma, you can better see the dilemma. The dilemma arises as each prisoner contemplates the consequences of denying. Each prisoner knows that if both of them deny, they will receive only a 2-year sentence for stealing the car. But neither has any way of knowing that his accomplice will deny. Each poses the following questions: Should I deny and rely on my accomplice to deny so that we will both get only 2 years? Or should I confess in the hope of getting just 1 year (provided that my accomplice denies), knowing that if my accomplice does confess, we will both get 3 years in prison? The dilemma is resolved by finding the equilibrium of the game.

TABLE 14.1

Prisoners' Dilemma Payoff Matrix

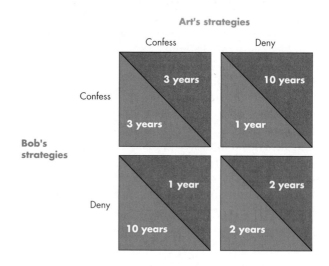

Each square shows the payoffs for the two players, Art and Bob, for each possible pair of actions. In each square, the red triangle shows Art's payoff and the blue triangle shows Bob's. For example, if both confess, the payoffs are in the top left square. The equilibrium of the game is for both players to confess, and each gets a 3-year sentence.

A Bad Outcome For the prisoners, the equilibrium of the game, with each confessing, is not the best outcome. If neither of them confesses, each gets only 2 years for the lesser crime. Isn't there some way in which this better outcome can be achieved? It seems that there is not, because the players cannot communicate with each other. Each player can put himself in the other player's place, and so each player can figure out that there is a dominant strategy for each of them. The prisoners are indeed in a dilemma. Each knows that he can serve 2 years only if he can trust the other to deny. But each prisoner also knows that it is not in the other's best interest to deny. So each prisoner knows that he must confess, thereby delivering a bad outcome for both.

Let's now see how we can use the ideas we've just developed to understand a host of economic situations such as price fixing, price wars, and other aspects of the behavior of firms in oligopoly.

An Oligopoly Price-Fixing Game

TO UNDERSTAND HOW OLIGOPOLIES FIX PRICES, we're going to study a special case of oligopoly called duopoly. **Duopoly** is a market structure in which two producers compete with each other. You can probably find some examples of duopoly in your city. Many cities have only two suppliers of milk, two local newspapers, two taxi companies, two car rental firms, two copy centers, or two college bookstores. But the main reason for studying duopoly is not its realism. It is because it captures the essence of oligopoly and yet is more revealing.

Our goal is to predict the prices charged and the quantities produced by the two firms. To pursue that goal, we're going to study the duopoly game.

Suppose that two firms, Trick and Gear, enter into a collusive agreement. A **collusive agreement** is an agreement between two (or more) producers to restrict output in order to raise prices and profits. Such an agreement is illegal in the United States and is undertaken in secret. A group of firms that has entered into a collusive agreement to restrict output and increase prices and profits is called a **cartel**. The strategies that firms in a cartel can pursue are to:

- Comply
- Cheat

Complying simply means sticking to the agreement. Cheating means breaking the agreement in a manner designed to benefit the cheating firm.

Because each firm has two strategies, there are four possible combinations of actions for the two firms:

- Both firms comply.
- Both firms cheat.
- Trick complies and Gear cheats.
- Gear complies and Trick cheats.

We'll begin by describing the cost and demand conditions in a duopoly industry.

Cost and Demand Conditions

Trick and Gear face identical costs, and Fig. 14.8(a) shows their average total cost curve (*ATC*) and marginal cost curve (*MC*). Figure 14.8(b) shows the market demand curve for switchgears (*D*). Each firm produces an identical switchgear product, so one firm's switchgear is a perfect substitute for the other's. The price of each firm's product, therefore, is identical. And the higher the price, the smaller is the quantity demanded.

This industry is a natural duopoly. Two firms can produce this good at a lower cost than either one firm or three firms can. For each firm, average total cost is at its minimum when production is 3,000 units a week. And when price equals minimum average total cost, the total quantity demanded is 6,000 units a week. So two firms can just supply that quantity.

FIGURE 14.8

Costs and Demand

(a) Individual firm   **(b) Industry**

The average total cost curve for each firm is *ATC*, and the marginal cost curve is *MC* (part a). Minimum average total cost is at $6,000 a unit, and it occurs at an output of 3,000 units a week. Part (b) shows the industry demand curve. At a price of $6,000, the quantity demanded is 6,000 units per week. The two firms can produce this output at the lowest possible average cost. If the market had one firm, it would be profitable for another to enter. If the market had three firms, one would exit. There is room for just two firms in this industry. It is a natural duopoly.

Colluding to Maximize Profits

Let's begin by working out the payoffs to the two firms if they collude to make the maximum industry profit by acting like a monopoly. The calculations that the two firms will perform are exactly the same calculations that a monopoly performs. (You can refresh your memory of these calculations by looking at Chapter 13, pp. 268–269.) The only thing that the duopolists must do that is additional to what a monopolist must do is to agree on how much of the total output each of them will produce.

Figure 14.9 shows the price and quantity that maximize industry profit for the duopolists. Part (a) shows the situation for each firm, and part (b) shows the situation for the industry as a whole. The curve labeled MR is the industry marginal revenue curve. This marginal revenue curve is exactly like that of a single-price monopoly. The curve labeled MC_I is the industry marginal cost curve if each firm produces the same output. That curve is constructed by adding together the outputs of the two firms at each level of marginal cost. That is, at each level of marginal cost, industry output is twice as much as the output of each firm. Thus the curve MC_I in part (b) is twice as far to the right as the curve MC in part (a).

To maximize industry profit, the duopolists agree to restrict output to the rate that makes the industry marginal cost and marginal revenue equal. That output rate, as shown in part (b), is 4,000 switchgears a week.

The highest price for which the 4,000 switchgears can be sold is $9,000 each. This is the price that Trick and Gear agree to charge.

To hold the price at $9,000 a unit, production must not exceed 4,000 units a week. So Trick and Gear must agree on production levels for each of them that totals 4,000 units a week. Let's suppose that they agree to split the market equally so that each firm produces 2,000 switchgears a week. Because the firms are identical, this division is the most likely.

The average total cost (ATC) of producing 2,000 switchgears a week is $8,000, so the profit per unit is $1,000 and economic profit is $2 million (2,000 units × $1,000 per unit). The economic profit of each firm is represented by the blue rectangle in Fig. 14.9(a).

We have just described one possible outcome for a duopoly game: The two firms collude to produce the monopoly profit-maximizing output and divide that output equally between themselves. From the industry point of view, this solution is identical to a monopoly. A duopoly that operates in this way is indistinguishable from a monopoly. The economic profit that is made by a monopoly is the maximum total profit that can be made by colluding duopolists.

But with price greater than marginal cost, either firm might think of trying to increase profit by cheating on the agreement and producing more than the agreed amount. Let's see what happens if one of the firms does cheat in this way.

FIGURE 14.9

Colluding to Make Monopoly Profits

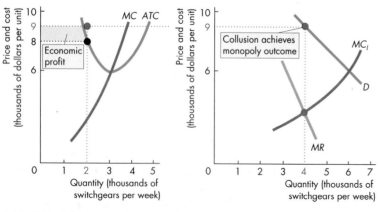

(a) Individual firm   (b) Industry

The industry marginal cost curve, MC_I (part b) is the horizontal sum of the two firms' marginal cost curves, MC (part a). The industry marginal revenue curve is MR. To maximize profit, the firms produce 4,000 units a week (the quantity at which marginal revenue equals marginal cost). They sell that output for $9,000 a unit. Each firm produces 2,000 units a week. Average total cost is $8,000 a unit, so each firm makes an economic profit of $2 million (blue rectangle)—2,000 units multiplied by $1,000 profit a unit.

One Firm Cheats on a Collusive Agreement

To set the stage for cheating on their agreement, Trick convinces Gear that demand has decreased and that it cannot sell 2,000 units a week. Trick tells Gear that it plans to cut its price in order to sell the agreed 2,000 units each week. Because the two firms produce an identical product, Gear matches Trick's price cut but still produces only 2,000 units a week.

In fact, there has been no decrease in demand. Trick plans to increase output, which it knows will lower the price, and Trick wants to ensure that Gear's output remains at the agreed level.

Figure 14.10 illustrates the consequences of Trick cheating. Suppose that Trick (the cheat) increases output to 3,000 units a week (part b). If Gear (the complier) sticks to the agreement to produce only 2,000 units a week (part a), total output is 5,000 a week, and given market demand in part (c), the price falls to $7,500 a unit.

Gear continues to produce 2,000 units a week at a cost of $8,000 a unit and incurs a loss of $500 a unit, or $1 million a week. This economic loss is the red rectangle in part (a). Trick produces 3,000 units a

week at an average total cost of $6,000. With a price of $7,500, Trick makes a profit of $1,500 a unit and therefore an economic profit of $4.5 million. This economic profit is the blue rectangle in part (b).

We've now described a second possible outcome for the duopoly game: One of the firms cheats on the collusive agreement. In this case, the industry output is larger than the monopoly output and the industry price is lower than the monopoly price. The total economic profit made by the industry is smaller than the monopoly economic profit. Trick (the cheat) makes an economic profit of $4.5 million, and Gear (the complier) incurs an economic loss of $1 million. The industry makes an economic profit of $3.5 million, which is $0.5 million less than the economic profit a monopoly would make. But the profit is distributed unevenly. Trick makes a bigger economic profit while Gear incurs an economic loss.

A similar outcome would arise if Gear cheated and Trick complied with the agreement. The industry profit and price would be the same, but in this case Gear (the cheat) would make an economic profit of $4.5 million and Trick (the complier) would incur an economic loss of $1 million.

Let's next see what happens if both firms cheat.

FIGURE 14.10

One Firm Cheats

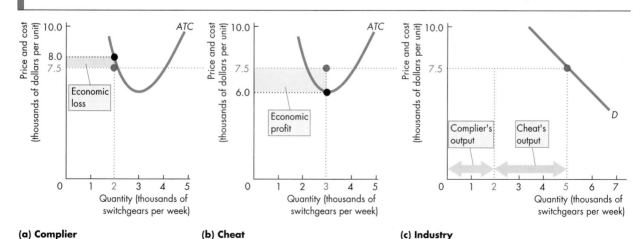

(a) Complier **(b) Cheat** **(c) Industry**

One firm, shown in part (a), complies with the agreement and produces 2,000 units. The other firm, shown in part (b), cheats on the agreement and increases its output to 3,000 units. Given the market demand curve, shown in part (c), and with a total production of 5,000 units a week, the price falls to

$7,500. At this price, the complier in part (a) incurs an economic loss of $1 million ($500 per unit × 2,000 units), shown by the red rectangle. In part (b), the cheat makes an economic profit of $4.5 million ($1,500 per unit × 3,000 units), shown as the blue rectangle.

Both Firms Cheat

Suppose that instead of just one firm cheating on the collusive agreement, both firms cheat. In particular, suppose that each firm behaves in exactly the same way as the cheating firm that we have just analyzed. Each tells the other that it is unable to sell its output at the going price and that it plans to cut its price. But because both firms cheat, each will propose a successively lower price. As long as price exceeds marginal cost, each firm has an incentive to increase its production—to cheat. Only when price equals marginal cost is there no further incentive to cheat. This situation arises when the price has reached $6,000. At this price, marginal cost equals price. Also, price equals minimum average total cost. At a price less than $6,000, each firm incurs an economic loss. At a price of $6,000, each firm covers all its costs and makes zero economic profit (makes normal profit). Also, at a price of $6,000, each firm wants to produce 3,000 units a week, so the industry output is 6,000 units a week. Given the demand conditions, 6,000 units can be sold at a price of $6,000 each.

Figure 14.11 illustrates the situation just described. Each firm, shown in part (a), produces 3,000 units a week, and at this output level, average total cost is a minimum ($6,000 per unit). The market as a whole, shown in part (b), operates at the point at which the demand curve (D) intersects the industry marginal cost curve. This marginal cost curve is constructed as the horizontal sum of the marginal

cost curves of the two firms. Each firm has lowered its price and increased its output to try to gain an advantage over the other firm. Each has pushed this process as far as it can without incurring an economic loss.

We have now described a third possible outcome of this duopoly game: Both firms cheat. If both firms cheat on the collusive agreement, the output of each firm is 3,000 units a week and the price is $6,000. Each firm makes zero economic profit.

The Payoff Matrix

Now that we have described the strategies and payoffs in the duopoly game, let's summarize the strategies and the payoffs in the form of the game's payoff matrix and then calculate the equilibrium.

Table 14.2 sets out the payoff matrix for this game. It is constructed in exactly the same way as the payoff matrix for the prisoners' dilemma in Table 14.1. The squares show the payoffs for the two firms—Gear and Trick. In this case, the payoffs are profits. (In the case of the prisoners' dilemma, the payoffs were losses.)

The table shows that if both firms cheat (top left), they achieve the perfectly competitive outcome—each firm makes zero economic profit. If both firms comply (bottom right), the industry makes the monopoly profit and each firm earns an economic profit of $2 million. The top right and bottom left squares show what happens if one firm

---

FIGURE 14.11

Both Firms Cheat

(a) Individual firm

(b) Industry

If both firms cheat by increasing production, the collusive agreement collapses. The limit to the collapse is the competitive equilibrium. Neither firm will cut price below $6,000 (minimum average total cost), for to do so results in economic losses. In part (a), both firms produce 3,000 units a week at an average total cost of $6,000 a unit. In part (b), with a total production of 6,000 units, the price falls to $6,000. Each firm now makes zero economic profit because price equals average total cost. The output and price are the ones that would prevail in a competitive industry.

TABLE 14.2

Duopoly Payoff Matrix

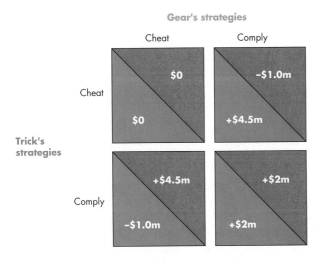

Each square shows the payoffs from a pair of actions. For example, if both firms comply with the collusive agreement, the payoffs are recorded in the bottom right square. The red triangle shows Gear's payoff, and the blue triangle shows Trick's. The equilibrium is a Nash equilibrium in which both firms cheat.

cheats while the other complies. The firm that cheats collects an economic profit of $4.5 million, and the one that complies incurs a loss of $1 million.

This duopoly game is like the prisoners' dilemma that we examined earlier in this chapter; it is a duopolists' dilemma.

Equilibrium of the Duopolists' Dilemma

What do the firms do? Do they comply or cheat? To answer these questions, we must find the equilibrium of the duopoly dilemma.

Look at things from Gear's point of view. Gear reasons as follows: Suppose that Trick cheats. If I comply, I will incur an economic loss of $1 million. If I also cheat, I will make zero economic profit. Zero is better than *minus* $1 million, so I'm better off if I cheat. Now suppose Trick complies. If I cheat, I will make an economic profit of $4.5 million; and if I comply, I will make an economic profit of $2 million. A $4.5 million profit is better than a $2 million

profit, so I'm better off if I cheat. So regardless of whether Trick cheats or complies, it pays Gear to cheat. Cheating is Gear's dominant strategy.

Trick comes to the same conclusion as Gear because the two firms face an identical situation. So both firms cheat. The equilibrium of the duopoly game is that both firms cheat. And although the industry has only two firms, the price and quantity are the same as in a competitive industry and each firm makes zero economic profit.

Although we have done this analysis for only two firms, it would not make any difference (other than to increase the amount of arithmetic) if we were to play the game with three, four, or more firms. In other words, although we have analyzed duopoly, the game theory approach can also be used to analyze oligopoly. The analysis of oligopoly is much harder, but the essential ideas that we have learned also apply to oligopoly.

Repeated Games

The games we've studied are played just once. In contrast, most real-world games get played repeatedly. This fact suggests that real-world duopolists might find some way of learning to cooperate so that their efforts to collude are more effective.

If a game is played repeatedly, one player has the opportunity to penalize the other player for previous "bad" behavior. If Gear cheats this week, perhaps Trick will cheat next week. Before Gear cheats this week, won't it take account of the possibility of Trick cheating next week? What is the equilibrium of this more complicated prisoners' dilemma game when it is repeated indefinitely?

Actually, there is more than one possible equilibrium. One is the Nash equilibrium that we have just analyzed. Both players cheat, and each makes zero economic profit forever. In such a situation, it will never pay one of the players to start complying unilaterally; because to do so would result in a loss for that player and a profit for the other. The price and quantity remain at the competitive levels forever. But another equilibrium, called a cooperative equilibrium, is possible. A **cooperative equilibrium** is an equilibrium in which the players make and share the monopoly profit.

A cooperative equilibrium may occur if each player knows that the other player will punish cheating. There are two extremes of punishment. The smallest penalty that one player can impose on the other is what is called "tit for tat." A *tit-for-tat strategy* is one in which a player cooperates in the current period if the other player cooperated in the previous period but cheats in the current period if the other player cheated in the previous period. The most severe form of punishment that one player can impose on the other arises in what is called a trigger strategy. A *trigger strategy* is one in which a player cooperates if the other player cooperates but plays the Nash equilibrium strategy forever thereafter if the other player cheats.

In the duopoly game between Gear and Trick, a tit-for-tat strategy keeps both players cooperating and earning monopoly profits. Let's see why.

If both firms stick to the collusive agreement in period 1, each makes an economic profit of $2 million. Suppose that Trick contemplates cheating in period 2. The cheating produces a quick $4.5 million economic profit and inflicts a $1 million economic loss on Gear. Adding up the profits over two periods of play, Trick comes out ahead by cheating ($6.5 million compared with $4 million if it did not cheat). The next period, Gear punishes Trick with its tit-for-tat response and cheats. But Trick must cooperate to induce Gear to cooperate again in period 4. Gear now makes an economic profit of $4.5 million, and Trick incurs an economic loss of $1 million. Adding up the profits over three periods of play, Trick would have made more profit by cooperating. In that case, its economic profit would have been $6 million compared with $5.5 million from cheating and generating Gear's tit-for-tat response.

What is true for Trick is also true for Gear. Because each firm makes a larger profit by sticking with the collusive agreement, both firms do so and the monopoly price, quantity, and profit prevail.

In reality, whether a cartel works like a one-play game or a repeated game depends primarily on the number of players and the ease of detecting and punishing cheating. The larger the number of players, the harder it is to maintain a cartel.

Games and Price Wars

The theory of price and output determination under duopoly can help us understand real-world behavior and, in particular, price wars. Some price wars can be interpreted as the implementation of a tit-for-tat strategy. We've seen that with a tit-for-tat strategy in place, firms have an incentive to stick to the monopoly price. But fluctuations in demand lead to fluctuations

in the monopoly price, and sometimes, when the price changes, it might seem to one of the firms that the price has fallen because the other has cheated. In this case, a price war will break out. The price war will end only when each firm has satisfied itself that the other is ready to cooperate again. There will be cycles of price wars and the restoration of collusive agreements. Fluctuations in the world price of oil can be interpreted in this way.

Some price wars arise from the entry of a small number of firms into an industry that had previously been a monopoly. Although the industry has a small number of firms, the firms are in a prisoners' dilemma, and they cannot impose effective penalties for price cutting. The behavior of prices and outputs in the computer chip industry during 1995 and 1996 can be explained in this way. Until 1995, the market for Pentium chips for IBM-compatible computers was dominated by one firm, Intel Corporation, which was able to make maximum economic profit by producing the quantity of chips at which marginal cost equaled marginal revenue. The price of Intel's chips was set to ensure that the quantity demanded equaled the quantity produced. Then in 1995 and 1996, with the entry of a small number of new firms, the industry became an oligopoly. If the firms had maintained Intel's price and shared the market, together they could have made economic profits equal to Intel's profit. But the firms were in a prisoners' dilemma. So prices tumbled closer to competitive levels.

R E V I E W   Q U I Z

- Why does a collusive agreement to restrict output and raise price create a game like the prisoners' dilemma?
- What creates an incentive for firms in a collusive agreement to cheat and increase production?
- What is the equilibrium strategy for each firm in a prisoners' dilemma and why do the firms not collude?
- If a prisoners' dilemma game is played repeatedly, what punishment strategies might the players employ and how does playing the game repeatedly change the equilibrium?

The game theory approach can be extended to deal with a much wider range of choices that firms face. Let's look at some other oligopoly games.

Other Oligopoly Games

FIRMS MUST DECIDE WHETHER TO MOUNT expensive advertising campaigns; whether to modify their product; whether to make their product more reliable (the more reliable a product, usually, the more expensive it is to produce but the more people are willing to pay for it); whether to price discriminate and, if so, among which groups of customers and to what degree; whether to undertake a large research and development (R&D) effort aimed at lowering production costs; or whether to enter or leave an industry. All of these choices can be analyzed by using game theory. The basic method that you have studied can be applied to these problems by working out the payoff for each of the alternative strategies and then finding the equilibrium of the game.

We'll look at two examples: first an R&D game and second an entry-deterrence game.

An R&D Game

Disposable diapers were first marketed in 1966. The two market leaders from the start of this industry have been Procter & Gamble (makers of Pampers) and Kimberly-Clark (makers of Huggies). Procter & Gamble has about 40 percent of the total market, and Kimberly-Clark has about 33 percent. When the disposable diaper was first introduced in 1966, it had to be cost-effective in competition with reusable, laundered diapers. A costly research and development effort resulted in the development of machines that could make disposable diapers at a low enough cost to achieve that initial competitive edge. But as the industry has matured, a large number of firms have tried to get into the business and take market share away from the two industry leaders, and the industry leaders themselves have battled each other to maintain or increase their own market share.

During the early 1990s, Kimberly-Clark was the first to introduce Velcro closures. And in 1996, Procter & Gamble was the first to introduce "breathable" diapers into the U.S. market. The key to success in this industry (or any industry) is designing products that people value highly relative to the cost of producing them. The firm that develops the most highly valued product and also develops the least-cost technology for producing it gains a competitive edge, undercutting the rest of the market, increasing its market share, and

increasing its profit. But the research and development effort that must be undertaken to achieve product improvements and cost reductions is itself costly. This cost of research and development must be deducted from the profit resulting from the increased market share that lower costs achieve. If no firm does R&D, every firm can be better off, but if one firm initiates the R&D activity, all must follow.

Each firm is in a research and development dilemma situation that is similar to the game played by Art and Bob. Although the two firms play an ongoing game against each other, it has more in common with the one-play game than with a repeated game. The reason is that research and development is a long-term process. Effort is repeated, but payoffs occur only infrequently and with uncertainty.

Table 14.3 illustrates the dilemma (with hypothetical numbers) for the R&D game that Kimberly-Clark and Procter & Gamble are playing. Each firm

---

TABLE 14.3

Pampers Versus Huggies: An R&D Game

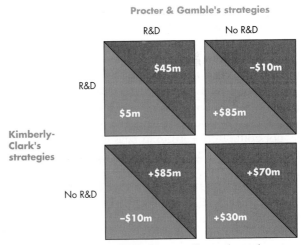

If both firms undertake R&D, their payoffs are those shown in the top left square. If neither firm undertakes R&D, their payoffs are in the bottom right square. When one firm undertakes R&D and the other one does not, their payoffs are in the top right and bottom left squares. The red triangle shows Procter & Gamble's payoff, and the blue triangle shows Kimberly-Clark's. The dominant strategy equilibrium for this game is for both firms to undertake R&D. The structure of this game is the same as that of the prisoners' dilemma.

has two strategies: to spend $25 million a year on R&D or to spend nothing on R&D. If neither firm spends on R&D, they make a joint profit of $100 million: $30 million for Kimberly-Clark and $70 million for Procter & Gamble (bottom right square of the payoff matrix). If each firm conducts R&D, market shares are maintained but each firm's profit is lower by the amount spent on R&D (top left square of the payoff matrix). If Kimberly-Clark pays for R&D but Procter & Gamble does not, Kimberly-Clark gains a large part of Procter & Gamble's market. Kimberly-Clark profits, and Procter & Gamble loses (top right square of the payoff matrix). Finally, if Procter & Gamble conducts R&D and Kimberly-Clark does not, Procter & Gamble gains market share from Kimberly-Clark, increasing its profit, while Kimberly-Clark incurs a loss (bottom left square).

Confronted with the payoff matrix in Table 14.3, the two firms calculate their best strategies. Kimberly-Clark reasons as follows: If Procter & Gamble does not undertake R&D, we will make $85 million if we do and $30 million if we do not; so it pays us to do R&D. If Procter & Gamble conducts R&D, we will lose $10 million if we don't and make $5 million if we do. Again, R&D pays off. Thus conducting R&D is a dominant strategy for Kimberly-Clark. It pays, regardless of Procter & Gamble's decision.

Procter & Gamble reasons similarly: If Kimberly-Clark does not undertake R&D, we will make $70 million if we follow suit and $85 million if we conduct R&D. It therefore pays to conduct R&D. If Kimberly-Clark does undertake R&D, we will make $45 million by doing the same and lose $10 million by not doing R&D. Again, it pays us to conduct R&D. So for Procter & Gamble, R&D is also a dominant strategy.

Because R&D is a dominant strategy for both players, it is the Nash equilibrium. The outcome of this game is that both firms conduct R&D. They make less profit than they would if they could collude to achieve the cooperative outcome of no R&D.

The real-world situation has more players than Kimberly-Clark and Procter & Gamble. A large number of other firms share a small portion of the market, all of them ready to eat into the market share of Procter & Gamble and Kimberly-Clark. So the R&D effort by these two firms not only serves the purpose of maintaining shares in their own battle, but also helps to keep barriers to entry high enough to preserve their joint market share.

Let's now study an entry-deterrence game in which a firm tries to prevent other firms from entering an industry. Such a game is played in a type of market called a contestable market.

Contestable Markets

A **contestable market** is a market in which one firm (or a small number of firms) operates but in which both entry and exit are free, so the firm (or firms) in the market faces competition from *potential* entrants. Examples of contestable markets are routes served by airlines and by barge companies that operate on the major waterways. These markets are contestable because even though only one or a few firms actually operate on a particular air route or river, other firms could enter those markets if an opportunity for economic profit arose and could exit those markets if the opportunity for economic profit disappeared. The potential entrance prevents the firm (or few firms) from making an economic profit.

If the HHI is used to determine the degree of competition, a contestable market appears to be uncompetitive. But a contestable market behaves as if it were perfectly competitive. You can see why by thinking about a game that we'll call an entry-deterrence game.

Entry-Deterrence Game

In the entry-deterrence game we'll study, there are two players. One player is Agile Air, the only firm operating on a particular route. The other player is Wanabe Inc., a potential entrant that is making a normal profit in its current business. The strategies for Agile Air are to set its price at the monopoly profit-maximizing level or at the competitive (zero economic profit) level. The strategies for Wanabe are to enter and set a price just below that of Agile or to not enter.

Table 14.4 shows the payoffs for the two firms. If Wanabe does not enter, Agile earns a normal profit by setting a competitive price or earns maximum monopoly profit (a positive economic profit) by setting the monopoly price. If Wanabe does enter and undercuts Agile's price, Agile incurs an economic loss regardless of whether it sets its price at the competitive or monopoly level. The reason is that Wanabe takes the market with the lower price, so Agile incurs a cost but has zero revenue. If Agile sets a competitive price, Wanabe earns a normal profit if it does not enter or incurs an economic loss if it enters and

TABLE 14.4
Agile Versus Wanabe: An Entry-Deterrence Game

Agile's strategies

Agile is the only firm in a contestable market. If Agile sets the monopoly price, Wanabe earns an economic profit by entering and undercutting Agile's price or a normal profit by not entering. So if Agile sets the price at the monopoly level, Wanabe will enter. If Agile sets the competitive price, Wanabe earns a normal profit if it does not enter or incurs an economic loss if it does enter. So if Agile sets the price at the competitive level, Wanabe will not enter. With entry, Agile incurs an economic loss regardless of the price it sets. The Nash equilibrium of this game is for Agile to set the competitive price, for Wanabe not to enter, and for both firms to make normal profit.

undercuts Agile by setting a price that is less than average total cost. If Agile sets the monopoly price, Wanabe earns a positive economic profit by entering or a normal profit by not entering.

The Nash equilibrium for this game is a competitive price at which Agile Air earns a normal profit and Wanabe does not enter. If Agile sets the monopoly price, Wanabe would enter and, by undercutting Agile's price, would take all the business, leaving Agile with an economic loss equal to total cost. Agile avoids this outcome by sticking with the competitive price and deterring Wanabe from entering.

Limit Pricing **Limit pricing** is the practice of charging a price below the monopoly profit-maximizing price and producing a quantity greater than that

at which marginal revenue equals marginal cost in order to deter entry. The game that we've just studied is an example of limit pricing, but the practice is more general. For example, a firm can use limit pricing to try to convince potential entrants that its own costs are so low that new entrants will incur an economic loss if they enter the industry. To see how this works, let's go back to Agile and Wanabe.

Wanabe knows the current market price but does not know Agile's costs and profit. It can infer those costs, though. Suppose Wanabe believes that marginal revenue is 50 percent of price. If the price is $100, then Wanabe estimates that marginal revenue is $50. Wanabe might assume that Agile is maximizing profit by setting marginal revenue equal to marginal cost. Given this assumption, Wanabe estimates Agile's marginal cost to be $50. If Wanabe's marginal cost is greater than $50, it can't compete with Agile, so it will drop the idea of entering this industry. But if its marginal cost is less than $50, it might be able to enter the industry and also drive Agile out.

Recognizing that Wanabe reasons in this way, Agile might decide to use limit pricing to send a false but possibly believable signal to Wanabe. Agile might cut its price to (say) $80 to make Wanabe believe that its marginal cost is only $40 (50 percent of $80). The lower Wanabe believes Agile's marginal cost to be, the less likely is Wanabe to enter. The strategic use of limit pricing makes it possible, in some situations, for a firm (or group of firms) to maintain a monopoly or collusive oligopoly and limit entry.

◆ The two market structures you've studied in this chapter—monopolistic competition and oligopoly—are the most common ones you encounter in real-world markets. *Reading Between the Lines* on pages 306–307 shows you monopolistic competition in action and the excess capacity it creates for airlines.

A key element in our study of markets for goods and services is the behavior of firms' costs. Costs are determined by technology and by the prices of productive resources. We have treated resource prices as given. We are now going to see how resource prices are themselves determined. Resource prices interact with the goods market that we have just studied in two ways. First, they determine the firm's production costs. Second, they determine household incomes and therefore influence the demand for goods and services. Resource prices also affect the distribution of income. We study each of these interactions in the next three chapters.

Monopolistic Competition in the Air

THE DALLAS MORNING NEWS, JANUARY 2, 1999

Capacity Growth to Benefit Air Travelers

By Terry Maxon /
The Dallas Morning News

The prosperity of the late 1990s may have clouded some airline executives' short-term memory.

Hundreds of airplanes ordered during the recent profitable years soon will roll off the assembly line, adding thousands of potential seats to airlines' schedules. At the same time, demand from passengers probably won't grow as fast, analysts say.

Airlines will be left to fly with more empty seats or cut fares. Either way, airline profits get squeezed, but travelers win.

"This is something we've seen coming from years away, quite literally," said airline analyst Sam Buttrick, of Paine Webber Inc. "With too much capacity sloshing around, ... it's going to put a damper" on earnings.

Or as American Airlines Inc. chairman Donald J. Carty joked last week: "It's the capacity, stupid." ...

But what's bad for airline profits can be good for consumers.

In the early 1990s, airlines offered frequent fare sales with deep cuts to lure people onto airplanes. That could happen again, analysts said.

Essence of the Story

■ A few years ago, when profits were high, the airlines ordered hundreds of new airplanes.

■ Many of these planes will be delivered during 1999.

■ The demand for air travel is predicted to increase by less than the increase in airline capacity.

■ Airlines will have more excess capacity or will cut fares.

■ Airline profits will fall.

■ Consumers will get lower prices and more empty seats.

■ The market for air travel is an example of monopolistic competition.

■ Figure 1 shows the situation facing an airline before the delivery of new airplanes described in the news article. The average total cost curve is ATC_0, the marginal cost curve is MC_0, the demand curve is D, and the marginal revenue curve is MR.

■ To maximize profit, the airline operates at the intersection of the marginal revenue and marginal cost curves. It sells 10 million travel miles a year for a price of 20 cents per mile.

■ The airline earns an economic profit shown by the blue rectangle.

■ Capacity output occurs where ATC_0 is minimized. So the airline operates with excess capacity.

■ Despite having some excess capacity, faced with an economic profit and anticipating further increases in demand, the airline ordered some new planes to be delivered a few years in the future.

■ But when the new planes were delivered, demand had not increased as anticipated.

■ Figure 2 shows the effect of the new planes with (an assumed) no change in demand.

■ The new planes increase the airline's capacity and put the airline on a new average total cost curve and marginal cost curve. These new curves are ATC_1 and MC_1, respectively, in Fig. 2.

■ At the higher output levels that the airline anticipated when it ordered the new planes, average total cost is lower on ATC_1 than it is on ATC_0. (See pp. 230–231 for an explanation of the cost curves for different plant sizes.)

■ But at the low output levels at which the airline must operate, average total cost is higher on ATC_1 than it is on ATC_0.

■ To maximize profit (at the intersection of the marginal revenue and marginal cost curves), the airline increases output to 12 million travel miles a year and cuts the price to 18 cents per mile.

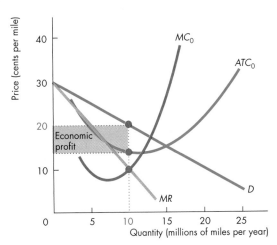

Figure 1 Before the expansion

Figure 2 After expansion

■ The airline now earns zero economic profit (an assumption).

■ Capacity output occurs where ATC_1 is minimized, at 15 million miles a year. So the airline operates with even more excess capacity than before.

■ Eventually, when demand increases, the airline might again make a positive economic profit. But more entry and expansion will keep competing that economic profit away.

SUMMARY

KEY POINTS

Monopolistic Competition (pp. 286–287)

- Monopolistic competition occurs when a large number of firms compete with each other on product quality, price, and marketing.

Output and Price in Monopolistic Competition (pp. 288–290)

- Firms in monopolistic competition face downward-sloping demand curves and produce the quantity at which marginal revenue equals marginal cost.
- Entry and exit result in zero economic profit and excess capacity in long-run equilibrium.

Product Development and Marketing (pp. 290–292)

- Firms in monopolistic competition innovate and develop new products to maintain economic profit.
- Advertising expenditures increase total cost, but they might lower average total cost if they increase the quantity sold by enough.
- Advertising expenditures might increase demand, but they might also decrease the demand facing a firm by increasing competition.
- Whether monopolistic competition is inefficient depends on the value we place on product variety.

Oligopoly (pp. 293–294)

- If rivals match price cuts but do not match price hikes, they face a kinked demand curve and change prices only when large cost changes occur.
- If one firms dominates a market, it acts like a monopoly and the small firms take its price as given and act like perfectly competitive firms.

Game Theory (pp. 295–296)

- Game theory is a method of analyzing strategic behavior.
- In a prisoners' dilemma, two prisoners acting in their own interest harm their joint interest.

An Oligopoly Price-Fixing Game (pp. 297–302)

- An oligopoly (duopoly) price-fixing game is a prisoners' dilemma.
- The firms might collude, one firm might cheat, or both firms might cheat.
- In a one-play game, both firms cheat and output and price are the same as in perfect competition.
- In a repeated game, a punishment strategy can produce a cooperative equilibrium in which price and output are the same as in a monopoly.

Other Oligopoly Games (pp. 303–305)

- A firm's decisions about whether to enter or leave an industry, how much to spend selling the product, whether to modify its product, and whether to undertake research and development can be studied by using game theory.

KEY FIGURES AND TABLE

KEY TERMS

PROBLEMS

*1. The figure shows the situation facing Lite and Kool Inc., a producer of running shoes.

a. What quantity does Lite and Kool produce?
b. What does it charge?
c. How much profit does Lite and Kool make?

2. The figure shows the situation facing Well Done Inc., a producer of steak sauce.

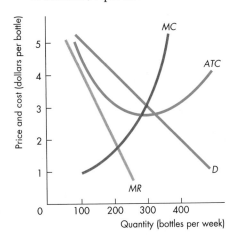

a. What quantity does Well Done produce?
b. What does it charge?
c. How much profit does Well Done make?

*3. A firm in monopolistic competition produces running shoes. If it spends nothing on advertising, it can sell no shoes at $100 a pair, and for each $10 cut in price, the quantity of shoes it can sell increases by 25 pairs a day so at $20 a pair, it can sell 200 pairs a day. The firm's total fixed cost is $4,000 a day. Its average variable cost and marginal cost are a constant $20 per pair. If the firm spends $3,000 a day on advertising, it can double the quantity of shoes sold at each price.

a. If the firm doesn't advertise, what is the quantity of shoes produced and what is the price per pair?
b. What is the firm's economic profit or economic loss?
c. If the firm does advertise, what is the quantity of shoes produced and what is the price per pair?
d. What is the firm's economic profit or economic loss?
e. Will the firm advertise or not? Why?

4. The firm in problem 3 has the same demand and costs as before if it does not advertise. But it hires a new advertising agency. If the firm spends $3,000 a day on advertising with the new agency, it can double the amount that consumers are willing to pay at each quantity demanded.

a. If the firm hires the new agency, what is the quantity of shoes produced and what is the price per pair?
b. What is the firm's economic profit or economic loss?
c. Will the firm advertise or not? Why?
d. What is the firm's economic profit in the long run?

*5. A firm with a kinked demand curve experiences an increase in its fixed costs. Explain the effects on the firm's price, output, and economic profit/loss.

6. A firm with a kinked demand curve experiences an increase in its variable cost. Explain the effects on the firm's price, output, and economic profit/loss.

*7. An industry with one very large firm and 100 very small firms experiences an increase in the demand for its product. Use the dominant firm model to explain the effects on the price, output, and economic profit of

a. The large firm
b. A typical small firm

8. An industry with one very large firm and 100 very small firms experiences an increase in total variable cost. Use the dominant firm model to

explain the effects on the price, output, and economic profit of

   a. The large firm

   b. A typical small firm

*9. Consider the following game: The game has two players, and each player is asked a question. The players can answer the question honestly, or they can lie. If both answer honestly, each receives a payoff of $100. If one answers honestly and the other lies, the liar gains at the expense of the honest player. In that event, the liar receives a payoff of $500 and the honest player gets nothing. If both lie, then each receives a payoff of $50.

   a. Describe this game in terms of its players, strategies, and payoffs.

   b. Construct the payoff matrix.

   c. What is the equilibrium for this game?

10. Describe the game known as the prisoners' dilemma. In describing the game:

   a. Make up a story that motivates the game.

   b. Work out a payoff matrix.

   c. Describe how the equilibrium of the game is arrived at.

*11. Two firms, Soapy and Sudsies, are the only producers of soap powder. They collude and agree to share the market equally. If neither firm cheats on the agreement, each makes $1 million economic profit. If either firm cheats, the cheater increases its economic profit to $1.5 million while the firm that abides by the agreement incurs an economic loss of $0.5 million. Neither firm can police the other's actions.

   a. What is the economic profit for each firm if both cheat?

   b. Construct the payoff matrix of a game that is played just once.

   c. Describe the best strategy for each firm in a game that is played once.

   d. What is the equilibrium if the game is played once?

   e. If this duopoly game can be played many times, describe some of the strategies that each firm might adopt.

12. Two firms, Faster and Quicker, are the only two producers of sports cars on an island that has no contact with the outside world. The firms collude and agree to share the market equally. If neither firm cheats on the agreement, each firm makes $3 million economic profit. If either

firm cheats, the cheater can increase its economic profit to $4.5 million, while the firm that abides by the agreement incurs an economic loss of $1 million. Neither firm has any way of policing the actions of the other.

   a. What is the economic profit for each firm if they both cheat?

   b. What is the payoff matrix of a game that is played just once?

   c. Describe the best strategy for each firm in a game that is played once.

   d. What is the equilibrium if the game is played once?

   e. If this game can be played many times, what are two strategies that could be adopted?

CRITICAL THINKING

 1. Study *Reading Between the Lines* on pp. 306–307 and then answer the following questions:

   a. Why are the airlines an example of monopolistic competition?

   b. How does an airline determine the price per mile and the number of travel miles to sell?

   c. Can the airlines earn economic profits in the long run? Why or why not?

   d. In addition to cutting prices, what other actions might the airlines take when faced with an increase in capacity? (Hint: Think about advertising and other selling efforts.)

   e. Could the airlines collude to increase their profits? Explain the difficulties they face, the benefits they would receive, and the costs to the consumer from such an action.

2. Suppose that Netscape and Microsoft each develop their own versions of an amazing new Web browser that allows advertisers to target consumers with great precision. Also, the new browser is easier and more fun to use than existing browsers. Each firm is trying to decide whether to sell the browser or to give it away free. What are the likely benefits from each action and which is likely to occur? Explain.

 3. Why do Coca-Cola Company and PepsiCo spend huge amounts on advertising? Do they benefit? Does the consumer benefit? Explain your answer.

Managing Change

Our economy is constantly changing. Every year, new goods appear and old ones disappear. New firms are born and old ones die. This process of change is initiated and managed by firms operating in markets. When a new product is invented, just one or two firms sell it initially. For example, when the personal computer first became available, there was an Apple or an IBM. The IBM-PC had just one operating system, DOS, made by Microsoft. One firm, Intel, made the chip that ran the IBM-PC. These are examples of industries in which the producer has market power to determine the price of the product and the quantity produced. The extreme case of a single producer that cannot be challenged by new competitors is *monopoly*, which Chapter 13 explained. ◆ But not all industries with just one producer are monopolies. In many cases, the firm that is first to produce a new good faces severe competition from new rivals. One firm facing potential competition is the case of a *contestable market*. If demand increases and makes space for more than one firm, an industry becomes increasingly competitive. Even with just two rivals, the industry changes its face in a dramatic way. *Duopoly*—the case of just two producers—illustrates this dramatic change. The two firms must pay close attention to each other's production and prices and must predict the effects of their own actions on the actions of the other firm. We call this situation one of *strategic interdependence*. As the number of rivals grows, the industry becomes an *oligopoly*, a market in which a small number of firms devise strategies and pay close attention to the strategies of their competitors. ◆ With the continued arrival of new firms in an industry, the market eventually becomes competitive. Competition might be limited because each firm produces its own special version or brand of a good. This case is called *monopolistic competition* because it has elements of both monopoly and competition. Chapter 14 explored the behavior of firms in all of these types of markets that lie between monopoly at the one extreme and perfect competition at the other. ◆ When competition is extreme—the case that we call *perfect competition*—the market changes again in a dramatic way. Now the firm is unable to influence price. Chapter 12 explained this case. ◆ Often, an industry that is competitive becomes less so as the bigger and more successful firms in the industry begin to swallow up the smaller firms, either by driving them out of business or by acquiring their assets. Through this process, an industry might return to oligopoly or even monopoly. You can see such a movement in the auto and banking industries today. ◆ By studying firms and markets, we gain a deeper understanding of the forces that allocate scarce resources and begin to see the anatomy of the invisible hand. ◆ Many economists have advanced our understanding of these forces and we'll now meet two of them. John von Neumann pioneered the idea of game theory. And Avinash Dixit is one of today's leading students of strategic behavior.

The Economist

John von Neumann *was one of the great minds of the twentieth century. Born in Budapest, Hungary, in 1903, Johnny, as he was known, showed early mathematical brilliance. His first mathematical publication was an article that grew out of a lesson with his tutor, which he wrote at the age of 18! But it was at the age of 25, in 1928, that von Neumann published the article that began a flood of research on game theory—a flood that has still not subsided today. In that article, he proved that in a zero-sum game (like sharing a pie), there exists a best strategy for each player.*

Von Neumann invented the computer and built the first modern practical computer, and he worked on the "Manhattan Project," which developed the atomic bomb at Los Alamos, New Mexico, during World War II.

Von Neumann believed that the social sciences would progress only if they used mathematical tools. But he believed that they needed different tools from those developed from the physical sciences.

"Real life consists of bluffing, of little tactics of deception, of asking yourself what is the other man going to think I mean to do."

JOHN VON NEUMANN, *told to Jacob Bronowski (in a London taxi) and reported in* The Ascent of Man

The Issues

It is not surprising that firms with market power will charge higher prices than those charged by competitive firms. But how much higher?

This question has puzzled generations of economists. Adam Smith said, "The price of a monopoly is upon every occasion the highest which can be got."

But he was wrong. Antoine-Augustin Cournot (see p. 150) first worked out the price a monopoly will charge. It is not the "highest which can be got" but the price that maximizes profit. Cournot's work was not appreciated until almost a century later when Joan Robinson explained how a monopoly sets its price.

Questions about monopoly became urgent and practical during the 1870s, a time when rapid technological change and falling transportation costs enabled huge monopolies to emerge in the United States. Monopolies dominated oil, steel, railroads, tobacco, and even sugar. Industrial empires grew ever larger.

The success of the nineteenth century monopolies led to the creation of our antitrust laws—laws that limit the use of monopoly power. Those laws have been used to prevent monopolies from being set up and to break up existing monopolies. They were used during the 1960s to end a conspiracy between General Electric, Westinghouse, and other firms when they colluded to fix their prices instead of competing with each other. The laws were used during the 1980s to bring greater competition to long-distance telecommunication. But in spite of antitrust laws, near monopolies still exist. Among the most prominent today are those in computer chips and operating systems. Like their forerunners, today's near monopolies make huge profits. But unlike the situation in the nineteenth century, the technological change taking place today is strengthening the forces of competition. Today's information technologies are creating substitutes for services that previously had none. Direct satellite TV is competing with cable, and new phone companies are competing with the traditional phone monopolies.

Then

Ruthless greed, exploitation of both workers and customers—these are the traditional images of monopolies and the effects of their power. These images appeared to be an accurate description during the 1880s, when monopolies stood at their peak of power and influence. One monopolist, John D. Rockefeller, Sr., built his giant Standard Oil Company, which by 1879 was refining 90 percent of the nation's oil and controlling its entire pipeline capacity.

Now

Despite antitrust laws that regulate monopolies, they still exist. One is the monopoly in cable television. In many cities, one firm decides which channels viewers will receive and the price they will pay. During the 1980s, with the advent of satellite technology and specialist cable program producers such as CNN and HBO, the cable companies expanded their offerings. At the same time, they steadily increased prices and their businesses became very profitable. But the very technologies that made cable television profitable are now challenging its market power. Direct satellite TV services are eroding cable's monopoly and bringing greater competition to this market.

Today, many economists who work on microeconomics use the ideas that John von Neumann pioneered. Game theory is the tool of choice. One economist who has made good use of this tool (and many other tools) is Avinash Dixit of Princeton University, whom you can meet on the following pages.

Avinash K. Dixit

is the Sherrerd University Professor of Economics at Princeton University. Born in 1944 in Bombay, India, he was an undergraduate at the University of Cambridge, England, and a graduate student at MIT.

Professor Dixit has worked on a wide range of economic problems but his most widely known work is his 1991 book Thinking Strategically *(with Barry J. Nalebuff), which became an international best seller. This book explains how to use game theory in business, politics, and even in social and family situations. Professor Dixit has also*

Avinash Dixit

explained how a firm establishes and maintains a dominant market position. He has revolutionized the way we think about irreversible decisions—decisions on which we can't go back (or can only reverse at great cost). Michael Parkin talked with Professor Dixit about these issues.

Professor Dixit, what is game theory and how do economists use it?
Game theory is a framework for thinking about decisions when your best choice depends on what someone else is choosing and vice versa. Such interdependence is called strategic interaction. For example, a chess player making an opening move with the white pieces must calculate how the opponent

with the black pieces will respond, knowing in turn that black is taking into account how white will respond at the next move, and so on. The outcome for each player depends on the actions of the other player, and each player makes his or her actions based on awareness of this interdependence.

Strategic interactions occur for either of two reasons. The first arises in small groups of people, firms, or nations where the choices of each have a significant impact on the others. The classic example in economics is an industry with a small number of firms, such as the U.S. auto industry. Before the 1970s, three major auto firms existed in the United States: General Motors, Ford, and Chrysler. Each firm had to decide which vehicles to produce, how to price them, and how many people to employ. While making these decisions, the firm also had to take into account the likely responses to these decisions by the other two firms. In international relations, war or peace among major powers hinges upon similar calculations by each nation's leaders of the interests and responses of others.

The second reason strategic interactions occur is if the market for a product or service extends over time or is of uncertain quality. Consider, for example, that someone is interested in having a home built and needs a contractor. He or she can choose from among many contractors, and a contractor can similarly choose from among numerous potential clients. But once a choice is made, the contractor and client become linked in a bilateral relationship. The builder might procrastinate or do a poor quality job, and the client might be slow with future payments. In

314

anticipation of these problems, a contract is negotiated, monitored, and enforced.

> We frequently play games in which the opponent is not another person but ourselves or, more accurately, our future self. Your future self is going to give in to temptations of the moment and do things you know would be really bad for you—eat more, exercise less, or study less diligently.

Can you give some everyday examples of how game theory helps a person to think strategically and make a better decision?
We frequently play games in which the opponent is not another person but ourselves or, more accurately, our future self. Your future self is going to give in to temptations of the moment and do things you know would be really bad for you—eat more, exercise less, or study less diligently. You can defeat this "opponent" by taking actions right now that diminish your future self's freedom of action. For example, you could join a group where other members will pressure you into keeping your current good resolutions to diet and exercise and study. In game theory, such actions are called "commitments." Finding good devices of commitment is a very important kind of strategy we all have to practice in our daily lives.

Another very important class of games is that of "no-win" interactions, which are best avoided altogether or resolved by prior

negotiation. In game theory, these interactions are typically "prisoners' dilemma" or "chicken" games, in which each person's pursuit of private advantage can lead to mutual harm. The nuclear arms race between the United States and the Soviet Union was the most dramatic example. Each country thought that a hundred more missiles would give it a decisive edge. The result of this thinking was very costly escalation of weapons with no net advantage to either country.

How do firms such as Microsoft and Intel use strategic thinking to dominate their markets?
Firms can become dominant or powerful in their markets for many reasons. First, a firm can be much better than others, producing a higher-quality product and selling it at a lower price. Second, a firm can take predatory strategic actions that increase and sustain its own dominance. For example, it can preemptively install capacity that exceeds what its current production would justify. This acts as a credible demonstration of its willingness to produce more and fight a price war and thereby deters other firms from entering or growing. And third, a product might have such strong economies of scale that the market is most efficiently served by just one firm, but which one emerges in this position can be a matter of historical accident. In practice, all three factors may be present—a firm may get an initial stroke of good luck, then use superior technology or management to lever it into a dominant position, and finally use predatory practices to preserve such a position.

All three factors operated in the computer industry. Both processor chips and operating systems have very large initial design costs but low costs of production or duplication of each copy thereafter. Thus we have good reasons to expect the markets to be dominated by one or a few firms. Which ones?

In the case of Microsoft and Intel, the fact that IBM chose them for its first PC clearly launched them into a favorable position. In the summer of 1980, IBM needed an operating system for their original personal computer. The obvious choice was CP-M, developed by Digital Research in California. The IBM team flew out to see Digital's chief, Gary Kildall. But he forgot the appointment and went flying in his small plane. In his absence, his wife wouldn't sign IBM's nondisclosure agreement. The IBM team left and then went on to Seattle to see Bill Gates, whose Basic language program they also wanted. Hearing that IBM needed an operating system, Gates bought one called QDOS—Quick and Dirty Operating System—from another local company, turned it into MS-DOS, and sold it to IBM as PC-DOS. The rest is history. This was a historical accident par excellence.

Microsoft and Intel made the most of the advantage they got from dealing with IBM. But the reason for their near-total dominance of the industry is a matter of controversy. The Microsoft-lovers argue that for the majority of business and home PC users, the company has delivered a good product at a good price. Microsoft-haters allege predation. They say

Microsoft has used unfair strategies to make it impossible for others to compete. For example, Microsoft insists on contracts with suppliers of DOS-Windows PCs whereby the suppliers have to pay Microsoft a royalty for each unit they ship, whether or not it has a Microsoft operating system. I suspect there is some truth on both sides.

Can you explain your key insight about irreversible investment decisions?

If an action cannot be reversed, or can be reversed only at a great cost, you are more cautious about taking it. Two conditions create this scenario. The first is uncertainty. You can never be entirely sure what the future will bring, but the passage of time and active searching reveals further information. The second is a window of opportunity. Most decisions can be postponed.

Waiting gives you an "option" that is very similar to a financial option—the right but not the obligation to do something in the future if conditions are right then. You can either buy or sell stock at various times. If the future brings new information that shows the action be to undesirable, then the waiting has enabled you to avoid a mistake. If the new information reaffirms the desirability of the action, then you can go ahead, having lost only the benefit that would have flowed from the action for the few weeks' or months' delay.

Your choice of a major or of an area of specialization in gradu-

ate school is a good application of this principle. Nuclear physics may appear to be an attractive career at one point in time and finance or law at another, but conditions change. There is much to be said for acquiring a broad set of flexible skills of wide applicability while learning more about your own interests and the prospects of particular career paths and delaying irreversible specialization.

Who are the giant economists of the past whose ideas have been most fruitful in your work?

I have drawn inspiration and knowledge from the work of so many great economists that it is very difficult to pick one or two. But if forced, I would choose Paul Samuelson and Thomas Schelling. Samuelson's *Foundations of Economic Analysis* and *Economics* were the first two books I read on the subject, Samuelson was one of my teachers in graduate school, and almost all my research has been influenced by the fundamental principles and techniques of optimization and equilibrium that I learned from him.

Thomas Schelling's books, most particularly *The Strategy of Conflict* and *Micromotives and Macrobehavior*, have been immensely influential for my thinking. You can learn about the formalism of game theory from dry mathematical articles and books, but to appreciate the importance of game theory for almost all aspects of life—interactions in the family, social

groups, business, and international relations—you have to read Schelling.

> Economics teaches us the fundamentals of decision making—to be clear about objectives, recognize constraints and thereby opportunity costs, handle uncertainty, and know how to update information in the light of new observations.

What is the case for majoring in economics today? What are the profits from an economics degree?

In very practical terms, an economics major is a good background for professional graduate training in law and business. But perhaps more important, economics is among the "broad set of flexible skills of wide applicability" that I recommended earlier. Economics teaches us the fundamentals of decision making—to be clear about objectives, recognize constraints and thereby opportunity costs, handle uncertainty, and know how to update information in the light of new observations. The techniques that are used in such analysis—mathematics, probability, and statistics—are also useful for many other applications. Studying economics is buying an option that can be exercised later in many kinds of careers and many walks of life.

Chapter 15

Demand and Supply in Resource Markets

Many Happy Returns

It might not be your birthday, and even if it is, chances are you are spending most of it working. But at the end of the week or month (or, if you're devoting all your time to college, when you graduate), you will receive the *returns* from your labor. Those returns vary a lot. Pedro Lopez, who spends his chilly winter days in a small container suspended from the top of Chicago's John Hancock Tower cleaning windows, makes a happy return of $12 an hour. Katie Couric, who hosts a 2-hour morning show each weekday, makes a very happy return of $7 million a year. Students working at what have been called "McJobs"—serving fast food or laboring in the fields of southern California—earn just a few dollars an hour. Why aren't *all* jobs well paid? ◆ Most of us have little trouble spending our pay. But most of us do manage to save some of what we earn. What determines the amount of saving that people do and the returns they make on that saving? How do the returns on saving influence the allocation of savings across the many industries and activities that use our capital resources? ◆ Some people receive income from supplying land, but the amount earned varies enormously with the land's location and quality. For example, an acre of farmland in Iowa rents for about $1,000 a year, while a block on Chicago's "Magnificent Mile" rents for several million dollars a year. What determines the rent that people are willing to pay for different blocks of land? Why are rents so enormously high in big cities and so relatively low in the great farming regions of the nation?

◆ In this chapter we study the markets for productive resources—labor, capital, land, and entrepreneurship—and learn how their prices and people's incomes are determined.

After studying this chapter, you will be able to:

- ■ Explain how firms choose the quantities of labor, capital, and natural resources to employ

- ■ Explain how people choose the quantities of labor, capital, and natural resources to supply

- ■ Explain how wages, interest, and natural resource prices are determined in competitive resource markets

- ■ Explain the concept of economic rent and distinguish between economic rent and opportunity cost

Resource Prices and Incomes

GOODS AND SERVICES ARE PRODUCED BY USING the four economic resources: *labor, capital, land,* and *entrepreneurship.* (These resources are defined in Chapter 3, p. 36.) Incomes are determined by *resource prices*—the *wage* rate for labor, the *interest* rate for capital, the *rental* rate for land, and the rate of *normal profit* for entrepreneurship—and the quantities of resources used.

In addition to the four resource incomes, a residual income, *economic profit* (or *economic loss*) is paid to (or borne by) firms' owners. For a small firm, the owner is usually the entrepreneur. For a large corporation, the owners are the stockholders, who supply capital.

An Overview of a Competitive Resource Market

We're going to learn how competitive resource markets determine the prices, quantities used, and incomes of productive resources. The tool that we use is the demand and supply model. The quantity demanded of a resource depends on its price, and the law of demand applies to resources just as it does to goods and services. The lower the price of a resource, other things remaining the same, the greater is the quantity demanded. Figure 15.1 shows the demand curve for a resource as the curve labeled *D*.

The quantity supplied of a resource also depends on its price. With a possible exception that we'll identify later in this chapter, the law of supply applies to resources. The higher the price of a resource, other things remaining the same, the greater is the quantity supplied of the resource. Figure 15.1 shows the supply curve of a resource as the curve labeled *S*.

The equilibrium resource price is determined at the point of intersection of the demand and supply curves. In Fig. 15.1, the price is *PR* and the quantity used is *QR*.

The income earned by the resource is its price multiplied by the quantity used. In Fig. 15.1, the resource income equals the area of the blue rectangle. This income is the total income received by the factor. Each person who supplies the factor receives the factor price multiplied by the quantity supplied by that person. Changes in demand and supply change the equilibrium price and quantity and change income.

An increase in demand shifts the demand curve rightward and increases price, quantity, and income. An increase in supply shifts the supply curve rightward and decreases price. The quantity used increases, and the income of the resource can increase, decrease, or remain constant. The change in income that results from a change in supply depends on the elasticity of demand for the resource. If demand is elastic, income rises; if demand is inelastic, income falls; and if demand is unit elastic, income remains constant (see Chapter 5, pp. 92–93).

The rest of this chapter explores the influences on the demand for and supply of productive resources. It also studies the influences on the elasticities of supply and demand for resources. These elasticities have major effects on resource prices, quantities used, and incomes.

We begin with the market for labor. But most of what we learn about the labor market also applies to the other resource markets that we study later in the chapter.

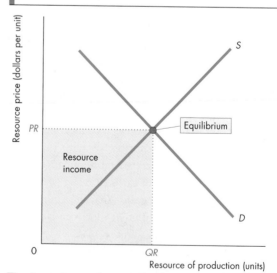

FIGURE 15.1

Demand and Supply in a Resource Market

The demand curve for a productive resource (*D*) slopes downward, and the supply curve (*S*) slopes upward. Where the demand and supply curves intersect, the resource price (*PR*) and the quantity of a resource used (*QR*) are determined. The resource income is the product of the resource price and the quantity of the resource, as represented by the blue rectangle.

Labor Markets

FOR MOST OF US, THE LABOR MARKET IS OUR ONLY source of income. And in recent years, many people have had a tough time. But over the years, both wages and the quantity of labor have moved steadily upward. Figure 15.2(a) shows the record since 1960. Using 1992 dollars to remove the effects of inflation, total compensation per hour of work increased by 90 percent from $10 in 1960 to more than $19 in 1998. Over the same period, the quantity of labor employed increased by 79 percent from 127 billion hours in 1960 to 227 billion hours in 1998.

Figure 15.2(b) shows why wages and employment increased. The demand for labor increased from LD_{60} to LD_{98} and this increase was much larger than the increase in supply from LS_{60} to LS_{98}.

A lot of diversity lies behind the average wage rate and the aggregate quantity of labor. During the 1980s and 1990s, some wages grew much more rapidly than the average and others fell. To understand changes in the labor market, we must probe the forces that influence the demand for labor and the supply of labor. This chapter studies these forces (and Chapter 16 takes a deeper look at them). We begin on the demand side of the labor market.

The Demand for Labor

The demand for labor is a derived demand. A **derived demand** is a demand for a productive resource, which is *derived* from the demand for the goods and services produced by the resource. The derived demand for labor (and the other resources demanded by firms) is driven by the firm's objective, which is to maximize profit.

You learned in Chapters 12, 13, and 14 that a profit-maximizing firm produces the output at which marginal cost equals marginal revenue. This principle holds true for all firms, regardless of whether they operate in perfect competition, monopolistic competition, oligopoly, or monopoly.

A firm that maximizes profit hires the quantity of labor that can produce the profit-maximizing output. What is that quantity of labor? And how does it change as the wage rate changes? We can answer these questions by comparing the *marginal* revenue earned by hiring one more worker with the *marginal* cost of that worker. Let's look first at the marginal revenue side of this comparison.

FIGURE 15.2

Labor Market Trends in the United States

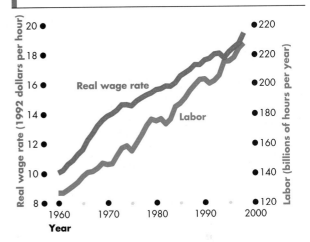

(a) Labor and wage rate

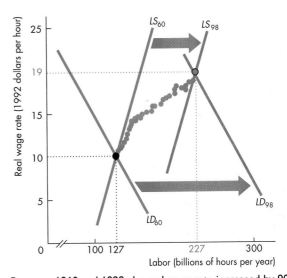

Between 1960 and 1998, the real wage rate increased by 90 percent and the quantity of labor employed increased by 79 percent. Part (a) shows these increases. Each dot in Part (b) shows the real wage rate and the quantity of labor in each year from 1960 to 1998. Part (b) shows the changes in demand and supply that have generated the trends. The demand for labor increased from LD_{60} to LD_{98}, and the supply of labor increased from LS_{60} to LS_{98}. Demand increased by more than supply, so both the real wage rate and the quantity of labor employed increased.

Source: Economic Report of the President, 1998 and author's assumptions.

Marginal Revenue Product

The change in total revenue that results from employing one more unit of labor is called the **marginal revenue product** of labor. Table 15.1 shows you how to calculate marginal revenue product for a perfectly competitive firm.

The first two columns show the total product schedule for Max's Wash 'n' Wax car wash service. The numbers tell us how the number of car washes per hour varies as the quantity of labor varies. The third column shows the *marginal product of labor*—the change in total product that results from a one-unit increase in the quantity of labor employed. (Look back at p. 221 for a quick refresher on these concepts.)

The car wash market in which Max operates is perfectly competitive, and he can sell as many washes as he chooses at $4 a wash, the (assumed) market price. So Max's *marginal revenue* is $4 a wash.

Given this information, we can now calculate *marginal revenue product* (fourth column). It equals marginal product multiplied by marginal revenue. For example, the marginal product of hiring a second worker is 4 car washes an hour, and because marginal revenue is $4 a wash, the marginal revenue product of the second worker is $16 (4 washes at $4 each).

The last two columns of Table 15.1 show an alternative way to calculate the marginal revenue product of labor. Total revenue is equal to total product multiplied by price. For example, two workers produce 9 washes per hour and generate a total revenue of $36 (9 washes at $4 each). One worker produces 5 washes per hour and generates a total revenue of $20 (5 washes at $4 each). Marginal revenue product, in the sixth column, is the change in total revenue from hiring one more worker. When the second worker is hired, total revenue increases from $20 to $36, an increase of $16. So the marginal revenue product of the second worker is $16, which agrees with our previous calculation.

Diminishing Marginal Revenue Product As the quantity of labor increases, marginal revenue product diminishes. For a firm in perfect competition, marginal revenue product diminishes because marginal product diminishes. For a monopoly (or in monopolistic competition or oligopoly), marginal revenue product diminishes for a second reason. When more labor is hired and total product increases, the firm must cut its price to sell the extra product. So marginal product *and* marginal revenue decrease, both of which bring decreasing marginal revenue product.

TABLE 15.1

Marginal Revenue Product at Max's Wash 'n' Wax

	Quantity of labor (L) (workers)	Total product (TP) (car washes per hour)	Marginal product ($MP = \Delta TP/\Delta L$) (additional washes per worker)	Marginal revenue product ($MRP = MR \times MP$) (additional dollars per worker)	Total revenue ($TR = P \times TP$) (dollars)	Marginal revenue product ($MRP = \Delta TR/\Delta L$) (additional dollars per worker)
a	0	0			0	
			5	20		16
b	1	5			20	
			4	16		16
c	2	9			36	
			3	12		12
d	3	12			48	
			2	8		8
e	4	14			56	
			1	4		4
f	5	15			60	

The car wash market is perfectly competitive and the price is $4 a wash. Marginal revenue is also $4 a wash. Marginal revenue product equals marginal product (column 3) multiplied by marginal revenue. For example, the marginal product of the second worker is 4 washes and marginal revenue is $4 a wash. So the marginal revenue product of the second worker (in column 4) is $16. Alternatively, if Max hires 1 worker (row b), total product is 5 washes an hour and total revenue is $20 (column 5). If he hires 2 workers (row c), total product is 9 washes an hour and total revenue is $36. By hiring the second worker, total revenue rises by $16—the marginal revenue product of labor is $16.

The Labor Demand Curve

Figure 15.3 shows how the labor demand curve is derived from the marginal revenue product curve. The *marginal revenue product curve* graphs the marginal revenue product of a resource at each quantity of the resource hired. Figure 15.3(a) illustrates the marginal revenue product curve for workers employed by Max. The horizontal axis measures the number of workers that Max hires, and the vertical axis measures the marginal revenue product of labor. The blue bars show the marginal revenue product of labor as Max employs more workers. These bars correspond to the numbers in Table 15.1. The curve labeled *MRP* is Max's marginal revenue product curve.

A firm's marginal revenue product curve is also its demand for labor curve. Figure 15.3(b) shows Max's demand for labor curve (*D*). The horizontal axis measures the number of workers hired—the same as in part (a). The vertical axis measures the wage rate in dollars per hour. In Fig. 15.3(a), when Max increases the quantity of labor employed from 2 workers an hour to 3 workers an hour, his marginal revenue product is $12 an hour. In Fig. 15.3(b), at a wage rate of $12 an hour, Max hires 3 workers an hour.

The marginal revenue product curve is also the demand for labor curve because the firm hires the profit-maximizing quantity of labor. If the wage rate is less than marginal revenue product, the firm can increase its profit by employing one more worker. Conversely, if the wage rate is greater than marginal revenue product, the firm can increase its profit by employing one fewer worker. But if the wage rate equals marginal revenue product, then the firm cannot increase its profit by changing the number of workers it employs. The firm is making the maximum possible profit. Thus the quantity of labor demanded by the firm is such that the wage rate equals the marginal revenue product of labor.

Because the marginal revenue product curve is also the demand curve, and because marginal revenue product diminishes as the quantity of labor employed increases, the demand for labor curve slopes downward. The lower the wage rate, other things remaining the same, the more workers a firm hires.

When we studied a firm's output decision, we discovered that a condition for maximum profit is that marginal revenue equals marginal cost. We've now discovered another condition for maximum profit: Marginal revenue product of a resource equals the resource's price. Let's study the connection between these two conditions.

FIGURE 15.3

The Demand for Labor at Max's Wash 'n' Wax

(a) Marginal revenue product

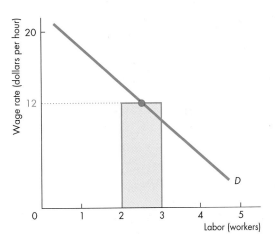

(b) Demand for labor

Max's Wash 'n' Wax operates in a perfectly competitive car wash market and can sell any quantity of washes at $4 a wash. The blue bars in part (a) represent the firm's marginal revenue product of labor. They are based on the numbers in Table 15.1. The orange line is the firm's marginal revenue product of labor curve. Part (b) shows Max's demand for labor curve. This curve is identical to Max's marginal revenue product curve. Max demands the quantity of labor that makes the wage rate equal to the marginal revenue product of labor. The demand for labor curve slopes downward because marginal revenue product diminishes as the quantity of labor employed increases.

Equivalence of Two Conditions for Profit Maximization

Profit is maximized when at the quantity of labor hired, *marginal revenue product* equals the wage rate and when at the output produced, *marginal revenue* equals *marginal cost.*

These two conditions for maximum profit are equivalent. The quantity of labor that maximizes profit produces the output that maximizes profit.

To see the equivalence of the two conditions for maximum profit, first recall that

Marginal revenue product = Marginal revenue × Marginal product.

If we call marginal revenue product *MRP*, marginal revenue *MR*, and marginal product *MP*,

$$MRP = MR \times MP.$$

If we call the wage rate *W*, the first condition for maximum profit is

$$MRP = W.$$

But *MRP* = *MR* × *MP*, so

$$MR \times MP = W.$$

This equation tells us that when profit is maximized, marginal revenue multiplied by marginal product equals the wage rate.

Divide the last equation by marginal product, *MP*, to obtain

$$MR = W \div MP.$$

This equation states that when profit is maximized, marginal revenue equals the wage rate divided by the marginal product of labor.

The wage rate divided by the marginal product of labor equals marginal cost. It costs the firm *W* to hire one more hour of labor. But the labor produces *MP* units of output. So the cost of producing one of those units of output, which is marginal cost, is *W* divided by *MP*.

If we call marginal cost *MC*, then

$$MR = MC,$$

which is the second condition for maximum profit.

Because the first condition for maximum profit implies the second condition, these two conditions are equivalent.

Table 15.2 summarizes the reasoning and calculations that show the equivalence between the two conditions for maximum profit.

TABLE 15.2

Two Conditions for Maximum Profit

Symbols

Marginal product	**MP**
Marginal revenue	**MR**
Marginal cost	**MC**
Marginal revenue product	**MRP**
Resource price	**PR**

Two Conditions for Maximum Profit

1.   **MR = MC**   2.   **MRP = PR**

Equivalence of Conditions

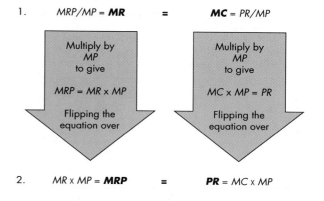

The two conditions for maximum profit are that marginal revenue (MR) equals marginal cost (MC) and marginal revenue product (MRP) equals the price of the resource (PR). These two conditions are equivalent because marginal revenue product (MRP) equals marginal revenue (MR) multiplied by marginal product (MP) and the resource price (PR) equals marginal cost (MC) multiplied by marginal product (MP).

Max's Numbers Check the numbers for Max's Wash 'n' Wax and confirm that the conditions you've just examined work. Max's profit-maximizing labor decision is to hire 3 workers if the wage rate is $12 an hour. When Max hires 3 hours of labor, marginal product is 3 washes per hour. Max sells the 3 washes an hour for a marginal revenue of $4 a wash. So marginal revenue product is 3 washes multiplied by $4 a wash, which equals $12 per hour. At a wage rate of $12 an hour, Max is maximizing profit.

Equivalently, Max's marginal cost is $12 an hour divided by 3 washes per hour, which equals $4 per wash. At a marginal revenue of $4 a wash, Max is maximizing profit.

You've discovered that the law of demand applies for labor just as it does for goods and services. Other things remaining the same, the lower the wage rate (the price of labor), the greater is the quantity of labor demanded.

Let's now study the influences that change the demand for labor and shift the demand for labor curve.

Changes in the Demand for Labor

The demand for labor depends on three factors:

1. The price of the firm's output
2. The prices of other productive resources
3. Technology

The higher the price of a firm's output, the greater is its demand for labor. The price of output affects the demand for labor through its influence on marginal revenue product. A higher price for the firm's output increases marginal revenue, which, in turn, increases the marginal revenue product of labor. A change in the price of a firm's output leads to a shift in the firm's demand for labor curve. If the price of the firm's output increases, the demand for labor increases, and the demand for labor curve shifts rightward.

The other two influences affect the *long-run demand for labor*, which is the relationship between the wage rate and the quantity of labor demanded when all resources can be varied. In contrast, the *short-run demand for labor* is the relationship between the wage rate and the quantity of labor demanded when the quantities of the other resources are fixed and labor is the only variable resource. In the long run, a change in the relative price of productive resources—such as the relative price of labor and capital—leads to a substitution away from the resource whose relative price has increased and toward the resource whose relative price has decreased. So if the price of capital

decreases relative to that of labor, the firm substitutes capital for labor and increases the quantity of capital demanded.

But the demand for labor might increase or decrease. If the lower price of capital increases the scale of production by enough, the demand for labor increases. Otherwise, the demand for labor decreases.

Finally, a new technology that changes the marginal product of labor changes the demand for labor. For example, the electronic telephone exchange has decreased the demand for telephone operators. This same new technology has increased the demand for telephone engineers. Again, these effects are felt in the long run when the firm adjusts all its resources and incorporates new technologies into its production process. Table 15.3 summarizes the influences on a firm's demand for labor.

We saw in Fig. 15.3 that the demand for labor has increased over time and the demand curve has shifted rightward. We can now give some of the reasons for this increase in demand. Advances in technology and investment in new capital increase the marginal product of labor and increase the demand for labor.

TABLE 15.3

A Firm's Demand for Labor

The Law of Demand

(Movements along the demand curve for labor)

The quantity of labor demanded by a firm

Decreases if:	*Increases if:*
■ The wage rate increases	■ The wage rate decreases

Changes in Demand

(Shifts in the demand curve for labor)

A firm's demand for labor

Decreases if:	*Increases if:*
■ The firm's output price decreases	■ The firm's output price increases
■ A new technology decreases the marginal product of labor	■ A new technology increases the marginal product of labor

(Changes in the prices of other resources have an ambiguous effect on the demand for labor.)

Market Demand

So far, we've studied the demand for labor by an individual firm. The market demand for labor is the total demand by all firms. The market demand for labor curve is derived (similarly to the market demand curve for any good or service) by adding together the quantities demanded by all firms at each wage rate. Because a firm's demand for labor curve slopes downward, so does the market demand curve.

Elasticity of Demand for Labor

The elasticity of demand for labor measures the responsiveness of the quantity of labor demanded to the wage rate. This elasticity is important because it tells us how labor income changes when the supply of labor changes. An increase in supply (other things remaining the same) brings a lower wage rate. If demand is inelastic, an increase in supply decreases labor income. But if demand is elastic, an increase in supply brings a lower wage rate and increases labor income. And if the demand for labor is unit elastic, a change in supply leaves labor income unchanged.

The demand for labor is less elastic in the short run, when only labor can be varied, than in the long run, when labor and other resources can be varied. The elasticity of demand for labor depends on:

- The labor intensity of the production process
- The elasticity of demand for the product
- The substitutability of capital for labor

Labor Intensity A labor-intensive production process is one that uses a lot of labor and little capital. Home building is an example. The greater the degree of labor intensity, the more elastic is the demand for labor. To see why, first suppose that wages are 90 percent of total cost. A 10 percent increase in the wage rate increases total cost by 9 percent. Firms will be sensitive to such a large change in total cost, so if wages increase, firms will decrease the quantity of labor demanded by a relatively large amount. But if wages are 10 percent of total cost, a 10 percent increase in the wage rate increases total cost by only 1 percent. Firms will be less sensitive to this increase in cost, so if wages increase in this case, firms will decrease the quantity of labor demanded by a relatively small amount.

The Elasticity of Demand for the Product The greater the elasticity of demand for the good, the larger is the elasticity of demand for the labor used to produce it. An increase in the wage rate increases marginal cost and decreases the supply of the good. The decrease in the supply of the good increases the price of the good and decreases the quantity demanded of the good and the quantities of the resources used to produce it. The greater the elasticity of demand for the good, the larger is the decrease in the quantity demanded of the good, and so the larger is the decrease in the quantities of the productive resources used to produce it.

The Substitutability of Capital for Labor The more easily capital can be used instead of labor in production, the more elastic is the long-run demand for labor. For example, it is easy to use robots rather than assembly line workers in car factories and to use grape-picking machines for labor in vineyards. So the long-run demand for these types of labor is more elastic. At the other extreme, it is difficult (but possible) to substitute computers for newspaper reporters, bank loan officers, and teachers. So the long-run demand for these types of labor is less elastic.

Let's now turn from the demand side of the labor market to the supply side and examine the decisions that people make about how to allocate time between working and other activities.

The Supply of Labor

People can allocate their time to two broad activities: labor supply and leisure. (Leisure is a catchall. It includes all activities other that supplying labor.) For most people, leisure is more enjoyable than supplying labor. We'll look at Jill's labor supply decision. Like most people, Jill enjoys her leisure time, and she would be pleased if she didn't have to spend her weekends working a supermarket checkout line.

But Jill has chosen to work weekends. The reason is that she is offered a wage rate that exceeds her *reservation wage*. Jill's reservation wage is the lowest wage at which she is willing to supply labor. If the wage rate exceeds her reservation wage, she supplies some labor. But how much labor does she supply? The quantity of labor that Jill supplies depends on the wage rate.

Substitution Effect Other things remaining the same, the higher the wage rate she is offered, at least over a range, the greater is the quantity of labor that Jill supplies. The reason is that Jill's wage rate is her *opportunity cost of leisure*. If she quits work an hour early to catch a movie, the cost of that extra hour of leisure is the wage rate that Jill forgoes. The higher the wage rate, the less willing Jill is to forgo the income and take the extra leisure time. This tendency for a higher wage rate to induce Jill to work longer hours is a *substitution effect*.

But there is also an *income effect* that works in the opposite direction to the substitution effect.

Income Effect The higher Jill's wage rate, the larger is her income. A larger income, other things remaining the same, induces Jill to increase her demand for most goods. Leisure is one of those goods. Because an increase in income creates an increase in the demand for leisure, it also creates a decrease in the quantity of labor supplied.

Backward-Bending Supply of Labor Curve As the wage rate rises, the substitution effect brings an increase in the quantity of labor supplied while the income effect brings a decrease in the quantity of labor supplied. At low wage rates, the substitution effect is larger than the income effect, so as the wage

rate rises, people supply more labor. But as the wage rate continues to rise, the income effect eventually becomes larger than the substitution effect and the quantity of labor supplied decreases. The labor supply curve is *backward bending*.

Figure 15.4(a) shows the labor supply curves for Jill, Jack, and Kelly. Each labor supply curve is backward bending but the three people have different reservation wage rates.

Market Supply The market supply of labor curve is the sum of the individual supply curves. Figure 15.4(b) shows the market supply curve (S_M) derived from the supply curves of Jill, Jack, and Kelly (S_A, S_B, S_C) in Fig. 15.4(a). At wage rates of less than $1 an hour, no one supplies any labor. At a wage rate of $1 an hour, Jill works but Jack and Kelly don't. As the wage rate increases and reaches $7 an hour, all three of them work. The market supply curve S_M eventually bends backward, but it has a long upward-sloping section.

Changes in the Supply of Labor The supply of labor changes when influences other than the wage rate changes. The key factors that change the supply of labor and that have increased it over the years are:

FIGURE 15.4

The Supply of Labor

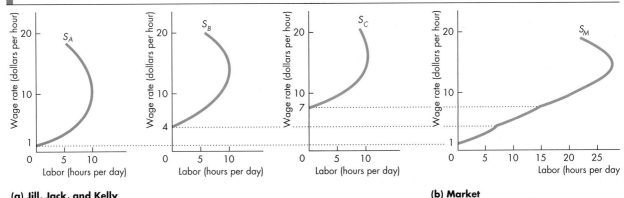

(a) Jill, Jack, and Kelly

(b) Market

Part (a) shows the labor supply curves of Jill (S_A), Jack (S_B), and Kelly (S_C). Each person has a reservation wage below which he or she will supply no labor. As the wage rises, the quantity of labor supplied increases to a maximum. If the wage continues to rise, the quantity of labor supplied begins to decrease. Each

person's supply curve eventually bends backward. Part (b) shows how, by adding the quantities of labor supplied by each person at each wage rate, we derive the market supply curve of labor (S_M). The market supply curve has a long upward-sloping region before it bends backward.

- Adult population
- Technological change and capital accumulation in home production

An increase in the adult population increases the supply of labor. Also, an increase in capital in home production (of meals, laundry services, and cleaning services) increases the supply of labor. These factors that have increased the supply of labor have shifted the labor supply curve rightward.

Let's now build on what we've learned about the demand for labor and the supply of labor and study labor market equilibrium and the trends in wage rates and employment.

Labor Market Equilibrium

Wages and employment are determined by equilibrium in the labor market. You saw in Fig. 15.2 that the wage rate and employment have both increased over the years. You can now explain why.

Trends in the Demand for Labor The demand for labor has *increased* because of technological change and the accumulation of capital, and the demand for labor curve has shifted steadily rightward.

Many people are surprised that technological change and capital accumulation *increase* the demand for labor. They see new technologies *destroying jobs*, not creating them. Downsizing became a catchword of the 1990s as the computer and information age took hold and eliminated millions of "good" jobs, even of managers. So how can it be that technological change *creates* jobs and increases the demand for labor?

Technological change destroys some jobs and creates others. But it creates more jobs than it destroys, and *on the average* the new jobs pay more than the old ones did. But to benefit from the advances in technology, people must acquire new skills and change their jobs. For example, during the past 15 years, the demand for typists has fallen almost to zero. But the demand for people who can type (on a computer rather than a typewriter) and do other things as well has increased. And the output of these people is worth more than that of a typist. So the demand for people with typing (and other) skills has increased.

Trends in the Supply of Labor The supply of labor has increased because of population growth and technological change and capital accumulation in the home. The mechanization of home production of

fast-food preparation services (the freezer and the microwave oven) and laundry services (the automatic washer and dryer and drip dry clothing) has decreased the time spent on activities that once were full-time jobs inside the home and has led to a large increase in the supply of labor. As a result, the supply of labor has steadily increased, but at a slower pace than the demand for labor.

Trends in Equilibrium Because technological advances and capital accumulation have increased demand by more than population growth and technological change in home production has increased supply, both wages and employment have increased. But not everyone has shared in the advancing prosperity that comes from higher wage rates. Some groups have been left behind, and some have even seen their wage rates fall. Why?

Two key reasons can be identified. First, technological change affects the marginal productivity of different groups in different ways. High-skilled computer-literate workers have benefited from the information revolution while low-skilled workers have suffered. The demand for the services of the first group has increased, and the demand for the services of the second group has decreased. (Draw a supply and demand figure, and you will see that these changes widen the wage difference between the two groups.) Second, international competition has lowered the marginal revenue product of low-skilled workers and so decreased the demand for their labor. We look further at skill differences in Chapter 16 and at trends in the distribution of income in Chapter 17.

R E V I E W   Q U I Z

- Why do we call the demand for labor a *derived demand*? From what is it derived?
- What is the distinction between marginal revenue product and marginal revenue? Provide an example that illustrates the distinction.
- When a firm's marginal revenue product equals the wage rate, marginal revenue also equals marginal cost. Why? Provide a numerical example different from that in the text.
- What determines the amount of labor that households plan to supply?
- Describe and explain the trends in wage rates and employment.

Capital Markets

CAPITAL MARKETS ARE THE CHANNELS THROUGH which firms obtain *financial* resources to buy *physical* capital resources. These financial resources come from saving. The *price of capital*, which adjusts to make the quantity of capital supplied equal to the quantity demanded, is the interest rate.

For most of us, capital markets are where we make our biggest ticket transactions. We borrow in a capital market to buy a home. And we lend in capital markets to build up a fund on which to live when we retire. Do the rates of return in capital markets increase as wage rates do? Figure 15.5(a) answers this question by showing the record since 1960. Measuring interest rates as *real* interest rates, which means that we subtract the loss in the value of money from inflation, the rate of return has fluctuated. It averaged around 3 percent a year in the 1960s, became negative in the 1970s, climbed to almost 9 percent in 1984, and steadied at around 5 percent in the 1990s. Over the same period, the quantity of capital employed increased steadily. In 1998, it stood at around $22 trillion (1992 dollars), up by 175 percent from its 1960 level.

Figure 15.5(b) shows why these changes in the capital market occurred. Demand increased from KD_{60} to KD_{98}, and this increase was similar to the increase in supply from KS_{60} to KS_{98}. To understand changes in the capital market, we must again probe the forces of demand and supply. Many of the ideas that you've already met in your study of demand and supply in the labor market apply to the capital market as well. But there are some special features of capital. Its main special feature is that in the capital market, people must compare *present* costs with *future* benefits. Let's discover how these comparisons are made by studying the demand for capital.

The Demand for Capital

A firm's demand for *financial* capital stems from its demand for *physical* capital, and the amount that a firm plans to borrow in a given time period is determined by its planned investment—purchases of new capital. This decision is driven by its attempt to maximize profit. As a firm increases the quantity of capital employed, other things remaining the same, the marginal revenue product of capital eventually diminishes. To maximize profit, a firm increases its

---

FIGURE 15.5

Capital Market Trends in the United States

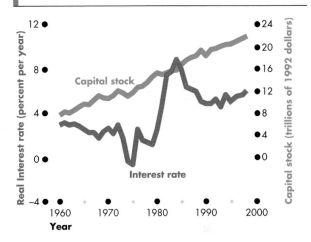

(a) Capital stock and interest rate

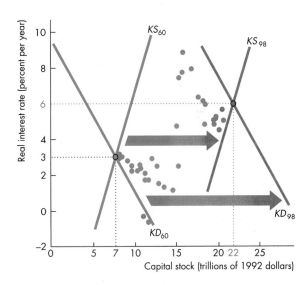

(b) Changes in demand and supply in the capital market

The real interest rate (the interest rate adjusted for inflation) fluctuated between a negative return in 1974 and 1975 and a high of almost 9 percent in 1984. It was steady at 3 percent in the 1960s and 5 percent in the 1990s. During the same period, the quantity of capital employed increased by 175 percent. Part (a) shows this record. Part (b) shows the changes in demand and supply that have generated the changes in the capital market. The demand for capital increased from KD_{60} to KD_{98} and the supply of capital increased from KS_{60} to KS_{98}.

plant size and uses more capital if the marginal revenue product of capital exceeds the cost of capital. But the marginal revenue product comes in the future, and capital must be paid for in the present. So the firm must convert *future* marginal revenue products into a *present value* so that it can be compared with the price of a new piece of capital equipment.

To make this conversion, we use the technique of discounting.

Discounting and Present Value

Discounting is converting a future amount of money to a present value. And the **present value** of a future amount of money is the amount that, if invested today, will grow to be as large as that future amount when the interest that it will earn is taken into account.

The easiest way to understand discounting and present value is to begin with the relationship between an amount invested today, the interest that it earns, and the amount that it will grow to in the future. The future amount is equal to the present amount (present value) plus the interest it will accumulate in the future. That is,

Future amount = Present value + Interest income.

The interest income is equal to the present value multiplied by the interest rate, r, so

Future amount = Present value + ($r \times$ Present value)

or

Future amount = Present value $\times (1 + r)$.

If you have $100 today and the interest rate is 10 percent a year ($r = 0.1$), one year from today you will have $110—the original $100 plus $10 interest. Check that the above formula delivers that answer: $100 \times 1.1 = \$110$.

The formula that we have just used calculates a future amount one year from today from the present value and an interest rate. To calculate the present value, we just work backward. Instead of multiplying the present value by $(1 + r)$, we divide the future amount by $(1 + r)$. That is,

$$\text{Present value} = \frac{\text{Future amount}}{(1 + r)}.$$

You can use this formula to calculate present value. This calculation of present value is called discounting. Let's check that we can use the present value formula by calculating the present value of $110 one year from now when the interest rate is 10 percent a

year. You'll be able to guess that the answer is $100 because we just calculated that $100 invested today at 10 percent a year becomes $110 in one year. Thus it follows immediately that the present value of $110 in one year's time is $100. But let's use the formula. Putting the numbers into the above formula, we have

$$\text{Present value} = \frac{\$110}{(1 + 0.1)}$$

$$= \frac{\$110}{1.1} = \$100.$$

Calculating the present value of an amount of money one year from now is the easiest case. But we can also calculate the present value of an amount any number of years in the future. As an example, let's see how we calculate the present value of an amount of money that will be available two years from now.

Suppose that you invest $100 today for two years at an interest rate of 10 percent a year. The money will earn $10 in the first year, which means that by the end of the first year, you will have $110. If the interest of $10 is invested, then the interest earned in the second year will be a further $10 on the original $100 plus $1 on the $10 interest. Thus the total interest earned in the second year will be $11. The total interest earned overall will be $21 ($10 in the first year and $11 in the second year). After two years, you will have $121. From the definition of present value, you can see that the present value of $121 two years hence is $100. That is, $100 is the present amount that, if invested at an interest rate of 10 percent a year, will grow to $121 two years from now.

To calculate the present value of an amount of money two years in the future, we use the formula

$$\text{Present value} = \frac{\text{Amount of money two years in future}}{(1 + r)^2}.$$

Use this formula to calculate the present value of $121 two years from now at an interest rate of 10 percent a year. With these numbers, the formula gives

$$\text{Present value} = \frac{\$121}{(1 + 0.1)^2}$$

$$= \frac{\$121}{(1.1)^2}$$

$$= \frac{\$121}{1.21}$$

$$= \$100.$$

We can calculate the present value of an amount of money any number of years in the future by using a formula based on the two that we've already used. The general formula is

$$\text{Present value} = \frac{\text{Amount of money}\ n\ \text{years in future}}{(1 + r)^n}.$$

For example, if the interest rate is 10 percent a year, $100 to be received 10 years from now has a present value of $38.55. That is, if $38.55 is invested today at an interest rate of 10 percent, it will accumulate to $100 in 10 years. (You might check that calculation on your pocket calculator.)

You've seen how to calculate the present value of an amount of money one year in the future, two years in the future, and n years in the future. Most practical applications of present value calculate the present value of a sequence of future amounts of money that spread over several years. To calculate the present value of a sequence of amounts over several years, we use the formula you have learned and apply it to each year. We then sum the present values for each year to find the present value of the sequence of amounts.

For example, suppose that a firm expects to receive $100 a year for each of the next five years. And suppose that the interest rate is 10 percent per year (0.1 per year). The present value (PV) of these five payments of $100 each is calculated by using the following formula:

$$PV = \frac{\$100}{1.1} + \frac{\$100}{1.1^2} + \frac{\$100}{1.1^3} + \frac{\$100}{1.1^4} + \frac{\$100}{1.1^5},$$

which equals

$$PV = \$100.00 + \$90.91 + \$82.64 + \$75.13 + \$68.30$$

$$= \$416.98.$$

You can see that the firm receives $500 over five years. But because the money arrives in the future, it is not worth $500 today. Its present value is only $416.98. And the farther in the future it arrives, the smaller is its present value. The $100 received one year in the future is worth $90.91 today. And the $100 received five years in the future is worth only $68.30 today.

Let's now see how a firm uses the concept of present value to achieve an efficient use of capital.

The Present Value of a Computer We'll see how a firm decides how much capital to buy by calculating the present value of a new computer.

Tina runs Taxfile, Inc., a firm that sells advice to taxpayers. Tina is considering buying a new computer that costs $10,000. The computer has a life of two years, after which it will be worthless. If Tina buys the computer, she will pay $10,000 now and she expects to generate business that will bring in an additional $5,900 at the end of each of the next two years.

To calculate the present value, PV, of the marginal revenue product of a new computer, Tina calculates

$$PV = \frac{MRP_1}{(1 + r)} + \frac{MRP_2}{(1 + r)^2}.$$

Here, MRP_1 is the marginal revenue product received by Tina at the end of the first year. It is converted to a present value by dividing it by $(1 + r)$, where r is the interest rate (expressed as a proportion). The term MRP_2 is the marginal revenue product received at the end of the second year. It is converted to a present value by dividing it by $(1 + r)^2$.

If Tina can borrow or lend at an interest rate of 4 percent a year, the present value of her marginal revenue product is given by

$$PV = \frac{\$5,900}{(1 + 0.04)} + \frac{\$5,900}{(1 + 0.04)^2}$$

$$PV = \$5,673 + \$5,455$$

$$PV = \$11,128.$$

The present value (PV) of $5,900 one year in the future is $5,900 divided by 1.04 (4 percent as a proportion is 0.04). The present value of $5,900 two years in the future is $5,900 divided by $(1.04)^2$. Tina works out those two present values and then adds them to get the present value of the future flow of marginal revenue product, which is $11,128.

Table 15.4, parts (a) and (b), summarizes the data and the calculations we've just made. Review these calculations and make sure you understand them.

Tina's Decision to Buy Tina decides whether to buy the computer by comparing the present value of its future flow of marginal revenue product with its purchase price. She makes this comparison by calculating the net present value (NPV) of the computer. **Net present value** is the present value of the future flow of marginal revenue product generated by the capital minus the cost of the capital. If net present value is positive, the firm buys additional capital. If the net present value is negative, the firm does not buy additional capital. Table 15.4(c) shows the

---

TABLE 15.4

Net Present Value of an Investment—Taxfile, Inc.

(a) Data

Price of computer	$10,000
Life of computer	2 years
Marginal revenue product	$5,900 at end of each year
Interest rate	4% a year

(b) Present value of the flow of marginal revenue product

$$PV = \frac{MRP_1}{(1+r)} + \frac{MRP_2}{(1+r)^2}$$

$$= \frac{\$5,900}{1.04} + \frac{\$5,900}{(1.04)^2}$$

$$= \$5,673 + \$5,455$$

$$= \$11,128.$$

(c) Net present value of investment

$NPV = PV$ of marginal revenue product − Cost of computer

$$= \$11,128 - \$10,000$$

$$= \$1,128.$$

---

calculation of Tina's net present value of a computer. The net present value is $1,128—greater than zero—so Tina buys the computer.

Tina can buy any number of computers that cost $10,000 and have a life of two years. But like all other factors of production, capital is subject to diminishing marginal returns. The greater the amount of capital employed, the smaller is its marginal revenue product. So if Tina buys a second computer or a third one, she gets successively smaller marginal revenue products from the additional machines.

Table 15.5(a) sets out Tina's marginal revenue products for one, two, and three computers. The marginal revenue product of one computer (the case just reviewed) is $5,900 a year. The marginal revenue product of a second computer is $5,600 a year, and the marginal revenue product of a third computer is

$5,300 a year. Table 15.5(b) shows the calculations of the present values of the marginal revenue products of the first, second, and third computers.

You've seen that with an interest rate of 4 percent a year, the net present value of one computer is positive. At an interest rate of 4 percent a year, the present value of the marginal revenue product of a second computer is $10,562, which exceeds its price by $562. So Tina buys a second computer. But at an interest rate of 4 percent a year, the present value of the marginal revenue product of a third computer is $9,996, which is $4 less than the price of the computer. So Tina does not buy a third computer.

A Change in the Interest Rate We've seen that at an interest rate of 4 percent a year, Tina buys two computers but not three. Suppose that the interest rate is 8 percent a year. In this case, the present value of the first computer is $10,521 (see Table 15.5b), so Tina still buys one computer because it has a positive net present value. At an interest rate of 8 percent a year, the net present value of the second computer is $9,986, which is less than $10,000, the price of the computer. So at an interest rate of 8 percent a year, Tina buys only one computer.

Suppose that the interest rate is even higher, at 12 percent a year. In this case, the present value of the marginal revenue product of one computer is $9,971 (see Table 15.5b). At this interest rate, Tina buys no computers.

These calculations trace Taxfile's demand schedule for capital, which shows the value of computers demanded by Taxfile at each interest rate. Other things remaining the same, as the interest rate rises, the quantity of capital demanded decreases. The higher the interest rate, the smaller is the quantity of *physical* capital demanded. But to finance the purchase of *physical* capital, firms demand *financial* capital. So the higher the interest rate, the smaller is the quantity of *financial* capital demanded.

Demand Curve for Capital

The quantity of capital demanded by a firm depends on the marginal revenue product of capital and the interest rate. A firm's demand curve for capital shows the relationship between the quantity of capital demanded by the firm and the interest rate, other things remaining the same. The market demand

TABLE 15.5

Taxfile's Investment Decision

(a) Data

Price of computer	$10,000
Life of computer	2 years
Marginal revenue product:	
Using 1 computer	$5,900 a year
Using 2 computers	$5,600 a year
Using 3 computers	$5,300 a year

(b) Present value of the flow of marginal revenue product

If r = 0.04 (4% a year):

Using 1 computer: $PV = \dfrac{\$5,900}{1.04} + \dfrac{\$5,900}{(1.04)^2} = \$11,128.$

Using 2 computers: $PV = \dfrac{\$5,600}{1.04} + \dfrac{\$5,600}{(1.04)^2} = \$10,562.$

Using 3 computers: $PV = \dfrac{\$5,300}{1.04} + \dfrac{\$5,300}{(1.04)^2} = \$9,996.$

If r = 0.08 (8% a year):

Using 1 computer: $PV = \dfrac{\$5,900}{1.08} + \dfrac{\$5,900}{(1.08)^2} = \$10,521.$

Using 2 computers: $PV = \dfrac{\$5,600}{1.08} + \dfrac{\$5,600}{(1.08)^2} = \$9,986.$

If r = 0.12 (12% a year):

Using 1 computer: $PV = \dfrac{\$5,900}{1.12} + \dfrac{\$5,900}{(1.12)^2} = \$9,971.$

---

curve (as in Fig. 15.5b) shows the relationship between the total quantity of capital demanded and the interest rate, other things remaining the same.

Changes in the Demand for Capital Figure 15.5(b) shows that the demand for capital has increased steadily over the years. The demand for capital changes when expectations about the future marginal revenue product of capital change. An increase in the expected marginal revenue product of capital increases the demand of capital. Two main factors

that change the marginal revenue product of capital and bring changes in the demand for capital are:

1. Population growth
2. Technological change

An increase in the population increases the demand for all goods and services and so increases the demand for the capital that produces them. Advances in technology increase the demand for some types of capital and decrease the demand for other types. For example, the development of diesel engines for railroad transportation decreased the demand for steam engines and increased the demand for diesel engines. In this case, the railroad industry's overall demand for capital did not change much. In contrast, the development of desktop computers increased the demand for office computing equipment, decreased the demand for electric typewriters, and increased the overall demand for capital in the office.

Let's now turn to the supply side of the capital market.

The Supply of Capital

The quantity of capital supplied results from people's saving decisions. The main factors that determine saving are:

- Income
- Expected future income
- Interest rate

Income Saving is the act of converting *current* income into *future* consumption. Usually, the higher a person's income, the more he or she plans to consume both in the present and in the future. But to increase *future* consumption, the person must save. So, other things remaining the same, the higher a person's income, the more he or she saves. The relationship between saving and income is remarkably stable. Most people save a constant proportion of their income.

Expected Future Income Because a major reason for saving is to increase future consumption, the amount that a person saves depends not only on its current income but also on his or her *expected future income*. If a person's current income is high and expected future income is low, he or she will have a high level of saving. But if the person's current income is low and expected future income is high, he or she will have a low (perhaps even negative) level of saving.

Young people (especially students) usually have low current incomes compared with their expected future income. To smooth out consumption over their lifetime, young people consume more than they earn and incur debts. Such people have a negative amount of saving. In middle age, most people's incomes reach their peak. At this stage in life, saving is at its maximum. After retirement, people spend part of the wealth they have accumulated during their working lives.

Interest Rate A dollar saved today grows into a dollar plus interest tomorrow. The higher the interest rate, the greater is the amount that a dollar saved today becomes in the future. Thus the higher the interest rate, the greater is the opportunity cost of current consumption. With a higher opportunity cost of current consumption, people cut their consumption and increase their saving.

Supply Curve of Capital

The supply curve of capital (like that in Fig. 15.5b) shows the relationship between the quantity of capital supplied and the interest rate, other things remaining the same. An increase in the interest rate brings an increase in the quantity of capital supplied and a movement along the supply curve. The supply of capital is inelastic in the short run but probably quite elastic in the long run. The reason is that in any given year, the total amount of saving is small relative to the stock of capital in existence. So even a large change in the amount of saving brings only a small change in the quantity of capital supplied.

Changes in the Supply of Capital The main influences on the supply of capital are the size and age distribution of the population and the level of income.

Other things remaining the same, an increase in the population or an increase in income brings an increase in the supply of capital. Also, other things remaining the same, the larger the proportion of middle-aged people, the higher is the amount of saving. The reason is that middle-aged people do most of the saving as they build up a pension fund to provide a retirement income. Any one of the factors that

increases the supply of capital shifts the supply curve of capital rightward.

Let's now use what we've learned about the demand for and supply of capital and see how the interest rate is determined.

The Interest Rate

Saving plans and investment plans are coordinated through capital markets, and the real interest rate adjusts to make these plans compatible.

Figure 15.6 shows the capital market. Initially, the demand for capital is KD_0, and the supply of capital is KS_0. The equilibrium real interest rate is 6 percent a year, and the quantity of capital is $10 trillion. If the interest rate exceeds 6 percent a year, the quantity of capital supplied exceeds the quantity of capital demanded and the interest rate falls. And if the interest rate is less than 6 percent a year, the quantity of

FIGURE 15.6

Capital Market Equilibrium

Initially, the demand for capital is KD_0, and the supply of capital is KS_0. The equilibrium interest rate is 6 percent a year, and the capital stock is $10 trillion. Over time, both demand and supply increase to KD_1 and KS_1 respectively. The capital stock increases, but the real interest rate is constant. Demand and supply increase because they are influenced by common factors.

capital demanded exceeds the quantity of capital supplied and the interest rate rises.

Over time, both the demand for capital and the supply of capital increase. The demand curve shifts rightward to KD_1, and the supply curve also shifts rightward, to KS_1. Both curves shift because the same forces influence both. Population growth increases both demand and supply. Technological advances increase demand and bring higher incomes, which in turn increase supply. Because both demand and supply increase over time, the quantity of capital trends upward and the real interest rate has no trend.

Although the real interest rate does not follow a rising or falling trend, it does fluctuate, as you can see in Fig. 15.5(a). The reason is that the demand for capital and the supply of capital do not change in lockstep. Sometimes, rapid technological change brings an increase in the demand for capital *before* it brings rising incomes that increase the supply of capital. When this sequence of events occurs, the real interest rate rises. The 1990s appeared to be such a time, as you can see in Fig. 15.5(a).

At other times, the demand for capital grows slowly or even decreases temporarily. In this situation, supply outgrows demand and the real interest rate falls. Figure 15.5(a) shows that 1975 was one of these times.

R E V I E W   Q U I Z

- What is discounting and how is it used to calculate a present value? When might you want to calculate a present value to make a decision?
- How does a firm compare the future marginal revenue product of capital with the current cost of capital?
- What are the main influences on a firm's demand for capital?
- What are the main influences on the supply of capital?
- What have been the main trends in the quantity of capital and interest rates? How can we explain these trends by using the demand for capital and the supply of capital?

The lessons that we've just learned about capital markets can be used to understand the prices of exhaustible natural resource prices. Let's see how.

Land and Exhaustible Natural Resource Markets

LAND IS THE QUANTITY OF NATURAL RESOURCES. All natural resources are called *land,* and they fall into two categories:

- Nonexhaustible
- Exhaustible

Nonexhaustible natural resources are natural resources that can be used repeatedly. Examples are land (in its everyday sense), rivers, lakes, and rain.

Exhaustible natural resources are natural resources that can be used only once and that cannot be replaced once they have been used. Examples are coal, natural gas, and oil—the hydrocarbon fuels.

The demand for a natural resource as an input into production is based on the same principle of marginal revenue product as the demand for labor (and the demand for capital). But the supply of a natural resource is special. Let's look first at the supply of a nonexhaustible natural resource.

The Supply of Land (Nonexhaustible Natural Resource)

The quantity of land and other nonexhaustible natural resources available is fixed. The quantity supplied cannot be changed by individual decisions. People can vary the amount of land they own. But when one person buys some land, another person sells it. The aggregate quantity of land supplied of any particular type and in any particular location is fixed, regardless of the decisions of any individual. This fact means that the supply of each particular piece of land is perfectly inelastic. Figure 15.7 illustrates such a supply. Regardless of the rent available, the quantity of land supplied on Chicago's "Magnificent Mile" is a fixed number of square feet.

Because the supply of land is fixed regardless of its price, price is determined by demand. The greater the demand for a specific piece of land, the higher is its price.

Expensive land can be, and is, used more intensively than inexpensive land. For example, high-rise buildings enable land to be used more intensively. However, to use land more intensively, it has to be combined with another productive resource—capital. Increasing the amount of capital per block of land does not change the supply of land itself.

FIGURE 15.7
The Supply of Land

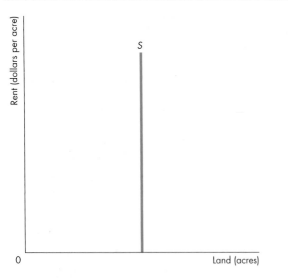

The supply of a given piece of land is perfectly inelastic. No matter what the rent, no more land than the quantity that exists can be supplied.

Although the supply of each type of land is fixed and its supply is perfectly inelastic, each individual firm, operating in competitive land markets, faces an elastic supply of land. For example, Fifth Avenue in New York City has a fixed amount of land, but Doubleday, the bookstore, could rent some space from Saks, the department store. Each firm can rent the quantity of land that it demands at the going rent, as determined in the marketplace. Thus provided that land markets are competitive, firms are price takers in these markets, just as they are in the markets for other productive resources.

The Supply of an Exhaustible Natural Resource

The *stock* of a natural resource is the quantity in existence at a given time. This quantity is fixed and is independent of the price of the resource. The *known* stock of a natural resource is the quantity that has been discovered. This quantity increases over time because advances in technology enable ever less accessible sources to be discovered. Both of these *stock* concepts influence the price of a natural resource.

But the influence is indirect. The direct influence on price is the rate at which the resource is supplied for use in production—called the *flow* supply.

The flow supply of an exhaustible natural resource is *perfectly elastic* at a price that equals the present value of the expected price next period.

To see why, think about the economic choices of Saudi Arabia, a country that possesses a large inventory of oil. Saudi Arabia can sell an additional billion barrels of oil right now and use the income it receives to buy U.S. bonds. Or it can keep the billion barrels in the ground and sell them next year. If it sells the oil and buys U.S. bonds, it earns the interest rate on the bonds. If it keeps the oil and sells it next year, it earns the price increase or loses the price decrease between now and next year.

If Saudi Arabia expects the price to rise next year by a percentage that equals the current interest rate, the price that it expects next year equals $(1 + r)$ multiplied by this year's price. For example, if this year's price is $12 a barrel and the interest rate is 5 percent $(r = 0.5)$, then next year's expected price is $1.05 \times$ $12, which equals $12.60 a barrel.

With the price expected to rise to $12.60 next year, Saudi Arabia is indifferent between selling now for $12 and not selling now but waiting until next year and selling for $12.60. It expects to make the same return either way. So, at $12 a barrel, Saudi Arabia will sell whatever quantity is demanded.

But if Saudi Arabia expects the price to rise next year by a percentage that exceeds the current interest rate, it expects to make a bigger return by hanging on to the oil than it can make from selling the oil and buying bonds. So it keeps the oil and sells none. And if it expects the price to rise next year by a percentage that is less than the current interest rate, the bond gives a bigger return than the oil so it sells as much oil as it can.

Recall the idea of discounting and present value. The minimum price at which Saudi Arabia is willing to sell oil is the present value of the expected future price. At this price, it will sell as much oil as buyers demand. So its supply is perfectly elastic.

Price and the Hotelling Principle

Figure 15.8 shows the equilibrium in a natural resource market. Because supply is perfectly elastic at the present value of next period's expected price, the actual price of the natural resource equals the present value of next period's expected price. Also, because the current price is the present value of the expected

An Exhaustible Natural Resource Market

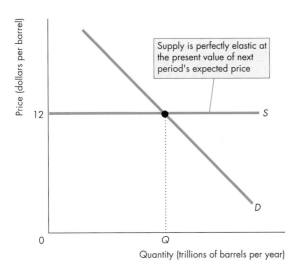

The supply of an exhaustible natural resource is perfectly elastic at the *present value* of next period's expected price. The demand for an exhaustible natural resource is determined by its marginal revenue product. The price is determined by supply and equals the *present value* of next period's expected price.

Falling Resource Prices

The prices of metals (here an average of the prices of aluminum, copper, iron ore, lead, manganese, nickel, silver, tin, and zinc) have tended to fall over time, not rise as predicted by the Hotelling Principle. The reason is that unanticipated advances in technology have decreased the cost of extracting metals and greatly increased the exploitable known reserves.

Source: International Financial Statistics, International Monetary Fund, Washington, D.C. (various issues).

future price, the price of the resource is expected to rise at a rate equal to the interest rate.

The proposition that the price of a resource is expected to rise at a rate equal to the interest rate is called the *Hotelling Principle.* It was first realized by Harold Hotelling, a mathematician and economist at Columbia University. But as Fig. 15.9 shows, *actual* prices do not follow the path of *expected* prices predicted by the Hotelling Principle. Why do natural resource prices sometimes fall rather than follow their expected path and increase over time?

The key reason is that the future is unpredictable. Expected technological change is reflected in the price of a natural resource. But a previously unexpected new technology that leads to the discovery or the more efficient use of an exhaustible natural resource causes its price to fall. Over the years, as technology has advanced, we have become more efficient in our use of exhaustible resources. And we haven't just become more efficient. We've become more efficient that we expected to.

REVIEW QUIZ

- Why is the price of a *nonexhaustible* natural resource such as land perfectly inelastic?
- At what price is the flow supply of an exhaustible natural resource perfectly elastic and why?
- Why is the price of an exhaustible natural resource expected to rise at a rate equal to the interest rate?
- Why do the prices of exhaustible resources not follow the path predicted by the Hotelling principle?

People supply resources to earn an income. But some people earn enormous incomes. Are such incomes necessary to induce people to work and supply other resources? Let's now answer this question.

Income, Economic Rent, and Opportunity Cost

YOU'VE NOW SEEN HOW RESOURCE PRICES ARE determined by the interaction of demand and supply. And you've seen that demand is determined by marginal productivity and supply is determined by the resources available and by people's choices about their use. The interaction of demand and supply in resource markets determines who receives a large income and who receives a small income.

Large and Small Incomes

A national morning show host earns a large income because she has a high marginal revenue product—reflected in the demand for her services—and few people have the combination of talents needed for this kind of job —reflected in the supply. Equilibrium occurs at a high wage rate and a small quantity employed.

People who work at McJobs earn a low wage rate because they have a low marginal revenue product—reflected in the demand—and many people are able and willing to supply their labor for these jobs. Equilibrium occurs at a low wage rate and a large quantity employed.

If the demand for morning show hosts increases, their incomes increase by a large amount and the number of morning show hosts barely changes. If the demand for workers in McJobs increases, the number of people doing these jobs increases by a large amount and the wage rate barely changes.

Another difference between a morning show host and a fast-food cook is that if the morning show host is hit with a pay cut, she will probably still supply her services, but if a fast-food cook is hit with a pay cut, he will probably quit. This difference arises from the interesting distinction between economic rent and opportunity cost.

Economic Rent and Opportunity Cost

The total income of a productive resource is made up of its economic rent and its opportunity cost. **Economic rent** is the income received by the owner of a resource over and above the amount required to induce that owner to offer the resource for use. Any productive resource can receive an economic rent. The income that is required to induce the supply of a productive resource is the opportunity cost of using a productive resource—the value of the resource in its next best use.

Figure 15.10(a) illustrates the way in which a resource income has an economic rent and opportunity cost component. The figure shows the market for a productive resource. It could be *any* productive resource—labor, capital, or land—but we'll suppose that it is labor. The demand curve is D, and its supply curve is S. The wage rate is W, and the quantity employed is C. The income earned is the sum of the yellow and green areas. The yellow area below the supply curve measures opportunity cost, and the green area above the supply curve but below the resource price measures economic rent.

To see why the area below the supply curve measures opportunity cost, recall that a supply curve can be interpreted in two different ways. It shows the quantity supplied at a given price, and it shows the minimum price at which a given quantity is willingly supplied. If suppliers receive only the minimum amount required to induce them to supply each unit of the productive resource, they will be paid a different price for each unit. The prices will trace the supply curve, and the income received is entirely opportunity cost—the yellow area in Fig. 15.10(a).

The concept of economic rent is similar to the concept of consumer surplus that you met in Chapter 6 (p. 111). Recall that consumer surplus is the maximum price someone is willing to pay, as indicated by the demand curve, minus the price paid. In a parallel sense, economic rent is the price a person receives for the use of a resource minus the minimum price at which a given quantity of the resource is willingly supplied.

Economic rent is not the same thing as the "rent" that a farmer pays for the use of some land or the "rent" that you pay for your apartment. Everyday "rent" is a price paid for the services of land or a building. *Economic rent* is a component of the income received by any productive resource.

The portion of the income of a productive resource that consists of economic rent depends on the elasticity of the supply of the productive resource. When the supply of a productive resource is perfectly inelastic, its entire income is economic rent. Most of the income of Garth Brooks and Pearl Jam is economic rent. Also, a large part of the income of a major league baseball player is economic rent. When the supply of a productive resource is perfectly elastic, none of its income is economic rent.

FIGURE 15.10
Economic Rent and Opportunity Cost

handwritten: transfer earnings = what you would be earning now (subtracted from current wage?)

(a) General case   **(b) All economic rent**   **(c) All opportunity cost**

When a resource supply curve slopes upward—the general case—as in part (a), part of the resource income is economic rent (green) and part is opportunity cost (yellow). When the supply of a productive resource is perfectly inelastic (the supply curve is vertical), as in part (b), the entire resource income is economic rent. When the supply of the productive resource is perfectly elastic, as in part (c), the resource's entire income is opportunity cost.

Most of the income of a baby-sitter is opportunity cost. In general, when the supply curve is neither perfectly elastic nor perfectly inelastic, like that illustrated in Fig. 15.10(a), some part of the resource income is economic rent and the other part is opportunity cost.

Figure 15.10, parts (b) and (c), shows the other two possibilities. Part (b) shows the market for a particular parcel of land in New York City. The quantity of land is fixed in size at *L* acres. Therefore the supply curve of the land is vertical—perfectly inelastic. Suppose that the demand curve in Fig. 15.10(b) shows the marginal revenue product of this block of land. Then it commands a rent of *R*. The entire income accruing to the owner of the land is the green area in the figure. This income is *economic rent*.

Figure 15.10(c) shows the market for a productive resource that is in perfectly elastic supply. An example of such a market might be that for low-skilled labor in a poor country such as India or China. In those countries, large amounts of labor flock to the cities and are available for work at the going wage rate (in this case, *W*). Thus in these situations, the supply of labor is almost perfectly elastic. The entire income earned by this labor is the yellow area. This income is *opportunity cost*. They receive no economic rent.

REVIEW QUIZ

- Why does Katie Couric earn a larger income than does a baby sitter?
- What is the distinction between an economic rent and an opportunity cost?
- Was the income that the Chicago Bulls paid to Michael Jordan an economic rent or compensation for his opportunity cost?
- Is a Big Mac more expensive in Manhattan than in Little Rock because rents are higher in Manhattan or are rents higher in Manhattan because people are willing to pay more there for a Big Mac?

Reading Between the Lines on pp. 338–339 looks at the market for basketball players. The next chapter studies labor markets more closely and explains differences in wage rates among high-skilled and low-skilled workers, males and females, and racial and ethnic minorities. Chapter 17 looks at how the market economy distributes income and at efforts by governments to redistribute income and modify the market outcome.

The Market for Basketball Players

THE NEW YORK TIMES, JANUARY 7, 1999

With Little Time on Clock, NBA and Players Settle

By MIKE WISE

NEW YORK—National Basketball Association players and owners brought an end to the most calamitous and costly labor dispute in league history Wednesday, agreeing to an 11th-hour deal that saved the season only a day before the owners were to vote on canceling it. ...

The crux of the disagreement for the past six months has been how to divide the $2 billion in annual revenue that the league generates. Although both sides made some concessions at the end, the league achieved its main goal of containing the contracts of high-salaried players, and received some unprecedented concessions from the union.

It insisted on and received a maximum salary provision, and no other professional sport has a limit on individual salaries. It also eliminated some of the crippling loopholes to its salary cap that had sent salaries skyrocketing in the last five years, and it refused to yield to the union's request for a greater percentage of revenue.

In the end, the union was left to try to hold onto some of the terms that had provided its players the highest average salary in pro sports, $2.6 million. It also achieved its stated priority of significantly

bettering the economic position of its middle-class players, those making around the median salary of $1.3 million.

THE DEAL

MAXIMUM SALARY

Ranging from $9 million for players with 1 to 6 years' experience to $14 million for veterans with 10 years of experience. No other sport has a cap on individual salaries.

PERCENTAGE OF REVENUE

The players will receive 55 percent of revenues toward their salaries in years 4, 5, and 6 of the contract. There is no fixed percentage for years 1 through 3.

SALARY INCREASES

The maximum salary increase will be 10 percent. Free agents who re-sign with their own team can receive up to 12 percent.

The union will receive 55 percent of total revenue toward salaries in the last three years of the deal. That was less than the players had hoped for, and the feeling among many of them was that they had given in to many of the league's demands at the last moment. Still, it was better than the prospect of no season and many more millions of dollars in lost paychecks. ...

Essence of the Story

■ The National Basketball Association players and owners agreed to a new contract in January 1999 and ended a six-month dispute.

■ The disagreement was over how to divide the $2 billion in annual revenue that the league generates.

■ The players will receive 55 percent of revenues toward their salaries in years 4, 5, and 6 of the contract. There is no fixed percentage for years 1 through 3.

■ The maximum salary will range from $9 million for players with 1 to 6 years of experience to $14 million for players with 10 years of experience.

■ The maximum salary increase will be 10 percent except for free agents who re-sign with their own team; they can receive up to 12 percent.

Economic Analysis

■ Basketball players are a special productive resource. The supply of top players' services is limited because they are extraordinarily talented and other people cannot replicate the special things that they do.

■ Figure 1 shows the marginal revenue product of players. The best players have a marginal revenue product that exceeds $20 million a year. The marginal revenue product of several players exceeds $10 million a year.

■ The marginal revenue product of players is the demand for players in a competitive labor market.

■ Figure 2 shows how the market for basketball players would work if it were competitive. The demand curve, *D*, is derived from the marginal revenue product curve in Fig. 1.

■ The supply is *S*. Supply is (assumed to be) elastic at a low salary rate up to 420 players and perfectly inelastic at 420 players.

■ This supply curve reflects two facts. First, the opportunity cost of playing basketball for most players is low—probably less than $100,000 a year. Second, the number of people who can play the game at the skill level that generates these high marginal revenue products is limited to a few hundred. (There are around 420 players in the 29 NBA teams.)

■ A competitive market might deliver a salary of $1 million a year. In this case, the total salary bill would be $420 million a year.

■ The total revenue of the NBA is $2 billion a year, so the competitive salary (on the assumptions just made) would be 21 percent of total revenue. Most of the players' income is economic rent.

■ Figure 3 shows how the players do better than the competitive market outcome and capture more economic rent by negotiating an agreement with the owners.

■ In Figure 3, the players take 55 percent of the total revenue and the highest-paid player earns a salary of $14 million a year. The green steps show other salary levels.

Figure 1 **The marginal revenue product of basketball players**

Figure 2 **A competitive market for basketball players**

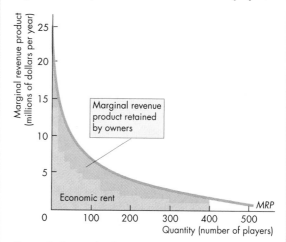

Figure 3 **A rent-sharing contract**

SUMMARY

KEY POINTS

Resource Prices and Incomes (p. 318)

- An increase in the demand for a productive resource increases its price and total income; a decrease in the demand for a productive resource decreases its price and total income.
- An increase in the supply of a productive resource increases the quantity used but decreases price and might increase or decrease its total income depending on whether demand is elastic or inelastic.

Labor Markets (pp. 319–326)

- The demand for labor is determined by the marginal revenue product of labor.
- The demand for labor increases if the price of the firm's output rises or if technological change and capital accumulation increase marginal product.
- The elasticity of demand for labor depends on the labor intensity of production, the elasticity of demand for the product, and the ease with which labor can be substituted for capital.
- The quantity of labor supplied increases as the real wage rate increases but at high wage rates, the supply curve eventually bends backward.
- The supply of labor increases with population growth and with technological change and capital accumulation in home production.
- Real wages and employment increase because demand increases by more than supply.

Capital Markets (pp. 327–333)

- To make an investment decision, a firm compares the *present value* of the marginal revenue product of capital with the price of capital.
- Population growth and technological change increase the demand for capital.
- The higher the interest rate, the greater are the level of saving and quantity of capital supplied.
- The supply of capital increases as incomes increase.
- Capital market equilibrium determines interest rates.

Land and Exhaustible Natural Resource Markets (pp. 333–335)

- The demand for a natural resource is determined by its marginal revenue product.
- The supply of land is inelastic.
- The supply of an exhaustible natural resource is perfectly elastic at a price equal to the present value of the expected future price.
- The price of an exhaustible natural resource is expected to rise at a rate equal to the interest rate but fluctuates and sometimes falls.

Incomes, Economic Rent, and Opportunity cost (pp. 336–337)

- Economic rent is the income received by a resource owner over and above the amount needed to induce the owner to supply the productive resource for use.
- The rest of a resource's income is opportunity cost.
- When the supply of a resource is perfectly inelastic, its entire income is economic rent; when supply is perfectly elastic, the entire income is opportunity cost.

KEY FIGURES AND TABLES ◆

KEY TERMS

PROBLEMS

*1. The figure illustrates the market for blueberry pickers:

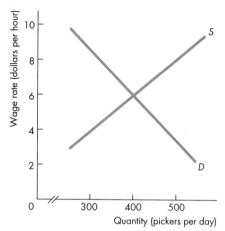

a. What is the wage rate paid to blueberry pickers?
b. How many blueberry pickers get hired?
c. What is the income received by blueberry pickers?

2. In problem 1, if the demand for blueberry pickers increases by 100 a day,
   a. What is the new wage rate paid to the pickers?
   b. How many additional pickers get hired?
   c. What is the total income paid to pickers?

*3. Wanda owns a fish shop. She employs students to sort and pack the fish. Students can pack the following amounts of fish in an hour:

Number of students	Quantity of fish (pounds)
1	20
2	50
3	90
4	120
5	145
6	165
7	180
8	190

Wanda can sell her fish for 50¢ a pound, and the wage rate of packers is $7.50 an hour.
a. Calculate the marginal product of the students and draw the marginal product curve.

b. Calculate the marginal revenue product of the students and draw the marginal revenue product curve.
c. Find Wanda's demand for labor curve.
d. How many students does Wanda employ?

4. Barry makes party ice. He employs workers to bag the ice who can produce the following quantities in an hour:

Number of workers	Quantity of ice (bags)
1	40
2	100
3	180
4	240
5	290
6	330
7	360
8	380

Barry can sell ice for 25¢ a bag, and the wage rate of baggers is $5.00 an hour.
a. Calculate the marginal product of the workers and draw the marginal product curve.
b. Calculate the marginal revenue product of the workers and draw the marginal revenue product curve.
c. Find Barry's demand for labor curve.
d. How much ice does Barry sell?

*5. Back at Wanda's fish shop described in problem 3, the price of fish falls to 33.33¢ a pound but fish packers' wages remain at $7.50 an hour.
   a. What happens to Wanda's marginal product?
   b. What happens to her marginal revenue product?
   c. What happens to her demand for labor curve?
   d. What happens to the number of students that she employs?

6. Back at Barry's party ice shop described in problem 4, the price of party ice falls to 10¢ a bag but baggers' wages remain at $5.00 an hour.
   a. What happens to Barry's marginal product?
   b. What happens to his marginal revenue product?
   c. What happens to his demand for labor curve?
   d. What happens to the number of students that he employs?

*7. Back at Wanda's fish shop described in problem 3, packers' wages increase to $10 an hour but the price of fish remains at 50¢ a pound.
    a. What happens to marginal revenue product?
    b. What happens to Wanda's demand for labor curve?
    c. How many students does Wanda employ?

8. Back at Barry's party ice shop described in problem 4, baggers' wages increase to $10 an hour but the price of ice remains at 25¢ a bag.
    a. What happens to marginal revenue product?
    b. What happens to Barry's demand for labor curve?
    c. How many baggers does Barry employ?

*9. Use the information in problem 5 to calculate Wanda's marginal revenue, marginal cost, and marginal revenue product. Show that when Wanda is making maximum profit, marginal cost equals marginal revenue and marginal revenue product equals the wage rate.

10. Use the information in problem 6 to calculate Barry's marginal revenue, marginal cost, and marginal revenue product. Show that when Barry is making maximum profit, marginal cost equals marginal revenue and marginal revenue product equals the wage rate.

*11. Venus makes Firecrackers, which she sells in December each year for New Year's celebrations. She must decide how many firecracker production lines to install. Each production line costs $1 million and operates for only two years after which it must be replaced. With one production line, Venus expects to sell $590,000 worth of firecrackers a year. With two production lines, she expects to sell $1,150,000 worth of firecrackers each year. And with three production lines, she expects to sell $1,680,000 worth of firecrackers a year. The interest rate is 5 percent a year. How many production lines does Venus install? Explain your answer.

12. Vulcan Balloon Rides must decide how many balloons to operate. Each balloon costs $10,000 and must be replaced after three years of service. With one balloon, Vulcan expects to sell $5,900 worth of rides a year. With two balloons, it expects to sell $11,500 worth of rides each year. And with three balloons, it expects to sell $16,800 worth of rides a year. The interest

rate is 8 percent a year. How many balloons does Vulcan operate? Explain your answer.

*13. Greg has found an oil well in his back yard. A geologist estimates that a total of 10 million barrels can be pumped for a pumping cost of a dollar a barrel. The price of oil is $20 a barrel. How much oil does Greg sell each year? If you can't predict how much he will sell, what extra information would you need to be able to do so?

14. Orley has a wine cellar in which he keeps choice wines from around the world. What does Orley expect to happen to the prices of the wines he keeps in his cellar? Explain your answer. How does Orley decide which wine to drink and when to drink it?

*15. In problem 1, show on the figure the blueberry pickers'
    a. Economic rent.
    b. Opportunity cost.

16. In problem 2, draw a figure to show the blueberry pickers'
    a. Economic rent.
    b. Opportunity cost.

CRITICAL THINKING

1. 1. Study *Reading Between the Lines* on pp. 338–339 and answer the following questions:
    a. Why did the basketball players strike?
    b. Why don't the players sign a deal that gives them their entire marginal revenue product?
    c. Why do you think Michael Jordan retired? What does his retirement tell you about his opportunity cost of playing?
    d. Why didn't the Bulls offer Michael Jordan a deal that he couldn't refuse?

2. "We are running out of natural resources and must take urgent action to conserve our precious reserves." "There is no shortage of resources that the market cannot cope with." Debate these two views. List the pros and cons for each.

3. Why do we keep finding new reserves of oil? Why don't we do once-and-for-all a big survey that catalogs the earth's entire inventory of natural resources?

16

Labor Markets

As you well know, college is not just a party. Those exams and problem sets require a lot of time and effort. Are they worth the sweat that goes into them? What is the payoff? Is it sufficient to make up for the years of tuition, room and board, and lost wages? (You could, after all, be working for pay now instead of slogging through this economics course.) ◆ Many workers belong to labor unions. Usually, union workers earn a higher wage than nonunion workers in comparable jobs. Why? How are unions able to get higher wages for their members than the wages that nonunion workers are paid? ◆ Among the most visible and persistent differences in earnings are those between men and women and between whites and minorities. White men, on the average, earn incomes that are one third higher than the incomes earned by black men and white women. Black men and white women earn more,

The Sweat of Our Brows

in descending order, than Hispanic men, black women, and Hispanic women, who earn only 58 cents for each dollar earned by the average white man. Certainly, a lot of individuals defy the averages. But why do minorities and women so consistently earn less than white men? Is it because of discrimination and exploitation? Or is it because of economic factors? Or is it a combination of the two? ◆ Equal pay legislation has resulted in comparable-worth programs that try to ensure that jobs of equivalent value receive the same pay regardless of the pay set by the market. Can comparable-worth programs bring economic help to women and minorities? ◆ We hear a lot these days about immigration. How does immigration affect the economic well-being of both immigrants and native Americans?

◆ In this chapter, we answer questions such as these by continuing our study of labor markets. We study the effects of education and training, labor unions, gender and race, comparable-worth laws, and immigration.

After studying this chapter, you will be able to:

■ Explain why college graduates earn more, on the average, than high school graduates

■ Explain why union workers earn higher wages than nonunion workers

■ Explain why, on the average, men earn more than women and whites earn more than minorities

■ Predict the effects of a comparable-worth program

■ Explain the effects of immigration on the wages of immigrants and native Americans

Skill Differentials

EVERYONE IS SKILLED, BUT THE VALUE THE market places on different types of skills varies a great deal. So differences in skills lead to large differences in earnings. For example, a clerk in a law firm earns less than a tenth of the earnings of the attorney he assists. An operating room assistant earns less than a tenth of the earnings of the surgeon she works with. Differences in skills arise partly from differences in education and partly from differences in on-the-job training. Differences in earnings between workers with varying levels of education and training can be explained by using a model of competitive labor markets. In the real world, there are many different levels and varieties of education and training. To keep our analysis as clear as possible, we'll study a model economy with two different skill levels and two types of labor: high-skilled labor and low-skilled labor. We'll study the demand for and supply of these two types of labor and see why there is a difference in their wages and what determines that difference. Let's begin by looking at the demand for the two types of labor.

The Demand for High-Skilled and Low-Skilled Labor

High-skilled workers can perform a variety of tasks that low-skilled workers would perform badly or perhaps could not even perform at all. Imagine an untrained, inexperienced person performing surgery or piloting an airplane. High-skilled workers have a higher marginal revenue product than low-skilled workers. As we learned in Chapter 15, a firm's demand for labor curve is the same as the marginal revenue product of labor curve.

Figure 16.1(a) shows the demand curves for high-skilled (D_H) and low-skilled labor (D_L). At any given level of employment, firms are willing to pay a higher wage rate to a high-skilled worker than to a low-skilled worker. The gap between the two wage rates measures the marginal revenue product of skill—for example, at an employment level of 2,000 hours, firms are willing to pay $12.50 for a high-skilled worker and only $5 for an low-skilled worker, a difference of $7.50 an hour. Thus the marginal revenue product of skill is $7.50 an hour.

The Supply of High-Skilled and Low-Skilled Labor

Skills are costly to acquire. Furthermore, a worker usually pays the cost of acquiring a skill before bene-fiting from a higher wage. For example, attending college usually leads to a higher income, but the higher income is not earned until after graduation. These facts imply that the acquisition of a skill is an investment. To emphasize the investment nature of acquiring a skill, we call that activity an investment in human capital. **Human capital** is the accumu-lated skill and knowledge of human beings.

The opportunity cost of acquiring a skill includes actual expenditures on such things as tuition and room and board and also a cost in the form of lost or reduced earnings while the skill is being acquired. When a person goes to school full time, that cost is the total earnings forgone. However, some people acquire skills on the job. Such skill acquisition is called on-the-job training. Usually, a worker undergo-ing on-the-job training is paid a lower wage than one doing a comparable job but not undergoing training. In such a case, the cost of acquiring the skill is the dif-ference between the wage paid to a person not being trained and that paid to a person being trained.

Supply Curves of High-Skilled and Low-Skilled Labor
The position of the supply curve of high-skilled workers reflects the cost of acquiring the skill. Figure 16.1(b) shows two supply curves: one for high-skilled workers and the other for low-skilled workers. The supply curve for high-skilled workers is S_H, and that for low-skilled workers is S_L.

The high-skilled workers' supply curve lies above the low-skilled workers' supply curve. The vertical distance between the two supply curves is the com-pensation that high-skilled workers require for the cost of acquiring the skill. For example, suppose that the quantity of low-skilled labor supplied is 2,000 hours at a wage rate of $5 an hour. This wage rate compensates the low-skilled workers mainly for their time on the job. Consider next the supply of high-skilled workers. To induce 2,000 hours of high-skilled labor to be supplied, firms must pay a wage rate of $8.50 an hour. This wage rate for high-skilled labor is higher than that for low-skilled labor because high-skilled labor must be compensated not only for the time on the job but also for the time and other costs of acquiring the skill.

FIGURE 16.1

Skill Differentials

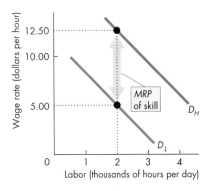

(a) Demand for high-skilled and low-skilled labor

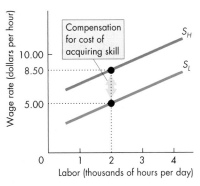

(b) Supply of high-skilled and low-skilled labor

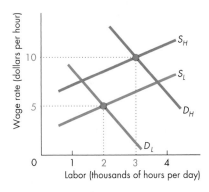

(c) Markets for high-skilled and low-skilled labor

Part (a) illustrates the marginal revenue product of skill. Low-skilled workers have a marginal revenue product that gives rise to the demand curve marked D_L. High-skilled workers have a higher marginal revenue product than low-skilled workers. Therefore the demand curve for high-skilled workers, D_H, lies to the right of D_L. The vertical distance between these two curves is the marginal revenue product of the skill.

Part (b) shows the effects of the cost of acquiring skills on the supply curves of labor. The supply curve for low-skilled

workers is S_L. The supply curve for high-skilled workers is S_H. The vertical distance between these two curves is the required compensation for the cost of acquiring a skill.

Part (c) shows the equilibrium employment and the wage differential. Low-skilled workers earn a wage rate of $5 an hour, and 2,000 hours of low-skilled labor are employed. High-skilled workers earn a wage rate of $10, and 3,000 hours of high-skilled labor are employed. The wage rate for high-skilled workers always exceeds that for low-skilled workers.

Wage Rates of High-Skilled and Low-Skilled Labor

To work out the wage rates of high-skilled and low-skilled labor, we have to bring together the effects of skill on the demand and supply of labor.

Figure 16.1(c) shows the demand curves and the supply curves for high-skilled and low-skilled labor. These curves are exactly the same as those plotted in parts (a) and (b). Equilibrium occurs in the market for low-skilled labor where the supply and demand curves for low-skilled labor intersect. The equilibrium wage rate is $5 an hour, and the quantity of low-skilled labor employed is 2,000 hours. Equilibrium in the market for high-skilled workers occurs where the supply and demand curves for high-skilled workers intersect. The equilibrium wage rate is $10 an hour, and the quantity of high-skilled labor employed is 3,000 hours.

As you can see in part (c), the equilibrium wage rate of high-skilled labor is higher than that of low-skilled labor. This outcome occurs for two reasons: First, high-skilled labor has a higher marginal revenue product than low-skilled labor, so at a given wage rate, the quantity of high-skilled labor demanded exceeds that of low-skilled labor. Second, skills are costly to acquire, so at a given wage rate, the quantity of high-skilled labor supplied is less than that of low-skilled labor. The wage differential (in this case, $5 an hour) depends on both the marginal revenue product of the skill and the cost of acquiring it. The higher the marginal revenue product of the skill, the larger is the vertical distance between the demand curves. The more costly it is to acquire a skill, the larger is the vertical distance between the supply curves. The higher the marginal revenue product of the skill and the more costly it is to acquire, the larger is the wage differential between high-skilled and low-skilled workers.

Do Education and Training Pay?

Figure 16.2 shows that there are large and persistent differences in earnings based on the degree of education and training. This figure also highlights the second main source of earnings differences: age. Age is strongly correlated with experience and the degree of on-the-job training a person has had. So as a person gets older, up to middle age, earnings increase.

Rates of return on high school and college education have been estimated to be in the range of 5 to 10 percent a year after allowing for inflation, which suggest that a college degree is a better investment than almost any other that a person can undertake.

Education is an important source of earnings differences. But there are others, and one of them is labor unions. Let's see how unions affect wages and why union wages tend to exceed nonunion wages.

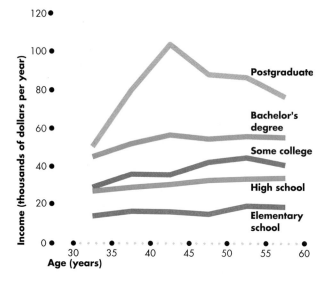

FIGURE 16.2
Education and Earnings

Earnings of male employees at various ages and with varying school levels are shown. Earnings increase with length of education. For postgraduates, earnings peak in the middle forties. For other groups, earnings peak in the middle fifties. These differences show the importance of experience and education in influencing skill differentials.

Source: U.S. Bureau of the Census, *Money Income in the United States 1995* and *Current Population Reports Consumer Income*, Series P-60, (1996).

Union-Nonunion Wage Differentials

WAGE DIFFERENTIALS CAN ARISE FROM MONOPOLY power in the labor market. Just as monopoly producers can restrict output and raise price, so a monopoly owner of a resource can restrict supply and raise the price of the resource.

The main source of monopoly power in the labor market is the labor union. A **labor union** is an organized group of workers whose purpose it is to increase wages and influence other job conditions for its members. The union seeks to restrict competition and, as a result, increases the price at which labor is traded.

There are two main types of union: craft unions and industrial unions. A **craft union** is a group of workers who have a similar range of skills but work for many different firms in many different industries and regions. Examples are the carpenters' union and the electrical workers union (IBEW). An **industrial union** is a group of workers who have a variety of skills and job types but work for the same industry. The United Auto Workers (UAW) and the United Steelworkers of America (USWA) are industrial unions.

Most unions are members of the AFL-CIO. The AFL-CIO was created in 1955 when two labor organizations combined: the American Federation of Labor (AFL), which was founded in 1886 to organize craft unions, and the Congress of Industrial Organizations (CIO), founded in 1938 to organize industrial unions. The AFL-CIO provides many services to member unions, such as training union organizers and acting as a national voice in the media and in the political arena.

Unions vary enormously in size. Craft unions are the smallest, and industrial unions are the biggest. Figure 16.3 shows the 12 largest unions in the United States—measured by number of members. Union strength peaked in the 1950s, when 35 percent of the nonagricultural work force belonged to unions. That percentage has declined steadily since 1955 and is now only 12 percent. Changes in union membership, however, have been uneven. Some unions have declined dramatically, while others, especially those in the government sector such as the American Federation of State, County and Municipal Employees, have increased in strength.

Union organization is based on a subdivision known as the local. The *local* is a subunit of a union

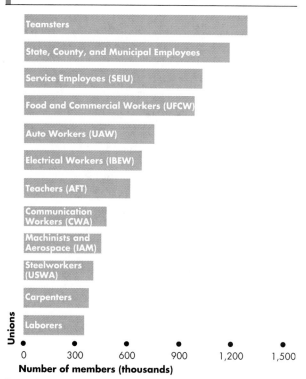

FIGURE 16.3
Unions with the
Largest Membership

Teamsters

State, County, and Municipal Employees

Service Employees (SEIU)

Food and Commercial Workers (UFCW)

Auto Workers (UAW)

Electrical Workers (IBEW)

Teachers (AFT)

Communication Workers (CWA)

Machinists and Aerospace (IAM)

Steelworkers (USWA)

Carpenters

Laborers

Unions

0   300   600   900   1,200   1,500

Number of members (thousands)

Each of the 12 largest labor unions in the United States, shown here, has more than 350,000 members.

Source: U.S. Bureau of the Census, *Statistical Abstract of the United States: 1996,* 116th edition, p. 436, Table 682.

that organizes the individual workers. In craft unions, the local is based on a geographical area; in industrial unions, the local is based on a plant or an individual firm.

There are three possible forms of organization for a local: an open shop, a closed shop, or a union shop. An *open shop* is an arrangement in which workers can be employed without joining the union—there is no union restriction on who can work in the "shop." A *closed shop* is an arrangement in which only union members can be employed by a firm. Closed shops have been illegal since the passage of the Taft-Hartley Act in 1947. A *union shop* is an arrangement in which a firm can hire nonunion workers, but in order for such workers to remain employed, they must join the union within a brief period specified by the union.

Union shops are illegal in the 20 states that have passed right-to-work laws. A *right-to-work law* allows an individual to work at any firm without joining a union.

Unions negotiate with employers or their representatives in a process called **collective bargaining**. The main weapons available to the union and the employer in collective bargaining are the strike, the lockout, and the use of replacement workers. A *strike* is a group decision to refuse to work under prevailing conditions. A *lockout* is a firm's refusal to operate its plant and employ its workers. Each party uses the threat of a strike, lockout, or the use of replacement workers to try to get an agreement in its own favor. Sometimes, when the two parties in the collective bargaining process cannot agree on the wage rate or other conditions of employment, they agree to submit their disagreement to binding arbitration. *Binding arbitration* is a process in which a third party—an arbitrator—determines wages and other employment conditions on behalf of the negotiating parties.

Although they are not labor unions in a legal sense, professional associations act similarly to labor unions. A *professional association* is an organized group of professional workers such as lawyers, dentists, or physicians (an example of which is the American Medical Association—AMA). Professional associations control entry into the professions and license practitioners, ensuring the adherence to minimum standards of competence. But they also influence the compensation and other labor market conditions of their members.

Union's Objectives and Constraints

A union has three broad objectives that it strives to achieve for its members:

1. To increase compensation
2. To improve working conditions
3. To expand job opportunities

Each of these objectives contains a series of more detailed goals. For example, in seeking to increase members' compensation, a union operates on a variety of fronts: wage rates, fringe benefits, retirement pay, and such things as vacation allowances. In seeking to improve working conditions, a union is concerned with occupational health and safety as well as the environmental quality of the workplace. In seeking to expand job opportunities, a union tries to get greater job security for existing union members and to find ways of creating additional jobs for them.

A union's ability to pursue its objectives is restricted by two sets of constraints—one on the supply side of the labor market and the other on the demand side. On the supply side, the union's activities are limited by how well it can restrict nonunion workers from offering their labor in the same market as union labor. The larger the fraction of the work force controlled by the union, the more effective the union can be in this regard. It is difficult for unions to operate in markets where there is an abundant supply of willing nonunion labor. For example, the market for farm labor in southern California is very tough for a union to organize because of the ready flow of nonunion, often illegal, labor from Mexico. At the other extreme, unions in the construction industry can better pursue their goals because they can influence the number of people who can obtain skills as electricians, plasterers, and carpenters. The professional associations of dentists and physicians are best able to restrict the supply of dentists and physicians. These groups control the number of qualified workers by controlling either the examinations that new entrants must pass or entrance into professional degree programs.

On the demand side of the labor market, the union faces a tradeoff that arises from firms' profit-maximizing decisions. Because labor demand curves slope downward, anything a union does that increases the wage rate or other employment costs decreases the quantity of labor demanded.

Despite the difficulties they face, unions do operate in competitive labor markets. Let's see how they do so.

Unions in a Competitive Labor Market

When a union operates in an otherwise competitive labor market, it seeks to increase wages and other compensation and to limit employment reductions by increasing demand for the labor of its members. That is, the union tries to take actions that shift the demand curve for its members' labor rightward.

Figure 16.4 illustrates a competitive labor market that a union enters. The demand curve is D_C, and the supply curve is S_C. Before the union enters the market, the wage rate is $7 an hour and 100 hours of labor are employed.

Now suppose that a union is formed to organize the workers in this market. The union can attempt to increase wages in this market in two ways. It can

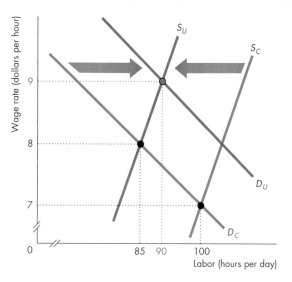

FIGURE 16.4

A Union in a Competitive Labor Market

In a competitive labor market, the demand curve is D_C and the supply curve is S_C. Competitive equilibrium occurs at a wage rate of $7 an hour with 100 hours employed. By restricting employment below the competitive level, the union shifts the supply of labor to S_U. If the union can do no more than that, the wage rate will increase to $8 an hour, but employment will fall to 85 hours. If the union can increase the demand for labor (by increasing the demand for the good produced by union members or by raising the price of substitute labor) and shift the demand curve to D_U, then it can increase the wage rate still higher, to $9 an hour, and achieve employment of 90 hours.

try to restrict the supply of labor, or it can try to stimulate the demand for labor. First, look at what happens if the union has sufficient control over the supply of labor to be able to artificially restrict that supply below its competitive level—to S_U. If that is all the union is able to do, employment falls to 85 hours of labor and the wage rate rises to $8 an hour. The union simply picks its preferred position along the demand curve that defines the tradeoff it faces between employment and wages.

You can see that if the union can only restrict the supply of labor, it raises the wage rate but decreases the number of jobs available. Because of this outcome unions try to increase the demand for labor and shift the demand curve rightward. Let's see what they might do to achieve this outcome.

How Unions Try to Change the Demand for Labor

Unless a union can take actions that change the demand for the labor that it represents, it has to accept the fact that a higher wage rate can be obtained only at the price of lower employment.

The union tries to operate on the demand for labor in two ways. First, it tries to make the demand for union labor less elastic. Second, it tries to increase the demand for union labor. Making the demand for labor less elastic does not eliminate the tradeoff between employment and wages, but it does make the tradeoff less unfavorable. If a union can make the demand for labor less elastic, it can increase the wage rate at a lower cost in terms of lost employment opportunities. But if the union can increase the demand for labor, it might even be able to increase both the wage rate and the employment opportunities of its members.

Some of the methods used by a union to increase the demand for the labor of its members are to:

- Increase the marginal product of union members
- Encourage import restrictions *compet^n*
- Support minimum wage laws *–? other wages inflate rel. to min. wage.*
- Support immigration restrictions
- Increase demand for the good produced

Unions try to increase the marginal product of their members, which in turn increases the demand for their labor, by organizing and sponsoring training schemes, by encouraging apprenticeship and other on-the-job training activities, and by professional certification.

One of the best examples of import restrictions is the support by the United Auto Workers union (UAW) for import restrictions on foreign cars.

Unions support minimum wage laws to increase the cost of employing low-skilled labor. An increase in the wage rate of low-skilled labor leads to a decrease in the quantity demanded of low-skilled labor and to an increase in demand for high-skilled union labor, a substitute for low-skilled labor.

Restrictive immigration laws decrease the supply and increase the wage rate of low-skilled workers. As a result, the demand for high-skilled union labor increases.

Because the demand for labor is a derived demand, an increase in the demand for the good produced increases the demand for union labor. The best examples of attempts by unions in this activity are in the textile and auto industries. The garment workers' union urges us to buy union-made clothes, and the UAW asks us to buy only American cars made by union workers.

Figure 16.4 illustrates the effects of an increase in the demand for the labor of a union's members. If the union can also take steps that increase the demand for labor to D_U, it can achieve an even bigger increase in the wage rate with a smaller fall in employment. By maintaining the restricted labor supply at S_U, the union increases the wage rate to $9 an hour and achieves an employment level of 90 hours of labor.

Because a union restricts the supply of labor in the market in which it operates, its actions increase the supply of labor in nonunion markets. Workers who can't get union jobs must look elsewhere for work. This increase in supply in nonunion markets lowers the wage rate in those markets and further widens the union-nonunion wage differential.

The Scale of Union-Nonunion Wage Differentials

We have seen that unions can influence the wage rate by restricting the supply of labor and increasing the demand for labor. How much of a difference to wage rates do unions make in practice?

Union wage rates are, on the average, 30 percent higher than nonunion wage rates. In mining and financial services, union and nonunion wages are similar. In services, manufacturing, and transportation, the differential is between 11 and 19 percent. In wholesale and retail trades, the differential is 28 percent, and in construction, it is 65 percent.

But these union-nonunion wage differentials don't give a true measure of the effects of unions. In some industries, union wages are higher than nonunion wages because union members do jobs that involve greater skill. Even without a union, those workers receive a higher wage. To calculate the effects of unions, we have to examine the wages of unionized and nonunionized workers who do nearly identical work. The evidence suggests that after allowing for skill differentials, the union-nonunion wage differential lies between 10 percent and 25 percent. For example, airline pilots who belong to the Air Line

Pilots' Association earn about 25 percent more than nonunion pilots with the same level of skill.

Let's now turn our attention to the case in which employers have considerable influence in the labor market.

Monopsony

A **monopsony** is a market in which there is a single buyer. This market type is unusual but it does exist. With the growth of large-scale production over the last century, large manufacturing plants such as coal mines, steel and textile mills, and car manufacturers became the major employer in some regions, and in some places a single firm employed almost all the labor. Today, in some parts of the country, managed health-care organizations are the major employer of health-care professionals. These firms have monopsony power.

In monopsony, the employer determines the wage rate and pays the lowest wage at which it can attract the labor it plans to hire. A monopsony makes a bigger profit than a group of firms that compete with each other for their labor. Let's find out how they achieve this outcome.

Like all firms, a monopsony has a downward-sloping marginal revenue product curve, which is *MRP* in Fig. 16.5. This curve tells us the extra revenue the monopsony receives by selling the output produced by an extra hour of labor. The supply of labor curve is *S*. This curve tells us how many hours are supplied at each wage rate. It also tells us the minimum wage for which a given quantity of labor is willing to work.

A monopsony recognizes that to hire more labor, it must pay a higher wage; equivalently, by hiring less labor, it can pay a lower wage. Because a monopsony controls the wage rate, the marginal cost of labor exceeds the wage rate. The marginal cost of labor is shown by the curve *MCL*. The relationship between the marginal cost of labor curve and the supply curve is similar to the relationship between the marginal cost and average cost curves that you studied in Chapter 11. The supply curve is like the average cost of labor curve. In Fig. 16.5, the firm can hire 49 hours of labor for a wage rate of just below $4.90 an hour. The firm's total labor cost is $240. But suppose that the firm hires 50 hours of labor. It can hire the 50 hours of labor for $5 an hour. The total cost of labor is now $250 an hour. So, hiring the 50th hour of labor increases the cost of labor from $240 to $250, which

FIGURE 16.5

A Monopsony Labor Market

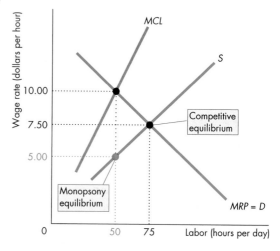

A monopsony is a market structure in which there is a single buyer. A monopsony in the labor market has marginal revenue product curve *MRP* and faces a labor curve *S*. The marginal cost of labor curve is *MCL*. Making the marginal cost of labor equal to marginal revenue product maximizes profit. The monopsony hires 50 hours of labor and pays the lowest wage for which that labor will work, which is $5 an hour.

is a $10 increase. The marginal cost of labor is $10 an hour. The curve *MCL* shows the $10 marginal cost of hiring the 50th hour of labor.

To calculate the profit-maximizing quantity of labor to hire, the firm sets the marginal cost of labor equal to the marginal revenue product of labor. That is, the firm wants the cost of the last worker hired to equal the extra total revenue brought in. In Fig. 16.5, this outcome occurs when the monopsony employs 50 hours of labor. What is the wage rate that the monopsony pays? To hire 50 hours of labor, the firm must pay $5 an hour, as shown by the supply of labor curve. So each worker is paid $5 an hour. But the marginal revenue product of labor is $10 an hour, which means that the firm makes an economic profit of $5 on the last hour of labor that it hires. Compare this outcome with that in a competitive labor market. If the labor market shown in Fig. 16.5 were competitive, equilibrium would occur at the point of intersection of the demand curve and the supply curve. The wage rate would be $7.50 an hour, and 75 hours of labor a day would be employed. So, compared with a competitive labor market, a monopsony decreases both the wage rate and the level of employment.

The ability of a monopsony to lower the wage rate and employment level and make an economic profit depends on the elasticity of the labor supply. The more elastic the supply of labor, the less opportunity a monopsony has to cut wages and employment and make an economic profit.

Monopsony Tendencies   Today, monopsony is rare. Workers can commute long distances to a job, so most people have more than one potential employer. But firms that are dominant employers in isolated communities do face an upward-sloping supply of labor curve and so have a marginal cost of labor that exceeds the wage rate. But in such situations, there is also, usually, a union. Let's see how unions and monopsonies interact.

Monopsony and Unions   When we studied monopoly in Chapter 13, we discovered that a single seller in a market is able to determine the price in that market. We have just studied monopsony—a market with a single buyer—and discovered that in such a market, the buyer is able to determine the price. Suppose that a union starts to operate in a monopsony labor market. A union is like a monopoly. It controls the supply of labor and acts like a single seller of labor. If the union (monopoly seller) faces a monopsony buyer, the situation is one of **bilateral monopoly**. In bilateral monopoly, the wage rate is determined by bargaining between the two sides. Let's study the bargaining process.

In Fig. 16.5, if the monopsony is free to determine the wage rate and the level of employment, it hires 50 hours of labor for a wage rate of $5 an hour. But suppose that a union represents the workers and can, if necessary, call a strike. Also suppose that the union agrees to maintain employment at 50 hours but seeks the highest wage rate the employer can be forced to pay. That wage rate is $10 an hour. That is, the wage rate equals the marginal revenue product of labor. It is unlikely that the union will get the wage rate up to $10 an hour. But it is also unlikely that the firm will keep the wage rate down to $5 an hour. The monopsony firm and the union bargain over the wage rate, and the result is an outcome between $10 an hour (the maximum that the union can achieve) and $5 an hour (the minimum that the firm can achieve).

The actual outcome of the bargaining depends on the costs that each party can inflict on the other as a result of a failure to agree on the wage rate. The

firm can lock out its workers and threaten to use replacement workers, and the workers can shut the plant by striking. Each party knows the other's strength and knows what it will lose if it does not agree to the other's demands. If the two parties are equally strong and they realize it, they will split the difference and agree to a wage rate of $7.50 an hour. If one party is stronger than the other—and both parties know that—the agreed wage will favor the stronger party. Usually, an agreement is reached without a strike or a lockout. The threat—knowledge that such an event can occur—is usually enough to bring the bargaining parties to an agreement. But when a strike or lockout does occur, it is often because one party has misjudged the costs each party can inflict on the other.

Minimum wage laws have interesting effects in monopsony labor markets. Let's study these effects.

Monopsony and the Minimum Wage

In a competitive labor market, a minimum wage that exceeds the equilibrium wage decreases employment (see Chapter 7, pp. 133–134). In a monopsony labor market, a minimum wage can *increase* both the wage rate and employment. Let's see how.

Figure 16.6 shows a monopsony labor market in which the wage rate is $5 an hour and 50 hours of labor are employed. A minimum wage law is passed that requires employers to pay at least $7.50 an hour. The monopsony in Fig. 16.6 now faces a perfectly elastic supply of labor at $7.50 an hour up to 75 hours. Above 75 hours, a higher wage than $7.50 an hour must be paid to hire additional hours of labor. Because the wage rate is a fixed $7.50 an hour up to 75 hours, the marginal cost of labor is also constant at $7.50 up to 75 hours. Beyond 75 hours, the marginal cost of labor rises above $7.50 an hour. To maximize profit, the monopsony sets the marginal cost of labor equal to its marginal revenue product. That is, the monopsony hires 75 hours of labor at $7.50 an hour. The minimum wage law has made the supply of labor perfectly elastic and made the marginal cost of labor the same as the wage rate up to 75 hours. The law has not affected the supply of labor curve or the marginal cost of labor at employment levels above 75 hours. The minimum wage law has succeeded in raising the wage rate by $2.50 an hour and increasing the amount of labor employed by 25 hours a day.

FIGURE 16.6
Minimum Wage in Monopsony

In a monopsony labor market, the wage rate is $5 an hour and 50 hours are hired. If a minimum wage law increases the wage rate to $7.50 an hour, employment increases to 75 hours.

R E V I E W   Q U I Z

- Why are the wage rates of high-skilled workers greater than those of low-skilled workers?
- What are the main methods that labor unions use to increase the wage rates of their members above the levels of nonunion wages rates?
- What is a monopsony and why is a monopsony able to pay a lower wage rate than a competitive firm?
- What is the effect of a minimum wage in a monopsony? What is the effect of a minimum wage in a competitive labor market? Why are the two effects different?

You now understand two sources of wage differentials: skill differentials and the actions of labor unions. These two sources of wage differences are easy to see and to analyze. The third source of wage differentials, sex and race, is harder to explain but it is the most sensitive of the sources of income differentials.

Wage Differentials Between Sexes and Races

THE OBJECTIVE OF THIS SECTION IS TO SHOW you how to use economic analysis to address a controversial and emotionally charged issue. Figure 16.7 gives a quick view of the earnings differences that exist between the sexes and the races and also shows how those differences have evolved since 1955. The wages of each race and sex group are expressed as a percentage of the wages of white men. In 1997, the most recent year for which we have data, these percentages ranged from 75 for white women to 53 for women of Hispanic origin.

Why do the differentials shown in Fig. 16.7 exist? Do they arise because there is discrimination against women and members of minority races, or is there some other explanation? These controversial questions generate an enormous amount of passion. It is not my

FIGURE 16.7
Sex and Race Differentials

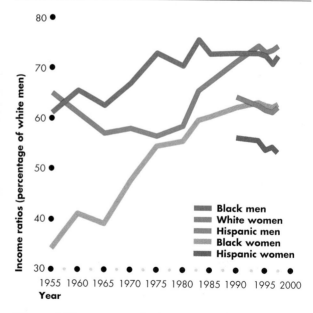

Wages of different race and sex groups are shown as percentages of white male wages. These differentials have persisted over many years, but their magnitudes have changed.

Source: U.S. Bureau of the Census, *Statistical Abstract of the United States: 1998,* 118th edition.

intention to make you angry, but that might happen as an unintended consequence of this discussion.

We are going to examine four possible explanations for earnings differences:

- Job types *e.g. secretary (low pay) vs. trash collectors (higher)*
- Discrimination
- Differences in human capital
- Differences in the degree of specialization

Job Types

Some of the sex differences in wages arise because men and women do different jobs and the jobs that men do are better paid. But today, greater numbers of women are entering jobs such as those of bus driver, police officer, and construction worker, traditionally done by men. The trend is strongest in professions such as architecture, medicine, law, and accounting. The percentage of enrollments in university courses in these subjects for women has increased from less than 20 percent in 1970 to as high as 50 percent today.

But many women and minorities earn less than white men even when they do the same job. One possible reason is discrimination. Let's see how discrimination might affect wage rates.

Discrimination

Suppose that black females and white males have identical abilities as investment advisors. Figure 16.8 shows the supply curves of black females, S_{BF} (in part a), and of white males, S_{WM} (in part b). The marginal revenue product of investment advisors, as shown by the two curves labeled *MRP* in parts (a) and (b), is the same for both groups.

If everyone is free of prejudice about race and sex, the market determines a wage rate of $40,000 a year for both groups of investment advisors. But if the customers of investment houses are prejudiced against women and minorities, this prejudice is reflected in wages and employment.

Suppose that the marginal revenue product of the black females, when discriminated against, is MRP_{DA}, where *DA* stands for "discriminated against." Suppose that the marginal revenue product for white males, the group discriminated in favor of, is MRP_{DF}, where *DF* stands for "discriminated in favor of." With these marginal revenue product curves, black females earn $20,000 a year, and only 1,000 will work as investment advisors. White males earn $60,000 a year, and 3,000 of them will work as investment advisors.

FIGURE 16.8

Discrimination

(a) Black females

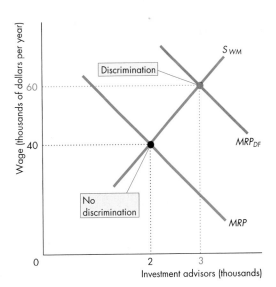

(b) White males

With no discrimination, the wage rate is $40,000 a year and 2,000 of each group are hired. With discrimination against blacks and women, the marginal revenue product curve in part (a) is MRP_{DA} and in part (b) it is MRP_{DF}. The wage rate for black women falls to $20,000 a year, and only 1,000 are employed. The wage rate for white men rises to $60,000 a year, and 3,000 are employed.

Economists disagree about whether prejudice actually causes wage differentials, and one line of reasoning suggests that it does not. In the example you've just studied, customers who buy from white men pay a higher service charge for investment advice than do the customers who buy from black women. This price difference acts as an incentive to encourage people who are prejudiced to buy from the people against whom they are prejudiced. This force could be so strong as to eliminate the effects of discrimination altogether. Suppose, as is true in manufacturing, that a firm's customers never meet its workers. If such a firm discriminates against women or minorities, it cannot compete with firms that hire these groups because its costs are higher than those of the nonprejudiced firms. So only those firms that do not discriminate survive in a competitive industry.

Let's now turn to the third source of wage differences: differences in human capital.

Differences in Human Capital

The more human capital a person possesses, the more that person earns, other things being equal. We measure human capital by using three indicators, which are:

1. Years of schooling
2. Years of work experience
3. Number of job interruptions

A larger proportion of men (25 percent) than women (20 percent) have completed 4 years of college. And a larger proportion of whites (24 percent) than blacks (13 percent) have completed a BA degree or higher. These differences in education levels among the sexes and the races are becoming smaller. But they have not yet been eliminated.

The more years of work and the fewer job interruptions a person has had, the higher is the person's wage, other things being equal. Interruptions to a career reduce the effectiveness of job experience and bring lower incomes. Historically, job interruptions are more serious for women than for men because women's careers have been interrupted for bearing and rearing children. This factor is a possible source of lower wages, on the average, for women. But maternity leave and day-care facilities are making career interruptions for women less common.

A final source of earnings differences, the relative degree of specialization of women and men, affects women's incomes adversely.

Differences in the Degree of Specialization

Couples must choose how to allocate their time between working for a wage and doing jobs in the home such as cooking, cleaning, shopping, organizing vacations and, most important, bearing and rearing children. Let's look at the choices of Bob and Sue.

Bob might specialize in earning an income and Sue in taking care of the home. Or Sue might specialize in earning an income and Bob in taking care of the home. Or both of them might earn an income and share home production jobs.

The allocation they choose depends on their preferences and on the earning potential of each of them. The choice of an increasing number of households is for each person to diversify between earning an income and doing some home chores. But in most households, Bob will specialize in earning an income and Sue will both earn an income and take care of the home. It seems likely that with this allocation, Bob will earn more than Sue. If Sue devotes time and effort to ensuring Bob's mental and physical well-being, the quality of Bob's market labor will be higher than if he were diversified. If the roles were reversed, Sue would be able to supply market labor that earns more than Bob.

To test whether the degree of specialization accounts for earnings differentials between the sexes, economists have studied two groups: "never married" men and "never married" women. The available evidence suggests that, on the average, when they have the same amount of human capital—measured by years of schooling, work experience, and career interruptions—the wages of these two groups are not significantly different.

R E V I E W Q U I Z

- What are the possible reasons for wage rate differences between the sexes and the races?
- How might differences in the degree of specialization result in the wage rates earned by men being higher than those earned by women?

Because labor markets bring unequal incomes, governments intervene in these markets to modify the wages and employment levels that they determine. One potentially far-reaching intervention is comparable-worth laws. Let's see how these laws work.

Comparable-Worth Laws

CONGRESS PASSED THE EQUAL PAY ACT IN 1963 and the Civil Rights Act in 1964. These acts require equal pay for equal work. They are attempts to remove the most blatant forms of discrimination between men and women and between whites and minorities. But many people believe that these acts do not go far enough. In their view, getting paid the *same* wage for doing the *same* job is just the first step that has to be taken. What's important is that jobs that are *comparable*—require the same levels of skills and responsibilities—receive the *same* wages, regardless of whether the jobs are done by men or women or by blacks or whites. Paying the same wage for different jobs that are judged to be comparable is called *comparable worth*.

Figure 16.9 shows how comparable-worth laws work. Part (a) shows the market for oil rig operators, and part (b) shows the market for school teachers. The marginal revenue product curves (MRP_R and

MRP_T) and the supply curves (S_R and S_T) are shown for each type of labor. Competition generates a wage rate W_R for oil rig operators and W_T for teachers.

Suppose it is decided that these two jobs are of comparable worth and that the courts enforce a wage rate of W_C for both groups. What happens? First, there is a shortage of oil rig operators. Oil rig companies are able to hire only S_R workers at the wage rate W_C. They cut back their production or build more expensive labor-saving oil rigs. Also the number of teachers employed decreases. But this decrease occurs because school boards demand fewer teachers. At the higher wage W_C, school boards demand only D_T teachers. The quantity of teachers supplied is S_T, and the difference between S_T and D_T is the number of unemployed teachers looking for jobs. These teachers eventually accept nonteaching jobs (which they don't like as much as teaching jobs), quite likely at a lower rate of pay than that of teachers.

Although comparable-worth laws can eliminate wage differences, they can do so only by incurring costly unintended consequences. They limit job

FIGURE 16.9
The Problem with Comparable Worth

(a) Market for oil rig operators

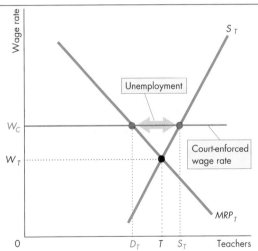

(b) Market for teachers

Part (a) shows the demand for and supply of oil rig operators, MRP_R and S_R, and part (b) shows the demand for and supply of school teachers, MRP_T and S_T. The competitive equilibrium wage rate for oil rig operators is W_R, and that for teachers is W_T. If an evaluation of the two jobs finds that they have comparable worth and rules that the wage rate W_C be paid to

both types of workers, such a wage creates a shortage of oil rig operators and a surplus of teachers. Oil producers search for labor-saving ways of producing oil (that are more expensive), and teachers search for other jobs (that are less desirable to them and probably are less well paid).

opportunities and create unemployment among workers whose wages they raise. And they make it hard for employers to hire workers whose wages are held down. Only in the rare case of a monopsonistic labor market does equalizing wage rates not create permanent surpluses and shortages of skills. In this situation, a comparable-worth law works in a similar way to a minimum wage law.

Effective Wage Policies

We have now surveyed the major sources of wage differentials, and one stands out: the level of education. People with postgraduate degrees earn much more than college graduates, who in turn earn much more than high school graduates, who in turn earn more than people who have not completed high school. This source of differences in earnings is the main one on which an effective policy can operate.

By pursuing the most effective education available in grade school, high school, and college and university, people can equip themselves with human capital that brings significantly higher earnings. But in today's rapidly changing world, education and human capital accumulation must be an ongoing enterprise. The most successful workers are those who are able to repeatedly retool and actively embrace each new technological advance. The least successful are those who get locked into a particular technology and are unable or unwilling to adapt when that technology becomes redundant.

So an effective wage policy is one that emphasizes the importance of ongoing education and training.

R E V I E W   Q U I Z

- What is a comparable-worth law and what does it seek to achieve?
- Do comparable-worth laws eliminate wage differences? What other effects do comparable-worth laws have that benefit or harm lower-paid workers?
- What is the most effective policy that can eliminate wage differentials between men and women and between whites and minorities?

We're now going to turn to the final topic of this chapter: immigration.

Immigration

SIXTY MILLION PEOPLE, OR 1.2 PERCENT OF THE world's current population, have migrated from the country in which they were born. And close to one third of these immigrants live in the United States.[1] We'll study four questions about U.S. immigration:

- How many people immigrate into the United States, where do they come from, and what skills do they bring?
- How does immigration affect employment and wage rates of native-born Americans?
- How do new immigrants perform in the United States?
- What are the effects of immigrants on the government budget?

Scale, Origin, and Skills of U.S. Immigrants

Almost 800,000 legal immigrants have arrived in the United States during each of the last few years. More than a quarter of these new immigrants, plus a further 200,000 to 300,000 a year, have come from Mexico.

The scale and pattern of immigration have changed over the years. Figure 16.10(a) shows that immigration was huge during the late nineteenth century and the first 30 years of the twentieth century. It fell during the 1930s and 1940s but built up again after World War II. By the 1980s, a new large wave of immigration was under way.

Figure 16.10(b) shows that before World War II, most immigration was either directly from Europe or indirectly from Europe via Canada. But gradually, over the decades, Asia, Mexico, and other American countries replaced Europe and Canada as the places of origin of new immigrants.

The skills that immigrants bring with them vary enormously. But the averages are interesting and important. We can measure skills of immigrants in two ways, by earnings and education levels. Based on earnings, newly arrived immigrants are less productive, on the average, than native Americans. And over the years, they have been getting less skilled relative

---

[1]This section on immigration draws extensively on George J. Borjas, "The Economics of Immigration," *Journal of Economic Literature,* Vol. XXXII (December 1994). pp. 1667–1717.

FIGURE 16.10

The Scale and Sources of U.S. Immigration

(a) Amount of immigration

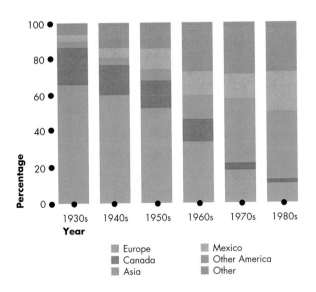

Europe
Canada
Asia
Mexico
Other America
Other

(b) Region of origin of immigrants

Part (a) shows the scale of immigration into the United States, decade by decade, since the 1880s. After a big wave during the 50 years to 1930, immigration decreased. A new wave began after World War II, which continued to rise through the 1980s. Before 1930, almost all the immigrants came from Europe. But over the years, Asia and other American countries have replaced Europe as the main source of new immigrants.

to native Americans. New immigrants who arrived during the 1960s earned 17 percent less than comparable Americans. Those who arrived during the 1970s earned 28 percent less than native Americans. And those who arrived during the 1980s earned 32 percent less than native Americans. Based on education levels, immigrants are also becoming less skilled, relative to native Americans. The percentage of immigrants who have not completed high school has decreased, but only slightly, and stands at almost 40 percent. In contrast, the high school dropout rate for native Americans has decreased from 40 percent in 1970 to less than 15 percent today.

At the other end of the education spectrum, the percentage of immigrants who are college graduates has increased somewhat, but the percentage of native American college graduates has increased faster.

To summarize the anatomy of U.S. immigrants: They are increasingly from Asia and Latin America, and their skill level is lower than that of native Americans and has been getting relatively lower.

Immigrants and the Labor Market

Immigration increases the supply of labor. By so doing, it lowers the wage rates of existing workers. At the same time, it decreases the supply of labor and raises wage rates in the country the immigrants are leaving. Figure 16.11 shows these effects in the labor markets of the United States (part a) and Mexico (part b). The demand for labor in the United States is LD_{US}, and in Mexico, it is LD_M. Before immigration takes place, 125 million workers in the United States earn $15 an hour and 50 million workers in Mexico earn $1 an hour. (The numbers are hypothetical.)

With free movement, Mexicans enter the United States as long as, by doing so, they can increase their incomes. In this example, the labor force of the United States increases to 150 million and the wage rate falls to $8 an hour. In Mexico, the labor force decreases to 25 million and the wage rate rises to $8 an hour. When the wage rates are the same, there is no incentive for anyone to migrate between the two countries.

The outcome shown in Fig. 16.11 would be unlikely to occur because people would not vote for an open border immigration law. Instead, we vote for immigration laws that prevent the free movement of people and so prevent the outcome shown in Fig. 16.11.

But does immigration move wage rates in the directions shown in the figure? Does it lower the wages of existing workers? The answer is ambiguous.

FIGURE 16.11

Immigration and the Labor Market

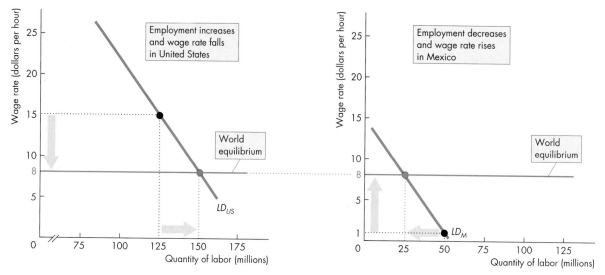

(a) The U.S. labor market

(b) The Mexican labor market

Part (a) shows the labor market in the United States. The demand for labor is LD_{US}, and with 125 million workers, the wage rate is $15 an hour. Part (b) shows the labor market in Mexico. The demand for labor is LD_M, and with 50 million workers, the wage rate is $1 an hour. With free movement of people between the two countries, people leave Mexico and migrate to the United States. Employment increases and the wage rate falls in the United States, and employment decreases and the wage rate rises in Mexico. The world equilibrium occurs when the wage rate is equal in the two countries, at $8 an hour.

It might lower wages. But it might raise them. Either way, the effect is probably small.

According to George Borjas, a leading authority on this topic, immigration might be partly responsible for the fall in the earnings of low-skilled Americans during the 1980s.

There are several reasons why immigration does not have the dramatic effect on domestic wages that Fig. 16.11 shows. First, immigrants bring not only a supply of labor but also a demand for goods and services. Consequently, firms expand and the demand for labor increases. This increase in the demand for labor limits the extent to which the wage rate falls. Second, some immigrants bring capital with them. This additional capital is invested in businesses and brings an increase in the demand for labor. Third, immigrants are not necessarily *substitutes* for domestic labor. They might be *complements* with it. For example, a shortage of low-skilled labor might cause a firm to close down and lay off its high-skilled workers.

Immigration might restore the ability of the firm to operate profitably and enable it to hire again.

For these three reasons, the effect of immigration on wage rates is smaller than the direct effect shown in Fig. 16.11.

Let's next look at the economic fortunes of the immigrants themselves.

How Do New Immigrants Perform in the United States?

We've seen that when a new immigrant arrives in the United States, he or she earns less, on the average, than similarly qualified native Americans. We've also seen that this earnings gap has been widening and is today close to one third. But what happens to immigrants in the years that follow their arrival?

The answer depends on when the immigrant arrived, the number of years elapsed since arriving, the ethnicity, and the language skills of the immigrant.

As a rule, immigrants' earnings grow more rapidly than the earnings of native Americans. That is, there is a tendency for immigrants' earnings to converge on and even to surpass the earnings of similar native Americans. But this tendency was stronger in the past than it is today. By 1990, immigrants who had arrived in the United States before 1970 had, on the average, reached income levels equal to those of native Americans. Those who had arrived before 1950 had income levels that averaged 26 percent *more* than the incomes of native Americans.

For more recent immigrant groups, there is still a tendency for incomes to grow faster than those of non-immigrants. But the starting gap is now so wide and the speed of convergence so slow that many new immigrants will never earn as much as their native equivalents.

This tendency for the immigrant to perform less well than a native American is more pronounced among Hispanic immigrants than among other ethnic groups. But it is also present among Asian immigrants.

Because the immigrant groups that perform least well are from countries in which English is not a major language, language skills might be playing a role. Studies of the influence of language on earnings agree with this suspicion. It has been estimated that immigrants who are proficient in the English language earn 17 percent more, on the average, than immigrants who are not proficient in English. This estimate, combined with the fact that an increasing percentage of immigrants have no English, explains some of the tendency for the most recent wave of immigrants to converge to non-immigrant earnings levels at a slower speed than that of earlier waves.

If the current group of immigrants might not catch up with the earnings of native Americans, what are the prospects for their children? Will they complete the convergence process? We do not know enough to be able to answer this question. But we do know that there is a strong correlation between the earnings of new immigrant families and the earnings of their children. Because of this correlation, there is a possiblity that convergence will continue to be slow.

Immigrants and the Government Budget

Since the mid-1960s, the United States has created a huge social welfare safety net. Do immigrants benefit more from our social programs than they contribute to them?

Immigrants have qualified for welfare assistance in increasing numbers over the past 20 years. In 1970, 6 percent of all native households and 5.9 percent of all immigrant households received some form of welfare. By 1990, these percentages were 7.4 for native households and 9.1 for immigrant households. Partly as a reaction to this trend, Congress passed legislation making it more difficult for immigrants to qualify for welfare and this new law might change the trend.

But there are huge differences in the extent to which different groups of immigrants use welfare. Those who rely most heavily on it are new immigrants from Cambodia, Laos, the Dominican Republic, and Vietnam.

But immigrants pay taxes. And their total tax payments are much greater than their welfare receipts. Data from the 1990 Census tell us that immigrants pay $85 billion in taxes and receive $24 billion in welfare benefits. Immigrants also impose other hard-to-quantify costs on the government, so we cannot say for sure what the net cost or benefit of immigration is for the government's budget.

R E V I E W   Q U I Z

- Where do most of the immigrants to the United States come from? Has the number of immigrants increased or decreased in recent years?
- How does immigration influence wage rates? Is the effect small or large?
- How do the wage rates and skills of new immigrants compare with those of people who have been in the United States for some time?
- Do recent immigrants rely more on welfare than earlier waves of immigrants did? Why might this be so?

◆ *Reading Between the Lines* on pages 360–361 returns to the U.S. labor markets and looks at Navy's problem in enlisting the number of sailors that it demands. It examines different ways in which a labor market can cope with a shortage and achieve equilibrium.

In the next chapter, we're going to examine the distributions of income and wealth that result from the operation of labor markets and the markets for other productive resources.

A Labor Market in Action

THE NEW YORK TIMES, JANUARY 16, 1999

Enlistments Falling, Navy Lowers Education Standard

Facing a shortage of sailors at sea, the Navy announced today that it would have to lower educational standards for new recruits as part of a series of initiatives to increase enlistments. Since the end of the cold war, the Navy has required that 95 percent of new recruits have a high school diploma, but for the first time in a decade, it will require no more than 90 percent. ...

The difficulty in recruiting—which has also hit the Army and, to a lesser extent, the Air Force and the Marine Corps—has forced the Navy to send ships to sea with less than full crews. In recent weeks, the Navy disclosed today, it has had as many as 22,000 empty positions—or bunks—in its 327-ship fleet. ...

The services attribute the shortages in new recruits to a variety of factors, from a booming economy and low unemployment rate to the fact that 70 percent of young people go straight to college after finishing high school, compared with less than half a decade ago.

But the Navy's response is certain to provoke criticism that the service is lowering the standards of its enlisted sailors. The Army faced sharp attacks from Congress when it announced a similar change two years ago. The Marine Corps continues to require at least 95 percent of enlistees to have diplomas. The Air Force also has a minimum standard of 90 percent but for the last 15 years has never fallen below 99 percent. ...

The Navy, with 372,000 officers and enlisted personnel, needs 160,000 sailors to fill its ships at sea. The shortages have left some ships, including aircraft carriers and submarines, at less than 90 percent strength.

Essence of the Story

■ The Navy needs 160,000 sailors to fill its ships at sea but is unable to recruit this number and is 22,000 short.

■ Faced with this shortage, the Navy announced plans to lower educational standards for new recruits.

■ In the future, only 90 percent of new recruits will be required to have a high school diploma, down from the previous requirement of 95 percent of recruits.

■ The Navy says that the shortage of new recruits arises because the unemployment rate is low and 70 percent of young people go straight to college after finishing high school, more than double the rate of a decade ago.

■ But the Navy's decision is expected to provoke criticism of the falling standards.

■ Figure 1 shows the current predicament of the Navy in the market for sailors.

■ The Navy's demand for sailors is determined by their marginal revenue product and is shown by the demand curve *D*.

■ The supply of sailors is determined by the decisions of high school students and high school graduates and is shown by the supply curve *S*.

■ The current wage rate of new recruits averages $11,000 a year. (This information is not provided in the news article.)

■ At the current wage rate, the quantity of labor demanded is 160,000 sailors, which is the quantity reported in the news article. The news article also reports a shortage of 22,000 sailors. So we can infer that the quantity of labor supplied at the current wage rate is 138,000 sailors.

■ The Navy raises the wage rate or lowers the recruiting standards.

■ Figure 2 shows what happens if the Navy raises the wage rate. The wage rises to the equilibrium level, which is $12,000 (an assumption). The quantity demanded decreases, and the quantity supplied increases.

■ Figure 3 shows what happens if the Navy lowers the recruiting standards. Supply increases, and the supply curve shifts rightward. A lower educational standard decreases marginal product. The Navy reorganizes some tasks, the demand for sailors decreases, and the demand curve shifts leftward. The equilibrium quantity decreases to 150,000 sailors.

You're The Voter

■ Would you vote for the lowering of recruiting standards in the Navy? Why or why not?

■ Would you vote for an increase in funding for the Navy to enable it to offer a higher wage rate? Explain.

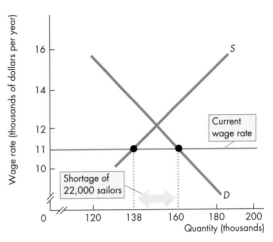

Figure 1 The Navy's predicament

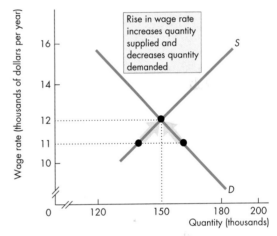

Figure 2 Solution 1: Raise the wage rate

Figure 3 Solution 2: Lower the standards required

SUMMARY

KEY POINTS

Skill Differentials (pp. 344–346)

- Skill differentials arise from differences in marginal revenue products and because skills are costly to acquire.
- Wage rates of high-skilled and low-skilled labor are determined by demand and supply in the two labor markets.

Union-Nonunion Wage Differentials (pp. 346–352)

- Labor unions influence wages by controlling the supply of labor.
- In competitive labor markets, unions obtain higher wages only at the expense of lower employment, but they try to influence the demand for labor.
- In a monopsony a union can increase the wage rate without sacrificing employment.
- Bilateral monopoly occurs when a union confronts a single buyer of labor. The wage rate is determined by bargaining between the two parties.
- Union workers earn 10 to 25 percent more than comparable nonunion workers.

Wage Differentials Between Sexes and Races (pp. 352–354)

- Earnings differentials between men and women and between whites and minorities arise from differences in types of jobs, discrimination, differences in human capital, and differences in degree of specialization.
- Well-paid jobs are more likely to be held by white men than by women and minorities. But discrimination is hard to measure objectively.
- Historically, white males have had more human capital than other groups. Human capital differences arising from schooling differences have been falling but they have not been eliminated.
- Differentials based on work experience have kept women's pay below that for men because women's careers have traditionally been interrupted more frequently than those of men. This difference is smaller today than in the past.

- Differentials arising from different degrees of specialization are probably important and might persist. Men have traditionally been more specialized in market activity, on the average, than women.

Comparable-Worth Laws (pp. 355–356)

- Comparable-worth laws determine wages by using objective characteristics rather than what the market will pay to assess the value of different types of jobs.
- Determining wages through comparable worth will result in a decrease in the number of people employed in jobs on which the market places a lower value and shortages of workers that the market values more highly.

Immigration (pp. 356–359)

- U.S. immigration has followed waves. A big increase occurred during the 1970s and 1980s. The origin of immigrants has shifted from Europe to Asia and Latin America. Immigrants have become less skilled than in the past.
- Immigration lowers wage rates but only slightly.
- Immigrants enter with low earnings but in the past their earnings have converged on those of native Americans. This convergence has slowed. Immigrants now use welfare more than in the past.

KEY FIGURES

KEY TERMS

PROBLEMS

*1. The demand for and supply of low-skilled labor are given by the following figure:

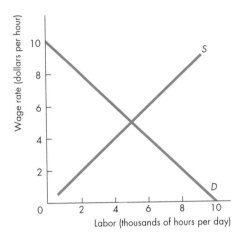

Workers can be trained—can obtain a skill—and their marginal productivity doubles. (The marginal product at each employment level is twice the marginal product of a low-skilled worker.) But the cost of acquiring the skill adds $2 an hour to the wage that must be offered to attract high-skilled labor. What is:

a. The wage rate of low-skilled labor?
b. The quantity of low-skilled labor employed?
c. The wage rate of high-skilled labor?
d. The quantity of high-skilled labor employed?

2. The demand for and supply of low-skilled labor are given by the following figure:

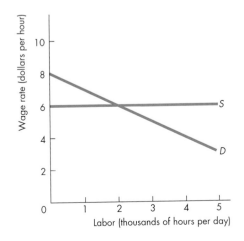

Workers can be trained—can obtain a skill—and their marginal productivity increases by $5 an hour. (The marginal product at each employment level is $5 greater than that of a low-skilled worker.) The cost of acquiring the skill adds $3 an hour to the wage that must be offered to attract high-skilled labor. What is:

a. The wage rate of low-skilled labor?
b. The quantity of low-skilled labor employed?
c. The wage rate of high-skilled labor?
d. The quantity of high-skilled labor employed?
e. Why does the wage rate increase by exactly the cost of acquiring the skill?

*3. Suppose in problem 1 that high-skilled workers become unionized and the union restricts the amount of high-skilled labor to 5,000 hours. What is:

a. The wage rate of high-skilled workers?
b. The wage differential between low- and high-skilled workers?

4. Suppose in problem 2 that high-skilled workers become unionized and the union restricts the amount of high-skilled labor to 2,000 hours. What is:

a. The wage rate of high-skilled workers?
b. The wage differential between low- and high-skilled workers?

*5. If in problem 1, the government introduces a minimum wage rate of $6 an hour for low-skilled workers

a. What is the wage rate paid to low-skilled workers?
b. How many hours of low-skilled labor gets hired each day?

6. If in problem 2, the government introduces a minimum wage rate of $8 an hour for low-skilled workers

a. What is the wage rate paid to low-skilled workers?
b. How many hours of low-skilled labor gets hired each day?

*7. A monopsony gold-mining firm operates in an isolated part of the Amazon basin. The table shows the firm's labor supply schedule (columns 1 and 2) and total product schedule (columns 2 and 3). The price of gold is $1.40 per grain.

Wage rate (dollars per day)	Workers (number per day)	Quantity of gold produced (grains per day)
5	0	0
6	1	10
7	2	25
8	3	45
9	4	60
10	5	70
11	6	75

a. What wage rate does the company pay?
b. How many workers does the gold mine hire?
c. What is the marginal revenue product at the quantity of labor employed?

8. A monopsony logging firm operates in an isolated part of the Alaska. The table shows the firm's labor supply schedule (columns 1 and 2) and total product schedule (columns 2 and 3). The price of logs is $1.50 per ton.

Wage rate (dollars per day)	Workers (number per day)	Quantity of logs produced (tons per day)
2.50	0	0
3.00	1	7
3.50	2	13
4.00	3	18
4.50	4	22
5.00	5	25
5.50	6	27

a. What wage rate does the company pay?
b. How many workers does the logging firm hire?
c. What is the marginal revenue product at the quantity of labor employed?

*9. In problem 7, explain the effects of a court-enforced wage rate above the equilibrium wage rate on employment and unemployment.

10. In problem 8, explain the effects of the arrival of new immigrants on the demand for labor, the supply of labor, and the wage rate.

CRITICAL THINKING

1. Study the *Reading Between the Lines* on pp. 360–361 and then answer the following questions:
   a. What problem did the Navy face in the labor market at the time the news article was written?
   b. What was the Navy's proposed solution?
   c. Explain the predicted effects of the Navy's proposed solution.
   d. Describe the changes that might occur on a Navy ship after the adoption of lower recruiting standards. (Hint: Be imaginative. Think about the types of jobs that a person who has not graduated from high school might not be able to do well that a high school graduate can handle.)
   e. Explain the market solution to the Navy's problem.
   f. Describe the changes that might occur on a Navy ship if the wage rises to the equilibrium level with no change in recruiting standards. (Hint: Think about how a ship might cope with fewer sailors.)

2. Use the link on the Parkin Web site to visit the AFL-CIO and look at the "Don't Buy List." Choose an item on this list that interests you and explain why the AFL-CIO recommends a boycott of this item. Explain how not buying this item increases either the wage rate or employment level of union members.

3. Use the link on the Parkin Web site to visit the Bureau of Labor Statistics (BLS) and obtain data for the past three months on usual weekly earnings and the level of employment.
   a. What has happened to earnings and employment during the past three months?
   b. Try to explain the changes by using the tools of demand and supply.

4. "Wages should be determined on the basis of what is fair." Debate this proposition. Set out the cases for and against. Then determine and explain your verdict.

5. Suppose that all nations permitted free migration. Which nations would be the biggest suppliers of immigrants and why? Which nations would attract most immigrants and why? Describe the world economy 10 years after the start of this process.

Chapter 17

Inequality, Redistribution, and Health Care

Fifty-three stories above Manhattan is a penthouse with unobstructed views of Central Park, the Hudson River, and the city skyline. Its price? $4 million. "Now, you can be one of the enviable few to fly Around the World by Supersonic Concorde ... for just $32,000 per person," trumpets an advertisement in *The New Yorker*. Not quite within view of the $4 million penthouse, but not far from it, is Fort Washington Armory in Upper Manhattan. What was opened as a temporary shelter in 1981 permanently houses close to 1,000 men who sleep in one football-field-sized room. These men live on the edge of despair and in fear of AIDS and other life-threatening diseases. ◆ Why are some people exceedingly rich while others are very poor and own almost nothing? Are the rich getting richer and the poor getting poorer? Does the information we have about the inequality of income and wealth in the United States paint an accurate picture or a misleading one? How do taxes and social security, welfare, and health-care programs influence economic inequality?

Riches and Rags

◆ In this chapter, we study economic inequality—its extent, its sources, and its potential remedies. We look at taxes and government programs that redistribute incomes and study their effects on economic inequality in the United States. We also study the different ways in which health care can be delivered and their effects on economic efficiency and equality. Let's begin by looking at some facts about economic inequality.

After studying this chapter, you will be able to:

- Describe the inequality in income and wealth in the United States

- Explain why wealth inequality is greater than income inequality

- Explain how economic inequality arises

- Explain the effects of taxes and social security and welfare programs on economic inequality

- Explain the effects of health-care reform on economic inequality

Economic Inequality in the United States

WE STUDY INEQUALITY BY LOOKING AT THE distribution of income and the distribution of wealth. A household's income is the amount that it receives in a given period. A household's wealth is the value of the things it owns at a point in time. We measure income inequality by looking at the percentage of total income received by a given percentage of households. And we can measure wealth inequality by looking at the percentage of total wealth owned by a given percentage of households.

In 1997, the average U.S. household income, before tax and not counting government transfers, was close to $50,000. But there was considerable inequality around that number. The poorest 20 percent of households received 3.6 percent of total income while the richest 20 percent received 49.4 percent of total income.

The wealth distribution is even more unequal. Average household wealth in 1992 was $193,000. But the poorest 90 percent of households owned about one third of total wealth. The next 9 percent owned another third of total wealth. And the wealthiest 1 percent of households owned the remaining one third of total wealth.

Lorenz Curves

Figure 17.1 shows the distributions of income and wealth. The table divides households into five groups, called *quintiles*, that range from the lowest income (row *a*) to highest income (row *e*). It shows the percentages of income of each of these groups. For example, row *a* tells us that the lowest quintile of households receives 3.6 percent of total income. The table also shows the *cumulative* percentages of households and income. For example, row *b* tells us that the lowest two quintiles (lowest 40 percent) of households receive 12.5 percent of total income (3.6 percent for the lowest quintile and 8.9 percent for the next lowest). The data on cumulative income shares are illustrated by a Lorenz curve. A **Lorenz curve** graphs the cumulative percentage of income against the cumulative percentage of households.

If income were distributed equally to every household, the cumulative percentages of income received by the cumulative percentages of households

FIGURE 17.1

Lorenz Curves for Income and Wealth

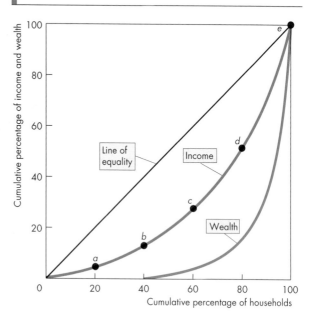

	Households		Income		Wealth	
	Percentage	Cumulative percentage	Percentage	Cumulative percentage	Percentage	Cumulative percentage
a Lowest 20	20	20	3.6	3.6	0	0
b Second 20	40	40	8.9	12.5	0	0
c Third 20	60	60	15.0	27.5	4	4
d Fourth 20	80	80	23.2	50.7	11	15
e Highest 20	100	100	49.4	100.0	85	100

The cumulative percentages of income and wealth are graphed against the cumulative percentage of households. If income and wealth were distributed equally, each 20 percent of households would have 20 percent of the income and wealth—the line of equality. Points *a* through *e* on the Lorenz curve for income correspond to the rows of the table. The Lorenz curves show that income and wealth are unequally distributed and wealth more unequally distributed than income. (Note there is a rounding approximation in the data.)

Sources: U.S. Bureau of the Census, Current Population Reports, P-60-200, *Money Income in the United States (With Separate Data on Valuation of Noncash Benefits),* U.S. Government Printing Office, Washington, D.C., 1998, and Robert D. Avery and Arthur B. Kennickell, "Measurement of Household Saving Obtained from First Differencing Wealth Estimates" (Washington, D.C.: Federal Reserve Board, February 1990).

would fall along the straight line labeled "Line of equality." The actual distribution of income is shown by the Lorenz curve labeled "Income." The closer the Lorenz curve is to the line of equality, the more equal is the distribution.

Figure 17.1 also shows a Lorenz curve for wealth. This curve is based on the distribution described in the table. Total wealth is divided approximately equally between the wealthiest 1 percent, the next 9 percent, and the other 90 percent of households.

You can see from the two Lorenz curves in Fig. 17.1 that the Lorenz curve for wealth is much farther away from the line of equality than the Lorenz curve for income is, so the distribution of wealth is much more unequal than the distribution of income.

Inequality over Time

Figure 17.2 shows how the distribution of income has changed since 1970.

- The share of income received by the richest 20 percent of households has increased.
- The share of income received by all four other groups of households has decreased.

The higher-income groups have gained because rapid technological change has increased the return to education. The lower-income groups have suffered for a variety of reasons; one of them is increased international mobility and competition that are keeping down the wages of the low skilled. The trends that are visible in Fig. 17.2 are real, but they are exaggerated after 1989 and more so after 1994 by a change in the method of measuring large incomes.

Who Are the Rich and the Poor?

The lowest-income household in the United States today is likely to be a black woman over 65 years of age who lives alone somewhere in the South and has fewer than eight years of elementary school education. The highest-income household in the United States today is likely to be a college-educated white married couple between 45 and 54 years of age living together with two children somewhere in the West.

These snapshot profiles are the extremes in Fig. 17.3. That figure illustrates the importance of education, size of household, marital status, age of householder, race, and region of residence in influencing the size of a household's income. The range of variation

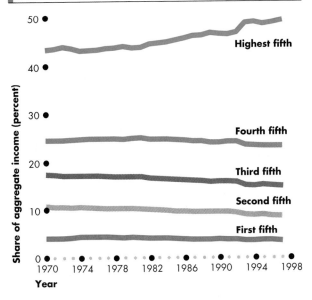

FIGURE 17.2

Trends in the Distribution of Income: 1950–1997

The distribution of income in the United States became more unequal between 1970 and 1997. The percentage of income earned by the highest fifth increased steadily through the 1970s and 1980s and sharply during the 1990s.

Source: U.S. Bureau of the Census, Current Population Reports, P-60-200, *Money Income in the United States (With Separate Data on Valuation of Noncash Benefits),* and Current Population Reports, *Consumer Income,* P-60-168 U.S. Government Printing Office, Washington, D.C, 1990 and 1998.

associated with education is the largest. On the average, people who have not completed grade 9 earn $15,400 a year, while people with a bachelor's degree or more earn an average of $60,000 a year. Four-person households have incomes that average more than $51,000 while one-person households have an average income of about $18,000. Single females, on the average, have incomes of $16,400 a year, while married couples earn an average joint income of $50,000 a year. The oldest and youngest households have lower incomes than middle-aged households. Black households have an average income of $23,500, while white households have an average income of just over $38,000. Finally, incomes are lowest in the South and highest in the Northeast. But incomes in the West and the Midwest are close to those in the Northeast and much higher than incomes in the South.

FIGURE 17.3

The Distribution of Income by Selected Household Characteristics in 1997

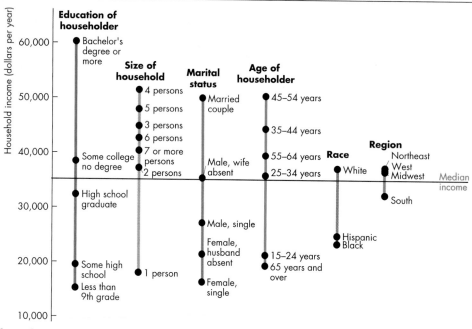

Education is the single biggest factor affecting household income distribution, but size of household, marital status, and age of householder are also important. Race and region of residence also play a role.

Sources: *Statistical Abstract of the United States: 1998*, 118th edition Table 740.

Poverty

Households at the low end of the income distribution are so poor that they are considered to be living in poverty. **Poverty** is a state in which a household's income is too low to be able to buy the quantities of food, shelter, and clothing that are deemed necessary. Poverty is a relative concept. Millions of people living in Africa and Asia survive on incomes of less than $400 a year. In the United States, the poverty level is calculated each year by the Social Security Administration. In 1997, the poverty level for a four-person household was an income of $16,813. In that year, 35.6 million Americans lived in households that had incomes below the poverty level. Many of these households benefited from Medicare and Medicaid, two government programs that benefit the poorest households and lift some of them above the poverty level.

The distribution of poverty by race is unequal: 11 percent of white households, 27.1 percent of Hispanic origin households, and 26.5 percent of black households are below the poverty level. Poverty is also influenced by household status. Almost 32 percent of households in which the householder is a female and no husband is present are below the poverty level, while fewer than 12 percent of other households are.

Poverty rates in the United States are falling, and especially for black families.

REVIEW QUIZ

- Which is distributed more unequally: income or wealth?
- Has the distribution of income become more equal or more unequal?
- Which group of households has experienced the largest increase in income share during the past 20 years?
- The influences on a household's income are age of householder, education of members, household size, marital status, race, and region of residence. Rank the items in decreasing order of importance.

Comparing Like with Like

To DETERMINE THE DEGREE OF INEQUALITY, we compare one person's economic situation with another person's. But what is the correct measure of a person's economic situation? Is it income or is it wealth? And is it *annual* income, the measure we've used so far in this chapter, or income over a longer time period—for example, over a family's lifetime?

Wealth Versus Income

Wealth is a stock of assets, and income is the flow of earnings that results from the stock of wealth. Suppose that a person owns assets worth $1 million—has a wealth of $1 million. If the rate of return on assets is 5 percent a year, then this person receives an income of $50,000 a year from those assets. We can describe this person's economic condition by using either the wealth of $1 million or the income of $50,000. When the rate of return is 5 percent a year, $1 million of wealth equals $50,000 of income in perpetuity. Wealth and income are simply different ways of looking at the same thing.

But in Fig. 17.1, the distribution of wealth is much more unequal than the distribution of income. Why? It is because the wealth data measure tangible assets and exclude the value of human capital while the income data measure income from both tangible assets and human capital.

Table 17.1 illustrates the consequence of omitting human capital from the wealth data. Lee has twice the wealth and twice the income of Peter. But Lee's human capital is less than Peter's—$200,000 compared with $499,000. And Lee's income from human capital of $10,000 is less than Peter's income from human capital of $24,950. Lee's nonhuman capital is larger than Peter's—$800,000 compared with $1,000. And Lee's income from nonhuman capital of $40,000 is larger than Peter's income from nonhuman capital of $50.

The national wealth and income surveys record their incomes of $50,000 and $25,000, respectively, which indicate that Lee is twice as well off as Peter. And they record their tangible assets of $800,000 and $1,000, respectively, which indicate that Lee is 800 times as wealthy as Peter. Because the national survey of wealth excludes human capital, the income distribution is a more accurate measure of economic inequality than the wealth distribution.

TABLE 17.1

Capital, Wealth, and Income

	Lee		Peter	
	Wealth	**Income**	**Wealth**	**Income**
Human capital	200,000	10,000	499,000	24,950
Nonhuman capital	800,000	40,000	1,000	50
Total	$1,000,000	$50,000	$500,000	$25,000

When wealth is measured to include the value of human capital as well as nonhuman capital, the distribution of income and the distribution of wealth display the same degree of inequality.

Annual or Lifetime Income and Wealth?

A typical family's income changes over time. It starts out low, grows to a peak when the family's workers reach retirement age, and then falls after retirement. Also, a typical family's wealth changes over time. Like income, it starts out low, grows to a peak at the point of retirement, and falls after retirement.

Suppose we look at three families that have identical lifetime incomes. One family is young, one is middle aged, and one is retired. The middle-aged family has the highest income and wealth, the retired family has the lowest, and the young family falls in the middle. The distributions of annual income and wealth in a given year are unequal, but the distributions of lifetime income and wealth are equal. So some of the measured inequality arises from the fact that different families are at different stages in the life cycle. Inequality of annual incomes overstates the degree of lifetime inequality.

R E V I E W   Q U I Z

- Is the distribution of income or the distribution of wealth the more accurate indicator of the degree of inequality? Why is one of these a better measure than the other?
- Is the distribution of lifetime income or the distribution of annual income the more accurate indicator of the degree of inequality? Why is one of these a better measure than the other?

Let's look at the sources of economic inequality.

Resource Prices, Endowments, and Choices

A FAMILY'S INCOME DEPENDS ON THREE THINGS:

- Resource prices
- Resource endowments
- Choices

The distribution of income depends on the distribution of these three things across the population. The first two are outside our individual control and are determined by market forces and by history. From the viewpoint of each one of us, they appear to be determined by luck. The last item is under individual control. We make choices that influence our incomes. Let's look at the three factors that influence incomes.

Resource Prices

Everyone faces the same interest rates in capital markets, but people face differing wage rates in the labor market. And the labor market is the biggest single source of income for most people. To what extent do variations in wage rates account for the unequal distribution of income? The answer is that they do to some extent, but wage differences cannot account for all the inequality. High-skilled workers earn about 3.5 times as much as low-skilled workers. Highly paid professionals earn about 3 times as much as high-skilled workers. So the highest-paid professionals earn around 10 times what the least skilled are paid.

Differences in resource endowments are another.

Resource Endowments

There is a large amount of variety in a family's endowments of capital and of human abilities. Differences in capital make a big contribution to differences in incomes. But so do differences in ability.

Physical and mental abilities (some inherited, some learned) have a normal, or bell-shaped, distribution—like the distribution of heights. The distribution of ability across individuals is a major source of inequality in income and wealth. But it is not the only source. If it were, the distributions of income and wealth would look like the bell-shaped curve that describes the distribution of heights. In fact, these distributions are skewed toward high incomes and look like the curve in Fig. 17.4. This figure shows income on the horizontal axis and the percentage of households receiving each income on the vertical axis. In 1997, the median household income—the income that separates households into two groups of equal size—was $37,000. The most common income—called the mode income—is less than the median income. The mean income—also called the average income—is greater than the median income and in 1997 was $50,000. A skewed distribution like the one shown in Fig. 17.4 is one in which many more families have incomes below the average than above it, a large number of families have low incomes, and a small number of families have high incomes. The distribution of (nonhuman) wealth has a shape similar to that of the distribution of income but is even more skewed.

The skewed distribution of income cannot be explained by the bell-shaped distribution of individual abilities. It results from the choices that people make.

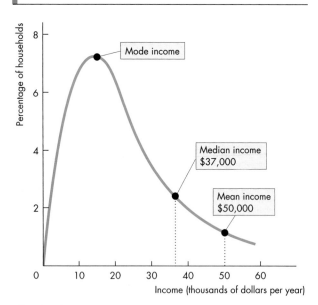

FIGURE 17.4

The Distribution of Income

The distribution of income is unequal and is not symmetric around the mean income. There are many more households with incomes below the mean income than above it. Also, the distribution has a long, thin upper tail representing a small number of households that earn very large incomes.

Choices

While many poor families feel trapped and do not have many options open to them, a family's income and wealth depend partly on the choices that its members make. You are going to discover that the choices people make exaggerate the differences among them and make the distribution of income more unequal than the distribution of abilities, as well as making the distribution of income skewed.

Wages and the Supply of Labor   Other things remaining the same, the quantity of labor that a person supplies usually increases as that person's wage rate increases. A person who has a low wage rate chooses to work fewer hours than a person who has a high wage rate.

Because the quantity of labor supplied increases as the wage rate increases, the distribution of income is more unequal than the distribution of hourly wages and skewed, like the one shown in Fig. 17.4. People whose wage rates are below the average tend to work fewer hours than the average, and their incomes bunch together below the average. People whose wage rates are above the average tend to work more hours than the average, and their incomes stretch out above the average.

Saving and Bequests   Another choice that results in unequal distributions in income and wealth is the decision to save and make bequests. A *bequest* is a gift from one generation to the next. The higher a family's income, the more that family tends to save and accumulate wealth across generations.

Saving and bequests are not inevitably a source of increased inequality. If a family saves to redistribute an uneven income over the life cycle and enable consumption to be constant, the act of saving decreases the degree of inequality. If a lucky generation that has a high income saves a large amount and makes a bequest to a generation that is unlucky, this act of saving also decreases the degree of inequality. But two features of bequests make intergenerational transfers of wealth a source of increased inequality:

■ Debts cannot be bequeathed
■ Mating is assortative

Debts Cannot Be Bequeathed   Although a person may die with debts that exceed assets—with negative wealth—debts cannot be forced onto other family members. Because a zero inheritance is the smallest inheritance that anyone can receive, bequests can only add to future generations' wealth and income potential.

Most people inherit nothing or a very small amount. A few people inherit enormous fortunes. As a result, bequests make the distribution of income persistently more unequal than the distribution of ability and job skills. A family that is poor in one generation is more likely to be poor in the next. A family that is wealthy in one generation is likely to be wealthy in the next. But there is a tendency for income and wealth to converge, across generations, to the average. Although there can be long runs of good luck or bad luck, or good judgment or bad judgment, such long runs are uncommon across generations. But a feature of human behavior slows the convergence of wealth to the average and makes inequalities persist—assortative mating.

Assortative Mating   *Assortative mating* is the tendency for people to marry within their own socioeconomic class. In the vernacular, "like attracts like." Although there is a good deal of folklore that "opposites attract," perhaps such Cinderella tales appeal to us because they are so rare in reality. Marriage partners tend to have similar socioeconomic characteristics. Wealthy individuals seek wealthy partners. The consequence of assortative mating is that inherited wealth becomes more unequally distributed.

REVIEW QUIZ

■ What role do wage rates, endowments, and choices play in creating income inequality?
■ What is the main reason that wage rates are unequal?
■ If the distribution of endowments is bell shaped, what makes the distribution of income skewed?
■ Which choices that people make generate the skew in the distribution of income?
■ How do bequests and assortative mating make the distribution of wealth more unequal and skewed?

We've now examined why inequality exists. Next, we're going to see how taxes and government programs redistribute income and wealth.

Income Redistribution

The three main ways that governments in the United States redistribute income are:

- Income taxes
- Income maintenance programs
- Subsidized services

Income Taxes

Income taxes may be progressive, regressive, or proportional. A **progressive income tax** is one that taxes income at a marginal rate that increases with the level of income. The term "marginal," applied to income tax rates, refers to the fraction of the last dollar earned that is paid in taxes. A **regressive income tax** is one that taxes income at a marginal rate that decreases with the level of income. A **proportional income tax** (also called a *flat-rate income tax*) is one that taxes income at a constant rate, regardless of the level of income.

The tax rates that apply in the United States are composed of two parts: federal and state taxes. Some cities, such as New York City, also have an income tax. There is variety in the detailed tax arrangements in the individual states, but the tax system, at both the federal and state levels, is progressive. The poorest working households receive money from the government through an earned income tax credit. The middle-income households pay 15 percent of each additional dollar they earn, and successively richer households pay 28 percent and 31 percent of each additional dollar earned.

Income Maintenance Programs

Three main types of programs redistribute income by making direct payments (in cash, services, or vouchers) to people in the lower part of the income distribution. They are:

- Social security programs
- Unemployment compensation
- Welfare programs

Social Security   The main social security program is OASDHI—Old Age, Survivors, Disability, and Health Insurance. Monthly cash payments to retired or disabled workers or their surviving spouses and children are paid for by compulsory payroll taxes on both employers and employees. In 1998, total social security expenditure was more than $350 billion, and 41 million people received an average monthly social security check of $721.

The other component of social security is Medicare, which provides hospital and health insurance for the elderly and disabled.

Unemployment Compensation   To provide an income to unemployed workers, every state has established an unemployment compensation program. Under these programs, a tax is paid based on the income of each covered worker and such a worker receives a benefit when he or she becomes unemployed. The details of the benefits vary from state to state.

Welfare Programs   The purpose of welfare is to provide incomes for people who do not qualify for social security or unemployment compensation. They are

1. Supplementary Security Income (SSI) program, designed to help the neediest elderly, disabled, and blind people
2. Temporary Assistance for Needy Households (TANF) program, designed to help households who have inadequate financial resources
3. Food Stamp program, designed to help the poorest households obtain a basic diet
4. Medicaid, designed to cover the costs of medical care for households receiving help under the SSI and TANF programs

Subsidized Services

A great deal of redistribution takes place in the United States through the provision of subsidized services—services provided by the government at prices far below the cost of production. The taxpayers who consume these goods and services receive a transfer in kind from the taxpayers who do not consume them. The two most important areas in which this form of redistribution takes place are education—both kindergarten through grade 12 and college and university—and health care.

In 1998–99, students enrolled in the University of California system paid annual tuition fees of $3,766. The cost of providing a year's education at the

University of California at Berkeley or San Diego in 1998–99 was $15,000. So households with a member enrolled in these institutions received a benefit from the government of more than $11,000 a year.

Government provision of health-care services has grown to equal the scale of private provision. Programs such as Medicaid and Medicare bring high-quality and high-cost health care to millions of people who earn too little to buy such services themselves.

The Scale of Income Redistribution

A household's income in the absence of government redistribution is called *market income.* We can measure the scale of income redistribution by calculating the percentage of market income paid in taxes and the percentage received in benefits at each income level. The data available include redistribution through taxes and cash and noncash benefits to welfare recipients. They do not include the value of subsidized services such as college, which might decrease the total amount of redistribution from the rich to the poor.

Figure. 17.5 shows the scale of redistribution. The blue Lorenz curve describes the market distribution of income. It is the same as that in Fig. 17.1. The red Lorenz curve shows the distribution of income after all taxes and benefits including Medicaid and Medicare benefits. The distribution after taxes and benefits is much less unequal than the market distribution. The lowest 20 percent of households receive only 3.6 percent of market income but 13 percent of income after taxes and benefits. The highest 20 percent of households receive 49.4 percent of market income but only 31 percent of income after taxes. Redistribution increases the share of total income received by the lowest 60 percent of households. It decreases the share of total income received by the highest 40 percent of households.

Another measure of the scale of redistribution is provided by the sources of income at different points of the income distribution. The poorest 20 percent of households receive more than 70 percent of their income from the government. The second 20 percent receive 43 percent of their income from the government. In contrast, the richest 20 percent receive almost nothing from the government but receive a third of their income from capital—interest and dividends from financial assets. The proportion of income from capital for the other 80 percent of households is remarkably constant at about 8 percent.

FIGURE 17.5

Income Redistribution

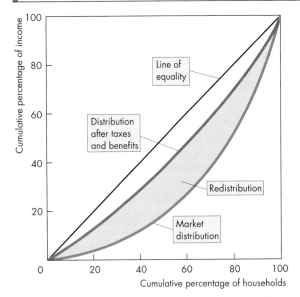

Taxes and income maintenance programs reduce the degree of inequality that the market generates. In 1997, the 20 percent of households with the lowest incomes received net benefits that increased their share of total income from 3.6 percent to 13 percent. The 20 percent of households with the highest incomes paid taxes that decreased their share of total income from 49.4 percent to 31 percent of total income.

Sources: U.S. Bureau of the Census, Current Population Reports, P–60–193, *Money Income in the United States (With Separate Data on Valuation of Noncash Benefits),* U.S. Government Printing Office, Washington, D.C, 1998, and the author's calculations.

The Big Tradeoff

The redistribution of income creates what has been called the **big tradeoff**, a tradeoff between equity and efficiency. The big tradeoff arises because redistribution uses scarce resources and weakens incentives.

A dollar collected from a rich person does not translate into a dollar received by a poor person. Some of it gets used up in the process of redistribution. Tax-collecting agencies such as the Internal Revenue Service and welfare-administering agencies (as well as tax accountants and lawyers) use skilled labor, computers, and other scarce resources to do their work. The bigger the scale of redistribution, the greater is the opportunity cost of administering it.

But the cost of collecting taxes and making welfare payments is a small part of the total cost of redistribution. A bigger cost arises from the inefficiency—deadweight loss—of taxes and benefits. Greater equality can be achieved only by taxing productive activities such as work and saving. Taxing people's income from their work and saving lowers the after-tax income they receive. This lower income makes them work and save less, which in turn result in smaller output and less consumption not only for the rich who pay the taxes but also for the poor who receive the benefits.

It is not only taxpayers who face weaker incentives to work. Benefit recipients also face weaker incentives. In fact, under the welfare arrangements that prevailed before the 1996 reforms, the weakest incentives to work were those faced by families that benefited from welfare. When a welfare recipient got a job, benefits were withdrawn and eligibility for programs like Medicaid ended, so the family in effect paid a tax of more than 100 percent on its earnings. This arrangement locked poor families in a welfare trap.

So the scale and methods of income redistribution must pay close attention to the incentive effects of taxes and benefits. Let's look at the way lawmakers are tackling the big tradeoff today.

A Major Welfare Challenge

The poorest people in the United States (see pp. 367–368) are young women who have not completed high school, have a child (or children), live without a partner, and are more likely black or Hispanic than white. These young women and their children present a major welfare challenge.

First, their numbers are large. In 1992 (the most recent year for which census data are available), there were 10 million single-mother families. This number is almost 30 percent of families with never-married children under 21. In 1991 (again the most recent year with census data), these families were owed $18 billion in child support. Of this amount, $6 billion was not paid and a quarter of the women received no support from their absent partners.

The long-term solution to the poverty problem that these people face is education and job training—acquiring human capital. The short-term solution is welfare. But welfare must be designed to minimize the disincentive to pursue the long-term goal. This is what the current welfare program in the United States tries to do.

Passed in 1996, *The Personal Responsibility and Work Opportunities Reconciliation Act* created the Temporary Assistance for Needy Families (TANF) program. TANF is a block grant paid to the states to administer payments to individuals. It is not an open-ended entitlement program. An adult member of a family receiving assistance must either work or perform community service. And there is a five-year limit for assistance.

These measures go a long way toward removing some serious poverty problems while being sensitive to the potential inefficiency of welfare. But they don't go as far as some economists want to go. Let's look at a more radical reform of welfare: the negative income tax.

Negative Income Tax

A negative income tax is *not* on the political agenda. But it is popular among economists, and it is the subject of several real-world experiments.

A **negative income tax** gives every family a *guaranteed minimum annual income* and taxes *all* income above the guaranteed minimum at a fixed *marginal tax rate*. Suppose the guaranteed minimum annual income is $10,000 and the marginal tax rate is 25 percent. A family with no market income receives the $10,000 guaranteed minimum income from the government. This family "pays" income tax of *minus* $10,000, hence the name *negative* income tax. A family with a market income of $40,000 also receives the $10,000 guaranteed minimum income from the government. But it also pays $10,000—25 percent of its market income—to the government. So this family pays no income tax. It has the break-even income. Families with a market income of between zero and $40,000 "pay" a negative income tax. They receive more from the government than they pay. A family with a market income of $60,000 receives the $10,000 guaranteed minimum income from the government, but it pays $15,000—25 percent of its market income—to the government. So this family pays income tax of $5,000. All families with incomes greater than $40,000 pay income tax to the government.

Figure 17.6 illustrates a negative income tax and compares it with our pre-1996 arrangements. In both parts of the figure, the horizontal axis measures *market income* and the vertical axis measures income *after* taxes are paid and benefits are received. The 45° line shows the hypothetical case of "no redistribution."

FIGURE 17.6

Comparing Traditional Programs and a Negative Income Tax

(a) Current redistribution arrangements

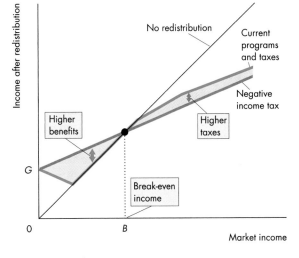

(b) A negative income tax

Part (a) shows traditional redistribution arrangements—the blue curve. Benefits of *G* are paid to those with no income. As incomes increase from zero to *A*, benefits are withdrawn, *lowering* income after redistribution below *G* and creating a welfare trap—the gray triangle. As incomes increase from *A* to *C*, there is no redistribution. As incomes increase above *C*, income taxes are paid at successively higher rates.

In part (b), a negative income tax gives a guaranteed annual income of *G* and decreases benefits at the same rate as the tax rate on incomes. The red line shows how market incomes translate into income after redistribution. Families with market incomes below *B*, the break-even income, receive net benefits. Those with market incomes above *B* pay net taxes.

Part (a) shows traditional redistribution arrangements—the blue curve. Benefits of *G* are paid to those with no income. As incomes increase from zero to *A*, benefits are withdrawn. This arrangement creates a *welfare trap*, shown as the gray triangle. It does not pay a person to work if the income he or she can earn is less than *A*. Over the income range *A* to *C*, each additional dollar of market income increases income after redistribution by a dollar. At incomes greater than *C*, income taxes are paid and at successively higher rates, so income after redistribution is smaller than market income.

Part (b) shows the negative income tax. The guaranteed annual income is *G*, and the break-even income is *B*. Families with market incomes below *B* receive an additional net benefit (blue area), and those with incomes above *B* pay additional taxes (red area). A negative income tax removes the welfare trap and gives greater encouragement to low-income families to seek more employment, even at a low

wage. It also overcomes many of the other problems arising from existing income maintenance programs.

R E V I E W   Q U I Z

- What are the four methods that governments in the United States use to redistribute income?
- How large is the scale of redistribution in the United States?
- What is the major welfare challenge and how is it being tackled in the United States today?
- What problem is a negative income tax designed to solve? Why don't we have a negative income tax?

Health and the cost of health care are major sources of inequality, and we now study the economics of health care and health-care reform.

Health-Care Reform

EXPENDITURE PER PERSON ON HEALTH CARE IS greater in the United States than in any other country. Also, the percentage of total income spent on health care in the United States exceeds that of any other country. An American who has a good job and the comprehensive health insurance that goes with it enjoys a high degree of security and receives the highest-quality health care. Let's look at the scale of spending on health care and at who does the spending.

Total spending on health care in the United States was 14 percent of total income in 1998 and, at its current trend, would reach 20 percent of total income by the early 2000s. The government meets 47 percent of the total health-care cost, and this share has increased from 25 percent in 1965, as Fig. 17.7

FIGURE 17.7

Who Pays for Health Care?

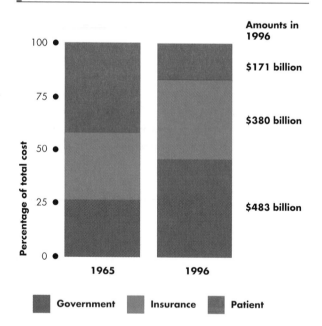

Government pays 47 percent of the total cost of health care, up from 26 percent in 1965. The direct payments by patients declined from 42 percent of the total in 1965 to 17 percent in 1996.

Source: U.S. Bureau of the Census, *Statistical Abstract of the United States: 1998,* 118th edition, Table 164.

shows. The government's share of the cost is made up of its expenditures on Medicare and Medicaid ($356 billion in 1996) and the premiums it pays to private health-care insurance companies for government employees. The other 53 percent of the cost of health care is met by private health-care insurance (up from 25 percent of total payments in 1965 to 37 percent in 1991) and by direct payments by patients (*down* from 42 percent of total payments in 1965 to 17 percent in 1996).

Despite our large commitment of resources and our high quality of care, many people perceive health care in the United States to be in crisis. Why? There are two main problem areas:

1. Health-care costs appear to be out of control.
2. Private health-care insurance does not cover everyone.

Let's take a closer look at these problems.

Problem of Health-Care Costs

Health-care costs have increased more rapidly than consumer prices, on the average, as Fig. 17.8 shows. Two separate factors create the gap between the rate of increase in health-care costs and average price increases: the health-care cost gap.

First, health care is a labor-intensive personal service with limited scope for labor-saving technological change. Health-care labor costs—wage rates of medical workers from surgeons to janitors—generally increase at a faster rate than do average prices, and because there is limited scope for labor-saving changes in health-care technology, these higher labor costs are reflected in higher costs for the final health-care product.

Second, the main effect of the technological change that does take place in health care is to improve the quality of the product. For example, the applications of computer technology and advances in drugs have broadened the range of conditions that can be treated. But the cost of using new technologies to treat previously untreatable conditions steadily rises. Both sources of the health-care cost gap can be expected to persist.

Figure 17.9 shows the market for health care. Initially (say in 1980), the demand curve was D_0, the supply curve was S_0, the quantity was Q_0, and the price was P_0. Increasing incomes, longer life spans, and advances in the medical conditions that can be treated increase the demand for health-care

The Rising Cost of Health Care

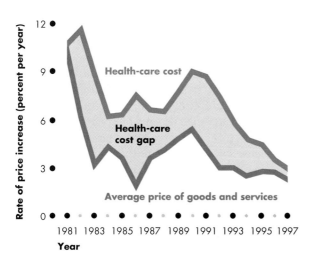

The cost of health care has increased much faster than the average price of other goods and services. The reasons are that health care is a labor-intensive industry—a personal service industry—so labor costs increase and quality improvements have changed the nature of the product and increased its cost.

Source: Statistical Abstract of the United States: 1998, 118th edition Table 179.

The Market for Health Care

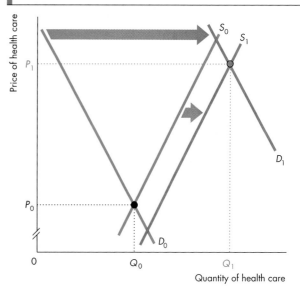

Initially (say in 1980), demand was D_0, supply was S_0, the quantity was Q_0, and the price was P_0. Increasing incomes and technological advances that expand the range of conditions that can be treated increase demand and shift the demand curve rightward to D_1. Advancing technology also increases supply, but increasing wages and more costly equipment and drugs counteract this increase in supply. The net result is that the supply curve shifts rightward to S_1. The quantity increases by a moderate amount, to Q_1, and the price increases steeply, to P_1.

services, and the demand curve shifts rightward from D_0 to D_1. Technological advances in health care have increased supply of health-care services. But the increase in supply is smaller than the increase in demand because some factors have worked to decrease supply. One of these factors is the increasing wage rates of health-care workers; another is the increasing cost of ever more sophisticated health-care technologies. The net effect of the positive and negative influences on supply is a rightward shift in the supply curve to S_1. The quantity of health care has increased to Q_1—and the price has risen to P_1—a relatively large increase.

The forces at work that produce the changes shown in Fig. 17.9 do not appear to be temporary, and they may be expected to bring similar changes in the future.

Health-Care Insurance

More than 50 percent of the health-care dollar is spent on less than 10 percent of the population. Another 30 percent is spent on 20 percent of the population. Health-care spending on the healthiest 70 percent of people is less than 20 percent of total health-care cost.

Because the costs are high and the frequency of use is low, most people choose to finance their health care by insurance. But health-care insurance, like all types of insurance, faces two problems: *moral hazard* and *adverse selection*.[1] Moral hazard in health insurance is the tendency for people who are covered by

---

[1] These problems and other aspects of insurance are explained more fully in Chapter 21, pp. 453–454.

insurance to use more health services or to be less careful about avoiding health risks than they otherwise would. Adverse selection in health insurance is the tendency for people who know they have a greater chance than the average of falling ill to be the ones most likely to buy health insurance.

For example, a person might buy insurance only a few days before going on a ski trip to Colorado (adverse selection). Covered by insurance, this person makes a faster run down the ski slope, knowing that the cost of fixing a broken ankle will be borne, in part, by the insurance company (moral hazard).

But the main adverse selection and moral hazard problems do not arise from reckless young skiers. They arise from the decisions of cautious physicians who elect to perform tests and procedures that are demanded by equally cautious patients only because someone else is paying for them.

Insurance companies set their premium levels sufficiently high to cover claims arising from people who have been adversely selected and who face moral hazard. But to attract profitable business from low-risk customers, insurance companies give preference to the healthy and employed. They also limit the coverage of preexisting conditions and claims arising from major illness. The result is that many people are uninsured or are insured for minor problems but not for catastrophic illness.

Reform Proposals

Health-care reform is a major political issue. Almost always, when some feature of the economy is not working the way people want it to, some people reach the conclusion that the government must step in to deal with the problem and others reach the opposite conclusion and identify existing government intervention as the source of the problem. So it is with health care. We'll end our brief study of the economics of health care by examining a range of alternative proposals for improving the performance of the health-care sector.

A Bigger Role for Government? The world is rich in examples of health-care systems in which government plays a major role. The most complete such example is next door, in Canada.

Each province of Canada (a province is a bit like a state) administers a comprehensive health insurance program. The resources that the health-care sector

uses are paid for by taxes. Some of these taxes are called Health Insurance Contributions, but funds from the general income tax are also used to pay the health-care bill.

The government is the sole provider of health-care services. It runs the hospitals, pays the doctors and other health-care professionals, and buys drugs for people with low incomes. People choose their family doctor, but the family doctor assigns people to specialists and hospitals.

Private health care is illegal in Canada. No one is permitted to offer services outside the government program, and no health-care provider is permitted to charge a fee greater than the one prescribed by the government. Doctors ration procedures for which there is an excess demand by lengthening waiting lines.

The wealthiest Canadians bypass the government system by purchasing health-care services in the United States (and occasionally Europe). Other Canadians complain but put up with services that are becoming more inadequate.

Britain and Australia are two other countries that are famed for their government-operated health care systems. In each of these countries, the government provides tax-funded health care at a zero price (or very low price) to anyone who demands it. At the same time, private insurers, doctors, and hospitals compete with the government sector. In Australia, people are provided with a tax incentive to buy private insurance and, in effect, opt out of the state scheme.

If health care is operated as a branch of government and financed with taxes, tax rates must continually rise to pay for the health care that people demand. There are two reasons why taxes must keep rising. First, as our incomes increase, we choose to spend a larger proportion of income on health. (Health care has a high *income elasticity* of demand.) Second, advances in health-care technology keep expanding the range of feasible treatments. But the cost of new technologies does not fall as quickly as our demand to use them rises. The combination of these factors means that if the government is to be the sole provider of health-care services, taxes must forever keep rising.

Make the Private Health-Care Market Work Better?
Many Republicans want to scale back the federal government's funding of health-care services. Proposals have been made to cut the projected increase by $270 billion from Medicare over a seven-year period. People who can afford to buy their own health care would no longer be eligible for Medicare, and people

would be given incentives to switch from high-cost fee-for-service providers to lower-cost managed-care providers.

The hope is that by cutting the scale of public expenditure, health-care costs would rise less quickly. There is evidence that this is a realistic hope. Removing the effects of inflation, the cost of Medicaid and Medicare has increased more than fourfold since 1970, while the cost of private health care has less than doubled.

By providing tax incentives that encourage employers to buy medical insurance, the government has made the private part of health care less efficient. Although *employers* buy medical insurance, it is the *employees* who pay for it. The compensation package, which consists of wages plus medical insurance, is determined by the forces of demand and supply. The amount that employers spend buying medical insurance is subtracted from the total compensation to determine the amount to be paid as wages.

But the income tax laws interact with employer-provided medical insurance to create a big problem. Employees pay income tax on their wages but not on the value of their medical insurance. So suppose a firm and its workers are negotiating a new compensation package. Will wages rise by $100 per employee, or will medical insurance premiums rise by $100 per employee to improve the quality of medical insurance? (Improved medical insurance might take the form of a lower deductible or a wider coverage.)

If a firm's labor cost is going to increase by $100 per employee, the firm doesn't care whether it pays the $100 in higher wages or in improved health insurance. But the employees care. Because wages are taxed, an extra $100 in wages translates into around $60 in disposable income. So employees must compare the value of improved health insurance that costs $100 with an additional $60 of disposable income. If the value employees place on improved medical insurance that costs $100 exceeds $60, they will opt for the insurance rather than the higher wages. If employers were not permitted to shelter the benefits from income tax in this way, wages would be higher and people would decide for themselves how much medical insurance coverage to buy.

There would be a strengthened incentive to buy insurance at a lower cost with a larger deductible and smaller range of coverage. With a larger deductible, people would have a stronger incentive to economize on medical treatments and the moral hazard and adverse selection problems would be lessened.

But the fundamental problem is that rising health-care costs stem from forces that are going to persist. Advances in health-care technology can be expected to keep the demand for health care increasing briskly. And the increasing cost of applying new medical technologies and steadily rising wage rates for skilled health-care workers can be expected to keep supply growing more slowly than demand. The result: The price that balances the quantities demanded and supplied will continue to increase faster than the average rise in prices.

REVIEW QUIZ

- What are the main problems with health care in the United States?
- Why do health-care costs increase more quickly than average prices?
- What are the *moral hazard* and *adverse selection* problems faced by providers of health insurance? Provide some examples of each.
- How do some other countries deal with health care? Do they offer any lessons to the United States?
- How might the market for health care be made to work better in the United States?

We've examined economic inequality in the United States, and we've seen that there is a large amount of inequality across families and individuals. Some of that inequality arises from comparing families at different stages in the life cycle. But even if we take a lifetime view, inequality remains. Some of that inequality arises from differences in wage rates. And economic choices accentuate those differences.

We've also seen that inequality has been increasing. *Reading Between the Lines* on pages 380–381 looks at the widening gap between the rich and the poor in the United States today.

We've seen that actions in the political marketplace redistribute income to alleviate the worst aspects of poverty. Our next task is to look more fully at the ways in which government actions modify the outcome of the market economy. We look at sources of market failure and the ways in which government actions aim to overcome it. We also look at what is called the political marketplace and the potential for it to fail too.

The Changing Income Distribution

THE NEW YORK TIMES, JANUARY 4, 1999

... *Problems Tarnishing a Robust Economy*

BY MICHAEL M. WEINSTEIN

It might seem churlish to find fault with a best-in-a-generation economy. Unemployment and inflation rates are at record lows, and low-paid workers are, for the first time in decades, receiving wage increases that outpace price increases. But despite the benefits of a temporarily buoyant economy, deep-seated problems remain.

Frank Levy, an economist at the Massachusetts Institute of Technology, notes that the best time to tackle problems is when the economy is flush. He points to increasing inequality at a time of stagnating wages in his new book, "The New Dollars and Dreams" (Russell Sage Foundation, 1998). Borrowing a phrase from Sen. Daniel Patrick Moynihan, D-N.Y., Levy warns against "defining deviancy down—accepting economic outcomes as normal today that would have been seen as pathological 10 or 20 years ago." ...

A study by Sheldon Danziger of the University of Michigan shows that from 1969 to 1997, when the earnings of college graduates rose briskly, the inflation-adjusted median earnings of white male high-school graduates 25 to 34 fell nearly 30 percent. An economy that was supposed to lift everyone to new highs of income and consumption instead pushed the least skilled workers down.

Danziger points to a stunning statistic: the earnings of these less skilled white workers fell so far that they earned less in 1997 than their black counterparts, a notoriously underpaid group, had earned almost 30 years earlier. And those black male high-school graduates fared almost as badly. From 1969 to 1997, their inflation-adjusted earnings fell 25 percent.

Levy's data show that the richest one-half of 1 percent of American taxpayers account for about 11 percent of aggregate income, and about 5 percent of households take home 20 percent of total income. The share of income captured by the bottom 60 percent of households is falling. Only college graduates, about a quarter of the work force, are racking up significant wage gains.

There is substantial evidence that the nature of technology in an information-intensive era is stacked in favor of workers with college-level verbal and math skills. That leaves at least half of the work force behind.

Essence of the Story

■ Sheldon Danziger of the University of Michigan says that from 1969 to 1997, the earnings of college graduates rose quickly but the inflation-adjusted earnings of white male high-school graduates were less in 1997 than the earnings of black male high-school graduates in 1969.

■ Frank Levy of MIT says that the richest ½ percent of American taxpayers earn 11 percent of total income, 5 percent of households earn 20 percent of total income, and the income share of the bottom 60 percent of households is falling.

■ Only people with college degrees are experiencing significant wage increases.

■ Technology in the information-intensive age favors workers with college-level verbal and math skills.

■ Figure 1 shows the Lorenz curve suggested by the news article (and other data in Fig. 17.1 on p. 366). The curve shows great inequality, even among the rich.

■ Figure 2 shows why the incomes of high school graduates have fallen. In 1969, the supply curve was S_{69} and the demand curve was D_{69}. The market was in equilibrium at quantity Q_0 and annual wages of $10,000.

■ Between 1969 and 1997, an increase in the population increased the supply of high school graduate labor. The supply curve shifted rightward to S_{97}.

■ The demand for high school graduate labor also increased but by a small amount. The increase in demand was small because advances in technology displaced high school graduate labor with machines. The demand curve shifted rightward to D_{97}.

■ In 1997, the market for high school graduate labor was in equilibrium at a wage of $7,000 a year (adjusted for inflation).

■ Figure 3 shows why the incomes of college graduates increased during recent years.

■ The technological advances that have decreased the demand for high school graduate labor have increased the demand for college graduates. The demand curve shifted rightward from D_{69} to D_{97}.

■ The increase in population and the increase in the number of people completing college have increased the supply of college graduates. But the increase in supply was smaller than the increase in demand. The supply curve shifted rightward from S_{69} to S_{97}.

■ The equilibrium wage rate of college graduates increased from $50,000 to $70,000 a year (adjusted for inflation).

■ The wage gap between the two groups will begin to narrow if high school graduates acquire more skills and if further technological change increases the demand for high school graduates.

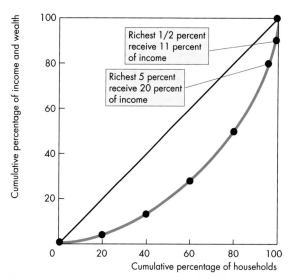

Figure 1 Great inequality, even among the rich

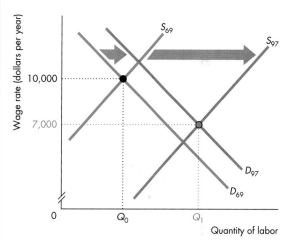

Figure 2 The market for high school graduates

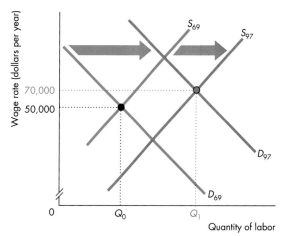

Figure 3 The market for college graduates

381

SUMMARY

KEY POINTS

Economic Inequality in the United States (pp. 366–368)

- The richest 1 percent of Americans own almost one third of the total wealth in the country.
- Income is distributed less unevenly than wealth. Throughout the 1970s, 1980s, and 1990s, inequality increased.
- The poorest people in the United States are single black women over 65 years of age with less than eight years of schooling who live in the South. The richest people live in the West and are college-educated, middle-aged, white families in which husband and wife live together.

Comparing Like with Like (p. 369)

- The distribution of wealth exaggerates the degree of inequality because it excludes human capital.
- The distributions of annual income and wealth exaggerate lifetime inequality because they do not take the life cycle into account.

Resource Prices, Endowments, and Choices (pp. 370–371)

- Differences in income and wealth arise from differences in resource prices, endowments, and choices.
- People who face high wage rates generally work longer than those who face low wage rates, so the distribution of income becomes more unequal and more skewed than the distribution of wage rates.

Income Redistribution (pp. 372–375)

- Governments redistribute income through income taxes, income maintenance programs, and provision of subsidized services.
- Income taxes are progressive.
- Redistribution creates a "big tradeoff" between equity and efficiency, which arises because the process of redistribution uses resources and weakens incentives to work and save.

- Traditional income maintenance programs create a welfare trap that discourages work, so poverty is persistent. Reforms seek to lessen the severity of the welfare trap. A more radical negative income tax reform would encourage people on welfare to find work.

Health-Care Reform (pp. 376–379)

- Total spending on health care in the United States is 14 percent of total income (45 percent met by the government, 35 percent by private insurance payments, and 20 percent by direct payments by patients.)
- Health-care costs have increased more rapidly than consumer prices.
- Health-care insurance faces moral hazard—the tendency for people who are insured to take greater risks—and adverse selection—the tendency for people with the greatest chance of making an insurance claim to be the ones who buy insurance.
- Some people suggest that health-care reform requires greater government intervention, as in Canada, Britain, and Australia; others say that market forces need strengthening.

KEY FIGURES

KEY TERMS

PROBLEMS

*1. You are provided with the following information about income shares in an economy:

Percentage of households	Income shares (percent)
Lowest 20%	5
Second 20%	11
Third 20%	17
Fourth 20%	24
Highest 20%	43

a. Draw the Lorenz curve for income in this economy.

b. Compare the distribution of income in this economy with that in the United States. Is U.S. income distributed more equally or less equally than that in the economy described in the table?

2. You are provided with the following information about wealth shares in an economy:

Percentage of households	Wealth shares (percent)
Lowest 20%	0
Second 20%	1
Third 20%	3
Fourth 20%	11
Highest 20%	85

a. Draw the Lorenz curve for wealth in this economy.

b. Compare the distribution of wealth in this economy with that in the United States. Is U.S. wealth distributed more equally or less equally than that in the economy described in the table?

c. Explain which of the two variables—income in problem 1 or wealth in problem 2—is more unequally distributed.

*3. Imagine an economy with five people who are identical in all respects. Each lives for 70 years. For the first 14 of those years, they earn no income. For the next 35 years, they work and earn $30,000 a year from their work. For their remaining years, they are retired and have no income from labor. To make the arithmetic easy, let's suppose that the interest rate in this economy is zero; the individuals consume all their income during their lifetime and at a constant annual rate. What are the distributions of income and wealth in this economy if the individuals have the following ages:

a. All are 45

b. 25, 35, 45, 55, 65

Does case (a) have greater inequality than case (b)?

4. In the economy described in problem 3, there is a "baby boom." Two people who were born in the same year are now 25. One person is 35, one is 45, one is 55, and no one is 65. What are the distributions of income and wealth:

a. This year?

b. 10 years in the future?

c. 20 years in the future?

d. 30 years in the future?

e. 40 years in the future?

f. Comment on and explain the changes in the distributions of income and wealth in this economy.

*5. An economy consists of 10 people, each of whom has the following labor supply schedule:

Wage rate (dollars per hour)	Hours worked per day
1	1
2	2
3	4
4	6
5	8

The people differ in ability and earn different wage rates. The distribution of *wage rates* is as follows:

Wage rate (dollars per hour)	Number of people
1	1
2	2
3	4
4	2
5	1

a. Calculate the average wage rate.

b. Calculate the ratio of the highest to the lowest wage rate.

c. Calculate the average daily income.

d. Calculate the ratio of the highest to the lowest daily income.

e. Sketch the distribution of hourly wage rates.

f. Sketch the distribution of daily incomes.

g. What important lesson is illustrated by this problem?

6. In the economy described in problem 5, the productivity of low-skilled labor falls and that of high-skilled labor rises. Consequently, the distribution of *wage rates* changes to the following:

Wage rate (dollars per hour)	Number of people
0	1
1	2
3	4
5	2
6	1

The labor supply schedule is the same as in problem 5. For this changed situation:
a. Calculate the average wage rate.
b. Calculate the ratio of the highest to the lowest wage rate.
c. Calculate the average daily income.
d. Calculate the ratio of the highest to the lowest daily income.
e. Sketch the distribution of hourly wage rates.
f. Sketch the distribution of daily incomes.
g. What important lesson is illustrated by comparing the economy in this problem with the one in problem 5?

*7. The table shows the distribution of market income in an economy.

Percentage of households	Income (millions of dollars)
Lowest 20%	5
Second 20%	10
Third 20%	18
Fourth 20%	28
Highest 20%	39

The government redistributes income by collecting income taxes and paying benefits shown in the following table:

Percentage of households	Income taxes (percent of income)	Benefits (millions of dollars)
Lowest 20%	0	10
Second 20%	10	8
Third 20%	15	3
Fourth 20%	20	0
Highest 20%	30	0

a. Draw the Lorenz curve for this economy after taxes and benefits.
b. Is the scale of redistribution of income in this economy greater or smaller than in the United States?

8. In the economy described in problem 7, the government replaces its existing taxes and benefits with a negative income tax. What changes do you expect to occur in the economy?

CRITICAL THINKING

1. Study *Reading Between the Lines* on pp. 380-381, and then:
   a. Describe the main facts about the distribution of income reported in the news article.
   b. Explain how you think the tax system and the welfare system change the situation described in the news article?
   c. Use the link on the Parkin Web site to visit the Employment Policy Foundation and read the article on "tracking 'same families' over time." How does what you learn here change your interpretation of the news article?

2. Use the link on the Parkin Web site to visit the U.S. Census Bureau. Obtain data on poverty and income distribution for your own state (or county if the data are available). Then:
   a. Describe the main facts about poverty and the distribution of income in your state (county).
   b. Compare the situation in your state (county) with that in the rest of the country.
   c. Explain why you think your state (county) is performing better/worse than the nation as a whole?

3. Use the link on the Parkin Web site to visit the National Governors' Association. Obtain information on *The Personal Responsibility and Work Opportunity Reconciliation Act* of 1996. Then describe and evaluate the Act. In what ways do you think the 1996 law improves on the programs that it replaces?

Understanding Resource Markets

For Whom?

During the past 35 years, the rich have been getting richer and the poor poorer. This trend is new. From the end of World War II until 1965, the poor got richer at a faster pace than the rich and the gap between rich and poor narrowed a bit. What are the forces that generate these trends? The answer to this question is the forces of demand and supply in resource markets. These forces determine wages, interest rates, and the prices of land and natural resources. These forces also determine people's incomes. ◆ The three categories of resources are human, capital, and natural. Human resources include labor, human capital, and entrepreneurship. The income of labor and human capital depends on wage rates and employment levels, which are determined in labor markets. The income from capital depends on interest rates and the amount of capital, which are determined in capital markets. The income from natural resources depends on prices and quantities that are determined in natural resource markets. Only the return to entrepreneurship is not determined directly in a market. That return is normal profit plus economic profit, and it depends on how successful each entrepreneur is in the business that he or she runs. ◆ The chapters in this part study the forces at play in resource markets and explain how those forces have led to changes in the distribution of income. ◆ The overview of all the resource markets in Chapter 15 explained how the demand for resources results from the profit-maximizing decisions of firms. You studied these decisions from a different angle in Chapters 10–14, where you learned how firms choose their profit-maximizing output and price. Chapter 15 explained how a firm's profit-maximizing decisions determine its demand for productive resources. It also explained how resource supply decisions are made and how equilibrium in resource markets determines resource prices and the incomes of resource owners. ◆ Some of the biggest incomes earned by superstars are a surplus that we call *economic rent*. ◆ Chapter 15 used labor resources and the labor market as its main example. But it also looked at some special features of capital markets and natural resource markets. ◆ Chapter 16 looked more closely at the labor market and studied the main sources of differences among people's wages. ◆ Chapter 17 studied the distribution of income. This chapter took you right back to the fundamentals of economics and answered one of the big economic questions: Who gets to consume the goods and services that are produced? ◆ Many outstanding economists have advanced our understanding of resource markets and the role they play in helping to resolve the conflict between the demands of humans and the resources available. One of them is Thomas Robert Malthus, whom you can meet on the following page. You can also enjoy the insights of Claudia Goldin, a professor of economics at Harvard University and a prominent contemporary labor economist.

The Economist

Thomas Robert Malthus

(1766–1834), an English clergyman and economist, was an extremely influential social scientist. In his best-selling Essay on the Principle of Population, *published in 1798, he predicted that population growth would outstrip food production and said that wars, famine, and disease were inevitable unless population growth was held in check by what he called "moral restraint." By "moral restraint," he meant marrying at a late age and living a celibate life. He married at the age of 38 a wife of 27, marriage ages that he recommended for others. Malthus's ideas were regarded as too radical in their day. And they led Thomas Carlyle, a contemporary thinker, to dub economics the "dismal science." But the ideas of Malthus had a profound influence on Charles Darwin, who got the key idea that led him to the theory of natural selection from reading the* Essay on the Principle of Population. *And David Ricardo and the classical economists were strongly influenced by Malthus's ideas.*

"The passion between the sexes has appeared in every age to be so nearly the same, that it may always be considered, in algebraic language as a given quantity."

THOMAS ROBERT MALTHUS
An Essay on the Principle of Population

The Issues

Is there a limit to economic growth, or can we expand production and population without effective limit? Thomas Malthus gave one of the most influential answers to these questions in 1798. He reasoned that population, unchecked, would grow at a geometric rate—1, 2, 4, 8, 16 … —while the food supply would grow at an arithmetic rate—1, 2, 3, 4, 5 … . To prevent the population from outstripping the available food supply, there would be periodic wars, famines, and plagues. In Malthus's view, only what he called moral restraint could prevent such periodic disasters.

As industrialization proceeded through the nineteenth century, Malthus's idea came to be applied to all natural resources, especially those that are exhaustible.

Modern-day Malthusians believe that his basic idea is correct and that it applies not only to food but also to every natural resource. In time, these prophets of doom believe, we will be reduced to the subsistence level that Malthus predicted. He was a few centuries out in his predictions but not dead wrong.

One modern-day Malthusian is ecologist Paul Ehrlich, who believes that we are sitting on a "population bomb." Governments must, says Ehrlich, limit both population growth and the resources that may be used each year.

In 1931, Harold Hotelling developed a theory of natural resources with different predictions from those of Malthus. The Hotelling Principle is that the relative price of an exhaustible natural resources will steadily rise, bringing a decline in the quantity used and an increase in the use of substitute resources.

Julian Simon (who died in 1998) challenged both the Malthusian gloom and the Hotelling Principle. He believed that people are the "ultimate resource" and predicted that a rising population lessens the pressure on natural resources. A bigger population provides a larger number of resourceful people who can work out more efficient ways of using scarce resources. As these solutions are found, the prices of exhaustible resources actually fall. To demonstrate his point, in 1980, Simon bet Ehrlich that the prices of five metals—copper, chrome, nickel, tin, and tungsten—would fall during the 1980s. Simon won the bet!

Then

No matter whether it is agricultural land, an exhaustible natural resource, or the space in the center of Chicago, and no matter whether it is 1998 or, as shown here, 1892, there is a limit to what is available, and we persistently push against that limit. Economists see urban congestion as a consequence of the value of doing business in the city center relative to the cost. They see the price mechanism, bringing ever-higher rents and prices of raw materials, as the means of allocating and rationing scarce natural resources. Malthusians, in contrast, explain congestion as the consequence of population pressure, and they see population control as the solution.

Now

In Tokyo, the pressure on space is so great that in some residential neighborhoods, a parking space costs $1,700 a month. To economize on this expensive space—and to lower the cost of car ownership and hence boost the sale of new cars—Honda, Nissan, and Toyota, three of Japan's big car producers, have developed a parking machine that enables two cars to occupy the space of one. The most basic of these machines costs a mere $10,000—less than 6 months' parking fees.

Malthus developed his ideas about population growth in a world in which women played a limited role in the economy. Malthus did not consider the opportunity cost of women's time a factor to be considered in predicting trends in the birth rate and population growth. But today, the opportunity cost of women's time is a crucial factor because women play an expanded role in the labor force. One woman who has made significant contributions to our knowledge of labor markets and the role of women in those markets is Claudia Goldin. You can meet Professor Goldin on the following pages.

Talking with

Claudia Goldin, *born in New York City, was an undergraduate at Cornell University and a graduate student at the University of Chicago, where she obtained her Ph.D. in 1972. Now Professor of Economics at Harvard University and Program Director at the National Bureau of Economic Research, Dr. Goldin is one of the world's foremost scholars. Her work combines economic history and labor economics and has investigated a wide range of important problems such as slavery in the American South, strategic factors in American economic development during the nineteenth century, and the evolution of labor markets during the twentieth century. She has studied the effects of technological change and the role of women in the labor market. Not only a brilliant research economist, Professor Goldin has received honors for her undergraduate teaching.*

Michael Parkin talked with Professor Goldin about her research and about trends in the U.S. labor markets.

Professor Goldin, why and how did you get into economics?
I entered Cornell University from the Bronx High School of Science intending to be a microbiologist, but I first wanted to acquire a strong liberal arts education. Economics appealed to me because of its rigor, its internal

Claudia Goldin

consistency, and, most of all, its relevance. But only after I took economics from Fred Kahn (who later, as head of the Civil Aeronautics Board, deregulated the airline industry) did I decide to major in the subject. I traded the laboratory of the scientist for that of the social scientist. Ours, I should add, is more challenging because we have to devise controlled experiments from already existing data.

In 1896, 18 percent of women were in the labor force; in 1996, 58 percent were in the labor force. What have been the driving forces behind this substantial change?
In 1896, most of the 18 percent were young, single, foreign-born, and black. Women generally worked for pay only before they married, although black women and poor women worked regardless of their marital status and age. In 1896, fewer than 5 percent of all married women were in the paid labor force. Therefore the question is why have married and adult women entered the labor force in such large numbers in the past 100 years. Contrary to popular opinion, the first large increase in married women's employment did not occur during the resurgence of feminism in the late 1960s, nor did it occur among the younger age groups. The large initial movement into the labor force occurred during the 1940s and 1950s among women older than 40 years. A host of long-run factors had been operating to reduce the time demands of women in their homes. These include the markedly reduced birth rate and the appearance of market goods substituting for those produced within the home, such as factory-made bread and clothing.

How do you explain the timing and the extent of the explosion in women's employment?

It was rooted in two changes earlier in the century. Between 1915 and 1930, the proportion of all Americans graduating from high school vastly increased, and at the same time, there was a surge in the demand for educated labor in the burgeoning clerical and sales sectors. Young women entered these jobs in droves in the 1920s but generally exited when they married. After World War II, rising wages and an increased demand

for labor drew these women back into the labor force. Younger married women were raising the baby boom of the 1950s and were less willing to trade the household for the marketplace. The shift of employment from manufacturing to office and sales work from 1920 to 1950 was an important factor in enabling adult and married women to work for pay. And the generation of older women in the 1950s, who had the requisite education for these jobs, was ripe for this monumental change in employment. They, not the young

women of their era, were the real pioneers in women's employment. But the trailblazers did not view these changes as part of a larger social movement.

In the 1970s and 1980s, younger women greatly increased their participation in the labor force, and in the 1980s, even women with infants expanded their employment. In short, rising real wages, falling relative prices of market substitutes for home-produced goods, a declining demand for goods within the home, and a shift of jobs from blue collar to white collar led women to enter the labor force. But the timing of the changes suggests that various norms and institutional rigidities had to be broken down for the long-run forces to operate. These were accomplished first during the 1940s and 1950s.

What have we learned from your work and the work of other labor economists about the sources of persistent wage differences between men and women?

From the mid-1950s to 1980, the ratio of female to male full-time, weekly (median) earnings was constant at about 0.60. Women as a group made little if any noticeable progress relative to men. But from 1981 to the present, the ratio increased by approximately 16 percentage points to 0.76. The analysis of the period of stability and the subsequent period of a narrowing gap reveals much about the sources of gender differences in earnings. The factors that economists group under the heading of "human capital" are most relevant. When working women's job expe-

rience and education advanced on those of men, their relative earnings increased, and when these factors remained constant compared with those of men, women's relative earnings were stable. The aspirations and expectations of teenaged girls are another factor. These young women formed far more realistic expectations in the 1970s than in the 1960s, when they severely underestimated their future participation in the labor force. Young women today are in a much better position to prepare themselves for a lifetime of labor market work than were their elders. We also know that in the 1980s, the returns to education and job experience increased for women relative to men. We aren't certain why this has been the case. Some of the increase could be due to better education or women's greater willingness to undertake more demanding jobs. But we cannot dismiss the notion that the labor market became more gender-neutral in the 1980s, and we also cannot dismiss the role of policy interventions in making it so.

What trend do we observe in the wage differences between blacks and whites?

Similar forces have operated over the long run to narrow differences in earnings between white and black males and between white and black females. In 1940, the ratio of the earnings of black men to white men was astoundingly low—0.43—but by 1980, it was 0.73. Among college graduate men about 35 years old, the increase was even greater—from 0.45 in 1940 to 0.81 in 1980. On the average, black women have made greater progress relative to white women than have black men relative to white men.

What caused these extraordinary changes?

There were two compelling factors—educational changes, including advances in the quality of the education of black Americans, and the movement of blacks from the low-wage South to the higher-wage North. But there were critical junctures in this history. Two occurred during World Wars I and II and led to the greater integration of blacks into the white-dominated manufacturing sector and to an enormous migration to the North. The third occurred during the mid-1960s, when the Civil Rights Act led to further inroads by blacks into the higher-wage manufacturing sector. Unfortunately, some of the gains made since World War I were reversed in the 1980s. I don't mean that we have turned the clock back with regard to education and prejudice. The 1980s were a period of widening inequality in which the lower-educated and the manufacturing sector in particular lost a tremendous amount of ground, and black Americans are still disproportionately represented in these two groups.

What have been the main effects of affirmative action programs? Have they helped or hindered the progress of women and minorities?

Affirmative action is a complex doctrine under which federal contractors, that is, firms that sell goods or services to the federal government, have target levels for the hiring and promotion of women and minorities. There are direct effects from affirmative

action programs and, possibly, indirect effects. Most scholarly work has been focused on the direct effects and finds that affirmative action programs have increased the employment and earnings of minorities. There is little evidence, however, that the programs have served to increase the employment and earnings of women. The indirect effects are more difficult to quantify.

Let's look at the economics profession, for example. Far fewer women than men major in economics, so it isn't surprising that women are vastly underrepresented as teachers and researchers in the field. If we want to know whether having more women economics professors would encourage more female undergraduates to major in economics—that is, if there is a "role model effect"—we could test whether female enrollments increase when women teach the basic economics courses, such as principles. If so, we can make a case for affirmative action as a means of increasing the pool of candidates for a field and thus increasing the future employment of the group even in the absence of further affirmative action. Another possible indirect effect has been the subject of considerable controversy and forms the basis of the conservative attack on the programs. It is that women and minorities get hired or promoted under affirmative action when they should not have been. Such actions will then reinforce discriminatory views of women and minorities as being incompetent at particular jobs and can, in addition, make both groups more complacent and less competitive. I know of no hard evidence to substantiate such claims.

What are the most important labor market problems that we don't understand and that the next generation of economists will work on and possibly solve?

A pressing problem today is why the wage structure and distribution of earnings widened so substantially during the past 10 or 15 years. We need to know more about the interaction among education, inherent ability, and new technologies, such as the computer revolution. What makes some individuals more able to adapt while others are left behind? What types of educational and training interventions will help workers make the transition?

> The labor market isn't yet structured or ready for the egalitarian family.

Returning to gender differences in the workplace, I wonder whether the gap in earnings can ever be eliminated, given the structure of jobs and the division of labor in the home. If women are still expected to raise children and do a disproportionate share of household work, they will not advance with men in the labor market. Even if individual husbands and wives would like to create the egalitarian home, the husband is likely to confront considerable problems if he asks his employer for family leave, shorter hours, or a flexible schedule, even at greatly reduced pay. The labor market isn't yet structured or ready for the egalitarian family. I see this restructuring of the workplace as a major issue facing the next generation of labor economists.

Chapter 18

Market Failure and Public Choice

In 1996, the federal, state, and local governments in the United States employed more than 19 million people and spent $2.4 trillion. Independent government agencies employed yet another million people. Do we need this much government? Is government, as conservatives sometimes suggest, too big? Is government "the problem"? Or, despite its enormous size, is government too small to do all the things it must attend to? Is government, as liberals sometimes suggest, not contributing enough to economic life? ◆ Government touches many aspects of our lives. It is present at our birth, supporting the hospitals in which we are born and helping to train the doctors and nurses who deliver us. It is present throughout our education, support-

Government— the Solution or the Problem?

ing schools and colleges and helping to train our teachers. It is present throughout our working lives, taxing our incomes, regulating our work environment, and paying us benefits when we are unemployed. It is present throughout our retirement, paying us a small income and, when we die, taxing our bequests. And government provides services such as the enforcement of law and order and the provision of national defense. But the government does not make all our choices. We decide what work to do, how much to save, and what to spend our income on. Why does the government participate in some aspects of our lives but not others? ◆ Almost everyone, from the poor single mother to the wealthy taxpayer, grumbles about government services. Why is the bureaucracy so unpopular? And what determines the scale on which public services are provided?

◇ We begin our study of governments and markets by describing the government sector and explaining how, in the absence of a government, the market economy fails to achieve an efficient allocation of resources. We also explain how the scale of government is determined.

After studying this chapter, you will be able to:

- Explain how the economic role for government arises from market failure and inequality

- Distinguish between public goods and private goods and explain the free-rider problem

- Explain how the quantity of public goods is determined

- Explain why most of the government's revenue comes from income taxes and why income taxes are progressive

- Explain why some goods are taxed at a much higher rate than others

The Economic Theory of Government

THE ECONOMIC THEORY OF GOVERNMENT SEEKS to predict the economic actions that governments take and the consequences of those actions. Governments exist to help people cope with scarcity and provide a nonmarket mechanism for allocating scarce resources. Four economic problems that governments help people to cope with are:

- Public goods
- Monopoly
- Externalities
- Economic inequality

Public Goods

Some goods and services are consumed either by everyone or by no one. Examples are national defense, law and order, and sewage and waste disposal services. National defense systems cannot isolate individuals and refuse to protect them. Airborne diseases from untreated sewage do not favor some people and hit others. A good or service that is consumed either by everyone or by no one is called a **public good**.

The market economy fails to deliver the efficient quantity of public goods because of a free-rider problem. Everyone tries to free ride on everyone else because the good is available to all whether they pay for it or not. We'll study public goods and the free-rider problem later in this chapter.

Monopoly

Monopoly and *rent seeking* prevent the allocation of resources from being efficient. Every business tries to maximize profit, and when a monopoly exists, it can increase profit by restricting output and increasing price. Until fairly recently, for example, AT&T had a monopoly on long-distance telephone services, and the quantity of long-distance services was much smaller and the price much higher than they are today. Since the breakup of AT&T, the quantity of long-distance calls has exploded.

Some monopolies arise from *legal barriers to entry*—barriers to entry created by governments—but a major activity of government is to regulate

monopoly and to enforce laws that prevent cartels and other restrictions on competition. We study these regulations and laws in Chapter 19.

Externalities

An **externality** is a cost or benefit that arises from an economic transaction and that falls on people who do not participate in that transaction. For example, when a chemical factory (legally) dumps its waste into a river and kills the fish, it imposes an external cost on the members of a fishing club who fish downstream. External costs and benefits are not usually taken into account by the people whose actions create them. For example, when the chemical factory decides whether to dump waste into the river, it does not take the fishing club's views into account. When a homeowner fills her garden with spring bulbs, she generates an external benefit for all the passersby. In deciding how much to spend on this lavish display, she takes into account only the benefits accruing to herself. We study externalities in Chapter 20.

These three problems from which government economic activity arises create an *inefficient* use of resources, a situation called **market failure.** When market failure occurs, the market produces too many of some goods and services and too few of some others. In these cases, the cost of producing a good does not equal the value people place on it. By reallocating resources, it is possible to make some people better off while making no one worse off. So some government activity is an attempt to modify the market outcome so as to moderate the effects of market failure.

Economic Inequality

Government economic activity also arises because an unregulated market economy delivers what most people regard as an unfair distribution of income. To lessen the degree of inequality, governments tax some people and pay benefits to others. You studied inequality and redistribution in Chapter 17. In this chapter, we look further at taxes and try to explain why the income tax is progressive and why some goods are taxed at extremely high rates.

Before we begin to study each of these problems from which government activity arises, let's look at the arena in which governments operate—the "political marketplace."

Public Choice and the Political Marketplace

Government is a complex organization made up of millions of individuals, each with his or her *own* economic objective. Government policy is the outcome of the choices made by these individuals. To analyze these choices, economists have developed a *public choice theory* of the political marketplace. The actors in the political marketplace are:

■ Voters
■ Politicians
■ Bureaucrats

Figure 18.1 illustrates the choices and interactions of these actors. Let's look at each in turn.

Voters Voters are the consumers in the political marketplace. In markets for goods and services, people express their preferences by their willingness to pay. In the political marketplace, they express their preferences by their votes, campaign contributions, and lobbying activity. Public choice theory assumes that people support the policies they believe will make them better off and oppose the policies they believe will make them worse off. It is voters' *perceptions* rather than reality that guide their choices.

Politicians Politicians are the entrepreneurs of the political marketplace. Public choice theory assumes that the objective of a politician is to get elected and to remain in office. Votes to a politician are like economic profit to a firm. To get enough votes, politicians propose policies that they expect will appeal to a majority of voters.

Bureaucrats Bureaucrats are the hired officials in government departments. They are the producers or firms in the political marketplace. Public choice theory assumes that bureaucrats aim to maximize their own utility and that to achieve this objective, they try to maximize the budget of their department.

The bigger the budget of a department, the greater is the prestige of its chief and the larger is the opportunity for promotion for people farther down the bureaucratic ladder. So all the members of a department have an interest in maximizing the department's budget. To maximize their budgets, bureaucrats devise programs that they expect will appeal to politicians and they help politicians to explain their programs to voters.

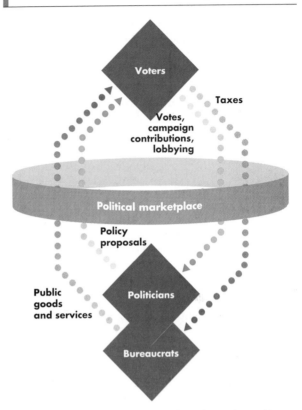

FIGURE 18.1

The Political Marketplace

Voters express their demands for policies by voting, making campaign contributions, and lobbying. Politicians propose policies to appeal to a majority of voters. Bureaucrats try to maximize the budgets of their departments. A political equilibrium emerges in which no group can improve its position by making a different choice.

Political Equilibrium

Voters, politicians, and bureaucrats make choices to best further their own objectives. But each group is constrained by the preferences of the other groups and by what is technologically feasible. The outcome that results from the choices of voters, politicians, and bureaucrats is a **political equilibrium**, which is a situation in which all their choices are compatible and in which no group can improve its position by making a different choice. Let's see how voters, politicians, and bureaucrats interact to determine the quantity of public goods.

Public Goods and the Free-Rider Problem

WHY DOES THE GOVERNMENT PROVIDE GOODS and services such as national defense and public health? Why don't we buy our national defense from North Pole Protection, Inc., a private firm that competes for our dollars in the marketplace in the same way that McDonald's and Coca-Cola do? The answer to these questions lies in the free-rider problem created by public goods. Let's explore this problem. We begin by looking at the nature of a public good.

Public Goods

A *public good* is a good or service that can be consumed simultaneously by everyone and from which no one can be excluded. The first feature of a public good is called nonrivalry. A good is *nonrival* if the consumption by one person does not decrease the consumption by another person. An example is watching a television show. The opposite of nonrival is rival. A good is *rival* if the consumption by one person decreases the consumption by another person. An example is eating a hotdog.

The second feature of a public good is that it is nonexcludable. A good is *nonexcludable* if it is impossible, or extremely costly, to prevent someone from benefiting from a good. An example is national defense. It would be difficult to exclude someone from being defended. The opposite of nonexcludable is excludable. A good is *excludable* if it is possible to prevent a person from enjoying the benefits of a good. An example is cable television. Cable companies can ensure that only those people who have paid the fee receive programs.

Figure 18.2 classifies goods according to these two criteria and gives examples of goods in each category. National defense is a *pure* public good. One person's consumption of the security provided by our national defense system does not decrease the security of someone else—defense is nonrival. And the military cannot select those whom it will protect and those whom it will leave exposed to threats—defense is nonexcludable.

Many goods have a public element but are not pure public goods. An example is a highway. A highway is nonrival until it becomes congested. One more car on a highway with plenty of space does not

FIGURE 18.2
Public Goods and Private Goods

	Rival	Nonrival
Excludable	**Pure private goods** Food Car House	**Excludable and nonrival** Cable television Bridge Highway
Non-excludable	**Nonexcludable and rival** Fish in the ocean Air	**Pure public goods** Lighthouse National defense

A pure public good (bottom right) is one for which consumption is nonrival and from which it is impossible to exclude a consumer. Pure public goods pose a free-rider problem. A pure private good (top left) is one for which consumption is rival and from which consumers can be excluded. Some goods are nonexcludable but are rival (bottom left), and some goods are nonrival but are excludable (top right).

Source: Adapted from and inspired by E. S. Savas, *Privatizing the Public Sector,* Chatham House Publishers, Inc., Chatham, NJ, 1982, p. 34.

reduce anyone else's consumption of transportation services. But once the highway becomes congested, one extra vehicle lowers the quality of the service available to everyone else—it becomes rival like a private good. Also, users can be excluded from a highway by tollgates. Another example is fish in the ocean. Ocean fish are rival because a fish taken by one person is not available for anyone else. Ocean fish are also nonexcludable because it is difficult to prevent people from catching them.

The Free-Rider Problem

Public goods create a free-rider problem. A **free rider** is a person who consumes a good without paying for it. Public goods create a *free-rider problem* because the quantity of the good that a person is able to consume is not influenced by the amount the person pays for the good. So no one has an incentive to pay for a public good. Let's look more closely at the free-rider problem by studying an example.

The Benefit of a Public Good

Suppose that for its defense, a country must launch some surveillance satellites. The benefit provided by a satellite is the *value* of its services. The value of a *private* good is the maximum amount that a *person* is willing to pay for one more unit, which is shown by the person's demand curve. The value of a *public* good is the maximum amount that all the *people* are willing to pay for one more unit of it.

To calculate the value placed on a public good, we use the concepts of total benefit and marginal benefit. *Total benefit* is the dollar value that a person places on a given level of provision of a public good. The greater the quantity of a public good, the larger is a person's total benefit. *Marginal benefit* is the increase in total benefit that results from a one-unit increase in the quantity of a public good.

Figure 18.3 shows the marginal benefit that arises from defense satellites for a society with just two members, Lisa and Max. Lisa's and Max's marginal benefits are graphed as MB_L and MB_M, respectively, in parts (a) and (b) of the figure. The marginal benefit from a public good is similar to the marginal benefit from a private good—its magnitude diminishes as the quantity of the good increases. For Lisa, the marginal benefit from the first satellite is $80, and from the second it is $60. By the time 4 satellites are deployed, Lisa's marginal benefit is zero. For Max, the marginal benefit from the first satellite is $50, and from the second it is $40. By the time 4 satellites are deployed, Max perceives only $10 worth of marginal benefit.

Part (c) shows the economy's marginal benefit curve, *MB*. An individual's marginal benefit curve for a public good is similar to the individual's demand curve for a private good. But the economy's marginal benefit curve for a public good is different from the market demand curve for a private good. To obtain the market demand curve for a private good, we sum the quantities demanded by all individuals at each price—we sum the individual demand curves horizontally (see Chapter 8, p. 165). But to find the economy's marginal benefit curve of a public good, we sum the marginal benefits of each individual at each quantity—we sum the individual marginal benefit curves *vertically*. The resulting marginal benefit for the economy made up of Lisa and Max is the economy's marginal benefit curve graphed in part (c)—the curve *MB*. Lisa's marginal benefit from the first satellite gets added to Max's marginal benefit from the first satellite because they *both* enjoy security from the first satellite.

FIGURE 18.3

Benefits of a Public Good

(a) Lisa's marginal benefit

(b) Max's marginal benefit

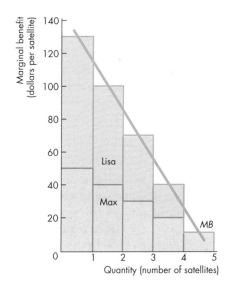

(c) Economy's marginal benefit

The marginal benefit to the economy at each quantity of the public good is the sum of the marginal benefits of all individuals. The marginal benefit curves are MB_L for Lisa, MB_M for Max, and *MB* for the economy.

The Efficient Quantity of a Public Good

An economy with two people would not buy any satellites—because the total benefit falls far short of the cost. But an economy with 250 million people might. To determine the efficient quantity, we need to take the cost as well as the benefit into account.

The cost of a satellite is based on technology and the prices of the resources used to produce it (just like the cost of producing sweaters, which you studied in Chapter 11).

Figure 18.4 sets out the benefits and costs. The second and third columns of the table show the total and marginal benefits. The next two columns show the total and marginal cost of producing satellites. The final column shows net benefit. Total benefit, *TB,* and total cost, *TC,* are graphed in part (a) of the figure.

The efficient quantity is the one that maximizes *net benefit*—total benefit minus total cost—and occurs when 2 satellites are provided.

The fundamental principles of marginal analysis that you have used to explain how consumers maximize utility and how firms maximize profit can also be used to calculate the efficient scale of provision of a public good. Figure 18.4(b) shows this alternative approach. The marginal benefit curve is *MB,* and the marginal cost curve is *MC.* When marginal benefit exceeds marginal cost, net benefit increases if the quantity produced increases. When marginal cost exceeds marginal benefit, net benefit increases if the quantity produced decreases. Marginal benefit equals marginal cost with 2 satellites. So making marginal cost equal to marginal benefit maximizes net benefit and uses resources efficiently.

Private Provision

We have now worked out the quantity of satellites that maximizes net benefit. Would a private firm—North Pole Protection, Inc.—deliver that quantity? It would not. To do so, it would have to collect $15 billion to cover its costs—or $60 from each of the 250 million people in the economy. But no one would have an incentive to buy his or her share of the satellite system. Everyone would reason as follows: The number of satellites provided by North Pole Protection, Inc., is not affected by my $60. But my own private consumption is greater if I free ride and do not pay my share of the cost of the satellite system. If I do not pay, I enjoy the same level of security and

I can buy more private goods. Therefore I will spend my $60 on other goods and free ride on the public good. This is the free-rider problem.

If everyone reasons the same way, North Pole Protection has zero revenue and so provides no satellites. Because two satellites is the efficient level, private provision is inefficient.

Public Provision

Suppose there are two political parties, the Hawks and the Doves, that agree with each other on all issues except for the quantity of satellites. The Hawks would like to provide 4 satellites at a cost of $50 billion, with benefits of $50 billion and a net benefit of zero, as shown in Fig. 18.4. The Doves would like to provide 1 satellite at a cost of $5 billion, a benefit of $20 billion, and a net benefit of $15 billion—see Fig. 18.4.

Before deciding on their policy proposals, the two political parties do a "what-if" analysis. Each party reasons as follows. If each party offers the satellite program it wants—Hawks 4 satellites and Doves 1 satellite—the voters will see that they will get a net benefit of $15 billion from the Doves and zero net benefit from the Hawks, and the Doves will win the election.

Contemplating this outcome, the Hawks realize that their party is too hawkish to get elected. They figure that they must scale back their proposal to 2 satellites. At this level of provision, total cost is $15 billion, total benefit is $35 billion, and net benefit is $20 billion. If the Doves stick with 1 satellite, the Hawks will win the election.

But contemplating this outcome, the Doves realize that they must match the Hawks. They too propose to provide 2 satellites on exactly the same terms as the Hawks. If the two parties offer the same number of satellites, the voters are indifferent between the parties. They flip coins to decide their votes, and each party receives around 50 percent of the vote.

The result of the politicians' "what-if" analysis is that each party offers 2 satellites, so regardless of who wins the election, this is the quantity of satellites installed. And this quantity is efficient. It maximizes the perceived net benefit of the voters. Thus in this example, competition in the political marketplace results in the efficient provision of a public good. But for this outcome to occur, voters must be well informed and evaluate the alternatives. But as you will see below, they do not always have an incentive to achieve this outcome.

FIGURE 18.4

The Efficient Quantity of a Public Good

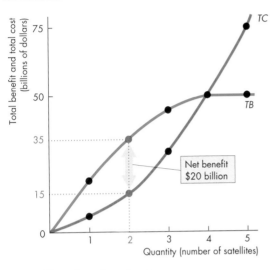

(a) Total benefit and total cost

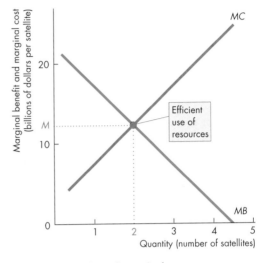

(b) Marginal benefit and marginal cost

Quantity (number of satellites)	Total benefit (billions of dollars)	Marginal benefit (billions of dollars per satellite)	Total cost (billions of dollars)	Marginal cost (billions of dollars per satellite)	Net benefit (billions of dollars)
0	0		0		0
		20		5	
1	20		5		15
		15		10	
2	35		15		20
		10		15	
3	45		30		15
		5		20	
4	50		50		0
		0		25	
5	50		75		−25

Net benefit—the vertical distance between total benefit, *TB*, and total cost, *TC*—is maximized when 2 satellites are installed (part a) and where marginal benefit, *MB*, equals marginal cost, *MC* (part b). The Doves would like to provide 1 satellite, and the Hawks would like to provide 4. But each party recognizes that its only hope of being elected is to provide 2 satellites—the quantity that maximizes net benefit and so leaves no room for the other party to improve on.

The Principle of Minimum Differentiation   In the example we've just studied, both parties propose identical policies. This tendency toward identical policies is an example of the **principle of minimum differentiation**, which is the tendency for competitors to make themselves identical to appeal to the maximum number of clients or voters. This principle not only describes the behavior of political parties but also explains why fast food restaurants cluster in the same block and even why new auto models share similar features. If McDonald's opens a restaurant in a new location, it is likely that Burger King will open next door to McDonald's rather than a mile down the road. If Chrysler designs a new van with a sliding door on the driver's side, most likely Ford will too.

The Role of Bureaucrats

We have analyzed the behavior of politicians but not that of the bureaucrats who translate the choices of the politicians into programs and who control the day-to-day activities that deliver public goods. Let's now see how the economic choices of bureaucrats influence the political equilibrium.

To do so, we'll stick with the previous example. We've seen that competition between two political parties delivers the efficient quantity of satellites. But will the Defense Department—the Pentagon—cooperate and accept this outcome?

Suppose the objective of the Pentagon is to maximize the defense budget. With 2 satellites being provided at minimum cost, the defense budget is $15 billion (see Fig. 18.4). To increase its budget, the Pentagon might do two things. First, it might try to persuade the politicians that 2 satellites cost more than $15 billion. As Fig. 18.5 shows, if possible, the Pentagon would like to convince Congress that 2 satellites cost $35 billion—the entire benefit. Second, and pressing its position even more strongly, the Pentagon might argue for more satellites. It might press for 4 satellites and a budget of $50 billion. In this situation, total benefit and total cost are equal and net benefit is zero.

The Pentagon wants to maximize its budget, but won't the politicians prevent it from doing so because the Pentagon's preferred outcome costs votes? They will if voters are well informed and know what is best for them. But voters might be rationally ignorant. In this case, well-informed interest groups might enable the Pentagon to achieve its objective.

Rational Ignorance

A principle of public choice theory is that it is rational for a voter to be ignorant about an issue unless that issue has a perceptible effect on the voter's income. **Rational ignorance** is the decision *not* to acquire information because the cost of doing so exceeds the expected benefit. For example, each voter knows that he or she can make virtually no difference to the defense policy of the U.S. government. Each voter also knows that it would take an enormous amount of time and effort to become even moderately well informed about alternative defense technologies. So voters remain relatively uninformed about the technicalities of defense issues. (Though we are using

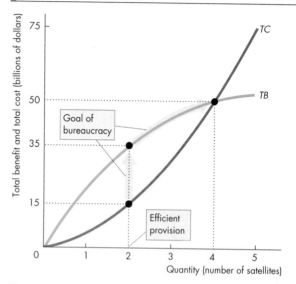

FIGURE 18.5

Bureaucratic Overprovision

The goal of a bureaucracy is to maximize its budget. A bureaucracy that maximizes its budget will seek to increase its budget so that its total cost equals total benefit and then to use its budget to expand output and expenditure. Here, the Pentagon tries to get $35 billion to provide 2 satellites. It would like to increase the quantity of satellites to 4 with a budget of $50 billion.

defense policy as an example, the same applies to all aspects of government economic activity.)

All voters are consumers of national defense. But not all voters are producers of national defense. Only a small number are in this latter category. Voters who own or work for firms that produce satellites have a direct personal interest in defense because it affects their incomes. These voters have an incentive to become well informed about defense issues and to operate a political lobby aimed at furthering their own interests. In collaboration with the defense bureaucracy, these voters exert a larger influence than do the relatively uninformed voters who only consume this public good.

When the rationality of the uninformed voter and special interest groups are taken into account, the political equilibrium provides public goods in excess of the efficient quantity. So in the satellite example, 3 or 4 satellites might be installed rather than the efficient quantity, which is 2 satellites.

Two Types of Political Equilibrium

We've seen that two types of political equilibrium are possible: efficient and inefficient. These two types of political equilibrium correspond to two theories of government:

■ Public interest theory
■ Public choice theory

Public Interest Theory Public interest theory predicts that governments make choices that achieve efficiency. This outcome occurs in a perfect political system in which voters are fully informed about the effects of policies and refuse to vote for outcomes that can be improved upon.

Public Choice Theory Public choice theory predicts that governments make choices that result in inefficiency. This outcome occurs in political markets in which voters are rationally ignorant and base their votes only on issues that they know affect their own net benefit. Voters pay more attention to their interests as producers than their interests as consumers, and public officials also act in their own best interest. The result is *government failure* that parallels market failure.

Why Government Is Large and Grows

Now that we know how the quantity of public goods is determined, we can explain part of the reason for the growth of government. Government grows, in part, because the demand for some public goods increases at a faster rate than the demand for private goods. There are two possible reasons for this growth:

■ Voter preferences
■ Inefficient overprovision

Voter Preferences The growth of government can be explained by voter preferences in the following way. As voters' incomes increase (as they usually do in most years), the demand for many public goods increases more quickly than income. (Technically, the *income elasticity of demand* for many public goods is greater than 1—see Chapter 5, pp. 96–97.) Many (and the most expensive) public goods are in this category. They include transportation systems such as highways, airports, and air-traffic control systems; public health; education; and national defense. If

politicians did not support increases in expenditures on these items, they would not get elected.

Inefficient Overprovision Inefficient overprovision might explain the *size* of government but not its *growth rate*. It (possibly) explains why government is *larger* than its efficient scale, but it does not explain why governments use an increasing proportion of total resources.

Voters Strike Back

If government grows too large, relative to what voters are willing to accept, there might be a voter backlash against government programs and a large bureaucracy. Electoral success during the 1990s at the state and federal level required politicians of all parties to embrace smaller, leaner, and more efficient government as part of their platform.

Another way in which voters—and politicians—can try to counter the tendency of bureaucrats to expand their budgets is to privatize the *production* of public goods. Government *provision* of a public good does not automatically imply that a government-operated bureau must *produce* the good. Garbage collection (public good) is often done by a private firm, and experiments are being conducted with private fire departments and even private prisons.

R E V I E W   Q U I Z

■ What is the free-rider problem and why does it make the private provision of a public good inefficient?
■ Under what conditions will competition among politicians for votes result in an efficient quantity of a public good?
■ How do rationally ignorant voters and budget-maximizing bureaucrats prevent competition in the political marketplace from producing the efficient quantity of a public good? Do they result in too much or too little public provision of public goods?

We've now seen how voters, politicians, and bureaucrats interact to determine the quantity of a public good. But public goods are paid for with taxes. Taxes also redistribute income. How does the political marketplace determine the scale and variety of taxes that we pay?

Taxes

TAXES GENERATE THE FINANCIAL RESOURCES that governments use to provide voters with public goods and other benefits. Five types of taxes are used:

- Income taxes
- Social Security taxes
- Sales taxes
- Property taxes
- Excise taxes

Figure 18.6 shows the relative amounts raised by these five types of tax in 1998. Income taxes are the biggest tax source and raised 52 percent of tax revenues in 1998. Social Security taxes are the next biggest revenue source, and they raised 24 percent of total taxes in 1998. State sales taxes and local government property taxes each raise about 10 percent of total taxes. Finally, excise taxes raise a small amount of government revenue. Although they raise a small amount of revenue, excise taxes have a big impact on some markets, as you'll discover later in this chapter. Let's take a closer look at each type of tax.

FIGURE 18.6

Government Tax Revenues

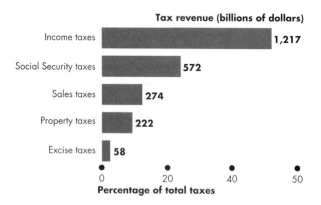

Almost a half of government revenues comes from income taxes. Almost a third comes from Social Security taxes. Excise taxes bring in a small amount of revenue, but these taxes have big effects on a small number of markets.

Source: Federal Budget Historical Table 2.1 and *Economic Report of the President,* 1999.

Income Taxes

Income taxes are paid on personal incomes and corporate profits. In 1998, the personal income tax raised $829 billion for the federal government and another $160 billion for state and local governments. Corporate profits taxes raised $190 billion for the federal government and $30 billion for the state governments. We'll look first at the effects of personal income taxes and then at corporate profits taxes.

Personal Income Tax   The amount of income tax that a person pays depends on her or his *taxable income,* which equals total income minus a *personal exemption* and a *standard deduction* or other allowable deductions. In 1998, the personal exemption was $2,700 and the standard deduction was $4,250 for a single person. So for such a person, taxable income equals total income minus $6,950.

The *tax rate* (percent) depends on the income level and for a single person increases according to the scale:

$0 to $25,350	15 percent
$25,351 to $61,400	28 percent
$61,401 to $128,100	31 percent
$128,101 to $278,450	36 percent
Over $278,450	39.6 percent

The percentages in this list are marginal tax rates. A **marginal tax rate** is the percentage of an additional dollar of income that is paid in tax. For example if taxable income increases from $25,000 to $25,001, the additional tax paid is 15 cents and the marginal tax rate is 15 percent. If income increases from $278,450 to $278,451, the additional tax paid is 39.6 cents and the marginal tax rate is 39.6 percent.

The **average tax rate** is the percentage of income that is paid in tax. The average tax rate is less than the marginal tax rate. For example, suppose a single person earns $50,000 in a year. Tax paid is zero on the first $6,950 plus $3,803 (15 percent) on the next $25,350, plus $4,956 (28 percent) on the remaining $17,700. Total taxes equal $8,759, which is 17.5 percent of $50,000. The average tax rate is 17.5 percent.

If the average tax rate increases as income increases, the tax is a *progressive tax.* The personal income tax is a progressive tax. To see this feature of the income tax, calculate another average tax rate for someone whose income is $100,000 a year. Tax paid is zero on the first $6,950 plus $3,803 (15 percent) on the next $25,350, plus $10,094 (28 percent) on the next $36,050, plus $9,182 on the remaining $31,650.

Total taxes equal $23,708, which is 23.7 percent of $100,000. The average tax rate is 23.7 percent.

A progressive tax contrasts with a *proportional tax*, which has the same average tax rate at all income levels, and a *regressive tax*, which has a decreasing average tax rate as income increases.

The Effect of Income Taxes   Figure 18.7 shows how the income tax affects labor markets. Part (a) shows the market for low-wage workers and part (b) shows the market for high-wage workers. These labor markets are competitive, and with no income taxes, they work just like all the other competitive markets you have studied. The demand curves are *LD*, and the supply curves are *LS* (in both parts of the figure). Both groups work 40 hours a week. Low-wage workers earn $9.50 an hour, and high-wage workers earn $175 an hour. What happens when an income tax is introduced?

If low-wage workers are willing to supply 40 hours a week for $9.50 an hour when there is no tax, then they are willing to supply that same quantity in the face of a 15 percent tax only if the wage rises to $11.18 an hour. That is, they want to get the $9.50 an hour they received before plus the 15 percent tax that they now must pay to the government. So the supply of labor decreases because the amount received from work is lowered by the amount of income tax paid. The acceptable wage rate at each level of employment rises by the amount of the tax that must be paid. For low-wage workers who face a tax rate of 15 percent, the supply curve shifts to *LS + tax*. The equilibrium wage rate rises to $10 an hour, but the after-tax wage rate falls to $8.50 an hour. Employment falls to 36 hours a week.

For high-wage workers who face a tax rate of 39.6 percent, the supply curve shifts to *LS + tax*. The equilibrium wage rate rises to $200 an hour, and the after-tax wage rate falls to $121 an hour. Employment falls to 32 hours a week. The decrease in employment of high-wage workers is larger than that of low-wage workers because of the differences in the marginal tax rates they each face.

FIGURE 18.7
The Effects of Income Taxes

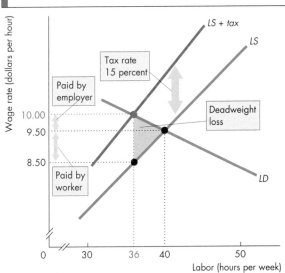

(a) Lowest income tax rate

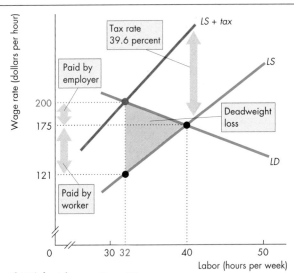

(b) Highest income tax rate

The demand for labor is *LD*, and with no income taxes, the supply of labor is *LS* (both parts). In part (a), low-wage workers earn $9.50 an hour and each works 40 hours a week. In part (b), high-wage workers earn $175 an hour and each works 40 hours a week. An income tax decreases the supply of labor and the labor supply curve shifts leftward. For low-wage workers in part (a), whose marginal tax rate is 15 percent, supply decreases to *LS + tax*. Employment falls to 36 hours a week. For high-wage workers in part (b), whose marginal tax rate is 39.6 percent, supply decreases to *LS + tax*. Employment falls to 32 hours a week. The deadweight loss from the high marginal tax rate on high-wage workers is much larger than that from the low marginal tax rate on low-wage workers.

Notice that the income tax is paid by both the employer and the worker. In the case of low-wage workers, the employer pays an extra 50 cents an hour and the worker pays $1 an hour. In the case of high-wage workers, employers pay an extra $25 an hour and workers pay $54 an hour. The exact split depends on the elasticities of demand and supply.

Notice also the difference in the *deadweight loss* for the two groups. (Check Chapter 6, pp. 116–117, if you need a refresher on the concept of deadweight loss.) The deadweight loss is much larger for the high-wage workers than for the low-wage workers.

Why Do We Have a Progressive Income Tax? We have a progressive income tax because it is part of the political equilibrium. A majority of voters support it, so politicians who also support it get elected.

The economic model that predicts progressive income taxes is called the *median voter* model. The core idea of the median voter model is that political parties pursue policies that are most likely to attract the support of the median voter. The median voter is the one in the middle—one half of the population lies on one side and one half on the other. So a political party must win the support of the median voter if it is to win an election. Let's see how the median voter model predicts a progressive income tax.

Imagine that government programs benefit everyone equally and are paid for by a proportional income tax. Everyone pays the same percentage of their income. In this situation, there is a redistribution from high-income voters to low-income voters. Everyone benefits equally, but because high-income voters have larger incomes, they pay larger taxes.

Is this situation the best one possible for the median voter? It is not. Suppose that instead of using a proportional tax, the marginal tax rate is lowered for low-income voters and increased for high-income voters—a progressive tax. Low-income voters are now better off, and high-income voters are worse off. Low-income voters will support this change, and high-income voters will oppose it. But there are many more low-income voters than high-income voters, so the low-income voters win.

The median voter is a low-income voter. In fact, because the distribution of income is skewed, the median voter has a smaller income than the average income (see Fig. 17.4 on pp. 370). This fact raises an interesting question: Why doesn't the median voter support taxes that skim off all income above the average and redistribute it to everyone with a below-average income. This tax would be so progressive that

it would result in equal incomes after taxes and transfers were paid.

The answer is that such high taxes would discourage effort and saving to the point that the median voter would be worse off with such a radical redistribution than under the arrangements that prevail today.

Let's now look at corporate profits taxes.

Corporate Profits Tax In popular discussions of taxes, corporate profits taxes are seen as a free source of revenue for the government. Taxing people is bad, but taxing corporations is just fine.

It turns out that taxing corporations is very inefficient. We use an inefficient tax because it redistributes income in favor of the median voter, just like the income tax. Let's see why taxing corporate profits is inefficient.

First, the tax is misnamed. It is only partly a tax on economic profit. It is mainly a tax on the income from capital. Taxing the income from capital works like taxing the income from labor except for two critical differences: The supply of capital is highly (perhaps perfectly) elastic, and the quantity of capital influences the productivity of labor and wage income. Because the supply of capital is highly elastic, the tax is fully borne by firms and the quantity of capital decreases. With a smaller capital stock than we would otherwise have, the productivity of labor and incomes are lower than they would otherwise be.

Social Security Taxes

Social Security taxes are the contributions paid by employers and employees to provide social security benefits, unemployment compensation, and health and disability benefits to workers (see Chapter 17, p. 372).

Unions lobby to get employers to pay a bigger share of these taxes, and employers' organizations lobby to get workers to pay a bigger share of them. But this lobbying effort is not worth much because who *really* pays these taxes depends in no way on who writes the checks. It depends on the elasticities of demand and supply for labor.

Figure 18.8 shows you why. In both parts of the figure, the demand curve *LD* and the supply curve *LS* are identical. With no Social Security tax, the quantity of labor employed is QL^* and the wage rate is W^*.

A Social Security tax is now introduced. In Fig. 18.8(a), the employee pays the tax; in Fig. 18.8(b), the employer pays. When the employee pays, supply decreases and the supply of labor curve shifts leftward to $LS + tax$. The vertical distance between the supply curve LS and the new supply curve $LS + tax$ is the amount of the tax. The wage rate rises to WC, the after-tax wage rate falls to WT, and employment decreases to QL_0.

When the employer pays (in Fig. 18.8b), demand decreases and the demand for labor curve shifts leftward to $LD - tax$. The vertical distance between the demand curve LD and the new demand curve $LD - tax$ is the amount of the tax. The wage rate falls to WT, but the cost of labor rises to WC and employment decreases to QL_0.

So regardless of which side of the market is taxed, the outcome is identical. If the demand for labor is perfectly inelastic or if the supply of labor is perfectly elastic, the employer pays the entire tax. And if the demand for labor is perfectly elastic or if the supply of labor is perfectly inelastic, the employee pays the entire tax. These cases are exactly like those for the sales tax that you studied in Chapter 7 on pp. 135–138.

Sales Taxes

Sales taxes are the taxes levied by state governments on a wide range of goods and services. We studied the effects of these taxes in Chapter 7. There is one feature of these taxes, though, that we need to note. They are *regressive*. The reason they are regressive is that saving increases with income and sales taxes are paid only on the part of income that is spent.

Suppose, for example, that the sales tax is 8 percent. A family with an income of $20,000 that spends all its income pays $1,600 in sales tax. Its average tax rate is 8 percent. A family with an income of $100,000 that spends $60,000 and saves $40,000 pays sales taxes of $4,800 (8 percent of $60,000). So this family's average tax rate is 4.8 percent.

If the sales tax is regressive, why is it supported by the median voter? It is the entire tax code that matters, not an individual tax. So a regressive sales tax is voted for only as part of an overall tax regime that is progressive.

Property Taxes

Property taxes are collected by local governments and are used to provide local public goods. A **local public good** is a public good that is consumed by all the people who live in a particular area. Examples of local public goods are parks, museums, and safe neighborhoods.

FIGURE 18.8
Social Security Taxes

(a) Tax on employees

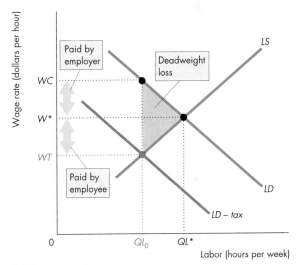

(b) Tax on employers

The labor demand curve is LD, and the supply curve is LS. With no Social Security taxes, the quantity of labor employed is QL^* and the wage rate is W^* (in both parts). In part (a), employees pay the Social Security tax. Supply decreases, and the supply of labor curve shifts leftward to $LS + tax$. The wage rate rises to WC, the after-tax wage rate falls to WT, and employment decreases to QL_0. In part (b), employers pay the Social Security tax. Demand decreases, and the demand for labor curve shifts leftward to $LD - tax$. The wage rate falls to WT, but the cost of labor rises to WC and employment decreases to QL_0. The outcome is identical in both cases.

There is a much closer connection between property taxes paid and benefits received than in the case of federal and state taxes. This close connection makes property taxes similar to a price for local services. Because of this connection, property taxes change both the demand for and supply of property in a neighborhood. A higher property tax lowers supply, but improved local public goods increase demand. So some neighborhoods have high taxes and high-quality local government services, and other neighborhoods have low taxes and low-quality services. Both can exist in the political equilibrium.

Excise Taxes

An **excise tax** is a tax on the sale of a particular commodity. The total amount raised by these taxes is small, but they have a big impact on some markets. Let's study the effects of an excise tax by considering the tax on gasoline shown in Fig. 18.9. The demand curve for gasoline is D, and the supply curve is S. If there is no tax on gasoline, its price is 60¢ a gallon and 400 million gallons of gasoline a day are bought and sold.

Now suppose that a tax is imposed on gasoline at the rate of 60¢ a gallon. As a result of the tax, the supply of gasoline decreases and the supply curve shifts leftward. The magnitude of the shift is such that the vertical distance between the original and the new supply curve is the amount of the tax. The new supply curve is the red curve, $S + tax$. The new supply curve intersects the demand curve at 300 million gallons a day and $1.10 a gallon. This situation is the new equilibrium after the imposition of the tax.

The excise tax creates a deadweight loss made up of the loss of consumer surplus and the loss of producer surplus. The dollar value of that loss is $30 million a day. Because 300 million gallons of gasoline are sold each day and the tax is 60¢ a gallon, total revenue from the gasoline tax is $180 million a day (300 million gallons multiplied by 60¢ a gallon). So to raise tax revenue of $180 million dollars a day by using the gasoline tax, a deadweight loss of $30 million a day—one sixth of the tax revenue—is incurred.

One of the main influences on the deadweight loss arising from an excise tax is the elasticity of demand for the commodity. The demand for gasoline is fairly inelastic. As a consequence, when a tax is imposed, the quantity demanded falls by a smaller percentage than the percentage rise in price.

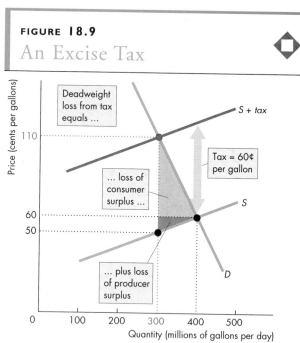

FIGURE 18.9
An Excise Tax

The demand curve for gasoline is D, and the supply curve is S. In the absence of any taxes, gasoline will sell for 60¢ a gallon and 400 million gallons a day will be bought and sold. When a tax of 60¢ a gallon is imposed, the supply curve shifts leftward to become the curve $S + tax$. The new equilibrium price is $1.10 a gallon, and 300 million gallons a day are bought and sold. The excise tax creates a deadweight loss represented by the gray triangle. The tax revenue collected is 60¢ a gallon on 300 million gallons, which is $180 million a day. The deadweight loss from the tax is $30 million a day. That is, to raise tax revenue of $180 million a day, a deadweight loss of $30 million a day is incurred.

To see the importance of the elasticity of demand, let's consider a different commodity—orange juice. So that we can make a quick and direct comparison, let's assume that the orange juice market is exactly as big as the market for gasoline. Figure 18.10 illustrates this market. The demand curve for orange juice is D, and the supply curve is S. Orange juice is not taxed, and so the price of orange juice is 60¢ a gallon—where the supply curve and the demand curve intersect—and the quantity of orange juice is 400 million gallons a day.

Now suppose that the government contemplates abolishing the gasoline tax and taxing orange juice instead. The demand for orange juice is more elastic than the demand for gasoline. It has many good substitutes in the form of other fruit juices. The government wants to raise $180 million a day so that its

FIGURE 18.10

Why We Don't Tax Orange Juice

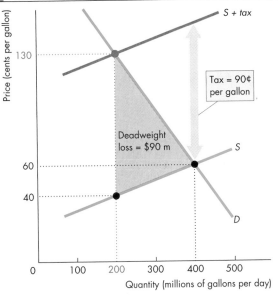

The demand curve for orange juice is D, and the supply curve is S. The equilibrium price is 60¢ a gallon, and 400 million gallons of juice a day are traded. To raise $180 million of tax revenue, a tax of 90¢ a gallon will have to be imposed. The introduction of this tax shifts the supply curve to S + tax. The price rises to $1.30 a gallon, and the quantity bought and sold falls to 200 million gallons a day. The deadweight loss is represented by the gray triangle and equals $90 million a day. The deadweight loss from taxing orange juice is much larger than that from taxing gasoline (Fig. 18.9) because the demand for orange juice is much more elastic than the demand for gasoline. Items that have a low elasticity of demand are taxed more heavily than items that have a high elasticity of demand.

it collects a total revenue of $180 million a day—exactly the amount that it requires.

But what is the deadweight loss in this case? The answer can be seen by looking at the gray triangle in Fig. 18.10. The magnitude of that deadweight loss is $90 million. Notice how much bigger the deadweight loss is from taxing orange juice than from taxing gasoline. In the case of orange juice, the deadweight loss is one half the revenue raised, while in the case of gasoline, it is only one sixth. What accounts for this difference? The supply curves are identical in each case, and the examples were also set up to ensure that the initial no-tax prices and quantities were identical. The difference between the two cases is the elasticity of demand: In the case of gasoline, the quantity demanded falls by only 25 percent when the price almost doubles. In the case of orange juice, the quantity demanded falls by 50 percent when the price only slightly more than doubles.

You can see why taxing orange juice is not on the political agenda of any of the major parties. Vote-seeking politicians seek out taxes that benefit the median voter. Other things being equal, this means that they try to minimize the deadweight loss of raising a given amount of revenue. Equivalently, they tax items with poor substitutes more heavily than items with close substitutes.

R E V I E W   Q U I Z

- How do income taxes influence employment and efficiency? Why are income taxes progressive?
- Can Congress make employers pay a larger share of the Social Security tax?
- Why do some neighborhoods have high taxes and high-quality services and others have low taxes and low-quality services?
- Why does the government impose excise taxes at high rates on goods that have a low elasticity of demand?

◆ *Reading Between the Lines* on pages 406–407 looks at the politically sensitive market for day-care services. It shows how this market can be influenced by subsidies (that work like taxes but bring lower prices). And it asks whether increasing the quantity of day-care services is efficient. In the next two chapters, we are going to look at government economic actions in the face of monopolies and externalities.

total revenue is not affected by this tax change. The government's economists, armed with their statistical estimates of the demand and supply curves for orange juice that appear in Fig. 18.10, work out that a tax of 90¢ a gallon will do the job. With such a tax, the supply curve shifts leftward to become the curve labeled S + tax. This new supply curve intersects the demand curve at a price of $1.30 a gallon and at a quantity of 200 million gallons a day. The price at which suppliers are willing to produce 200 million gallons a day is 40¢ a gallon. The government collects a tax of 90¢ a gallon on 200 million gallons a day, so

The Politics and Economics of Day Care

T H E   W A L L   S T R E E T   J O U R N A L ,   March 30, 1999

Bills to Improve Day Care Gain In Augusta

By Carol Gentry

AUGUSTA, Maine—A raft of new child-care measures, including tax breaks, low-interest loans and scholarships, have won near-unanimous support in committees and are speeding toward passage in the Legislature.

The nine bills sponsored by Sen. Susan Longley, a Democrat from rural Liberty, are the private-sector component of a massive child-care initiative called Start ME Right that aims to expand the overwhelmed system and improve its quality. Start ME Right calls for $26 million in public-sector spending over two years, a significant commitment in a state where child-care issues have long been relegated to the back burner in favor of business development and job growth. That means it's likely to face a bruising fight in the Appropriations Committee next month.

But most of Sen. Longley's bills call for little or no new state spending. Instead they invite business interests to join children's advocates in pushing for child-care solutions and tinker with tax breaks to spur improvements in child-care services. And by framing child care as a central economic development issue, Sen. Longley has gotten the attention of conservative lawmakers and built a broad coalition in support of her bills.

"Child care is the third-largest industry in our state, and we haven't been treating it like a business," she says. "It's hugely important, both for the child and family and for the development of the state."

...

As things stand now, Maine puts a smaller percentage of its tax dollars into child care than any other New England state, says Lee Parker, director of Bath-Brunswick Child Care Services, a child-care agency.

...

Children's advocates are hoping that Sen. Longley's emphasis on the economic development angle will resonate with Gov. King, who has been focusing heavily on business-recruiting efforts during his five years in office.

Says Ms. Parker: "If we're going to attract business here, we have to be able to say it's a crackerjack place to raise your kids."

Essence of the Story

■ Start ME Right, Maine's child-care program, seeks $26 million in public spending. This spending increase does not have unanimous support.

■ But almost all of the legislators (liberal Democrats, conservative Republicans, and independents) support nine bills sponsored by Senator Susan Longley.

■ Senator Longley's bills call for little new state spending but seek to expand and improve the quality of child care by the use of tax breaks, low-interest loans, and scholarships.

■ Senator Longley says that child care is the third largest industry in Maine, and it is important for both the child and family and for the economic development of the state.

Economic Analysis

■ Day-care service is a *private* good, not a *public* good. But it is a politically sensitive good because it influences the work choices and incomes of parents.

■ Figure 1 shows the labor market problem confronting two people who are identical in all ways except that one has a young child and the other does not. The supply curve of labor for the person with no child is S_N. The supply curve of labor for the parent is S_C.

■ The parent's labor supply curve requires a higher wage at each quantity supplied to meet the cost of child care (assumed to be $4 an hour).

■ If the market wage faced by these two people is $8 an hour, the parent stays at home and the nonparent works a 30-hour week and earns $240 a week.

■ If child-care services are subsidized, more parents will decide to work.

■ Figure 2 shows how a subsidy influences the market for child-care services. The demand curve is *D*, and the supply curve is *S*. With no subsidy, the price of child care is $5 an hour and 4 million places are available.

■ If child-care service providers receive a subsidy of $2 an hour, the supply curve shifts downward by the amount of the subsidy. The price falls to $4 an hour, and the number of places available increases to 6 million.

■ Figure 3 emphasizes that the provision of more child-care services is not a free lunch. The opportunity cost is the other goods and services forgone—here the move from *a* to *b* costs 6 units of other goods and services.

■ The economic marketplace would deliver outcome *a*. The political marketplace might deliver outcome *b*.

You're The Voter

■ Should governments provide free day care on demand? Why or why not?

■ Should the cost of day care be fully tax deductible? Why or why not?

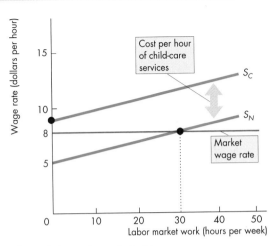

Figure 1 Parent's work decision

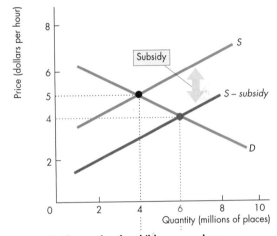

Figure 2 The market for child-care services

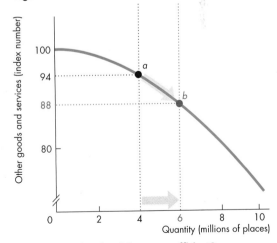

Figure 3 No free lunch but more efficient?

SUMMARY

KEY POINTS

The Economic Theory of Government
(pp. 392–393)

- Government exists to provide public goods, regulate monopoly, cope with externalities, and reduce economic inequality.
- Public choice theory explains how voters, politicians, and bureaucrats interact in a political marketplace.

Public Goods and the Free-Rider Problem
(pp. 394–399)

- A public good is a good or service that is consumed by everyone and that is *nonrival* and *nonexcludable*.
- A public good creates a *free-rider* problem—no one has an incentive to pay their share of the cost of providing a public good.
- The efficient level of provision of a public good is that at which net benefit is maximized. Equivalently, it is the level at which marginal benefit equals marginal cost.
- Competition between political parties, each of which tries to appeal to the maximum number of voters, can lead to the efficient scale of provision of a public good and to both parties proposing the same policies—the principle of minimum differentiation.
- Bureaucrats try to maximize their budgets, and if voters are rationally ignorant, producer interests may result in voting to support taxes that provide public goods in quantities that exceed those that maximize net benefit.

Taxes (pp. 400–405)

- Government revenue comes from income taxes, payroll taxes, sales taxes, property taxes, and excise taxes.
- Income taxes decrease the level of employment and create a deadweight loss.

- Taxes can be progressive (the average tax rate rises with income), proportional (the average tax rate is constant), or regressive (the average tax rate falls with income).
- Income taxes are progressive because this arrangement is in the interest of the median voter.
- Payroll taxes are paid by the employer and the employee (and sales taxes are paid by the buyer and the seller) in amounts that depend on the elasticities of demand and supply.
- Property taxes change both demand and supply and can result in neighborhoods with high taxes and high-quality services and with low taxes and low-quality services.
- Excise taxes at high rates on commodities such as gasoline create a smaller deadweight loss than would taxes on commodities with more elastic demands.

KEY FIGURES

KEY TERMS

PROBLEMS

*1. You are provided with the following information about a sewage disposal system that a city of 1 million people is considering installing:

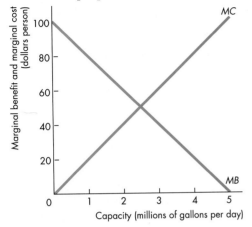

a. What is the capacity that achieves maximum net benefit?
b. How much will each person have to pay in taxes to pay for the efficient capacity level?
c. What is the political equilibrium if voters are well informed?
d. What is the political equilibrium if voters are rationally ignorant and bureaucrats achieve the highest attainable budget?

2. You are provided with the following information about a mosquito control program:

Quantity (square miles sprayed per day)	Marginal cost (dollars per day)	Marginal benefit (dollars per day)
0	0	0
1	1,000	5,000
2	2,000	4,000
3	3,000	3,000
4	4,000	2,000
5	5,000	1,000

a. What is the quantity of spraying that achieves maximum net benefit?
b. What is the total tax revenue needed to pay for the efficient quantity of spraying?
c. What is the political equilibrium if voters are well informed?
d. What is the political equilibrium if voters are rationally ignorant and bureaucrats achieve the highest attainable budget?

*3. An economy has two groups of people, A and B. The population consists of 80 percent A-types and 20 percent B-types. A-types have a perfectly elastic supply of labor at a wage rate of $10 an hour. B-types have a perfectly inelastic supply of labor, and their equilibrium wage rate is $100 an hour.
a. What kinds of tax arrangements do you predict this economy will adopt?
b. Analyze the labor market in this economy and explain what will happen to the wage rates and employment levels of the two groups when the taxes you predict in your answer to part (a) are introduced.

4. Suppose that in the economy described in problem 3, the proportion of A-types is 20 percent and the proportion of B-types is 80. Everything else remains the same.
a. Now what kinds of tax arrangements do you predict the economy will adopt?
b. Analyze the labor market in this economy and explain what will happen to the wage rates and employment levels of the two groups when the taxes you predict in your answer to part (a) are introduced.
c. Compare the economy in problem 3 with the economy in this problem. Which economy more closely resembles our actual economy?

*5. An economy has a competitive labor market, which is described by the following demand schedule and supply schedule:

Wage Rate (dollars per hour)	Quantity demanded (hours per week)	Quantity supplied (hours per week)
20	0	50
16	15	40
12	30	30
8	45	20
4	60	10
0	75	0

a. What are the equilibrium wage rate and hours of work done?
b. If a $4 an hour Social Security tax is imposed on employers:
   (i) What is the new wage rate?
   (ii) What is the new number of hours worked?

(iii) What is the after-tax wage rate?

(iv) What is the tax revenue?

(v) What is the deadweight loss?

6. In the economy described in problem 5, the Social Security tax on employers is eliminated and a new Social Security tax of $4 is imposed on employees.
   a. What is the new wage rate?
   b. What is the new number of hours worked?
   c. What is the after-tax wage rate?
   d. What is the tax revenue?
   e. What is the deadweight loss?
   f. Compare the situation in problem 5 with that in this problem and explain the similarities and differences in the two situations.

*7. In a competitive market for cookies:

Price (dollars per pound)	Quantity demanded (pounds per month)	Quantity supplied (pounds per month)
10	0	28
8	4	24
6	8	20
4	12	16
2	16	12

   a. Find the equilibrium price and quantity.
   b. If cookies are taxed $2 a pound:
      (i) What is the new price of cookies?
      (ii) What is the new quantity bought?
      (iii) What is the tax revenue?
      (iv) What is the deadweight loss?

8. In the competitive market for cookies in problem 7, the government wants to change the tax to the one that brings in the greatest possible amount of revenue.
   a. What is that tax rate?
   b. What is the new price of cookies?
   c. What is the new quantity bought?
   d. What is the tax revenue?
   e. What is the deadweight loss?

CRITICAL THINKING

1. Study *Reading Between the Lines* on pp. 406–407, and then:
   a. Describe the measures that Senator Longley proposes and predict their effects on child-care services and labor markets in Maine.
   b. Why do people generally agree that increasing the quantity of child-care services above the quantity that the marketplace would deliver is a good thing? (Hint: Think about who benefits from child-care services other than the parent and child.)
   c. Do you think it is efficient to increase the quantity of child-care services above the quantity that the market would deliver?

2. Use the links on the Parkin Web site to obtain information about child-care services.
   a. How has the quantity of child-care services changed in recent years?
   b. How much does the average family spend on child care?
   c. What percentage of family income is spent on child care by a family with a monthly income of (i) $4,500 or more, (ii) $3,000 to $4,499, (iii) $1,200 to $2,999, and (iv) less than $1,200.

3. Your local city council believes that by installing computers to control the traffic signals, it can improve the speed of traffic flow. The bigger the computer the council buys, the better job it can do. The officials who are working on the proposal want to determine the scale of the system that will win them the most votes. The city bureaucrats want to maximize the budget. Suppose that you are an economist who is observing this public choice. Your job is to calculate the quantity of this public good that uses resources efficiently.
   a. What data would you need to reach your own conclusions?
   b. What does the public choice theory predict will be the quantity chosen?
   c. How could you, as an informed voter, attempt to influence the choice?
   d. What does the public interest theory predict will be the quantity chosen?

19

Regulation and Antitrust Law

When you consume water or local telephone service you usually buy from a regulated monopoly. Why are the industries that produce these items regulated? How are they regulated? Do the regulations work in the public interest—the interest of all consumers and producers—or do they serve special interests—the interests of particular groups of consumers or producers? ◆ Cable TV has been on a regulatory roller coaster. It was initially regulated, but in 1984 it was deregulated. After deregulation, the profits of cable TV firms soared and in 1992, Congress re-regulated the industry only to deregulate it yet again in 1996. Why has cable TV been deregulated, re-regulated, and then deregulated again? ◆ Some years ago, PepsiCo and 7-Up wanted to merge. Coca-Cola and Dr Pepper also wanted to merge. But the government blocked these mergers with its antitrust laws. It used these same laws to break up the American Telephone and Telegraph Company (AT&T). This action brought competition into the market for long-distance telephone service and permitted previously struggling firms such as MCI and Sprint to expand and flourish. The government has also used its antitrust laws to punish Archer Daniel Midland for price fixing, to permit Boeing and McDonnell Douglas to merge their aircraft building businesses, and to permit mergers of big banks. These same laws will determine whether Microsoft has monopolized the markets for computer operating systems and Web browsers. What are antitrust laws? How have they evolved over the years? How are they used today? Do they serve the public interest or the special interests of producers?

Public Interest or Special Interests?

◆ This chapter studies government regulation. It draws on your earlier study of how markets work and on your knowledge of consumer surplus and producer surplus. It shows how consumers and producers can redistribute the gains from trade in the political marketplace, and it identifies who stands to win and who stands to lose from government regulation.

After studying this chapter, you will be able to:

- Define regulation and antitrust law

- Distinguish between the public interest and capture theories of regulation

- Explain how regulation affects prices, outputs, profits, and the distribution of the gains from trade between consumers and producers

- Explain how antitrust law has been applied in a number of landmark cases

- Explain how antitrust law is used today

Market Intervention

THE GOVERNMENT INTERVENES IN MONOPOLISTIC and oligopolistic markets to influence prices, quantities produced, and the distribution of the gains from economic activity. It intervenes in two main ways:

- Regulation
- Antitrust law

Regulation

Regulation consists of rules administered by a government agency to influence economic activity by determining prices, product standards and types, and the conditions under which new firms may enter an industry. To implement its regulations, the government establishes agencies to oversee the regulations and ensure their enforcement. The first national regulatory agency to be set up in the United States was the Interstate Commerce Commission (ICC), established in 1887. Over the years since then, up to the late 1970s, regulation of the economy grew until, at its peak, almost a quarter of the nation's output was produced by regulated industries. Regulation applied to banking and financial services, telecommunications, gas and electric utilities, railroads, trucking, airlines and buses, many agricultural products, and even haircutting and braiding. Since the late 1970s, there has been a tendency to deregulate the U.S. economy.

Deregulation is the process of removing restrictions on prices, product standards and types, and entry conditions. In recent years, deregulation has occurred in domestic air transportation, telephone service, interstate trucking, and banking and financial services. Cable TV was deregulated in 1984, re-regulated in 1992, and deregulated again in 1996.

Antitrust Law

An **antitrust law** is a law that regulates and prohibits certain kinds of market behavior, such as price fixing, monopoly, and monopolistic practices. Antitrust law is enacted by Congress and enforced through the judicial system. Lawsuits under the antitrust laws may be initiated either by government agencies or by injured private parties.

The main thrust of antitrust law is the prohibition of monopoly practices of restricting output to achieve higher prices and profits. The first antitrust law—the Sherman Act—was passed in 1890. Successive acts and amendments have strengthened and refined the body of antitrust law. Antitrust law (like all law) depends as much on the decisions of the courts and of the Supreme Court as on the statutes passed by Congress. Over the 100 years since the passage of the Sherman Act, there have been some interesting changes in the court's interpretation of the law and in how vigorously the law has been enforced. We'll study these later in this chapter.

To understand why the government intervenes in the markets for goods and services and to work out the effects of its interventions, we need to identify the gains and losses that government actions can create. These gains and losses are the consumer surpluses and producer surpluses associated with different output levels and prices. We first study the economics of regulation.

Economic Theory of Regulation

THE ECONOMIC THEORY OF REGULATION IS part of the broader theory of public choice that is explained in Chapter 18. Here, we apply public choice theory to regulation. We'll examine the demand for government actions, the supply of those actions, and the political equilibrium that emerges.

Demand for Regulation

People and firms demand regulation that makes them better off. They express this demand through political activity—voting, lobbying, and making campaign contributions. But engaging in political activity is costly, so people demand political action only if the benefit that they individually receive from such action exceeds their individual costs in obtaining it. The four main factors that affect the demand for regulation are:

1. Consumer surplus per buyer
2. Number of buyers
3. Producer surplus per firm
4. Number of firms

The larger the consumer surplus per buyer that results from regulation, the greater is the demand for regulation by buyers. Also, as the number of buyers increases, so does the demand for regulation. But numbers alone do not necessarily translate into an effective political force. The larger the number of buyers, the greater is the cost of organizing them, so the demand for regulation does not increase proportionately with the number of buyers.

The larger the producer surplus per firm that arises from a particular regulation, the larger is the demand for that regulation by firms. Also, as the number of firms that might benefit from some regulation increases, so does the demand for that regulation. But again, large numbers do not necessarily mean an effective political force. The larger the number of firms, the greater is the cost of organizing them.

For a given consumer or producer surplus, the smaller the number of households or firms that share the surplus, the larger is the demand for the regulation that creates the surplus.

Supply of Regulation

Politicians and bureaucrats supply regulation. According to public choice theory, politicians choose policies that appeal to a majority of voters, thereby enabling themselves to achieve and maintain office. Bureaucrats support policies that maximize their budgets (see Chapter 18, p. 398). Given these objectives of politicians and bureaucrats, the supply of regulation depends on the following three factors:

1. Consumer surplus generated per buyer
2. Producer surplus generated per firm
3. The number of voters benefited

The larger the consumer surplus per buyer or producer surplus per firm generated and the larger the number of people affected by a regulation, the greater is the tendency for politicians to supply that regulation. If regulation benefits a large number of people by enough for it to be noticed and if the recipients know the source of the benefits, that regulation appeals to politicians and is supplied. If regulation benefits a *small* number of people by a large amount per person, that regulation also appeals to politicians, provided that its costs are spread widely and are not easily identified. If regulation benefits a large number of people but by too small an amount

per person to be noticed, that regulation does not appeal to politicians and is not supplied.

Political Equilibrium

In equilibrium, the regulation that exists is such that no interest group finds it worthwhile to use additional resources to press for changes and no group of politicians finds it worthwhile to offer different regulations. Being in a political equilibrium is not the same thing as everyone being in agreement. Lobby groups will devote resources to trying to change regulations that are already in place. Others will devote resources to maintaining the existing regulations. But no one will find it worthwhile to *increase* the resources they are devoting to such activities. Also, political parties might not agree with each other. Some support the existing regulations, and others propose different regulations. In equilibrium, no one wants to change the proposals that they are making.

What will a political equilibrium look like? The answer depends on whether the regulation serves the public interest or the interest of the producer. Let's look at these two possibilities.

Public Interest Theory   The **public interest theory** is that regulations are supplied to satisfy the demand of consumers and producers to maximize total surplus—that is, to attain allocative efficiency. The public interest theory implies that the political process relentlessly seeks out deadweight loss and introduces regulations that eliminate it. For example, where monopoly practices exist, the political process will introduce price regulations to ensure that outputs increase and prices fall to their competitive levels.

Capture Theory   The **capture theory** is that the regulations are supplied to satisfy the demand of producers to maximize producer surplus—that is, to maximize economic profit. The key idea of the capture theory is that the cost of regulation is high and only those regulations that increase the surplus of small, easily identified groups and that have low organization costs are supplied by the political process. Such regulations are supplied even if they impose costs on others, provided that those costs are spread thinly and widely enough that they do not decrease votes.

The predictions of the capture theory are less clear-cut than those of the public interest theory. The capture theory predicts that regulations give large and visible benefits to cohesive interest groups and impose small costs on everyone else. Those costs per person are so small that no one finds it worthwhile to incur the cost of organizing an interest group to avoid them.

Whichever theory of regulation is correct, according to public choice theory, the political system delivers the amounts and types of regulations that best further the electoral success of politicians. Because producer-oriented and consumer-oriented regulation are in conflict with each other, the political process can't satisfy both groups in any particular industry. Only one group can win. This makes the regulatory actions of government a bit like a unique product—for example, a painting by Leonardo da Vinci. There is only one original, and it will be sold to just one buyer. Normally, a unique commodity is sold at auction; the highest bidder takes the prize. Equilibrium in the regulatory process is similar: The suppliers satisfy the demands of the highest bidder. If the producer demand offers a bigger return to the politicians, either directly through votes or indirectly through campaign contributions, then the producers' interests will be served. If the consumer demand translates into a larger number of votes, then the consumers' interests will be served by regulation.

R E V I E W   Q U I Z

- How do consumers and producers express their demand for regulation? What are their objectives? What are the costs of expressing a demand for regulation?
- When politicians and bureaucrats supply regulation, what are they trying to achieve? Do politicians and bureaucrats have the same objectives?
- What is a political equilibrium? When does the political equilibrium achieve economy efficiency? When does the political equilibrium serve the interests of producers?

We have now completed our study of the *theory* of regulation in the marketplace. Let's turn our attention to the regulations that exist in our economy today. Which theory of regulation best explains these real-world regulations? Which regulations are in the public interest and which are in the interest of producers?

Regulation and Deregulation

THE PAST 20 YEARS HAVE SEEN DRAMATIC changes in the way in which the U.S. economy is regulated by government. We're going to examine some of these changes. To begin, we'll look at what is regulated and also at the scope of regulation. Then we'll turn to the regulatory process and examine how regulators control prices and other aspects of market behavior. Finally, we'll tackle the more difficult and controversial questions: Why do we regulate some things but not others? Who benefits from the regulations that we have—consumers or producers?

The Scope of Regulation

The first federal regulatory agency, the Interstate Commerce Commission (ICC), was set up in 1887 to control prices, routes, and the quality of service of interstate railroads. Its scope later covered trucking lines, bus lines, water carriers, and, in more recent years, oil pipelines. Following the establishment of the ICC, the federal regulatory environment remained static until the years of the Great Depression. Then, in the 1930s, more agencies were established—the Federal Power Commission, the Federal Communications Commission, the Securities and Exchange Commission, the Federal Maritime Commission, the Federal Deposit Insurance Corporation, and, in 1938, the Civil Aeronautical Agency, which was replaced in 1940 by the Civil Aeronautics Board. There was a further lull until the establishment during the 1970s of the Copyright Royalty Tribunal and the Federal Energy Regulatory Commission. In addition to these, there are many state and local regulatory commissions.

In the mid-1970s, almost one quarter of the economy was subject to some form of regulation. Heavily regulated industries—those subject both to price regulation and to regulation of entry of new firms—were electricity, natural gas, telephones, airlines, highway freight services, and railroads.

During the 1980s and 1990s, a deregulation process stimulated competition in broadcasting, telecommunications, banking and finance, and all forms of transportation (air, rail, and road, passengers, and freight.)

What exactly do regulatory agencies do? How do they regulate?

The Regulatory Process

Though regulatory agencies vary in size and scope and in the detailed aspects of economic life that they control, all agencies have features in common.

First, the bureaucrats who are the key decision makers in a regulatory agency are appointed by the administration or Congress in the case of federal agencies and by state and local governments. In addition, all agencies have a permanent bureaucracy made up of experts in the industry being regulated and often recruited from the regulated firms. Agencies have financial resources, voted by Congress or state or local legislatures, to cover the costs of their operations.

Second, each agency adopts a set of practices or operating rules for controlling prices and other aspects of economic performance. These rules and practices are based on well-defined physical and financial accounting procedures, but they are extremely complicated in practice and hard to administer.

In a regulated industry, individual firms are usually free to determine the technology that they will use in production. But they are not free to determine the prices at which they will sell their output, the quantities that they will sell, or the markets that they will serve. The regulatory agency grants certification to a company to serve a particular market and with a particular line of products, and it determines the level and structure of prices that will be charged. In some cases, the agency also determines the quantity that firms may produce.

To analyze the way in which regulation works, it is convenient to distinguish between the regulation of natural monopoly and the regulation of cartels. Let's begin with the regulation of natural monopoly.

Natural Monopoly

Natural monopoly was defined in Chapter 13 (p. 264) as an industry in which one firm can supply the entire market at a lower cost than two or more firms can. Examples of natural monopolies include local distribution of cable television signals, electricity and gas, and urban rail services. For these activities, most of the costs are fixed and the larger the output, the lower its average total cost. It is much more expensive to have two or more competing sets of wires, pipes,

and train lines serving every neighborhood than it is to have a single set. (Whether an industry is a natural monopoly changes over time as technology changes. With the introduction of fiber-optic cables, telephone companies and cable television companies can compete with each other in both markets, so what was once a natural monopoly is gradually becoming a more competitive industry. Direct satellite TV is also beginning to break the cable monopoly.)

Let's consider the example of cable TV, which is shown in Fig. 19.1. The demand curve for cable TV is *D*. The cable TV company's marginal cost curve is *MC*. That marginal cost curve is (assumed to be) horizontal at $10 per household per month—that is, the cost of providing each additional household with a month of cable programming is $10. The cable company has a heavy investment in satellite receiving dishes, cables, and control equipment and so has high fixed costs. These fixed costs are part of the company's average total cost curve, shown as *ATC*. The average total cost curve slopes downward because as the number of households served increases, the fixed cost is spread over a larger number of households. (To refresh your memory on the average total cost curve, take a quick look at Chapter 11, p. 226.)

Regulation in the Public Interest How will cable TV be regulated, according to the public interest theory? In the public interest theory, regulation maximizes total surplus, which occurs if marginal cost equals price. As you can see in Fig. 19.1, that outcome occurs if the price is regulated at $10 per household per month and if 8 million households are served. Such a regulation is called a marginal cost pricing rule. A **marginal cost pricing rule** sets price equal to marginal cost. It maximizes total surplus in the regulated industry.

A natural monopoly that is regulated to set price equal to marginal cost incurs an economic loss. Because its average total cost curve is falling, marginal cost is below average total cost. Because price equals marginal cost, price is below average total cost. Average total cost minus price is the loss per unit produced. It's pretty obvious that a cable TV company that is required to use a marginal cost pricing rule will not stay in business for long. How can a company cover its costs and, at the same time, obey a marginal cost pricing rule?

One possibility is price discrimination (see Chapter 13, pp. 273–276). Another possibility is to use a two-part price (called a *two-part tariff*). For example, local telephone companies can charge consumers a monthly fee for being connected to the telephone system and then charge a price equal to marginal cost for each local call. A cable TV operator can charge a one-time connection fee that covers its fixed cost and then charge a monthly fee equal to marginal cost.

If a natural monopoly cannot cover its total cost from its customers and if the government wants it to follow a marginal cost pricing rule, the government must give the firm a subsidy. In this case, the government raises the revenue for the subsidy by taxing some other activity. But as we saw in Chapter 18, taxes themselves generate deadweight loss. Thus the deadweight loss resulting from additional taxes must be subtracted from the efficiency gained by forcing the natural monopoly to adopt a marginal cost pricing rule.

It is possible that deadweight loss will be minimized by permitting the natural monopoly to charge a higher price than marginal cost rather than by taxing some other sector of the economy to subsidize the natural monopoly. Such a pricing arrangement is called an average cost pricing rule. An **average cost pricing rule** sets price equal to average total cost. Figure 19.2 shows the average cost pricing solution. The cable TV operator charges $15 a month and serves 6 million households. A deadweight loss arises, which is shown by the gray triangle in the figure.

Capturing the Regulator What does the capture theory predict about the regulation of this industry? According to the capture theory, regulation serves the interests of the producer, which means getting the regulator to set the price equal to the monopoly's

---

FIGURE 19.1

Natural Monopoly: Marginal Cost Pricing

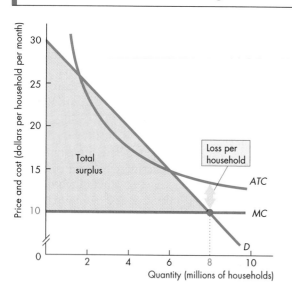

A natural monopoly is a firm that can supply the entire market at a lower price than two or more firms can. A cable TV operator faces the demand curve D. The firm's marginal cost is constant at $10 per household per month, as shown by the curve labeled MC. Fixed costs are large, and the average total cost curve, which includes average fixed cost, is shown as ATC. A marginal cost pricing rule that maximizes total surplus sets the price at $10 a month, with 8 million households being served. The resulting consumer surplus is shown as the green area. The firm incurs a loss on each household, indicated by the red arrow. To remain in business, the firm must price discriminate, use a two-part tariff, or receive a subsidy.

FIGURE 19.2

Natural Monopoly: Average Cost Pricing

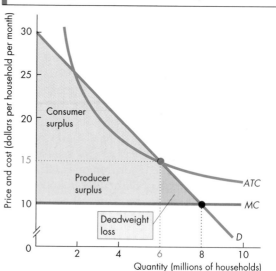

Average cost pricing sets price equal to average total cost. The cable TV operator charges $15 a month and serves 6 million households. In this situation, the firm breaks even— average total cost equals price. Deadweight loss, shown by the gray triangle, is generated. Consumer surplus is reduced to the green area.

unregulated price. To work out the price that achieves this goal, we need to look at the relationship between marginal revenue and marginal cost. A monopoly maximizes profit by producing the output at which marginal revenue equals marginal cost. The monopoly's marginal revenue curve in Fig. 19.3 is the curve *MR*. Marginal revenue equals marginal cost when output is 4 million households. The monopoly charges a price of $20 a month and makes the profit shown by the blue area. Thus a regulation that best serves the interest of the producer will set the price at this level.

But how can a producer go about obtaining regulation that results in this monopoly profit-maximizing outcome? To answer this question, we need to look at the way in which agencies determine a regulated price. A key method used is called rate of return regulation.

FIGURE 19.3

Natural Monopoly: Profit Maximization

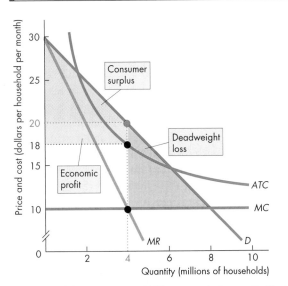

The cable TV operator would like to maximize profit. To do so, marginal revenue (*MR*) is made equal to marginal cost. At a price of $20 a month, 4 million households buy cable service. Consumer surplus is reduced to the green triangle. The deadweight loss increases to the gray triangle. The monopoly makes the profit shown by the blue rectangle. If the producer can capture the regulator, the outcome will be the situation shown here.

Rate of Return Regulation   Rate of return regulation determines a regulated price by setting the price at a level that enables the regulated firm to earn a specified target percent return on its capital. The target rate of return is determined with reference to what is normal in competitive industries. This rate of return is part of the opportunity cost of the natural monopolist and is included in the firm's average total cost. By examining the firm's total cost, including the normal rate of return on capital, the regulator attempts to determine the price at which average total cost is covered. Thus rate of return regulation is equivalent to average cost pricing.

In Fig. 19.2, average cost pricing results in a regulated price of $15 a month with 6 million households being served. Thus rate of return regulation, based on a correct assessment of the producer's average total cost curve, results in a price that favors the consumer and does not enable the producer to maximize monopoly profit. The special interest group will have failed to capture the regulator, and the outcome will be closer to that predicted by the public interest theory of regulation.

But there is a feature of many real-world situations that the above analysis does not take into account: the ability of the monopoly firm to mislead the regulator about its true costs.

Inflating Costs   The managers of a firm might be able to inflate the firm's costs by spending part of the firm's revenue on inputs that are not strictly required for the production of the good. By this device, the firm's apparent costs exceed the true costs. On-the-job luxury in the form of sumptuous office suites, limousines, free baseball tickets (disguised as public relations expenses), company jets, lavish international travel, and entertainment are all ways in which managers can inflate costs.

If the cable TV operator manages to inflate its costs and persuade the regulator that its true average total cost curve is that shown as *ATC (inflated)* in Fig. 19.4, then the regulator, applying the normal rate of return principle, will regulate the price at $20 a month. In this example, the price and quantity will be the same as those under unregulated monopoly. It might be impossible for firms to inflate their costs by as much as the amount shown in the figure. But to the extent that costs can be inflated, the apparent average total cost curve lies somewhere between the true *ATC* curve and *ATC (inflated)*. The greater the ability of the firm to pad its costs in this way, the

FIGURE 19.4

Natural Monopoly: Inflating Costs

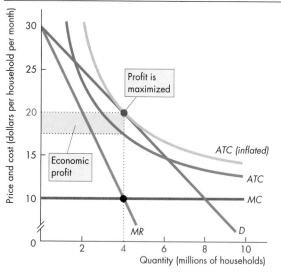

If the cable TV operator is able to inflate its costs to *ATC (inflated)* and persuade the regulator that these are genuine minimum costs of production, rate of return regulation results in a price of $20 a month—the profit-maximizing price. To the extent that the producer can inflate costs above average total cost, the price rises, output falls, and deadweight loss increases. The profit is captured by the managers, not the shareholders (owners) of the firm.

more closely its profit (measured in economic terms) approaches the maximum possible. The shareholders of this firm don't receive this economic profit because it gets used up in baseball tickets, luxury offices, and the other actions taken by the firm's managers to inflate the company's costs.

Incentive Regulation and Deregulation Partly for the reasons we've just examined, rate of return regulation is increasingly being replaced by incentive regulation schemes. An **incentive regulation scheme** is a type of regulation that gives a firm an incentive to operate efficiently and keep costs under control. Today, a majority of states have adopted incentive regulation schemes for telecommunications rather than traditional rate of return regulation. These new schemes take two main forms: price caps (adopted in California, New Jersey, Oregon, and Rhode Island) and earnings sharing plans (adopted in Colorado,

Connecticut, Florida, Georgia, Kentucky, Tennessee, and Texas). Under a price cap regulation, the regulators set the maximum price that may be charged and hold that cap (adjusted for inflation) for several years. If profits are considered too high, the price cap will be lowered. Under earnings-sharing regulation, if profits rise above a certain level, they must be shared with the firm's customers. There is some evidence that under these types of regulations, local telephone companies are attempting to cut costs.

Sometimes, technological change occurs that destroys a natural monopoly. When this happens, deregulation and the introduction competition are possible. Technologies that permit many gas and electricity producers to share a common distribution network is an example.

Public Interest or Capture?

It is not clear whether actual regulation produces prices and quantities that more closely correspond with the predictions of capture theory or with public interest theory. One thing is clear, however. Price regulation does not require natural monopolies to use the marginal cost pricing rule. If it did, most natural monopolies would make losses and receive hefty government subsidies to enable them to remain in business. But there are even exceptions to this conclusion. For example, many local telephone companies do appear to use marginal cost pricing for local telephone calls. They cover their total cost by charging a flat fee each month for being connected to their telephone system but then permitting each call to be made at its marginal cost—zero or something very close to it.

A test of whether natural monopoly regulation is in the public interest or the interest of the producer is to examine the rates of return earned by regulated natural monopolies. If those rates of return are significantly higher than those in the rest of the economy, then, to some degree, the regulator might have been captured by the producer. If the rates of return in the regulated monopoly industries are similar to those in the rest of the economy, then we cannot tell for sure whether the regulator has been captured or not, for we cannot know the extent to which costs have been inflated by the managers of the regulated firms.

Table 19.1 shows rates of return in regulated natural monopolies as well as the economy's average rate of return. In the 1960s, rates of return in regulated natural monopolies were somewhat below the economy

Rates of Return in Regulated Monopolies

Industry	Years 1962–69	1970–77
Electricity	3.2	6.1
Gas	3.3	8.2
Railroad	5.1	7.2
Average of above	3.9	7.2
Economy average	6.6	5.1

Source: Paul W. MacAvoy, *The Regulated Industries and the Economy* (New York: W.W. Norton, 1979), 49–60.

average; in the 1970s, those returns exceeded the economy average. Overall, the rates of return achieved by regulated natural monopolies were not very different from those in the rest of the economy. We can conclude from these data either that natural monopoly regulation does, to some degree, serve the public interest or that natural monopoly managers inflate their costs by amounts sufficiently large to disguise the fact that they have captured the regulator and that the public interest is not being served.

A final test of whether regulation of natural monopoly is in the public interest or the producers' interest is

Gains from Deregulating Natural Monopolies

Industry	Consumer surplus	Producer surplus	Total surplus
	(billions of 1990 dollars)		
Railroads	8.5	3.2	11.7
Telecommunications	1.2	0.0	1.2
Cable television	0.8	0.0	0.8
Total	10.5	3.2	13.7

Source: Clifford Winston, "Economic Deregulation: Days of Reckoning for Microeconomists," *Journal of Economic Literature*, XXXI, September 1993, pp. 1263–1289, and the author's calculations.

to study the changes in consumer surplus and producer surplus following deregulation. Microeconomists have researched this issue, and Table 19.2 summarizes their conclusions. In the case of railroad deregulation, which occurred during the 1980s, both consumers and producers gained, and by large amounts. The gains from deregulation of telecommunications and cable television were smaller and accrued only to consumers. These findings suggest that railroad regulation hurt everyone, while regulation of telecommunications and cable television hurt only consumers.

We've now examined the regulation of natural monopoly. Let's next turn to regulation in oligopolistic industries—the regulation of cartels.

Cartel Regulation

A *cartel* is a collusive agreement among a number of firms that is designed to restrict output and achieve a higher profit for the cartel's members. Cartels are illegal in the United States and in most other countries. But international cartels can sometimes operate legally, such as the international cartel of oil producers known as OPEC (the Organization of Petroleum Exporting Countries).

Illegal cartels can arise in oligopolistic industries. An oligopoly is a market structure in which a small number of firms compete with each other. We studied oligopoly (and duopoly—two firms competing for a market) in Chapter 14. There we saw that if firms manage to collude and behave like a monopoly, they can set the same price and sell the same total quantity as a monopoly firm would. But we also discovered that in such a situation, each firm will be tempted to cheat, increasing its own output and profit at the expense of the other firms. A possible result of such cheating on the collusive agreement is the unraveling of the monopoly equilibrium and the emergence of a competitive outcome with zero economic profit for producers. Such an outcome benefits consumers at the expense of producers.

How is oligopoly regulated? Does regulation prevent monopoly practices or does it encourage those practices?

According to the public interest theory, oligopoly is regulated to ensure a competitive outcome. Consider, for example, the market for trucking tomatoes from the San Joaquin Valley to Los Angeles, illustrated in Fig. 19.5. The market demand curve for trips is *D*. The industry marginal cost curve—and the competitive supply curve—is *MC*. Public interest regulation will regulate the price of a trip at $20, and there will be 300 trips a week.

How would this industry be regulated according to the capture theory? Regulation that is in the producer interest will maximize profit. To find the outcome in this case, we need to determine the price and quantity when marginal cost equals marginal revenue. The marginal revenue curve is *MR*. So marginal cost equals marginal revenue at 200 trips a week. The price of a trip is $30.

One way of achieving this outcome is to place an output limit on each firm in the industry. If there are 10 trucking companies, an output limit of 20 trips per company ensures that the total number of trips in a week is 200. Penalties can be imposed to ensure that no single producer exceeds its output limit.

All the firms in the industry would support this type of regulation because it helps to prevent cheating and to maintain a monopoly outcome. Each firm knows that without effectively enforced production quotas, every firm has an incentive to increase output. (For each firm, price exceeds marginal cost, so a greater output brings a larger profit.) So each firm wants a method of preventing output from increasing above the industry profit-maximizing level, and the quotas enforced by regulation achieve this end. With this type of cartel regulation, the regulator enables a cartel to operate legally and in its own best interest.

What does cartel regulation do in practice? Some regulation has benefited the producer. When the Interstate Commerce Commission regulated trucking, producers persistently earned economic profits. Also, by forming a strong labor union, truck drivers captured a large part of the producer surplus.

Some regulation has benefited both the producer and the consumer. When the Civil Aeronautics Board regulated the airlines, they earned economic profits, but they competed by offering high-cost services that benefited consumers and eventually eroded profits.

Table 19.3 provides some evidence in support of the conclusion that regulation increased profits in trucking and airlines. If regulation ensured a competitive outcome, rates of return in regulated oligopolies would be no higher than those in the economy as a whole. As the numbers in Table 19.3 show, rates of return in airlines and trucking were close to twice the economy average rate of return in the 1960s. In the 1970s, the rate of return in trucking remained higher than the economy average (although by a smaller

---

FIGURE 19.5
Collusive Oligopoly

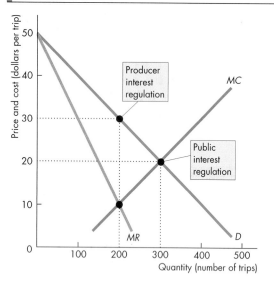

Ten trucking firms transport tomatoes from the San Joaquin Valley to Los Angeles. The demand curve is *D*, and the industry marginal cost curve is *MC*. Under competition, the *MC* curve is the industry supply curve. If the industry is competitive, the price of a trip will be $20 and 300 trips will be made each week. Producers will demand regulation that restricts entry and limits output to 200 trips a week, where industry marginal revenue (*MR*) is equal to industry marginal cost (*MC*). This regulation raises the price to $30 a trip and results in each producer making maximum profit—as if it is a monopoly.

TABLE 19.3
Rates of Return in Regulated Oligopolies

Industry	Years	
	1962–69	1970–77
Airlines	12.8	3.0
Trucking	13.6	8.1
Economy average	6.6	5.1

Source: Paul W. MacAvoy, *The Regulated Industries and the Economy* (New York: W.W. Norton, 1979), 49–60.

margin than had prevailed in the 1960s). Airline rates of return in the 1970s fell to below the economy average. The overall picture that emerges from examining data on rates of return is mixed. The regulation of oligopoly does not always result in higher profit, but there are many situations in which it does.

Further evidence on oligopoly regulation can be obtained from the performance of prices and profit following deregulation. If, following deregulation, prices and profit fall, then, to some degree, the regulation must have been serving the interest of the producer.

In contrast, if, following deregulation, prices and profits remain constant or increase, then the regulation may be presumed to have been serving the public interest. Because there has been a substantial amount of deregulation in recent years, we can use this test of oligopoly regulation to see which of the two theories better fits the facts.

The evidence is mixed, but in the cases of the airlines and trucking, the two main oligopolies that have been deregulated, prices fell and there was a large increase in the volume of business. Table 19.4 summarizes the estimated effects of deregulation of airlines and trucking on consumer surplus, producer surplus, and total surplus. Most of the gains were in consumer surplus. In the case of the airlines, there was a gain in producer surplus as well.

But the table shows that in the trucking industry, producer surplus decreased by almost $5 billion a year. This outcome implies that the regulation benefited the producer by restricting competition and enabling prices to exceed their competitive levels.

Making Predictions

Most industries have a few producers and many consumers. In this situation, public choice theory predicts that regulation protects producer interests and that politicians are rewarded with campaign contributions rather than votes. But there are situations in which the consumer interest has prevailed. There are also cases in which the balance has switched from producer to consumer, as seen in the deregulation process that began in the late 1970s.

Deregulation has occurred for three main reasons. First, economists have become more confident and vocal in predicting gains from deregulation. Second, a large increase in energy prices in the 1970s increased the cost of regulation borne by consumers. These price hikes made route regulation in the transportation sector extremely costly and changed the balance in favor of consumers in the political equilibrium. Third, technological change ended some natural monopolies. New technologies enable small producers to offer low-cost long-distance telephone services. These producers want a share of the business—and profit—of AT&T. Furthermore, as communication technology improve, the cost of communication falls and the cost of organizing larger groups of consumers also falls.

If this line of reasoning is correct, there will be more public interest regulation and deregulation in the future.

TABLE 19.4
Gains from Deregulating Oligopolies

Industry	Consumer surplus	Producer surplus	Total surplus
	(billions of 1990 dollars)		
Airlines	11.8	4.9	16.7
Trucking	15.4	−4.8	10.6
Total	27.2	0.1	27.3

Source: Clifford Winston, "Economic Deregulation: Days of Reckoning for Microeconomists," *Journal of Economic Literature,* XXXI, September 1993, pp. 1263–1289, and the author's calculations.

REVIEW QUIZ

- When did regulation begin in the United States, what was regulated, and when did regulation reach its peak?
- Why does natural monopoly need to be regulated?
- What pricing rule enables a natural monopoly to operate in the public interest and why is that rule difficult to implement?
- What pricing rule is typically used to regulate a natural monopoly and what problems does it create?
- What is incentive regulation and how does it work?
- How might cartels be regulated in the public interest?

Let's now leave regulation and turn to the other method of intervention in markets: antitrust law.

Antitrust Law

ANTITRUST LAW PROVIDES AN ALTERNATIVE WAY in which the government may influence the marketplace. As in the case of regulation, antitrust law can be formulated in the public interest, to maximize total surplus, or in private interests, to maximize the surpluses of particular special interest groups such as producers.

The Antitrust Laws

The antitrust laws are easily summarized. The first antitrust law, the Sherman Act, was passed in 1890 in an atmosphere of outrage and disgust at the actions and practices of J.P. Morgan, John D. Rockefeller, and W.H. Vanderbilt—the so-called robber barons. Ironically, the most lurid stories of the actions of these great American capitalists are not of their monopolization and exploitation of consumers but of their sharp practices against each other. Nevertheless, monopolies did emerge—for example, the spectacular control of the oil industry by John D. Rockefeller.

A wave of mergers at the turn of the century produced stronger antitrust laws. The Clayton Act of 1914 supplemented the Sherman Act, and the Federal Trade Commission, an agency charged with enforcing the antitrust laws, was created.

Table 19.5 summarizes the two main provisions of the Sherman Act. Section 1 of the Act is precise.

TABLE 19.5	

The Sherman Act of 1890

Section 1:

Every contract, combination in the form of trust or otherwise, or conspiracy, in restraint of trade or commerce among the several States, or with foreign nations, is hereby declared to be illegal.

Section 2.

Every person who shall monopolize, or attempt to monopolize, or combine or conspire with any other person or persons, to monopolize any part of the trade or commerce among the several States, or with foreign nations, shall be deemed guilty of a felony

TABLE 19.6	

The Clayton Act and Its Amendments

Clayton Act	1914
Robinson-Patman Act	1936
Celler-Kefauver Act	1950

These Acts prohibit the following practices *only* if they substantially lessen competition or create monopoly:

1. Price discrimination
2. Contracts that require other goods to be bought from the same firm (called tying arrangements)
3. Contracts that require a firm to buy all its requirements of a particular item from a single firm (called requirements contracts)
4. Contracts that prevent a firm from selling competing items (called exclusive dealing)
5. Contracts that prevent a buyer from reselling a product outside a specified area (called territorial confinement)
6. Acquiring a competitor's shares or assets
7. Becoming a director of a competing firm

Conspiring with others to restrict competition is illegal. But section 2 is general and imprecise. Just what is an "attempt to monopolize"? The Clayton Act and its two amendments, the Robinson-Patman Act of 1936 and Celler-Kefauver of 1950, which outlaw specific practices, provided greater precision. Table 19.6 describes these practices and summarizes the main provisions of these three Acts.

Landmark Antitrust Cases

The real force of any law arises from its interpretation. The interpretation of the antitrust laws has been clear on price fixing (section 1 of the Sherman Act) but less clear on attempts to monopolize (section 2 of the Sherman Act and the Clayton Act) and rulings have fluctuated between favoring producers and consumers. Table 19.7 summarizes the landmark cases.

Price Fixing Court decisions have made *any* price fixing deal a violation of Section 1 of the Sherman Act. Taking someone's life is a serious offense. But it is not always a violation of the murder law. In contrast, price fixing is always a violation of the antitrust law. Accidents and other involuntary causes of death are recognized as reasons not to convict someone of murder. But if the Justice Department can prove the existence of price fixing, a defendant can offer no acceptable excuse.

A 1927 case against *Trenton Potteries Company* and others first established this hard line, which is known as the *per se* interpretation of the law. The court ruled that an agreement between Trenton Potteries and others to fix the prices of sanitary pottery violated the Sherman Act even if the prices themselves were reasonable. Price fixing *per se* (in and of itself) is a violation of the law.

In 1961, General Electric, Westinghouse, and other electrical component manufacturers were found guilty of a price-fixing conspiracy. This case was the first one in which the executives (rather than the company itself) were fined and jailed.

A recent costly example that illustrates this strict interpretation of the law is that of Archer Daniels Midland. In 1996, this firm, which is a major producer of agricultural products, was fined $100 million for conspiring with foreign producers to fix the prices of lysine and citric acid, two additives that are used in various food products.

Attempts to Monopolize   The most important early antitrust cases were those involving the American Tobacco Company and Standard Oil Company, which were decided in 1911. These two companies were found guilty of violations under the Sherman Act and ordered to divest themselves of large holdings in other companies. The breakup of John D. Rockefeller's Standard Oil Company resulted in the creation of the oil companies that today are household names, such as Amoco, Chevron, Exxon, and Sohio.

In finding these companies to be in violation of the provisions of the Sherman Act, the Supreme Court enunciated the "rule of reason." The rule of reason states that monopoly arising from mergers and agreements among firms is not necessarily illegal. Only if there is an unreasonable restraint of trade does the arrangement violate the provisions of the Sherman Act.

TABLE 19.7

Landmark Antitrust Cases

Case	Year	Verdict and consequence
1. Price Fixing		
Trenton Potteries Company	1927	*Guilty:* Agreement to fix prices was *per se* a violation of the Sherman Act, regardless of whether the prices themselves are "reasonable."
General Electric, Westinghouse, and others	1961	*Guilty:* Price-fixing conspiracy; executives fined and jailed.
Archer Daniels Midland	1996	*Guilty:* Price-fixing conspiracy; fined $100 million.
2. Attempts to Monopolize?		
American Tobacco Co. and *Standard Oil Co.*	1911	*Guilty:* Ordered to divest themselves of large holdings in other companies; "rule of reason" enunciated—only *unreasonable* combinations guilty under Sherman Act.
U.S. Steel Co.	1920	*Not guilty:* Although U.S. Steel had a very large market share (near monopoly), mere "size alone is not an offense"; application of the "rule of reason."
Alcoa	1945	*Guilty:* Too big—had too large a share of the market.
Aspen Skiing	1985	*Guilty:* Owner of three of the four downhill ski facilities refused to offer an all-Aspen ticket and share revenues on a use-basis with the owner of the other facility.
Spectrum Sports	1993	*Not guilty:* Although Spectrum Sports was the national distributor of sorbothane (used in athletic products), no evidence was present that the company had attempted to monopolize the relevant market.

The rule of reason was widely regarded as removing the force of the Sherman Act itself. This view was reinforced in 1920 when U.S. Steel Company was acquitted of violations under the act even though it had a very large (more than 50 percent) share of the U.S. steel market. Applying the "rule of reason," the court declared that "size alone is not an offense."

In a case that some people interpreted as challenging the "rule of reason," the *Alcoa* case, decided in 1945, Alcoa was judged to be in violation of the antitrust law because it was too big. It had too large a share of the aluminum market. This relatively tough interpretation of the law continued through the late 1960s.

Of the many other cases concerning the attempt to monopolize, we look at two interesting and relatively recent ones. During the 1970s, the Aspen Skiing Company, which owned three of the four downhill ski facilities in Aspen, offered an all-Aspen ticket and shared the revenues with Aspen Highlands Skiing Corp. that owned the fourth facility. Revenues were split based on a survey of users. In 1977, Aspen Skiing refused to offer the all-Aspen ticket unless Aspen Highland agreed to accept a low fixed share of the revenue. The all-Aspen ticket was not offered, and Aspen Highland lost business. The court held that the Aspen Skiing Company was attempting to monopolize.

When Spectrum Sports became the national distributor of sorbothane athletic products, (sorbothane is a shock-absorber), some injured companies alleged that Spectrum had attempted to monopolize. The court held that Spectrum could not be held to have attempted to monopolize absent evidence that it had engaged in monopoly practices.

Today's Showcase: The United States Versus Microsoft

Microsoft has been charged with specific violations of the antitrust laws, and in 1998 a trial of these charges began.

The Case Against Microsoft The claims against Microsoft are that the firm:

1. Possesses monopoly power in the market for PC operating systems.
2. Uses below-cost pricing (called predatory pricing) and tying arrangements to achieve a monopoly in the market for Web browsers.
3. Uses other anticompetitive practices to strengthen its monopoly in these two markets.

Microsoft, it is claimed, operates behind barriers to entry that arise from economies of scale and network economies. Microsoft's average total cost falls as production increases (economies of scale) because the costs of developing software are large but are a fixed cost while the marginal cost of one copy of Windows is small. The benefit to Windows users increases as the number of users increases (network economies) because with more users, the range of Windows applications expands.

When Microsoft entered the Internet browser market with Internet Explorer (IE), it offered it for a zero price. This is viewed as predatory pricing—an attempt to drive out the competition and monopolize a market. Microsoft now has integrated IE with Windows 98, which means that no one using this operating system needs a separate browser such as Netscape Communicator. Microsoft's critics claim that this practice is illegal product tying.

Microsoft's Response Microsoft challenges all these claims. It says that although Windows dominates today, it is vulnerable to new operating systems. It also claims that integrating Internet Explorer with Windows 98 provides a product of greater consumer value. It is not tying. It is one product.

Microsoft will be the subject of ongoing investigation, and you should try to keep track of developments.

Merger Rules

The Federal Trade Commission (FTC) uses guidelines to determine which mergers it will examine and possibly block based on the Herfindahl-Hirschman index (HHI), which is explained in Chapter 10 (p. 208). A market in which the HHI is less than 1,000 is regarded as competitive. An index between 1,000 and 1,800 indicates a moderately concentrated market, and a merger in this market that would increase the index by 100 points is examined by the FTC. An index above 1,800 indicates a concentrated market, and a merger in this market that would increase the index by 50 points is examined. Figure 19.6(a) summarizes these guidelines.

The FTC used these guidelines to analyze two recently proposed mergers in the market for soft drinks. In 1986, PepsiCo announced its intention to buy 7-Up for $380 million. A month later, Coca-Cola said it would buy Dr Pepper for $470 million.

FIGURE 19.6

The HHI Merger Guidelines

(a) The merger guidelines

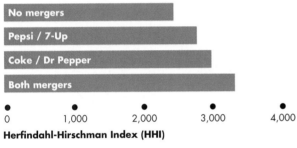

(b) Product mergers in soft drinks

The FTC scrutinizes proposed mergers if the HHI exceeds 1,000. Proposed mergers between producers of carbonated soft drinks were blocked in 1986 by application of these guidelines.

Whether this market is concentrated depends on how it is defined. The market for *all* soft drinks, which includes *carbonated* drinks marketed by these four companies plus *fruit juices* and *bottled water*, has an HHI of 120, so it is highly competitive. But the market for *carbonated* soft drinks is highly concentrated. Coca-Cola has a 39 percent share, PepsiCo has 28 percent, Dr Pepper is next with 7 percent, then comes 7-Up with 6 percent. One other producer, RJR, has a 5 percent market share. So the five largest firms in this market have an 85 percent market share. If we assume that the other 15 percent of the market consists of 15 firms, each with a 1 percent market share, the Herfindahl-Hirschman index is

$$HHI = 39^2 + 28^2 + 7^2 + 6^2 + 5^2 + 15 = 2,430.$$

With an HHI of this magnitude, a merger that increases the index by 50 points is examined by the FTC. Figure 19.6(b) shows how the HHI would have changed with the mergers. The PepsiCo and 7-Up merger would have increased the index by more than 300 points, the Coca-Cola and Dr Pepper merger would have increased it by more than 500 points, and both mergers together would have increased the index by almost 800 points. The FTC decided to define the market narrowly and, with increases of these magnitudes, blocked the mergers.

Public or Special Interest?

It is clear from the historical contexts in which antitrust law has evolved that its intent has been to protect and pursue the public interest and restrain the profit-seeking and anticompetitive actions of producers. But it is also clear from the above brief history of antitrust legislation and cases that, from time to time, the interest of the producer has had an influence on the way in which the law has been interpreted and applied. Nevertheless, the overall thrust of antitrust law appears to have been directed toward achieving efficiency and therefore to serving the public interest.

R E V I E W   Q U I Z

- What are the four Acts of Congress that make up our antitrust laws? When were these laws enacted?
- When is price fixing not a violation of the antitrust laws?
- What is an attempt to monopolize an industry?
- Name three antitrust cases that involve price fixing. What did the court decide?

◆ We've reviewed the public interest and capture theories of government intervention. And we've seen that regulators do sometimes get captured by the regulated and work against the interest of consumers. But this outcome does not always occur.

In *Reading Between the Lines*, on pages 426–427, you can see a recent example of antitrust law being used to penalize fixing in an attempt to protect the public interest.

Price Fixing

THE NEW YORK TIMES, OCTOBER 15, 1996

Archer Daniels Agrees to Big Fine for Price Fixing

BY KURT EICHENWALD

The Archer Daniels Midland Company, long one of the country's most powerful corporations, agreed to plead guilty to conspiring with competitors to fix the prices of two agricultural products and pay $100 million in fines, the company announced yesterday.

The fine is by far the largest ever obtained by the Justice Department in a criminal price-fixing case, eclipsing the next highest by almost seven times. ...

In the plea, Archer Daniels—a food processing giant that advertises itself as the "Supermarket to the World"—will admit that it fixed prices of lysine, a feed additive, and citric acid, an organic acid used in various foods and beverages.

Under the deal, Archer Daniels will pay $70 million in fines for fixing lysine prices and $30 million for the citric acid case. ...

"The $100 million fine is shareholder assets that are being squandered to pay for criminal activity that never should have occurred," said James E. Burton, chief executive of the California Public Employees Retirement System, one of the nation's largest pension funds and an investor in Archer Daniels. ...

The company's financial power means that Archer Daniels will be able to pay its $100 million in fines—as well as another $90 million it has agreed to pay to settle class action suits relating to the investigation—without feeling much pain. The company has more than $1.3 billion in cash and liquid securities on hand; its profits last year approached $700 million and its businesses continue to boom. ...

Essence of the Story

- Archer Daniels Midland (ADM) paid fines totaling $100 million for fixing the prices of lysine and citric acid.

- The fine is seven times larger than the previous largest.

- One large investor in ADM complained that the fine was squandering shareholder assets.

- With $1.3 billion in cash and liquid assets and a profit of close to $700 million a year, ADM was easily able to pay the fine.

Economic Analysis

■ Here, we'll focus on fixing the price of lysine, for which ADM paid a $70 million fine.

■ First, a few technical facts. Lysine is an amino acid that is essential in the diets of most animals.

■ Animal food such as soybeanmeal contain lysine, but corn is deficient in lysine. So animals can be fed soybeanmeal or corn supplemented with lysine.

■ Now to the economics. Cost-conscious farmers use the least-cost diet. They buy lysine only if corn plus lysine costs less than soybeanmeal. So the price of lysine cannot rise much above the gap between the price of soybeanmeal and the price of corn.

■ The figure shows the (worldwide) market for lysine. The demand curve, D, is highly elastic because lysine competes with soybeanmeal.

■ The marginal cost of lysine is MC. In a competitive market, the marginal cost curve is the supply curve, S.

■ Equilibrium in a competitive market occurs at the quantity Q_C and the price P_C.

■ If the producers of lysine collude to fix the price, and if they act like a monopoly, their marginal revenue curve is MR in the figure.

■ To maximize economic profit, the firms fix the price at P_M, the highest price at which they can sell Q_M, the quantity at which marginal revenue equals marginal cost. The firms allocate the total output Q_M among themselves.

■ This action brings gains to producers—their economic profit increases by the blue area in the figure.

■ This action imposes costs on consumers because it decreases consumer surplus and also creates deadweight loss, the gray area in the figure.

■ The fine imposed on ADM decreases its profit and returns some of the loss to the taxpayers (consumers).

■ Some ADM stockholders say that their assets are being used to pay the fine. This claim is not exactly correct. The illegal price fixing increased ADM's profit, which boosted its share price and benefited its stockholders. The fine corrects this situation.

■ It is not known if the fine is large enough to wipe out the gains from price fixing or to leave ADM and its stockholders with a net gain from illegal actions.

■ But what is known is that the deadweight loss from price fixing is lost forever. No fine can restore this loss.

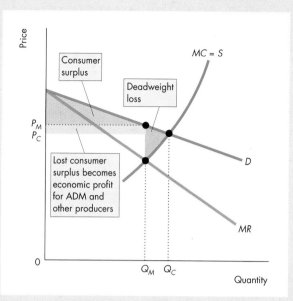

You're The Voter

■ The largest fine for price fixing before the ADM fine was $15 million, imposed on Dyno Nobel for price fixing. Is the ADM fine is too large, too small, or about right? Explain.

■ Price fixing is punishable by fines or by possibly jailing the people found responsible. This news article reports only the fine on ADM. But in January 1997, a Chicago federal grand jury indicted three former top executives of ADM, along with a Japanese executive, for conspiring to fix prices and allocate sales in the worldwide market for lysine. How would you use economic reasoning to decide which penalty is likely to be more effective (a) to deter price fixing and (b) to compensate those who lose from it?

SUMMARY

KEY POINTS

Market Intervention (p. 412)

- Governments intervene in monopoly and oligopoly markets with regulation and antitrust law.

Economic Theory of Regulation (pp. 412–414)

- Consumers and producers express their demand for the regulation by voting, lobbying, and making campaign contributions.
- The larger the surplus per person generated by a regulation, the greater the number of gainers, and the smaller the number of losers, the larger is the demand for the regulation.
- Regulation is supplied by politicians, who pursue votes and bureaucrats who pursue large budgets.
- The larger the surplus per person generated and the larger the number of people affected by it, the larger is the supply of regulation.
- Public interest theory predicts that regulation maximizes total surplus. Capture theory predicts that regulation maximizes producer surplus.

Regulation and Deregulation (pp. 414–421)

- Federal regulation began in 1887 (with the Interstate Commerce Commission) and expanded until the mid-1970s, since when much deregulation has occurred.
- Regulation is conducted by agencies that are controlled by politically appointed bureaucrats and staffed by a permanent bureaucracy of experts.
- Regulation has often had little effect on profits, and deregulation has often brought gains for consumers and producers.

Antitrust Law (pp. 422–425)

- Antitrust law is an alternative way in which the government can control monopoly and monopolistic practices.
- The first antitrust law, the Sherman Act, was passed in 1890, and the law was strengthened in 1914 when the Clayton Act was passed and the Federal Trade Commission was created.

- All price-fixing agreements are violations of the Sherman Act, and no acceptable excuse exists.
- The first landmark cases (against the American Tobacco Company and Standard Oil Company) established the "rule of reason," which held that an attempt to monopolize is illegal; monopoly itself is not illegal.
- The Federal Trade Commission uses guidelines to determine which mergers to examine and possibly block based on the Herfindahl-Hirschman Index.
- The intent of antitrust law is to protect the public interest. This intent has been served most of the time. But sometimes the interest of the producer has influenced the way in which the law has been interpreted and applied.

KEY FIGURES AND TABLES ◆

KEY TERMS

Antitrust law, 412
Average cost pricing rule, 416
Capture theory, 413
Incentive regulation scheme, 418
Marginal cost pricing rule, 415
Public interest theory, 413
Rate of return regulation, 417
Regulation, 412

P R O B L E M S

*1. Elixir Springs, Inc., is an unregulated natural monopoly that bottles Elixir, a unique health product with no substitutes. The total fixed cost incurred by Elixir Springs is $150,000, and its marginal cost is 10¢ a bottle. The figure illustrates the demand for Elixir.

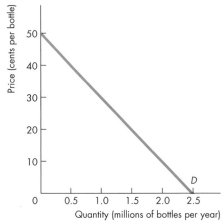

a. What is the price of a bottle of Elixir?
b. How many bottles does Elixir Springs sell?
c. Does Elixir Springs maximize total surplus or producer surplus?

2. Cascade Springs, Inc., is a natural monopoly that bottles water from a spring high in the Rocky Mountains. The total fixed cost that it incurs is $120,000, and its marginal cost is 20 cents a bottle. The figure illustrates the demand for Cascade Springs bottled water.

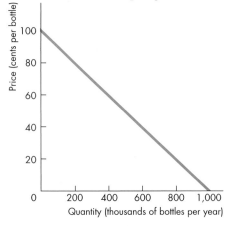

a. What is the price of Cascade Springs water?
b. How many bottles does Cascade Springs sell?
c. Does Cascade Springs maximize total surplus or producer surplus?

*3. The government regulates Elixir Springs in problem 1 by imposing a marginal cost pricing rule.
a. What is the price of a bottle of Elixir?
b. How many bottles does Elixir Springs sell?
c. What is Elixir Springs' economic profit?
d. What is the consumer surplus?
e. Is the regulation in the public interest? Explain.

4. The government regulates Cascade Springs in problem 2 by imposing a marginal cost pricing rule.
a. What is the price of Cascade Springs water?
b. How many bottles does Cascade Springs sell?
c. What is the economic profit?
d. What is the consumer surplus?
e. Is the regulation in the public interest? Explain.

*5. The government regulates Elixir Springs in problem 1 by imposing an average cost pricing rule.
a. What is the price of a bottle of Elixir?
b. How many bottles does Elixir Springs sell?
c. What is Elixir Springs' economic profit?
d. What is the consumer surplus?
e. Is the regulation in the public interest? Explain.

6. The government regulates Cascade Springs in problem 2 by imposing an average cost pricing rule.
a. What is the price of Cascade Springs water?
b. How many bottles does Cascade Springs sell?
c. What is the economic profit?
d. What is the consumer surplus?
e. Is the regulation in the public interest? Explain.

*7. Two airlines share an international route.

The figure shows the market demand curve for trips on this route and the marginal cost curve that each firm faces. This air route is regulated.

a. What is the price of a trip and what is the number of trips per day if the regulation is in the public interest?

b. What is the price of a trip and what is the number of trips per day if the airlines capture the regulator?

c. What is the deadweight loss in part (b)?

d. What do you need to know to predict whether the regulation is in the public interest or the producer interest?

8. Two phone companies offer local calls in an area. The figure shows the market demand curve for calls and the marginal costs curves of each firm. These firms are regulated.

a. What is the price of a call and what is the number of calls per day if the regulation is in the public interest?

b. What is the price of a call and what is the number of calls per day if the phone companies capture the regulator?

c. What is the deadweight loss in part (b)?

d. What do you need to know to predict whether the regulation is in the public interest or the producer interest?

*9. Explain the difference between regulation and antitrust law. What types of situations do each apply to? Give an example of the use of each.

10. Describe the difference between the way in which the two parts of the Sherman Act have been applied. Why do you think one part has been interpreted more strictly than the other?

CRITICAL THINKING

1. Study *Reading Between the Lines* on pp. 426–427, and then answer the following questions:

a. To what charges did Archer Daniels Midland plead guilty?

b. Why is price fixing a problem? Who gains and who loses?

c. Why is it likely that the demand for lysine is highly elastic? What effect does the elasticity of demand have on a firm's ability to increase price in a price-fixing agreement?

d. What is citric acid used for? Is it likely that the demand for citric acid is highly elastic?

e. Critically evaluate the claim of James E. Burton.

f. Try to think of some different ways in which price fixing can be prevented. Use economic reasoning to explain why each method you have thought of will work.

2. Why is the Department of Justice concerned about the practices of Microsoft? What provision of the antitrust laws is Microsoft alleged to have violated? What is Microsoft's response?

3. What regulatory problems if any, are created by new technologies that enable people to connect to the Internet using a cable modem (and cable television lines) and make long-distance calls over the Internet?

4. Use the link on the Parkin Web site to visit the Federal Trade Commission, where you can obtain information about Intel, the computer chip maker.

a. What was the FTC's problem with Intel?

b. What did Intel agree to do?

c. Explain how Intel's agreement will influence the price, quantity, and consumer and producer surplus in the market for computer chips.

5. Use the link on the Parkin Web site to visit the Department of Justice on the World Wide Web and go to the page on press releases for 1997. Read the press release on price fixing by California crab catchers.

a. Explain how the price of crabs was fixed.

b. Explain what the Department of Justice did about the problem.

Chapter 20

Externalities, the Environment, and Knowledge

We burn huge quantities of fossil fuels—coal, natural gas, and oil—that cause acid rain and possibly global warming. The persistent and large-scale use of chlorofluorocarbons (CFCs) may have caused irreparable damage to the earth's ozone layer, thereby exposing us to additional ultraviolet rays, which increase the incidence of skin cancer. We dump toxic waste into rivers, lakes, and oceans. These environmental issues are simultaneously everybody's problem and nobody's problem. What, if anything, can government do to protect our environment? How can government action help us to take account of the damage that we cause others every time we turn on our heating or air conditioning systems? ◆ Almost every day, we hear about a new discovery—in medicine, engineering, chemistry, physics, or even economics. The advance of knowledge seems boundless. And more and more people are learning more and more of what is already known. The stock of knowledge—what is known and how many people know it—is increasing, apparently without bound. We are getting smarter. But is our stock of knowledge advancing fast enough? Are we spending enough on research and development? Do we spend enough on education? Do enough people remain in school for long enough? Would we be better off if we spent more on research and education?

Greener and Smarter

◇ In this chapter, we study the problems that arise because many of our actions create externalities. They affect other people, for ill or good, in ways that we do not usually take into account when we make our own economic choices. We study two big areas—the environment and the accumulation of knowledge—in which these problems are especially important. Externalities are a major source of *market failure*. When market failure occurs, we must either live with the inefficiency it creates or try to achieve greater efficiency by making some *public choices*. This chapter studies these choices. It begins by looking at external costs that affect the environment.

After studying this chapter, you will be able to:

- **Explain how property rights can sometimes overcome externalities**

- **Explain how emission charges, marketable permits, and taxes can be used to achieve efficiency in the face of external costs**

- **Explain how subsidies can be used to achieve efficiency in the face of external benefits**

- **Explain how scholarships, below-cost tuition, and research grants make the quantity of education and invention more efficient**

- **Explain how patents increase efficiency**

Economics of the Environment

ENVIRONMENTAL PROBLEMS ARE NOT NEW, AND they are not restricted to rich industrial countries. Preindustrial towns and cities in Europe had severe sewage disposal problems that created cholera epidemics and plagues that killed tens of millions of people. Nor is the desire to find solutions to environmental problems new. The development in the fourteenth century of pure water supplies and of garbage and sewage disposal are examples of early contributions to improving the quality of the environment.

Popular discussions of the environment usually pay little attention to economics. They focus on physical aspects of the environment, not costs and benefits. A common assumption is that if people's actions cause *any* environmental degradation, those actions must cease. In contrast, an economic study of the environment emphasizes costs and benefits. An economist talks about the efficient amount of pollution or environmental damage. This emphasis on costs and benefits does not mean that economists, as citizens, do not share the same goals as others and value a healthy environment. Nor does it mean that economists have the right answers and everyone else has the wrong ones (or vice versa). Economics provides a set of tools and principles that clarify the issues. It does not provide an agreed list of solutions. The starting point for an economic analysis of the environment is the demand for a healthy environment.

The Demand for Environmental Quality

The demand for a clean and healthy environment is greater today than it has ever been. We express our demand for a better environment in several ways. We join organizations that lobby for environmental regulations and policies. We vote for politicians who support the environmental policies that we want to see implemented. (All politicians at least pay lip service to the environment today.) We buy "green" products and avoid hazardous products, even if we pay a bit more to do so. And we pay higher housing costs and commuting costs to live in pleasant neighborhoods.

The demand for a cleaner environment has grown for two main reasons. First, as our incomes increase, we demand a larger range of goods and services, and one of these "goods" is a high-quality environment. We value clean air, unspoiled natural scenery, and wildlife, and we are willing and able to pay for them.

Second, as our knowledge of the effects of our actions on the environment grows, we are able to take measures that improve the environment. For example, now that we know how sulfur dioxide causes acid rain and how clearing rain forests destroys natural stores of carbon dioxide, we are able, in principle, to design measures that limit these problems.

Let's look at the range of environmental problems that have been identified and the actions that create those problems.

The Sources of Environmental Problems

Environmental problems arise from pollution of the air, water, and land, and these individual sources of pollution interact through the *ecosystem.*

Air Pollution Figure 20.1(a) shows the five economic activities that create most of our air pollution. It also shows the relative contributions of each activity. More than two thirds of air pollution comes from road transportation and industrial processes. Only one sixth arises from electric power generation.

A common belief is that air pollution is getting worse. On many fronts, as we will see later in this chapter, *global* air pollution *is* getting worse. But air pollution in the United States is getting less severe for most substances. Figure 20.1(b) shows the trends in the concentrations of six air pollutants. While lead has been almost eliminated from our air and sulfur dioxide, carbon monoxide, and suspended particulates have been reduced substantially, levels of other pollutants have remained more stable.

While the facts about the sources and trends in air pollution are not in doubt, there is considerable disagreement among scientists about the *effects* of air pollution. The least controversial problem is *acid rain,* which is caused by sulfur dioxide and nitrogen oxide emissions from coal- and oil-fired generators of electric utilities. Acid rain begins with air pollution, leads to water pollution, and damages vegetation.

More controversial are airborne substances (suspended particulates) such as lead from leaded gasoline. Some scientists believe that in sufficiently large concentrations, these substances (189 of which have currently been identified) cause cancer and other life-threatening conditions.

FIGURE 20.1

Air Pollution

4%	Solid waste disposal
12%	Other fuel combustion
16%	Electric utilities
25%	Industrial processes
43%	Road transportation

(a) Sources of emission

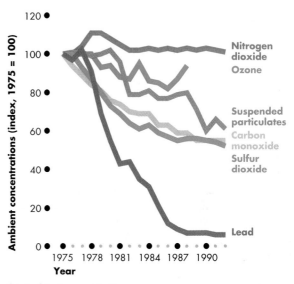

(b) Ambient concentrations

Part (a) shows that road transportation is the largest source of air pollution, followed by industrial processes and electric utilities. Part (b) shows that lead has almost been eliminated from our air and concentrations of carbon monoxide, sulfur dioxide, and suspended particulates have decreased. But nitrogen dioxide and ozone levels have persisted at close to their 1975 levels.

Source: U.S. Environmental Protection Agency, *National Air Quality and Emissions Trends Report,* 1996.

Even more controversial is *global warming,* which some scientists believe results from the carbon dioxide emissions of road transportation and electric utilities, methane created by cows and other livestock, and nitrous oxide emissions of electric utilities and from fertilizers. The earth's average temperature has increased over the past 100 years, but most of the increase occurred *before* 1940. Determining what causes changes in the earth's temperature and separating out the effect of carbon dioxide and other factors are proving to be very difficult.

Equally controversial is the problem of *ozone layer depletion,* which some scientists believe results from chlorofluorocarbons (CFCs) from refrigeration equipment and (in the past) aerosols. There is no doubt that a hole in the ozone layer exists over Antarctica and that the ozone layer protects us from cancer-causing ultraviolet rays from the sun. But how our industrial activity influences the ozone layer is simply not understood at this time.

One air pollution problem has almost been eliminated: lead from gasoline. In part, this happened because the cost of living without leaded gasoline, it turns out, is not high. But sulfur dioxide and the so-called greenhouse gases are a much tougher problem to tackle. Their alternatives are costly or have environmental problems of their own. The major sources of these pollutants are road vehicles and electric utilities. Road vehicles can be made "greener" in a variety of ways. One is with new fuels—some alternatives that are being investigated are alcohol, natural gas, propane and butane, and hydrogen. Another way of making cars and trucks "greener" is to change the chemistry of gasoline. Refiners are working on reformulations of gasoline that cut tailpipe emissions. Similarly, electric power can be generated in cleaner ways by harnessing solar power, tidal power, or geothermal power. Technically possible, these methods are more costly than conventional carbon-fueled generators. Another alternative is nuclear power. This method is good for air pollution but bad for land and water pollution because there is no known safe method of disposing of spent nuclear fuel.

Water Pollution   The largest sources of water pollution are the dumping of industrial waste and treated sewage in lakes and rivers and the runoff from fertilizers. A more dramatic source is the accidental spilling of crude oil into the oceans such as the *Exxon Valdez* spill in Alaska in 1989 and an even larger spill in the Russian Arctic in 1994. The most frightening is the dumping of nuclear waste into the ocean by the former Soviet Union.

There are two main alternatives to polluting the waterways and oceans. One is the chemical processing of waste to render it inert or biodegradable. The other, in wide use for nuclear waste, is to use land sites for storage in secure containers.

Land Pollution   Land pollution arises from dumping toxic waste products. Ordinary household garbage does not pose a pollution problem unless dumped garbage seeps into the water supply. This possibility increases as less-suitable landfill sites are used. It is estimated that 80 percent of existing landfills will be full by 2010. Some regions (New York, New Jersey, and other East Coast states) and some countries (Japan and the Netherlands) are seeking less costly alternatives to landfill, such as recycling and incineration. Recycling is an apparently attractive alternative, but it requires an investment in new technologies to be effective. Incineration is a high-cost alternative to landfill, and it produces air pollution. These alternatives are not free, and they become efficient only when the cost of using landfill is high.

We've seen that the demand for a high-quality environment has grown, and we've described the range of environmental problems. Let's now look at the ways in which these problems can be handled. We'll begin by looking at property rights and how they relate to environmental externalities.

Absence of Property Rights and Environmental Externalities

Externalities arise because of an *absence* of property rights. **Property rights** are social arrangements that govern the ownership, use, and disposal of resources, goods, and services. In modern societies, a property right is a legally established title that is enforceable in the courts.

Property rights are absent when externalities arise. No one owns the air, the rivers, and the oceans. So it is no one's private business to ensure that these resources are used in an efficient way. In fact, there is an incentive to use them more than if there were property rights.

Figure 20.2 shows an environmental externality in the absence of property rights. A chemical factory upstream from a fishing club must decide how to dispose of its waste.

The factory's marginal benefit curve, *MB*, tells us the benefit to the factory of an additional ton of waste dumped into the river. The *MB* curve is also the firm's demand curve for the use of the river, which is a productive resource. The demand for a resource slopes downward because of the law of diminishing returns (see Chapter 15, pp. 320–321).

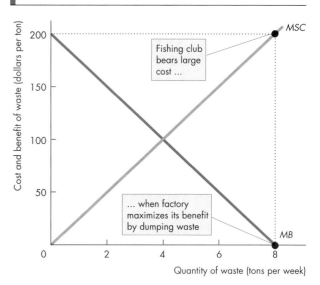

FIGURE 20.2

An Externality

A chemical factory's marginal benefit from dumping its waste into a river is *MB*, and a fishing club's marginal cost of having waste dumped is *MSC*. With no property rights, the factory maximizes total benefit by dumping 8 tons a week, the quantity at which the marginal benefit of dumping equals the marginal cost (zero). With this quantity of waste, the fishing club bears a marginal cost of $200 per ton. This outcome is inefficient because marginal social cost exceeds marginal benefit.

Marginal social cost is the marginal cost incurred by the producer of a good—marginal private cost—plus the marginal cost imposed on others—the external cost. The factory bears no cost of dumping. All the costs are borne by the fishing club. The marginal social cost curve, *MSC*, tells us the cost borne by the club when one additional ton of waste is dumped into the river. Marginal cost increases as the quantity dumped increases.

If no one owns the river, the factory dumps the amount of waste that maximizes *its own* total benefit. Its marginal cost is zero (along the *x*-axis), so it dumps 8 tons a week, the quantity that makes marginal benefit zero. The marginal social cost of the waste, which is borne by the fishing club, is $200 a ton. Marginal cost exceeds marginal benefit, so the outcome is inefficient.

Property Rights and the Coase Theorem

Sometimes it is possible to correct an externality by establishing a property right where one does not currently exist. For example, suppose that the chemical factory owns the river. The fishing club must pay the factory for the right to fish in the river. But the price that the club is willing to pay depends on the number and quality of fish, which in turn depend on how much waste the factory dumps in the river. The greater the amount of pollution, the smaller is the amount the fishing club is willing to pay for the right to fish. The chemical factory is now confronted with the cost of its pollution decision. It might still decide to pollute, but if it does, it faces the opportunity cost of its actions—forgone revenue from the fishing club.

Alternatively, suppose that the fishing club owns the river. Now the factory must pay a fee to the fishing club for the right to dump its waste. The more waste it dumps (equivalently, the more fish it kills), the more it must pay. Again, the factory faces an opportunity cost for the pollution it creates.

Does it matter how property rights are assigned? Does it matter whether the polluter or the victim of the pollution owns the resource that might be polluted? At first thought, ownership seems crucial. And until 1960, that is what everyone thought—including economists who had thought about the problem for longer than a few minutes. But in 1960, Ronald Coase had a remarkable insight, now called the Coase theorem. The **Coase theorem** is the proposition

that if property rights exist and transactions costs are low, private transactions are efficient. Equivalently, with property rights and low transactions costs, there are no externalities. All the costs and benefits are taken into account by the transacting parties. So it doesn't matter how the property rights are assigned.

Figure 20.3 illustrates the Coase theorem. As before, the demand curve for dumping waste is the factory's marginal benefit curve, *MB*. This curve tells us what the factory is willing to pay to dump. With property rights in place, the *MSC* curve is the fishing club's supply curve of river use to the firm. It tells us what the club's members must be paid if they are to put up with inferior fishing and supply the firm with a permit to dump.

The efficient level of waste is 4 tons a week. At this level, the club bears a cost of $100 for the last

FIGURE 20.3

The Coase Theorem

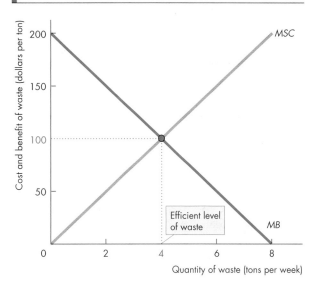

Pollution of a river imposes a marginal social cost, *MSC*, on the victim and provides a marginal benefit, *MB*, to the polluter. The efficient amount of pollution is the quantity that makes marginal benefit equal to marginal social cost—in this example, 4 tons per week. If the polluter owns the river, the victim will pay $400 a week ($100 a ton × 4 tons a week) to the polluter for the assurance that pollution will not exceed 4 tons a week. If the victim owns the river, the polluter will pay $400 for pollution rights to dump 4 tons a week.

ton dumped into the river, and the factory gets a benefit of that amount. If waste disposal is restricted below 4 tons a week, an increase in waste disposal benefits the factory more than it costs the club. The factory can pay the club to put up with more waste disposal, and both the club and the factory can gain. If waste disposal exceeds 4 tons a week, an increase in waste disposal costs the club more than it benefits the factory. The club can now pay the factory to cut its waste disposal, and again, both the club and the factory can gain. Only when the level of waste disposal is 4 tons a week can neither party do any better. This is the efficient level of waste disposal.

The amount of waste disposal is the same regardless of who owns the river. If the factory owns it, the club pays $400 for fishing rights and for an agreement that waste disposal will not exceed 4 tons a week. If the club owns the river, the factory pays $400 for the right to dump 4 tons of waste a week. In both cases, the amount of waste disposal is the efficient amount.

Property rights work if transactions costs are low. The factory and the fishing club can negotiate the deal that produces the efficient outcome. But in many situations, transactions costs are high and property rights cannot be enforced. Imagine the transactions costs if the 50 million people who live in the northeastern part of the United States and Canada tried to negotiate an agreement with the 20,000 factories that emit sulfur dioxide and cause acid rain! In this type of case, governments use alternative methods of coping with externalities. They use:

1. Emission charges
2. Marketable permits
3. Taxes

In the United States, the federal government has established an agency, the Environmental Protection Agency (EPA), to coordinate and administer the nation's environment policies. Let's look at the tools available to the EPA and see how they work.

Emission Charges

Emission charges are a method of using the market to achieve efficiency, even in the face of externalities. The government (or the regulatory agency established by the government) sets the emission charges, which are, in effect, a price per unit of pollution. The more pollution a firm creates, the more it pays in emission

charges. This method of dealing with environmental externalities has been used only modestly in the United States, but it is common in Europe. For example, in France, Germany, and the Netherlands, water polluters pay a waste disposal charge.

To work out the emission charge that achieves efficiency, the regulator must determine the marginal social cost and marginal *social* benefit of pollution. **Marginal social benefit** is the marginal benefit received by the buyer of a good—marginal private benefit—plus the marginal benefit to others—the external benefit. To achieve efficiency, the price per unit of pollution must be set to make the marginal social cost of the pollution equal to its marginal social benefit.

Figure 20.4 illustrates an efficient emissions charge. The marginal benefit of pollution is *MB* and accrues to the polluters—there is no *external* benefit. The marginal social cost of pollution is *MSC* and is

FIGURE 20.4

Emission Charges

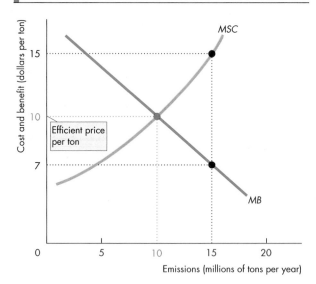

Electric utilities obtain marginal benefits from sulfur dioxide emissions of *MB*, and everyone else bears a marginal social cost of *MSC*. The efficient level of pollution—10 million tons a year in this example—is achieved by imposing an emission charge on the utilities of $10 a ton. If the emission charge is set too low, at $7 a ton, the resulting amount of pollution is greater than the efficient amount—at 15 million tons a year in this example. In this case, the marginal social cost is $15 a ton and it exceeds the marginal benefit of $7 a ton.

entirely an external cost. The efficient level of sulfur dioxide emissions is 10 million tons a year, which is achieved with an emission charge of $10 per ton. At this price, polluters do not find it worthwhile to buy the permission to pollute in excess of 10 million tons a year.

In practice, it is hard to determine the marginal benefit of pollution. And the people who are best informed about the marginal benefit, the polluters, have an incentive to mislead the regulators about the benefit. As a result, if a pollution charge is used, the most likely outcome is for the price to be set too low. For example, in Fig. 20.4, the price might be set at $7 per ton. At this price, polluters find it worthwhile to pay for 15 million tons a year. At this level of pollution, the marginal social cost is $15 a ton, and the amount of pollution exceeds the efficient level.

One way of overcoming excess pollution is to impose a quantitative limit. The most sophisticated way of doing this is with quantitative limits that firms can buy and sell—with marketable permits. Let's look at this alternative.

Marketable Permits

Instead of imposing emission charges on polluters, each potential polluter might be given a pollution limit. To achieve efficiency, marginal benefit and marginal cost must be assessed just as in the case of emission charges. Provided that these benefit-cost calculations are correct, the same efficient outcome can be achieved with quantitative limits as with emission charges. But in the case of quantitative limits, a cap must be set for each polluter. To set these caps at their efficient levels, the marginal benefit of *each* producer must be assessed. If firm *H* has a higher marginal benefit than firm *L*, an efficiency gain can be achieved by decreasing the cap of firm *L* and increasing that of firm *H*. It is virtually impossible to determine the marginal benefits of each firm, so in practice, quantitative restrictions cannot be allocated to each producer in an efficient way.

Marketable permits are a clever way of overcoming the need for the regulator to know every firm's marginal benefit schedule. Each firm can be allocated a permit to emit a certain amount of pollution, and firms may buy and sell such permits. Firms that have low marginal benefits from sulfur dioxide emissions will be willing to sell their permits to other firms that have a high marginal benefit. If the market in permits

is competitive, the price at which firms trade permits makes the marginal benefit of pollution equal for all firms. And if the correct number of permits has been allotted, the outcome can be efficient.

The Market for Emissions in the United States

Markets for emission permits have operated in the United States since the Environmental Protection Agency first implemented air quality programs following the passage of the Clean Air Act in 1970.

Trading in lead pollution permits became common during the 1980s, and this marketable permit program has been rated a success. It enabled lead to be virtually eliminated from the atmosphere of the United States (see Figure 20.1b). But this success might not easily translate to other situations because lead pollution has some special features. First, most lead pollution came from a single source, leaded gasoline. Second, lead in gasoline is easily monitored. Third, the objective of the program was clear: eliminate lead in gasoline.

The EPA is now considering using marketable permits to promote efficiency in the control of chlorofluorocarbons, the gases that are believed to damage the ozone layer.

Taxes and External Costs

Taxes can be used to provide incentives for producers or consumers to cut back on an activity that creates external costs. To see how taxes work, consider the market for transportation services.

The costs borne by the producers of transportation services are not the only costs. External costs arise from the airborne particulates and greenhouse gases caused by vehicle emissions. Further, one person's decision to use a highway imposes congestion costs on others. These costs also are external costs. When all the external marginal costs are added to the marginal cost faced by the producer, we obtain the marginal social cost of transportation.

Figure 20.5 shows the market for transportation services. The demand curve, *D*, is also the marginal benefit curve, *MB*. This curve tells us how much consumers value each different quantity of transportation services. The curve *MC* measures the marginal *private* cost of producing transportation services—the costs directly incurred by the producers of these services. The curve *MSC* measures the marginal *social* cost, which sums the external costs and private costs.

FIGURE 20.5

Taxes and Pollution

The demand curve for road transportation services is also the marginal benefit curve (D = MB). The marginal private cost curve is MC. If the market is unregulated, output is Q_0 vehicle-miles and the price is P_0 per vehicle-mile. Marginal social cost is SC_0 per vehicle-mile. Because of congestion and pollution, the marginal social cost exceeds the marginal private cost. Marginal social cost is shown by curve MSC. If the government imposes a tax so that producers of transportation services must pay the marginal social cost, the MSC curve becomes the relevant marginal cost curve for suppliers' decisions. The price increases to P_1 per vehicle-mile, and the quantity decreases to Q_1 vehicle-miles. Allocative efficiency is achieved.

If the transportation market is competitive and unregulated, the equilibrium will be at the price P_0 and quantity Q_0. Road users will balance their own marginal cost, MC, against their own marginal benefit, MB, and travel Q_0 vehicle-miles at a price (and cost) of P_0 per mile. At this scale of transportation services, the marginal social cost is SC_0. The marginal social cost minus the marginal private cost, $SC_0 - P_0$, is the marginal cost imposed on others—the marginal external cost.

Suppose the government taxes road transportation and that it sets the tax equal to the external marginal cost. By imposing such a tax, the government makes the suppliers of transportation services incur a marginal cost equal to the marginal social cost. That

is, the marginal private cost plus the tax equals the marginal social cost. The market supply curve is now the same as the MSC curve. The price rises to P_1 per vehicle-mile, and at this price, people travel Q_1 vehicle-miles. The marginal cost of the resources used in producing Q_1 vehicle-miles is C_1, and the marginal external cost is P_1 minus C_1. That marginal external cost is paid by the consumer through the tax.

The situation at the price P_1 and the quantity Q_1 is efficient. At a quantity greater than Q_1, marginal social cost exceeds marginal benefit, so net benefit increases by decreasing the quantity of transportation services. At a quantity less than Q_1, marginal benefit exceeds marginal social cost, so net benefit increases by increasing the quantity of transportation services.

A Carbon Fuel Tax? A tax can be imposed on any activity that creates external costs. For example, we could tax *all* air-polluting activities. Because the carbon fuels that we use to power our vehicles and generate our electric power are a major source of pollution, why don't we have a broad-based tax on all activities that burn carbon fuel and set the tax rate high enough to give a large reduction in carbon emissions?

The question becomes even more pressing when we consider not only the current levels of greenhouse gases but also their projected future levels. In 1995, annual carbon emissions worldwide were a staggering 6.8 billion tons. By 2050, with current policies, that annual total is predicted to be 24 billion tons.

Uncertainty About Global Warming Part of the reason we do not have a high, broad-based, carbon fuel tax is that the scientific evidence that carbon emissions produce global warming is not accepted by everyone. Climatologists are uncertain about how carbon emissions translate into atmospheric concentrations—about how the *flow* of emissions translates into a *stock* of pollution. The main uncertainty arises because carbon drains from the atmosphere into the oceans and vegetation at a rate that is not well understood. Climatologists are also uncertain about the connection between carbon concentration and temperature. And economists are uncertain about how a temperature increase translates into economic costs and benefits. Some economists believe that the costs and benefits are almost zero, while others believe that a temperature increase of 5.4 degrees Fahrenheit by 2050 will reduce the total output of goods and services by 20 percent.

Present Cost and Future Benefit   Another factor weighing against a large change in fuel use is that the costs would be borne now, while the benefits, if any, would accrue many years in the future. To compare future benefits with current costs, we must use an interest rate. If the interest rate is 1 percent a year, a dollar today becomes $2.70 in 100 years. If the interest rate is 5 percent a year, a dollar today becomes more than $131.50 in 100 years. So at an interest rate of 1 percent a year, it is worth spending $1 million in 1997 on pollution control to avoid $2.7 million in environmental damage in 2097. At an interest rate of 5 percent a year, it is worth spending $1 million today only if this expenditure avoids $131.5 million in environmental damage in 2097.

Because large uncertain future benefits are needed to justify small current costs, a general tax on carbon fuels is not a high priority on the political agenda.

International Factors   A final factor against a large change in fuel use is the international pattern of the use of carbon fuels. Right now, carbon pollution comes in even doses from the industrial countries and the developing countries. But by 2050, three quarters of the carbon pollution will come from the developing countries (if the trends persist).

One reason for the high pollution rate in some developing countries (notably China, Russia, and other Eastern European countries) is that their governments *subsidize* the use of coal or oil. These subsidies lower producers' marginal costs and encourage the use of fuels. The result is that the quantity of carbon fuels consumed exceeds the efficient quantity—and by a large amount. It is estimated that by 2050, these subsidies will induce annual global carbon emissions of some 10 billion tons—about two fifths of total emissions. If the subsidies were removed, global emissions in 2050 would be 10 billion tons a year less.

A Global Warming Dilemma

With the high output rate of greenhouse gases in the developing world, the United States and the other industrial countries are faced with a global warming dilemma (like the prisoners' dilemma in Chapter 14, pp. 295–296). Decreasing pollution is costly and might bring benefits. But the benefits depend on actions being taken by all countries to limit pollution. If one country acts alone, it bears the cost of limiting pollution and gets almost no benefits. So it

is worthwhile taking steps to limit global pollution only if all nations act together.

Table 20.1 shows the global warming dilemma faced by the United States and the developing countries. The numbers are hypothetical. Each country (we'll call the developing countries a country) has two possible policies: to control carbon emissions or to pollute. If each country pollutes, it receives a zero net return (by assumption), shown in the top left square in the table. If both countries control emissions, each pays the cost and gets the benefit. Its net return is $25 billion, as shown in the bottom right square of the table. If the United States controls emissions but the developing countries do not, the United States alone bears the cost and all countries enjoy a lower level of pollution. In this example, the United States pays $50 billion more than it benefits and the developing countries benefit by $50 billion more than they pay, as shown in the top right corner of the table. Finally, if the developing countries control emissions and the United States does not, the developing countries bear the cost and the United States

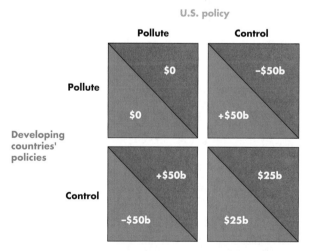

TABLE 20.1

A Global Warming Dilemma

If the United States and developing countries both pollute, the top left square shows their payoffs. If both countries control pollution, the bottom right square shows their payoffs. When one country pollutes and the other one does not, the top right and bottom left squares show their payoffs. The outcome of this game is for both countries to pollute. The structure of this game is the same as that of the prisoners' dilemma.

shares the gains. The developing countries lose $50 billion and the United States gains this amount, as shown in the bottom left corner of the table.

Confronted with these possible payoffs, the United States and the developing countries decide their policies. Each country reasons as follows: If the other country does not control emissions, we break even if we pollute and we lose $50 billion if we control our emissions. Conclusion: Each country is better off individually by polluting. So no one controls emissions, and pollution continues unabated.

Treaties and International Agreements

To break the dilemma, international agreements—treaties—might be negotiated. But such treaties must have incentives for countries to comply with their agreements. Otherwise, even with a treaty, the situation remains as we've just described and illustrated in Table 20.1.

One such international agreement is the *climate convention* that came into effect on March 21, 1994. This convention is an agreement among 60 countries to limit their output of greenhouse gases. But the convention does not have economic teeth. The poorer countries are merely asked to list their sources of greenhouse gases. The rich countries must show how, by 2000, they will return to their 1990 emissions levels.

R E V I E W   Q U I Z

- Why do externalities prevent markets from being efficient?
- How can an externality be eliminated by assigning property rights? How does this method of coping with an externality work?
- How do emission charges and pollution limits work to deal with externalities? Is one preferred over the other?
- How do taxes help us to cope with externalities? At what level must a pollution tax be set if it is to induce firms to produce the efficient quantity of pollution?
- What are the problems that arise when an externality goes beyond the scope of one country?

Economics of Knowledge

KNOWLEDGE, THE THINGS PEOPLE KNOW AND understand, has a profound effect on the economy. The economics of knowledge is an attempt to understand that effect. It is also an attempt to understand the process of knowledge accumulation and the incentives people face to discover, to learn, and to pass on what they know to others. It is an economic analysis of the scientific and engineering processes that lead to the discovery and development of new technologies. And it is a study of the education process of teaching and learning.

You can think of knowledge as being both a consumer good and a factor of production. The demand for knowledge—the willingness to pay to acquire knowledge—depends on the marginal benefit it provides to its possessor. As a consumer good, knowledge provides utility, and this is one source of its marginal benefit. As a factor of production—part of the stock of capital—knowledge increases productivity, and this is another source of its marginal benefit.

Knowledge clearly creates benefits for its possessor. It might also create external benefits. When children learn the basics of reading, writing, and numbers in grade school, they are equipping themselves to be better citizens, better able to communicate and interact with each other. The process continues through high school and college. But when people make decisions about how much schooling to undertake, they undervalue the external benefits that it creates.

External benefits also arise from research and development activities that lead to the creation of new knowledge. Once someone has worked out how to do something, others can copy the basic idea. They do have to work to copy an idea, so they face an opportunity cost. But they do not usually have to pay the person who made the discovery to use it. When Isaac Newton worked out the formulas for calculating the rate of response of one variable to another—calculus—everyone was free to use his method. When a spreadsheet program called VisiCalc was invented, others were free to copy the basic idea. Lotus Corporation developed its 1-2-3 and later Microsoft created Excel, and both became highly successful, but they did not pay for the key idea first used in VisiCalc. When the first shopping mall was built and found to be a successful way of arranging retailing, everyone was free to copy the idea, and malls spread like mushrooms.

When people make decisions about the quantity of education to undertake or the amount of research and development to do, they balance the *private* marginal costs against the private marginal benefits. They undervalue the external benefits. As a result, if we were to leave education and research and development to unregulated market forces, we would get too little of these activities. To deliver them in efficient quantities, we make public choices through governments to modify the market outcome.

Three devices that governments can use to achieve an efficient allocation of resources in the presence of the external benefits from education and research and development are:

- Subsidies
- Below-cost provision
- Patents and copyrights

Subsidies

A **subsidy** is a payment made by the government to producers that depends on the level of output. By subsidizing private activities, government can in principle encourage private decisions to be taken in the public interest. A government subsidy program might alternatively enable private producers to capture resources for themselves. Although subsidies cannot be guaranteed to work successfully, we'll study an example in which they do achieve their desired goal.

Figure 20.6 shows how subsidizing education can increase the amount of education undertaken and achieve an efficient allocation. Suppose that the marginal cost of producing a student-year of college education is a constant $20,000. We'll assume that all these costs are borne by the colleges and that there are no external costs. The marginal social cost is the same as the colleges' marginal cost and is shown by the curve *MC*. The maximum price that students (or parents) are willing to pay for an additional year of college determines the marginal private benefit curve and the demand curve for education. That curve is *D = MB*. In this example, a competitive market in private college education results in 20 million students being enrolled in college with tuition at $20,000 a year.

Suppose that the external benefit—the benefit derived by people other than those who receive the education—results in marginal social benefits described by the curve *MSB*. An efficient allocation occurs when marginal social cost equals marginal social benefit. In the example in Fig. 20.6, this equality occurs when 40

million students are enrolled in college. One way of getting 40 million students in college is to subsidize private colleges. In the example, a subsidy of $15,000 per student per year paid to the colleges does the job. With a subsidy of $15,000 and a marginal cost of $20,000, colleges earn an economic profit if the annual tuition exceeds $5,000. Competition among the colleges would drive the tuition down to $5,000, and at this price, 40 million students would enroll in college. So a subsidy can achieve an efficient outcome.

The lessons in this example can be applied to stimulating the rate of increase in the stock of

FIGURE 20.6

The Efficient Quantity of Education

The demand curve for education measures the marginal private benefit of education (*D = MB*). The curve *MC* shows the marginal cost of education—in this example, $20,000 per student-year. If education is provided in a competitive market, tuition is $20,000 a year and 20 million students enroll. Education produces an external benefit, and adding the external benefit to the marginal private benefit gives marginal social benefit, *MSB*. Education has no external costs, so *MC* is also the marginal social cost of education. An efficient outcome is achieved if the government provides education services to 40 million students a year, which is achieved by either subsidizing private colleges or providing education below cost in public colleges. In this example, students pay an annual tuition of $5,000 and the government pays a subsidy of $15,000.

knowledge—research and development. By subsidizing these activities, the government can move the allocation of resources toward a more efficient outcome. The mechanism that the government uses for this purpose is a research and development grant. In 1997, through the National Science Foundation, the government made research and development grants to universities and federally funded research and development centers of more than $2.5 billion.

Another way to achieve an efficient amount of education or research and development is through public provision below cost.

Below-Cost Provision

Instead of subsidizing private colleges, the government can establish its own colleges (public colleges) that provide schooling below cost. And instead of subsidizing research and development in industry and the universities, the government can establish its own research facilities and make discoveries available to others. Let's see how this approach works by returning to the example in Fig. 20.6.

By establishing public colleges with places for 40 million students, the government can supply the efficient quantity of college education. To ensure that this number of places is taken up, the public colleges would charge a tuition, in this example, of $5,000 a student per year. The government provides this tuition below its marginal cost of $20,000 a student per year. At this price, the number of people who choose to attend college makes the marginal social benefit of education equal to its marginal social cost.

We've now looked at two examples of how government action can help market participants take account of the external benefits deriving from education to achieve an outcome different from that of a private unregulated market. In reality, governments use both methods of encouraging an efficient quantity of education. They subsidize private colleges and universities, and they run their own institutions and sell their services at below cost. But in education, the public sector is by far the larger. In research and development, subsidies to the private sector are far larger than the government direct provision.

Patents and Copyrights

Knowledge may well be the only factor of production that does not display *diminishing marginal productivity*.

More knowledge (about the right things) makes people more productive. And there seems to be no tendency for the additional productivity from additional knowledge to diminish.

For example, in just 15 years, advances in knowledge about microprocessors have given us a sequence of processor chips that has made our personal computers increasingly powerful. Each advance in knowledge about how to design and manufacture a processor chip has brought apparently ever-larger increments in performance and productivity. Similarly, each advance in knowledge about how to design and build an airplane has brought apparently ever larger increments in performance: Orville and Wilbur Wright's "Flyer 1" was a one-seat plane that could hop a farmer's field. The Lockheed Constellation was an airplane that could fly 120 passengers from New York to London, but with two refueling stops in Newfoundland and Ireland. The latest version of the Boeing 747 can carry 400 people nonstop from Los Angeles to Sydney or New York to Tokyo (flights of 7,500 miles that take 13 1/2 hours). Similar examples can be found again and again in fields as diverse as agriculture, biogenetics, communications, engineering, entertainment, medicine, and publishing.

A key reason why the stock of knowledge increases without diminishing returns is the sheer number of different techniques that can in principle be tried. Paul Romer explains this fact with an amazing example. Suppose, says Romer,

> that to make a finished good, 20 different parts have to be attached to a frame, one at a time. A worker could proceed in numerical order, attaching part one first, then part two. … Or the worker could proceed in some other order, starting with part 10, then adding part seven. … With 20 parts, a standard (but incredible) calculation shows that there are about 10^{18} different sequences one can use for assembling the final good. This number is larger than the total number of seconds that have elapsed since the big bang created the universe, so we can be confident that in all activities, only a very small fraction of the possible sequences have ever been tried.[1]

[1]From Paul Romer, "Ideas and Things," in *The Future Surveyed*, supplement to *The Economist*, 11 September, 1993, pp. 71–72. The "standard calculation" that Romer refers to is the number of ways of selecting and arranging in order 20 objects from 20 objects—also called the number of permutations of 20 objects

Think about all the processes, all the products, and all the different bits and pieces that go into each, and you can see that we have only begun to scratch around the edges of what is possible.

Because knowledge is productive and creates external benefits, it is necessary to use public policies to ensure that those who develop new ideas face incentives that encourage an efficient level of effort. The main way of creating the right incentives is to provide the creators of knowledge with property rights in their discoveries—called **intellectual property rights**. The legal device for creating intellectual property rights is the patent or copyright. A **patent** or **copyright** is a government-sanctioned exclusive right granted to the inventor of a good, service, or productive process to produce, use, and sell the invention for a given number of years. A patent enables the developer of a new idea to prevent, for a limited number of years, others from benefiting freely from an invention. But to obtain the protection of the law, an inventor must make knowledge of the invention public.

Although patents encourage invention and innovation, they do so at an economic cost. While a patent is in place, its holder is a monopolist. And monopoly is another type of market failure. To maximize profit, a monopoly (patent holder) produces the quantity at which marginal cost equals marginal revenue. The monopoly sets the price above marginal cost and equal to the highest price at which the profit-maximizing quantity can be sold. In this situation, consumers value the good more highly (are willing to pay more for one more unit of it) than its marginal cost. So the quantity of the good available is less than the efficient quantity.

But without a patent, the effort to develop new goods, services, or processes is diminished and the flow of new inventions is slowed. So the efficient outcome is a compromise that balances the benefits of more inventions against the cost of temporary monopoly power in newly invented activities.

---

20 at a time. This number is *factorial* 20, or 20! = 20 × 19 × 18 × ... × 2 × 1 = $10^{18.4}$. A standard theory (challenged by observations made by the Hubble Space Telescope in 1994) is that a big bang started the universe 15 billion years, or $10^{17.7}$ seconds, ago. Although $10^{18.4}$ and $10^{17.7}$ look similar, $10^{18.4}$ is *five* times as large as $10^{17.7}$, so if you started trying alternative sequences at the moment of the big bang and took only one second per trial, you would still have tried only one fifth of the possibilities. Amazing?

R E V I E W   Q U I Z

- What is special about knowledge as a consumer good and as a factor of production that creates external benefits?
- What are the external benefits that arise from education and from research and development?
- How might governments use subsidies, below-cost provision, and patents and copyrights to achieve an efficient amount of research and development?
- How might governments use subsidies or below-cost provision to deliver an efficient amount of education?
- Why might knowledge be special in *not* displaying diminishing returns?
- If patents and copyrights can stimulate research, why don't we just award unlimited patents and copyrights to inventors and other creators of new knowledge?

◆ *Reading Between the Lines* on pages 444–445 looks at the challenge to intellectual property rights presented by digital information technologies. As you study this problem, try to reflect on all the topics you've learned about in your study of *microeconomics*. You've learned how all economic problems arise from scarcity, that scarcity forces choices, and that choice implies cost—opportunity cost. Prices (*relative prices*) are opportunity costs and are determined by the interactions of buyers and sellers in markets. People choose what to buy and what resources to sell to maximize utility. Firms choose what to sell and what resources to buy to maximize profit. People and firms interact in markets. But the resulting equilibrium might be inefficient and might be viewed as creating too much inequality. By providing public goods, redistributing income, curbing monopoly power, and coping with externalities, public choice modifies the market outcome.

The next chapter studies some problems for the market economy that arise from uncertainty and incomplete information. But unlike the cases we've studied here, the market does a good job of coping with these problems, as you're about to discover.

Protecting Intellectual Property Rights

T H E   N E W   Y O R K   T I M E S ,   DECEMBER 2, 1996

160 Nations to Weigh Revisions of International Copyright Laws

BY PETER H. LEWIS

Copyright laws are under technological siege. Intended to insure both a financial return to those who create everything from poetry to computer software and reasonable public access to such material, the current laws may be unequal to the task.

Copies of the latest Madonna song, a computer spreadsheet or a telephone directory can all be duplicated and distributed on the Internet at the click of a computer mouse, often with little regard for the legal rights of the owners of their copyrights.

Now, for the first time in the age of the personal computer and the Internet, copyright experts from 160 countries are gathering in Switzerland today to begin to write new international treaties protecting intellectual property in the digital age...

Delegates to the World Intellectual Property Organization diplomatic conference in Geneva,... hope to agree on one or more global pacts to update copyright laws for an era in which anything that can be copyrighted can be digitized, and anything that can be digitized can be distributed almost instantly around the world.

The United States ... delegation, led by Bruce Lehman, the Commissioner of Patents and Trademarks, will offer three proposals to protect literary and artistic works, music recordings and data bases from unauthorized use. ...

Supporters of the American proposals say ... that changes in international copyright law are needed to halt the growing international trend to pirate billions of dollars worth of intellectual property. Without stronger protections, they argue, there will be no incentive to develop new material to sate the appetite of the emerging global information infrastructure. ...

"The central premise of the Administration is that creators of intellectual property will be wary of the electronic marketplace unless the law gives them protection, but I would differ," said Richard B. Hovey, director of the Digital Equipment Corporation's corporate technology and strategy group.

Mr. Hovey said his company and others are already developing hardware and software methods for preventing unauthorized duplication, transmission or playback of copyrighted materials, including not just text and graphics, but also video, audio and multimedia. ...

Essence of the Story

- Copyright laws are difficult to enforce in the digital information age when music and other material can be duplicated and distributed on the Internet.

- Changes in international copyright law are required to stop growing international pirating of intellectual property.

- Without stronger protection, there will be no incentive to develop new material.

- Copyright experts are writing new international treaties that protect intellectual property.

- Digital Equipment Corporation is trying to use the new technologies to prevent unauthorized duplication and protect inventors and authors without a change in the law.

■ A copyright gives the inventor of a good, service, or productive process the exclusive right to produce, use, and sell the invention for a given number of years.

■ During the life of the copyright, the inventor is a monopolist.

■ Figure 1 shows what happens when copyright law is violated. It uses the example of a recording of a Madonna song. The demand for a copy of the song is shown by the demand curve, D.

■ The marginal cost of making one more copy of the Madonna song is constant and is shown by the marginal cost curve, MC.

■ If people freely copy the Madonna song, the marginal cost curve becomes the supply curve in a competitive market.

■ The number of copies made is Q_C, and the price is P_C, which equals marginal cost.

■ This outcome appears to be efficient. Marginal cost equals marginal benefit, and the gains from trade are maximized.

■ But this outcome is not efficient. In fact, it is not even feasible because Madonna has no incentive to record her songs. Without Madonna, there is nothing to copy. The quantity is zero, and the consumer surplus is zero.

■ An enforced copyright law can improve on this situation. Figure 2 shows you how. Again, the demand curve is D, and the marginal cost curve is MC.

■ By being granted a copyright on her song, Madonna becomes a monopolist. Madonna's marginal revenue curve is MR, and she maximizes profit by authorizing Q_{CR} copies to be made, which sell for P_{CR}.

■ The market appears to be inefficient because a deadweight loss, the gray area in Fig. 2, is created.

■ This deadweight loss is unavoidable. But in the long run, it disappears when the life of the copyright ends and the market becomes competitive.

■ The blue area in Fig. 2 shows Madonna's economic profit during the life of her copyright. It is this gain that encourages her to sing and create material that is worth copying.

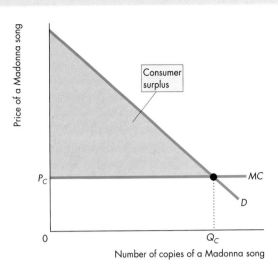

Figure 1 When copyright law is violated

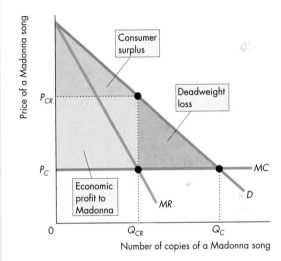

Figure 2 How a copyright works

■ How would you write the copyright law?

■ How many years' protection would you give the inventor or creator of a new good or service such as a Madonna song?

■ How would you suggest that violators of copyright law be penalized? Use economic reasoning and the concept of efficiency to develop your answers.

SUMMARY

KEY POINTS

Economics of the Environment (pp. 432–440)

- Popular discussion of the environment frames the debate in terms of right and wrong, but economists emphasize costs and benefits and a need to find a way to balance the two.

- The demand for environmental policies has grown because incomes and awareness of the connection between actions and the environment have grown.

- Air pollution arises from road transportation, electric utilities, and industrial processes. In the United States, the trends in most types of air pollution are downward.

- Externalities (environmental and others) arise when property rights are absent. Sometimes it is possible to overcome an externality by assigning a property right.

- The Coase theorem states that if property rights exist and transactions costs are low, private transactions are efficient—there are no externalities. In this case, the same efficient amount of pollution is achieved regardless of *who* has the property right—the polluter or the victim.

- When property rights cannot be assigned, governments might overcome environmental externalities by using emission charges, marketable permits, or taxes.

- Marketable permits were used successfully to virtually eliminate lead from our air.

- Global externalities, such as greenhouse gases and substances that deplete the earth's ozone layer, can be overcome only by international action. Each country acting alone has insufficient incentive to act in the interest of the world as a whole. But there is a great deal of scientific uncertainty and disagreement about the effects of greenhouse gases and ozone depletion, and in the face of this uncertainty, international resolve to act is weak.

- The world is locked in a type of prisoners' dilemma game, in which it is in every country's self-interest to let other countries carry the costs of environmental policies.

Economics of Knowledge (pp. 440–443)

- Knowledge is both a consumer good and a factor of production that creates external benefits.

- External benefits from education—passing on existing knowledge to others—arise because the basic reading, writing, and number skills equip people to interact and communicate more effectively.

- External benefits from research and development—creating and applying new knowledge—arise because once someone has worked out how to do something, others can copy the basic idea.

- To enable the efficient amount of education and innovation to take place, we make public choices through governments to modify the market outcome.

- Three devices are available to governments: subsidies, below-cost provision, and patents and copyrights.

- Subsidies to private schools or the provision of public education below cost can achieve an efficient provision of education.

- Patents and copyrights create intellectual property rights and increase the incentive to innovate. But they do so by creating a temporary monopoly, the cost of which must be balanced against the benefit of more inventive activity.

KEY FIGURES

KEY TERMS

PROBLEMS

*1. A pesticide maker can dump waste into a lake or truck it to a safe storage place. The marginal cost of trucking is a $100 a ton. A trout farm uses the lake, and the table shows how its profit depends on the quantity of waste dumped.

Quantity of waste (tons per week)	Trout farm profit (dollars per week)
0	1,000
1	950
2	875
3	775
4	650
5	500
6	325
7	125

a. What is the efficient amount of waste to be dumped into the lake?
b. If the trout farm owns the lake, how much waste is dumped and how much does the pesticide maker pay to the farmer per ton?
c. If the pesticide maker owns the lake, how much waste is dumped and how much rent does the farmer pay the factory for the use of the lake?

2. A steel smelter is located at the edge of a residential area. The table shows the cost of cutting the pollution of the smelter. It also shows the property taxes that people are willing to pay at different levels of pollution.

Pollution cut (percentage)	Property taxes willingly paid (dollars per day)	Total cost of pollution cut (dollars per day)
0	0	0
10	150	10
20	285	25
30	405	45
40	510	70
50	600	100
60	675	135
70	735	175
80	780	220
90	810	270
100	825	325

Assume that the increase in property taxes that people are willing to pay measures the change in total benefit of cleaner air that results from a change in the percentage decrease in pollution.
a. What is the efficient percentage decrease in pollution?
b. With no regulation of pollution, how much pollution will there be?
c. If the city owns the smelter, how much pollution will there be?
d. If the city is a company town owned by the steel smelter, how much pollution will there be?

*3. Back at the pesticide plant and trout farm described in problem 1, suppose that no one owns the lake and that the government introduces a pollution tax.
a. What is the tax per ton of waste dumped that will achieve an efficient outcome?
b. Explain the connection between the answer to this problem and the answer to problem 1.

4. Back at the steel-smelting city in problem 2, suppose that the city government introduces a pollution tax.
a. What is the tax per percentage of waste dumped that will achieve an efficient outcome?
b. Explain the connection between the answer to this problem and the answer to problem 2.

*5. Using the information provided in problem 1, suppose that no one owns the lake and that the government issues marketable pollution permits to both the farmer and the factory. Each may dump the same amount of waste in the lake, and the total that may be dumped is the efficient amount.
a. What is the quantity that may be dumped into the lake?
b. What is the market price of a permit? Who buys and who sells?
c. What is the connection between the answer to this problem and the answers to problems 1 and 3?

6. Using the information given in problem 2, suppose that the city government issues marketable pollution permits to citizens and the smelter. Each may pollute the air by the same percentage, and the total is the efficient amount.

a. What is the percentage of pollution?
b. What is the market price of a permit? Who buys and who sells?
c. What is the connection between the answer to this problem and the answers to problems 2 and 4?

*7. The marginal cost of educating a student is $4,000 a year and is constant. The figure shows the marginal private benefit curve.

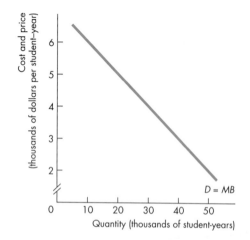

a. With no government involvement and if the schools are competitive, how many students are enrolled and what is the tuition?
b. The external benefit from education is $2,000 per student-year and is constant. If the government provides the efficient amount of education, how many school places does it offer and what is the tuition?

8. A technological advance cuts the marginal cost of educating a student to $2,000 a year and is constant. The marginal private benefit is the same as in problem 7. The external benefit from education increases to $4,000 per student-year and is constant.
a. With no government involvement and if the schools are competitive, how many students are enrolled and what is the tuition?
b. If the government provides the efficient amount of education, how many school places does it offer and what is the tuition?
c. Compare the outcomes in problem 8 with those in problem 7. Explain the differences between the two situations.

CRITICAL THINKING

1. After you have studied *Reading Between the Lines* on pp. 444–445, answer the following questions:
a. Do copyright laws create an efficient or an inefficient outcome?
b. What are the pros and cons of a long copyright period?
c. How could a further technological advance that makes unauthorized copying impossible change copyright law? Who would need protecting from whom in this situation?

2. Use the links on the Parkin Web site to get two viewpoints on global warming. Then answer these questions:
a. What are the benefits and costs of greenhouse gas emissions?
b. Do you think the environmentalists are correct in the view that greenhouse gas emissions must be cut or do you think the costs of reducing greenhouse gas emissions exceed the benefits?
c. If greenhouse gas emissions are to be reduced, should reductions be achieved by assigning quotas or by using the price mechanism?

3. To decrease the amount of overfishing in their territorial waters, the governments of Iceland and New Zealand have introduced private property rights with an allocation of Individual Transferable Quotas (ITQs). To check out the effects of this system, use the link on the Parkin Web site to visit the Fraser Institute in Vancouver. Then answer the following questions:
a. Would the introduction of ITQs in the United States help to replenish U.S. fish stocks?
b. Explain why ITQs give an incentive to not overfish.
c. Who would oppose ITQs and why?

4. Some political leaders want stronger tax incentives to encourage more people to go to college and to remain in college for longer. What are the economic arguments in favor of such a change in incentives? What are the arguments against such a change? Where do you come out on this issue and why?

Chapter 21

Uncertainty and Information

Life is like a lottery. You work hard in school, but what will the payoff be? Will you get an interesting, high-paying job or a miserable, low-paying one? You set up a small summer business and work hard at it. But will you make enough income to keep you in school next year or will you get wiped out? How do people make a decision when they don't know its consequences? ◆ As you drive across an intersection on a green light, you see a car on your left that's still moving. Will it stop or will it run the red light? You buy insurance against such a risk, and insurance companies gain from your business. Why are we willing to buy insurance at prices that leave insurance companies with a gain? ◆ Buying a new car—or a used car—is fun, but it's also scary. You could get stuck with a lemon. And cars are not unique. Just about every complicated product you buy could be defective. How do car dealers and retailers induce us to buy what might turn out to be a lemon? ◆ People keep some of their wealth in the bank, some in mutual funds, some in bonds, and some in stocks. Some of these ways of holding wealth have a high return, and some have a low return. Why don't people put all their wealth in the place that has the highest return? Why does it pay to diversify?

Lotteries and Lemons

◆ In this chapter, we answer questions such as these. We'll begin by explaining how people make decisions when they're uncertain about the consequences. We'll see how it pays to buy insurance, even if its price leaves the insurance company with a profit. We'll explain why we use scarce resources to generate and disseminate information. And we'll look at transactions in a variety of markets in which uncertainty and the cost of acquiring information play important roles. ◆ A recurring theme of economics is that markets help people to use their scarce resources efficiently. Uncertainty and incomplete information are possible reasons why markets might fail to achieve efficiency. But markets do an amazing job of coping with these problems.

After studying this chapter, you will be able to:

- Explain how people make decisions when they are uncertain about the consequences

- Explain why people buy insurance and how insurance companies make a profit

- Explain why buyers search and sellers advertise

- Explain how markets cope with private information

- Explain how people use financial markets to lower risk

Uncertainty and Risk

ALTHOUGH WE LIVE IN AN UNCERTAIN WORLD, we rarely ask what uncertainty is. Yet to explain how we make decisions and do business with each other in an uncertain world, we need to think more deeply about uncertainty. What exactly is uncertainty? We also live in a risky world. Is risk the same as uncertainty? Let's begin by defining uncertainty and risk and distinguishing between them.

Uncertainty is a situation in which more than one event may occur but we don't know which one. For example, when farmers plant their crops, they are uncertain about the weather during the growing season.

In ordinary speech, risk is the probability of incurring a loss (or some other misfortune). In economics, **risk** is a situation in which more than one outcome may occur and the *probability* of each possible outcome can be estimated. A *probability* is a number between 0 and 1 that measures the chance of some possible event occurring. A 0 probability means that the event will not happen. A probability of 1 means that the event will occur for sure—with certainty. A probability of 0.5 means that the event is just as likely to occur as not. An example is the probability of a tossed coin falling heads. In a large number of tosses, about half of them will be heads and the other half tails.

Sometimes, probabilities can be measured. For example, the probability that a tossed coin will come down heads is based on the fact that in a large number of tosses, half are heads and half are tails; the probability that an automobile in Chicago in 1998 will be involved in an accident can be estimated by using police and insurance records of previous accidents; the probability that you will win a lottery can be estimated by dividing the number of tickets you have bought by the total number of tickets bought.

Some situations cannot be described by using probabilities based on past observed events. These situations may be unique events, such as the introduction of a new product. How much will sell and at what price? Because the product is new, there is no previous experience on which to base a probability. But the questions can be answered by looking at past experience with *similar* new products, supported by some judgments. Such judgments are called *subjective probabilities*.

Regardless of whether the probability of some event occurring is based on actual data or judgments—or even guesses—we can use probability to study the way in which people make decisions in the face of uncertainty. The first step in doing this is to describe how people assess the cost of risk.

Measuring the Cost of Risk

Some people are more willing to bear risk than others, but almost everyone prefers less risk to more, other things remaining the same. We measure people's attitudes toward risk by using their utility of wealth schedules and curves. The **utility of wealth** is the amount of utility a person attaches to a given amount of wealth. The greater a person's wealth, other things remaining the same, the higher is the person's total utility. Greater wealth brings higher total utility, but as wealth increases, each additional unit of wealth increases total utility by a smaller amount. That is, the *marginal utility of wealth diminishes.*

Figure 21.1 sets out Tania's utility of wealth schedule and curve. Each point *a* through *e* on Tania's utility of wealth curve corresponds to the row of the table identified by the same letter. You can see that as her wealth increases, so does her total utility of wealth. You can also see that her marginal utility of wealth diminishes. When wealth increases from $3,000 to $6,000, total utility increases by 20 units, but when wealth increases by a further $3,000 to $9,000, total utility increases by only 10 units.

We can use Tania's utility of wealth curve to measure her cost of risk. Let's see how Tania evaluates two summer jobs that involve different amounts of risk.

One job, working as a painter, pays enough for her to save $5,000 by the end of the summer. There is no uncertainty about the income from this job and hence no risk. If Tania takes this job, by the end of the summer her wealth will be $5,000. The other job, working as a telemarketer selling subscriptions to a magazine, is risky. If she takes this job, her wealth at the end of the summer depends entirely on her success at selling. She might be a good salesperson or a poor one. A good salesperson makes $9,000 in a summer, and a poor one makes $3,000. Tania has never tried telemarketing, so she doesn't know how successful she'll be. She assumes that she has an equal chance—a probability of 0.5—of making either $3,000 or $9,000. Which outcome does Tania

FIGURE 21.1
The Utility of Wealth

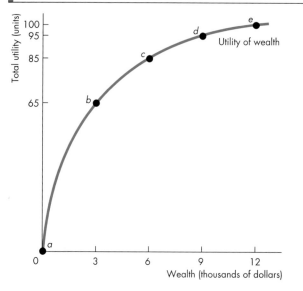

	Wealth (thousands of dollars)	Total utility (units)	Marginal utility (units)
a	0	0	
			65
b	3	65	
			20
c	6	85	
			10
d	9	95	
			5
e	12	100	

The table shows Tania's utility of wealth schedule, and the figure shows her utility of wealth curve. Utility increases as wealth increases, but the marginal utility of wealth diminishes.

prefer: $5,000 for sure from the painting job or a 50 percent chance of either $3,000 or $9,000 from the telemarketing job?

When there is uncertainty, people do not know the *actual* utility they will get from taking a particular action. But it is possible to calculate the utility they *expect* to get. **Expected utility** is the average utility arising from all possible outcomes. So, to choose her summer job, Tania calculates the expected utility from each job. Figure 21.2 shows how she does this.

FIGURE 21.2
Choice Under Uncertainty

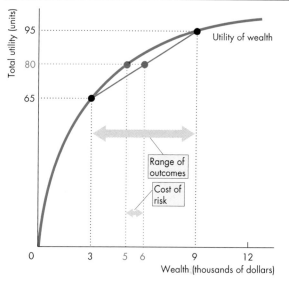

If Tania's wealth is $5,000 and she faces no risk, her utility is 80 units. If she faces an equal probability of having $9,000 with a utility of 95 or $3,000 with a utility of 65, her expected wealth is $6,000. But her expected utility is 80 units—the same as with $5,000 and no uncertainty. Tania is indifferent between these two alternatives. Tania's extra $1,000 of expected wealth is just enough to offset her extra risk.

If Tania takes the painting job, she has $5,000 of wealth and 80 units of utility. There is no uncertainty, so her expected utility equals her actual utility—80 units. But suppose she takes the telemarketing job. If she makes $9,000, her utility is 95 units, and if she makes $3,000, her utility is 65 units. Tania's *expected income* is the average of these two outcomes and is $6,000—($9,000 × 0.5) + ($3,000 × 0.5). This average is called a *weighted average*, the weights being the probabilities of each outcome (both 0.5 in this case). Tania's *expected utility* is the average of these two possible total utilities and is 80 units—(95 × 0.5) + (65 × 0.5).

Tania chooses the job that maximizes her expected utility. In this case, the two alternatives give the same expected utility—80 units—so she is indifferent between them. She is equally likely to take either job. The difference between Tania's expected wealth of $6,000 from the risky job and $5,000 from the no-risk job—$1,000—is just large enough to off-set the additional risk that Tania faces.

The calculations that we've just done enable us to measure Tania's cost of risk. The cost of risk is the amount by which expected wealth must be increased to give the same expected utility as a no-risk situation. In Tania's case, the cost of the risk arising from an uncertain income of $3,000 or $9,000 is $1,000.

If the amount Tania can make from painting remains at $5,000 and the expected income from telemarketing also remains constant while its range of uncertainty increases, Tania will take the painting job. To see this conclusion, suppose that good tele-marketers make $12,000 and poor ones make nothing. The average income from telemarketing is unchanged at $6,000, but the range of uncertainty has increased. The table in Fig. 21.1 shows that Tania gets 100 units of utility from a wealth of $12,000 and zero units of utility from a wealth of zero. Thus in this case, Tania's expected utility from telemarketing is 50 units—(100 × 0.5) + (0 × 0.5). Because the expected utility from telemarketing is now less than that from painting, she chooses painting.

Risk Aversion and Risk Neutrality

There is a huge difference between Bill Parcells, head coach of the New York Jets, who favors a cautious running game, and Jim Kelly, former quarterback of the Buffalo Bills, who favored a risky passing game. They have different attitudes toward risk. Bill is more *risk averse* than is Jim. Tania is also *risk averse*. The shape of the utility of wealth curve tells us about the attitude toward risk—about the person's degree of *risk aversion*. The more rapidly a person's marginal utility of wealth diminishes, the more risk averse that person is. You can see this fact best by considering the case of *risk neutrality*. A risk-neutral person cares only about *expected wealth* and doesn't mind how much uncertainty there is.

Figure 21.3 shows the utility of wealth curve of a risk-neutral person. It is a straight line, and the marginal utility of wealth is constant. If this person has an expected wealth of $6,000, expected utility is 50 units regardless of the range of uncertainty around that average. An equal probability of having $3,000 or $9,000 gives the same expected utility as a certain $6,000. When Tania's risk increased to this range, she needed an extra $1,000. This person does not. Even if the range of risk becomes $0 to $12,000, the risk-neutral person still gets the same expected utility as a certain $6,000 gives. Most real people are risk averse,

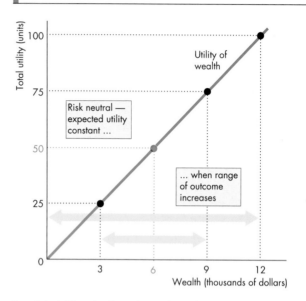

FIGURE 21.3

Risk Neutrality

People's dislike of risk implies a diminishing marginal utility of wealth. A (hypothetical) risk-neutral person has a linear utility of wealth curve and a constant marginal utility of wealth. For a risk-neutral person, expected utility does not depend on the range of uncertainty, and the cost of risk is zero.

and their utility of wealth curves look like Tania's. But the case of risk neutrality illustrates the importance and the consequences of the shape of the utility of wealth curve for a person's degree of risk aversion.

REVIEW QUIZ

- How do people make decisions when they are faced with uncertain outcomes? What do they try to achieve?
- How can we measure the cost of risk?
- What determines the amount that someone would be willing to pay to avoid risk? Is the cost of risk the same for everyone?
- What is a *risk-neutral* person and how much would such a person pay to avoid risk?

Most people are risk averse. Let's now see how insurance enables them to reduce the risk they face.

Insurance

ONE WAY OF REDUCING THE RISK WE FACE IS TO buy insurance. How does insurance reduce risk? Why do people buy insurance? And what determines the amount we spend on insurance? Before we answer these questions, let's look at the insurance industry in the United States today.

Insurance Industry in the United States

We spend close to 15 percent of our income, on the average, on private insurance. That's as much as we spend on housing and more than we spend on cars and food. In addition, we buy insurance through our taxes in the form of social security and unemployment insurance. When we buy private insurance, we enter into an agreement with an insurance company to pay an agreed price—called a *premium*—in exchange for benefits to be paid to us if some specified event occurs. The three main types of insurance we buy are:

■ Life insurance

■ Health insurance

■ Property and casualty insurance

Life Insurance   Life insurance reduces the risk of financial loss in the event of death. Almost 80 percent of households in the United States have life insurance, and the average amount of coverage is $110,000 per household. More than 2,400 companies supply life insurance, and the total premiums paid in a year are more than $450 billion. As you can see in Fig. 21.4, life insurance has been the greatest source of private insurance business in recent years.

Health Insurance   Health insurance reduces the risk of financial loss in the event of illness. It can provide funds to cover both lost earnings and the cost of medical care. Private health insurance is growing rapidly and is profitable. Figure 21.4 shows that it is almost as large as life insurance.

Property and Casualty Insurance   Property and casualty insurance reduces the risk of financial loss in the event of an accident involving damage to persons or property. It includes auto insurance—its biggest component—workers' compensation; fire, earthquake, and professional malpractice insurance;

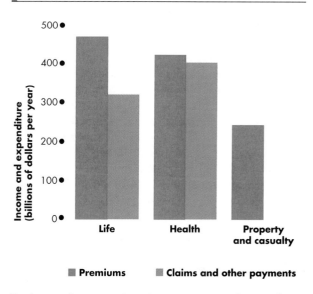

FIGURE 21.4

The Insurance Industry

Total expenditure on private insurance is more than a trillion dollars a year. Most is spent on life insurance and health insurance.

Source: U.S. Bureau of the Census, *Statistical Abstract of the United States 1995*, 115th edition (Washington, D.C., 1995), Tables 150, 840, 841, and 843–845 and the author's assumptions and calculations.

and a host of smaller items. Figure 21.4 shows that we spend almost $250 billion a year on these types of insurance.

How Insurance Works

Insurance works by pooling risks. It is possible and profitable because people are risk averse. The probability of any one person having a serious auto accident is small, but the cost of an accident to the person involved is enormous. For a large population, the probability of one person having an accident is the proportion of the population that does have an accident. Because this probability can be estimated, the total cost of accidents can be predicted. An insurance company can pool the risks of a large population and share the costs. It does so by collecting premiums from everyone and paying out benefits to those who suffer a loss. If the insurance company does its calculations correctly, it collects at least as much in premiums as it pays out in benefits and operating costs.

To see why people buy insurance and why it is profitable, let's consider an example. Dan has the utility of wealth curve shown in Fig. 21.5. He owns a car worth $10,000, and that is his only wealth. If there is no risk of his having an accident, his utility will be 100 units. But there is a 10 percent chance (a probability of 0.1) that he will have an accident within a year. Suppose Dan does not buy insurance. If he does have an accident, his car is worthless, and with no insurance, he has no wealth and no utility. Because the probability of an accident is 0.1, the probability of *not* having an accident is 0.9. Dan's expected wealth, therefore, is $9,000 ($10,000 × 0.9 + $0 × 0.1), and his expected utility is 90 units (100 × 0.9 + 0 × 0.1).

Given his utility of wealth curve, Dan has 90 units of utility if his wealth is $7,000 and he faces no

uncertainty. That is, Dan's utility of a guaranteed wealth of $7,000 is the same as his utility of a 90 percent chance of having wealth of $10,000 and a 10 percent chance of having nothing. If the cost of an insurance policy that pays out in the event of an accident is less than $3,000 ($10,000 − $7,000), Dan will buy the policy. Thus Dan has a demand for auto insurance at premiums less than $3,000.

Suppose there are lots of people like Dan, each with a $10,000 car and each with a 10 percent chance of having an accident within the year. If an insurance company agrees to pay each person who has an accident $10,000, the company will pay out $10,000 to one tenth of the population, or an average of $1,000 per person. This amount is the insurance company's minimum premium for such insurance. It is less than the value of insurance to Dan because Dan is risk averse. He is willing to pay something to reduce the risk he faces.

Now suppose that the insurance company's operating expenses are a further $1,000 and that it offers insurance for $2,000. The company now covers all its costs—the amounts paid out to policyholders for their losses plus the company's operating expenses. Dan—and all the other people like him—will maximize their utility by buying this insurance.

FIGURE 21.5
The Gains from Insurance

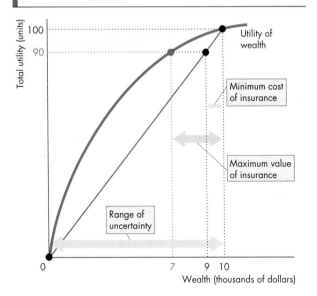

Dan has a car valued at $10,000 that gives him a utility of 100 units, but there is a 0.1 probability that he will have an accident, making his car worthless (wealth and utility equal to zero). With no insurance, his expected wealth is $9,000 and his expected utility is 90 units. His guaranteed wealth is $7,000. Dan will pay up to $3,000 for insurance. If an insurance company can offer Dan insurance for $1,000, there is a potential gain from insurance for both Dan and the insurance company.

REVIEW QUIZ

- What types of insurance do we buy and how large a percentage of our incomes do we spend on it (on the average)?
- How does insurance work? How can people avoid unwanted outcomes by insuring against them?
- How can an insurance company offer people a deal worth taking? Why don't the amounts paid in by insurers only just cover the amounts paid out by insurance companies to claimants?

Much of the uncertainty that we face arises from ignorance. We just don't know all the things we could benefit from knowing. But knowledge or information is not free. And government intervention is of little use in dealing with this problem. Governments usually are even less well informed than buyers and sellers. Faced with incomplete information, we must make decisions about how much information to acquire. Let's now study the choices we make about obtaining information and how markets cope with incomplete information.

Information

$\llcorner$ WE SPEND A HUGE QUANTITY OF OUR SCARCE resources on economic information. **Economic information** includes data on the prices, quantities, and qualities of goods and services and resources.

In the models of perfect competition, monopoly, and monopolistic competition, information is free. Everyone has all the information he or she needs. Households are completely informed about the prices of the goods and services they buy and the factors of production they sell. Similarly, firms are completely informed about consumers' preferences and about the prices and products of other firms.

In contrast, information is scarce in the real world. If it were not, we wouldn't need *The Wall Street Journal* and CNN. And we wouldn't need to shop around for bargains or spend time looking for a job. The opportunity cost of economic information—the cost of acquiring information on prices, quantities, and qualities of goods and services and resources—is called **information cost**.

The fact that many economic models ignore information costs does not make these models useless. They give us insights into the forces generating trends in prices and quantities over periods long enough for information limits not to be important. But to understand how markets work hour by hour and day by day, we must take information problems into account. Let's look at some of the consequences of information cost.

Searching for Price Information

When many firms sell the same good or service, there is a range of prices and buyers want to find the lowest price. But searching takes time and is costly. So buyers must balance the expected gain from further search against the cost of further search. To perform this balancing act, buyers use a decision rule called the *optimal-search rule*—or *optimal-stopping rule*. The optimal-search rule is:

■ Search for a lower price until the expected marginal benefit of additional search equals the marginal cost of search.

■ When the expected marginal benefit from additional search is less than or equal to the marginal cost, stop searching and buy.

To implement the optimal-search rule, each buyer chooses her or his own reservation price. The buyer's **reservation price** is the highest price that the buyer is willing to pay for a good. The buyer will continue to search for a lower price if the lowest price so far found exceeds the reservation price but will stop searching and buy if the lowest price found is less than or equal to the reservation price. At the buyer's reservation price, the expected marginal benefit of search equals the marginal cost of search.

Figure 21.6 illustrates the optimal-search rule. Suppose you've decided to buy a used Mazda Miata. Your marginal cost of search is $\$C$ per dealer visited and is shown by the horizontal orange line in the figure. This cost includes the value of your time, which is the amount that you could have earned by working instead of cruising around used car lots, and the amount spent on transportation and advice. Your expected marginal benefit of visiting one more dealer

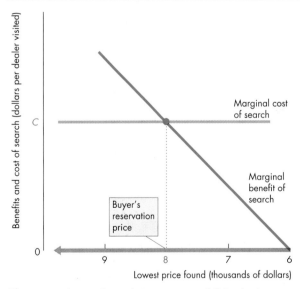

FIGURE 21.6

Optimal-Search Rule

The marginal cost of search is constant at $\$C$. As the lowest price found (measured from right to left on the horizontal axis) declines, the expected marginal benefit of further search diminishes. The lowest price found at which the marginal cost equals the expected marginal benefit is the reservation price. The optimal-search rule is to search until the reservation price is found and then buy at that lowest found price.

depends on the lowest price that you've found. The lower the price you've already found, the lower is your expected marginal benefit of visiting one more dealer, as shown by the blue curve in the figure.

The price at which expected marginal benefit equals marginal cost is your reservation price—$8,000 in the figure. If you find a price equal to or below your reservation price, you stop searching and buy. If you find a price that exceeds your reservation price, you continue to search for a lower price. Individual shoppers differ in their marginal cost of search and so have different reservation prices. As a result, identical items can be found selling for a range of prices.

A Real Car Shopping Trip Real car shoppers are confronted with a much bigger problem than the one we've just studied. There are many more dimensions of the car they are looking for than its price. They could spend almost forever gathering information about the alternatives. But at some point in their search, they decide they've done enough looking and make a decision to buy. Your imaginary shopping trip to buy a used Mazda Miata rationalizes their decision. Real shoppers think, "The benefits I expect from further search are insufficient to make it worth going on with the process." They don't do the calculations we've just done—at least, not explicitly—but their actions can be explained by those calculations. But buyers are not alone in creating information. Sellers do a lot of it too—in the form of advertising. Let's see what the effects of advertising are.

Advertising

Advertising constantly surrounds us—on television, radio, and billboards and in newspapers and magazines—and costs billions of dollars. How do firms decide how much to spend on advertising? Does advertising create information, or does it just persuade us to buy things we don't really want? What does it do to prices?

Advertising for Profit Maximization A firm's advertising decision is part of its overall profit-maximization strategy. Firms in perfect competition don't advertise because everyone has all the information there is. But firms selling differentiated products in monopolistic competition and firms locked in the struggle of survival in oligopoly advertise a lot.

The amount of advertising undertaken by firms in monopolistic competition is such that the marginal revenue product of advertising equals its marginal cost. The amount of advertising undertaken by firms in oligopoly is determined by the game they are playing. If that game is a *prisoners' dilemma*, they might spend amounts that lower their combined profits, but they can't avoid advertising without being wiped out by other firms in the industry.

Persuasion or Information Much advertising is designed to persuade us that the product being advertised is the best in its class. For example, the Pepsi advertisement tells us that Pepsi is really better than Coke. The Coca-Cola advertisement tells us that Coke is really better than Pepsi. But advertising also informs. It provides information about the quality and price of a good or service.

Does advertising mainly persuade or mainly inform? The answer varies for different goods and different types of markets. Goods whose quality can be assessed *before* they are bought are called *search goods*. Typically, the advertising of search goods mainly informs—gives information about price, quality, and location of suppliers. Examples of such goods are gasoline, basic foods, and household goods. Goods whose quality can be assessed only *after* they are bought are called *experience goods*. Typically, the advertising of experience goods mainly persuades—encourages the consumer to buy now and make a judgment later about quality, based on experience with the good. Examples of such goods are cigarettes, alcoholic beverages, and perfume.

Because most advertising involves experience goods, it is likely that advertising is more often persuasive rather than merely informative. But persuasive advertising doesn't necessarily harm the consumer. It might result in lower prices.

Advertising and Prices Does advertising increase the price of the good advertised? Your immediate response is "Of course it does!" But this conclusion is not always correct. Advertising can lower prices for two different reasons. First, *informative advertising* can lower prices because it increases competition by telling potential buyers about alternative sources of supply. Second, if advertising enables firms to increase their output and reap economies of scale, it is possible that the price of the good will be lower with advertising than without it, provided that there is sufficient competition to prevent firms from restricting output.

- What types of economic information do people find useful?
- Why is economic information scarce and how do people economize on its use?
- How do you decide when to stop searching for a lower-priced item to buy?
- What actions do sellers take to increase the information that potential buyers might use and that would encourage them to buy?
- Does advertising always raise costs and raise prices? How might advertising lower costs and prices?

Private Information

SO FAR WE HAVE LOOKED AT SITUATIONS IN which information is available to everyone and can be obtained with an expenditure of resources. But not all situations are like this. For example, someone might have private information. **Private information** is information that is available to one person but too costly for anyone else to obtain.

Private information affects many economic transactions. One is your knowledge about your driving. You know much more than your auto insurance company does about how carefully and defensively you drive. Another is your knowledge about your work effort. You know far more than your employer about how hard you work. Yet another is your knowledge about the quality of your car. You know whether it's a lemon. But the person to whom you are about to sell it does not and can't find out until after he or she has purchased it from you.

Private information creates two problems:

1. Moral hazard
2. Adverse selection

Moral hazard exists when one of the parties to an agreement has an incentive *after the agreement is made* to act in a manner that brings additional benefits to himself or herself at the expense of the other party. Moral hazard arises because it is too costly for the injured party to monitor the actions of the advantaged party. For example, Jackie hires Mitch as a salesperson and pays him a fixed wage regardless of his sales. Mitch faces a moral hazard. He has an incentive to put in the least possible effort, benefiting himself and lowering Jackie's profits. For this reason, salespeople are usually paid by a formula that makes their income higher the greater is the volume (or value) of their sales.

Adverse selection is the tendency for people to enter into agreements in which they can use their private information to their own advantage and to the disadvantage of the less informed party. For example, if Jackie offers salespeople a fixed wage, she will attract lazy salespeople. Hardworking salespeople will prefer *not* to work for Jackie because they can earn more by working for someone who pays by results. The fixed-wage contract adversely selects those with private information (knowledge about their work habits) who can use that knowledge to their own advantage and to the disadvantage of the other party.

A variety of devices have evolved that enable markets to function in the face of moral hazard and adverse selection. We've just seen one, the use of incentive payments for salespeople. Let's look at some more and also see how moral hazard and adverse selection influence three real-world markets:

- The market for used cars
- The market for loans
- The market for insurance

The Market for Used Cars

When a person buys a car, it might turn out to be a lemon. If the car is a lemon, it is worth less to the buyer and to everyone else than if it has no defects. Does the used car market have two prices reflecting these two values—a low price for lemons and a higher price for cars without defects? It does not. To see why, let's look at a used car market, first with no dealer warranties and second with warranties.

Used Cars Without Warranties   To make the points as clearly as possible, we'll make some extreme assumptions. There are just two kinds of cars: lemons and those without defects. A lemon is worth $1,000 both to its current owner and to anyone who buys it. A car without defects is worth $5,000 to its current and potential future owners. Whether a car is a lemon is private information that is available only to the current owner. Buyers of used cars can't tell whether they are buying a lemon until *after* they have bought the car and learned as much about it as its current owner knows. There are no dealer warranties.

Because buyers can't tell the difference between a lemon and a good car, they are willing to pay only one price for a used car. What is that price? Are they willing to pay $5,000, the value of a good car? They are not, because there is at least some probability that they are buying a lemon worth only $1,000. If buyers are not willing to pay $5,000 for a used car, are the owners of good cars willing to sell? They are not, because a good car is worth $5,000 to them, so they hang onto their cars. Only the owners of lemons are willing to sell—as long as the price is $1,000 or higher. But, reason the buyers, if only the owners of lemons are selling, all the used cars available are lemons, so the maximum price worth paying is $1,000. Thus the market for used cars is a market for lemons, and the price is $1,000.

Moral hazard exists in the car market because sellers have an incentive to claim that lemons are good cars. But, given the assumptions in the above description of the car market, no one believes such claims. Adverse selection exists, resulting in only lemons actually being traded. The market for used cars is not working well. Good used cars just don't get bought and sold, but people want to be able to buy and sell good used cars. How can they do so? The answer is by introducing warranties into the market.

Used Cars with Warranties Buyers of used cars can't tell a lemon from a good car, but car dealers sometimes can. For example, they might have regularly serviced the car. They know, therefore, whether they are buying a lemon or a good car and can offer $1,000 for lemons and $5,000 for good cars.[1] But how can they convince buyers that it is worth paying $5,000 for what might be a lemon? The answer is by giving a guarantee in the form of a warranty. The dealer *signals* which cars are good ones and which are lemons. A **signal** is an action taken outside a market that conveys information that can be used by that market. There are many examples of signals, one of which is students' grades. Your grade acts as a *signal* to potential employers.

In the case of the used cars, dealers take actions in the market for car repairs that can be used by the market for cars. For each good car sold, the dealer gives a warranty. The dealer agrees to pay the costs of repairing the car if it turns out to have a defect. Cars with a warranty are good; cars without a warranty are lemons.

Why do buyers believe the signal? It is because the cost of sending a false signal is high. A dealer who gives a warranty on a lemon ends up paying the high cost of repairs—and risks gaining a bad reputation. A dealer who gives a warranty only on good cars has no repair costs and a reputation that gets better and better. It pays to send an accurate signal. It is rational, therefore, for buyers to believe the signal. Warranties break the lemon problem and enable the used car market to function with two prices, one for lemons and one for good cars.

The Market for Loans

The market for bank loans is one in which private information plays a crucial role. Let's see how.

The quantity of loans demanded by borrowers depends on the interest rate. The lower the interest rate, the greater is the quantity of loans demanded—the demand curve for loans is downward-sloping. The supply of loans by banks and other lenders depends on the cost of lending. This cost has two parts. One is interest, and this interest cost is determined in the market for bank deposits—the market in which the banks borrow the funds that they lend. The other part of the cost of lending is the cost of bad loans—loans that are not repaid—called the default cost. The interest cost of a loan is the same for all borrowers. The default cost of a loan depends on the quality of the borrower.

Suppose that borrowers fall into two classes: low-risk and high-risk. Low-risk borrowers seldom default on their debts and then only for reasons beyond their control. For example, a firm might borrow to finance a project that fails and be unable to repay the bank. High-risk borrowers take high risks with the money they borrow and frequently default on their loans. For example, a firm might borrow to speculate in high-risk mineral prospecting that has a very small chance of paying off.

If banks can separate borrowers into risk categories, they supply loans to low-risk borrowers at one interest rate and to high-risk borrowers at another, higher interest rate. Real banks do this as much as possible. But they cannot always separate their borrowers. They have no sure way of knowing whether they are lending to a low-risk or a high-risk borrower.

---

[1] In this example, to keep the numbers simple, we'll ignore dealers' profit margins and other costs of doing business and suppose that dealers buy cars for the same price as they sell them. The principles are the same with dealers' profit margins.

So the banks charge the same interest rate to both low-risk and high-risk borrowers. If they offered loans to everyone at the low-risk interest rate, borrowers would face moral hazard and the banks would attract a lot of high-risk borrowers—adverse selection. Most borrowers would default, and the banks would incur economic losses. If the banks offered loans to everyone at the high-risk interest rate, most low-risk borrowers, with whom the banks would like to do profitable business, would be unwilling to borrow.

Faced with moral hazard and adverse selection, banks use *signals* to discriminate between borrowers, and they *ration* or limit loans to amounts below the amounts demanded. To restrict the amounts they are willing to lend to borrowers, banks use signals such as length of time in a job, ownership of a home, marital status, age, and business record.

Figure 21.7 shows how the market for loans works in the face of moral hazard and adverse selection. The demand for loans is *D*, and the supply is *S*. The supply curve is horizontal—perfectly elastic supply—because it is assumed that banks have access to a large quantity of funds that have a constant marginal cost of *r*. With no loan limits, the interest rate is *r* and the quantity of loans is *Q*. Because of moral hazard and adverse selection, the banks set loan limits based on signals and restrict the total loans to *L*. At the interest rate *r*, there is an excess demand for loans. A bank cannot increase its profit by making more loans because it can't identify the type of borrower taking the loans. Because the signals used mean that more high-risk borrowers are unsatisfied than low-risk borrowers, it is likely that additional loans will be biased toward high-risk (and high-cost) borrowers.

The Market for Insurance

People who buy insurance face a moral hazard problem, and insurance companies face an adverse selection problem. The moral hazard problem is that a person with insurance coverage for a loss has less incentive than an uninsured person to avoid such a loss. For example, a business with fire insurance has less incentive to take precautions against fire, such as installing a fire alarm or sprinkler system, than a business with no fire insurance does. The adverse selection problem is that people who face greater risks are more likely to buy insurance. For example, a person with a family history of serious illness is more likely to buy health insurance than is a person with a family history of good health.

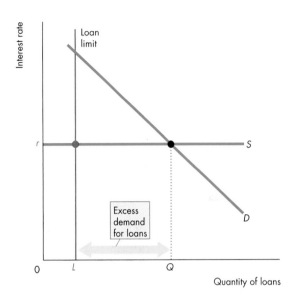

FIGURE 21.7

The Market for Loans

If a bank supplied loans on demand at the going interest rate *r*, the quantity of loans would be *Q*, but most of the loans would be taken by high-risk borrowers. Banks use signals to distinguish between low-risk and high-risk borrowers, and they limit the total loans to *L* and ration them. Banks have no incentive to increase interest rates and increase the quantity of loans because the additional loans would be to high-risk borrowers.

Insurance companies have an incentive to find ways around the moral hazard and adverse selection problems. By doing so, they can lower premiums and increase the amount of business they do. Real-world insurance markets have developed a variety of devices for overcoming or at least moderating these private information problems. Let's see how signals work in markets for insurance by looking at the example of auto insurance.

One of the clearest signals a person can give an auto insurance company is her or his driving record. Suppose that Dan is a good driver and rarely has an accident. If he can demonstrate to the insurance company that his driving record is impeccable over a long enough period, then the insurance company will recognize him as a good driver. Dan will work hard at establishing a reputation as a good driver because he will be able to get his insurance at a lower price.

If all drivers, good and bad alike, can establish good records, then simply having a good record will not convey any information. For the signal to be informative, it must be difficult for bad drivers to fake low risk by having a good record. The signals used in car insurance are the "no-claim" bonuses that drivers accumulate when they do not make an insurance claim.

Another device that insurance companies use is the deductible. A deductible is the amount of a loss that the insured person agrees to bear. For example, most auto insurance policies have the insured person paying the first few hundred dollars worth of damage. The premium varies with the deductible, and the decrease in the premium is more than proportionate to the increase in the deductible. By offering insurance with full coverage—no deductible—on terms that are attractive only to the highest-risk people and by offering coverage with a deductible on more favorable terms that are attractive to other people, insurance companies can do profitable business with everyone. High-risk people choose policies with low deductibles and high premiums; low-risk people choose policies with high deductibles and low premiums.

R E V I E W   Q U I Z

- How does private information create moral hazard and adverse selection?
- How do markets for cars use warranties to cope with private information?
- How do markets for insurance use no-claim bonuses to cope with private information?

Managing Risk in Financial Markets

RISK IS A DOMINANT FEATURE OF MARKETS FOR stocks and bonds—indeed for any asset whose price fluctuates. One thing people do to cope with risky asset prices is diversify their asset holdings.

Diversification to Lower Risk

The idea that diversification lowers risk is very natural. It is just an application of not putting all one's eggs into the same basket. How exactly does diversification reduce risk? The best way to answer this question is to consider an example.

Suppose there are two risky projects that you can undertake. Each involves investing $100,000. The two projects are independent of each other, but they both promise the same degree of risk and return.

On each project, you will either make $50,000 or lose $25,000, and the chance that either of these will happen is 50 percent. The expected return on each project is ($50,000 × 0.5) + (−$25,000 × 0.5), which is $12,500. But because the two projects are completely independent, the outcome of one project in no way influences the outcome of the other.

Undiversified   Suppose you risk everything, investing the $100,000 in either Project 1 or Project 2. You will either make $50,000 or lose $25,000. Because the probability of each of these outcomes is 50 percent, your expected return is the average of these two outcomes—an expected return of $12,500. But in this case in which only one project is chosen, there is no chance that you will actually make a return of $12,500.

Diversified   Suppose instead that you diversify by putting 50 percent of your money into Project 1 and 50 percent into Project 2. (Someone else is putting up the other money in these two projects.) Because the two projects are independent, you now have *four* possible returns:

1. Lose $12,500 on each project, and your return is −$25,000.
2. Make $25,000 on Project 1 and lose $12,500 on Project 2, and your return is $12,500.
3. Lose $12,500 on Project 1 and make $25,000 on Project 2, and your return is $12,500.
4. Make $25,000 on each project, and your return is $50,000.

Each of these four possible outcomes is equally probable—each has a 25 percent chance of occurring. You have lowered the chance that you will earn $50,000, but you have also lowered the chance that you will lose $25,000. And you have increased the chance that you will actually make your expected return of $12,500. By diversifying your portfolio of assets, you have reduced its riskiness while maintaining an expected return of $12,500.

If you are risk averse—if your utility of wealth curve looks like Tania's, which you studied earlier in this chapter—you'll prefer the diversified portfolio to the one that is not diversified. That is, your *expected utility* with a diversified set of assets is greater.

A common way to diversify is to buy stocks in different corporations. Let's look at the market in which these stocks are traded.

The Stock Market

The prices of the stocks are determined by demand and supply. But demand and supply in the stock market is dominated by one thing: the expected future price. If the price of a stock today is higher than the expected price tomorrow, people will sell the stock today. If the price of a stock today is less than its expected price tomorrow, people will buy the stock today. As a result of such trading, today's price equals tomorrow's expected price, and so today's price embodies all the relevant information that is available about the stock. A market in which the actual price embodies all currently available relevant information is called an **efficient market**.

In an efficient market, it is impossible to forecast changes in price. Why? If your forecast is that the price is going to rise tomorrow, you will buy now. Your action of buying today is an increase in demand today and increases *today's* price. It's true that your action—the action of a single trader—is not going to make much difference to a huge market like the New York Stock Exchange. But if traders in general expect a higher price tomorrow and they all act today on the basis of that expectation, then today's price will rise. It will keep on rising until it reaches the expected future price, because only at that price do traders see no profit in buying more stock today.

There is an apparent paradox about efficient markets. Markets are efficient because people try to make a profit. They seek a profit by buying at a low price and selling at a high price. But the very act of buying and selling to make a profit means that the market price moves to equal its expected future value. When it has done that, no one, not even those who are seeking to profit, can *predictably* make a profit. Every profit opportunity seen by traders leads to an action that produces a price change that removes the profit opportunity for others. Even the probability of an intergalactic attack on New York City is taken into account in determining stock market prices—see the cartoon.

"Drat! I suppose the market has already discounted this, too."

Drawing by Lorenz; © 1986 *The New Yorker Magazine, Inc.*

Thus an efficient market has two features:

1. Its price equals the expected future price and embodies all the available information.
2. No forecastable profit opportunities are available.

The key thing to understand about an efficient market such as the stock market is that if something can be anticipated, it will be, and the anticipation of a future event will affect the *current* price of a stock.

Volatility in Stock Prices If the price of a stock equals its expected future price, why is the stock market so volatile? It is volatile because expectations are volatile. They depend on the information available. As new information becomes available, stock traders form new expectations about the future state of the economy and, in turn, new expectations of future stock prices. New information comes randomly, so prices change randomly.

◆ We've seen how people cope with uncertainty and how markets work when there are information problems. *Reading Between the Lines* on pages 462–463 looks one more time at the problem of picking a portfolio and shows how a person's attitude toward risk influences the type of portfolio selected.

The next part of this book studies *macroeconomics*. It builds on what you learned in Chapter 3 about production possibilities and shows how economic growth expands these possibilities. It also studies fluctuations in production, employment, and prices.

A Tradeoff Between Risk and Return

THE NEW YORK TIMES, NOVEMBER 15, 1998

Diversified Pillows for Resting Easy in Storms

BY JONATHAN FUERBRINGER

"We are not trying to hit home runs," said Benjamin Thorndike, lead portfolio manager of the Scudder Pathway Series of funds. "We are trying to do well and sleep well at night."

That's a diversified money manager talking about an investment style that has not always fared well in an era of double-digit annual gains in the Dow Jones industrial average and the Standard & Poor's 500-stock index. ...

The idea is simple. If your investments are spread around—in stocks, in bonds, in foreign stocks, in different kinds of bonds and different kinds of stocks—you have a good chance of getting a cushioning rise in one area while another is plunging. In the third quarter, for example, the return from government and corporate bonds was 4 percent while the Dow, the S&P 500 and the Nasdaq index fell 10 percent or more.

Diversification is not the way to big stock returns because it reduces risk in exchange for lower returns. But it is a way to survive the volatile swings of the stock market, which have become much more common over the last year.

Investors should "find the comfort zone" between return and risk, said Gary Brinson, chief executive of Brinson Partners, which manages a diversified mutual fund. Diversification, he said, means "the path of that return is much less bumpy." ...

But deciding to be diversified is not enough. Investors must decide how much risk to take on, which means looking closely at the mix of investments in their fund or portfolio.

Essence of the Story

■ If investments are spread around in different kinds of bonds and stocks, returns are lower but risk is also lower.

■ Investors need to find the combination of return and risk that makes them comfortable—that enables them to sleep well.

■ Some investors are comfortable taking big risks in exchange for a chance of a big return. Other investors are comfortable only if they invest cautiously.

■ In Fig. 1, a cautious investor sleeps well. This person has wealth of $100,000, and the utility of this wealth is 100 (on the index number scale used in Fig. 1).

■ This person has an opportunity to invest $10,000 in a business venture. There is a 50 percent chance that the business succeeds and pays out $20,000. And there is a 50 percent chance that the business fails and the $10,000 is lost.

■ Expected wealth is $105,000 (0.5 multiplied by $90,000 plus 0.5 multiplied by $120,000). Expected utility is 101 (0.5 multiplied by 91 plus 0.5 multiplied by 111). The investment increases expected utility. So this person sleeps well!

■ In Fig. 2, a cautious investor is beyond the comfort zone. Here the person has $20,000 to invest. There is a 50 percent chance that the business succeeds and pays out $40,000. And there is a 50 percent chance that the business fails and the $20,000 is lost.

■ Expected wealth is $110,000 (0.5 multiplied by $80,000 plus 0.5 multiplied by $140,000). But expected utility is only 98 (0.5 multiplied by 78 plus 0.5 multiplied by 118). Expected wealth increases, but expected utility decreases. The cautious investor is beyond the comfort zone and will not make this investment.

■ Figure 3 shows the case of an investor who is comfortable with a risky investment strategy.

■ This person has $50,000 to invest. There is a 50 percent chance that the business succeeds and pays out $100,000. And there is a 50 percent chance that the business fails and the entire $50,000 is lost. This opportunity is more risky than the one that the cautious investor rejected in Fig. 2.

■ Expected wealth is $125,000 (0.5 multiplied by $50,000 plus 0.5 multiplied by $200,000). Expected utility is 116 (0.5 multiplied by 52 plus 0.5 multiplied by 180). Expected wealth increases and expected utility increases. This person feels better off pursuing this risky opportunity than passing it up.

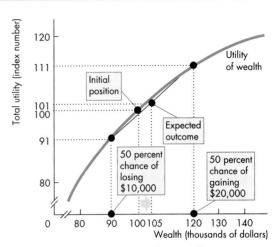

Figure 1 A cautious investor sleeps well

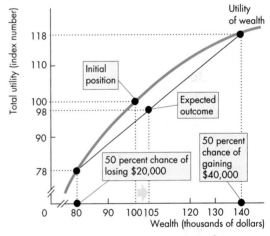

Figure 2 Beyond a cautious investor's comfort zone

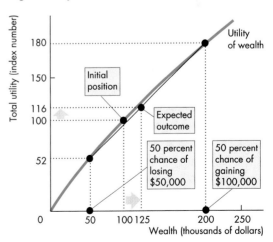

Figure 3 In a high-risk investor's comfort zone

S U M M A R Y

KEY POINTS

Uncertainty and Risk (pp. 450–452)

■ Uncertainty is a situation in which more than one event may occur but we don't know which one.

■ Risk is uncertainty with probabilities attached to outcomes.

■ A person's attitude toward risk, called the degree of risk aversion, is described by a utility of wealth schedule and curve.

■ Faced with uncertainty, people choose the action that maximizes expected utility.

Insurance (pp. 453–454)

■ We spend 15 percent of our income on insurance to reduce the risk we face.

■ The three main types of insurance are life, health, and property and casualty.

■ By pooling risks, insurance companies can reduce the risks people face (from insured activities) at a lower cost than the value placed on the lower risk.

Information (pp. 455–457)

■ Buyers search for the least-cost source of supply and stop when the expected marginal benefit of search equals the marginal cost of search.

■ The price at which the search stops is less than or equal to the buyer's reservation price.

■ Advertising provides information, and it might increase prices or decrease them.

■ Advertising can lower prices because it increases competition or extends economies of scale.

Private Information (pp. 457–460)

■ Private information is one person's knowledge that is too costly for anyone else to discover.

■ Private information creates the problems of moral hazard (the use of private information to the advantage of the informed and the disadvantage of the uninformed) and adverse selection (the tendency for people to enter into agreements in which they can use their private information to their own advantage and to the disadvantage of the less informed party).

■ Devices that enable markets to function in the face of moral hazard and adverse selection are incentive payments, guarantees such as warranties, rationing, and signals.

Managing Risk in Financial Markets (pp. 460–461)

■ Risk can be reduced by diversifying asset holdings, thereby combining the returns on projects that are independent of each other.

■ A common way to diversify is to buy stocks in different corporations. Stock prices are determined by the expected future price of the stock.

■ Expectations about future stock prices are based on all the information that is available and regarded as relevant.

■ A market in which the price equals the expected price is an efficient market.

KEY FIGURES

KEY TERMS

PROBLEMS

*1. The figure shows Lee's utility of wealth curve.

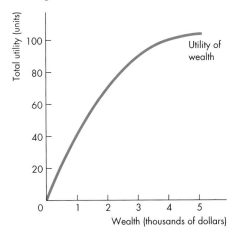

Lee is offered a job as a salesperson in which there is a 50 percent chance that she will make $4,000 a month and a 50 percent chance that she will make nothing.
a. What is Lee's expected income from taking this job?
b. What is Lee's expected utility from taking this job?
c. How much (approximately) would another firm have to offer Lee with certainty to persuade her not to take the risky sales job?

2. The figure shows Colleen's utility of wealth curve.

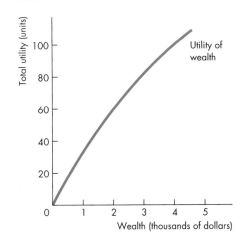

Just like Lee in problem 1, Colleen is offered a job as a salesperson in which there is a 50 percent chance that she will make $4,000 a month and a 50 percent chance that she will make nothing.
a. What is Colleen's expected income from taking this job?
b. What is Colleen's expected utility from taking this job?
c. How much (approximately) would another firm have to offer Colleen with certainty to persuade her not to take the risky sales job?
d. Explain who is more likely to be willing to take this risky job, Lee or Colleen.

*3. Jimmy and Zenda have the following utility of wealth schedules:

Wealth	Jimmy's utility	Zenda's utility
0	0	0
100	200	512
200	300	640
300	350	672
400	375	678
500	387	681
600	393	683
700	396	684

Who is more risk averse, Jimmy or Zenda?

4. Suppose that Jimmy and Zenda in problem 3 have $400 each and that each sees a business project that involves committing the entire $400 to the project. They reckon that the project could return $600 (a profit of $200) with a probability of 0.85 or $200 (a loss of $200) with a probability of 0.15. Who goes for the project and who hangs onto the initial $400?

*5. Lee in problem 1 has built a small weekend shack on a steep, unstable hillside. She spent all her wealth, which is $5,000, on this project. There is a 75 percent chance that the house will be washed down the hill and be worthless. How much is Lee willing to pay for an insurance policy that pays her $5,000 if the house is washed away?

6. Colleen in problem 2 has built a small weekend shack right next to Lee's (of problem 1). Colleen has spent all her wealth, which is $4,000, on this project. There is a 75 percent chance that the house will be washed down the hill and be worthless. How much is Colleen willing to pay for an insurance policy that pays her $4,000 if the house is washed away?

*7. Lee in problem 1 is shopping for a new car. She plans to borrow the money to pay for the car from the bank. Describe in detail the search problems that Lee faces. What information does she find useful? How does she obtain it? How does she make her decisions?

8. Lee in problem 1 is shopping for a new car. She plans to borrow the money to pay for the car from the bank. Describe in detail the moral hazard and adverse selection problems that Lee faces. What arrangements is she likely to encounter that are designed to cope with these problems?

CRITICAL THINKING

1. Study *Reading Between the Lines* on pp. 462–463 and then answer the following questions:
   a. Why is it rational for some people to take big risks and for other people to be cautious?
   b. Who makes more money on the average: the cautious investor or the one who takes bigger risks? Why?
   c. Why do you think pension funds hold a mixture of stocks and bonds?

2. Use the links on the Parkin Web site to obtain information on the prices of three stocks that interest you.
   a. Describe the change in the prices of these stocks over the past month.
   b. If you had invested $1,000 in each of these stocks (a total of $3,000) one month ago, how much would your initial investment be worth today?
   c. If you had $3,000 to invest, would you use some of it to buy these stocks? How much would you put in each? How much would you keep in cash?
   d. Form a group with other students and compare your answers to part (c). Which one of you is the most risk averse? Which of you is the least risk averse? Explain your answer.

3. Why do you think it is not possible to buy insurance against having to put up with a low-paying, miserable job? Explain why a market in insurance of this type would not work.

4. Although you can't buy insurance against the risk of being sold a lemon, the market does give you some protection. How? What are the main ways in which markets overcome the lemon problem?

5. Grades send signals to potential employers. Explain why you are better served or worse served by a professor who demands high standards for an A than by one who always ensures that 20 percent of the class gets an A.

6. Merck discovers a new drug that is expected to bring big profits. What happens to the price of Merck's stock? Why wouldn't people put all their wealth into Merck's stock?

We, the People, ...

Thomas Jefferson knew that creating a government of the people, by the people, and for the people was a huge enterprise and one that could easily go wrong. Creating a constitution that made despotic and tyrannical rule impossible was relatively easy. The founding fathers did their best to practice sound economics. They designed a sophisticated system of incentives—of carrots and sticks—to make the government responsive to public opinion and to limit the ability of individual special interests to gain at the expense of the majority. But they were not able to create a constitution that effectively blocks the ability of special interest groups to capture the consumer and producer surpluses that result from specialization and exchange. ◆ We have created a system of government to deal with four economic problems. The market economy would produce too small a quantity of those public goods and services that we must consume together, such as national defense and air-traffic control. It enables monopoly to restrict production and charge too high a price. It produces too large a quantity of some goods and services, the production of which creates pollution. And it generates a distribution of income and wealth that most people believe is too unequal. So we need a government to help cope with these economic problems. But as the founding fathers knew would happen, when governments get involved in the economy, people try to steer the government's actions in directions that bring personal gains at the expense of the general interest. ◆ The four chapters in this part explained the problems with which the market has a hard time coping. Chapter 18 overviewed the entire range of problems and studied one of these problems, public goods, more deeply. Chapter 19 studied antitrust law and the regulation of natural monopoly. And Chapter 20 dealt with externalities. It examined the external costs imposed by pollution and the external benefits that come from education and research. It described some of the ways in which externalities can be dealt with. And it explained that one way of coping with externalities is to strengthen the market and "internalize" the externalities rather than to intervene in the market. Chapter 21 is different from the other three. It looked at the problems of uncertainty and incomplete information and the problems that markets have in the face of these problems. But it also showed you that the market does cope with these problems remarkably well. ◆ Many economists have thought long and hard about the problems discussed in this part. But none has had as profound an effect on our ideas in this area as Ronald Coase, whom you can meet on the following page. You can also meet Walter Williams of George Mason University, another major contributor to our understanding of market failure and government intervention.

The Economist

Ronald Coase *(1910–), was born in England and educated at the London School of Economics, where he was deeply influenced by his teacher, Arnold Plant, and by the issues of his youth: communist central planning versus free markets. Professor Coase has lived in the United States since 1951. He first visited America as a 20-year-old on a traveling scholarship during the depths of the Great Depression. It was on this visit, and before he had completed his bachelor's degree, that he conceived the ideas that 60 years later were to earn him the 1991 Nobel Prize for Economic Science. He discovered and clarified the significance of transaction costs and property rights for the functioning of the economy. Ronald Coase has revolutionized the way we think about property rights and externalities and has opened up the growing field of law and economics.*

"The question to be decided is: is the value of fish lost greater or less than the value of the product which contamination of the stream makes possible?"

RONALD H. COASE
The Problem of Social Cost

The Issues

As knowledge accumulates, we are becoming more sensitive to environmental externalities. We are also developing more sensitive methods of dealing with them. But all the methods involve a public choice.

Urban smog, which is both unpleasant and dangerous to breathe, forms when sunlight reacts with emissions from the tailpipes of automobiles. Because of this external cost of auto exhaust, we set emission standards and tax gasoline. Emission standards increase the cost of a car, and gasoline taxes increase the cost of the marginal mile traveled. The higher costs decrease the quantity demanded of road transportation and so decrease the amount of pollution it creates. Is the value of cleaner urban air worth the higher cost of transportation? The public choices of voters, regulators, and lawmakers answer this question.

Acid rain, which imposes a cost on everyone who lives in its path, falls from sulfur-laden clouds produced by electric utility smokestacks. This external cost is being tackled with a market solution. This solution is marketable permits, the price and allocation of which are determined by the forces of supply and demand. Private choices determine the demand for pollution permits, but a public choice determines the supply.

As cars stream onto an urban freeway during the morning rush hour, the highway clogs and becomes an expensive parking lot. Each rush hour traveler imposes external costs on all the others. Today, road users bear private congestion costs but do not face a share of the external congestion costs that they create. But a market solution to this problem is now technologically feasible. It is a solution that charges road users a fee similar to a toll that varies with time of day and degree of congestion. Confronted with the social marginal cost of their actions, each road user makes a choice and the market for highway space is efficient. Here, a public choice to use a market solution leaves the final decision about the degree of congestion to private choices.

Then

Chester Jackson, a Lake Erie fisherman, recalls that when he began fishing on the lake, boats didn't carry drinking water. Fishermen drank from the lake. Speaking after World War II, Jackson observed, "Can't do that today. Those chemicals in there would kill you." Farmers used chemicals, such as the insecticide DDT that got carried into the lake by runoff. Industrial waste and trash were also dumped in the lake in large quantities. As a result, Lake Erie became badly polluted during the 1940s and became incapable of sustaining a viable fish stock.

Now

Today, Lake Erie supports a fishing industry, just as it did in the 1930s. No longer treated as a garbage dump for chemicals, the lake is regenerating its ecosystem. Fertilizers and insecticides are now recognized as products that have potential externalities, and their external effects are assessed by the Environmental Protection Agency before new versions are put into widespread use. Dumping industrial waste into rivers and lakes is now subject to much more stringent regulations and penalties. Lake Erie's externalities have been dealt with by one of the methods available: government regulation.

Walter Williams, whom you can meet on the following pages, has done much to improve our understanding of public policy and the problems of government intervention in the economy.

Talking with

Walter E. Williams *is*

Professor of Economics at George Mason University in Fairfax, Virginia. Born in Philadelphia, Pennsylvania, in 1936, Professor Williams was an undergraduate at California State University at Los Angeles and a graduate student at UCLA, where he obtained his Ph.D. in 1972.

Professor Williams's research covers a wide area, but his major work is on labor markets, discrimination, and market failure. He has lectured throughout the world, including the University of Capetown during the 1980s, where he learned first-hand the lessons of apartheid. Professor Williams is a member of the prestigious Mont Pelerin Society, an international organization of free market economists. Its membership includes six Nobel Laureates: Milton Friedman, Friedrich Hayek, George Stigler, James Buchanan, Gary Becker, and Ronald Coase.

Michael Parkin talked with Professor Williams about his work, how it connects with the ideas of other great economists, and the insights they offer us in facing today's problems.

Walter E. Williams

Professor Williams, what attracted you to economics?

Like many undergraduate students of the 1960s, I was concerned with public policy that focused on the betterment of mankind and tackled issues such as urban decay, poverty, unemployment, and discrimination. At the time, it seemed that social sciences like sociology and psychology were the ideal tools to analyze these important social issues. That was until by pure chance a particular sociology class was filled, and so I substituted an introductory economics class. As a consequence of not being good at the deductive logic of economics, plus several classroom disputes with the professor on topics such as income distribution and racial discrimination, I wound up getting a "D." However, I was sufficiently interested in economics that I took two economics classes the following semester, earning an "A" in both. Ultimately, I changed my major to economics and earned a B.A. from California State University at Los Angeles and later earned a Ph.D. in Economics from UCLA.

You and I first met in Capetown, South Africa, in 1980, when we were both visiting professors at the University of Capetown. What are the big economic lessons that the experience of South Africa teaches about the proper role of government in economic life?

When we first met in Capetown, apartheid was very much a part of South Africa. I was very impressed with the economic lessons of apartheid, so much so that I ultimately wrote a book in 1992 entitled *South Africa's War Against Capitalism.* The biggest lesson from South Africa's experience is that the free market does not confer privileges based on race. The free market instead uses economic factors such as prices and productivity. If people wish to indulge their preferences for noneconomic factors such as race, sex, and nationality, the free market exacts a price. South African whites knew this very well and found that if they wanted privileges, they needed the extensive government apparatus of coercion and control that became known as apartheid. Labor laws such as those that reserved certain jobs for whites stand as unambiguous evidence that the market would not discriminate in employment to the extent whites wished. If it would have, there would have been no need for racially restrictive laws.

> The biggest lesson from South Africa's experience is that the free market cannot be trusted to confer privileges based on race. The free market instead uses economic factors such as prices and productivity.

What do you identify as the major sources of market failure that need government action today?

Many alleged instances of "market failure" are the result of ill-defined property rights. That is surely the case in instances of air and water pollution. In those instances, a case can be made for efficient government intervention. Government can ban the polluting activity, assign pollution taxes, or assign pollution rights that can be bought and sold in the market. Many economists agree that the last is a more efficient method of dealing with the external costs of pollution. We should also recognize that government decision makers do not hold property rights to the resources they control. Since they

are not residual claimants to either the costs or benefits they create, we cannot expect to see the kinds of forces, such as the threat of bankruptcy, that create the kind of operational efficiency we see in the market. In other words, since a politician's personal wealth is not at stake, when he makes decisions, he will be far more shortsighted than his counterpart in the private sector.

Has deregulation of telecommunications and air transportation done its job? Has deregulation brought problems that were not expected?

By any objective measure, the deregulation of the telecommunications and transportation industries has done its job. Consumers pay lower prices and receive higher quality and a more varied set of services than was the case before deregulation. Deregulation of airlines led to cheaper fares, which in turn led to more Americans traveling by air. To the extent that statistics show that air travel is far safer than highway travel, the deregulation has actually saved thousands of lives. With the deregulation of the telephone industry, we see the greater use of services such as faxes, modems, electronic transactions, and the Internet that would have been impossible with the regulatory heavy hand of government. The remaining problem in these industries is that deregulation has not gone far enough: in the case of transportation, privatization of the airports and air traffic control, and in the case of telecommunications, complete auctioning of the airwaves to new and existing firms in the communications industry.

Do we have a monopoly problem in the new information industries? Microsoft? Intel? The Internet? Why and what do we need to do about it?

Often a monopoly is the most efficient method of organization. Monopolies are not inherently good or bad. After all, the institution of marriage is essentially one of a monopolistic structure: It hopes to limit competition. Obviously, the participants guess there are some gains from limited competition. If you read the Ten Commandments, you will see that the first two, presumably the most important, are: Thou shalt have none other gods before me, and thou shalt not make any graven image. In other words, there cannot be any substitutes for God—surely a monopoly arrangement!

Monopoly is a problem when government creates monopolies, whether the monopoly is private or public. Classic government-created monopolies are those in education, postal services, and rail services that limit consumer choices and are not subject to the corrective forces of the marketplace when they do not serve their customers properly. Such insulation does not apply in the cases of Microsoft and Intel.

What are the main forms of discrimination that economic policy can correct and what is your assessment of the progress made in the United States during the past decade?

First, we need to come up with an operational and useful definition of discrimination. I think discrimination can be best described solely as the act of choice. Scarcity implies choice. When one chooses one activity or person, he or she must necessarily choose against some other activity or person. For example, when the student chooses to major in economics, he or she must necessarily choose—or discriminate—against other majors. When someone chooses a spouse, he or she must discriminate against other potential spouses.

When one modifies the word "discrimination" with the word "sex" or "race," one is merely specifying an attribute upon which a choice is made. What most people call discrimination is more properly called preference indulgence. As such, the preference for Burgundy wine over Bordeaux wine does not conceptually differ from a person's preference for a white spouse, white employee, or white renter. In other words, there are no commonly accepted criteria to say whether the preference for one good or set of physical attributes is better or more righteous than another.

Preference indulgence becomes a moral and economic problem when government is used. For example, any principle of liberty suggests that a person has the right to sell his house to whomever he pleases, but that principle does not allow him to use state coercion to force his neighbor to act likewise. When there is public provision of a good such as schools, libraries, or golf courses, that fact implies that every member of the public has the right to use the good in question. While racial or sexual preference indulgence may be offensive, the true test of one's commitment

to freedom of association does not come when we permit people to associate as we see fit. The true test of that commitment comes when we allow people to associate in ways we deem offensive.

The best thing that government can do in the area of racial or sex discrimination is not to subsidize it through laws that regulate prices such as minimum wages and rent control and other regulatory laws such as occupational and business licensure. Minimum wages deny people the right to bid lower prices for their labor services. Rent control laws deny them the right to bid higher prices for rental services. Licensure laws allow incumbent practitioners to establish arbitrary, capricious, legally binding occupational and business entry standards.

The power to bid lower prices for what one sells or higher prices for what one buys is the most effective way for people deemed less preferred—minorities, women, and foreigners—to compete with others. Price controls prevent that competition. Similarly, voluntary mutually satisfactory exchange permits effective competition with people deemed more preferred.

Who are the great economists of the past who have inspired you most? What principal idea has proved crucial in your own thinking?
Frederic Bastiat's works, *The Law* and *Economic Sophisms*, have been my major sources of inspiration. But Friedrich Hayek's many works have played a major part as well. Both shared the vision that the uglier portions of mankind's history features arbitrary abuse and

control by a powerful government. If liberty is to emerge and survive, government must be limited to the legitimate and moral functions of government. For the most part, those functions lie principally in the areas of protection of the individual from coercion by others and the protection of his property, including his person. Evidence shows that where individuals have a greater measure of liberty, there is a higher level of prosperity and wealth accumulation. But prosperity and wealth should be viewed as a secondary benefit of liberty. Liberty is morally superior, and its primary benefit lies in its respect for the individual.

> Evidence shows that where individuals have a greater measure of liberty, there is a higher level of prosperity and wealth accumulation.

What do you say to an undergraduate who wants to know whether it is worth majoring in economics?
Economics is a way of thinking and, as such, a powerful tool of analysis that has broad application. Economic theory can be usefully applied in any discussion where there is an issue of benefits versus the cost of human action. Economists have a broad range of employment choices from working in business, government, research, and educational institutions. Moreover, among social scientists, economists tend to be the more highly paid.

Chapter 22

A First Look at Macroeconomics

During the past 100 years, the quantity of goods and services produced in the nation's farms, factories, shops, and offices has expanded more than twentyfold. As a result, we have a much higher living standard than our grandparents had. Will production always expand? Will your world be more prosperous than today's? ◆ For most of us, a high standard of living means finding a good job. What kind of job will you find when you graduate? Will you have lots of choice, or will you face a labor market with a high unemployment rate in which jobs are hard to find? ◆ A high standard of living means being able to afford to buy life's necessities and some fun. If prices rise too quickly, some people get left behind and must trim what they buy. Prices have increased slowly over the past few years. But can we count on them rising slowly in the future? What will the dollar buy next year? What will it buy in 10 years when you are paying off your student loan? And what will it buy in 50 years when you are spending your life's savings in retirement? ◆ Every year from 1970 to 1997, the government has spent more than it has raised in taxes. And most years, we have imported more goods and services from the rest of the world than we have exported to it. We have experienced large and persistent government and international deficits. How will these deficits affect your future? ◆ To keep production expanding and prevent an economic slowdown, the federal government and the Federal Reserve Board—the nation's financial managers—take policy actions. What kinds of actions do they take? How do their actions influence production, jobs, prices, and the ability of Americans to compete in the global marketplace?

◆ These are the questions of macroeconomics. The macroeconomic events through which we are now living are tumultuous and exciting. With what you learn in these chapters, you will be able to understand these events, the policy challenges they bring, and the political debate they stir. You will be able to prepare yourself better for your world, the economic world that you will enter when you graduate and in which you will earn your living.

What Will Your World Be Like?

After studying this chapter, you will be able to:

■ Describe the origins of macroeconomics and the problems it deals with

■ Describe the long-term trends and short-term fluctuations in economic growth, unemployment, inflation, and government and international deficits

■ Explain why economic growth, unemployment, inflation, and deficits matter

■ Identify the macroeconomic policy challenges and describe the tools available for meeting them

Origins and Issues of Macroeconomics

ECONOMISTS BEGAN TO STUDY LONG-TERM economic growth, inflation, and international payments as long ago as the 1750s, and this work was the origin of macroeconomics. But modern macroeconomics did not emerge until the **Great Depression**, a decade (1929–1939) of high unemployment and stagnant production throughout the world economy. In the Depression's worst year, 1933, the production of U.S. farms, factories, shops, and offices was only 70 percent of its 1929 level and 25 percent of the labor force was unemployed. These were years of human misery on a scale that is hard to imagine today. They were also years of extreme pessimism about the ability of the market economy to work properly. Many people believed that private ownership, free markets, and democratic political institutions could not survive.

The science of economics had no solutions to the Great Depression. The major alternative system of central planning and socialism seemed increasingly attractive. It was in this climate of economic depression and political and intellectual turmoil that modern macroeconomics emerged with the publication in 1936 of John Maynard Keynes' *The General Theory of Employment, Interest, and Money* (see p. 466).

Short-Term Versus Long-Term Goals

Keynes' theory was that depression and high unemployment result from insufficient private spending and that to cure these problems, the government must increase its spending. Keynes' focused primarily on the *short term*. He wanted to cure an immediate problem almost regardless of the *long-term* consequences of the cure. "In the long run," said Keynes, "we're all dead."

But Keynes believed that after his cure for depression had restored the economy to a normal condition, the long-term problems of inflation and slow economic growth would return. And he suspected that his cure for depression, increased government spending, might trigger inflation and might lower the long-term growth rate of production. With a lower long-term growth rate, the economy would create fewer jobs. If this outcome did occur, a policy aimed at lowering unemployment in the short run might end up increasing it in the long run.

By the late 1960s and through the 1970s, Keynes' predictions became a reality. Inflation increased, economic growth slowed down, and in some countries, unemployment became persistently high. The causes of these developments are complex. But they point to an inescapable conclusion: The long-term problems of inflation, slow growth, and persistent unemployment and the short-term problems of depression and economic fluctuations intertwine and are most usefully studied together. So although macroeconomics was reborn during the Great Depression, it has now returned to its older tradition. Today, macroeconomics studies long-term economic growth and inflation as well as short-term business fluctuations and unemployment.

The Road Ahead

There is no unique way to study macroeconomics. Because its rebirth was a product of depression, the common practice for many years was to pay most attention to short-term output fluctuations and unemployment but to never completely lose sight of the long-term issues. When a rapid inflation emerged during the 1970s, this topic returned to prominence. During the 1980s, when long-term growth slowed in the United States and other rich industrial countries but exploded in East Asia, economists redirected their energy toward economic growth. During the 1990s, as information technologies continue to shrink the globe, the international dimension of macroeconomics has become more prominent. The result of these developments is that modern macroeconomics is a broad subject that studies all the issues we've just identified: long-term economic growth, unemployment, and inflation. It also studies two new problems: the government budget and international deficits.

Over the past 40 years, economists have developed a clearer understanding of the forces that determine macroeconomic performance and have devised policies that they hope will improve this performance. Your main goal is to become familiar with the theories of macroeconomics and the policies they make possible. To set you on your path toward this goal, we're going to take a first look at economic growth, unemployment, inflation, and surpluses and deficits and learn why these macroeconomic phenomena merit our attention.

Economic Growth

YOUR PARENTS ARE RICHER THAN YOUR GRAND-parents were when they were young. But are you going to be richer than your parents? And are your children going to be richer than you? The answers depend on the rate of economic growth.

Economic growth is the expansion of the economy's production possibilities. It can be pictured as an outward shift of the production possibility frontier (*PPF*)—see Chapter 3, pp. 43–44.

We measure economic growth by the increase in real gross domestic product. **Real gross domestic product** (also called **real GDP**) is the value of the total production of all the nation's farms, factories, shops, and offices linked back to the prices of a single year. Real GDP in the United States is currently linked back to the prices of 1992 (called 1992 dollars). We link back to the dollar prices of a single year to eliminate the influence of *inflation*—the increase in prices—and determine how much production has grown from one year to another. (Real GDP is explained more fully in Chapter 23 on pp. 498–501.)

Real GDP is not a perfect measure of total production because it does not include everything that is produced. It excludes the things we produce for ourselves at home (preparing meals, doing laundry, house painting, gardening, and so on). It also excludes production that people hide to avoid taxes or because it is illegal—the underground economy. But despite its shortcomings, real GDP is the best measure of total production available. Let's see what it tells us about economic growth in the United States.

Economic Growth in the United States

Figure 22.1 shows real GDP in the United States since 1960 and highlights two features of economic growth:

- The growth of potential GDP
- Fluctuations of real GDP around potential GDP

The Growth of Potential GDP   When all the economy's resources are fully employed, the value of production is called **potential GDP**. Real GDP fluctuates around potential GDP, and the rate of long-term economic growth is measured by the growth rate of potential GDP. It is shown by the steepness of the potential GDP line (the black line) in Fig. 22.1.

During the 1960s, real GDP grew at an unusually rapid rate of 4.4 percent a year. But the growth rate of output per person slowed during the 1970s, a phenomenon called the **productivity growth slowdown**. Real GDP began to grow more rapidly during the late 1980s and through the 1990s. But the high growth rate of the 1960s did not return.

Why did the productivity growth slowdown occur? This question is controversial. One possible cause is a sharp rise in the relative price of energy. How this factor might have slowed productivity growth is explored in Chapter 28 on pp. 614. Whatever its cause, the productivity growth slowdown means that we all have smaller incomes today than we would have had if the economy had continued to grow at its 1960s rate.

Let's now look at GDP fluctuations.

FIGURE 22.1

Economic Growth in the United States

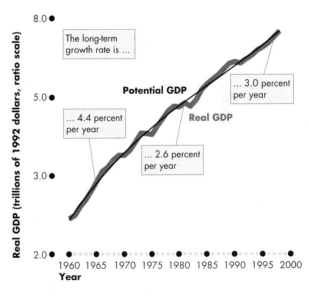

The long-term economic growth rate, measured by the growth of potential GDP, was 4.4 percent a year during the 1960s but slowed to 2.6 percent a year during the 1970s. Growth speeded up again during the 1980s and 1990s but did not return to its 1960s rate. Real GDP fluctuates around potential GDP.

Source: U.S. Department of Commerce, *National Income and Product Accounts of the United States.*

Fluctuations Around Potential GDP   Real GDP fluctuates around potential GDP in a business cycle. A **business cycle** is the periodic but irregular up-and-down movement in production. It is measured by fluctuations in real GDP around potential GDP. When real GDP is less than potential GDP, some resources are underused. For example, some labor is unemployed and capital is underutilized. When real GDP is greater than potential GDP, resources are being *over*used. Many people work longer hours than they are willing to put up with in the long run, capital is worked so intensively that it is not maintained in prime working order, delivery times lengthen, bottlenecks occur, and backorders increase.

Business cycles are not regular, predictable, or repeating cycles like the phases of the moon. Their timing changes unpredictably. But cycles do have some things in common. Every business cycle has two phases:

1. A recession
2. An expansion

and two turning points:

1. A peak
2. A trough

Figure 22.2 shows the most recent business cycle in the United States. A **recession** is a period during which real GDP decreases—the growth rate of real GDP is negative—for at least two successive quarters. The most recent recession began in the third quarter of 1990 and ended in the first quarter of 1991. An **expansion** is a period during which real GDP increases. The most recent expansion began in the second quarter of 1991 and was still in progress during 1999. If this expansion continues through January 2000, it will become the longest expansion on record. An earlier expansion ended with the onset of recession in the second quarter of 1990.

When a business cycle expansion ends and a recession begins, the turning point is called a *peak*. The most recent peak occurred in the second quarter of 1990. When a business cycle recession ends and a recovery begins, the turning point is called a *trough*. The most recent trough occurred in the first quarter of 1991.

FIGURE 22.2
The Most Recent U.S. Business Cycle

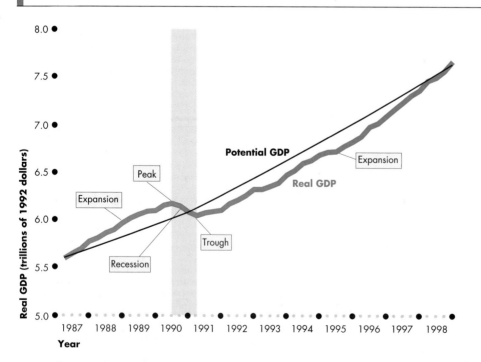

A business cycle has two phases: recession and expansion. The most recent recession (highlighted) ran from the third quarter of 1990 through the first quarter of 1991. Then a new expansion began in the second quarter of 1991. A business cycle has two turning points, a peak and a trough. In the most recent business cycle, the peak occurred in the second quarter of 1990 and the trough occurred in the first quarter of 1991.

The Recent Recession in Historical Perspective

The recession of 1990–1991 seemed severe while we were passing through it, but compared with earlier recessions, it was mild. You can see how mild it was by looking at Fig. 22.3, which shows a longer history of U.S. economic growth. The biggest decrease in real GDP occurred during the Great Depression of the 1930s. A large decrease also occurred in 1946 and 1947, immediately after World War II. In more recent times, severe recessions occurred during the mid-1970s, following oil price hikes by the Organization of Petroleum Exporting Countries (OPEC), and during the early 1980s.

Each of these economic downturns was more severe than that in 1990–1991. But you can see that the Great Depression was much more severe than anything that followed it. This episode was so extreme that we don't call it a recession. We call it a *depression*.

This last truly great depression occurred before governments started taking policy actions to stabilize the economy. It also occurred before the birth of modern macroeconomics. Is the absence of another great depression a sign that macroeconomics has contributed to economic stability? Some people believe it

is. Others doubt it. We'll evaluate these opinions on a number of occasions in this book.

We've looked at real GDP growth and fluctuations in the United States. But is the U.S. experience typical? Do other countries share our experience? Let's see whether they do.

Economic Growth Around the World

A country might have a rapid growth rate of real GDP, but it might also have a rapid population growth rate. To compare growth rates over time and across countries, we use the growth rate of real GDP *per person*. Real GDP per person is real GDP divided by the population. For example, U.S. real GDP in 1998 was $7,550 billion, and the population of the United States was 271.8 million. So U.S. real GDP per person was $7,550 billion divided by 271.8 million, which equals $27,778.

Figure 22.4 shows real GDP per person between 1962 and 1998 for the world's three largest economies: the United States, Japan, and Germany.

FIGURE 22.3

Long-Term Economic Growth in the United States

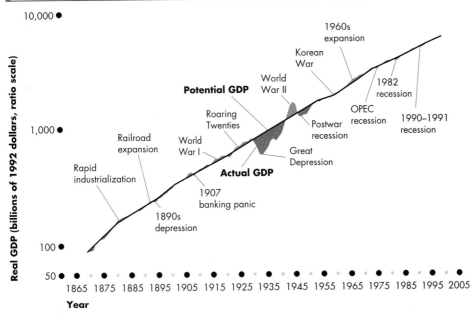

The thin black line shows potential GDP. Along this line, real GDP grew at an average rate of 3.3 percent a year between 1870 and 1994. The blue areas show when real GDP was above potential GDP, and the red areas show when it was below potential GDP. During some periods, such as World War II, real GDP expanded quickly. During other periods, such as the Great Depression and more recently in 1975 (following the OPEC oil price hike), 1982, and 1990–1991, real GDP declined.

Sources: 1869–1928, Christina D. Romer, "The Prewar Business Cycle Reconsidered: New Estimates of Gross National Product, 1869–1908," *Journal of Political Economy* 97, (1989) 1–37. 1929–1996, U.S. Department of Commerce, *National Income and Product Accounts of the United States.*

In these countries, four features of the paths of real GDP per person stand out:

- Similar 1970s growth slowdowns
- Similar business cycles before 1990
- Different business cycles in 1990s
- Different long-term growth trends

Similar 1970s Growth Slowdowns   U. S. real GDP per person grew at a rate of 2.9 percent a year from 1960 through 1973, but slowed to 1.3 percent a year between 1974 and 1988. For the same periods, Germany's growth slowed from 3.5 percent a year to 2 percent a year and Japan's growth slowed from 8.5 percent a year to 3.1 percent a year.

Similar Business Cycles Before 1990   Each of the three big economies had an expansion running from the early or mid-1960s through 1973, a recession from 1973 to 1975, an expansion through 1979, another recession in the early 1980s, and a long expansion through the rest of the 1980s.

Different Business Cycles in 1990s   The 1990s saw the United States in a long and strong business cycle expansion. But the decade brought severe recession in Japan and only moderate expansion in Germany. This divergence of business cycle experience is relatively uncommon and creates a concern that recession in Japan and the rest of Asia might spread.

Different Long-Term Growth Trends   Perhaps the most striking feature of Fig. 22.4 is the variation in the long-term growth rates of the three big economies. In 1960, real GDP per person in the United States was 50 percent greater than that in Germany and more than three times that of Japan.

During the 1960s, Japan's production streaked upward like a rocket departing Cape Canaveral. When U.S. long-term growth of real GDP per person was 2.9 percent a year, Germany's was 3.5 percent a year, and Japan's was an astonishing 8.5 percent a year. The differences in long-term growth trends survived the productivity growth slowdown of the 1970s. But Japan's economic growth disappeared in the 1990s.

FIGURE 22.4

Economic Growth in the Three Largest Economies

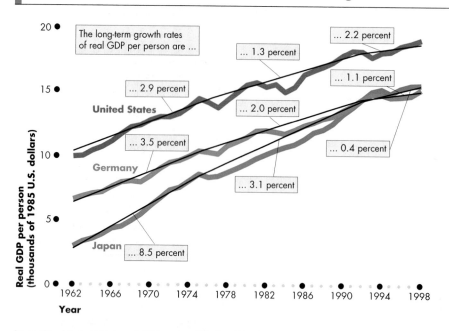

Economic growth in three large economies, the United States, Germany, and Japan, has followed a similar pattern. The growth rate in all three countries slowed during the 1970s, and each country has had similar business cycles. But Japan has grown fastest, and Germany too has grown faster than the United States.

Sources: The data for 1960 through 1992 are from "The Penn World Table," *Quarterly Journal of Economics,* May 1991, pp. 327–368. New computer disk supplement (Mark 5.6a). The data use comparable international relative prices converted to 1985 U.S. dollars. The data for 1993–1998 are from International Monetary Fund, *World Economic Outlook,* Washington, D.C., October 1998, p. 145.

Because it achieved such a high growth rate before 1990, Japan narrowed the gap between its own real GDP per person and that of the United States and it overtook Germany. But Japan's slow growth of the 1990s reversed these changes. During the 1990s, its real GDP per person fell below Germany's and fell further behind that of the United States.

Figure 22.5 compares the growth of the U.S. economy with that of several other countries and regions since 1980. Among the advanced economies (the red bars), the European Union has grown the slowest and the other advanced economies have grown fastest. Among the developing economies (the green bars) the most rapid growth has occurred in Asia, where the average growth rate has exceeded 7 percent a year. The slowest growing developing countries are in Africa and the Western Hemisphere (Central and South America). The transition economies (purple bars) have grown slowest. These are countries such as Russia and the other countries of Central Europe that are making a transition from a state managed economy to a market economy. Production has been shrinking severely in these countries.

World average growth (the blue bar) has been just over 3 percent a year. The U.S. growth rate is slightly below the world average and much below the growth rates that the developing economies of Asia have achieved.

Benefits and Costs of Economic Growth

What are the benefits and costs of economic growth? Does it matter whether the long-term growth rate slows as it did during the 1970s?

The main benefit of long-term economic growth is expanded consumption possibilities, including more health care for the poor and elderly, more cancer and AIDS research, more space research and exploration, better roads, and more and better housing. We can even have cleaner lakes, more trees, and cleaner air by devoting more resources to environmental problems.

When the long-term growth rate slows, some of these benefits are lost, and the loss can be large. For example, if long-term growth had not slowed in the United States during the 1970s, real GDP in 1996 would have been $8,650 billion, or $32,600 per person. Instead, it was $6,903 billion, or $26,000 per person. So if the long-term trend of the 1960s

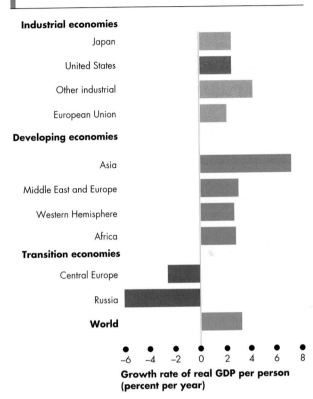

FIGURE 22.5

Growth Rates Around the World

Since 1980, the growth rate of real GDP has been lower in the United States than in some other advanced economies. The developing economies of Asia have had the most rapid growth rates and those of Central Europe and Russia have had the slowest growth.

Source: International Monetary Fund, *World Economic Outlook*, Washington, D.C., October 1998, p. 145.

had persisted, as a nation we would have had $1,750 billion more to spend. Each person (on the average) would have had $6,600 more. If the government had taken one third of this extra income, it could have provided more health care, education, day-care services, highways, space shuttle launches and space stations with no decrease in its provision of other goods and services, and its budget would be in a huge surplus. At the same time, you might have had another $4,400 a year to spend on whatever pleased you.

The main cost of economic growth is forgone consumption. To sustain a high growth rate, resources must be devoted to advancing technology and accumulating capital rather than to producing goods and services for current consumption. But this cost brings the benefit of greater consumption in the future.

Two other possible costs of faster growth are a more rapid depletion of exhaustible natural resources such as oil and natural gas and increased pollution of the air, rivers, and oceans. But neither of these two costs is inevitable. The technological advances that bring economic growth help us to economize on natural resources and to clean up the environment. For example, more efficient auto engines cut gasoline use and tailpipe emissions.

A fourth possible cost of faster growth is more frequent job changes and more frequent moves from one region of the country to another. For example, during the 1990s, the South expanded and people migrated there from the Northeast and Midwest.

The pace of economic growth is determined by the choices that people make to balance the benefits and costs of economic growth. You'll study these choices and their consequences in Chapters 27 and 28.

R E V I E W   Q U I Z

- What is economic growth and how is the long-term economic growth rate measured?
- What is the distinction between real GDP and *potential* GDP?
- What is a business cycle and what are its phases?
- What is a *recession*?
- In what phase of the business cycle was the U.S. economy during 1998?
- What happened to U.S. productivity growth during the 1970s?
- What are the similarities and differences in growth among the major economies?
- What are the benefits and the costs of long-term economic growth?

We've seen that real GDP grows and that it fluctuates over the business cycle. The business cycle brings fluctuations in jobs and unemployment. Let's now examine these macroeconomic problems.

Jobs and Unemployment

WHAT KIND OF LABOR MARKET WILL YOU ENTER when you graduate? Will there be plenty of good jobs to choose from, or will there be so much unemployment that you will be forced to take a low-paying job that doesn't use your education? The answer depends, to a large degree, on the total number of jobs available and on the unemployment rate.

Jobs

The U.S. economy is an incredible job-creating machine. In 1999, 133 million people had jobs. That number is 16 million more than in 1989 and 35 million more than in 1979. Every year, on the average, the U.S. economy creates an *additional* 1.8 million jobs.

During the past four years, the economy has created 7.8 million jobs. Most of these jobs are in the service industries. Jobs in manufacturing shrink each year as we become more efficient and as we buy more of our consumer goods from cheaper foreign sources of supply.

The pace of job creation and destruction is not constant. It fluctuates over the business cycle. More jobs are destroyed than created during a recession, so the number of jobs decreases. But more jobs are created than destroyed during an expansion, so the number of jobs increases. For example, during the recession of 1990–1991, the number of jobs fell by more than 1 million, but through the expansion that followed, 2 million jobs were created each year. During the expansion of the 1980s, jobs were created at an even faster pace of 2.5 million jobs each year.

Unemployment

Not everyone who wants a job can find one. On any one day in a normal or average year, 7 million people are unemployed, and during a recession or depression, unemployment rises above this level. For example, in the recession of 1991, almost 9 million people were looking for jobs. In the booming economic conditions of 1999, the number of job seekers fell to 6 million.

These unemployment numbers are large. The number of people unemployed during a recession is equivalent to the population of Los Angeles. And in a boom, the number is equivalent to the population of Chicago!

In order to place the number of unemployed people in perspective we use a measure called the **unemployment rate**, which is the number of unemployed people expressed as a percentage of all the people who have a job or are looking for one. (The concept of the unemployment rate along with some other labor market measures is explained more fully in Chapter 24 on pp. 519–520.)

The unemployment rate is not a perfect measure of the underutilization of labor for two main reasons. First, it excludes people who are so discouraged that they've given up the effort to find work. Second, the unemployment rate measures unemployed people rather than unemployed labor hours. So it doesn't tell us about the numbers of part-time workers who want full-time jobs. Despite these two limitations, the unemployment rate is the best available measure of underused labor resources. Let's look at some facts about the unemployment rate.

Unemployment in the United States

Figure 22.6 shows the unemployment rate in the United States from 1929 through 1998. Three features stand out. First, during the Great Depression of the 1930s, the unemployment rate climbed to an all-time high of 25 percent in 1933 and remained high throughout the 1930s. After 1934, the official rate probably overstates unemployment because it counts as unemployed the people who had make-work jobs created by governments.

Second, although in recent years we have not experienced anything as devastating as the Great Depression, we have seen some high unemployment rates during recessions. Figure 22.6 highlights three of them: the OPEC recession of the mid-1970s, the 1982 recession, and the 1990–1991 recession.

Third, unemployment never falls to zero. In the period since the Great Depression, the average unemployment rate has been close to 6 percent.

How does U.S. unemployment compare with unemployment in other countries?

FIGURE 22.6

Unemployment in the United States

Unemployment is a persistent feature of economic life, but its rate varies. At its worst—during the Great Depression—25 percent of the labor force was unemployed. Even in recent recessions, the unemployment rate climbed toward 10 percent. Between the late 1960s and 1982, there was a general tendency for the unemployment rate to increase. The unemployment rate has remained below its peak during the 1982 recession and has fallen during the 1990s.

Source: *Economic Report of the President*, 1999.

Unemployment Around the World

Figure 22.7 shows the unemployment rate in Canada, Western Europe, and Japan and compares those unemployment rates with that of the United States. Over the period shown in this figure, U.S. unemployment averaged 6.5 percent, much higher than Japanese unemployment, which averaged 2.7 percent, but lower than Canadian unemployment, which averaged 9.5 percent, and European unemployment, which averaged 9.3 percent.

U.S. unemployment fluctuates over the business cycle. It increases during a recession and decreases during an expansion. Like U.S. unemployment, Canadian and European unemployment increase during recessions and decrease during expansions. The cycles in Canadian unemployment are similar to those in U.S. unemployment, but the European cycle is out of phase with the U.S. cycle. Also, European unemployment was on a rising trend through the 1980s. In contrast with the other countries, Japanese unemployment has remained remarkably stable.

We've looked at some facts about unemployment in the United States and in other countries. Let's now look at some of the consequences of unemployment that make it the serious problem that it is.

Why Unemployment Is a Problem

Unemployment is a serious economic, social, and personal problem for two main reasons:

- Lost production and incomes
- Lost human capital

Lost Production and Incomes   The loss of a job brings an immediate loss of income and production. These losses are devastating for the people who bear them and make unemployment a frightening prospect for everyone. Unemployment insurance creates a safety net, but it does not provide the same living standard as having a job provides.

Lost Human Capital   Prolonged unemployment can permanently damage a person's job prospects. For example, a manager loses his job when his employer downsizes. Short of income, he becomes a taxi driver. After a year in this work, he discovers that he can't compete with new MBA graduates. He eventually gets hired as a manager but in a small firm and at a low wage. He has lost some of his human capital.

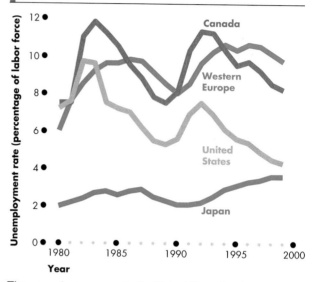

FIGURE 22.7
Unemployment in Industrial Economies

The unemployment rate in the United States has been lower than that in Canada and Western Europe but higher than that in Japan. The cycles in Canadian unemployment are similar to those in the United States. Western European unemployment has a cycle that is out of phase with the U.S. unemployment cycle. Unemployment in Japan has drifted upward in recent years.

Source: World Economic Outlook, October 1998. International Monetary Fund, Washington, D.C, p. 149.

The costs of unemployment are spread unequally, which makes unemployment a political as well as a serious economic problem.

REVIEW   QUIZ

- What is unemployment?
- What have been the main trends and cycles in the unemployment rate in the United States since 1929?
- How does unemployment in the United States compare with unemployment in Canada, Europe, and Japan?
- What are the main costs of unemployment that make it a serious problem?

Let's turn to the third major problem: inflation.

Inflation

COMPUTER PRICES FALL STEADILY. TICKET PRICES for ball games rise steadily. In microeconomics, we try to explain these individual price changes. But in macroeconomics, we are interested in prices *on the average* that we call the **price level**. And we measure the price level by using an index number called the *Consumer Price Index* (CPI). The CPI tells us how the average price of all the goods and services bought by a typical urban household changes from month to month. (The CPI and another measure of the price level are explained in Chapter 23, p. 503).

The price level might be rising, falling, or stable. If the price level is rising, we have inflation. **Inflation** is a process of rising prices. We measure the *inflation rate* as the percentage change in the price level.

In December 1998, the CPI was 163, and in December 1997, it was 160.5, so the change in the price level during 1998 was 2.5. Expressing this change as a percentage of the CPI in December 1997 gives the inflation rate during 1998 as 1.6 percent.

Inflation in the United States

Figure 22.8 shows the U.S. inflation rate from 1962 through 1996. You can see from this figure that during the early 1960s, the inflation rate was between 1 and 2 percent a year. Inflation began to increase in the late 1960s at the time of the Vietnam War. But the largest increases occurred in 1974 and 1980, years in which the actions of the Organization of Petroleum Exporting Countries (OPEC) resulted in exceptionally large increases in the price of oil. Inflation was brought under control in the early 1980s when Federal Reserve chairman Paul Volcker pushed interest rates up and people cut back on their spending. Since 1983, inflation has been relatively mild, and during the 1990s, its rate fell yet further.

The inflation rate rises and falls over the years, but it rarely becomes negative. If the inflation rate is negative, the price *level* is falling and we have **deflation**. Since the 1930s, the price level has generally risen—the inflation rate has been positive. Thus even when the inflation rate is low, as it was in 1961 and 1986, the price level is rising.

FIGURE 22.8
Inflation in the United States

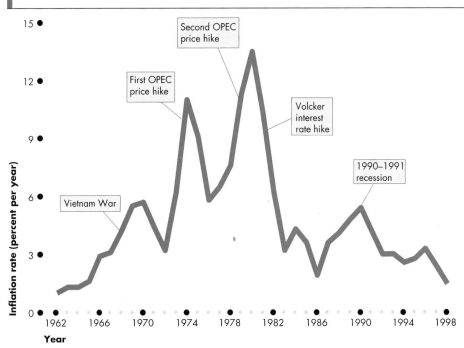

Inflation is a persistent feature of economic life in the United States. The inflation rate was low in the first half of the 1960s, but it increased during the Vietnam War years. It increased further with the OPEC oil price hikes but eventually declined in the early 1980s because of policy actions taken by the Federal Reserve. Since 1983, inflation has been mild, and during the 1990s, it has fallen further.

Source: *Economic Report of the President*, 1999.

Inflation Around the World

Figure 22.9 shows inflation around the world since 1978. It also shows the U.S. inflation rate in a broader perspective. Part (a) shows that the U.S. inflation rate has been similar to that of other industrial countries. You can also see that all the industrial countries shared the burst of double-digit inflation during the 1970s and the fall in inflation during the 1980s. Part (b) shows that the average inflation rate of industrial countries has been very low compared with that of the developing counties. Among the developing countries, the most extreme inflation in recent times has occurred in the former Yugoslavia, where its rate has exceeded 6,000 percent per year.

Is Inflation a Problem?

If inflation were predictable, it would not be much of a problem. But inflation is not predictable. Unpredictable inflation makes the economy behave a bit like a casino in which some people gain and some lose and no one can predict where the gains and losses will fall. Gains and losses occur because of unpredictable changes in the value of money. Money is used as a measuring rod of value in the transactions that we undertake. Borrowers and lenders, workers and employers, all make contracts in terms of money. If the value of money varies unpredictably over time, then the amounts *really* paid and received—the quantity of goods that the money will buy—also fluctuate unpredictably. Measuring value with a measuring rod whose units vary is a bit like trying to measure a piece of cloth with an elastic ruler. The size of the cloth depends on how much the ruler is stretched.

In a period of rapid, unpredictable inflation, resources get diverted from productive activities to forecasting inflation. It becomes more profitable to forecast the inflation rate correctly than to invent a new product. Doctors, lawyers, accountants, farmers—just about everyone—can make themselves better off, not by specializing in the profession for which they have been trained but by spending more of their time dabbling as amateur economists and inflation forecasters and managing their investment portfolios.

From a social perspective, this diversion of talent resulting from inflation is like throwing scarce resources onto the garbage heap. This waste of resources is a cost of inflation.

FIGURE 22.9

Inflation Around the World

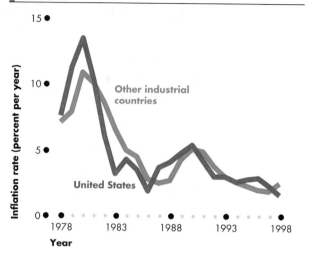

(a) The United States and other industrial countries

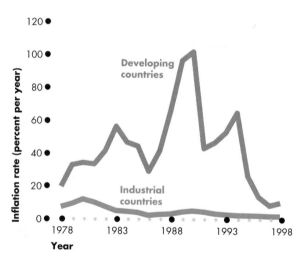

(b) Industrial countries and developing countries

Inflation in the United States is similar to that in the other industrial countries. Compared with the developing countries, inflation in the industrial countries is low.

Sources: International Monetary Fund, *International Financial Statistics Yearbook 1997,* Washington, D.C., 1997 and *World Economic Outlook,* International Monetary Fund, Washington, D.C, October 1998, p. 156.

The most serious type of inflation is called *hyperinflation*—an inflation rate that exceeds 50 percent a month. At the height of a hyperinflation, workers are often paid twice a day because money loses its value so quickly. As soon as workers are paid, they rush out to spend their wages before they lose too much value.

Hyperinflation is rare but there have been some spectacular examples of it. Several European countries experienced hyperinflation during the 1920s after World War I and again during the 1940s after World War II. But hyperinflation is more than just a historical curiosity. It occurs in today's world. In 1994, the African nation of Zaire had a hyperinflation that peaked at a *monthly* inflation rate of 76 percent. Also in 1994, Brazil almost reached the hyperinflation stratosphere with a monthly inflation rate of 40 percent. A cup of coffee that cost 15 cruzeiros in 1980 cost 22 *billion* cruzeiros in 1994.

Inflation imposes costs, but getting rid of inflation is also costly. Policies that lower the inflation rate increase the unemployment rate. Most economists think the increase in the unemployment rate that accompanies a fall in the inflation rate is temporary. But some economists say that higher unemployment is a permanent cost of low inflation. The cost of lowering inflation must be evaluated when an anti-inflation policy is pursued. You will learn more about inflation and the costs of curing it in Chapter 33.

R E V I E W   Q U I Z

- What is inflation and how does it influence the value of money?
- How is inflation measured?
- What has been the U.S. inflation record since 1962?
- How does inflation in the United States compare with inflation in other industrial countries and in developing countries?
- What are some of the costs of inflation that make it a serious economic problem?

Now that we've studied economic growth and fluctuations, unemployment, and inflation, let's turn to the fourth macroeconomic problem: deficits. What happens when a government spends more than it collects in taxes? And what happens when a nation buys more from other countries that it sells to them? Do governments and nations face the problem that you and I would face if we spent more than we earned? Do they run out of funds? Let's look at these questions.

Surpluses and Deficits

IN 1998, FOR THE FIRST TIME IN ALMOST 30 years, the U.S. federal government had a budget surplus. At the same time, the United States had a large international deficit. What are the government budget surplus and the nation's international deficit?

Government Budget Surplus and Deficit

If a government collects more in taxes than it spends, it has a surplus—a **government budget surplus**. If a government spends more than it collects in taxes, it has a deficit—a **government budget deficit**. The U.S. federal government had a surplus in 1998.

Figure 22.10(a) shows the federal government budget surplus and deficit measured as a percentage of GDP since 1962. (The concept of GDP, which is explained more fully in Chapter 23, pp. 494–497, equals total income in the economy.)

We measure the budget surplus or deficit as a percentage of GDP so that we can compare the surplus or deficit in one year with that in another year. You can think of this measure as the number of cents of surplus or deficit per dollar of income earned by an average person.

The government had a budget surplus in 1969 and again in 1998. In every year from 1970 through 1997, the government had a deficit that fluctuated and swelled during recessions. From 1980 through 1995, the deficit was never less than 2 percent of GDP.

Since 1992, the government deficit has been shrinking and a surplus emerged in 1998. In 1998, the government budget surplus was almost 1 percent of GDP and in 1999 and beyond, it is projected to become larger.

International Deficit

When we import goods and services from the rest of the world, we make payments to foreigners. When we export goods and services to the rest of the world, we receive payments from foreigners. If our imports exceed our exports, we have an international deficit.

Figure 22.10(b) shows the history of the international deficit of the United States since 1962. The figure shows the balance on the **current account**, which includes our exports minus our imports but

FIGURE 22.10

Government Budget and International Deficits

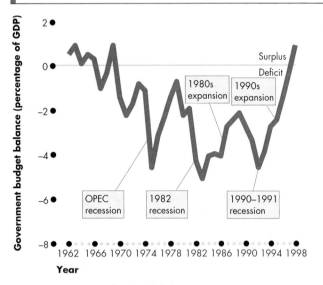

(a) U.S. government budget deficit

(b) U.S. international deficit

In part (a), the federal government deficit increased as a percentage of GDP before 1982 and shrank after 1982. A surplus emerged in 1998. In part (b), the U.S. current account shows the balance of our exports minus our imports. Until the early 1980s, our current account was generally in surplus. During the expansion of the 1980s, a large international deficit emerged. The deficit almost disappeared during the 1990–1991 recession, but it reappeared during the 1990s expansion.

Sources: The government budget balance is the U.S. federal government's budget deficit, *Economic Report of the President,* 1999. The international balance is the current account balance, U.S. Department of Commerce, *Survey of Current Business,* March 1999.

also takes interest payments paid to and received from the rest of the world into account. To compare one year with another, the figure shows the current account as a percentage of GDP. The U.S. current account deficit has fluctuated, and since 1980, it has ranged from close to zero to almost 4 percent of GDP. Our imports have usually exceeded our exports.

Do Deficits Matter?

Why do deficits cause anxiety? What happens when a government cannot cover its spending with taxes or when a country buys more from other countries than it sells to them?

If you spend more than you earn, you have a deficit. And to cover your deficit, you have to borrow. But when you borrow, you must pay interest on your debt. Just like you, if a government or a nation has a deficit, it must borrow. And like you, the government and the nation must pay interest on their debts.

Whether borrowing and paying out huge amounts of interest are a good idea depends on what the borrowed funds are used for. If you borrow to finance a vacation, you must eventually tighten your belt, cut spending, and repay your debt as well as pay interest on the debt. But if you borrow to invest in a business that earns a large profit, you might be able to repay your debt and pay the interest on it while continuing to increase your spending. It is the same with a government and a nation. A government or a nation that borrows to increase its consumption might be heading for trouble later. But a government or a nation that borrows to buy assets that earn a profit might be making a sound investment.

You will learn more about government budget deficits in Chapter 30 and about the international current account deficit in Chapter 37.

- What determines a government's budget deficit?
- How has the U.S. federal government deficit evolved since the 1960s?
- What is a country's international deficit?
- How has the U.S. international deficit changed since the 1960s?

Macroeconomic Policy Challenges and Tools

FROM THE TIME OF ADAM SMITH'S *THE WEALTH of Nations* in 1776 until the publication of Keynes' *General Theory of Employment, Interest, and Money* in 1936, it was widely believed that the only economic role for government was to enforce property rights. The economy behaves best, it was believed, if the government leaves people free to pursue their own best interests. The macroeconomics of Keynes challenged this view. Keynes' central point was that the economy will not fix itself and that government actions are needed to achieve and maintain full employment. The U.S. government declared full employment as a policy goal soon after World War II ended.

Policy Challenges and Tools

Today, the five widely agreed challenges for macroeconomic policy are to:

1. Boost economic growth
2. Stabilize the business cycle
3. Reduce unemployment
4. Keep inflation low
5. Reduce the government and international deficits

But how can we do all these things? What are the tools available to pursue the macroeconomic policy challenges? Macroeconomic policy tools are divided into two broad categories:

- Fiscal policy
- Monetary policy

Fiscal Policy Making changes in taxes and government spending is called **fiscal policy**. This range of policy actions is under the control of the federal government. Fiscal policy can be used to try to boost long-term growth by creating incentives that encourage saving, investment, and technological change. Fiscal policy can also be used to try to smooth out the business cycle. When the economy is in a recession, the government might cut taxes or increase its spending. Conversely, when the economy is in a rapid expansion, the government might increase taxes or cut its spending in an attempt to slow real GDP growth and prevent inflation from increasing. Fiscal policy is discussed in Chapter 30.

Monetary Policy Changing interest rates and the amount of money in the economy is called **monetary policy**. These actions are under the control of the Federal Reserve (the Fed). The principal aim of monetary policy is to keep inflation in check. To achieve this objective, the Fed prevents the quantity of money from expanding too rapidly. Monetary policy can also be used to smooth the business cycle. When the economy is in recession, the Fed might lower interest rates and inject money into the economy. And when the economy is in a rapid expansion, the Fed might increase interest rates in an attempt to slow real GDP growth and prevent the inflation from increasing. Monetary policy is discussed in Chapters 31 and 32.

- What are the main challenges of macroeconomic policy?
- What are the main tools of macroeconomic policy?
- Can you distinguish between fiscal policy and monetary policy?

◆ In your study of macroeconomics, you will learn what is currently known about the causes of economic growth, business cycles, unemployment, inflation, and government and international deficits and about the policy choices and challenges that the government and the Fed face. *Reading Between the Lines* on pp. 488–489 looks at the state of the U.S. macroeconomy in 1998 and examines the long expansion, falling unemployment, and low inflation of the 1990s.

Economy Watching

C N N f n , MARCH 31, 1999

GDP grew 6% in 4Q 1998

NEW YORK (CNNfn)—In case there was need for another reminder, 1998 ended on a high note for the U.S. economy, as the government confirmed Wednesday that its broadest measure of goods and services rose to record levels during the fourth quarter last year.

In its second and final revision, the Commerce Department said Wednesday that fourth-quarter GDP rose 6 percent. That's down incrementally from February's 6.1 percent revision and up from the 5.6 percent expansion originally reported.

Wednesday's number, the highest since the second quarter of 1996, confirmed the buoyancy of a domestic economy that grew last year with little inflation and despite overseas slowdowns.

"We know the economy's been strong," said Robert Brusca, chief economist at Nikko Securities. For the full year 1998, GDP grew 3.9 percent, matching 1997's growth for the strongest annual performance since 1984, when the economy expanded 7 percent.

The GDP price deflator, a closely watched inflation gauge, was revised back up to 0.8 percent from 0.7 percent. It was the smallest quarterly gain in prices in nearly four decades, since a 0.6 percent rise in the third quarter of 1959.

...

Despite vigorous economic growth, corporate profits after taxes contracted for a second straight quarter by 1 percent in last year's fourth quarter. Profits for all of 1998 fell 2.2 percent to $477.7 billion—the first year company profits declined since 1989, when they fell 4.8 percent.

Looking ahead, analysts generally forecast 1999's economy growing at a slower pace of about 3.5 percent. Brusca said 1999 GDP will hinge upon the stock market's performance and the prospects for rising inflation, which thus far remains tame.

Essence of the Story

■ The Commerce Department originally, in January 1999, estimated that GDP had grown by 5.6 percent (annual rate) in the fourth quarter of 1998. In February, it revised the estimate upward to 6.1 percent, and in March, it provided the final (and last) revision and estimated a growth rate of 6 percent.

■ This growth rate is the highest since the second quarter of 1996.

■ Inflation during the fourth quarter of 1998 was estimated to be 0.8 percent a year, its lowest level since 1959.

■ Company profits after taxes decreased by 1 percent during the fourth quarter of 1998 and decreased by 2.2 percent for the whole of 1998, the first year of falling company profits since 1989.

Economic Analysis

■ Figure 1 shows the expansions in real GDP since 1921. The longest expansion lasted for almost 10 years during the 1960s. The 1990s expansion is now the second longest. If it persists through March 2000, it will exceed the length of the 1960s expansion.

■ Figure 2 shows the 1990s expansion. Real GDP started out below potential GDP in the recession of 1990–1991. Real GDP expanded, and by 1996, it was close to potential GDP. Both real GDP and potential GDP have grown at a similar rate since 1996.

■ Figure 3 shows the unemployment rate during the 1990s expansion. Unemployment peaked in 1992, fell quickly through 1994, and continued to fall through 1998.

■ Figure 4 shows the inflation rate during the 1990s expansion. Beginning at almost 5 percent a year, the inflation rate has fallen to around 1 percent a year, its lowest level since the 1960s.

■ Expansions that last as long as the 1990s expansion are rare, and the current expansion will at some time come to an end. But we cannot predict when.

■ The news article says that company profits decreased in 1998 and that the last time they decreased was 1989. The last recession began in June 1990.

■ The next recession will begin when some *currently unforeseeable* event brings a fall in spending and a surge in layoffs. In the past, such events have occurred on the average every four years but with a range that runs from one year to ten years.

Figure 1 Expansion since 1921

Figure 2 Real GDP

Figure 3 Unemployment

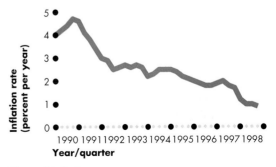

Figure 4 Inflation

SUMMARY

KEY POINTS

Origins and Issues of Macroeconomics (p. 474)

■ Macroeconomics studies economic growth and fluctuations, unemployment, inflation, and surpluses and deficits.

Economic Growth (pp. 475–480)

■ Economic growth is the expansion of potential GDP. Real GDP fluctuates around potential GDP in a business cycle.

■ Countries have similar productivity growth slowdowns and business cycles but different long-term trends in potential GDP.

■ The main benefit of long-term economic growth is higher future consumption, and the main cost is lower current consumption.

Jobs and Unemployment (pp. 480–482)

■ The U.S. economy creates 1.8 million jobs a year, but unemployment persists.

■ Unemployment increases during a recession and decreases during an expansion. The U.S. unemployment rate is lower than that in Canada and Western Europe but higher than that in Japan.

■ Unemployment can permanently damage a person's job prospects.

Inflation (pp. 483–485)

■ Inflation, a process of rising prices, is measured by the percentage change in the CPI.

■ Inflation is a problem because it lowers the value of money and makes money less useful as a measuring rod of value.

Surpluses and Deficits (pp. 485–487)

■ When its tax receipts exceed spending, a government has a budget surplus. When its spending exceeds tax receipts, a government has a budget deficit.

■ When imports exceed exports, a nation has an international deficit.

■ Deficits are financed by borrowing.

Macroeconomic Policy Challenges and Tools (p. 487)

■ The macroeconomic policy challenge is to use fiscal policy and monetary policy to boost long-term growth, stabilize the business cycle, lower unemployment, tame inflation, and prevent large deficits.

KEY FIGURES

KEY TERMS

P R O B L E M S

💻 *1. Use Variable Graphing in Chapter 22 of *Economics in Action* to answer the following questions. In which country in 1992 was
    a. The growth rate of real GDP highest: the United States, France, Japan, or Canada?
    b. The unemployment rate highest: the United States, Japan, the United Kingdom, or Canada?
    c. The inflation rate lowest: the United States, Germany, the United Kingdom, or Canada?
    d. The government budget deficit (as a percentage of GDP) largest: the United States, Japan, the United Kingdom, or Canada?

💻 2. Use Variable Graphing in Chapter 22 in the *Economics in Action* to answer the following questions. In which country in 1996 was
    a. The growth rate of real GDP highest: The United States, France, Japan, or Canada?
    b. The unemployment rate lowest: the United States, Japan, the United Kingdom, or Canada?
    c. The inflation rate lowest: the United States, Finland, Ireland, or Canada?
    d. The government budget deficit (as a percentage of GDP) smallest: the United States, Australia, Ireland, or Canada?
    e. Is it possible to say in which country consumption possibilities are growing faster? Why or why not?

*3. The figure shows real GDP growth rate in India and Pakistan from 1989 to 1996.

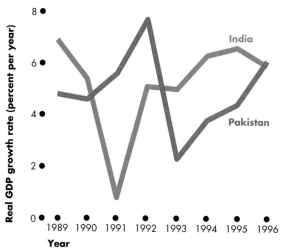

In which years did economic growth in
    a. India increase? And in which year was growth fastest?
    b. Pakistan decrease? And in which year was growth slowest?
    c. Compare the paths of economic growth in India and Pakistan during this period.

4. The figure shows real GDP per person in Australia and Japan from 1989 to 1996.

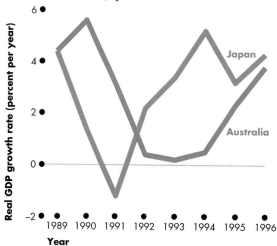

In which years did economic growth in
    a. Australia increase? And in which year was growth fastest?
    b. Japan decrease? And in which year was growth slowest?
    c. Compare the paths of economic growth in Australia and Japan during this period.

*5. The figure shows real GDP in Germany from the first quarter of 1991 to the second quarter of 1994.

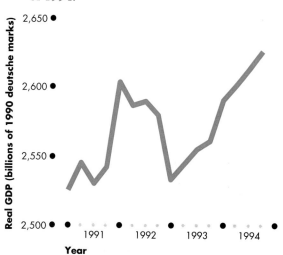

a. How many recessions did Germany experience during this period?

b. In which quarters, if any, did Germany experience a business cycle peak?

c. In which quarters, if any, did Germany experience a business cycle trough?

d. In which quarters, if any, did Germany experience an expansion?

6. Use the links on the Parkin Web site to obtain data on quarterly real GDP for the United States since the fourth quarter of 1998 and update Fig. 22.2. Use what you have discovered to answer the following questions:

a. Is the U.S. economy now in a recession or an expansion?

b. If the economy is still in an expansion, how long has the expansion lasted? If the economy is now in recession, how long the economy been in recession?

c. During the last year, has the growth rate sped up or slowed?

*7. Use Variable Graphing in Chapter 22 in the *Economics in Action* to answer the following questions. Which country, in 1988, had

a. The largest budget deficit: the United States, Japan, the United Kingdom, or Canada?

b. A current account surplus: the United States, Japan, Germany, or Canada?

8. Use Variable Graphing in Chapter 22 in the *Economics in Action* to answer the following questions. Which country, in 1988, had

a. The largest budget surplus: the United States, Japan, the United Kingdom, or Canada?

b. The largest current account deficit: the United States, Japan, Germany, or Canada?

*9. Use Variable Graphing in Chapter 22 in the *Economics in Action* to make a scatter diagram of inflation and unemployment in the United States.

a. Describe the relationship.

b. Do you think that low unemployment brings an increase in the inflation rate?

10. Use Variable Graphing in Chapter 22 in the *Economics in Action* to make a scatter diagram of the government budget deficit as a percentage of GDP and the unemployment rate.

a. Describe the relationship.

b. Do you think that low unemployment brings a decrease in the budget deficit?

CRITICAL THINKING

1. Study *Reading Between the Lines* on pp. 488–489 and then answer the following questions:

a. When did the most recent expansion begin?

b. How long has the most recent expansion lasted? Is it an unusually long expansion? Compare the length of the most recent expansion with those of other expansions since World War II and before World War II?

c. Can you think of convincing reasons why the 1990s expansion has been a long one?

2. Use the links on the Parkin Web site to obtain the latest data on real GDP, unemployment, and inflation.

a. Update the figures on pages 476, 481, and 483.

b. What dangers does the U.S. economy face today?

c. What actions, if any, do you think might be needed to keep the economy strong?

3. Use the links on the Parkin Web site to obtain data on unemployment in your home state.

a. Compare unemployment in your home state with that in the United States as a whole.

b. Why do you think your state might have a higher or a lower unemployment rate than the U.S. average?

4. Use the links on the Parkin Web site to obtain data on the Consumer Price Index for the large city that you live closest to.

a. Compare the inflation rate in your chosen city with that in the United States as a whole.

b. Compare the inflation rate in your chosen city with that in other large cities.

5. Use the links on the Parkin Web site to obtain data on each of the following variables for the United States for the most recent period. Describe how the variables have changed over the last year.

a. The unemployment rate

b. The inflation rate

c. The government budget deficit

d. The international deficit?

Chapter 23

Measuring GDP, Economic Growth, and Inflation

Economic Barometers

When Motorola contemplates spending $1 billion developing a cellular telephone system in China, it pays close attention to forecasts of China's real GDP. When AT&T plans to expand its fiber-optic network, it uses forecasts of long-term growth in the U.S. economy. The outcomes of many business decisions turn on the quality of forecasts of economic conditions. ◆ A key input for making economic forecasts is Gross Domestic Product, or GDP, which is like a barometer of a nation's economy. Economists pore over the numbers, looking at past trends and seeking patterns that might give a glimpse of the future. How do economic statisticians add up all the production of the country to arrive at the number called GDP? What exactly *is* GDP? ◆ Most of the time, our economy grows, but sometimes it shrinks. To reveal the rate of growth (or shrinkage), we must remove the effects of inflation on GDP and assess how *real* GDP is changing. How do we remove the inflation component of GDP to reveal real GDP? ◆ Some countries are rich while others are poor and only now are in the process of developing their industries and reaching their productive potential. How do we compare incomes in one country with incomes in another? How can we make international comparisons of GDP? ◆ From economists to homemakers, all types of people pay close attention to another economic barometer, the Consumer Price Index, or CPI. The Department of Labor publishes new figures each month, and analysts in newspapers and on TV quickly leap to conclusions about the causes of recent changes in prices and the prospects for future changes. How does the government determine the CPI? How well does it measure a consumer's living costs and the inflation rate?

◆ In this chapter, you will find out how economic statisticians measure GDP, the price level, and real GDP. You will also learn how they measure the economic growth rate and the inflation rate and about the limitations of these measures.

After studying this chapter, you will be able to:

■ Explain why aggregate income, expenditure, and product are equal

■ Explain how we measure **GDP**

■ Explain how we measure the price level using the Consumer Price Index (CPI)

■ Explain how we measure *real* **GDP** and the **GDP deflator**

■ Explain how we use real **GDP** to measure economic growth and describe the limitations of our measure

■ Explain how we use the **CPI** and the **GDP deflator** to measure inflation and describe the limitations of our measures

Gross Domestic Product

WHAT EXACTLY IS GDP, HOW IS IT CALCULATED, what does it mean, and why do we care about it? You are going to discover the answers to these questions in this chapter. First, what *is* GDP? **GDP**, or **gross domestic product**, is the value of the *aggregate* production of goods and services in a country during a given time period—usually a year. The GDP of the United States, which measures the value of aggregate production in the United States during a year, was $8,511 billion in 1998.

How is GDP calculated? In a nutshell, GDP is calculated by valuing everything that is produced and adding all the values together. But precisely *what* is valued and *how* it is valued? To answer these questions, you need to understand two fundamental principles of economic accounting:

- The distinction between flows and stocks
- The equality of income, expenditure, and the value of production

Flows and Stocks

To keep track of our personal economic transactions and the economic transactions of a country, we distinguish between flows and stocks. A **flow** is a quantity per unit of time. The water that is running from an open faucet into a bathtub is a flow. So are the number of CDs that you buy during a month and the amount of income that you earn during a month. GDP is a flow. It is the value of the goods and services produced in a country *during a given time period*.

A **stock** is a quantity that exists at a point in time. The water in a bathtub is a stock. So are the number of CDs that you own and the amount of money in your savings account.

Capital and Investment The key macroeconomic stock is capital. **Capital** is the plant, equipment, buildings, and inventories of raw materials and semifinished goods that are used to produce other goods and services. The amount of capital in the economy exerts a big influence on GDP. Two flows change the stock of capital: investment and depreciation. Investment is the purchase of new capital. It increases the stock of capital. (Investment includes additions to inventories.) **Depreciation** is the decrease in the stock of capital that results from wear and tear and obsolescence. Another

name for depreciation is *capital consumption*. The total amount spent on adding to the stock of capital and on replacing depreciated capital is called **gross investment**. The amount spent on adding to the stock of capital is called **net investment**. Net investment equals gross investment minus depreciation.

Figure 23.1 illustrates these concepts. On January 1, 2000, Tom's Tapes, Inc. had 3 machines. This quantity was its initial capital. During 2000, Tom's scrapped an older machine. This quantity is its depreciation. After depreciation, Tom's stock of capital was down to 2 machines. But also during 2000, Tom's bought 2 new machines. This amount is its gross investment. By December 31, 2000, Tom's Tapes had 4 machines, so its capital had increased by 1 machine. This amount is Tom's net investment. Tom's net investment equals its gross investment (the

---

FIGURE 23.1

Capital and Investment

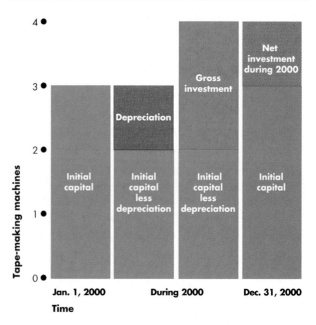

Tom's Tapes has a capital stock at the end of 2000 that equals its capital stock at the beginning of the year plus its net investment. Net investment is equal to gross investment less depreciation. Tom's gross investment is the 2 new machines bought during the year, and its depreciation is the 1 machine that Tom's scrapped during the year.

purchase of 2 new machines) minus its depreciation (1 machine scrapped).

The example of Tom's Tapes factory can be applied to the economy as a whole. The nation's capital stock decreases because capital depreciates and increases because of gross investment. The change in the nation's capital stock from one year to the next equals its net investment.

Wealth and Saving Another macroeconomic stock is **wealth**, which is the value of all the things that people own. What people *own*, a stock, is related to what they *earn*, a flow. People *earn* an *income*, which is the amount they receive during a given time period from supplying the services of resources. Income that is left after paying taxes is either consumed or saved. **Consumption expenditure** is the amount spent on consumption goods and services. **Saving** is the amount of income remaining after meeting consumption expenditures. Saving adds to wealth, and dissaving (negative saving) decreases wealth.

For example, suppose that at the end of the school year, you have $250 in a savings account and some textbooks that are worth $300. That's all you own. Your wealth is $550. Suppose that you take a summer job and earn an income of $5,000. You are extremely careful and spend only $1,000 through the summer on consumption goods and services. At the end of the summer, when school starts again, you have $4,250 in your savings account. Your wealth is now $4,550. Your wealth has increased by $4,000, which equals your saving of $4,000. Your saving of $4,000 equals your income of $5,000 minus your consumption expenditure of $1,000.

National wealth and national saving work just like this personal example. The wealth of a nation at the start of a year equals its wealth at the start of the previous year plus its saving during the year. Its saving equals its income minus its consumption expenditure.

We'll make the idea of the nation's income and consumption expenditure more precise a bit later in this chapter. Before doing so, let's see what the stocks and flows that we've just learned about imply for the recurring theme of macroeconomics: short-term fluctuations in actual real GDP and long-term growth in potential GDP.

The Short Term Meets the Long Term You saw in Chapter 22 that potential GDP grows incessantly, year after year. You also saw that actual real GDP grows and fluctuates around potential GDP. The

stocks and flows that you've just studied influence *both* the long-term growth in potential GDP and the short-term fluctuations in actual GDP. One of the reasons why potential GDP grows is that the capital stock grows. One of the reasons that real GDP fluctuates is that investment fluctuates. So capital and investment as well as wealth and saving are part of the key to understanding the growth of potential GDP and the fluctuations of real GDP.

The flows of investment and saving together with the flows of income and consumption expenditure interact in a circular flow of income and expenditure. In this circular flow, income equals expenditure, which also equals the value of production. This amazing equality is the foundation on which a nation's economic accounts are built and from which its GDP is measured.

Income, Expenditure, and the Value of Production

To see that for the economy as a whole, income equals expenditure and also equals the value of production, we study the circular flow of income and expenditure.

Figure 23.2 illustrates the circular flow of income and expenditure. In the figure, the economy consists of four sectors: households, firms, governments, and the rest of the world (the purple diamonds). It has three types of markets: resource markets, goods (and services) markets, and financial markets. Focus first on households and firms.

Households and Firms Households sell and firms buy the services of labor, capital, land, and entrepreneurship in resource markets. For these resource services, firms pay income to households: wages for labor services, interest for the use of capital, rent for the use of land, and profits for entrepreneurship. Firms' retained earnings—profits that are not distributed to households—are also part of the household sector's income. You can think of retained earnings as being income that households save and lend back to firms. Figure 23.2 shows the *aggregate income* received by all households in payment for the services of resources by the blue dots labeled *Y*.

Firms sell and households buy consumer goods and services—such as popcorn and soda, movies and chocolate bars, microwave ovens and inline skates, dental and dry cleaning services—in the markets for goods and services. The total payment that households make for these goods and services is *consumption*

FIGURE 23.2

The Circular Flow of Income and Expenditure

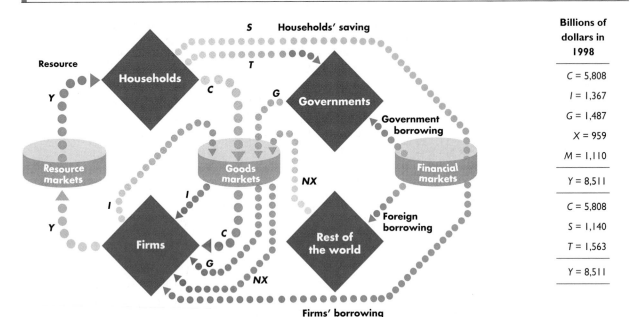

Billions of dollars in 1998
C = 5,808
I = 1,367
G = 1,487
X = 959
M = 1,110
Y = 8,511
C = 5,808
S = 1,140
T = 1,563
Y = 8,511

In the circular flow of income and expenditure, households receive incomes (Y) from firms (blue flow) and make consumption expenditures (C); firms make investment expenditures (I); governments purchase goods and services (G); the rest of the world purchases net exports (NX)—(red flows). Aggregate income (blue flow) equals aggregate expenditure (red flows). Households' saving (S) and net taxes (T) leak from the circular flow. Firms borrow to finance their investment expenditures, and governments and the rest of the world borrow to finance their deficits or lend their surpluses (green flows). The values shown are for 1998.

Source: U.S. Department of Commerce, *Survey of Current Business* (April 1999).

expenditure. Figure 23.2 shows consumption expenditure by the red dots labeled *C*.

Firms buy and sell new capital equipment in the goods market. For example, IBM sells 1,000 PCs to General Motors, or Boeing sells an airplane to United Airlines. Some of what firms produce might not be sold at all and is added to inventory. For example, if GM produces 1,000 cars and sells 950 of them, the other 50 cars remain unsold and GM's inventory of cars increases by 50. When a firm adds unsold output to inventory, we can think of the firm as buying goods from itself. The purchase of new plant, equipment, and buildings and the additions to inventories are **investment**.

Figure 23.2 shows investment by the red dots labeled *I*. Notice that in the figure, investment flows from firms through the goods markets and back to firms. Some firms produce capital goods, and other

firms buy them (and firms "buy" inventories from themselves).

Firms finance their investment by borrowing from households in financial markets. Households' saving flows into financial markets, and firms' borrowing flows out of financial markets. Figure 23.2 shows these flows by the green dots labeled "Households' saving" or *S* and "Firms' borrowing." These flows are neither income nor expenditure. Income is a payment for the services of a resource, and expenditure is a payment for goods or services.

Governments Governments buy goods and services, called **government purchases**, from firms. In Fig. 23.2 these government purchases are shown as the red flow *G*. Governments use taxes to pay for their purchases. Figure 23.2 shows taxes as net taxes by the green dots labeled *T*. **Net taxes** are equal to

TABLE 23.1

GDP: The Expenditure Approach

Item	Symbol	Amount in 1998 (billions of dollars)	Percentage of GDP
Personal consumption expenditures	C	5,808	68.2
Gross private domestic investment	I	1,367	16.1
Government purchases of goods and services	G	1,487	17.5
Net exports of goods and services	NX	−151	−1.8
Gross domestic product	Y	8,511	100.0

The expenditure approach measures GDP by adding together personal consumption expenditures (*C*), gross private domestic investment (*I*), government purchases of goods and services (*G*), and net exports (*NX*). In 1998, GDP measured by the expenditure approach was $8,509 billion. Two thirds of aggregate expenditure is on personal consumption goods and services.

Source: U.S. Department of Commerce, *Survey of Current Business* (April 1999).

Gross private domestic investment is expenditure on capital equipment and buildings by firms and expenditure on new homes by households. It also includes the change in business inventories.

Government purchases of goods and services are the purchases of goods and services by all levels of government. This item includes expenditures on national defense and garbage collection. But it does *not* include *transfer payments*. These payments, such as medical aid and social security benefits, are not purchases of goods and services. They are transfers of funds from government to households.

Net exports of goods and services are the value of exports minus the value of imports. This item includes computers that IBM sells to Volkswagen, the German car producer (a U.S. export), and Japanese VCRs that Circuit City buys from Japan (a U.S. import).

Table 23.1 shows the relative importance of the four items of aggregate expenditure. The largest component is personal consumption expenditures, and the smallest is net exports (negative in 1998).

Expenditures Not in GDP Aggregate expenditure, which equals GDP, does not include all the things that people and businesses buy. To distinguish total expenditure on GDP from other items of spending, we call the expenditure included in GDP *final expenditure*. Spending that is not part of final expenditure and not part of GDP includes the purchase of:

- Intermediate goods and services
- Used goods
- Financial assets

Intermediate goods and services are the goods and services that firms buy from each other and use as inputs in the goods and services that they eventually sell to final users. When Dell Corp. buys computer chips from Intel Corp., it buys an intermediate good. A Dell computer is a final good, but an Intel chip is an intermediate good. To count the expenditure on intermediate goods and services as well as the expenditure on the final good involves counting the same thing twice—called *double counting*.

A good can sometimes be an intermediate good and sometimes a final good. For example, the ice cream that you buy on a hot summer day is a final good, but the ice cream that a diner buys and uses to make sundaes is an intermediate good. Whether a good is intermediate or final depends on what it is used for, not on what it is.

Expenditure on *used goods* is not part of GDP because these goods were counted as part of GDP in the period in which they were produced and in which they were new goods. For example, a 1990 automobile was part of GDP in 1990. If the car is traded on the used car market in 1998, the amount paid for the car is not part of GDP in 1998.

Firms often sell *financial assets* such as bonds and stocks to finance purchases of newly produced capital goods. The expenditure on newly produced capital goods is part of GDP, but the expenditure on financial securities is not. GDP includes the amount spent on new capital, not the amount spent on pieces of paper.

Let's look at the second way of measuring GDP, the income approach.

The Income Approach

The *income approach* measures GDP by summing the incomes that firms pay households for the resources they hire: wages for labor, interest for capital, rent for land, and profits for entrepreneurship. Let's see how the income approach works.

The *National Income and Product Accounts* divide incomes into five categories:

1. Compensation of employees
2. Net interest
3. Rental income
4. Corporate profits
5. Proprietors' income

Compensation of employees is the payment for labor services. It includes net wages and salaries (called "take-home pay") that workers receive plus taxes withheld on earnings plus fringe benefits such as social security and pension fund contributions.

Net interest is the interest households receive on loans they make minus the interest households pay on their own borrowing.

Rental income is the payment for the use of land and other rented inputs. It includes payments for rented housing and imputed rent for owner-occupied housing. (Imputed rent is an estimate of what home-owners would pay to rent the housing they own and use themselves. By including this item in the national income accounts, we measure the total value of housing services, whether they are owned or rented.)

Corporate profits are the profits of corporations. Some of these profits are paid to households in the form of dividends, and some are retained by corporations as undistributed profits. They are all income.

Proprietors' income is a mixture of the previous four items. It is difficult to split the income earned by the owner-operator of a business into compensation for labor, payment for the use of capital, and profit, so the national income accounts lump all these items into a single category.

Table 23.2 shows these five incomes and their relative magnitudes. Compensation of employees is the largest income category.

The sum of these five categories of incomes is called *net domestic income at factor cost.* The term *factor cost* is used because *factor of production* is another name for a productive resource. But *net domestic income at factor cost* is not GDP. We must make two further adjustments to get to GDP, one from *factor cost* to *market prices* and another from *net* product to *gross* product.

Factor Cost to Market Prices When we add up all the final expenditures on goods and services, we arrive at a total called domestic product at *market prices.* These expenditures are valued at the market prices that people pay for the various goods and services. Another way of valuing goods and services is at factor cost. *Factor cost* is the value of a good or service measured by adding together the costs of all the resources used to produce it. If the only economic transaction were between households and firms—if there were no government taxes or subsidies—the market price and factor cost values would be the same. But the presence of indirect taxes and subsidies makes these two methods of valuation differ.

An *indirect tax* is a tax paid by consumers when they buy goods and services. (In contrast, a *direct tax* is a tax on income.) State sales taxes and taxes on alcohol, gasoline, and tobacco products are indirect

---

TABLE 23.2

GDP: The Income Approach

Item	Amount in 1998 (billions of dollars)	Percentage of GDP
Compensation of employees	4,981	58.5
Net interest	449	5.3
Rental income	163	1.9
Corporate profits	825	9.7
Proprietors' income	577	6.8
Indirect taxes *less* Subsidies	608	7.1
Capital consumption (depreciation)	908	10.7
Gross domestic product	8,511	100.0

The sum of all incomes plus indirect taxes less subsidies equals net domestic income. GDP equals net domestic income plus capital consumption (depreciation). In 1998, GDP measured by the income approach was $8,511 billion.

Source: U.S. Department of Commerce, *Survey of Current Business* (April 1999).

taxes. Because of indirect taxes, consumers pay more for some goods and services than producers receive. Market price exceeds factor cost. For example, if the sales tax is 7 percent, when you buy a $1 chocolate bar you pay $1.07. The factor cost of the chocolate bar including profit is $1. The market price is $1.07.

A *subsidy* is a payment by the government to a producer. Payments made to grain growers and dairy farmers are subsidies. Because of subsidies, consumers pay less for some goods and services than producers receive. Factor cost exceeds market price.

To get from factor cost to market price, we add indirect taxes and subtract subsidies. Making this adjustment brings us one step closer to GDP, but it does not quite get us there. We must make one further adjustment.

Net Domestic Product to Gross Domestic Product

What do the words *gross* and *net* mean? *Gross* means *before* subtracting *depreciation*—the decrease in the value of the capital stock that results from wear and tear and obsolescence. *Net* means *after* subtracting depreciation.

Gross investment is a component of aggregate expenditure. So total expenditure includes depreciation and is a gross measure. The *net profit* of businesses—profit *after* subtracting depreciation—is a component of aggregate incomes. So total income excludes depreciation and is a net measure.

To get *gross* domestic product from the income approach, we must add depreciation to aggregate income.

Table 23.2 summarizes these calculations and shows how the income approach leads to the same estimate of GDP as the expenditure approach after the adjustments that we've just described have been made.

Valuing the Output of Industries

The methods used to measure GDP can also be used to measure the contribution that an industry makes to GDP. But to measure the value of production of an individual industry, we count only the value added by that industry. **Value added** is the value of a firm's production minus the value of the *intermediate goods* that the firm buys from other firms. Equivalently, it is the sum of the incomes (including profits) paid to the resources used by the firm.

Figure 23.3 illustrates value added by looking at the brief life of a loaf of bread. It starts with the

farmer, who grows the wheat. The farmer hires labor, capital, and land and pays wages, interest, and rent for these resources. The farmer also earns a profit. The entire value of the wheat produced is the farmer's value added. The miller buys wheat from the farmer and turns it into flour. The miller hires labor and capital, pays wages and interest, and earns a profit. The miller has now added value to the wheat bought from the farmer. The baker buys flour from the miller. The price of the flour includes the value added by both the farmer and the miller. The baker adds more value by turning the flour into bread. The grocer buys the bread from the baker. The price paid by the grocer includes the value added by the farmer, the miller, and the baker. At this stage, the value of the loaf is its *wholesale* value. The grocer adds further value by

FIGURE 23.3

Value Added and Final Expenditure

A consumer's expenditure on bread (the green bar) is equal to the sum of the value added at each stage in its production (the red bars). The blue bars illustrate intermediate expenditure. Intermediate expenditure, for example the amount paid by the baker for the purchase of flour from the miller, equals the value added by the farmer and the miller. So to include intermediate expenditure and final expenditure double counts some value added.

making the loaf available at a convenient place and time. The consumer buys the bread for a price—its *market price*—that includes the value added by the farmer, the miller, the baker, and the grocer.

Final Goods and Intermediate Goods To value output, we count only *value added* because the sum of the value added at each stage of production equals expenditure on the *final good*. By using value added, we avoid double counting. In the above example, the only thing that has been produced and consumed is a loaf of bread—shown by the green bar in Fig. 23.3. The value added at each stage is shown by the red bars, and the sum of the red bars equals the green bar. The transactions involving intermediate goods,

shown by the blue bars, are not part of value added and are not counted as part of the value of output or of GDP.

Aggregate Expenditure, Income, and GDP You've seen that aggregate expenditure equals aggregate income. And you've seen that the Department of Commerce uses both aggregate expenditure and aggregate income to measure GDP. Why does it use two approaches when they are supposed to be the same? The answer is that although the two concepts of the value of aggregate production are identical, the actual measurements, which are based on samples of information, give slightly different answers. The expenditure approach uses data from surveys of retail stores, house building, and business investment; the accounts of the federal, state, and local government; customs records; and many other sources. The income approach uses data supplied by the Internal Revenue Service. None of these sources gives a complete coverage of all the items that make up aggregate expenditure and aggregate income. So by using the two approaches, the Department of Commerce can check one aggregate against the other. The small discrepancy between the approaches is used to adjust both approaches to make them equal.

Figure 23.4 shows this equality between the approaches to measuring GDP and summarizes the expenditure, income, and product concepts.

FIGURE 23.4

Aggregate Expenditure, Output, and Income

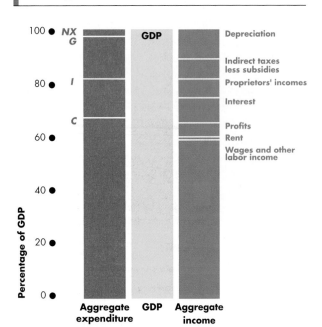

The red bar illustrates the components of aggregate expenditure as well as their relative magnitudes. Net exports, the smallest component, is shown here as a positive quantity, but in some years it is negative. The green bar illustrates the components of aggregate income and their relative magnitudes. The figure illustrates the equality between aggregate expenditure, aggregate income, and GDP (the yellow bar).

R E V I E W   Q U I Z

- What is the expenditure approach to measuring GDP?
- What is the income approach to measuring GDP?
- What is the distinction between expenditure on final goods and expenditure on intermediate goods?
- What is value added? How is it calculated?

So far, in our study of GDP and its measurement, we've been concerned with the dollar value of GDP and its components. But the dollar value of GDP can change either because prices change or because there is a change in the volume of goods and services produced—a change in *real* GDP. Let's now see how we measure the price level and distinguish between the dollar value and the real value of GDP.

The Price Level and Real GDP

THE PRICE LEVEL IS THE AVERAGE LEVEL OF PRICES measured by a *price index*. The best known price index in the United States is the Consumer Price Index. Let's see how this price index is calculated.

The Consumer Price Index

The **Consumer Price Index (CPI)** measures the average level of prices of the goods and services that a typical urban family buys. The Bureau of Labor Statistics (BLS) calculates the CPI every month.

To construct the CPI, the BLS first selects a base period (currently the three-year period 1993–1995) and surveys consumer spending patterns to determine the "basket" of goods and services that people bought in the base period. That basket contains around 400 different goods and services. Then, every month, the BLS sends observers to more than 50 urban centers to record the prices of the 400 items. The CPI is calculated by valuing the basket at the current month's prices and expressing its value as a percentage of the value of the same basket in the base period.

Table 23.3 shows a simplified example of the CPI calculation. Here, the basket contains only three goods and services: oranges, haircuts, and bus rides. The table shows the quantities in the base period and the prices in the base period and the current period. In the base period, a typical consumer buys 100 bus rides at $1.40 each and spends $140 on bus rides. Expenditure on oranges and haircuts is worked out in the same way. Total expenditure is the sum of expenditures on the three goods, which is $210.

To calculate the CPI for the current period, we need only discover the prices of the goods in the current period. Suppose that the prices are those shown in Table 23.3 under "Current period." We can now calculate the current period's value of the basket. For example, the current price of oranges is $1.20 per pound, so the current period's value of the oranges in the basket (5 pounds) is 5 multiplied by $1.20, which is $6. The quantities of haircuts and bus rides are valued at the current period's prices in a similar way. The total value of the base-period basket in the current period is $231.

The CPI is the ratio of the current period's value of the base period's basket to the base period's value, multiplied by 100. In Table 23.3, the CPI is 110 in the current period. The current period's price of the basket is 10 percent higher than it was in the base period.

The CPI is just one of two types of price index. An alternative price index uses the *current-period basket* of goods and services and values them at both the base period's prices and the current period's prices.

TABLE 23.3

The Consumer Price Index: A Simplified Calculation

Base-period basket	Base period		Current period	
	Price	Expenditure	Price	Value of basket
5 pounds of oranges	$ 0.80/pound	$ 4	$ 1.20/pound	$ 6
6 haircuts	$ 11.00 each	$ 66	$ 12.50 each	$ 75
100 bus rides	$ 1.40 each	$ 140	$ 1.50 each	$ 150
Total expenditure		$210		$231
CPI	$\dfrac{\$210.00}{\$210.00} \times 100 = 100$		$\dfrac{\$231.00}{\$210.00} \times 100 = 110$	

A fixed base-period basket of goods—5 pounds of oranges, 6 haircuts, and 100 bus rides—is valued in the base period at $210. Prices change, and that same basket is valued at $231 in the current period. The CPI is equal to the current-period value of the basket divided by the base-period value of the basket, multiplied by 100. In the base period, the CPI is 100, and in the current period, the CPI is 110.

A Current-Period Basket Price Index

Table 23.4 shows how to calculate price index that uses a current-period basket. In the *current* period, a typical consumer buys 136 bus rides at $1.50 each and spends $204 on bus rides. Expenditure on oranges and haircuts is worked out in the same way. Total expenditure in the current period is $270.10.

We can calculate the base period's value of the current-period basket by valuing it at the base period's prices. For example, the base period's price of oranges is 80¢ per pound, so the base period's value of the oranges in the basket (3 pounds) is 3 multiplied by 80¢, which is $2.40. The current-period quantities of haircuts and bus rides are valued at the base period's prices in a similar way. The total value of the current-period basket in the base period is $247.80.

The current-period basket price index is the ratio of the current period's expenditure to the base period's value of the basket, multiplied by 100. In Table 23.4, the price index is 109 in the current period. The current period's price of the current-period basket is 9 percent higher than it was in the base period.

The price index that uses current-period quantities increases by less than the CPI, which uses base-period quantities. The reason is that consumers make substitutions when prices change. Here, consumers buy fewer oranges and haircuts and more bus rides.

Real GDP

Real gross domestic product (**real GDP**) is GDP valued in the prices of a base year. Currently, 1992 is the base year for real GDP calculations in the United States. To calculate real GDP, we begin with GDP in the base year and then use a **chain-weighted output index**, to calculate the growth of real GDP from one year to the next. Real GDP each year is linked to the preceding year's real GDP, all the way back to the base year.

An *output* index is a *quantity* index. It compares the quantities in two periods using the prices of one of the periods. (A *price* index, in contrast, compares the prices in two periods using the quantities of one of the periods.) To learn how to calculate an *output* index, let's use the same simplified situation that Tables 23.3 and 23.4 describe.

In Table 23.3, the value of the base period's quantities at the base-period prices is $210. In Table 23.4, the value of the current period's quantities at the base-period prices is $247.80. In these two value calculations, the prices are the same but the quantities are different. To calculate an output index (a quantity index), express the current period's quantities valued at base-period prices as a percentage of the base period's quantities valued at the base-period prices. The quantity index number is $247.80 ÷ $210 × 100 = 118. Using the base-period prices, the

---

TABLE 23.4

A Current-Period Basket Price Index

Current-period basket	Base period		Current period	
	Price	Value of basket	Price	Expenditure
3 pounds of oranges	$ 0.80/pound	$2.40	$ 1.20/pound	$3.60
5 haircuts	$ 11.00 each	$55.00	$ 12.50 each	$62.50
136 bus rides	$ 1.40 each	$190.40	$ 1.50 each	$204.00
Total expenditure		$247.80		$270.10
Price Index	$\frac{\$247.80}{\$247.80} \times 100 = 100$		$\frac{\$270.10}{\$247.80} \times 100 = 109$	

A fixed current-period basket of goods—3 pounds of oranges, 5 haircuts, and 136 bus rides—is valued in the current period at $270.10. In the base period, that same basket is valued at $247.80. A price index that uses the current-period basket is equal to the current-period value of the basket divided by the base-period value of the basket, multiplied by 100. In the base period, the price index is 100, and in the current period, the price index is 109.

quantity of goods and services is 18 percent higher in the current period than in the base period.

Just as we can calculate two price indexes, we can also calculate two quantity indexes. The second quantity index uses the current-period prices. In Table 23.3, the value of the base period's quantities at current-period prices is $231. In Table 23.4, the value of the current period's quantities at current-period prices is $270.10. In these two value calculations, the prices are the same but the quantities are different. To calculate an output index (a quantity index), express the current period's quantities valued at current-period prices as a percentage of the base period's quantities valued at the current-period prices. The quantity index number is $270.10 ÷ $231 × 100 = 116.9. So using the current-period prices, the quantity of goods and services increased 16.9 percent between the base period and the current period.

The Department of Commerce uses an average of *both* of these quantity indexes to calculate real GDP. The average is a special one called a *geometric mean*, which is the square root of the product of the two indexes. In this simplified example, the average index number is 117.5. If we multiply last period's real GDP by this number (and divide by 100), we get this period's real GDP.

The GDP Deflator

The CPI is a popular index, but it includes only consumer prices. In macroeconomics, we use a broader index called the **GDP deflator**, which measures the average level of prices of all the goods and services that are included in GDP. To calculate the GDP deflator, we use the formula

$$\text{GDP deflator} = \frac{\text{GDP}}{\text{Real GDP}} \times 100.$$

GDP, also called **nominal GDP** for emphasis, is the value of the current period's production in current-period prices. Real GDP is the value of the current period's production in base-period prices. So the GDP deflator is a current-period basket price index. Unlike the CPI, the weights for the GDP deflator are constantly changing.

You can think of GDP as a balloon that is blown up by growing production and rising prices. In Fig. 23.5, the GDP deflator lets the inflation air out of the nominal GDP balloon—the contribution of ris-

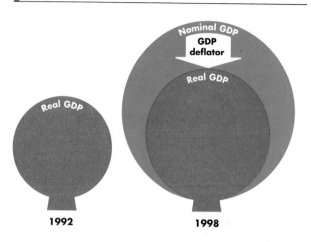

FIGURE 23.5

The U.S. GDP Balloon

Part of the rise in GDP comes from inflation and part from increased production—an increase in real GDP. The GDP deflator lets some air out of the GDP balloon so that we can see the extent to which production has grown.

ing prices—so that we can see what has happened to *real* GDP. The red balloon for 1992 shows real GDP in that year. The green balloon shows *nominal* GDP in 1998. The red balloon for 1998 shows real GDP for that year. To see real GDP in 1998, we *deflate* nominal GDP using the GDP deflator.

R E V I E W   Q U I Z

- What is the CPI and how is it calculated?
- What is a current-period basket price index?
- How are real GDP and the GDP deflator calculated?
- How does the CPI differ from the GDP deflator?

You now know how to calculate real GDP and the price level. Your next task is to learn how to use these measures to calculate economic growth and inflation. We also look at some limitations of real GDP as a measure of economic growth. And we look at some potential biases in the CPI as a measure of inflation.

Measuring Economic Growth

WE USE ESTIMATES OF REAL GDP TO CALCULATE the economic growth rate. The **economic growth rate** is the percentage change in the quantity of goods and services produced from one year to the next. To calculate the economic growth rate, we use the formula

$$\text{Economic growth rate} = \frac{\text{Real GDP this year} - \text{Real GDP last year}}{\text{Real GDP last year}} \times 100.$$

For example, real GDP was \$7,552 in 1998 and \$7,270 in 1997. So the economic growth rate (percent per year) during 1998 was

$$\text{Economic growth rate} = \frac{(\$7{,}552 - \$7{,}270)}{\$7{,}270} \times 100$$

$$= 3.7 \text{ percent per year.}$$

We want to measure the economic growth rate so that we may make:

- Economic welfare comparisons
- International comparisons
- Business cycle forecasts

Although the real GDP growth rate is used for these three purposes, it is not a perfect measure for any of them. But nor is it a totally misleading measure. We'll evaluate the limitations of real GDP and its growth rate in each of the three cases.

Economic Welfare Comparisons

Economic welfare is a comprehensive measure of the general state of economic well-being. Economic welfare improves when the production of *all* the goods and services grows. The goods and services that make up real GDP growth are only a part of all the items that influence economic welfare.

Today, because of real GDP growth, real GDP per person in the United States of \$28,000 is twice what it was in 1963. But are we twice as well off? Does this growth of real GDP provide a full and accurate measure of the change in economic welfare?

It does not. The reason is that economic welfare depends on many other factors that are not measured by real GDP or that are not measured accurately by real GDP. Some of these factors are:

- Over adjustment for inflation
- Household production
- Underground economic activity
- Health and life expectancy
- Leisure time
- Environment quality
- Political freedom and social justice

Over Adjustment for Inflation The price indexes used to measure inflation give an upward-biased estimate of true inflation. (We learn about the sources of this bias on pp. 510-511.) If we overestimate the rise in prices, we underestimate of the growth of real GDP. When car prices rise because cars have gotten better (safer, more fuel efficient, more comfortable), the CPI and the GDP deflator count the price increase as inflation. So what is really an increase in production is counted as an increase in price rather than an increase in real GDP. It is deflated away by the wrongly measured higher price level. The magnitude of this bias is probably less than 1 percentage point a year, but its exact magnitude is not known.

Household Production An enormous amount of production takes place every day in our homes. Preparing meals, cleaning the kitchen, changing a light bulb, cutting the grass, washing the car, and helping a high school student with homework are all examples of productive activities that do not involve market transactions and are not counted as part of GDP.

If these activities grew at the same rate as real GDP, not measuring them would not be a problem. But it is likely that market production, which is part of GDP, is increasingly replacing household production, which is not part of GDP. Two trends point in this direction. One is the number of people who have jobs, which has increased from 57 percent in 1970 to 64 percent in 1998. The other is the trend in the purchase of traditionally home-produced goods and services in the market. For example, more and more families now eat in fast-food restaurants—one of the fastest-growing industries in the United States—and use day-care services. This trend means that an increasing proportion of food preparation and child care that were part of household production are now measured as part of GDP. So real GDP grows more rapidly than does real GDP plus home production.

Underground Economic Activity   The *underground economy* is the part of the economy that is purposely hidden from the view of the government in order to avoid taxes and regulations or because the goods and services being produced are illegal. Because underground economic activity is unreported, it is omitted from GDP.

The underground economy is easy to describe, even if it is hard to measure. It includes the production and distribution of illegal drugs, production that uses illegal labor that is paid less than the minimum wage, and jobs done for cash to avoid paying income taxes. This last category might be quite large and includes tips earned by cab drivers, hairdressers, and hotel and restaurant workers.

Estimates of the scale of the underground economy range between 9 and 30 percent of GDP ($770 billion to $2,550 billion) in the United States and much more in some countries. It is particularly large in some Eastern European countries that are making a transition from communist economic planning to a market economy.

Provided that the underground economy is a reasonably stable proportion of the total economy, the growth rate of real GDP still gives a useful estimate of changes in economic welfare. But sometimes, production shifts from the underground economy to the rest of the economy, and sometimes it shifts the other way. The underground economy expands relative to the rest of the economy if taxes become especially high or if regulations become especially restrictive. And the underground economy shrinks relative to the rest of the economy if the burdens of taxes and regulations are eased. During the 1980s, when tax rates were cut, there was an increase in the reporting of previously hidden income and tax revenues increased. So some part (but probably a very small part) of the expansion of real GDP during the 1980s represented a shift from the underground economy rather than an increase in production.

Health and Life Expectancy   Good health and a long life—the hopes of everyone—do not show up in real GDP, at least not directly. A higher real GDP does enable us to spend more on medical research, health care, a good diet, and exercise equipment. And as real GDP has increased, our life expectancy has lengthened—from 70 years at the end of World War II to approaching 80 years today. Infant deaths and death in childbirth, two fearful scourges of the nineteenth century, have almost been eliminated.

But we face new health and life expectancy problems every year. AIDS and drug abuse are taking young lives at a rate that causes serious concern. When we take these negative influences into account, we see that real GDP growth overstates the improvements in economic welfare.

Leisure Time   Leisure time is an economic good that adds to our economic welfare. Other things being equal, the more leisure we have, the better off we are. Our working time is valued as part of GDP, but our leisure time is not. Yet from the point of view of economic welfare, that leisure time must be at least as valuable to us as the wage that we earn on the last hour worked. If it was not, we would work instead of taking the leisure. Over the years, leisure time has steadily increased. The workweek has become shorter, more people take early retirement, and the number of vacation days has increased. These improvements in economic well-being are not reflected in real GDP.

Environment Quality   Economic activity directly influences the quality of the environment. The burning of hydrocarbon fuels is the most visible activity that damages our environment. But it is not the only example. The depletion of exhaustible resources, the mass clearing of forests, and the pollution of lakes and rivers are other major environmental consequences of industrial production.

Resources that are used to protect the environment are valued as part of GDP. For example, the value of catalytic converters that help to protect the atmosphere from automobile emissions is part of GDP. But if we did not use such pieces of equipment and instead polluted the atmosphere, we would not count the deteriorating air that we were breathing as a negative part of GDP.

An industrial society possibly produces more atmospheric pollution than an agricultural society does. But such pollution does not always increase as we become wealthier. One of the things that wealthy people value is a clean environment, and they devote resources to protecting it. Compare the pollution that was discovered in East Germany in the late 1980s with pollution in the United States. East Germany, a relatively poor country, polluted its rivers, lakes, and atmosphere in a way that is unimaginable in the United States or in wealthy West Germany.

Political Freedom and Social Justice   Most people value political freedoms such as those provided by the U.S. Constitution. And they value social justice or fairness—equality of opportunity and of access to social security safety nets that protect people from the extremes of misfortune.

A country might have a very large real GDP per person but have limited political freedom and equity. For example, a small elite might enjoy political liberty and extreme wealth while the vast majority are effectively enslaved and live in abject poverty. Such an economy would generally be regarded as having less economic welfare than one that had the same amount of real GDP but in which political freedoms were enjoyed by everyone. Today, China has rapid real GDP growth but limited political freedoms, while Russia has a decreasing real GDP and an emerging democratic political system. Economists have no easy way to determine which of these countries is better off.

The Bottom Line Do we get the wrong message about the growth in economic welfare by looking at the growth of real GDP? The influences omitted from real GDP are probably important and could be large. Developing countries have a larger underground economy and a larger amount of household production than do developed countries. So as an economy develops and grows, part of the apparent growth might reflect a switch from underground to regular production and from home production to market production. This measurement error overstates the rate of economic growth and the improvement in economic welfare.

Other influences on living standards include the amount of leisure time available, the quality of the environment, the security of jobs and homes, the safety of city streets, and so on. It is possible to construct broader measures that combine the many influences that contribute to human happiness. Real GDP will be one element in those broader measures, but it will by no means be the whole of them.

International Comparisons

All the problems we've just reviewed affect economic welfare of every country, so to make international comparisons of economic welfare, factors additional to real GDP must be used. But real GDP comparisons are major components of international welfare comparisons and two special problems arise in making these comparisons. First, the real GDP of one country must be converted into the same currency units as the real GDP of the other country. Second,

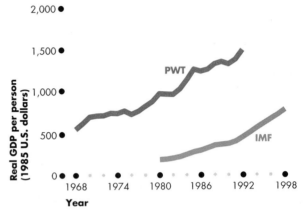

FIGURE 23.6

Two Views of Real GDP in China

According to the official statistics of the International Monetary Fund (IMF) and the World Bank, China is a poor developing country. But according to an alternative view, Penn World Table (PWT), which is based on purchasing power prices, China has a real GDP more than 3.3 times the official view and has the world's third largest total production.

Sources: IMF, *International Financial Statistics Yearbook*, 1998, Washington, D.C., World Bank, *World Development Report, 1998*, Washington, D.C.; "The Penn World Table (Mark 5.5): An Expanded Set of International Comparisons, 1950–1988," *Quarterly Journal of Economics*, May 1991, pp. 327–368; new computer diskette, Mark 5.6a, 1995; and the author's calculations.

the same prices must be used to value the goods and services in the countries being compared. Let's look at these two problems by using a striking example, a comparison of the United States and China.

In 1992 (the most recent year for which we can make this comparison), GDP per person in the United States was $24,451. The official Chinese statistics published by the International Monetary Fund (IMF) say that GDP per person in China in 1992 was 2,402 yuan. (The yuan is the currency of China.) On the average, during 1992, $1 U.S. was worth 5.762 yuan. If we use this exchange rate to convert Chinese yuan into U.S. dollars, we get a value of $417.

The official comparison of China and the United States makes China look extremely poor. In 1992, GDP per person in the United States was 59 times that in China.

Figure 23.6 shows the official story of real GDP in China between 1980 and 1998. But Fig. 23.6 also shows another story. It shows an estimate of real GDP per person in China that is much larger than the official measure. Let's see how this alternative measurement is made.

GDP in the United States is measured by using prices that prevail in the United States. China's GDP is measured by using prices that prevail in China. But the relative prices in the two countries are very different. Some goods that are expensive in the United States cost very little in China. These items get a small weight in China's real GDP. If, instead of using China's prices, all the goods and services produced in China are valued at the prices prevailing in the United States, then a more valid comparison can be made of GDP in the two countries. Such a comparison uses prices called *purchasing power parity prices.*

Robert Summers and Alan Heston, economists in the Center for International Comparisons at the University of Pennsylvania, have used purchasing power parity prices to construct real GDP data for more than one hundred countries. These data, which are published in the Penn World Table (PWT), tell a remarkable story about China. The PWT data use 1985 as the base year, so they are measured in 1985 dollars. According to the Penn World Table, in 1992, real GDP per person in the United States was 12 times that of China, not the 59 times shown in the official data.

Figure 23.6 shows the PWT view of China and compares it with the official view. The difference in the two views arises from the prices used. The official statistics use Chinese prices, while the PWT data use purchasing power parity prices.

Despite large differences in estimates of the *level* of China's real GDP, there is much less doubt about its growth rate. The economy of China is expanding at an extraordinary rate, and it is for this reason that most businesses are paying a great deal of attention to the prospects of expanding their activities in China and the other Asian economies.

U.S. real GDP is measured quite reliably. But China's is not. The alternative measures of China's real GDP are somewhat unreliable, and the truth about GDP in China is not known.

Business Cycle Forecasts

When the Fed decides to raise interest rates to slow an expansion that it believes is too strong, it looks at the latest estimates of real GDP and inflation. But

suppose that for the reasons that we've just discussed, real GDP is mismeasured. Does this mismeasurement hamper our ability to identify the phases of the business cycle? It does not. The reason is that although the omissions from real GDP do change over time, they probably do not change in a systematic way with the business cycle. So inaccurate measurement of real GDP does not necessarily cause a wrong assessment of the phase of the business cycle.

The fluctuations in economic activity measured by real GDP tell a reasonably accurate story about the phase of the business cycle that the economy is in. When real GDP grows, the economy is in a business cycle expansion; when real GDP shrinks (for two quarters), the economy is in a recession. Also, as real GDP fluctuates, so do employment and unemployment.

But real GDP fluctuations probably exaggerate or overstate the fluctuations in total production and economic welfare. The reason is that when business activity slows in a recession, household production increases, and so does leisure time. When business activity speeds up in an expansion, household production and leisure time decrease. Because household production and leisure time increase in a recession and decrease in an expansion, real GDP fluctuations tend to overstate the fluctuations in total production and in economic welfare. But the directions of change of real GDP, total production, and economic welfare are probably the same.

R E V I E W   Q U I Z

- Does real GDP measure economic welfare? If not, why not?
- Does real GDP measure total production of goods and services? If not, what are the main omissions?
- How can we make valid international comparisons of real GDP?
- Does the growth of real GDP measure the long-term growth rate accurately?
- Do the fluctuations in real GDP measure the business cycle accurately?

Let's now see how we use the CPI data to measure inflation and learn about the limitations of our measurement of this important feature of our economy.

Measuring Inflation

A MAJOR PURPOSE OF THE CPI IS TO MEASURE inflation, and the measure is put to practical use. For example, it is used to determine cost of living adjustments to Social Security payments and changes in tax brackets—the income ranges over which different income tax rates apply. The data generated by the CPI survey are also used, along with other information, in the calculations of real GDP, nominal GDP, and the GDP deflator.

The **inflation rate** is the percentage change in the price level from one year to the next. To calculate the inflation rate, we use the formula

$$\text{Inflation rate} = \frac{(\text{CPI this year} - \text{CPI last year})}{\text{CPI last year}} \times 100.$$

For example, the CPI was 164 in December 1998 and 161.3 in December 1997. So the inflation rate during 1998 was

$$\text{Inflation rate} = \frac{(164 - 161.3)}{161.3} \times 100.$$

$$= 1.67 \text{ percent per year.}$$

An alternative measure of inflation replaces the CPI with the GDP deflator in the formula above.

How different are the two measures of inflation based on the CPI and the GDP deflator? And how good a measure of inflation do these index numbers provide?

Figure 23.7 answers the first question. The average inflation rate over the period shown is 4.9 percent a year for the CPI and 4.8 percent a year for the GDP deflator. So on the average, the two measures are similar. But the CPI fluctuates more than the GDP deflator. Worse, *both* measures of inflation probably overstate the inflation rate, and especially the CPI.

The Biased CPI

The main sources of bias in the CPI are:

■ New goods bias
■ Quality change bias
■ Commodity substitution bias
■ Outlet substitution bias

FIGURE 23.7

Two Measures of Inflation

The CPI and the GDP deflator have similar averages over the period shown here—4.9 percent a year for the CPI and 4.8 percent a year for the GDP deflator—but the CPI fluctuates more than the GDP deflator, and both measures probably overstate the inflation rate.

Source: Economic Report of the President, 1999.

New Goods Bias New goods keep replacing old goods. For example, PCs have replaced typewriters. If you want to compare the price level in 1998 with that in 1978, you must somehow compare the price of a computer today with that of a typewriter in 1978. Because PCs are more expensive than typewriters, the arrival of these new goods puts an upward bias into the CPI and its inflation rate.

Quality Change Bias Cars, CD players, and many other items get better every year. Part of the rise in the prices of these items is a payment for improved quality and is not inflation. But the CPI counts the price rise as inflation and so overstates inflation.

Commodity Substitution Bias Changes in relative prices lead consumers to change the items they buy. For example, if the price of beef rises and the price of chicken remains unchanged, people buy more chicken and less beef. Suppose they switch from beef to chicken on a scale that provides the same amount of protein and the same enjoyment as before and costs the same as before. Because the CPI ignores the substitution, it says the price of protein has increased when in fact it is constant.

Outlet Substitution Bias   When confronted with higher prices, people use discount stores more frequently and convenience stores less frequently. This phenomenon is called *outlet substitution*. The CPI surveys do not monitor outlet substitutions.

The Magnitude of the Bias

You've reviewed the sources of bias in the CPI. But how big is the bias? This question was tackled in 1996 by a Congressional Advisory Commission on the Consumer Price Index, chaired by Michael Boskin, an economics professor at Stanford University. This commission said that the CPI overstates inflation by 1.1 percentage points a year. That is, if the CPI reports that inflation is 3.1 percent a year, most likely inflation is actually 2 percent a year.

Reducing the Bias   To reduce the bias in the CPI, the Bureau of Labor Statistics has decided to undertake consumer spending surveys at more frequent intervals and to revise the basket used for calculating the CPI every 2 years.

Some Consequences of the Bias

The bias in the CPI has three main consequences. It

- Distorts private contracts
- Increases government outlays
- Biased estimates of real earnings

Many private agreements, such as wage contracts, are linked to the CPI. For example, a firm and its workers might agree to a 3-year wage deal that increases the wage rate by 2 percent a year *plus* the percentage increase in the CPI. Such a deal ends up giving the workers more real income than the firm intended.

Close to a third of federal government outlays are linked directly to the CPI. And while a bias of 1 percent a year seems small, accumulated over a decade, it adds up to almost a trillion dollars of additional expenditures.

According to official government statistics, since 1973, real hourly earnings in manufacturing industry have *fallen* by 13 percent. If the CPI is adjusted for the bias estimated by the Boskin Commission, this picture is transformed into one in which real earnings have *increased* by 13 percent!

Is the GDP Deflator Biased?

The GDP deflator is calculated from nominal GDP and the chain-linked estimate of real GDP growth. In principle, real GDP includes new goods and quality improvements. It is also based on people's actual expenditures and so reflects substitutions of both commodities and retail outlets. So in principle, the GDP deflator is not subject to the biases of the CPI. But in practice, the GDP deflator suffers from some of the CPI's problems. To arrive at its estimate of real GDP, the Commerce Department does not directly measure the physical quantities produced. Instead, it estimates quantities by dividing expenditures by price indexes. And one of these price indexes is the CPI. So the biased CPI injects a bias into the GDP deflator.

R E V I E W   Q U I Z

- What are the four main ways in which the CPI is an upward-biased measure of the price level?
- By how much is the CPI estimated to overstate the inflation rate? Is the amount the same in all countries?
- Why might the GDP deflator be a biased measure of the price level?
- What are the main problems that arise from a bias in the measurement of the price level?

◆ You've now studied the methods used to measure GDP, economic growth, and inflation. And you've learned about some of the limitations of these measures. Your next task, in Chapter 24, is to study the methods used to measure employment and unemployment and other indicators of economic health in labor markets.

Before you embark on this next topic, spend a few minutes with *Reading Between the Lines* on pp. 512–513, which explores the consequences of the bias in the CPI for the measurement of real GDP and real hourly earnings. You'll be surprised by the numbers.

Correcting the CPI Bias

THE NEW YORK TIMES, DECEMBER 1, 1996

Sorry, Wrong Numbers So Maybe It Wasn't the Economy

BY FLOYD NORRIS

Economic statistics are thrust into the news every day, with a portentous exactitude that can send Wall Street soaring or reeling, influence Government policy, even sway elections. Did consumer prices rise one-tenth of a percent more than was expected? Was economic growth a half percentage point less than people had been hoping?

But what if the statistics are wrong? And what if they are consistently wrong in the same direction? Over time, that can produce a very distorted picture of the economy, with unfortunate effects brought about not by the economy but by our perceptions of it and with those perceptions having effects of their own. ...

This week a commission headed by Michael Boskin, the Stanford economist and former adviser to President Bush, will report to the Senate Finance Committee that inflation, as measured by the Consumer Price Index, has been rising at a far slower pace than we had thought. Economists who have studied the issue now generally agree that inflation has been overstated, although some argue that the error is relatively small and may not make a significant difference.

The commission was appointed last year because of serious doubts about how changes in benefits and tax brackets, which have a major effect on the deficit, are calculated. A conclusion that the Consumer Price Index [CPI] has been overstated could lead to efforts to reduce the automatic increases in certain benefits, notably Social Security. That's sure to provoke a fight.

But perhaps even more important are changes that may be necessary in our view of the economy for the last two decades. For much of that time, even as America came roaring back into a preeminent position in technological leadership and the stock market zoomed, economists have been looking at statistics that showed a weak economy. And politicians have been trying to address public angst over economic decline. ...

Leonard Nakamura, an economist with the Federal Reserve Bank of Philadelphia, is known for his work on inflation. ... His estimates of the overstatement are among the largest ... at about 1.25 percent annually in the mid-1970s, rising to about 2.75 percent now. ...

Essence of the Story

■ Economic statistics can influence stock markets and government policy, and, if inaccurate, economic statistics can produce a distorted picture of the economy.

■ In December 1996, a commission headed by Michael Boskin reported to the Senate Finance Committee that the CPI overstates the inflation rate.

■ Economists generally agree that the CPI overstates the inflation rate but are uncertain about the magnitude of the overstatement.

■ For the last 20 years, technology has advanced and the stock prices have increased, but economic statistics have shown slow economic growth.

■ Leonard Nakamura, an economist at the Federal Reserve Bank of Philadelphia, says the economic statistics are wrong and that inflation has been overstated—by 1.25 percent a year during the mid-1970s to 2.75 percent a year in 1996.

■ Leonard Nakamura, a research economist at the Federal Reserve Bank of Philadelphia, believes that inflation has been overstated for at least 20 years. He says that the overstatement was approximately 1.25 percent annually during the mid-1970s, rising to approximately 2.75 percent annually by the mid-1990s.

■ Figure 1 shows Mr. Nakamura's estimate of the Consumer Price Index. His index equals 100 in 1975. According to Mr. Nakamura, the price level doubled between 1975 and 1996, not tripled as has been reported in the official data.

■ If we accept Mr. Nakamura's revised price level, we must change other economic indicators that are expressed in constant dollars.

■ Figure 2 shows the implications of Mr. Nakamura's assumptions for real GDP. According to his new inflation figures, real GDP has increased by twice as much as reported in the official data.

■ Figure 3 shows the impact of the new view of prices on real hourly earnings. The official view is that since 1975, real hourly earnings have *decreased* by 9 percent. The new view is that real hourly earnings have *increased* by 35 percent!

■ Mr. Nakamura's views are toward the upper end of the range of what economists believe, but they are not outrageous. He could be correct. If he is correct, the U.S. economy is in even better shape than Alan Greenspan, President Clinton, and many other leading public commentators dared to believe.

■ As a taxpayer and voter, do you care whether the government's economic statistics are accurate?

■ Try to think of reasons why is matters *to you* that the official statistics are accurate.

■ Would you be willing to see government funds diverted from some existing use and spent on data gathering and processing to get better measures of prices, real GDP, and real earnings?

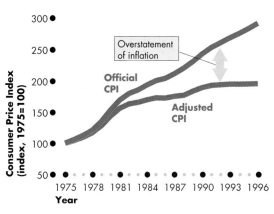

Figure 1 Consumer Price Index

Figure 2 Real GDP

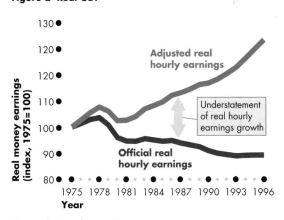

Figure 3 Hourly earnings

513

SUMMARY

KEY POINTS

Gross Domestic Product (pp. 494–498)

■ Gross domestic product (GDP), which is the value of total production in a country during a given period, is calculated by using the circular flow of income and expenditure.

■ Aggregate expenditure on goods and services equals aggregate income and GDP.

Measuring U.S. GDP (pp. 498–502)

■ Because aggregate expenditure, aggregate income, and the value of aggregate production are equal, we can measure GDP by using the expenditure approach or the income approach.

■ The expenditure approach sums consumption expenditure, investment, government purchases of goods and services, and net exports.

■ The income approach sums wages, interest, rent, and profit (and indirect taxes and depreciation).

The Price Level and Real GDP (pp. 503–505)

■ The Consumer Price Index (CPI) is an index number that measures average price of goods and services typically consumed by American families.

■ Real GDP is measured by a chain-weighted output index that compares the value of production each year with its value at the previous year's prices.

■ The GDP deflator measures the price level based on the prices of the items that make up GDP.

Measuring Economic Growth (pp. 506–509)

■ We measure the economic growth rate as the percentage change in real GDP.

■ Real GDP growth is not a perfect measure of economic growth because it excludes quality improvements, household production, the underground economy, environmental damage, health and life expectancy, leisure time, political freedom, and social justice.

■ The growth rate of real GDP gives a good indication of the phases of the business cycle.

Measuring Inflation (pp. 510–511)

■ We measure the inflation rate as the percentage change in the CPI (or GDP deflator).

■ The CPI is biased upward because it does not take proper account of the effects of changes in spending patterns.

■ Attempts are being made to reduce the CPI bias.

KEY FIGURES AND TABLES

KEY TERMS

PROBLEMS

*1. Martha owns a copy shop that has 5 copiers. One copier wears out each year and is replaced. In addition, this year Martha will expand her business to 7 copiers. Calculate Martha's initial capital stock, depreciation, gross investment, net investment, and final capital stock.

2. Wendy operates a weaving shop with 10 looms. One loom wears out each year and is replaced. But this year, Wendy will expand her business to 12 looms. Calculate Wendy's initial capital stock, depreciation, gross investment, net investment, and final capital stock.

*3. The figure shows the flows of income and expenditure on Lotus Island. During 1997, A was $10 million, B was $30 million, C was $12 million, D was $15 million, and E was $3 million. Calculate:

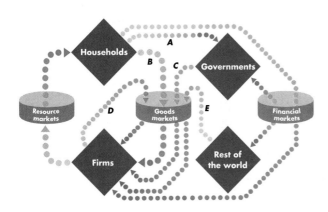

a. Aggregate expenditure.
b. Aggregate income.
c. GDP.
d. Government budget deficit.
e. Household saving.
f. Government saving.
g. Foreign borrowing.
h. National saving.

4. In problem 3, during 1998, A was $10 million, B was $50 million, C was $15 million, D was $15 million, and E was –$5 million. Calculate the quantities in problem 3 during 1998.

*5. The transactions in Ecoland last year were:

Item	Dollars
Wages paid to labor	800,000
Consumption expenditure	600,000
Taxes	250,000
Transfer payments	50,000
Profits	200,000
Investment	250,000
Government purchases	200,000
Exports	300,000
Saving	300,000
Imports	250,000

a. Calculate Ecoland's GDP.
b. Did you use the expenditure approach or the incomes approach to make this calculation?
c. How is investment financed?

6. The transactions in Highland last year were:

Item	Dollars
Wages paid to labor	800,000
Consumption expenditure	650,000
Net taxes	200,000
Profits	250,000
Investment	300,000
Government purchases	250,000
Exports	250,000
Saving	200,000
Imports	300,000

a. Calculate Highland's GDP.
b. What extra information do you need to calculate net domestic product?
c. Where does Highland get the funds to finance its investment?

*7. A typical family on Sandy Island consumes only juice and cloth. Last year, which was the base year, the family spent $40 on juice and $25 on cloth. In the base year, juice was $4 a bottle and cloth was $5 a length. In the current year, juice is $4 a bottle and cloth is $6 a length. Calculate:
a. The basket used in the CPI.
b. The CPI in the current year.
c. The inflation rate in the current year.

8. A typical family on Lizard Island consumes only mangoes and nuts. Last year, which was the base year, the family spent $60 on nuts and $10 on mangoes. In the base year, mangoes were $1 each and nuts were $3 a bag. In the

current year, mangoes are $1.50 each and nuts are $4 a bag. Calculate:

a. The basket used in the CPI.
b. The CPI in the current year.
c. The inflation rate in the current year.

*9. Bananaland produces only bananas and sunscreen. The base year is 1997, and the tables give the quantities produced and the prices.

	Quantity	
Good	**1997**	**1998**
Bananas	1,000 bunches	1,100 bunches
Sunscreen	500 bottles	525 bottles

	Price	
Good	**1997**	**1998**
Bananas	$2 a bunch	$3 a bunch
Sunscreen	$10 a bottle	$8 a bottle

Calculate Bananaland's:

a. GDP and real GDP in 1997 and 1998.
b. Growth rate of real GDP in 1998.
c. GDP deflator in 1998.

10. Sea Island produces only lobsters and crabs. The base year is 1997, and the tables give the quantities produced and the prices.

	Quantity	
Good	**1997**	**1998**
Lobsters	1,000	1,100
Crabs	500	525

	Price	
Good	**1997**	**1998**
Lobsters	$20 each	$25 each
Crabs	$10 each	$12 each

Calculate Sea Island's:

a. GDP and real GDP in 1997 and 1998.
b. Growth rate of real GDP in 1998.
c. GDP deflator in 1998.

CRITICAL THINKING

1. Study *Reading Between the Lines* on pp. 512–513 and then answer the following questions:

   a. How large does Mr. Nakamura believe the bias in the CPI to be?
   b. How does Mr. Nakamura's estimate of the CPI bias compare with that of the Boskin commission?
   c. Write a brief description of the U.S. economy since 1975 based on the view of the official statistics and based on the view of Mr. Nakamura.
   d. If Mr. Nakamura's view of the economy is correct, how different does economic growth look during the terms of Presidents Carter, Reagan, Bush, and Clinton compared with each other and compared with the official data?
   e. Should Social Security benefits be linked to the measured CPI or to an estimate of the true CPI? Why or why not?
   f. What difference, if any, do you think there would be in the distribution of income between workers and business owners if the bias in the CPI had been discovered 10 years ago? Explain your answer.

2. Use the link on the Parkin Web site to visit the Federal Reserve Economic Data (FRED) Web site at the Federal Reserve Bank of St. Louis. There you can obtain the latest data on real GDP, nominal GDP, and the GDP deflator as well as the data for the previous year.

   a. What was the GDP deflator in the most recent year?
   b. What was the GDP deflator in the previous year?
   c. What is the inflation rate as measured by the GDP deflator between these two years?
   d. What was real GDP in the most recent year?
   e. What was real GDP in the previous year?
   f. What is the real GDP growth rate between these two years?
   g. Check that, for the data you have obtained, nominal GDP divided by real GDP equals the GDP deflator.

Chapter 24

Measuring Employment and Unemployment

Vital Signs

Each month, we chart the course of the unemployment rate as a measure of U.S. economic health. How do we measure unemployment? What does it tell us? Is it a reliable vital sign for the economy? ◆ June 1992 was a month in which unemployment peaked at almost 10 million. How can such a large number of people be unemployed? How do people become unemployed? Do most of them get fired, or do most quit their jobs to look for better ones? How long do spells of unemployment last for most people—a week, two weeks, or several months? And how does the length of unemployment spells vary over the business cycle? ◆ You probably know that unemployment is more common among young people than among older people. It is also more common among minorities than among whites. Why are some groups more frequently unemployed than others? ◆ We also chart every month the number of people working. This number fluctuates as the unemployment rate fluctuates, but it also trends upward. At the start of 1999, more than 130 million people in the United States had jobs. What does this vital sign tell us about the health of the U.S. economy? Does the number of jobs grow quickly enough to keep pace with increases in the population? ◆ Yet other signs of economic health are the hours people work and the wages they receive. Are work hours growing as quickly as the number of people with jobs? Are most of the new jobs full time or part time? Also, are most new jobs high-wage or low-wage jobs?

◇ These are the questions we study in this chapter. You will discover that a lot of ideas that people have about the U.S. labor market are just plain wrong. The economy has created millions of jobs, including good jobs that pay high wages and provide good benefits. But most people have seen a slowdown in their rate of wage increase, and many have seen their wages fall. We begin by looking at the key labor market indicators and the way they are measured.

After studying this chapter, you will be able to:

- Define the unemployment rate, the labor force participation rate, the employment-to-population ratio, and aggregate hours

- Describe the trends and fluctuations in the indicators of labor market performance

- Describe the sources of unemployment, its duration, and the groups that are most affected by it

- Describe the relationship between employment, unemployment, and real GDP

Employment and Wages

For most of us, the labor market is the source of almost all our income. We become concerned when jobs are hard to find. And we become more relaxed when jobs are plentiful. We also care about the kinds of jobs that are available. We want good jobs, which means we want well-paid and interesting jobs. In this chapter, we study the way that economists track the health of the labor market.

Population Survey

Every month, the U.S. Census Bureau surveys 60,000 households and asks a series of questions about the age and job market status of its members. This survey is called the Current Population Survey. The Census Bureau uses the answers to describe the anatomy of the labor force.

Figure 24.1 shows the population categories used by the Census Bureau and the relationships among the categories. It divides the population into two groups: the working-age population and others who are too young to work or who live in institutions and are unable to work. The **working-age population** is the total number of people aged 16 years and over who are not in jail, hospital, or some other form of institutional care. The Census Bureau divides the working-age population into two groups: those in the labor force and those not in the labor force. It also divides the labor force into two groups: the employed and the unemployed. So the **labor force** is the sum of the employed and the unemployed.

To be counted as employed in the Current Population Survey, a person must have either a full-time job or a part-time job. To be counted as *un*employed, a person must be available for work and must be in one of three categories:

1. Without work but has made specific efforts to find a job within the previous four weeks
2. Waiting to be called back to a job from which he or she has been laid off
3. Waiting to start a new job within 30 days

Anyone surveyed who satisfies one of these three criteria is counted as unemployed. People in the working-age population who are neither employed nor unemployed are classified as not in the labor force.

FIGURE 24.1

Population Labor Force Categories

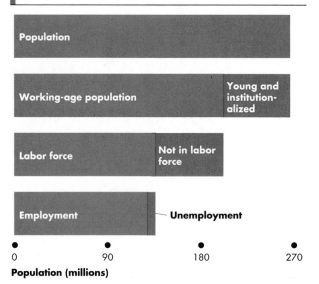

The population is divided into the working-age population and the young and institutionalized. The working-age population is divided into the labor force and those not in the labor force. The labor force is divided into the employed and the unemployed.

Source: Economic Report of the President, 1999.

In 1998, the population of the United States was 270.2 million. There were 65 million people under 16 years of age or living in institutions. The working-age population was 205.2 million. Of this number, 67.5 million were not in the labor force. Most of these people were in school full time or had retired from work. The remaining 137.7 million people made up the U.S. labor force. Of these, 131.5 million were employed and 6.2 million were unemployed.

Three Labor Market Indicators

The Census Bureau calculates three indicators of the state of the labor market, which are shown in Fig. 24.2. They are:

- The unemployment rate
- The labor force participation rate
- The employment-to-population ratio

The Unemployment Rate   The amount of unemployment is an indicator of the extent to which people who want jobs can't find them. The **unemployment rate** is the percentage of the people in the labor force who are unemployed. That is,

$$\text{Unemployment rate} = \frac{\text{Number of people unemployed}}{\text{Labor force}} \times 100,$$

and

$$\text{Labor force} = \text{Number of people employed} + \text{Number of people unemployed}.$$

In 1998, the number of people employed was 131.5 million and the number unemployed was 6.2 million. By using the above equations, you can verify that the labor force was 137.7 million (131.5 million plus 6.2 million) and the unemployment rate was 4.5 percent (6.2 million divided by 137.7 million, multiplied by 100).

Figure 24.2 shows the unemployment rate (orange line) and two other labor market indicators between 1960 and 1998. The average unemployment rate has been 6 percent, and it reached peak values during the OPEC recession and the recessions of 1982 and 1990—1991.

The Labor Force Participation Rate   The number of people who join the labor force is an indicator of the willingness of people of working age to take jobs. The **labor force participation rate** is the percentage of the working-age population who are members of the labor force. That is,

$$\frac{\text{Labor force}}{\text{participation rate}} = \frac{\text{Labor force}}{\text{Working-age population}} \times 100.$$

In 1998, the labor force was 137.7 million and the working-age population was 205.2 million. By using the above equation, you can calculate the labor force participation rate. It was 67.1 percent (137.7 million divided by 205.2 million, multiplied by 100).

The labor force participation rate (graphed in red and plotted on the left scale) has followed an upward trend and has increased from 59 percent during the early 1960s to 67 percent during the 1990s. It has also had some mild fluctuations. They result from unsuccessful job seekers becoming discouraged

FIGURE 24.2

Employment, Unemployment, and the Labor Force: 1960–1998

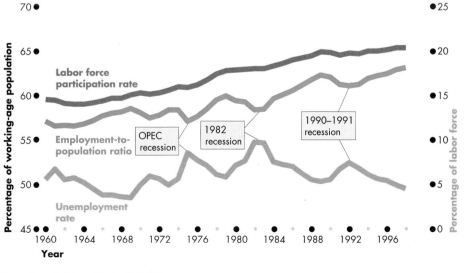

The unemployment rate increases in recessions and decreases in expansions. The labor force participation rate and the employment-to-population ratio have upward trends and fluctuate with the business cycle. The employment-to-population ratio fluctuates more than the labor force participation rate and reflects cyclical fluctuations in the unemployment rate. Fluctuations in the labor force participation rate arise mainly because of discouraged workers.

Source: Economic Report of the President, 1999.

workers. **Discouraged workers** are people who are available and willing to work but have not made specific efforts to find a job within the previous four weeks. These workers often temporarily leave the labor force during a recession and reenter during an expansion and become active job seekers.

The Employment-to-Population Ratio   The number of people of working age who have jobs is an indicator of both the availability of jobs and the degree of match between people's skills and jobs. The **employment-to-population ratio** is the percentage of people of working age who have jobs. That is,

$$\text{Employment-to-population ratio} = \frac{\text{Number of people employed}}{\text{Working-age population}} \times 100.$$

In 1998, employment was 131.5 million and the working-age population was 205.2 million. By using the above equation, you can calculate the employment-to-population ratio. It was 64.1 percent (131.5 million divided by 205.2 million, multiplied by 100).

The employment-to-population ratio (graphed in blue and plotted against the left scale) has increased from 55 percent during the early 1960s to 64 percent in 1998. The increase in the employment-to-population ratio means that the U.S. economy has created jobs at a faster rate than the working-age population has grown. This labor market indicator also fluctuates, and its fluctuations coincide with but are opposite to those in the unemployment rate. It falls during a recession and increases during an expansion.

Why have the labor force participation rate and the employment-to-population ratio increased? The main reason is an increase in the number of women in the labor force. Figure 24.3 shows this increase. Between 1960 and 1998, the female labor force participation rate increased from 38 percent to 60 percent. Shorter work hours, higher productivity, and an increased emphasis on white-collar jobs have expanded the job opportunities and wages available to women. At the same time, technological advances have increased productivity in the home and freed up women's time to take jobs outside the home.

Figure 24.3 also shows another remarkable trend in the U.S. labor force: The labor force participation rate and the employment-to-population ratio for men have *decreased*. Between 1960 and 1998, the male labor force participation rate decreased from

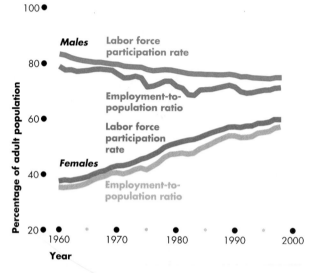

FIGURE 24.3

The Changing Face of the Labor Market

The upward trends in the labor force participation rate and the employment-to-population ratio are accounted for mainly by the increasing participation of women in the labor market. The male labor force participation rate and employment-to-population ratio have decreased.

Source: *Economic Report of the President*, 1999.

83 percent to 75 percent. It has decreased because increasing numbers of men are remaining in school longer and because some are retiring earlier.

Aggregate Hours

The three labor market indicators that we've just examined are useful signs of the health of the economy and directly measure what matters to most people: jobs. But they don't tell us the quantity of labor used to produce GDP, and we cannot use them to calculate the productivity of labor. The productivity of labor is significant because it influences the wages people earn.

The reason why the number of people employed does not measure the quantity of labor employed is that jobs are not all the same. People in part-time jobs might work just a few hours a week. People in full-time jobs work around 35 to 40 hours a week.

And some people regularly work overtime. For example, a 7-11 convenience store might hire six students who work three hours a day each. Another 7-11 store might hire two full-time workers who work nine hours a day each. The number of people employed in these two stores is eight, but the total hours worked by six of the eight is the same as the hours worked by the other two. To determine the total amount of labor used to produce GDP, we measure labor in hours rather than in jobs. **Aggregate hours** are the total number of hours worked by all the people employed, both full time and part time, during a year.

Figure 24.4(a) shows aggregate hours in the U.S. economy from 1960 to 1998. Like the employment-to-population ratio, aggregate hours have an upward trend. But aggregate hours have not grown as quickly as have the number of people employed. Between 1960 and 1998 the number of people employed in the U.S. economy increased by 100 percent. During that same period, aggregate hours increased by only 80 percent. Why the difference? Because average hours per worker decreased.

Figure 24.4(b) shows average hours per worker. After hovering at almost 39 hours a week during the early 1960s, average hours per worker decreased to about 34 hours a week during the 1990s. This shortening of the average workweek has arisen partly because of a decrease in the average hours worked by full-time workers but mainly because the number of part-time jobs has increased faster than the number of full-time jobs.

Fluctuations in aggregate hours and average hours per worker line up with the business cycle. Figure 24.4 highlights the past three recessions, during which aggregate hours decreased and average hours per worker decreased more quickly than trend.

Wage Rates

The **real wage rate** is the quantity of goods and services that an hour's work can buy. It is equal to the money wage rate (dollars per hour) divided by the price level. If we use the GDP deflator to measure the price level, the real wage rate is expressed in 1992 dollars because the GDP deflator is 100 in 1992. The real wage is a significant economic variable because it measures the reward for labor.

What has happened to the real wage rate in the United States? Figure 24.5 answers this question. It shows four measures of the average hourly real wage rate in the U.S. economy between 1960 and 1998.

FIGURE 24.4

Aggregate Hours: 1960–1998

(a) Aggregate hours

(b) Average weekly hours per person

Aggregate hours (part a) measure the total labor used to produce real GDP more accurately than does the number of people employed because an increasing proportion of jobs are part time. Between 1960 and 1998, aggregate hours increased by an average of 1.5 percent a year. Fluctuations in aggregate hours coincide with business cycle fluctuations. Aggregate hours have increased at a slower rate than the number of jobs because the average workweek has shortened (part b).

Source: Economic Report of the President, 1999, and the author's calculations.

FIGURE 24.5
Real Wage Rates: 1960–1998

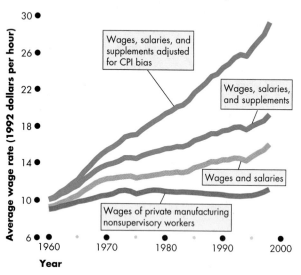

The average hourly real wage rate of private manufacturing nonsupervisory workers peaked in 1978, fell through 1993, then increased again to exceed the 1978 level. Broader measures of the average hourly real wage rate increased. All the official measures show a productivity growth slowdown during the 1970s. An unofficial view is that inflation has been overestimated by 1.1 percent a year and the real wage rate has increased at roughly a constant rate.

Source: *Economic Report of the President,* 1999, and the author's calculations and assumptions.

The first measure of the real wage rate is the Department of Labor's calculation of the average hourly earnings of private manufacturing nonsupervisory workers. This measure increased to a maximum of $11.16 in 1978 (in 1992 dollars) and then followed a fifteen-year downward trend.

The second measure of the real wage rate is calculated by dividing total wages and salaries in the national income accounts by aggregate hours. This measure is broader than the first and includes the incomes of all types of labor, whether their rate of pay is calculated by the hour or not. This broader measure did not follow a downward trend, but its growth rate slowed during the mid-1970s and remained low through the early 1980s. It then speeded up during the late 1980s and 1990s.

An increasing proportion of labor compensation takes the form of fringe benefits such as pension contributions and the payment by employers of health insurance premiums. Figure 24.5 shows a third measure of the hourly real wage rate that reflects this trend. It is *total labor compensation*—wages, salaries, and supplements—divided by aggregate hours. This measure is the most comprehensive one available, and it shows that the real wage rate has increased. But it also shows that no matter how we measure the wage rate, the productivity growth slowdown also slowed real wage rate growth.

The decline in the average wage rate of manufacturing nonsupervisory workers and the slowdown in the growth rate of the broader measures of the average wage rate coincide with the *productivity growth slowdown* that you saw in Chapter 22. This productivity growth slowdown is the main reason for this behavior of average real wage rates. But whether this slowdown actually occurred depends on what actually happened to the price level. The three measures of real wages that we've just described are based on the official measure of inflation. If inflation has been overestimated by the 1.1 percent that the Boskin Commission (see Chapter 23, p. 511) estimates it has, then real wages have grown at a constant rate, as shown by the fourth line in Fig. 24.5.

REVIEW   QUIZ

- What are the trends in the labor force participation rate, the employment-to-population ratio, and the unemployment rate?
- How do the labor force participation rate, the employment-to-population ratio, and the unemployment rate fluctuate over the business cycle?
- Has the female labor force participation rate been similar to or different from the male labor force participation rate?
- How have aggregate hours changed?
- How have average hourly real wage rates changed since 1970?

You've now seen how we measure employment, unemployment, and wage rates. Your next task is to study the anatomy of unemployment and see why it never disappears, even at full employment.

Unemployment and Full Employment

How do people become unemployed, how long do they remain unemployed, and who is at greatest risk to become unemployed? Let's answer these questions by looking at the anatomy of unemployment.

The Anatomy of Unemployment

People become unemployed if they:

1. Lose their jobs and search for another job
2. Leave their jobs and search for another job
3. Enter or reenter the labor force to search for a job

People end a spell of unemployment if they:

1. Are hired or recalled
2. Withdraw from the labor force

People who are laid off, either permanently or temporarily, from their jobs are called **job losers**. Some job losers become unemployed, but some immediately withdraw from the labor force. People who voluntarily quit their jobs are called **job leavers**. Like job losers, some job leavers become unemployed and search for a better job, while others withdraw from the labor force temporarily or permanently retire from work. People who enter or reenter the labor force are called **entrants** and **reentrants**. Entrants are mainly people who have just left school. Some entrants get a job right away and are never unemployed, but many spend time searching for their first job, and during this period, they are unemployed. Reentrants are people who have previously withdrawn from the labor force. Most of these people are formerly discouraged workers. Figure 24.6 shows these labor market flows.

Let's see how much unemployment arises from the three different ways in which people can become unemployed.

The Sources of Unemployment Figure 24.7 shows unemployment by reason for becoming unemployed. Job losers are the biggest source of unemployment. Also, their number fluctuates a great deal. In the recession of 1990–1991, on any given day, more than

FIGURE **24.6**

Labor Market Flows

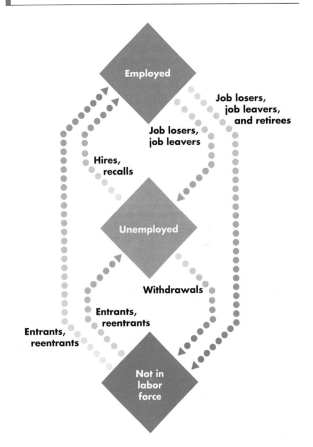

Unemployment results from employed people losing or leaving their jobs (job losers and job leavers) and from people entering the labor force (entrants and reentrants). Unemployment ends because people get hired or recalled or because they withdraw from the labor force.

5 million of the 9.4 million people who were unemployed were job losers. In contrast, in 1998, only 2.8 million of the 6.2 million people who were unemployed were job losers.

Entrants and reentrants also are a large component of the unemployed, and their number fluctuates mildly. On any given day, between 2.5 million and 3 million unemployed people are entrants and reentrants.

Job leavers are the smallest and most stable source of unemployment. On any given day, fewer than 1 million people are unemployed because they

FIGURE 24.7
Unemployment by Reasons

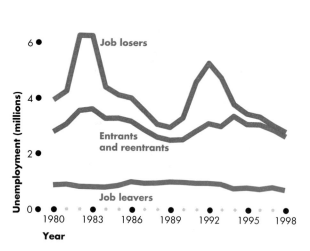

Everyone who is unemployed is either a job loser, a job leaver, or an entrant or reentrant into the labor force. Most of the unemployment that exists results from job loss. The number of job losers fluctuates more closely with the business cycle than do the numbers of job leavers and entrants and reentrants. Entrants and reentrants are the second most commonly unemployed people. Their number fluctuates with the business cycle because of discouraged workers. Job leavers are the least common unemployed people.

Source: Economic Report of the President, 1999.

FIGURE 24.8
Unemployment by Duration

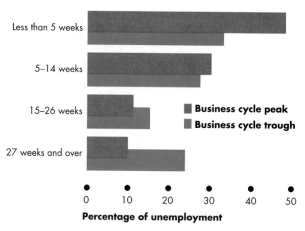

In the business cycle peak of 1989, when the unemployment rate was 5.3 percent, 49 percent of unemployment lasted for less than 5 weeks and 30 percent lasted for 5 to 14 weeks. So 79 percent of unemployment lasted for less than 15 weeks, and 21 percent lasted for 15 weeks or more. In the business cycle trough of 1983, when the unemployment rate was 9.7 percent, 33 percent of unemployment lasted for less than 5 weeks and 27 percent lasted for 5 to 14 weeks. So 60 percent of unemployment lasted for less than 15 weeks, and 40 percent lasted for 15 weeks or more.

Source: Economic Report of the President, 1999.

are job leavers. The number of job leavers is remarkably constant, although to the extent that it fluctuates, it does so in line with the business cycle: A slightly larger number of people leave their jobs in good times than in bad times.

The Duration of Unemployment Some people are unemployed for a week or two, and others are unemployed for periods of a year or more. The longer the spell of unemployment, the greater the personal cost to the unemployed. The average duration of unemployment varies over the business cycle. Figure 24.8 compares the duration of unemployment in a business cycle peak in 1989, when the unemployment rate was low, with that at the business cycle trough of 1983, when the unemployment rate was high. In 1989, when the unemployment rate hit a low of 5.3 percent, almost 50 percent of the unemployed were in that state for less

than 5 weeks and only 21 percent of the unemployed were jobless for longer than 15 weeks. In 1983, when unemployment reached a high of 9.7 percent, only 33 percent of the unemployed found a new job in less than 5 weeks and 40 percent were unemployed for more than 15 weeks. At both low and high unemployment rates, about 30 percent of the unemployed take between 5 weeks and 14 weeks to find a job.

The Demographics of Unemployment Figure 24.9 shows unemployment for different demographic groups. The figure shows that high unemployment rates occur among young workers and also among blacks. In the business cycle trough in 1992, the unemployment rate of black teenagers was almost 40 percent. Even in 1998, when the unemployment rate was 4.5 percent, the black teenage rate was 30 percent. The unemployment rates for white teenagers are less than half those of black teenagers. The racial

FIGURE **24.9**

Unemployment by Demographic Group

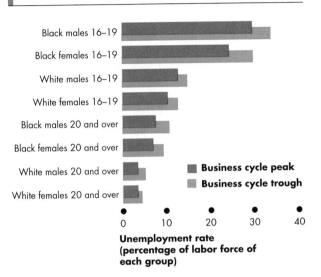

Black teenagers experience unemployment rates that average three times those of white teenagers, and the unemployment rates of teenagers are much higher than those of people aged 20 years and over. Even in a business cycle trough, when unemployment is at its highest rate, only 6 percent of whites aged 20 years and over are unemployed.

Source: Economic Report of the President, 1999.

differences also exist for workers aged 20 years and over. The highest unemployment rates that whites 20 years and over experience are less than the lowest rates experienced by the other groups.

Why are unemployment rates of teenagers so high? There are three reasons. First, young people are still in the process of discovering what they are good at and trying different lines of work. So they leave their jobs more frequently than older workers do. Second, firms sometimes hire teenagers on a short-term or trial basis. So the rate of job loss is higher for teenagers than for other people. Third, most teenagers are not in the labor force but are in school. This fact means that the percentage of the teenage population that is unemployed is much lower than the percentage of the teenage labor force that is unemployed. In 1998, for example, 1.2 million teenagers were unemployed and 7.5 million were employed. So the teenage unemployment rate (all races) was 14 percent. But 11.6 million teenagers were in school.

Teenage unemployment as a percentage of the teenage labor force plus the school population was 6 percent. That is, 14 percent of the teenage labor force or 6 percent of the teenage population is unemployed.

Types of Unemployment

Unemployment is classified into three types that are based on its causes. They are:

■ Frictional
■ Structural
■ Cyclical

Frictional Unemployment **Frictional unemployment** is the unemployment that arises from normal labor turnover—from people entering and leaving the labor force and from the ongoing creation and destruction of jobs. Frictional unemployment is a permanent and healthy phenomenon in a dynamic, growing economy.

The unending flow of people into and out of the labor force and the processes of job creation and job destruction create the need for people to search for jobs and for businesses to search for workers. Always there are businesses with unfilled jobs and people seeking jobs. Look in your local newspaper, and you will see that there are always some jobs being advertised. Businesses don't usually hire the first person who applies for a job, and unemployed people don't usually take the first job that comes their way. Instead, both firms and workers spend time searching out what they believe will be the best match available. By this process of search, people can match their own skills and interests with the available jobs and find a satisfying job and income. While these unemployed people are searching, they are frictionally unemployed.

The amount of frictional unemployment depends on the rate at which people enter and reenter the labor force and on the rate at which jobs are created and destroyed. During the 1970s, the amount of frictional unemployment increased as a consequence of the postwar baby boom that began during the late 1940s. By the late 1970s, the baby boom had created a bulge in the number of people leaving school. As these people entered the labor force, the amount of frictional unemployment increased.

The amount of frictional unemployment is influenced by unemployment benefits. The greater the number of unemployed people covered by unemployment insurance and the more generous the unemployment insurance and the more generous the unemployment benefit they receive, the longer is the average time taken in job search and the greater is the amount of frictional unemployment. In the United States in 1998, 36 percent of the unemployed received unemployment benefit. And the average benefit check was $167 a week. Canada and Western Europe have more generous benefits than those in the United States and have higher unemployment rates.

Structural Unemployment **Structural unemployment** is the unemployment that arises when changes in technology or international competition change the skills needed to perform jobs or change the locations of jobs. Structural unemployment usually lasts longer than frictional unemployment because workers must usually retrain and possibly relocate to find a job. For example, when a steel plant in Gary, Indiana, is automated, some jobs in that city are destroyed. Meanwhile, new jobs for security guards, life-insurance salespeople, and retail clerks are created in Chicago, Indianapolis, and other cities. The unemployed former steelworkers remain unemployed for several months until they move, retrain, and get one of these jobs. Structural unemployment is painful, especially for older workers for whom the best available option might be to retire early but with a lower income than they had expected.

At some times the amount of structural unemployment is modest. At other times it is large, and at such times, structural unemployment can become a serious long-term problem. It was especially large during the late 1970s and early 1980s. During those years, oil price hikes and an increasingly competitive international environment destroyed jobs in traditional U.S. industries, such as auto and steel, and created jobs in new industries, such as electronics and bioengineering, as well as in banking and insurance. Structural unemployment was also present during the early 1990s as many businesses and governments "downsized."

Cyclical Unemployment **Cyclical unemployment** is the fluctuating unemployment over the business cycle. Cyclical unemployment increases during a recession and decreases during an expansion. An autoworker who is laid off because the economy is in a recession and who gets rehired some months later when the expansion begins has experienced cyclical unemployment.

Full Employment

There is always *some* unemployment—someone looking for a job or laid off and waiting to be recalled. So what do we mean by *full employment*? **Full employment** occurs when there is no cyclical unemployment or, equivalently, when all the unemployment is frictional and structural. The divergence of the unemployment rate from full employment is cyclical unemployment. The unemployment rate at full employment is called the **natural rate of unemployment**.

There can be a lot of unemployment at full employment, and the term "full employment" is an example of a technical economic term that does not correspond with everyday language. The term "natural rate of unemployment" is another example of a technical economic term that does not correspond with everyday language. For most people—especially for unemployed workers—there is nothing *natural* about unemployment.

So, why are do economists call a situation with a lot of unemployment one of full employment? And why is the unemployment at full employment called "natural"?

The reason is that the complex mechanism that we call the U.S. economy undergoes constant changes in its players, structure, and direction. This process of change creates frictions and dislocations that are unavoidable. And they create unemployment.

In 1998, the U.S. economy employed 131 million people. More than 2.5 million retired during that year and more than 3 million new workers entered the labor force. All these people worked in some 20 million businesses, some of which downsized or failed and others of which expanded. All these people and businesses produced goods and services valued at more than $8 trillion.

Figure 24.10 illustrates full employment and cyclical unemployment in the United States between 1980 and 1998. Part (a) shows the fluctuations of real GDP around potential GDP. Part (b) shows fluctuations in the unemployment rate around the natural rate. Notice that cyclical unemployment is positive at a business cycle trough but is *negative* at a business cycle peak. At the cycle peak, total unemployment is less than the sum of frictional and structural unemployment.

In Fig. 24.10 the unemployment rate fluctuates around the natural rate of unemployment (part b) as real GDP fluctuates around potential GDP (part a).

FIGURE 24.10
Unemployment and Real GDP

(a) Real GDP

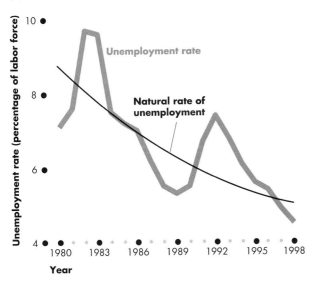

(b)

As real GDP fluctuates around potential GDP (part a), the unemployment rate fluctuates around the natural rate of unemployment (part b). In the deep recession of 1982, unemployment reached almost 10 percent. In the milder recession of 1990–1991, the unemployment rate peaked at less than 8 percent. The natural rate of unemployment decreased during the 1980s and 1990s.

Source: Economic Report of the President, 1999, and the author's assumptions.

When there is full employment and the rate equals the natural rate of unemployment, real GDP equals potential GDP. When the unemployment rate is less than the natural rate of unemployment, real GDP is greater than potential GDP. And when the unemployment rate is greater than the natural rate of unemployment, real GDP is less than potential GDP.

There is not much controversy about the existence of a natural rate of unemployment. Nor is there much controversy that it changes. The natural rate of unemployment arises from the existence of frictional and structural unemployment, and it fluctuates because the frictions and the amount of structural change fluctuate. But economists don't agree about the size of the natural rate of unemployment and the extent to which it fluctuates. Some economists believe that the natural rate of unemployment fluctuates frequently and that at times of rapid demographic and technological change, its rate can be high. Others think that it changes slowly.

In Fig. 24.10(b), the natural rate of unemployment is 8.5 percent in 1980 and it falls steadily through the 1980s and 1990s to less than 5 percent by 1999. This estimate of the natural rate of unemployment in the United States is one that many, but not all economists would accept.

R E V I E W   Q U I Z

- What are the categories of people who become unemployed?
- Can you define *frictional* unemployment, *structural* unemployment, and *cyclical* unemployment and provide an example of each type of unemployment?
- What is the *natural rate of unemployment*?

◆ You now know how we measure the key macroeconomic variables—real GDP, the price level, employment, and unemployment. And you understand the link between employment and real GDP. *Reading Between the Lines* on pp. 528–529, looks at the U.S. labor market today.

Your next task is to study the forces that determine real GDP and the price level (and employment and unemployment). You'll begin this task by learning about the *aggregate supply–aggregate demand model.* This aggregate model serves as a backdrop against which to place your further study of the forces that determine economic growth, unemployment, and inflation.

Technological Change and Jobs

THE WASHINGTON POST, DECEMBER 5, 1998

Jobless Rate Falls Despite Layoff Plans

John M. Berry

The nation's unemployment rate fell to 4.4 percent last month, as stronger-than-expected hiring by builders, retailers, restaurants and other service providers more than offset layoffs by manufacturers, the government reported yesterday.

The gain of 267,000 payroll jobs in November, which was much greater than many analysts had anticipated, showed that the nation's labor markets remained strong despite the recent flurry of corporate layoff announcements. ...

"The U.S. growth story remains a tale of two economies, with the manufacturing sector shedding 47,000 jobs in November, purchasing agents reporting the weakest factory conditions since February 1996 and (new factory) orders dropping in October," said Bill Dudley, chief economist at Goldman Sachs & Co. in New York.

More than compensating for those job losses were a jump of 55,000 jobs at firms providing business services, including temporary help, and of 47,000 in construction.

Unusually strong holiday hiring boosted retail trade employment by 65,000 jobs, the Labor Department said. ...

Bill Parks, a special assistant to the commissioner of labor statistics, ... (says) ... that each month's labor market report is "a snapshot of the net effects of the movements of millions of people into and out of" employment, unemployment and the labor force itself. ...

For example, the department's figures for 1997 show that about 13.5 million people make such movements in a typical month. That's almost one of every 10 people in the labor force—which consists of those who are working or seeking a job.

Last month's "snapshot" showed that the civilian labor force increased by 277,000, to 138.3 million. Compared with October, when the unemployment rate was 4.6 percent, an additional 477,000 people got jobs last month, while 6.1 million were unemployed, a drop of 200,000. But those were the "net" changes resulting from those millions of decisions.

Essence of the Story

■ In November 1998, the civilian labor force increased by 277,000 to 138.3 million.

■ An additional 477,000 people got jobs, but employment increased by only 267,000. (210,000 people who had jobs became unemployed.)

■ Unemployment decreased by 200,000 to 6.1 million, an unemployment rate of 4.4 percent.

■ The Department of Labor estimates that one of every 10 people in the labor force changes their labor market status in a typical month.

■ In November 1998, the number of jobs in manufacturing decreased by 47,000, but the number of jobs in business services increased by 55,000, in construction by 47,000, and in retail trade by 65,000.

Economic Analysis

■ The labor market is in a constant state of churning. Millions of decisions each month result in small *net* changes in the labor force, employment, and unemployment.

■ Figure 1 shows the rate of job destruction in U.S. manufacturing industries between 1980 and 1993. These data are compiled infrequently and are not yet available beyond 1993. But the available data tell us a lot.

■ The rate of job destruction fluctuates with the business cycle. But on the average, about 1 percent of jobs get destroyed each month.

■ Much of the job destruction arises because technological advances enable companies to produce more output with fewer workers. This process has been going on almost uninterrupted since the Industrial Revolution began around 1760.

■ At the normal rate of job destruction, more than a million people lose their jobs each month.

■ When a large employer cuts jobs, the news media pays attention. But when a small employer cuts jobs or creates jobs, the media does not usually notice.

■ Because most of the newly created jobs are in small businesses, they go unreported. Consequently, the media often creates the impression that jobs are only being destroyed. This news article does not give this wrong impression. It puts job losses and gains in their proper perspective.

■ Job cuts are serious for the people whom they affect. But they would be even more serious if jobs were not being created in even larger numbers.

■ Figure 1 also shows the rate of job creation and the net change in the number of jobs in manufacturing. In most years, more jobs have been destroyed than created in the manufacturing industries. But (not shown in the figure) more jobs have been created in other sectors such as business services, construction, and retail trade, than the number lost in manufacturing.

■ Technological change creates more jobs than it destroys. It increases the productivity of labor and leads to an increase in the demand for labor.

■ Figure 2 shows the total amount of job creation and job destruction in manufacturing and the relationship between this number and the

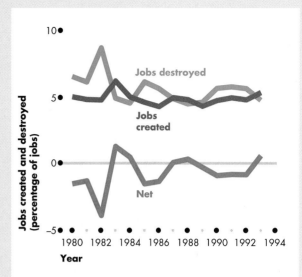

Figure 1 Job creation and destruction rates

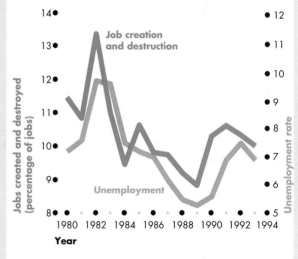

Figure 2 Job creation and destruction and unemployment

Source: Steven J. Davis, John Haltiwanger, and Scott Schuh, *Job Creation and Job Destruction*, Cambridge: MIT Press 1996. Professor Davis kindly updated to 1993.

unemployment rate. It shows that the total amount of job creation and job destruction fluctuates in line with fluctuations in the unemployment rate.

You're The Voter

■ What policy actions, if any, can the government take to protect people from job losses?

■ List all the policy actions you can think of and attach to each policy its pros and cons.

529

SUMMARY

KEY POINTS

Employment and Wages (pp. 518–522)

- The labor force participation rate and the employment-to-population ratio have an upward trend and fluctuate with the business cycle.
- The labor force participation rate has increased for females and decreased for males.
- Aggregate hours have an upward trend, and they fluctuate with the business cycle.
- Based on the CPI, real hourly wage rates in manufacturing fell after 1973. Broader real wage measures did not fall, but their growth rates slowed.

Unemployment and Full Employment (pp. 523–527)

- People are constantly entering and leaving the state of unemployment.
- The duration of unemployment fluctuates over the business cycle. But the demographic patterns of unemployment are constant.
- Unemployment can be frictional, structural, and cyclical.
- When all the unemployment is frictional and structural, unemployment is at its natural rate and there is *full employment*. The natural rate of unemployment fluctuates because of fluctuations in frictional and structural unemployment.

KEY FIGURES

KEY TERMS

PROBLEMS

*1. The Bureau of Labor Statistics reported the following data for December 1997:
Labor force: 137,169,000
Employment: 130,777,000
Working-age population: 204,020,000
Calculate for that month the
a. Unemployment rate
b. Labor force participation rate
c. Employment-to-population ratio

2. The Bureau of Labor Statistics reported the following data for December 1998:
Labor force: 138,547,000
Employment: 132,526,000
Working-age population: 206,270,000
Calculate for that month the
a. Unemployment rate
b. Labor force participation rate
c. Employment-to-population ratio

*3. During 1997, the working-age population increased by 2,287,000, employment increased by 2,878,000, and the labor force increased by 2,109,000. Use these numbers and the data in problem 1 to calculate the change in unemployment and the change in the number of discouraged workers during 1997.

4. During 1998, the working-age population increased by 2,172,000 employment increased by 1,888,000, and the labor force increased by 1,461,000. Use these numbers and the data in problem 2 to calculate the change in unemployment and the change in the number of discouraged workers during 1998.

*5. In August 1994, the unemployment rate was 10.1 percent. In August 1995, the unemployment rate was 9.6 percent. Use this information to predict what happened between August 1994 and August 1995 to the numbers of
a. Job losers and job leavers
b. Labor force entrants and re-entrants

6. In January 1998, the unemployment rate was 4.6 percent. In January 1999, the unemployment rate was 4.3 percent. Use these numbers to predict what happened in 1998 to the numbers of
a. Job losers and job leavers
b. Labor force entrants and re-entrants

*7. The figure shows the numbers of working-age people who were employed, unemployed, and not in the labor force in Labecon in July 1997 and the labor market flows during August 1997.

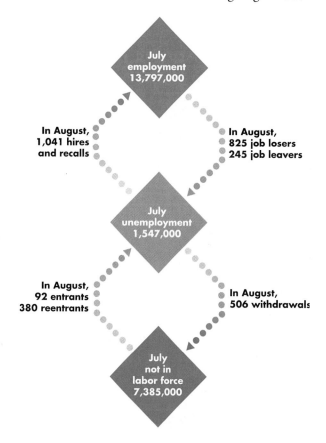

Calculate for July 1997:
a. The labor force
b. The unemployment rate
c. The working-age population
d. The employment-to-population ratio

Calculate for the end of August 1997:
e. The number of people unemployed
f. The number of people employed
g. The labor force
h. The unemployment rate
i. The employment-to-population ratio if the labor force participation rate is 65.5 percent

8. The figure shows the numbers of working-age people who were employed, unemployed, and not in the labor force in Ecolab in July 1998 and the labor market flows during August 1998.

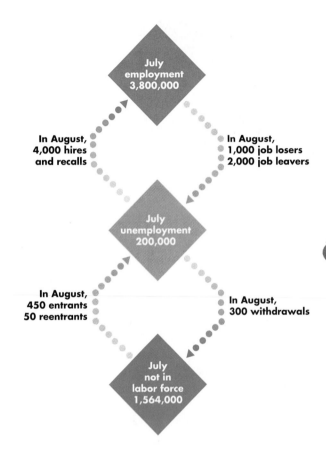

Calculate for July 1998:
a. The labor force
b. The unemployment rate
c. The working-age population
d. The employment-to-population ratio

Calculate for the end of August 1998:
e. The number of people unemployed
f. The number of people employed
g. The labor force
h. The unemployment rate
i. The employment-to-population ratio if the labor force participation rate is 60 percent

*9. Describe the main features of the labor market at the peak of business cycle.

10. Describe the main features of the labor market at the trough of business cycle.

CRITICAL THINKING

1. Study *Reading Between the Lines* on pp. 528–529 and then answer the following questions:
   a. What types of jobs have been destroyed and created in the United States in the past 15 years?
   b. What types of businesses create jobs and what types of business destroy jobs?
   c. Do all the jobs created get reported in the newspapers? Explain why or why not.
   d. Do all the jobs destroyed get reported in the newspapers? Explain why or why not.
   e. What information would you need to determine whether the job losses reported will create frictional, structural, or cyclical unemployment?
   f. Which fluctuates more: the rate of job creation or the rate of job destruction?

2. Use the link on the Parkin Web site to visit the Bureau of Labor Statistics and find labor market data for your own state.
   a. What have been the trends in employment, unemployment, and labor force participation in your own state during the past two years?
   b. On the basis of what you know about your own region, how would you set about explaining these trends?
   c. Try to identify the industries that have expanded most and those that have shrunk.
   d. What are the problems in your state labor market that you think need state government action to resolve?
   e. What actions do you think your state government must take to resolve them? Use the demand and supply model of the labor market to answer this question and to make predictions about the effects of the actions you prescribe.
   f. Compare the labor market performance of your own state with that of the nation as a whole.
   g. If your state is performing better than the national average, to what do you attribute the success? If your state is performing worse than the national average, to what do you attribute its problems? What federal actions are needed in your state labor market?

Chapter 25

Aggregate Supply and Aggregate Demand

During the past 30 years, U.S. real GDP has more than doubled. In fact, a doubling of real GDP every 30 years has been routine. What forces drive our economy to grow? ◆ At the same time that real GDP has grown, we've experienced first a rise and then a fall in inflation. In 1967, U.S. prices were rising at a rate of 3 percent a year. In 1981, the peak inflation year, prices increased by 10 percent. Today, the inflation rate stands at less than 2 percent a year. The result of all this inflation is that you need $400 today to buy what $100 bought in 1967. What causes inflation? And why did its rate explode during the 1970s? ◆ Our economy does not expand at a constant pace. Instead, it ebbs and flows over the business cycle. For example, we had a recession during 1990 and early 1991. For half a year, real GDP decreased. Then began a long period of expansion that was still in progress in 1999. What makes real GDP grow at an uneven pace? Why does growth sometimes speed up, and why does real GDP sometimes shrink? ◆ When economic growth speeds up in Asia and Europe, we benefit because we sell more goods and services abroad. And when economic growth slows in the rest of the world, we suffer because the demand for our goods and services decreases. But some influences on our economy are home made and stem from the actions of the government and the Federal Reserve Board (the Fed) in Washington. How do events in the rest of the world and the policy actions of the government and the Fed affect production and prices?

◆ To answer these questions, we need a *model* of real GDP and the price level. Our main task in this chapter is to study such a model: the *aggregate supply—aggregate demand model*. Our second task is to use the aggregate supply—aggregate demand (or *AS-AD*) model to answer the questions we've just posed. You'll discover that this model enables us to understand the forces that make our economy expand, that bring inflation, and that cause business cycle fluctuations. You will also find that this model is a useful tool with which to organize your entire study of macroeconomics.

What Makes Our Garden Grow?

After studying this chapter, you will be able to:

- Explain what determines aggregate supply

- Explain what determines aggregate demand

- Explain macroeconomic equilibrium

- Explain the effects of changes in aggregate supply and aggregate demand on economic growth, inflation, and business cycles

- Explain U.S. economic growth, inflation, and business cycles by using the *AS-AD* model.

Aggregate Supply

THE AGGREGATE SUPPLY-AGGREGATE DEMAND model enables us to understand three features of macroeconomic performance:

- Growth of potential GDP
- Inflation
- Business cycle fluctuations

The model uses the concepts of *aggregate* supply and *aggregate* demand to determine *real GDP* and the *price level* (the *GDP deflator*). We begin by looking at the limits to production that influence aggregate supply.

Aggregate Supply Fundamentals

The *quantity of real GDP supplied* (Y) depends on:

- The quantity of labor (N)
- The quantity of capital (K)
- The state of technology (T)

The influence of these three factors on the quantity of real GDP supplied are described by the **aggregate production function**, which is written as the equation:

$$Y = F(N, K, T).$$

In words, the quantity of real GDP supplied is determined by (is a function F of) the quantities of labor and capital and of the state of technology. The larger are N, K, or T, the greater is Y.

At any given time, the quantity of capital and the state of technology are fixed. They depend on decisions that were made in the past. The population is also fixed. But the quantity of labor is not fixed. It depends on decisions made by people and firms about the supply of and demand for labor.

The labor market can be in any one of three states: at full employment, above full employment, or below full employment.

Even at full employment, there are always some people looking for jobs and some firms looking for people to hire. The reason is that there is a constant churning of the labor market. Every day, some jobs are destroyed as businesses reorganize or fail. Some jobs are created as new businesses start up or existing ones expand. Some workers decide, for any of a thousand personal reasons, to quit their jobs. And other people decide to start looking for a job. This constant churning in the labor market prevents unemployment from ever disappearing. The unemployment rate at full employment is called the **natural rate of unemployment**.

Another way to think about full employment is as a state of the labor market in which the quantity of labor demanded equals the quantity supplied. Firms demand labor only if it is profitable to do so. And the lower the wage rate, which is the cost of labor, the greater is the quantity of labor demanded. People supply labor only if doing so is the most valuable use of their time. And the higher the wage rate, which is the return to labor, the greater is the quantity of labor supplied. The wage rate that makes the quantity of labor demanded equal to the quantity of labor supplied is the equilibrium wage rate. At this wage rate there is full employment. (You can study the labor market at full employment further in Chapter 26 on pp. 570–572).

The quantity of real GDP supplied at full employment is **potential GDP**, which depends on the full-employment quantity of labor, the quantity of capital, and the state of technology. Over the business cycle, employment fluctuates around full employment and real GDP fluctuates around potential GDP.

To study aggregate supply in different states of the labor market, we distinguish two time frames:

- Long-run aggregate supply
- Short-run aggregate supply

Long-Run Aggregate Supply

The economy is constantly bombarded by events that move real GDP away from potential GDP and, equivalently, that move the unemployment rate away from full employment. Following such an event, forces operate to take real GDP back toward potential GDP and restore full employment. The **macroeconomic long run** is a time frame that is sufficiently long for these forces to have done their work so that real GDP equals potential GDP and full employment prevails.

The **long-run aggregate supply curve** is the relationship between the quantity of real GDP supplied and the price level in the long run when real GDP equals potential GDP. Figure 25.1 shows this relationship as vertical line labeled *LAS*. Along the long-run aggregate supply curve, as the price level changes, real GDP remains at potential GDP, which in Fig. 25.1 is $7 trillion. The long-run aggregate

FIGURE 25.1
Long-Run Aggregate Supply

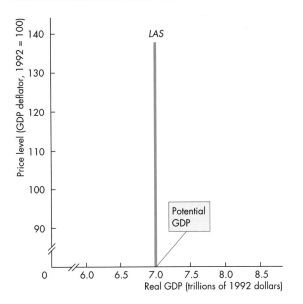

The long-run aggregate supply (*LAS*) curve shows the relation-ship between potential GDP and the price level. Potential GDP is independent of the price level, so the *LAS* curve is vertical at potential GDP.

supply curve is always vertical and is located at poten-tial GDP.

The long-run aggregate supply curve is vertical because potential GDP is independent of the price level. The reason for this independence is that a move-ment along the *LAS* curve is accompanied by a change in *two* sets of prices: the prices of goods and services—the price level—and the prices of productive resources. A 10 percent increase in the prices of goods and ser-vices is matched by a 10 percent increase in wage rates and other resource prices. That is, the price level, wage rate, and other resource prices all change by the same percentage, and *relative prices* and the *real wage rate* remain constant. When the price level changes but relative prices and the real wage rate remain constant, real GDP also remains constant.

Production at a Pepsi Plant   You can see why real GDP remains constant when all prices change by the same percentage by thinking about production

decisions at a Pepsi bottling plant. The plant is pro-ducing the quantity of Pepsi that maximizes profit. The plant can increase production, but only by incur-ring a higher *marginal cost* (see Chapter 3, pp. 40–41). So the firm has no incentive to change production.

Short-Run Aggregate Supply

The **macroeconomic short run** is a period during which real GDP has fallen below or risen above potential GDP. At the same time, the unemployment rate has risen above or fallen below the natural rate.

The **short-run aggregate supply curve** is the relationship between the quantity of real GDP supplied and the price level in the short run when the money wage rate, other resource prices, and potential GDP remain constant. Figure 25.2 shows a short-run aggregate supply curve as the upward-sloping curve labeled *SAS*. This curve is based on the short-run aggregate supply schedule, and each point on the aggregate supply curve corresponds to a row of the aggregate supply schedule. For example, point *a* on the short-run aggregate supply curve and row *a* of the schedule tell us that if the price level is 100, the quantity of real GDP supplied is $6 trillion.

At point *c*, the price level is 110 and the quantity of real GDP supplied is $7 trillion, which equals potential GDP. If the price level is higher than 110, real GDP exceeds potential GDP; if the price level is below 110, real GDP is less than potential GDP.

Back at the Pepsi Plant   You can see why the short-run aggregate supply curve slopes upward by return-ing to the Pepsi bottling plant. The plant produces the quantity that maximizes profit. If the price of Pepsi rises and wage rates and other costs don't change, the *relative price* of Pepsi rises and the firm has an incentive to increase its production. The higher relative price of Pepsi covers the higher mar-ginal cost of producing more Pepsi, so the firm increases production.

Similarly, if the price of Pepsi falls and wage rates and other costs don't change, the lower relative price is not sufficient to cover the marginal cost of Pepsi, so the firm decreases production.

Again, what's true for Pepsi bottlers is true for the producers of all goods and services. So when the price level rises and the money wage rate and other resource prices remain constant, the quantity of real GDP supplied increases.

FIGURE 25.2

Short-Run Aggregate Supply

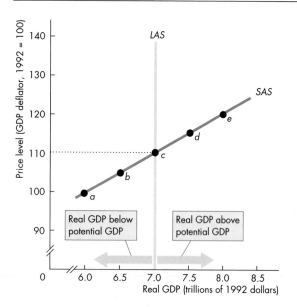

	Price Level (GDP deflator)	Real GDP (trillions of 1992 dollars)
a	100	6.0
b	105	6.5
c	110	7.0
d	115	7.5
e	120	8.0

The short-run aggregate supply (SAS) curve shows the relationship between the quantity of real GDP supplied and the price level when the money wage rate, other resource prices, and potential GDP are constant. The short-run aggregate supply curve SAS is based on the schedule in the table. The short-run aggregate supply curve is upward-sloping because firms' costs increase as the rate of output increases, so a higher price is needed, relative to the prices of productive resources, and bring forth an increase in the quantity produced. On the SAS curve, when the price level is 110, real GDP equals potential GDP. If the price level is greater than 110, real GDP exceeds potential GDP; if the price level is below 110, real GDP is less than potential GDP.

Movements Along the *LAS* and *SAS* Curves

Figure 25.3 summarizes what you've just learned about the *LAS* and *SAS* curves. When the price level, the money wage rate, and other resource prices rise by the same percentage, relative prices remain constant and real GDP remains at potential GDP. There is a *movement along* the *LAS* curve.

When the price level rises but the money wage rate and other resource prices remain constant, the quantity of real GDP supplied increases and there is a *movement along* the *SAS* curve.

Let's next study the influences that bring changes in aggregate supply.

FIGURE 25.3

Movements Along the Aggregate Supply Curves

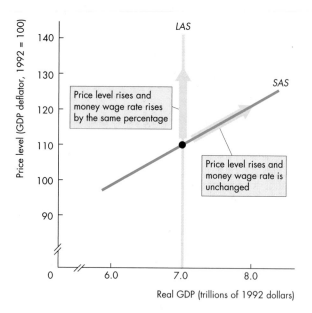

A rise in the price level with no change in the money wage rate and other resource prices brings an increase in the quantity of real GDP supplied and a movement along the short-run aggregate supply curve. A rise in the price level with equal percentage rises in the money wage rate and other resource prices keeps the quantity of real GDP supplied constant and brings a movement along the long-run aggregate supply curve.

Changes in Aggregate Supply

You've just seen that a change in the price level brings a movement along the aggregate supply curves but it does not change aggregate supply. Aggregate supply changes when influences on production plans other than the price level change. Let's begin by looking at factors that change potential GDP.

Changes in Potential GDP When potential GDP changes, both long-run aggregate supply and short-run aggregate supply change. Potential GDP changes for three reasons:

1. Change in the full-employment quantity of labor
2. Change in the quantity of capital
3. Advance in technology

An increase in the full-employment quantity of labor, an increase in the quantity of capital, or an advance in technology increases potential GDP. And an increase in potential GDP changes both long-run aggregate supply and short-run aggregate supply.

Figure 25.4 shows these effects of a change in potential GDP. Initially, the long-run aggregate supply curve is LAS_0 and the short-run aggregate supply curve is SAS_0. If an increase in the quantity of capital or a technological advance increases potential GDP to $8 trillion, long-run aggregate supply increases and the long-run aggregate supply curve shifts rightward to LAS_1. Short-run aggregate supply also increases, and the short-run aggregate supply curve shifts rightward to SAS_1.

Let's look more closely at the influences on potential GDP and the aggregate supply curves.

A Change in the Full-Employment Quantity of Labor A Pepsi bottling plant that employs 100 workers bottles more Pepsi than an otherwise identical plant that employs 10 workers. The same is true for the economy as a whole. The larger the quantity of labor employed, the greater is real GDP.

Over time, potential GDP increases because the labor force increases. But (with constant capital and technology) *potential* GDP increases only if the full-employment quantity of labor increases. Fluctuations in employment over the business cycle bring fluctuations in real GDP. But these changes in real GDP are fluctuations around potential GDP. They are not changes in potential GDP and long-run aggregate supply.

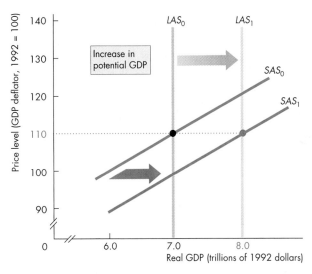

FIGURE 25.4

A Change in Potential GDP

An increase in potential GDP increases both long-run aggregate supply and short-run aggregate supply and shifts both aggregate supply curves rightward from LAS_0 to LAS_1 and from SAS_0 to SAS_1.

A Change in the Quantity of Capital A Pepsi plant with two production lines bottles more Pepsi than an otherwise identical plant that has only one production line. For the economy, the larger the quantity of capital, the more productive is the labor force and the greater is its potential GDP. Potential GDP per person in the capital-rich United States is vastly greater than that in capital-poor China or Russia.

Capital includes *human capital*. One Pepsi plant is managed by an economics major with an MBA and has a labor force with an average of 10 years experience. This plant produces a much larger output than an otherwise identical plant that is managed by someone with no business training or experience and has a young labor force that is new to bottling. The first plant has a greater amount of human capital than the second. For the economy as a whole, the larger the quantity of *human capital*—the skills that people have acquired in school and through on-the-job training—the greater is potential GDP.

An Advance in Technology A Pepsi plant that has pre–computer age machines produces less than one that uses the latest robot technology. Technological change enables firms to produce more from any given amount of inputs. So even with fixed quantities of labor and capital, improvements in technology increase potential GDP.

Technological advances are by far the most important source of increased production over the past two centuries. Because of technological advances, one farmer in the United States today can feed 100 people, and one auto worker can produce almost 14 cars and trucks in a year.

Let's now look at the effects of changes of money wages.

Changes in Money Wages and Other Resource Prices

When the money wage rate or the money prices of other resources such as the price of oil changes, short-run aggregate supply changes but long-run aggregate supply does not change.

Figure 25.5 shows the effect on aggregate supply of an increase in the money wage rate. Initially, the short-run aggregate supply curve is SAS_0. A rise in the money wage rate *decreases* short-run aggregate supply and shifts the short-run aggregate supply curve leftward to SAS_2.

Money wages (and resource prices) affect short-run aggregate supply because they change firms' costs. The higher the money wage rate, the higher are firms' costs and the smaller is the quantity that firms are willing to supply at each price level. So an increase in the money wage rate decreases short-run aggregate supply.

Changes in the money wage rate do not change long-run aggregate supply because on the *LAS* curve, a change in the money wage rate is accompanied by an equal percentage change in the price level. With no change in *relative* prices, firms have no incentive to change production and real GDP remains constant at potential GDP.

In Fig. 25.5, the vertical distance between the original *SAS* curve and the new *SAS* curve is determined by the percentage change in the money wage rate. That is, the percentage increase in the price level between point *a* and point *b* equals the percentage increase in the money wage rate.

Because potential GDP does not change when the money wage rate changes, long-run aggregate supply does not change. The long-run aggregate supply curve remains at *LAS*.

FIGURE 25.5

A Change in the Money Wage Rate

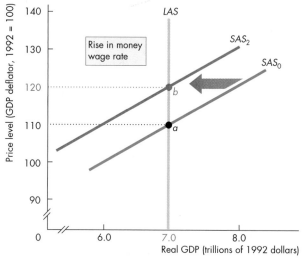

A rise in the money wage rate decreases short-run aggregate supply and shifts the short-run aggregate supply curve leftward from SAS_0 to SAS_2. A rise in the money wage rate does not change potential GDP, so the long-run aggregate supply curve does not shift.

REVIEW QUIZ

- If the price level rises and if the money wage rate also rises by the same percentage, what happens to the quantity of real GDP supplied? Along which aggregate supply curve does the economy move?

- If the price level rises and the money wage rate remains constant, what happens to the quantity of real GDP supplied? Along which aggregate supply curve does the economy move?

- If potential GDP increases, what happens to aggregate supply? Is there a shift of or a movement along the *LAS* curve and the *SAS* curve?

- If the money wage rate rises and potential GDP remains the same, what happens to aggregate supply? Is there a shift of or a movement along the *LAS* curve and the *SAS* curve?

Aggregate Demand

THE QUANTITY OF REAL GDP DEMANDED IS THE sum of the real consumption expenditure (C), investment (I), government purchases (G), and exports (X) minus imports (M). That is,

$$Y = C + I + G + X - M.$$

The *quantity of real GDP demanded* is the total amount of final goods and services produced in the United States that people, businesses, governments, and foreigners plan to buy. What determines these buying plans?

Buying plans depend on many factors. Some of the main ones are:

- The price level
- Expectations
- Fiscal policy and monetary policy
- The world economy

We first focus on the relationship between the quantity of real GDP demanded and the price level. To study this relationship, we hold constant all other influences on buying plans. We then ask: How does the quantity of real GDP demanded vary as the price level varies?

The Aggregate Demand Curve

Other things remaining the same, the higher the price level, the smaller is the quantity of real GDP demanded. This relationship between the quantity of real GDP demanded and the price level is called **aggregate demand**. Aggregate demand is described by an *aggregate demand schedule* and an *aggregate demand curve*.

Figure 25.6 shows an aggregate demand curve (*AD*) and an aggregate demand schedule. Each point on the *AD* curve corresponds to a row of the schedule. For example, point c' on the *AD* curve and row c' of the schedule tell us that if the price level is 110, the quantity of real GDP demanded is $7 trillion.

The aggregate demand curve slopes downward for two reasons:

- Wealth effect
- Substitution effects

FIGURE 25.6

Aggregate Demand

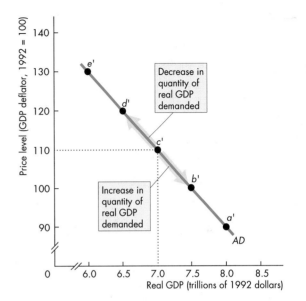

	Price Level (GDP deflator)	Real GDP (trillions of 1992 dollars)
a'	90	8.0
b'	100	7.5
c'	110	7.0
d'	120	6.5
e'	130	6.0

The aggregate demand curve (*AD*) shows the relationship between the quantity of real GDP demanded and the price level. The aggregate demand curve is based on the schedule in the table. Each point a' through e' on the curve corresponds to the row in the table identified by the same letter. Thus when the price level is 110, the quantity of real GDP demanded is $7.0 trillion, shown by point c' in the figure.

Wealth Effect When the price level rises but other things remain the same, *real* wealth decreases. Real wealth is the amount of money in the bank, bonds, stocks, and other assets that people own, measured not in dollars but in terms of the goods and services that this money, bonds, and stock will buy.

People save and hold money, bonds, and stocks for many reasons. One reason is to build up funds for college expenses. Another reason is to build up enough funds to meet possible medical or other big bills. But the biggest reason is to build up enough funds to provide a retirement income.

If the price level rises, real wealth decreases. People then try to restore their wealth. To do so, they must increase saving and, equivalently, decrease consumption. Such a decrease in consumption is a decrease in aggregate demand.

Maria's Wealth Effect   You can see how the wealth effect works by thinking about Maria's buying plans. Maria lives in Moscow, Russia. She has worked hard all summer and saved 20,000 rubles (the ruble is the currency of Russia), which she plans to spend attending graduate school when she's finished her economics degree. So Maria's wealth is 20,000 rubles. Maria has a part-time job, and her income from this job pays her current expenses. The price level in Russia rises by 100 percent, and now Maria needs 40,000 rubles to buy what 20,000 once bought. To try to make up some of the fall in value of her savings, Maria saves even more and cuts her current spending to the bare minimum.

Substitution Effects   When the price level rises and other things remain the same, interest rates rise. But the basic reason for the rise in the interest rate is easy to see. A rise in the price level decreases the real value of the money in people's pockets and bank accounts. With a smaller amount of real money around, banks and other lenders can get a higher interest rate on loans. But faced with higher interest rates, people and businesses delay plans to buy new capital and consumer durable goods and cut back on spending.

This substitution effect involves substituting goods in the future for goods in the present and is called an *intertemporal* substitution effect—a substitution across time. Saving increases to increase future consumption.

To see this intertemporal substitution effect more clearly, think about your own plan to buy a new computer. At an interest rate of 5 percent a year, you might borrow $2,000 and buy the new machine you've been researching. But at an interest rate of 10 percent a year, you might decide the payments would be too high. You don't abandon your plan to buy the computer, but you decide to delay your purchase.

A second substitution effect works through international prices. When the U.S. price level rises and other things remain the same, some of those other things are the prices in other countries. So a rise in the U.S. price level makes U.S.-made goods and services more expensive relative to foreign-made goods and services. This change in relative prices encourages people to spend less on U.S.-made items and more on foreign-made items. For example, if the U.S. price level rises relative to the Canadian price level, Canadians buy fewer U.S.-made cars (U.S. exports decrease) and Americans buy more Canadian-made cars (U.S. imports increase). U.S. real GDP decreases.

Maria's Substitution Effects   In Moscow, Russia, Maria makes some substitutions. She was planning on trading in her old motor scooter and getting a new one. But with a higher price level, and faced with higher interest rates, she decides to make her old scooter last one more year. Also, with the prices of Russian goods sharply increasing, Maria substitutes a low cost dress made in Malaysia for the Russian-made dress she had originally planned to buy.

Changes in the Quantity of Real GDP Demanded
When the price level changes and other things remain the same, the quantity of real GDP demanded changes. Such a change is shown by a movement along the aggregate demand curve. The arrows in Fig. 25.6 illustrate changes in the quantity of real GDP demanded.

We've now seen how the quantity of real GDP demanded changes when the price level changes. How do other influences on buying plans affect aggregate demand?

Changes in Aggregate Demand

A change in any factor that influences buying plans other than the price level brings a change in aggregate demand. The main factors are:

- Expectations
- Fiscal policy and monetary policy
- The world economy

Expectations   Expectations about future incomes, inflation, and profits influence buying plans today. An increase in expected future income increases the amount of consumption goods (especially big-ticket items such as cars) that people plan to buy today and increases aggregate demand.

An increase in the expected future inflation rate increases aggregate demand because people decide to buy more goods and services at today's relatively lower prices. An increase in expected future profit increases the investment that firms plan to undertake today and increases aggregate demand.

Fiscal Policy and Monetary Policy   The government's attempt to influence the economy by setting and changing taxes, transfer payments, and government purchases is called **fiscal policy**. A decrease in taxes or an increase in transfer payments—unemployment benefits, social security benefits, and welfare payments—with no change in government purchases increases aggregate demand. Both of these influences operate by increasing households' *disposable* income. **Disposable income** is aggregate income minus taxes plus transfer payments. The greater the disposable income, the greater is the quantity of consumption goods and services that households plan to buy and the greater is aggregate demand.

Government purchases of goods and services are one component of aggregate demand. So if taxes and transfer payments don't change but the government plans to buy more spy satellites and highways, aggregate demand increases.

Monetary policy consists of changes in interest rates and in the quantity of money in the economy. The quantity of money is determined by the Fed and by the banks (in a process described in Chapters 31 and 32). An increase in the quantity of money in the economy increases aggregate demand. To see why money affects aggregate demand, imagine that the Fed borrows the army's helicopters, loads them with millions of new $10 bills, and sprinkles them like confetti across the nation. People gather the newly available money and plan to spend some of it. So the quantity of goods and services demanded increases. But people don't plan to spend all the new money. They plan to save some of it and lend it to others through the banks. Interest rates fall, and with lower interest rates, people plan to buy more consumer durables and firms plan to increase their investment.

The World Economy   Two main world economy influences on aggregate demand are the foreign exchange rate and foreign income. The *foreign exchange rate* is the amount of a foreign currency that you can buy with a U.S. dollar. Other things remaining the same, a rise in the foreign exchange

FIGURE 25.7

Changes in Aggregate Demand

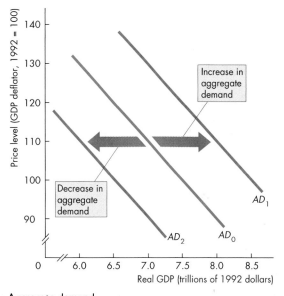

Aggregate demand

Decreases if

- Expected future incomes, inflation, or profits decrease

- Fiscal policy decreases government purchases, increases taxes, or decreases transfer payments

- Monetary policy decreases the quantity of money and increases interest rates

- The exchange rate increases or foreign income decreases

Increases if

- Expected future incomes, inflation, or profits increase

- Fiscal policy increases government purchases, decreases taxes, or increases transfer payments

- Monetary policy increases the quantity of money and decreases interest rates

- The exchange rate decreases or foreign income increases

rate decreases aggregate demand. To see how the foreign exchange rate influences aggregate demand, suppose that $1 exchanges for 100 Japanese yen. A Fujitsu phone (made in Japan) costs 12,500 yen, and an equivalent Motorola phone (made in the

United States) costs $110. In U.S. dollars, the Fujitsu phone costs $125, so people around the world buy the cheaper U.S. phone. Now suppose the exchange rate rises to 125 yen. At 125 yen per dollar, the Fujitsu phone costs $100 and is now cheaper than the Motorola phone. People will switch from the U.S. phone to the Japanese phone. U.S. exports will decrease and U.S. imports will increase, so U.S. aggregate demand will decrease.

An increase in foreign income increases U.S. exports and increases U.S. aggregate demand. For example, an increase in income in Japan and Germany increases the purchases of U.S.-made goods and services that Japanese and German consumers and producers plan to make.

Shifts of the Aggregate Demand Curve   When aggregate demand changes, the aggregate demand curve shifts. Figure 25.7 shows two changes in aggregate demand and summarizes the factors bringing about such changes.

The aggregate demand curve shifts rightward, from AD_0 to AD_1, when expected future incomes, inflation, or profits increase, government purchases on goods and services increase, taxes are cut, transfer payments increase, the quantity of money increases and interest rates fall, the foreign exchange rate falls, or foreign income increases. The aggregate demand curve shifts leftward, from AD_0 to AD_2, when expected future incomes, inflation, or profits decrease, government purchases of goods and services decrease, taxes increase, transfer payments decrease, the quantity of money decreases and interest rates rise, the foreign exchange rate rises, or foreign income decreases.

R E V I E W   Q U I Z

- What does the aggregate demand curve show and what factors change and what factors remain the same when there is a movement along the aggregate demand curve?
- Why does the aggregate demand curve slope downward?
- How do changes in expectations, fiscal policy and monetary policy, and the world economy change aggregate demand and shift the aggregate demand curve?

Macroeconomic Equilibrium

THE PURPOSE OF THE AGGREGATE SUPPLY—aggregate demand model is to explain changes in real GDP and the price level. To achieve this purpose, we combine aggregate supply and aggregate demand and determine macroeconomic equilibrium. There is a macroeconomic equilibrium for each of the time frames for aggregate supply: a long-run equilibrium and a short-run equilibrium. Long-run equilibrium is the state toward which the economy is heading. Short-run equilibrium is the normal state of the economy as it fluctuates around potential GDP.

We'll begin our study of macroeconomic equilibrium by looking first at the short run.

Short-Run Macroeconomic Equilibrium

The aggregate demand curve tells us the quantity of real GDP demanded at each price level, and the short-run aggregate supply curve tells us the quantity of real GDP supplied at each price level. **Short-run macroeconomic equilibrium** occurs when the quantity of real GDP demanded equals the quantity of real GDP supplied. That is, short-run equilibrium occurs at the point of intersection of the AD curve and the SAS curve. Figure 25.8 shows such an equilibrium at a price level of 110 and real GDP of $7 trillion (points c and c').

To see why this position is the equilibrium, think about what happens if the price level is something other than 110. Suppose, for example, that the price level is 120 and that real GDP is $8 trillion (at point e) on the SAS curve. The quantity of real GDP demanded is less than $8 trillion, so firms are unable to sell all their output. Unwanted inventories pile up, and firms cut both production and prices. Production and prices are cut until firms can sell all their output. This situation occurs only when real GDP is $7 trillion and the price level is 110.

Now suppose the price level is 100 and real GDP is $6 trillion (at point a) on the SAS curve. The quantity of real GDP demanded exceeds $6 trillion, so firms are unable to meet the demand for their output. Inventories decrease, and customers clamor for goods and services. So firms increase production and raise prices. Production and prices increase until firms can

FIGURE 25.8
Short-Run Equilibrium

Short-run macroeconomic equilibrium occurs when real GDP demanded equals real GDP supplied—at the intersection of the aggregate demand curve (*AD*) and the short-run aggregate supply curve (*SAS*). Here, such an equilibrium occurs at points *c* and *c'*, where the price level is 110 and real GDP is $7 trillion. If the price level is 120 and real GDP is $8 trillion (point *e*), firms will not be able to sell all their output. They will decrease production and cut prices. If the price level is 100 and real GDP is $6 trillion (point *a*), people will not be able to buy all the goods and services they demand. Firms will increase production and raise their prices. Only when the price level is 110 and real GDP is $7 trillion can firms sell all that they produce and people buy all that they demand. This is the short-run macroeconomic equilibrium.

meet demand. This situation occurs only when real GDP is $7 trillion and the price level is 110.

In short-run equilibrium, the money wage rate is fixed. It does not adjust to bring full employment. So in the short run, real GDP can be greater than or less than potential GDP. But in the long run, the money wage rate does adjust and real GDP moves toward potential GDP. We are going to study this adjustment process. But first, let's look at the economy in long-run equilibrium.

Long-Run Macroeconomic Equilibrium

Long-run macroeconomic equilibrium occurs when real GDP equals potential GDP—equivalently, when the economy is on its *long-run* aggregate supply curve. Figure 25.9 shows long-run equilibrium, which occurs at the intersection of the aggregate demand curve and the long-run aggregate supply curve (the blue curves). Long-run equilibrium comes about because the money wage rate adjusts. Potential GDP and aggregate demand determine the price level, and the price level influences the money wage rate. In long-run equilibrium, the money wage rate has adjusted to put the (green) short-run aggregate supply through the long-run equilibrium point.

We'll look at this adjustment process later in this chapter. But first, let's use the *AS-AD* model to study economic growth and inflation.

FIGURE 25.9
Long-Run Equilibrium

In long-run macroeconomic equilibrium, real GDP equals potential GDP. So long-run equilibrium occurs where the aggregate demand curve intersects the long-run aggregate demand curve. In the long run, aggregate demand determines the price level and has no effect on real GDP. The money wage rate adjusts in the long run, so the *SAS* curve intersects the *LAS* curve at the long-run equilibrium price level.

Economic Growth and Inflation

Economic growth occurs because, over time, the quantity of labor grows, capital is accumulated, and technology advances. These changes increase potential GDP and shift the long-run aggregate supply curve rightward. Figure 25.10 shows such a shift. The growth rate of potential GDP is determined by the pace at which labor grows, capital is accumulated, and technology advances.

Inflation occurs when, over time, aggregate demand increases by more than long-run aggregate supply. That is, inflation occurs if the aggregate demand curve shifts rightward by more than the rightward shift in the long-run aggregate supply curve. Figure 25.10 shows such shifts.

If aggregate demand increased at the same pace as long-run aggregate supply, we would experience real GDP growth with no inflation.

In the long run, the main influence on aggregate demand is the growth rate of the quantity of money. At times when the quantity of money increases rapidly, aggregate demand increases quickly and the inflation rate is high. When the growth rate of the quantity of money slows, other things remaining the same, the inflation rate eventually decreases.

Our economy experiences growth and inflation, like that shown in Fig. 25.10. But it does not experience *steady* growth and *steady* inflation. Real GDP fluctuates around potential GDP in a business cycle, and inflation also fluctuates. When we study the business cycle, we ignore economic growth. By doing so, we can see the business cycle more clearly.

Business Cycles

The business cycle occurs because aggregate demand and short-run aggregate supply fluctuate but the money wage rate does not adjust quickly enough to keep real GDP at potential GDP. Figure 25.11 shows three types of short-run equilibrium.

Figure 25.11(a) shows a below full-employment equilibrium. A **below full-employment equilibrium** is a macroeconomic equilibrium in which potential GDP exceeds real GDP. The amount by which potential GDP exceeds real GDP is called a **recessionary gap**. This name reminds us that a gap has opened up between potential GDP and real GDP either because the economy has experienced a recession or because real GDP, while growing, has grown more slowly than potential GDP.

The below full-employment equilibrium shown in Fig. 25.11(a) occurs where the aggregate demand curve AD_0 intersects short-run aggregate supply curve SAS_0 at a real GDP of $6.8 trillion and a price level of 110. The recessionary gap is $0.2 trillion. The U.S. economy was in a situation similar to that shown in Fig. 25.11(a) in the early 1980s and again in the early 1990s. In those years, real GDP was less than potential GDP.

Figure 25.11(b) is an example of *long-run equilibrium* in which real GDP equals potential GDP. In this example, the equilibrium occurs where the aggregate demand curve AD_1 intersects the short-run aggregate supply curve SAS_1 at an actual and potential GDP of $7 trillion. The U.S. economy was in a situation such as that shown in Fig. 25.11(b) in 1999.

Figure 25.11(c) shows an above full-employment equilibrium. An **above full-employment equilibrium** is a macroeconomic equilibrium in which real

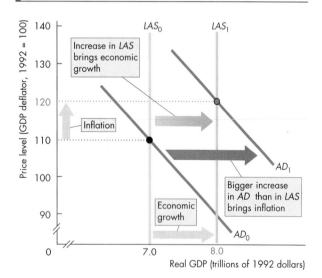

FIGURE 25.10

Economic Growth and Inflation

Economic growth is the persistent increase in potential GDP. Economic growth is shown as an ongoing rightward movement in the *LAS* curve. Inflation is the persistent rise in the price level. Inflation occurs when aggregate demand increases by more than the increase in long-run aggregate supply.

GDP exceeds potential GDP. The amount by which real GDP exceeds potential GDP is called an **inflationary gap**. This name reminds us that a gap has opened up between real GDP and potential GDP and that this gap creates inflationary pressure.

The above full-employment equilibrium shown in Fig. 25.11(c) occurs where the aggregate demand curve AD_2 intersects the short-run aggregate supply curve SAS_2 at a real GDP of $7.2 trillion and a price level of 110. There is an inflationary gap of $0.2

trillion. The U.S. economy was in a situation similar to that depicted in Fig. 25.11(c) in 1988–1990.

The economy moves from one type of equilibrium to another as a result of fluctuations in aggregate demand and in short-run aggregate supply. These fluctuations produce fluctuations in real GDP and the price level. Figure 25.11(d) shows how real GDP fluctuates around potential GDP.

Let's now look at some of the sources of these fluctuations around potential GDP.

FIGURE 25.11

The Business Cycle

(a) Below full-employment equilibrium

(b) Long-run equilibrium

(c) Above full-employment equilibrium

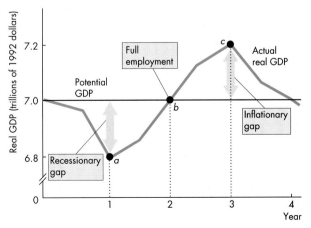

(d) Fluctuations in real GDP

Part (a) shows a below full-employment equilibrium in year 1; part (b) shows a long-run equilibrium in year 2; part (c) shows an above full-employment equilibrium in year 3. Part (d) shows how real GDP fluctuates around potential GDP in a business cycle. In year 1, there is a recessionary gap and the economy is at point a (in parts a and d). In year 2, there is long-run equilibrium and the economy is at point b (in parts b and d). In year 3, there is an inflationary gap and the economy is at point c (in parts c and d).

Fluctuations in Aggregate Demand

One reason real GDP fluctuates around potential GDP is that aggregate demand fluctuates. Let's see what happens when aggregate demand increases.

Figure 25.12(a) shows an economy in long-run equilibrium. The aggregate demand curve is AD_0, the short-run aggregate supply curve is SAS_0, and the long-run aggregate supply curve is LAS. Real GDP equals potential GDP at $7 trillion, and the price level is 110.

Now suppose that the world economy expands and that the demand for U.S.-made goods increases in Japan and Europe. The increase in U.S. exports increases aggregate demand, and the aggregate demand curve shifts rightward from AD_0 to AD_1 in Fig. 25.12(a).

Faced with an increase in demand, firms increase production and raise prices. Real GDP increases to $7.5 trillion, and the price level rises to 115. The economy is now in an above full-employment equilibrium. Real GDP exceeds potential GDP, there is an inflationary gap.

The increase in aggregate demand has increased the prices of all goods and services. Faced with higher prices, firms have increased their output rates. At this stage, prices of goods and services have increased but wage rates have not changed. (Recall that as we move along a short-run aggregate supply curve, wage rates are constant.)

The economy cannot produce in excess of potential GDP forever. Why not? What are the forces at work that bring real GDP back to potential GDP?

Because the price level has increased and wage rates are unchanged, workers have experienced a fall in the buying power of their wages and firms' profits have increased. In these circumstances, workers demand higher wages and firms, anxious to maintain their employment and output levels, meet those demands. If firms do not raise wage rates, they will either lose workers or have to hire less productive ones.

As wage rates rise, the short-run aggregate supply curve begins to shift leftward. In Fig. 25.12(b), the short-run aggregate supply curve moves from SAS_0

FIGURE 25.12

An Increase in Aggregate Demand

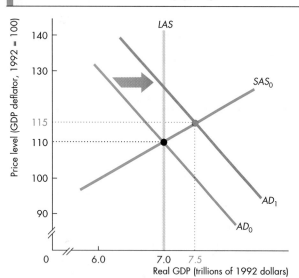

(a) Short-run effect

An increase in aggregate demand shifts the aggregate demand curve from AD_0 to AD_1. In the short-run equilibrium, real GDP is $7.5 trillion and the price level rises to 115 in part (a). In this situation, there is an inflationary gap. The money wage rate rises, and the short-run aggregate supply curve shifts

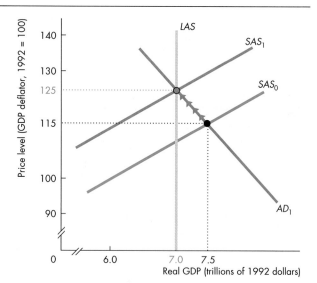

(b) Long-run effect

leftward from SAS_0 to SAS_1 in part (b). As it shifts, it intersects the aggregate demand curve AD_1 at higher price levels and lower real GDP levels. Eventually, the price level rises to 125 and real GDP decreases to $7.0 trillion—potential GDP.

toward SAS_1. The rise in wages and the shift in the SAS curve produce a sequence of new equilibrium positions. Along the adjustment path, real GDP falls and the price level rises. The economy moves up along its aggregate demand curve as shown by the arrowheads in the figure.

Eventually, wage rates rise by the same percentage as the price level. At this time, the aggregate demand curve AD_1 intersects SAS_1 at a new long-run equilibrium. The price level has risen to 125, and real GDP is back where it started, at potential GDP.

A decrease in aggregate demand has similar but opposite effects to those of an increase in aggregate demand. That is, a decrease in aggregate demand shifts the aggregate demand curve leftward. Real GDP decreases to less than potential GDP, and a recessionary gap emerges. Firms cut prices. The lower price level increases the purchasing power of wages and increases firms' costs relative to their output prices because wages remain unchanged. Eventually, the slack economy leads to falling wage rates and the short-run aggregate supply curve shifts rightward. But wage rates change slowly, so real GDP slowly returns to potential GDP and the price level falls slowly.

Let's now work out how real GDP and the price level change when aggregate supply changes.

Fluctuations in Aggregate Supply

Fluctuations in short-run aggregate supply can bring fluctuations in real GDP around potential GDP. Suppose that initially real GDP equals potential GDP. Then there is a large but temporary rise in the price of oil. What happens to real GDP and the price level?

Figure 25.13 answers this question. The aggregate demand curve is AD_0, the short-run aggregate supply curve is SAS_0, and the long-run aggregate supply curve is LAS. Equilibrium real GDP is $7 trillion, which equals potential GDP, and the price level is 110. Then the price of oil rises. Faced with higher energy and transportation costs, firms decrease production. Short-run aggregate supply decreases, and the short-run aggregate supply curve shifts leftward to SAS_1. The price level rises to 120, and real GDP decreases to $6.5 trillion. Because real GDP decreases, the economy experiences recession. Because the price level increases, the economy experiences inflation. A combination of recession and inflation, called *stagflation*, actually occurred in the United States in the mid-1970s and early 1980s. But events like this are not common.

FIGURE 25.13

A Decrease in Aggregate Supply

An increase in the price of oil decreases short-run aggregate supply and shifts the short-run aggregate supply curve from SAS_0 to SAS_1. Real GDP decreases from $7.0 trillion to $6.5 trillion, and the price level rises from 110 to 120. The economy experiences both recession and inflation—stagflation.

REVIEW QUIZ

- Does economic growth result from increases in aggregate demand, short-run aggregate supply, or long-run aggregate supply?
- Does inflation result from increases in aggregate demand, short-run aggregate supply, or long-run aggregate supply?
- Can you describe three types of short-run macroeconomic equilibrium?
- How do fluctuations in aggregate demand and short-run aggregate supply bring fluctuations in real GDP around potential GDP?

Let's put our new knowledge of aggregate supply and aggregate demand to work and see how we can explain recent U.S. macroeconomic performance.

U.S. Economic Growth, Inflation, and Cycles

THE ECONOMY IS CONTINUALLY CHANGING. IF you imagine the economy as a video, then an aggregate supply–aggregate demand figure such as Fig. 25.13 is a freeze-frame. We're going to run the video—an instant replay—but keep our finger on the freeze-frame button and look at some important parts of the previous action. Let's run the video from 1960.

Figure 25.14 shows the state of the economy in 1960 at the point of intersection of its aggregate demand curve AD_{60} and short-run aggregate supply curve SAS_{60}. Real GDP was $2.3 trillion, and the GDP deflator was 23 (about a fifth of its 1998 level). In 1960, real GDP equaled potential GDP—the economy was on its long-run aggregate supply curve, LAS_{60}.

By 1998, the economy had reached the point marked by the intersection of aggregate demand curve AD_{98} and short-run aggregate supply curve SAS_{98}. Real GDP was $7.6 trillion, and the GDP deflator was 113. The LAS curve assumes that potential GDP in 1998 was $7.6 trillion. The path traced by the blue and red dots shows three key features:

- Economic growth
- Inflation
- Business cycles

Economic Growth

Over the years, real GDP grows—shown in Fig. 25.14 by the rightward movement of the points. The faster real GDP grows, the larger is the horizontal distance between successive dots in the figure. The forces that generate economic growth are those that increase potential GDP. Potential GDP grows because the quantity of labor grows, we accumulate physical capital and human capital, and our technologies advance.

These forces that bring economic growth were stronger during the early 1970s and mid-1980s than at other times. During the late 1970s, growth was slow.

FIGURE 25.14

Aggregate Supply and Aggregate Demand: 1960–1998

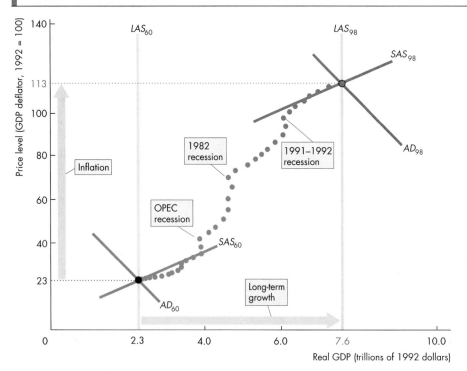

Each point shows the GDP deflator and real GDP in a given year. In 1960, these variables were determined by the aggregate demand curve AD_{60} and the short-run aggregate supply curve SAS_{60}. Each point is generated by the gradual shifting of the AD and SAS curves. By 1998, the curves were AD_{98} and SAS_{98}. Real GDP grew, and the price level increased. Real GDP grew quickly and inflation was moderate during the 1960s; real GDP growth sagged in 1974–1975 and again in 1982. Inflation was rapid during the 1970s but slowed after the 1982 recession. The period from 1982 to 1989 was one of strong, persistent expansion. A recession began in 1991, and a further strong and sustained expansion then followed.

Source: U.S. Department of Commerce, *Survey of Current Business*, (March 1999) and the author's assumptions.

Inflation

The price level rises over the years—shown in Fig. 25.14 by the upward movement of the points. The larger the rise in the price level, the larger is the vertical distance between successive dots in the figure. The main force generating the persistent increase in the price level is a tendency for aggregate demand to increase at a faster pace than the increase in long-run aggregate supply. All of the factors that increase aggregate demand and shift the aggregate demand curve influence the pace of inflation. But one factor—the growth of the quantity of money—is the main source of *persistent* increases in aggregate demand and persistent inflation.

Business Cycles

Over the years, the economy grows and shrinks in cycles—shown in Fig. 25.14 by the wavelike pattern made by the points, with the recessions highlighted. The cycles arise because both the expansion of short-run aggregate supply and the growth of aggregate demand do not proceed at a fixed, steady pace. Although the economy has cycles, recessions do not usually follow quickly on the heels of their predecessors; "double-dip" recessions like the one in the cartoon are rare.

The Evolving Economy: 1960–1998

During the 1960s, real GDP growth was rapid and inflation was low. This was a period of rapid increases in aggregate supply and of moderate increases in aggregate demand.

The mid-1970s were years of rapid inflation and recession—of stagflation. The major source of these developments was a series of massive oil price increases that shifted the short-run aggregate supply curve leftward and rapid increases in the quantity of money that shifted the aggregate demand curve rightward. Recession occurred because the short-run aggregate supply curve shifted leftward at a faster pace than the aggregate demand curve shifted rightward.

The rest of the 1970s saw high inflation—the price level increased quickly—and only moderate growth in real GDP. By 1980, inflation was a major problem and the Fed decided to take strong action against it. It permitted interest rates to rise to previously unknown levels. Consequently, aggregate demand decreased. By 1982, the decrease in aggregate demand put the economy in a deep recession.

"Please stand by for a series of tones. The first indicates the official end of the recession, the second indicates prosperity, and the third the return of the recession."

Drawing by Mankoff; © 1991 *The New Yorker Magazine, Inc.*

During the years 1982 to 1990, capital accumulation and steady technological advance resulted in a sustained rightward shift of the long-run aggregate supply curve. Wage growth was moderate, and the short-run aggregate supply curve also shifted rightward. Aggregate demand growth kept pace with the growth of aggregate supply. Sustained but steady growth in aggregate supply and aggregate demand kept real GDP growing and inflation steady. The economy moved from a recession with real GDP less than potential GDP in 1982 to above full-employment in 1990. It was in this condition when a decrease in aggregate demand led to the 1991 recession. The economy again embarked on a path of expansion through 1998. The expansion took real GDP to a level that probably exceeded potential GDP and took employment to above-full employment.

◆ The aggregate supply–aggregate demand model explains economic growth, inflation, and the business cycle. The model is a useful one because it enables us to keep our eye on the big picture. But it lacks detail. It does not tell us as much as we need to know about the deeper forces that lie behind aggregate supply and aggregate demand. The chapters that follow begin to fill in the details. We begin with the supply side and study the forces that make our economy grow. But before you embark on this next stage, take a look at *Reading Between the Lines* on pages 550–551, which gives you a look at the U.S. economy in 1999.

Aggregate Supply and Aggregate Demand in Action

C N N f n ,   MARCH 30, 1999

Economy Full-Steam Ahead

By staff writer Steven Radwell

NEW YORK—The American economy, the big engine that could, has made the rest of the world green with envy for most of this decade and 1999 is shaping up as no exception.

Most forecasters expect growth of 3 percent or better this year with little inflation—a mix that has Federal Reserve Chairman Alan Greenspan and many other forecasters scratching their heads. Traditional economic theory says growth of 3 to 4 percent—seen in four of the last five years—should have pushed wages and prices sharply higher by now, but inflation is all but absent after eight years of growth, the longest peace time expansion in the history of the United States. ...

Is there an end in sight? Most forecasters say not yet, though many see growth slowing in 2000. Some others say there is about a one-in-three chance of a recession next year.

"As long as Alan Greenspan's not frowning, I'm not too worried," said David Blitzer, chief economist at Standard & Poor's, who sees strong corporate and consumer spending, the solid job market and low inflation adding up to GDP growth of about 3.6 percent this year, up from his earlier forecast of 3.1 percent.

... Productivity, an important measure of output per worker, grew at a 4.6 percent rate in the fourth quarter, the fastest rise in six years and something Fed Chairman Greenspan considers crucial if economic growth is going to continue with low inflation. ...

"I don't believe the business cycle has been conquered. There'll (eventually) be another recession," (said Blitzer) ..., noting it will be more like the 1990–1991 downturn than the 1981–1982 recession, when unemployment rose to 10.7 percent, the highest since the Great Depression, and interest rates touched 20 percent, levels unseen in the United States since the Civil War. ...

Essence of the Story

■ At the beginning of 1999, most economic forecasters expected real GDP to grow by 3 percent or more during 1999 and to slow during 2000. A few forecasters predicted a recession for 2000.

■ Traditional economic theory predicts that growth of 3 to 4 percent maintained for several years will push wages and prices sharply higher. But inflation has remained low after eight years of growth.

■ Productivity growth is the key to expansion with low inflation.

■ There will eventually be another recession, but it will be more like the mild 1990–1991 recession rather than the severe 1981–1982 recession.

■ In 1998, U.S. real GDP grew by 4.2 percent to $7.6 trillion and the price level (which equaled 100 in 1992) increased by only 1 percent to 113.

■ No one can forecast next year's real GDP and price level. And no one knows for sure the current level of potential GDP. But at the beginning of 1999, most forecasters believed that real GDP would continue to grow with low inflation during 1999. A minority believed that a recession would occur in 1999.

■ Figure 1 shows the majority view. Real GDP ($7.6 trillion) and the price level (113) are determined at the intersection of the aggregate demand curve, AD_{98} and the short-run aggregate supply curve SAS_{98}. Potential GDP in 1998 was $7.6 trillion so the long-run aggregate supply curve was LAS_{98}.

■ During 1999, potential GDP was expected to grow by 3 percent to $7.8 trillion so the long-run aggregate supply curve shifts rightward to LAS_{99}. Aggregate demand was expected to increase to AD_{99} and short-run aggregate supply to SAS_{99}. Real GDP was expected to grow by 3 percent and the price level to rise by less than 1 percent.

■ Figure 2 shows a minority view of the U.S. economy in 1999. Potential GDP is $7.5 trillion on long-run aggregate supply curve LAS in 1999. This LAS curve assumes that the growth rate of potential GDP has been around its historical average rate.

■ Aggregate demand was expected to remain at level AD through 1999. At the beginning of 1999, real GDP is $7.6 trillion and there was an inflationary gap.

■ With an inflationary gap, wage rates were expected to rise more rapidly and the SAS curve was expected to shift leftward to SAS_{99}.

■ Real GDP was expected to shrink to $7.5 trillion and the inflation rate will increase.

■ Real GDP was expected to decrease for at least two quarters, so a recession was forecasted. But the recession was expected to be mild, and the pickup in the inflation rate modest

Figure 1 Expansion continues

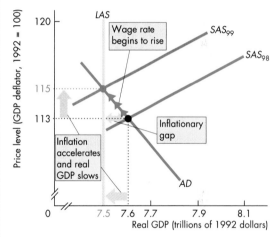

Figure 2 Recession ?

You're The Voter

■ Do you think the Fed should increase interest rates to keep inflation in check? Or do you think the Fed should cut interest rates to prevent a recession? Explain your answer.

■ Do you think the federal government should cut taxes to prevent a recession? Explain your answer.

SUMMARY

KEY POINTS

Aggregate Supply (pp. 534–538)

- In the long run, the quantity of real GDP supplied is potential GDP, which is independent of the price level. The long-run aggregate supply curve is vertical.
- In the short run, the money wage rate is constant, so a rise in the price level increases the quantity of real GDP supplied. The short-run aggregate supply curve is upward sloping.
- A change in potential GDP changes both long-run and short-run aggregate supply. A change in the money wage rate or resource prices changes only short-run aggregate supply.

Aggregate Demand (pp. 539–542)

- A rise in the price level decreases the quantity of real GDP demanded, other things remaining the same.
- The reason is that the higher price level decreases the quantity of *real* wealth, raises the interest rate, and raises the cost of domestic goods compared with foreign goods.
- Changes in expected future incomes, profits, and inflation, changes in fiscal policy and monetary policy, and changes in world real GDP and the foreign exchange rate change aggregate demand.

Macroeconomic Equilibrium (pp. 542–547)

- In the short run, real GDP and the price level are determined by aggregate demand and short-run aggregate supply.
- In the long run, real GDP equals potential GDP and aggregate demand determines the price level and the money wage rate.
- Economic growth occurs because potential GDP increases.
- Inflation occurs because aggregate demand grows more quickly than potential GDP.
- Business cycles occur because aggregate demand and aggregate supply fluctuate.

U.S. Economic Growth, Inflation, and Cycles (pp. 548–549)

- U.S. potential GDP grew fastest during the 1960s and mid-1980s and slowest during the 1970s.
- U.S. inflation persists because aggregate demand grows faster than potential GDP.
- U.S. business cycles occur because aggregate supply and aggregate demand change at an uneven pace.

KEY FIGURES

KEY TERMS

PROBLEMS

💻 *1. The following events occur that influence the economy of Toughtimes:
- ■ A deep recession hits the world economy.
- ■ Oil prices rise sharply.
- ■ Businesses expect huge losses in the near future.
  - a. Explain the separate effects of each of these events on real GDP and the price level in Toughtimes, starting from a position of long-run equilibrium.
  - b. Explain the combined effects of these events on real GDP and the price level in Toughtimes, starting from a position of long-run equilibrium.
  - c. Explain what the Toughtimes government and central bank can do to overcome the problems faced by the economy.

2. The following events occur that influence the economy of Coolland:
- ■ A strong expansion in the world economy.
- ■ Businesses expect huge profits in the near future.
- ■ The Coolland government cuts its expenditure.
  - a. Explain the separate effects of each of these events on real GDP and the price level in Coolland, starting from a position of long-run equilibrium.
  - b. Explain the combined effects of these events on real GDP and the price level in Coolland, starting from a position of long-run equilibrium.
  - c. Explain why the Coolland government or central bank might want to take action to influence the Coolland economy.

💻 *3. The economy of Mainland has the following aggregate demand and supply schedules:

Price level	Real GDP demanded	Real GDP supplied in the short run
	(billions of 1992 dollars)	
90	450	350
100	400	400
110	350	450
120	300	500
130	250	550
140	200	600

a. In a figure, plot the aggregate demand curve and the short-run aggregate supply curve.
b. What are the values of real GDP and the price level in Mainland in a short-run macroeconomic equilibrium?
c. Mainland's potential GDP is $500 billion. Plot the long-run aggregate supply curve in the same figure in which you answered part (a).

4. The economy of Miniland has the following aggregate demand and supply schedules:

Price level	Real GDP demanded	Real GDP supplied in the short run
	(billions of 1992 dollars)	
90	600	150
100	500	200
110	400	250
120	300	300
130	200	350
140	100	400

a. In a figure, plot the aggregate demand curve and the short-run aggregate supply curve.
b. What are the values of real GDP and the price level in Miniland in a short-run macroeconomic equilibrium?
c. Miniland's potential GDP is $250 billion. Plot the long-run aggregate supply curve in the same figure in which you answered part (a).

💻 *5. In problem 3, aggregate demand is increased by $100 billion. How do real GDP and the price level change in the short run?

6. In problem 4, aggregate demand is decreased by $150 billion. How do real GDP and the price level change in the short run?

💻 *7. In problem 3, aggregate supply decreases by $100 billion. What now is the short-run macroeconomic equilibrium?

8. In problem 4, aggregate supply increases by $150 billion. What now is the short-run macroeconomic equilibrium?

*9. In the economy shown in the figure, initially the short-run aggregate supply is SAS_0 and aggregate demand is AD_0. Then some events change aggregate demand, and the aggregate demand curve shifts rightward to AD_1. Later, some other events change aggregate supply and shifts the short-run aggregate supply curve leftward to SAS_1.

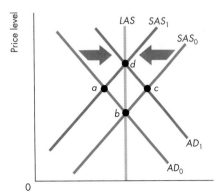

a. What is the equilibrium point after the change in aggregate demand?
b. What is the equilibrium point after the change in aggregate supply?
c. What events could have changed aggregate demand from AD_0 to AD_1?
d. What events could have changed aggregate supply from SAS_0 to SAS_1?

10. In the economy shown in the figure, initially long-run aggregate supply is LAS_0, short-run aggregate supply is SAS_0, and aggregate demand is AD_0. Then some events change aggregate supply, and the aggregate supply curves shifts rightward to LAS_1 and SAS_1.

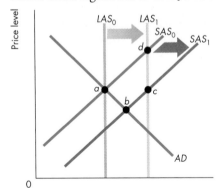

a. What is the equilibrium point after the change in aggregate supply?
b. What events could have changed long-run aggregate supply from LAS_0 to LAS_1?
c. What events could have changed short-run aggregate supply from SAS_0 to SAS_1?
d. After the increase in aggregate demand but before the increase in aggregate supply, is real GDP greater than or less than potential GDP?
e. What change in aggregate demand will make real GDP equal to potential GDP?

CRITICAL THINKING

1. After you have studied the forecasts for the U.S. economy during 1999 in *Reading Between the Lines* on pp. 550–551, answer the following questions:
   a. What were most economists predicting for the U.S. economy during 1999? Why?
   b. Why might some economists have thought that an inflationary gap existed at the beginning of 1999?
   c. Use the *AS-AD* model to show the economy in 1999 if the Fed cuts interest rates.
   d. Use the *AS-AD* model to show the economy in 1999 if the Fed raises interest rates.

2. Use the links on the Parkin Web site to obtain the latest data on real GDP and the price level. Then:
   a. Create a figure similar to those on p. 551 to interpret the latest numbers.
   b. In light of the events that occurred during 1999, which of the two figures on p. 551 is the more likely description of the U.S. economy at the end of 1999? Explain.

3. You are the President's economic advisor and have the following forecasts of aggregate demand and aggregate supply for next year:

Price level	Real GDP demanded	Real GDP supplied	Potential GDP
	(trillions of 1992 dollars)		
100	8.3	5.3	7
105	7.8	6.3	7
110	7.3	7.3	7
115	6.8	8.3	7

This year, real GDP is $6.8 trillion, potential GDP is also $6.8 trillion, and the price level is 107. The President wants answers to the following questions:
   a. What is your forecast of next year's real GDP?
   b. What is your forecast of next year's price level?
   c. What is your forecast of the inflation rate?
   d. What is your forecast of the growth rate of real GDP?
   e. What is your forecast of the growth rate of potential GDP?
   f. Will there be a recessionary gap or an inflationary gap? By how much?

Understanding the Themes of Macroeconomics

Macroeconomics is a large and controversial subject that is interlaced with political ideological disputes. And it is a field in which charlatans as well as serious thinkers have much to say. This page is a map that looks back at the road you've just traveled and forward at the path you will take from here. ◆ You began your study of macroeconomics with the core questions of the subject. What are the causes of:

The Big Picture

- Economic growth?
- Business cycles?
- Unemployment?
- Inflation?

In Chapter 22, you took your first look at each of these questions. You learned some facts about economic growth, business cycles, unemployment, and inflation in the United States and around the world. ◆ In Chapter 23, you learned how we measure the economy's output and the price level. These measures are used to calculate the rate of economic growth, business cycle fluctuations, and inflation. You discovered that making these measurements is not straightforward and that small measurement errors can have a big effect of our perceptions about how we are doing. ◆ In Chapter 24, you learned how we measure the state of the labor market—the levels of employment and unemployment and wages. And in Chapter 25, you studied the macroeconomic version of supply and demand—*aggregate supply* and *aggregate demand*. You saw that the aggregate supply–aggregate demand model is the big picture model. It explains both the long-term trends in economic growth and inflation and the short-term business cycle fluctuations in production, jobs, and inflation. ◆ The chapters that lie ahead of you look behind aggregate supply and aggregate demand. First, in Chapters 26 through 28, you study aggregate supply and economic growth. This material is so central to the oldest question in macroeconomics that Adam Smith tried to answer. You'll begin in Chapter 26 by looking at the economy at full employment and study the forces that determine potential GDP and make it change. In Chapter 27, you will study the role played by saving and investment in increasing the amount of capital and creating economic growth. Then, in Chapter 28, you will study the growth process and the roles of capital accumulation and technological change in bringing economic growth about. ◆ Second, in Chapters 29 through 35, you will study aggregate demand, inflation, and deflation. This material is central to the macroeconomics that Keynes developed as a response to the Great Depression. Here you will learn about economic fluctuations and the policies that might limit their severity. ◆ Before continuing your study of macroeconomics, spend a few minutes with John Maynard Keynes and Jean Baptiste Say, the leading scholars who developed this subject. And spend a few minutes with today's leading macroeconomist, Robert E. Lucas, Jr. of the University of Chicago.

The Economist

John Maynard Keynes,

born in England in 1883, was one of the outstanding minds of the twentieth century. He wrote on probability as well as economics, represented Britain at the Versailles peace conference at the end of World War I, was a master speculator on international financial markets (an activity he conducted from bed every morning and which made and lost him several fortunes), and played a prominent role in creating the International Monetary Fund. He was a member of the Bloomsbury Group, a circle of outstanding artists and writers that included E. M. Forster, Bertrand Russell, and Virginia Woolf. Keynes was a controversial and quick-witted figure. A critic once complained that Keynes had changed his opinion on some matter, to which Keynes retorted: "When I discover I am wrong, I change my mind. What do you do?"

"The ideas of economists and political philosophers, both when they are right and when they are wrong, are more powerful than is commonly understood. Indeed the world is ruled by little else."

JOHN MAYNARD KEYNES
The General Theory of Employment, Interest, and Money

The Issues

During the Industrial Revolution, as technological change created new jobs and destroyed old ones, people began to wonder whether the economy could create enough jobs and sufficient demand to buy all the things that the new industrial economy could produce.

Jean-Baptiste Say argued that production creates incomes that are sufficient to buy everything that is produced—supply creates its own demand—an idea that came to be called *Say's Law.*

Say and Keynes would have had a lot to disagree about. Jean-Baptiste Say, born in Lyon, France, in 1767 (he was 9 years old when Adam Smith's *Wealth of Nations* was published), suffered the wrath of Napoleon for his views on government and the economy. In today's world, Say would be leading a radical conservative charge for a smaller and leaner government. Say was the most famous economist of his era on both sides of the Atlantic. His book, *Traité d'économie politique (A Treatise in Political Economy),* published in 1803, became a best-selling university economics textbook in both Europe and North America.

As the Great Depression of the 1930s became more severe and more prolonged, Say's Law looked less and less relevant. John Maynard Keynes revolutionized macroeconomic thinking by turning Say's Law on its head, arguing that production does not depend on supply. Instead, it depends on what people are willing to buy—on demand. Or as Keynes put it, production depends on *effective demand.* It is possible, argued Keynes, for people to refuse to spend all of their incomes. If businesses fail to spend on new capital the amount that people plan to save, demand might be less than supply. In this situation, resources might go unemployed and remain unemployed indefinitely.

The influence of Keynes persists even today, more than 60 years after the publication of his main work. But during the past 20 years, Nobel Laureate Robert E. Lucas, Jr., with significant contributions from a list of outstanding macroeconomists too long to name, has further revolutionized macroeconomics. Today, we know a lot about economic growth, unemployment, inflation, and business cycles. And we know how to use fiscal policy and monetary policy to improve macroeconomic performance. But we don't yet have all the answers. Macroeconomics remains a field of lively controversy and exciting research.

Then

In 1776, James Hargreaves, an English weaver and carpenter, developed a simple hand-operated machine called a spinning jenny (pictured here). Using this machine, a person could spin 80 threads at once. Thousands of hand-wheel spinners, operators of machines that could spin only one thread, lost their jobs. They protested by wrecking spinning jennies. In the long run, the displaced hand-wheel spinners found work, often in factories that manufactured the machines that had destroyed their previous jobs. From the earliest days of the Industrial Revolution to the present day, people have lost their jobs as new technologies have automated what human effort had previously been needed to accomplish.

Now

Advances in computer technology have made it possible for us to dial our own telephone calls to any part of the world and get connected in a flash. A task that was once performed by telephone operators, who made connections along copper wires, is now performed faster and more reliably by computers along fiber-optic cables. Just as the Industrial Revolution transformed the textile industry, so today's Information Revolution is transforming the telecommunications industry. In the process, the mix of jobs is changing. There are fewer jobs for telephone operators but more jobs for telephone systems designers, builders, managers, and marketers. In the long run, as people spend the income they earn in their changing jobs, supply creates its own demand, just as Say predicted. But does supply create its own demand in the short run, when displaced workers are unemployed?

Keynes and Robert E. Lucas, Jr, would have had plenty of disagreements too. Lucas, of the University of Chicago, has led a revolution in macroeconomics that has enabled economists to build model (artificial) economies that display properties similar to those of the actual economy and to use these models to study the effects of alternative policies on macroeconomic performance. A cornerstone of the new macroeconomics is the idea of "rational expectations"—people use all the available information to make economic forecasts. This information includes theories about how the economy works. Lucas, like Say, believes that it is easier for government intervention to do harm than good. Said Lucas, "I don't want to manage the U.S. economy. And I don't think anybody else should take the job either." You can meet Professor Lucas on the following pages.

Talking with

Robert E. Lucas, Jr.,

is a professor of economics at the University of Chicago, a position he has held since 1975. Professor Lucas was born in Yakima, Washington, in 1937. He earned his B.A. and his Ph.D. from the University of Chicago in 1959 and 1963, respectively.

In 1995, Professor Lucas received the Nobel Prize for Economic Science for his work on developing the theory of rational expectations. Challenging the Keynesian theories of economic fluctuations, this new macroeconomic theory is based on the hypothesis that people and businesses make rational decisions based on rational expectations and markets reconcile individual decisions by balancing supply and demand, even in a recession.

Michael Parkin spoke with Professor Lucas about rational expectations macroeconomics, his views of economic policy, and the legacy of Keynes.

Robert E. Lucas, Jr.

Why are you an economist?
I grew up in a family where everyone talked about politics and economics every night at dinner. So I've been concerned with social questions as long as I can remember. My experience as an undergraduate history major confirmed my belief in the importance of economic forces.

You applied the idea of rational expectations to macroeconomics and to expectations about inflation. How has that hypothesis changed the way we think about things?
It ties down a loose end that shouldn't have been there. Any important economic decision depends on what you think about the future. Rational expectations is a way of dealing with that.

What do you see as the chief criticism of the rational expectations hypothesis?
Here's the genuine difficulty people have with the idea. You would never discover the idea of rational expectations by introspection. Rational expectations describes something that has to be true of the outcome of a much more complicated underlying process. But it doesn't describe the actual thought process people use in trying to figure out the future. Our behavior is adaptive. We try some mode of behavior. If it's successful, we do it again. If not, we try something else. Rational expectations describes the situation when you've got it right.

Can you give an example?
In economics, we're mostly concerned about repetitive events and decisions of some consequence. Our capitalist economy has been operating under pretty much the same laws for 200 years now. People aren't reacting to every monetary contraction as if it's the first time it ever happened: That is just inconceivable. I think people have developed certain ways of living with regular events as best they can.

One of the most significant developments in macroeconomics in recent years has been real business cycle

558

theory. How do you evaluate this approach?

Real business cycle theory asks what the time path of the economy's GDP or employment would be under the best possible macroeconomic policy. The early authors of this approach asked themselves what fraction of the actual variation in GDP you could account for if you restricted yourself to the fluctuations in the rate of technological change. Their initial answer was: All of it, that there is nothing left over for traditional macroeconomic theory to account for. I don't think that can be right.

For example, you can't account for something like the events of 1929 to 1933, when real output fell by a quarter in four years, as if it resulted from the changes in the rate at which technology was decaying. The Depression didn't occur because production techniques got worse. But real business cycle theory has shown us that real forces are much more important than we had thought and that the questions addressed by traditional macroeconomics are not as important as we once thought. That's the important message.

How can we introduce monetary forces into a macroeconomic model that at the same time pays serious attention to real forces, one that shows fluctuations in price as well as in output?

This question is the subject of my Nobel Lecture, "Monetary Neutrality." I think it is the central question of macroeconomics, but it remains unresolved today, as it did when David Hume first addressed it in the eighteenth century.

Your early work focused primarily on short-term macroeconomic problems. For the past 10 years, you've increasingly devoted your life to thinking about long-term growth. Why has your work changed in that direction?

When I began taking economics courses in the early 1960s, the Great Depression of the 1930s was a key topic of discussion for all my professors. The study of macroeconomics was, at that time, the study of how to prevent depressions and how to get out of them. The United States has not had a serious depression since the 1930s, and we should not be surprised that macroeconomic study has switched from a depression focus to a growth focus. If you ask what determines our income today relative to what it was in the 1960s, 99 percent of the answer is economic growth.

> If you ask what determines our income today relative to what it was in the 1960s, 99 percent of the answer is economic growth.

What can we bring to the study of growth today that Smith couldn't bring to it when he tried to figure out what caused the wealth of nations?

When Adam Smith wrote about the wealth of nations, he was thinking about a world in which no country had ever experienced sustained growth in living standards. Some countries had higher *levels* of income than others, and Smith was interested in understanding why those differences existed. But Smith never observed or imagined a country where production could grow at 3 percent per year for a century and more. Smith also lacked good data, by modern standards. We now have tremendous data sets on income and the growth of income for the richest and poorest countries. During the past 10 years, growth theory has evolved from being the study of the United States, the United Kingdom, and a few other very wealthy economies to being the comparative study of rich and poor economies. The hope is that the same general theoretical principles will apply to both.

There's about a 25 to 1 difference between the United States and India in per capita production. How do you explain that difference?

Only a small fraction can be explained by the differences in physical capital. U.S. workers have better equipment than Indian workers, and that's certainly a factor in making them more productive, but a much more important factor is human capital. The level of education and training of the U.S. worker is much higher than the typical Indian worker. Once human capital is introduced—and placed at the center of growth theory—a lot of things start falling into place and it becomes much easier to understand the enormous differences in incomes.

> People aren't reacting to every monetary contraction as if it's the first time it ever happened.

559

How do you explain the astonishing growth rates of per capita incomes in East Asia compared with the 1 to 2 percent growth rates of North America?

The countries of East Asia are catching up with those of Europe and North America. The Industrial Revolution has opened them up to trade with the more advanced countries of the world. East Asia is experiencing annual growth rates of 6 to 8 percent. Nothing like that ever occurred in the United States or the United Kingdom, the countries that were leaders from the start of the Industrial Revolution. East Asian countries are rapidly learning technology that took decades to produce.

You were a student of Milton Friedman, the architect of the movement called monetarism. How do you distinguish this approach from the kind of macroeconomics that you are responsible for creating?

I'm not that big on the distinction. I think of myself as a monetarist. But the term does refer to several different things. One aspect of what people call monetarism is just an emphasis on the quantity of some money as a determinant of prices and of economic activity. In some ways, I think that revolution has been so successful that it doesn't seem like a revolution any more. In this day

and age, no one talks about the price level, exchange rates, or interest rates without talking about the quantity of money. In that sense, we're all monetarists. The second aspect of monetarism

> Economics is a great major.
> ... economics is a good
> pre–almost anything major.

is a hostility toward the government's continual management of the economy. The role of government, in a monetarist perspective, is to make its own behavior on fiscal or monetary policy simple and predictable and then just to let the system operate without fine tuning. That view, I think, is absolutely right.

In recent years, we've experienced the biggest peacetime government budget deficit ever. How have you viewed the deficit over the years?

I was a deficit alarmist in the early years of the Reagan administration because I thought the deficits would be inflationary. Well, that just hasn't happened. I've become more sympathetic to people like Larry Kotlikoff, who argued that the deficit just doesn't measure anything we care about, since things like future social security liabilities are arbitrarily excluded.

What for you is the legacy of Keynes?

Keynes' influence was almost entirely political. He wrote *The General Theory* in the 1930s at a time when many of the major countries were in the process of moving away from liberal democracy and capitalism toward fascism in Germany and Italy and toward Communism in Russia. These countries appeared to deal better with the depression of the 1930s than countries like ours that stayed with liberal institutions. Keynes' message in *The General Theory* is that we can deal with depressions within the framework of a basically capitalistic economy and liberal democratic institutions. This is an important message to get across.

The intellectual forefathers of modern macroeconomics are, for me, the classical economists, Smith and Ricardo, the neoclassical work of Marshall, and the generation of our teachers, Arrow, Friedman, and Samuelson.

Would you advise undergraduates to major in economics?

Economics is a great major. I feel economics is a good pre–almost anything major. Most of the economics majors at the University of Chicago will go to law school, professional school, or work for a while. Our students have a lot of electives to choose from; they have a broad, liberal arts education.

Chapter 26

The Economy at Full Employment

Production and Jobs

In 1943, at the height of World War II, total production in the United States was a staggering 83 percent higher than it had been just four years earlier. How could production increase by such a large amount in such a short time? ◆ Over longer periods, we gradually become more productive and our incomes grow. On the average, each hour that we worked in 1998 earned us 70 percent more than it did in 1960. Despite setbacks during the past few years, the economies of Japan and China have expanded more rapidly than ours has and incomes in these countries have grown more quickly than ours. What makes production and incomes grow over the years? ◆ What are the forces that determine employment, wage rates, and real GDP when our economy is at full employment? ◆ Our population grows every year. Some of this population growth comes from immigration. What effect does population size have on employment, wage rates, and potential GDP? ◆ We also hear a lot about the importance of increasing our national saving to invest in new capital, about the importance of education, and about the need to support science and technology. How do capital accumulation, education, and advances in technology influence employment, wage rates, and potential GDP? ◆ When we talk about full employment, we don't mean that there is *no* unemployment. What determines the amount of unemployment when the economy is at full employment?

◆ In this chapter, we study the economy at full employment. We'll study the relationship between production and employment and learn about the forces that determine the quantity of employment. We'll also discover how changes in population, capital, and technology influence employment and incomes. And we'll learn about the forces that create unemployment when the economy is at full employment.

After studying this chapter, you will be able to:

■ Describe the relationship between the quantity of labor employed and real GDP

■ Explain what determines the demand for labor and the supply of labor

■ Explain what determines employment, the real wage rate, and potential GDP

■ Explain the influences on employment, the real wage rate, and potential GDP of an increase in the population, an increase in capital, and an advance in technology

■ Explain what determines unemployment when the economy is at full employment

Real GDP and Employment

To PRODUCE MORE OUTPUT, WE MUST USE MORE inputs. We can increase real GDP by employing more labor, increasing the quantity of capital, or developing technologies that are more productive. In the short term, the quantity of capital and the state of technology are fixed. So to increase real GDP in the short term, we must increase the quantity of labor employed. Let's look at the relationship between real GDP and the quantity of labor employed.

Production Possibilities

When you studied the limits to production in Chapter 3 (see pp. 37–38), you learned about the **production possibility frontier**, which is the boundary between those combinations of goods and services that can be produced and those that cannot. We can think about the production possibility frontier for any pair of goods or services when we hold the quantities of all other goods and services constant. Let's think about the production possibility frontier between two special items—real GDP and the quantity of leisure time.

Real GDP is a measure of the final goods and services produced in the economy in a given time period (see Chapter 23, pp. 494–497). We measure real GDP as a number of 1992 dollars, but the measure is a *real* one. Real GDP is not a pile of dollars. It is a pile of goods and services. Think of it as a number of big shopping carts filled with goods and services. Each cart contains some of each of the different goods and services produced, and one cartload of items costs $1 billion. To say that real GDP is $7,000 billion means that real GDP is 7,000 big shopping carts of goods and services.

The quantity of leisure time is the number of hours we spend not working. It is the time we spend playing sports, seeing movies, and hanging out with friends. Leisure time is a special type of good or service.

Each hour that we spent pursuing fun could have been an hour that we spent at work. So when the quantity of leisure time increases by one hour, the quantity of labor employed decreases by one hour. If we spent all our time having fun rather than working, we would not produce anything. Real GDP would be zero. The more leisure time we forgo to work, the greater is the quantity of labor employed and the greater is real GDP.

The relationship between leisure time and real GDP is a *production possibility frontier*. Figure 26.1(a) shows an example of this frontier. Here, an economy has 450 billion hours of leisure time available. If people use all these hours to pursue leisure, no labor is employed and real GDP is zero. As people forgo leisure and work more, real GDP increases. If people spent 200 billion hours working and took 250 billion hours in leisure, real GDP would be $7 trillion at point *a*. If people spent all the available hours working, real GDP would be $10 trillion.

The bowed-out *PPF* displays increasing opportunity cost. In this case, the opportunity cost of a given amount of real GDP is the amount of leisure time forgone to produce the real GDP. The additional hours of leisure forgone to produce a given additional amount of real GDP increases as real GDP increases. The reason is that we use the most productive labor first, and as we use more labor, we use increasingly less productive labor.

The Production Function

The **production function** is the relationship between real GDP and the quantity of labor employed when all other influences on production remain the same. The production function shows how real GDP varies as the quantity of labor employed varies, other things remaining the same.

Because one more hour of labor employed means one less hour of leisure, the production function is like a mirror image of the leisure time-real GDP *PPF*. Figure 26.1(b) shows the production function for the economy whose *PPF* is shown in Fig. 26.1(a). You can see that when the quantity of labor employed is zero, real GDP is also zero. And as the quantity of labor employed increases, so does real GDP. When 200 billion labor hours are employed, real GDP is $7 trillion (at point *a*).

A decrease in leisure hours and the corresponding increases in the quantity of labor employed and real GDP bring a movement along the production possibility frontier and along the production function. The arrows along the *PPF* and production function in Fig. 26.1 show these movements. Such movements occurred when employment and real GDP surged during the first four years of World War II.

But the increase in real GDP during World War II changed for an additional reason. Labor became more productive. Let's study the influences on the productivity of labor.

FIGURE 26.1

Production Possibilities and the Production Function

(a) Production possibility frontier

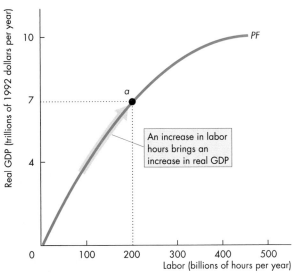

(b) Production function

On the production possibility frontier in part (a) if we enjoy 450 billion hours of leisure, we produce no real GDP. If we forgo 200 billion hours of leisure time and spend 250 billion hours on leisure, we produce a real GDP of $7 trillion, at point *a*.

The production function in part (b) is like a mirror image of the *PPF*. At point *a* on the production function, we use 200 billion hours of labor to produce $7 trillion of real GDP.

Changes in Productivity

When we talk about *productivity*, we usually mean the labor productivity. **Labor productivity** is real GDP per hour of labor. Three factors influence labor productivity:

- Physical capital
- Human capital
- Technology

Physical Capital   A farm worker equipped with only a stick and primitive tools can cultivate almost no land and grow barely enough food to feed a single family. One equipped with a steel plow pulled by an animal can cultivate more land and produce enough food to feed a small village. One equipped with a modern tractor, plow, and harvester can cultivate thousands of acres and produce enough food to feed hundreds of people.

By using physical capital on our farms and in our factories, shops, and offices, we enormously increase labor productivity. And the more physical capital we use, the greater is our labor productivity, other things remaining the same.

Human Capital   An economy's **human capital** is the knowledge and skill that people have obtained from education and on-the-job training.

The average college graduate has a greater amount of human capital than the average high school graduate possesses. Consequently, the college graduate is able to perform some tasks that are beyond the ability of the high school graduate. The college graduate is more productive. For the nation as a whole, the greater the amount of schooling completed by its citizens, the greater is its real GDP, other things remaining the same.

Regardless of how much schooling a person has completed, not much production is accomplished on the first day at work. Learning about the new work environment consumes the newly hired worker's time. But as time passes and experience accumulates, the worker becomes more productive. We call this activity of on-the-job education **learning-by-doing**.

Learning-by-doing can bring incredible increases in labor productivity. The more experienced the work force, the greater is its labor productivity, and, other things remaining the same, the greater is real GDP.

World War II provides a carefully documented example of the importance of this source of increase in labor productivity. In the shipyards that produced transport vessels called *Liberty ships*, labor productivity increased by an astonishing 30 percent purely as a result of learning-by-doing.

Technology A student equipped with a pen can complete a readable page of writing in perhaps 10 minutes. This same task takes 5 minutes with a typewriter and 2 minutes with a computer. Traveling on foot from New York to Los Angeles takes a person (a fit person!) more than 100 days. In a car, the trip takes a comfortable 5 days. And in an airplane, the trip takes 5 hours. These are examples of the enormous impact of technology on productivity. Imagine the profound effect of these advances in technology on the productivity of a movie director who works in New York and Los Angeles!

Shift in the Production Function

Any influence on production that increases labor productivity shifts the production function upward. Real GDP increases at each level of labor hours. In Fig. 26.2(a), the production function is initially PF_0. Then an increase in physical capital and human capital and an advance in technology occur. The production function shifts upward to PF_1.

At each quantity of labor employed, real GDP is greater on the new production function than it was on the original one. For example, at 200 billion hours in Fig. 26.2(a), real GDP increases from $7 trillion (point *a*) to $9 trillion (point *b*).

Figure 26.2(b) shows how the production function in the United States has shifted upward between 1980 and 1998. Along the production function PF_{98}, labor productivity is 38 percent greater than on PF_{80}. Labor productivity in the United States increases by almost 2 percent a year.

R E V I E W   Q U I Z

- What is the relationship between the leisure hours–real GDP *PPF* and the production function?
- What does the bowed-out shape of the leisure hours–real GDP *PPF* imply about the opportunity cost of real GDP and why is the *PPF* bowed out?
- Why does the production function shift upward when capital increases and technology advances?

FIGURE 26.2

An Increase in Labor Productivity

(a) An increase in labor productivity

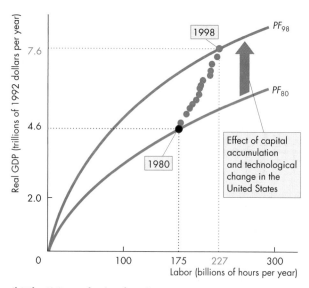

(b) The U.S. production function

The production function is initially PF_0 and 200 billion labor hours produces a real GDP of $7 trillion (point *a*). An increase in capital or an advance in technology that increases labor productivity shifts the production function upward to PF_1 and 200 billion labor hours produces a real GDP of $9 trillion (point *b*). U.S. real GDP has increased (part b) because labor has become more productive and the quantity of labor has increased.

The Labor Market and Aggregate Supply

YOU'VE SEEN THAT IN A GIVEN YEAR, WITH A given amount of physical and human capital and given technology, real GDP depends on the quantity of labor hours employed. To produce more real GDP, we must employ more labor hours. The labor market determines the quantity of labor hours employed and the quantity of real GDP supplied. We'll learn how by studying:

■ The demand for labor
■ The supply of labor
■ Labor market equilibrium
■ Aggregate supply

The Demand for Labor

The **quantity of labor demanded** is the labor hours hired by all the firms in the economy. The **demand for labor** is the relationship between the quantity of labor demanded and the real wage rate when all other influences on firms' hiring plans remain the same. The **real wage rate** is the quantity of goods and services that an hour of labor earns. In contrast, the **money wage rate** is the number of dollars that an hour of labor earns. A real wage rate is equal to a money wage rate divided by the price of a good. For the economy as a whole, the average real wage rate equals the average money wage rate divided by the price level multiplied by 100. So we express the real wage rate in constant dollars. (Today, we express this real wage rate in 1992 dollars.)

The *real* wage rate influences the quantity of labor demanded because what matters to firms is not the number of dollars they pay (the money wage rate) but how much output they must sell to earn those dollars.

We can represent the demand for labor as either a demand schedule or a demand curve. The table in Fig. 26.3 shows part of a demand for labor schedule. It tells us the quantity of labor demanded at three different real wage rates. For example, if the real wage rate falls from $30 an hour to $25 an hour, the qua￼ tity of labor demanded increases from 150 bil￼ hours a year to 200 billion hours a year. (Y￼ find these numbers in rows *a* and *b* of the

The demand for labor curve is *LD*. Po￼ and *c* on the curve correspond to rows *a*, *b* the demand schedule.

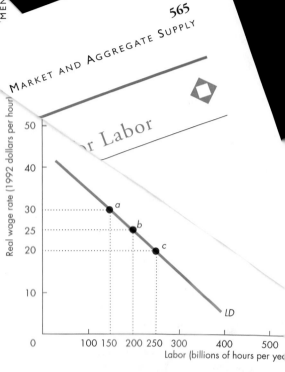

r Labor

	Real wage rate (1992 dollars per hour)	Quantity of labor demanded (billions of hours per year)
a	30	150
b	25	200
c	20	250

The table shows part of a demand for labor schedule. P￼ ￼ *b*, and *c* on the demand for labor curve correspond￼￼er is rows of the table. The lower the real wage rat￼ the quantity of labor demanded.

demanded
￼ses? That is, why
Why does the qu￼ ￼e slope downward? To
increase as the real ￼st first return to the
does the dema￼ ￼arn about the marginal
answer the￼**of Labor** The **marginal**
produc￼ ￼is the additional real GDP pro-
pro￼ ￼ional hour of labor when all other
pro￼ ￼duction remain the same. We calcu-
￼nal product of labor as the change in
￼vided by the change in the quantity of
￼loyed. Figure 26.4(a) shows some marginal
￼ calculations and Fig. 26.4(b) shows the mar-
Product curve.

...to 200

In Fig. 26.4(a)... ...rillion, an
employed increas... ...al product of labor
billion hours, a... ($3 trillion) divided
GDP increase... ...y of labor employed
increase of $... is $30 an hour.
equals the i... ...of labor employed increases
by the inc... ...rs to 300 billion hours, an
(100 bill... ...llion hours, real GDP increases
W... ...h to $9 trillion, an increase of $2 tril-
from ... ...arginal product of labor equals the
incre... ...n real GDP ($2 trillion) divided by the
fro... ase in the quantity of labor employed (100 bil-
lic... hours), which is $20 an hour.

In Fig. 26.4(b), as the quantity of labor
...ployed increases, the marginal product of labor
...inishes. Between 100 billion and 200 billion (at
...) billion), marginal product is $30 an hour. And
...ween 200 billion and 300 billion (at 250 billion),
...rginal product is $20 an hour.

...ninishing Marginal Product   The marginal prod-
... of labor diminishes as the quantity of labor
...ployed increases because all the labor, both the old
...d the new, work with the same fixed amount of
...ysical capital and given technology. As more labor
...urs are hired, the physical capital is worked more
...ensively, and more breakdowns and bottlenecks
...se. Eventually, as more labor hours are hired, work-
...s ... in each other's way and output increases barely
...at al...

T...
its the d...inishing marginal product of labor lim-
...for labor.

Diminishin...
Labor   Fir...
Each hour of...al Product and the Demand for
and adds to co...usiness to maximize profits.
produces more o... firm hires increases output
labor costs. Margi... n extra hour of labor
rate. But each additi... real wage that the
additional output tha... eeds the real wage
ginal product of labor ...eds the real wage
As a firm hires more ...r produces less
output from an extra hour ...ur—the mar-
that hour of labor costs. At t...
uct equals the real wage rate. I... extra
marginal product exceeds the re... at
more hour and the real wage rate... at
ginal product. In either case, profit...d-

FIGURE 26.4

Marginal Product and the Demand for Labor

(a) Calculating marginal product

(b) The marginal product curve

An increase in labor from 100 billion to 200 billion hours increases real GDP by $3 trillion. The marginal product of labor is $30 an hour. An increase from 200 billion to 300 billion hours increases real GDP by $2 trillion. Marginal product is $20 an hour. At point *a* on the *MP* curve, marginal product is $30 an hour at 150 billion hours (midpoint between 100 billion and 200 billion). The *MP* curve is the demand for labor curve.

Because marginal product diminishes as the quantity of labor employed increases, the lower the real wage rate, the greater is the quantity of labor that a firm can profitably hire. The marginal product curve is the same as the demand for labor curve.

You might gain a clearer understand of the demand for labor by looking at an example.

The Demand for Labor in a Soda Factory   Suppose that when a soda factory employs one additional hour of labor, output increases by 11 bottles. Marginal product is 11 bottles an hour. If the money wage rate is $5.50 an hour and soda sells for 50¢ a bottle, the real wage rate is 11 bottles an hour. (We calculate the real wage rate as the money wage rate of $5.50 an hour divided by a price of 50¢ a bottle, which equals a real wage rate of 11 bottles an hour.) Because marginal product diminishes, we know that if the firm did not hire this hour of labor, marginal product would exceed 11 bottles. Because the firm can hire the hour of labor for a real wage rate of 11 bottles, it just pays the firm to do so.

If the price of soda remains at 50¢ a bottle and the money wage rate falls to $5.00 an hour, the real wage rate falls to 10 bottles an hour and the firm increases the quantity of labor demanded.

Similarly, if the money wage rate remains at $5.50 an hour and the price of soda rises to 55¢ a bottle, the real wage rate falls to 10 bottles an hour and the firm increases the quantity of labor demanded.

When the firm pays a real wage rate equal to the marginal product of labor, it is maximizing profit.

Changes in the Demand for Labor   When the marginal product of labor changes, the demand for labor changes and the demand curve for labor shifts. You've seen that an increase in capital (both physical and human) and an advance in technology that increase productivity shift the production function upward. These same forces increase the demand for labor and shift the demand for labor curve rightward.

The Supply of Labor

The **quantity of labor supplied** is the number of labor hours that all the households in the economy plan to work. The **supply of labor** is the relationship between the quantity of labor supplied and the real wage rate when all other influences on work plans remain the same.

The table in Fig. 26.5 shows a supply of labor schedule. It tells us the quantity of labor supplied at three different real wage rates. For example, if the real wage rate rises from $11 an hour (row *a*) to $25 an hour (row *b*), the quantity of labor supplied increases from 150 billion hours a year to 200 billion hours a year. The curve *LS* is a supply of labor curve. Points *a*, *b*, and *c* on the curve correspond to rows *a*, *b*, and *c* of the supply schedule.

The *real* wage rate influences the quantity of labor supplied because what matters to people is not the number of dollars they earn (the money wage rate) but what those dollars will buy.

The quantity of labor supplied increases as the real wage rate increases for two reasons:

FIGURE 26.5
The Supply of Labor

	Real wage rate (1992 dollars per hour)	Quantity of labor supplied (billions of hours per year)
a	11	150
b	25	200
c	45	250

The table shows part of a supply of labor schedule. Points *a*, *b*, and *c* on the supply of labor curve correspond to the rows of the table. The higher the real wage rate, the greater is the quantity of labor supplied.

- Hours per person increase
- Labor force participation increases

Hours Per Person   In choosing how many hours to work, a household considers the opportunity cost of not working. This opportunity cost is the real wage rate. The higher the real wage rate, the greater is the opportunity cost of taking leisure and not working. And as the opportunity cost of taking leisure rises, other things remaining the same, the more the household chooses to work.

But other things don't remain the same. The higher the real wage rate, the greater is the household's income. And the higher the household's income, the more it wants to consume. One item that it wants to consume more of is leisure.

So a rise in the real wage rate has two opposing effects. By increasing the opportunity cost of leisure, it makes the household want to consume less leisure and to work more. And by increasing the household's income, it makes the household want to consume more leisure and to work fewer hours. For most households, the opportunity cost effect is stronger than the income effect. So the higher the real wage rate, the greater is the amount of work that the household chooses to do.

Labor Force Participation   Some people have productive opportunities outside the labor force. These people choose to work only if the real wage rate exceeds the value of these other productive activities. For example, a parent might spend time caring for her or his child. The alternative is day care. The parent will choose to work only if he or she can earn enough per hour to pay the cost of child care and have enough left to make the work effort worthwhile. The higher the real wage rate, the more likely it is that a parent will choose to work and so the greater is the labor force participation rate.

Labor Supply Response   The quantity of labor supplied increases as the real wage rate rises. But the quantity of labor supplied is not highly responsive to the real wage rate. A large percentage change in the real wage rate brings a small percentage change in the quantity of labor supplied.

Let's now see how the labor market determines employment, the real wage rate, and potential GDP.

Labor Market Equilibrium

The forces of supply and demand operate in labor markets just as they do in the markets for goods and services. The price of labor is the real wage rate. A rise in the real wage rate eliminates a shortage of labor by decreasing the quantity demanded and increasing the quantity supplied. A fall in the real wage rate eliminates a surplus of labor by increasing the quantity demanded and decreasing the quantity supplied. If there is neither a shortage nor a surplus, the labor market is in equilibrium.

In macroeconomics, we study the economy-wide labor market to determine the total quantity of labor employed and the average real wage rate.

Labor Market Equilibrium   Figure 26.6(a) shows a labor market in equilibrium. The demand curve *LD* and the supply curve *LS* are the same as those in Fig. 26.3 and Fig. 26.5.

If the real wage rate exceeds $25 an hour, the quantity of labor supplied exceeds the quantity demanded and there is a surplus of labor. In this situation, the real wage rate falls.

If the real wage rate is less than $25 an hour, the quantity of labor demanded exceeds the quantity supplied and there is a shortage of labor. In this situation, the real wage rate rises.

If the real wage rate is $25 an hour, the quantity of labor demanded equals the quantity supplied and there is neither a shortage nor a surplus of labor. In this situation, the labor market is in equilibrium and the real wage rate remains constant. The equilibrium level of employment is 200 billion hours a year. This equilibrium is *full-employment equilibrium*.

Potential GDP   You've seen that the quantity of real GDP depends on the quantity of labor employed. The production function tells us how much real GDP a given amount of employment can produce. At the equilibrium level of employment, there is full employment. And the level of real GDP at full employment is **potential GDP**. So the equilibrium level of employment produces potential GDP.

Figure 26.6(b) shows potential GDP. The equilibrium level of employment in Fig. 26.6(a) is 200 billion hours. The production function in Fig. 26.6(b) tells us that 200 billion hours of labor can produce a real GDP of $7 trillion. This amount is potential GDP.

FIGURE 26.6

The Labor Market and Potential GDP

(a) The labor market

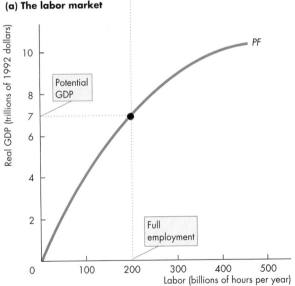

(b) Potential GDP

Full employment occurs (part a) when the quantity of labor demanded equals the quantity of labor supplied. The equilibrium real wage rate is $25 an hour, and employment is 200 billion hours a year.

Part (b) shows how potential GDP is determined. It is the quantity of real GDP determined by the production function and the full-employment quantity of labor.

Aggregate Supply

The **long-run aggregate supply curve** is the relationship between the quantity of real GDP supplied and the price level when real GDP equals potential GDP. Figure 26.7 shows this relationship as the vertical *LAS* curve. Along the long-run aggregate supply curve, as the price level changes, the money wage rate also changes to keep the real wage rate at the full-employment equilibrium level in Fig. 26.6(a). With no change in the real wage rate and no change in employment, real GDP remains at potential GDP.

The **short-run aggregate supply curve** is the relationship between the quantity of real GDP supplied and the price level when the money wage rate and potential GDP remain constant. Figure 26.7

FIGURE 26.7

The Aggregate Supply Curves

A rise in the price level with a rise in the money wage rate that keeps the real wage rate at its full-employment equilibrium level keeps the quantity of real GDP supplied at potential GDP—a movement along the long-run aggregate supply curve. A rise in the price level with no change in the money wage rate lowers the real wage rate and brings an increase in employment and in the quantity of real GDP supplied—a movement along the short-run aggregate supply curve.

shows a short-run aggregate supply curve as the upward-sloping *SAS* curve. Along the short-run aggregate supply curve, as the price level rises, the money wage rate remains fixed, so the real wage rate *falls*. In Fig. 26.6, when the real wage rate falls, the quantity of labor demanded increases and real GDP increases.

When the economy is at a point on its short-run aggregate supply curve above potential GDP, the real wage rate is below the full-employment equilibrium level. And when the economy is at a point on the short-run aggregate supply curve below potential GDP, the real wage rate is above the full-employment equilibrium level. In both cases, the quantity of labor that firms employ departs from the quantity that households would like to supply.

Production is efficient in the sense that the economy operates on its production possibility frontier. But production is inefficient in the sense that the economy operates at the wrong point on the frontier. When the real wage rate is below the full-employment equilibrium, people do too much work and produce too much real GDP. When the real wage rate is above the full-employment equilibrium, people do too little work and produce too little real GDP.

When the real wage rate departs from its full-employment equilibrium level, the resulting shortage or surplus of labor brings market forces into play that move the real wage rate and quantity of labor employed back toward their full-employment levels.

R E V I E W   Q U I Z

- Why does a rise in the real wage rate bring a decrease in the quantity of labor demanded, other things remaining the same?
- Why does a rise in the real wage rate bring an increase in the quantity of labor supplied, other things remaining the same?
- What happens in the labor market if the real wage rate is above or below the full-employment level?
- How is potential GDP determined?
- What is the relationship between the labor market and long-run aggregate supply?
- What is the relationship between the labor market and short-run aggregate supply?

You studied the forces that determine full-employment real wages, employment, and potential GDP. Let's now look at *changes* in full-employment equilibrium.

Changes in Potential GDP

REAL GDP WILL INCREASE IF:

1. The economy recovers from recession
2. Potential GDP increases

Recovery from recession means the economy moves along the real GDP–leisure *PPF* from a point at which real GDP and employment are too low to the full-employment equilibrium point. Equivalently, the economy moves along the short-run aggregate supply curve. Economists have a lot to say about such a move. And you can learn about this type of short-run change in real GDP in Chapters 29–35.

Increasing potential GDP means expanding production possibilities. We're going to study such an expansion in the rest of this chapter and in Chapters 27 and 28. We begin this process here by examining two influences on potential GDP:

- An increase in population
- An increase in labor productivity

An Increase in Population

As the population increases and the additional people reach working age, the supply of labor increases. With more labor available, the economy's production possibilities expand.

But does the expansion of production possibilities mean that potential GDP increases? And does it mean that potential GDP *per person* increases?

The answers to these questions have intrigued economists for many years. And they cause heated political debate today. In China, for example, families are under enormous pressure to limit the number of children they have. In some other countries, France is an example, the government encourages large families. We can study the effects of an increase in population by using the model of the full-employment economy in Fig. 26.8.

In Fig. 26.8(a), the demand for labor is *LD* and initially the supply of labor is LS_0. At full employment, the real wage rate is $25 an hour and the level of employment is 200 billion hours a year. In Fig. 26.8(b), the production function (*PF*) shows that with 200 billion hours of labor employed, potential GDP is $7 trillion. We're now going to work out what happens when the population increases.

FIGURE 26.8
An Increase in Population

(a) The labor market

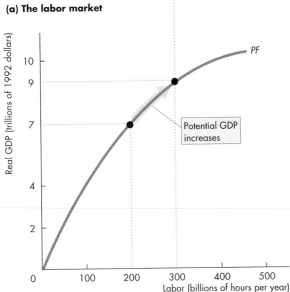

(b) Potential GDP

An increase in population increases the supply of labor and shifts the supply curve rightward (in part a). The real wage rate falls, and the quantity of labor employed at full employment increases. In part (b), the increase in full-employment equilibrium employment increases potential GDP. Because the marginal product of labor diminishes, the increased population produces a greater potential GDP but a smaller potential GDP per hour of work.

An increase in the population increases the number of people of working age and the supply of labor increases. The labor supply curve shifts rightward to LS_1. At a real wage rate of $25 an hour, there is now a surplus of labor. So the real wage rate falls. In this example, it falls until it reaches $15 an hour. At $15 an hour, the quantity of labor demanded equals the quantity of labor supplied. Equilibrium employment increases to 300 billion hours a year.

Figure 26.8(b) shows the effect of the increase in equilibrium employment on real GDP. As the full-employment quantity of labor increases from 200 billion hours to 300 billion hours, potential GDP increases from $7 trillion to $9 trillion.

So at full employment, an increase in population increases employment, increases potential GDP, and lowers the real wage rate.

An increase in population also decreases potential GDP per hour of work. You can see this decrease by dividing potential GDP by total labor hours. Initially, with potential GDP at $7 trillion and labor hours at 200 billion, potential GDP per hour of work was $35. With the increase in population, potential GDP is $9 trillion and labor hours are 300 billion. Potential GDP per hour of work is $30. Diminishing returns is the source of the decrease in potential GDP per hour of work.

You've seen that an increase in population increases potential GDP and decreases potential GDP per work hour. Some economists challenge this conclusion and argue that people are the ultimate economic resource. They claim that a larger population brings forth a greater amount of scientific discovery and technological advance. Consequently, these economists argue, an increase in population never takes place in isolation. It is always accompanied by an increase in labor productivity. Let's now look at the effects of this influence on potential GDP.

An Increase in Labor Productivity

We've seen that three factors increase labor productivity:

- An increase in physical capital
- An increase in human capital
- An advance in technology

The quantity of physical capital increases over time because of saving and investment. We study the factors that influence saving and investment decisions in Chapter 27. Human capital increases because of education and on-the-job training and experience. And technology advances because of research and development efforts. We study the way all these forces interact to determine the growth rate of potential GDP in Chapter 28.

Here, we study the *effects* of an increase in physical capital, an increase in human capital, or an advance in technology on the labor market and potential GDP. We'll see how potential GDP, employment, and the real wage rate change when any of these three influences on labor productivity changes.

An Increase in Physical Capital   If the quantity of physical capital increases, labor productivity increases. With labor being more productive, the economy's production possibilities expand. How does such an expansion of production possibilities change the equilibrium real wage rate, employment, and potential GDP?

The additional capital increases the real GDP that each quantity of labor can produce. It also increases the marginal product of labor and so increases the demand for labor. Some physical capital replaces some types of labor. So the demand for those types of labor decreases when capital increases. But an increase in physical capital creates a demand for the types of labor that build, sell, and maintain the additional capital. The increases in demand for labor are always larger than the decreases in demand and the economy-wide demand for labor increases.

With an increase in the economy-wide demand for labor, the real wage rate rises and the quantity of labor supplied increases. Equilibrium employment increases.

Potential GDP now increases for two reasons. First, a given level of employment produces more real GDP. Second, equilibrium employment increases.

An Increase in Human Capital   If the quantity of human capital increases, labor productivity increases. Again, with labor being more productive, the economy's production possibilities expand. And this expansion of production possibilities changes the equilibrium real wage rate, employment, and potential GDP in a similar manner to the effects of a change in physical capital.

An Advance in Technology   As technology advances, labor productivity increases. And exactly as in the case of an increase in capital, the economy's production possibilities expand. Again, just as in the case of an increase in capital, the new technology increases

the real GDP that each quantity of labor can produce and increases the marginal product of labor and the demand for labor.

With an increase in the demand for labor, the real wage rate rises, the quantity of labor supplied increases, and equilibrium employment increases. And again, potential GDP increases because a given level of employment produces more real GDP and because equilibrium employment increases.

Illustrating the Effects of an Increase in Labor Productivity   Figure 26.9 shows the effects of an increase in labor productivity that results from an increase in capital or an advance in technology. In part (a), the demand for labor initially is LD_0 and the supply of labor is LS. The real wage rate is $25 an hour, and full employment is 200 billion hours a year.

In part (b), the production function initially is PF_0. With 200 billion hours of labor employed, potential GDP is $7 trillion.

Now an increase in capital or an advance in technology increases the productivity of labor. In Fig. 26.9(a), the demand for labor increases and the demand curve shifts rightward to LD_1. In Fig. 26.9(b), the productivity of labor increases and the production function shifts upward to PF_1.

In Fig. 26.9(a), at the original real wage rate of $25 an hour, there is now a shortage of labor. So the real wage rate rises. In this example, it keeps rising until it reaches $35 an hour. At $35 an hour, the quantity of labor demanded equals the quantity of labor supplied and full employment increases to 220 billion hours a year.

Figure 26.9(b) shows the effects of the increase in full employment combined with the new production function on potential GDP. As employment increases from 200 billion hours to 220 billion hours, potential increases from $7 trillion to $10 trillion.

Potential GDP per hour of work also increases. You can see this increase by dividing potential GDP by total labor hours. Initially, with potential GDP at $7 trillion and labor hours at 200 billion, potential GDP per hour of work was $35. With the increase in labor productivity, potential GDP is $10 trillion and labor hours are 220 billion, so potential GDP per hour of work is $45.45.

We've just studied the effects of a change in population and an increase in labor productivity separately. In reality, these changes occur together. We can see the combined effects by examining an episode in the life of the U.S. economy.

FIGURE 26.9

An Increase in Labor Productivity

(a) The labor market

(b) Potential GDP

An increase in labor productivity shifts the demand for labor curve rightward from LD_0 to LD_1 (part a) and the production function upward from PF_0 to PF_1 (part b). The real wage rate rises from $25 to $35 an hour, and full employment increases from 200 billion to 220 billion hours. Potential GDP increases from $7 trillion to $10 trillion. Potential GDP increases because labor becomes more productive and full employment increases.

Population and Productivity in the United States

The U.S. economy was close to full employment in 1998. It was also close to full employment 14 years earlier, in 1984. We're going to compare these two years and look at the forces that moved the economy from one full-employment equilibrium to another.

In 1984, real GDP in the United States was $5.1 trillion, employment was 185 billion hours, and the real wage rate was $16 an hour. (We are using 1992 dollars.)

By 1998, real GDP had increased to $7.6 trillion, labor hours had increased to 227 billion, and the real wage rate had risen to $19 an hour. (Again, we are using 1992 dollars.)

The factors that you've just studied—an increase in population, an increase in physical and human capital, and advances in technology—brought these changes.

Population Increase In 1984, the working-age population of the United States was 176 million. By 1998, this number had increased to 205 million. The 1998 working-age population was 16 percent greater than the 1984 population. Recall that labor hours were 185 billion in 1984. A 16 percent increase would take labor hours in 1998 to 215 billion. But labor hours actually increased to 227 billion. Why? The answer is that an increase in capital and advances in technology increased labor productivity, which increased the labor force participation rate.

Capital Increase In 1984, the capital stock in the United States was estimated to be $16 trillion (1992 dollars). By 1998, the capital stock had increased to $22 trillion. This increase in capital increased labor productivity. But the increase in capital was not the only influence on labor productivity. Technological advances also occurred.

Technological Advances In 1984, we were just getting into the information revolution. Personal computers were around, but they were slow, had little memory, and had no hard drive. The Internet existed as a tool used by academic researchers for e-mail and file transfers, but no one had imagined the World Wide Web. Telephones couldn't remember numbers and record messages. Communication was slower and more costly than it was to become by 1998.

Production processes were beginning to be computerized but on a limited scale. Banks equipped

FIGURE 26.10

Full Employment in the United States: 1984 and 1998

(a) The labor market

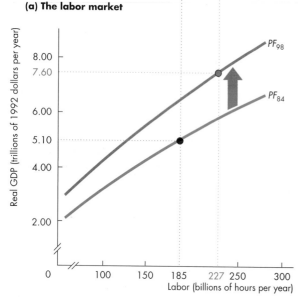

(b) The U.S. production function in 1984 and 1998

In 1984, the real wage rate was $16 an hour and the quantity of labor employed was 185 billion hours at the intersection of LD_{84} and LS_{84} (part a). Potential GDP was $5.1 trillion on PF_{84} (part b). By 1998, the real wage rate had increased to $19 an hour and the quantity of labor employed had increased to 227 billion hours at the intersection of LD_{98} and LS_{98} (part a). Potential GDP had increased to $7.6 trillion on PF_{98} (part b).

with ATMs were in the future. Supermarkets with laser scanners were only a dream. Robots in car factories and coal mines were still unknown. The biotechnology sector had still to be developed. The combined effects of capital accumulation and technological advance have made our farms and factories, shops, and offices more productive.

Figure 26.10 shows their effects along with the effects of the increase in population that occurred. In 1984, the demand for labor curve was LD_{84}, the supply of labor curve was LS_{84}, the full-employment real wage rate of $16 an hour and 185 billion hours of labor were employed. The production function in 1984 was PF_{84}. With 185 billion hours of labor employed, real GDP (and potential GDP) was $5.1 trillion.

By 1998, the increase in population had increased the working-age population by 16 percent. This increase in population increased the supply of labor and shifted the labor supply curve rightward to LS_{98}.

The accumulation of capital and advances in technology increased labor productivity. The demand for labor increased, and the demand for labor curve shifted rightward to LD_{98}. And the production function shifted upward to PF_{98}.

The real wage rate increased to $19 an hour, and employment increased to 227 billion hours. At this quantity of labor, real GDP (and potential GDP) increased to $7.6 trillion.

So in the United States, the effects of an increase in capital and advances in technology have been larger than the effects of increases in population. The forces that increase labor productivity have been sufficiently strong to overcome the effects of an increasing population.

R E V I E W   Q U I Z

- When the population increases but nothing else changes, why does real GDP per hour of work decrease?
- How does an increase in capital change the real wage rate, full employment, and potential GDP?
- How do advances in technology change the real wage rate, full employment, and potential GDP?
- If, as some people suggest, capital accumulation and technological change always accompany an increase in population, is it possible for potential GDP per hour of work to decrease?

Unemployment at Full Employment

SO FAR, WE'VE FOCUSED ON THE FORCES THAT determine the real wage rate, the quantity of labor employed, and potential GDP. And we've studied the effects of changes in population, capital, and technology on these variables. We're now going to bring unemployment into the picture.

In Chapter 24 (pp. 518–520), we learned how unemployment is measured. We *described* how people become unemployed—they lose jobs, leave jobs, and enter or reenter the labor force—and we *classified* unemployment—it can be frictional, structural, and cyclical. We also learned that we call the unemployment rate at full employment the **natural rate of unemployment**.

But measuring, describing, and classifying unemployment do not *explain* it. Why is there always some unemployment? Why does its rate fluctuate? Why was the unemployment rate lower during the 1960s and the late 1990s than during the 1980s and early 1990s?

The forces that make the unemployment rate fluctuate around the natural rate take some time to explain, and we study these forces in Chapters 29–35. Here, we look at the churning economy and the reasons why we have unemployment at full employment.

Unemployment is ever present for two broad reasons:

■ Job search
■ Job rationing

Job Search

Job search is the activity of looking for an acceptable vacant job. There are always some people who have not yet found a suitable job and who are actively searching for one. The reason is that the labor market is in a constant state of change. The failure of existing businesses destroys jobs. The expansion of existing businesses and the startup of new businesses that use new technologies and develop new markets create jobs. As people pass through different stages of life, some enter or reenter the labor market. Still others leave their jobs to look for better ones, and others retire. This constant churning in the labor market

means that there are always some people looking for jobs. These people are the unemployed.

The amount of job search depends on a number of factors, one of which is the real wage rate. In Figure 26.11, when the real wage rate is $25 an hour, the economy is at a full-employment equilibrium. The amount of job search that takes place at this wage rate generates unemployment at the natural rate. If the real wage rate is above the full-employment equilibrium, for example at $35 an hour, there is a surplus of labor. At this higher real wage rate, more job search takes place and the unemployment rate rises above the natural rate. If the real wage rate is below the full-employment equilibrium, for example at $15 an hour, there is a shortage of labor. At this real wage rate, less job search takes place and the unemployment rate falls below the natural rate.

The market forces of supply and demand move the real wage rate toward the full-employment equilibrium. These same forces move the amount of job search toward the level that creates unemployment at the natural rate.

But other influences on the amount of job search bring changes, over time, in the natural rate of unemployment. The main sources of these changes are:

■ Demographic change
■ Unemployment compensation
■ Structural change

Demographic Change An increase in the proportion of the population that is of working age brings an increase in the entry rate into the labor force and an increase in the unemployment rate. This factor has been important in the U.S. labor market in recent years. The bulge in the birth rate that occurred in the late 1940s and the 1950s increased the proportion of new entrants into the labor force during the 1970s and brought an increase in the unemployment rate.

As the birth rate declined, the bulge moved into higher age groups and the proportion of new entrants declined during the 1980s. During this period, the natural rate of unemployment decreased.

Another demographic trend is an increase in the number of households with two paid workers. When unemployment comes to one of these workers, it is possible, with income still flowing in, to take longer to find a new job. This factor might have increased frictional unemployment.

FIGURE 26.11
Job Search Unemployment

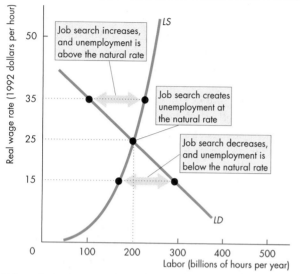

When the real wage rate is at its full-employment level—$25 an hour in this example—job search puts unemployment at the natural rate. If the real wage rate is above the full-employment level, there is a surplus of labor. Job search increases, and unemployment rises above the natural rate. If the real wage rate is below the full-employment level, there is a shortage of labor. Job search decreases, and unemployment falls below the natural rate.

Unemployment Compensation The length of time that an unemployed person spends searching for a job depends, in part, on the opportunity cost of job search. An unemployed person who receives no unemployment insurance benefits faces a high opportunity cost of job search. In this situation, search is likely to be short and the person is likely to accept a less attractive job rather than continue a costly search process. An unemployed person who receives generous unemployment insurance benefits faces a low opportunity cost of job search. In this situation, search is likely to be prolonged. The unemployed worker will continue to search for an ideal job.

The extension of unemployment benefits to larger groups of workers during the late 1960s and 1970s lowered the opportunity cost of job search. Consequently, the amount of job search and the natural rate of unemployment increased during those years.

Structural Change Labor market flows and unemployment are influenced by the pace and direction of technological change. Sometimes, technological change brings a *structural slump*, a condition in which some industries die and some regions suffer while other industries are born and other regions flourish. When these events occur, labor turnover is high—the flows between employment and unemployment increase and the number of people unemployed increases. The decline of industries in the "Rust Belt" and the rapid expansion of industries in the "Sun Belt" illustrate the effects of technological change and were a source of the increase in unemployment during the 1970s and early 1980s. While these changes were taking place, the natural rate of unemployment increased.

Job Rationing

You've learned that markets *allocate* scarce resources by adjusting the market price to make buying plans and selling plans agree. Another word that has a meaning similar to that of "allocate" is "ration." Markets *ration* scarce resources by adjusting prices. In the labor market, the real wage rate rations employment and therefore rations jobs. Changes in the real wage rate keep the number of people seeking work and the number of jobs available in balance.

But the real wage rate is not the only possible instrument for rationing jobs. And in some industries, the real wage rate is set above the market equilibrium level. **Job rationing** is the practice of paying a real wage rate above the equilibrium level and then rationing jobs by some method.

Two reasons why the real wage rate might be set above the equilibrium level are:

■ Efficiency wage
■ Minimum wage

Efficiency Wage It is costly for a firm to pay its workers more than the market wage rate. But to do so also brings benefits. An **efficiency wage** is a real wage rate that is set above the full-employment equilibrium wage rate and that balances the costs and benefits of this higher wage rate to maximize the firm's profit.

The cost of paying a higher wage rate is direct. It is the addition to the firm's wage bill. The benefits of paying a higher wage rate are indirect.

First, a firm that pays a high wage rate can attract the most productive workers. Second, the firm can get greater productivity from its work force if it threatens to fire those who do not perform at the desired standard. The threat of losing a well-paid job stimulates greater work effort. Third, workers are less likely to quit their jobs, so the firm faces a lower rate of labor turnover and lower training costs. Fourth, the firm's recruiting costs are lower. The firm always faces a steady stream of available new workers.

Faced with benefits and costs, a firm offers a wage rate that balances productivity gains from the higher wage rate against its additional cost. This wage rate maximizes the firm's profit and is the efficiency wage.

The Minimum Wage A **minimum wage** is the lowest wage rate at which a firm may legally hire labor. If the minimum wage is set *below* the equilibrium wage, the minimum wage has no effect. The minimum wage and market forces are not in conflict. But if a minimum wage is set *above* the equilibrium wage, the minimum wage is in conflict with the market forces and does have some effects on the labor market.

The minimum wage in the United States is set by the federal government's Fair Labor Standards Act. Some state governments have passed state minimum wage laws that exceed the federal minimum. In 1999, the minimum wage is $5.15 an hour. The minimum wage increases from time to time and has fluctuated between 35 percent and more than 50 percent of the average wage of production workers.

Job Rationing and Unemployment

Regardless of the reason, if the real wage rate is set above the equilibrium level, the natural rate of unemployment increases. The above-equilibrium real wage rate decreases the quantity of labor demanded and increases the quantity of labor supplied. So even at full employment, the quantity of labor supplied exceeds the quantity of labor demanded.

The surplus of labor is an addition to the amount of unemployment. The unemployment that results from a nonmarket wage rate and job rationing increases the natural rate of unemployment because it is added to the job search that takes place at full-employment equilibrium.

Economists broadly agree that efficiency wages can create persistent unemployment. Most economists believe that the minimum wage contributes to

unemployment, especially among low-skilled young workers. But David Card of the University of California at Berkeley and Alan Krueger of Princeton University have challenged this view. And the challenge has been rebutted.

Card and Krueger say that an increase in the minimum wage works like an efficiency wage. It makes workers more productive and less likely to quit. Most economists remain skeptical about this suggestion. If higher wage rates make workers more productive and reduce labor turnover, why don't firms freely pay the wage rates that encourage the correct work habits? Daniel Hamermesh of the University of Texas at Austin says that firms anticipate increases in the minimum wage and cut employment *before* they occur. Looking for the effects of an increase in the minimum wage *after* it has occurred misses its effects. Finis Welch of Texas A&M University and Kevin Murphy of the University of Chicago say that regional differences in economic growth, not changes in the minimum wage, explain the facts that Card and Krueger found.

R E V I E W   Q U I Z

- Why does the economy experience unemployment at full employment?
- Why does the natural rate of unemployment fluctuate?
- What is job rationing and why does it occur?
- How does an efficiency wage influence the real wage rate, employment, and unemployment?
- How does the minimum wage create unemployment?

♦ In this chapter, you've seen how the economy operates at full employment. *Reading Between the Lines* on pp. 578–579 looks at recent productivity gains in the United States. In the next two chapters, we study the rate of growth of the full-employment economy. In Chapter 27, we study decisions by firms to increase the amount of capital they employ and the decisions by households about the amount to save to finance capital accumulation. Then in Chapter 28, we study the interactions of capital accumulation, technological change, and population growth in the process of economic growth.

Productivity and Real Wages in the United States

THE WASHINGTON POST, FEBRUARY 10, 1999

Productivity Gains Give Wages a Boost

JOHN M. BERRY

Strong economic growth last year gave a healthy boost to labor productivity, allowing firms to give their workers solid pay increases while raising the prices of what they produced only slightly, the Labor Department reported yesterday.

Gains in productivity—the amount of goods and services produced for each hour worked—are a key ingredient in raising the nation's living standards. Consider this arithmetic:

Last year businesses other than farms increased their workers' compensation 4.2 percent while raising the prices they charged only 0.7 percent. The companies could do that without clobbering their profits because productivity gains offset 2.2 percentage points of that difference. And other cost-saving actions reduced non-labor costs by 1.4 percent on each unit of output.

The overall result was a combination that's hard to beat. The firms eked out a small increase in profit on each unit sold, workers' real pay went up 2.6 percent faster than consumer prices, and inflation went down. (The Labor Department uses the consumer price index, which rose 1.6 percent last year, to adjust compensation for inflation.)

However, many analysts and policymakers are questioning whether such good news is likely to continue for long.

Many economists believe that better education and on-the-job training, major investments in computers and other information processing technology and improved management may have increased the long-term trend in productivity growth in the United States. But even the optimists generally believe that trend is still much closer to the 1.3 percent annual productivity gain of the past two decades than last year's 2.2 percent increase. Over the past five years, for example, the average has been 1.4 percent.

Usually, productivity spurts along with economic growth, with the gain slowing markedly when growth slows. That's exactly what many forecasters expect to happen this year as growth tapers to a 2 percent to 3 percent pace from last year's 4 percent. One consequence could be higher inflation and smaller inflation-adjusted pay gains. ...

Essence of the Story

■ Labor productivity in businesses other than farms increased in 1998 by 2.2 percent. Wages increased by 4.2 percent while prices increased by only 0.7 percent. Non-labor costs per unit of output fell by 1.4 percent, and profits increased.

■ For the economy as a whole, profits increased slightly, real wages rose by 2.6 percent, and inflation fell to 1.6 percent.

■ Many economists think that better education and on-the-job training, investment in information technologies, and improved management may have increased the long-term trend in productivity growth.

■ But most believe that the trend growth rate is closer to the 1.3 percent annual productivity gain of the past two decades than to the 2.2 percent gain of 1998.

Economic Analysis

■ Figure 1 shows what happened in the labor market during 1998 in the United States.

■ In 1997, the demand for labor curve was LD_{97} and the supply of labor curve was LS_{97}.

■ The labor market was in equilibrium with 224 billion hours of labor employed at an average real wage rate of $18.74 (measured in 1992 dollars).

■ During 1998, technological change and capital accumulation increased the marginal product of labor. The demand for labor increased, and the demand curve shifted rightward to LD_{98}.

■ Because the working-age population increased by 1 percent, the supply of labor increased by this percentage. The supply of labor curve shifted rightward to LS_{98}.

■ The increase in the demand for labor was large compared to the increase in the supply of labor. Employment increased to 227 billion hours, and the real wage rate increased to $19.43.

■ Figure 2 shows the effect of the increase in labor productivity on the production function.

■ In 1997, the production function was PF_{97}. With employment at 224 billion hours, real GDP was $7.3 trillion. Real GDP per hour of work was $32.77 (in 1992 dollars).

■ The same technological change and capital accumulation that increased the demand for labor shifted the production function upward to PF_{98} in 1998. With employment at 227 billion hours, real GDP was $7.6 trillion. Real GDP per hour of work was $33.21.

■ The increase in real GDP per hour of work is the broadest and best measure of labor productivity. On this measure, labor productivity increased by 1.3 percent in 1998—equal to the annual productivity increase of the past two decades.

■ Real GDP grew by 2.8 percent in 1998 because employment increased by 1.5 percent.

■ The growth rate of labor productivity in the business sector reported in the news article is greater than the rate for the economy as a whole.

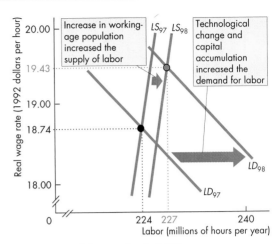

Figure 1 The labor market in 1998

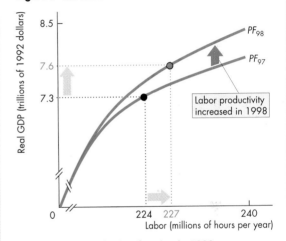

Figure 2 The production function in 1998

SUMMARY

KEY POINTS

Real GDP and Employment (pp. 562–564)

- To produce real GDP, we must forgo leisure time.
- As the quantity of labor increases, real GDP increases.
- Labor productivity increases if physical capital or human capital increases or if technology advances.

The Labor Market and Aggregate Supply (pp. 565–570)

- The quantity of labor demanded increases as the real wage rate falls, other things remaining the same.
- The diminishing marginal product of labor is the reason the quantity of labor demanded increases as the real wage rate falls.
- The quantity of labor supplied increases as the real wage rate rises, other things remaining the same.
- At full-employment equilibrium, the quantity of labor demanded equals the quantity of labor supplied.
- Potential GDP is real GDP produced by the full-employment quantity of labor.
- Along the long-run aggregate supply curve, the real wage rate is constant at its full-employment level. Along the short-run aggregate supply curve, the real wage rate, employment, and real GDP change.

Changes in Potential GDP (pp. 570–574)

- An increase in population increases the supply of labor, lowers the real wage rate, increases the quantity of labor employed, and increases potential GDP. It decreases potential GDP per hour of work.
- An increase in capital or an advance in technology increases labor productivity. It shifts the production function upward and the demand for labor curve rightward. The real wage rate rises, the quantity of labor employed increases, and potential GDP increases.

Unemployment at Full Employment (pp. 575–577)

- The unemployment rate at full employment is the natural rate of unemployment.
- Unemployment is ever present because of job search and job rationing.
- Job-search unemployment is influenced by demographic change, unemployment compensation, and structural change.
- Job-rationing unemployment arises from efficiency wages and the minimum wage.

KEY FIGURES

KEY TERMS

PROBLEMS

🖥 *1. Robinson Crusoe lives on a desert island on the equator. He has 12 hours of daylight every day to allocate between leisure and work. The table shows seven alternative combinations of leisure and real GDP in the economy of Crusoe:

Possibility	Leisure (hours per day)	Real GDP ($ per day)
a	12	0
b	10	10
c	8	18
d	6	24
e	4	28
f	2	30
g	0	30

  a. Make a graph of Crusoe's *PPF* for leisure and real GDP.

  b. Make a table and a graph of Crusoe's production function.

  c. Find the marginal product of labor for Crusoe at different quantities of labor.

2. The people of Nautica have 100 hours every day to allocate between leisure and work. The table shows the opportunity cost of real GDP in terms of leisure time forgone in the economy of Nautica:

Possibility	Leisure (hours per day)	Opportunity cost of leisure ($ of real GDP per hour)
a	0	0
b	20	5
c	40	10
d	60	15
e	80	20
f	100	25

  a. Make a table and a graph of Nautica's *PPF* for leisure and real GDP.

  b. Make a table and a graph of Nautica's production function.

  c. Find the marginal product of labor for Nautica at different quantities of labor.

🖥 *3. Use the information provided in problem 1 about the economy of Crusoe. Also, use the information that Crusoe must earn $4.50 an hour. If he earns less than this amount, he does not have enough food on which to live. He has no interest in earning more than $4.50 an hour. At a real wage rate of $4.50 an hour, he is willing to work any number of hours between zero and the total available to him.

  a. Make a table that shows Crusoe's demand for labor schedule and draw Crusoe's demand for labor curve.

  b. Make a table that shows Crusoe's supply of labor schedule and draw Crusoe's supply of labor curve.

  c. What is the full-employment equilibrium real wage rate and quantity of labor in Crusoe's economy?

  d. Find Crusoe's potential GDP.

4. Use the information provided in problem 2 about the economy of Nautica. Also, use the information that the people of Nautica are willing to work 20 hours a day for a real wage rate of $10 an hour. And for each 50¢ an hour *increase* in the real wage, they are willing to work an *additional* hour a day.

  a. Make a table that shows Nautica's demand for labor schedule and draw Nautica's demand for labor curve.

  b. Make a table that shows Nautica's supply of labor schedule and draw Nautica's supply of labor curve.

  c. Find the full-employment equilibrium real wage rate and quantity of labor in Nautica's economy.

  d. Find Nautica's potential GDP.

🖥 *5. Crusoe, whose economy is described in problems 1 and 3, gets a bright idea. He diverts a stream and increases his food production by 50 percent. That is, each hour that he works produces 50 percent more real GDP than before.

  a. Make a table that shows Crusoe's new production function and new demand for labor schedule.

  b. Find the new full-employment equilibrium real wage rate and quantity of labor in Crusoe's economy.

  c. Find Crusoe's new potential GDP.

  d. Explain and interpret the results you obtained in parts (a), (b), and (c).

6. Nautica's economy, described in problems 2 and 4, experiences a surge in its population. The supply of labor increases, and 50 percent more hours are supplied at each real wage rate.

a. Make a table that shows Nautica's new supply of labor schedule.
b. Find the new full-employment equilibrium real wage rate and quantity of labor in Nautica's economy.
c. Find Nautica's new potential GDP.
d. Explain and interpret the results you obtained in parts (a), (b), and (c).

*7. The figure describes the labor market on Cocoa Island. In addition (not shown in the figure), a survey tell us that when Cocoa Island is at full employment, people spend 1,000 hours a day in job search.

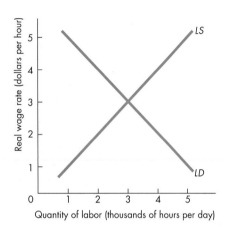

a. Find the full-employment equilibrium real wage rate and quantity of labor employed.
b. Find potential GDP in Cocoa Island. (Hint: The demand for labor curve tells you the *marginal* product of labor. How do we calculate the marginal product of labor?)
c. Calculate the natural rate of unemployment in Cocoa Island.

8. On Cocoa Island described in the figure and in problem 7, the government introduces a minimum wage of $4 an hour.
a. Find the new equilibrium real wage rate and quantity of labor employed.
b. What now is potential GDP in Cocoa Island?
c. Calculate the new natural rate of unemployment in Cocoa Island.
d. How much of the unemployment results from the minimum wage?

CRITICAL THINKING

1. Study the news article about productivity growth in the United States in *Reading Between the Lines* on pp. 578–579 and then answer the following questions:
   a. By how much did labor productivity grow in the business sector in 1998?
   b. By how much did real wages increase?
   c. What, according to the news article, caused the increase in labor productivity?
   d. Was the growth rate of labor productivity for the economy as a whole greater or smaller than that for the business sector? What do you think accounts for the difference?
   e. Why does employment increase by a relatively small amount while the real wage rate increases by a relatively large amount?

2. Visit the Parkin Web site and use the links provided to obtain information about the economy of Russia during the 1990s. Try to figure out what has happened to the production possibility frontier and production function and to the demand for labor and supply of labor in Russia during the 1990s. Describe the Russian economy during these years, using only the concepts and tools that you have learned about in this chapter.

3. Visit the Parkin Web site and use the links provided to obtain information about the economy of China during the 1990s. Try to figure out what has happened to the production possibility frontier and production function and to the demand for labor and supply of labor in China during the 1990s. Describe the Chinese economy during these years, using only the concepts and tools that you have learned about in this chapter.

4. You are working for the President's Council of Economic Advisors and must write a memo for the President that provides a checklist of policy initiatives that will increase potential GDP. Be as imaginative as possible, but justify each of your suggestions with reference to the concepts and tools that you have learned about in this chapter.

Chapter 27

Capital, Investment, and Saving

The 1996 Olympic Games in Atlanta were watched, as they happened, by more than two billion people (two fifths of the world's population). This media event was made possible by an enormous investment in a global video network. An even larger investment in a vast network of computers, telecommunications equipment, and databases enables a grade school student in Alice Springs, Australia, to click her mouse button and surf the Internet or send an e-mail message to her "pen-friend" in Akron, Ohio. How do businesses make the investment decisions that create the amazing tools that are building a global village? ◆ Each one of us decides how much income to save and how much to spend on consumption goods and services. Some of us spend everything we earn and can't wait for the next payday to come around. Others of us save large amounts of income. How do people make their saving decisions? ◆ Investment and saving decisions combine to determine interest rates and the long-term growth of potential GDP. Fluctuations in investment create cycles in real GDP. How do investment and saving decisions influence the interest rate you pay on your credit card balance and the interest rate you'll pay when you take a mortgage to buy a home? How do they influence the size of your pension when you retire?

Building the Global Village

◆ In this chapter, we study the decisions that determine the amount of capital in the economy and the return—the interest rate—that capital earns. When you have completed your study of this topic, you will be ready to learn about the forces that make potential GDP grow, which are explained in Chapter 28. ◆ We begin by looking at some facts about investment, capital, and interest rates in the United States and around the world.

After studying this chapter, you will be able to:

- Describe the growth and fluctuations of investment and the capital stock
- Describe the fluctuations in the real interest rate
- Explain how investment decisions are made
- Explain how household saving decisions are made
- Explain how investment and saving determine the real interest rate
- Explain how government influences the real interest rate, saving, and investment
- Explain how international borrowing and lending are determined

Capital and Interest

POTENTIAL GDP DEPENDS ON THE QUANTITIES of our productive resources. One of these resources is the economy's **capital stock**, which is the total quantity of plant, equipment, buildings, and inventories. The capital stock includes business capital such as auto assembly lines and supermarkets together with the inventories that businesses carry. It includes houses and apartments. And it includes government-owned *social infrastructure capital* such as the courts and the justice system that establish and enforce property rights, highways, dams and canals, schools and state universities, and national defense systems. All of these types of capital contribute to our production possibilities and potential GDP.

The size of the capital stock is a consequence of our *investment decisions.* The purchase of new capital, called **gross investment**, increases the capital stock. The wearing out and scrapping of capital, called **depreciation**, decreases the capital stock. The capital stock changes by the amount of **net investment**, which equals gross investment minus depreciation (see Chapter 23, p. 494). Investment, like the capital stock, includes private and government components. Private investment is business investment plus purchases of new homes and additions to inventories. Government investment is the part of government purchases that creates social infrastructure capital.

People decide how much investment to undertake, and these decisions help to determine the rate at which potential GDP grows. This chapter explains these decisions. We begin by looking at the facts about investment and the capital stock.

Investment and Capital

Figure 27.1(a) shows gross investment and depreciation. In recession years such as 1975, 1982, and 1991, gross investment decreases, and in the expansion years, it grows quickly. Depreciation also grows and fluctuates but it does not line up neatly with the business cycle. In Fig. 27.1(a), the vertical distance between the two lines shows net investment (gross investment minus depreciation). Net investment fluctuates like gross investment.

Figure 27.1(b) provides a more direct view of net investment, which fluctuates with the business cycle, and the capital stock, which grows steadily every year.

FIGURE 27.1

Investment and the Capital Stock: 1970–1998

(a) Investment

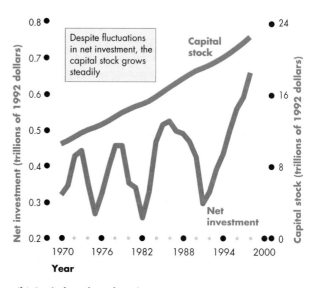

(b) Capital stock and net investment

Net investment fluctuates between $0.25 trillion a year in a recession and $0.65 trillion a year in an expansion. The capital stock grew steadily to $22 trillion in 1998.

Source: U.S. Department of Commerce, *National Income and Product Accounts of the United States* and *The Capital Stock of the United States,* and author's assumptions and calculations.

The capital stock increased from $10 trillion in 1970 to $22 trillion in 1998. The growth *rate* of the capital stock slows during the recessions, but the growth rate has always been positive because net investment has always been positive. When net investment increases during an expansion, the capital stock grows at about 3 percent a year, but on the average, the capital stock grows at around 2.5 percent per year.

Investment Around the World

Figure 27.2 compares investment in the United States with that in other parts of the world. Here, investment includes both business investment and government investment. And so that we can make comparisons, we measure investment as a percentage of GDP—called the investment rate.

Figure 27.2 shows that the investment rate in the United States has fluctuated and, throughout

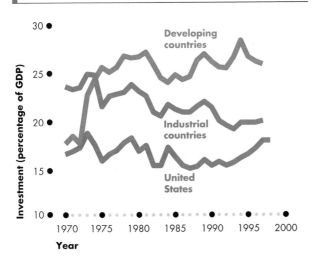

FIGURE 27.2

Investment in the United States and World: 1970–1998

Investment in the United States fluctuates between 15 percent and 19 percent of GDP. The United States has invested a smaller percentage of GDP than many other countries have. Since 1975, the developing countries have invested a larger percentage of GDP than have the industrial countries.

Sources: U.S. Department of Commerce, National Income and Product Accounts of the United States and International Financial Statistics, Yearbook, 1998.

the period shown in the figure, has been less than the investment rate in the other industrial countries and the developing countries. The industrial countries are Canada, Japan, Australia, New Zealand, and 18 rich countries in Western Europe. The developing countries comprise the rest of the world.

Investment in the industrial countries has fluctuated and has been on a downward trend. Investment in the developing countries has fluctuated and has followed two distinct trends: a strong upward trend from 1970 through 1976 and a moderate upward trend through the 1980s and 1990s. Since 1975, the investment rate in the developing countries has exceeded that in the industrial countries.

Within the developing economies, those in Asia (such as China, Korea, Taiwan, and Malaysia) have the highest investment rates and those in Africa and Central and South America have the lowest investment rates. But most of these countries have higher investment rates than that of the United States.

Interest Rates

When we studied labor in Chapter 24, we discovered that both the quantity of labor and the real wage rate per hour of labor have increased over the years. We've seen that the capital stock has grown steadily over time. But what has happened to the return on capital? Has it grown also? To find out, we must first define the return on capital.

The return on capital is the **real interest rate**, which is equal to the *nominal* interest rate adjusted for inflation. The nominal interest rate is the interest rate expressed in terms of money.

The real interest rate is approximately equal to the nominal interest rate minus the inflation rate. The exact calculation allows for the change in the purchasing power of the interest as well as the amount of the loan.[1]

Here, we'll work with the approximate formula. Suppose the nominal interest rate is 6 percent a year and there is no inflation. The real interest rate is also 6 percent a year.

Now suppose the inflation rate is 4 percent a year. In this situation, prices are rising and money is

---

[1] To calculate the *exact* real interest rate, use the formula: *real interest rate = nominal interest rate − inflation rate* divided by (1 + *inflation rate*/100). If the nominal interest rate is 10 percent and the inflation rate is 4 percent, the real interest rate is (10 − 4) ÷ (1 + 0.04) = 5.77 percent. The lower the inflation rate, the better is the approximation.

losing value at a rate of 4 percent a year. If the real interest rate remains at 6 percent a year, the nominal interest rate must rise to 10 percent a year.

To see why the nominal interest rate is 10 percent when inflation is 4 percent and the real interest rate is 6 percent, think about the following example. You borrow $1,000 for one year. If the real interest rate is 6 percent a year, the people who loaned you the money must be able to buy goods and services valued in today's prices at $1,060 when you repay them. But after a year in which prices rise by 4 percent, they need $1,100 to buy the goods and services that today cost $1,060. So if you pay them $1,100, you are only paying them $1,060 in today's prices and the *real* interest paid is $60—6 percent a year.

In the world economy, there are thousands of different interest rates. The real interest rate at which homebuyers and risky businesses can borrow is higher than the rate at which large corporations can borrow. And large corporations pay a higher interest rate than the U.S. government pays. But all real interest rates tend to move up and down together.

One real interest rate that fluctuates with many others is the real interest rate at which big U.S. corporations borrow. This rate is higher than that at which the U.S government can borrow but lower than the rate that you must pay on a bank loan or credit card balance. But it moves up and down in the same way as all these other interest rates.

Figure 27.3 shows the real interest rate paid by big U.S. corporations from 1970 through 1998. The average real interest rate during these years is 4 percent a year. The real interest rate does not rise steadily like the real wage rate rises. It fluctuates around a constant level.

Four subperiods are striking:

1. The 1970s—low (and negative in 1975)
2. Between 1980 and 1985—increased to exceed 8 percent a year
3. Between 1985 and 1989—decreased to about 5 percent a year
4. The 1990s—steady between 4 percent and 6 percent a year

The 1970s were years of economic turmoil that resulted from huge oil price hikes. The 1980s began with a deep recession but then went into a long expansion. The 1990s also began in recession and then had a long expansion. We'll learn in this chapter *why* these events influenced the real interest rate.

FIGURE 27.3

The Real Interest Rate

The real interest rate (here, the rate at which big U.S. corporations can borrow) was low during the 1970s and negative in 1975. It increased strongly between 1980 and 1984 and then decreased through 1989. It remained relatively steady at between 4 percent and 6 percent a year during the 1990s.

Source: Economic Report of the President, 1999, and the author's calculations.

R E V I E W   Q U I Z

■ What are the relationships among gross investment, net investment, depreciation, and the capital stock?

■ Provide some examples of private capital and of government social infrastructure capital.

■ Which item fluctuates most and which fluctuates least: net investment, depreciation, or the capital stock?

■ How does the U. S. investment rate (percentage of GDP invested) compare with the investment rates in other industrial countries and in the developing countries?

■ What is the return on capital and how has it changed over the past 30 years? Is the return ever negative?

We are now going to study businesses investment decisions and learn what determines the demand for new capital.

Investment Decisions

INVESTMENT CONSISTS OF PRIVATE INVESTMENT and government investment. We'll look at the role of government later in this chapter and first focus on private investment decisions.

How does Chrysler decide how much to spend on a new car assembly plant? How does AT&T decide how much to spend on fiber-optic cables? Business investment decisions are influenced by:

- The expected profit rate
- The real interest rate

To decide whether to invest in a new assembly line, Chrysler compares the expected profit rate with the real interest rate. The real interest rate is the opportunity cost of an investment. Let's look more closely at the expected profit rate and the real interest rate.

The Expected Profit Rate

Other things remaining the same, the greater the expected profit rate from new capital, the greater is the amount of investment.

Imagine that Chrysler is trying to decide whether to build a new $100 million automobile assembly line that will produce cars for one year and then be scrapped. Chrysler expects a net revenue of $120 million from operating the plant. Net revenue is equal to total revenue from sales minus the cost of labor and materials. The firm's expected profit from this assembly line is $20 million, which equals $120 million (net revenue) minus $100 million (cost of the plant). The expected *profit rate* is 20 percent a year—($20 million ÷ $100 million) × 100.

Of the many influences on the expected profit rate, the three that stand out are:

1. The phase of the business cycle
2. Advances in technology
3. Taxes

The phase of the business cycle influences the expected profit rate because sales fluctuate over the business cycle. In an expansion, an increase in sales brings a higher profit rate. In a recession, a decrease in sales brings a lower profit rate.

As technologies advance, profit expectations change. When a new technology first becomes available, firms expect to be on a learning curve and so expect a modest profit rate from the new technology. But as firms gain experience with a new technology, they expect costs to fall and the profit rate to increase.

It is the *after-tax* profit rate that a firm receives, so changes in tax rates influence the firm's after-tax profit rate. Firms go to extreme lengths to avoid taxes, and for multinational firms, the decision about *where* to invest often turns on the effect of taxes on profit.

The Real Interest Rate

Other things remaining the same, the lower the real interest rate, the greater is the amount of investment.

The funds used to finance investment might be borrowed, or they might be the financial resources of the firm's owners (the firm's retained earnings). But regardless of the source of the funds, the opportunity cost of the funds is the real interest rate. The real interest paid on borrowed funds is an obvious cost. The real interest rate is also the cost of using retained earnings because these funds could be loaned to another firm. The real interest income forgone is the opportunity cost of using retained earnings to finance an investment project.

In the Chrysler example, the expected profit rate is 20 percent a year. So it is profitable for Chrysler to invest as long as the real interest rate is less than 20 percent a year. That is, at real interest rates below 20 percent a year, Chrysler will build this assembly line, and at real interest rates in excess of 20 percent a year, it will not. Some projects are profitable at higher real interest rates, but other projects are profitable only at low real interest rates. Consequently, the higher the real interest rate, the smaller is the number of projects that are worth undertaking and the smaller is the amount of investment.

We summarize the influences on investment decisions in an investment demand curve.

Investment Demand

If the real interest rate rises, other things remaining the same, investment decreases. The table in Fig. 27.4 shows an example of this relationship. It lists the levels of investment that occur at three real interest rates and with three expected profit rates. The relationship between investment and the real interest rate, other things remaining the same, is called **investment demand**.

Figure 27.4(a) shows an investment demand curve when the expected profit rate is average. Each point (*a* through *c*) corresponds to a row in the table. If the real interest rate is 6 percent a year, investment is $1 trillion. A change in the real interest rate brings a movement along the investment demand curve. If the real interest rate rises to 8 percent a year, investment decreases to $0.8 trillion; there is a movement up the investment demand curve. If the real interest rate falls to 4 percent a year, investment increases to $1.2 trillion; there is a movement down the investment demand curve.

Figure 27.4(b) shows how investment demand depends on the expected rate of profit. When firms expect an average profit rate, the investment demand curve is ID_0, the same as in part (a). But when the expected profit rate increases, investment demand increases and the investment demand curve shifts rightward to ID_1. When the expected profit rate decreases, investment demand decreases and the investment demand curve shifts leftward to ID_2. Fluctuations in the expected profit rate are the main source of fluctuations in investment demand.

Let's now see how the investment demand curve helps us to understand the changes in investment in the United States.

FIGURE 27.4

Investment Demand

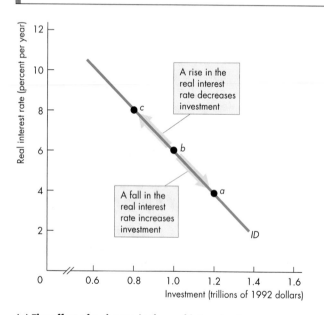

(a) The effect of a change in the real interest rate

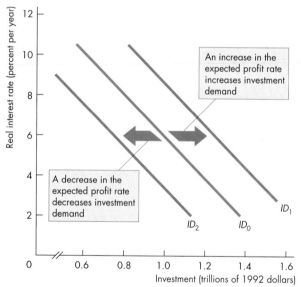

(b) The effect of a change in the expected profit rate

		Investment (trillions of 1992 dollars)		
	Real interest rate (percent per year)	**Expected profit rate**		
		Low	**Average**	**High**
a	4	1.0	1.2	1.4
b	6	0.8	1.0	1.2
c	8	0.6	0.8	1.0

The table shows the level of investment for three different expected profit rates—low, average, and high—and three different interest rates. When the real interest rate is 6 percent a year and the expected profit rate is average, investment is $1.0 trillion. Part (a) shows the investment demand curve, *ID*, for an average expected profit rate. A change in the interest rate brings a movement along the investment demand curve. In part (b), a high expected profit rate shifts the curve rightward to ID_1 and a low expected profit rate shifts it leftward to ID_2.

Investment Demand in the United States

Fluctuations in the real interest rate and in the expected profit rate bring fluctuations in investment. Figure 27.5 shows the relative importance of these two factors in the United States. The blue dots show net investment and the real interest rate each year

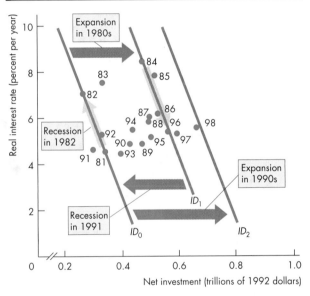

FIGURE 27.5

Investment Demand in the United States

The blue dots show net investment and the real interest rate in the United States for each year between 1981 and 1998. When the expected profit rate was low in the recession of the early 1980s, the investment demand curve was ID_0. Then, as the real interest rate increased in 1982, investment decreased. During the 1980s, the expected profit rate increased and the investment demand curve shifted rightward. By 1984, it had shifted to ID_1. Then, as the real interest rate fell during 1985 and 1986, investment increased. When the expected profit rate decreased in the late 1980s and the recession of 1991, the investment demand curve shifted leftward to ID_0. Then as the expected profit rate increased again through 1998, the investment demand curve shifted rightward through ID_1 to ID_2. Both swings in profit expectations and changes in interest rates bring fluctuations in net investment.

Source: Figures 27.1, 27.3, and the author's assumptions.

from 1981 to 1998. The curves labeled ID_0, ID_1, and ID_2 are three U.S. investment demand curves.

During the early 1980s, the investment demand curve was ID_0. A rise in the interest rate in 1982 brought a decrease in investment and a movement along the investment demand curve. The expected profit rate increased during the expansion of 1983 and 1984, and investment demand increased. The investment demand curve shifted rightward to ID_1. Between 1984 and 1986, the real interest rate fell and there was a movement downward along the investment demand curve ID_1.

During the late 1980s, profit expectations decreased and investment demand decreased. By 1991, the investment demand curve had shifted leftward back to ID_0. The expected profit rate increased again during the expansion of the 1990s and investment demand increased. By 1996, the investment demand curve had shifted rightward to ID_1 and by 1998, to ID_2.

You can see in Fig. 27.5 that investment fluctuates for two reasons: The real interest rate changes, which brings movements along an investment demand curve, and the expected profit rate changes, which shifts the investment demand curve.

R E V I E W   Q U I Z

- If the real interest rate falls and other things remain the same, what happens to investment? If the real interest rate rises and other things remain the same, what happens to investment? How would you use an investment demand curve to illustrate these events?

- If the expected profit rate increases and other things remain the same, what happens to investment? If the expected profit rate decreases and other things remain the same, what happens to investment? How would you illustrate these events using an investment demand curve?

- In which years have changes in the real interest rate changed U.S. investment and in which years have changes in other factors had the larger influence on U.S. investment?

Next, we study the decisions that create the funds that finance investment: saving and consumption decisions.

Saving Decisions

PRIVATE INVESTMENT IS FINANCED BY NATIONAL saving and by borrowing from the rest of the world (see Chapter 23, p. 498). **National saving** is the sum of private saving and government saving. We first study private saving. Later in the chapter, we'll see how government actions influence the saving decisions.

Households must decide how to allocate their *disposable income* between saving and consumption. Of the many factors that influence a household's saving decision, the more important ones are:

- The real interest rate
- Disposable income
- Purchasing power of net assets
- Expected future income

The Real Interest Rate

Other things remaining the same, the lower the real interest rate, the smaller is the amount of saving and the greater is the amount of consumption. The real interest rate is the opportunity cost of consumption. A dollar consumed is a dollar not saved, so the interest that could have been earned on that saving is forgone. This opportunity cost arises regardless of whether a person is a lender or a borrower. For a lender, saving less this year means receiving less interest next year. For a borrower, saving less this year means paying less off a loan this year and paying more interest next year.

You can see why the real interest rate influences saving by thinking about student loans. If the real interest rate on student loans jumped to 20 percent a year, students would save more (buying cheaper food and finding lower-rent accommodations) to pay off their loans as quickly as possible. If the real interest rate on student loans fell to 1 percent a year, students would save less and take larger loans.

Disposable Income

The greater a household's disposable income, other things remaining the same, the greater is its saving. For example, a student works during the summer and earns a disposable income of $10,000. She spends the entire $10,000 on consumption during the year and saves nothing. When she graduates as an economics major, her disposable income jumps to $20,000 a year. She now saves $4,000 and spends $16,000 on consumption. The increase in disposable income of $10,000 has increased saving by $4,000.

Purchasing Power of Net Assets

A household's assets are what it *owns*, and its debts are what it *owes*. A household's *net assets* are its assets minus its debts. The purchasing power of a household's net assets is the *real* value of its net assets. It is the quantity of goods and services that its net assets can buy. The greater the purchasing power of a household's net assets, other things remaining the same, the less is its saving.

Patty is a department store executive who earns a disposable income of $30,000 a year. She has been saving and now has $15,000 in the bank and no debts. Patty's colleague, Tony, also earns a disposable income of $30,000, but he has no money in the bank. Patty decides that this year, she will take a vacation and save only $1,000. But Tony decides to skip a vacation and save $5,000.

Expected Future Income

The lower a household's expected future income, other things remaining the same, the greater is its saving. That is, if two households have the same disposable income in the current year, the household with the larger expected future income will spend a larger portion of current disposable income on consumption goods and services.

Look at Patty and Tony again. Patty has just been promoted and will receive a $10,000 pay raise next year. Tony has just been told that he will be laid off at the end of the year. On receiving this news, Patty buys a new car—increases her consumption expenditure—and Tony sells his car and takes the bus—decreases his consumption expenditure.

Every young household expects to have a higher future income for some years and then to have a lower income during retirement. Because of this pattern of income over the life cycle, young people save a small amount, middle-aged people save a lot, and retired people gradually spend their accumulated savings.

We've studied households' saving decisions so that we can see how their saving decisions interact with firms' investment decisions to determine the real interest rate, investment, and saving. The next step is to learn about the saving supply curve.

Saving Supply

If the real interest rate rises, other things remaining the same, saving increases. The relationship between saving and the real interest rate, other things remaining the same, is called **saving supply**.

Figure 27.6 illustrates saving supply. The table shows a saving supply schedule, and the graph shows the saving supply curve. The points *a* through *c* on the saving supply curve *SS* in Fig. 27.6(a) correspond to the rows of the table. For example, point *b* indicates that when the real interest rate is 6 percent a year, saving is $1.0 trillion. If the real interest rate

rises from 6 percent a year to 8 percent a year, saving increases from $1 trillion to $1.1 trillion and there is a movement along the saving supply curve from *b* to *c*. If the real interest rate falls from 6 percent a year to 4 percent a year, saving decreases from $1 trillion to $0.9 trillion and there is a movement along the saving supply curve from *b* to *a*.

Along the saving supply curve, all other influences on saving remain the same. A change in any influence on saving other than the real interest rate changes saving supply and shifts the saving supply curve. An increase in disposable income, a decrease in the purchasing power of net assets, or a decrease

FIGURE 27.6
Saving Supply

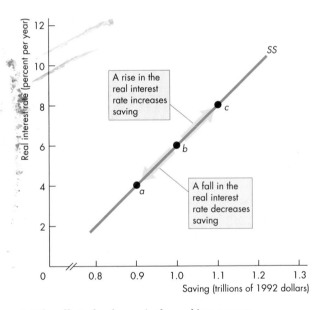

(a) The effect of a change in the real interest rate

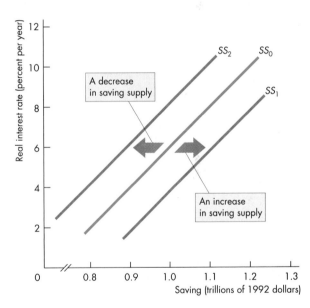

(b) The effects of other influences on saving

The table shows saving at three real interest rates. Part (a) shows the saving supply curve. Along the saving supply curve, the real interest rate changes but all other influences on saving remain the same. In part (b) an increase in disposable income (or a decrease in the purchasing power of net assets or a decrease in expected future income) increases saving and shifts the saving supply curve rightward from SS_0 to SS_1. A decrease in disposable income (or an increase in the purchasing power of net assets or an increase in expected future income) decreases saving and shifts the saving supply curve leftward from SS_0 to SS_2.

	Real interest rate (percent per year)	Saving (trillions of 1992 dollars)
a	4	0.9
b	6	1.0
c	8	1.1

in expected future income increases saving supply and shifts the saving supply curve rightward from SS_0 to SS_1. Changes in these factors in the opposite direction decrease saving and shift the saving supply curve leftward from SS_0 to SS_2.

Let's now see how the saving supply curve helps us to understand changes in saving in the United States.

Saving Supply in the United States

Fluctuations in the real interest rate, disposable income, the purchasing power of net assets, and expected future income change saving. Figure 27.7 shows the relative importance of these factors in the United States. The blue dots show net private saving and the real interest rate each year from 1980 to 1998. The curves labeled SS_0, and SS_1 are two U.S. saving supply curves.

The saving supply curve shows that when the real interest rate rises, saving increases. For example, between 1980 and 1983, the real interest rate rose and saving increased. But a large change in the real interest rate brings only a small change in saving.

The saving supply curve shifts rightward over time and by 1995, it was SS_1. Increasing disposable income is the main factor that increases saving and shifts the saving supply curve rightward.

Increases in the purchasing power of net assets and expected future income decrease saving. During the 1980s, with a booming stock market and increasing personal wealth, the purchasing power of net assets and expected future incomes both increased. Expectations of continued rapid economic expansion, which increased expected future incomes, reinforced the effect of increasing personal wealth. The result was an increase in consumption expenditure that almost equaled the increase in disposable income and the increase in saving was small.

In some years, such as 1998, a rising stock market and rising expected future income were so strong that saving decreased. In these years, the saving supply curve shifts leftward.

But on the average, rising disposable income has increased saving supply and the rightward shifts in the saving supply curve have been greater than the leftward shifts.

We've now studied the decisions that determine investment and saving and seen that both sets of decisions depend on the real interest rate. Next, we're going to see how the real interest rate, investment, and saving are simultaneously determined.

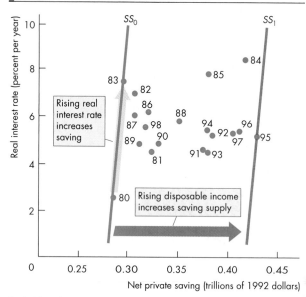

FIGURE 27.7

Saving Supply in the United States: 1980–1998

Each blue dot shows net private saving and the real interest rate for a particular year from 1980 through 1998. The blue curve SS_0 is an estimate of the saving supply curve for 1980. As disposable income increased, saving supply increased and the saving supply curve shifted rightward through SS_1 to SS_2. But in some years, the supply of saving decreases because a rising stock market and rising expected future income encourage consumption and discourage saving.

Source: U.S. Department of Commerce, *National Income and Product Accounts of the United States,* Figure 27.3, and the author's assumptions.

REVIEW QUIZ

- How do the real interest rate, disposable income, the purchasing power of net assets, and expectations of future income influence saving?
- If the real interest rate falls and other things remain the same, what happens to saving? If the real interest rate rises and other things remain the same, what happens to saving? How would you illustrate these events using a saving supply curve?
- How has the U.S. saving supply curve shifted in recent years and what have been the main reasons for the shifts?

Equilibrium in the World Economy

WE ARE NOW GOING TO SEE HOW INVESTMENT decisions and saving decisions determine the real interest rate. To do so, we study the economy of the entire world. The reason is that there is a single world capital market. Capital is free to roam the globe and seek the highest possible real rate of return. In 1998, for example, loans from the rest of the world to the developing countries and countries in transition were $2.1 trillion. So the saving of one country is not always used to finance the investment of that country.

Real interest rates are not the same in every country because some countries are riskier than others. The riskier countries have higher real interest rates. But interest rates move up and down together. If two countries with equal risk had different interest rates, people would want to borrow in the country with a low interest rate and lend in the country with a high interest rate. But no one would want to lend in the country with a low interest rate, so its interest rate would rise. And no one would want to borrow in the country with a high interest rate, so its interest rate would fall. Interest rates would quickly become equal in the two countries. The real interest rate in the world economy is determined by global investment and global saving.

Determining the Real Interest Rate

In Fig. 27.8, the world investment demand curve is *ID* and the world saving supply curve is *SS*. The higher the real interest rate, the greater is the amount of saving and the smaller is the amount of investment.

In the figure, when the real interest rate exceeds 6 percent a year, saving exceeds investment. Borrowers have an easy time finding the loans they want, but lenders are unable to lend all the funds they have available. The real interest rate falls, and as it does so, investment increases and saving decreases. The interest rate continues to fall until saving equals investment.

Alternatively, when the interest rate is less than 6 percent a year, saving is less than investment. Borrowers can't find the loans they want, but lenders are able to lend all the funds they have available. So the real interest rate rises. As the real interest rate rises, investment decreases and saving increases. The interest rate continues to rise as long as saving exceeds investment.

FIGURE 27.8

Equilibrium in the World Capital Market

	Real interest rate (percent per year)	Investment	Saving
		(trillions of 1992 dollars)	
a	4	12	9
b	6	10	10
c	8	8	11

The table shows world investment and saving at three interest rates, and the figure shows the world investment demand curve, *ID*, and world saving supply curve, *SS*. If the real interest rate is 4 percent a year, investment exceeds saving. There is a shortage of saving, and the real interest rate rises. If the real interest rate is 8 percent a year, investment is less than saving. There is a surplus of saving, and the real interest rate falls. When the real interest rate is 6 percent a year, investment equals saving. There is neither a shortage nor a surplus of saving, and the real interest rate is at its equilibrium level.

The real interest rate changes and is pulled toward an equilibrium level. In Fig. 27.8, this equilibrium is 6 percent a year. At this interest rate, there is neither a surplus nor a shortage of saving. Investors can get the funds they demand, and savers can lend all the funds they have available. The plans of savers and investors are consistent with each other.

Let's use the global saving supply and investment demand curves to explain changes in the real interest rate in the world economy.

Explaining Changes in the Real Interest Rate

In 1998, the real interest rate paid on long-term loans by the biggest and safest U.S. corporations was about 6 percent a year. It was more than 6 percent a year for homebuyers and risky businesses. Fourteen years earlier in 1984, the real interest rate reached a peak level for big companies of 8 percent a year. In contrast, 23 years earlier in 1975, the real interest rate was *negative*. Big companies could borrow at about 9 percent

a year, and the inflation rate was about 10 percent a year. So the real interest rate was close to *minus* 1 percent a year.

Figure 27.9 explains why these changes in the real interest rate occurred. In 1973 (in part a), the saving supply curve was SS_{73} and the investment demand curve was ID_{73}. The real interest rate was 2 percent a year, and the amount of saving and investment in the world economy was $4 trillion.

Between 1973 and 1975, world saving supply increased and the world saving supply curve shifted rightward to SS_{75}. The main reason for this increase was a huge rise in the price of oil, which increased the incomes and saving of oil producers and exporters.

At the same time, world investment demand collapsed and the world investment demand curve

---

FIGURE 27.9

Explaining Changes in the Real Interest Rate

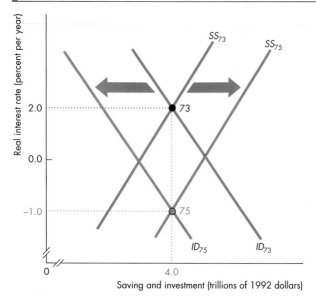

(a) Onset of growth slowdown

(b) 1975–1998

In 1973 (part a), world saving supply was SS_{73}, world investment demand was ID_{73}, and the real interest rate was 2 percent a year. A large increase in the world price of oil increased world saving supply and decreased world investment demand. By 1975, saving supply was SS_{75}, investment demand was ID_{75}, and the real interest rate was negative. By 1984 (part b), a

strong expansion increased investment demand to ID_{84}, but saving supply increased to only SS_{84}. The real interest rate increased to 8 percent a year. After 1984, saving supply increased by more than investment demand, and by 1998, the saving supply was SS_{98}, the investment demand was ID_{98}, and the real interest rate was 6 percent a year.

Sources: International Monetary Fund, *World Economic Outlook,* (Washington D.C., October 1998); International Monetary Fund, *International Financial Statistics, Yearbook,* (Washington D.C., 1998); *Economic Report of the President,* 1999; and the author's assumptions, calculations, and approximations.

shifted leftward to ID_{75}. The reason was that same oil price shock that increased saving supply. On the demand side of the capital market, oil users and importers faced steep cost increases and a collapse of profits, which decreased investment demand.

So by 1975, world saving supply had increased and world investment demand had decreased. The real interest rate fell to –1 percent a year.

Figure 27.9(b) takes up the story at this point. Gradually, investment demand recovered and, except for severe recession in 1982, increased each year. By 1984, the investment demand curve had shifted rightward to ID_{84}. Through these same years, saving supply increased slowly. The reasons for slow saving growth are complex. But one factor at work, which we examine later in this chapter, was the emergence of large government deficits, which must be subtracted from private saving to determine total saving. The combination of a large increase in investment demand and a small increase in saving supply increased the real interest rate to 8 percent a year in 1984, and world investment and world saving increased to $6 trillion.

The rest of the 1980s and the 1990s saw a growth in the supply of saving relative to the increase in investment demand. By 1998, the investment demand curve had shifted rightward to ID_{98} and the saving supply curve had shifted to SS_{98}. Because of these changes, the real interest rate fell to 6 percent a year.

R E V I E W   Q U I Z

- How is the real interest rate is determined? Why is it determined in the *world* capital market?
- What event simultaneously increased saving supply and decreased investment demand in 1973–1974. What was the effect on the real interest rate?
- What were the trends in world investment demand, world saving supply, and the real interest rate during the 1980s? Can you explain the trends?
- What were the trends in world investment demand, world saving supply, and the real interest rate during the late 1980s and 1990s? Can you explain the trends?

So far in our study of investment, saving, and the real interest rate, we've ignored government saving. Let's now bring government saving into the picture.

The Role of Government

PART OF THE CAPITAL STOCK ARISES FROM government investment. And investment is financed by total saving, which is made up of private saving plus government saving. So government actions influence investment demand, saving supply, and the real interest rate. In order to complete our study of the forces that determine the quantity of capital and the real interest rate, we must investigate the role played by governments.

But because the real interest rate is determined in the *world* capital market, it is the *aggregate* investment and *aggregate* saving of all governments that matters, not the investment and saving of one government.

Most governments are tiny and many U.S. corporations have a bigger impact on the world capital market than do some governments. Even the biggest governments have a relatively small impact on the world capital market. For example, the saving of the U. S. government is less than 1 percent of world saving.

But governments in total are large. The saving of world total government is close to 10 percent of world total saving. And the direction of that saving is negative. World total government saving is *negative!*

Let's see why government saving is negative and how government investment and saving influence total investment demand, saving supply, and the real interest rate.

Government Budgets

You learned in Chapter 23, (pp. 498–499) that GDP equals the sum of consumption expenditure, C, investment, I, government purchases, G, and net exports. We'll ignore net exports for the moment and consider only a closed economy (such as the world economy). So, in a closed economy,

$$GDP = C + I + G.$$

GDP also equals the sum of consumption expenditure, saving, S, and net taxes, T. That is,

$$GDP = C + S + T.$$

By combining these two ways of looking at GDP, you can see that:

$$I = S + T - G.$$

- If net taxes, *T*, exceed government purchases, *G*, the government has a budget surplus and government saving is positive.
- If government purchases exceed net taxes, the government has a budget deficit and government saving is negative.

When the government has a budget surplus, it contributes toward financing investment. Its saving must be added to private saving. But when the government has a budget deficit, it competes with businesses for private saving. In this situation, government saving must be subtracted from private saving.

Government saving can influence the world capital market in two ways, one direct and one indirect. We'll begin with the direct effect.

Direct Effect of Government Saving

Figure 27.10 shows the direct effect of government saving for the case in which government saving is negative—governments have a deficit. The world investment demand curve, *ID*, is the same as that in Fig. 27.8. The *private* saving supply curve, *PS*, shows the relationship between private saving and the real interest rate. The world saving supply curve *SS* shows the sum of private saving and government saving.

The horizontal distance between the private saving curve and the world saving supply curve is government saving. In this example, government saving is a negative $2 trillion. That is, the governments of all the nations have a total budget deficit of $2 trillion. (This number is larger than the actual total government deficit in the world economy in 1998.)

The effect of government negative saving, which is also called *dissaving*, is to decrease world saving and increase the real interest rate. Investment decreases. In this example, with a government deficit of $2 trillion, the world saving supply curve shifts leftward, and the real interest rate rises from 6 percent a year to 7 percent a year. Investment decreases from $10 trillion to $9 trillion.

Investment does not decrease by the full amount of the government deficit because the higher real interest rate induces an increase in private saving. In this example, private saving increases by $1 trillion to $11 trillion. In reality, the increase in private saving might be quite small, at least in the short term.

The tendency for a government budget deficit to decrease investment is called a **crowding-out effect**. By raising the real interest rate, the government

FIGURE 27.10

A Crowding-Out Effect

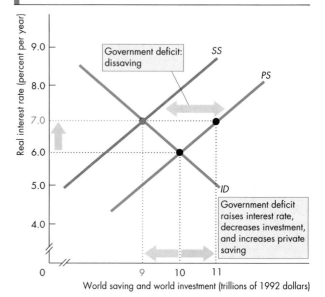

The world investment demand curve is *ID*, and the world private saving supply curve is *PS*. With balanced government budgets, the real interest rate is 6 percent a year and investment equals saving at $10 trillion a year. A government budget deficit is negative government saving (dissaving). We subtract the government deficit from private saving to determine the world saving supply curve *SS*. The real interest rate rises, investment decreases (is crowded out), and private saving increases.

deficit crowds out private investment and slows the rate of economic growth.

A government surplus has the opposite effect: It increases world saving supply, lowers the real interest rate, and stimulates investment and economic growth.

We've just studied the direct effect of government saving on the world capital market. But there is an indirect effect that we must also take into account.

Indirect Effect of Government Saving

Government saving has an indirect effect on the world capital market because it influences private saving. In the crowding-out story we've just told, the *quantity of private saving* changes because the real interest rate changes. There is a movement along the *PS* curve. But private saving supply does not change. That is, the *PS* curve does not shift. The indirect effect arises from the possibility that a change in government saving changes private saving supply and shifts the *PS* curve. In an extreme version of this effect, private saving changes to offset the government deficit and the deficit has no effect on the real interest rate or investment. Let's look at this extreme case.

The Barro-Ricardo Effect So named because it was first suggested by the English economist David Ricardo in the eighteenth century and refined by Robert J. Barro of Harvard University during the 1980s, the Barro-Ricardo effect holds that a government budget deficit has no effect on the real interest rate or investment. Another way of stating this view is that financing government purchases by taxes or by borrowing is equivalent.

The reasoning behind the Barro-Ricardo effect is the following. A government that runs a deficit must sell bonds to pay for the goods and services that are not paid for by taxes. And the government must pay interest on those bonds. It must also collect more taxes *in the future* to pay the interest on the larger quantity of bonds that are outstanding. Taxpayers are rational and have good foresight. They can see that their taxes will be higher in the future, so their disposable income will be smaller. With a smaller expected future disposable income, saving increases. And if taxpayers want to neutralize the effects of the government deficit on their own consumption plans, they increase their saving by the same amount that the government is dissaving through its deficit.

Figure 27.11 shows this outcome. Initially, the government has a balanced budget—neither a deficit nor a surplus—so the world saving supply curve *SS* is the private saving supply curve PS_0. With world investment demand *ID*, the equilibrium real interest rate is 6 percent a year and investment and saving are $10 trillion.

Governments now run deficits that total $2 trillion. But these deficits induce an increase in private saving. In Fig. 27.11, the increase in private saving equals the government deficit. So the private saving supply curve shifts rightward to PS_1. But the world saving supply curve *SS* remains unchanged, and the real interest rate remains at 6 percent a year. Investment also remains at $10 trillion a year. Private saving increases by $2 trillion to $12 trillion.

The outcome shown in Fig. 27.11 is extreme and probably does not actually occur. Taxpayers probably respond in the *direction* suggested by Ricardo and Barro but not in the *amount* they suggest. So the effect of government deficits probably lies between

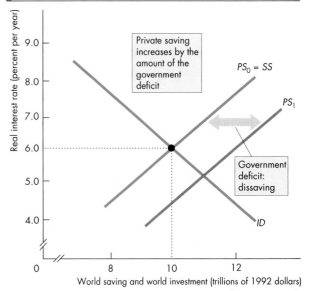

FIGURE 27.11

A Barro-Ricardo Effect

The world investment demand curve is *ID*, and initially, the world saving supply curve *SS* is the same as the private saving supply curve, PS_0. With balanced government budgets, the real interest rate is 5 percent a year and investment equals saving at $10 trillion a year. A government budget deficit induces an increase in private saving to PS_1, but the world saving supply curve remains at *SS*. The real interest rate, investment, and *total* saving remain constant.

the two cases shown in Figs. 27.10 and 27.11. That is, a government deficit increases the real interest rate and partly crowds out investment, but it also induces a partial increase in private saving in anticipation of lean times later when the tax bill rises to pay the interest on a rising debt.

Government Deficits Today

Government deficits have been large in recent years and have probably been responsible for the high real interest rates of the 1990s. Figure 27.12 shows the deficits of the United States, the other advanced countries, and the developing and transitional countries from 1990 through 1998 and the projected deficits for 1999. During the early 1990s, deficits in the United States and the other advanced countries increased to more than 4 percent of GDP. But after

FIGURE 27.12

Government Surpluses and Deficits

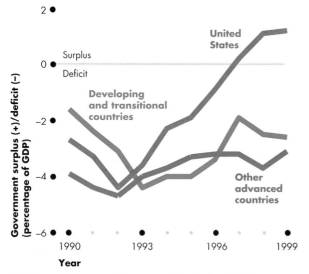

A U.S. government surplus emerged in the late 1990s after a long run of deficits. Government budget deficits in the other advanced countries and the developing and transition countries have shrunk slightly since the early 1990s but deficits persist.

Source: International Monetary Fund, *World Economic Outlook,* (Washington D.C., October 1998).

1993, government deficits in the advanced countries decreased, and spectacularly so in the United States, where by the late 1990s a surplus emerged.

Government deficits in the developing countries and transitional countries (the countries of central and eastern Europe that are introducing market economies and private enterprise) have also persisted but have fallen somewhat through the 1990s. These countries have decreased their deficits because doing so has been a condition for receiving loans, most notably from the International Monetary Fund. (To learn about the International Monetary Fund, see Talking with Stanley Fischer on pp. 866–870.)

During the 1990s, real interest rates were higher than average. The reason is that world investment demand was high relative to world saving supply. During the 1990s, investment opportunities were large and saving rates were low compared with average times. Figure 27.3 shows that real interest rates averaged 4 percent between 1970 and 1995. But even this number is above the long-term average, which

over the past 100 years is 2 percent a year. If government deficits continue to decrease, real interest rates will also decrease (other things remaining the same).

R E V I E W   Q U I Z

- How is world saving influenced by private saving, taxes, and government purchases?
- How does an increase in aggregate budget deficit of all governments change private saving, total saving, investment, and the real interest rate?
- How did government deficits influence world saving and world investment during the 1990s?

Saving and Investment in the National Economy

SAVING SUPPLY AND INVESTMENT DEMAND IN the world economy determine the world real interest rate. At the equilibrium real interest rate, world saving equals world investment.

Although saving equals investment in the world economy, it does not necessarily do so in a national economy. In a nation, investment is financed by *national* saving plus borrowing from the rest of the world (see Chapter 23, p. 498). Nations in which investment exceeds national saving borrow from the rest of the world, and nations in which national saving exceeds investment lend to the rest of the world. For the world as a whole, international borrowing equals international lending.

But as you also learned in Chapter 23, a nation's international lending equals its net exports. So a nation that has a net export surplus is also one that lends to the rest of the world. A nation whose imports exceed its exports has negative net exports and borrows from the rest of the world. Whether a nation has a surplus or deficit in its international trade depends on whether its national saving exceeds or falls short of its investment.

Let's take a closer look at the role played by national saving and investment decisions and see how they determine international borrowing. There are two channels of influence to consider.

First, each nation contributes to world saving and investment and so influences the world real interest rate. The larger the country, the greater is that influence. For example, investment and saving decisions in the United States, the European Union, and Japan have a big impact on world investment demand and world saving supply. So they have a big influence on the world real interest rate. The investment and saving of other nations individually have a small impact on world investment demand and world saving supply. So they have a negligible influence on the world real interest rate.

Second, a nation's saving and investment decisions, along with the world real interest rate, determine the amount the nation borrows from or lends to the rest of the world. They also, equivalently, determine a nation's net exports.

Figure 27.13 shows the determination of a nation's international borrowing and net exports. The nation's investment demand curve is *ID*, and its saving supply curve (including any government saving) is *SS*. The world real interest rate is 6 percent a year. At this real interest rate, investment is $1.5 trillion and saving is $1.0 trillion. International borrowing fills the gap between investment and saving. In the example in Fig. 27.13, investment exceeds saving, so the nation borrows from the rest of the world. If, at the world real interest rate, saving exceeds investment, the nation lends to the rest of the world.

Government Saving and International Borrowing

The greater the amount of government saving, other things remaining the same, the greater is national saving. And the greater the national saving, the smaller is international borrowing (or the larger is international lending). An increase in the government deficit decreases national saving and increases international borrowing.

You can now see why U.S. net exports have been negative for the past 20 years. It is because U.S. national saving has been less than investment. Government dissaving (a government budget deficit) has contributed to the shortfall. A low private saving rate has also contributed.

You can also see that one popular view about the U.S. budget deficit is incorrect. Because the capital market is a global market and the U.S. government is a small player, the U.S. government deficit cannot cause much damage to growth by crowding out investment. But it does damage the growth of U.S disposable incomes because it increases international borrowing and increases the interest payments that we must make to the rest of the world.

FIGURE 27.13

Saving, Investment, and International Borrowing

A nation's investment demand curve is *ID*, and its saving supply curve (including government saving) is *SS*. The world real interest rate is 6 percent a year. At this interest rate, investment, which is $1.5 trillion, exceeds saving, which is $1.0 trillion. The nation borrows $0.5 trillion from the rest of the world.

R E V I E W   Q U I Z

- If, in a country, investment exceeds saving at the world real interest rate, does that country have positive or negative net exports? Does it lend to or borrow from the rest of the world?
- Does an increase in a government's deficit crowd out investment? Explain why or why not.

◆ In this chapter, we've seen that the quantity of capital depends on investment and saving, and we've seen how the real interest rate is determined in the world capital market. Your next task is to see how technological change brings capital accumulation and economic growth.

Before embarking on this task, take a look at *Reading Between the Lines* on pp. 600–601, which examines the private saving performance of the United States in recent years.

Saving in the United States

THE WALL STREET JOURNAL, FEBRUARY 4, 1999

The Economy Is Safe From a 'Savings Crisis'

By MICKEY D. LEVY

A specter is haunting our economic boom—the specter of low personal savings. As measured by the Department of Commerce, the rate of personal savings, which averaged 7.7% in the 1960s and 1970s and 7% in the 1980s, fell steadily toward zero in the 1990s, and even turned negative during parts of 1998.

But these concerns are largely misplaced, for they rely on an incomplete picture of the economy. The rate of personal savings is a very limited measure, and although it has fallen, the stock of household wealth has soared, while gross national savings have actually risen as a share of gross domestic product. The relatively modest rise in the current-account deficit (the amount by which national investment exceeds national savings) as a share of the economy is attribut-able to continued strong gross investment with high expected rates of return, and has been consistent with a firm dollar. And while the recent strong growth in consumption seems unsustainable, the fundamentals do not point toward collapse.

A comprehensive measure of savings would capture all changes in the stock of wealth. But the rate of personal savings, measured for national income purposes, is calculated as the ratio of disposable personal income (income minus taxes) minus consumption to disposable personal income. As such, it excludes key sources of savings: business savings and the appreciation of stock values, rising housing values and even the appreciation of individual retirement accounts. Nor does it include personal claims on private pensions and other forms of deferred compensation.

Essence of the Story

- The rate of *personal* saving measured in the national income accounts fell toward zero during the 1990s.

- The personal saving rate excludes business saving and the increase in stock values, house values, and individual retirement accounts.

- A full measure of saving equals the change in the stock of wealth.

- The falling saving rate is not a problem because the measured saving rate ignores the fact that the stock of household wealth has increased.

- The current account deficit, which is the amount by which national investment exceeds national saving, has increased because a high expected rate of return has increased investment.

Economic Analysis

■ Figure 1 shows the falling saving rate in the United States. Two measures, the gross saving rate and the personal saving rate, show a similar downward trend after 1980. But after 1993, while the personal rate continued to decrease, the national saving rate began to increase. The news article notes this fact.

■ The personal saving rate depends on the real interest rate, the purchasing power of net assets, and expected future income.

■ The higher the real interest rate, the greater is the saving rate, other things remaining the same. The real interest rate was higher during the 1980s and 1990s than during the 1970s. So this influence has lessened the decrease in the saving rate.

■ The greater the purchasing power of net assets, other things remaining the same, the smaller is the saving rate. As the news article notes, a full measure of saving includes the change in the value of net assets.

■ So when the value of net assets increases, saving properly measured has increased, and households feel comfortable increasing the percentage of disposable income consumed. The measured saving rate decreases.

■ A large increase in stock market values has increased the value of net assets and decreased the saving rate.

■ The higher is expected future income, other things remaining the same, the smaller is the saving rate. This factor, too, has probably decreased the saving rate as people have come to expect more rapid economic growth during the 1990s.

■ One consequence of the decreased saving rate is a decrease in world saving and a higher real interest rate.

■ Other consequences are a larger amount of U.S. borrowing from the rest of the world and imports that exceed exports.

■ Figure 2 shows how an increasing amount of U.S. investment has been financed by foreign borrowing.

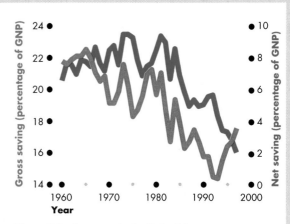

Figure 1 Saving rates in the United States

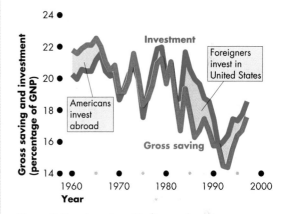

Figure 2 How investment is financed in the United States

You're The Voter

■ What do you think the federal government should do about the low U.S. saving rate?

■ Can you think of any tax reforms that might increase saving?

■ How do you think Social Security and Medicare might influence personal saving?

■ Would you vote for tax incentives, a cut in Social Security, neither, or both, and why?

SUMMARY

KEY POINTS

Capital and Interest (pp. 584–586)

- The capital stock grows steadily because net investment is usually positive.
- The return on capital is the real interest rate—the nominal interest rate adjusted for inflation.

Investment Decisions (pp. 587–589)

- Other things remaining the same, the lower the real interest rate or the higher the expected profit rate, the greater is the amount of investment.
- Investment demand is the relationship between investment and the real interest rate, other things remaining the same. Investment demand changes when the expected profit rate changes.

Saving Decisions (pp. 590–592)

- Other things remaining the same, the higher the real interest rates, the greater is saving.
- Saving supply is the relationship between saving and the real interest rate, other things remaining the same.
- Saving supply changes when disposable income, the purchasing power of net assets, or expected future income changes.

Equilibrium in the World Economy (pp. 593–595)

- Because capital is free to move internationally to seek the highest possible real rate of return, the real interest rate is determined in a global market.
- The equilibrium real interest rate makes world saving equal to world investment.

The Role of Government (pp. 595–598)

- National saving equals private saving plus government saving.
- Government saving equals net taxes minus government purchases.
- A government budget deficit might increase the real interest rate and crowd out private investment.

- A government budget deficit might also increase private saving supply because it decreases expected future disposable income.

Saving and Investment in the National Economy (pp. 598–599)

- In the national economy, foreign borrowing fills the gap between national saving and investment.
- An increase in the government budget deficit of a country decreases national saving and increases foreign borrowing, but it does not decrease investment.

KEY FIGURES

KEY TERMS

PROBLEMS

*1. A cellular phone assembly plant costs $10 million and has a life of one year. The firm will have to hire labor at a cost of $3 million and buy parts and fuel at a cost of a further $3 million. If the firm builds the plant, it will be able to produce cellular telephones that will sell for a total revenue of $17 million. Does it pay the firm to invest in this new production line at the following real interest rates:
   a.   5 percent a year?
   b.   10 percent a year?
   c.   15 percent a year?

2. A natural gas deposit contains gas that can be pumped out in one year and sold for a total revenue of $40 million. It will take a $36 million investment in equipment and pipelines to access the gas and deliver it to the buyers. Does it pay to undertake this investment at the following real interest rates:
   a.   5 percent a year?
   b.   10 percent a year?
   c.   15 percent a year?

*3. In 1999, the Batman family (Batman and Robin) had a disposable income of $50,000, net assets of $100,000, and an expected future income of $50,000 a year. At an interest rate of 4 percent a year, the Batmans would save $10,000. At an interest rate of 6 percent a year, they would save $12,500. And at an interest rate of 8 percent a year, they would save $15,000.
   a.   Draw a graph of the Batman family's saving supply curve for 1999.
   b.   In 2000, everything remained the same as the year before except that the Batmans expected their future income to rise to $60,000 a year. Show the influence of this change on the Batman family's saving supply curve.
   c.   In 2001, everything remained the same as the year before except that the Batmans' disposable income increased to the $60,000 a year they expected it would the year before. The Batmans now expect their income to remain at $60,000 a year. Show the influence of this change on the Batman family's saving supply curve.

4. It is now 2002, and the Batman family has net assets of $120,000. Its disposable income is $60,000, and its expected future income is also $60,000 a year. The Batmans will save $15,000 at an interest rate of 6 percent a year. If the interest rate falls to 4 percent a year, they will cut their saving to $10,000. And if the interest rate rises to 8 percent a year, they will increase their saving to $20,000.
   a.   Draw a graph of the Batman family's saving supply curve for 2002.
   b.   In 2002, the stock market boomed and the Batmans' net assets increased by 50 percent. Indicate the direction of influence of this change on the Batman family's saving supply curve.
   c.   In 2003, the stock market crashed and the Batmans' net assets were wiped out. Indicate the direction of influence of this change on the Batman family's saving supply curve.

*5. The year is 3053. The economy of Planet Earth, still isolated from all other planets, has the following saving supply and investment demand:

Real interest rate (percent per year)	Saving	Investment (trillions of 3050 dollars)
4	2	7
5	6	6
6	10	5
7	14	4
8	18	3

Planet Earth's government budget is balanced.
   a.   What is the equilibrium real interest rate?
   b.   What is equilibrium investment?
   c.   What is equilibrium saving?

6. The year is 3053. The economy of Alpha Centura, still isolated from all other planets, has the following saving supply and investment demand:

Real interest rate (percent per year)	Saving	Investment (trillions of 3050 zips)
4	1	16
5	3	13
6	5	10
7	7	7
8	9	4

Alpha Centura's government budget is balanced.
  a. What is the equilibrium real interest rate?
  b. What is equilibrium investment?
  c. What is equilibrium saving?

*7. The government of Planet Earth spends big on a space program and incurs a deficit of 5 trillion dollars. But the citizens of Planet Earth have a long memory and remember the Ricardo-Barro principle, which they apply to their saving and spending decisions.
  a. What is the new equilibrium real interest rate?
  b. What are the new equilibrium investment and saving?

8. The government of Alpha Centura spends big on a space program and incurs a deficit of 5 trillion zips. The citizens of Alpha Centura have never heard of David Ricardo and Robert Barro, so they keep spending as if there were no government deficit.
  a. What is the new equilibrium real interest rate?
  b. What are the new equilibrium investment and saving?

*9. The space programs of Alpha Centura and Planet Earth pay off. The Alpha Centurans and Earth people discover each other and begin to pursue intergalactic economic trade, borrowing, and lending. They establish a common currency: 1 zip equals one dollar. They terminate their government deficits and return to the levels of saving and investment described in problems 5 and 6.
  a. What is the real interest rate in the galactic economy?
  b. What is the level of galactic investment?
  c. What is the level of galactic saving?
  d. Do investment and saving on Alpha Centura increase or decrease?

10. In the galactic economy consisting of Alpha Centura and Planet Earth described in problem 9,
  a. Do investment and saving on Planet Earth increase or decrease?
  b. Do investment and saving on Alpha Centura increase or decrease?
  c. Which planet borrows from the other and how much?

CRITICAL THINKING

1. Study *Reading Between the Lines* on pp. 600–601 and then answer the following questions:
  a. What has happened to the personal saving rate in the United States during the past 30 years?
  b. What has happened to the national saving rate in the United States during the past 30 years?
  c. What are the main reasons you can think of that might account for the patterns that you describe in your answers to parts (a) and (b)?
  d. What are the likely effects of a decrease in U.S. saving supply? Explain the effects on national saving, investment, the world real interest rate, and U.S. international borrowing and lending.
  e. If the U.S. saving rate increases during the 2000s, how will that change influence the quantity of U.S. and world capital by 2010?

2. Suppose that the U.S. government cuts the tax rate on business profits.
  a. How do you think this tax cut will influence firms' investment plans?
  b. How will the tax cut influence personal saving decisions?
  c. How will the tax cut influence the real interest rate?
  d. How will the tax cut influence U.S. international borrowing?

For each part, draw a figure to illustrate the effects. Then think about and answer the following questions:
  e. Who would benefit from such a tax cut?
  f. Who would pay for such a tax cut?
  g. On balance, do you favor or oppose such a tax cut? Why?

3. Use the link on the Parkin Web site to obtain data on government budget deficits from the latest *World Economic Outlook* published by the International Monetary Fund.
  a. What are the trends in these deficits? Are they the same as or different from those in Fig. 27.12 on p. 598?
  b. What influence do you expect these deficits to have on the real interest rate and investment next year?

Chapter 28

Economic Growth

Real GDP *per person* in the United States more than doubled between 1960 and 1998. If you live in a dorm, chances are it was built during the 1960s and equipped with two electricity outlets, one for a desk lamp and one for a bedside lamp. Today, with the help of a power bar (or two), your room bulges with a television and VCR, CD player, microwave, refrigerator, coffee maker, toaster, computer—and the list goes on. What has brought about this growth in production and incomes? What can be done to speed up economic growth? ◆ We see greater extremes of economic growth if we look at modern Asia. On the banks of the Li River in Southern China, Songman Yang breeds cormorants, amazing birds

Transforming People's Lives

that he trains to fish and to deliver their catch to a basket on his simple bamboo raft. Songman's work, the capital equipment and technology he uses, and the income he earns are similar to those of his ancestors going back some 2,000 years. Yet all around Songman, in China's bustling villages, towns, and cities, people are participating in an economic miracle. They are creating businesses, investing in new technologies, developing local and global markets, and experiencing income growth of more than 6 percent a year. Despite a slowdown in 1998, similar rapid economic growth has taken place in Hong Kong, South Korea, and Taiwan. In these countries, real GDP doubled *three times*—an eightfold increase—between 1960 and 1998. Why have incomes in these Asian economies grown so rapidly? What makes an economic miracle?

◆ In this chapter, we study the forces that make real GDP grow, that make some countries grow faster than others, and that make our own growth rate sometimes slow down and sometimes speed up. We'll also look at policies for achieving faster economic growth.

After studying this chapter, you will be able to:

- Describe the long-term growth trends in the United States and other countries and regions
- Identify the main sources of long-term or real GDP growth
- Explain the productivity growth slowdown in the United States during the 1970s
- Explain the rapid economic growth rates being achieved in East Asia
- Explain the theories of economic growth
- Describe the policies that might be used to speed up economic growth

Long-Term Growth Trends

THE LONG-TERM GROWTH TRENDS THAT WE
study in this chapter are the trends in *potential GDP*.
We are interested in long-term growth primarily
because it brings rising incomes *per person*. So we begin
by looking at some facts about the level and growth
rate of real GDP per person in the United States and
around the world. Let's look first at real GDP per person in the United States over the past hundred years.

Growth in the U.S. Economy

Figure 28.1 shows real GDP per person in the United
States for the hundred years from 1898 to 1998. The
average growth rate over this period is 2 percent a year.
But the long-term growth rate has varied from a low
of 1.1 percent a year between 1973 and 1984 to a high
of 3 percent a year during the 1920s and the 1960s.

Figure 28.1 shows you the recent productivity
growth slowdown in a longer perspective. It also shows
that productivity growth slowdowns have occurred
before. The early years of the 1900s and the mid-1950s
had even slower growth than we have today. The
rapid growth of the 1960s was not unusual either.
The decade of the 1920s was a period of similarly
rapid growth.

In the middle of the graph are two extraordinary
events: the Great Depression of the 1930s and World
War II of the 1940s. The fall in real GDP during the
Depression and the bulge during the war obscure any
changes in the long-term growth trend that might
have occurred within these years. But between 1930
and 1950, averaging out the Depression and the war,
the long-term growth rate was 2.2 percent a year.

A major goal of this chapter is to explain why our
economy grows and why the long-term growth rate
varies. A related goal is to explain variations in the
economic growth rate across countries. Let's look at
some facts about these variations.

FIGURE 28.1

A Hundred Years of Economic Growth in the United States

During the 100 years from
1898–1998, real GDP per
person in the United States
grew by 2 percent a year,
on the average. The growth
rate was above average during the 1920s, 1960s, and
1983–1998 and it was below
average in 1903–1920, the
1950s, and 1973–1983.

Source: Christina D. Romer "The Prewar Business Cycle Reconsidered: New Estimates of Gross National Product, 1869–1908," *Journal of Political Economy* Vol. 97 (1989);
National Income and Product Accounts of the United States; Historical Statistics of the United States Colonial Times to 1957 (U.S. Department of Commerce, 1960); and
Economic Report of the President, 1999.

Real GDP Growth in the World Economy

Figure 28.2 shows real GDP per person in the United States and in other countries between 1960 and 1998. (The data shown in this figure are in 1985 dollars.) Part (a) looks at the richest countries. The United States has the highest real GDP per person.

In 1998, Canada had the second highest real GDP per person and Japan the third highest. Before the 1990s, both of these countries grew faster than the United States and were catching up. Japan also grew faster than the Europe Big 4 (France, Germany, Italy, and the United Kingdom) and overtook them in the mid-1980s. The Europe Big 4 also grew faster than United States but only by a small margin.

Not all countries are growing faster than, and catching up with, the United States. Figure 28.2(b) looks at some of these. Western Europe (other than the Big 4) grew faster than the United States before 1975, slowed to the U.S. growth rate during the 1980s, and fell behind during the 1990s. After a brief period of catch-up, the former Communist countries of Central Europe fell increasingly behind the United States and by 1998, they were as far behind as they had been 30 years earlier.

Africa and Central and South America have persistently grown more slowly than the United States. Real GDP per person in Central and South America slipped from a comparative high of 30 percent of the U.S. level of real GDP per person in 1980 to 23 percent in 1998. Africa slipped from 8 percent of the U.S. level of real GDP per person in 1960 to 6 percent in 1998.

FIGURE 28.2

Economic Growth Around the World: Catch-Up or Not?

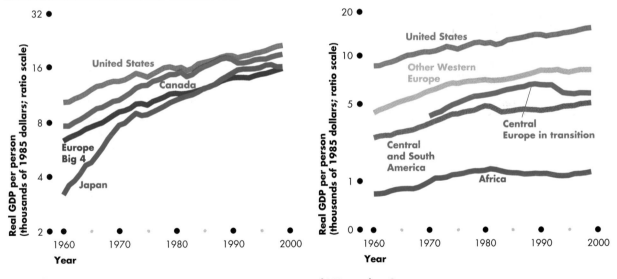

(a) Catch up?

(b) No catch up?

Real GDP per person has grown throughout the world economy. Among the rich industrial countries (part a), real GDP growth has been faster in Canada, the Europe Big 4 (France, Germany, Italy, and the United Kingdom), and Japan than in the United States and they are catching up. The most spectacular growth was in Japan during the 1960s. Real GDP per person in

Canada has also become closest to the U.S. real GDP per person. Among a wider range of countries (part b), there is little sign of catch-up. The gaps between the levels of real GDP per person in the United States, other Western European countries, Central Europe, Central and South America, and Africa have remained remarkably constant.

Sources: 1960–1992, Robert Summers and Alan Heston, New Computer Diskette (Mark 5.6a), January 15, 1995, distributed by the National Bureau of Economic Research to update "The Penn World Table: An Expanded Set of International Comparisons, 1950–1988," *Quarterly Journal of Economics*, May 1991, 327–368; 1993–1998, International Monetary Fund, *World Economic Outlook*, (Washington D.C., October 1998).

Taking both parts of Fig. 28.2 together, we can see that the catch-up in real GDP per person that is visible in part (a) is not a global phenomenon.

Hong Kong, Korea, Singapore, and Taiwan were in the headlines in 1998 because, along with some other Asian countries, they experienced a recession. But as Fig. 28.3 shows, their long-term growth has been spectacular. In 1960, these countries had levels of real GDP per person that ranged from one tenth to one quarter that in the United States. By 1998, two of them (Hong Kong and Singapore) had caught the United States and the other two were close behind.

FIGURE 28.3
Catch-Up in Asia

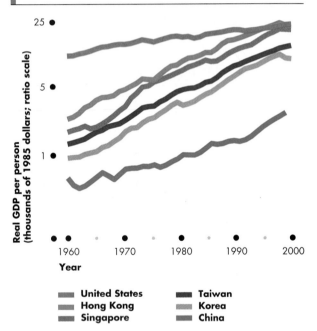

The clearest examples of catch-up have occurred in five economies in Asia. After starting out in 1960 with real GDP per person as little as one tenth of that in the United States, Hong Kong, Korea, Singapore, and Taiwan have substantially narrowed the gap on the United States. And from being a very poor developing country in 1960, China's real GDP per person now exceeds that of Hong Kong in 1960. China is growing at a rate that is enabling it to continue to catch up with the United States.

Sources: 1960–1992, Robert Summers and Alan Heston, New Computer Diskette (Mark 5.5), June 15, 1993, distributed by the National Bureau of Economic Research to update "The Penn World Table (Mark 5): An Expanded Set of International Comparisons, 1950–1988," *Quarterly Journal of Economics*, May 1991, 327–368; 1993–1998, *World Economic Outlook*, International Monetary Fund, Washington D.C., October, 1998.

Figure 28.3 also shows that China is catching up, but more slowly and from a very long way behind. In 1960, China's real GDP per person was one twentieth that of the United States, but by 1998 it was one eighth.

The four small Asian countries shown in Fig. 28.3 are like fast trains running on the same track at similar speeds and with a roughly constant gap between them. Hong Kong is the lead train and runs about 10 years in front of Taiwan, which is the last train. Real GDP per person in Taiwan in 1990 was similar to that in Hong Kong in 1980, ten years earlier. Between 1960 and 1999, Hong Kong transformed itself from a poor developing country into one of the world's richest countries.

China is now doing what Hong Kong has done. If China continues its rapid growth, the world economy will become a dramatically different place—China is equivalent to more than 200 countries the size of Hong Kong. Whether China will continue on its current path of rapid growth is impossible to predict.

R E V I E W　　Q U I Z

- What is the average rate of economic growth in the United States over the past 100 years? In which periods was growth the most rapid and in which was it the slowest?

- Describe the gaps between real GDP per person in the United States and other countries. For which countries are the gaps narrowing? For which countries are the gaps widening? And for which countries are the gaps remaining unchanged?

- Compare the growth rates and levels of real GDP per person in Hong Kong, Korea, Singapore, Taiwan, China, and the United States. How far is China behind the other Asian economies?

The facts about economic growth in the United States and around the world raise some big questions that we're now going to answer. We'll study the causes of economic growth in three stages. First, we'll look at the preconditions for growth and the activities that sustain it. Second, we'll learn how economists measure the relative contributions of the sources of growth—an activity called *growth accounting*. And third, we'll study three theories of economic growth that seek to explain how the influences on growth interact to determine the growth rate.

The Causes of Economic Growth: A First Look

MOST HUMAN SOCIETIES HAVE LIVED FOR centuries and even thousands of years like Songman Yang, with no economic growth. The key reason is that they have lacked some fundamental social institutions and arrangements that are essential preconditions for economic growth. Let's see what these preconditions are.

Preconditions for Economic Growth

The most basic precondition for economic growth is an appropriate *incentive* system. Three institutions are crucial to the creation of incentives. They are:

1. Markets
2. Property rights
3. Monetary exchange

Markets enable buyers and sellers to get information and to do business with each other, and market prices send signals to buyers and sellers that create incentives to increase or decrease the quantities demanded and supplied. Markets enable people to specialize and trade and to save and invest. But for markets to work, we need property rights and monetary exchange.

Property rights are the social arrangements that govern the ownership, use, and disposal of resources and goods and services. They include the rights to physical property (land, buildings, and capital equipment), to financial property (claims by one person against another), and to intellectual property (such as inventions). Clearly established and enforced property rights give people an assurance that a capricious government will not confiscate their income or savings.

Monetary exchange facilitates transactions of all kinds, including the orderly transfer of private property from one person to another. Property rights and monetary exchange create incentives for people to specialize and trade, to save and invest, and to discover new technologies.

No unique political system is necessary to deliver the preconditions for economic growth. Liberal democracy, founded on the fundamental principle of the rule of law, is the system that does the best job. It provides a solid base on which property rights can be established and enforced. But authoritarian political systems have sometimes provided an environment in which economic growth has occurred.

Early human societies, based on hunting and gathering, did not experience economic growth because they lacked these preconditions. Economic growth began when societies evolved the three key institutions that create incentives. But the presence of an incentive system and the institutions that create it does not guarantee that economic growth will occur. It permits economic growth but does not make that growth inevitable.

The simplest way in which growth happens when the appropriate incentive system exists is that people begin to specialize in the activities at which they have a comparative advantage and trade with each other. You saw in Chapter 3 how everyone can gain from such activity. By specializing and trading, everyone can acquire goods and services at the lowest possible cost. Equivalently, people can obtain a greater volume of goods and services from their labor.

As an economy moves from one with little specialization to one that reaps the gains from specialization and exchange, its production and consumption grow. Real GDP per person increases, and the standard of living rises.

But for growth to be persistent, people must face incentives that encourage them to pursue three activities that generate ongoing economic growth. These activities are:

- Saving and investment in new capital
- Investment in human capital
- Discovery of new technologies

These three sources of growth, which interact with each other, are the primary sources of the extraordinary growth in productivity during the past 200 years. Let's look at each in turn.

Saving and Investment in New Capital

Saving and investment in new capital increase the amount of capital per worker and increase real GDP per hour of labor—labor productivity. Labor productivity took the most dramatic upturn when the amount of capital per worker increased during the Industrial Revolution. Production processes that use hand tools can create beautiful objects, but production methods that use large amounts of capital per worker, such as auto plant assembly lines, are much more productive.

The accumulation of capital on farms, in textile factories, in iron foundries and steel mills, in coal mines, on building sites, in chemical plants, in auto plants, in banks and insurance companies, and in shopping malls has added incredibly to the productivity of our economy. The next time you see a movie that's set in the Old West, look carefully at the small amount of capital around. Try to imagine how productive you would be in such circumstances compared with your productivity today.

Investment in Human Capital

Human capital—the accumulated skill and knowledge of human beings—is the most fundamental source of economic growth. It is a source of both increased productivity and technological advance.

The development of one of the most basic human skills—writing—was the source of some of the earliest major gains in productivity. The ability to keep written records made it possible to reap ever-larger gains from specialization and exchange. Imagine how hard it would be to do any kind of business if all the accounts, invoices, and agreements existed only in people's memories.

Later, the development of mathematics laid the foundation for the eventual extension of knowledge about physical forces and chemical and biological processes. This base of scientific knowledge was the foundation for the technological advances of the Industrial Revolution 200 years ago and of today's Information Revolution.

But much human capital that is extremely productive is much more humble. It takes the form of millions of individuals learning and repetitively doing simple production tasks and becoming remarkably more productive in the tasks.

One carefully studied example illustrates the importance of this kind of human capital. Between 1941 and 1944 (during World War II), U.S. ship-yards produced some 2,500 units of a cargo ship, called the Liberty Ship, to a standardized design. In 1941, it took 1.2 million person-hours to build a ship. By 1942, it took 600,000, and by 1943, it took only 500,000. Not much change occurred in the capital employed during these years. But an enormous amount of human capital was accumulated. Thousands of workers and managers learned from experience and accumulated human capital that more than doubled their productivity in 2 years.

Discovery of New Technologies

Saving and investment in new capital and the accumulation of human capital have made a large contribution to economic growth. But the contribution of technological change—of the discovery and the application of new technologies and new goods—has made an even greater contribution.

People are many times more productive today than they were a hundred years ago. We are not more productive because we have more steam engines per person and more horse-drawn carriages per person. Rather, it is because we have the engines and transportation equipment that use technologies that were unknown a hundred years ago and that are more productive than the old technologies were. Technological change makes an enormous contribution to our increased productivity. It arises from formal research and development programs and from informal trial and error, and it involves discovering new ways of getting more out of our resources.

To reap the benefits of technological change, capital must increase. Some of the most powerful and far-reaching fundamental technologies are embodied in human capital—for example, language, writing, and mathematics. But most technologies are embodied in physical capital. For example, to reap the benefits of the internal combustion engine, millions of horse-drawn carriages and horses had to be replaced by automobiles; more recently, to reap the benefits of computerized word processing, millions of type-writers had to be replaced by PCs and printers.

R E V I E W   Q U I Z

- What economic activities that lead to economic growth do markets, property rights, and monetary exchange facilitate?
- What are the roles of saving and investment in new capital, the growth of human capital, and the discovery of new technologies in economic growth?
- Provide some examples of how human capital has created new technologies that are embodied in both human and physical capital.

What is the quantitative contribution of the sources of economic growth? To answer this question, economists use growth accounting.

Growth Accounting

THE QUANTITY OF REAL GDP SUPPLIED (Y) depends on three factors:

1. The quantity of labor (N)
2. The quantity of capital (K)
3. The state of technology (T)

The purpose of **growth accounting** is to calculate how much real GDP growth results from growth of labor and capital and how much is attributable to technological change.

The key tool of growth accounting is the **aggregate production function**, which is written as the equation:

$$Y = F(N, K, T).$$

In words, the quantity of real GDP supplied is determined by (is a function F of) the quantities of labor and capital and of the state of technology. The larger N, K, or T, the greater is Y. And the faster N and K grow and the faster T advances, the faster Y grows.

So understanding what makes labor and capital grow and technology advance is the key to understanding economic growth. Labor growth depends primarily on population growth. And the growth rate of capital and the pace of technological advance determine the growth rate of labor productivity.

Labor Productivity

Labor productivity is real GDP per hour of work. It is calculated by dividing real GDP by aggregate labor hours. That is, labor productivity equals Y divided by N.

Labor productivity determines how much income an hour of labor generates. Figure 28.4 shows labor productivity for the period 1960–1998. You can see in this figure that productivity growth was most rapid during the 1960s and that it slowed down in 1973. You can also see that it speeded up again after 1983, but not to the pace of the 1960s.

Why did productivity grow fastest during the 1960s? Why did it slow down during the 1970s and then speed up again after 1983? Growth accounting answers these questions by dividing the growth in

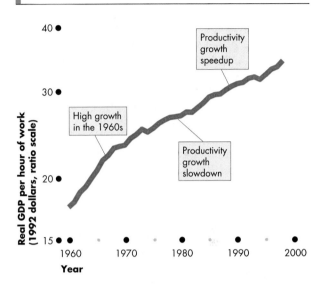

FIGURE 28.4

Real GDP per Hour of Work

Real GDP divided by aggregate hours equals real GDP per hour of work, which is a broad measure of productivity. During the 1960s, the productivity growth rate was high. It slowed during the 1970s and speeded up again after 1983.

Sources: U.S. Department of Commerce, *National Income and Product Accounts of the United States* (Washington, D.C.: U.S. Government Printing Office); U.S. Department of Labor, *Current Population Survey* (Washington, D.C.: U.S. Government Printing Office).

labor productivity into two components and then measuring the contribution of each. The components are:

- Growth in capital per hour of work
- Technological change

Technological change includes everything that contributes to labor productivity growth that is not included in growth in capital per hour. In particular, it includes human capital growth. Human capital growth and technological change are intimately related. Technology advances because knowledge advances. And knowledge is part of human capital. So "technological change" is a broad catchall concept.

The analytical engine of growth accounting is a relationship called the productivity function. Let's learn about this relationship and see how it is used.

The Productivity Function

The **productivity function** is a relationship that shows how real GDP per hour of labor changes as the amount of capital per hour of labor changes with a given state of technology. Figure 28.5 illustrates the productivity function. Capital per hour of work is measured on the *x*-axis, and real GDP per hour of work is measured on the *y*-axis. The figure shows *two* productivity functions. One is the curve labeled PF_0, and the other is the curve labeled PF_1.

An increase in the quantity of capital per hour of labor increases real GDP per hour of labor, which is shown by a movement along a productivity function. For example, on PF_0, when capital per hour of labor is $30, real GDP per hour of labor is $20. If capital per hour of labor increases to $60, real GDP per hour of labor increases to $25.

Technological change increases the amount of GDP per hour of labor that can be produced by a given amount of capital per hour of labor. It is shown by an upward shift of the productivity function. For example, if capital per hour of work is $30 and a technological change increases real GDP per hour of work from $20 to $25, the productivity function shifts upward from PF_0 to PF_1 in Fig. 28.5. Similarly, if capital per hour of work is $60, the same technological change increases real GDP per hour of work from $25 to $32 and shifts the productivity function upward from PF_0 to PF_1.

To calculate the contributions of capital growth and technological change to productivity growth, we need to know the shape and slope of the productivity function. The shape of the productivity function reflects a fundamental economic law—the law of diminishing returns. The **law of diminishing returns** states that as the quantity of one input increases with the quantities of all other inputs remaining the same, output increases but by ever smaller increments. For example, in a factory that has a given amount of capital, as more labor is hired, production increases. But each *additional* hour of labor produces less *additional* output than the previous hour produced. Two typists working with one computer type fewer than twice as many pages per day as one typist working with one computer.

Applied to capital, the law of diminishing returns states that if a given number of hours of labor use more capital (with the same technology), the *additional* output that results from the *additional* capital gets smaller as the amount of capital increases. One

FIGURE 28.5

How Productivity Grows

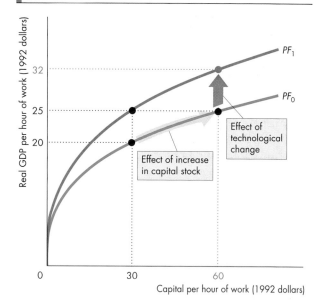

Productivity is measured by real GDP per hour of work, and it can grow for two reasons: (1) Capital per hour of work increases, and (2) technological advances occur. The productivity function, PF_0, shows the effects of an increase in capital per hour of work on productivity. Here, when capital per hour of work increases from $30 to $60, real GDP per hour of work increases from $20 to $25 along the productivity curve PF_0. Technological advance shifts the productivity function upward. Here, an advance in technology shifts the productivity function from PF_0 to PF_1. With this technological advance, real GDP per hour of work increases from $25 to $32 when there is $60 of capital per hour of work.

typist working with two computers types fewer than twice as many pages per day as one typist working with one computer. More generally, one hour of labor working with $60 of capital produces less than twice the output of one hour of labor working with $30 of capital. But how much less? The answer is given by the *one third rule*.

The One Third Rule Robert Solow of MIT estimated a production function from U.S. data. He discovered that on the average, with no change in technology, a 1 percent increase in capital per hour of labor brings a *one third of 1 percent* increase in real GDP per hour of labor. This one third rule is used to calculate the contributions of an increase in capital per hour of work and technological change to the growth of real GDP. Let's do such a calculation.

Suppose that capital per hour of work grows by 3 percent a year and real GDP per hour of work grows by 2.5 percent a year. The one third rule tells us that capital growth has contributed one third of 3 percent, which is 1 percent. The rest of the 2.5 percent growth of real GDP comes from technological change. That is, technological change has contributed 1.5 percent, which is the 2.5 percent growth of real GDP per hour of work minus the estimated 1 percent contribution of capital growth.

Accounting for the Productivity Growth Slowdown and Speedup

We can use the one third rule to study U.S. productivity growth and the productivity growth slowdown. Figure 28.6 tells the story, starting in 1960.

1960 to 1973 In 1960, capital per hour of work was $56 and real GDP per hour of work was $18 at the point marked 60 on PF_0. During the next 13 years, real GDP per hour of work expanded by 40 percent to $25. At the same time, capital per hour of work increased by 30 percent to $74. With no change in technology, the economy would have moved to point a on PF_0 in Fig. 28.6, where real GDP per hour of work has increased by 10 percent ($1/3$ of 30 percent). But rapid technological change shifted the productivity curve upward to PF_1 and the economy moved to the point marked 73 on that curve.

1973 to 1983 During the 11 years from 1973 to 1983, real GDP per hour of work expanded by 8 percent to $27. At the same time, capital per hour of work increased by 15 percent to $86. With no change in technology, the economy would have moved to point b on PF_1 in Fig. 28.6, where real GDP per hour of work has increased by 5 percent ($1/3$ of 15 percent). But a tiny amount of technological change shifted the productivity curve upward to PF_2 and the economy moved to the point marked 83 on that curve.

We've now isolated the reason for the productivity growth slowdown. It occurred because the contribution of technological change to real GDP growth slowed.

1983 to 1998 During the 16 years from 1983 to 1998, real GDP per hour of work expanded by 22 percent to $33. At the same time, capital per hour of work increased by 14 percent to $98. With no change

FIGURE 28.6

Growth Accounting and the Productivity Growth Slowdown

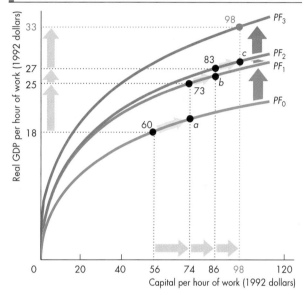

Between 1960 and 1973, which was a period of rapid productivity growth, capital per hour of work increased from $56 to $74, and technological progress shifted the productivity function upward from PF_0 to PF_1. Between 1973 and 1983, when potential GDP grew slowly, capital per hour of work increased from $74 to $86 and the productivity function barely shifted to PF_2. The effect of technological change was offset by oil price shocks. Between 1983 and 1998, capital per hour of work increased from $86 to $98, and technological progress shifted the productivity function upward from PF_2 to PF_3. Although productivity growth was not as rapid as in the 1960s, the productivity growth rate did increase.

Sources: U.S. Department of Commerce, *National Income and Product Accounts of the United States* (Washington, D.C.: U.S. Government Printing Office); U.S. Department of Labor, *Current Population Survey* (Washington, D.C.: U.S. Government Printing Office); and the author's calculations.

in technology, the economy would have moved to point c on PF_2 in Fig. 28.6, where real GDP per hour of work has increased by 4.5 percent ($1/3$ of 14 percent). But a return of more rapid technological change shifted the productivity curve upward to PF_3 and the economy moved to the point marked 98 on that curve. Although technological change resumed, its pace was slower than during the 1960s.

Technological Change During the Productivity Growth Slowdown

Technological change did not stop during the productivity growth slowdown. But its focus changed from increasing productivity to coping with:

- Energy price shocks
- The environment

Energy Price Shocks   Energy price increases that occurred in 1973–1974 and in 1979–1980 diverted research efforts toward saving energy rather than increasing productivity. Airplanes became more fuel efficient, but they didn't operate with smaller crews. Real GDP per gallon of fuel increased faster, but real GDP per hour of labor increased more slowly.

The Environment   The 1970s saw an expansion of laws and resources devoted to protecting the environment and improving the quality of the workplace. The benefits of these actions—cleaner air and water and safer factories—are not counted as real GDP. So the growth of these benefits is not measured as part of productivity growth.

Achieving Faster Growth

Growth accounting tells us that to achieve faster economic growth, we must either increase the growth rate of capital per hour of work or increase the pace of technological advance (which includes improving human capital). The main suggestions for achieving these objectives are:

- Stimulate saving
- Stimulate research and development
- Target high-technology industries
- Encourage international trade
- Improve the quality of education

Stimulate Saving   Saving finances investment, which brings capital accumulation. So stimulating saving can stimulate economic growth. The East Asian economies have the highest growth rates and saving rates. Some African economies have the lowest growth rates and saving rates.

Tax incentives can increase saving. Individual Retirement Accounts (IRAs) are an example of a tax incentive to save. Economists claim that a tax on consumption rather than on income provides the best saving incentive.

Stimulate Research and Development   Everyone can use the fruits of *basic* research and development efforts. For example, all biotechnology firms can use advances in gene-splicing technology. Because basic inventions can be copied, the inventor's profit is limited, and the market allocates too few resources to this activity.

Governments can direct public funds toward financing basic research, but this solution is not foolproof. It requires a mechanism for allocating the public funds to their highest-valued use. The National Science Foundation is one possibly efficient channel for allocating public funds to the universities to finance and stimulate basic research.

Target High-Technology Industries   Some people say that by providing public funds to high-technology firms and industries, a country can become the first to exploit a new technology and can earn above-average profits for a period while others are busy catching up. This strategy is risky and just as likely to use resources inefficiently as to speed growth.

Encourage International Trade   Free international trade stimulates growth by extracting all the available gains from specialization and exchange. The fastest-growing nations today are those with the fastest-growing exports and imports.

Improve the Quality of Education   The free market produces too little education because it brings benefits beyond those valued by the people who receive the education. By funding basic education and by ensuring high standards in basic skills such as language, mathematics, and science, governments can contribute to a nation's growth potential. Education can also be stimulated and improved by using tax incentives to encourage improved private provision.

R E V I E W   Q U I Z

- Explain the *one third* rule, and explain how it is used in growth accounting to isolate the contributions of capital growth and technological change to productivity growth.
- Explain how growth accounting can be used to provide information about the factors that contributed to the productivity growth slowdown of the 1970s. What does growth accounting tell us about why the slowdown occurred?

Growth Theories

WE'VE SEEN THAT REAL GDP GROWS WHEN THE quantities of labor and capital (which includes human capital) grow and when technology advances. Does this mean that the growth of labor and capital and technological advances *cause* economic growth? It might. But there are other possibilities. *One* of these factors might be the cause of real GDP growth and the others, the *effect*. We must try to discover how the influences on economic growth interact with each other to make some economies grow quickly and others grow slowly. And we must probe the reasons why a country's long-term growth rate sometimes speeds up and sometimes slows.

Growth theories are designed to study the interactions among the several factors that contribute to growth and to disentangle cause and effect. They are also designed to enable us to study the way in which the different factors influence each other.

Growth theories are also designed to be universal. They are not theories about the growth of poor countries only or rich countries only. They are theories about why and how poor countries become rich and rich countries continue to get richer.

We're going to study three theories of economic growth, each of which gives some insights about the process of economic growth. But none provides a definite answer to the basic questions: What causes economic growth and why do growth rates vary? Economics has some way to go before it can provide a definite answer to these most important of questions. The three growth theories that we study are:

- Classical growth theory
- Neoclassical growth theory
- New growth theory

Classical Growth Theory

Classical growth theory is the view that real GDP growth is temporary and that when real GDP per person rises above the subsistence level, a population explosion eventually brings real GDP per person back to the subsistence level. Adam Smith, Thomas Robert Malthus, and David Ricardo, the leading economists of the late eighteenth century and early nineteenth century, proposed this theory, but the view is most closely associated with the name of Malthus and is sometimes called the *Malthusian theory*.

Many people today are Malthusians! They say that if today's global population of 5 billion explodes to 11 billion by 2200, we will run out of resources and return to a primitive standard of living. We must act, say the Malthusians, to contain the population growth.

The Basic Idea To understand the basic idea of classical growth theory, let's transport ourselves back to the world of 1776, when Adam Smith is first explaining the idea. Most of the 2.5 million people who live in the newly independent United States of America work on farms or on their own land and perform their tasks using simple tools and animal power. They earn an average of 2 shillings (a bit less than $12 dollars in today's money) for working a 10-hour day.

Then advances in farming technology bring new types of plows and seeds that increase farm productivity. As farm productivity increases, farm production increases and some farm workers move from the land to the cities, where they get work producing and selling the expanding range of farm equipment. Incomes rise, and the people seem to be prospering. But will the prosperity last? Classical growth theory says that it will not.

Advances in technology—in both agriculture and industry—lead to an investment in new capital, which makes labor more productive. More and more businesses start up and hire the now more productive labor. The greater demand for labor raises the real wage rate and increases employment.

At this stage, economic growth has occurred and everyone has benefited from it. Real GDP has increased, and the real wage rate has increased. But the classical economists believe that this new situation can't last because it will induce a population explosion.

Classical Theory of Population Growth When the classical economists were developing their ideas about population growth, an unprecedented population explosion was under way. In Britain and other Western European countries, improvements in diet and hygiene had lowered the death rate while the birth rate remained high. For several decades, population growth was extremely rapid. For example, after being relatively stable for several centuries, the population of Britain increased by 40 percent between 1750 and 1800 and by a further 50 percent between 1800 and 1830. At the same time, an estimated 1 million people (about 20 percent of the 1750 population) left

Britain for America and Australia before 1800, and outward migration continued on a similar scale through the nineteenth century. These facts are the empirical basis for the classical theory of population growth.

To explain the high rate of population growth, the classical economists used the idea of a **subsistence real wage rate**, which is the minimum real wage rate needed to maintain life. If the actual real wage rate is less than the subsistence real wage rate, some people cannot survive and the population decreases. In classical theory, when the real wage rate exceeds the subsistence real wage rate, the population grows. But an increasing population increases the quantity of labor and brings diminishing returns to labor. So labor productivity eventually decreases. This dismal implication led to economics being called the *dismal science.* The dismal implication is that no matter how much technological change occurs, real wage rates are always pushed back toward the subsistence level.

Figure 28.7 illustrates the classical growth theory. Part (a) shows the situation before growth begins. The labor demand curve is LD_0, and the labor supply curve is LS_0. There is equilibrium in the labor market: The quantity of labor demanded equals the quantity supplied at a real wage rate of 2 shillings a day and 2 million people are employed. The subsistence real wage rate is (by assumption) 2 shillings a day. (We will use constant 1776 prices to keep this example in its historical context.)

Figure 28.7(a) also shows what happens when growth begins. Technological change and investment in new capital that make labor more productive increase the demand for labor, and the demand curve shifts rightward to LD_1. With this greater demand for labor, the real wage rate rises to 4 shillings a day, and this higher wage rate brings an increase in the quantity of labor supplied (a movement along the labor supply curve). Now 3 million people are employed.

Figure 28.7(b) shows what happens next, according to the Malthusians. The actual real wage rate, at the intersection of LS_0 and LD_1, is now 4 shillings a day. Because the actual real wage rate exceeds the subsistence real wage rate of 2 shillings a day, the population grows and the labor supply increases. The labor supply curve shifts rightward to LS_1. As it does so, the real wage rate falls and the quantity of labor demanded increases. Eventually, in the absence of further technological change, the economy comes to rest at the subsistence real wage rate of 2 shillings a day and 5 million people are employed.

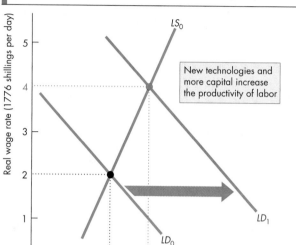

FIGURE 28.7

Classical Growth Theory

(a) Growth begins

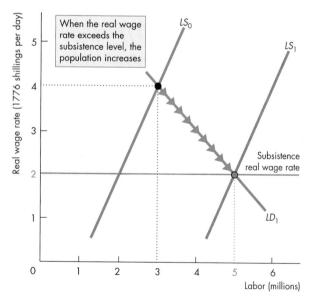

(b) A dismal outcome

Initially, 2 million people earn 2 shillings a day. The demand for labor increases to LD_1. The real wage rate rises to 4 shillings a day, and employment increases to 3 million (part a). With above subsistence real wages, the population increases. The labor supply curve shifts rightward toward LS_1. The real wage falls and the quantity of labor employed increases. Population growth stops when the subsistence real wage returns.

The economy has grown, real GDP has increased, but a larger population is earning only the subsistence real wage rate.

The classical growth theory, with its focus on the labor market and population, makes technological change and capital accumulation the engines of growth. But the classical theory ignores any influences that real GDP growth might have on the capital stock, investment, saving, and interest rates. The neoclassical theory corrects this omission. It demotes the labor market and places it in the background. Instead, it puts capital, investment, saving, and the interest rate at center stage. It explores the interactions among these capital market variables and the level and growth rate of real GDP. Let's now study neoclassical growth theory.

Neoclassical Growth Theory

Neoclassical growth theory is the proposition that that real GDP per person grows because technological change induces a level of saving and investment that makes capital per person grow. Growth ends if technological change stops.

Robert Solow of MIT suggested the most popular version of neoclassical growth theory during the 1950s. But Frank Ramsey of Cambridge University in England first developed this theory during the 1920s.

Neoclassical theory's big break with its classical predecessor is its view about population growth. So we'll begin our account of neoclassical theory by examining its views about population growth.

The Neoclassical Economics of Population Growth

The population explosion of eighteenth century Europe that created the classical theory of population eventually ended. The birth rate fell, and while the population continued to increase, its rate of increase became moderate. This slowdown in population growth seemed to make the classical theory increasingly less relevant. It also eventually led to the development of a modern economic theory of population growth.

The modern view is that although the population growth rate is influenced by economic factors, the influence is not a simple and mechanical one like that proposed by the classical economists. Key among the economic influences on population growth is the opportunity cost of a woman's time. As women's wage rates increase and their job opportunities expand, the opportunity cost of having children increases. Faced with a higher opportunity cost, families choose to have a smaller number of children and the birth rate falls.

A second economic influence works on the death rate. The technological advance that brings increased productivity and increased incomes brings advances in health care that extends lives.

So two opposing economic forces influence population growth. As incomes increase, the birth rate decreases and the death rate decreases. It turns out that these opposing forces are almost offsetting, so to a good approximation, the rate of population growth is independent of the rate of economic growth.

This modern view of population growth and the historical trends that support it contradict the views of the classical economists. It also calls into question the modern doomsday conclusion that we will be one day swamped with too many people for the planet to feed.

Neoclassical growth theory adopts this modern view of population growth. Forces other than real GDP and its growth rate determine population growth.

Technological Change In the neoclassical theory, the rate of technological change influences the rate of economic growth, but economic growth does not influence the pace of technological change. It is assumed that technological change results from chance. When we get lucky, we have rapid technological change, and when bad luck strikes, the pace of technological advance slows.

The Basic Idea To understand the basic ideal of neoclassical growth theory, imagine the world of the mid-1950s, when Robert Solow is explaining his idea. Americans are enjoying post World War II prosperity. Income per person is around $12,000 a year in today's money. The population is growing at about 1 percent a year. People are saving and investing about 20 percent of their incomes. But income per person is not growing much.

Then technology begins to advance at a more rapid pace across a range of activities. The transistor revolutionizes an emerging electronics industry. New plastics revolutionize the manufacture of household appliances. Jet airliners start to replace piston-engine airplanes and speed transportation. Elvis revolutionizes popular music by inventing rock!

These technological advances bring new profit opportunities. Businesses expand, and new businesses are created to exploit the newly available profitable technologies. Investment and saving increase. The economy enjoys new levels of prosperity and growth. But will the prosperity last? And will the growth last? Neoclassical growth theory says that the prosperity will last but the growth will not unless technology keeps advancing.

According to the neoclassical growth theory, the prosperity will persist because there is no classical population growth induced to lower wages.

But growth will stop if technology stops advancing for two related reasons. First, high profit rates that result from technological change bring increased investment and capital accumulation. But second, capital accumulation eventually results in diminishing returns that lower the return on capital, and that eventually decreases saving and slows the rate of capital accumulation.

Figure 28.8 illustrates neoclassical growth theory. In part (a), the investment demand curve is ID_0 and the saving supply curve is SS_0. (See Chapter 27, pp. 588 and 591 for a refresher.) Equilibrium occurs at the point of intersection of ID_0 and SS_0 where the real interest rate is 4 percent a year and saving and investment equal $1 trillion a year. Suppose that this amount of investment is sufficient to replace depreciated capital. Net investment is zero, and the capital stock is constant. Real GDP per person is also constant.

Now a technological advance increases the productivity of capital and increases the expected profit rate. So investment demand increases, and the investment demand curve shifts rightward to ID_1. The real interest rate rises to 6 percent a year, and saving and investment increase to $1.5 trillion. Net investment is now positive, the capital stock is increasing, and real GDP is growing.

Now that real GDP is growing, rising disposable income and an increasing capital stock induce changes in saving and investment— the saving supply curve and the investment demand curve shift. We cannot keep track of all these changes by using the investment demand–saving supply figure. Instead, we look at two related demand and supply curves: the demand for and the supply of the *stock* of capital.

Investment demand is the demand for *newly produced* capital during a given time period. The demand for the *stock* of capital is the quantity of capital that people and businesses would like to have available for use at the end of a period. It is equal to the capital stock at the beginning of a period *plus* investment demand during the period.

Similarly, saving supply is the supply of funds to buy newly produced capital in a given time period. And the supply of the *stock* of capital is the quantity of funds (wealth) that people and businesses plan to

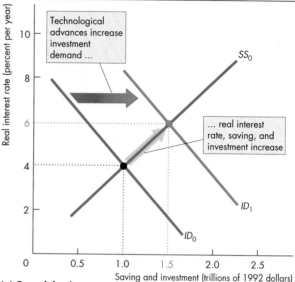

FIGURE 28.8

Neoclassical Growth Theory

Technological advances increase investment demand ...

... real interest rate, saving, and investment increase

(a) Growth begins

When the real interest rate exceeds the target rate, saving and investment increase the supply of capital

(b) Growth ends

Initially, investment is $1 trillion a year, the real interest rate is 4 percent a year, and the capital stock is $10 trillion. A technological advance increases investment demand to ID_1 and increases the demand for capital to KD_1. The real interest rate rises to 6 percent a year, investment increases to $1.5 trillion (part a), and the capital stock grows (part b). The KS curve shifts rightward toward KS_1 and the real interest rate falls. When the real interest rate equals the target rate, the capital stock is $15 trillion and growth ends.

own at the end of a period. It is equal to the quantity at the beginning of a period *plus* saving supply during the period.

Figure 28.8(b) shows the demand for the stock of capital KD_0. The lower the real interest rate, the greater is the quantity of capital demanded. This demand curve slopes downward for the same reason that the investment demand curve slopes downward.

At a given moment, the quantity of capital is given. It is the vertical line KS_0. In the long run, the supply of capital depends on saving decision.

Target Rate and Long-Run Saving   The neoclassical theory holds that if the real interest rate exceeds a *target rate*, the supply of capital increases; if the real interest rate is less than a target rate, the supply of capital decreases; and if the real interest rate equals a target rate, the supply of capital is constant. In Fig. 28.8(b), the target real interest rate is 4 percent a year and the long-run capital supply curve is LKS. If the real interest rate exceeds 4 percent a year, saving is positive, and the quantity of capital supplied persistently increases. And if the real interest rate is less than 4 percent a year, saving is negative, and the quantity of capital supplied persistently decreases. (Negative saving occurs and capital decreases when capital is not replaced as it wears out.)

Initially, equilibrium is at point *a*, where KD_0 and KS_0 intersect and where the real interest rate is 4 percent a year—its target rate. The capital stock is $10 trillion. Neoclassical growth begins from this point.

A technological advance now increases the productivity of capital, and the demand for capital curve shifts rightward to KD_1. The expected rate of profit increases. As a result, investment demand increases (shown in Fig. 28.8a). With greater investment, the supply of capital increases and the KS curve begins to shift rightward. As it does so, the real interest rate falls.

The capital stock continues to increase and the real interest rate continues to fall until the economy reaches point *b* in Fig. 28.8(b). Here, the real interest rate is back at its target rate of 4 percent a year and the capital stock has grown to $15 trillion. With no further growth of the capital stock, real GDP stops growing, and in the absence of another technological advance, growth ends.

Throughout the process you've just studied, real GDP grows but the growth rate gradually decreases and eventually ends. Ongoing technology advances are constantly increasing the demand for capital, raising the real interest rate, and inducing the saving that

increases the capital stock. The process repeats as long as technology advances and creates ongoing long-term economic growth. The growth rate fluctuates because technological progress occurs at a variable rate.

A Problem with Neoclassical Growth Theory   All economies have access to the same technologies, and capital is free to roam the globe seeking the highest available real interest rate. So neoclassical growth theory implies that growth rates and income levels per person around the globe will converge. While there is some sign of convergence among the rich countries (shown in Fig. 28.2a), convergence is slow, and it does not appear to be imminent for all countries (as we saw in Fig. 28.2b).

New growth theory attempts to overcome this shortcoming of neoclassical growth theory. It also attempts to explain how the rate of technological progress is determined.

New Growth Theory

New growth theory holds that real GDP per person grows because of the choices people make in the pursuit of profit and that growth can persist indefinitely. Paul Romer of Stanford University developed this theory during the 1980s, but the ideas go back to work by Joseph Schumpeter during the 1930s and 1940s.

The theory begins with two facts about market economies:

- Discoveries result from choices.
- Discoveries bring profit and competition destroys profit.

Discoveries and Choices   When people discover a new product or technique, they think of themselves as being lucky. They are right. But the pace at which new discoveries are made—and at which technology advances—is not determined by chance. It depends on how many people are looking for a new technology and how intensively they are looking.

Discoveries and Profits   Profit is the spur to technological change. The forces of competition squeeze profits, so to increase profit, people constantly seek either lower-cost methods of production or new and better products for which people are willing to pay a higher price. Inventors can maintain a profit for several years by taking out a patent or copyright. But eventually, a new discovery is copied, and profits disappear.

Two further facts play a key role in the new growth theory. They are:

■ Discoveries can be used by many people at the same time.
■ Physical activities can be replicated.

Discoveries Used by All   Once a profitable new discovery has been made, everyone can use it. And one person's use of a new discovery does not prevent others from using it. This fact means that as the benefits of a new discovery spread, free resources become available. These resources are free because nothing is given up when they are used. They have a zero opportunity cost.

Replicating Activities   Production activities can be replicated. For example, there might be two, three, or fifty-three identical firms making fiber-optic cable using an identical assembly line and production technique. If one firm increases its capital and output, that firm experiences diminishing returns. But the economy can increase its capital and output by adding another identical fiber-cable factory and the economy does not experience diminishing returns.

The assumption that capital does *not* experience diminishing returns is the central novel proposition of the new growth theory. And the implication of this simple and appealing idea is astonishing. In the neoclassical theory, with its diminishing returns to capital, as capital is accumulated, the real interest rate gradually falls until it equals the target real interest rate. At this point, growth stops. But the new growth theory has no such growth-stopping mechanism. As capital accumulates, the real interest rate is unaffected. It can remain above the target real interest rate indefinitely. Real GDP per person grows indefinitely as long as people can undertake research and development that yields a higher real interest rate than the target rate.

New growth theory sees the economy as a kind of perpetual motion mechanism. Economic growth is driven by our insatiable wants, which lead us to pursue profit and innovate. The result of this process is new and better products. But new and better products result in new firms starting up and old firms going out of business. In this process, jobs are created and destroyed. The outcome is new and better jobs, more leisure, and more consumption. But our insatiable wants are still there, so the process continues, going round and round a circle of wants, profits, innovation, and new products.

The growth rate depends on people's ability to innovate and the real interest rate. Over the years, this ability has changed. The invention of language and writing (the two most basic human capital tools), and later the development of the scientific method and the establishment of universities and research institutions, brought a huge increase in the real interest rate. Today, a deeper understanding of genes is bringing profit in a growing biotechnology industry. And astonishing advances in computer technology are creating an explosion of profit opportunities in a wide range of new information age industries.

Figure 28.9 illustrates new growth theory. Like Fig. 28.8(b), it shows the demand for and supply of the *stock* of capital. But unlike Fig. 28.8(b), here the marginal product of capital does not diminish as the quantity of capital increases. The demand curve for capital is horizontal at the real interest rate that equals the expected rate of profit. This expected profit rate does not change as the stock of capital changes. The horizontal demand for capital curve captures the special feature of the new growth theory that produces its novel prediction.

The supply of capital is fixed in the short run and is shown by a vertical supply curve such as KS_0. The long-run capital supply curve is horizontal at the target real interest rate and is LKS.

Initially, the real interest rate is 2 percent a year, and the line KD_0 in Fig. 28.9 shows the demand for capital. This real interest rate is below the target rate, so no one has an incentive to save. The economy is stuck at point a.

The development of basic human capital tools such as mathematics and physics increases the return to capital and innovation, and the demand for capital curve shifts upward to KD_1. The real interest rate now exceeds the target rate, and there is an incentive to save and invest. So investment and saving increase, and the quantity of capital grows. As it does so, the supply of capital curve shifts rightward through KS_0, KS_1, KS_2, KS_3, and so on. The capital stock grows, real GDP grows, and because there are no diminishing returns to capital, the real interest rate remains constant. Economic growth continues indefinitely as long as the real interest rate exceeds the target rate.

Figure 28.9 shows the process we've just described. The target real interest rate is 4 percent a year, and the real interest rate is 6 percent a year.

FIGURE 28.9

New Growth Theory

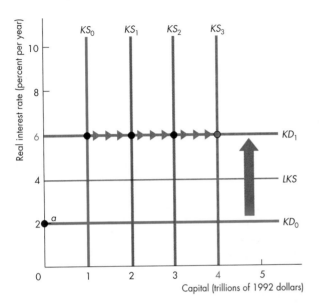

In new growth theory, economic growth results from incentives to innovate and from capital that does not experience diminishing returns. Initially, the real interest rate is 2 percent a year and the demand for capital is KD_0. The stock of capital is zero, and the economy is stuck at point a. The development of the scientific method increases the real interest rate to 6 percent a year, and the demand for capital increases to KD_1. With a real interest rate greater than the target real interest rate, saving increases and the supply of capital increases. The capital supply curve shifts rightward successively through KS_0, KS_1, KS_2, KS_3, and so on. As capital grows, real GDP grows, but the real interest rate does not fall because there are no diminishing returns. Real GDP growth continues indefinitely.

With positive saving, the capital supply curve shifts rightward indefinitely. The speed with which it shifts rightward depends on the extent to which the real interest rate exceeds the target rate. The higher the real interest rate, the more it exceeds that target rate and the faster the capital supply curve shifts rightward. So the faster the economy grows.

Sorting Out the Theories

Which theory is correct? Probably none is exactly correct. But they all teach us something of value. The classical theory reminds us that our physical resources are limited and that with no advances in technology, we must eventually hit diminishing returns. Neoclassical theory reaches essentially the same conclusion, but not because of a population explosion. Instead, it emphasizes potentially diminishing returns to capital and reminds us that we cannot necessarily keep growth going just by accumulating capital. New growth theory emphasizes the possible capacity of human resources to innovate at a pace that offsets diminishing returns.

R E V I E W   Q U I Z

- What is the central idea of classical growth theory that leads to the dismal outcome?
- Explain the mechanism at work in the classical growth theory and describe the role played by diminishing returns.
- What, according to the neoclassical growth theory, is the fundamental cause of economic growth?
- What is the key proposition of the new growth theory that makes growth persist? Is the proposition believable? Is the conclusion believable?

◆ Economic growth is the single most decisive factor in influencing a country's living standard, but it is not the only one. Another is the extent to which the country fully employs its scarce resources, especially its labor. In recent years, the United States has enjoyed full employment and steady growth. But the business cycle is almost certainly not dead. And unemployment has become a severe problem for many countries. In Part 9, we study the fluctuations of real GDP and employment and unemployment around their long-term trends. But before embarking on this new topic, take a look at *Reading Between the Lines* on pages 622–623 and see how the Internet is contributing to the growth of our economy today.

Growth in the Internet Economy

Essence of the Story

■ Stock prices increased during April 1999 to record levels, and the Dow Jones industrial average closed above 10,000.

■ The biggest gains were concentrated in technology and Internet stocks such as IBM, Microsoft, Intel, Lucent, America Online, Yahoo, and providers of financial services.

■ Yahoo had one of the biggest price increases—up $39.38 to $219.13—when the company announced plans to develop services for hand-held devices and television-based Internet appliances.

■ A report that more individual investors are switching from traditional stockbrokers to Internet trading also boosted Internet stock prices.

THE NEW YORK TIMES, APRIL 5, 1999

Tech Stocks Fuel Market Gain

NEW YORK—The stock market's torrid affair with technology and Internet companies continued Monday, lifting the three main gauges of stock market performance to records, with the Dow Jones industrial average closing above 10,000 for the second time ever.

Among the biggest gainers was Internet portal Yahoo, which jumped $39.38 to $219.13 on news that the company plans to extend its reach beyond personal computers to hand-held devices and television-based Internet appliances like WebTV.

The Internet sector got an extra boost from a report that more individual investors are turning to the Internet to trade, casting aside their reliance on traditional stock brokers.

"The Internet stocks are running the show," said Barry Hyman, market strategist at Ehrenkrantz, King & Nussbaum. ...

For the most part, the biggest gains were concentrated among the largest and best-known leaders of a select group of industries, from IBM and Microsoft to Intel, Lucent and America Online. Several financial-services stocks also soared. ...

■ The extraordinary growth of stock prices, especially for Internet firms, is based on the equally extraordinary growth of the Internet.

■ And the growth of the Internet is one aspect of the growth of the U.S. and global economies during the 1990s.

■ Figure 1 shows the growth of the Internet on two measures. One measure is the number of host computers, which grew from 1.3 million in 1993 to 43.2 million in 1999, a growth rate of 5.0 percent *per month*. This growth rate doubles the size of the Internet every 14 months!

■ The other measure is consumer expenditure on the Internet, which increased 10-fold between 1990 and 1998.

■ The growth of the Internet is one element in overall economic growth in the United States.

■ Figure 2 shows real GDP from 1987 to 1998. The growth rate of real GDP was 2.06 percent a year between 1987 and 1992 (before the Internet took off). It was 3.26 percent a year between 1993 and 1998 (after the Internet took off).

■ Although real GDP growth increased after 1993, it is too early to tell whether potential GDP growth has increased as well. In 1992, the economy was still recovering from the 1990–1991 recession and the unemployment rate was more than 7 percent. By 1996, the unemployment rate had fallen to 5.5 percent. We will not be able to say whether the *growth rate* of potential GDP has increased until we can see the current business cycle in a longer-term perspective.

■ Although we cannot determine whether the *growth rate* of potential GDP has increased, it is undeniable that the Internet has had a positive effect on the *level* of potential GDP.

■ The new technologies that are helping the Internet to grow are available for everyone to use. And the opportunity cost of using these technologies is low.

■ Also, the human capital and physical capital that the Internet uses are probably not yet experiencing diminishing returns and perhaps will not do so for a long time.

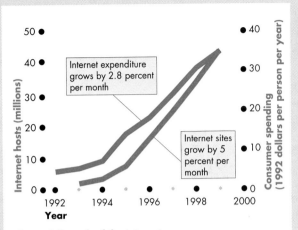

Figure 1 Growth of the Internet

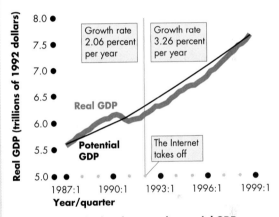

Figure 2 Growth of real GDP and potential GDP

■ It is possible that these new technologies have increased the rate of profit. If they have done so, they might have created a new growth environment in which the U.S. economy will expand at a more rapid rate than it did previously.

■ The evidence is not yet present in the GDP data. But current estimates of real GDP might understate its true growth rate.

SUMMARY

KEY POINTS

Long-Term Growth Trends (pp. 606–608)

- Between 1895 and 1998, real GDP per person in the United States grew at an average rate of 2 percent a year. Growth was fastest during the 1920s and 1960s.

- The real GDP gaps between the United States and Africa as well as Central and South America have widened. The gaps between the United States and Hong Kong, Korea, Taiwan, and China have narrowed.

The Causes of Economic Growth: A First Look (pp. 609–610)

- Economic growth requires an *incentive* system created by markets, property rights, and monetary exchange.

- Economic growth occurs when people save, invest in physical and human capital, and discover new technologies.

Growth Accounting (pp. 611–614)

- Growth accounting measures the contributions of capital accumulation and technological change to productivity growth.

- Growth accounting uses the productivity function and the *one third rule:* A 1 percent increase in capital per hour of work brings a 1/3 percent increase in real GDP per hour of work.

- During the productivity growth slowdown of the 1970s, technological change made no contribution to real GDP growth.

- It might be possible to achieve faster growth by stimulating saving, subsidizing research and development, targeting (and possibly subsidizing) high-technology industries, and encouraging more international trade.

Growth Theories (pp. 615–621)

- In classical theory, when technological advances increase real GDP per person above the *subsistence* level, a population explosion brings diminishing returns to labor and real GDP per person returns to the subsistence level.

- In neoclassical growth theory, when technological advances increase saving and investment, an increase in the capital stock brings diminishing returns to capital, and eventually, without further technological change, the capital stock and real GDP per person stop growing.

- In new growth theory, when technological advances increase saving and investment, an increase in the capital stock *does not* bring diminishing returns to capital and growth persists indefinitely.

KEY FIGURES

KEY TERMS

PROBLEMS

💻 *1. The following information has been discovered about the economy of Longland: The economy's productivity function is:

Capital per hour of work (1997 dollars per hour)	Real GDP per hour of work (1997 dollars per hour)
10	3.80
20	5.70
30	7.13
40	8.31
50	9.35
60	10.29
70	11.14
80	11.94

Does this economy conform to the one third rule? If so, explain why. If not, explain why not and explain what rule, if any, it does conform to. Explain how you would do the growth accounting for this economy.

2. The following information has been discovered about the economy of Flatland: The economy's productivity function is:

Capital per hour of work (1997 dollars per hour)	Real GDP per hour of work (1997 dollars per hour)
10	3.00
20	3.75
30	4.22
40	4.57
50	4.86
60	5.10
70	5.31
80	5.50

Does this economy conform to the one third rule? If so, explain why. If not, explain why not and explain what rule, if any, it does conform to. Explain how you would do the growth accounting for this economy.

💻 *3. In Longland, described in problem 1, capital per hour of work in 1999 was $40 and real GDP per hour of work was $8.31. In 2001, capital per hour of work had increased to $50 and real GDP per hour of work had increased to $10.29 an hour.

  a. Does Longland experience diminishing returns? Explain why or why not.

  b. Use growth accounting to find the contribution of the change in capital between 1999 and 2001 to the growth of productivity in Longland.

  c. Use growth accounting to find the contribution of technological change between 1999 and 2001 to the growth of productivity in Longland.

4. In Flatland, described in problem 2, capital per hour of work in 1999 was $30 and real GDP per hour of work was $4.22. In 2001, capital per hour of work had increased to $60 and real GDP per hour of work had increased to $6.37 an hour.

  a. Does Flatland experience diminishing returns? Explain why or why not.

  b. Use growth accounting to find the contribution of the change in capital between 1999 and 2001 to the growth of productivity in Flatland.

  c. Use growth accounting to find the contribution of technological change between 1999 and 2001 to the growth of productivity in Flatland.

💻 *5. The following information has been discovered about the economy of Cape Despair. The subsistence real wage rate is $7 an hour. Whenever the real wage rate rises above this level, the population grows; when the real wage rate falls below this level, the population falls. With its current population, the demand and supply schedules for labor in Cape Despair are as follows:

Real wage rate (1992 dollars per hour)	Quantity of labor demanded (billions of hours per year)	Quantity of labor supplied (billions of hours per year)
3	8	4
5	7	5
7	6	6
9	5	7
11	4	8
13	3	9
15	2	10
17	1	11

Initially, the labor force of Cape Despair is constant, and the real wage is at its subsistence level. Then a technological advance increases the amount that firms are willing to pay for labor by $2 at each level of employment.

a. What is the initial level of employment and real wage rate in Cape Despair?

b. What happens to the real wage rate immediately following the technological advance?

c. What happens to the population growth rate following the technological advance?

d. What is the employment level when Cape Despair returns to a long-run equilibrium?

6. Martha's Island is an economy that behaves according to the neoclassical growth model. The economy is in long-run equilibrium and is described in the following table.

Real interest rate (percent per year)	Quantity of capital demanded (billions of dollars)	Quantity of capital (billions of dollars)
1	9	7
2	8	7
3	7	7
4	6	7
5	5	7
6	4	7
7	3	7
8	2	7

a. What is the real interest rate on Martha's Island?

b. What is the target rate?

A technological advance increases the demand for capital by $2 billion at each real interest rate.

c. What is the real interest rate immediately following the technological advance?

d. What is the real interest rate and quantity of capital when Martha's Island returns to a long-run equilibrium?

*7. Romeria is a country that behaves according to the predictions of new growth theory. The target real interest rate is 3 percent a year. A technological advance increases the demand for capital and raises the real interest rate to 5 percent a year. Describe the events that happen in Romeria and contrast them with the events in Martha's Island in problem 6.

8. Suppose that in Romeria, which is described in problem 7, technological advance slows and the real interest rate falls to 3 percent a year. Describe what happens in Romeria.

CRITICAL THINKING

1. After studying *Reading Between the Lines* on pp. 622–623, answer the following questions:

a. How quickly is the Internet growing in comparison with the growth of real GDP?

b. Are the measures of growth of the Internet in Figure 1 comparable with the measure of the growth of real GDP in Figure 2? (Hint: Think about what real GDP measures.)

c. What information about growth of the Internet would you need to determine the contribution of the Internet to real GDP?

d. Suppose that the arrival of the Internet increases the growth rate of potential GDP. What, according to each of the three economic growth theories—classical, neoclassical, and new—will happen in the longer term?

2. Use the link on the Parkin Web site to visit the Penn World Table and obtain data on real GDP per person for the United States, China, South Africa, and Mexico since 1960.

a. Draw a graph of the data.

b. Which country has the lowest real GDP per person and which has the highest?

c. Which country has experienced the fastest growth rate since 1960 and which has experienced the slowest?

d. Explain why the growth rates in these four countries are ranked on the order you have discovered?

e. Return to the Penn World Table Web site and obtain data for any four other countries that interest you. Describe and explain the patterns that you find for these countries.

3. Write a memo to your member of Congress in which you set out the policies you believe the U.S. government must follow to speed up the growth rate of real GDP in the United States. Explain how each policy would work.

4. Is faster economic growth always a good thing? Argue the case for faster growth and for slower growth, and then reach a conclusion on whether growth should be increased or decreased.

Understanding Aggregate Supply and Economic Growth

Expanding the Frontier

Economics is about how we cope with scarcity. We cope by making choices that balance marginal benefits and marginal costs so that we use our scarce resources efficiently. ◆ These choices determine how much work we do, how hard we work at school to learn the mental skills that form our human capital and that determine the kinds of jobs we get and the incomes we earn; and how much we save for future big-ticket expenditures. These choices also determine how much businesses and governments spend on new capital—on auto assembly lines, computers and fiber cables for improved Internet services, shopping malls, highways, bridges, and tunnels; and how intensively existing capital and natural resources are used and therefore how quickly they wear out or are used up. Most significant of all, these choices determine the problems that scientists, engineers, and other inventors work on to develop new technologies. ◆ All the choices we've just described determine two vital measures of economic performance:

- Real GDP
- Economic growth

Real GDP is determined by the quantity of labor, the quantity of capital, and the state of technological knowledge. And economic growth—the growth rate of real GDP—is determined by growth in the quantity of labor, capital accumulation, and technological advances. ◆ Economic growth, maintained at a steady rate over a number of decades, is the single most powerful influence on any society. It brings a transformation that continues to amaze thoughtful people. Economic growth that is maintained at a rapid rate can transform a society in years, not decades. Such transformations are taking place right now in many Asian countries. These transformations are economic miracles. ◆ The three chapters in this part studied the miracle of rapid economic growth and the forces that shape our capacity to produce goods and services. ◆ Chapter 26 explained how potential GDP and the full-employment quantity of labor, employment, and unemployment are determined by equilibrium in the labor market. ◆ Chapter 27 explained how capital accumulation results from saving and investment decisions that are coordinated in a global capital market. Some countries don't save enough to pay for the capital they accumulate; others save more than they need. And the international capital market moves savings to the places in which they obtain the highest available real interest rate. ◆ Chapter 28 studied the process of economic growth in the fast-growing economies of Asia and the United States. It explained how growth is influenced by technological change and the incentives that stimulate it. ◆ Modern ideas about economic growth owe much to two economists, Joseph Schumpeter and Paul Romer, whom you can meet on the following pages.

The Economist

Joseph Schumpeter,

the son of a textile factory owner, was born in Austria in 1883. He moved from Austria to Germany during the tumultuous 1920s when those two countries experienced hyperinflation. In 1932, in the depths of the Great Depression, he came to the United States and became a professor of economics at Harvard University.

This creative economic thinker wrote about economic growth and development, business cycles, political systems, and economic biography. He was a person of strong opinions who expressed them strongly and delighted in verbal battles.

Schumpeter has become the unwitting founder of modern growth theory. He saw the development and diffusion of new technologies by profit-seeking entrepreneurs as the source of economic progress. But he saw economic progress as a process of creative destruction—the creation of new profit opportunities and the destruction of currently profitable businesses. For Schumpeter, economic growth and the business cycle were a single phenomenon.

When Schumpeter died, in 1950, he had achieved his self-expressed life ambition: He was regarded as the world's greatest economist.

> "Economic progress, in capitalist society, means turmoil."
>
> JOSEPH SCHUMPETER
> *Capitalism, Socialism, and Democracy*

The Issues

Technological change, capital accumulation, and population growth all interact to produce economic growth. But what is cause and what is effect? And can we expect productivity and income per person to keep growing?

The classical economists of the eighteenth and nineteenth centuries believed that technological advances and capital accumulation were the engines of growth. But they also believed that no matter how successful people were at inventing more productive technologies and investing in new capital, they were destined to live at the subsistence level. These economists based their conclusion on the belief that productivity growth causes population growth, which in turn causes productivity to decline. These classical economists believed that whenever economic growth raises incomes above the subsistence level, the population will increase. They went on to reason that the increase in population brings diminishing returns that lower productivity. As a result, incomes must always return to the subsistence level. Only when incomes are at the subsistence level is population growth held in check.

A new approach, called neoclassical growth theory, was developed by Robert Solow of MIT, during the 1950s. Solow, who was one of Schumpeter's students, received the Nobel Prize for Economic Science for this work.

Solow challenged the conclusions of the classical economists. But the new theories of economic growth developed during the 1980s and 1990s went further. They stand the classical belief on its head. Today's theory of population

628

growth is that rising income slows the population growth rate because it increases the opportunity cost of having children and lowers the opportunity cost of investing in children and equipping them with more human capital, which makes them more productive. Productivity and income grow because technology advances, and the scope for further productivity growth, which is stimulated by the search for profit, is practically unlimited.

Then

In 1830, a strong and experienced farm worker could harvest three acres of wheat in a day. The only capital employed was a scythe to cut the wheat, which had been used since Roman times, and a cradle on which the stalks were laid, which had been invented by Flemish farmers in the fifteenth century. With newly developed horse-drawn plows, harrows, and planters, farmers could plant more wheat than they could harvest. But despite big efforts, no one had been able to make a machine that could replicate the swing of a scythe. Then in 1831, 22-year-old Cyrus McCormick built a machine that worked. It scared the horse that pulled it, but it did in a matter of hours what three men could accomplish in a day. Technological change has increased productivity on farms and brought economic growth. Do the facts about productivity growth mean that the classical economists, who believed that diminishing returns would push us relentlessly back to a subsistence living standard, were wrong?

Now

Today's technologies are expanding our horizons beyond the confines of our planet and are expanding our minds. Geosynchronous satellites bring us global television, voice and data communication, and more accurate weather forecasts, which, incidentally, increase agricultural productivity. In the foreseeable future, we might have superconductors that revolutionize the use of electric power, virtual reality theme parks and training facilities, pollution-free hydrogen cars, wristwatch telephones, and optical computers that we can talk to. Equipped with these new technologies, our ability to create yet more dazzling technologies increases. Technological change begets technological change in an (apparently) unending process and makes us ever more productive and brings ever higher incomes.

Today's revolution in the way economists think about economic growth has been led by Paul Romer, a professor of economics at Stanford University, whom you can meet on the following pages.

Paul Romer *is Professor of Economics at the Graduate School of Business at Stanford University and the Royal Bank Fellow of the Canadian Institute for Advanced Research. Born in 1955 in Denver, Colorado, he earned his B.S. in Mathematics (1977) and his Ph.D. in Economics (1983) from the University of Chicago. Professor Romer has transformed the way economists think about economic growth. He believes that sustained economic growth arises from competition among firms. Firms try to increase their profits by devoting resources to creating new products and developing new ways of making existing products.*

Michael Parkin talked with Professor Romer about his work, how he was influenced by Joseph Schumpeter and Robert Solow, and the insights economic growth offers us.

Professor Romer, why did you decide to become an economist?
As an undergraduate, I studied math and physics and was interested in becoming a cosmologist. During my senior year, I concluded that job prospects in physics were not very promising, so I decided to go to law school. I was an undergraduate at the

Paul Romer

University of Chicago, where the law and economics movement first emerged. In the fall of my senior year, I took my first economics course to prepare for law school. My economics professor, Sam Peltzman, presented a simple piece of economic analysis that changed my life. He argued that the demand for economists was likely to grow for decades. The government, which employs economists, would grow in size. Businesses that deal with the government would want their own economists. The legal profession that serves businesses would also need more economists. Because of all these demands, many students would want to take economics courses. This meant that there would be many job openings for economists at universities. Moreover, he claimed, being a professor of economics was a lot like being a cosmologist and far more fun than being a lawyer. I could take fragmentary bits of evidence and try to make sense of them using mathematical equations. So I tore up my law school applications, applied to graduate school in economics, and never looked back.

What are the truly important lessons about the causes of economic growth?
As a physics major, I felt that the description economists used for growth violated a basic law of physics: the conservation of mass. Economists seemed to be saying that GDP, the output of a nation, was a bunch of stuff that was "produced" and that the quantity of stuff produced has grown steadily over time and will continue to do so. But this can't be right. We have the same amount of stuff, or elements from the periodic table, that we had 100,000 years ago because there are many more

people now. In terms of kilograms of matter per person, we know that we are vastly poorer than our ancestors were 100,000 years ago. Yet we clearly have a higher standard of living. How could this be? This basic question indicates that thinking about growth as a production process that generates stuff is a dead-end. Instead, economic growth has to be about rearranging the fixed amount of matter that we have to work with and making new combinations that seem a lot more valuable. The key insight is that economic growth comes from increases in value, not increases in the amount of matter.

Can you give us an example of an increase in value?
For tens of thousands of years, we treated iron oxide, ordinary rust, like dirt. When we lived in caves, we learned how to use it as a pigment for decorating cave walls. We took the low-value dirt and put it to the higher-valued use of making cave paintings. Later, we learned how to extract the iron from iron ore to make bridges and rails. Later still, we learned how to arrange the iron atoms together with carbon atoms and make steel. Recently, we learned how to take iron oxide and put it on magnetic tape and use it to store sound and pictures. The iron, oxygen, and carbon atoms have always been here. We have a higher standard of living because we have learned how to arrange these atoms in ways that we find more valuable.

What kind of policy implications does this kind of thinking lead to?
Policy makers must encourage institutions to become more efficient at discovering new recipes to rearrange matter. Consider the transistor as an example. We take silicon and mix it with a few impurities and some metal in just the right way, and we get a computer chip worth thousands of times what the raw ingredients were worth. Research grants, subsidies for education, and institutions like the nonprofit private university encourage the production of new recipes or ideas. But so do venture capitalists who help new-technology startups, competitive markets that allow the firms with better instructions or ideas to quickly displace existing firms,

> We take silicon and mix it with a few impurities and some metal in just the right way, and we get a computer chip worth thousands of times what the raw ingredients were worth.

and labor laws that let inefficient firms lay off workers when more efficient new firms come on the scene. We must let firms like Digital Electronics or Wang Computers shrink, maybe even fail, if we want to make room for new firms like Intel to enter the scene and thrive.

Were the classical economists wrong in their view that population growth and diminishing returns are the dominant long-term influences on production and incomes? Or is the current global population explosion part of a process that will ultimately prove them correct?
Classical economists like Malthus and Ricardo were right when they argued that we have a fixed amount of natural resources to work with. Malthus pointed out that resource scarcity will lead to falling standards of living if we continue to work with the same set of recipes or instructions for using our resources. Where he went wrong was in assuming that there was little scope for us to find new recipes for taking resources such as land, water, carbon dioxide, nitrogen, and sunshine and converting them into carbohydrates and proteins that we can eat.

The classical economists got half of the story right. We do live in a world with scarce resources. They missed the other half. There is an incomprehensibly large number of different formulas we can use to recombine these scarce resources into things we value, such as protein or entertainment.

Scarcity is a very important part of economics and our lives. For example, we know that there is an absolute limit on the number of people who can live on the earth. One way or another, we know that the rate of population growth will slow down. It's only a question of how and when. But will this ultimately lead to a period when standards of living fall as Malthus predicted? I doubt it. As countries get rich, population growth slows. As a larger fraction of the worldwide population becomes educated, these people will help us to discover new things, like plants that are more efficient at taking carbon dioxide out of the atmosphere, and more efficient distribution systems. Thus standards of living for all humans will continue to improve.

During the past decade, China and several other economies in East Asia have experienced rapid, unheralded growth rates. Why? These countries took some of the recipes, formulas, and instructions for generating value that already existed in the advanced countries of the world and put them to use within their borders. It's the same process that the Japanese followed after the Meiji restoration at the end of the last century. These countries noticed that other people in the world knew a lot about how to create value and realized that by trading with these people, they could share in the gains.

What lessons from East Asia can, in principle, be applied in Africa and Central Europe? The basic insight is that there are huge potential gains from trade. Poor countries can supply their natural and human resources. Rich countries can supply their know-how. When these are combined, everyone can be better off. The challenge is for a country to arrange its laws and institutions so that both sides can profitably engage in trade. If there are barriers to trade or if the government cannot protect basic property rights and prevent crime, trade can't take place. For example, the Japanese have been able to borrow many ideas about manufacturing and design and even to improve on some of these ideas. But because they have barriers that limit entry of foreign firms into the retail sector, they still waste vast quantities of resources on a very inefficient distribution system.

What does today's thinking about economic growth owe to Joseph Schumpeter and Robert Solow? Schumpeter worked at a time before most economists had learned to work with equations. He coined the phrase "creative destruction," which describes the process by which companies like Wang shrink or go out of business when new firms come in. He also described in words how important monopoly profits are in the process of innovation. There were many other economists, including Alfred Marshall, who described these same issues in verbal terms and also struggled to express these ideas in terms of equations.

Robert Solow was part of the post–World War II generation of economists who truly mastered the use of equations and wrote eloquently using both words and equations. As a result, his ideas have been far more influential than Schumpeter's. Many economists in the 1950s were trying to get a grasp on the economic effects of knowledge, formulas, recipes, and instructions. Solow called these things "technology" and gave us a wonderfully concise and workable way to think about how technology interacts with other economic inputs such as capital and labor. He also linked the methods that he and several economists were using to measure technology with this framework for thinking about the behavior of the economy as a whole. His work on growth was a masterful piece of invention, synthesis, and exposition.

Recent economists have taken Solow's mathematical framework and extended it to bring in some of the elements that Schumpeter described in words, like creative destruction and monopoly power. One of the great things about ideas is that they build on each other. In Isaac Newton's famous phrase, those of us working on growth today are "able to see farther because we stand on the shoulders of giants." Newton was another person who was pretty good with equations and could turn a good phrase.

Is economics a worthwhile subject to major in? What can one do with an economics degree? Economics is an excellent training ground for developing mathematical and verbal skills. But students should supplement the courses in

> If you can learn how to write readable prose and use the basic tools of mathematics, you can do almost anything.

economics with courses in mathematics and science that force them to practice working with equations, graphs, and numbers. There is no substitute for such practice. Innate ability is far less important than most students think.

They should also take courses that force them to write, revise, and edit. I took an English course in college that taught me the basics of how to edit, and it is one of the best investments I made. You can't tell what you will end up doing or what skills you will need later in life. But if you can learn how to write readable prose and use the basic tools of mathematics, you can do almost anything.

Chapter 29

Expenditure Multipliers

In the Red Rocks Amphitheater in Denver, Bonnie Raitt sings into a microphone in a barely audible whisper. Moving to a louder passage, she increases the volume of her voice and now, through the magic of electronic amplification, booms across the stadium, drowning out every other sound. ◆ Dennis Archer, the mayor of Detroit, and a secretary are being driven to a business meeting along one of the city's less well-repaired highways. (There are some badly potholed highways in Detroit.) The car's wheels are bouncing and vibrating over some of the worst highways in the nation, but its passengers are completely undisturbed and the secretary's notes are written without a ripple, thanks to the car's efficient shock absorbers. ◆ Investment and exports fluctuate like the volume of Bonnie Raitt's voice and the uneven surface of a Detroit highway. How does the economy react to those fluctuations? Does it react like Dennis Archer's limousine, absorbing the shocks and providing a smooth ride for the economy's passengers? Or does it behave like Bonnie Raitt's amplifier, blowing up the fluctuations and spreading them out to affect the many millions of participants in an economic rock concert?

Amplifier or Shock Absorber?

◆ You will explore these questions in this chapter. You will learn how a recession or a recovery begins when a change in investment or exports triggers a larger change in *aggregate* expenditure and real GDP—like Bonnie Raitt's amplifier. You will also learn how imports and income taxes have lowered the power of the amplifier. Finally, you will discover that in contrast to the initial amplification effect, the economy's shock absorbers, which are price and wage changes, pull real GDP back toward potential GDP. ◆ To achieve these objectives, we use a model called the *aggregate expenditure model*. This model explains changes in aggregate expenditure in a very short time frame during which prices do not change.

After studying this chapter, you will be able to:

■ Explain how expenditure plans are determined

■ Explain how real GDP is determined when the price level is fixed

■ Explain the multiplier

■ Explain how imports and taxes influence the multiplier

■ Explain how recessions and expansions begin

■ Explain the relationship between aggregate expenditure and aggregate demand

■ Explain how the multiplier gets smaller as the price level changes

Fixed Prices and Expenditure Plans

MOST FIRMS ARE LIKE YOUR LOCAL SUPERMARKET. They set their prices, advertise their products and services, and sell the quantities their customers are willing to buy. If firms persistently sell a greater quantity than they plan to and are constantly running out of inventory, they eventually raise their prices. And if firms persistently sell a smaller quantity than they plan to and have inventories piling up, they eventually cut their prices. But in the very short term, their prices are fixed. They hold the prices they have set, and the quantities they sell depend on demand, not supply.

The Aggregate Implications of Fixed Prices

Fixed prices have two immediate implications for the economy as a whole:

1. Because each firm's price is fixed, the *price level* is fixed.

2. Because demand determines the quantities that each firm sells, *aggregate demand* determines the aggregate quantity of goods and services sold, which equals real GDP.

So to understand the fluctuations in real GDP when the price level is fixed, we must understand aggregate demand fluctuations. The aggregate expenditure model explains fluctuations in aggregate demand by identifying the forces that determine expenditure plans.

Expenditure Plans

The components of aggregate expenditure are:

- Consumption expenditure
- Investment
- Government purchases of goods and services
- Net exports (exports *minus* imports)

These four components of aggregate expenditure sum to real GDP (see Chapter 23, pp. 498–499).
Aggregate planned expenditure is equal to *planned* consumption expenditure plus *planned* investment plus *planned* government purchases plus *planned* exports minus *planned* imports.

In the very short term, *planned* investment, *planned* government purchases, and *planned* exports are fixed. But *planned* consumption expenditure and *planned* imports are not fixed. They depend on the level of real GDP itself.

A Two-Way Link Between Aggregate Expenditure and GDP Because real GDP influences consumption expenditure and imports and because consumption expenditure and imports are components of aggregate expenditure, there is a two-way link between aggregate expenditure and GDP. Other things remaining the same:

- An increase in real GDP increases aggregate planned expenditure.
- An increase in aggregate expenditure increases real GDP.

You are going to learn how this two-way link between aggregate expenditure and real GDP determines real GDP when the price level is fixed. The starting point is to consider the first piece of the two-way link: the influence of real GDP on planned consumption expenditure and saving.

Consumption Function and Saving Function

Several factors influence consumption expenditure and saving. The more important ones are:

- Real interest rate
- Disposable income
- Purchasing power of net assets
- Expected future income

Chapter 27 (see p. 592) explains how these factors influence consumption expenditure and saving. The second factor, **disposable income**, is aggregate income minus taxes plus transfer payments. And aggregate income equals real GDP. So to explore the two-way link between real GDP and planned consumption expenditure, our focus here is on the relationship between consumption expenditure and disposable income when the other factors are constant.

Consumption and Saving Plans The table in Fig. 29.1 shows an example of the relationship among planned consumption expenditure, planned saving, and disposable income. It lists the consumption expenditure and the saving that people plan to undertake at each level of disposable income. Notice that at each level of disposable income, consumption expenditure plus saving always equals disposable income. The reason is that households can only consume or save their disposable income. So planned consumption plus planned saving always equals disposable income.

The relationship between consumption expenditure and disposable income, other things remaining the same, is called the **consumption function.** The relationship between saving and disposable income, other things remaining the same, is called the **saving function**. Let's begin by studying the consumption function.

FIGURE **29.1**

Consumption Function and Saving Function

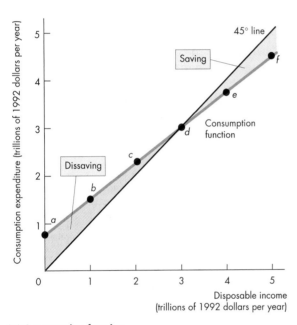

(a) Consumption function

(b) Saving function

	Disposable income	Planned consumption expenditure	Planned saving
		(trillions of 1992 dollars per year)	
a	0	0.75	−0.75
b	1	1.50	−0.50
c	2	2.25	−0.25
d	3	3.00	0
e	4	3.75	0.25
f	5	4.50	0.50

The table shows consumption expenditure and saving plans at various levels of disposable income. Part (a) of the figure shows the relationship between consumption expenditure and disposable income (the consumption function). The height of the consumption function measures consumption expenditure at each level of disposable income. Part (b) shows the relationship between saving and disposable income (the saving function). The height of the saving function measures saving at each level of disposable income. Points a through f on the consumption and saving functions correspond to the rows of the table. The height of the 45° line in part (a) measures disposable income. So, along the 45° line, consumption expenditure equals disposable income. Consumption expenditure plus saving equals disposable income. When the consumption function is above the 45° line, saving is negative (dissaving occurs). When the consumption function is below the 45° line, saving is positive. At the point where the consumption function intersects the 45° line, all disposable income is consumed and saving is zero.

Consumption Function Figure 29.1(a) shows a consumption function. The *y*-axis measures consumption expenditure, and the *x*-axis measures disposable income. Along the consumption function, the points labeled *a* through *f* correspond to the rows of the table. For example, point *e* shows that when disposable income is $4 trillion, consumption expenditure is $3.75 trillion. Along the consumption function, as disposable income increases, consumption expenditure also increases.

At point *a* on the consumption function, consumption expenditure is $0.75 trillion even though disposable income is zero. This consumption expenditure is called *autonomous consumption*, and it is the amount of consumption expenditure that would take place in the short run, even if people had no current income. Consumption expenditure in excess of this amount is called *induced consumption*, which is expenditure that is induced by an increase in disposable income.

45° Line Figure 29.1(a) also contains a 45° line, the height of which measures disposable income. At each point on this line, consumption expenditure equals disposable income. In the range over which the consumption function lies above the 45° line—between *a* and *d*—consumption expenditure exceeds disposable income. In the range over which the consumption function lies below the 45° line—between *d* and *f*—consumption expenditure is less than disposable income. And at the point at which the consumption function intersects the 45° line—at point *d*—consumption expenditure equals disposable income.

Saving Function Figure 29.1(b) shows a saving function. The *x*-axis is exactly the same as that in part (a). The *y*-axis measures saving. Again, the points marked *a* through *f* correspond to the rows of the table. For example, point *e* shows that when disposable income is $4 trillion, saving is $0.25 trillion. Along the saving function, as disposable income increases, saving also increases. At disposable income less than $3 trillion (point *d*), saving is negative. Negative saving is called *dissaving*. At disposable income greater than $3 trillion, saving is positive, and at $3 trillion, saving is zero.

Notice the connection between the two parts of Fig. 29.1. When consumption expenditure exceeds disposable income in part (a), saving is negative in part (b). When disposable income exceeds consumption expenditure in part (a), saving is positive in part (b). And when consumption expenditure equals disposable income in part (a), saving is zero in part (b).

When saving is negative (when consumption expenditure exceeds disposable income), past savings are used to pay for current consumption. Such a situation cannot last forever, but it can occur if disposable income falls temporarily.

Marginal Propensities to Consume and Save

The extent to which consumption expenditure changes when disposable income changes depends on the marginal propensity to consume. The **marginal propensity to consume** (*MPC*) is the fraction of a *change* in disposable income that is consumed. It is calculated as the *change* in consumption expenditure (ΔC) divided by the *change* in disposable income (ΔYD) that brought it about. That is,

$$MPC = \frac{\Delta C}{\Delta YD}.$$

In the table in Fig. 29.1, when disposable income increases from $3 trillion to $4 trillion, consumption expenditure increases from $3 trillion to $3.75 trillion. The $1 trillion increase in disposable income increases consumption expenditure by $0.75 trillion. The *MPC* is $0.75 trillion divided by $1 trillion, which equals 0.75.

The **marginal propensity to save** (*MPS*) is the fraction of a *change* in disposable income that is saved. It is calculated as the *change* in saving (ΔS) divided by the *change* in disposable income (ΔYD) that brought it about. That is,

$$MPS = \frac{\Delta S}{\Delta YD}.$$

In the table in Fig. 29.1, an increase in disposable income from $3 trillion to $4 trillion increases saving from zero to $0.25 trillion. The $1 trillion increase in disposable income increases saving by $0.25 trillion. The *MPS* is $0.25 trillion divided by $1 trillion, which equals 0.25.

The marginal propensity to consume plus the marginal propensity to save always equals 1. They sum to 1 because consumption expenditure and saving exhaust disposable income. Part of each dollar increase in disposable income is consumed, and the remaining part is saved. You can see that these two marginal propensities sum to 1 by using the equation

$$\Delta C + \Delta S = \Delta YD.$$

Divide both sides of the equation by the change in disposable income to obtain

$$\frac{\Delta C}{\Delta YD} + \frac{\Delta S}{\Delta YD} = 1.$$

$\Delta C/\Delta YD$ is the *marginal propensity to consume* (*MPC*), and $\Delta S/\Delta YD$ is the *marginal propensity to save* (*MPS*), so

$$MPC + MPS = 1.$$

Slopes and Marginal Propensities

The slopes of the consumption function and the saving function are the marginal propensities to consume and save. Figure 29.2(a) shows the *MPC* as the slope of the consumption function. A $1 trillion increase in disposable income from $3 trillion to $4 trillion is the base of the red triangle. The increase in consumption expenditure that results from this increase in income is $0.75 trillion and is the height of the triangle. The slope of the consumption function is given by the formula "slope equals rise over run" and is $0.75 trillion divided by $1 trillion, which equals 0.75—the *MPC*.

Figure 29.2(b) shows the *MPS* as the slope of the saving function. A $1 trillion increase in disposable income from $3 trillion to $4 trillion (the base of the red triangle) increases saving by $0.25 trillion (the height of the triangle). The slope of the saving function is $0.25 trillion divided by $1 trillion, which equals 0.25—the *MPS*.

Other Influences on Consumption Expenditure and Saving

You've seen that a change in disposable income leads to changes in consumption expenditure and saving. A change in disposable income brings movements along the consumption function and saving function.

FIGURE 29.2

Marginal Propensities to Consume and Save

(a) Consumption function

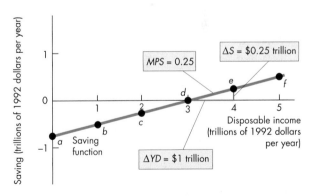

(b) Saving function

The marginal propensity to consume, *MPC*, is equal to the change in consumption expenditure divided by the change in disposable income, other things remaining the same. It is measured by the slope of the consumption function. In part (a), the *MPC* is 0.75. The marginal propensity to save, *MPS*, is equal to the change in saving divided by the change in disposable income, other things remaining the same. It is measured by the slope of the saving function. In part (b), the *MPS* is 0.25.

Along the consumption function and saving function, all other influences on consumption expenditure and saving (such as the real interest rate, expected future income, and the purchasing power net assets) are fixed. A change in any of these other influences shifts both the consumption function and the saving function.

When the real interest rate falls or when the purchasing power of net assets or expected future income increases, consumption expenditure increases and saving decreases. Figure 29.3 shows the effects of these changes on the consumption function and the saving function. The consumption function shifts upward from CF_0 to CF_1, and the saving function shifts downward from SF_0 to SF_1. Such shifts commonly occur during the expansion phase of the business cycle because, at such times, expected future income increases.

When the real interest rate rises or when the purchasing power of net assets or expected future income decreases, consumption expenditure decreases and saving increases. Figure 29.3 also shows the effects of these changes on the consumption function and the saving function. The consumption function shifts downward from CF_0 to CF_2, and the saving function shifts upward from SF_0 to SF_2. Such shifts often occur when a recession begins because at such a time, expected future income decreases.

We've studied the theory of the consumption function. Let's now see how that theory applies to the U.S. economy.

The U.S. Consumption Function

Figure 29.4 shows the U.S. consumption function. Each point identified by a blue dot represents consumption expenditure and disposable income for a particular year. (The dots are for the years 1970–1998, and the even-numbered years are identified in the figure.) The line labeled CF_0 is an estimate of the U.S. consumption function in 1970, and the line labeled CF_1 is an estimate of the U.S. consumption function in 1998.

The slope of the consumption function in Fig. 29.4 is 0.75, which means that a $1 trillion increase in disposable income brings a $0.75 trillion increase in consumption expenditure. This slope, which is an estimate of the marginal propensity to consume, is an assumption that is in the middle of the range of values that economists have estimated for the marginal propensity to consume.

FIGURE 29.3

Shifts in the Consumption and Saving Functions

(a) Consumption function

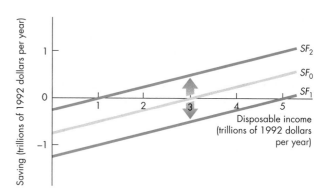

(b) Saving function

A fall in the real interest rate, an increase in the purchasing power of net assets, or an increase in expected future income increases consumption expenditure and decreases saving. It shifts the consumption function upward from CF_0 to CF_1 and shifts the saving function downward from SF_0 to SF_1. A rise in the real interest rate or a decrease in either the purchasing power of net assets or expected future income shifts the consumption function downward from CF_0 to CF_2 and shifts the saving function upward from SF_0 to SF_2.

FIGURE 29.4

The U.S. Consumption Function

Each blue dot shows consumption expenditure and disposable income for a particular year. The lines CF_0 and CF_1 are estimates of the U.S. consumption function in 1970 and 1998, respectively. Here, the (assumed) marginal propensity to consume is 0.75.

The consumption function shifts upward over time as other influences on consumption expenditure. Of these other influences, the real interest rate and the purchasing power of net assets fluctuate and so bring upward and downward shifts in the consumption function. But rising expected future income brings a steady upward shift in the consumption function. As the consumption function shifts upward, autonomous consumption expenditure increases.

Consumption as a Function of Real GDP

You've seen that consumption expenditure changes when disposable income changes. Disposable income changes when either real GDP changes or net taxes change. If tax rates don't change, real GDP is the only influence on disposable income. So consumption depends not only on disposable income but also on real GDP. We use this link between consumption

and real GDP to determine equilibrium expenditure. But before we do so, we need to look at one further component of aggregate expenditure: imports. Like consumption expenditure, imports are influenced by real GDP.

Import Function

U.S. imports are determined by many factors, but in the short run, one factor dominates: U.S. real GDP. Other things remaining the same, the greater the U.S. real GDP, the larger is the quantity of U.S. imports.

The relationship between imports and real GDP is determined by the marginal propensity to import. The **marginal propensity to import** is the fraction of an increase in real GDP that is spent on imports. It is calculated as the change in imports divided by the change in real GDP that brought it about, other things remaining the same. For example, if a $1 trillion increase in real GDP increases imports by $0.25 trillion, the marginal propensity to import is 0.25.

In recent years, since the North American Free Trade Agreement was implemented, U.S. imports have surged. For example, in 1998, real GDP increased by $280 billion and imports increased by $120 billion. Other factors also influenced imports in 1998, but the marginal propensity to import in that year was probably larger than 0.2. The U.S. marginal propensity to import has been increasing.

R E V I E W   Q U I Z

- Which components of aggregate expenditure are influenced by real GDP?
- Define the marginal propensity to consume. What is your estimate of your own marginal propensity to consume? After you graduate, will it change? Why?
- How do we calculate the effects of real GDP on consumption expenditure and imports by using the marginal propensity to consume and the marginal propensity to import?

Real GDP influences consumption and imports. But consumption and imports along with investment, government purchases, and exports influence real GDP. Your next task is to study this second piece of the two-way link between aggregate expenditure and real GDP and see how all the components of aggregate planned expenditure interact to determine real GDP.

Real GDP with a Fixed Price Level

YOU ARE NOW GOING TO DISCOVER HOW AGGRE-gate expenditure plans interact to determine real GDP when the price level is fixed. First, we will study the relationship between aggregate planned expenditure and real GDP. Second, we'll learn about the key distinction between *planned* expenditure and *actual*

expenditure. And third, we'll study equilibrium expenditure, a situation in which aggregate planned expenditure and actual expenditure are equal.

The relationship between aggregate planned expenditure and real GDP can be described by either an aggregate expenditure schedule or an aggregate expenditure curve. The *aggregate expenditure schedule* lists aggregate planned expenditure generated at each level of real GDP. The *aggregate expenditure curve* is a graph of the aggregate expenditure schedule.

FIGURE 29.5

Aggregate Planned Expenditure

The aggregate expenditure schedule shows the relationship between aggregate planned expenditure and real GDP. Aggregate planned expenditure is the sum of planned consumption expenditure, investment, government purchases of goods and services, and exports minus imports. For example, in row *b* of the table, when real GDP is $2 trillion, planned consumption expenditure is $2.25 trillion, planned investment is $0.5 trillion, planned government purchases of goods and services are $0.55 trillion, planned exports are $1.2 trillion, and planned imports are $0.5 trillion. Thus when real GDP is $2 trillion, aggregate planned expenditure is $4 trillion ($2.25 + $0.5 + $0.55 + $1.2 − $0.5). The schedule shows that aggregate planned expenditure increases as real GDP increases. This relationship is graphed as the aggregate expenditure curve *AE*, the line *af*. The components of aggregate expenditure that increase with real GDP are consumption expenditure and imports. The other components—investment, government purchases, and exports—do not vary with real GDP.

		Planned expenditure					
	Real GDP (Y)	**Consumption expenditure** (C)	**Investment** (I)	**Government purchases** (G)	**Exports** (X)	**Imports** (M)	**Aggregate planned expenditure** (AE = C + I + G + X − M)
				(trillions of 1992 dollars)			
a	0	0.75	0.5	0.55	1.2	0.0	3
b	2	2.25	0.5	0.55	1.2	0.5	4
c	4	3.75	0.5	0.55	1.2	1.0	5
d	6	5.25	0.5	0.55	1.2	1.5	6
e	8	6.75	0.5	0.55	1.2	2.0	7
f	10	8.25	0.5	0.55	1.2	2.5	8

Aggregate Planned Expenditure and Real GDP

The table in Fig. 29.5 sets out an aggregate expenditure schedule together with the components of aggregate planned expenditure. To calculate aggregate planned expenditure at a given real GDP, we add the various components together. The first column of the table shows real GDP, and the second column shows the consumption expenditure generated by each level of real GDP. A $2 trillion increase in real GDP generates a $1.50 trillion increase in consumption expenditure—the MPC is 0.75.

The next two columns show investment and government purchases of goods and services. Investment depends on the real interest rate and the expected rate of profit (see Chapter 27, p. 589). At a given point in time, these factors generate a particular level of investment. Suppose this level of investment is $0.5 trillion. Also, suppose that government purchases of goods and services are $0.55 trillion.

The next two columns show exports and imports. Exports are influenced by events in the rest of the world, prices of foreign-made goods and services relative to the prices of similar U.S.-made goods and services, and foreign exchange rates. But exports are not directly affected by real GDP in the United States. Exports are a constant $1.2 trillion. Imports increase as real GDP increases. A $2 trillion increase in real GDP generates a $0.5 trillion increase in imports—the marginal propensity to import is 0.25.

The final column shows aggregate planned expenditure—the sum of planned consumption expenditure, investment, government purchases of goods and services, and exports minus imports.

Figure 29.5 plots an aggregate expenditure curve. Real GDP is shown on the x-axis, and aggregate planned expenditure is shown on the y-axis. The aggregate expenditure curve is the red line AE. Points a through f on that curve correspond to the rows of the table. The AE curve is a graph of aggregate planned expenditure (the last column) plotted against real GDP (the first column).

Figure 29.5 also shows the components of aggregate expenditure. The constant components—investment (I), government purchases of goods and services (G), and exports (X)—are shown by the horizontal lines in the figure. Consumption expenditure (C) is the vertical gap between the lines labeled $I + G + X$ and $I + G + X + C$.

To construct the AE curve, subtract imports (M) from the $I + G + X + C$ line. Aggregate expenditure is expenditure on U.S.-made goods and services. But the components of aggregate expenditure—C, I, and G—include expenditure on imported goods and services. For example, a student's purchase of a new motor bike is part of consumption expenditure. But if that motor bike is a Honda made in Japan, expenditure on it must be subtracted from consumption expenditure to find out how much is spent on goods and services produced in the United States—on U.S. real GDP. Money paid to Honda for motor bike imports from Japan does not add to aggregate expenditure on U.S.-made goods and services.

Figure 29.5 shows that aggregate planned expenditure increases as real GDP increases. But as real GDP increases, only some of the components of aggregate planned expenditure increase. These components are consumption expenditure and imports. The sum of the components of aggregate expenditure that vary with real GDP is called **induced expenditure**. The sum of the components of aggregate expenditure that are not influenced by real GDP is called **autonomous expenditure**. The components of autonomous expenditure are investment, government purchases, exports, and autonomous consumption—that part of consumption expenditure that does not vary with real GDP. That is, autonomous expenditure is equal to the level of aggregate planned expenditure when real GDP is zero. In Fig. 29.5, autonomous expenditure is $3 trillion. And as real GDP increases from zero to $2 trillion, aggregate expenditure increases from $3 trillion to $4 trillion. Induced expenditure is $1 trillion—$4 trillion minus $3 trillion.

The aggregate expenditure curve summarizes the relationship between aggregate *planned* expenditure and real GDP. But what determines the point on the aggregate expenditure curve at which the economy operates? What determines *actual* aggregate expenditure?

Actual Expenditure, Planned Expenditure, and Real GDP

Actual aggregate expenditure is always equal to real GDP, as we saw in Chapter 23 (p. 497). But aggregate *planned* expenditure is not necessarily equal to actual aggregate expenditure and therefore is not necessarily equal to real GDP. How can actual expenditure and planned expenditure differ from each other? Why don't expenditure plans get implemented? The main reason is that firms might end up with more inventories than planned or with less inventories than planned. People carry out their consumption expenditure plans, the government implements its planned purchases of goods and services, and net exports are as planned. Firms carry out their plans to purchase new buildings, plant, and equipment. But one component

of investment is the change in firms' inventories of goods. If aggregate planned expenditure is less than real GDP, firms don't sell all the goods they produce and they end up with inventories they hadn't planned. If aggregate planned expenditure exceeds real GDP, firms sell more than they produce and inventories decrease below the level that firms had planned.

FIGURE 29.6

Equilibrium Expenditure

(a) Equilibrium expenditure

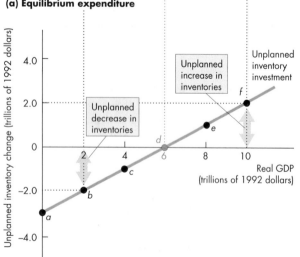

(b) Unplanned inventory changes

	Real GDP (Y)	Aggregate planned expenditure (AE)	Unplanned inventory change (Y – AE)
		(trillions of 1992 dollars)	
a	0	3	–3
b	2	4	–2
c	4	5	–1
d	6	6	0
e	8	7	1
f	10	8	2

The table shows expenditure plans at different levels of real GDP. When real GDP is $6 trillion, aggregate planned expenditure equals real GDP. Part (a) of the figure illustrates equilibrium expenditure, which occurs when aggregate planned expenditure equals real GDP at the intersection of the 45° line and the *AE* curve. Part (b) of the figure shows the forces that bring about equilibrium expenditure. When aggregate planned expenditure exceeds real GDP, inventories decrease— for example, point *b* in both parts of the figure. Firms increase production, and real GDP increases. When aggregate planned expenditure is less than real GDP, inventories increase—for example, point *f* in both parts of the figure. Firms decrease production, and real GDP decreases. When aggregate planned expenditure equals real GDP, there are no unplanned inventory changes and real GDP remains constant at equilibrium expenditure.

Equilibrium Expenditure

Equilibrium expenditure is the level of aggregate expenditure that occurs when aggregate *planned* expenditure equals real GDP. It is a level of aggregate expenditure and real GDP at which everyone's spending plans are fulfilled. When the price level is fixed, equilibrium expenditure determines real GDP. When aggregate planned expenditure and actual aggregate expenditure are unequal, a process of convergence toward equilibrium expenditure occurs. And throughout this convergence process, real GDP adjusts. Let's examine equilibrium expenditure and the process that brings it about.

Figure 29.6(a) illustrates equilibrium expenditure. The table sets out aggregate planned expenditure at various levels of real GDP. These values are plotted as points *a* through *f* along the *AE* curve. The 45° line shows all the points at which aggregate planned expenditure equals real GDP. Thus where the *AE* curve lies above the 45° line, aggregate planned expenditure exceeds real GDP; where the *AE* curve lies below the 45° line, aggregate planned expenditure is less than real GDP; and where the *AE* curve intersects the 45° line, aggregate planned expenditure equals real GDP. Point *d* illustrates equilibrium expenditure. At this point, real GDP is $6 trillion.

Convergence to Equilibrium

What are the forces that move aggregate expenditure toward its equilibrium level? To answer this question, we must look at a situation in which aggregate expenditure is away from its equilibrium level. Suppose that in Fig. 29.6, real GDP is $2 trillion. With real GDP at $2 trillion, actual aggregate expenditure is also $2 trillion. But aggregate *planned* expenditure is $4 trillion (point *b* in Fig. 29.6a). Aggregate planned expenditure exceeds *actual* expenditure. When people spend $4 trillion and firms produce goods and services worth $2 trillion, firms' inventories fall by $2 trillion (point *b* in Fig. 29.6b). Because the change in inventories is part of investment, *actual* investment is $2 trillion less than *planned* investment.

Real GDP doesn't remain at $2 trillion for very long. Firms have inventory targets based on their sales. When inventories fall below target, firms increase production to restore inventories to the target level. To increase inventories, firms hire additional labor and increase production. Suppose that they

increase production in the next period by $2 trillion. Real GDP increases by $2.0 trillion to $4.0 trillion. But again, aggregate planned expenditure exceeds real GDP. When real GDP is $4.0 trillion, aggregate planned expenditure is $5 trillion (point *c* in Fig. 29.6a). Again, inventories decrease, but this time by less than before. With real GDP of $4.0 trillion and aggregate planned expenditure of $5 trillion, inventories decrease by $1 trillion (point *c* in Fig. 29.6b). Again, firms hire additional labor, and production increases; real GDP increases yet further.

The process that we have just described—planned expenditure exceeds real GDP, inventories decrease, and production increases—ends when real GDP has reached $6 trillion. At this real GDP, there is an equilibrium. There are no unplanned inventory changes, and firms do not change their production.

You can do an experiment similar to the one we've just done but starting with a level of real GDP greater than equilibrium expenditure. In this case, planned expenditure is less than actual expenditure, inventories pile up, and firms cut production. As before, real GDP keeps on changing (decreasing this time) until it reaches its equilibrium level of $6.0 trillion.

REVIEW QUIZ

- What is the relationship between aggregate planned expenditure and real GDP in expenditure equilibrium?
- How does equilibrium expenditure come about? What adjusts to achieve equilibrium?
- If real GDP and aggregate expenditure are less than their equilibrium levels, what happens to firms' inventories? How do firms change their production? And what happens to real GDP?
- If real GDP and aggregate expenditure are greater than their equilibrium levels, what happens to firms' inventories? How do firms change their production? And what happens to real GDP?

We've learned that when the price level is fixed, real GDP is determined by equilibrium expenditure. And we have seen how unplanned changes in inventories and the production response they generate bring a convergence toward equilibrium. We're now going to study *changes* in equilibrium and discover an economic amplifier called the *multiplier*.

The Multiplier

INVESTMENT AND EXPORTS CAN CHANGE FOR many reasons. A fall in the real interest rate might induce firms to increase their planned investment. A wave of innovation, such as occurred with the spread of multimedia computers in the 1990s, might increase expected future profits and lead firms to increase their planned investment. An economic boom in Western Europe and Japan might lead to a large increase in their expenditure on U.S.-produced goods and services—on U.S. exports. These are all examples of increases in autonomous expenditure.

When autonomous expenditure increases, aggregate expenditure increases, and so does equilibrium expenditure and real GDP. But the increase in real GDP is *larger* than the change in autonomous expenditure. The **multiplier** is the amount by which a change in autonomous expenditure is magnified or multiplied to determine the change in equilibrium expenditure and real GDP.

It is easiest to get the basic idea of the multiplier if we work with an example economy in which there are no income taxes and no imports. So we'll first assume that these factors are absent. Then, when you understand the basic idea, we'll bring these factors back into play and see what difference they make to the multiplier.

The Basic Idea of the Multiplier

Suppose that investment increases. The additional expenditure by businesses means that aggregate expenditure and real GDP increase. The increase in real GDP increases disposable income and with no income taxes, real GDP and disposable income increase by the same amount. The increase in disposable income brings an increase in consumption expenditure. And the increased consumption expenditure adds even more to aggregate expenditure. Real GDP and disposable income increase further, and so does consumption expenditure. The initial increase in investment brings an even bigger increase in aggregate expenditure because it induces an increase in consumption expenditure. The magnitude of the increase in aggregate expenditure that results from an increase in autonomous expenditure is determined by the *multiplier*.

The table in Fig. 29.7 sets out aggregate planned expenditure. Initially, when real GDP is $5 trillion,

aggregate planned expenditure is $5.25 trillion. For each $1 trillion increase in real GDP, aggregate planned expenditure increases by $0.75 trillion. This aggregate expenditure schedule is shown in the figure as the aggregate expenditure curve AE_0. Initially, equilibrium expenditure is $6 trillion. You can see this equilibrium in row *b* of the table and in the figure where the curve AE_0 intersects the 45° line at the point marked *b*.

Now suppose that autonomous expenditure increases by $0.5 trillion. What happens to equilibrium expenditure? You can see the answer in Fig. 29.7. When this increase in autonomous expenditure is added to the original aggregate planned expenditure, aggregate planned expenditure increases by $0.5 trillion at each level of real GDP. The new aggregate expenditure curve is AE_1. The new equilibrium expenditure, highlighted in the table (row *d'*), occurs where AE_1 intersects the 45° line and is $8 trillion (point *d'*). At this real GDP, aggregate planned expenditure equals real GDP.

The Multiplier Effect

In Fig. 29.7, the increase in autonomous expenditure of $0.5 trillion increases equilibrium expenditure by $2 trillion. That is, the change in autonomous expenditure leads, like Bonnie Raitt's music-making equipment, to an amplified change in equilibrium expenditure. This amplified change is the *multiplier effect*—equilibrium expenditure increases by *more than* the increase in autonomous expenditure. The multiplier is greater than 1.

Initially, when autonomous expenditure increases, aggregate planned expenditure exceeds real GDP. As a result, inventories decrease. Firms respond by increasing production so as to restore their inventories to the target level. As production increases, so does real GDP. With a higher level of real GDP, *induced expenditure* increases. Thus equilibrium expenditure increases by the sum of the initial increase in autonomous expenditure and the increase in induced expenditure. In this example, induced expenditure increases by $1.5 trillion, so equilibrium expenditure increases by $2 trillion.

Although we have just analyzed the effects of an *increase* in autonomous expenditure, the same analysis applies to a decrease in autonomous expenditure. If initially the aggregate expenditure curve is AE_1, equilibrium expenditure and real GDP are $8

FIGURE 29.7

The Multiplier

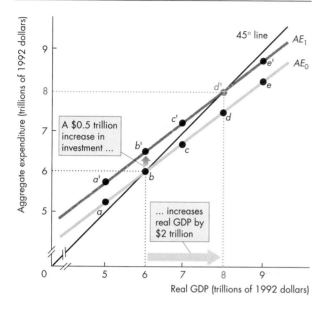

Real GDP (Y)	Aggregate planned expenditure			
	Original (AE₀)		New (AE₁)	
	(trillions of 1992 dollars)			
5	a	5.25	a'	5.75
6	b	6.00	b'	6.50
7	c	6.75	c'	7.25
8	d	7.50	d'	8.00
9	e	8.25	e'	8.75

A $0.5 trillion increase in autonomous expenditure shifts the AE curve upward by $0.5 trillion from AE_0 to AE_1. Equilibrium expenditure increases by $2 trillion, from $6 trillion to $8 trillion. The increase in equilibrium expenditure is 4 times the increase in autonomous expenditure, so the multiplier is 4.

trillion. A decrease in autonomous expenditure of $0.5 trillion shifts the aggregate expenditure curve downward by $0.5 trillion to AE_0. Equilibrium expenditure decreases from $8 trillion to $6 trillion. The decrease in equilibrium expenditure ($2 trillion) is larger than the decrease in autonomous expenditure that brought it about ($0.5 trillion). The multiplier is 4.

Why Is the Multiplier Greater Than 1?

We've seen that equilibrium expenditure increases by more than the increase in autonomous expenditure. This makes the multiplier greater than 1. How come? Why does equilibrium expenditure increase by more than the increase in autonomous expenditure?

The multiplier is greater than 1 because of induced expenditure—an increase in autonomous expenditure *induces* further increases in expenditure. If General Motors spends $10 million on a new car assembly line, aggregate expenditure and real GDP immediately increase by $10 million. But that is not the end of the story. Engineers and construction workers now have more income, and they spend part of the extra income on cars, microwave ovens, vacations, and a host of other goods and services. Real GDP now rises by the initial $10 million plus the extra consumption expenditure induced by the $10 million increase in income. The producers of cars, microwave ovens, vacations, and other goods now have increased incomes, and they, in turn, spend part of the increase in their incomes on consumption goods and services. Additional income induces additional expenditure, which creates additional income.

We have seen that a change in autonomous expenditure has a multiplier effect on real GDP. But how big is the multiplier effect?

The Size of the Multiplier

Suppose that the economy is in a recession. Profit prospects start to look better, and firms are making plans for large increases in investment. The world economy is also heading toward expansion, and exports are increasing. The question on everyone's lips is: How strong will the expansion be? This is a hard question to answer. But an important ingredient in the answer is working out the size of the multiplier.

The *multiplier* is the amount by which a change in autonomous expenditure is multiplied to determine the change in equilibrium expenditure that it generates. To calculate the multiplier, we divide the change in equilibrium expenditure by the change in autonomous expenditure. Let's calculate the multiplier for the example in Fig. 29.7. Initially, equilibrium expenditure is $6 trillion. Then autonomous expenditure increases by $0.5 trillion, and equilibrium expenditure increases by $2 trillion to $8 trillion.

The multiplier is

$$\text{Multiplier} = \frac{\text{Change in equilibrium expenditure}}{\text{Change in autonomous expenditure}}$$

$$= \frac{\$2 \text{ trillion}}{\$0.5 \text{ trillion}} = 4.$$

The Multiplier and the Marginal Propensity to Consume and Save

What determines the magnitude of the multiplier? The answer is the marginal propensity to consume. The larger is the marginal propensity to consume, the larger is the multiplier. To see why, let's do a calculation.

Aggregate expenditure and real GDP change because consumption expenditure changes and investment changes. The change in real GDP (ΔY) equals the change in consumption expenditure (ΔC) plus the change in investment (ΔI). That is,

$$\Delta Y = \Delta C + \Delta I.$$

But the change in consumption expenditure is determined by the change in real GDP and the marginal propensity to consume. It is

$$\Delta C = MPC \times \Delta Y.$$

Now substitute $MPC \times \Delta Y$ for ΔC in the previous equation to give

$$\Delta Y = (MPC \times \Delta Y) + \Delta I.$$

Now solve for ΔY as

$$(1 - MPC) \times \Delta Y = \Delta I.$$

and rearranging gives

$$\Delta Y = \frac{\Delta I}{(1 - MPC)}$$

Finally, divide both sides of the previous equation by ΔI to give

$$\text{Multiplier} = \frac{\Delta Y}{\Delta I} = \frac{1}{(1 - MPC)}.$$

Using the numbers for Fig. 29.7, the *MPC* is 0.75 so the multiplier is

$$\text{Multiplier} = \frac{1}{(1 - 0.75)} = \frac{1}{0.25} = 4.$$

There is another formula for the multiplier. Because the marginal propensity to consume (*MPC*) plus the marginal propensity to save (*MPS*) sum to 1, the term (1 − *MPC*) equals *MPS*. Therefore another formula for the multiplier is

$$\text{Multiplier} = \frac{1}{MPS}.$$

Again using the numbers in Fig. 29.7, we have

$$\text{Multiplier} = \frac{1}{0.25} = 4.$$

Because the marginal propensity to save (*MPS*) is a fraction—a number between 0 and 1—the multiplier is greater than 1.

Figure 29.8 illustrates the multiplier process. In round 1, autonomous expenditure increases by $0.5 trillion (shown by the green bar). At this time, induced expenditure does not change, so aggregate expenditure and real GDP increase by $0.5 trillion. In round 2, the larger real GDP induces more consumption expenditure. Induced expenditure increases by 0.75 times the increase in real GDP, so the increase in real GDP of $0.5 trillion induces a further increase in expenditure of $0.375 trillion. This change in induced expenditure (the green bar in round 2), when added to the previous increase in expenditure (the blue bar in round 2), increases aggregate expenditure and real GDP by $0.875 trillion. The round 2 increase in real GDP induces a round 3 increase in expenditure. The process repeats through successive rounds. Each increase in real GDP is 0.75 times the previous increase. The cumulative increase in real GDP gradually approaches $2 trillion.

So far, we've ignored imports and income taxes. Let's now see how these two factors influence the multiplier.

Imports and Income Taxes

The multiplier is determined, in general, not only by the marginal propensity to consume but also by the marginal propensity to import and by the marginal tax rate. Imports make the multiplier smaller than it otherwise would be. To see why, think about what

FIGURE 29.8
The Multiplier Process

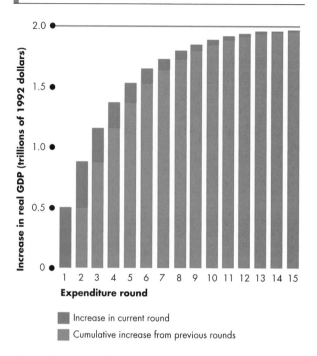

■ Increase in current round

■ Cumulative increase from previous rounds

Autonomous expenditure increases in round 1 by $0.5 trillion. As a result, real GDP increases by the same amount. With a marginal propensity to consume of 0.75, each additional dollar of real GDP induces an additional 0.75 of a dollar of aggregate expenditure. The round 1 increase in real GDP induces an increase in consumption expenditure of $0.375 trillion in round 2. At the end of round 2, real GDP has increased by $0.875 trillion. The extra $0.375 trillion of real GDP in round 2 induces a further increase in consumption expenditure of $0.281 trillion in round 3. Real GDP increases yet further to $1.156 trillion. This process continues with real GDP increasing by ever-smaller amounts. When the process comes to an end, real GDP has increased by a total of $2 trillion.

happens following an increase in investment. An increase in investment increases real GDP, which in turn increases consumption expenditure. But part of the increase in investment and consumption expenditure is expenditure on imported goods and services, not U.S.-produced goods and services. Only expenditure on U.S.-produced goods and services increases U.S. real GDP. The larger the marginal propensity to import, the smaller is the change in U.S. real GDP.

Income taxes also make the multiplier smaller than it otherwise would be. Again, think about what happens following an increase in investment. An increase in investment increases real GDP. But because income taxes increase, disposable income increases by less than the increase in real GDP. Consequently, consumption expenditure increases by less than it would do if taxes had not changed. The larger is the marginal tax rate, the smaller is the change in disposable income and real GDP.

The marginal propensity to import and the marginal tax rate together with the marginal propensity to consume determine the multiplier. And their combined influence depends on the slope of the *AE* curve. The multiplier is equal to 1 divided by 1 minus the slope of the *AE* curve. Figure 29.9 compares two situations. In Fig. 29.9(a), there are no imports and no taxes. The slope of the *AE* curve equals the marginal propensity to consume, which is 0.75, and the multiplier is 4. In Fig. 29.9(b), imports and income taxes decrease the slope of the *AE* curve to 0.5. In this case, the multiplier is 2.

Over time, the value of the multiplier changes as tax rates change and as the marginal propensity to consume and the marginal propensity to import change. These ongoing changes make the multiplier hard to predict. But they do not change the fundamental fact that an initial change in autonomous expenditure leads to a magnified change in aggregate expenditure and real GDP.

Now that we've studied the multiplier and the factors that influence its magnitude, let's use what we've learned to gain some insights into business cycle turning points.

Business Cycle Turning Points

At business cycle turning points, the economy moves from expansion to recession or from recession to expansion. Economists understand these turning points as seismologists understand earthquakes. They know quite a lot about the forces and mechanisms that produce them, but they can't predict them. The forces that bring business cycle turning points are the swings in autonomous expenditure such as investment and exports. The mechanism that gives momentum to the economy's new direction is the multiplier. Let's use what we've now learned to examine these turning points.

FIGURE **29.9**

The Multiplier and the Slope of the *AE* Curve

(a) Multiplier is 4

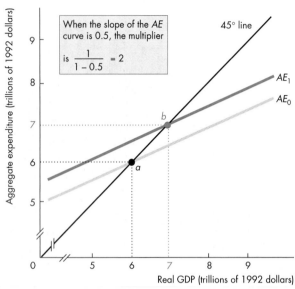

(b) Multiplier is 2

Imports and income taxes make the *AE* curve less steep and reduce the value of the multiplier. In part (a), with no imports and income taxes, the slope of the *AE* curve is 0.75 (the marginal propensity to consume) and the multiplier is 4. But with

imports and income taxes, the slope of the *AE* curve is less than the marginal propensity to consume. In part (b), the slope of the *AE* curve is 0.5. In this case, the multiplier is 2.

An Expansion Begins An expansion is triggered by an increase in autonomous expenditure that increases aggregate planned expenditure. At the moment the economy turns the corner into expansion, aggregate planned expenditure exceeds real GDP. In this situation, firms see their inventories taking an unplanned dive. The expansion now begins. To meet their inventory targets, firms increase production, and real GDP begins to increase. This initial increase in real GDP brings higher incomes that stimulate consumption expenditure. The multiplier process kicks in, and the expansion picks up speed.

A Recession Begins The process we've just described works in reverse at a business cycle peak. A recession is triggered by a decrease in autonomous expenditure that decreases aggregate planned expenditure. At the moment the economy turns the corner into recession, real GDP exceeds aggregate planned

expenditure. In this situation, firms see unplanned inventories piling up. The recession now begins. To reduce their inventories, firms cut production, and real GDP begins to decrease. This initial decrease in real GDP brings lower incomes that cut consumption expenditure. The multiplier process reinforces the initial cut in autonomous expenditure, and the recession takes hold.

The Next U.S. Recession? Since 1991, the U.S. economy has been in a business cycle expansion. The last real GDP trough was in the first quarter of 1991. The science of macroeconomics cannot predict when the next recession will begin. A recession seemed possible in 1995 following a rapid buildup of inventories during 1994. But firms planned this inventory buildup. At the beginning of 1999, there was still no immediate prospect of the next recession. But it will surely come. And when it does, the mechanism you've just studied will operate.

- What is the multiplier? What does it determine? Why does it matter?
- How do the marginal propensity to consume, the marginal propensity to import, and the marginal tax rate influence the multiplier?
- How do fluctuations in autonomous expenditure influence real GDP? If autonomous expenditure decreases, which phase of the business cycle does the economy enter?

The economy's potholes are changes in investment and exports. And the economy does not operate like the shock absorbers on Dennis Archer's car. While the price level is fixed, the effects of the economic potholes are not smoothed out. Instead, they are amplified like Bonnie Raitt's voice. But we've considered only the adjustments in spending that occur in the very short term when the price level is fixed. What happens after a long enough time lapse for the price level to change? Let's answer this question.

The Multiplier and the Price Level

WHEN FIRMS CAN'T KEEP UP WITH SALES AND their inventories fall below target, they increase production, but at some point, they raise their prices. Similarly, when firms find unwanted inventories piling up, they decrease production, but eventually, they cut their prices. So far, we've studied the macroeconomic consequences of firms changing their production levels when their sales change, but we haven't looked at the effects of price changes. When individual firms change their prices, the economy's price level changes.

To study the simultaneous determination of real GDP and the price level, we use the *aggregate supply–aggregate demand model*, which is explained in Chapter 25. But to understand how aggregate demand adjusts, we need to work out the connection between the aggregate supply–aggregate demand model and the equilibrium expenditure model that we've used in this chapter. The key to understanding the relationship between these two models is the distinction between the aggregate *expenditure* and aggregate *demand*.

Aggregate Expenditure and Aggregate Demand

The aggregate expenditure curve is the relationship between the aggregate planned expenditure and real GDP, all other influences on aggregate planned expenditure remaining the same. The aggregate demand curve is the relationship between the aggregate quantity of goods and services demanded and the price level, all other influences on aggregate demand remaining the same. Let's explore the links between these two relationships.

Aggregate Expenditure and the Price Level

When the price level changes, aggregate planned expenditure changes and the quantity of real GDP demanded changes. The aggregate demand curve slopes downward. Why? There are two main reasons:

1. Wealth effect
2. Substitution effects

Wealth Effect Other things remaining the same, the higher the price level, the smaller is the purchasing power of people's assets. For example, suppose you have $100 in the bank and the price level is 110. If the price level rises to 130, your $100 buys fewer goods and services. You are less wealthy. With less wealth, you will probably want to try to spend a bit less and save a bit more. Aggregate planned expenditure is lower the higher the price level, other things remaining the same.

Substitution Effects A rise in the price level today, other things remaining the same, makes current goods and services more costly relative to future goods and services and results in a delay in purchases—an *intertemporal substitution*. A rise in the price level, other things remaining the same, makes U.S.-produced goods more expensive relative to foreign-produced goods and services and increases imports and decreases exports—an *international substitution*.

When the price level rises, each of these effects reduces aggregate planned expenditure at each level of real GDP. As a result, when the price level rises, the aggregate expenditure curve shifts downward. A fall in the price level has the opposite effect. When the price level falls, the aggregate expenditure curve shifts upward.

Figure 29.10(a) shows the shifts of the *AE* curve. When the price level is 110, the aggregate expenditure curve is AE_0, which intersects the 45° line at point *b*. Equilibrium expenditure is $7 trillion. If the price level increases to 130, the aggregate expenditure curve shifts downward to AE_1, which intersects the 45° line at point *a*. Equilibrium expenditure is $6 trillion. If the price level decreases to 90, the aggregate expenditure curve shifts upward to AE_2, which intersects the 45° line at point *c*. Equilibrium expenditure is $8 trillion.

We've just seen that when the price level changes, other things remaining the same, the aggregate expenditure curve shifts and the equilibrium expenditure changes. And when the price level changes, other things remaining the same, there is a movement along the aggregate demand curve. Figure 29.10(b) shows these movements along the aggregate demand curve. At a price level of 110, the aggregate quantity of goods and services demanded is $7 trillion—point *b* on the aggregate demand curve *AD*. If the price level rises to 130, the aggregate quantity of goods and services demanded decreases to $6 trillion. There is a movement along the aggregate demand curve to point *a*. If the price level falls to 90, the aggregate quantity of goods and services demanded increases to $8 trillion. There is a movement along the aggregate demand curve to point *c*.

Each point on the aggregate demand curve corresponds to a point of equilibrium expenditure. The equilibrium expenditure points *a*, *b*, and *c* in Fig. 29.10(a) correspond to the points *a*, *b*, and *c* on the aggregate demand curve in Fig. 29.10(b).

When the price level changes, other things remaining the same, the aggregate expenditure curve shifts and there is a movement along the aggregate demand curve. When any other influence on aggregate planned expenditure changes, *both* the aggregate expenditure curve and the aggregate demand curve shift. For example, an increase in investment or in exports increases both aggregate planned expenditure and aggregate demand and shifts both the *AE* curve and the *AD* curve. Figure 29.11 illustrates the effect of such an increase.

Initially, the aggregate expenditure curve is AE_0 in part (a) and the aggregate demand curve is AD_0 in part (b). The price is 110, real GDP is $7 trillion, and the economy is at point *a* in both parts of the figure. Now suppose that investment increases by $1 trillion. At a constant price level of 110, the aggregate expenditure curve shifts upward to AE_1. This curve intersects the 45° line at an equilibrium

FIGURE 29.10

Aggregate Demand

(a) Equilibrium expenditure

(b) Aggregate demand

A change in the price level shifts the *AE* curve and results in a *movement along* the *AD* curve. When the price level is 110, the *AE* curve is AE_0, and equilibrium expenditure is $7 trillion at point *b*. When the price level rises to 130, the *AE* curve is AE_1, and equilibrium expenditure is $6 trillion at point *a*. When the price level falls to 90, the *AE* curve is AE_2, and equilibrium expenditure is $8 trillion at point *c*. Points *a*, *b*, and *c* on the *AD* curve in part (b) correspond to the equilibrium expenditure points *a*, *b*, and *c* in part (a).

FIGURE 29.11

A Change in
Aggregate Demand

(a) Aggregate expenditure

(b) Aggregate demand

The price level is 110. When the aggregate expenditure curve is AE_0 (part a), the aggregate demand curve is AD_0 (part b). An increase in autonomous expenditure shifts the AE curve upward to AE_1. In the new equilibrium, real GDP is $9 trillion (at b). Because the quantity of real GDP demanded at a price level of 110 increases to $9 trillion, the AD curve shifts rightward to AD_1.

expenditure of $9 trillion (point b). This equilibrium expenditure of $9 trillion is the aggregate quantity of goods and services demanded at a price level of 110, as shown by point b in part (b). Point b lies on a new aggregate demand curve. The aggregate demand curve has shifted rightward to AD_1.

But how do we know by how much the AD curve shifts? The multiplier determines the answer. The larger the multiplier, the larger is the shift in the aggregate demand curve that results from a given change in autonomous expenditure. In this example, the multiplier is 2. A $1 trillion increase in investment produces a $2 trillion increase in the aggregate quantity of goods and services demanded at each price level. That is, a $1 trillion increase in autonomous expenditure shifts the aggregate demand curve rightward by $2 trillion.

A decrease in autonomous expenditure shifts the aggregate expenditure curve downward and shifts the aggregate demand curve leftward. You can see these effects by reversing the change that we've just studied. Suppose that the economy is initially at point b on the aggregate expenditure curve AE_1 and the aggregate demand curve AD_1. A decrease in autonomous expenditure shifts the aggregate planned expenditure curve downward to AE_0. The aggregate quantity of goods and services demanded falls from $9 trillion to $7 trillion, and the aggregate demand curve shifts leftward to AD_0.

Let's summarize what we have just discovered:

If some factor other than a change in the price level increases autonomous expenditure, the AE curve shifts upward and the AD curve shifts rightward.

The size of the AD curve shift depends on the change in autonomous expenditure and the multiplier.

Equilibrium Real GDP and the Price Level

In Chapter 25, we learned that aggregate demand and short-run aggregate supply determine equilibrium real GDP and the price level. We've now put aggregate demand under a more powerful microscope and have discovered that a change in investment (or in any component of autonomous expenditure) changes aggregate demand and shifts the aggregate demand curve. The magnitude of the shift depends on the multiplier. But whether a change in autonomous expenditure results ultimately in a change in real

GDP, a change in the price level, or a combination of the two depends on aggregate supply. There are two time frames to consider, the short run and the long run. First we'll see what happens in the short run.

An Increase in Aggregate Demand in the Short Run

Figure 29.12 describes the economy. In part (a), the aggregate expenditure curve is AE_0, and equilibrium expenditure is $7 trillion—point a. In part (b), aggregate demand is AD_0, and the short-run aggregate supply curve is SAS. (Look at Chapter 25 if you need to refresh your understanding of this curve.) Equilibrium is at point a, where the aggregate demand and short-run aggregate supply curves intersect. The price level is 110, and real GDP is $7 trillion.

Now suppose that investment increases by $1 trillion. With the price level fixed at 110, the aggregate expenditure curve shifts upward to AE_1. Equilibrium expenditure increases to $9 trillion—point b in part (a). In part (b), the aggregate demand curve shifts rightward by $2 trillion, from AD_0 to AD_1. How far the aggregate demand curve shifts is determined by the multiplier when the price level is fixed. But with this new aggregate demand curve, the price level does not remain fixed. The price level rises, and as it does so, the aggregate expenditure curve shifts downward. The short-run equilibrium occurs when the aggregate expenditure curve has shifted downward to AE_2 and the new aggregate demand curve, AD_1, intersects the short-run aggregate supply curve. Real GDP is $8.6 trillion, and the price level is 116 (at point c).

When price level effects are taken into account, the increase in investment still has a multiplier effect on real GDP, but the effect is smaller than it would be if the price level were fixed. The steeper the slope of the short-run aggregate supply curve, the larger is the increase in the price level and the smaller is the multiplier effect on real GDP.

An Increase in Aggregate Demand in the Long Run

Figure 29.13 illustrates the long-run effect of an increase in aggregate demand. In the long run, real GDP equals potential GDP and there is full employment. Potential GDP is $7 trillion, and the long-run aggregate supply curve is LAS. Initially, the economy is at point a (parts a and b).

Investment increases by $1 trillion. The aggregate expenditure curve shifts to AE_1, and the aggregate demand curve shifts to AD_1. With no change in the price level, the economy would move to point b

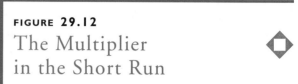

FIGURE 29.12

The Multiplier in the Short Run

(a) Aggregate expenditure

(b) Aggregate demand

An increase in investment shifts the AE curve from AE_0 to AE_1 (part a) and the AD curve from AD_0 to AD_1 (part b). The price level does not remain at 110 but rises. The higher price level shifts the AE curve downward from AE_1 to AE_2. The economy moves to point c in both parts. In the short run, the multiplier effect is smaller than when the price level is fixed.

FIGURE 29.13

The Multiplier in the Long Run

(a) Aggregate expenditure

(b) Aggregate demand

Starting from point *a*, an increase in investment shifts the *AE* curve to AE_1 and the *AD* curve to AD_1. In the short run, the economy moves to point *c*. In the long run, the money wage rate rises, the *SAS* curve shifts to SAS_1, the *AE* curve shifts back to AE_0, the price level rises, and real GDP falls. The economy moves to point *a'*, and in the long run, the multiplier is zero.

and real GDP would increase to $9 trillion. But in the short run, the price level rises to 116 and real GDP increases to only $8.6 trillion. With the higher price level, the *AE* curve shifts from AE_1 to AE_2. The economy is now in a short-run equilibrium at point *c*. Real GDP is now above potential GDP. The labor force is more than fully employed, and shortages of labor increase the money wage rate. The higher money wage rate increases costs, which decreases short-run aggregate supply and shifts the *SAS* curve leftward to SAS_1. The price level rises further, and real GDP decreases. There is a movement along AD_1, and the *AE* curve shifts downward from AE_2 toward AE_0. When the money wage rate and the price level have increased by the same percentage, real GDP is again equal to potential GDP and the economy is at point *a'*. In the long run, the multiplier is zero.

You are now ready to build on what you've learned about expenditure fluctuations and study the roles of fiscal policy and monetary policy in smoothing the business cycle. In Chapter 30, we study fiscal policy—government purchases, taxes, and the surplus or deficit on the government's budget— and in Chapters 31 and 32, we study monetary policy—interest rates and the quantity of money. But before you leave the current topic, look at *Reading Between the Lines* on pages 654–655 and see the expenditure multiplier you've studied in this chapter at work in the U.S. economy.

A Local Multiplier

THE SEATTLE TIMES, DECEMBER 4, 1998

Will Cuts at Boeing Multiply Hard Times for Area?

MICHELE MATASSA FLORES

We hear it all the time, a refrain that sounds as much like a prep-school cheer as solid economic analysis.

"For every Boeing job, 2.8 more are created around Washington state."

"Seattle will lose 1,800 jobs if the Mariners leave town."

"Cultural/arts organizations create more than 8,800 jobs in the county each year."

Such numbers, called "multipliers," typically are cited with precision and certainty, as if they're sure-fire ways to measure economic impact. In fact, they are inexact and controversial, a fact that could be underscored next year when Boeing begins laying off thousands of workers.

One of the most debatable things about so-called multiplier effects is whether they work in reverse, as a company cuts jobs instead of adding them.

If multipliers do work in reverse, then Boeing's imminent elimination of an estimated 30,000 Puget Sound jobs in the next two years will cost the state more than 114,000 jobs. Everyone from a line worker at an airplane-parts supplier to a clerk at the corner Safeway could be at risk.

But there's a catch.

"They are just numbers. It ought to work the same way going down as it does going up," said Paul Sommers, a regional economist and head of the Northwest Policy Center at the University of Washington. "But there seems to be some stickiness on the way down."

Here's why:

— Some employees facing lay-offs will instead take early retire-ment, maintaining enough income to continue making house pay-ments, buying food and clothing and eating out, supporting the spin-off jobs cited in multiplier studies.

— Laid-off workers are eligible for unemployment compensation, so they, too, can continue spending money. Some live off their savings for a while instead of cutting back their spending.

— Companies that do lose business often postpone or avoid their own layoffs, hoping instead to ride out the slump.

— Often, there are hiring booms under way in other indus-tries, smoothing the ripples caused by the layoffs. ...

Essence of the Story

■ A claim in Washing-ton State is that one Boeing job creates 2.8 additional jobs in the state—a multiplier effect.

■ If the Boeing multi-plier works in reverse, then Boeing's elimina-tion of 30,000 jobs will cost the state more than 114,000 jobs.

■ According to econo-mist Paul Sommers of the University of Wash-ington, the multiplier is smaller on the way down. Spending levels are maintained because:
  - Some employees fac-ing layoffs take early retirement.
  - Laid-off workers receive unemploy-ment compensation.
  - Companies that lose business postpone or avoid layoffs.
  - Hiring booms in other industries coun-teract layoffs in other industries.

■ This news article highlights several confusions about multipliers.

■ The first confusion is about what initiates an economic change and what gets multiplied.

■ In the expenditure model, the initiator of change is a change in *autonomous* expenditure. The change in autonomous expenditure is multiplied to determine the change in aggregate expenditure.

■ Figure 1 shows the autonomous expenditure multiplier for the state of Washington on the assumption that the multiplier is 2.8, the value in the news article for the so-called Boeing multiplier.

■ In Fig. 1, the Washington state aggregate expenditure curve is initially AE_0 and gross state product (GSP) is $160 billion, where the AE_0 curve intersects the 45° line.

■ A $10 billion decrease in autonomous expenditure shifts the AE curve downward to AE_1. Equilibrium expenditure decreases to $132 billion, a decrease of $28 billion.

■ The decrease in equilibrium expenditure is 2.8 times the decrease in autonomous expenditure. An AE curve with a slope of 0.643 delivers this multiplier. (Check that $1/(1 - 0.643) = 2.8$.)

■ As Washington's GSP is decreasing, firms are laying off workers. One of these firms might be Boeing. And the change in employment in Washington divided by the change in employment at Boeing is the "Boeing multiplier."

■ If the change in expenditure that brings the change in the Boeing labor force is *autonomous*, then the Boeing multiplier is relevant for determining the change in total employment. But if the change in expenditure that brings the change in the Boeing labor force is *induced*, then the Boeing multiplier is irrelevant.

■ The news article asks whether the multiplier is the same in both directions.

■ The answer for the autonomous expenditure multiplier is that it is the same in both directions because the slope of the AE curve determines the outcome. And this slope is the same for an increase as it is for a decrease in expenditure.

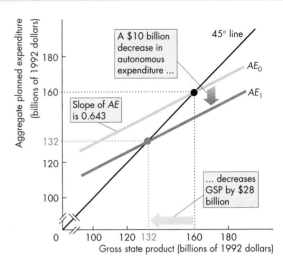

Figure 1 A multiplier of 2.8

■ The reasons attributed to economist Paul Sommers of the University of Washington why the multiplier is smaller on the way down apply with equal force on the way up.

■ In bad times, some employees facing layoffs take early retirement; and in good times some employees considering retirement postpone it.

■ In bad times, laid-off workers receive unemployment compensation; and in good times, previously laid off workers go back to work.

■ In bad times, companies that lose business postpone or avoid layoffs; and in good times, companies that gain business first use the slack in their existing work force before hiring again.

■ In both bad times and good times, hiring booms in some industries counteract layoffs in other industries.

■ These are all reasons why the multiplier is small, not reasons why its value is different for expansions and recessions. And for these reasons, it is most unlikely that the Washington state multiplier is as large as 2.8.

MATHEMATICAL NOTE

The Algebra of the Multiplier

THIS NOTE EXPLAINS THE MULTIPLIER IN GREATER detail than that presented on p. 646. We begin by defining the symbols we need:

- Aggregate planned expenditure, AE
- Real GDP, Y
- Consumption expenditure, C
- Investment, I
- Government purchases, G
- Exports, X
- Imports, M
- Net taxes, T
- Disposable income, YD
- Autonomous consumption expenditure, a
- Marginal propensity to consume, b
- Marginal propensity to import, m
- Marginal tax rate, t
- Autonomous expenditure, A

Aggregate Expenditure

Aggregate planned expenditure (AE) is the sum of the planned amounts of consumption expenditure (C), investment (I), government purchases (G), and exports (X) minus the planned amount of imports (M). That is

$$AE = C + I + G + X - M.$$

Consumption Function   Consumption expenditure (C) depends on disposable income (YD), and we write the consumption function as

$$C = a + bYD.$$

Disposable income (YD) equals real GDP minus net taxes ($Y - T$). So by replacing YD with ($Y - T$), the consumption function becomes

$$C = a + b(Y - T).$$

Net taxes equal real GDP (Y) multiplied by the marginal tax rate (t). That is,

$$T = tY.$$

Use this equation in the previous one to obtain

$$C = a + b(1 - t)Y.$$

This equation describes consumption expenditure as a function of real GDP.

Import Function   Imports depend on real GDP, and the import function is

$$M = mY.$$

Aggregate Expenditure Curve   Use the consumption function and the import function to replace C and M in the aggregate planned expenditure equation. That is,

$$AE = a + b(1 - t)Y + I + G + X - mY.$$

Collect the terms on the right side of the equation that involve Y to obtain

$$AE = [a + I + G + X] + [b(1 - t) - m]Y.$$

Autonomous expenditure (A) is $[a + I + G + X]$, and the slope of the AE curve is $[b(1 - t)] - m$. So the equation for the AE curve, which is shown in the following figure, is

$$AE = A + [b(1 - t) - m]Y.$$

Equilibrium Expenditure

Equilibrium expenditure occurs when aggregate planned expenditure (AE) equals real GDP (Y). That is,

$$AE = Y.$$

In the figure below, the scales of the x-axis (real GDP) and the y-axis (aggregate planned expenditure) are identical, so the 45° line shows the points at which aggregate planned expenditure equals real GDP. That is, the 45° line is the line along which $AE = Y$.

The figure shows the point of equilibrium expenditure at the intersection of the AE curve and the 45° line.

To calculate equilibrium expenditure and real GDP, we solve the equations for the AE curve and the 45° line for the two unknown quantities AE and Y. So, starting with

$$AE = A + [b(1 - t) - m]Y$$

$$AE = Y,$$

replace AE with Y in the AE equation to obtain

$$Y = A + [b(1 - t) - m]Y.$$

The solution for Y is

$$Y = \frac{1}{1 - [b(1 - t) - m]} A.$$

The Multiplier

The multiplier equals the change in equilibrium expenditure and real GDP (Y) that results from a change in autonomous expenditure (A) divided by the change in autonomous expenditure.

A change in autonomous expenditure (ΔA) leads to a change in equilibrium expenditure and real GDP (ΔY), which is given by

$$\Delta Y = \frac{1}{1 - [b(1 - t) - m]} \Delta A.$$

$$\text{Multiplier} = \frac{1}{1 - [b(1 - t) - m]}.$$

The size of the multiplier depends on the slope of the AE curve $b(1 - t) - m$. The larger the slope, the larger is the multiplier. So the multiplier is larger,

- The greater the marginal propensity to consume (b)
- The smaller the marginal tax rate (t)
- The smaller the marginal propensity to import (m)

An economy with no imports and no marginal taxes has $m = 0$ and $t = 0$. In this special case, the multiplier equals $1/(1 - b)$. If b is 0.75, then the multiplier is 4, as shown in the following figure. In an economy with $b = 0.75$, $t = 0.2$, and $m = 0.1$, the multiplier is 1 divided by 1 minus 0.75(1 − 0.2) − 0.1, which equals 2. Make up some more examples to show the effects of b, t, and m on the multiplier.

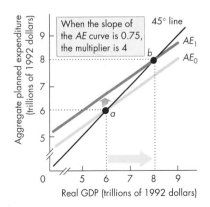

SUMMARY

KEY POINTS

Fixed Prices and Expenditure Plans
(pp. 634–639)

- When the price level is fixed, expenditure plans determine real GDP.
- Consumption expenditure is determined by disposable income, and the marginal propensity to consume (*MPC*) determines the change in consumption expenditure brought about by a change in disposable income. Real GDP determines disposable income.
- Imports are determined by real GDP, and the marginal propensity to import determines the change in imports brought about by a change in real GDP.

Real GDP with a Fixed Price Level
(pp. 640–643)

- Aggregate *planned* expenditure depends on real GDP.
- Equilibrium expenditure occurs when aggregate planned expenditure equals actual expenditure and real GDP.

The Multiplier (pp. 644–649)

- The multiplier is the magnified effect of a change in autonomous expenditure on real GDP.
- The multiplier is influenced by the marginal propensity to consume, the marginal propensity to import, and the marginal income tax rate.

The Multiplier and the Price Level
(pp. 649–653)

- The aggregate demand curve is the relationship between the quantity of real GDP demanded and the price level, other things remaining the same.
- The aggregate expenditure curve is the relationship between aggregate planned expenditure and real GDP, other things remaining the same.

- At a given price level, there is a given aggregate expenditure curve. A change in the price level changes aggregate planned expenditure and shifts the aggregate expenditure curve. A change in the price level also creates a movement along the aggregate demand curve.
- A change in autonomous expenditure that is not caused by a change in the price level shifts the aggregate expenditure curve and shifts the aggregate demand curve. The magnitude of the shift of the aggregate demand curve depends on the multiplier and on the change in autonomous expenditure.
- The multiplier decreases as the price level changes, and in the long run the multiplier is zero.

KEY FIGURES

KEY TERMS

PROBLEMS

*1. You are given the following information about the economy of Heron Island:

Disposable income (millions of dollars per year)	Consumption expenditure (millions of dollars per year)
0	5
10	10
20	15
30	20
40	25

Calculate Heron Island's:
a. Marginal propensity to consume.
b. Saving at each level of disposable income.
c. Marginal propensity to save.

2. You are given the following information about the economy of Spendthrift Island:

Disposable income (millions of dollars per year)	Saving (millions of dollars per year)
0	−100
500	−50
1,000	0
1,500	50
2,000	100
2,500	150
3,000	200

Calculate Spendthrift Island's:
a. Marginal propensity to save.
b. Consumption at each level of disposable income.
c. Marginal propensity to consume.
d. Why is the island called Spendthrift?

*3. Turtle Island has no imports or exports, the people of Turtle Island pay no incomes taxes, and the price level is fixed. The figure illustrates the components of aggregate planned expenditure on Turtle Island.

On Turtle Island, what is:
a. Autonomous expenditure?
b. The marginal propensity to consume?
c. Aggregate planned expenditure when real GDP is $6 billion?
d. Happening to inventories if real GDP is $4 billion?
e. Happening to inventories if real GDP is $6 billion?
f. The multiplier?

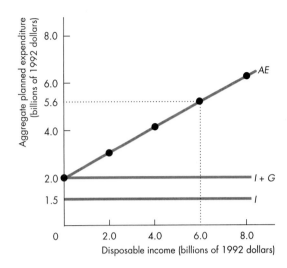

4. The spreadsheet lists the components of aggregate planned expenditure in Spice Bay. The numbers are in billions of cloves, the currency of the Bay.

	A	B	C	D	E	F	G
1		Y	C	I	G	X	M
2	a	100	110	50	60	60	15
3	b	200	170	50	60	60	30
4	c	300	230	50	60	60	45
5	d	400	290	50	60	60	60
6	e	500	350	50	60	60	75
7	f	600	410	50	60	60	90

In Spice Bay, what is:
a. Autonomous expenditure?
b. The marginal propensity to consume?
c. Aggregate planned expenditure when real GDP is 200 billion cloves?
d. Happening to inventories if real GDP is 200 billion cloves?
e. Happening to inventories if real GDP is 500 billion cloves?
f. The multiplier in Spice Bay?

*5. In the economy of Zeeland: Autonomous consumption expenditure is $100 billion, and the marginal propensity to consume is 0.9. Investment is $460 billion, government purchases of goods and services are $400 billion, and net taxes are a constant $400 billion—they do not vary with income. Zeeland has no imports or exports.
a. What is the consumption function?
b. What is the equation that describes the aggregate expenditure curve?

c. Calculate equilibrium expenditure.
d. If investment falls to $360 billion, what is the change in equilibrium expenditure and what is the size of the multiplier?

6. You are given the following information about the economy of Antarctica: Autonomous consumption expenditure is $1 billion, and the marginal propensity to consume is 0.95. Investment is $4 billion, government purchases of goods and services are $4 billion, and net taxes are a constant $4 billion—they do not vary with income.
a. What is the consumption function?
b. What is the equation that describes the aggregate expenditure curve?
c. Calculate equilibrium expenditure.
d. If investment falls to $3 billion, what is the change in equilibrium expenditure and what is the size of the multiplier?

*7. Suppose that in problem 5 the price level is 100 and real GDP equals potential GDP. If investment increases by $100 billion,
a. What happens to the quantity of real GDP demanded?
b. In the short run, does equilibrium real GDP increase by more than, less than, or the same amount as the increase in the quantity of real GDP demanded?
c. In the long run, does equilibrium real GDP increase by more than, less than, or the same amount as the increase in the quantity of real GDP demanded?
d. In the short run, does the price level in Zeeland rise, fall, or remain unchanged? In the long run, does the price level in Zeeland rise, fall, or remain unchanged?

8. Suppose that in problem 6 the price level is 100 and real GDP equals potential GDP. If investment increases by $1 billion,
a. What happens to the quantity of real GDP demanded?
b. In the long run, does equilibrium real GDP increase by more than, less than, or the same amount as the increase in the quantity of real GDP demanded?
c. In the short run, does the price level in Antarctica rise, fall, or remain unchanged?

CRITICAL THINKING

1. Study *Reading Between the Lines* on pp. 654–655, and then answer the following questions:
a. What does the news article say about the magnitude and stability of the Boeing multiplier?
b. What is the distinction between autonomous expenditure and induced expenditure?
c. Do you think the changes in expenditure that change employment at Boeing are typically changes in autonomous expenditure, changes in induced expenditure, or a mixture of the two. (Hint: Think about what Boeing produces and who its customers are.)
d. Why does it matter whether the change in expenditure that changes Boeing's employment is autonomous or induced?
e. What information do you need to be able to predict the Boeing multiplier?
f. Think of other big firms in other regions that might have a multiplier effect.

2. Use the link on the Parkin Web site to visit the Penn World Table and obtain data on real GDP per person and consumption as a percentage of real GDP for the United States, China, South Africa, and Mexico since 1960.
a. In a spreadsheet, multiply your real GDP data by the consumption percentage and divide by 100 to obtain data on real consumption expenditure per person.
b. Make graphs like Fig. 29.4 on p. 639 that show the relationship between consumption and real GDP for these four countries.
c. On the basis of the numbers you've obtained, in which country do you expect the multiplier to be largest (other things remaining the same)?
d. What other data would you need to be able to calculate the multipliers for these countries?
e. You are a research assistant in the office of the President's Council of Economic Advisors. The President wants only 250 words of crisp, clear, jargon-free explanation together with a lively example of the power and limitations of the multiplier. You are asked to draft this note.

Chapter 30

Fiscal Policy

In 1999, the federal government planned to spend $1,868 billion, or 23 cents of every dollar that Americans earn. What are the effects of government spending on the economy? Does it create jobs? Or does it destroy them? And does a dollar spent by the government on goods and services have the same effect as a dollar spent by someone else? ◆ Although the federal government planned to *spend* 23 cents of every dollar earned, it did not plan to tax us by that amount. Its plans were for tax revenues of $1,987 billion or 24 cents of every dollar earned. What are the effects of taxes on the economy? Do taxes harm employment and economic growth? ◆ The plan to have tax revenues fall short of expenditures is not new on Capitol Hill. The last time the federal government budget was in surplus was 1969. Over the 30 years since then, and using constant 1992 dollars, the federal govern-

Balancing Acts on Capitol Hill

ment's debt has increased from $1,000 billion to $3,250 billion. If these numbers are too big to mean anything, divide them by the U.S. population to find *your* share. Government debt per person was more than $12,000 in 1999. Does it matter if the government doesn't balance its books? What are the effects of an ongoing government deficit and accumulating debt? Does it slow economic growth? Does it impose a burden on future generations—on you and your children? What must be done to balance the budget? Can spending cuts do it? Or must taxes be increased? Or can spending be cut so severely that taxes can also be cut?

◆ These are the fiscal policy issues that you will study in this chapter. We'll begin by describing the federal budget and the process of creating it. We'll also look at the recent history of the budget. We'll then use the multiplier analysis of Chapter 29 and the aggregate supply–aggregate demand model of Chapter 25 to study the effects of the budget on the economy.

After studying this chapter, you will be able to:

- Describe the federal budget process
- Describe the recent history of federal expenditures, tax revenues, and the budget deficit
- Distinguish between automatic and discretionary fiscal policy
- Define and explain the fiscal policy multipliers
- Explain the effects of fiscal policy in the short run and in the long run
- Distinguish between and explain the demand-side and supply-side effects of fiscal policy

The Federal Budget

THE ANNUAL STATEMENT OF THE EXPENDITURES and tax revenues of the government of the United States together with the laws and regulations that approve and support those expenditures and taxes make up the **federal budget**. The federal budget has two purposes:

1. To finance the activities of the federal government
2. To stabilize the economy

The first purpose of the federal budget was its only purpose before the Great Depression years of the 1930s. The second purpose of the federal budget arose as a reaction to the Great Depression. The use of the federal budget to achieve macroeconomic objectives such as full employment, sustained economic growth, and price level stability is called **fiscal policy**. It is on this second purpose that we focus in this chapter.

The Institutions and Laws

Fiscal policy is made by the President and Congress on an annual time line that is shown in Figure 30.1.

The Roles of the President and Congress   The President *proposes* a budget to Congress each February and, after Congress has passed the budget acts in September, either signs those acts into law or vetoes them. The President approves or vetoes the *entire* budget bill. He does not have the veto power to eliminate specific items in a budget bill and approve others—known as a *line-item veto*. Many state governors have a line-item veto authority, and Congress attempted to grant this power to the President in 1996. But a Supreme Court ruling of 1998 declared the line-item veto for the President unconstitutional. Although the President proposes and ultimately approves the budget, the task of making the tough decisions on spending and taxes rests with Congress.

Congress begins its work on the budget with the President's proposal. The House of Representatives and the Senate develop their own budget ideas in their respective House and Senate Budget Committees. Formal conferences between the two houses eventually resolve differences of view, and a series of spending acts and an overall budget act are usually passed by both houses before the start of the fiscal year. A *fiscal*

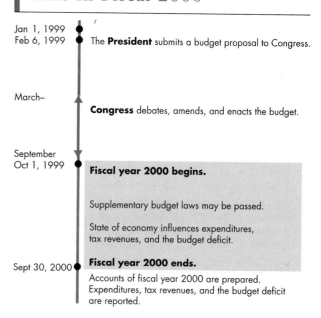

FIGURE 30.1

The Federal Budget Time Line in Fiscal 2000

Jan 1, 1999
Feb 6, 1999   The **President** submits a budget proposal to Congress.

March–   **Congress** debates, amends, and enacts the budget.

September
Oct 1, 1999   **Fiscal year 2000 begins.**

Supplementary budget laws may be passed.

State of economy influences expenditures, tax revenues, and the budget deficit.

Sept 30, 2000   **Fiscal year 2000 ends.**
Accounts of fiscal year 2000 are prepared. Expenditures, tax revenues, and the budget deficit are reported.

The federal budget process begins with the President's proposals in February. Congress debates and amends these proposals and enacts a budget before the start of the fiscal year on October 1. The President signs the budget acts into law or vetoes them. Throughout the fiscal year, Congress might pass supplementary budget laws. The budget outcome is calculated after the fiscal year ends on September 30.

year is a year that runs from October 1 to September 30 in the next calendar year. *Fiscal 2000* is the fiscal year that *begins* on October 1, 1999.

During a fiscal year, Congress often passes supplementary budget laws, and the budget outcome is influenced by the evolving state of the economy. For example, if a recession begins, tax revenues fall and welfare payments increase.

The Employment Act of 1946   Fiscal policy operates within the framework of the **Employment Act of 1946**, in which Congress declared that

> it is the continuing policy and responsibility of the Federal Government to use all practicable means … to coordinate and utilize all its plans, functions, and resources … to promote maximum employment, production, and purchasing power.

This act recognized a role for government actions to keep unemployment low, keep the economy expanding, and keep inflation in check. The *Full Employment and Balanced Growth Act of 1978*, more commonly known as the *Humphrey-Hawkins Act*, went further than the 1946 employment act and set a specific target of 4 percent for the unemployment rate. But this target has never been treated as an unwavering policy goal. Under the 1946 Act, the President must describe the current economic situation and the policies he believes are needed in an annual *Economic Report of the President*, which is written by the Council of Economic Advisers.

The Council of Economic Advisers   The President's **Council of Economic Advisers** (CEA) was established in 1946 by the Employment Act. The Council consists of a Chair and two other members, all of whom are economists on a 1- or 2-year leave from their regular university or public service jobs. In 1999, the Chair of President Clinton's Council of Economic Advisers was Janet Yellen of the University of California at Berkeley. The Council monitors the economy and keeps the President and the public well informed about the current state of the economy and the best available forecasts of where it is heading. This economic intelligence activity is one source of data that informs the budget-making process.

Let's look at the most recent federal budget.

Highlights of the 2000 Budget

Table 30.1 shows the main items in the federal budget proposed by President Clinton for 2000. The numbers are projected amounts for the fiscal year beginning on October 1, 1999—fiscal 2000. Notice the three main parts of the table: *tax revenues* are the government's receipts, *expenditures* are the government's outlays, and the *surplus* is the amount by which the government's tax revenues exceed its expenditures.

Tax Revenues   Tax revenues were projected to be $1,987 billion in fiscal 2000. These revenues come from four sources:

1. Personal income taxes
2. Social insurance taxes
3. Corporate income taxes
4. Indirect taxes

The largest source of revenue is *personal income taxes*, which in 2000 are expected to be $926 billion. These are the taxes paid by individuals on their incomes. The second largest source is *social insurance taxes*. These are the taxes paid by workers and their employers to finance the government's social insurance programs. Third in size are *corporate income taxes*. These are the taxes paid by companies on their profits. Finally, the smallest source of federal revenue comes from what are called *indirect taxes*. These are taxes on the sale of gasoline, alcoholic drinks, and a few other items.

Expenditures   Expenditures are classified in three categories:

1. Transfer payments
2. Purchases of goods and services
3. Debt interest

The largest item of expenditure, *transfer payments*, are payments to individuals, businesses, other levels of government, and the rest of the world. In 2000, this item is expected to be $1,868 billion. It includes Social Security benefits, Medicare and Medicaid, unemployment checks, welfare payments, farm

TABLE 30.1

Federal Budget in Fiscal 2000

Item	Projections (billions of dollars)	
Tax Revenues	**1,987**	
Personal income taxes		926
Social insurance taxes		738
Corporate income taxes		211
Indirect taxes		112
Expenditures	**1,868**	
Transfer payments		1,189
Purchases of goods and services		477
Debt interest		202
Surplus	**119**	

Source: Budget of the United States Government, Fiscal Year 2000, Table 14.1, Federal Transactions in the National Income and Product Accounts.

subsidies, grants to state and local governments, aid to developing countries, and dues to international organizations such as the United Nations. Transfer payments, especially those on Medicare and Medicaid, are sources of persistent growth in government expenditures and are a major source of concern and political debate.

Purchases of goods and services are expenditures on final goods and services, and in 2000, they are expected to total $477 billion. These expenditures, which include those on national defense, the NASA space program, research on cures for AIDS, computers for the Internal Revenue Service, government cars and trucks, federal highways, and dams, have decreased in recent years. This component of the federal budget is *government purchases of goods and services* that appears in the circular flow of expenditure and income and in the National Income and Product Accounts (see Chapter 23, pp. 498–499).

Debt interest is the interest on the government debt. In 2000, this item is expected to be $202 billion—some 11 percent of total expenditure. This interest payment is large because the government has a debt of more $3 trillion, which has arisen from many years of budget deficits during the 1970s, 1980s, and 1990s.

Surplus The government's budget balance is equal to its tax revenues minus its expenditures. That is,

Budget balance = Tax revenues – Expenditures.

If tax revenues exceed expenditures, the government has a **budget surplus**. If expenditures exceed tax revenues, the government has a **budget deficit**. If tax revenues equal expenditures, the government has a **balanced budget**. In fiscal 2000, with projected expenditures of $1,868 billion and tax revenues of $1,987 billion, the government projected a budget surplus of $119 billion.

Big numbers like these are hard to visualize and hard to compare over time. To get a better sense of the magnitude of taxes, spending, and the surplus, we often express them as percentages of GDP. Expressing them in this way lets us to see how large government is relative to the size of the economy and also helps us to study *changes* in the scale of government over time.

How typical is the federal budget of 2000? Let's look at its recent history.

The Budget in Historical Perspective

Figure 30.2 shows the government's tax revenues, expenditures, and budget surplus or deficit since 1980. Through 1997, there was a budget deficit. The deficit was about 2 percent of GDP in 1980 and

---

FIGURE 30.2

The Budget Deficit

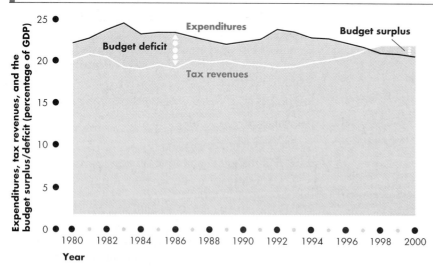

The figure records the federal government's expenditures, tax revenues, and budget surplus/deficit from 1980 through 2000. During the 1980s, a large and persistent budget deficit arose from the combination of a decrease in tax revenues and an increase in expenditures. In 1998, rising revenues and falling expenditures (as percentages of GDP) created a budget surplus.

Source: *Budget of the United States Government, Fiscal Year 2000,* Table 14.2, Federal Transactions in the National Income and Product Accounts.

1981, but it then increased and reached a peak in 1983 of 5.2 percent of GDP. It declined from 1983 through 1989 but climbed again during the 1990–1991 recession. During the 1990s expansion, the deficit gradually shrank and in 1998, the first surplus since 1969 emerged.

Why did the budget deficit grow during the 1980s and eventually vanish in the late 1990s? The answer lies in the changes in expenditures and tax revenues. But which components of expenditures and

tax revenues changed to swell and then shrink the deficit? Let's look at tax revenues and expenditures in a bit more detail.

Tax Revenues Figure 30.3(a) shows the components of tax revenues as percentages of GDP between 1980 and 2000. Cuts in corporate and personal income taxes lowered total tax revenues between 1981 and 1986. The decline resulted from tax cuts passed during 1981. From 1986 through 1991, tax

---

FIGURE 30.3

Federal Government Tax Revenues and Expenditures

(a) Tax revenues

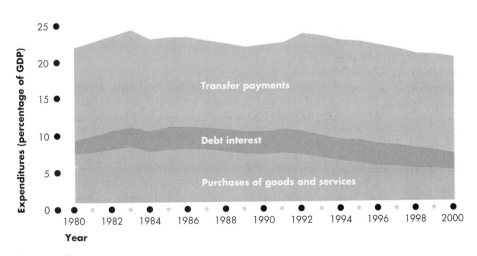

(b) Expenditures

In part (a), revenues from personal and corporate income taxes decreased during the early 1980s and revenues from personal income taxes increased during the 1990s. The other components of tax revenues remained steady.

In part (b), purchases of goods and services increased during the early 1980s and decreased through the 1990s. Transfer payments increased during the early 1980s. Debt interest increased steadily during the 1980s as the budget deficit fed on itself and then decreased during the 1990s as the deficit shrank and interest rates fell.

Source: Budget of the United States Government, Fiscal Year 2000, Table 14.2, Federal Transactions in the National Income and Product Accounts.

revenues did not change much as a percentage of GDP. But rising personal income taxes increased total tax revenues through the 1990s.

Expenditures   Figure 30.3(b) shows the components of government expenditures as percentages of GDP between 1980 and 2000. Total expenditures increased sharply between 1980 and 1983 and then declined slightly through 1989 before increasing again through 1992. After 1992, total expenditures decreased steadily. Purchases of goods and services decreased most during the 1990s. Debt interest increased most during the 1980s and contributed to the decrease in expenditures during the 1990s. To understand why, we need to see the connection between the government budget surplus or deficit and government debt.

Surplus, Deficit, and Debt   The government borrows when it has a budget deficit and makes repayments when it has a budget surplus. **Government debt** is the total amount that the government has borrowed. It is the sum of past deficits minus the sum of past surpluses. When the government has a budget deficit, its debt increases. And if a budget deficit persists, as it did during the 1980s, the deficit feeds itself. The deficit leads to increased borrowing; increased borrowing leads to larger interest payments; and larger interest payments lead to a larger deficit. That is the story of the increasing deficit of the 1980s.

Figure 30.4 shows the history of government debt since 1940. At the end of World War II, debt (as a percentage of GDP) was at an all-time high of 109 percent. Huge wartime deficits had increased debt to the point that it exceeded real GDP. Budget surpluses and rapid economic growth lowered the debt to GDP ratio through 1974, by which time it stood at 24 percent. Small deficits increased the debt to GDP ratio slightly through the 1970s, and large deficits increased it dramatically during the 1980s and through the 1990–1991 recession. The growth rate of the debt to GDP ratio slowed as the economy expanded during the mid-1990s and began to fall when the government budget went into surplus in the late 1990s.

Debt and Capital   Businesses and individuals incur debts to buy capital—assets that yield a return. In fact, the main point of debt is to enable people to buy assets that will earn a return that exceeds the interest paid on the debt. The government is similar to individuals and businesses in this regard. Much

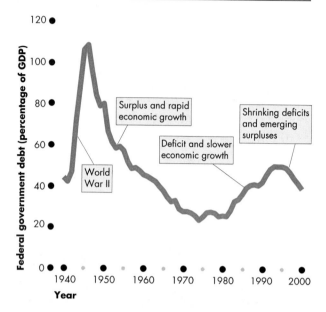

FIGURE 30.4

The Federal Government Debt

Federal government debt (the accumulation of past budget deficits less past budget surpluses) was more than 100 percent of GDP at the end of World War II. Debt as a percentage of GDP fell through 1974 but then started to increase. After a further brief decline during the late 1970s, it exploded during the 1980s and continued to increase through 1995, after which it began to fall.

Source: Budget of the United States Government, Fiscal Year 2000, Table 7.1, Federal Debt.

government expenditure is on public assets that yield a return. Highways, major irrigation schemes, public schools and universities, public libraries, and the stock of national defense capital all yield a social rate of return that probably far exceeds the interest rate the government pays on its debt.

But total government debt, which is almost $4 trillion, is more than twice the value of the public capital stock. So some government debt has been incurred to finance public consumption expenditure (such as foreign travel for diplomats). This expenditure does not have an ongoing social return.

How does the U. S. government budget balance compare with those in other countries?

The Budget Surplus in Global Perspective

Is the United States unusual in running a budget surplus? Do other countries have budget surpluses or do they have budget deficits? Figure 30.5 answers these questions. In today's world, almost all countries have budget deficits. To compare countries, we measure the budget surplus or deficit as a percentage of GDP. The biggest deficit relative to GDP is found in Japan, where the budget deficit exceeds 5 percent of GDP. The rest of Asia and the Middle East also have large deficits. The smallest deficits relative to GDP are found in the European Union.

FIGURE 30.5

Government Budgets Around the World in 1999

Governments in most countries have budget deficits. The largest ones are in Japan followed by the Middle East and the rest of Asia. The United States, Canada, and a few other advanced economies have surpluses.

Source: World Economic Outlook, October 1998, International Monetary Fund, Washington, D.C., Tables A15 and A20.

The United States and a small group of other countries that include Canada, Australia, Ireland, and some Scandinavian countries are relatively unusual in having budget *surpluses.*

State and Local Budgets

The *total government* sector of the United States includes state and local governments as well as the federal government. In 1998, when federal government expenditures were $1,750 billion, state and local expenditures were more than $1,000 billion. Most of these expenditures were on public schools, colleges, and universities ($350 billion); local police and fire services; and roads.

It is the total government sector that influences the aggregate economy. But state and local budgets are not designed, as the federal budget is, with the specific goal of stabilizing the aggregate economy. On the contrary, sometimes, when the aggregate economy needs an injection of additional expenditures, state and local governments cut their expenditures and deficits. Such changes in expenditures occurred during the 1990–1991 recession when many states both cut their expenditures and increased taxes.

R E V I E W   Q U I Z

- What is fiscal policy, who makes it, and what is it designed to influence?
- What special role does the President play in creating fiscal policy?
- What is the time line for the U.S. federal budget each year? When does a fiscal year begin and end?
- Is the U.S. federal government budget today in surplus or deficit?

Now that you know what the federal budget is and what the main items of revenue and expenditure are, it is time to study the *effects* of fiscal policy. We'll begin by learning about its effects on expenditure plans when the price level is fixed. You will see that fiscal policy has multiplier effects like the expenditure multipliers explained in Chapter 29. Then we'll study the influences of fiscal policy on both aggregate demand and aggregate supply and look at its short-run and long-run effects on real GDP and the price level.

Fiscal Policy Multipliers

FISCAL POLICY ACTIONS CAN BE EITHER AUTOMATIC or discretionary. **Automatic fiscal policy** is a change in fiscal policy that is triggered by the state of the economy. For example, an increase in unemployment triggers an *automatic* increase in payments to the unemployed. A fall in income triggers an *automatic* decrease in tax receipts. That is, this type of fiscal policy adjusts automatically. **Discretionary fiscal policy** is a policy action that is initiated by an act of Congress. It requires a change in tax laws or in some spending program. For example, an increase in the income tax rate and an increase in defense spending are discretionary fiscal policy actions. That is, discretionary fiscal policy is a deliberate policy action.

We begin by studying the effects of *discretionary* changes in government spending and taxes. To focus on the essentials, we'll initially study a model economy that is simpler than the one in which we live. In our model economy, there is no international trade and the taxes are all lump sum. **Lump-sum taxes** are taxes that do not vary with real GDP. The government fixes them, and they change when the government changes them. But they do not vary automatically with the state of the economy.

The main example of a lump-sum tax is the *property tax.* This tax varies across individuals and depends on the value of the property a person occupies. But unlike the income tax, it does not change simply because a person's income changes.

We use lump-sum taxes in our model economy because they make the principles we are studying easier to understand. Once we've grasped the principles, we'll explore our real economy with its international trade and income taxes—taxes that *do* vary with real GDP.

Like our real economy, the model economy we study is bombarded by spending fluctuations. Business investment in new building, plant and equipment, and inventories fluctuates because of swings in profit expectations and interest rates. These fluctuations set up multiplier effects that start a recession or an expansion. If a recession takes hold, unemployment increases and incomes fall. If an expansion becomes too strong, inflationary pressures build up. To minimize the effects of these swings in spending, the government might change either its purchases of goods and services or taxes. By changing either of these items, the government can influence aggregate expenditure and real GDP. But it also changes its budget deficit or surplus. An alternative fiscal policy action is to change both purchases and taxes together so that the budget balance does not change. We are going to study the initial effects of these discretionary fiscal policy actions in the very short run when the price level is fixed. Each of these actions creates a multiplier effect on real GDP. These multipliers are:

- The government purchases multiplier
- The lump-sum tax multiplier

The Government Purchases Multiplier

The **government purchases multiplier** is the magnification effect of a change in government purchases of goods and services on equilibrium expenditure and real GDP.

Government purchases are a component of aggregate expenditure. So when government purchases change, aggregate expenditure and real GDP change. The change in real GDP induces a change in consumption expenditure, which brings a further change in aggregate expenditure. A multiplier process ensues. This multiplier process is like the one described in Chapter 29 (pp. 644–649). Let's look at an example.

Cape Canaveral Multiplier Before the National Aeronautics and Space Administration (NASA) built a major space launching facility at Cape Canaveral in Florida in the 1960s, the Cape was a quiet place. The injection of government purchases to build the space launching and research facility created jobs in the region. Because construction workers and NASA workers spent most of their incomes locally, consumption expenditure increased. Retail stores and hotels and motels opened and hired yet more people and, in the process, created yet bigger incomes. These incomes were also spent in the area, so spending and incomes rose still further. Eventually, expenditures and incomes stopped rising but remained at their new higher levels.

The Size of the Multiplier Table 30.2 illustrates the government purchases multiplier with a numerical example. The first column lists various possible levels of real GDP. Our task is to find equilibrium expenditure and the change in real GDP when government purchases change. The second column shows taxes.

TABLE 30.2

The Government Purchases Multiplier

	Real GDP (Y)	Taxes (T)	Disposable income (Y – T)	Consumption expenditure (C)	Investment (I)	Initial government purchases (G)	Initial aggregate planned expenditure (C + I + G)	Increase in government purchases (ΔG)	New aggregate planned expenditure (C + I + G + ΔG)
					(trillions of dollars)				
a	5.0	0.5	4.5	3.75	1.0	0.5	5.25	0.5	5.75
b	6.0	0.5	5.5	4.50	1.0	0.5	6.00	0.5	6.50
c	7.0	0.5	6.5	5.25	1.0	0.5	6.75	0.5	7.25
d	8.0	0.5	7.5	6.00	1.0	0.5	7.50	0.5	8.00
e	9.0	0.5	8.5	6.75	1.0	0.5	8.25	0.5	8.75

They are fixed at $0.5 trillion, regardless of the level of real GDP. (This is an assumption that keeps your attention on the key idea and makes the calculations easier to do.) The third column calculates disposable income. Because taxes are a lump sum, disposable income equals real GDP minus the $0.5 trillion of taxes. For example, in row *b*, real GDP is $6 trillion and disposable income is $5.5 trillion. The next column shows consumption expenditure. In this example, the *marginal propensity to consume* is 0.75. That is, a $1 increase in disposable income brings a 75-cent increase in consumption expenditure. Check this fact by calculating the increase in consumption expenditure when disposable income increases by $1 trillion from row *b* to row *c*. Consumption expenditure increases by $0.75 trillion. The next column shows investment, which is a constant of $1 trillion. The next column shows the initial level of government purchases, which is $0.5 trillion. Aggregate planned expenditure is the sum of consumption expenditure, investment, and government purchases.

Equilibrium expenditure and real GDP occur when aggregate planned expenditure equals actual expenditure. In this example, equilibrium expenditure is $6 trillion (highlighted in row *b* of the table.)

The final two columns of the table show what happens when government purchases increase by $0.5 trillion to $1 trillion. Aggregate planned expenditure increases by $0.5 trillion at each level of real GDP. At the initial real GDP of $6 trillion (row *b*), aggregate planned expenditure increases to $6.5 trillion.

Because aggregate planned expenditure now exceeds real GDP, inventories decrease and firms increase production. Output, incomes, and expenditure increase. Increased incomes induce a further increase in expenditure. But the induced increase in aggregate planned expenditure is less than the increase in income, and eventually a new equilibrium is reached. The new equilibrium is at a real GDP of $8 trillion (highlighted in row *d*).

A $0.5 trillion increase in government purchases has increased equilibrium expenditure and real GDP by $2 trillion. Therefore the government purchases multiplier is 4. The size of the multiplier depends on the marginal propensity to consume, which in this example is 0.75. The following formula shows the connection between the government purchases multiplier and the marginal propensity to consume (*MPC*):

$$\text{Government purchases multiplier} = \frac{1}{1 - MPC}.$$

Let's check this formula by using the numbers in the above example. The marginal propensity to consume is 0.75, so the government purchases multiplier is 4.

Figure 30.6 illustrates the government purchases multiplier. Initially, aggregate planned expenditure is shown by the curve labeled AE_0. The points on this curve, labeled *a* through *e*, correspond with the rows of Table 30.2. This aggregate expenditure curve intersects the 45° line at the equilibrium level of real GDP, which is $6 trillion.

FIGURE 30.6

The Government Purchases Multiplier

A $0.5 trillion increase in government purchases shifts the *AE* curve upward by $0.5 trillion ...

... and increases real GDP by $2 trillion. The government purchases multiplier is

$$\frac{1}{(1 - 0.75)} = 4$$

Initially, the aggregate expenditure curve is AE_0 and real GDP is $6 trillion (at point *b*). An increase in government purchases of $0.5 trillion increases aggregate planned expenditure at each level of real GDP by $0.5 trillion. The aggregate expenditure curve shifts upward from AE_0 to AE_1—a parallel shift. At the initial real GDP of $6 trillion, aggregate planned expenditure is now $6.5 trillion. Because aggregate planned expenditure is greater than real GDP, real GDP increases. The new equilibrium is reached when real GDP is $8 trillion—the point at which the AE_1 curve intersects the 45° line (at *d'*). In this example, the government purchases multiplier is 4.

When government purchases increase by $0.5 trillion, the aggregate expenditure curve shifts upward by that amount to AE_1. With this new aggregate expenditure curve, equilibrium real GDP increases to $8 trillion. The increase in real GDP is 4 times the increase in government purchases. The government purchases multiplier is 4.

You've seen that in the very short term, when the price level is fixed, an increase in government purchases increases real GDP. But to produce more output, more people must be employed. So in the short term, an increase in government purchases can create jobs.

Increasing its purchases of goods and services is one way in which the government can try to stimulate the economy. A second way in which the government might act to increase real GDP in the very short run is by decreasing lump-sum taxes. Let's see how this action works.

The Lump-Sum Tax Multiplier

The **lump-sum tax multiplier** is the magnification effect of a change in lump-sum taxes on equilibrium expenditure and real GDP. An *increase* in taxes *decreases* disposable income, which *decreases* consumption expenditure. The amount by which consumption expenditure initially changes is determined by the marginal propensity to consume. In our example, the marginal propensity to consume is 0.75, so a $1 tax cut increases disposable income by $1 and increases aggregate expenditure initially by 75 cents.

This initial change in aggregate expenditure has a multiplier just like the government purchases multiplier. We've seen that the government purchases multiplier is $1/(1 - MPC)$. Because a tax *increase* leads to a *decrease* in expenditure, the lump-sum tax multiplier is *negative*. And because a change in lump-sum taxes changes aggregate expenditure initially by only MPC multiplied by the tax change, the lump-sum tax multiplier is equal to

$$\text{Lump-sum tax multiplier} = \frac{-MPC}{1 - MPC}.$$

In our example, the marginal propensity to consume is 3/4, so the lump-sum tax multiplier is

$$\text{Lump-sum tax multiplier} = \frac{-\dfrac{3}{4}}{1 - \dfrac{3}{4}} = -3.$$

Figure 30.7 illustrates the lump-sum tax multiplier. Initially, the aggregate expenditure curve is AE_0, and equilibrium expenditure is $8 trillion. Taxes increase by $1 trillion, and disposable income falls by that amount. With a marginal propensity to consume of 3/4, aggregate expenditure decreases initially by $0.75 trillion and the aggregate expenditure curve shifts downward by that amount to AE_1. Equilibrium expenditure and real GDP fall by $3 trillion to $5 trillion. The lump-sum tax multiplier is −3.

FIGURE 30.7
The Lump-Sum Tax Multiplier

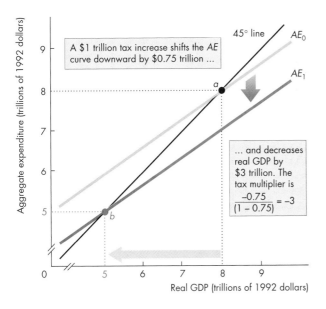

A $1 trillion tax increase shifts the AE curve downward by $0.75 trillion ...

... and decreases real GDP by $3 trillion. The tax multiplier is
$$\frac{-0.75}{(1-0.75)} = -3$$

Initially, the aggregate expenditure curve is AE_0 and equilibrium expenditure is $8 trillion. The marginal propensity to consume is 0.75. Lump-sum taxes increase by $1 trillion, so disposable income falls by $1 trillion. The decrease in aggregate expenditure is found by multiplying this change in disposable income by the marginal propensity to consume and is $1 trillion x 0.75 = $0.75 trillion. The aggregate expenditure curve shifts *downward* by this amount to AE_1. Equilibrium expenditure decreases by $3 trillion, from $8 trillion to $5 trillion. The lump-sum tax multiplier is –3.

Lump-Sum Transfer Payments   The lump-sum tax multiplier also tells us the effects of a change in lump-sum transfer payments. Transfer payments are like negative taxes, so an increase in transfer payments works like a decrease in taxes. Because the tax multiplier is negative, a decrease in taxes increases expenditure. An increase in transfer payments also increases expenditure. So the lump-sum transfer payments multiplier is positive. It is

$$\frac{\text{Lump-sum transfer}}{\text{payments multiplier}} = \frac{MPC}{1-MPC}.$$

Induced Taxes and Entitlement Spending

In the examples we've studied so far, taxes are lump-sum taxes. But in reality, net taxes (taxes minus transfer payments) vary with the state of the economy.

On the revenue side of the budget, tax laws define tax *rates* to be paid, not tax *dollars* to be paid. Tax *dollars* paid depend on tax *rates* and incomes. But incomes vary with real GDP, so tax *revenues* depend on real GDP. Taxes that vary with real GDP are called **induced taxes.** When the economy expands, induced taxes increase because real GDP increases. When the economy is in a recession, induced taxes decrease because real GDP decreases.

On the outlay side of the budget, the government creates programs that entitle suitably qualified people and businesses to receive benefits. The spending on such programs is called **entitlement spending,** and it results in transfer payments that depend on the economic state of individual citizens and businesses. When the economy is in a recession, unemployment is high, the number of people experiencing economic hardship increases, and a larger number of firms and farms experience hard times. Entitlement spending increases. When the economy expands, entitlement spending decreases.

Induced taxes and entitlement payments decrease the multiplier effects of changes in government purchases and lump-sum taxes. The reason is that they weaken the link between real GDP and disposable income and so dampen the effect of a change in real GDP on consumption expenditure. When real GDP increases, induced taxes increase and entitlement payments decrease, so disposable income does not increase by as much as the increase in real GDP. As a result, consumption expenditure does not increase by as much as it otherwise would have done and the multiplier effect is reduced.

The extent to which induced taxes and entitlement payments decrease the multiplier depends on the *marginal tax rate*. The marginal tax rate is the proportion of an additional dollar of real GDP that flows to the government in net taxes (taxes minus transfer payments). The higher the marginal tax rate, the larger is the proportion of an additional dollar of real GDP that is paid to the government and the smaller is the induced change in consumption expenditure. The smaller the change in consumption expenditure induced by a change in real GDP, the smaller is the multiplier effect of a change in government purchases or lump-sum taxes.

International Trade and Fiscal Policy Multipliers

Not all expenditure in the United States is on U.S.-produced goods and services. Some of it is on imports—on foreign-produced goods and services. Imports affect the fiscal policy multipliers in exactly the same way that they influence the expenditure multiplier, as explained in Chapter 29 (see pp. 646–647), and there is no new principle involved. The extent to which an additional dollar of real GDP is spent on imports is determined by the *marginal propensity to import.* Expenditure on imports does not generate U.S. real GDP and does not lead to an increase in U.S. consumption expenditure. The larger the marginal propensity to import, the smaller is the increase in consumption expenditure induced by an increase in real GDP and the smaller are the government purchases and lump-sum tax multipliers.

So far, we've studied *discretionary* fiscal policy. Let's now look at *automatic* stabilizers.

Automatic Stabilizers

Automatic stabilizers are mechanisms that stabilize real GDP without explicit action by the government. Their name is borrowed from engineering and conjures up images of shock absorbers, thermostats, and sophisticated devices that keep airplanes and ships steady in turbulent air and seas. Automatic fiscal stabilizers are a consequence of income taxes and transfer payments that automatically fluctuate with real GDP. If real GDP begins to decrease, tax revenues fall and transfer payments rise. These changes in taxes and transfer payments affect the economy and the government's budget deficit. Let's study the budget deficit over the business cycle.

Budget Deficit Over the Business Cycle Figure 30.8 shows the business cycle and fluctuations in the budget deficit since 1975. Part (a) shows the fluctuations of real GDP around potential GDP. Part (b) shows the federal budget deficit. Both parts highlight recessions by shading those periods. By comparing the two parts of the figure, you can see the relationship between the business cycle and the budget deficit. As a rule, when the economy is in the expansion phase of a business cycle, the budget deficit declines. (In the figure, a declining deficit means a deficit that is getting closer to zero.) As the expansion slows before the recession begins, the budget deficit

FIGURE 30.8

The Business Cycle and the Budget Deficit

(a) Growth and recessions

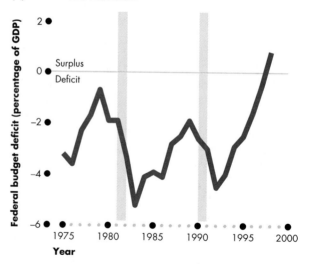

(b) Federal budget deficit

As real GDP fluctuates around potential GDP (part a), the budget deficit fluctuates (part b). During a recession (shaded years), tax revenues decrease, transfer payments increase, and the budget deficit increases. The deficit also increases *before* a recession as real GDP growth slows and *after* a recession before real GDP growth speeds up.

Source: *Economic Report of the President,* 1999, and the author's calculations.

increases. It continues to increase during the recession and for a further period after the recession is over. Then, when the expansion is well under way, the budget deficit declines again.

The budget deficit fluctuates with the business cycle because both tax revenues and expenditures fluctuate with real GDP. As real GDP increases during an expansion, tax revenues increase and transfer payments decrease, so the budget deficit automatically decreases. As real GDP decreases during a recession, tax revenues decrease and transfer payments increase, so the budget deficit automatically increases.

Fluctuations in investment and exports have a multiplier effect on real GDP. But automatic fluctuations in tax revenues (and the budget deficit) act as an automatic stabilizer. They decrease the swings in disposable income and make the multiplier effect smaller. They dampen both expansions and recessions.

Cyclical and Structural Balances   Because the government budget balance fluctuates with the business cycle, we need a method of measuring the balance that tells us whether it is a temporary cyclical phenomenon or a persistent phenomenon. A temporary and cyclical surplus or deficit vanishes when full employment returns. A persistent surplus or deficit requires government action to remove it.

To determine whether the budget balance is temporary and cyclical or persistent, economists have developed the concepts of the structural budget balance and the cyclical budget balance. The **structural surplus or deficit** is the budget balance that would occur if the economy were at full employment and real GDP equalled potential GDP. The **cyclical surplus or deficit** is the actual surplus or deficit minus the structural surplus or deficit. That is, the cyclical surplus or deficit is the part of the budget balance that arises purely because real GDP does not equal potential GDP.

For example, suppose there is a budget deficit of $100 billion. And suppose that economists have determined that there is a structural deficit of $25 billion. Then there is a cyclical deficit of $75 billion.

Figure 30.9 illustrates the concepts of cyclical surplus or deficit and structural surplus or deficit. The blue curve shows government expenditures. The expenditures curve slopes downward because the higher the level of real GDP, the smaller is the level of transfer payments and so the smaller is the level of government expenditures. The green curve shows tax revenues. The tax revenues curve slopes upward

FIGURE 30.9

Cyclical and Structural Surpluses and Deficits

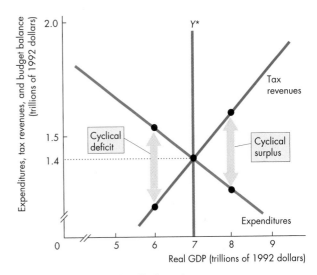

(a) Cyclical deficit and cyclical surplus

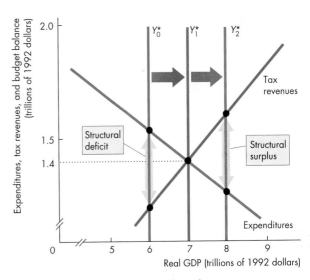

(b) Structural deficit and structural surplus

In part (a), potential GDP is $7 trillion. When real GDP is less than potential GDP, the budget is in a *cyclical deficit*. When real GDP exceeds potential GDP, the budget is in a *cyclical surplus*. The government has a *balanced budget* when real GDP equals potential GDP. In part (b), when potential GDP is $6 trillion, there is a *structural deficit*. But when potential GDP is $8 trillion, there is a *structural surplus*.

because most components of tax revenues increase as incomes and real GDP increase.

In Fig. 30.9(a), potential GDP is $7 trillion. If real GDP equals potential GDP, the government has a *balanced budget*. Expenditures and tax revenues each equal $1.4 trillion. If real GDP is less than potential GDP, expenditures exceed tax revenues and there is a *cyclical deficit*. If real GDP is greater than potential GDP, expenditures are less than tax revenues and there is a *cyclical surplus*.

In Fig. 30.9(b), potential GDP grows but the tax revenue curve and the expenditure curve do not change. When potential GDP is $6 trillion, there is a *structural deficit*. When potential GDP grows to $7 trillion, there is a *structural balance* of zero (neither a deficit nor a surplus). And when potential GDP grows to $8 trillion, there is a *structural surplus*.

The U.S. federal budget was in a structural deficit starting in the mid-1970s and through the mid-1990s. That is, even if the economy had been at full employment, the budget would have been in deficit. Worse, the structural deficit was so large that even at the peak of a business cycle, the budget was in deficit.

At the end of the 1990s, a budget surplus was emerging. But it is not yet clear that this surplus is structural. The economy was above full employment, so the surplus could be cyclical.

R E V I E W   Q U I Z

- What are the government purchases multiplier and the lump-sum tax multiplier? How do these multiplier effects work?
- Which multiplier effect is larger, that of a change in government purchases or that of a change in lump-sum taxes? Why is one larger than the other?
- How do income taxes and international trade influence the size of the fiscal policy multipliers?
- How do income taxes and entitlement programs work as automatic stabilizers to dampen the business cycle?
- How do we tell whether a budget deficit needs government action to remove it?

Your next task is to see how, with the passage of more time and with some price level adjustments, these multiplier effects change.

Fiscal Policy Multipliers and the Price Level

WE'VE SEEN HOW REAL GDP RESPONDS TO changes in fiscal policy when the price level is fixed and all the adjustments that take place are in spending, income, and production. The period over which this response occurs is very short. Once production starts to change, regardless of whether it increases or decreases, prices also start to change. The price level and real GDP change together, and the economy moves to a new short-run equilibrium.

To study the simultaneous changes in real GDP and the price level that result from fiscal policy, we use the aggregate supply–aggregate demand model of Chapter 25. In the long run, both the price level and the money wage rate respond to fiscal policy. As these further changes take place, the economy gradually moves toward a new long-run equilibrium. We also use the aggregate supply–aggregate demand model to study these adjustments.

We begin by looking at the effects of fiscal policy on aggregate demand and the aggregate demand curve.

Fiscal Policy and Aggregate Demand

You learned about the relationship between aggregate demand, aggregate expenditure, and equilibrium expenditure in Chapter 29. You are now going to use what you learned there to work out what happens to aggregate demand, the price level, real GDP, and jobs when fiscal policy changes. We'll start by looking at the effects of a change in fiscal policy on aggregate demand.

Figure 30.10 shows the effects of an increase in government purchases on aggregate demand. Initially, the aggregate expenditure curve is AE_0 in part (a), and the aggregate demand curve is AD_0 in part (b). The price level is 110, real GDP is $7 trillion, and the economy is at point a in both parts of the figure. Now suppose that government purchases increase by $0.5 trillion. At a constant price level of 110, the aggregate expenditure curve shifts upward to AE_1. This curve intersects the 45° line at an equilibrium expenditure of $9 trillion at point b. This amount is the aggregate quantity of goods and services demanded at a price level of 110, as shown by point b in part (b). Point b

FIGURE 30.10

Government Purchases
and Aggregate Demand

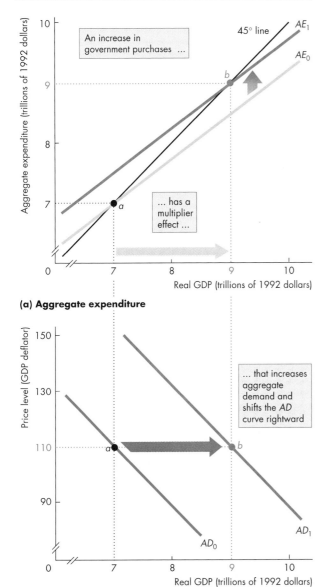

(a) Aggregate expenditure

(b) Aggregate demand

The price level is 110, aggregate planned expenditure is AE_0 (part a), and aggregate demand is AD_0 (part b). An increase in government purchases shifts the AE curve to AE_1 and equilibrium real GDP increases to $9 trillion. The aggregate demand curve shifts rightward to AD_1.

lies on a new aggregate demand curve. The aggregate demand curve has shifted rightward to AD_1.

The government purchases multiplier determines the distance by which the aggregate demand curve shifts rightward. The larger the multiplier, the larger is the shift in the aggregate demand curve resulting from a given change in government purchases. In this example, a $0.5 trillion increase in government purchases produces a $2 trillion increase in the aggregate quantity of goods and services demanded at each price level. The multiplier is 4. So the $0.5 trillion increase in government purchases shifts the aggregate demand curve rightward by $2 trillion.

Figure 30.10 shows the effects of an increase in government purchases. But a similar effect occurs for *any* expansionary fiscal policy. An **expansionary fiscal policy** is an increase in government purchases or a decrease in tax revenues. But the distance the AD curve shifts is smaller for a tax cut than for a government purchases increase of the same size.

Figure 30.10 can also be used to illustrate the effects of a **contractionary fiscal policy**—a decrease in government purchases or an increase in tax revenues. In this case, start at point *b* in each part of the figure and decrease government purchases or increase taxes. Aggregate demand decreases from AD_1 to AD_0.

Equilibrium GDP and the Price Level in the Short Run We've seen how an increase in government purchases increases aggregate demand. Let's now see how it changes real GDP and the price level. Figure 30.11(a) describes the economy. Aggregate demand is AD_0, and the short-run aggregate supply curve is *SAS*. (Check back to Chapter 25 if you need to refresh your understanding of the *SAS* curve.) Equilibrium is at point *a*, where the aggregate demand and short-run aggregate supply curves intersect. The price level is 110, and real GDP is $7 trillion.

An increase in government purchases of $0.5 trillion shifts the aggregate demand curve rightward from AD_0 to AD_1. While the price level is fixed at 110, the economy moves toward point *b* and real GDP increases toward $9 trillion. But during the adjustment process, the price level does not remain constant. It gradually rises, and the economy moves along the short-run aggregate supply curve to the point of intersection of the short-run aggregate supply curve and the new aggregate demand curve—point *c*. The price level rises to 116, and real GDP increases to only $8.6 trillion.

FIGURE 30.11

Fiscal Policy, Real GDP, and the Price Level

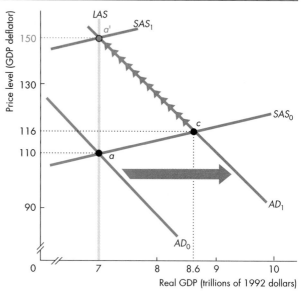

(a) Fiscal policy with unemployment

An increase in government purchases shifts the *AD* curve from AD_0 to AD_1. With a fixed price level, the economy would have moved to point *b*. But the price level rises, and in the short run, the economy moves to point *c*. The price level increases to 116, and real GDP increases to $8.6 trillion.

(b) Fiscal policy with full employment

At point *c*, real GDP exceeds potential GDP and unemployment is below the natural rate. The wage rate rises, and short-run aggregate supply decreases. The *SAS* curve shifts leftward to SAS_1, and in the long run, the economy moves to point *a'*. The price level rises to 150, and real GDP returns to $7 trillion.

When we take the price level effect into account, the increase in government purchases still has a multiplier effect on real GDP, but the effect is smaller than it would be if the price level remained constant. Also, the steeper the slope of the short-run aggregate supply curve, the larger is the increase in the price level, the smaller is the increase in real GDP, and the smaller is the government purchases multiplier. But the multiplier is not zero.

In the long run, real GDP equals potential GDP—the economy is at full-employment equilibrium. When real GDP equals potential GDP, an increase in aggregate demand has the same short-run effect as we've just worked out, but its long-run effect is different. The increase in aggregate demand raises the price level, but in the long run, it leaves real GDP unchanged at potential GDP.

To study this case, let's see what happens if the government embarks on an expansionary fiscal policy when real GDP equals potential GDP.

Fiscal Expansion at Potential GDP

Suppose that real GDP is equal to potential GDP, which means that unemployment is equal to the natural rate of unemployment. But suppose also that the unemployment rate and the natural rate are high and that most people, including the government, mistakenly think that the unemployment rate exceeds the natural rate. In this situation, the government tries to lower the unemployment rate by using an expansionary fiscal policy.

Figure 30.11(b) shows the effect of an expansionary fiscal policy when real GDP equals potential GDP. In this example, potential GDP is $7 trillion. Aggregate demand increases, and the aggregate demand curve shifts rightward from AD_0 to AD_1. The short-run equilibrium, point *c*, is an above full-employment equilibrium. The labor force is more than fully employed, and there are shortages of labor.

Money wage rates begin to increase. Higher money wage rates increase costs, and short-run aggregate supply decreases. The *SAS* curve begins to shift leftward from SAS_0 to SAS_1. The economy moves up the aggregate demand curve AD_1 toward point a'.

Eventually, when all adjustments to wage rates and the price level have been made, the price level is 150 and real GDP is again at potential GDP of $7 trillion. The multiplier in the long run is zero. There has been a temporary decrease in the unemployment rate during the process you've just looked at, but not a permanent decrease. But the price level rise is permanent.

Limitations of Fiscal Policy

Because the short-run fiscal policy multipliers are not zero, expansionary fiscal policy can be used to increase real GDP and decrease the unemployment rate in a recession. Contractionary fiscal policy can also be used if the economy is overheating to decrease real GDP and help to keep inflation in check. But the use of fiscal policy is limited by two factors.

First, the legislative process is slow, which means that it is difficult to take fiscal policy actions in a timely way. The economy might be able to benefit from fiscal stimulation right now, but it will take Congress many months to act. By then, the economy might need an entirely different fiscal medicine.

Second, it is not always easy to tell whether real GDP is below (or above) potential GDP. A change in aggregate demand can move real GDP away from potential GDP, or a change in aggregate supply can change real GDP and change potential GDP. This difficulty is a serious one because, as you've seen, fiscal stimulation at full employment leads to a rise in the price level and has no long-run effect on real GDP.

R E V I E W   Q U I Z

- How do changes in the price level influence the multiplier effects of fiscal policy on real GDP?
- What are the long-run effects of fiscal policy on real GDP and the price level when initially real GDP equals potential GDP?

So far in this chapter, we've ignored any potential effects of fiscal policy on aggregate supply. Yet many economists believe that the supply-side effects of fiscal policy are large. Let's now look at these effects.

Fiscal Policy and Aggregate Supply

DURING THE 1980S, WHEN RONALD REAGAN WAS President, a group of economists known as *supply-siders* became prominent. Supply-siders believed that tax cuts would strengthen incentives and increase aggregate supply. George Bush called their ideas "voodoo economics," and many other people are skeptical about supply-siders' claims. But these claims remain part of the political debate today. They are the main rationale for a flat tax that some economists and politicians have advocated.

Using the concepts of the *AS-AD* model, the supply-siders' claim is that tax cuts increase potential GDP. Is this claim correct?

There is no disagreement among economists that taxes create disincentives and decrease potential GDP. The disagreements are about numbers. Supply-siders say the effects are large. Others suspect that the effects are small, possibly too small to bother about.

Let's study the effects of taxes on potential GDP and then see how the supply effects and demand effects together influence real GDP and the price level.

Fiscal Policy and Potential GDP

Potential GDP depends on the full-employment quantity of labor, the quantity of capital, and the state of technology. Taxes can influence all three of these factors. The main tax to consider is the income tax. By taxing the incomes people earn when they work or save, the government weakens the incentives to work and save. The result is a smaller quantity of labor and capital and a lower potential GDP. Also, the income tax weakens the incentive to develop new technologies that increase income. So the pace of technological change might be slowed, which slows the growth rate of potential GDP. Let's look at the effect of the income tax on both the quantity of labor and the quantity of capital.

Labor and the Income Tax   The quantity of labor is determined by demand and supply in the labor market (see Chapter 26, pp. 570–571). Figure 30.12(a) shows a labor market. The demand for labor is *LD*, and the supply is *LS*. With no income tax, this labor market achieves equilibrium at a real wage rate of $14 an hour and 230 billion hours of labor per year are employed.

FIGURE 30.12

Supply-Side Effects of the Income Tax

(a) The labor market

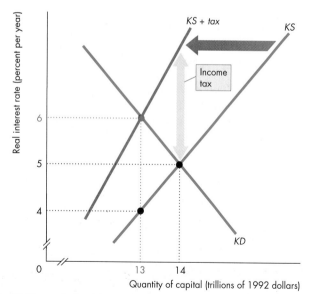

(b) The capital market

In part (a), the income tax shifts the supply of labor curve, LS, leftward to LS + tax. The before-tax wage rate rises, the after-tax wage rate falls, and the quantity of labor employed decreases. In part (b), the income tax shifts the supply of capital curve, KS, leftward to KS + tax. The before-tax interest rate rises, the after-tax interest rate falls, and the quantity of capital decreases. With less labor and less capital, potential GDP falls.

Now suppose an income tax is introduced. The income tax weakens the incentive to work and decreases the supply of labor. The supply curve shifts leftward to *LS + tax*. With this new lower supply of labor, the *before-tax* wage rate rises to $15 an hour and the quantity of labor employed decreases to 210 billion hours a year. The before-tax wage rate rises, but the *after-tax* wage rate falls. In Fig. 30.12(a), it falls to $10 an hour.

Capital and the Income Tax The quantity of capital is determined by demand and supply in the capital market (see Chapter 27, pp. 593–595). Figure 30.12(b) shows the capital market. The demand for capital is *KD*, and the supply is *KS*. With no income tax, the capital market achieves equilibrium at a real interest rate of 5 percent a year and $14 trillion of capital is available.

Now consider the effects of a tax on income from capital. The income tax, which weakens the incentive to save, decreases the supply of capital. The supply curve shifts leftward to *KS + tax*. The *before-tax* interest rate rises to 6 percent a year, and the quantity of capital decreases to $13 trillion. The before-tax interest rate rises, but the *after-tax* interest rate falls. In Fig. 30.12, it falls to 4 percent a year.

Potential GDP and *LAS* Because the income tax decreases the equilibrium quantities of labor and capital, it also decreases potential GDP. But potential GDP determines long-run aggregate supply. So the income tax decreases long-run aggregate supply and shifts the *LAS* curve leftward.

Supply Effects and Demand Effects

Let's now bring the supply effects and demand effects of fiscal policy together. Figure 30.13(a) shows the most likely effects of a tax cut. The tax cut increases aggregate demand and shifts the *AD* curve rightward, just as before. But a tax cut that increases the incentive to work and save also increases aggregate supply. It shifts the long-run and short-run aggregate supply curves rightward. Here we focus on the short-run and show the effect on the *SAS* curve, which shifts rightward to *SAS*₁. In this example, the tax cut has a large effect on aggregate demand and a small effect on aggregate supply. The aggregate demand curve shifts rightward by a larger amount than the rightward shift in the short-run aggregate supply curve. The outcome is a rise in the price level and an increase in real GDP.

FIGURE 30.13

Two Views of the Supply-Side Effects of Fiscal Policy

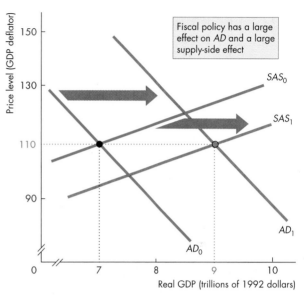

(a) The traditional view

A tax cut increases aggregate demand and shifts the AD curve rightward from AD_0 to AD_1 (both parts). Such a policy change also has a supply-side effect. If the supply-side effect is small, the SAS curve shifts rightward from SAS_0 to SAS_1 in part (a). The demand-side effect dominates the supply-side effect, real GDP increases, and the price level rises.

(b) The supply-side view

If the supply-side effect of a tax cut is large, the SAS curve shifts to SAS_1 in part (b). In this case, the supply-side effect is as large as the demand-side effect. Real GDP increases, and the price level remains constant. But if the supply-side effect were larger than the demand-side effect, the price level would actually fall.

But notice that the price level rises by *less* and real GDP increases by *more* than would occur if there were no supply-side effects.

Figure 30.13(b) shows the effects that supply-siders believe to occur. A tax cut still has a large effect on aggregate demand, but it has a similarly large effect on aggregate supply. The aggregate demand curve and the short-run aggregate supply curve shift rightward by similar amounts. In this particular case, the price level remains constant and real GDP increases. A slightly larger increase in aggregate supply would have brought a fall in the price level, a possibility that some supply-siders believe could occur.

The general point that everyone agrees with is that a tax cut that strengthens incentives increases real GDP by more and is less inflationary than an equal-sized expansionary fiscal policy that does not change incentives or that weakens them.

> ### R E V I E W   Q U I Z
>
> ■ What are the incentive effects that the income tax has on the supply of labor and the supply of capital and how would a cut in the income tax rate affect potential GDP?
>
> ■ Because a tax cut increases both aggregate supply and aggregate demand, can we tell whether a tax cut increases or decreases real GDP and the price level?

◆ You've seen how fiscal policy influences real GDP and potential GDP. *Reading Between the Lines* on pp. 680–681 looks at U.S. fiscal policy in 1999. Your next task is to study monetary policy. We begin by describing the monetary system of a modern economy.

Deficit and Debts

THE NEW YORK TIMES, JANUARY 31, 1999

The Deficit's Gone, but Not the National Debt

By RICHARD W. STEVENSON

WASHINGTON—The Federal budget deficit is gone, transformed by a strong economy into a string of projected surpluses that should grow larger for years to come—at least by the reckoning that passes for fiscal forecasting in Washington.

Eliminating the deficit is hardly the end of the Government's financial troubles, however, and it marks the beginning of a new debate over how fiscal policy should be used to shape the nation's future.

It's like a family that after spending more than it earns month after month suddenly finds itself bringing in more than it spends— great news, to be sure, but a turnaround that still leaves the family with the debt it ran up during the hard times and the choice of whether to pay it off.

Washington was never in much danger of maxing out its credit cards. But the national debt was built up over decades of deficit spending—the Federal Government has not run steady surpluses since the 1920's—and it remains an economic millstone of considerable proportions. Only now do Congress and the White House have the luxury of debating what to do about it. ...

"Debt reduction ultimately gets trumped in a political process by Government spending," said John F. Cogan, a senior fellow at the Hoover Institution and a former budget official in the Reagan and Bush Administrations. "Achieving a sustained policy of debt reduction is very difficult, to say the least."

There are several ways to measure the national debt, but the most meaningful is to look at the debt held by the public—the individuals, Wall Street firms and banks from around the world that bought bonds sold by the Treasury Department. There is currently $3.7 trillion in public debt outstanding, which is equal to 45 percent of the economy's total output. ...

In economic terms, the question of whether debt reduction should be a higher priority than tax cuts or spending increases is an easy call. Most economists agree that paying down the national debt is the surest way to spur more savings and investment, create more jobs, improve productivity and generally enable the economy to grow faster. ...

Essence of the Story

■ The federal budget is in surplus, but the federal government has a large debt.

■ The debt held by the public was $3.7 trillion or 45 percent of GDP in January 1999.

■ The national debt was built up over decades of deficit spending, and it is a large economic millstone.

■ Most economists agree that decreasing the national debt will increase saving and investment, create jobs, increase productivity, and increase the economic growth rate.

■ But politically, it is difficult to achieve a sustained commitment to deficit reduction.

■ To increase the pace at which we pay down the national debt, the government must either increase taxes or cut purchases of goods and services.

■ The short-run effects of paying down the debt work in the opposite direction to the long-run effects.

■ Figure 1 shows the short-run effects. Initially, the aggregate planned expenditure curve is AE_0. Equilibrium expenditure and real GDP are $7.6 trillion, where the AE curve intersects the 45° line. Potential GDP is also $7.6 trillion (an assumption).

■ Now the federal government decides to step up the pace at which it pays down the debt. It raises taxes and cuts its purchases of goods and services. The AE curve shifts downward to AE_1. Real GDP decreases, and the economy moves to below full employment.

■ The outcome in Fig. 1 is temporary. The price level rises less quickly, the real interest rate falls, and the economy returns to full employment.

■ With a lower real interest rate, investment increases and economic growth increases.

■ Figure 2 shows the long-run effect after 10 years—in 2009—if the economic growth rate increases from 3 percent a year to 4 percent a year.

■ With growth at 3 percent a year, potential GDP increases to $10.2 trillion by 2009. With growth at 4 percent a year, potential GDP increases to $11.2 trillion by 2009.

■ To be at full employment in 2009, aggregate expenditure must be AE_0 if potential GDP is $10.2 trillion and AE_1 if potential GDP is $11.2 trillion.

■ The level of investment is greater on AE_1 than on AE_0 and it is this fact that enables the economy to expand more rapidly and achieve the greater level of potential GDP.

■ The effect of the deficit on growth is probably small. Economists are not as much in agreement on the relationship between the deficit and growth as the news article suggests. And most economists do not think the debt is a millstone.

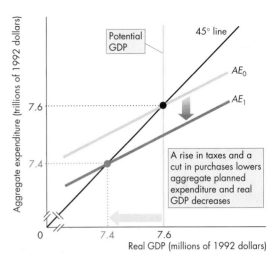

Figure 1 The short-run effect of paying down the debt

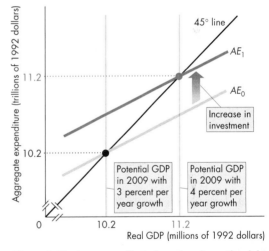

Figure 2 The long-run effect of paying down the debt

■ Do you think that the debt should be paid down faster than the government plans? Why or why not?

■ Do you think that the debt should be paid down more slowly than the government plans? Why or why not?

■ Do you think that the debt should be paid down with a greater emphasis on tax increases than on spending cuts? Why or why not?

MATHEMATICAL NOTE
The Algebra of the Fiscal Policy Multipliers

THIS MATHEMATICAL NOTE DERIVES FORMULAS FOR the fiscal policy multipliers. We begin by defining the symbols we need:

- Aggregate planned expenditure, AE
- Real GDP, Y
- Consumption expenditure, C
- Investment, I
- Government purchases, G
- Exports, X
- Imports, M
- Net taxes, T
- Autonomous consumption expenditure, a
- Lump-sum taxes, T_a
- Lump-sum transfer payments, T_r
- Marginal propensity to consume, b
- Marginal propensity to import, m
- Marginal tax rate, t
- Autonomous expenditure, A

Equilibrium Expenditure

Aggregate planned expenditure is

$$AE = C + I + G + X - M.$$

The consumption function is

$$C = a + b(Y - T).$$

Net taxes equals lump-sum taxes minus lump-sum transfer payments plus induced taxes, which is

$$T = T_a - T_r + tY.$$

Use the last equation in the consumption function to give consumption expenditure as a function of GDP

$$C = a - bT_a + bT_r + b(1 - t)Y.$$

The import function is

$$M = mY.$$

Use the consumption function and the import function to replace C and M in the aggregate planned expenditure equation to obtain

$$AE = a - bT_a + bT_r + b(1 - t)Y + I + G + X - mY.$$

Collect the terms on the right side of the equation that involve Y to obtain

$$AE = [a - bT_a + bT_r + I + G + X] + [b(1 - t) - m]Y.$$

Autonomous expenditure (A) is given by

$$A = a - bT_a + bT_r + I + G + X,$$

so

$$AE = A + [b(1 - t) - m]Y.$$

Equilibrium expenditure occurs when aggregate planned expenditure (AE) equals real GDP (Y). That is,

$$AE = Y.$$

To calculate equilibrium expenditure, we solve the equation

$$Y = A + [b(1 - t) - m]Y$$

to obtain

$$Y = \frac{1}{1 - [b(1 - t) - m]}A.$$

Government Purchases Multiplier

The government purchases multiplier equals the change in equilibrium expenditure (Y) that results from a change in government purchases (G) divided by the change in government purchases. Because autonomous expenditure is equal to

$$A = a - bT_a + bT_r + I + G + X,$$

the change in government purchases changes autonomous expenditure such that

$$\Delta A = \Delta G.$$

The government purchases multiplier is found by working out the change in Y that results from the change in A. You can see from the solution for Y that

$$\Delta Y = \frac{1}{1 - [b(1 - t) - m]}\Delta G.$$

The government purchases multiplier equals

$$\frac{1}{1 - [b(1 - t) - m]}.$$

In an economy in which $t = 0$ and $m = 0$, the government purchases multiplier is $1/(1 - b)$. With $b = 0.75$, the government purchases multiplier equals 4, as part (a) of the figure shows. Make up some examples and use the above formula to show how b, m, and t influence the government purchases multiplier.

Lump-Sum Taxes Multiplier

The lump-sum taxes multiplier equals the change in equilibrium expenditure (Y) that results from a change in lump-sum taxes (T_a) divided by the change in lump-sum taxes. Because autonomous expenditure is equal to

$$A = a - b T_a + b T_r + I + G + X,$$

the change in lump-sum taxes changes autonomous expenditure such that

$$\Delta A = -b \Delta T_a.$$

You can see from the solution for equilibrium expenditure Y that

$$\Delta Y = \frac{-b}{1 - [b(1 - t) - m]} \Delta T_a.$$

The lump-sum taxes multiplier equals

$$\frac{-b}{1 - [b(1 - t) - m]}.$$

In an economy in which $t = 0$ and $m = 0$, the lump-sum taxes multiplier is $-b/(1 - b)$. With $b = 0.75$, the lump-sum tax multiplier equals -3, as part (b) of the

figure shows. Make up some examples and use the above formula to show how b, m, and t influence the lump-sum tax multiplier.

Lump-Sum Transfer Payments Multiplier

The lump-sum transfer payments multiplier equals the change in equilibrium expenditure (Y) that results from a change in lump-sum transfer payments (T_r) divided by the change in lump-sum transfer payments. Because autonomous expenditure is equal to

$$A = a - b T_a + b T_r + I + G + X,$$

the change in lump-sum transfer payments changes autonomous expenditure such that

$$\Delta A = b \Delta T_r.$$

This amount equals minus the change in autonomous expenditures when $\Delta T_a = \Delta T_r$. So the lump-sum transfer payments multiplier equals minus the lump-sum taxes multiplier. The lump-sum transfer payments multiplier equals

$$\frac{b}{1 - [b(1 - t) - m]}.$$

In an economy in which $t = 0$ and $m = 0$, the lump-sum transfer payments multiplier is $b/(1 - b)$. With $b = 0.75$, the lump-sum transfer payments multiplier equals 3, as part (c) of the figure shows. Make up some examples and use the above formula to show how b, m, and t influence the lump-sum transfer payments multiplier.

(a) Government purchases multiplier

(b) Lump-sum tax multiplier

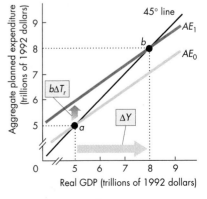

(c) Lump-sum transfer payments multiplier

SUMMARY

KEY POINTS

The Federal Budget (pp. 662–667)

- The federal budget finances the activities of the government and is used to stabilize real GDP.
- Federal tax revenues come from personal income taxes, social insurance taxes, corporate income taxes, and indirect taxes. Federal expenditures include transfer payments, purchases of goods and services, and debt interest.
- When tax revenues exceed government expenditures, the government has a budget surplus.

Fiscal Policy Multipliers (pp. 668–674)

- Fiscal policy actions are discretionary or automatic.
- The government purchases multiplier equals $1/(1 - MPC)$. The lump-sum tax multiplier equals $-MPC/(1 - MPC)$. The transfer payments multiplier is equal in magnitude to the lump-sum tax multiplier but is positive.
- Income taxes and entitlement payments bring fluctuations in tax revenues and transfer payments over the business cycle and act as automatic stabilizers.

Fiscal Policy Multipliers and the Price Level (pp. 674–677)

- An expansionary fiscal policy increases aggregate demand and shifts the aggregate demand curve rightward. It increases real GDP and raises the price level. (A contractionary fiscal policy has the opposite effects.)
- Price level changes dampen fiscal policy multiplier effects.
- At potential GDP, an expansionary fiscal policy raises the price level and in the long run leaves real GDP unchanged. The fiscal policy multipliers in the long run are zero.

Fiscal Policy and Aggregate Supply (pp. 677–679)

- Fiscal policy has supply-side effects because the increases in taxes weaken the incentives to work, save, and invest.
- A tax cut increases both aggregate demand and aggregate supply. It increases real GDP but has an ambiguous effect on the price level.

KEY FIGURES

KEY TERMS

PROBLEMS

*1. In the economy of Zap, the marginal propensity to consume is 0.9. Investment is $50 billion, government purchases of goods and services are $40 billion, and lump-sum taxes are $40 billion. Zap has no exports and no imports.
   a. The government cuts its purchases of goods and services to $30 billion. What is the change in equilibrium expenditure?
   b. What is the value of the government purchases multiplier?
   c. The government continues to purchase $40 billion worth of goods and services and cuts lump-sum taxes to $30 billion. What is the change in equilibrium expenditure?
   d. What is the value of the tax multiplier?
   e. The government simultaneously cuts both its purchases of goods and services and taxes to $30 billion. What is the change in equilibrium expenditure? Why does equilibrium expenditure decrease?

2. In the economy of Zip, the marginal propensity to consume is 0.8. Investment is $60 billion, government purchases of goods and services are $50 billion, and lump-sum taxes are $60 billion. Zip has no exports and no imports.
   a. The government increases its purchases of goods and services to $60 billion. What is the change in equilibrium expenditure?
   b. What is the value of the government purchases multiplier?
   c. The government continues to purchase $60 billion worth of goods and services and increases lump-sum taxes to $70 billion. What is the change in equilibrium expenditure?
   d. What is the value of the tax multiplier?
   e. The government simultaneously increases its purchases of goods and services and taxes by $10 billion. What is the change in equilibrium expenditure? Why does equilibrium expenditure increase?

*3. Suppose that the price level in the economy of Zap, as described in problem 1, is 100. The economy is also at full employment.
   a. If the government of Zap increases its purchases of goods and services by $10 billion, what happens to the quantity of real GDP demanded?
   b. How does Zap's aggregate demand curve change? Draw a two-part diagram that is similar to Fig. 30.10 to illustrate the change in both the *AE* curve and the *AD* curve.
   c. In the short run, does equilibrium real GDP increase by more than, less than, or the same amount as the increase in the quantity of real GDP demanded?
   d. In the long run, does equilibrium real GDP increase by more than, less than, or the same amount as the increase in the quantity of real GDP demanded?
   e. In the short run, does the price level in Zap rise, fall, or remain unchanged?
   f. In the long run, does the price level in Zap rise, fall, or remain unchanged?

4. Suppose that the price level in the economy of Zip, as described in problem 1, is 100. The economy is also at full employment.
   a. If the government of Zip decreases its purchases of goods and services by $5 billion, what happens to the quantity of real GDP demanded?
   b. How does Zip's aggregate demand curve change? Draw a two-part diagram that is similar to Fig. 30.10 to illustrate the change in both the *AE* curve and the *AD* curve.
   c. In the short run, does equilibrium real GDP decrease by more than, less than, or the same amount as the increase in the quantity of real GDP demanded?
   d. In the short run, does the price level in Zip rise, fall, or remain unchanged?
   e. Why does real GDP in the short term decrease by a smaller amount than the decrease in aggregate demand?

*5. The figure shows expenditures and tax revenues of the government of Dreamland. Potential GDP is $40 million.

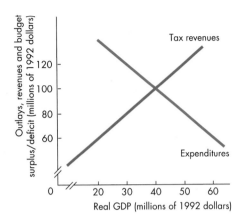

a. What is the government's budget balance if real GDP is $40 million?
b. Does Dreamland have a structural surplus or deficit if its real GDP is $40 million? What is its size? Explain why.
c. What is the government's budget balance if real GDP is $30 million?
d. If Dreamland's real GDP is $30 million, does Dreamland have a structural surplus or deficit? What is its size? Explain why.
e. If Dreamland's real GDP is $50 million, does Dreamland have a structural surplus or deficit? What is its size? Explain why.

6. In problem 5, if Dreamland's real GDP is $50 million,
a. What is the government's budget balance?
b. Does Dreamland have a structural surplus? What is its size? Explain why.
c. What is the government's budget balance if potential GDP is $30 million?
d. If Dreamland's potential GDP is $30 million, does Dreamland have a structural surplus or deficit? What is its size? Explain why.
e. What would Dreamland's real GDP have to be for it to have neither a structural deficit/surplus nor a cyclical deficit/surplus if its potential GDP is $40 million.

CRITICAL THINKING

 1 Study *Reading Between the Lines* on pp. 680–681 and then:
a. Explain the short-run effects of paying down the national debt at a more rapid pace.
b. Explain the long-run effects of paying down the national debt at a more rapid pace.
c. Use the link on the Parkin Web site to obtain data on the federal government's more recent budget and compare the projected deficit with the projection one year earlier. Do the data support or reject the views of John Cogan reported in the news article?
d. Use the link on the Parkin Web site to obtain data on the federal government's debt and economic growth. Do the data support or reject the view that is attributed to "most economists" in the news article: That the debt is a millstone and cutting it will speed economic growth?

2. Thinking about the supply-side effects of tax cuts:
a. What would be the main effects of lower income tax rates on the level of potential GDP?
b. How would lower income taxes influence the real wage rate and the real interest rate?
c. What are the main costs of lower income taxes?

 3. Use the links of the Parkin Web site to visit the National Center for Policy Analysis Idea House and study any two flat tax plans that are described there. When you have studied these plans, answer the following questions:
a. What are the main features of the two plans?
b. What do you predict would be the main effects of each proposal?
c. Which proposal appeals most to you and why?

 4. Use the link on the Parkin Web site to obtain data on the amounts of government expenditure in the main industrial countries. Then use the fiscal policy multiplier analysis that you've learned about in this chapter to predict which countries have strong automatic stabilizers and which have a weak one. Explain the reasons for your predictions.

Chapter 31

Money

Money, like fire and the wheel, has been around for a very long time. An incredible array of items have served as money. Wampum (beads made from shells) was used by North American Indians, whale's teeth were used by Fijians, and tobacco was used by early American colonists. Cakes of salt served as money in Ethiopia and Tibet. Today, when we want to buy something, we use coins or bills, write a check, or present a credit card. Tomorrow, we'll use a "smart card" that keeps track of spending and that our pocket computer can read. Are all these things money? ◆ When we deposit some coins or notes into a bank, is that still money? And what happens when the bank lends the money in our deposit account to someone else? How can we get our money back if it's been lent out? Does lending by banks create money—out of thin air? ◆ In the 1970s, you had either a savings deposit that earned interest or a checking deposit that did not. Today, there are accounts that provide the convenience of a checking deposit and the income of a savings deposit. Why were these new kinds of bank deposits introduced? ◆ During the 1970s, the quantity of money in the United States increased quickly, but during the 1980s and 1990s, it increased at a slower pace. In Russia and in some Latin American countries, the quantity of money increased at an extremely rapid pace during the early 1990s, but the pace has slowed in recent years. Does the rate of increase in the quantity of money matter? What are the effects of an increasing quantity of money on our economy?

Money Makes the World Go Around

◇ In this chapter, we'll study that useful invention: money. We'll look at its functions and the way it is measured in the United States today. We'll explain how banks and other financial institutions create money. Finally, we'll examine the effects of money on the economy.

After studying this chapter, you will be able to:

- **Define money and describe its functions**
- **Explain the economic functions of banks and other financial institutions**
- **Describe the financial innovations of the 1980s and 1990s**
- **Explain how banks create money**
- **Explain why the quantity of money is an important economic magnitude**
- **Explain the quantity theory of money**

What Is Money?

WHAT DO WAMPUM, TOBACCO, AND NICKELS AND dimes have in common? Why are they all examples of money? To answer these questions, we need a definition of money. **Money** is any commodity or token that is generally acceptable as the means of payment. A **means of payment** is a method of settling a debt. When a payment has been made, there is no remaining obligation between the parties to a transaction. So what wampum, tobacco, and nickels and dimes have in common is that they have served (or still do serve) as the means of payment. But money has three other functions:

- Medium of exchange
- Unit of account
- Store of value

Medium of Exchange

A *medium of exchange* is an object that is generally accepted in exchange for goods and services. Money acts as such a medium. Without money, it would be necessary to exchange goods and services directly for other goods and services—an exchange called **barter**. For example, if you want to buy a hamburger, you offer the paperback novel you've just finished reading in exchange for it. Barter requires a *double coincidence of wants*, a situation that occurs when Erika wants to buy what Kazia wants to sell and Kazia wants to buy what Erika wants to sell. To get your hamburger, you must find someone who's selling hamburgers and who wants your paperback novel. Money guarantees that there is a double coincidence of wants because people with something to sell will always accept money in exchange for it. Money acts as a lubricant that smoothes the mechanism of exchange.

Unit of Account

A *unit of account* is an agreed measure for stating the prices of goods and services. To get the most out of your budget, you have to figure out whether seeing one more movie is worth its opportunity cost. But that cost is not dollars and cents. It is the number of ice-cream cones, sodas, and cups of coffee that you must give up. It's easy to do such calculations when

all these goods have prices in terms of dollars and cents (see Table 31.1). If a movie costs $6 and a six-pack of soda costs $3, you know right away that seeing one movie costs you 2 six-packs of soda. If jelly beans are 50¢ a pack, a movie costs 12 packs of jelly beans. You need only one calculation to figure out the opportunity cost of any pair of goods and services.

But imagine how troublesome it would be if your local movie theater posted its price as 2 six-packs of soda, and if the convenience store posted the price of a six-pack of soda as 2 ice-cream cones, and if the ice-cream shop posted the price of a cone as 3 packs of jelly beans, and if the candy store priced a pack of jelly beans as 2 cups of coffee! Now how much running around and calculating do you have to do to figure out how much that movie is going to cost you

---

TABLE 31.1

The Unit of Account Function of Money Simplifies Price Comparisons

Good	Price in money units	Price in units of another good
Movie	$6.00 each	2 six-packs of soda
Soda	$3.00 per six-pack	2 ice-cream cones
Ice cream	$1.50 per cone	3 packs of jelly beans
Jelly beans	$0.50 per pack	2 cups of coffee
Coffee	$0.25 per cup	1 local phone call

Money as a unit of account: The price of a movie is $6 and the price of a cup of coffee is 25¢, so the opportunity cost of a movie is 24 cups of coffee ($6.00 ÷ 25¢ = 24).

No unit of account: You go to a movie theater and learn that the price of a movie is 2 six-packs of soda. You go to a candy store and learn that a pack of jelly beans costs 2 cups of coffee. But how many cups of coffee does seeing a movie cost you? To answer that question, you go to the convenience store and find that a six-pack of soda costs 2 ice-cream cones. Now you head for the ice-cream shop, where an ice-cream cone costs 3 packs of jelly beans. Now you get out your pocket calculator: 1 movie costs 2 six-packs of soda, or 4 ice-cream cones, or 12 packs of jelly beans, or 24 cups of coffee!

in terms of the soda, ice cream, jelly beans, or coffee that you must give up to see it? You get the answer for soda right away from the sign posted on the movie theater. But for all the other goods, you're going to have to visit many different stores to establish the price of each commodity in terms of another and then calculate prices in units that are relevant for your own decision. Cover up the column labeled "price in money units" in Table 31.1 and see how hard it is to figure out the number of local phone calls it costs to see one movie. It's enough to make a person swear off movies! How much simpler it is if all the prices are expressed in dollars and cents.

Store of Value

Any commodity or token that can be held and exchanged later for goods and services is called a *store of value*. Money acts as a store of value. If it did not, it would not be acceptable in exchange for goods and services. The more stable the value of a commodity or token, the better it can act as a store of value, and the more useful it is as money. No store of value is completely safe. The value of a physical object, such as a house, a car, or a work of art, fluctuates over time. The value of commodities and tokens used as money also fluctuate, and when there is inflation, they persistently fall in value.

Money in the United States Today

In the United States today, money consists of:

- Currency
- Deposits at banks and other financial institutions

Currency The bills and coins that we use in the United States today are known as **currency**. Bills are money because the government declares them so with the words "This note is legal tender for all debts, public and private." You can see these words on every dollar bill.

Deposits Deposits at banks and other financial institutions such as savings and loan associations (S&Ls) are also money. Deposits are money because they can be converted into currency and because they are used to settle debts.

Official Measures of Money The two main official measures of money in the United States today are known as M1 and M2. Figure 31.1 shows the items that make up these two measures. **M1** consists of currency and traveler's checks plus checking deposits owned by individuals and businesses. M1 does *not* include currency held by banks, and it does not include currency and checking deposits owned by the U.S. government. **M2** consists of M1 plus savings deposits, time deposits, money market mutual funds, and other deposits. (There is a third official measure of money, M3, which consists of M2 plus large-scale time deposits and term deposits.)

FIGURE 31.1
Two Measures of Money

	$ billions in 1998
M2	4,194
Money market mutual funds and other deposits	681
Time deposits	953
Savings deposits	1,485
M1	1,075
Checking deposits	629
Currency and traveler's checks	446

M1
- Currency held outside banks and traveler's checks
- Checking deposits at commercial banks, S&Ls, savings banks, and credit unions

M2
- M1
- Savings deposits
- Time deposits
- Money market mutual funds and other deposits

Source: Economic Report of the President, 1999.

Are M1 and M2 Really Money? Money is the means of payment. So the test of whether an asset is money is whether it serves as a means of payment. Currency passes the test. But what about deposits? Checking deposits are money because they can be transferred from one person to another by writing a check. Such a transfer of ownership is equivalent to handing over currency. Because M1 consists of currency plus checking deposits and each of these is a means of payment, *M1 is money.*

But what about M2? Some of the savings deposits in M2 are just as much a means of payment as the checking deposits in M1. You can use the ATM at the grocery store checkout or gas station and transfer funds directly from your saving account to pay for your purchase. But other saving deposits are not means of payment. These deposits are known as *liquid assets.* **Liquidity** is the property of being instantly convertible into a means of payment with little loss in value. Because most of the deposits in M2 are quickly and easily converted into currency or checking deposits, they are operationally similar to M1, but they are not means of payment.

Deposits Are Money but Checks Are Not In defining money, we include, along with currency, deposits at banks and other financial institutions. But we do not count the checks that people write as money. Why are deposits money and checks not?

To see why deposits are money but checks are not, think about what happens when Colleen buys some roller blades for $200 from Rocky's Rollers. When Colleen goes to Rocky's shop, she has $500 in her deposit account at the Laser Bank. Rocky has $1,000 in his deposit account—at the same bank, as it happens. The total deposits of these two people is $1,500. Colleen writes a check for $200. Rocky takes the check to the bank right away and deposits it. Rocky's bank balance rises from $1,000 to $1,200, and Colleen's balance falls from $500 to $300. The total deposits of Colleen and Rocky are still the same as before: $1,500. Rocky now has $200 more, and Colleen has $200 less than before.

This transaction has transferred money from Colleen to Rocky. The check itself was never money. There wasn't an extra $200 worth of money while the check was in circulation. The check instructs the bank to transfer money from Colleen to Rocky.

In the example, Colleen and Rocky use the same bank. The same story, but with additional steps, describes what happens if Colleen and Rocky use different banks. Rocky's bank credits the check to Rocky's account and then takes the check to a check-clearing center. The check is then sent to Colleen's bank, which pays Rocky's bank $200 and then debits Colleen's account $200. This process can take a few days, but the principles are the same as when two people use the same bank.

Credit Cards Are Not Money So checks are not money. But what about credit cards? Isn't having a credit card in your wallet and presenting the card to pay for your roller blades the same thing as using money? Why aren't credit cards somehow valued and counted as part of the quantity of money?

When you pay by check, you are frequently asked to prove your identity by showing your driver's license. It would never occur to you to think of your driver's license as money. It's just an ID card. A credit card is also an ID card but one that lets you take a loan at the instant you buy something. When you sign a credit card sales slip, you are saying, "I agree to pay for these goods when the credit card company bills me." Once you get your statement from the credit card company, you must make the minimum payment due (or clear your balance). To make that payment, you need money—you need to have currency or a checking deposit to pay the credit card company. So although you use a credit card when you buy something, the credit card is not the *means of payment*, and it is not money.

REVIEW QUIZ

- What makes something money? What functions does money perform? Why do you think packets of chewing gum don't serve as money?
- What are the problems that arise when a commodity is used as money?
- What are the main components of money in the United States today?
- What are the official measures of money? Are all the measures really money?
- Why are checks and credit cards not money?

We've seen that the main component of money in the United States is deposits at banks and other financial institutions. Let's take a closer look at these institutions.

Financial Intermediaries

A FIRM THAT TAKES DEPOSITS FROM HOUSEHOLDS and firms and makes loans to other households and firms is called a **financial intermediary**. The deposits of three types of financial intermediaries make up the nation's money:

- Commercial banks
- Thrift institutions
- Money market mutual funds

Commercial Banks

A **commercial bank** is a firm, licensed by the Comptroller of the Currency (in the U.S. Treasury) or by a state agency to receive deposits and make loans. Close to 13,000 commercial banks operate in the United States today. A commercial bank's business is summarized in its balance sheet.

A bank's *balance sheet* lists its assets, liabilities, and net worth. *Assets* are what the bank *owns*, *liabilities* are what the bank *owes*, and *net worth*, which is equal to assets minus liabilities, is the value of the bank to its stockholders—its owners. A bank's balance sheet is described by the equation

Assets = Liabilities + Net worth.

Among a bank's liabilities are the deposits that are part of the nation's money. Your deposit at the bank is a liability to your bank (and an asset to you) because the bank must repay your deposit (and sometimes the interest on it, too) whenever you decide to take your money out of the bank.

Profit and Prudence: A Balancing Act   The aim of a bank is to maximize the net worth of its stockholders. To achieve this objective, the interest rate at which a bank lends exceeds the interest rate at which it borrows. But a bank must perform a delicate balancing act. Lending is risky, and the more deposits a bank ties up in high-risk, high-interest rate loans, the bigger is its chance of not being able to repay its depositors. And if depositors perceive a high risk of not being repaid, they withdraw their funds and create a crisis for the bank. So a bank must be prudent in the way it uses its deposits, balancing security for the depositors against profit for its stockholders.

Reserves and Loans   To achieve security for its depositors, a bank divides its funds into two parts: reserves and loans. **Reserves** are cash in a bank's vault plus its deposits at Federal Reserve banks. (We'll study the Federal Reserve banks in Chapter 32.) The cash in a bank's vaults is a reserve to meet its depositor's demand for currency. It keeps the ATM replenished every time you and your friends have raided it for cash for a midnight pizza. The account of a bank at the Federal Reserve is similar to your own bank account. Commercial banks use these accounts to receive and make payments. A commercial bank deposits cash into or draws cash out of its account at the Federal Reserve and writes checks on that account to settle debts with other banks.

If a bank kept all its deposits as reserves, it wouldn't make any profit. In fact, it keeps only a small fraction of its funds in reserves and lends the rest. A bank has three types of assets. They are as follows:

1. *Liquid assets* are U.S. government Treasury bills and commercial bills. These assets are the banks' first line of defense if they need cash. They can be sold and instantly converted into cash with virtually no risk of loss. Because liquid assets are virtually risk free, they have a low interest rate.

2. *Investment securities* are longer-term U.S. government bonds and other bonds. These assets can be sold quickly and converted into cash but at prices that fluctuate. Because their prices fluctuate, these assets are riskier than liquid assets, but they also have a higher interest rate.

3. *Loans* are commitments of fixed amounts of money for agreed-upon periods of time. Most banks' loans are made to corporations to finance the purchase of capital equipment and inventories and to households—personal loans—to finance consumer durable goods, such as cars or boats. The outstanding balances on credit card accounts are also bank loans. Loans are the riskiest assets of a bank because they cannot be converted into cash until they are due to be repaid. And some borrowers default and never repay. Because they are the riskiest of a bank's assets, they also carry the highest interest rate.

Commercial bank deposits are one component of the nation's money. But thrift institutions and money market mutual funds also take deposits that form part—an increasing part—of the nation's money. We'll now describe the other institutions whose deposits form part of the nation's money.

Thrift Institutions

The **thrift institutions** are:

- Savings and loan associations
- Savings banks
- Credit unions

Savings and Loan Associations   A **savings and loan association** (S&L) is a financial intermediary that receives checking deposits and savings deposits and that makes personal, commercial, and home-purchase loans.

Savings Banks   A **savings bank** is a financial intermediary that accepts savings deposits and makes mostly mortgage loans. Some savings banks (called *mutual* savings banks) are owned by their depositors.

Credit Unions   A **credit union** is a financial intermediary owned by a social or economic group, such as a firm's employees, that accepts savings deposits and makes mostly consumer loans.

Money Market Mutual Funds

A **money market mutual fund** is a financial institution that obtains funds by selling shares and uses these funds to buy liquid assets such as U.S. Treasury bills. Money market mutual fund shares act like bank deposits. Shareholders can write checks on their money market mutual fund accounts. But there are restrictions on most of these accounts. For example, the minimum deposit accepted might be $2,500, and the smallest check a depositor is permitted to write might be $500.

The Economic Functions of Financial Intermediaries

All financial intermediaries make a profit from the spread between the interest rate they pay on deposits and the interest rate at which they lend. Why can financial intermediaries get deposits at a low interest rate and lend at a higher one? What services do they perform that make their depositors willing to put up with a low interest rate and their borrowers willing to pay a higher one?

Financial intermediaries provide four main services that people are willing to pay for:

- Creating liquidity
- Minimizing the cost of obtaining funds
- Minimizing the cost of monitoring borrowers
- Pooling risk

Creating Liquidity   Financial intermediaries create liquidity. *Liquid* assets are those that are easily and with certainty convertible into money. Some of the liabilities of financial intermediaries are themselves money; others are highly liquid assets that are easily converted into money.

Financial intermediaries create liquidity by borrowing short and lending long. Borrowing short means taking deposits but standing ready to repay them on short notice (and on even no notice in the case of checking deposits). Lending long means making loan commitments for a prearranged, and often quite long, period of time. For example, when a person makes a deposit with a savings and loan association, that deposit can be withdrawn at any time. But the S&L makes a lending commitment for perhaps more than 20 years to a homebuyer.

Minimizing the Cost of Borrowing   Finding someone from whom to borrow can be a costly business. Imagine how troublesome it would be if there were no financial intermediaries. A firm that was looking for $1 million to buy a new production plant would probably have to hunt around for several dozen people from whom to borrow in order to acquire enough funds for its capital project. Financial intermediaries lower those costs. The firm needing $1 million can go to a single financial intermediary to obtain those funds. The financial intermediary has to borrow from a large number of people, but it's not doing that just for this one firm and the million dollars it wants to borrow. The financial intermediary can establish an organization that is capable of raising funds from a large number of depositors and can spread the cost of this activity over a large number of borrowers.

Minimizing the Cost of Monitoring Borrowers   Lending money is a risky business. There's always a danger that the borrower might not repay. Most of the money lent gets used by firms to invest in projects that they hope will return a profit. But sometimes those hopes are not fulfilled. Checking up on the activities of a borrower and ensuring that the best possible decisions are being made for making a profit and avoiding a loss are costly and specialized activities. Imagine how costly it would be if each household that lent money to a firm had to incur the costs of monitoring that firm directly. By depositing funds with a financial intermediary, households avoid those costs. The financial intermediary performs the monitoring activity by using specialized resources that have a much lower cost than what each household would incur if it had to undertake the activity individually.

Pooling Risk   As we noted above, lending money is risky. There is always a chance of not being repaid—of default. Lending to a large number of different individuals can reduce the risk of default. In such a situation, if one person defaults on a loan, it is a nuisance but not a disaster. In contrast, if only one person borrows and that person defaults on the loan, the entire loan is a write-off. Financial intermediaries enable people to pool risk in an efficient way. Thousands of people lend money to any one financial intermediary, and, in turn, the financial intermediary re-lends the money to hundreds, perhaps thousands, of individual firms. If any one firm defaults on its loan, that default is spread across all the depositors with the intermediary, and no individual depositor is left exposed to a high degree of risk.

REVIEW QUIZ

- What are the functions of commercial banks, savings and loan associations, savings banks and credit unions, and money market mutual funds? What functions do they have in common and how do they differ from each other?
- What is liquidity and how do financial intermediaries create it?
- How do financial intermediaries lower the cost of borrowing and lending and of monitoring borrowers?
- How do financial intermediaries pool risks?

We are interested in banks and other financial intermediaries because they create money. But these firms are highly regulated, and this regulation limits their ability to create money. So next, we'll examine these regulations. We'll also look at the deregulation and innovation that have occurred in the financial sector during the past 20 years.

Financial Regulation, Deregulation, and Innovation

FINANCIAL INTERMEDIARIES ARE HIGHLY REGULATED institutions. But regulation is not static, and in the 1980s, some important changes in their regulation as well as deregulation took place. Also, the institutions are not static. In their pursuit of profit, they constantly seek lower-cost ways of obtaining funds, monitoring borrowers, pooling risk, and creating liquidity. They also are inventive in seeking ways to avoid the costs imposed on them by financial regulation. Let's look at regulation, deregulation, and innovation in the financial sector in recent years.

Financial Regulation

Financial intermediaries face two types of regulation:
- Deposit insurance
- Balance sheet rules

Deposit Insurance   The deposits of most financial intermediaries are insured by the Federal Deposit Insurance Corporation (FDIC). The FDIC is a federal agency that receives its income from compulsory insurance premiums paid by commercial banks and other financial intermediaries. The FDIC operates two separate insurance funds: the Bank Insurance Fund (BIF), which insures deposits in commercial banks, and the Saving Association Insurance Fund (SAIF), which insures the deposits of S&Ls, savings banks, and credit unions. Each of these funds insures deposits of up to $100,000.

The existence of deposit insurance provides protection for depositors in the event that a financial intermediary fails. But it also limits the incentive for the owner of a financial intermediary to make safe investments and loans. Some economists believe that deposit insurance played an important role in creating a crisis for S&Ls during the 1980s. Depositors did not worry about risk because their deposits were insured. The S&L owners made high-risk loans because they knew they were making a one-way bet. If their loans paid off, they made a high rate of return. If they failed and could not meet their obligations to the depositors, the insurance fund would step in. Bad loans were good business!

Because of this type of problem, all financial intermediaries face regulation of their balance sheets.

Balance Sheet Rules The most important balance sheet regulations are:

- Capital requirements
- Reserve requirements
- Deposit rules
- Lending rules

Capital requirements are the minimum amount of an owner's own financial resources that must be put into an intermediary. This amount must be sufficiently large to discourage owners from making loans that are too risky.

Reserve requirements are rules setting out the minimum percentages of deposits that must be held in currency or other safe, liquid assets. These minimum percentages vary across the different types of intermediaries and deposits; they are largest for checking deposits and smallest for long-term savings deposits.

Deposit rules are restrictions on the different types of deposits that an intermediary can accept. These are the rules that historically have created the sharpest distinctions between the various institutions. For example, in the past, commercial banks provided checking accounts while other institutions provided only savings accounts.

Lending rules are restrictions on the proportions of different types of loans that an intermediary may make. Like deposit rules, these rules also helped to create sharp distinctions between the various institutions. Before 1980, commercial banks were the only intermediaries that were permitted to make commercial loans, and S&Ls and savings banks were restricted to making mostly mortgage loans to home buyers.

Deregulation in the 1980s

In 1980, Congress passed the Depository Institutions' Deregulation and Monetary Control Act (DIDMCA). The DIDMCA removed many of the distinctions between commercial banks and other financial intermediaries. It permitted nonbank financial intermediaries to compete with commercial banks in a wider range of lending business. At the same time, it permitted the payment of interest on checking deposits so that NOW accounts and ATS accounts could be offered by all deposit-taking institutions—

banks and nonbanks.[1] It also extended the powers of the Federal Reserve to place reserve requirements on *all* depository institutions. Despite the general direction of deregulation, this move brought a greater measure of central control over the financial system than had previously existed and represented a strengthening of the Fed's control.

The ability of S&Ls and savings banks to compete for lending business with commercial banks was further strengthened in 1982 with the passage of the Garn–St. Germain Depository Institutions Act. This legislation further eased restrictions on the scale of commercial lending that S&Ls and savings banks could undertake.

Deregulation in the 1990s

The most significant deregulation during the 1990s is the Riegle–Neal Interstate Banking and Branching Efficiency Act of 1994. This law permits U.S. banks for the first time to establish branches in any state.

Large changes have occurred in the structure of the banking industry because of this new law. The most visible are the wave of mergers of large banks and the appearance on the American banking scene of some major international banks. These changes will make the U.S. banking industry more efficient.

Financial Innovation

The development of new financial products—of new ways of borrowing and lending—is called **financial innovation**. The aim of financial innovation is to lower the cost of deposits or to increase the return from lending or, more simply, to increase the profit from financial intermediation. There are three main influences on financial innovation:

- Economic environment
- Technology
- Regulation

The pace of financial innovation was remarkable during the 1980s and 1990s, and all three of these forces played a role.

---

[1] A NOW account is a Negotiable Order of Withdrawal account; "negotiable order of withdrawal" is another name for a check. An ATS account is an Automatic-Transfer Savings account—a savings account that is linked to a checking account. Funds are automatically transferred between the two accounts.

Economic Environment   Some of the innovation was a response to high inflation and high interest rates of the late 1970s and early 1980s. An important example is the development of variable interest rate mortgages. Traditionally, house purchases have been financed by mortgage loans at a guaranteed interest rate. Rising interest rates brought rising borrowing costs for S&Ls, and because they were committed to fixed interest rates on their mortgages, the industry incurred severe losses. The creation of variable interest rate mortgages has taken some of the risk out of long-term lending for house purchases.

Technology   Other financial innovations resulted from technological change, most notably that associated with the decreased cost of computing and long-distance communication. The spread in the use of credit cards and the development of international financial markets—for example, the increased importance of Eurodollars—are consequences of technological change.[2]

Regulation   A good deal of financial innovation takes place to avoid regulation. For example, Regulation Q, which prevented banks from paying interest on checking deposits, gave the impetus to devising new types of deposits on which checks could be written and interest paid, thereby getting around the regulation.

Deregulation, Innovation, and Money

Deregulation and financial innovation that have led to the development of new types of deposit accounts have brought important changes in the composition of the nation's money. In 1960, M1 consisted of only currency and checking deposits at commercial banks. In the 1990s, other new types of checking deposits have expanded while traditional checking deposits have declined. Similar changes have taken place in the composition of M2. Savings deposits have declined, while time deposits and money market mutual funds have expanded.

---

[2]Eurodollars are U.S. dollar bank accounts held in other countries, mainly in Europe. They were "invented" during the 1960s when the Soviet Union wanted the security and convenience of holding funds in U.S. dollars but were unwilling to place deposits in U.S. banks.

R E V I E W   Q U I Z

- Is everyone free to open a bank, take deposits, and make loans with no restrictions on these activities? What are the main restrictions that regulators impose on banks? Why?
- Did the financial deregulation of the 1980s make commercial banks more like or less like other financial institutions?
- What are the main factors that constantly stimulate financial intermediaries to develop new financial products and services?
- What have deregulation and financial innovation done to the composition of the nation's money?

We're now ready to learn how banks create money. In the following section, we'll use the term *banks* to refer to all the depository institutions whose deposits are part of the money supply. Let's see how money gets created.

How Banks Create Money

BANKS CREATE MONEY. BUT THIS DOESN'T MEAN that they have smoke-filled back rooms in which counterfeiters are busily working. Remember, most money is deposits, not currency. What banks create is deposits, and they do so by making loans. But the amount of deposits they can create is limited by their reserves.

Reserves: Actual and Required

We've seen that banks don't have $100 in bills for every $100 that people have deposited with them. In fact, a typical bank today has reserves of $6.00 for every $100 of deposits. No need for panic. These reserve levels are adequate for ordinary business needs.

The fraction of a bank's total deposits that are held in reserves is called the **reserve ratio**. The reserve ratio changes when a bank's customers make a deposit or withdrawal. Making a deposit increases the reserve ratio, and making a withdrawal decreases the reserve ratio.

The **required reserve ratio** is the ratio of reserves to deposits that banks are required, by regulation, to hold. A bank's *required reserves* are equal to its deposits multiplied by the required reserve ratio. Actual reserves minus required reserves are **excess reserves**. Whenever banks have excess reserves, they are able to create money.

To see how banks create money, we'll look at two model banking systems. In the first, there is only one bank; in the second, there are many banks.

Creating Deposits by Making Loans in a One-Bank Economy

In the model banking system that we'll study first, there is only one bank and its required reserve ratio is 25 percent. That is, for each dollar deposited, the bank keeps 25¢ in reserves and lends the rest. The balance sheet of One-and-Only Bank is shown in Fig. 31.2(a). On January 1, its deposits are $400 million and its reserves are 25 percent of this amount—$100 million. Its loans are equal to deposits minus reserves and are $300 million.

The story begins with Al Capone, who has decided to end his career of crime. He has been holding all his money in currency and has a nest egg of $1 million. On January 2, Al decides to put his $1 million on deposit at the One-and-Only Bank. On the day that Al makes his deposit, the One-and-Only Bank's balance sheet changes. The new situation is shown in Fig. 31.2(b). The bank now has $101 million in reserves and $401 million in deposits. It still has loans of $300 million.

The bank now has *excess reserves*. With reserves of $101 million, the bank would like to have deposits of $404 million and loans of $303 million. Because it is the One-and-Only Bank, the manager knows that the reserves will remain at $101 million. That is, she knows that when she makes a loan, the amount lent remains on deposit at the One-and-Only Bank. She knows, for example, that all the suppliers of Sky's-the-Limit Construction are also depositors of One-and-Only. So she knows that if she makes the loan that Sky's-the-Limit has just requested, the deposit she lends will never leave One-and-Only. When Sky's-the-Limit uses part of its new loan to pay $100,000 to I-Dig-It Excavating Company for some excavations, the One-and-Only Bank simply moves the funds from Sky's-the-Limit's checking account to I-Dig-It's checking account.

So on January 3, the manager of One-and-Only calls Sky's-the-Limit's accountant and offers to lend the maximum that she can. How much does she lend? She lends $3 million. By lending $3 million, One-and-Only's balance sheet changes to the one shown in Fig. 31.2(c). Loans increase by $3 million to $303 million. The loan shows up in Sky's-the-Limit's deposit initially, and total deposits increase to $404 million—$400 million plus Al Capone's deposit of $1 million plus the newly created deposit of $3 million. The bank now has no excess reserves and has reached the limit of its ability to create money.

FIGURE 31.2

Creating Money at the One-and-Only Bank

(a) Balance sheet on January 1

Assets (millions of dollars)		**Liabilities** (millions of dollars)	
Reserves	$100	Deposits	$400
Loans	$300		
Total	$400	Total	$400

(b) Balance sheet on January 2

Assets (millions of dollars)		**Liabilities** (millions of dollars)	
Reserves	$101	Deposits	$401
Loans	$300		
Total	$401	Total	$401

(c) Balance sheet on January 3

Assets (millions of dollars)		**Liabilities** (millions of dollars)	
Reserves	$101	Deposits	$404
Loans	$303		
Total	$404	Total	$404

In part (a) the One-and-Only Bank has deposits of $400 million, loans of $300 million, and reserves of $100 million. The bank's required reserve ratio is 25 percent. When the bank receives a deposit of $1 million (part b), it has excess reserves. It lends $3 million and creates a further $3 million of deposits. Deposits increase by $3 million, and loans increase by $3 million (in part c).

The Deposit Multiplier

The **deposit multiplier** is the amount by which an increase in bank reserves is multiplied to calculate the increase in bank deposits. That is,

$$\text{Deposit multiplier} = \frac{\text{Change in deposits}}{\text{Change in reserves}}.$$

In the example we've just worked through, the deposit multiplier is 4. The $1 million increase in reserves created a $4 million increase in deposits. The deposit multiplier is linked to the required reserve ratio by the following equation:

$$\text{Deposit multiplier} = \frac{1}{\text{Required reserve ratio}}.$$

In the example, the required reserve ratio is 25 percent, or 0.25. That is,

$$\text{Deposit multiplier} = \frac{1}{0.25}$$

$$= 4.$$

Creating Deposits by Making Loans with Many Banks

If you told the loan officer at your own bank that she creates money, she wouldn't believe you. Bankers see themselves as lending the money they receive from others, not creating money. But in fact, even though each bank lends only what it receives, the banking *system* creates money. To see how, let's look at another example.

Figure 31.3 is going to keep track of what is happening in the process of money creation by a banking system in which each bank has a required reserve ratio of 25 percent. The process begins when Art decides to decrease his currency holding and put $100,000 on deposit. Now Art's bank has $100,000 of new deposits and $100,000 of additional reserves. With a required reserve ratio of 25 percent, the bank keeps $25,000 on reserve and lends $75,000 to Amy. Amy writes a check for $75,000 to buy a copy-shop franchise from Barb. At this point, Art's bank has a new deposit of $100,000, new loans of $75,000, and new reserves of $25,000. You can see this situation in Fig. 31.3 as the first row of the "running tally."

For Art's bank, that is the end of the story. But it's not the end of the story for the entire banking system. Barb deposits her check for $75,000 in another bank, which has an increase in deposits and reserves of $75,000. This bank puts 25 percent of its increase in deposits ($18,750) into reserve and lends $56,250 to Bob. And Bob writes a check to Carl to pay off a business loan. The current state of play is seen in the second row of the "running tally" in Fig. 31.3. Now total bank reserves have increased by $43,750 ($25,000 plus $18,750), total loans have increased by $131,250 ($75,000 plus $56,250), and total deposits have increased by $175,000 ($100,000 plus $75,000).

When Carl takes his check to his bank, its deposits and reserves increase by $56,250, $14,063 of which it keeps in reserve and $42,187 of which it lends. This process continues until there are no excess reserves in the banking system. But the process takes a lot of further steps. One additional step is shown in Fig. 31.3. The figure also shows the final tallies—reserves increase by $100,000, loans increase by $300,000, and deposits increase by $400,000.

The sequence in Fig. 31.3 is the first four stages of the process. To figure out the entire process, look closely at the numbers in the figure. At each stage, the loan is 75 percent (0.75) of the previous loan and the deposit is 0.75 of the previous deposit. Call that proportion L ($L = 0.75$). The complete sequence is

$$1 + L + L^2 + L^3 + \dots .$$

Remember, L is a fraction, so at each stage in this sequence, the amount of new loans gets smaller. The total number of loans made at the end of the process is the above sum, which is[3]

$$\frac{1}{(1 - L)}.$$

---

[3]Both here and in the expenditure multiplier process in Chapter 29, the sequence of values is called a convergent geometric series. To find the sum of a series such as this, begin by calling the sum S. Then write out the sum as

$$S = 1 + L + L^2 + L^3 + \dots .$$

Multiply by L to get

$$LS = L + L^2 + L^3 + \dots$$

and then subtract the second equation from the first to get

$$S(1 - L) = 1$$

or

$$S = \frac{1}{(1 - L)}.$$

FIGURE 31.3

The Multiple Creation of Bank Deposits

The sequence

Deposit
$100,000

Reserve
$25,000

Loan
$75,000

Deposit
$75,000

Reserve
$18,750

Loan
$56,250

Deposit
$56,250

Reserve
$14,063

Loan
$42,187

Deposit
$42,187

Reserve
$10,547

Loan
$31,640

and
so on ...

The running tally

Reserves	Loans	Deposits
$25,000	$75,000	$100,000
$43,750	$131,250	$175,000
$57,813	$173,437	$231,250
$68,360	$205,077	$273,437
•	•	•
•	•	•
▼	▼	▼
$100,000	$300,000	$400,000

When a bank receives deposits, it keeps 25 percent in reserves and lends 75 percent. The amount lent becomes a new deposit at another bank. The next bank in the sequence keeps 25 percent and lends 75 percent, and the process continues until the banking system has created enough deposits to eliminate its excess reserves. The running tally tells us the amounts of deposits and loans created at each stage. At the end of the process, an additional $100,000 of reserves creates an additional $400,000 of deposits.

If we use the numbers from the example, the total increase in deposits is

$100,000 + 75,000 + 56,250 + 42,190 + ...

= $100,000 (1 + 0.75 + 0.5625 + 0.4219 + ...)

= $100,000 (1 + 0.75 + 0.75^2 + 0.75^3 + ...)

$$= \$100,000 \times \frac{1}{(1 - 0.75)}$$

$$= \$100,000 \times \frac{1}{(0.25)}$$

= $100,000 × 4

By using the same method, you can check that the totals for reserves and loans are the ones shown in Fig. 31.3.

So even though each bank lends only the money it receives, the banking system as a whole does create money by making loans. The amount created is exactly the same in a multibank system as in a one-bank system.

The Deposit Multiplier in the United States   The deposit multiplier in the United States works in the same way as the deposit multiplier we've just worked out for a model economy. But the deposit multiplier in the United States differs from the one we've just calculated for three reasons. First, the required reserve ratio of U.S. banks is smaller than the 25 percent we used here. Second, U.S. banks sometimes choose to hold excess reserves. Third, not all the loans made by banks return to them in the form of reserves. Some of the loans remain outside the banks and are held as currency. The smaller required reserve ratio makes the U.S. multiplier larger than the multiplier in the above example. But the other two factors make the U.S. multiplier smaller.

REVIEW QUIZ

- How do banks create deposits by making loans, and what are the factors that limit the amount of deposits and loans they can create?
- A bank manager tells you that he doesn't create money. He just lends the money that people deposit in the bank. How do you explain to him that he's wrong and that he does create money?
- If the banks receive new deposits of $100 million, what determines the total change in deposits that the banking system can create?

Now that we know what money is and how banks create it, let's see how the amount of money created by the banks influences the economy. We'll discover that this influence is powerful.

Money, Real GDP, and the Price Level

YOU NOW KNOW THAT IN A MODERN ECONOMY such as that of the United States today, most of the money is bank deposits. You've seen that banks actually create money by making loans. Does the quantity of money created by the banking and financial system matter? What effect does money have? Does it matter whether the quantity of money increases quickly or slowly? How does the quantity of money influence real GDP, the price level, and the inflation rate? Can a country increase its real GDP just by increasing the quantity of money?

We're going to answer these questions first by using the aggregate supply–aggregate demand model, which explains how money affects real GDP and the price level in the short run. Then we're going to study a theory called the quantity theory of money, which explains how money growth influences inflation in the long run. We'll also look at some historical and international evidence on the relationship between money growth and inflation.

The Short-Run Effects of a Change in the Quantity of Money

Figure 31.4 illustrates the *AS-AD* model that explains how real GDP and the price level are determined in the short run. (For a full explanation of the *AS-AD* model, see Chapter 25, pp. 542–543.) We are going to use this model to study the short-run effects of a change in the quantity of money on real GDP and the price level. Potential GDP is $7 trillion, and the long-run aggregate supply curve is *LAS*. The short-run aggregate supply curve is *SAS*. Initially, the aggregate demand curve is AD_0. Equilibrium real GDP is $6.8 trillion, and the price level is 107 at the intersection of the *AD* curve and the *SAS* curve.

FIGURE 31.4

Short-Run Effects of Change in Quantity of Money

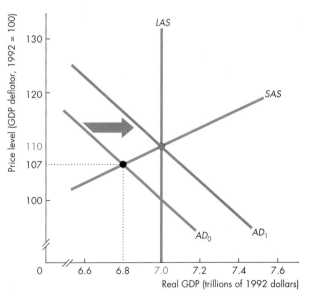

Real GDP is less than potential GDP. An increase in the quantity of money increases aggregate demand and shifts the aggregate demand curve rightward from AD_0 to AD_1. The price level rises to 110, and real GDP expands to $7 trillion. The increase in the quantity of money increases real GDP to potential GDP.

Banks, flush with excess reserves, make loans, and the loans create money. This increase results from the process of money creation we've just studied. With more money in their bank accounts and more loans, people plan to increase their consumption expenditure and businesses plan to increase their investment. Aggregate demand increases, and the aggregate demand curve shifts rightward to AD_1. A new equilibrium emerges at the intersection point of AD_1 and SAS. Real GDP expands to $7 trillion, and the price level rises to 110. Real GDP now equals potential GDP, and there is full employment. This increase in the quantity of money has increased both real GDP and the price level.

Now imagine the reverse situation. Real GDP is initially $7 trillion, and the price level is 110 at the intersection point of AD_1 and SAS. The quantity of money *decreases*. With *less* money in their bank accounts, people and businesses plan to decrease their expenditures. Aggregate demand decreases, and the aggregate demand curve shifts leftward to AD_0. A recession occurs as real GDP shrinks to $6.8 trillion, and the price level falls to 107.

These influences of the quantity of money on real GDP and the price level are *short-run* effects. In the long run, a change in the quantity of money, perhaps surprisingly, has no effect on real GDP. All its effects are on the price level. Let's see why this outcome occurs.

The Long-Run Effects of a Change in the Quantity of Money

Figure 31.5 explains how real GDP and the price level are determined in both the short run and the long run. Again, potential GDP is $7 trillion and the long-run aggregate supply curve is *LAS*. The short-run aggregate supply curve is SAS_1. Initially, the aggregate demand curve is AD_1. Equilibrium real GDP is $7 trillion, and the price level is 110. So real GDP equals potential GDP, and there is full employment.

Now suppose the quantity of money increases. Aggregate demand increases, and the aggregate demand curve shifts rightward to AD_2. The new short-run equilibrium is at the intersection point of AD_2 and SAS_1. The price level rises to 113, and real GDP expands to $7.2 trillion. This short-run adjustment has put real GDP above potential GDP and has decreased unemployment below the natural rate. A

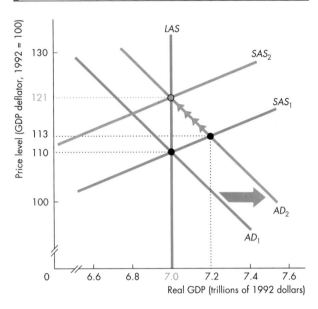

FIGURE 31.5

Long-Run Effects of Change in Quantity of Money

Real GDP equals potential GDP. An increase in the quantity of money shifts the aggregate demand curve from AD_1 to AD_2. In the short run, the price level rises to 113, and real GDP increases to $7.2 trillion. Real GDP exceeds potential GDP, and the money wage rate rises. Short-run aggregate supply decreases, and the SAS curve shifts leftward from SAS_1 to SAS_2. Real GDP returns to potential GDP, and the price level rises to 121. In the long run, the increase in the quantity of money increases the price level and has no effect on real GDP.

shortage of labor makes the money wage rate rise. As the money wage rate rises, short-run aggregate supply decreases and the SAS curve shifts leftward toward SAS_2. As short-run aggregate supply decreases, the price level rises to 121 and real GDP decreases back to potential GDP at $7 trillion.

Thus from one full-employment equilibrium to another, an increase in the quantity of money increases the price level and has no effect on real GDP. This relationship between the quantity of money and the price level at full employment is made more precise by the quantity theory of money, which tells us about the quantitative link between money growth and inflation.

The Quantity Theory of Money

The **quantity theory of money** is the proposition that in the long run, an increase in the quantity of money brings an equal percentage increase in the price level. The original basis of the quantity theory of money is a concept known as *the velocity of circulation* and an equation called *the equation of exchange*.

The **velocity of circulation** is the average number of times a dollar of money is used annually to buy the goods and services that make up GDP. GDP is equal to the price level (P) multiplied by real GDP (Y); that is,

$$GDP = PY.$$

Call the quantity of money M. The velocity of circulation, V, is determined by the equation

$$V = PY/M.$$

For example, if GDP is $6.0 trillion and the quantity of money is $3 trillion, the velocity of circulation is

2. On the average, each dollar of money circulates twice in its use to purchase the final goods and services that make up GDP; that is, each dollar of money is used twice in a year to buy GDP.

Figure 31.6 shows the velocity of circulation of both M1 and M2, the two main official definitions of money since 1960. You can see that the velocity of circulation of M1 increased through 1980 and fluctuated during the 1980s and 1990s. In contrast, the velocity of circulation of M2 has been remarkably stable. The reason why the velocity of M1 has increased is that deregulation and financial innovation have created new types of deposits and payments technologies that are substitutes for M1. As a result, the quantity of M1 per dollar of GDP has decreased, and equivalently, the velocity of circulation of M1 has increased. The reason why the velocity of M2 has been almost constant is that the new types of deposits that have replaced M1 are part of M2. So the ratio of M2 to GDP and the velocity of circulation of M2 have been much more stable.

FIGURE 31.6

The Velocity of Circulation in the United States: 1960–1998

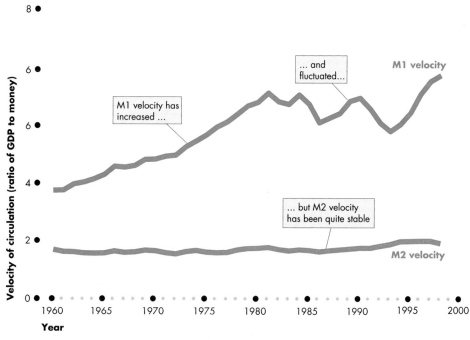

The velocity of circulation of M1 has increased over the years because financial innovation has developed M1 substitutes. The velocity of circulation of M2 has been relatively stable because the M1 substitutes that have resulted from financial innovation are new types of deposits that are part of M2.

Source: Economic Report of the President, 1999.

The **equation of exchange** states that the quantity of money (M) multiplied by the velocity of circulation (V) equals GDP, or

$$MV = PY.$$

Given the definition of the velocity of circulation, this equation is always true—it is true by definition. With M equal to $3 trillion and V equal to 2, MV is equal to $6.0 trillion, the value of GDP.

The equation of exchange becomes the quantity theory of money by making two assumptions:

1. The velocity of circulation is not influenced by the quantity of money.
2. Potential GDP is not influenced by the quantity of money.

If these two assumptions are true, the equation of exchange tells us that a change in the quantity of money brings about an equal proportional change in the price level. You can see why by solving the equation of exchange for the price level. Dividing both sides of the equation by real GDP (Y) gives

$$P = (V/Y)M.$$

In the long run, real GDP (Y) equals potential GDP, so if potential GDP and velocity are not influenced by the quantity of money, the relationship between the change in the price level (ΔP) and the change in the quantity of money (ΔM) is

$$\Delta P = (V/Y)\,\Delta M.$$

Divide this equation by the previous one, $P = (V/Y)M$, to get

$$\Delta P/P = \Delta M/M.$$

($\Delta P/P$) is the proportional increase in the price level, and ($\Delta M/M$) is the proportional increase in the quantity of money. So this equation is the quantity theory of money: In the long run, the percentage increase in the price level equals the percentage increase in the quantity of money.

The Quantity Theory and the *AS-AD* Model

The quantity theory of money can be interpreted in terms of the *AS-AD* model. The aggregate demand curve is a relationship between the quantity of real GDP demanded (Y) and the price level (P), other things remaining constant. We can obtain such a

relationship from the equation of exchange,

$$MV = PY.$$

Dividing both sides of this equation by real GDP (Y) gives

$$P = MV/Y.$$

This equation may be interpreted as describing an aggregate demand curve. In Chapter 25 (pp. 539–540), you saw that the aggregate demand curve slopes downward: As the price level increases, the quantity of real GDP demanded decreases. The above equation also shows such a relationship between the price level and the quantity of real GDP demanded. For a given quantity of money (M) and a given velocity of circulation (V), the higher the price level (P), the smaller is the quantity of real GDP demanded (Y).

In general, when the quantity of money changes, the velocity of circulation might also change. But the quantity theory asserts that velocity is not influenced by the quantity of money. If this assumption is correct, an increase in the quantity of money increases aggregate demand and shifts the aggregate demand curve upward by the same amount as the percentage change in the quantity of money.

The quantity theory of money also asserts that real GDP, which in the long run equals potential GDP, is not influenced by the quantity of money. This assertion is true in the *AS-AD* model in the long run when the economy is on its long-run aggregate supply curve. Figure 31.5 shows the quantity theory result in the *AS-AD* model. Initially, the economy is on the long-run aggregate supply curve *LAS* and at the intersection of the aggregate demand curve AD_1 and the short-run aggregate supply curve SAS_1. A 10 percent increase in the quantity of money shifts the aggregate demand curve from AD_1 to AD_2. This shift, measured by the vertical distance between the two demand curves, is 10 percent. In the long run, wages rise (also by 10 percent) and shift the *SAS* curve leftward to SAS_2. A new long-run equilibrium occurs at the intersection of AD_2 and SAS_2. Real GDP remains at potential GDP of $7 trillion, and the price level rises to 121. The new price level is 10 percent higher than the initial one ($121 - 110 = 11$, which is 10 percent of 110).

So the *AS-AD* model predicts the same outcome as the quantity theory of money. The *AS-AD* model also predicts a less precise relationship between the quantity of money and the price level in the short run than in the long run. For example, Fig. 31.4 shows that if we start out at a below-full employment equilibrium, an increase in the quantity of money increases real GDP. In this case, a 10 percent increase in the money supply increases the price level from 107 to 110—a 2.8 percent increase. That is, the price level increases by a smaller percentage than the percentage increase in the quantity of money.

How good a theory is the quantity theory of money? Let's answer this question by looking at the relationship between money and the price level, both historically and internationally.

Historical Evidence on the Quantity Theory of Money

The percentage increase in the price level is the inflation rate, and the percentage increase in the quantity of money is the money supply growth rate. So the quantity theory predictions can be cast in terms of money growth and inflation. The quantity theory predicts that at a given level of potential GDP and in the long run, the inflation rate will equal the money growth rate. But over time, potential GDP expands. Taking this expansion into account, the quantity theory predicts that in the long run, the inflation rate will equal the money growth rate minus the growth rate of potential GDP.

We can test the quantity theory of money by looking at the historical relationship between money growth and inflation in the United States. Figure 31.7 shows two views of this relationship for the years between 1930 and 1998. In both parts of the figure, the inflation rate is the percentage change in the GDP deflator, and the two alternative money growth rates are based on M1 and M2. Part (a) shows year-to-year changes in money and the price level. These changes show the short-run relationship between money growth and inflation. Part (b) shows decade average changes. These changes average out the year-to-year fluctuations and enable us to see the long-run relationship between the variables. If the quantity theory is a reasonable guide to reality, there should be a strong correlation between inflation and money growth in the decade average data and a weak correlation in the year-to-year data.

The data are broadly consistent with the quantity theory. The money growth rate and the inflation rate are correlated, but the relationship is not precise. During World War II, money growth increased sharply while inflation remained low. After the war, inflation exploded while money growth remained

steady. Between 1950 and 1998, the inflation rate fluctuated less than the fluctuations in the money growth rate. The year-to-year fluctuations in money growth and inflation, which contain short-run influences (in part a), show a weak correlation, and the decade average fluctuations in money growth and inflation (in part b) show a stronger correlation.

International Evidence on the Quantity Theory of Money

Another way to test the quantity theory of money is to look at the cross-country relationship between money growth and inflation. Figure 31.8 shows this relationship for 60 countries during the 1980s. By looking at a decade average, we again are smoothing out the short-run effects of money growth and focusing on the long-run effects. There is in these data an unmistakable tendency for high money growth to be associated with high inflation. The evidence is strongest for the high-inflation countries, which are shown in Fig. 31.8(a), but it is also present for the low-inflation countries, which are shown in Fig. 31.8(b).

Correlation, Causation, and Other Influences

Both the historical evidence for the United States and the international data tell us that in the long run, money growth and inflation are correlated. But the correlation between money growth and inflation does not tell us that money growth causes inflation. Money growth might cause inflation; inflation might cause money growth; or some third variable might simultaneously cause inflation and money growth.

According to the quantity theory and according to the *AS-AD* model, causation runs from money growth to inflation. But neither theory denies the possibility that at different times and places, causation might run in the other direction or that some third factor might be the root cause of both rapid money growth and inflation. One possible third factor is a large and persistent government budget deficit that gets financed by creating money.

But some occasions give us an opportunity to test our assumptions about causation. One of these is World War II and the years immediately following it. Rapid money growth during the war years was accompanied by controls that held prices down during

FIGURE 31.7
Money Growth and Inflation in the United States

(a) Year-to-year change in money supply and the price level

Year-to-year fluctuations in money growth and inflation (part a) are loosely correlated, but decade average fluctuations in money growth and inflation (part b) are closely correlated. The burst of postwar inflation was caused by rapid money growth during World War II, and the rise in inflation during the 1970s was caused by more rapid money growth during the 1960s.

(b) Decade average change in money supply and the price level

Sources: *Historical Statistics of the United States, Economic Report of the President,* 1999, and the author's calculations.

FIGURE 31.8
Money Growth and Inflation in the World Economy

(a) All countries

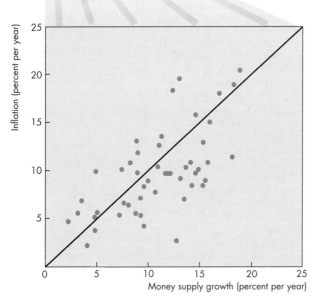

(b) Low-inflation countries

Inflation and money growth in 60 countries (in part a) and low-inflation countries (in part b) show a clear positive relationship between money growth and inflation.

Source: Federal Reserve Bank of St. Louis, Review, May/June 1988, p. 15.

the war but allowed them to rise immediately after the war. The inflationary consequences of wartime money growth were delayed by price controls but not removed. It is inconceivable that this was an example of reverse causation—of postwar inflation causing wartime money growth. Another is the late 1960s and 1970s. Rapid money growth that began during the 1960s almost certainly caused the high and persistent inflation of the 1970s. The combination of historical and international correlations between money growth and inflation and independent evidence about the direction of causation leads to the conclusion that the quantity theory is correct in the long run. It explains the long-term fundamental source of inflation. But the quantity theory is not correct in the short run. To understand the short-term fluctuations in inflation, the joint effects of a change in the quantity of money on real GDP, the velocity of circulation, and the price level must be explained. The *AS-AD* model provides this explanation. It also points to the possibility of other factors that influence both aggregate supply and aggregate demand influencing the inflation rate independently of the money growth rate in the short run.

R E V I E W   Q U I Z

- Do the short-run effects of an increase in the quantity of money on the price level and real GDP differ from the long-run effects? If so, what are the differences? Why are there different effects?
- What is the quantity theory of money? Are the predictions of the quantity theory in conflict with the predictions of the *AS-AD* model?
- Do the long-run historical evidence and the international evidence on the relationship between money growth and inflation support the quantity theory?

Before you leave the subject of this chapter, look at *Reading Between the Lines* on pp. 706–707 and see the quantity theory in action in Brazil. In the next chapter, we'll learn how the Fed influences the quantity of money and interest rates in its attempt to steer the course of the economy. Then, in Chapter 33, we'll return to the problem of inflation and explore more deeply its causes and consequences and ways of keeping it under control.

The Quantity Theory in Action

THE WALL STREET JOURNAL, JANUARY 22, 1999

Brazilians Brace Again for Inflation ...

BY WALL STREET JOURNAL STAFF REPORTERS PETER FRITSCH IN SAO PAULO AND MATT MOFFETT IN RIO DE JANEIRO

Campaigning for re-election last year, Brazilian President Fernando Henrique Cardoso popped in on the Peres Bakery, outside Brasilia, and noted with deep satisfaction that the price of a French roll had barely budged since his last visit three years earlier.

But next week, bakery owner Arnaldo Peres will raise the price of that French roll somewhere between 20% and 50%, saying that half the flour he uses comes from Argentina and is more expensive since last week's devaluation of the Brazilian real.

Mr. Cardoso's hard-won victory over inflation—which relied on an artificially inflated local currency—is being put to the test like never before. Vendors are giving in to old temptations, and bread winners are bracing for the effects of higher prices and climbing interest rates, already the world's most severe. And Mr. Peres isn't alone out there.

Already, memories of the Brazilian hyperinflation of the early 1990s—rivaling in ferocity that of Germany's Weimar Republic in the 1920s—appear to be stirring some shopkeepers to action. In local supermarkets, the price of Chilean salmon fillets are up nearly 30% this week. The cost of a bus ticket in São Paulo went up 15% the very day Brazil first moved to devalue its currency on Jan. 13. At São Paulo's vast produce market known as Ceagesp, the prices of domestic papaya and watermelon are up 8% over the past week, with vegetables up an average 24%. Ceagesp attributes the sudden rises to a pinch in supply due to heavy rains this month, but most Brazilians are skeptical of such explanations.

Stopping by the Rio Sul supermarket in Rio de Janeiro yesterday, housewife Fernanda Almeida says she tucked an extra package of rice in her shopping cart in case prices rise in the near future. "It said on the television news that the price could be going up, so I decided to be prepared," she said. In one São Paulo market, the price of a bag of black beans is up 33% from last week. ...

Essence of the Story

■ During the early 1990s, Brazil had a hyperinflation that rivaled that of Germany during the 1920s.

■ President Cardoso lowered Brazil's inflation, and price increases have been modest for the past three years. But inflation seemed set to take off again in January 1999.

■ Some price increases in one week: salmon fillets, almost 30 percent; a bus ticket in São Paulo, 15 percent; papaya and watermelon, 8 percent; vegetables, an average of 24 percent.

■ A São Paolo produce market official says that prices have increased because heavy rains have decreased supply. Most Brazilians do not believe this explanation.

■ Shoppers are buying larger quantities than normal in anticipation of higher prices.

Economic Analysis

■ Brazil had a serious inflation during the early 1990s. But it was not a hyperinflation and was not even close to the inflation that Germany experienced during the 1920s.

■ Figure 1 shows the inflation rate in Brazil between 1975 and 1999.

■ Note that the numbers for the growth rates are *thousands* of percent per year!

■ Hyperinflation is defined as an inflation rate greater than 50 percent per month, or 12,875 percent per year. Germany's inflation during the 1920s *exceeded* this rate!

■ Brazil has not had hyperinflation, but its inflation rate has been high and reached almost 3,000 percent a year in 1993.

■ Also, as you can see from the figure, money growth and inflation tend to move in a similar direction.

■ The quantity theory of money can be used to explain the movements in money growth and inflation.

■ When inflation is as high and variable as it was in Brazil during the early 1990s and people fear that such inflation

might occur again, money ceases to work well as a medium of exchange, a unit of account, or a store of value.

■ As a result, people don't want to hold money. They prefer to hold goods like the rice that Fernanda Almeida bought in the news article. So the velocity of circulation increases.

■ The higher the inflation rate, the more quickly people try to spend their income and the higher is the velocity of circulation. Figure 2 shows that in low-inflation Japan, the velocity of circulation is lower than that in high-inflation Brazil. And in hyperinflation Zaire, the velocity of circulation is even higher than in Brazil.

■ Brazil's money supply grows rapidly in some years not because the government is trying to cause inflation but because it has no other way of getting the funds that it needs to meet its expenditures. The government deficit is financed by printing money.

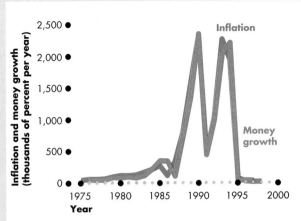

Figure 1 Inflation and money growth in Brazil

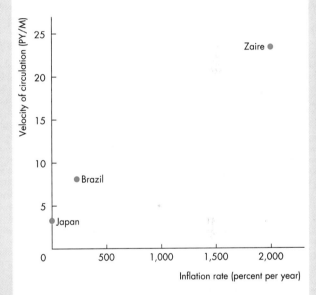

Figure 2 Inflation and velocity

SUMMARY

KEY POINTS

What Is Money? (pp. 688–690)

- Money is the means of payment, a medium of exchange, a unit of account, and a store of value.
- M1 consists of currency, travelers' checks, and checking deposits), and M2 consists of M1 plus savings deposits, time deposits, and money market mutual funds.

Financial Intermediaries (pp. 691–693)

- Commercial banks, thrift institutions (S&Ls, savings banks, and credit unions) and money market mutual funds are financial intermediaries whose liabilities are money.
- Financial intermediaries provide four main economic services: They create liquidity, minimize the cost of obtaining funds, minimize the cost of monitoring borrowers, and pool risks.

Financial Regulation, Deregulation, and Innovation (pp. 693–695)

- Financial regulation to protect depositors includes deposit insurance, minimum capital rules, and required reserves.
- Deregulation during the 1980s removed the distinctions between banks and nonbank intermediaries.
- The search for profit leads to the creation of new types of deposits and loans, which change the composition of the nation's money supply.

How Banks Create Money (pp. 695–699)

- Banks create money by making loans.
- The total quantity of deposits that can be supported by a given amount of reserves (the deposit multiplier) is determined by the required reserve ratio.

Money, Real GDP, and the Price Level (pp. 699–705)

- An increase in the quantity of money increases aggregate demand and, in the short run, increases both the price level and real GDP.
- In the long run, an increase in the quantity of money brings increases in the price level and no change in real GDP.
- Like the *AS-AD* model, the quantity theory of money predicts no long-run relationship between money and real GDP.

KEY FIGURES

KEY TERMS

P R O B L E M S

*1. In the United States today, money includes which of the following items?
   a. Federal Reserve banknotes in the Bank of America's cash machines
   b. Your Visa card
   c. The quarters inside public phones
   d. U.S. dollar bills in your wallet
   e. The check you have just written to pay for your rent
   f. The loan you took out last August to pay for your school fees

2. Which of the following items are money? Which are deposit money?
   a. Checking deposits at Citicorp
   b. IBM stock held by individuals
   c. The Susan B. Anthony dollar coin
   d. U.S. government securities
   e. NOW accounts
   Explain your answer by referring to the three basic functions of money.

*3. Sara withdraws $1,000 from her savings account at the Lucky S&L, keeps $50 in cash, and deposits the balance in her checking account at the Bank of Illinois. What is the immediate change in M1 and M2?

4. Monica takes $10,000 from her savings account at the Bank of Alaska and puts the funds into her money market mutual fund. What is the immediate change in M1 and M2?

*5. The commercial banks in Zap have:

Reserves	$250 million
Loans	$1,000 million
Deposits	$2,000 million
Total assets	$2,500 million

   a. Construct the commercial banks' balance sheet. If you are missing any assets, call them "other assets"; if you are missing any liabilities, call them "other liabilities."
   b. Calculate the banks' reserve ratio.
   c. If banks hold no excess reserves, calculate the deposit multiplier.

6. The commercial banks in Zip have:

Reserves	$125 million
Loans	$1,875 million
Deposits	$2,000 million
Total assets	$2,100 million

   a. Construct the commercial banks' balance sheet. If you are missing any assets, call them "other assets"; if you are missing any liabilities, call them "other liabilities."
   b. Calculate the banks' reserve ratio.
   c. If banks hold no excess reserves, calculate the deposit multiplier.

*7. An immigrant arrives in New Transylvania with $1,200. The $1,200 is deposited in a bank. All the banks in Transylvania have a required reserve ratio of 10 percent, and they have no excess reserves when the immigrant arrives.
   a. What is the initial increase in the quantity of money in New Transylvania?
   b. What is the initial increase in the quantity of bank deposits when the immigrant arrives?
   c. How much does the immigrant's bank lend out initially?
   d. Calculate the amount lent and the amount of deposits created if all the funds lent in (c) are returned to the banking system in the form of deposits.
   e. By how much has the quantity of money increased after the banks have made 20 loans?
   f. What is the total increase in the quantity of money, in bank loans, and in bank deposits when the process comes to an end?

8. An Internet thief in Chicago steals $100,000 from a bank in Buenos Aires, Argentina. He transfers the funds to a bank account in Chicago. The Chicago bank has a required reserve ratio of 5 percent, and it has no excess reserves when the transfer occurs.
   a. What is the initial increase in the quantity of money in the United States?
   b. What is the initial increase in the quantity of bank deposits when the theft occurs?
   c. How much does the thief's bank lend out?
   d. Calculate the amount lent and the amount of deposits created if all the funds lent in (c) are returned to the banking system in the form of deposits.
   e. By how much has the quantity of money increased after the banks have made 2 rounds of loans?
   f. What is the total increase in the quantity of money, in bank loans, and in bank deposits when the process comes to an end?

*9. Slowcon is a country in which the quantity theory of money operates in the long run but not in the short run. Slowcon has some unemployment when banks begin to make new loans and increase the quantity of money.
   a. What is the effect of the banks' actions on aggregate demand?
   b. What are the effects of the banks' actions on real GDP and the price level in the short run?
   c. What are the effects of the banks' actions on real GDP and the price level in the long run?

10. Banks in Indonesia make bad loans that don't get repaid, and several banks fail. The banks' customers lose their deposits.
   a. What is the effect of the bank failures on the quantity of money?
   b. What is the effect of the bank failures on aggregate demand?
   c. What are the effects of the bank failures on real GDP and the price level in the short run?
   d. What are the effects of the bank failures on real GDP and the price level in the long run?

*11. Quantecon is a country in which the quantity theory of money operates. The country has a constant population, capital stock, and technology. In year 1, real GDP was $400 million, the price level was 200, and the velocity of circulation of money was 20. In year 2, the quantity of money was 20 percent higher than in year 1.
   a. What was the quantity of money in year 1?
   b. What was the quantity of money in year 2?
   c. What was the price level in year 2?
   d. What was the level of real GDP in year 2?
   e. What was the velocity of circulation in year 2?

12. In Quantecon, described in problem 11, in year 3, the quantity of money falls to one fifth of its year 2 level.
   a. What is the quantity of money in year 3?
   b. What is the price level in year 3?
   c. What is the level of real GDP in year 3?
   d. What is the velocity of circulation in year 3?
   e. If it takes more than one year for the full quantity theory effect to occur, what do you predict happens to real GDP in Quantecon in year 3? Why?

CRITICAL THINKING

1. Study *Reading Between the Lines* on pp. 706–707 and then answer the following questions:
   a. What, according to the news article, were Brazilians expecting to happen to the inflation rate in January 1999?
   b. Use the link on the Parkin Web site to obtain data on Brazil's inflation since January 1999. Were the people's expectations correct?
   c. How do Brazilians protect themselves from a falling value of the real (Brazil's money)?
   d. Why has Brazil's inflation rate been higher than its money supply growth rate in some years? Does this fact contradict the quantity theory of money?

2. When rapid inflation in Brazil causes the real (Brazil's money) to lose its ability to function as money, which of the following commodities do you think would most likely take the place of the real in the Brazilian economy and why?
   a. Tractor parts
   b. Packs of cigarettes
   c. Loaves of bread
   d. Impressionist paintings
   e. Baseball trading cards

3. Use the link on the Parkin Web site to visit Mark Bernkopf's Central Banking Resource Center. Read the short article on Electronic Cash and also read "The End of Cash" by James Gleick (first published in the *New York Times Magazine* on June 16, 1996). Then answer the following questions:
   a. What is e-cash?
   b. Mark Bernkopf asks: "Will 'e-cash' enable private currencies to overturn the ability of governments to make monetary policy?" Will it? Why or why not?
   c. When you buy an item on the Internet and pay by using a form of e-cash, are you using money? Explain why or why not.
   d. In your opinion, is the concern about e-cash a real concern or hype?

Chapter 32

Monetary Policy

In 1987, William Greider's *Secrets of the Temple: How the Federal Reserve Runs the Country* made the *New York Times* best-seller list. This book was popular partly because it was (and is) a good read and partly because it let its reader in on some secrets— the secrets of the mysterious Fed. What exactly is the Fed? What tools does it possess? And how does it use them? ◆ One thing the Fed does is to manage the nation's money. The amount of money in existence is surprisingly large. An unknown quantity of U.S. bills circulates abroad, especially in Russia and the rest of Eastern Europe. But there are enough coins and bills circulating in the United States today for every person to have a wallet stuffed with more than $1,000. In addition, enough money is deposited in banks and other financial institutions for every person to have a deposit of more than $12,500. What determines the amount of currency and bank deposits in existence? How does the Fed change the amount of money floating around the economy? And why do individuals and businesses hold so much money? ◆ In 1997 and 1998, financial markets in some Asian economies were under stress. Banks collapsed and currencies sank. People feared contagion. Would the Asian problems spread to the United States? Anxious to maintain calm and keep the economy expanding, the Fed gradually lowered interest rates through 1998. Would the Fed keep on lowering interest rates through 1999 or would it increase interest rates to choke off inflation? How does the Fed change interest rates? How do interest rates influence the economy? How do higher interest rates keep inflation in check?

Temple of Secrets

◆ In this chapter, you will learn about the Fed and monetary policy. You will learn how the Fed influences interest rates and how interest rates influence the economy. You'll discover that interest rates depend, in part, on the amount of money in existence. You will also discover how the Fed influences the quantity of money to influence interest rates as it attempts to smooth the business cycle and keep inflation in check.

After studying this chapter, you will be able to:

- Describe the structure of the Federal Reserve System (the Fed)

- Describe the tools used by the Fed to conduct its monetary policy

- Explain what an open market operation is and how it works

- Explain how an open market operation changes the money supply

- Explain what determines the demand for money

- Explain how the Fed influences interest rates

- Explain how interest rates influence the economy

The Federal Reserve System

THE CENTRAL BANK OF THE UNITED STATES IS the **Federal Reserve System**. A **central bank** is a bank's bank and a public authority that regulates a nation's financial institutions and markets. As the banks' bank, the Fed provides banking services to commercial banks such as Citibank and the Bank of America. A central bank is not a citizens' bank. That is, the Fed does not provide general banking services for businesses and individual citizens.

The Fed conducts the nation's **monetary policy**, which means that it adjusts the quantity of money in circulation. The Fed's goals are to keep inflation in check, maintain full employment, moderate the business cycle, and contribute toward achieving long-term growth. Complete success in the pursuit of these goals is impossible, and the Fed's more modest goal is to improve the performance of the economy and to get closer to the goals than a "hands off" approach would achieve. Whether the Fed succeeds in improving economic performance is a matter on which there is a range of opinion.

This chapter examines the tools available to the Fed in its conduct of monetary policy and looks at the effects of the Fed's actions on the economy. We begin by describing the structure of the Fed.

The Structure of the Federal Reserve System

The key elements in the structure of the Federal Reserve System are:

- The Board of Governors
- The Regional Federal Reserve Banks
- The Federal Open Market Committee

The Board of Governors The Board of Governors has seven members, who are appointed by the President of the United States and confirmed by the Senate, each for a 14-year term. The terms are staggered so that one seat on the board becomes vacant every two years. The President appoints one of the board members as Chairman for a term of four years, which is renewable.

The Federal Reserve Banks There are 12 Federal Reserve banks, one for each of 12 Federal Reserve districts shown in Fig. 32.1. Each Federal Reserve

bank has nine directors. Three of the directors are appointed by the Board of Governors and each of the other six are elected by the commercial banks in their Federal Reserve district. The directors of the regional Federal Reserve banks appoint the bank's president, and the Board of Governors approves this appointment.

The Federal Reserve Bank of New York (known as the New York Fed) occupies a special place in the Federal Reserve System because it implements some of the Fed's most important policy decisions.

The Federal Open Market Committee The **Federal Open Market Committee** (FOMC) is the main policy-making organ of the Federal Reserve System. The FOMC consists of the following voting members:

- The chairman and other six members of the Board of Governors
- The president of the Federal Reserve Bank of New York
- The presidents of the other regional Federal Reserve banks (of whom, on a yearly rotating basis, only four vote)

The FOMC meets approximately every six weeks to review the state of the economy and to decide the actions to be carried out by the New York Fed.

The Fed's Power Center

A description of the formal structure of the Fed gives the impression that power in the Fed resides with the Board of Governors. In practice, it is the chairman of the Board of Governors who has the largest influence on the Fed's monetary policy actions, and some remarkable individuals have held this position. One of these is Paul Volcker, who was appointed in 1979 by President Carter and reappointed in 1983 by President Reagan. Volcker eradicated inflation but helped to create one of the most severe postwar recessions. Another is Alan Greenspan, who was appointed by President Reagan in 1987 and reappointed by President Bush in 1992 and again for another term by President Clinton in 1996.

The chairman's power and influence stem from three sources. First, it is the chairman who controls the agenda and who dominates the meetings of the FOMC. Second, day-to-day contact with a large staff of economists and other technical experts provides the chairman with detailed background briefings on monetary policy issues. Third, the chairman is the spokesperson for the Fed and the Fed's

FIGURE 32.1

The Federal Reserve System

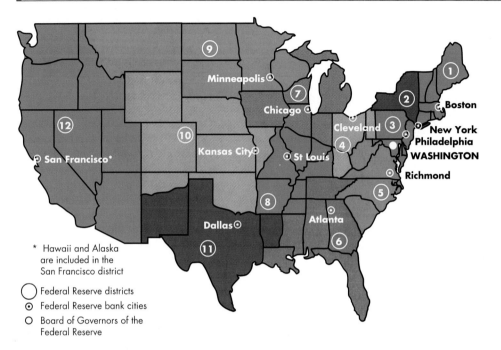

The nation is divided into 12 Federal Reserve districts, each having a Federal Reserve bank. (Some of the larger districts also have branch banks.) The Board of Governors of the Federal Reserve System is located in Washington, D.C.

* Hawaii and Alaska are included in the San Francisco district

◯ Federal Reserve districts
◉ Federal Reserve bank cities
◯ Board of Governors of the Federal Reserve

Source: *Federal Reserve Bulletin*, published monthly.

---

main point of contact with the President and government and with foreign central banks and governments.

The Fed's Policy Tools

The Federal Reserve System has many responsibilities, but we'll examine its single most important one: regulating the amount of money floating around in the United States. How does the Fed control the money supply? It does so by adjusting the reserves of the banking system. It is also by adjusting the reserves of the banking system and by standing ready to make loans to banks that the Fed is able to prevent bank failures. The Fed uses three main policy tools to achieve its objectives:

■ Required reserve ratios
■ Discount rate
■ Open market operations

Required Reserve Ratios   All depository institutions in the United States are required to hold a minimum

percentage of deposits as reserves. This minimum percentage is known as a *required reserve ratio*. The Fed determines a required reserve ratio for each type of deposit. In 1997, banks were required to hold minimum reserves equal to 3 percent of checking deposits up to $49 million and 10 percent of these deposits in excess of $49 million. The required reserves on other types of deposits were zero.

Discount Rate   The **discount rate** is the interest rate at which the Fed stands ready to lend reserves to commercial banks. A change in the discount rate is proposed to the FOMC by the Board of Directors of at least one of the 12 Federal Reserve banks and is approved by the Board of Governors.

Open Market Operations   An **open market operation** is the purchase or sale of government securities—U.S. Treasury bills and bonds—by the Federal Reserve System in the open market. When the Fed conducts an open market operation, it makes a transaction with a bank or some other business but it does not transact with the federal government.

The structure and policy tools of the Federal Reserve System are summarized in Fig. 32.2. To understand how open market operations work, we need to know about the Fed's balance sheet.

The Fed's Balance Sheet

The balance sheet of the Federal Reserve System for December 1998 is set out in Table 32.1. The assets on the left side are what the Fed owns, and the liabilities on the right side are what it owes. The Fed's three main assets are:

1. Gold and foreign exchange
2. U.S. government securities
3. Loans to banks

The Fed's holdings of gold and foreign exchange are its international reserves. Most of the Fed's foreign exchange consists of deposits by the Fed at other central banks. The Fed's holdings of U.S. government securities are the backing for dollar bills and banks' deposits at the Fed. The Fed sometimes makes loans to banks on which the Fed charges them the discount rate. (These loans were negligible in December 1998.)

The Fed's two main liabilities are:

1. Federal Reserve notes in circulation
2. Banks' deposits

The Federal Reserve notes in circulation are the dollar bills that we use in our daily transactions. Some of these bills are in circulation with the public; others are in the tills and vaults of banks and other financial institutions. Banks' deposits are the deposits of commercial banks, which are part of the reserves of those banks.

You might be wondering why Federal Reserve notes are considered a liability of the Fed. When bank notes were invented, they gave their owner a claim on the gold reserves of the issuing bank. Such notes were *convertible paper money.* The holder of such a note could convert the note on demand into gold (or some other commodity such as silver) at a guaranteed price. Thus when a bank issued a note, it was holding itself liable to convert that note into gold or silver. Modern bank notes are nonconvertible. A *nonconvertible note* is a bank note that is not convertible into any commodity and that obtains its value by government fiat—hence the term "fiat money." Such notes are the legal liability of the bank that issues them, and they are backed by holdings of securities and loans. Federal Reserve notes are backed by the Fed's holdings of U.S. government securities.

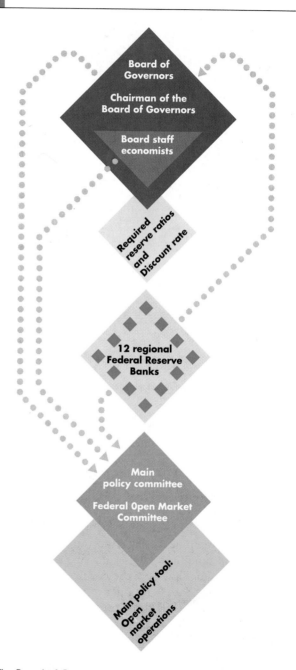

FIGURE **32.2**

The Structure of the Fed

Board of Governors

Chairman of the Board of Governors

Board staff economists

Required reserve ratios and Discount rate

12 regional Federal Reserve Banks

Main policy committee Federal Open Market Committee

Main policy tool: Open market operations

The Board of Governors sets required reserve ratios and, on the proposal of the 12 Federal Reserve banks, sets the discount rate. The Board of Governors and presidents of the regional Federal Reserve banks sit on the FOMC to determine open market operations.

TABLE 32.1
The Fed's Balance Sheet, December 1998

Assets (billions of dollars)		Liabilities (billions of dollars)	
Gold and foreign exchange	65	Federal Reserve notes	481
U.S. government securities	463	Banks' deposits	27
Loans to banks	0	Other liabilities (net)	20
Total assets	528	Total liabilities	528

Source: Federal Reserve Bulletin (March 1999).

The Fed's liabilities, together with coins in circulation (coins are issued by the Treasury and are not liabilities of the Fed), make up the monetary base. That is, the **monetary base** is the sum of Federal Reserve notes, coins, and banks' deposits at the Fed. The monetary base is so called because it acts like a base that supports the nation's money supply. The larger the monetary base, the greater is the quantity of money.

REVIEW QUIZ

- What is the central bank of the United States and what functions does it perform?
- Who appoints the Fed board members and chairman and for how long do they serve?
- What is special about the Federal Reserve Bank of New York?
- Can you name the three policy tools that the Fed uses?
- What is the Federal Open Market Committee and what are its main functions?
- How often does the FOMC meet?

Next, we're going to see how the Fed controls the money supply. We'll see how the Fed's monetary policy instruments change the monetary base and how changes in the monetary base change the quantity of money in circulation.

Controlling the Money Supply

THE FED CONSTANTLY MONITORS AND ADJUSTS the quantity of money in the economy. To change the quantity of money, the Fed can use any of its three tools: required reserve ratios, the discount rate, and open market operations. Required reserve ratios are changed infrequently. The discount rate and open market operations are used more frequently. Let's see how these tools work.

How Required Reserve Ratios Work

When the Fed *increases* the required reserve ratio, the banks must hold more reserves. To increase their reserves, the banks must *decrease* their lending, which *decreases* the quantity of money. When the Fed *decreases* the required reserve ratio, the banks may hold less reserves. To decrease their reserves, the banks *increase* their lending, which *increases* the quantity of money.

How the Discount Rate Works

When the Fed *increases* the discount rate, the banks must pay a higher price for any reserves that they borrow from the Fed. Faced with higher cost of reserves, the banks try to get by with smaller reserves. But with a given required reserve ratio, the banks must also *decrease* their lending to decrease their borrowed reserves. So the quantity of money *decreases*. When the Fed *decreases* the discount rate, the banks pay a lower price for any reserves that they borrow from the Fed. Faced with lower cost of reserves, the banks are willing to borrow more reserves and *increase* their lending. So the quantity of money *increases*.

How an Open Market Operation Works

When the Fed *buys* securities in an open market operation, bank reserves *increase,* banks *increase* their lending, and the quantity of money *increases*. When the Fed *sells* securities in an open market operation, bank reserves *decrease*, banks *decrease* their lending, and the quantity of money *decreases*. Open market operations are used more frequently than the other two tools and are the most complex in their operation. So we'll study this tool in greater detail than the other two.

The key to understanding how an open market operation works is to see how it changes the reserves of the banking system. We'll trace the effects of an open market operation when the Fed *buys* securities. (The effects of a sale of securities are the reverse of what we'll see here.)

The Fed Buys Securities Suppose the Fed buys $100 million of U.S. government securities in the open market. There are two cases to consider: when the Fed buys from a commercial bank and when it buys from the public (a person or business that is not a commercial bank). The outcome is essentially the same in either case, but you might need to be convinced of this fact, so we'll study the two cases, starting with the simplest case, in which the Fed buys from a commercial bank.

Buys from Commercial Bank When the Fed buys $100 million of securities from the Manhattan Commercial Bank, two things happen:

1. The Manhattan Commercial Bank has $100 million less securities, and the Fed has $100 million more securities.
2. The Fed pays for the securities by crediting the Manhattan Commercial Bank's deposit account at the Fed with $100 million.

Figure 32.3(a) shows the effects of these actions on the balance sheets of the Fed and the Manhattan Commercial Bank. Ownership of the securities passes from the commercial bank to the Fed, so the bank's assets decrease by $100 million and the Fed's assets increase by $100 million, as shown by the blue arrow running from the Manhattan Commercial Bank to the Fed. The Fed pays for the securities by crediting the Manhattan Commercial Bank's deposit account—its reserves—at the Fed with $100 million, as shown by the green arrow running from the Fed to the Manhattan Commercial Bank. This action increases the monetary base and increases the reserves of the banking system.

The Fed's assets increase by $100 million, and its liabilities also increase by $100 million. The commercial bank's total assets remain constant, but their composition changes. Its holdings of government securities decrease by $100 million, and its deposits at the Fed increase by $100 million. So the bank has additional reserves, which it can use to make loans.

FIGURE 32.3

The Fed Buys Securities in the Open Market

(a) The Fed buys securities from a commercial bank

The Federal Reserve Bank of New York

Assets		Liabilities
Securities +$100		Reserves of Manhattan Commercial Bank +$100
The Fed buys securities from a commercial bank ...	... and pays for the securities by increasing the reserves of the commercial bank	

The Manhattan Commercial Bank

Assets		Liabilities
Securities −$100		
Reserves +$100		

(b) The Fed buys securities from the public

The Federal Reserve Bank of New York

Assets		Liabilities
Securities +$100		Reserves of Manhattan Commercial Bank +$100
The Fed buys securities from Goldman Sachs, a member of the general public ...		

Goldman Sachs

Assets		Liabilities
Securities −$100		... and pays for the securities by writing a check that is deposited to Goldman Sachs's account at the Manhattan Commercial Bank and that increases the reserves of the commercial banks
Deposits at Manhattan Commercial Bank +$100		

The Manhattan Commercial Bank

Assets		Liabilities
Reserves +$100		Goldman Sachs's deposit +$100

We've just seen that when the Fed buys government securities from a bank, the bank's reserves increase. But what happens if the Fed buys government securities from the public—say, from Goldman Sachs, a financial services company?

Buys from Public When the Fed buys $100 million of securities from Goldman Sachs, three things happen:

1. Goldman Sachs has $100 million less securities, and the Fed has $100 million more securities.
2. The Fed pays for the securities with a check for $100 million drawn on itself, which Goldman Sachs deposits in its account at the Manhattan Commercial Bank.
3. The Manhattan Commercial Bank collects payment of this check from the Fed, and $100 million is deposited in Manhattan's deposit account at the Fed.

Figure 32.3(b) shows the effects of these actions on the balance sheets of the Fed, Goldman Sachs, and the Manhattan Commercial Bank. Ownership of the securities passes from Goldman Sachs to the Fed, so Goldman Sachs's assets decrease by $100 million and the Fed's assets increase by $100 million, as shown by the blue arrow running from Goldman Sachs to the Fed. The Fed pays for the securities with a check payable to Goldman Sachs, which Goldman Sachs deposits in the Manhattan Commercial Bank. This payment increases Manhattan's reserves by $100 million, as shown by green arrow running from the Fed to Manhattan Commercial Bank. It also increases Goldman Sachs's deposit at the Manhattan Commercial Bank by $100 million, as shown by the red arrow running from the Manhattan Commercial Bank to Goldman Sachs. Just as when the Fed buys from a bank, this action increases the monetary base and increases the reserves of the banking system.

Again, the Fed's assets increase by $100 million, and its liabilities also increase by $100 million. Goldman Sachs has the same total assets as before, but their composition has changed. It now has more money and fewer securities. The Manhattan Commercial Bank's total assets increase, and so do its liabilities. Its deposits at the Fed—its reserves—increase by $100 million, and its deposit liability to Goldman Sachs increases by $100 million. Because its reserves have increased by the same amount as its deposits, the bank has excess reserves, which it can use to make loans.

We've studied what happens when the Fed *buys* government securities from either a bank or the public. When the Fed *sells* securities, all the transactions and events you've just studied work in reverse. (Trace the process again but with the Fed selling and the banks or public buying securities.)

The effects of an open market operation on the balance sheets of the Fed and the banks that we've just described are not the end of the story—they are just the beginning.

A change in bank reserves that results from an open market operation has ripple effects through the economy. First, it has a multiplier effect on the quantity of money. Second, it changes interest rates. Third, it changes aggregate expenditure and real GDP.

We are going to study these ripple effects in the rest of this chapter. We begin by studying the multiplier effect of an open market operation on the quantity of money. To do so, we build on the link between bank reserves and bank deposits that you studied in Chapter 31. But first we must learn about a related link between bank reserves and the monetary base.

Bank Reserves, the Monetary Base, and the Money Multiplier

An open market purchase that increases bank reserves also increases the monetary base. The increase in the monetary base equals the amount of the open market purchase and, initially it equals the increase in bank reserves. To see why, recall that the *monetary base* is the sum of Federal Reserve notes, coins, and banks' deposits at the Fed. An open market purchase increases the banks' deposits at the Fed—part of banks' reserves—by the amount of the open market purchase. Nothing else changes, so the monetary base increases by the amount of the open market purchase.

But when the banks use the new reserves to make loans, bank deposits and currency held outside the banks increase. An increase in currency held outside the banks is called a **currency drain**. A currency drain does not change the monetary base. Bank reserves decrease, currency increases, and the monetary base remains the same. But a currency drain decreases the amount of money that banks can create from a given increase in the monetary base.

The amount of money that banks can create from a given increase in the monetary base is determined by the **money multiplier**, which is the amount by which a change in the monetary base is multiplied to determine the resulting change in the quantity of money. Let's now look at the money multiplier.

The Multiplier Effect of an Open Market Operation

Figure 32.4 shows the multiplier effect of an open market purchase of securities from the banks. Initially, the banks' reserves increase but the quantity of money does not change. The banks have excess reserves, and the following sequence of events takes place:

- Banks lend excess reserves.
- The money supply increases.
- New deposits are used to make payments.
- Some of the new money is held as currency— a *currency drain*.
- Some of the new money remains on deposit in banks.
- Banks' required reserves increase.
- Excess reserves decrease but remain positive.

The sequence repeats in a series of rounds, but each round begins with a smaller quantity of excess reserves

than did the previous one. The process continues until excess reserves have finally been eliminated.

Figure 32.5 keeps track of the increases in reserves, loans, deposits, currency, and money that results from an open market operation of $100,000. In this figure, the *currency drain* is 33.33 percent and the *required reserve ratio* is 10 percent. These numbers are assumed to keep the arithmetic simple.

The Fed buys $100,000 of securities from the banks. The banks' reserves increase by this amount, but deposits do not change. The banks have excess reserves of $100,000, and they lend those reserves. When the banks lend $100,000 of excess reserves, $66,667 remains in the banks as deposits and $33,333 drains off and is held outside the banks as currency. The quantity of money has now increased by $100,000—the increase in deposits plus the increase in currency holdings.

The increased bank deposits of $66,667 generates an increase in required reserves of 10 percent of that amount, which is $6,667. Actual reserves have

---

FIGURE 32.4

A Round in the Multiplier Process Following an Open Market Operation

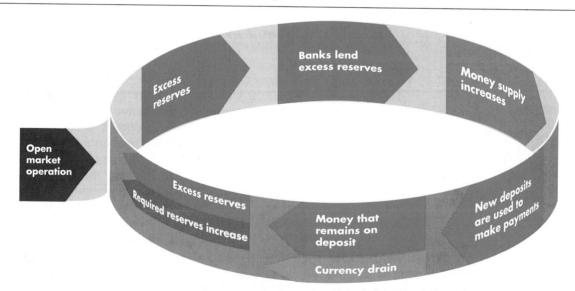

An open market operation increases bank reserves and creates excess reserves. Banks lend the excess reserves, and new loans are used to make payments. Households and firms receiving payments keep some of the receipts in the form of currency— a currency drain—and place the rest on deposit in banks. The

increase in bank deposits increases banks' reserves but also increases banks' required reserves. Required reserves increase by less than actual reserves, so the banks still have some excess reserves, though less than before. The process repeats until excess reserves have been eliminated.

FIGURE 32.5

The Multiplier Effect of an Open Market Operation

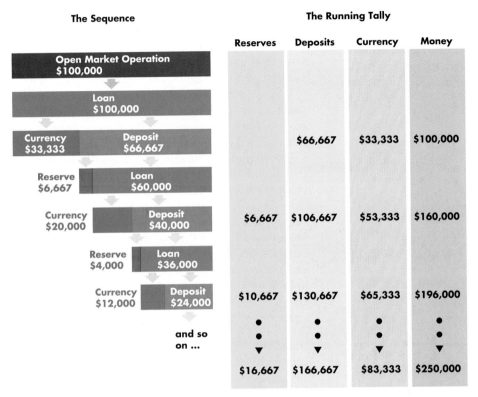

When the Fed provides the banks with $100,000 of additional reserves in an open market operation, the banks lend those reserves. Of the amount lent, $33,333 (33.33 percent) leaves the banks in a currency drain and $66,667 remains on deposit. With additional deposits, required reserves increase by $6,667 (10 percent required reserve ratio) and the banks lend $60,000. Of this amount, $20,000 leaves the banks in a currency drain and $40,000 remains on deposit. The process repeats until the banks have created enough deposits to eliminate their excess reserves. An additional $100,000 of reserves creates $250,000 of money.

---

increased by the same amount as the increase in deposits—$66,667. So the banks now have excess reserves of $60,000. At this stage, we have gone once around the circle shown in Fig. 32.4. The process we've just described repeats but begins with excess reserves of $60,000. Figure 32.5 shows the next two rounds. At the end of the process, the quantity of money has increased by a multiple of the increase in the monetary base. In this case, the increase is $250,000, which is 2.5 times the increase in the monetary base.

An open market *sale* works similarly to an open market purchase, but it *decreases* the quantity of money. (Trace the process again but with the Fed selling and the banks or public buying securities.)

When the Fed undertakes an open market operation, it is trying to influence the course of the economy. But the Fed's influence is indirect. You've now studied the initial effect of the Fed's actions, which is to change the quantity of money.

When the Fed changes the quantity of money, interest rates change. To see why, we must study the demand for money.

The Demand for Money

THE AMOUNT OF MONEY WE RECEIVE EACH WEEK in payment for our labor is income—a flow. The amount of money that we hold in our wallet or in a deposit account at the bank is an inventory—a stock. There is no limit to how much income we would like to receive each week. But there is a limit to how big an inventory of money each of us would like to hold on to and not spend.

The Influences on Money Holding

The quantity of money that people choose to hold depends on four main factors:

- The price level
- The interest rate
- Real GDP
- Financial innovation

Let's look at each of them.

The Price Level   The quantity of money measured in dollars is called the quantity of *nominal money*. The quantity of nominal money demanded is proportional to the price level, other things remaining the same. That is, if the price level (GDP deflator) increases by 10 percent, people will want to hold 10 percent more nominal money than before, other things being equal. What matters is not the number of dollars that you hold but their buying power. If you hold $20 to buy your weekly movies and soda, you will increase your money holding to $22 if the prices of movies and soda—and your wage rate—increase by 10 percent.

The quantity of money measured in constant dollars (for example, in 1992 dollars) is called *real money*. Real money is equal to nominal money divided by the price level. It is the quantity of money measured in terms of what it will buy. In the above example, when the price level rises by 10 percent and you increase your average cash holding by 10 percent, you are keeping your *real* cash holding constant. Your $22 at the new price level buys the same quantity of goods and is the same quantity of *real money* as your $20 at the original price level. The quantity of real money held does not depend on the price level.

The Interest Rate   A fundamental principle of economics is that as the opportunity cost of something increases, people try to find substitutes for it. Money is no exception. The higher the opportunity cost of holding money, other things being equal, the lower is the quantity of real money demanded. But what is the opportunity cost of holding money? It is the interest rate that you must forgo on other assets that you could hold instead of money minus the interest rate that you can earn by holding money.

The interest rate that you earn on currency and some checking deposits is zero. So the opportunity cost of holding these items is the interest rate on other assets such as a savings bond or Treasury bill. By holding money instead, you forgo the interest that you otherwise would have received. This forgone interest is the opportunity cost of holding money.

Money loses value because of inflation. So why isn't the inflation rate part of the cost of holding money? It is: Other things being equal, the higher the expected inflation rate, the higher are interest rates and the higher, therefore, is the opportunity cost of holding money. (The forces that make interest rates change to reflect changes in the expected inflation rate are described in Chapter 33 on pp. 750–751.)

Real GDP   The quantity of money that households and firms plan to hold depends on the amount they are spending, and the quantity of money demanded in the economy as a whole depends on aggregate expenditure—real GDP.

Again, suppose that you hold an average of $20 to finance your weekly purchases of movies and soda. Now imagine that the prices of these goods and of all other goods remain constant but that your income increases. As a consequence, you now spend more, and you also keep a larger amount of money on hand to finance your higher volume of expenditure.

Financial Innovation   Technological change and the arrival of new financial products change the quantity of money held. The major financial innovations are the widespread use of:

1. Daily interest checking deposits
2. Automatic transfers between checking and savings deposits
3. Automatic teller machines
4. Credit cards

These innovations have occurred because of the development of computing power that has lowered the cost of calculations and record keeping.

We summarize the effects of the influences on money holding by using the demand for money curve.

The Demand for Money Curve

The *demand for money* is the relationship between the quantity of real money demanded and the interest rate, when all other influences on the amount of money that people wish to hold remain the same. Figure 32.6 shows a demand for money curve, *MD*. When the interest rate rises, everything else remaining the same, the opportunity cost of holding money rises and the quantity of money demanded decreases—there is a movement along the demand for money curve. Similarly, when the interest rate falls, the opportunity cost of holding money falls and the quantity of money demanded increases—there is a downward movement along the demand for money curve.

Shifts in the Demand Curve for Real Money

A change in real GDP or financial innovation changes the demand for money and shifts the demand curve for real money. Figure 32.7 illustrates the change in the demand for money. A decrease in real GDP decreases the demand for money and shifts the demand curve leftward from MD_0 to MD_1. An increase in real GDP has the opposite effect. It increases the demand for money and shifts the demand curve rightward from MD_0 to MD_2.

The influence of financial innovation on the demand for money curve is more complicated. It might increase the demand for some types of deposits, decrease the demand for others, and decrease the demand for currency. We'll look at the effects of financial innovation by studying the demand for money in the United States.

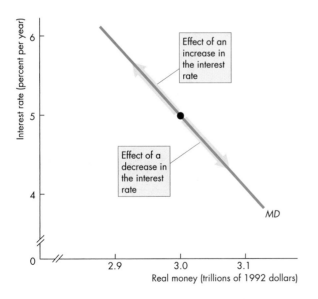

FIGURE 32.6
The Demand for Money

The demand for money curve, *MD*, shows the relationship between the quantity of money that people plan to hold and the interest rate, other things remaining the same. The interest rate is the opportunity cost of holding money. A change in the interest rate brings a movement along the demand curve.

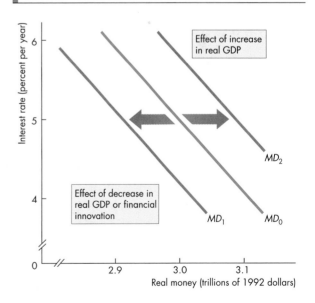

FIGURE 32.7
Changes in the Demand for Money

A decrease in real GDP decreases the demand for money and shifts the demand curve leftward from MD_0 to MD_1. An increase in real GDP increases the demand for money and shifts the demand curve rightward from MD_0 to MD_2. Financial innovation generally decreases the demand for money.

The Demand for Money in the United States

Figure 32.8 shows the relationship between the interest rate and the quantity of real money demanded in the United States between 1970 and 1998. Each dot shows the interest rate and the amount of real money held in a given year. In 1970, the demand for M1 (shown in part a) was MD_0. During the early 1970s, the spread of credit cards decreased the demand for M1 (currency and checking deposits) and shifted the demand for M1 curve leftward to MD_1. But over the years, real GDP growth increased the demand for M1 and by 1994 the demand for M1 curve had shifted rightward to MD_2. Further financial innovation arising from a continued increase in the use of credit

cards and the spread of ATMs decreased the demand for M1 and shifted the demand curve leftward again.

In 1970, the demand for M2 (shown in part b) was MD_0. The spread of credit cards that decreased the demand for M1 during the period did not decrease demand for M2. The reason is that many new financial products were M2 deposits. So from 1970 through 1989, the demand for M2 increased and the demand for M2 curve shifted rightward to MD_1. But between 1989 and 1994, innovations in financial products that compete with deposits of all kinds occurred and the demand for M2 decreased. The demand for M2 curve shifted leftward to MD_2. Finally, after 1994, the expanding economy brought rising real GDP. The demand for M2 increases again and the demand curve shifted rightward to MD_3.

FIGURE 32.8

The Demand for Money in the United States

(a) M1 demand

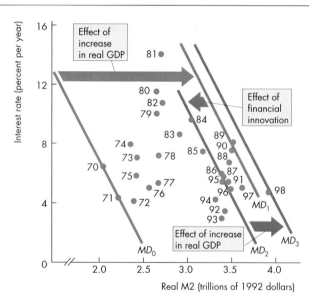

(b) M2 demand

The dots show the quantity of real money and the interest rate in each year between 1970 and 1998. In 1970, the demand for M1 was MD_0 in part (a). The demand for M1 decreased during the early 1970s because of financial innovation and the demand curve shifted leftward to MD_2. But real GDP growth increased the demand for M1 and by 1994, the demand curve had shifted rightward to MD_2. Further financial innovation decreased the demand for M1 in 1995 and 1998 and shifted the demand

curve leftward again to MD_3. In 1970, the demand for M2 curve was MD_0 in part (b). The growth of real GDP increased the demand for M2 and by 1989, the demand curve had shifted rightward to MD_1. During the early 1990s, new substitutes for M2 decreased the demand for M2 and the demand curve shifted leftward to MD_2. But during the late 1990s, rapid growth of real GDP increased the demand for M2 and the demand curve shifted rightward to MD_3.

Source: *Economic Report of the President*, 1999, and the author's calculations and assumptions.

- What are the main influences on the quantity of real money that people and businesses plan to hold?
- What does the demand for money curve show?
- How does an increase in the interest rate change the quantity of money demanded and how would you use the demand curve for real money to show the effects?
- How does an increase in real GDP change the demand for money and how would you use the demand curve for real money to show the effects?
- How have financial innovations changed the demand for M1 and M2?

We now know what determines the demand for money. And we've seen that a key factor is the interest rate—the opportunity cost of holding money. But what determines the interest rate? Let's find out.

Interest Rate Determination

AN INTEREST RATE IS THE PERCENTAGE YIELD on a financial security such as a *bond* or a *stock*. The higher the price of a financial asset, other things remaining the same, the lower is the interest rate. An example will make this relationship clear. Suppose the federal government sells a bond that promises to pay $10 a year. If the price of the bond is $100, the interest rate is 10 percent per year—$10 is 10 percent of $100. If the price of the bond is $50, the interest rate is 20 percent—$10 is 20 percent of $50. And if the price of the bond is $200, the interest rate is 5 percent—$10 is 5 percent of $200.

You've just seen the link between the price of a bond and the interest rate. People divide their wealth between bonds (and other interest-bearing financial assets) and money, and the amount they hold as money depends on the interest rate. We can study the forces that determine the interest rate in either the market for bonds or the market for money. Because the Fed can influence the *supply* of money, we focus on the market for money.

Money Market Equilibrium

The interest rate is determined by the supply of and demand for money. The quantity of money supplied is determined by the actions of the banking system and the Fed. On any given day, the supply of money is a fixed quantity. The *real* quantity of money supplied is equal to the nominal quantity supplied divided by the price level. At a given moment in time, there is a particular price level, and so the quantity of real money supplied is also a fixed amount. The supply curve of real money is shown in Fig. 32.9 as the vertical line labeled *MS*. The quantity of real money supplied is $3.0 trillion.

FIGURE 32.9
Money Market Equilibrium

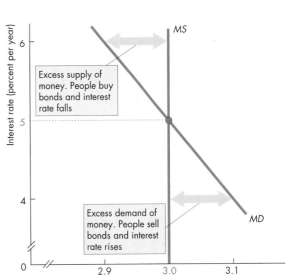

Money market equilibrium occurs when the interest rate has adjusted to make the quantity of real money demanded equal to the quantity supplied. Here, equilibrium occurs at an interest rate of 5 percent a year. At interest rates above 5 percent a year, the quantity of real money demanded is less than the quantity supplied, so people buy bonds and the interest rate falls. At interest rates below 5 percent a year, the quantity of real money demanded exceeds the quantity supplied, so people sell bonds and the interest rate rises. Only at 5 percent a year is the quantity of real money in existence willingly held.

On any given day, all the influences on the demand for money except for the interest rate are constant. But the lower the interest rate, the greater is the quantity of real money demanded. Figure 32.9 shows a demand for real money curve, MD.

Equilibrium   When the quantity of real money supplied equals the quantity of real money demanded, the money market is in equilibrium. Figure 32.9 illustrates equilibrium in the money market. Equilibrium is achieved by changes in the interest rate. If the interest rate is too high, people demand a smaller quantity of money than the quantity supplied. They are holding too much money. In this situation, they try to get rid of money by buying bonds. As they do so, the price of a bond rises and the interest rate falls to the equilibrium rate. Conversely, if the interest rate is too low, people demand a larger quantity of money than the quantity supplied. They are holding too little money. In this situation, they try to get more money by selling bonds. As they do so, the price of a bond falls and the interest rate rises to the equilibrium rate. Only when the interest rate is at the level at which people are holding the quantity of money supplied do they willingly hold the money and take no actions that change the interest rate.

Changing the Interest Rate

Suppose that the economy is overheating and the Fed fears inflation. It decides to take action to decrease aggregate demand and spending. To do so, it wants to raise interest rates and discourage borrowing and expenditure on goods and services. What does the Fed do?

The Fed sells securities in the open market. As it does so, it mops up bank reserves and induces the banks to cut their lending. The banks make a smaller quantity of new loans each day until the stock of loans outstanding has fallen to a level that is consistent with the new lower level of reserves. The money supply decreases.

Suppose that the Fed undertakes open market operations on a sufficiently large scale to decrease the money supply from $3.0 trillion to $2.9 trillion. As a consequence, the supply curve of real money shifts leftward, as shown in Fig. 32.10, from MS_0 to MS_1.

The demand for money is shown by MD. With an interest rate of 5 percent a year and $2.9 trillion of money in the economy, firms and households are now holding less money than they wish to hold. They attempt to increase their money holding by selling financial assets. As they do so, the price of a bond

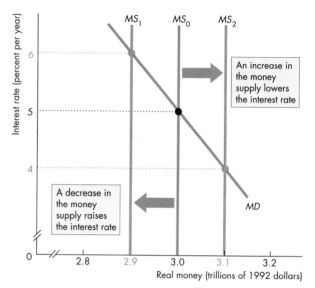

FIGURE 32.10

Interest Rate Changes

An open market sale of securities shifts the money supply curve leftward to MS_1, and the interest rate rises to 6 percent a year. An open market purchase of securities shifts the money supply curve rightward to MS_2, and the interest rate falls to 4 percent a year.

falls and the interest rate rises. When the interest rate has increased to 6 percent a year, people are willing to hold the smaller $2.9 trillion of money that the Fed and the banks have created.

Conversely, suppose that the Fed fears recession and decides to stimulate spending by increasing the money supply. If the Fed increases the real money supply to $3.1 trillion, the supply of real money curve shifts rightward from MS_0 to MS_2. The interest rate falls to 4 percent a year.

R E V I E W   Q U I Z

- How is the short-term interest rate determined?
- What do people do if they are holding more money than they plan to hold and what happens to the interest rate?
- What actions does the Fed take if it wants to increase the interest rate? What actions does the Fed take if it wants to decrease the interest rate?

Monetary Policy

YOU HAVE NOW LEARNED A GREAT DEAL ABOUT the Fed, the monetary policy actions it can take, and the effects of those actions on short-term interest rates. Most of the "secrets of the temple" have been revealed. But you are possibly thinking: All this sounds nice in theory, but does it really happen? Does the Fed actually do the things we've learned about in this chapter? Indeed, it does happen, sometimes with dramatic effect.

To see the Fed in action, we'll do two things. First, we'll look at the fluctuations in short-term interest rates in the United States since 1970 and see how the Fed has influenced those fluctuations. Second, we'll focus on two episodes in the life of the Fed. One is from the turbulent years of the early 1980s when the Fed was struggling to eradicate a stubborn inflation. The other is from the period since a stock market crash of 1987 during which the Fed tried to keep inflation in check without killing economic growth.

The Fed in Action

You've seen that the immediate effect of the Fed's actions is a change in the short-term interest rate. Figure 32.11 shows the course of four short-term interest rates since 1970:

1. The 3-month Treasury bill rate, which is the interest rate paid by the federal government on 3-month loans

2. The 6-month commercial bill rate, which is the interest rate paid by large corporations on 6-month loans

3. The discount rate, which is the interest rate charged to banks by the Fed when the banks borrow reserves

4. The federal funds rate, which is the interest rate that the banks charge each other on overnight loans of reserves

Notice how closely these four interest rates move together. The interest rate that the Fed directly controls is the discount rate, and the rate that it closely

FIGURE 32.11

Short-Term Interest Rates

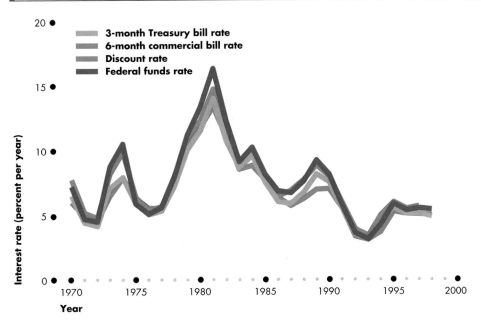

The Fed directly determines the discount rate (the rate at which the Fed lends reserves to banks) and closely monitors the federal funds rate (the rate at which banks lend reserves to each other). All short-term interest rates move up and down together, so the Fed influences all short-term rates such as the 3-month Treasury bill rate (the rate at which the federal government borrows in the short term) and the 6-month commercial bill rate (the rate at which big corporations borrow in the short term).

Source: *Economic Report of the President,* 1999

monitors is the federal funds rate, but because the short-term rates all move up and down together, the Fed is effectively able to influence all these rates.

Do short-term interest rates rise and fall in response to changes in the quantity of money, as the theory we've just studied predicts? Mostly they do, but not quite always. Figure 32.12 illustrates this connection. It shows the federal funds rate and a measure of the quantity of money. This measure of money is M2 expressed as a percentage of GDP. The reason for looking at M2 is that it is this measure of money that the Fed has placed greatest emphasis on. The reason for expressing M2 as a percentage of GDP is that we can see both the supply-side and demand-side effects on interest rates in a single measure. Interest rates rise if the quantity of money decreases. Interest rates also rise if the demand for money increases. But the demand for money increases if GDP increases. So the ratio of M2 to GDP decreases if either the supply of money decreases (M2 decreases) or the demand for money increases (GDP increases).

You can see by studying Fig. 32.12 that between 1970 and 1990, the rises and falls in the interest rate were exactly matched by decreases and increases in the ratio of M2 to GDP. An increase in the supply of money relative to the demand for money brought a fall in the interest rate (1970–1972, 1974–1977, and 1981–1986). A decrease in the supply of money relative to the demand for money brought a rise in the interest rate (1972–1974, 1977–1981, and 1986–1989).

You can also see in Fig. 32.12 that after 1990, the relationship between money and interest rates broke down. When the interest rate fell through 1993, the M2 to GDP ratio did not increase. The reason is that the demand for M2 fell because of the availability of some new substitute ways of holding wealth—bond and equity mutual funds. These funds were growing through the 1980s, but they grew more quickly during the 1990s, and their growth disturbed the traditional relationship between M2 and short-term interest rates. Consequently, after 1990, the Fed began to pay less attention to M2.

FIGURE 32.12
Money and Interest Rates

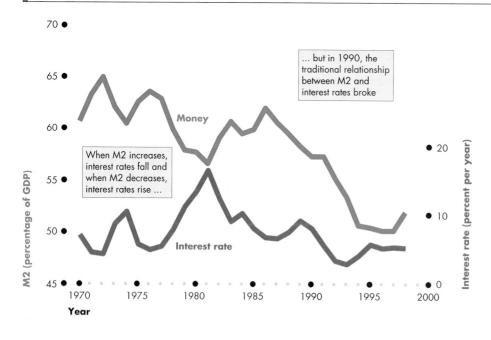

When the ratio of M2 to GDP (measured on the left scale) rises, either the supply of money increases or the demand for money decreases. The result, before 1990, is a fall in the federal funds rate (measured on the right scale). Similarly, when the ratio of M2 to GDP falls, either the supply of money has decreased or the demand for money has increased and (again before 1990) the federal funds rate rises. After 1990, the relationship between M2 and interest rates broke down because new substitutes for M2 decreased the demand for M2.

Source: *Economic Report of the President,* 1999, and the author's calculations.

You've now seen that we can explain short-term interest rate fluctuations as arising from fluctuations in the supply of money relative to the demand for money. But this relationship doesn't tell us whether actions by the Fed or fluctuations in GDP brought the fluctuations in the M2 to GDP ratio. Do the Fed's own actions move interest rates around? Let's look at the Fed in action.

Paul Volcker's Fed   At the start of Paul Volcker's term of office as chairman of the Fed, which began in August 1979, the United States was locked in the grips of double-digit inflation. Volcker ended that inflation. He did so by forcing interest rates sharply upward from 1979 through 1981. This increase in interest rates resulted from the Fed using open market operations and increases in the discount rate to keep the banks short of reserves, which in turn held back the growth in the supply of loans and of money relative to the growth in their demand.

As we saw in Fig. 32.10, to increase interest rates, the Fed has to cut the real money supply. In practice, because the economy is growing and because prices are rising, a *slowdown* in nominal money supply growth is enough to increase interest rates. It is not necessary to actually *cut* the nominal money supply.

When Volcker became chairman of the Fed, the money supply was growing at more than 8 percent a year. Volcker slowed down that money supply growth to 6.5 percent in 1981. As a result, interest rates increased. The Treasury bill rate—the rate at which the government borrows—increased from 10 percent to 14 percent. The rate at which big corporations borrow increased from 9 percent to 14 percent. Mortgage rates—the rates at which homebuyers borrow—increased from 11 percent to 15 percent. The economy went into recession. The money supply growth slowdown and interest rate hike cut back the growth rate of aggregate demand. Real GDP decreased, and the inflation rate fell.

Alan Greenspan's Fed   Alan Greenspan became chairman of the Fed in August 1987. In the two preceding years, the money supply had grown at a rapid pace, interest rates had tumbled, and the stock market had boomed. Then, suddenly and with no warning, stock prices fell, bringing fears of economic calamity and recession. This was Alan Greenspan's first test as Fed chairman.

The Fed's immediate reaction to the new situation was to emphasize the flexibility and sensitivity of the financial system and to make reserves plentiful to avoid any fear of a banking crisis. But as the months passed, it became increasingly clear that the economy was not heading for any kind of a recession. Unemployment continued to fall, income growth continued to be strong, and the fears that emerged were of inflation, not recession.

Seeking to avoid an upturn in inflation, the Fed slowed money growth and, just as Paul Volcker had done eight years earlier, forced interest rates sharply upward. Open market operations created a shortage of reserves and slowed the growth rate of the money supply. The slowdown in money supply growth had the effect implied by the model that you have been studying in this chapter. Interest rates increased throughout 1988. As 1989 advanced, concern about inflation remained, but renewed fears of recession returned, and interest rates were gradually lowered.

By 1990, recession had become a reality. At first, the Fed adopted a neutral position and waited for signs of recovery. But as the months passed and recovery seemed elusive, the Fed eventually began to cut interest rates. During 1991, interest rates fell by three percentage points as the Fed tried to stimulate aggregate demand.

By mid-1991, the recovery had begun and real GDP expanded. This expansion was to become one of the longest and strongest in history. The Fed helped to keep the expansion alive and to hold inflation in check. It did so by trying to anticipate unwanted deviations in either direction.

Through 1992 and 1993, the Fed permitted rapid money growth and kept interest rates low. During 1994, the Fed slowed money growth and pushed interest rates upward. It permitted interest rates to fall again during 1996 and nudged them up slightly in the first quarter of 1997.

Through most of 1997, the Fed's main concern was to hold inflation in check. But by the end of the year and throughout 1998, a different type of risk threatened. Economic growth was slowing in Asia. Japan and some other usually fast-growing economies were in deepening recession. Russia was in economic turmoil. Latin America was slowing. Even in parts of Europe, real GDP growth began to slow. At the same time, real GDP in the United States almost certainly exceeded potential GDP. So during 1998, the Fed tried to balance two opposing risks: inflation from the domestic economy and recession abroad. Eventually, the foreign risk dominated and the Fed engineered a series of interest rate cuts aimed at keeping the economy expanding.

Profiting by Predicting the Fed

Every day, the Fed influences interest rates by its open market operations. By buying securities and increasing the money supply, the Fed can lower interest rates; by selling securities and lowering the money supply, the Fed can increase interest rates. Sometimes such actions are taken to offset other influences and keep interest rates steady. At other times, the Fed moves interest rates up or down. The higher the interest rate, the lower is the price of a bond; the lower the interest rate, the higher is the price of a bond. Thus predicting interest rates is the same as predicting bond prices. Predicting that interest rates are going to fall is the same as predicting that bond prices are going to rise—a good time to buy bonds. Predicting that interest rates are going to rise is the same as predicting that bond prices are going to fall—a good time to sell bonds.

Because the Fed is the major player whose actions influence interest rates and bond prices, predicting the Fed is profitable and a good deal of effort goes into that activity. But people who anticipate that the Fed is about to increase the money supply buy bonds right away, pushing their prices upward and pushing interest rates downward *before* the Fed acts. Similarly, people who anticipate that the Fed is about to decrease the money supply sell bonds right away, pushing their prices downward and pushing interest rates upward before the Fed acts. In other words, bond prices and interest rates change as soon as the Fed's actions are foreseen. By the time the Fed actually takes its actions, if those actions are correctly foreseen, they have no effect. The effects occur in anticipation of the Fed's actions. Only changes in the money supply that are not foreseen change the interest rate at the time that those changes occur.

growth and inflation. The mechanism through which aggregate demand changes involves several channels. Higher interest rates bring a decrease in consumption expenditure and investment. Tighter bank credit brings fewer loans and reinforces the effects of higher interest rates on consumption expenditure and investment.

Higher interest rates bring an increase in the exchange rate that makes U.S. exports more expensive and makes imports less costly. So net exports decrease. The decreases in consumption, investment, and net exports all combine to decrease aggregate demand, which in turn slows the growth rate of real GDP and the inflation rate. Schematically, the effects of the Fed's actions ripple through the economy in the following way:

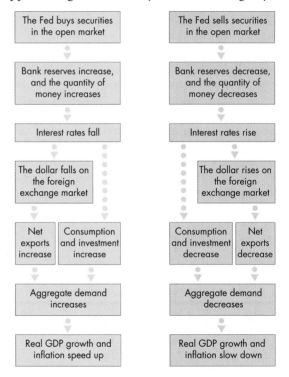

The Ripple Effects of Monetary Policy

You've now seen that the Fed's actions do indeed change interest rates and that the Fed tries to influence the course of the economy. These monetary policy measures work by changing aggregate demand. When the Fed slows money growth and pushes interest rates up, it decreases aggregate demand, which in turn slows both real GDP growth and inflation. When the Fed speeds money growth and lowers interest rates, it increases aggregate demand, which in turn speeds real GDP

Interest Rates and the Business Cycle

You've seen the connection between the Fed's actions and interest rates in Fig. 32.12. What about the ripple effects that we've just described? Do they really occur? Do changes in interest rates ultimately influence the real GDP growth rate? Yes they do. You can see these effects in Fig. 32.13. The blue line in this figure shows the short-term interest rate minus the long-term interest rate. The short-term interest rate is influenced by the Fed in the way that you studied

FIGURE 32.13
Interest Rates and Real GDP Growth

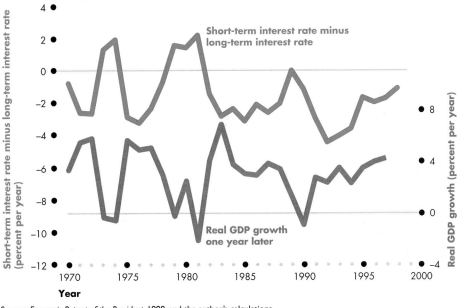

When the Fed increases short-term interest rates, the short-term interest rate rises above the long-term interest rate and, later, real GDP growth slows down. Similarly, when the Fed decreases short-term interest rates, the short-term interest rate falls below the long-term interest rate and, later, real GDP growth speeds up.

Source: *Economic Report of the President,* 1999, and the author's calculations.

earlier in this chapter. And changes in short-term rates have some influence on the long-term interest rate. But this influence is small, and the long-term interest rate is determined by saving and investment plans (see Chapter 27, pp. 593–595) and by long-term inflation expectations (see Chapter 33, pp. 750–751). The red line in Fig. 32.13 is the real GDP growth rate *one year later.* You can see that when short-term interest rates rise or long-term interest rates fall, the real GDP growth rate slows down in the following year. Long-term interest rates fluctuate less than short-term rates, so when short-term rates rise above long-term rates, it is because the Fed has pushed short-term rates upward. And when short-term rates fall below long-term rates, it is because the Fed has pushed short-term rates downward. So when the Fed stimulates aggregate demand (pushes short-term rates downward), the GDP growth rate speeds up, and when the Fed lowers aggregate demand (pushes short-term rates upward), the real GDP growth rate slows down. The inflation rate also increases and decreases in sympathy with these fluctuations in real GDP growth.

R E V I E W Q U I Z

- To which interest rates does the Fed pay the closest attention?
- Is there any relationship in the U.S. economy between fluctuations in short-term interest rates and fluctuations in the ratio of M2 to GDP?
- How do *un*anticipated and *anticipated* changes in the quantity of money influence interest rates?
- When the Fed lowers interest rates, what happens to aggregate demand, real GDP growth, and inflation?

◆ *Reading Between the Lines* on pages 730–731 looks at the Fed in action during 1999 and its decision to hold interest rates steady. Now that you know how the Fed determines the quantity of money and interest rates, we're going to explore the influence of money (and other factors) on inflation.

The Fed in Action

THE WALL STREET JOURNAL, MARCH 31, 1999

Fed Again Holds Steady on Rates As Growth, Low Inflation Continue

BY JACOB M. SCHLESINGER STAFF REPORTER OF *THE WALL STREET JOURNAL*

WASHINGTON—Federal Reserve policy makers once again left interest rates steady Tuesday and signaled that monetary policy is likely to remain on hold for a while.

The central bank's inaction stems both from the U.S. economy's current healthy performance and its uncertain future. With growth robust and inflation low, there's little that needs fixing. The risks, meanwhile, seem evenly balanced between dangers that would invite a rate increase, such as inflation sparked by tight labor markets, and those that would dictate a cut, such as a sharp slowdown induced by weakness overseas.

The stock market's lofty levels also complicate matters: A tightening of monetary policy could trigger a sharp correction that could slash consumer spending. A policy easing could further inflate what many Fed officials fear is a bubble, which some now concede was the result of the three quarter-point rate cuts last fall.

"I don't know what adjustments to monetary policy, if any, will be needed to help the economy on a trend of sustainable growth and benign inflation," Edward Boehne, president of the Federal Reserve Bank of Philadelphia, said in a speech earlier in March.

Financial markets widely anticipated the decision to leave the target for the federal-funds rate, the rate at which banks lend to each other overnight, at 4.75%. Immediately after Tuesday's 2:15 p.m. announcement, the Dow Jones Industrial Average, which had drifted lower throughout the morning, slipped slightly. It closed down 93.52 points at 9913.26.

HOLDING STEADY

The Federal Reserve's target for the federal-funds rate (left axis) and inflation, or the year-to-year percentage change in the consumer-price index (right axis)

Target rate

CPI (ex. food and energy)

Fed leaves rates unchanged

1996 '97 '98 '99

Sources: Datastream, Federal Reserve

Fed officials issued no public comment, as is customary when the central bank takes no action. At these meetings, Fed officials also debate their so-called policy directive, a consensus statement that declares whether the next rate move is more likely to be an increase or a decrease.

Essence of the Story

- The Federal Reserve decided to leave interest rates unchanged at its March 1999 meeting.

- This decision was widely expected.

- The Fed left interest rates unchanged because real GDP growth was strong and inflation was low, so nothing needed to be fixed.

- But the possibility that a tight labor market might bring renewed inflation and that a weak global economy might bring a recession made the future uncertain.

- If the Fed increased interest rates, the stock market might fall and bring a deep cut in consumer spending.

- If the Fed decreased interest rates, the stock market might rise even further.

Economic Analysis

■ Approximately every 6 weeks, the Fed's FOMC meets to review the state of the economy and set policy guidelines for open market operations (see p. 712). During 1998, the FOMC cut interest rates.

■ Figure 1 shows the economy in 1997 and 1998.

■ In 1997, real GDP was $7.3 trillion and the price level was 112, at the intersection of the aggregate demand curve AD_{97} and the short-run aggregate supply curve SAS_{97}. Real GDP was equal to potential GDP—the economy was on the long-run aggregate supply curve LAS_{97}.

■ By 1998, real GDP had increased to $7.6 trillion and the price level had increased to 113, at the intersection of the aggregate demand curve AD_{98} and the short-run aggregate supply curve SAS_{98}. Potential GDP had increased to $7.6 trillion (an assumption but a reasonable one). So in 1998, real GDP was greater than potential GDP.

■ Looking forward through 1999, the Fed was comfortable with the state of the U.S.

economy. Figure 2 shows the Fed's forecast of aggregate demand for 1999 as AD_{99} and the short-run aggregate supply curve as SAS_{99}. The Fed expected real GDP to grow to $7.7 trillion and the price level to rise to 114.

■ If aggregate demand turned out to be AD_0, we would have an inflationary gap. Inflation and real GDP would increase. To counter such an increase, the Fed might tighten the money supply and raise interest rates.

■ If aggregate demand turned out to be AD_1, we would have a deflationary gap. Inflation and real GDP would decrease. To counter such an outcome, the Fed might loosen the money supply and lower interest rates.

■ You can see the dilemma that the Fed faces every year. If aggregate demand increases by too much, the Fed must try to dampen the economy. If aggregate demand increases by too little, the Fed must try to stimulate the economy. But to be effective, the Fed must anticipate the change in aggregate demand correctly.

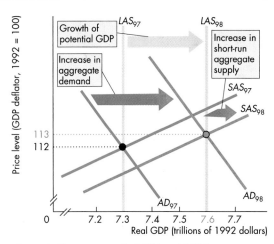

Figure 1 The economy in 1997 and 1998

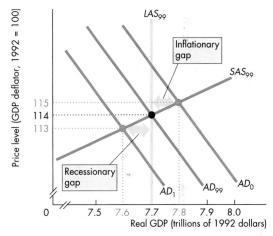

Figure 2 Some senarios for 1999

You're The Voter

■ Why did the Fed believe that no monetary policy action was needed in March 1999?

■ Did the Fed change interest rates during 1999? If so, by how much, in which direction, and why? If not, why not?

■ What, in your opinion, should the Fed do if a recession appears to be likely?

■ What, in your opinion, should the Fed do if inflation appears to be likely?

SUMMARY

KEY POINTS

The Federal Reserve System (pp. 712–715)

- The Federal Reserve System is the central bank of the United States.
- The Fed influences the economy by setting the required reserve ratio for banks, by setting the discount rate—the interest rate at which it is willing to lend reserves to the banking system—and by open market operations.

Controlling the Money Supply (pp. 715–719)

- By buying government securities in the market (an open market purchase), the Fed is able to increase the monetary base and the reserves available to banks.
- There follows an expansion of bank lending and the quantity of money increases.
- By selling government securities, the Fed is able to decrease the monetary base and bank reserves and decrease the quantity of money.

The Demand for Money (pp. 720–723)

- The quantity of money demanded is the amount of money that people plan to hold.
- The quantity of real money equals the quantity of nominal money divided by the price level.
- The quantity of real money demanded depends on the interest rate and real GDP. A higher interest rate induces a smaller quantity of real money demanded.

Interest Rate Determination (pp. 723–724)

- Changes in interest rates achieve equilibrium in the markets for money and financial assets.
- Money market equilibrium achieves an interest rate (and an asset price) that makes the quantity of real money available willingly held.
- If the quantity of real money is increased by the actions of the Fed, the interest rate falls and the prices of financial assets rise.

Monetary Policy (pp. 725–729)

- The Fed directly controls the discount rate and closely targets the federal funds rate, but all short-term rates fluctuate together and the Fed influences all short-term interest rates.
- People attempt to profit by predicting the actions of the Fed. To the extent that they can predict the Fed, interest rates and the price of financial assets move in anticipation of the Fed's actions rather than in response to them.
- Consequently, interest rates change when the Fed changes the money supply only if the Fed catches people by surprise. Anticipated changes in the money supply produce interest rate changes by themselves.
- When the Fed lowers interest rates, it increases aggregate demand, which speeds real GDP growth and inflation. And when the Fed raises interest rates, it decreases aggregate demand, which slows real GDP growth and inflation.

KEY FIGURES

KEY TERMS

PROBLEMS

1. You are given the following information about the economy of Nocoin: The banks have deposits of $300 billion. Their reserves are $15 billion, two thirds of which is in deposits with the central bank. There are $30 billion notes outside the banks. There are no coins!
   a. Calculate the monetary base.
   b. Calculate the money supply.
   c. Calculate the banks' reserve ratio as a percentage of deposits.
   d. Calculate the currency drain as a percentage of the money supply.

2. You are given the following information about the economy of Fredzone: The people and businesses in Fredzone have bank deposits of $500 billion and hold $100 billion in notes and coin. The banks hold deposits at the Fredzone Fed of $5 billion and they keep $5 billion in notes and coin in their vaults and ATM machines.
   a. Calculate the monetary base.
   b. Calculate the money supply.
   c. Calculate the banks' reserve ratio as a percentage of deposits.
   d. Calculate the currency drain as a percentage of the money supply.

*3. In problem 1, suppose that the Bank of Nocoin, the central bank, undertakes an open market purchase of securities of $1 billion. After the money multiplier process is complete, what is the new level of:
   a. The money supply?
   b. Currency in circulation?
   c. Bank deposits?
   d. Bank reserves?
   e. Why does the money supply change by more than the change in the monetary base?

4. In problem 2, suppose that the Fredzone Fed undertakes an open market sale of securities of $1 billion. After the money multiplier process is complete, what is the new level of:
   a. The money supply?
   b. Currency in circulation?
   c. Bank deposits?
   d. Bank reserves?
   e. Why does the money supply change by more than the change in the monetary base?

*5. The spreadsheet provides information about the demand for money in Miniland. Column A is the interest rate, R. Columns B, C, and D show the quantity of money demanded at three different levels of real GDP. Y_0 is $10 billion, Y_1 is $20 billion and Y_2 is $30 billion. The quantity of money supplied by the Miniland Fed is $3.0 billion. Initially, real GDP is $20 billion.

	A	B	C	D
1	R	Y_0	Y_1	Y_2
2	7	1.0	1.5	2.0
3	6	1.5	2.0	2.5
4	5	2.0	2.5	3.0
5	4	2.5	3.0	3.5
6	3	3.0	3.5	4.0
7	2	3.5	4.0	4.5
8	1	4.0	4.5	5.0

What happens in Miniland if the interest rate:
   a. Exceeds 4 percent a year?
   b. Is less than 4 percent a year?
   c. Equals 4 percent a year?

6. In problem 5, Miniland experiences a severe recession. Real GDP falls to $10 billion. The Miniland Fed takes no actions to change the quantity of money.
   a. What happens if the interest rate is 4 percent a year?
   b. What is the equilibrium interest rate?
   c. Compared with the situation In problem 5, does the interest rate in Miniland rise or fall? Why?

*7. In problem 5, Miniland experiences a severe business cycle. Real GDP rises to $30 billion and then falls to $10 billion. The Miniland Fed takes no actions to change the quantity of money. What happens to the interest rate in Miniland during the:
   a. Expansion phase of the cycle?
   b. Recession phase of the cycle?

8. In problem 5, financial innovation changes the demand for money. People now plan to hold $0.5 billion less than the numbers in the spreadsheet.
   a. What happens to the interest rate if the Miniland Fed takes no actions?
   b. What happens to the interest rate if the Miniland Fed decreases the quantity of money by $0.5 billion? Explain.

*9. The figure shows the demand for real money in Upland.
   a. Draw the supply of money curve if the interest rate in Upland is 3 percent a year.
   b. If the Upland Fed wants to lower the interest rate by 1 percentage point, by how much must it change the real money supply.

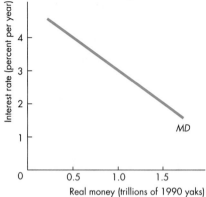

   c. Suppose that to change the quantity of money in part (b), the Upland Fed uses open market operations. Does it make an open market purchase or an open market sale of securities?

10. In Upland, a new smart card replaces currency and the demand for money changes. Also, the new smart card causes business to boom and real GDP increases.
   a. Using the figure for problem 9, draw a new demand for money curve that is consistent with the events just described.
   b. Suppose that the Upland Fed wants to prevent the interest rate from changing. What must it do to the supply of money?
   c. Does the Upland Fed make an open market purchase or an open market sale of securities?

*11. Starting from above full-employment equilibrium, briefly explain with the aid of a figure the short-run effect on the price level and real GDP of an open market purchase of securities by the Fed. Does such an action help to avoid inflation? Does such an action lower real GDP in the long run?

12. Starting from unemployment equilibrium, briefly explain with the aid of a figure the short-run effect on the price level and real GDP of an open market purchase of securities by the Fed. Does such an action help to avoid inflation? Does such an action lower real GDP in the long run?

CRITICAL THINKING

1. Study *Reading Between the Lines* on pp. 730–731 and then answer the following questions:
   a. Why did the Fed *not* change interest rates in March 1999?
   b. What does the Fed look at when it is deciding whether to change interest rates?
   c. What risks does the Fed face if it raises interest rates? What risks does it face if it does not raise interest rates? Which is the more risky in your opinion and why?
   d. When the Fed decides to raise interest rates, what actions does it take?

2. Could the Volcker Fed have brought inflation under control without creating a deep recession? If you think that the answer is "no," do you think that it was wise to lower inflation? If you think that the answer is "yes," what could the Fed have done differently?

 3. Use the links on the Parkin Web site to find the latest data on M1, M2, and a short-term interest rate as well as the latest minutes of the FOMC. Then answer the following questions.
   a. Is the Fed trying to slow economic growth or speed it up? How can you tell which?
   b. What open market operations do you think the Fed has undertaken during the past month?
   c. Skim the latest minutes of the FOMC and see whether you can discover the open market operations that are planned.
   d. In light of the Fed's recent actions, what ripple effects do you expect over the coming months?
   e. What do you think the effects of the Fed's recent actions will be on bond prices and stock prices?

4. Use the link on the Parkin Web site and look at the current economic conditions described in the Beige Book for your region of the United States. On the basis of the Fed's current description of the economic conditions in your region, do you predict that the Fed will raise interest rates, lower interest rates, or hold interest rates steady? Do you think that the Fed ought to raise interest rates, lower them, or hold them steady? Write a brief summary of your predictions and prescriptions and provide your reasons.

Chapter 33

Inflation

At the end of the third century A.D., Roman Emperor Diocletian struggled to contain an inflation that raised prices by more than 300 percent a year. At the end of the twentieth century, Russian President Boris Yeltsin struggled to contain a severe inflation that raised prices at a rate of close to 1,000 percent a year. But the most rapid recent inflations have been in Brazil, where the inflation rate hit 40 percent *per month* in 1994, and in Zaire, which had an inflation rate of 75 percent *per month*. What causes rapid inflation? ◆ In comparison with the cases just described, the United States has had remarkable price stability. Nevertheless, during the 1970s, the U.S. price level more than doubled—an inflation of more than 100 percent over the decade. Today, along with the other rich industrial countries, the United States has a low inflation rate of less than 2 percent a year. Why do some countries have a low inflation

From Rome to Russia

rate? And why did a more serious inflation break out in the United States during the 1970s? ◆ Most of life's big economic decisions—whether to buy or rent a home, whether to save more for retirement—turn on what is going to happen to inflation. Will inflation increase so our savings buy less? Will inflation decrease, making our debts harder to repay? To make good decisions, we need good forecasts of inflation, and not for just next year but for many years into the future. How do people try to forecast inflation? And how do expectations of inflation influence the economy? ◆ As the inflation rate rises and falls, the unemployment rate and interest rates also fluctuate. What are the links between inflation and the economy that make unemployment and interest rates fluctuate when inflation fluctuates?

◇ In this chapter, you will learn about the forces that generate inflation, the effects of inflation, and the way in which people try to forecast inflation. You will pull together several of the threads you have been following through your study of macroeconomics. And again, you will use the *AS-AD* model of Chapter 25. But first, let's recall what inflation is and how it is measured.

After studying this chapter, you will be able to:

■ Distinguish between inflation and a one-time rise in the price level

■ Explain the different ways in which inflation can be generated

■ Describe how people try to forecast inflation

■ Explain the short-run and long-run relationships between inflation and unemployment

■ Explain the short-run and long-run relationships between inflation and interest rates

Inflation and the Price Level

WE DON'T HAVE MUCH INFLATION TODAY, BUT during the 1970s it was a major problem. **Inflation** is a process in which the *price level is rising* and *money is losing value.*

If the price level rises persistently, then people need more and more money to make transactions. Incomes rise, so firms must pay out more in wages and other payments to resource owners. And prices rise, so consumers must take more money with them when they go shopping. But the value of money gets smaller and smaller.

A change in one price is not inflation. For example, if the price of hot dogs jumps to $25 and all other money prices fall slightly, so the price level remains constant, there is no inflation. Instead, the relative price of hot dogs has increased. If the price of hot dogs and all other prices rise by a similar percentage, there is inflation.

But a one-time jump in the price level is not inflation. Instead, inflation is an ongoing *process.* Figure 33.1 illustrates this distinction. The red line shows the price level rising continuously. That is inflation. The blue line shows a one-time jump in the price level. This economy is not experiencing inflation. Its price level is constant most of the time.

Inflation is a serious problem, and preventing inflation is the main task of monetary policy and the actions of the Fed. We are going to learn how inflation arises and see how we can avoid the situation shown in the cartoon. But first, let's see how we calculate the inflation rate.

To measure the inflation *rate,* we calculate the annual percentage change in the price level. For

"I told you the Fed should have tightened."

Drawing by Mankoff; © 1997 *The New Yorker Magazine, Inc.*

FIGURE 33.1
Inflation Versus a One-Time Rise in the Price Level

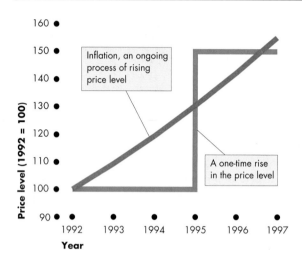

Along the red line, an economy experiences inflation because the price level is rising persistently. Along the blue line, an economy experiences a one-time rise in the price level.

example, if this year's price level is 126 and last year's price level was 120, the inflation rate is 5 percent per year. That is,

$$\text{Inflation rate} = \frac{126 - 120}{120} \times 100$$

$$= 5 \text{ percent per year.}$$

This equation shows the connection between the *inflation rate* and the *price level.* For a given price level last year, the higher the price level in the current year, the higher is the inflation rate. If the price level is *rising*, the inflation rate is *positive.* If the price level rises at a *faster* rate, the inflation rate *increases.* Also, the higher the new price level, the lower is the value of money, and the higher is the inflation rate.

Inflation can result from either an increase in aggregate demand or a decrease in aggregate supply. These two sources of impulses that can get inflation started are called:

1. Demand pull
2. Cost push

We'll first study a demand-pull inflation.

Demand-Pull Inflation

AN INFLATION THAT RESULTS FROM AN INITIAL increase in aggregate demand is called **demand-pull inflation**. Such an inflation can arise from any factor that increases aggregate demand such as an:

1. Increase in the money supply
2. Increase in government purchases
3. Increase in exports

Initial Effect of an Increase in Aggregate Demand

Suppose that last year the price level was 110 and real GDP was $7 trillion. Potential GDP was also $7 trillion. Figure 33.2(a) illustrates this situation. The aggregate demand curve is AD_0, the short-run

aggregate supply curve is SAS_0, and the long-run aggregate supply curve is LAS.

In the current year, aggregate demand increases to AD_1. Such a situation arises if, for example, the Fed loosens its grip on the money supply, or the government increases its purchases of goods and services, or exports increase.

With no change in potential GDP and no change in the money wage rate, the long-run aggregate supply curve and the short-run aggregate supply curve remain at LAS and SAS_0.

The price level and real GDP are determined at the point where the aggregate demand curve AD_1 intersects the short-run aggregate supply curve. The price level rises to 113, and real GDP increases above potential GDP to $7.5 trillion. The economy experiences a 2.7 percent rise in the price level (a price level of 113 compared with 110) and a rapid expansion of real GDP. Unemployment falls below the natural rate. The next step in the story is a rise in money wages.

FIGURE 33.2

A Demand-Pull Rise in the Price Level

(a) Initial effect

(b) Wages adjust

In part (a), the aggregate demand curve is AD_0, the short-run aggregate supply curve is SAS_0, and the long-run aggregate supply curve is LAS. The price level is 110, and real GDP is $7 trillion, its long-run level. Aggregate demand increases to AD_1 (because, for example, the Fed increases the money supply, or the government increases its purchases of goods and services, or exports increase). The new equilibrium occurs where AD_1 intersects SAS_0. The price level rises to 113, and real GDP increases to $7.5 trillion. In part (b), starting from above full employment, money wages begin to rise and the short-run aggregate supply curve shifts leftward toward SAS_1. The price level rises further, and real GDP returns to its long-run level.

Wage Response

Real GDP cannot remain above potential GDP forever. With unemployment below its natural rate, there is a shortage of labor. In this situation, the money wage rate begins to rise. As it does so, short-run aggregate supply decreases and the *SAS* curve starts to shift leftward. The price level rises further, and real GDP begins to decrease.

With no further change in aggregate demand—the aggregate demand curve remains at AD_1—this process ends when the short-run aggregate supply curve has shifted to SAS_1 in Fig. 33.2(b). At this time, the price level has increased to 121 and real GDP has returned to potential GDP of $7 trillion, the level from which it started.

A Demand-Pull Inflation Process

The process we've just studied eventually ends when, for a given increase in aggregate demand, the money wage rate has adjusted enough to restore the real wage rate to its full-employment level. We've studied a one-time rise in the price level like that described in Fig. 33.1(b). For inflation to proceed, aggregate demand must persistently increase.

The only way in which aggregate demand can persistently increase is if the quantity of money persistently increases. Suppose the government has a large budget deficit that it finances by selling bonds to the Fed. When the Fed buys these bonds, it creates more money. In this situation, aggregate demand increases year after year. The aggregate demand curve keeps shifting rightward. This persistent increase in aggregate demand puts continual upward pressure on the price level. The economy now experiences demand-pull inflation.

Figure 33.3 illustrates the process of demand-pull inflation. The starting point is the same as that shown in Fig. 33.2. The aggregate demand curve is AD_0, the short-run aggregate supply curve is SAS_0, and the long-run aggregate supply curve is *LAS*. Real GDP is $7 trillion, and the price level is 110. Aggregate demand increases, shifting the aggregate demand curve to AD_1. Real GDP increases to $7.5 trillion, and the price level rises to 113. The economy is at an above full-employment equilibrium. The money wage rate rises, shifting the short-run aggregate supply curve to SAS_1. The price level rises to 121, and real GDP returns to potential GDP.

FIGURE 33.3
A Demand-Pull Inflation Spiral

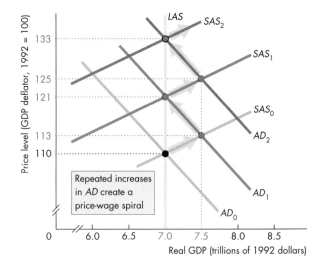

Each time the money supply increases, aggregate demand increases, and the aggregate demand curve shifts rightward from AD_0 to AD_1 to AD_2, and so on. Each time real GDP goes above potential GDP and unemployment goes below the natural rate, the money wage rate rises and the short-run aggregate supply curve shifts leftward from SAS_0 to SAS_1 to SAS_2, and so on. As aggregate demand continues to increase, the price level rises from 110 through 113, 121, 125, to 133, and so on. There is a perpetual demand-pull inflation. Real GDP fluctuates between $7 trillion and $7.5 trillion.

But the money supply increases again, and aggregate demand continues to increase. The aggregate demand curve shifts rightward to AD_2. The price level rises further to 125, and real GDP again exceeds potential GDP at $7.5 trillion. Yet again, the money wage rate rises and decreases short-run aggregate supply. The *SAS* curve shifts to SAS_2, and the price level rises further to 133. As the money supply continues to grow, aggregate demand increases and the price level rises in an ongoing demand-pull inflation process.

The process you have just studied generates inflation—an ongoing process of a rising price level.

Demand-Pull Inflation in Kalamazoo You may better understand the inflation process that we've just described by considering what is going on in an individual part of the economy, such as a Kalamazoo soda-bottling plant. Initially, when aggregate demand increases, the demand for soda increases and the price of soda rises. Faced with a higher price, the soda plant works overtime and increases production. Conditions are good for workers in Kalamazoo, and the soda factory finds it hard to hang onto its best people. To do so, it has to offer higher wages. As wages increase, so do the soda factory's costs.

What happens next depends on what happens to aggregate demand. If aggregate demand remains constant (as in Fig. 33.2b), the firm's costs are increasing but the price of soda is not increasing as quickly as its costs. Production is scaled back. Eventually, wages and costs increase by the same percentage as the price of soda. In real terms, the soda factory is in the same situation as initially—before the increase in aggregate demand. The plant produces the same amount of soda and employs the same amount of labor as before the increase in demand.

But if aggregate demand continues to increase, so does the demand for soda, and the price of soda rises at the same rate as wages. The soda factory continues to operate above full employment, and there is a persistent shortage of labor. Prices and wages chase each other upward in an unending spiral.

Demand-Pull Inflation in the United States   A demand-pull inflation like the one you've just studied occurred in the United States during the 1960s. In 1960, inflation was a moderate 2 percent a year, but its rate increased slowly to 3 percent by 1966. Then, in 1967, a large increase in government purchases on the Vietnam War and an increase in spending on social programs, together with an increase in the growth rate of the money supply, increased aggregate demand more quickly. Consequently, the rightward shift of the aggregate demand curve speeded up and the price level increased more quickly. Real GDP increased above potential GDP, and the unemployment rate fell below the natural rate.

With unemployment below the natural rate, the money wage rate started to rise more quickly and the short-run aggregate supply curve shifted leftward. The Fed responded with a further increase in the money supply growth rate, and a demand-pull inflation spiral unfolded. By 1970, the inflation rate had reached 6 percent a year.

For the next three years, aggregate demand continued to grow quickly and the inflation rate remained around 6 percent a year.

R E V I E W   Q U I Z

- How does demand-pull inflation begin? What are the initial effects of demand-pull inflation on real GDP and the price level?
- When real GDP increases to more than potential GDP, what happens to the money wage rate and short-run aggregate supply? How do real GDP and the price level respond?
- What must happen to create a demand-pull inflation spiral?

Next, let's see how shocks to aggregate supply can create cost-push inflation.

Cost-Push Inflation

AN INFLATION THAT RESULTS FROM AN INITIAL increase in costs is called **cost-push inflation**. The two main sources of increases in costs are:

1. An increase in money wage rates
2. An increase in the money prices of raw materials

At a given price level, the higher the cost of production, the smaller is the amount that firms are willing to produce. So if money wage rates rise or if the prices of raw materials (for example, oil) rise, firms decrease their supply of goods and services. Aggregate supply decreases, and the short-run aggregate supply curve shifts leftward.[1] Let's trace the effects of such a decrease in short-run aggregate supply on the price level and real GDP.

Initial Effect of a Decrease in Aggregate Supply

Suppose that last year the price level was 110 and real GDP was $7 trillion. Potential real GDP was also $7 trillion. Figure 33.4 illustrates this situation. The aggregate demand curve was AD_0, the short-run aggregate supply curve was SAS_0, and the long-run aggregate supply curve was LAS. In the current year, the

---

[1]Some cost-push forces, such as an increase in the price of oil accompanied by a decrease in the availability of oil, can also decrease long-run aggregate supply. We'll ignore such effects here and examine cost-push factors that change only short-run aggregate supply.

FIGURE 33.4

A Cost-Push Rise in the Price Level

Initially, the aggregate demand curve is AD_0, the short-run aggregate supply curve is SAS_0, and the long-run aggregate supply curve is LAS. A decrease in aggregate supply (for example, resulting from an increase in the world price of oil) shifts the short-run aggregate supply curve to SAS_1. The economy moves to the point where the short-run aggregate supply curve SAS_1 intersects the aggregate demand curve AD_0. The price level rises to 117, and real GDP decreases to $6.5 trillion. The economy experiences inflation and a contraction of real GDP—*stagflation*.

world's oil producers form a price-fixing organization that strengthens their market power and increases the relative price of oil. They raise the nominal price of oil, and this action decreases short-run aggregate supply. The short-run aggregate supply curve shifts leftward to SAS_1. The price level rises to 117, and real GDP decreases to $6.5 trillion. The combination of a rise in the price level and a decrease in real GDP is called **stagflation**.

This event is a one-time rise in the price level like that in Fig. 33.1(b). It is not inflation. In fact, a supply shock on its own cannot cause inflation. Something more must happen to enable a one-time supply shock to be converted into a process of money supply growth and ongoing inflation. The money supply must persistently increase. And it often does increase, as you will now see.

Aggregate Demand Response

When real GDP falls, the unemployment rate rises above the natural rate. In such a situation, there is usually an outcry of concern and a call for action to restore full employment. Suppose that the Fed increases the money supply. Aggregate demand increases. In Fig. 33.5, the aggregate demand curve shifts rightward to AD_1. The increase in aggregate demand has restored full employment. But the price level rises to 121, a 10 percent increase over the initial price level.

A Cost-Push Inflation Process

The oil producers now see the prices of everything that they buy increase by 10 percent. So they increase the price of oil again to restore its new high relative price. Figure 33.6 continues the story.

FIGURE 33.5

Aggregate Demand Response to Cost Push

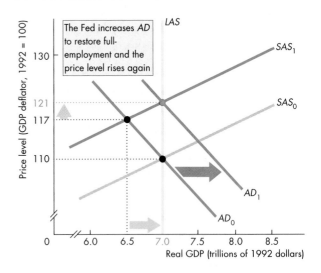

Following a cost-push increase in the price level, real GDP is below potential GDP and unemployment is above the natural rate. If the Fed responds by increasing aggregate demand to restore full employment, the aggregate demand curve shifts rightward to AD_1. The economy returns to full employment but at the expense of more inflation. The price level rises to 121.

The short-run aggregate supply curve now shifts to SAS_2, and another bout of stagflation ensues. The price level rises further to 129, and real GDP falls to $6.5 trillion. Unemployment increases above its natural rate. If the Fed responds yet again with an increase in the money supply, aggregate demand increases and the aggregate demand curve shifts to AD_2. The price level rises even higher—to 133—and full employment is again restored. A cost-push inflation spiral results. But if the Fed does not respond, the economy remains below full employment.

You can see that the Fed has a dilemma. If it increases the money supply to restore full employment, it invites another oil price hike that will call forth yet a further increase in the money supply. Inflation will

FIGURE 33.6

A Cost-Push
Inflation Spiral

When a cost increase (for example, an increase in the world oil price) decreases short-run aggregate supply from SAS_0 to SAS_1, the price level rises to 117 and real GDP decreases to $6.5 trillion. The Fed responds with an increase in the money supply that shifts the aggregate demand curve from AD_0 to AD_1. The price level rises again to 121, and real GDP returns to $7 trillion. A further cost increase occurs, which shifts the short-run aggregate supply curve again, this time to SAS_2. Stagflation is repeated, and the price level now rises to 129. The Fed responds again, and the cost-price inflation spiral continues.

rage along at a rate decided by the oil-exporting nations. If the Fed keeps the lid on money supply growth, real GDP remains below potential GDP.

Cost-Push Inflation in Kalamazoo What is going on in the Kalamazoo soda-bottling plant when the economy is experiencing cost-push inflation? When the oil price increases, so do the costs of bottling soda. These higher costs decrease the supply of soda, increasing its price and decreasing the quantity produced. The soda plant lays off some workers. This situation will persist until either the Fed increases aggregate demand or the price of oil falls. If the Fed increases aggregate demand, as it did in the mid-1970s, the demand for soda increases and so does its price. The higher price of soda brings higher profits, and the bottling plant increases its production. The soda factory rehires the laid-off workers.

Cost-Push Inflation in the United States A cost-push inflation like the one you've just studied occurred in the United States during the 1970s. It began in 1974 when the Organization for Petroleum Exporting Countries (OPEC) raised the price of oil fourfold. The higher oil price decreased aggregate supply, which caused the price level to rise more quickly and real GDP to shrink. The Fed then faced a dilemma. Would it increase the quantity of money and accommodate the cost-push forces or would it keep aggregate demand growth in check by limiting money growth? In 1975, 1976, and 1977, the Fed repeatedly allowed the money supply to grow quickly, and inflation proceeded at a rapid rate. In 1979 and 1980, OPEC was again able to push oil prices higher. On that occasion, the Fed decided not to respond to the oil price hike with an increase in the money supply. The result was a recession but also, eventually, a fall in inflation.

REVIEW QUIZ

- How does cost-push inflation begin? What are the initial effects of cost-push inflation on real GDP and the price level?
- What is *stagflation* and why does cost-push inflation cause stagflation?
- What must the Fed do to convert a one-time rise in the price level into a freewheeling cost-push inflation?

Effects of Inflation

Regardless of whether inflation is demand-pull or cost-push, the failure to correctly *anticipate* it results in unintended consequences. These unintended consequences impose costs in both labor markets and capital markets. Let's examine these costs.

Unanticipated Inflation in the Labor Market

Unanticipated inflation has two main consequences for the operation of the labor market:

- Redistribution of income
- Departure from full employment

Redistribution of Income   Unanticipated inflation redistributes income between employers and workers. Sometimes employers gain at the expense of workers, and sometimes they lose. If an unexpected increase in aggregate demand increases the inflation rate, then wages will not have been set high enough. Profits will be higher than expected, and wages will buy fewer goods than expected. In this case, employers gain at the expense of workers. But if aggregate demand is expected to increase at a rapid rate and it fails to do so, workers gain at the expense of employers. With a high inflation rate anticipated, wages are set too high and profits are squeezed. Redistribution between employers and workers creates an incentive for both firms and workers to try to forecast inflation correctly.

Departures from Full Employment   Redistribution brings gains to some and losses to others. But departures from full employment impose costs on everyone. To see why, let's return to the soda-bottling plant in Kalamazoo.

If the bottling plant and its workers do not anticipate inflation, but inflation occurs, the money wage rate does not rise to keep up with inflation. The real wage rate falls, and the firm tries to hire more labor and increase production. But because the real wage rate has fallen, the firm has a hard time attracting the labor it wants to employ. It pays overtime rates to its existing work force, and because it runs its plant at a faster pace, it incurs higher plant maintenance and parts replacement costs. But also, because the real wage rate has fallen, workers begin to quit the bottling plant to find jobs that pay a real wage rate that is closer to one that prevailed before the outbreak of inflation. This labor turnover imposes additional costs on the firm. So even though its production increases, the firm incurs additional costs, and its profits do not increase as much as they otherwise would. The workers incur additional costs of job search, and those who remain at the bottling plant wind up feeling cheated. They've worked overtime to produce the extra output, and when they come to spend their wages, they discover that prices have increased, so their wages buy a smaller quantity of goods and services than expected.

If the bottling plant and its workers anticipate a high inflation rate that does not occur, they increase the money wage rate by too much, and the real wage rate rises. At the higher real wage rate, the firm lays off some workers and the unemployment rate increases. Those workers who keep their jobs gain, but those who become unemployed lose. Also, the bottling plant loses because its output and profits fall.

Unanticipated Inflation in the Capital Market

Unanticipated inflation has two consequences for the operation of the capital market. They are:

- Redistribution of income
- Too much or too little lending and borrowing

Redistribution of Income   Unanticipated inflation redistributes income between borrowers and lenders. Sometimes borrowers gain at the expense of lenders, and sometimes they lose. When inflation is unexpected, interest rates are not set high enough to compensate lenders for the falling value of money. In this case, borrowers gain at the expense of lenders. But if inflation is expected and then fails to occur, interest rates are set too high. In this case, lenders gain at the expense of borrowers. Redistributions of income between borrowers and lenders create an incentive for both groups to try to forecast inflation correctly.

Too Much or Too Little Lending and Borrowing
If the inflation rate turns out to be either higher or lower than expected, the interest rate does not incorporate a correct allowance for the falling value of money and the real interest rate is either lower or higher than it otherwise would be. When the real

interest rate turns out to be too low, which occurs when inflation is *higher* than expected, borrowers wish they had borrowed more and lenders wish they had lent less. Both groups would have made different lending and borrowing decisions with greater foresight about the inflation rate. When the real interest rate turns out to be too high, which occurs when inflation is *lower* than expected, borrowers wish they had borrowed less and lenders wish they had lent more. Again, both groups would have made different lending and borrowing decisions with greater foresight about the inflation rate.

So unanticipated inflation imposes costs regardless of whether the inflation turns out to be higher or lower than anticipated. The presence of these costs gives everyone an incentive to forecast inflation correctly. Let's see how people go about this task.

Forecasting Inflation

Inflation is difficult to forecast. The reasons are, first, there are several sources of inflation—the demand-pull and cost-push sources you've just studied. Second, the speed with which a change in either aggregate demand or aggregate supply translates into a change in the price level varies. This speed of response also depends, as you will see below, on the extent to which the inflation is anticipated.

Because inflation is costly and difficult to forecast, people devote considerable resources to improving inflation forecasts. Some people specialize in forecasting, and others buy forecasts from specialists. The specialist forecasters are economists who work for public and private macroeconomic forecasting agencies and for banks, insurance companies, labor unions, and large corporations. The returns these specialists make depend on the quality of their forecasts, so they have a strong incentive to forecast as accurately as possible. The most accurate forecast possible is the one that is based on all the relevant information and is called a **rational expectation**.

A rational expectation is not necessarily a correct forecast. It is simply the best forecast available. It will often turn out to be wrong, but no other forecast that could have been made with the information available could be predicted to be better.

You've seen the effects of inflation when people fail to anticipate it. And you've seen why it pays to try to anticipate inflation. Let's now see what happens if inflation is correctly anticipated.

Anticipated Inflation

In the demand-pull and cost-push inflations that we studied earlier in this chapter, money wages are sticky. When aggregate demand increases, either to set off a demand-pull inflation or to accommodate cost-push inflation, the money wage does not change immediately. But if people correctly anticipate increases in aggregate demand, they will adjust money wage rates so as to keep up with anticipated inflation.

In this case, inflation proceeds with real GDP equal to potential GDP and unemployment equal to the natural rate. Figure 33.7 explains why. Suppose that last year the price level was 110 and real GDP was $7 trillion, which is also potential GDP. The aggregate demand curve was AD_0, the aggregate supply curve was SAS_0, and the long-run aggregate supply curve was LAS.

Suppose that potential GDP does not change, so the LAS curve does not shift. Also suppose that aggregate demand is expected to increase and that the expected aggregate demand curve for this year is AD_1. In anticipation of this increase in aggregate demand, money wage rates rise and the short-run aggregate supply curve shifts leftward. If the money wage rate rises by the same percentage as the price level rises, the short-run aggregate supply curve for next year is SAS_1.

If aggregate demand turns out to be the same as expected, the aggregate demand curve is AD_1, and with the short-run aggregate supply curve SAS_1 the actual price level is 121. Between last year and this year, the price level increased from 110 to 121 and the economy experienced an inflation rate of 10 percent, the same as the inflation rate that was anticipated. If this anticipated inflation continues, in the following year aggregate demand increases (as anticipated) and the aggregate demand curve shifts to AD_2. The money wage rate rises to reflect the anticipated inflation, and the short-run aggregate supply curve shifts to SAS_2. The price level rises by a further 10 percent to 133.

What has caused this inflation? The immediate answer is that because people expected inflation, wages were increased and prices increased. But the expectation was correct. Aggregate demand was expected to increase, and it did increase. Because aggregate demand was *expected* to increase from AD_0 to AD_1, the short-run aggregate supply curve shifted from SAS_0 to SAS_1. Because aggregate demand actually did increase by the amount that was expected, the actual aggregate demand curve shifted from AD_0

to AD_1. The combination of the anticipated and actual increases in aggregate demand produced an increase in the price level that was anticipated.

Only if aggregate demand growth is correctly forecasted does the economy follow the course described in Fig. 33.7. If the expected growth rate of aggregate demand is different from its actual growth rate, the expected aggregate demand curve shifts by an amount that is different from the actual aggregate demand curve. The inflation rate departs from its expected level, and to some extent, there is unanticipated inflation.

FIGURE **33.7**

Anticipated Inflation

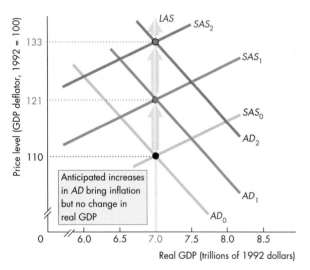

Potential real GDP is $7 trillion. Last year, aggregate demand was AD_0, and the short-run aggregate supply curve was SAS_0. The actual price level was the same as the expected price level—110. This year, aggregate demand is expected to increase to AD_1. The rational expectation of the price level changes from 110 to 121. As a result, wages rise and the short-run aggregate supply curve shifts to SAS_1. If aggregate demand actually increases as expected, the actual aggregate demand curve AD_1 is the same as the expected aggregate demand curve. Equilibrium occurs at a real GDP of $7 trillion and an actual price level of 121. The inflation is correctly anticipated. Next year the process continues with aggregate demand increasing as expected to AD_2 and wages rising to shift the short-run aggregate supply curve to SAS_2. Again, real GDP remains at $7 trillion, and the price level rises, as anticipated, to 133.

Unanticipated Inflation

When aggregate demand increases by *more* than expected, there is some unanticipated inflation that looks just like the demand-pull inflation that you studied earlier. Some inflation is expected, and the money wage rate is set to reflect that expectation. The SAS curve intersects the LAS curve at the expected price level. Aggregate demand then increases, but by more than expected. So the AD curve intersects the SAS curve at a level of real GDP that exceeds potential GDP. With real GDP above potential GDP and unemployment below the natural rate, the money wage rate rises. So the price level rises further. If aggregate demand increases again, a demand-pull inflation spiral unwinds.

When aggregate demand increases by *less* than expected, there is some unanticipated inflation that looks like the cost-push inflation that you studied earlier. Again, some inflation is expected, and the money wage rate is set to reflect that expectation. The SAS curve intersects the LAS curve at the expected price level. Aggregate demand then increases, but by less than expected. So the AD curve intersects the SAS curve at a level of real GDP below potential GDP. Aggregate demand increases to restore full employment. But if aggregate demand is expected to increase by more than it actually does, wages again rise, short-run aggregate supply again decreases, and a cost-push spiral unwinds.

We've seen that only when inflation is unanticipated does real GDP depart from potential GDP. When inflation is anticipated, real GDP remains at potential GDP. Does this mean that an anticipated inflation has no costs?

The Costs of Anticipated Inflation

The costs of an anticipated inflation depend on its rate. At a moderate rate of 2 or 3 percent a year, the cost is probably small. But as the anticipated inflation rate rises, so do its costs, and an anticipated inflation at a rapid rate can be extremely costly.

Anticipated inflation decreases potential GDP and slows economic growth. These adverse consequences arise for three major reasons:

■ Transactions costs
■ Tax effects
■ Increased uncertainty

Transactions Costs   The first transactions costs are known as the "boot leather costs." These are costs that arise from an increase in the velocity of circulation of money and an increase in the amount of running around that people do to try to avoid incurring losses from the falling value of money.

When money loses value at a rapid anticipated rate, it does not function well as a store of value and people try to avoid holding money. They spend their incomes as soon as they receive them, and firms pay out incomes—wages and dividends—as soon as they receive revenue from their sales. The velocity of circulation increases. During the 1920s, when inflation in Germany reached *hyperinflation* levels (rates more than 50 percent a month), wages were paid and spent twice in a single day!

The range of estimates of the boot leather costs is large. Some economists put the cost at close to zero. Others estimate it to be as much 2 percent of GDP for a 10 percent inflation. For a rapid inflation, these costs are much more.

The boot leather costs of inflation are just one of several transactions costs that are influenced by the inflation rate. At high anticipated inflation rates, people seek alternatives to money as a means of payment and use tokens and commodities or even barter, all of which are less efficient than money as a means of payment. For example, in Israel during the 1980s, when inflation reached 1,000 percent a year, the U.S. dollar started to replace the increasingly worthless shekel. Consequently, people had to keep track of the exchange rate between the shekel and the dollar hour by hour and had to engage in many additional and costly transactions in the foreign exchange market.

Because anticipated inflation increases transactions costs, it diverts resources from producing goods and services and it decreases potential GDP. The faster the anticipated inflation rate, the greater is the decrease in potential GDP and the further leftward does the *LAS* curve shift.

Tax Effects   Anticipated inflation interacts with the tax system and creates serious distortions in incentives. Its major effect is on real interest rates.

Anticipated inflation swells the dollar returns on investments. But dollar returns are taxed, so the effective tax rate rises. This effect becomes serious at even modest inflation rates. Let's consider an example.

Suppose the real interest rate is 4 percent a year and the tax rate is 50 percent. With no inflation, the nominal interest rate is also 4 percent a year and 50 percent of this rate is taxable. The real *after-tax* interest rate is 2 percent a year (50 percent of 4 percent). Now suppose the inflation rate is 4 percent a year, so the nominal interest rate is 8 percent a year. The nominal *after-tax* rate is 4 percent a year (50 percent of 8 percent). Now subtract the 4 percent inflation rate from this amount, and you see that the *real after-tax interest rate* is zero! The true tax rate on interest income is 100 percent.

The higher the inflation rate, the higher is the effective tax rate on income from capital. And the higher the tax rate, the higher is the interest rate paid by borrowers and the lower is the after-tax interest rate received by lenders (see Chapter 30, p. 678).

With a low after-tax real interest rate, the incentive to save is weakened and the saving rate falls. With a high cost of borrowing, the amount of investment decreases. And with a fall in saving and investment, the pace of capital accumulation slows and so does the long-term growth rate of real GDP.

Increased Uncertainty   When the inflation rate is high, there is increased uncertainty about the long-term inflation rate. Will inflation remain high for a long time or will price stability be restored? This increased uncertainty makes long-term planning difficult and gives people a shorter-term focus. Investment falls, and so the growth rate slows.

But this increased uncertainty also misallocates resources. Instead of concentrating on the activities at which they have a comparative advantage, people find it more profitable to search for ways of avoiding the losses that inflation inflicts. As a result, inventive talent that might otherwise work on productive innovations works on finding ways of profiting from the inflation instead.

The implications of inflation for economic growth have been estimated to be enormous. Peter Howitt of Ohio State University, building on work by Robert Barro of Harvard University, has estimated that if inflation is lowered from 3 percent a year to zero, the growth rate of real GDP will rise by between 0.06 and 0.09 percentage points a year. These numbers might seem small. But they are growth rates. After 30 years, real GDP would be 2.3 percent higher and the present value of all the future output would be 85 percent of current GDP—almost $6 trillion! In the rapid anticipated inflations of Brazil and Russia, the costs are much greater than the numbers given here.

┌───┐
│ **R E V I E W   Q U I Z**   │

■ What is a *rational expectation*? Are people who form rational expectations ever wrong?

■ Why do people forecast inflation and what information do they use to do so?

■ How does anticipated inflation occur?

■ What are the effects of a rapid anticipated inflation? Does anticipated inflation bring an increase in real GDP?
└───┘

You've seen that an increase in aggregate demand that is not fully anticipated increases both the price level and real GDP. It also decreases unemployment. Similarly, a decrease in aggregate demand that is not fully anticipated decreases the price level and real GDP. It also increases unemployment. Do these relationships mean that there is a tradeoff between inflation and unemployment? That is, does low unemployment always bring inflation and does low inflation bring high unemployment? We explore these questions next.

Inflation and Unemployment: The Phillips Curve

THE AGGREGATE SUPPLY–AGGREGATE DEMAND model focuses on the price level and real GDP. Knowing how these two variables change, we can work out what happens to the inflation rate and the unemployment rate. But the model does not place inflation and unemployment at the center of the stage.

A more direct way of studying inflation and unemployment uses a relationship called the Phillips curve. The Phillips curve approach uses the same basic ideas as the *AS-AD* model, but it focuses directly on inflation and unemployment. The Phillips curve is so named because New Zealand economist A.W. Phillips popularized it. A **Phillips curve** is a curve that shows a relationship between inflation and unemployment. There are two time frames for Phillips curves:

■ The short-run Phillips curve
■ The long-run Phillips curve

The Short-Run Phillips Curve

The **short-run Phillips curve** is a curve that shows the tradeoff between inflation and unemployment, holding constant:

1. The expected inflation rate
2. The natural unemployment rate

You've just seen what determines the expected inflation rate. The natural rate of unemployment and the factors that influence it are explained in Chapter 24 p. 526 and Chapter 26 pp. 575–577.

Figure 33.8 shows a short-run Phillips curve, *SRPC*. Suppose that the expected inflation rate is 10 percent a year and the natural unemployment rate is

---

FIGURE 33.8

A Short-Run Phillips Curve

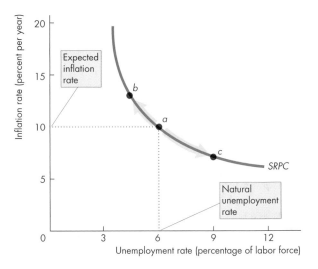

The short-run Phillips curve (*SRPC*) shows the relationship between inflation and unemployment at a given expected inflation rate and given natural unemployment rate. With an expected inflation rate of 10 percent a year and a natural unemployment rate of 6 percent, the short-run Phillips curve passes through point *a*. An unanticipated increase in aggregate demand lowers unemployment and increases inflation—a movement up the short-run Phillips curve. An unanticipated decrease in aggregate demand increases unemployment and lowers inflation—a movement down the short-run Phillips curve.

6 percent, point *a* in the figure. A short-run Phillips curve passes through this point. If inflation rises above its expected rate, unemployment falls below its natural rate. This joint movement in the inflation rate and the unemployment rate is illustrated as a movement up the short-run Phillips curve from point *a* to point *b* in the figure. Similarly, if inflation falls below its expected rate, unemployment rises above the natural rate. In this case there is movement down the short-run Phillips curve from point *a* to point *c*.

This negative relationship between inflation and unemployment along the short-run Phillips curve is explained by the aggregate supply–aggregate demand model. Figure 33.9 shows the connection between the two approaches. Initially, the aggregate demand curve is AD_0, the short-run aggregate supply curve is SAS_0, and the long-run aggregate supply curve is *LAS*. Real GDP is $7 trillion, and the price level is 100. Aggregate demand is expected to increase, and the aggregate demand curve is expected to shift rightward to AD_1. Anticipating this increase in aggregate demand, the money wage rate rises, which shifts the short-run aggregate supply curve to SAS_1. What happens to actual inflation and real GDP depends on the *actual* change in aggregate demand.

First, suppose that aggregate demand actually increases by the amount expected, so the aggregate demand curve shifts to AD_1. The price level rises from 100 to 110, and the inflation rate is an anticipated 10 percent a year. Real GDP remains at potential GDP, and unemployment remains at the natural rate. The economy moves to point *a* in Fig. 33.9, and it can equivalently be described as being at point *a* on the short-run Phillips curve in Fig. 33.8.

Alternatively, suppose that aggregate demand is expected to increase to AD_1 but actually increases by more than expected to AD_2. The price level now rises to 113, a 13 percent inflation rate. Real GDP increases above potential GDP, and unemployment falls below the natural rate. We can now describe the economy as moving to point *b* in Fig. 33.9 or at point *b* on the short-run Phillips curve in Fig. 33.8.

Finally, suppose that aggregate demand is expected to increase to AD_1 but actually remains at AD_0. The price level now rises to 107, a 7 percent inflation rate. Real GDP falls below potential GDP, and unemployment rises above the natural rate. We can now describe the economy as moving to point *c* in Fig. 33.9 or at point *c* on the short-run Phillips curve in Fig. 33.8.

FIGURE 33.9

AS-AD and the Short-Run Phillips Curve

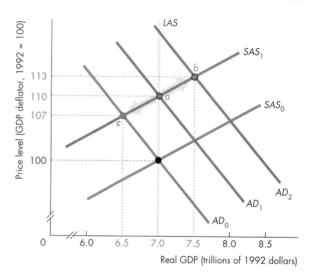

If aggregate demand is expected to increase and shift the aggregate demand curve from AD_0 to AD_1, then the money wage rate rises by an amount that shifts the short-run aggregate supply curve from SAS_0 to SAS_1. The price level rises to 110, a 10 percent rise, and the economy is at point *a* in this figure and at point *a* on the short-run Phillips curve in Fig. 33.8. If, with the same expectations, aggregate demand increases and shifts the aggregate demand curve from AD_0 to AD_2, the price level rises to 113, a 13 percent rise, and the economy is at point *b* in this figure and at point *b* on the short-run Phillips curve in Fig. 33.8. If, with the same expectations, aggregate demand does not change, the price level rises to 107, a 7 percent rise, and the economy is at point *c* in this figure and at point *c* on the short-run Phillips curve in Fig. 33.8.

The short-run Phillips curve is like the short-run aggregate supply curve. A movement along the *SAS* curve that brings a higher price level and an increase in real GDP is equivalent to a movement along the short-run Phillips curve that brings an increase in the inflation rate and a decrease in the unemployment rate. (Similarly, a movement along the *SAS* curve that brings a lower price level and a decrease in real GDP is equivalent to a movement along the short-run Phillips curve that brings a decrease in the inflation rate and an increase in the unemployment rate.)

The Long-Run Phillips Curve

The **long-run Phillips curve** shows the relationship between inflation and unemployment when the actual inflation rate equals the expected inflation rate. The long-run Phillips curve is vertical at the natural unemployment rate. In Fig. 33.10, it is the vertical line *LRPC*. The long-run Phillips curve tells us that any anticipated inflation rate is possible at the natural unemployment rate. This proposition is consistent with the *AS-AD* model, which predicts that when inflation is anticipated, real GDP equals potential GDP and unemployment is at the natural rate.

When the expected inflation rate changes, the short-run Phillips curve shifts but the long-run Phillips curve does not shift. If the expected inflation rate is 10 percent a year, the short-run Phillips curve is $SRPC_0$. If the expected inflation rate falls to 7

percent a year, the short-run Phillips curve shifts downward to $SRPC_1$. The distance by which the short-run Phillips curve shifts downward when the expected inflation rate falls is equal to the change in the expected inflation rate.

To see why the short-run Phillips curve shifts when the expected inflation rate changes, let's do a thought experiment. There is full employment, and a 10 percent a year anticipated inflation is raging. The Fed now begins an attack on inflation by slowing money supply growth. Aggregate demand growth slows, and the inflation rate falls to 7 percent a year. At first, this decrease in inflation is *un*anticipated, so wages continue to rise at their original rate. The short-run aggregate supply curve shifts leftward at the same pace as before. Real GDP falls, and unemployment increases. In Fig. 33.10, the economy moves from point *a* to point *c* on $SRPC_0$.

If the actual inflation rate remains steady at 7 percent a year, this rate eventually comes to be expected. As this happens, wage growth slows and the short-run aggregate supply curve shifts leftward less quickly. Eventually, it shifts leftward at the same pace at which the aggregate demand curve is shifting rightward. The actual inflation rate equals the expected inflation rate, and full employment is restored. Unemployment is back at its natural rate. In Fig. 33.10, the short-run Phillips curve has shifted from $SRPC_0$ to $SRPC_1$ and the economy is at point *d*.

An increase in the expected inflation rate has the opposite effect to that shown in Fig. 33.10. Another important source of shifts in the Phillips curve is a change in the natural rate of unemployment.

Changes in the Natural Unemployment Rate

The natural unemployment rate changes for many reasons (see Chapter 26, pp. 575–577). A change in the natural unemployment rate shifts both the short-run and long-run Phillips curves. Figure 33.11 illustrates such shifts. If the natural unemployment rate increases from 6 percent to 9 percent, the long-run Phillips curve shifts from $LRPC_0$ to $LRPC_1$, and if expected inflation is constant at 10 percent a year, the short-run Phillips curve shifts from $SRPC_0$ to $SRPC_1$. Because the expected inflation rate is constant, the short-run Phillips curve $SRPC_1$ intersects the long-run curve $LRPC_1$ (point *e*) at the same inflation rate at which the short-run Phillips curve $SRPC_0$ intersects the long-run curve $LRPC_0$ (point *a*).

FIGURE 33.10

Short-Run and Long-Run Phillips Curves

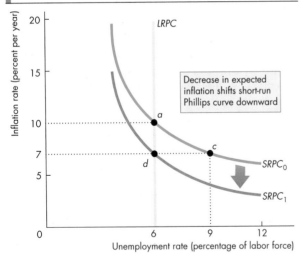

The long-run Phillips curve is *LRPC*, a vertical line at the natural unemployment rate. A fall in expected inflation shifts the short-run Phillips curve downward. For example, when the expected inflation rate falls from 10 percent a year to 7 percent a year, the short-run Phillips curve shifts downward from $SRPC_0$ and $SRPC_1$. The new short-run Phillips curve intersects the long-run Phillips curve at the new expected inflation rate—point *d*. With the original expected inflation rate (of 10 percent), an actual inflation rate of 7 percent a year would occur at an unemployment rate of 9 percent, at point *c*.

The U.S. Phillips Curve

Figure 33.12(a) is a scatter diagram of inflation and unemployment since 1960. The Phillips curve does not jump out of this figure. But we can interpret the data in terms of a shifting short-run Phillips curve as in Fig. 33.12(b). During the 1960s, the natural rate of unemployment was 5 percent and the expected inflation rate was 2 percent a year (point a), so the short-run Phillips curve was $SRPC_0$. During the 1970s and through 1981, the expected inflation rate and the natural unemployment rate increased and the short-run Phillips curve shifted rightward to $SRPC_1$, $SRPC_2$, and $SRPC_3$. During the 1980s and 1990s, the expected inflation rate and the natural unemployment rate decreased and the short-run Phillips curve shifted leftward. By the early 1990s, the curve was back at $SRPC_1$. And by 1996, the natural unemployment rate and the expected inflation rate were back around their 1960s levels, so the short-run Phillips curve was back at $SRPC_0$.

FIGURE 33.11
A Change in the Natural Unemployment Rate

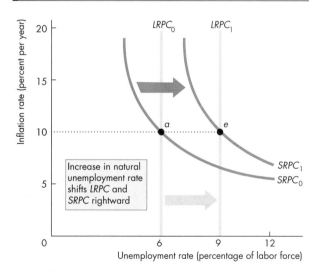

A change in the natural unemployment rate shifts both the short-run and long-run Phillips curves. Here the natural unemployment rate increases from 6 percent to 9 percent, and the two Phillips curves shift right to $SRPC_1$ and $LRPC_1$. The new long-run Phillips curve intersects the new short-run Phillips curve at the expected inflation rate—point e.

FIGURE 33.12
Phillips Curves in the United States

(a) Time sequence

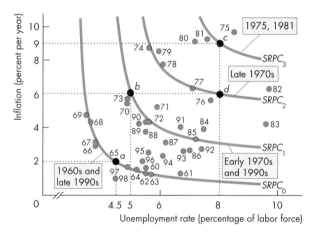

(b) Four Phillips curves

In part (a), each dot represents the combination of inflation and unemployment for a particular year in the United States. Part (b) interprets the data with a shifting short-run Phillips curve. The black dots a, b, c, and d, show the combination of the natural rate of unemployment and the expected inflation rate in different periods. The short-run Phillips curve was $SRPC_0$ during the 1960s and late 1990s. It was $SRPC_1$ during the early 1970s and 1990s, $SRPC_2$ during the late 1970s, and $SRPC_3$ (briefly) in 1975 and 1981.

Source: Economic Report of the President, 1999, and the author's calculations and assumptions.

- How would you illustrate an unanticipated change in the inflation rate by using the Phillips curve?
- What are the effects of an unanticipated increase in the inflation rate on the unemployment rate?
- If the expected inflation rate increases by 10 percentage points, how does the short-run Phillips curve change and how does the long-run Phillips curve change?
- If the natural unemployment rate increases, what happens to the short-run Phillips curve? What happens to the long-run Phillips curve? What happens to the expected inflation rate?
- Does the United States have a short-run Phillips curve? If so, has the U.S. short-run Phillips curve remained stable?
- Does the United States have a stable long-run Phillips curve?

So far, we've studied the effects of inflation on real GDP, real wages, employment, and unemployment. But inflation lowers the value of money and changes the real value of the amounts borrowed and repaid. As a result, interest rates are influenced by inflation. Let's see how.

Interest Rates and Inflation

TODAY, BUSINESSES IN THE UNITED STATES CAN borrow at interest rates of around 6 percent a year. Businesses in Russia pay interest rates of 60 percent a year and in Turkey, 80 percent a year. Although U.S. interest rates have never been as high as these two cases, during the 1980s, U.S. businesses faced interest rates of 16 percent a year or higher. Why do interest rates vary so much both across countries and over time? Part of the answer is because risk differences make *real interest rates* vary across countries (see Chapter 27, p. 593). But another part of the answer is that the inflation rate varies.

You can see in Fig. 33.13 that the higher the inflation rate, the higher is the nominal interest rate. This proposition is true for the United States over time (Fig. 33.13a) and for the world at a given time (Fig. 33.13b).

FIGURE 33.13
Inflation and the Interest Rate

(a) United States

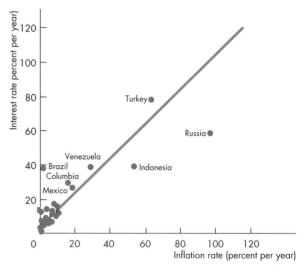

(b) Around the world

Other things remaining the same, the higher the inflation rate, the higher is the nominal interest rate. Part (a) shows this relationship between nominal interest rates and the inflation rate in the United States, and part (b) shows the relationship across a number of countries in 1999.

Source: Economic Report of the President, 1999 and The Economist, March 6, 1999.

How Interest Rates Are Determined

The *real* interest rate is determined by investment demand and saving supply in the global capital market. Investment demand and saving supply depend on the real interest rate. And the real interest rate adjusts to make investment plans and saving plans equal. (Chapter 27, pp. 593–595 explains the forces that determine the equilibrium real interest rate. National real interest rates vary around the world-average real interest rate because of national differences in risk.)

A *nominal* interest rate is determined by the demand for money and the supply of money in each nation's money market. The demand for money depends on the nominal interest rate and the supply of money is determined by the central bank's monetary policy—the Fed's monetary policy in the United States. And the nominal interest rate adjusts to make the quantity of money demanded equal to the quantity supplied. (Chapter 32, pp. 723–724 explains the forces that determine the equilibrium nominal interest rate.)

Why Inflation Influences the Nominal Interest Rate

Because the real interest rate is determined in the global capital market and nominal interest rates are determined in each nation's money market, there is no tight and mechanical link between the two interest rates. But, on the average, and other things remaining the same, a 1 percentage point rise in the inflation rate leads to a 1 percentage point rise in the nominal interest rate. Why? The answer is that the capital market and the money market are closely interconnected. The investment, saving, and demand for money decisions that people make are connected and the result is that the equilibrium nominal interest rate approximately equals the real interest rate plus the expected inflation rate.

To see why this relationship between the real interest rate and the nominal interest rate arises, think about the investment, saving, and demand for money decisions that people make. Imagine first that there is no inflation. Investment equals saving at a real interest rate of 6 percent a year. The demand for money equals the supply of money at a nominal interest rate of 6 percent a year. Walt Disney Corporation is willing to pay an interest rate of 6 percent a year to get the funds it needs to pay for its global investment in new theme parks. Sue and thousands of people like her are willing to save and lend Disney the amount it

needs for its theme parks if they can get a *real* return of 6 percent a year. (Sue is saving to buy a new car.) And Disney, Sue, and everyone else are willingly holding the quantity of (real) money supplied by the Fed.

Now imagine the inflation rate is a steady and expected 4 percent a year. All dollar amounts, including theme park profits and car prices are rising by 4 percent a year. If Disney was willing to pay a 6 percent interest rate when there was no inflation, it is now willing to pay 10 percent interest. Its profits are rising by 4 percent a year, so it is *really* paying only 6 percent. Similarly, if Sue was willing to lend at a 6 percent interest rate when there was no inflation, she is now willing to lend only if she gets a 10 percent interest rate. The price of the car Sue is planning on buying is rising by 4 percent a year, so she is *really* getting only a 6 percent interest rate.

Because borrowers are willing to pay the higher rate and lenders are willing to lend only if they receive the higher rate when inflation is anticipated, the *nominal interest rate* increases by an amount equal to the expected inflation rate. The *real interest rate* remains constant.

At a nominal interest rate of 10 percent a year, people are willingly holding the quantity of (real) money supplied by the Fed. This quantity is less than with zero inflation. The price level rises by more than the quantity of money and the real quantity of money decreases because of the increase in inflation.

R E V I E W   Q U I Z

- What is the relationship among the real interest rate, the nominal interest rate, and the inflation rate?
- Why does inflation change the nominal interest rate?

◆ *Reading Between the Lines* on pages 752–753 looks at the current low inflation in the United States and the Fed's actions to keep it that way.

You have now completed your study of inflation. This material, together with that on economic growth (Chapter 28), gives a good overview of the long-term problems that confront a modern economy such as that of the United States. Our task in the following chapter is to focus more sharply on the problems of short-term fluctuations and the business cycle.

Reading
Between
the Lines

Keeping Inflation Down

THE WALL STREET JOURNAL, APRIL 5, 1999

Unemployment Data Hints At a Slowing U.S. Economy

BY GLENN BURKINS STAFF REPORTER OF THE WALL STREET JOURNAL

WASHINGTON—The economy, which has been expanding at a rapid rate in recent years, may be slowing somewhat, the government's latest employment report suggests.

The jobless rate in March fell to 4.2%, its lowest level since 1970, from 4.4% in February, the Labor Department said Friday. But other signs suggest that the economy may finally be leveling off, vindicating the Federal Reserve's decision last week to leave interest rates alone. (All figures are seasonally adjusted.)

Only 46,000 nonfarm jobs were created in March, down from 297,000 in February, according to the government's employer survey. The index of aggregate hours worked, a rough indicator of gross domestic product, fell 0.5% in March after rising 0.5% in February. And manufacturing, after briefly showing signs of recovery, resumed its longer-term employment decline. ...

PAYROLL PARADOX

Joblessness Hits 29-Year Low, but Wages Rise More Slowly

Monthly unemployment rate (left axis) and year-to-year change in inflation-adjusted average hourly wages* (right axis)

Earnings growth slows for fourth straight month

Unemployment rate falls to 29-year low

In constant 1982 dollars   Source: Bureau of Labor Statistics

Despite the continuing tight labor market, wage gains remained moderate. Average hourly earnings of production or nonsupervisory workers on private nonfarm payrolls rose 0.2%, just three cents, in March to $13.09. Over the last 12 months, average hourly wages have risen 3.6%.

Rosanne Cahn, chief economist in the equity department at Credit Suisse First Boston, said she isn't surprised wage gains have come slowly. In part, she says, workers are putting in fewer overtime hours; that holds down the government's hourly wage figure. And despite a tight labor market, "workers are not organized to take advantage of their scarcity" by demanding higher pay, she added.

Ms Cahn says the unemployment rate would have to drop to at least 4%, and possibly much lower, before employers begin a "bidding war" for workers. ...

Essence of the Story

■ The unemployment rate in March 1999 was 4.2 percent, down from 4.4 percent in February, and at its lowest level since 1970.

■ But only 46,000 nonfarm jobs were created in March, down from 297,000 in February. The index of aggregate hours, which rose 0.5 percent in February, fell 0.5 percent in March. And employment in manufacturing fell.

■ Despite the tight labor market, wage increases were moderate.

■ Rosanne Cahn, an economist at Credit Suisse First Boston, said that the unemployment rate would have to drop to at least 4 percent, possibly lower, before wages begin to increase more quickly.

■ Figure 1 shows the inflation rate and the earnings growth rate from January 1997 to December 1998. Inflation was on a downward path through 1997 but was constant during 1998.

■ Figure 2 uses the Phillips curve to interpret the changes in inflation and unemployment.

■ In January 1997, the long-run Phillips curve was $LRPC_0$ at the (assumed) natural unemployment rate of 5.3 percent. The short-run Phillips curve was $SRPC_0$, and unemployment was at the natural rate.

■ Even if the natural rate of unemployment had remained constant, the short-run Phillips curve would have shifted downward to $SRPC_1$ because of a fall in the expected inflation rate.

■ But during 1997, the natural rate of unemployment decreased to (an assumed) 4.5 percent and the long-run Phillips curve shifted leftward to $LRPC_1$. The short-run Phillips curve also shifted leftward, to $SRPC_2$.

■ Through 1998, the unemployment rate was close to the natural rate.

■ It is possible that by the end of 1998 and the beginning of 1999, the unemployment rate was below the natural rate.

■ If the unemployment rate was below the natural rate at the beginning of 1999, the rate of inflation would be predicted to increase during 1999.

■ The view of Rosanne Cahn reported in the news article implies that she believes that the natural rate of unemployment is below 4 percent.

■ But whether inflation is going to continue to increase depends on how rapidly the money supply grows. The Fed is committed to maintaining noninflationary money growth, but Fig. 3 raises some questions about whether it is succeeding.

■ Between February 1997 and November 1998, the M2 growth rate increased. If the M2 growth rate in November 1998, which is close to 9 percent a year, is maintained, inflation will rise and probably to more than 5 percent a year.

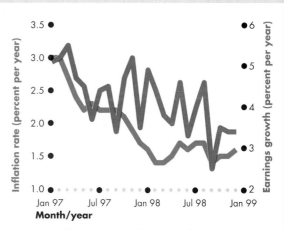

Figure 1 Inflation and earnings growth

Figure 2 Phillips curves

Figure 3 M2 money growth

SUMMARY

KEY POINTS

Inflation and the Price Level (p. 736)

- Inflation is a process of persistently rising prices and falling value of money.

Demand-Pull Inflation (pp. 737–739)

- Demand-pull inflation arises from increasing aggregate demand.
- Its main sources are increases in the money supply or in government purchases.

Cost-Push Inflation (pp. 739–741)

- Cost-push inflation can result from any factor that decreases aggregate supply.
- Its main sources are increasing wage rates and increasing prices of key raw materials.

Effects of Inflation (pp. 742–746)

- Inflation is costly when it is unanticipated because it creates inefficiencies and redistributes income and wealth.
- People try to anticipate inflation to avoid its costs.
- Forecasts of inflation based on all the available relevant information are called rational expectations.
- A moderate anticipated inflation has a small cost. But a rapid anticipated inflation is costly because it decreases potential GDP and slows growth.

Inflation and Unemployment: The Phillips Curve (pp. 746–750)

- The short-run Phillips curve shows the tradeoff between inflation and unemployment when the expected inflation rate and the natural unemployment rate are constant.
- The long-run Phillips curve, which is vertical, shows that when the actual inflation rate equals the expected inflation rate, the unemployment rate equals the natural unemployment rate.
- Unexpected changes in the inflation rate bring movements along the short-run Phillips curve.
- Changes in expected inflation shift the short-run Phillips curve.
- Changes in the natural unemployment rate shift both the short-run and long-run Phillips curves.

Interest Rates and Inflation (pp. 750–751)

- The higher the expected inflation rate, the higher is the nominal interest rate.
- As the anticipated inflation rate rises, borrowers willingly pay a higher interest rate and lenders successfully demand a higher interest rate.
- The nominal interest rate adjusts to equal the real interest rate plus the expected inflation rate.

KEY FIGURES

KEY TERMS

PROBLEMS

*1. The figure shows an economy's long-run aggregate supply curve, *LAS*; three aggregate demand curves AD_0, AD_1, and AD_2; and three short-run aggregate supply curves SAS_0, SAS_1, and SAS_2. The economy starts out on the curves AD_0 and SAS_0. Some events then occur that generate a demand-pull inflation.

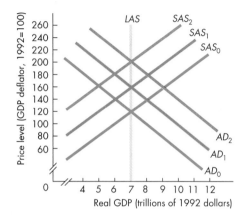

a. List the events that might cause demand-pull inflation.

b. Using the figure, describe the initial effects of demand-pull inflation.

c. Using the figure, describe what happens as a demand-pull inflation spiral unwinds.

2. In the economy described in problem 1, some events then occur that generate a cost-push inflation.

a. List the events that might cause cost-push inflation.

b. Using the figure, describe the initial effects of cost-push inflation.

c. Using the figure, describe what happens as a cost-push inflation spiral unwinds.

*3. In the economy described in problem 1, some events then occur that generate a perfectly anticipated inflation.

a. List the events that might cause a perfectly anticipated inflation.

b. Using the figure, describe the initial effects of anticipated inflation.

c. Using the figure, describe what happens as anticipated inflation proceeds.

4. In the economy described in problem 1, suppose that people anticipate deflation (a falling price level) but aggregate demand turns out not to change.

a. What happens to the short-run and long-run aggregate supply curves? (Draw some new curves if you need to.)

b. Using the figure, describe the initial effects of anticipated deflation.

c. Using the figure, describe what happens as it becomes obvious to everyone that the anticipated deflation is not going to occur.

*5. An economy has an unemployment rate of 4 percent and an inflation rate of 5 percent a year at point *a* in the figure. Some events then occur that move the economy to point *d*.

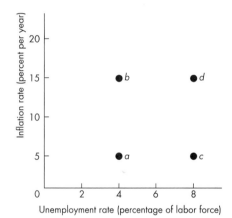

a. Describe the events that could move the economy from point *a* to point *d*.

b. Draw in the diagram the economy's short-run and long-run Phillips curves when the economy is at point *a*.

c. Draw in the diagram the economy's short-run and long-run Phillips curves when the economy is at point *d*.

6. In the economy described in problem 5, some events occur that move the economy from point *b* to point *c*.

a. Describe the events that could move the economy from point *b* to point *c*.

b. Draw in the diagram the economy's short-run and long-run Phillips curves when the economy is at point *b*.

c. Draw in the diagram the economy's short-run and long-run Phillips curves when the economy is at point *c*.

*7. In the economy described in problem 5, some events occur that move the economy in a clockwise loop from *a* to *b* to *d* to *c* and back to *a*.
   a. Describe the events that could create this sequence.
   b. Draw in the diagram the sequence of the economy's short-run and long-run Phillips curves.
   c. Has the economy experienced demand-pull inflation, cost-push inflation, anticipated inflation, or none of these?

8. In the economy described in problem 5, some events occur that move the economy in a counterclockwise loop from *a* to *c* to *d* to *b* and back to *a*.
   a. Describe the events that could create this sequence.
   b. Draw in the diagram the sequence of the economy's short-run and long-run Phillips curves.
   c. Has the economy experienced demand-pull inflation, cost-push inflation, anticipated inflation, or none of these?

*9. An economy with a natural unemployment rate of 4 percent and an expected inflation rate of 6 percent a year has the following inflation and unemployment history:

Year	Inflation rate (percent per year)	Unemployment rate (percent)
1999	10	2
2000	8	3
2001	6	4
2002	4	5
2003	2	6

   a. Draw a diagram of the economy's short-run and long-run Phillips curves.
   b. If the actual inflation rate rises from 6 percent a year to 8 percent a year, what is the change in the unemployment rate? Explain why it occurs.

10. For the economy described in problem 9, the natural unemployment rate rises to 5 percent and the expected inflation rate falls to 5 percent a year. Draw the new short-run and long-run Phillips curves in a diagram.

CRITICAL THINKING

 1. Study *Reading Between the Lines* on pp. 752–753 and use the link on the Parkin Web site to obtain the latest data on inflation, unemployment, and money growth. Then answer the following questions:
   a. What happened to the unemployment rate, the inflation rate, and the M2 money growth rate during the months following April 1999 when the news article was written?
   b. Do the events of 1999 support the view of Rosanne Cahn reported in the news article?
   c. Did the Fed keep the M2 money growth rate high, did it speed up the growth rate yet further, or did it slow the growth rate?
   d. Explain the likely effects of the Fed's monetary actions on the inflation rate and the unemployment rate through 1999.
   e. What do you think the Fed should be doing to interest rates and M2 money growth right now? Why?

2. If an inflation rate of 10 percent a year (like that we had during the 1970s) returned in the United States, who would benefit and who would lose?

3. "The Phillips curve is a menu from which the government must choose how much inflation and how much unemployment to buy." Evaluate this statement. Under what conditions is it true? Under what conditions is it false?

4. If the Fed aimed to use monetary policy to lower the unemployment rate to 2 percent, what do you predict would happen to:
   a. Unemployment in the short run?
   b. Unemployment in the long run?
   c. Inflation in the short run?
   d. Inflation in the long run?
   e. The short-run Phillips curve?
   f. The long-run Phillips curve?
   g. Potential GDP?
   h. The growth rate of potential GDP?

5. Use the link on the Parkin Web site to obtain the latest data on inflation, unemployment, and money growth in Japan, Germany, and Canada. Then:
   a. Interpret the data for each country in terms of shifting Phillips curves.
   b. Which country do you think has the lowest expected inflation rate? Why?

Understanding Aggregate Demand and Inflation

PART 9

Money Chasing Goods

Aggregate demand fluctuations bring recessions and expansions. If aggregate demand expands more rapidly than long-run aggregate supply, we get inflation. So understanding the forces that determine aggregate demand helps us to understand both the business cycle and inflation. ◆ It took economists a long time to achieve this knowledge, and we still don't know enough about aggregate demand to be able to forecast it more than a few months ahead. But we do know the basic factors that influence aggregate demand. And we know a lot about how those factors interact to send shock waves rippling through the economy. ◆ Fundamentally, aggregate demand is a monetary phenomenon. The quantity of money is the single most significant influence on aggregate demand. This insight was first outlined more than 200 years ago by David Hume, a Scottish philosopher and close friend of Adam Smith. Said Hume, "In every Kingdom into which money begins to flow in greater abundance than formerly, every thing takes a new face: labor and industry gain life; the merchant becomes more enterprising, the manufacturer more diligent and skilful, and even the farmer follows his plow with greater alacrity and attention." Milton Friedman and other economists known as *monetarists* also emphasize the central role of money. Money lies at the center of Keynes' theory of aggregate demand as well. But Keynes also called attention to the power of independent changes in government

purchases, taxes, and business investment to influence aggregate demand. In the modern world, we also recognize the effect of changes in exports on aggregate demand. ◆ The chapters in this part explain the factors that influence aggregate demand and help you to understand how they interact to bring multiplier effects on aggregate expenditure. Chapter 28 explained the effects of changes in business investment and the multiplier effect they have on consumption expenditure and aggregate expenditure. This chapter also explained how changes in business inventories trigger changes in production and incomes. Chapter 29 looked at fiscal policy and applied the model of Chapter 28 to study the effects of changes in government purchases and taxes. Chapter 30 brought money into the picture and explained exactly what money is and how banks create it. Chapter 31 showed how the Fed controls the quantity of money and thereby influences interest rates and expenditure. Chapter 32 returned to the aggregate supply–aggregate demand framework and explained inflation. It showed how the trends in inflation are determined by the trend in the money supply and how fluctuations in aggregate demand bring fluctuations in inflation, employment, and unemployment. ◆ Many economists have developed the insights you've learned in these chapters. One of the truly outstanding ones is Milton Friedman, whom you can meet on the next page. Another, and one of today's leading macroeconomists, is Bennett McCallum of Carnegie Mellon University, whom you can also meet on the following pages.

757

The Economist

Milton Friedman *was born into a poor immigrant family in New York City in 1912. He was an undergraduate at Rutgers and graduate student at Columbia University during the Great Depression. Today, Professor Friedman is a Senior Fellow at the Hoover Institution at Stanford University. But his reputation was built between 1946 and 1983, when he was a leading member of the "Chicago School," an approach to economics developed at the University of Chicago and based on the views that free markets allocate resources efficiently and that stable and low money supply growth delivers macroeconomic stability.*

Friedman has advanced our understanding of the forces that determine aggregate demand and clarified the effects of the quantity of money and for this work, he was awarded the (much overdue, in the opinion of his many admirers) 1977 Nobel Prize for Economic Science.

By reasoning from basic economic principles, Friedman predicted that persistent demand stimulation would not increase output but would cause inflation. When output growth slowed and inflation broke out in the 1970s, Friedman seemed like a prophet, and for a time, his policy prescription, known as monetarism, was embraced around the world.

> "Inflation is always and everywhere a monetary phenomenon."
>
> MILTON FRIEDMAN
> *The Counter-Revolution in Monetary Theory*

The Issues

The combination of history and economics has taught us a lot about the causes of inflation. Severe inflation—hyperinflation—arises from a breakdown of the normal fiscal policy processes at times of war or political upheaval. Tax revenues fall short of government spending, and newly printed money fills the gap between them. As inflation increases, the quantity of money that is needed to make payments increases, and a shortage of money can even result. So the rate of money growth increases yet further, and prices rise yet faster. Eventually, the monetary system collapses. Such was the experience of Germany during the 1920s and Brazil during the 1990s.

In earlier times, when commodities were used as money, inflation resulted from the discovery of new sources of money. The most recent occurrence of this type of inflation was at the end of the nineteenth century when gold, then used as money, was discovered in Australia, the Klondike, and South Africa.

In modern times, inflation has resulted from increases in the money supply that has accommodated increases in costs. The most dramatic such inflations occurred during the 1970s when the Fed and other central banks around the world accommodated oil price increases.

To avoid inflation, money supply growth must be held in check. But at times of severe cost pressure, central banks feel a strong tug in the direction of avoiding recession and accommodating the cost pressure.

Yet some countries have avoided inflation more effectively than others have. One source of success is central bank independence. In low-inflation countries, such as Germany and Japan, the central bank decides how much money to create and at what level to set interest rates, and does not take instructions from the government. In high-inflation countries, such as the United Kingdom and Italy, the central bank takes direct orders from the government about interest rates and money supply growth. The architects of a new monetary system for the European Community have noticed this connection between central bank independence and inflation, and they are modeling the European Central Bank on Germany's Bundesbank.

Then

When inflation is especially rapid, as it was in Germany in 1923, money becomes almost worthless. In Germany at that time, bank notes were more valuable as fire kindling than as money, and the sight of people burning Reichmarks was a common one. To avoid having to hold money for too long, wages were paid and spent twice a day. Banks took deposits and made loans, but at interest rates that compensated both depositors and the bank for the falling value of money—interest rates that could exceed 100 percent a month. The price of a dinner would increase during the course of an evening, making lingering over coffee a very expensive pastime.

Now

In 1994, Brazil had a computer-age hyperinflation, an inflation rate that was close to 50 percent a month. Banks installed ATMs on almost every street corner and refilled them several times an hour. Brazilians tried to avoid holding currency. As soon as they were paid, they went shopping and bought enough food to get them through to the next payday. Some shoppers filled as many as six carts on a single monthly trip to the supermarket. Also, instead of using currency, Brazilians used credit cards whenever possible. But they paid their card balances off quickly because the interest rate on unpaid balances was 50 percent a month. Only at such a high interest rate did it pay banks to lend to cardholders, because banks themselves were paying interest rates of 40 percent a month to induce depositors to keep their money in the bank.

Many economists today are working on aggregate demand and inflation. One distinguished contributor, whom you can meet on the following pages, is Bennett McCallum of Carnegie Mellon University.

Bennett T. McCallum

is Professor of Economics at Carnegie Mellon University. He was born in Poteet, Texas, in 1935. As an undergraduate, he attended Rice University, where he earned a degree in chemical engineering in 1958. He earned an MBA from Harvard Business School in 1963 and a Ph.D. in economics from Rice University in 1969.

Professor McCallum's research interests include monetary theory and policy, macroeconomic dynamics, and applied econometrics. Much of his research is aimed toward improving monetary policy, and Professor McCallum's advice is sought by central banks around the world.

Bennett T. McCallum

He has recently spent time at the Reserve Bank of New Zealand as well as the central bank of the Philippines.

Michael Parkin talked with Professor McCallum about his work, how it connects with the work of other great economists, and his insights on monetary policy.

Professor McCallum, how did you become interested in Economics?
I majored in chemical engineering in college and later worked for three years as a process design engineer for a petrochemical firm in Houston, Texas. Then, at my wife's urging, I earned an MBA at Harvard University. While attending

Harvard, I took as many economics, statistics, and operations research courses as possible. I enjoyed these courses and, as a result, decided to enroll in a Ph.D. program in economics.

What I found attractive about economics is its fascinating—even beautiful—theoretical structure combined with its emphasis on thinking analytically about public policy issues. The usual noneconomist approach to policy issues that one gets from the media and other sources seems to consist mostly of moralizing on the basis of the effects that a policy might have on some particular social group, which is very different from thinking analytically.

Many economists of your generation were heavily influenced by John Maynard Keynes. Looking back now on the work of Keynes, what do you think his legacy amounts to?
Keynes was by all accounts an exceptionally brilliant person and very good at his chosen subject of economics. But he was principally interested in the practical side of economics and government policy. During World War II, for instance, he contributed greatly to Britain's wartime finance policy and to the design of the Bretton Woods system that governed international monetary relations from 1945 to 1971. Thus for Keynes, economic theory was something that he did to persuade others of insights that he had. As a consequence, his theoretical work was, in my opinion, badly flawed. His famous *General Theory* contains numerous theoretical mistakes. It nevertheless did make a big contribution to the way that economic analysis is done, primarily by helping to persuade economists to be interested in short-run rather

> **What I found attractive about economics is its fascinating—even beautiful—theoretical structure combined with its emphasis on thinking analytically about public policy issues.**

than just long-run analysis. That was actually a major reorientation in thinking. It was like saying, "Hey, guys, let's pay attention to short-run effects. They're important."

Immediately following Keynes, economists began to emphasize that we can and should use fiscal policy to manipulate aggregate demand. What do we actually know about the ability of governments to manipulate aggregate expenditure using fiscal policy?

If there is a major sustained increase in government spending, starting from a deep recession such as in the 1930s, there will be major effects, as in 1940 to 1944. But if resources are fully employed, then the main real effect will be to shift consumption to the government from households and businesses. If, instead, the government imposes a tax change that's financed by bonds, by borrowing more or less, then the effects will be smaller. From a business cycle point of view, the most important fiscal policy considerations involve the automatic stabilizers, since, at least in the United States, the legislature typically isn't able to take actions promptly enough to be very helpful for any particular economic boom or slump.

What do we know about the Fed's ability to manipulate aggregate expenditure by using monetary policy?

The Fed can act much more quickly, and changes in its policy stance almost certainly affect nominal expenditures, or GDP in dollar terms. In other words, when the central bank pursues a more expansionary policy, the rate of aggregate expenditures will increase. But that is in money terms. What the real effects are depends on how wage and price adjustments occur, and our understanding in that respect is very far from complete. Indeed, my opinion is that the most serious weakness in our understanding of macro and monetary issues is the mechanism by which changes in monetary policy affect real variables such as employment or price-level-adjusted GDP. Although there is a lot of good work going on right now, we don't have agreement on the nature of the wage and price adjustment process.

Can we continue to use monetary policy to prevent inflation? If we can, how? And is Greenspan's current monetary policy on the right track?

Certainly monetary policy can be used to prevent inflation. You just cannot have a serious long-lasting inflation unless the central bank is creating money rapidly. As for gauging whether monetary policy is right or not, I think the best single measure is the rate of growth of the monetary base, by which we mean currency plus bank reserves.

As for recent federal reserve policy, I think it's been quite good over the period since Greenspan

became chairman, but nevertheless, I think that the United States would benefit from legislation stating that the prevention of inflation is the Fed's main objective. Currently, the law fails to state the main responsibility of the Fed. Although Greenspan has been quite consistent on this dimension himself, it's not a good idea to have a system that relies so much on the judgments of a single person. The next Fed chairman might not be so reasonable. Legislation clearly mandating prevention of inflation as the Fed's main responsibility would make it more difficult for Congress to pressure the Fed toward other objectives, which are less suitable.

What should the Fed be doing to minimize the risk of inflation and recession?

There's no question that Fed policies have substantial effects on output and employment, but these effects are temporary. From my perspective, the extent to which the Fed can usefully contribute to reducing cyclical fluctuation is rather limited. So I think the Fed should try to keep total spending, one measure of which would be nominal GDP, growing smoothly at a rate that is basically noninflationary. For example, if the objective is to keep inflation at about 2 percent per year, then the Fed ought to keep nominal GDP growing rather smoothly at about 4 1/2 percent (since real GDP will in any case grow at about 2 1/2 percent, on the average).

In conducting this policy, in which the Fed tightens or loosens depending on whether nominal GDP is growing faster or slower than 4 1/2 percent, you have to use some measure to determine whether you are in fact tightening or loosening, and I would favor looking at the growth rate of the monetary base. Now the Fed does not do that; instead, it looks at the federal funds interest rate. The problem with that approach is that from the perspective of short-run analysis, a high interest rate means tight money, but from the perspective of long-run analysis, a high interest rate reflects loose money (fast money growth). So gauging monetary conditions on the basis of an interest rate is a rather tricky and difficult thing to do. That's why I would prefer to look at a very narrow, controllable monetary measure, such as the monetary base.

What is your assessment of the U.S. deficit? Are deficits inflationary?
Government deficits per se are not all that important at the macroeconomic level. More important is the extent of goods and services that are consumed by the government, rather than the private sector. Deficits are going to be inflationary if the central bank responds to them by creating money in an attempt to keep interest rates from rising. This often happens, especially in countries with poorly developed tax systems. But in the United States, the Fed has not been printing money to finance the deficit. Instead, the Fed has forced the Treasury to finance the deficit by borrowing from the public. So we've not had an accommodating policy from the Fed, and as a result, we've not had much inflation. Much the same has been true in Europe and in many of the

developed economies over the last 10 to 15 years.

Who historically are the big contributors to our understanding of aggregate fluctuations? Who are today's big contributors?
There were several macroeconomists who took John Maynard Keynes' general body of reasoning and his idea of focusing on short-run phenomena and made something fairly coherent out them. Economists such as Patinkin, Modigliani, and Hicks developed Keynesian economics as opposed to thoughts that Keynes had himself begun with. What about before Keynes? His teacher, Alfred Marshall, viewed the generation of business cycles in a manner rather consistent with Keynes' views, but he did not give so much attention to that topic. Irving Fisher believed that if you stabilized price levels, it would tend to prevent the problems that create recessions. Marshall believed fairly much the same thing.

Robert Lucas has been easily the most productive economist of the last 25 years, certainly in the area of macroeconomics. Although his information-based theory of fluctuations has not prevailed, he nevertheless set the tone and direction for today's research.

There are two important lessons from Lucas's work. First, is the basic idea of rational expectations—that although people can't forecast the future perfectly, they can and do strive to avoid systematic expectational errors. This implies that in designing macroeconomic policy, governments should not rely on the presumption that people are going to make the same mistakes over and over again. The second main lesson

> I'm of the belief that an undergraduate should take subjects that are interesting to him or her. Find something that's enjoyable to you, that you're interested in, and then work hard on that.

from Lucas's work is that we should focus on long-run and long-lasting effects of policy actions rather than the temporary, short-term effects emphasized by the Keynesian approach of the 1950s and 1960s. We should try to design good institutions and good rules for policy making rather than being distracted by the alleged crisis of the day. In these teachings, as in many other ways, Lucas was further developing the general approach of Milton Friedman.

Is an economics major a good thing to pursue at the start of the new millenium?
Although only a small fraction of students studying economics will go on to become professional economists, it's an excellent subject to take for preparing for other careers—including business and the law—because of the disciplined, analytical thinking that it teaches.

I'm of the belief that an undergraduate should take subjects that are interesting to him or her. Find something that's enjoyable to you, that you're interested in, and then work hard on that. It doesn't have to be economics. What's unfortunate is for students to just go through the paces while they're undergraduates and miss the opportunity to gain a foundation in some field that will allow them to start off on an intellectually satisfying life.

Chapter 34

The Business Cycle

The 1920s were years of unprecedented prosperity for Americans.
After the horrors of World War I
(1914–1918), the economic machine was
back at work, producing such technological
marvels as cars and airplanes, telephones and vac-
uum cleaners. Houses and apartments were being built
at a frantic pace. Then, almost without warning, in
October 1929, came a devastating stock market crash.
Overnight, the values of stocks and shares traded on Wall Street
fell by 30 percent. During the four succeeding years, there followed
the most severe economic contraction in recorded history. By 1933,
real GDP had fallen by 30 percent, unemployment had increased to 25
percent of the labor force, and employment was down 20 percent.
What caused the Great Depression? ◆ By the standard of the Great
Depression, recent recessions have been mild.
But recessions have not gone away. Our economy has experienced 15 recessions since 1920
and 10 since the end of World War II in
1945. For 16 months, from November 1973
through March 1975, real GDP fell by 5 percent. It fell again in back-to-back recessions in
1980 and in 1981–1982. Most recently, real
GDP decreased for 8 months in 1990–1991. Between these recessions,
expansions took real GDP and income per person to new heights.
Since the 1990–1991 recession, real GDP has grown steadily. By the
end of 1998, it was some 25 percent higher than it had been in the
1990–1991 recession. What causes a repeating sequence of recessions
and expansions in our economy? Must what goes up always come
down? Will we have another recession? When?

◆ We are going to explore the business cycle in this chapter. You will
see how all the strands of macroeconomics that you've been following
come together and weave a complete picture of the forces and
mechanisms that generate economic growth and fluctuations in production, employment and unemployment, and inflation.

Must What Goes Up Always Come Down?

After studying this chapter, you will be able to:

- ◼ Distinguish among the different theories of the business cycle

- ◼ Explain the Keynesian and monetarist theories of the business cycle

- ◼ Explain the new classical and new Keynesian theories of the business cycle

- ◼ Explain real business cycle theory

- ◼ Describe the origins of and the mechanisms at work during two recent recessions and during the Great Depression

Cycle Patterns, Impulses, and Mechanisms

YOU'VE LOOKED AT THE BUSINESS CYCLE AT several points in your study of macroeconomics. You met it first in Chapter 22, which defines the phases of the cycle and describes its history. In Chapter 24, you saw how unemployment fluctuates over the business cycle. You learned about a framework for studying the business cycle—the aggregate supply–aggregate demand model—in Chapter 25. In Chapter 29, you focused on business cycle turning points and the inventory changes and expenditure multiplier effects that operate as the economy swings from expansion to recession and from recession to expansion. In Chapter 30, you studied the ways in which fiscal policy influences and is influenced by the business cycle. Finally, you saw in Chapters 31 through 33 how money influences economic fluctuations and how inflation and the business cycle intertwine.

You've also looked at another type of economic fluctuation: the productivity growth slowdown of the 1970s. This slowdown is not classified as a business cycle event, but it has some similarities. It is part of an overall process of economic growth, the pace of which fluctuates. The processes of growth and of the business cycle are intimately connected. In fact, according to one view, they are all manifestations of the same phenomenon.

This chapter brings all these strands in your previous study of macroeconomics together and gives you an opportunity both to review what you have learned and to put it to work in a focused way in interpreting and making sense of particular episodes in our economic history.

We'll get moving by first returning to the facts about the business cycle and looking at the complex patterns it makes.

Business Cycle Patterns

The business cycle is an irregular and nonrepeating up-and-down movement of business activity that takes place around a generally rising trend and that shows great diversity. Each recession, expansion, and turning point has been dated by the National Bureau of Economic Research (NBER). The NBER has identified 15 recessions and expansions since 1920. On the average, recessions have lasted for just over a

year and real GDP has fallen from peak to trough by more than 6 percent. Expansions have lasted for almost 4 years on the average, and real GDP has increased from trough to peak by an average of 22 percent. But these averages hide huge variations from one cycle to another.

Figure 34.1 shows the range of variation across the different recessions and expansions. It shows the total percentage change in real GDP during successive recessions and expansion. You can see that the Great Depression was much more severe than anything that followed it. Over a 43-month period, real GDP shrank by 33 percent. The second most severe recession was also in the 1930s. Another relatively severe recession occurred at the end of World War II in 1945. The only other recession that comes close to these is the OPEC recession of 1974–1975. A four-fold rise in the price of oil brought a 16-month and 5 percent fall in real GDP. The other recessions since 1950, including the most recent 1990–1991 recession, have been much milder than those of the 1930s. The biggest expansion occurred during World War II. But the other two big expansions were in the 1960s and 1980s. There is no correlation between the length of an expansion and the length of the preceding recession.

With this enormous diversity of experience, there is no simple explanation for the business cycle. Also, there is no (currently available) way of forecasting when the next turning point will come. But there is a body of theory about the business cycle that helps us to understand its causes. A good place to begin studying this theory is to distinguish the possible ways in which cycles can be created.

Cycle Impulses and Mechanisms

Cycles are a widespread physical phenomenon. In a tennis match, the ball cycles from one side of the court to the other and back again. Every day, the earth cycles from day to night and back to day. A child on a rocking horse creates a cycle as the horse swings back and forth.

The tennis ball cycle is the simplest. It is caused by the actions of the players. Each time the ball changes direction (at each turning point), the racket (an outside force) is applied. The day-night-day cycle is the most subtle. This cycle is caused by the rotation of the earth. No new force is applied each day to make the sun rise and set. It happens because of

FIGURE 34.1

Some Business Cycle Patterns

Recessions have lasted from 43 months during the Great Depression, when real GDP fell by 33 percent, to 6 months in 1980, when real GDP fell by 2.5 percent. The mildest recession lasted through most of 1970, when real GDP fell by 1 percent. Recessions have been less severe in the post–World War II period. Expansions have lasted from 6 months in 1980 to more than 100 months during the 1960s. Expansions have become longer and stronger during the post–World War II period.

Source: National Bureau of Economic Research and the author's calculations.

the design of the objects that interact to create the cycle. Nothing happens at a turning point (sunrise and sunset) that is any different from what is happening at other points except that the sun comes into or goes out of view. The child's rocking horse cycle is a combination of these two cases. To start the horse rocking, some outside force must be exerted (as in the tennis ball cycle). But once the horse is rocking, the to-and-fro cycle continues for some time with no further force being applied (as in the day-night-day cycle). The rocking horse cycle eventually dies out unless the horse is pushed again, and each time the horse is pushed, the cycle temporarily becomes more severe.

The economy is a bit like all three of these examples. It can be hit by shocks (like a tennis ball) that send it in one direction or another, it can cycle indefinitely (like the turning of day into night), and it can cycle in swings that get milder until another shock sets off a new burst of bigger swings (like a rocking horse). While none of these analogies is perfect, they all contain some insights into the business cycle.

Different theories of the cycle emphasize different outside forces (different tennis rackets) and different cycle mechanisms (different solar system and rocking horse designs).

Although there are several different theories of the business cycle, they all agree about one aspect of the cycle: the central role played by investment and the accumulation of capital.

The Central Role of Investment and Capital

Whatever the shocks are that hit the economy, they hit one crucial variable: investment. Recessions begin when investment in new capital slows down, and they turn into expansions when investment speeds up. Investment and capital interact like the spinning earth and the sun to create an ongoing cycle.

In an expansion, investment proceeds at a rapid rate and the capital stock grows quickly. But rapid capital growth means that the amount of capital per hour of labor is growing. Equipped with more capital, labor becomes more productive. But the *law of diminishing returns* begins to operate. The law of diminishing returns states that as the quantity of capital increases, with the quantity of labor remaining the same, the gain in productivity from the additional units of capital eventually diminishes. Diminishing returns to capital bring a fall in the profit rate, and with a lower profit rate, the incentive to invest weakens. As a result, investment eventually falls. When it falls by a large amount, recession begins.

In a recession, investment is low and the capital stock grows slowly. In a deep recession, the capital stock might actually fall. Slow capital growth (or even a falling capital stock) means that the amount of capital per hour of labor is falling. With a low amount of capital per hour of labor, businesses begin to see opportunities for profitable investment and the pace of investment eventually picks up. As it does so, recession turns into expansion.

The AS-AD Model

Investment and capital are a crucial part of the business cycle mechanism, but they are just one part. To study the broader business cycle mechanism, we need a broader framework. That framework is the *AS-AD* model of Chapter 25. All the theories of the business cycle can be described in terms of the *AS-AD* model. Theories differ both in what they identify as the impulse and in the cycle mechanism. But all theories can be thought of as making assumptions about the factors that make either aggregate supply or aggregate demand fluctuate and assumptions about how they interact with each other to create a business cycle. Business cycle impulses can affect either the supply side or the demand side of the economy or both. But there are no pure supply-side theories. We will classify all theories of the business cycle as either:

1. Aggregate demand theories
2. Real business cycle theory

We'll study the aggregate demand theories first. Then we'll study real business cycle theory, which is a more recent approach that isolates a shock that has both aggregate supply and aggregate demand effects.

Aggregate Demand Theories of the Business Cycle

THREE TYPES OF AGGREGATE DEMAND THEORY OF the business cycle have been proposed. They are:

- Keynesian theory
- Monetarist theory
- Rational expectations theories

Keynesian Theory

The **Keynesian theory of the business cycle** regards volatile expectations as the main source of economic fluctuations. This theory is distilled from Keynes' *General Theory of Employment, Interest, and Money*. We'll explore the Keynesian theory by looking at its main impulse and the mechanism that converts that impulse into a real GDP cycle.

Keynesian Impulse The *impulse* in the Keynesian theory of the business cycle is *expected future sales and profits*. A change in expected future sales and profits changes the demand for new capital and changes the level of investment.

Keynes had a sophisticated theory about *how* expected sales and profits are determined. He reasoned that these expectations would be volatile because most of the events that shape the future are unknown and impossible to forecast. So, he reasoned, news or even rumors about future tax rate changes, interest rate changes, advances in technology, global economic and political events, or any other of the thousands of relevant factors that influence sales and profits change expectations in ways that can't be quantified but that have large effects.

To emphasize the volatility and diversity of sources of changes in expected sales and profits, Keynes described these expectations as *animal spirits*. In using this term, Keynes was not saying that expectations are irrational. Rather, he meant that because future sales and profits are impossible to forecast, it might be rational to take a view about them based on rumors, guesses, intuition, and instinct. Further, it might be rational to *change* one's view of the future, perhaps radically, in the light of scraps of new information.

Keynesian Cycle Mechanism In the Keynesian theory, once a change in animal spirits has changed investment, a cycle mechanism begins to operate that has two key elements. First, the initial change in investment has a multiplier effect. The change in investment changes *aggregate* expenditure, real GDP, and disposable income. The change in disposable income changes consumption expenditure and aggregate demand changes by a multiple of the initial change in investment. (This mechanism is described in detail in Chapter 29, p. 646 and pp. 652–653.) The aggregate demand curve shifts rightward in an expansion and leftward in a recession.

The second element of the Keynesian cycle mechanism is the response of real GDP to a change in aggregate demand. The short-run aggregate supply curve is horizontal (or nearly so). With a horizontal *SAS* curve, swings in aggregate demand translate into swings in real GDP with no changes in the price level. But the short-run aggregate supply curve depends on the money wage rate. If the money wage rate is fixed (sticky), the *SAS* curve does not move. And if the money wage rate changes, the *SAS* curve shifts. In the Keynesian theory, the response of the money wage rate to changes in aggregate demand are *asymmetric*.

On the downside, when aggregate demand decreases and unemployment rises, the money wage rate does not change. It is completely rigid in the downward direction. With a decrease in aggregate demand and no change in the money wage rate, the economy gets stuck in a below full-employment equilibrium. No natural forces operate to restore full employment. The economy remains in that situation until animal spirits are lifted and investment increases.

On the upside, when aggregate demand increases and unemployment falls below the natural rate, the money wage rate rises quickly. It is flexible in the upward direction. At above full employment, the horizontal *SAS* curve plays no role and only the vertical *LAS* curve is relevant. With an increase in aggregate demand and an accompanying rise in the money wage rate, the price level rises quickly to eliminate the shortages and bring the economy back to full employment. The economy remains in that situation until animal spirits fall and investment and aggregate demand decrease.

Figures 34.2 and 34.3 illustrate the Keynesian theory of the business cycle by using the aggregate supply–aggregate demand model. In Fig. 34.2, the economy is initially at full employment (point *a*) on the long-run aggregate supply curve (*LAS*), the aggregate demand curve (*AD₀*), and the short-run

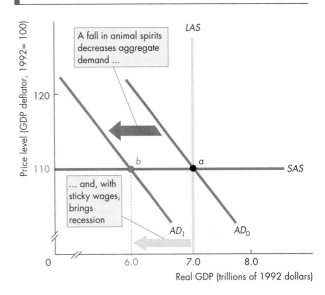

FIGURE 34.2

A Keynesian Recession

The economy is operating at point *a* at the intersection of the long-run aggregate supply curve (*LAS*), the short-run aggregate supply curve (*SAS*), and the aggregate demand curve (*AD₀*). A Keynesian recession begins when a fall in animal spirits causes investment demand to decrease. Aggregate demand decreases, and the *AD* curve shifts leftward to *AD₁*. With sticky money wages, real GDP decreases to $6 trillion and the price level does not change. The economy moves to point *b*.

aggregate supply curve (*SAS*). A fall in animal spirits decreases investment, and a multiplier process decreases aggregate demand. The aggregate demand curve shifts leftward to *AD₁*. With a fixed money wage rate, real GDP falls to $6 trillion and the economy moves to point *b*. Unemployment has increased and there is a surplus of labor. But the money wage rate does not fall, and the economy remains at point *b* until some force moves it away.

That force is shown in Fig. 34.3. Here, starting out at point *b*, a rise in animal spirits increases investment. The multiplier process kicks in, and aggregate demand increases. The *AD* curve shifts to *AD₂*, and real GDP begins to increase. An expansion is under way. As long as real GDP remains below potential GDP ($7 trillion in this example), the money wage rate and the price level remain constant. But real

FIGURE 34.3
A Keynesian Expansion

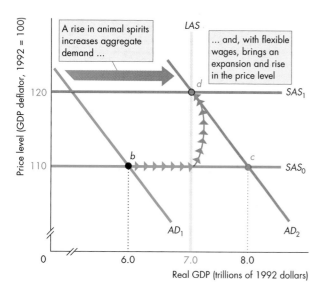

Starting at point b, a Keynesian expansion begins when a rise in animal spirits causes investment demand to increase. Aggregate demand increases, and the AD curve shifts rightward to AD_2. With sticky money wages, real GDP increases to \$7 trillion. But the economy does not go all the way to point c. When full employment is reached, the money wage rate rises and the SAS curve shifts upward toward SAS_1. The price level rises as the economy heads toward point d.

GDP never increases to point c, the point of intersection of SAS_0 and AD_2. The reason is that once real GDP exceeds potential GDP and unemployment falls below the natural rate, the money wage rate begins to rise and the SAS curve starts to shift upward toward SAS_1. As the money wage rate rises, the price level also rises and real GDP growth slows. The economy follows a path like the one shown by the arrows connecting point b, the initial equilibrium, with point d, the final equilibrium.

The Keynesian business cycle is mainly like a tennis match. It is caused by outside forces—animal spirits—that change direction and set off a process that ends at an equilibrium that must be hit again by the outside forces to disturb it.

Monetarist Theory

The **monetarist theory of the business cycle** regards fluctuations in the money stock as the main source of economic fluctuations. This theory is distilled from the writings of Milton Friedman and several other economists. We'll explore the monetarist theory as we did the Keynesian theory, by looking first at its main impulse and second at the mechanism that creates a cycle in real GDP.

Monetarist Impulse The *impulse* in the monetarist theory of the business cycle is the *growth rate of the quantity of money*. A speedup in money growth brings expansion, and a slowdown in money growth brings recession. The source of the change in the growth rate of the quantity of money is the monetary policy actions of the Fed.

Monetarist Cycle Mechanism In the monetarist theory, once the Fed has changed the money growth rate, a cycle mechanism begins to operate that, like the Keynesian mechanism, first affects aggregate demand. When the money growth rate increases, the quantity of real money in the economy increases. Interest rates fall, and real money balances increase. The foreign exchange rate also falls—the dollar loses value on the foreign exchange market. These initial financial market effects begin to spill over into other markets. Investment demand and exports increase, and consumers spend more on durable goods. These initial changes in expenditure have a multiplier effect, just as investment has in the Keynesian theory. Through these mechanisms, a speedup in money growth shifts the aggregate demand curve rightward and brings an expansion. Similarly, a slowdown in money growth shifts the aggregate demand curve leftward and brings a recession.

The second element of the monetarist cycle mechanism is the response of aggregate supply to a change in aggregate demand. The short-run aggregate supply curve is upward-sloping. With an upward-sloping SAS curve, swings in aggregate demand translate into swings in both real GDP and the price level. But monetarists believe that real GDP deviations from full employment are temporary in both directions.

In monetarist theory, the money wage rate is only *temporarily sticky*. When aggregate demand decreases and unemployment rises, the money wage rate eventually begins to fall. As the money wage rate falls, so does the price level and after a period of adjustment, full employment is restored. When aggregate demand increases and unemployment falls below the natural rate, the money wage rate begins to rise. As the money wage rate rises, so does the price level. And through a period of adjustment, real GDP returns to potential GDP and the unemployment rate returns to the natural rate.

Figure 34.4 illustrates the monetarist theory. In part (a), the economy is initially at full employment (point *a*) on the long-run aggregate supply curve (*LAS*), the aggregate demand curve (*AD*$_0$), and the short-run aggregate supply curve (*SAS*$_0$). A slow-down in the money growth rate decreases aggregate

demand and the aggregate demand curve shifts left-ward to *AD*$_1$. Real GDP decreases to $6.5 trillion, and the economy goes into recession (point *b*). Unemployment increases and there is a surplus of labor. The money wage rate begins to fall. As the money wage falls, the short-run aggregate supply curve starts to shift rightward toward *SAS*$_1$. The price level falls, and real GDP begins to expand as the economy moves to point *c*, its new full-employment equilibrium.

Figure 34.4(b) shows the effects of the opposite initial money shock—a speedup in money growth. Here, starting out at point *c*, a speedup in the money growth rate increases aggregate demand and shifts the

FIGURE 34.4
A Monetarist Business Cycle

(a) Recession

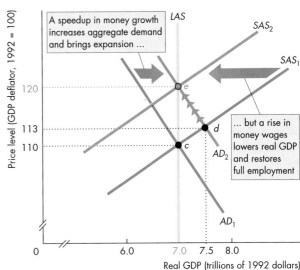

(b) Expansion

A monetarist recession begins when a slowdown in money growth decreases aggregate demand. The *AD* curve shifts left-ward from *AD*$_0$ to *AD*$_1$ (in part a). With sticky money wages, real GDP decreases to $6.5 trillion and the price level falls to 117 as the economy moves from point *a* to point *b*. With a surplus of labor, the money wage rate falls and the *SAS* curve shifts rightward to *SAS*$_1$. The price level falls further, and real GDP returns to potential GDP at point *c*.

Starting at point *c* (part b), a monetarist expansion begins when an increase in money growth increases aggregate demand and shifts the *AD* curve rightward to *AD*$_2$. With sticky money wages, real GDP rises to $7.5 trillion, the price level rises to 113, and the economy moves to point *d*. With a shortage of labor, the money wage rate rises and the *SAS* curve shifts toward *SAS*$_2$. The price level rises, and real GDP decreases to potential GDP as the economy heads toward point *e*.

AD curve to *AD*$_2$. Both real GDP and the price level increase as the economy moves to point *d*, the point of intersection of *SAS*$_1$ and *AD*$_2$. With real GDP above potential GDP and unemployment below the natural rate, the money wage rate begins to rise and the *SAS* curve starts to shift leftward toward *SAS*$_2$. As the money wage rate rises, the price level also rises and real GDP decreases. The economy moves from point *d* to point *e*, its new full-employment equilibrium.

The monetarist business cycle is like a rocking horse. It needs an outside force to get it going, but once going, it rocks back and forth (but just once). It doesn't matter in which direction the force initially hits. If it is a money growth slowdown, the economy cycles with a recession followed by expansion. If it is a money growth speedup, the economy cycles with an expansion followed by recession.

Rational Expectations Theories

A **rational expectation** is a forecast that is based on all the available relevant information (see Chapter 33, p. 743). Rational expectations theories of the business cycle are theories based on the view that money wages are determined by a rational expectation of the price level. Two distinctly different rational expectations theories of the cycle have been proposed. A **new classical theory of the business cycle** regards *unanticipated* fluctuations in aggregate demand as the main source of economic fluctuations. This theory is based on the work of Robert E. Lucas, Jr., (see pp. 555–560) and several other economists, including Thomas J. Sargent and Robert J. Barro. A different **new Keynesian theory of the business cycle** also regards *unanticipated* fluctuations in aggregate demand as the main source of economic fluctuations but it leaves room for *anticipated* demand fluctuations to play a role. We'll explore these theories as we did the Keynesian and monetarist theories, by looking first at the main impulse and second at the cycle mechanism.

Rational Expectations Impulse The *impulse* that distinguishes the rational expectations theories from the other aggregate demand theories of the business cycle is the *unanticipated change in aggregate demand*. A larger than anticipated increase in aggregate demand brings an expansion, and a smaller than anticipated increase in aggregate demand brings a recession. Any factor that influences aggregate demand—for example,

fiscal policy, monetary policy, or developments in the world economy that influence exports—whose change is not anticipated can bring a change in real GDP.

Rational Expectations Cycle Mechanisms To describe the rational expectations cycle mechanisms, we'll deal first with the new classical version. When aggregate demand decreases, if the money wage rate doesn't change, real GDP and the price level both decrease. The fall in the price level increases the *real* wage rate, and employment decreases and unemployment increases. In the new classical theory, these events occur only if the decrease in aggregate demand is not anticipated. If the decrease in aggregate demand *is* anticipated, the price level is expected to fall and both firms and workers will agree to a lower money wage rate. By doing so, they can prevent the real wage from rising and avoid a rise in the unemployment rate.

Similarly, if firms and workers anticipate an increase in aggregate demand, they expect the price level to rise and will agree to a higher money wage rate. By doing so, they can prevent the real wage rate from falling and avoid a fall in the unemployment rate below the natural rate.

Only fluctuations in aggregate demand that are unanticipated and not taken into account in wage agreements bring changes in real GDP. *Anticipated* changes in aggregate demand change the price level, but they leave real GDP and unemployment unchanged and do not create a business cycle.

New Keynesian economists, like new classical economists, believe that money wages are influenced by rational expectations of the price level. But new Keynesians emphasize the long-term nature of most wage contracts. They say that *today's* money wages are influenced by *yesterday's* rational expectations. These expectations, which were formed in the past, are based on old information that might now be known to be incorrect. After they have made a long-term wage agreement, both firms and workers might anticipate a change in aggregate demand, which they expect will change the price level. But because they are locked into their agreement, they are unable to change money wages. So money wages are sticky in the new Keynesian theory, and with sticky money wages, even an *anticipated* change in aggregate demand changes real GDP.

New classical economists believe that long-term contracts are renegotiated when conditions change to make them outdated. So they do not regard long-term contracts as an obstacle to money wage flexibility, provided that both parties to an agreement recognize the changed conditions. If both firms and workers expect the price level to change, they will change the agreed money wage rate to reflect that shared expectation. In this situation, anticipated changes in aggregate demand change the money wage rate and the price level and leave real GDP unchanged.

The distinctive feature of both versions of the rational expectations theory of the business cycle is the role of unanticipated changes in aggregate demand. Figure 34.5 illustrates the effect of unanticipated changes on real GDP and the price level.

Potential GDP is $7 trillion, and the long-run aggregate supply curve is *LAS*. Aggregate demand is expected to be *EAD*. Given potential GDP and *EAD*, the money wage rate is set at the level that is expected to bring full employment. At this money wage rate, the short-run aggregate supply curve is *SAS*. Imagine that initially aggregate demand equals expected aggregate demand, so there is full employment. Real GDP is $7 trillion, and the price level is 110. Then, unexpectedly, aggregate demand turns out to be less than expected and the aggregate demand curve shifts leftward to AD_0 (in Fig. 34.5a). Many different aggregate demand shocks, such as a slowdown in the money growth rate or a collapse of exports, could have caused this shift. A recession

---

FIGURE 34.5

A Rational Expectations Business Cycle

(a) Recession

(b) Expansion

The economy is expected to be at point *a* at the intersection of the long-run aggregate supply curve, *LAS*; the short-run aggregate supply curve, *SAS*; and the *expected* aggregate demand curve, *EAD*. A rational expectations recession begins when an unanticipated fall in aggregate demand shifts the *AD* curve leftward to AD_0. With money wage rates based on the expectation that aggregate demand will be *EAD*, real GDP falls to $6.5 trillion and the price level falls to 107 as the economy moves to point *b*. As long as aggregate demand is *expected* to

be *EAD*, there is no change in the money wage rate.

A rational expectations expansion begins when an unanticipated rise in aggregate demand shifts the *AD* curve rightward from AD_0 to AD_1. With money wage rates based on the expectation that aggregate demand will be *EAD*, real GDP increases to $7.5 trillion and the price level rises to 113 as the economy moves to point *c*. Again, as long as aggregate demand is *expected* to be *EAD*, there is no change in the money wage rate.

begins. Real GDP falls to $6.5 trillion, and the price level falls to 107. The economy moves to point b. Unemployment increases, and there is a surplus of labor. But aggregate demand is expected to be at EAD, so the money wage rate doesn't change and the short-run aggregate supply curve remains at SAS.

The recession ends when aggregate demand increases to its expected level. And a larger increase that takes aggregate demand to a level that exceeds EAD brings an expansion. In Fig. 34.5(b), the aggregate demand curve shifts rightward to AD_1. Such an increase in aggregate demand might be caused by a speedup in the money growth rate or an export boom. Real GDP now increases to $7.5 trillion, and the price level rises to 113. The economy moves to point c. Unemployment is now below the natural rate. But aggregate demand is expected to be at EAD, so the money wage rate doesn't change and the short-run aggregate supply curve remains at SAS.

Fluctuations in aggregate demand between AD_0 and AD_1 around expected aggregate demand EAD bring fluctuations in real GDP and the price level between points b and c.

The two versions of the rational expectations theory differ in their predictions about the effects of a change in expected aggregate demand. The new classical theory predicts that as soon as expected aggregate demand changes, the money wage rate also changes, so the SAS curve shifts. The new Keynesian theory predicts that the money wage rate changes only gradually when new contracts are made, so the SAS curve moves only slowly. This difference between the two theories is crucial for policy. According to the new classical theory, anticipated policy actions change the price level only and have no effect on real GDP and unemployment. The reason is that when policy is expected to change, the money wage rate changes, so the SAS curve shifts and offsets the effects of the policy action on real GDP. In contrast, in the new Keynesian theory, because the money wage rate changes only when new contracts are made, even anticipated policy actions change real GDP and can be used in an attempt to stabilize the cycle.

Like the monetarist business cycle, these rational expectations cycles are similar to rocking horses. They need an outside force to get them going, but once going, the economy rocks around its full employment point. The new classical horse rocks faster and comes to rest more quickly than the new Keynesian horse.

AS-AD General Theory

All the theories of the business cycle that we've considered can be viewed as particular cases of the more general AS-AD theory. In this more general theory, the impulses of both the Keynesian and monetarist theories can change aggregate demand. A multiplier effect makes aggregate demand change by more than any initial change in one of its components. The money wage rate can be viewed as responding to changes in the expected price level. Even if the money wage is flexible, it will change only to the extent that price level expectations change. As a result, the money wage rate will adjust gradually.

Although in all three types of business cycle theory that we've considered, the cycle is caused by fluctuations in aggregate demand, the possibility that an occasional aggregate supply shock might occur is not ruled out. A recession could occur because aggregate supply falls. For example, a widespread drought that cuts agricultural production could cause a recession in an economy that has a large agricultural sector. But these aggregate demand theories of the cycle regard aggregate supply shocks as rare rather than normal events. Aggregate demand fluctuations are the normal ongoing sources of fluctuations.

REVIEW QUIZ

- What, according to Keynesian theory, causes the business cycle? What are the roles of *animal spirits*, the multiplier, and sticky money wages in this theory?
- What, according to monetarist theory, causes the business cycle? What are the roles of the Fed and the money supply in this theory?
- What, according to new classical theory and new Keynesian theory, causes the business cycle? What are the roles of rational expectations and unanticipated fluctuations in aggregate demand in these theories?
- What are the differences between the new classical theory and the new Keynesian theory concerning the money wage rate over the business cycle?

A new theory of the business cycle challenges the mainstream and traditional aggregate demand theories that you've just studied. It is called the real business cycle theory. Let's look at this new cycle theory.

Real Business Cycle Theory

THE NEWEST THEORY OF THE BUSINESS CYCLE, known as **real business cycle theory** (or RBC theory), regards random fluctuations in productivity as the main source of economic fluctuations. These productivity fluctuations are assumed to result mainly from fluctuations in the pace of technological change, but they might also have other sources such as international disturbances, climate fluctuations, or natural disasters. The origins of real business cycle theory can be traced to the rational expectations revolution set off by Robert E. Lucas, Jr., but the first demonstration of the power of this theory was given by Edward Prescott and Finn Kydland and by John Long and Charles Plosser. Today, real business cycle theory is part of a broad research agenda called *dynamic general equilibrium analysis*, and hundreds of young macroeconomists do research on this topic.

Like our study of the aggregate demand theories, we'll explore RBC theory by looking first at its impulse and second at the mechanism that converts that impulse into a cycle in real GDP.

The RBC Impulse

The *impulse* in RBC theory is the *growth rate of productivity* that results from *technological change*. RBC theorists believe this impulse to be generated mainly by the process of research and development that leads to the creation and use of new technologies. Most of the time, technological change is steady and productivity grows at a moderate pace. But sometimes productivity growth speeds up and occasionally productivity *decreases*—labor becomes less productive, on the average.

A period of rapid productivity growth brings a strong business cycle expansion and a *decrease* in productivity triggers a recession.

It is easy to understand why technological change brings productivity growth. But how does it *decrease* productivity? All technological change eventually increases productivity. But if initially, technological change makes a sufficient amount of existing capital, especially human capital, obsolete, productivity temporarily decreases. At such a time, more jobs are destroyed than created and more businesses fail than start up.

FIGURE 34.6
The Real Business Cycle Impulse

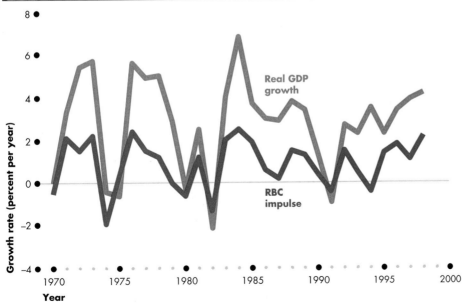

The real business cycle is caused by changes in technology that bring fluctuations in the growth rate of productivity. The fluctuations in productivity growth shown here are calculated by using growth accounting (the one third rule) to remove the contribution of capital accumulation to productivity growth. Productivity fluctuations are correlated with real GDP fluctuations. Economists are not sure what the productivity variable actually measures or what causes it to fluctuate.

Source: *Economic Report of the President*, 1999, and the author's calculations.

To isolate the RBC theory impulse, economists use growth accounting, which is explained in Chapter 28, pp. 613–616. Figure 34.6 shows the RBC impulse for the United States from 1970 to 1998. You can see that fluctuations in productivity growth are correlated with real GDP fluctuations. But this RBC impulse variable is a catch-all and no one knows what it actually measures or what causes it to fluctuate.

The RBC Mechanism

According to RBC theory, two immediate effects follow from a change in productivity that get an expansion or a contraction going:

1. Investment demand changes.
2. The demand for labor changes.

We'll study these effects and their consequences during a recession. In an expansion, they work in the direction opposite to what is described here.

Technological change makes some existing capital obsolete and temporarily decreases productivity. Firms expect the future profits to fall and see their labor productivity falling. With lower profit expectations, they cut back their purchases of new capital, and with lower labor productivity, they plan to lay off some workers. So the initial effect of a temporary fall in productivity is a decrease in investment demand and a decrease in the demand for labor.

Figure 34.7 illustrates these two initial effects of a decrease in productivity. Part (a) shows investment demand, ID, and saving supply, SS (both of which are explained in Chapter 27, pp. 589–590 and 593–594). Initially, investment demand is ID_0 and the equilibrium investment and saving are $1 trillion at a real interest rate of 6 percent a year. A decrease in productivity decreases investment demand and the ID curve shifts leftward to ID_1. The real interest rate falls to 4 percent, and investment and saving decrease to $0.7 trillion.

Part (b) shows the demand for labor, LD, and the supply of labor, LS (which are explained in Chapter 26, pp. 565–570). Initially, the demand for labor is LD_0, and equilibrium employment is 200 billion hours a year at a real wage rate of $15 an hour. The decrease in productivity decreases the demand for labor, and the LD curve shifts leftward to LD_1.

Before we can determine the new level of employment and real wage rate, we need to take a ripple effect into account—the key ripple effect in RBC theory.

The Key Decision: When to Work? According to RBC theory, people decide *when* to work by doing a cost-benefit calculation. They compare the return from working in the current period with the *expected* return from working in a later period. You make such a comparison every day in school. Suppose your goal in this course is to get an A. To achieve this goal, you work pretty hard most of the time. But during the few days before the midterm and final exams, you work especially hard. Why? Because you believe that the return from studying close to the exam is greater than the return from studying when the exam is a long time away. So during the term, you take time off for the movies and other leisure pursuits, but at exam time, you work every evening and weekend.

Real business cycle theory says that workers behave like you. They work fewer hours, sometimes zero hours, when the real wage rate is temporarily low, and they work more hours when the real wage rate is temporarily high. But to properly compare the current wage rate with the expected future wage rate, workers must use the real interest rate. If the real interest rate is 6 percent a year, a real wage of $1 an hour earned this week will become $1.06 a year from now. If the real wage rate is expected to be $1.05 an hour next year, today's real wage of $1 looks good. By working longer hours now and shorter hours a year from now, a person can get a 1 percent higher real wage rate. But suppose the real interest rate is 4 percent a year. In this case, $1 earned now is worth $1.04 next year. Working fewer hours now and more next year is the way to get a 1 percent higher real wage rate.

So the when-to-work decision depends on the real interest rate. The lower the real interest rate, other things remaining the same, the smaller is the supply of labor. Many economists believe this *intertemporal substitution* effect to be of negligible size. RBC theorists believe that the effect is large, and it is the key element in the RBC mechanism.

You saw in Fig. 34.7(a) that the decrease in investment demand lowers the real interest rate. This fall in the real interest rate lowers the return to current work and decreases the supply of labor. In Fig. 34.7(b), the labor supply curve shifts leftward to LS_1. The effect of a productivity shock on the demand for labor is larger than the effect of the fall in the real interest rate on the supply of labor. That is, the LD curve shifts farther leftward than does the LS curve. As a result, the real wage rate falls to $14.50 an hour and the level of employment falls to 195 billion hours. A recession has begun and is intensifying.

FIGURE 34.7
Capital and Labor Markets in a Real Business Cycle

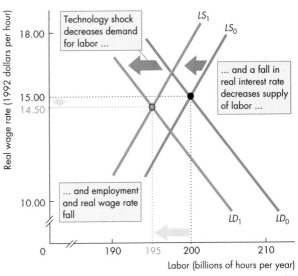

(a) Investment, saving, and interest rate

(b) Labor and wage rate

Saving supply is *SS* (part a), and initially, investment demand is ID_0. The real interest rate is 6 percent, and saving and investment are $1 trillion. In the labor market (part b), the demand for labor is LD_0 and the supply of labor is LS_0. The real wage rate is $15 an hour, and employment is 200 billion hours. A technological change temporarily decreases productivity, and both investment demand and the demand for labor decrease.

The two demand curves shift leftward to ID_1 and LD_1. In part (a), the real interest rate falls to 4 percent a year and investment and saving decrease. In part (b), the fall in the real interest rate decreases the supply of labor (the when-to-work decision) and the supply curve shifts leftward to LS_1. Employment falls to 195 billion hours, and the real wage rate falls to $14.50 an hour. A recession is under way.

Real GDP and the Price Level   The next part of the RBC story traces the consequences of the changes you've just seen for real GDP and the price level. With a decrease in employment, aggregate supply decreases, and with a decrease in investment demand, aggregate demand decreases. Figure 34.8 illustrates these effects, using the *AS-AD* framework. Initially, the long-run aggregate supply curve is LAS_0, and the aggregate demand curve is AD_0. The price level is 110, and real GDP is $7 trillion. There is no short-run aggregate supply curve in this figure because in RBC theory, the *SAS* curve has no meaning. The labor market moves relentlessly toward its equilibrium, and the money wage rate adjusts freely (either upward or downward) to ensure that the real wage rate keeps the quantity of labor demanded equal to the quantity supplied. In RBC theory, unemployment is always

at the natural rate, and the natural rate fluctuates over the business cycle because the amount of job search fluctuates.

The decrease in employment decreases total production and aggregate supply decreases. The *LAS* curve shifts leftward to LAS_1. The decrease in investment demand decreases aggregate demand, and the *AD* curve shifts leftward to AD_1. The price level falls to 107, and real GDP decreases to $6.8 trillion. The economy has gone through a recession.

What Happened to Money?   The name *real* business cycle theory is no accident. It reflects the central prediction of the theory. Real things, not nominal or monetary things, cause the business cycle. If the quantity of money changes, aggregate demand changes. But if there is no real change—with no

FIGURE 34.8

AS-AD in a Real
Business Cycle

Initially, the long-run aggregate supply curve is LAS_0 and the
aggregate demand curve is AD_0. Real GDP is $7 trillion (which
equals potential GDP), and the price level is 110. There is no
SAS curve in the real business cycle theory because the money
wage rate is flexible. The technological change described in
Fig. 34.7 temporarily decreases potential GDP, and the *LAS*
curve shifts leftward to LAS_1. The fall in investment demand
decreases aggregate demand, and the AD curve shifts leftward
to AD_1. Real GDP decreases to $6.8 trillion, and the price level
falls to 107. The economy has gone into recession.

change in the use of resources and no change in
potential GDP—the change in money changes only
the price level. In real business cycle theory, this outcome occurs because the aggregate supply curve is the
LAS curve, which pins real GDP down at potential
GD. So when *AD* changes, only the price level
changes.

Cycles and Growth The shock that drives the business cycle of RBC theory is the same as the force that
generates economic growth: technological change.
On the average, as technology advances, productivity
grows. But it grows at an uneven pace. You saw this
fact when you studied growth accounting in Chapter

28. There, we focused on slow-changing trends in
productivity growth. Real business cycle theory uses
the same idea but says that there are frequent shocks
to productivity that are mostly positive but that are
occasionally negative.

Criticisms of Real Business Cycle Theory

RBC theory is controversial, and when economists
discuss it, they often generate more heat than light.
Its detractors claim that its basic assumptions are just
too incredible. Money wages *are* sticky, they claim, so
to assume otherwise is at odds with a clear fact. Intertemporal substitution is too weak, they say, to account
for large fluctuations in labor supply and employment
with small real wage changes.

But what really kills the RBC story, say most
economists, is an implausible impulse. Technology
shocks are not capable of creating the swings in productivity that growth accounting reveals. These
swings in productivity are caused by something, they
concede, but they are as likely to be caused by *changes
in aggregate demand* as by technology. If the fluctuations in productivity are caused by aggregate demand
fluctuations, then the traditional demand theories are
needed to explain them. Fluctuations in productivity
do not cause the cycle but are caused by it!

Building on this theme, the critics point out that
the so-called productivity fluctuations that growth
accounting measures are correlated with changes in
the growth rate of money and other indicators of
changes in aggregate demand.

Defense of Real Business Cycle Theory

The defenders of RBC theory claim that the theory
works. It explains the macroeconomic facts about the
business cycle and is consistent with the facts about
economic growth. In effect, a single theory explains
both growth and cycles. The growth accounting exercise that explains slowly changing trends also explains
the more frequent business cycle swings. Its defenders
also claim that RBC theory is consistent with a wide
range of *micro*economic evidence about labor supply
decisions, labor demand and investment demand
decisions, and information on the distribution of
income between labor and capital.

RBC theorists acknowledge that money and the business cycle are correlated. That is, rapid money growth and expansion go together, and slow money growth and recession go together. But, they argue, causation does not run from money to real GDP as the traditional aggregate demand theories state. Instead, they view causation as running from real GDP to money—so-called reverse causation. In a recession, the initial fall in investment demand that lowers the interest rate decreases the demand for bank loans and lowers the profitability of banking. So banks increase their reserves and decrease their loans. The quantity of bank deposits and hence the quantity of money decrease. This reverse causation is responsible for the correlation between money growth and real GDP according to real business cycle theory.

Its defenders also argue that the RBC view is significant because it at least raises the possibility that the business cycle is efficient. The business cycle does not signal an economy that is misbehaving; it is business as usual. If this view is correct, it means that policy designed to smooth the cycle is misguided. Only by taking out the peaks can the troughs be smoothed out. But peaks are bursts of investment to take advantage of new technologies in a timely way. So smoothing the cycle means delaying the benefits of new technologies.

REVIEW QUIZ

- What, according to real business cycle theory, causes the business cycle? What is the role of fluctuations in the rate of technological change?
- How, according to real business cycle theory, does a fall in productivity growth influence investment demand, the real interest rate, the demand for labor, the supply of labor, employment, and the real wage rate?
- How, according to real business cycle theory, does a fall in productivity growth influence long-run aggregate supply, aggregate demand, real GDP, and the price level?

You've now reviewed the main theories of the business cycle. Your next task is to examine some actual business cycles. In pursuing this task, we will focus on the recession phase of the cycle. We'll do this mainly because it is the recessions that cause the most trouble. We begin by looking at two recent recessions.

Recessions and Expansions During the 1990s

THE 1990s HAVE BROUGHT SOME INTERESTING business cycle experience. In the United States, we had a brief recession during 1990–1991 followed by a period of sustained and at times rapid expansion. In contrast, Japan experienced a decade of slow growth and ended the decade in serious recession. In 1999, while the three fifths of the global economy that includes the United States, Canada, and Western Europe continued to expand vigorously, the other two fifths that includes Japan, some other East Asian countries, and Central Europe was in recession.

In the theories of the business cycle that you've studied, recessions and expansions can be triggered by a variety of forces, some on the aggregate demand side and some on the aggregate supply side. We'll study the shocks that triggered and the processes at work during some of these 1990s episodes. We'll focus on three situations:

- The U.S. recession of 1990–1991
- The U.S. expansion of the 1990s
- The Japanese recession

The U.S. Recession of 1990–1991

At the beginning of 1990, the U.S. economy was at full employment. The unemployment rate was just above 5 percent, and inflation was steady at 4 percent a year. But the events of 1990 disturbed this situation and ended what was then the longest peacetime expansion in U.S. history.

External Shock: The Gulf Crisis   The dominant event of 1990 was a political and military crisis in the Persian Gulf. Iraq's president Saddam Hussein invaded Kuwait, and the United States responded with massive air strikes against Iraq. The Gulf Crisis, as it was known, brought shocks to both aggregate demand and aggregate supply.

The main aggregate demand shock was a decrease in investment. The Gulf Crisis increased uncertainty and lowered expected sales and profits. Investment decreased between 1990 and 1991 by $80 billion. The decrease in investment brought an even greater decrease in aggregate demand because of the multiplier effect on consumption expenditure.

On the supply side, the Gulf Crisis threw the world energy markets into turmoil. Between April 1990 and October 1990, the price of crude oil more than doubled. This oil price increase also led to increases in the prices of other fuels and raw materials, and it decreased short-run aggregate supply.

Fiscal Policy and Monetary Policy   There were no major fiscal policy or monetary policy shocks to trigger the recession. Government purchases increased slightly to cope with the military consequences of the crisis. But this effect was small. Tax revenues decreased and the deficit increased as the normal automatic stabilizers began to operate (see Chapter 30, p. 672).

Monetary policy was unremarkable. The Fed slowed the M2 money growth rate from 4 percent in 1990 to 3 percent in 1991, but real interest rates were lowered. So if monetary policy played a role in this recession, it was in the direction of moderating it.

Aggregate Demand and Aggregate Supply   Figure 34.9 shows the events that started the 1990–1991 recession. In mid-1990, the economy was on aggregate demand curve AD_{90} and short-run aggregate supply curve SAS_{90} with real GDP at $6.14 trillion and the GDP deflator at 94. By mid-1991, the short-run aggregate supply curve had shifted to SAS_{91} and investment uncertainty had shifted the aggregate demand curve to AD_{91}. Real GDP had decreased to $6.08 trillion. The GDP deflator increased to 97, but the inflation rate slowed slightly from 4.3 percent a year in 1990 to 4 percent a year in 1991 and to 2.8 percent a year during 1992.

Labor Market and Productivity   As real GDP decreased, so did employment and aggregate hours. Unemployment increased, but the real wage rate did not change much. Labor productivity growth slowed to about half a percent and overall productivity decreased by more than half a percent during 1991.

After just eight months of contraction, the 1990s recession was over and the economy was expanding again.

The U.S. Expansion of the 1990s

By the end of 1998, the U.S. economy had completed 94 months of uninterrupted expansion and looked set to break the all-time record of 106 months recorded during the 1960s. Real GDP had grown by

FIGURE 34.9

The 1990–1991 Recession

In 1990, the economy was on its aggregate demand curve, AD_{90}, and its short-run aggregate supply curve, SAS_{90}, with real GDP at $6.14 trillion and a GDP deflator of 94. A large increase in oil prices decreased aggregate supply and shifted the short-run aggregate supply curve to SAS_{91}. Uncertainty surrounding the world economy lowered profit expectations, leading to a fall in investment and a decrease in aggregate demand. The aggregate demand curve shifted to AD_{91}. The combination of a decrease in both aggregate supply and aggregate demand puts the economy into recession.

23 percent during this period. What caused this long and strong expansion?

Productivity Growth in the Information Age   The most significant feature of the 1990s was an explosion in the use of the computer. The growth of the Internet is the single most visible consequence of this explosion. But it is just one of many transformations of economic life that has occurred during the 1990s.

The personal computer has changed the way we write, keep financial and other records, and communicate with each other. The microprocessor has revolutionized the way we listen to music, drive a car, use a camera, make a microwave dinner, and check out at the supermarket. It has revolutionized even more the way firms produce goods and services.

But the computer and related technologies are not the whole technological story of the 1990s. Biotechnology changed from being primarily a research activity to a commercial activity in this decade. It was also a decade in which personal services expanded enormously.

All this technological change created profit opportunities but required a large amount of investment to realize those profits. Also, most of the world shared in this technological revolution. And its global nature brought a large increase in U.S. exports.

Between 1991 and 1998, investment increased from $740 billion to $1,332 billion and exports increased from $600 billion to $985 billion (all 1992 dollars). An expansion of aggregate expenditure of this magnitude—almost a trillion dollars—with its multiplier effect on consumption expenditure brought a large increase in aggregate demand.

It also brought a correspondingly large increase in aggregate supply. The capital stock increased by almost $3 trillion (or almost 20 percent), and employment increased by more than 20 billion hours a year (or about 10 percent).

Fiscal Policy and Monetary Policy The expansion of the 1990s was to some degree made possible by the fiscal policy and monetary policy that accompanied it. The expansion was not caused by these policies, but they encouraged sustained real GDP growth.

Fiscal policy was restrained throughout the expansion. Government purchases of goods and services remained almost constant. Tax revenues increased early in the expansion because of a 1993 tax bill that increased some tax rates. But most of the rising tax revenues and falling transfer payments resulted from the growing economy. The result was that a deficit of $280 billion in 1992 was transformed into a surplus of $75 billion in 1998.

Monetary policy encouraged the expansion. The Fed kept the quantity of money (M2) growing at a low but steady rate that lowered inflation and interest rates throughout the expansion.

Aggregate Demand and Aggregate Supply During the Expansion Figure 34.10 shows the 1990s expansion using the *AS-AD* model. In 1991, the economy was on aggregate demand curve AD_{91} and short-run aggregate supply curve SAS_{91} with real GDP at $6.08 trillion and the GDP deflator at 97. The long-run

aggregate supply curve was LAS_{91}, and potential GDP exceeded real GDP. There was a recessionary gap. By 1998, capital accumulation, increased labor hours, and technological change had increased potential GDP to $7.6 trillion and the long-run aggregate supply curve had shifted to LAS_{98}. The large increase in investment demand and exports with their multiplier effects increased aggregate demand and the aggregate demand curve shifted to AD_{98}.

The increase in potential GDP increased short-run aggregate supply, but higher money wages decreased short-run aggregate supply. The net effect of these effects was a small decrease in short-run aggregate supply to SAS_{98}. Real GDP increased to $7.6 trillion—equal to potential GDP—and the price level increased to 113.

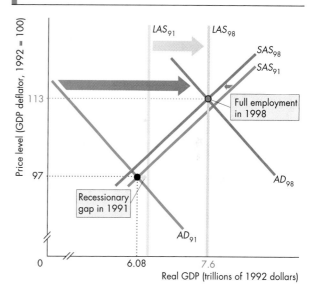

FIGURE 34.10
The 1990s Expansion

In 1991, the economy was on its aggregate demand curve, AD_{91}, and its short-run aggregate supply curve, SAS_{91}, with real GDP at $6.08 trillion and a GDP deflator of 97. Potential GDP (the *LAS* curve) exceeded real GDP by a recessionary gap. Technological advances increased both aggregate demand and aggregate supply. The aggregate demand curve shifted to AD_{98}, the long-run aggregate supply curve shifted to LAS_{98}, and the short-run aggregate supply curve shifted to SAS_{98}, The result of these shifts was an increase in real GDP to $7.6 trillion (equal to potential GDP) and an increase in the price level to 113.

A Real Business Cycle Expansion Phase   The description of the expansion of the 1990s that we've just reviewed looks exactly like the events that real business cycle theory predicts. A strong and sustained burst of technological change brought rising productivity. The result was an increase in investment demand, an increase in the demand for labor, and an increase in the supply of labor. The real interest rate increased, and the real wage rate increased but only slightly.

The expansion in the demand for labor and supply of labor brought a falling unemployment rate. The lower unemployment rate is a lower *natural* rate, not a sign that the economy is overheating.

The Stock Market During the Expansion   The U.S. stock market enjoyed extraordinary growth during the 1990s expansion. The real stock price (the Dow Jones Industrial Average corrected for inflation) increased moderately through 1994. It then exploded. Between 1995 and 1998, real stock prices increased by 130 percent.

The explanation for this huge increase in stock prices is not known with certainty. Some people believe it shows what Fed Chairman Alan Greenspan called "irrational exuberance." But it is possible to rationalize such a large stock price increase as the consequence of people believing that the trend growth rate of the economy has increased. If in 1994, people had been expecting a growth trend of 2 percent a year and if by the late 1990s they had revised this expectation upward to 4 percent a year, a more than doubling of stock prices would be feasible. But whether such a growth rate expectation is realistic is another matter.

While the U.S. economy continued to enjoy its longest peacetime expansion, some economies across the Pacific Ocean were in trouble. One that was in special trouble is Asia's largest economy, Japan. Let's look at the Japanese business cycle during the 1990s.

The Japanese Recession

Between 1992 and 1998, when real GDP in the United States expanded by more than 20 percent, Japan's real GDP expanded by a mere 6 percent—a growth rate of only 0.7 percent per year. By 1998, real GDP in Japan was shrinking at a near 5 percent annual rate.

Why did Japan experience such a low rate of economic growth during the 1990s and a recession in 1998? Several factors seem to have combined to produce Japan's problems. And these factors together with the fiscal policies and monetary policies that Japan has pursued provide valuable information

about the validity of the alternative theories of the business cycle that you studied earlier in this chapter.

The main factors that contributed to Japan's weak economy and ultimate recession were:

- Collapse of asset prices
- Fiscal policy
- Monetary policy
- Structural rigidities

Collapse of Asset Prices   During the second half of the 1980s, land prices and stock prices in Japan increased *threefold.* This increase was much larger than that in the United States and Europe. Asset prices increased for three main reasons.

First, investors believed that Japan's medium-term and long-term prospects were bright. Second, financial deregulation brought an increase of foreign investment into Japan. Japan's banks expanded loans to finance the purchase of assets whose prices were rising. Third, the Bank of Japan (the nation's central bank) lowered interest rates between 1985 and 1987 and permitted a rapid growth rate of money. The motivation for rapid monetary expansion was to prevent the yen from rising against the U.S. dollar in the foreign exchange market. (See Chapter 37, pp. 856–857 for an explanation of how monetary policy influences the foreign exchange rate.)

Asset prices collapsed in 1990. And the collapse created a wealth effect. Saving and consumption were not much affected by the decrease in wealth. But investment expenditure decreased sharply, and so did aggregate demand. With a lower investment rate, the capital stock and potential GDP grew more slowly.

Fiscal Policy   From 1991 through 1996, Japan pursued ambitious and substantial fiscal policies to stimulate the economy. In 1991, the government of Japan had a budget surplus equal to 3 percent of GDP. By 1996, this surplus had been transformed into a deficit equal to more than 7 percent of GDP. Six major *discretionary* actions occurred, which are detailed in Table 34.1, that added 12.9 percent to aggregate expenditure. With its associated multiplier effects, this represents an enormous increase in aggregate demand relative to what it would have been in the absence of stimulation. But the stimulation was not persistent during the 1990s.

The removal of temporary tax cuts and cuts in government investment expenditures *lowered* aggregate expenditure by 3 percent of real GDP in 1996–1997. This fiscal policy tightening decreased aggregate demand and contributed to the recession of 1998.

TABLE 34.1

Fiscal Stimulation in Japan

Date proposed	Total stimulation (percent of GDP)
August 1992	2.3
April 1993	2.8
September 1993	1.3
February 1994	3.2
September 1995	3.0
Mid-1996–mid-1997	–3.0
April 1998	3.3
Total	**12.9**

Monetary Policy   The Bank of Japan lowered its official interest rate (called the official discount rate, or ODR) from 6 percent in 1991 to 1.75 percent by the end of 1993 and to 0.5 percent by 1995. The ODR has remained at this level since 1995. Despite these large cuts in interest rates, a lower inflation rate meant that the real interest rate did not fall as much and so did not act as a stimulus to investment. Also, a strong yen limited the growth of export demand.

Since 1996, a weaker yen and lower real short-term interest rates have had a small but positive effect on aggregate demand in Japan.

Structural Problems   Market distortions in agriculture, transportation, retail and wholesale trades, and construction that protect inefficient farms and firms create a lack of competition and low productivity growth. Rich countries such as the United States, Canada, and those in Western Europe have experienced a process of de-industrialization as manufacturing processes have migrated to poorer countries and have been replaced by rapid expansion in the service sector. Japan has not shared this experience.

This aspect of Japan's economy goes to the core of the real business cycle explanation for fluctuations: fluctuations in the productivity growth rate. When viewed on the longer-term context, this factor might have been slowing Japan's growth rate for many years. Figure 34.11 shows Japan's steadily declining growth rate. Slower productivity growth works through the real business cycle mechanism described earlier in this chapter.

FIGURE 34.11

Japan's Sliding Growth Rate

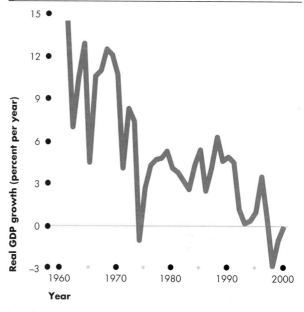

Japan's economic growth rate has been on a slide for many years. Growth of 10 percent a year during the 1960s was followed by growth of 4 percent a year during the 1970s and 1980s and by less than 1 percent a year during the 1990s.

Source: The Penn World Table: An Expanded Set of International Comparisons, 1950–1988, *Quarterly Journal of Economics,* May 1991, 327–368. 1993-1998, International Monetary Fund, *World Economic Outlook* (Washington D.C., October 1998).

R E V I E W   Q U I Z

- What events triggered the 1990–1991 recession in the United States? What role was played by external shocks and by policy? What mechanisms translated the shocks into a recession?
- What factors brought the long and strong expansion in the United States during the 1990s?
- What factors contributed to the slow growth and eventual recession in Japan during the 1990s?

You've now seen how business cycle theory can be used to interpret recessions and expansions during the 1990s. But can we use business cycle theory to explain the greatest of recessions—the Great Depression? Let's find out.

The Great Depression

THE LATE 1920s WERE YEARS OF ECONOMIC
boom. New houses and apartments were built on an
unprecedented scale, new firms were created, and the
capital stock of the nation expanded. At the beginning of 1929, U.S. real GDP exceeded potential
GDP and the unemployment rate was a low 3.2 percent. But as that eventful year unfolded, increasing
signs of economic weakness began to appear. The
most dramatic events occurred in October when the
stock market collapsed, losing more than one third of
its value in two weeks. The four years that followed
were years of monstrous economic depression.

Figure 34.12 shows the dimensions of the Great
Depression. On the eve of the Great Depression in
1929, the economy was on aggregate demand curve
AD_{29} and short-run aggregate supply curve SAS_{29}.
Real GDP was $1,028 billion (1992 dollars), and the
GDP deflator was 15.

In 1930, there was a widespread expectation that
the price level would fall, and the money wage rate fell.
With a lower money wage rate, the short-run aggregate supply curve shifted from SAS_{29} to SAS_{30}. But
increased pessimism and uncertainty decreased investment and the demand for consumer durables, and
aggregate demand decreased to AD_{30}. In 1930, real
GDP decreased to $936 billion (a 9 percent decrease)
and the price level fell to 14.6 (a 3 percent fall).

In a normal recession, the economy might have
remained below full employment for a year or so and
then started to expand. But the recession of 1930 was
not a normal one. In 1930 and the next two years,
the economy was further bombarded with huge negative demand shocks (the sources of which we'll look
at in a moment). The aggregate demand curve shifted
leftward all the way to AD_{33}. With a depressed economy, the price level was expected to fall and wages
fell in line with those expectations. The money wage
fell from 55¢ an hour in 1930 to 44¢ an hour by
1933. As a result of lower wages, the aggregate supply
curve shifted from SAS_{30} to SAS_{33}. But the size of the
shift of the short-run aggregate supply curve was
much less than the decrease in aggregate demand. As
a result, the aggregate demand curve and the short-
run aggregate supply curve intersected in 1933 at a
real GDP of $734 billion (a decrease of 29 percent
from 1929) and a GDP deflator of 11.4 (a decrease
of 24 percent from 1929).

FIGURE 34.12

The Great Depression

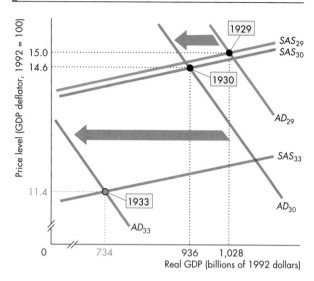

In 1929, real GDP was $1,028 billion and the GDP deflator
was 15—at the intersection of AD_{29} and SAS_{29}. Increased pessimism and uncertainty resulted in a decrease in investment
and aggregate demand decreased to AD_{30}. The money wage
rate decreased, so the short-run aggregate supply curve
shifted to SAS_{30}. Real GDP and the price level fell. In the next
three years, decreases in the money supply and investment
decreased aggregate demand, shifting the aggregate demand
curve to AD_{33}. Again, to some degree, the decrease in aggregate demand was anticipated, so wages fell and the short-run
aggregate supply curve shifted to SAS_{33}. By 1933, real GDP had
fallen to $734 billion (71 percent of its 1929 level) and the
GDP deflator had fallen to 11.4 (76 percent of its 1929 level).

Although the Great Depression brought enormous hardship, the distribution of that hardship was
uneven. Twenty-five percent of the work force had no
jobs at all. Also at that time, there were virtually no
organized social security and unemployment programs in place. So for many families there was virtually no income. But the pocketbooks of those who
kept their jobs barely noticed the Great Depression.
It is true that wages fell from 57¢ an hour in 1929 to
44¢ an hour in 1933. But at the same time, the price
level fell by a larger percentage, so real wages actually
increased. Thus people who had jobs became better
off during the Great Depression.

You can begin to appreciate the magnitude of the Great Depression if you compare it with the two recessions that we studied earlier in this chapter. Between 1973 and 1975, real GDP fell by 1.8 percent. From mid-1990 to mid-1991, it fell by 1.6 percent. A hypothetical 1999 Great Depression would lower real GDP by 30 percent, to less than its 1979 level.

Why the Great Depression Happened

The late 1920s were years of economic boom, but they were also years of increasing uncertainty. The main source of increased uncertainty was international. The world economy was going through tumultuous times. The patterns of world trade were changing as Britain, the traditional economic powerhouse of the world, began its period of relative economic decline and new economic powers such as Japan began to emerge. International currency fluctuations and the introduction of restrictive trade policies by many countries (see Chapter 36) further increased the uncertainty faced by firms. There was also domestic uncertainty arising from the fact that there had been such a strong boom in recent years, especially in the capital goods sector and housing. No one believed that this boom would last forever, but many people thought it had a lot farther to run and there was great uncertainty about how demand would change.

This environment of uncertainty led to a slowdown in consumer spending, especially on new homes and household appliances. By the fall of 1929, the uncertainty had reached a critical level and contributed to the stock market crash. The stock market crash, in turn, heightened people's fears about economic prospects in the foreseeable future. Fear fed fear. Investment collapsed. The building industry almost disappeared. An industry that had been operating flat out just two years earlier was now building virtually no new houses and apartments. It was this drop in investment and a drop in consumer spending on durables that led to the initial leftward shift of the aggregate demand curve from AD_{29} to AD_{30} in Fig. 34.12.

At this stage, what became the Great Depression was no worse than many previous recessions had been. What distinguishes the Great Depression from previous recessions are the events that followed between 1930 and 1933. But economists, even to

this day, have not come to agreement on how to interpret those events. One view, argued by Peter Temin,[1] is that spending continued to fall for a wide variety of reasons—including a continuation of increasing pessimism and uncertainty. According to Temin's view, the continued contraction resulted from a collapse of expenditure that was independent of the decrease in the quantity of money. The investment demand curve shifted leftward. Milton Friedman and Anna J. Schwartz have argued that the continuation of the contraction was almost exclusively the result of the subsequent worsening of financial and monetary conditions.[2] According to Friedman and Schwartz, it was a severe cut in the money supply that lowered aggregate demand, prolonging the contraction and deepening the depression.

Although there is disagreement about the causes of the contraction phase of the Great Depression, the disagreement is not about the elements at work but about the degree of importance attached to each. Everyone agrees that increased pessimism and uncertainty lowered investment demand, and everyone agrees that there was a massive contraction of the real money supply. Temin and his supporters assign primary importance to the fall in autonomous expenditure and secondary importance to the fall in the money supply. Friedman and Schwartz and their supporters assign primary responsibility to the money supply and regard the other factors as being of limited importance.

Let's look at the contraction of aggregate demand a bit more closely. Between 1930 and 1933, the nominal money supply decreased by 20 percent. This decrease in the money supply was not directly induced by the Fed's actions. The *monetary base* (currency in circulation and bank reserves) hardly fell at all. But the bank deposits component of the money supply suffered an enormous collapse. It did so primarily because a large number of banks failed. Before the Great Depression, fueled by increasing stock prices and booming business conditions, bank loans expanded. But after the stock market crash and the downturn, many borrowers found themselves in hard economic times. They could not pay the interest on

---

[1]Peter Temin, *Did Monetary Forces Cause the Great Depression?* (New York: W. W. Norton, 1976).
[2]Milton Friedman and Anna J. Schwartz developed this explanation in *A Monetary History of the United States: 1867–1960* (Princeton, N.J.: Princeton University Press, 1963), Chapter 7.

their loans, and they could not meet the agreed repayment schedules. Banks had deposits that exceeded the realistic value of the loans that they had made. When depositors withdrew funds from the banks, the banks lost reserves. Many of them simply couldn't meet their depositors' demands to be repaid.

Bank failures feed on themselves and create additional failures. Seeing banks fail, people become anxious to protect themselves and so take their money out of the banks. Such were the events of 1930. The quantity of notes and coins in circulation increased, and the volume of bank deposits declined. But the very action of taking money out of the bank to protect one's wealth accentuated the process of banking failure. Banks were increasingly short of cash and unable to meet their obligations.

What role did the stock market crash of 1929 play in producing the Great Depression? It certainly created an atmosphere of fear and panic and probably also contributed to the overall air of uncertainty that dampened investment spending. It also reduced the wealth of stockholders, encouraging them to cut back on their consumption spending. But the direct effect of the stock market crash on consumption, although a contributory factor to the Great Depression, was not the major source of the drop in aggregate demand. It was the collapse in investment arising from increased uncertainty that brought the 1930 decline in aggregate demand.

The stock market crash was a predictor of severe recession. It reflected the expectations of stockholders concerning future profit prospects. As those expectations became pessimistic, people sold their stocks. There were more sellers than buyers and the prices of stocks were bid lower and lower. That is, the behavior of the stock market was a consequence of expectations about future profitability, and those expectations were lowered as a result of increased uncertainty.

Can It Happen Again?

Because we have an incomplete understanding of the causes of the Great Depression, we cannot be sure whether such an event will happen again. The economic turmoil of the 1920s that preceded the Depression certainly can happen again. But there are some significant differences between the economy of the 1990s and that of the 1930s that make a severe depression much less likely today than it was 60 years ago. The most significant features of the economy

that make severe depression less likely today are:

- Bank deposit insurance
- The Fed's role as lender of last resort
- Taxes and government spending
- Multi-income families

Let's examine these in turn.

Bank Deposit Insurance As a result of the Great Depression, the federal government established, in the 1930s, the Federal Deposit Insurance Corporation (FDIC). The FDIC insures bank deposits for up to $100,000 per deposit, so most depositors need no longer fear bank failure. If a bank fails, the FDIC pays the deposit holders. With federally insured bank deposits, the key event that turned a fairly ordinary recession into the Great Depression is most unlikely to occur. It was the fear of bank failure that caused people to withdraw their deposits from banks. The aggregate consequence of these individually rational acts was to cause the very bank failures that were feared. With deposit insurance, most depositors have nothing to lose if a bank fails and so have no incentive to take actions that are likely to give rise to that failure.

Some recent events reinforce this conclusion. With massive failures of S&Ls in the 1980s and with bank failures in New England in 1990 and 1991, there was no tendency for depositors to panic and withdraw their funds in a self-reinforcing run on similar institutions.

Lender of Last Resort The Fed is the lender of last resort in the U.S. economy. If a single bank is short of reserves, it can borrow reserves from other banks. If the entire banking system is short of reserves, banks can borrow from the Fed. By making reserves available (at a suitable interest rate), the Fed is able to make the quantity of reserves in the banking system respond flexibly to the demand for those reserves. Bank failure can be prevented, or at least contained to cases in which bad management practices are the source of the problem. Widespread failures of the type that occurred in the Great Depression can be prevented.

It is now generally agreed that the Fed made a serious mistake in its handling of monetary policy during the Great Depression. With one eye on the international situation, the Fed *increased* the discount rate sharply from 1.5 percent to 3.5 percent just when the banks needed to borrow more. It was only long after the event, when Friedman and Schwartz examined the contraction years of the Great Depression, that economists came to realize that the Fed would have had to *decrease* the discount rate and *increase* the monetary base to have prevented the intensification of the contraction. Now that this lesson has been learned and there is such widespread agreement about the matter, there is at least some chance that the mistake will not be repeated.

The last time the Fed was confronted by a similar problem, though on a much smaller scale, was in October 1987. At that time, a severe stock market crash triggered fears of a new Great Depression. The Fed Chairman, Alan Greenspan, told the U.S. banking and financial community that the Fed had both the ability and the intent to maintain calm financial conditions and to supply sufficient reserves to ensure that the banking system did not begin to contract.

Taxes and Government Spending The government sector was a much smaller part of the economy in 1929 than it has become today. On the eve of that earlier recession, government purchases of goods and services were less than 9 percent of GDP. Today, government purchases exceed 20 percent of GDP. Government transfer payments were less than 6 percent of GDP in 1929. Today, they exceed 15 percent of GDP.

A larger level of government purchases of goods and services means that when recession hits, a large component of aggregate demand does not decline. But government transfer payments are the most sensitive economic stabilizer. When the economy goes into recession and depression, more people qualify for unemployment benefits and social security. As a consequence, although disposable income decreases, the extent of the decrease is moderated by the existence of such programs. Consumption expenditure, in turn, does not decline by as much as it would in the absence of such government programs. The limited decline in consumption spending further limits the overall decrease in aggregate expenditure, thereby limiting the magnitude of an economic downturn.

Multi-Income Families At the time of the Great Depression, families with more than one wage earner were much less common than they are today. The labor force participation rate in 1929 was around 55 percent. Today, it is 67 percent. Thus even if the unemployment rate increased to around 25 percent today, close to 50 percent of the adult population would actually have jobs. During the Great Depression, less than 40 percent of the adult population had work. Multi-income families have greater security than single-income families do. The chance of both (or all) income earners in a family losing their jobs simultaneously is much lower than the chance of a single earner losing work. With greater family income security, family consumption is likely to be less sensitive to fluctuations in family income that are seen as temporary. Thus when aggregate income falls, it might not induce a cut in consumption. For example, during the OPEC recession, as real GDP fell, personal consumption expenditure actually increased. In 1990–1991, when real GDP fell by $60 billion, consumption expenditure fell by only $26 billion.

For the four reasons we have just reviewed, it appears that the economy has better shock-absorbing characteristics today than it had in the 1920s and 1930s. Even if there is a collapse of confidence, leading to a fall in investment, today's shock absorbers will not translate that initial shock into the large and prolonged fall in real GDP and rise in unemployment that occurred more than 60 years ago.

Because the economy is now more immune to severe recession than it was in the 1930s, even a stock market crash of the magnitude that occurred in 1987 had barely noticeable effects on spending. A crash of a similar magnitude in 1929 resulted in the near collapse of housing investment and consumer durable purchases. In the period following the 1987 stock market crash, investment and spending on durable goods hardly changed.

None of this is to say that there might not be a deep recession or even a Great Depression in the future. But it would take a very severe shock to trigger one.

◆ We have now completed our study of the business cycle. Analysts use the theories you have studied to try to forecast the next business cycle turning point. You can see an example of this activity in *Reading Between the Lines* on pp. 786–787.

We have also completed our study of the science of macroeconomics and learned about the influences on long-term economic growth and inflation as well as the business cycle. We have discovered that these issues pose huge policy challenges. How can we speed up the rate of economic growth while at the same time keeping inflation low and avoiding big swings of the business cycle? Our task in the next chapter is to study these macroeconomic policy challenges.

Is Japan Recovering?

DOW JONES NEWSWIRES, WSJ INTERACTIVE, APRIL 9, 1999

Japan Sticks to Economic Growth Forecast for 1999

TOKYO (AP)—Japan's top economic official on Friday stood by the government's forecast of 0.5% growth for the coming year, despite signs that the country is not close to pulling out of recession.

Japan's economy shrank 0.8% in the last three months of 1998, and is expected to have shrunk for the second year in a row when statistics for the fiscal year ended March 31 emerge.

Independent analysts expect the economy to shrink yet again in the fiscal year that just began.

But Taichi Sakaiya, the director general of Japan's Economic Planning Agency, said the government's record spending and tax-cut program would spur the economy.

"Although I can't say it absolutely, I have considerable confidence" that the official growth target of 0.5% will be reached this fiscal year, Sakaiya told reporters.

The administration of Prime Minister Keizo Obuchi has pledged to avoid three fiscal years in a row of contraction.

The economy shrank 0.4% in the 1997-98 fiscal year and is expected to shrink more than 2% in the just-ended fiscal year.

Also Friday, Takafusa Shioya, the deputy director-general of the Economic Planning Agency, said there would probably not be any major changes in the agency's assessment of the economy in its next monthly report.

In its March report, the EPA described conditions as "extremely severe," but said the economy's "downward movement continues to slow to a halt."

A string of Japanese government officials have voiced optimism about the economy recently, declaring that it had hit its lowest point and would now begin to recover from its worst recession since World War II.

Foreign Minister Masahiko Komura was quoted as telling a group of four U.S. congressmen Friday that the Japanese economy "is poised to bottom out and to move upward." ...

Essence of the Story

■ Japan's real GDP shrank 0.4 percent* in the 1997–1998 fiscal year. (Japan's fiscal year runs from April 1 to March 31.) It is expected to shrink more than 2 percent in the 1998–1999 fiscal year.

■ In April 1999, independent economic forecasters were predicting that Japan's real GDP would shrink yet again during the 1999–2000 fiscal year.

■ But the Japanese government was committed to bringing an expansion in 1999–2000.

■ Several Japanese government officials declared that real GDP had hit its lowest point and that Japan would begin to recover from its worst recession since World War II.

*The news article seems to misreport this number. According to the official data, the economy shrank by 3.6 percent (or almost 4 percent) during fiscal year 1997-1998. The economic analysis on the next page uses this corrected number.

Economic Analysis

- Figure 1 shows how the Japanese economy got into its worst recession since World War II.

- We'll assume that before the recession began, in the first quarter of 1997 (1997, Q1), the Japanese economy was at full employment. We'll use index numbers to measure both real GDP and the price level with bases of 100 in 1997, Q1.

- In 1997, Q1, aggregate demand was AD_{97}, long-run aggregate supply was LAS_{97}, and short-run aggregate supply was SAS_{97}. The aggregate demand curve intersected the short-run aggregate supply curve at potential GDP on the long-run aggregate supply curve (by assumption).

- During the next two years, asset prices crashed, decreasing wealth. The decrease in wealth brought a large decrease in investment. So the aggregate demand curve shifted leftward to AD_{99}.

- At the same time, structural problems and widespread business failure decreased short-run aggregate supply. The short-run aggregate supply curve shifted leftward to SAS_{99}.

- Real GDP decreased over the two-year period by 6 percent to 94. The price level remained constant.

- Forecasts of where Japan is heading in 1999–2000 differ—but not by much.

- Figure 2 shows the range of disagreement.

- The Japanese government believes that it has done enough with tax cuts and spending increases (combined with the Bank of Japan's loose monetary policy) to make aggregate demand increase to AD_{00} (gov).

- The government probably also believes that short-run aggregate supply will increase to SAS_{00} (gov).

- If the government is correct, real GDP will increase during 1999 by about 0.5 percent.

- Independent economic forecasters believe that aggregate demand in Japan will decrease further in 1999 but by a small amount. Their forecast is that aggregate demand will decrease to AD_{00} (ind).

- These forecasters probably also believe that short-run aggregate supply will decrease to SAS_{00} (ind).

- If the independent forecasters are correct, real GDP will decrease during 1999 by about 1 percent.

- Although the independent forecasters and the Japanese government disagree on the *direction* of change of real GDP during 1999, the disagreement about the year-end *level* is within 2 percentage points. This range of disagreement is small relative to the range of uncertainty in macroeconomic forecasts.

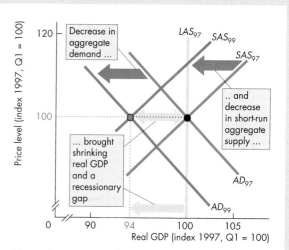

Figure 1 Japan goes into recession

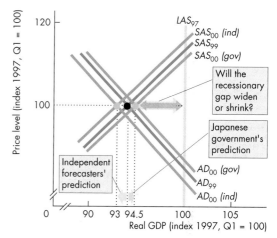

Figure 2 Predictions for 2000

787

SUMMARY

KEY POINTS

Cycle Patterns, Impulses, and Mechanisms (pp. 764–766)

- Since 1920, there have been 15 recessions and expansions.
- The Great Depression was the most severe contraction of real GDP, and the postwar recessions have been milder than the prewar recessions.

Aggregate Demand Theories of the Business Cycle (pp. 766–772)

- Keynesian business cycle theory identifies volatile expectations about future sales and profits as the main source of economic fluctuations.
- Monetarist business cycle theory identifies fluctuations in the money stock as the main source of economic fluctuations.
- Rational expectations theory identifies unanticipated fluctuations in aggregate demand as the main source of economic fluctuations.

Real Business Cycle Theory (pp. 773–777)

- In real business cycle (RBC) theory, economic fluctuations are caused by fluctuations in the influence of technological change on productivity growth.
- A temporary slowdown in the pace of technological change decreases investment demand and both the demand for labor and supply of labor.

Recessions and Expansions During the 1990s (pp. 777–781)

- The 1990–1991 recession resulted from the Gulf Crisis, which increased the price of oil—a decrease in aggregate supply—and a decrease in investment—a decrease in aggregate demand.
- The 1990s expansion resulted from a large increase in the rate of productivity growth that increased investment demand and the demand for and supply of labor and that increased both aggregate demand and aggregate supply.

- The Japanese slowdown and recession of the 1990s were triggered by an asset price collapse combined with structural problems. Policy stimulation occurred, but it was not sufficient to prevent recession, and a tightening of fiscal policy in 1996 and 1997 contributed to the 1998 recession.

The Great Depression (pp. 782–785)

- The Great Depression started with increased uncertainty, which brought a fall in investment (especially in housing) and spending on consumer durables.
- There then followed a near total collapse of the financial system. Banks failed and the money supply fell, resulting in a continued fall in aggregate demand.
- The Great Depression itself produced a series of reforms that make a repeat of such a depression much less likely.

KEY FIGURES

KEY TERMS

PROBLEMS

Use the figure for all the problems.

*1. The figure shows the economy of Virtual Reality. When the economy is in a long-run equilibrium, it is at points *b*, *f*, and *j*. When a recession occurs in Virtual Reality, the economy moves away from these points to one of the two other points identified in each of the three parts of the figure.
   a.   If the Keynesian theory is the correct explanation for the recession, to which points does the economy move?
   b.   If the monetarist theory is the correct explanation for the recession, to which points does the economy move?
   c.   If the new classical theory of the business cycle is the correct explanation for the recession, to which points does the economy move?
   d.   If the new Keynesian theory of the business cycle is the correct explanation for the recession, to which points does the economy move?
   e.   If real business cycle theory is the correct explanation for the recession, to which points does the economy move?

2. The figure shows the economy of Vital Signs. When the economy is in a long-run equilibrium, it is at points *a*, *e*, and *i*. When an expansion occurs in Vital Signs, the economy moves away from these points to one of the two other points identified in each of the three parts of the figure.
   a.   If the Keynesian theory is the correct explanation for the recession, to which points does the economy move?
   b.   If the monetarist theory is the correct explanation for the recession, to which points does the economy move?
   c.   If the new classical theory of the business cycle is the correct explanation for the recession, to which points does the economy move?
   d.   If the new Keynesian theory of the business cycle is the correct explanation for the recession, to which points does the economy move?

   e.   If real business cycle theory is the correct explanation for the recession, to which points does the economy move?

(a) Labor market

(b) AS-AD

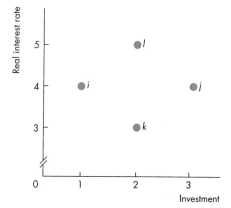

(c) Investment

*3. Suppose that when the recession occurs in Virtual Reality, the economy moves to *d*, *g*, and *k*. Which theory of the business cycle, if any, explains this outcome?

4. Suppose that when the expansion occurs in Vital Signs, the economy moves to *d*, *h*, and *l*. Which theory of the business cycle, if any, explains this outcome?

*5. Suppose that when the recession occurs in Virtual Reality, the economy moves to *c*, *g*, and *k*. Which theory of the business cycle, if any, explains this outcome?

6. Suppose that when the expansion occurs in Vital Signs, the economy moves to *c*, *h*, and *l*. Which theory of the business cycle, if any, explains this outcome?

*7. Suppose that when the recession occurs in Virtual Reality, the economy moves to *d*, *h*, and *k*. Which theory of the business cycle, if any, explains this outcome?

8. Suppose that when the expansion occurs in Vital Signs, the economy moves to *d*, *g*, and *l*. Which theory of the business cycle, if any, explains this outcome?

*9. Suppose that when the recession occurs in Virtual Reality, the economy moves to *c*, *h*, and *k*. Which theory of the business cycle, if any, explains this outcome?

10. Suppose that when the expansion occurs in Vital Signs, the economy moves to *c*, *g*, and *l*. Which theory of the business cycle, if any, explains this outcome?

*11. Suppose that when the recession occurs in Virtual Reality, the economy moves to *d*, *g*, and *l*. Which theory of the business cycle, if any, explains this outcome?

12. Suppose that when the expansion occurs in Vital Signs, the economy moves to *c*, *h*, and *k*. Which theory of the business cycle, if any, explains this outcome?

*13. Suppose that when the recession occurs in Virtual Reality, the economy moves to *c*, *g*, and *l*. Which theory of the business cycle, if any, explains this outcome?

14. Suppose that when the expansion occurs in Vital Signs, the economy moves to *d*, *h*, and *k*. Which theory of the business cycle, if any, explains this outcome?

CRITICAL THINKING

1. Study *Reading Between the Lines* on pp. 786–787 and use the links on the Parkin Web site to obtain the data on Japan's real GDP since the end of 1998. Then answer the following questions:

   a. Given the most recent data on Japan's real GDP, does it appear that the government of Japan or the independent forecasters had the correct view of where Japan was heading during 1999?

   b. Why did the official forecasters believe that Japan was on the road to recovery?

   c. What, according to the different theories of the business cycle, must happen if Japan is to enjoy a strong and sustained recovery?

   d. Can you detect any clues in the news article that tell you whether the Japanese government takes a Keynesian, monetarist, new classical, new Keynesian, or real business cycle view of Japan's recession?

   e. What policy actions, if any, do you think the government of Japan and the Bank of Japan need to take in 2000 to keep the Japanese economy growing and to prevent a new recession?

2. Describe the changes in real GDP, employment and unemployment, and the price level that occurred in the United States during the Great Depression years of 1929–1933.

3. Use the links on the Parkin Web site to obtain information about the current state of the U.S. economy. Then:

   a. List all of the features of the U.S. economy during the current year that you think are consistent with a pessimistic outlook for the next two years.

   b. List all of the features of the U.S. economy during the current year that you think are consistent with an optimistic outlook for the next two years.

   c. Describe how you think the U.S. economy is going to evolve over the next year or two. Explain your predictions, drawing on the pessimistic and optimistic factors that you listed in parts (a) and (b) and on your knowledge of macroeconomic theory.

35

Macroeconomic Policy Challenges

From 1991 through 1998, the U.S. economy performed well. Real GDP expanded by 3.2 percent a year, unemployment fell to 4.3 percent, the inflation rate fell to less than 2 percent a year, and a $280 billion federal government budget deficit in 1992 was turned into a $75 billion surplus in 1998. The United States was not alone in achieving a strong economic expansion. Real GDP in Canada grew by 3 percent a year, and despite a recession in 1998, the developing Asian countries expanded by 7.5 percent a year during the 1990s. ◆ But not all countries shared in this solid growth. Japan's real GDP expanded by less than 2 percent a year and shrank in 1998. In Russia, real GDP shrank for five successive years to less than two

What Can Policy Do?

thirds its 1990 level. ◆ These problems in Japan and Russia raised doubts about the future of the U.S. expansion. There were other questions about the U.S. economy: Had the potential GDP growth rate increased? Had the natural rate of unemployment decreased? Was real GDP above potential GDP? Was inflation about to increase? And when is the next recession coming? ◆ The

variety of macroeconomic performance raises questions about macroeconomic policy. Can policy improve performance? Specifically, can the federal government use its fiscal policy to speed up long-term growth, keep inflation in check, and maintain a low unemployment rate? Can the Fed use its monetary policy to achieve any of these ends? Are some policy goals better achieved by fiscal policy and some by monetary policy? What specific policy actions do the best job? Are some ways of conducting policy better than others?

◆ In this chapter, we're going to study the challenges of achieving the highest sustainable long-term growth rate and low unemployment while avoiding inflation. At the end of the chapter, you will have a deeper understanding of the macroeconomic policy problems that face the United States today and of the debates that surround us concerning those problems.

After studying this chapter, you will be able to:

- Describe the goals of macroeconomic policy and the main features of fiscal policy and monetary policy since 1960

- Explain how fiscal policy and monetary policy influence long-term economic growth

- Evaluate fixed-rule and feedback-rule policies to stabilize the business cycle

- Explain how fiscal policy influences the natural rate of unemployment

- Explain why lowering inflation usually brings recession

Policy Goals

MACROECONOMIC POLICY GOALS FALL INTO TWO big categories: domestic and international. We study international macroeconomic policy issues in Chapters 36 and 37. Here, we focus on domestic policy. The four main domestic macroeconomic policy goals are to:

- Achieve the highest sustainable rate of potential GDP growth
- Smooth out avoidable business cycle fluctuations
- Maintain low unemployment
- Maintain low inflation

Potential GDP Growth

Rapid sustained real GDP growth can make a profound contribution to economic well being. With a growth rate of 2 percent a year, it takes more than 30 years for production to double. With a growth rate of 5 percent a year, production more than doubles in just 15 years. And with a growth rate of 10 percent a year, as some Asian countries have achieved, production doubles in just 7 years. The limits to *sustainable* growth are determined by the availability of natural resources, by environmental considerations, and by the willingness of people to save and invest in new capital and new technologies rather than consume everything they produce.

How fast can the economy grow over the long term? Between 1988 and 1995, through one complete business cycle, potential GDP grew at a rate of 2 percent a year.[1] But the U.S. population grows at about 1 percent a year, so the growth rate of real GDP per person was 1 percent a year, which means that output per person doubles every 70 years. Most economists believe that the U.S. economy can maintain a long-term growth rate of potential GDP of 2.5 percent a year. This growth rate would double output per person every 48 years. A few economists believe that with the right policies, sustainable growth of 5 percent a year is possible. This growth rate would double output per person every 18 years, increase it more than sixfold over 48 years, and increase it more than twelvefold in 70 years. So increasing the long-term growth rate is of critical importance.

---

[1] This number and the other numbers in this paragraph are based on the official measure of real GDP. If we take inflation bias into account, the growth rates might be as much as 1 percent per year more than these.

The Business Cycle

Potential GDP probably does not grow at a constant rate. Fluctuations in the pace of technological advance and in the pace of investment in new capital bring fluctuations in potential GDP. So some fluctuations in real GDP represent fluctuations in potential GDP. But when real GDP grows less quickly than potential GDP, output is lost, and when real GDP grows more quickly than potential GDP, bottlenecks arise. Keeping real GDP growth steady and equal to potential GDP growth avoids these problems.

It is not known how smooth real GDP growth can be made. Real business cycle theory regards all the fluctuations in real GDP as fluctuations in potential GDP. The aggregate demand theories regard most of the fluctuations in real GDP as being avoidable deviations from potential GDP.

Unemployment

When real GDP growth slows, unemployment rises above the natural rate of unemployment. The higher the unemployment rate, the longer is the time taken by unemployed people to find jobs. Productive labor is wasted, and there is a slowdown in the accumulation of human capital. If high unemployment persists, serious psychological and social problems arise for the unemployed workers and their families.

When real GDP growth speeds up, unemployment decreases and falls below the natural rate of unemployment. The lower the unemployment rate, the harder it becomes for expanding industries to get the labor they need to keep growing. If extremely low unemployment persists, serious bottlenecks and production dislocations occur.

Keeping unemployment at the natural rate avoids both of these problems. But just what is the natural rate of unemployment? Assessments vary. The actual average unemployment rate over the most recent business cycle—1988 to 1998—was 5.7 percent. Most economists think the natural rate has fallen in recent years and would put it at somewhere between 4.5 percent and 5.5 percent today. Real business cycle theorists believe the natural rate fluctuates and always equals the actual unemployment rate.

If the natural rate of unemployment becomes high, then a goal of policy becomes lowering the natural rate itself. This goal is independent of smoothing the business cycle.

Inflation

When inflation fluctuates unpredictably, money becomes less useful as a measuring rod for conducting transactions. In extreme cases, it becomes useless and is abandoned as the means of payment. Borrowers and lenders and employers and workers must take on extra risks. Keeping the inflation rate steady and predictable avoids these problems.

What is the most desirable inflation rate? Some economists say that the *rate* of inflation doesn't matter much as long as the rate is *predictable*. But most economists believe that price stability, which they translate as an inflation rate between 0 and 3 percent a year, is desirable. The reason why zero is not the target is that some price increases are due to quality improvements—a measurement bias in the price index—so a *measured* inflation rate between 0 and 3 percent a year is equivalent to price stability.

FIGURE 35.1

Macroeconomic Performance: Real GDP and Inflation

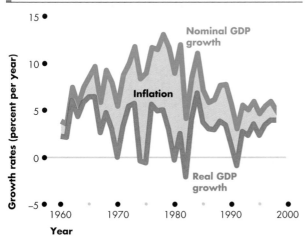

Real GDP growth and inflation fluctuate a great deal, and during the 1970s, inflation mushroomed (the height of the green shaded area) and real GDP growth slowed. This macroeconomic performance falls far short of the goals of a high and stable real GDP growth rate and low and predictable inflation.

Source: The Economic Report of the President, 1999.

The Two Core Policy Indicators: Real GDP Growth and Inflation

Although macroeconomic policy pursues the four goals we've just considered, the goals are not independent ones. Three of these goals—increasing the real GDP growth rate, smoothing the business cycle, and maintaining low unemployment—are linked together. Real GDP growth tells us directly about the long-term goal of high sustainable growth and the business cycle. It also has a strong link to unemployment. If growth becomes too rapid, unemployment falls below the natural rate, and if growth becomes too slow, unemployment rises above the natural rate. So keeping real GDP growing steadily at its maximum sustainable rate is equivalent to avoiding business fluctuations and keeping unemployment at the natural rate.

There are some connections between real GDP growth and inflation, but over the long run, these two variables are largely independent. So two variables, real GDP growth and inflation, are the core policy targets.

Policy performance, judged by the two core policy targets—real GDP growth and inflation—is shown in Fig. 35.1. Here the red line shows real GDP growth. Real GDP growth averaged 4 percent a year during the 1960s, but after 1970, the growth rate fell to less than 2.5 percent a year. Real GDP growth has fluctuated between a high of 6.8 percent in 1984 and a low of −2.1 percent in 1982. The height of the green shaded area shows inflation. The inflation rate was low during the 1960s, exploded during the 1970s, and then fell through the 1980s. During the 1990s, inflation returned to its 1960s level.

R E V I E W   Q U I Z

- Why does macroeconomic stabilization policy try to achieve the highest sustainable rate of potential GDP growth, small business cycle fluctuations, low unemployment, and low inflation?
- Can stabilization policy keep the unemployment rate below the natural rate?
- Why are real GDP growth and inflation the two core policy indicators?

We've examined the policy goals. Let's now look at the policy tools and the way they have been used.

Policy Tools and Performance

THE TOOLS THAT ARE USED TO TRY TO ACHIEVE macroeconomic performance objectives are fiscal policy and monetary policy. **Fiscal policy**, which is described in Chapter 30, is the use of the federal budget to achieve macroeconomic objectives. The detailed fiscal policy tools are tax rates, benefit rates, and government purchases of goods and services. These tools work by influencing aggregate supply and aggregate demand in the ways explained in Chapter 25. **Monetary policy**, which is described in Chapter 32, is the adjustment of the quantity of money in circulation and interest rates by the Federal Reserve (the Fed) to achieve macroeconomic objectives. These tools work by changing aggregate demand. How have the tools actually been used in the United States? Let's answer this question by summarizing the main directions of fiscal and monetary policy over the years since 1960.

Fiscal Policy Since 1960

Figure 35.2 gives a broad summary of fiscal policy since 1960. It shows the levels of government revenues and expenditures and the budget balance (each as a percentage of GDP). So that you can see the political context of fiscal policy, the figure also shows the terms of administrations and the names of the incumbent presidents.

Fiscal policy was mildly expansionary during the Kennedy years and strongly expansionary during the later Johnson years when the Vietnam War buildup occurred. During Nixon's presidency, spending growth was kept moderate. But under the pressure of the first OPEC oil shock, spending soared during Ford's presidency. The Carter years began with spending cuts, but then spending climbed to a new high. During the first Reagan term, spending continued to increase at first but it was later held in check, and then during the second Reagan term, spending was cut. During the Bush years, government purchases took an increased percentage of GDP but taxes took a smaller percentage. As the 1991 recession

---

FIGURE 35.2

The Fiscal Policy Record: A Summary

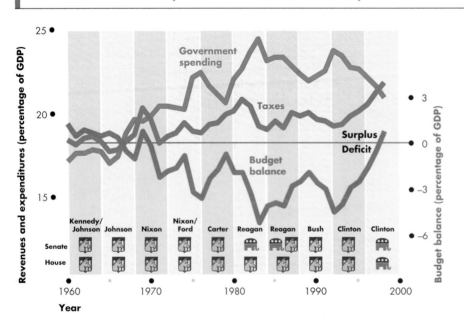

Fiscal policy is summarized here by the performance of government spending, taxes, and the budget balance. Spending has been on an upward trend, and because spending has increased more than taxes, a deficit has emerged. Cycles in spending and taxes have resulted in cycles in the deficit that often have been expansionary in the year before an election and contractionary in the year following an election.

Source: *Budget of the United States Government, Fiscal Year 2000*, Table 14.2, Federal Transactions in the National Income and Product Accounts, and *The Congressional Record*.

intensified and the 1992 election drew closer, tax cuts became the rage, especially in Congress, and revenues decreased. But a tax bill in 1993 increased taxes, so revenues increased during the Clinton presidency. At the same time, spending was held in check and decreased as a percentage of GDP.

The budget balance tells an interesting story. During the terms of Johnson, Nixon, and Ford and the first Reagan term, the budget deficit decreased in the immediate post-election year and increased as the next election approached. Through the Clinton years, the deficit decreased and a surplus emerged.

Monetary Policy Since 1960

Figure 35.3 shows three broad measures of monetary policy. They are the growth rate of M2, the federal funds rate, and the real federal funds rate. The M2 growth rate tells us how monetary policy was influencing an important determinant of aggregate demand. The federal funds rate tells us how the Fed was acting to change money growth. And the real federal funds rate tells us how the Fed was acting

on the opportunity cost of short-term funds that influences spending plans.

Figure 35.3 also identifies the election years, the presidents, and the Fed chairs. The Fed has had five chairs during this period. Notice that the term of a Fed chair does not coincide with the term of a president. William McChesney Martin was a long-serving chair whose term began in 1951. He retired in 1969 and was replaced by Arthur Burns, who served until 1977. William Miller had the shortest term and was replaced by Paul Volcker in 1979. The next chair, Alan Greenspan, was appointed by President Reagan in 1987 and has served under three presidents.

First, let's look at some of the monetary policy trends. During the 1960s, the M2 growth rate averaged 7 percent a year and ranged between a low of 4 percent in 1969 and a high of 9 percent in 1967. It then increased to average 10 percent a year between 1970 and 1983 and hit a peak of 14 percent in 1976. M2 growth fell steadily from 12 percent in 1983 to less than 1 percent in 1994 but then increased in 1995. The federal funds rate trended upward from 1960 through 1981 and then trended downward. The real federal funds rate fell through 1975 and

FIGURE 35.3

The Monetary Policy Record: A Summary

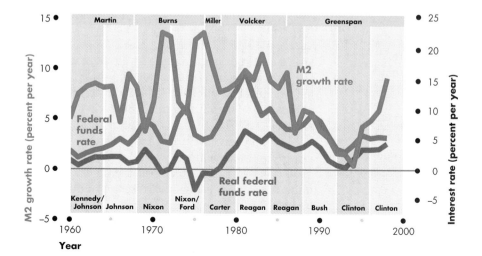

Here the growth rate of M2 and the federal funds rate summarizes the monetary policy record. Fluctuations in M2 growth have coincided with elections, the growth rate usually increasing in the year before an election. Important exceptions are 1979–1980 and 1991–1992, when monetary policy did not become expansionary and the incumbent President lost the election.

Source: The Economic Report of the President, 1999.

then increased and remained high through most of the 1980s. It fell during the early 1990s but then began to rise again through 1998.

The general upward trend in M2 growth brought the 1970s inflation, which brought rising *nominal* interest rates but, at first, falling real interest rates. The subsequent sharp downward trend in M2 growth brought falling inflation and falling nominal interest rates but was accompanied by high real interest rates.

Next, look at the cycles. The peaks and troughs in M2 growth more or less coincide with the opposite turning points in the federal funds rate. When the Fed cuts the federal funds rate, M2 growth speeds up; when the Fed increases the federal funds rate, M2 growth slows down. But notice also a remarkable fact about the monetary policy cycles. There is a tendency for the federal funds rate to rise and the M2 growth rate to decrease immediately following an election and for the federal funds rate to fall and the M2 growth rate to increase as the next election approaches. Usually, the incumbent president or his party's successor has won the election. There are two exceptions. In 1980, M2 growth increased, but not as quickly as the demand for money. Interest rates increased, the economy slowed, and Jimmy Carter lost his reelection bid. In 1992, M2 growth slowed, interest rates rose, and George Bush lost his reelection bids. A coincidence? Perhaps, but presidents take a keen interest in what the Fed is up to.

REVIEW QUIZ

- What were the main features and effects of fiscal policy during the terms of the various presidents from Kennedy in the 1960s to Clinton in the 1990s? What problems did fiscal policy respond to during the late 1960s and the 1970s?
- What were the main features and effects of monetary policy during each decade from the 1960s through the 1990s? In which periods was monetary policy inflationary? In which periods was it used to fight inflation?

You've now studied the goals of policy and seen the broad trends and cycles in fiscal and monetary policy. Let's now study the ways in which policy might be used better to achieve its goals. We'll begin by looking at long-term growth policy.

Long-Term Growth Policy

THE SOURCES OF THE LONG-TERM GROWTH OF potential GDP, which are explained in Chapter 28 (pp. 611–612), are the accumulation of physical and human capital and the advance of technology. Chapter 28 briefly examines the range of policies that might achieve faster growth. Here, we probe more deeply into the problem of boosting the long-term growth rate.

Monetary policy can contribute to long-term growth by keeping the inflation rate low. (Chapter 33, p. 744–745 explains some connections between inflation and growth.) Fiscal policy and other policies can also contribute to growth by influencing the private decisions on which long-term growth depends in three areas. All growth policies increase:

- National saving
- Investment in human capital
- Investment in new technologies

National Saving

National saving equals private saving plus government saving (see Chapter 23, p. 498). Figure 35.4 shows national saving and its private and government components since 1960. From 1960 through 1982, national saving (green line) fluctuated around an average of 20 percent of GDP. There then began a steady slide that saw national saving sink to 14 percent of GDP in 1993 before beginning to rise again. Private saving (blue line) actually increased as a percentage of GDP between 1960 and 1984, when it peaked at 22 percent of GDP. Government saving (the vertical gap between the blue line and the green line) was positive before 1975, became negative (government dissaving) during the 1980s, and returned to positive in 1997.

The data you have just examined are for *gross* saving. Each year, national wealth grows by the amount of *net* saving, which equals gross saving minus the value of capital that is scrapped during the year. Figure 35.4 shows U.S. net saving as a percentage of GDP. You can see that net saving (red line) followed a falling trend through 1993. The reason is that capital depreciated at an increasing rate. During the 1960s, depreciation ranged between 10 percent and 14 percent of GDP. This percentage edged upward and was around 12 percent by the mid-1990s. In the 1982 recession, it reached 14 percent of GDP. As a result of the fall in gross saving and the increase in the depreciation rate, net saving in the United States sank to an all-time low of 2.4 percent of GDP in 1993. But since 1993, the net saving rate has been rising.

U.S. investment, one of the engines of growth, is not limited by U.S. saving. The reason is that foreign saving can be harnessed to finance U.S. investment. But boosting the U.S. saving rate can help to bring faster real GDP growth for two reasons. First, the U.S. economy is a significant proportion of the world economy, so an increase in U.S. saving would increase world saving and bring lower real interest rates around the world. With lower real interest rates, investment would be boosted everywhere. The U.S. economy and the world economy could grow faster. Second, with more domestic saving, there might be an increase in

domestic investment in high-risk–high-return new technologies that could boost U.S. growth.

How can national saving be increased? The two points of attack are:

- Increasing government saving
- Increasing private saving

Increasing Government Saving   Government saving was negative between 1975 and 1996, and its average during the 1990s was –1.3 percent of GDP. But government saving increased after 1992 as the federal budget deficit was gradually eliminated and replaced by a surplus. Maintaining a federal budget surplus will be hard work and will be achieved only by resisting tax cuts and increases in expenditures on Social Security, Medicaid, and Medicare.

Increasing Private Saving   Private saving has fallen from its peak of the mid-1980s, but even in the low years of 1992 and 1993, private saving was the same percentage of GDP it had been in 1960. The main way in which government actions can boost private saving is by increasing the after-tax rate of return on saving. This is what government policy has sought to do, but on only one type of asset: individual retirement accounts (IRAs). By putting their savings into IRAs, people can avoid income tax on their interest income. But they cannot use their IRAs (without tax penalties) until they reach the age of 59 1/2. Also, there are limits (that were relaxed somewhat in 1997) to the amount that can be accumulated tax-free in an IRA.

Private saving probably could be stimulated more effectively by cutting taxes on interest income and capital gains (increases in asset values) and replacing the lost government revenue from such a tax cut with a national consumption tax or a national sales tax. Whether such restructuring of taxes is politically feasible or desirable is a question that goes beyond the scope of macroeconomics.

Private Saving and Inflation   Inflation erodes the value of money and other financial assets such as bonds, and uncertainty about future inflation discourages saving. One further policy, therefore, that increases the saving rate is a monetary policy that preserves stable prices and minimizes uncertainty about the future value of money. Chapter 33 (p. 744–745) spells out the broader connection between inflation and real GDP and explains why low inflation brings greater output and faster growth.

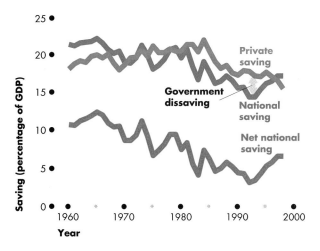

FIGURE 35.4

Saving Rates in the
United States: 1960–1998

U.S. national saving (green line) peaked in 1979 and has fallen since that year. Both government saving and private saving have contributed to the fall. U.S. net saving (red line) has fallen even faster than national saving and has been on a downward trend since the mid-1960s. It hit an all-time low of 2.4 percent of GDP in 1993. It has increased since then.

Source: The Economic Report of the President, 1999.

Investment in Human Capital

The accumulation of human capital plays a crucial role in economic growth, and two areas are relevant: schooling and on-the-job experience. Economic research shows that both schooling and on-the-job training pay. That is, on the average, the greater the number of years a person remains in school and the greater the number of years of work experience, the higher are that person's earnings. Furthermore, schooling and on-the-job experience yield one of the highest rates of return available.

If education and on-the-job training yield higher earnings, why does the government need a policy toward investment in human capital? Why can't people simply be left to get on with making their own decisions about how much human capital to acquire? The answer is that the *social* returns to human capital probably exceed the *private* returns. The extra productivity that comes from the *interactions* of well-educated and experienced people exceeds what each individual could achieve alone. So, left to ourselves, we would probably accumulate too little human capital. Let's look at some aspects of education and training policies.

Education and Training Policies Governments attempt to increase human capital by subsidizing schooling. They also help to set the standards of achievement for the school system.

The United States has achieved a high standard on some dimensions of schooling but not on all dimensions. For example, in 1998, 63 percent of high school graduates enrolled in postsecondary education (one of the highest percentages in the world) but 13 percent of high school students dropped out and did not graduate.

The Goals 2000: Educate America Act of 1994 and President Clinton's second term education initiative are examples of attempts to improve the quality of schooling. The 1994 Act pays special attention to improving each child's state of preparation for school and performance in school, especially in mathematics and science, two areas in which U.S. schoolchildren are not leading the world. A further feature of Goals 2000 is to improve college access, especially for adults who can benefit from retraining.

The scope for government training programs is limited, but the government can set an example as an employer and it can encourage best-practice training programs for workers.

Investment in New Technologies

Investment in new technologies is the third area in which policy can influence economic growth. As Chapter 28 explains, investment in new technologies is special for two reasons. First, it appears not to run into the problem of diminishing returns that plague the other types of capital and the other factors of production. Second, the benefits of new technologies spill over to influence all parts of the economy, not just the firms undertaking the investment. For these reasons, increasing the rate of investment in new technologies is a promising way of boosting long-term growth. But how can government policy influence the pace of technological change?

Government can fund and provide tax incentives for research and development activities. Through the National Science Foundation, the public universities, and various research establishments, governments fund a large amount of basic research. Also, the federal government encourages business research with a Research and Experiment Tax Credit (R&E credit). This credit is available to firms that spend more on research and development than some threshold amount. The idea is to stimulate more expenditure on these activities than would occur otherwise. The effectiveness of the R&E credit is not certain, but there is some evidence that it is a cost-effective way of boosting research.

REVIEW QUIZ

- Why do long-term growth policies focus on increasing saving and increasing investment in human capital and new technologies?
- What have been the trends in the U.S. net saving rate since the mid-1970s?
- What actions can the government take that might increase the saving rate?
- What actions can the government take that might increase the rate of investment in human capital?
- What actions can the government take that might increase investment in new technologies?

We've seen how government might use its fiscal and monetary policies to influence long-term growth. How can it influence the business cycle and unemployment? Let's now address this question.

Business Cycle and Unemployment Policy

MANY DIFFERENT FISCAL AND MONETARY POLICIES can be pursued to stabilize the business cycle and cyclical unemployment. But all these polices fall into three broad categories:

- Fixed-rule policies
- Feedback-rule policies
- Discretionary policies

Fixed-Rule Policies

A **fixed-rule policy** specifies an action to be pursued independently of the state of the economy. An everyday life example of a fixed rule is a stop sign. It says, "Stop regardless of the state of the road ahead— even if no other vehicle is trying to use the road." One fixed-rule policy, proposed by Milton Friedman, is to keep the quantity of money growing at a constant rate year in and year out, regardless of the state of the economy, to make the *average* inflation rate zero. Another fixed-rule policy is to balance the federal budget. Fixed rules are rarely followed in practice, but they have some merits in principle, and later in this chapter, we will study how they would work if they were pursued.

Feedback-Rule Policies

A **feedback-rule policy** specifies how policy actions respond to changes in the state of the economy. A yield sign is an everyday feedback rule. It says, "Stop if another vehicle is attempting to use the road ahead, but otherwise, proceed." A macroeconomic feedback-rule policy is one that changes the money supply, interest rates, or even tax rates in response to the state of the economy. Some feedback rules guide the actions of policy makers. For example, the Fed's Federal Open Market Committee used a feedback rule when it kept pushing interest rates ever higher through 1994 in response to persistently falling unemployment and strong real GDP growth. Other feedback-rule policies are automatic. Examples are the automatic increase in tax revenues and decrease in transfer payments during an expansion and the automatic decrease in tax revenues and increase in transfer payments during a recession.

Discretionary Policies

A **discretionary policy** responds to the state of the economy in a possibly unique way that uses all the information available, including perceived lessons from past "mistakes." An everyday discretionary policy occurs at an unmarked intersection. Each driver uses discretion in deciding whether to stop and how slowly to approach the intersection. Most macroeconomic policy actions have an element of discretion because every situation is to some degree unique. For example, through 1998, the Fed cut interest rates several times to maintain economic growth in the face of a sagging Asian economy. The Fed might have delayed cutting rates until it was sure that lower rates were needed and then cut them in larger increments. The Fed used discretion based on lessons it had learned from earlier expansions. But despite the fact that all policy actions have an element of discretion, they can be regarded as modifications of a basic feedback-rule policy.

We'll study the effects of business cycle policy by comparing the performance of real GDP and the price level under a fixed rule and a feedback rule. Because the business cycle can result from demand shocks or supply shocks, we need to consider these two cases. We'll begin by studying demand shocks.

Stabilizing Aggregate Demand Shocks

We'll study an economy that starts out at full employment and has no inflation. Figure 35.5 illustrates this situation. The economy is on aggregate demand curve AD_0 and short-run aggregate supply curve SAS. These curves intersect at a point on the long-run aggregate supply curve, LAS. The GDP deflator is 110, and real GDP is \$7 trillion. Now suppose that there is an unexpected and temporary decrease in aggregate demand. Let's see what happens.

Perhaps investment decreases because of a wave of pessimism about the future, or perhaps exports decrease because of a recession in the rest of the world. Regardless of the origin of the decrease in aggregate demand, the aggregate demand curve shifts leftward, to AD_1 in Fig. 35.5. Aggregate demand curve AD_1 intersects the short-run aggregate supply curve, SAS, at a GDP deflator of 105 and a real GDP of \$6.5 trillion. The economy is in a recession. Real GDP is less than potential GDP, and unemployment is above its natural rate.

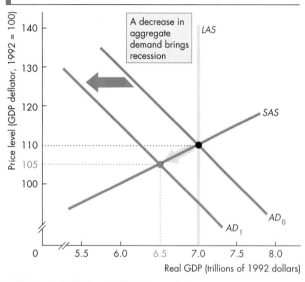

FIGURE 35.5

A Decrease in
Aggregate Demand

The economy starts out at full employment on aggregate demand curve AD_0 and short-run aggregate supply curve SAS, the two curves intersecting on the long-run aggregate supply curve, LAS. Real GDP is $7 trillion, and the GDP deflator is 110. A fall in aggregate demand (due to pessimism about future profits, for example) unexpectedly shifts the aggregate demand curve to AD_1. Real GDP falls to $6.5 trillion, and the GDP deflator falls to 105. The economy is in a recession.

Suppose that the decrease in aggregate demand from AD_0 to AD_1 is temporary. As confidence in the future improves, firms' investment picks up, or as economic expansion proceeds in the rest of the world, exports gradually increase. As a result, the aggregate demand curve gradually returns to AD_0, but it takes some time to do so.

We are going to work out how the economy responds under two alternative policies during the period in which aggregate demand gradually increases to its original level: a fixed rule and a feedback rule.

Fixed Rule: Monetarism   The fixed rule that we'll study here is one in which government purchases of goods and services, taxes, and the money supply remain constant. Neither fiscal policy nor monetary policy responds to the depressed economy. This is

the rule advocated by monetarists. A **monetarist** is an economist who believes that fluctuations in the money stock are the main source of economic fluctuations—the monetarist theory of the business cycle (see Chapter 34, p. 768).

Figure 35.6(a) illustrates the response of the economy under a fixed rule when the decrease in aggregate demand to AD_1 is *temporary*. Gradually, aggregate demand returns to its original level and the aggregate demand curve shifts rightward to AD_0. As it does so, real GDP and the GDP deflator gradually increase. The GDP deflator gradually returns to 110 and real GDP to $7 trillion, as shown in Fig. 35.6(a). Throughout this process, the economy experiences more rapid growth than usual but beginning from a state in which real GDP is less than potential GDP. Also throughout the adjustment, unemployment remains above the natural rate.

Figure 35.6(b) illustrates the response of the economy under a fixed rule when the decrease in aggregate demand to AD_1 is *permanent*. Gradually, with unemployment above the natural rate, the money wage rate falls and the short-run aggregate supply curve shifts rightward to SAS_1. As it does so, real GDP gradually increases and the GDP deflator falls. Real GDP gradually returns to potential GDP of $7 trillion, and the GDP deflator gradually falls to 95, as shown in Fig. 35.6(b). Again, throughout the adjustment, real GDP is less than potential GDP and unemployment exceeds the natural rate.

Let's contrast the adjustment under a fixed-rule policy with that under a feedback-rule policy.

Feedback Rule: Keynesian Activism   The feedback rule that we'll study is one in which government purchases of goods and services increase, tax rates decrease, and the money supply increases when real GDP falls below potential GDP. In other words, both fiscal policy and monetary policy become expansionary when real GDP is less than potential GDP. When real GDP exceeds potential GDP, both policies operate in reverse, becoming contractionary. This rule is advocated by Keynesian activists. A **Keynesian activist** is an economist who believes that fluctuations in aggregate demand combined with sticky wages (and/or sticky prices) are the main source of economic fluctuations—the Keynesian and new Keynesian theories of the business cycle (see Chapter 34, pp. 766–770).

Figure 35.6(c) illustrates the response of the economy under this feedback-rule policy. When aggregate demand decreases to AD_1, the expansionary fiscal and

FIGURE 35.6

Two Stabilization Policies: Aggregate Demand Shock

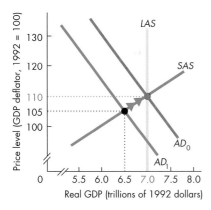

(a) Fixed rule: temporary demand shock

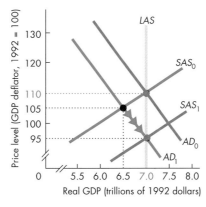

(b) Fixed rule: permanent demand shock

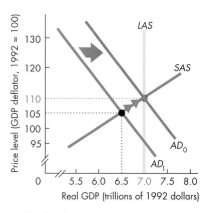

(c) Feedback rule

Aggregate demand has fallen from AD_0 to AD_1, and the economy is in a recession. Real GDP has fallen to $6.5 trillion, and the GDP deflator has fallen to 105. A fixed-rule stabilization policy (parts a and b) leaves aggregate demand at AD_1, so real GDP remains at $6.5 trillion and the GDP deflator remains at 105. If the aggregate demand shock is temporary (part a), aggregate demand subsequently returns to its original level and the aggregate demand curve shifts back to AD_0. As it does, real GDP increases back to $7 trillion and the GDP deflator increases to 110. If the demand shock is permanent (part b),

aggregate demand remains at AD_1. Eventually, because unemployment is above the natural rate, the money wage rate falls and the SAS curve shifts to SAS_1. The price level falls further (to a GDP deflator of 95), and real GDP returns to $7 trillion. Part (c) shows a feedback rule. With the economy in recession, expansionary fiscal and monetary policies increase aggregate demand and shift the aggregate demand curve from AD_1 to AD_0. Real GDP returns to $7 trillion and the GDP deflator returns 110.

monetary policies increase aggregate demand, shifting the aggregate demand curve immediately to AD_0. As other influences begin to increase aggregate demand, fiscal and monetary policies become contractionary and hold the aggregate demand curve steady at AD_0. Real GDP is held steady at $7 trillion, and the GDP deflator remains at 110.

The Two Rules Compared   Under a fixed-rule policy, the economy goes into a recession and stays there for as long as it takes for aggregate demand to increase again under its own steam. Only gradually does the aggregate demand curve return to its original position and the recession come to an end.

Under a feedback-rule policy, the economy is pulled out of its recession by the policy action. Once back at potential GDP, real GDP is held there by a gradual, policy-induced decrease in aggregate demand that exactly offsets the increase in aggregate demand coming from private spending decisions.

The price level and real GDP decrease and increase by exactly the same amounts under the two policies, but real GDP stays below potential GDP for longer with a fixed rule than it does with a feedback rule.

The Fed's Feedback Rule: 1992–1998   The Fed operates a feedback rule but also tries to anticipate events. At the end of 1992, real GDP was less than potential GDP and unemployment exceeded the natural rate. Through 1992 the Fed cut interest rates and speeded up money growth. By 1994, real GDP was close to and growing faster than potential GDP. To prevent inflation, the Fed increased interest rates and slowed money growth. As the economy slowed, during 1995, the Fed cut interest rates and speeded up money growth. Real GDP growth again speeded up in 1996. Again, in early 1997, the Fed applied the monetary brake. The economy did not slow in 1998, but because much of Asia was in recession, the Fed cut rates again to try to avoid a U.S. and global recession.

Are Feedback Rules Better?

Is a feedback rule better than a fixed rule? Can the government and the Fed use feedback rules to keep the economy close to full employment with a stable price level? Of course, unforecasted events—such as a collapse in business confidence—will hit the economy from time to time. But by responding with a change in tax rates, spending, interest rates, and money supply, can't the government and the Fed minimize the damage from such a shock? It appears to be so from our analysis, and the Fed did a pretty good job during 1992–1998.

Despite the apparent superiority of a feedback rule, many economists remain convinced that a fixed rule stabilizes aggregate demand more effectively than a feedback rule does. These economists assert that fixed rules are better than feedback rules because:

■ Potential GDP is not known.

■ Policy lags are longer than the forecast horizon.

■ Feedback-rule policies are less predictable than fixed-rule policies.

Knowledge of Potential GDP   To decide whether a feedback policy needs to stimulate or retard aggregate demand, it is necessary to determine whether real GDP is currently above or below potential GDP. But potential GDP is not known with certainty. It depends on a large number of factors, one of which is the level of employment when unemployment is at its natural rate. But uncertainty and disagreement exist about how the labor market works, so we can only estimate the natural rate of unemployment. As a result, there is uncertainty about the *direction* in which a feedback policy should be pushing the level of aggregate demand.

Policy Lags and the Forecast Horizon   The effects of policy actions taken today are spread out over the following two years or even more. But no one is able to forecast accurately that far ahead. The forecast horizon of the policy makers is less than 1 year. Further, it is not possible to predict the precise timing and magnitude of the effects of policy actions. Thus feedback policies that react to today's economy may be inappropriate for the state of the economy at that uncertain future date when the policy's effects are felt.

For example, suppose that today the economy is in recession. The Fed reacts with an increase in the money supply growth rate. When the Fed puts on the monetary accelerator, the first reaction is a fall in interest rates. Some time later, lower interest rates produce an increase in investment and the purchases of consumer durable goods. Some time still later, this increase in expenditure increases income; higher income in turn induces higher consumption expenditure. Later yet, the higher expenditure increases the demand for labor, and eventually, wages and prices rise. The industries and regions in which spending increases occur vary, and so does the impact on employment. It can take from 9 months to 2 years for an initial action by the Fed to cause a change in real GDP, employment, and the inflation rate.

By the time the Fed's actions are having their maximum effect, the economy has moved on to a new situation. Perhaps a world economic slowdown has added a new negative effect on aggregate demand that is offsetting the Fed's expansionary actions. Or perhaps a boost in business confidence has increased aggregate demand yet further, adding to the Fed's own expansionary policy. Whatever the situation, the Fed can take the appropriate actions today only if it can forecast those future shocks to aggregate demand.

Thus to smooth the fluctuations in aggregate demand, the Fed needs to take actions today, based on a forecast of what will be happening over a period stretching 2 or more years into the future. It is no use taking actions a year from today to influence the situation that then prevails. By then it will be too late.

If the Fed is good at economic forecasting and bases its policy actions on its forecasts, then the Fed can deliver the type of aggregate-demand-smoothing performance that we assumed in the model economy that we studied earlier in this chapter. But if the Fed takes policy actions that are based on today's economy rather than on the forecasted economy a year into the future, then those actions will often be inappropriate ones.

When unemployment is high and the Fed puts its foot on the accelerator, it speeds the economy back to full employment. But the Fed might not be able to see far enough ahead to know when to ease off the accelerator and gently tap the brake, holding the economy at its full-employment point. Usually, the Fed keeps its foot on the accelerator for too long, and after the Fed has taken its foot off the accelerator pedal, the economy races through the full-employment point and starts to experience shortages and inflationary pressures. Eventually, when inflation increases and unemployment falls below its natural rate, the Fed steps on the brake, pushing the economy back below full employment.

According to advocates of fixed rules, the Fed's own reactions to the current state of the economy is one of the major sources of fluctuations in aggregate demand and the major factor that people have to forecast to make their own economic choices.

During recent years, the Fed has tried to avoid the problems just described. In 1994, it increased interest rates early in the expansion and by small increments. In 1995, after real GDP growth slowed but before any signs of recession were on the horizon, the Fed began to cut interest rates. In 1997, before inflation turned seriously upward, the Fed squeezed the monetary brake. And in 1998, while the economy expanded strongly, the Fed cut rates to avoid the effects of the Asian recession. So the Fed's actions during 1992–1998 were gentler and better timed than in previous business cycles.

The problems for fiscal policy feedback rules are more severe than those for monetary policy because of the lags in the implementation of fiscal policy. The Fed can take actions relatively quickly. But before a fiscal policy action can be taken, the entire legislative process must be completed. Thus even before a fiscal policy action is implemented, the economy may have moved on to a new situation that calls for a different feedback policy from the one that is in the legislative pipeline.

Predictability of Policies To make decisions about long-term contracts for employment (wage contracts) and for borrowing and lending, people have to anticipate the future course of prices—the future inflation rate. To forecast the inflation rate, it is necessary to forecast aggregate demand. And to forecast aggregate demand, it is necessary to forecast the policy actions of the government and the Fed.

If the government and the Fed stick to rock-steady, fixed rules for tax rates, spending programs, and money supply growth, then policy itself cannot be a contributor to unexpected fluctuations in aggregate demand.

In contrast, when a feedback rule is being pursued, there is more scope for the policy actions to be unpredictable. The main reason is that feedback rules are not written down for all to see. Rather, they have to be inferred from the behavior of the government and the Fed.

Thus with a feedback policy, it is necessary to predict the variables to which the government and Fed react and the extent to which they react. Consequently, a feedback rule for fiscal and monetary

policies can create more unpredictable fluctuations in aggregate demand than a fixed rule can.

Economists disagree about whether those bigger fluctuations offset the potential stabilizing influence of the predictable changes the Fed makes. No agreed measurements have been made to settle this dispute. Nevertheless, the unpredictability of the Fed in its pursuit of feedback policies is an important fact of economic life. And the Fed does not always go out of its way to make its reactions clear. Even in Congressional testimony, Federal Reserve Board chairmen are reluctant to make the Fed's actions and intentions entirely plain. (It has been suggested that two former chairmen of the Federal Reserve Board, the pipe-puffing Arthur Burns and the cigar-puffing Paul Volcker, carried their own smokescreens around with them, as if to exemplify the Fed's mysteriousness and unpredictability. The nonsmoking Alan Greenspan seems to be running a more open and predictable Fed.)

It is not surprising that the Fed seeks to keep *some* of its actions behind a smokescreen. First, the Fed wants to maintain as much freedom of action as possible and so does not want to state with too great a precision the feedback rules that it will follow in any given circumstances. Second, the Fed is part of a political process and, although legally independent of the federal government, is not immune to subtle influence. For at least these two reasons, the Fed does not specify feedback rules as precisely as the one we've analyzed in this chapter. As a result, the Fed cannot deliver an economic performance that has the stability that we generated in the model economy.

To the extent that the Fed's actions are discretionary and unpredictable, they lead to unpredictable fluctuations in aggregate demand. These fluctuations, in turn, produce fluctuations in real GDP, employment, and unemployment.

If it is difficult for the Fed to pursue a predictable feedback stabilization policy, it is probably impossible for Congress to do so. The stabilization policy of Congress is formulated in terms of spending programs and tax laws. Because these programs and laws are the outcome of a political process that is constrained only by the Constitution, there can be no effective way in which a predictable feedback fiscal policy can be adhered to.

We reviewed three reasons why feedback-rule policies might not be more effective than fixed-rule policies in controlling aggregate demand. But there is a fourth reason why some economists prefer fixed rules: Not all shocks to the economy are on the demand side. Most advocates of feedback rules believe that most fluctuations do come from aggregate demand. Some advocates of fixed rules believe that aggregate supply fluctuations are the dominant ones. Let's now see how aggregate supply fluctuations affect the economy under a fixed rule and a feedback rule. We will also see why the economists who believe that aggregate supply fluctuations are the dominant ones also favor a fixed rule rather than a feedback rule.

Stabilizing Aggregate Supply Shocks

Real business cycle theorists believe that fluctuations in real GDP (and in employment and unemployment) are caused not by fluctuations in aggregate demand but by fluctuations in productivity growth. According to real business cycle theory, there is no useful distinction between long-run aggregate supply and short-run aggregate supply. Because wages are flexible, the labor market is always in equilibrium and unemployment is always at its natural rate. The vertical long-run aggregate supply curve is also the short-run aggregate supply curve. Fluctuations occur because of shifts in the long-run aggregate supply curve. Normally, the long-run aggregate supply curve shifts to the right—the economy expands. But the pace at which the long-run aggregate supply curve shifts to the right varies. Also, on occasion, the long-run aggregate supply curve shifts leftward, bringing a decrease in aggregate supply and a fall in real GDP.

If the real business cycle theory is correct, economic policy that influences the aggregate demand curve has no effect on real GDP. But it does affect the price level. If a feedback-rule policy is used to increase aggregate demand every time real GDP decreases, and if the real business cycle theory is correct, the feedback-rule policy will make price level fluctuations more severe than they otherwise would be. To see why, consider Fig. 35.7.

Imagine that the economy starts out on aggregate demand curve AD_0 and long-run aggregate supply curve LAS_0 at a GDP deflator of 110 and with real GDP equal to $7 trillion. Now suppose that the long-run aggregate supply curve shifts to LAS_1. An actual decrease in long-run aggregate supply can occur as a result of a severe drought or other natural catastrophe or perhaps as the result of a disruption of international trade such as the OPEC embargo of the 1970s.

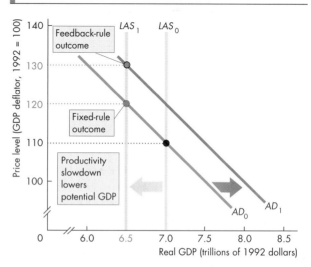

FIGURE 35.7

Responding to a Productivity Growth Slowdown

A productivity growth slowdown shifts the long-run aggregate supply curve from LAS_0 to LAS_1. Real GDP decreases to $6.5 trillion, and the GDP deflator rises to 120. With a fixed rule, there is no change in the money supply, taxes, or government spending; aggregate demand stays at AD_0; and that is the end of the matter. With a feedback rule, the Fed increases the money supply and the Congress cuts taxes or increases spending, intending to increase real GDP. Aggregate demand shifts to AD_1, but the result is an increase in the price level—the GDP deflator rises to 130—with no change in real GDP.

Fixed Rule   With a fixed rule, the fall in the long-run aggregate supply has no effect on the policies of the Fed or the government and no effect on aggregate demand. The aggregate demand curve remains AD_0. Real GDP decreases to $6.5 trillion, and the GDP deflator increases to 120.

Feedback Rule   Now suppose that the Fed and the government use feedback rules. In particular, suppose that when real GDP decreases, the Fed increases the money supply and Congress enacts a tax cut to increase aggregate demand. In this example, the money supply and tax cut shift the aggregate demand curve to AD_1. The policy goal is to bring real GDP back to $7 trillion. But the long-run aggregate supply curve has shifted, and so potential GDP has decreased to $6.5 trillion. The increase in aggregate demand cannot bring forth an increase in output if the economy does not have the capacity to produce that output. So real GDP stays at $6.5 trillion, but the price level rises still further—the GDP deflator goes to 130. You can see that in this case, the attempt to stabilize real GDP using a feedback-rule policy has no effect on real GDP but generates a substantial price level increase.

We've now seen some of the shortcomings of using feedback rules for stabilization policy. Some economists believe that these shortcomings are serious and want to constrain Congress and the Fed so that they use fixed rules. Others, regarding the potential advantages of feedback rules as greater than their costs, advocate the continued use of such policies but with an important modification that we'll now look at.

Nominal GDP Targeting

Nominal GDP targeting is an attempt to keep the growth rate of nominal GDP steady. This policy target was first proposed by a leading Keynesian activist, James Tobin of Yale University. It is a policy that recognizes the strengths of a fixed rule but that regards the monetarist fixed rule as inappropriate. Instead, nominal GDP targeting uses feedback rules for fiscal and monetary policy to hit a fixed nominal GDP growth target.

Because nominal GDP growth equals the real GDP growth rate plus the inflation rate, keeping nominal GDP growth steady does not directly target either real GDP growth or inflation. But nominal GDP usually grows quickly because the inflation rate is high. And nominal GDP usually grows slowly because real GDP growth is negative—the economy is in recession. So the idea is that, by keeping nominal GDP growth steady, both excessive inflation and severe recession might be avoided.

Nominal GDP targeting uses feedback rules. Expansionary fiscal and/or monetary actions increase aggregate demand when nominal GDP is below target and contractionary fiscal and/or monetary actions decrease aggregate demand when nominal GDP is above target. The main problem with nominal GDP targeting is that there are long and variable time lags between the identification of a need to change aggregate demand and the effects of the policy actions that are taken.

Natural Rate Policies

The business cycle and unemployment policies we've considered have been directed at smoothing the business cycle and minimizing *cyclical unemployment*. It is also possible to pursue policies aimed at lowering the natural rate of unemployment. But there are no costless ways of lowering the natural rate of unemployment. Let's look at two possible ways.

One policy tool is unemployment insurance. To lower the natural rate of unemployment, the government might reduce the unemployment benefit, or shorten the period for which benefits are paid, or restrict benefits to people who undertake training programs that increase the likelihood of their finding jobs. With reduced benefits, an unemployed person would spend less time looking for a job and would accept a job even if it were not a good match for the person's skills. But such a policy might create hardship and have a cost that exceeds the cost of a high natural rate of unemployment.

The government might lower the minimum real wage rate. It could achieve a cut in the minimum wage either by holding the minimum money wage rate constant and letting inflation cut the minimum real wage rate or by cutting the minimum money wage rate. A lower minimum wage increases the quantity of labor demanded and lowers unemployment. The government faces a tradeoff between real wages and unemployment.

R E V I E W   Q U I Z

- What is a fixed-rule fiscal policy and what is a fixed-rule monetary policy? Can you provide two examples of fixed rules in everyday life (other than those in the text)?
- What is a feedback-rule fiscal policy and what is a feedback-rule monetary policy? When might a feedback-rule policy be used? Can you provide two examples of feedback rules in everyday life (other than those in the text)?
- Why do some economists say that feedback rules do not necessarily deliver a better macroeconomic performance than fixed rules? Do you agree or disagree with them? Why?

We've studied growth policy and business cycle and unemployment policy. Let's now study inflation policy.

Inflation Policy

THERE ARE TWO INFLATION POLICY PROBLEMS. In times of price level stability, the problem is to prevent inflation from breaking out. In times of inflation, the problem is to reduce its rate and restore price stability. Preventing inflation from breaking out means avoiding both demand-pull and cost-push forces. Avoiding demand-pull inflation is the flip side of avoiding demand-driven recession and is achieved by stabilizing aggregate demand. So the business cycle and unemployment policy we've just studied is also an anti-inflation policy. But avoiding cost-push inflation raises some special issues that we need to consider. So we will look at two issues for inflation policy:

- Avoiding cost-push inflation
- Slowing inflation

Avoiding Cost-Push Inflation

Cost-push inflation is inflation that has its origins in cost increases. In 1973–1974 and again in 1979, the world oil price exploded. Cost shocks such as these become inflationary if they are accommodated by an increase in the quantity of money. Such an increase in the quantity of money can occur if a monetary policy feedback rule is used. A fixed-rule policy for the money stock makes cost-push inflation impossible. Let's see why.

Figure 35.8 shows the economy at full employment. Aggregate demand is AD_0, short-run aggregate supply is SAS_0, and long-run aggregate supply is LAS. Real GDP is $7 trillion, and the GDP deflator is 110. Now suppose that OPEC tries to gain a temporary advantage by increasing the price of oil. The short-run aggregate supply curve shifts leftward from SAS_0 to SAS_1.

FIGURE 35.8

Responding to an OPEC Oil Price Increase

(a) Fixed rule

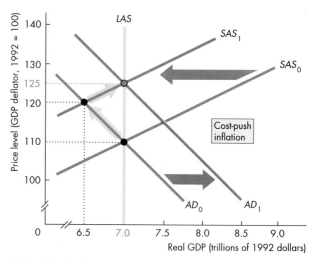

(b) Feedback rule

The economy starts out on AD_0 and SAS_0, with a GDP deflator of 110 and real GDP of $7 trillion. OPEC forces up the price of oil, and the short-run aggregate supply curve shifts to SAS_1. Real GDP decreases to $6.5 trillion, and the GDP deflator increases to 120. With a fixed-rule policy (part a), the Fed makes no change to aggregate demand. The economy stays in

a recession until resource prices fall and the economy returns to its original position. With a feedback-rule policy (part b), the Fed injects additional money and the aggregate demand curve shifts to AD_1. Real GDP returns to $7 trillion (potential GDP), but the GDP deflator increases to 125. The economy is set for another round of cost-push inflation.

Monetarist Fixed Rule Figure 35.8(a) shows what happens if the Fed follows a fixed rule for monetary policy and the government follows a fixed rule for fiscal policy. Suppose that the fixed rule is for zero money growth and no change in taxes or government purchases of goods and services. With these fixed rules, the Fed and the government pay no attention to the fact that there has been an increase in the price of oil. No policy actions are taken. The short-run aggregate supply curve has shifted to SAS_1, but the aggregate demand curve remains at AD_0. The GDP deflator rises to 120, and real GDP falls to $6.5 trillion. The economy has experienced *stagflation*. With unemployment above the natural rate, the money wage rate will eventually fall. The low level of real GDP and low sales will probably also bring a fall in the price of oil. These events will shift the short-run aggregate supply curve back to SAS_0. The GDP deflator will fall to 110, and real GDP will increase to $7 trillion. But this adjustment might take a long time.

Keynesian Feedback Rule Figure 35.8(b) shows what happens if the Fed and government operate a feedback rule. The starting point is the same as before—the economy is on SAS_0 and AD_0 with a GDP deflator of 110 and real GDP of $7 trillion. OPEC raises the price of oil, and the short-run aggregate supply curve shifts to SAS_1. Real GDP decreases to $6.5 trillion, and the price level rises to 120.

A feedback rule is followed. With potential GDP perceived to be $7 trillion and with actual real GDP at $6.5 trillion, the Fed pumps money into the economy and the government increases its spending and lowers taxes. Aggregate demand increases, and the aggregate demand curve shifts rightward to AD_1. The price level rises to 125, and real GDP returns to $7 trillion. The economy moves back to full employment but at a higher price level. The economy has experienced *cost-push inflation*.

The Fed responded in the way we've just described to the first wave of OPEC price increases in the mid-1970s. OPEC sees the same advantage in forcing up the price of oil again. A new rise in the price of oil decreases aggregate supply, and the short-run aggregate supply curve shifts leftward once more. The Fed chases it with an increase in aggregate demand, and the economy is in a freewheeling inflation. Realizing this danger, the Fed did *not* respond in the early 1980s to the second wave of OPEC price increases as it had done before. Instead, the Fed held firm and even slowed down the growth of aggregate demand

to further dampen the inflation consequences of OPEC's actions.

Incentives to Push Up Costs You can see that there are no checks on the incentives to push up *nominal* costs if the Fed accommodates price hikes. If some group sees a temporary gain from pushing up the price at which they are selling their resources and if the Fed always accommodates the increase to prevent unemployment and slack business conditions from emerging, then cost-push elements will have a free rein. But when the Fed pursues a fixed-rule policy, the incentive to attempt to steal a temporary advantage from a price increase is severely weakened. The cost of higher unemployment and lower output is a consequence that each group will have to face and recognize.

Thus a fixed rule can deliver steady inflation, while a feedback rule, in the face of cost-push pressures, leaves inflation free to rise and fall at the whim of whichever group believes a temporary advantage to be available from pushing up its price.

Slowing Inflation

So far, we've concentrated on *avoiding* inflation. But often the problem is not to avoid inflation but to tame it. The United States was in such a situation during the late 1970s and early 1980s. How can inflation, once it has set in, be cured? We'll look at two cases:

■ A surprise inflation reduction
■ A credible announced inflation reduction

A Surprise Inflation Reduction We'll use two equivalent approaches to study the problem of lowering inflation: the aggregate supply–aggregate demand model and the Phillips curve. The *AS-AD* model tells us about real GDP and the price level, while the Phillips curve, which is explained in Chapter 33 (pp. 746–748), lets us keep track of inflation and unemployment.

Figure 35.9 illustrates the economy at full employment with inflation raging at 10 percent a year. In part (a), the economy is on aggregate demand curve AD_0 and short-run aggregate supply curve SAS_0. Real GDP is $7 trillion, and the GDP deflator is 110. With real GDP equal to potential GDP on the *LAS* curve, the economy is at full employment. Equivalently, in part (b), the economy is on its long-run Phillips curve, *LRPC*, and short-run Phillips curve, $SRPC_0$. The

FIGURE 35.9

Lowering Inflation

(a) Aggregate demand and aggregate supply

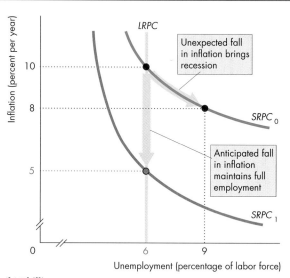

(b) Phillips curves

In part (a), aggregate demand is AD_0, short-run aggregate supply is SAS_0, and real GDP and potential GDP are $7 trillion on the long-run aggregate supply curve LAS. The aggregate demand curve is expected to shift and actually shifts to AD_1. The short-run aggregate supply curve shifts to SAS_1. The GDP deflator rises to 121, but real GDP remains at $7 trillion. Inflation is proceeding at 10 percent a year, and this inflation rate is anticipated. In part (b), which shows this same situation, the economy on the short-run Phillips curve $SRPC_0$ and on the long-run Phillips curve $LRPC$. Unemployment is at the natural rate of 6 percent, and inflation is 10 percent a year. An unex-

pected slowdown in aggregate demand growth means that the aggregate demand curve shifts from AD_0 to AD_2, real GDP falls to $6.5 trillion, and inflation slows to 8 percent (GDP deflator is 118.8). Unemployment rises to 9 percent as the economy slides down $SRPC_0$. An anticipated, credible, announced slowdown in aggregate demand growth means that when the aggregate demand curve shifts from AD_0 to AD_2, the short-run aggregate supply curve shifts from SAS_0 to SAS_2. The short-run Phillips curve shifts to $SRPC_1$. Inflation slows to 5 percent, real GDP remains at $7 trillion, and unemployment remains at its natural rate of 6 percent.

inflation rate of 10 percent a year is anticipated, so unemployment is at its natural rate, 6 percent of the labor force.

Next year, aggregate demand is *expected* to increase and the aggregate demand curve in Fig. 35.9(a) is expected to shift rightward from AD_0 to AD_1. In expectation of this increase in aggregate demand, wages increase to shift the short-run aggregate supply curve from SAS_0 to SAS_1. If expectations are fulfilled, the GDP deflator rises to 121—a 10 percent inflation—and real GDP remains at potential GDP. In part (b), the economy remains at its original position—unemployment is at the natural rate, and the inflation rate is 10 percent a year.

Now suppose that no one is expecting the Fed to change its policy, but the Fed actually tries to slow

inflation. It raises interest rates and slows money growth. Aggregate demand growth slows, and the aggregate demand curve (in part a) shifts rightward from AD_0 not to AD_1, as people expect, but only to AD_2.

With no change in the expected inflation rate, wage rates rise by the same amount as before and the short-run aggregate supply curve shifts leftward from SAS_0 to SAS_1. Real GDP decreases to $6.5 trillion, and the GDP deflator rises to 118.8—an inflation rate of 8 percent a year. In Fig. 35.9(b), the economy moves along the short-run Phillips curve $SRPC_0$ as unemployment rises to 9 percent and inflation falls to 8 percent a year. The Fed's policy has succeeded in slowing inflation but at the cost of recession. Real GDP is below potential GDP, and unemployment is above its natural rate.

A Credible Announced Inflation Reduction   Suppose that instead of simply slowing down the growth of aggregate demand, the Fed announces its intention ahead of its action and in a credible and convincing way so that its announcement is believed. That is, the Fed's policy is anticipated. Because the lower level of aggregate demand is expected, wages increase at a pace consistent with the lower level of aggregate demand. The short-run aggregate supply curve (in Fig. 35.9a) shifts leftward from SAS_0 but only to SAS_2. Aggregate demand increases by the amount expected, and the aggregate demand curve shifts from AD_0 to AD_2. The GDP deflator rises to 115.5—an inflation rate of 5 percent a year—and real GDP remains at potential GDP.

In Fig. 35.9(b), the lower expected inflation rate shifts the short-run Phillips curve downward to $SRPC_1$, and inflation falls to 5 percent a year, while unemployment remains at its natural rate of 6 percent.

A credible announced inflation reduction lowers inflation but with no accompanying loss of output or increase in unemployment.

Inflation Reduction in Practice

When the Fed in fact slowed inflation in 1981, we paid a high price. The Fed's policy action was unpredicted. It occurred in the face of wages that had been set at too high a level to be consistent with the growth of aggregate demand that the Fed subsequently allowed. The consequence was recession—a decrease in real GDP and a rise in unemployment. Could the Fed have lowered inflation without causing recession by telling people far enough ahead of time that it did indeed plan to lower inflation?

The answer appears to be no. The main reason is that people expect the Fed to behave in line with its record, not with its stated intentions. How many times have you told yourself that it is your firm intention to take off 10 unwanted pounds or to keep within your budget and put a few dollars away for a rainy day, only to discover that, despite your very best intentions, your old habits win out in the end?

To form expectations of the Fed's actions, people look at the Fed's past *actions*, not its stated intentions. On the basis of such observations—called Fed-watching—they try to work out what the Fed's policy is, to forecast its future actions, and to forecast the effects of those actions on aggregate demand and inflation. The Greenspan Fed, like the Volcker Fed that preceded it, has built a reputation for being anti-inflationary. That reputation is valuable because it helps the Fed to contain inflation and lowers the cost of eliminating inflation if it temporarily returns. The reason is that with a low expected inflation rate, the short-run Phillips curve is in a favorable position (like $SRPC_1$ in Fig. 35.9b). The Fed's actions during the 1990s have been designed to keep inflation expectations low and prevent the gains made during the 1980s recession from being eroded.

A Truly Independent Fed

A radical suggestion for strengthening the Fed's reputation as the guardian of price stability is to make the Fed more independent of government and to charge it with the single responsibility of achieving and maintaining price level stability. Some central banks are more independent than the Fed. The German and Swiss central banks are the best examples. Another example is the New Zealand central bank. All these central banks have the responsibility of stabilizing prices but not real GDP and of pursuing their objective without interference from the government. Recent research on central bank performance has strengthened the view that a more independent central bank can deliver a lower average inflation rate without creating either a higher unemployment rate or a lower real GDP growth rate.

R E V I E W   Q U I Z

- Why does a fixed rule provide more effective protection against a cost-push inflation than a feedback rule?
- Why does a recession usually result as inflation is being tamed?
- How does establishing a reputation of being an inflation fighter improve the Fed's ability to maintain low inflation and to lower the cost of fighting inflation?

◆ *Reading Between the Lines* on pp. 810–811 looks at the challenges the Fed faced in 1999 as it sought to keep the economy expanding but avoid renewed inflation.

You've now completed your study of macroeconomics. In the remaining chapters, we shift our focus to the international economy.

A Feedback Rule?

B A R R O N ' S   O N L I N E ,   April 12, 1999

The Fed Catches On

By John Liscio

At this stage of the economic expansion, a few things should be abundantly clear. First and foremost, inflation is simply not a threat. Look at any measure of it that tickles your fancy and the message is the same: Cost-push inflation sleeps with the fishes. ...

Productive investment in technology has eased capacity constraints and alleviated upward pressure on wage growth. It's a brave new world out there; and now even the Fed is warming up to it.

NO COST PUSH – NOT EVEN A GENTLE SHOVE

Capacity Utilization (Left scale)

Hourly Earnings (Right scale)

86% ... 4.5%
84 ... 4.0
82 ... 3.5
80 ... 3.0
78 ... 2.5 ... 2.0

1/94 7/94 1/95 7/95 1/96 7/96 1/97 7/97 1/98 7/98 1/99

BARRON'S/Briefing.com

...

Here is just a small taste of the Fed of the Future (from the minutes of the FOMC's February confab):

"With regard to the outlook for inflation, the members saw no evidence of accelerating price inflation despite high levels of business activity and very tight labor markets across most of the nation. Indeed, the conjuncture over an extended period of strong economic growth, very low rates of unemployment, and the absence of any buildup of inflation could not be explained in terms of normal historical relationships. While temporary factors, such as declining oil prices, had played a role in depressing inflation, the persistence of very low inflation under these conditions most likely also resulted from more lasting changes in economic relationships."...

By accepting these new economic relationships, Fed officials are making it clear that they will not raise rates until and unless inflation actually picks up. We have long been arguing that there will be no preemptive tightening, as the Fed no longer has any confidence that there is anything to preempt.

Essence of the Story

■ Inflation is not a threat in the United States.

■ The Fed says that there is "no evidence of accelerating price inflation despite high levels of business activity and very tight labor markets."

■ The Fed believes that there is a new relationship between inflation and unemployment.

■ The Fed will not raise interest rates until and unless inflation actually increases.

■ The Fed will not tighten monetary policy in anticipation of increased inflation because the Fed does not foresee inflation increasing.

Economic Analysis

■ This article argues that inflation is dead, that the economy is governed by new relationships, and that the Fed should not and likely will not act to raise interest rates in anticipation of renewed inflation but instead will wait until the inflation rate actually increases.

■ Waiting until the inflation rate increases and then reacting to it is an example of a feed-back-rule policy.

■ The belief that the economy is governed by new relationships is a belief that the growth rate of potential GDP has increased and that the natural rate of unemployment has decreased.

■ Both the growth rate of potential GDP and the natural unemployment rate change from time to time. The growth rate decreased and the natural rate increased during the 1970s. The growth rate increased and the natural rate decreased during the 1990s.

■ To pursue a feedback-rule policy, the Fed must estimate the growth rate of potential GDP so that it can estimate the position of the long-run aggregate supply curve.

■ Figure 1 shows how the economy will behave in 1999 if the Fed gets things right.

■ The Fed expects potential GDP to be $7.7 trillion. The long-run aggregate supply curve is expected to be LAS_{99}, and the short-run aggregate supply curve is expected to be SAS_{99}. The Fed holds interest rates steady and expects the aggregate demand curve to be AD_{99}.

■ If all these expectations are correct, real GDP increases and equals potential GDP and the price level rises, but at roughly the same rate as in 1998.

■ Figure 2 shows what happens in 1999 if the Fed gets potential GDP wrong. Here, potential GDP remains at $7.6 trillion.

■ The aggregate demand curve is AD_0, and the short-run aggregate supply curve is SAS_0. Initially, real GDP increases to $7.7 trillion and there is an inflationary gap.

■ Wage rates now begin to rise, and the SAS curve starts to shift left-ward. Inflation increases as the price level rises, and real GDP decreases.

■ Now that inflation has taken off, the Fed tight-ens its monetary policy by raising interest rates. Aggregate demand decreases, and the AD curve shifts leftward to AD_1. The Fed's action

limits inflation. The price level rises to 116 rather than 117. But the economy goes into recession.

■ Some economists believe that the scene just described will occur because the Fed has per-mitted the quantity of money to grow too quickly during 1998 and early 1999.

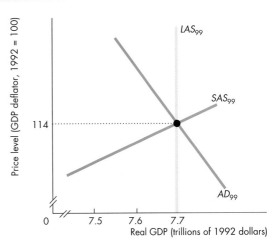

Figure 1 **The Fed gets it right**

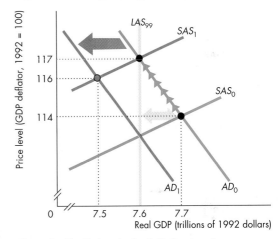

Figure 2 **The Fed waits for inflation to return**

811

SUMMARY

KEY POINTS

Policy Goals (pp. 792–793)

- The goals of macroeconomic policy are to achieve the highest sustainable rate of long-term real GDP growth, smooth unavoidable business cycle fluctuations, maintain low unemployment, and avoid inflation.

Policy Tools and Performance (pp. 794–796)

- Fiscal policy was expansionary during the Kennedy years, the late 1960s and early 1970s, and the early Reagan 1980s. It was contractionary during the Carter, later Reagan, and Clinton years.
- The M2 growth rate increased during the 1970s, peaked in 1976, and then fell.

Long-Term Growth Policy (pp. 796–798)

- Policies to increase the long-term growth rate focus on increasing saving and investment in human capital and new technologies.
- To increase the saving rate, government saving must increase or incentives for private saving must be strengthened by increasing after-tax returns.
- Human capital investment might be increased with improved education and by improving on-the-job training programs.
- Investment in new technologies can be encouraged by tax incentives.

Business Cycle and Unemployment Policy (pp. 799–805)

- In the face of an aggregate demand shock, a fixed-rule policy takes no action. Real GDP and the price level fluctuate.
- In the face of an aggregate demand shock, a feedback-rule policy takes offsetting fiscal and monetary action. An ideal feedback rule keeps the economy at full employment, with stable prices.
- Some economists say that a feedback rule creates fluctuations because it requires greater knowledge of the economy than we have, operates with time

lags that extend beyond the forecast horizon, and introduces unpredictability about policy reactions.

- In the face of a productivity growth slowdown, both rules have the same effect on output. A feedback rule brings a higher inflation rate than a fixed rule does.
- Nominal GDP targeting might avoid the extremes of inflation and recession.

Inflation Policy (pp. 806–809)

- A fixed rule minimizes the threat of cost-push inflation. A feedback rule validates cost-push inflation and leaves the price level and inflation rate free to move to wherever they are pushed.
- Inflation can be tamed, at little or no cost in terms of lost output or excessive unemployment, by slowing the growth of aggregate demand in a credible and predictable way. But usually, when inflation is slowed down, a recession occurs.

KEY FIGURES

KEY TERMS

PROBLEMS

*1. A productivity growth slowdown has occurred. Explain its possible origins and describe a policy package that is designed to speed up growth again.

2. A nation is experiencing a falling saving rate. Explain its possible origins and describe a policy package that is designed to increase the saving rate.

*3. The economy shown in the figure is initially on aggregate demand curve AD_0 and short-run aggregate supply curve SAS_0. Then aggregate demand decreases and the aggregate demand curve shifts leftward to AD_1.

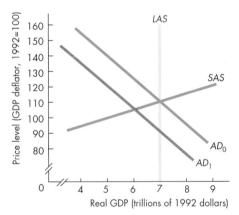

a. What are the initial equilibrium real GDP and price level?

b. If the decrease in aggregate demand is temporary and the government follows a fixed-rule fiscal policy, what happens to real GDP and the price level? Trace the immediate effects and the adjustment as aggregate demand returns to its original level.

c. If the decrease in aggregate demand is temporary and the government follows a feedback-rule fiscal policy, what happens to real GDP and the price level? Trace the immediate effects and the adjustment as aggregate demand returns to its original level.

d. If the decrease in aggregate demand is permanent and the government follows a fixed-rule fiscal policy, what happens to real GDP and the price level?

e. If the decrease in aggregate demand is permanent and the government follows a feedback-rule fiscal policy, what happens to real GDP and the price level?

4. The economy shown in the figure is initially on aggregate demand curve AD_0 and short-run aggregate supply curve SAS_0. Then short-run aggregate supply decreases and the short-run aggregate supply curve shifts leftward to SAS_1.

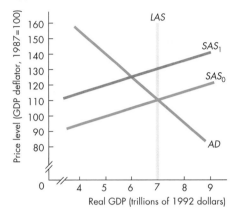

a. What are the initial equilibrium real GDP and price level?

b. What type of event could have caused the decrease in short-run aggregate supply?

c. If the government follows a fixed-rule monetary policy, what happens to real GDP and the price level? Trace the immediate effects and the adjustment as aggregate demand and short-run aggregate supply return to its original level.

d. If the government follows a feedback-rule monetary policy, what happens to real GDP and the price level? Trace the immediate effects and the adjustment as aggregate demand and short-run aggregate supply respond to the policy action.

*5. The economy is experiencing 10 percent inflation and 7 percent unemployment. Real GDP growth has sagged to 1 percent a year. The stock market has crashed.

a. Explain how the economy might have gotten into its current state.

b. Set out policies for the Fed and Congress to pursue that will lower inflation, lower unemployment, and speed real GDP growth.

c. Explain how and why your proposed policies will work.

6. The inflation rate has fallen to less than 1 percent a year, and the unemployment rate has fallen to less then 4 percent. Real GDP is growing at almost 5 percent a year. The stock market is at a record high.

a. Explain how the economy might have gotten into its current state.

b. Set out policies for the Fed and Congress to pursue that will lower inflation, lower unemployment, and speed real GDP growth.

c. Explain how and why your proposed policies will work.

*7. When the economies of Indonesia, Korea, Thailand, Malaya, and the Philippines entered into recession in 1997, the International Monetary Fund (IMF) made loans but only on condition that the recipients of the loans increased interest rates, raised taxes, and cut government expenditures.

a. Would you describe the IMF prescription as a feedback-rule policy or a fixed-rule policy?

b. What do you predict the effects of the IMF policies would be?

c. Do you have any criticisms of the IMF polices? What would you have required these countries to do? Why?

8. As the U.S. economy continued to expand and its stock market soared to new record levels during 1998, the Fed cut interest rates.

a. Would you describe the Fed's actions as a feedback-rule policy or a fixed-rule policy?

b. What do you predict the effects of the Fed's policies would be?

c. Do you have any criticisms of the Fed's polices? What monetary policy would you have pursued? Why?

CRITICAL THINKING

1. Study *Reading Between the Lines* on pp. 810–811 and then:

a. Describe the challenge faced by the Fed and explain why the challenge was particularly interesting during 1999.

b. In what state is the economy when the inflation rate increases?

c. What signs would you look for to determine whether inflation was about to take off?

d. What in your opinion does the Fed's challenge of 1999 tell us about the relative merits of a fixed-rule monetary policy and a feedback-rule monetary policy?

2. The economy is booming and inflation is beginning to rise, but it is widely agreed that a massive recession is just around the corner. Provide Congress with testimony that summarizes your opinion on whether a fixed-rule policy or a feedback-rule policy is better able to deal with the situation.

3. The economy is in a recession, and inflation is falling. It is widely agreed that a strong recovery is just around the corner. Provide the Fed with a memorandum that summarizes your opinion on whether a fixed-rule policy or a feedback-rule policy is better able to deal with the situation.

4. You have been hired to draw up an economic plan that will maximize the chance that the President will be re-elected.

a. What are the macroeconomic stabilization policy elements in that plan?

b. What do you have to make the economy do in an election year?

c. What policy actions would help the President achieve re-election?

(In dealing with this problem, be careful to take into account the effects of your proposed policy on expectations and the effects of those expectations on actual economic performance.)

 5. Use the link on the Parkin Web site to obtain the latest *Economic Report of the President*. Review Chapter 2 on Macroeconomic Policy and Performance. Write a summary and critique of this chapter.

Boom and Bust

To cure a disease, doctors must first understand how the disease responds to different treatments. It helps to understand the mechanisms that operate to cause the disease, but sometimes, a workable cure can be found even before the full story of the causes has been told. ◆ Curing economic ills is similar to curing our medical ills. We need to understand how the economy responds to the treatments we might prescribe for it. And sometimes, we want to try a cure even though we don't fully understand the reasons for the problem we're trying to control. ◆ You've seen how the pace of capital accumulation and technological change determine the long-term growth trend. You've learned how fluctuations around the long-term trend can be generated by changes in aggregate demand and aggregate supply. And you've learned about the key sources of fluctuations in aggregate demand and aggregate supply. ◆ The two chapters in this part have built on everything you've studied in macroeconomics. The central tool they use is the *AS-AD* model. But they use it to explain the big picture or grand vision that different schools of thought hold concerning the way the economy operates and what is important. ◆ In Chapter 34, we learned about alternative visions of the business cycle. All of these visions can be translated into the *AS-AD* model. And doing so helps us to compare and contrast the competing visions. But one

theory of the cycle, the new *real business cycle (RBC)* theory, is more at home with the demand and supply model of microeconomics (Chapter 4) than the *AS-AD* model. Most economists have not embraced the real business cycle approach. It is an extreme view. But the method that real business cycle theory uses is here to stay. This method is to build a (mathematical) model of the entire economy and then see, in a computer simulation, what kind of cycle the model creates. The economy on the computer is then calibrated to the real economy, and the cycles are compared. The computer model can be treated with a variety of "medications" and their effects observed. This new style of business cycle research cannot be explained in detail without using advanced mathematical ideas. But Chapter 33 explained the economics that underlies it and showed you the type of model that real business cycle theorists use. ◆ Chapter 34 described the policy debate and explained the alternative approaches that have been proposed to speed growth, smooth the business cycle, and contain inflation. Again, the *AS-AD* model was the workhorse that was used to compare the effects of alternative policy strategies. ◆ The economist you're going to meet on the following page, Irving Fisher, developed ideas about business cycles that have never been in the mainstream but that are becoming fashionable today. Frederic S. Mishkin has helped to refine modern business cycle theory and has worked as the senior research economist at the New York Fed.

815

The Economist

Irving Fisher *(1867-1947)*

ranks among the greatest American-born economists. The son of a Congregational minister who died as Irving was finishing high school, he paid his way through Yale and earned enough to keep his mother and younger brother by tutoring his fellow students.

Irving Fisher came to economics by way of mathematics. He was Yale's first Ph.D. student in pure economics, but in the math department!

The contributions that Fisher made to economics cover the entire subject. He is best known for his work on the quantity theory of money (Chapter 31, pp. 701–704) and the relation between interest rates and inflation (Chapter 33, pp. 750–751). But he also wrote on the business cycle. He believed that the Great Depression was caused because the fall in the price level increased the real burden of debts. He wrote from experience. He had borrowed heavily to buy stocks in the rising market of the late 1920s and lost a fortune of perhaps 10 million dollars in the crash of 1929.

"…in the great booms and depressions, … the two big bad actors are debt disturbances and price level disturbances."

IRVING FISHER
"*The Debt Deflation Theory of Depressions*"
ECONOMETRICA, 1933

The Issues

Economic activity has fluctuated between boom and bust for as long as we've had records. And understanding the sources of economic fluctuations has turned out to be difficult. One reason is that there are no simple patterns. Every new episode of the business cycle is different from its predecessor in some way. Some cycles are long and some short, some are mild and some severe, some begin in the United States and some abroad. We never know with any certainty when the next turning point (down or up) is coming or what will cause it. A second reason is that the apparent waste of resources during a recession or a depression seems to contradict the very foundation of economics: Resources are limited and people have unlimited wants—there is scarcity. A satisfactory theory of the business cycle must explain why scarce resources don't *always* get fully employed.

One theory is that recessions result from insufficient aggregate demand. The solution is to increase government spending, cut taxes, and cut interest rates. But demand stimulation must not be overdone. Countries that stimulate aggregate demand too much, such as the Brazil, find their economic growth rates sagging, unemployment rising, and inflation accelerating.

Today's new theory, real business cycle theory, predicts that fluctuations in aggregate demand have *no* effect on output and employment and change only the price level and inflation rate. But this theory ignores the *real* effects of financial collapse of the type that occurred in the 1930s. If banks fail on a large scale and people lose their wealth, other firms also begin to fail and jobs are destroyed. Unemployed people cut their spending, and output falls yet further. Demand stimulation might not be called for, but action to ensure that sound banks survive certainly is.

While economists are trying to understand the sources of the business cycle, the government and the Fed are doing the best they can to moderate the cycle. In the years since World War II, there appears to have been some success. Although the business cycle has not disappeared, it has become much less severe.

Then

What happens to the economy when people lose confidence in banks? They withdraw their funds. These withdrawals feed on themselves, creating a snowball of withdrawals and, eventually, panic. Short of funds with which to repay depositors, banks call in loans and previously sound businesses are faced with financial distress. They close down and lay off workers. And recession deepens and turns into depression. Bank failures and the resulting decline in the nation's supply of money and credit were a significant factor in deepening and prolonging the Great Depression. But they taught us the importance of stable financial institutions and gave rise to the establishment of federal deposit insurance to prevent future financial collapse.

Now

How can a building designed as a shop have no better use than to be boarded up and left empty? Not enough aggregate demand, say the Keynesians. Not so, say the real business cycle theorists. Technological change has reduced the building's current productivity as a shop to zero. But its expected future productivity is sufficiently high that it is not efficient to refit the building for some other purpose.

All unemployment, whether of buildings or people, can be explained in a similar way. For example, how can it be that during a recession, a person trained as a shop clerk is without work? Not enough aggregate demand is one answer. Another is that the current productivity of shop clerks is low but their expected future productivity is sufficiently high that it does not pay an unemployed clerk to retrain for a job that is currently available.

It is now almost 70 years since the Great Depression. Although we've had many recessions since then, none of them compare with the severity of that event. Some credit for avoiding another major depression must go to the Federal Reserve Board and the monetary policy it has pursued. Next you can meet Professor Frederic Mishkin of Columbia University and former vice-president and director of research at the Federal Reserve Bank of New York.

Frederic S. Mishkin

Frederic S. Mishkin

is the A. Barton Hepburn Professor of Economics in the Graduate School of Business at Columbia University. Professor Mishkin was born in New York City in 1951. He received his Ph.D. from MIT in 1976 and has taught at the University of Chicago, Northwestern University, Princeton University, and Columbia University. He has served as an executive vice-president and director of research at the Federal Reserve Bank of New York. Professor Mishkin's research focuses on monetary policy and its impact on financial markets and the aggregate economy. Michael Parkin talked with Professor Mishkin about his work, the role the Fed plays in monetary policy, and the legacy of Irving Fisher.

Why are you an economist?
The Great Depression was the most important event in my father's life, and we talked about it continually at the dinner table. We also talked about the stock market. These discussions piqued my interest in economics. When I went to college, I thought of becoming a physicist, but I realized that economics has many of same attributes. Both disciplines demand thinking logically and are consistently based on models. The real-world problems that were implicit

in the study of economics proved much more interesting to me then. I realized that economics was my calling, and in fact, it was one of the best choices I've ever made.

What are the most basic principles that you find yourself repeatedly returning to in your professional life, and especially in your life as the director of research at the New York Fed.
A key principle is that incentives are everything. Particularly in today's world, where you need creativity, you cannot motivate people to do good research by just commanding them. You instead need to motivate them by saying, "Do your own work, figure it out yourself, but, on the other hand, I'm going to give you the right incentives." A second principle is the concept of backward induction. If you think about where you want to be and work backwards, you are frequently way ahead of the game. Not only are these two concepts extremely useful in thinking about real-world economic problems, they've been absolutely invaluable to me in managing the Fed's research group of 150 people. We have an annual evaluation process followed by a salary review, and promotions are determined by how well people are doing and how well they respond to incentives.

Does the work of Federal Reserve banks directly contribute to the quality of the monetary policy that is developed?
In economics we never really have answers, but we are able to understand things better through research that initiates debate and makes good policy outcomes more likely. Many of the new

ideas that are published in the academic journals have helped to guide policy makers. I have stressed the value of basic research here at the Federal Reserve Bank of New York and have emphasized our need to be at the very frontier of ideas. We also have to make decisions from day to day that involves much more nitty-gritty research. For example, we have to forecast the economy and try to understand what's going on in the inflation process.

We are enjoying one of longest uninterrupted recoveries in U.S. economic history, and there's little sign of either serious inflation or a serious recession. To what do you attribute this successful run? What part do you think the Fed can take credit for, and where else would you allocate credit, if anywhere?
There's a fair amount of credit due to the Fed, but I'm going to use an adage that my mother always said to me, "It's better to be lucky than good, but it's even better to be good and lucky." The Fed has been both good and lucky. The "good" part is that the Fed has acted in accordance with the results of economic research that indicates that good monetary policy is forward looking. There are lags from monetary policy to inflation on the order of two to three years. This indicates that monetary policy actions today have little effect on today's inflation but are highly relevant to what will happen to

future inflation. We must look to the future if we are to promote a stable economic environment in which we have very low inflation. In February 1994, when the Fed started to raise interest rates, unemployment was close to the 7 percent range and inflation pressures were nonexistent. Yet, looking several years down the road, we realized that if we did not start to raise interest rates and tighten monetary policy, then we would eventually have an overheated

economy with inflation out of control. The preemptive policy of raising interest rates was extremely successful because it helped the inflation rate to stay very low, and the economy continued to grow at a sustainable pace. Another benefit of pursuing a preemptive policy is that markets and businesses understand that the central bank will be serious about controlling inflation. That produces a much more stable environment because businesses know they can't solve their problems by just raising prices. Instead, they have to be efficient and keep costs low. The Fed has also been "lucky." Even if the Fed is doing the right thing during a business cycle expansion, there may be a tendency for the economy to overheat a little bit and a little bit of inflation to occur. This has not happened. The economy is about as good as it can get, and that requires not only good policy but also some luck.

The traditional categories for discussing policy involve terms such as *rules*, *discretion*, and *fixed rules* versus *feedback rules*. Is that language of use in thinking about Fed policy?
I think that there's a problem with the dichotomy between rules and discretion. One part of the literature views rules as being critical to solving problems such as time inconsistency. Trying to do what looks good right now but not worrying about the future may result in a sequence of policies that lead to poor outcomes in the long run. You have to avoid the temptation to do what looks like the right thing today and ignore the long run. That's one of the reasons why people feel that rules are important. On the other hand, the criticism of rules is that they are too rigid, particularly for dealing with unexpected events. Rules can, in that situation, lead to a very bad outcome. An alternative is to pursue a policy that is basically constrained discretion. It's rulelike, but without a rigid rule. For example, inflation-targeting regimes that have been pursued in many countries throughout the world in recent years are neither a rule nor discretion. They are, instead, constrained discretion. My view is that a good monetary policy should always be rulelike; but, on the other hand, the idea of putting in fixed rules is probably not a good idea.

For the past 15 years the real business cycle research agenda has downplayed the role of money. How do you evaluate the recent real business cycle research program?

The real business cycle literature takes the view that monetary policy is not important to the actual short-term business cycle. I think that monetary policy is more important to the business cycle than real business cycle models give credit for. There is evidence that monetary policy has been important. For example, during the early 1980s, the Federal Reserve took very active steps to get inflation under control and the result was a quite severe recession, but eventually the tight monetary policy produced the right outcome, which was low inflation. I would also characterize the Great Depression as a period where monetary policy performed very poorly and contributed to the most severe economic contraction in the U.S. history. I think monetary policy actions were extremely important during that episode and extremely important during the period 1980 to 1982. On the other hand, real business cycle literature points out that the degree of control that monetary policy authorities can exert on the business cycle is indeed limited, and I am quite sympathetic to this view. The idea that the monetary authorities are able to tweak the business cycle at every turn is just not correct because the actual degree of certainty as to what will happen as a result of certain monetary policy actions is by no

means clear. The real business cycle literature has made people aware that monetary policy cannot be fully in control of what happens in the business cycle. On the other hand, I think that it's overstretching to say that monetary policy actions don't have real effects.

How can students help themselves to be more able to address interesting, real problems?

It is critical to get students to apply what they learn in class to their everyday lives. I tell my students that they must be reading newspapers such as *The Wall Street Journal*, *The Financial Times*, or *The New York Times* for business and financial news. I also tell students that they actually can use economic principles such as adverse selection and moral hazard to solve real-world problems every day. For example, if somebody's a rich person and is thinking about getting married, he or she faces an adverse selection problem: Does the other person love me because I'm wealthy rather than because I'm a lovable person?

In addition to managing the research group, I participate in the management committee of the bank. I've been able to actively contribute to the management of this bank because I can use economic principles to discuss what I think would be sensible solutions to problems. Economics is wonderful training for being able to solve many problems that hit you every day.

What, for you, is the legacy of Irving Fisher?

Irving Fisher is one of the extraordinary American economists. He's famous for the quantity theory of money, which is extremely useful in thinking about the importance of money to the economy. He was a pioneer whose work on interest rates is still valuable today in thinking about how to conduct monetary policy. He also did pathbreaking work for which he was not famous. For example, his paper "The Debt Deflation Theory of the Great Depression" has led to a much better understanding of financial crises in today's world.

What can an undergraduate gain from taking an economics course?

Economics is an important part of a liberal arts education and is essential for law and MBA students. For the first time in my life, I've actually been a manager, and one of the things that is really striking is how useful economic concepts have been to helping me to be effective. I now can go back to my MBA students and show them that many of these concepts are ones that I actually used in practice to make me a better manager.

Economics is not only useful in helping people become professionals, but also extremely useful in terms of making them better educated citizens. Yes, I do want to train people to help them be successful directly in their careers, but I also want to make them more successful, generally, as people. I think economics is a very powerful tool in achieving that.

Chapter 36

Trading with the World

Since ancient times, people have expanded their trading as far as technology allowed. Marco Polo opened up the silk route between Europe and China in the thirteenth century. Today, container ships laden with cars and machines and Boeing 747s stuffed with farm-fresh foods ply sea and air routes, carrying billions of dollars worth of goods. Why do people go to such great lengths to trade with those in other nations? ◆ Low-wage Mexico has entered into a free trade agreement with high-wage Canada and the United States—the North American Free Trade Agreement, or NAFTA. According to Texas billionaire Ross Perot, this agreement has caused a "giant sucking sound" and transferred jobs from Michigan to Mexico. Is Ross Perot right? How can we compete with a country that pays its workers a fraction of U.S. wages? Are there any industries, besides perhaps the Hollywood movie industry, in which we have an advantage? ◆ In 1930, Congress passed the Smoot-Hawley Act, which imposed a 45 percent tariff (rising to 60 percent by 1933) on one third of U.S. imports. This move provoked widespread retaliation and a tariff war among the world's major trading countries. After World War II, a process of trade liberalization brought about a gradual reduction of tariffs. What are the effects of tariffs on international trade? Why don't we have completely unrestricted international trade?

Silk Routes and Sucking Sounds

◆ In this chapter, we're going to learn about international trade. We'll discover how all nations can gain by specializing in producing the goods and services in which they have a comparative advantage and trading with other countries. We'll discover that *all* countries can compete, no matter how high their wages. We'll also explain why countries restrict trade.

After studying this chapter, you will be able to:

■ Describe the patterns in international trade

■ Explain comparative advantage and explain why all countries can gain from international trade

■ Explain how economies of scale and diversity of taste lead to gains from trade

■ Explain why trade restrictions reduce our imports, exports, and consumption possibilities

■ Explain the arguments used to justify trade restrictions and show how they are flawed

■ Explain why we have trade restrictions

Patterns and Trends in International Trade

THE GOODS AND SERVICES THAT WE BUY FROM people in other countries are called **imports**. The goods and services that we sell to people in other countries are called **exports**. What are the most important things that we import and export? Most people would probably guess that a rich nation such as the United States imports raw materials and exports manufactured goods. Although that is one feature of U.S. international trade, it is not its most important feature. The vast bulk of our exports *and* imports is manufactured goods. We sell foreigners earth-moving equipment, airplanes, supercomputers, and scientific equipment, and we buy televisions, VCRs, blue jeans, and T-shirts from them. Also, we are a major exporter of agricultural products and raw materials. We also import and export a huge volume of services.

Trade in Goods

Manufactured goods account for 50 percent of our exports and for 60 percent of our imports. Industrial materials (raw materials and semimanufactured items) account for 17 percent of our exports and for 20 percent of our imports, and agricultural products account for only 7 percent of our exports and 3 percent of our imports. Our largest individual export and import items are capital goods and autos.

But goods account for only 74 percent of our exports and 83 percent of our imports. The rest of our international trade is in services.

Trade in Services

You may be wondering how a country can "export" and "import" services. Here are some examples.

If you take a vacation in France and travel there on an Air France flight from New York, you import transportation services from France. The money you spend in France on hotel bills and restaurant meals is also a U.S. import of services. Similarly, the vacation taken by a French student in the United States counts as an U.S. export of services to France.

When we import TV sets from South Korea, the owner of the ship that transports them might be Greek and the company that insures them might be British. The payments that we make for the transportation

and insurance are U.S. imports of services. Similarly, when an American shipping company transports California wine to Tokyo, the transportation cost is an American export of a service to Japan. Our international trade in these types of services is large and growing.

Geographical Patterns

The United States has trading links with every part of the world, but Canada is our biggest single trading partner for both exports and imports. We buy 45 percent of our imports from Japan and other Asian countries such as China, Hong Kong, South Korea, and Taiwan, and we sell a similar percentage of our exports to Asia, Europe, Latin America, and Canada.

Trends in the Volume of Trade

In 1960, we exported less than 5 percent of total output and imported 4 1/2 percent of the goods and services that we bought. In 1998, we exported 11 percent of total output and imported 13 percent of the goods and services that we bought.

On the export side, capital goods, automobiles, food, and raw materials have remained large items and held a roughly constant share of total exports, but the composition of imports has changed. Food and raw material imports have fallen steadily. Imports of fuel increased dramatically during the 1970s but fell during the 1980s. Imports of machinery have grown, and today they approach 50 percent of total imports.

Balance of Trade and International Borrowing

The value of exports minus the value of imports is called the **balance of trade.** In 1998, the U.S. balance of trade was a negative $170 billion. Our imports were $170 billion more than our exports. When we import more than we export, as we did in 1998, we borrow from foreigners or sell some of our assets. When we export more than we import, we make loans to foreigners or buy some of their assets.

We study the *balance* of trade in Chapter 37. In this chapter, our goal is to understand the factors that influence the *volume* and *directions* of international trade rather than its balance. And the keys to this understanding are the concepts of opportunity cost and comparative advantage.

Opportunity Cost and Comparative Advantage

THE FUNDAMENTAL FORCE THAT GENERATES international trade is *comparative advantage*. And the basis of comparative advantage is divergent *opportunity costs*. You met these ideas in Chapter 3, when we learned about the gains from specialization and exchange between Tom and Nancy.

Tom and Nancy each specialize in producing just one good and then trade with each other. Most nations do not go to the extreme of specializing in a single good and importing everything else. Nonetheless, nations can increase the consumption of all goods if they redirect their scarce resources toward the production of those goods and services in which they have a comparative advantage.

To see how this outcome occurs, we'll apply the same basic ideas we learned in the case of Tom and Nancy to trade among nations. We'll begin by recalling how we can use the production possibility frontier to measure opportunity cost. Then we'll see how divergent opportunity costs bring comparative advantage and gains from trade for countries as well as for individuals even though no country completely specializes in the production of just one good.

Opportunity Cost in Farmland

Farmland (a fictitious country) can produce grain and cars at any point inside or along its production possibility frontier, *PPF*, shown in Fig. 36.1. (We're holding constant the output of all the other goods that Farmland produces.) The Farmers (the people of Farmland) are consuming all the grain and cars that they produce, and they are operating at point *a* in the figure. That is, Farmland is producing and consuming 15 billion bushels of grain and 8 million cars each year. What is the opportunity cost of a car in Farmland?

We can answer that question by calculating the slope of the production possibility frontier at point *a*. The magnitude of the slope of the frontier measures the opportunity cost of one good in terms of the other. To measure the slope of the frontier at point *a*, place a straight line tangential to the frontier at point *a* and calculate the slope of that straight line. Recall that the formula for the slope of a line is the change in the value of the variable measured on the *y*-axis divided by the change in the value of the variable measured on the *x*-axis as we move along the line.

Here, the variable measured on the *y*-axis is billions of bushels of grain, and the variable measured on the *x*-axis is millions of cars. So the slope is the change in the number of bushels of grain divided by the change in the number of cars.

As you can see from the red triangle at point *a* in the figure, if the number of cars produced increases by 2 million, grain production decreases by 18 billion bushels. Therefore the magnitude of the slope is 18 billion divided by 2 million, which equals 9,000. To get one more car, the people of Farmland must give up 9,000 bushels of grain. Thus the opportunity cost of 1 car is 9,000 bushels of grain. Equivalently, 9,000 bushels of grain cost 1 car. For the people of Farmland, these opportunity costs are the prices they face. The price of a car is 9,000 bushels of grain, and the price of 9,000 bushels of grain is 1 car.

FIGURE 36.1

Opportunity Cost in Farmland

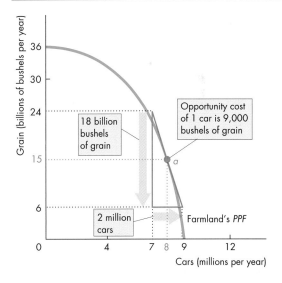

Farmland produces and consumes 15 billion bushels of grain and 8 million cars a year. That is, it produces and consumes at point *a* on its production possibility frontier. Opportunity cost is equal to the magnitude of the slope of the production possibility frontier. The red triangle tells us that at point *a*, 18 billion bushels of grain must be forgone to get 2 million cars. That is, at point *a*, 2 million cars cost 18 billion bushels of grain. Equivalently, 1 car costs 9,000 bushels of grain or 9,000 bushels cost 1 car.

Opportunity Cost in Mobilia

Figure 36.2 shows the production possibility frontier of Mobilia (another fictitious country). Like the Farmers, the Mobilians consume all the grain and cars that they produce. Mobilia consumes 18 billion bushels of grain a year and 4 million cars, at point a'.

Let's calculate the opportunity costs in Mobilia. At point a', the opportunity cost of a car is equal to the magnitude of the slope of the red line tangential to the production possibility frontier, *PPF*. You can see from the red triangle that the magnitude of the slope of Mobilia's production possibility frontier is 6 billion bushels of grain divided by 6 million cars, which equals 1,000 bushels of grain per car. To get one more car, the Mobilians must give up 1,000 bushels of grain. Thus the opportunity cost of 1 car is 1,000 bushels of grain, or, equivalently, the opportunity cost of 1,000 bushels of grain is 1 car. These are the prices faced in Mobilia.

FIGURE 36.2

Opportunity Cost in Mobilia

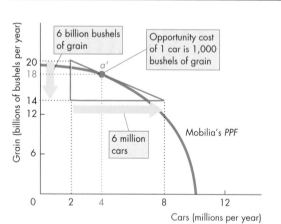

Mobilia produces and consumes 18 billion bushels of grain and 4 million cars a year. That is, it produces and consumes at point a' on its production possibility frontier. Opportunity cost is equal to the magnitude of the slope of the production possibility frontier. The red triangle tells us that at point a', 6 billion bushels of grain must be forgone to get 6 million cars. That is, at point a', the opportunity cost of 6 million cars is 6 billion bushels of grain. Equivalently, 1 car costs 1,000 bushels of grain or 1,000 bushels of grain cost 1 car.

Comparative Advantage

Cars are cheaper in Mobilia than in Farmland. One car costs 9,000 bushels of grain in Farmland but only 1,000 bushels of grain in Mobilia. But grain is cheaper in Farmland than in Mobilia—9,000 bushels of grain costs only 1 car in Farmland, while that same amount of grain costs 9 cars in Mobilia.

Mobilia has a comparative advantage in car production. Farmland has a comparative advantage in grain production. A country has a **comparative advantage** in producing a good if it can produce that good at a lower opportunity cost than any other country.

Let's see how opportunity cost differences and comparative advantage generate gains from international trade.

Gains from Trade

IF MOBILIA BOUGHT GRAIN FOR WHAT IT COSTS Farmland to produce it, then Mobilia could buy 9,000 bushels of grain for 1 car. That is much lower than the cost of growing grain in Mobilia, for there it costs 9 cars to produce 9,000 bushels of grain. If the Mobilians can buy grain at the low Farmland price, they will reap some gains.

If the Farmers can buy cars for what it costs Mobilia to produce them, they will be able to obtain a car for 1,000 bushels of grain. Because it costs 9,000 bushels of grain to produce a car in Farmland, the Farmers would gain from such an opportunity.

In this situation, it makes sense for Mobilians to buy their grain from Farmers and for Farmers to buy their cars from Mobilians. But at what price will Farmland and Mobilia engage in mutually beneficial international trade?

The Terms of Trade

The quantity of grain that Farmland must pay Mobilia for a car is Farmland's **terms of trade** with Mobilia. Because the United States exports and imports many different goods and services, we measure the terms of trade in the real world as an index number that averages the terms of trade over all the items we trade.

The forces of international supply and demand determine the terms of trade. Figure 36.3 illustrates these forces in the Farmland-Mobilia international car market. The quantity of cars *traded internationally* is measured on the *x*-axis. On the *y*-axis, we measure the

FIGURE 36.3

International Trade in Cars

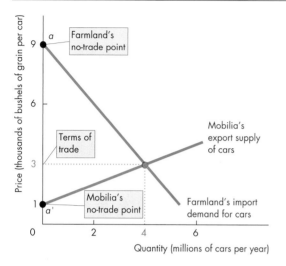

As the price of a car falls, the quantity of imports demanded by Farmland increases—Farmland's import demand curve for cars is downward sloping. As the price of a car rises, the quantity of cars supplied by Mobilia for export increases—Mobilia's export supply curve of cars is upward sloping. Without international trade, the price of a car is 9,000 bushels of grain in Farmland (point *a*) and 1,000 bushels of grain in Mobilia (point *a'*).

With free international trade, the price (terms of trade) is determined where the export supply curve intersects the import demand curve—3,000 bushels of grain per car. At that price, 4 million cars a year are imported by Farmland and exported by Mobilia. The value of grain exported by Farmland and imported by Mobilia is 12 billion bushels a year, the quantity required to pay for the cars imported.

price of a car. This price is expressed as the *terms of trade*—bushels of grain per car. If no international trade takes place, the price of a car in Farmland is 9,000 bushels of grain, its opportunity cost, as indicated by point *a* in the figure. Again, if no trade takes place, the price of a car in Mobilia is 1,000 bushels of grain, its opportunity cost, as indicated by point *a'* in the figure. The no-trade points *a* and *a'* in Fig. 36.3 correspond to the points identified by those same letters in Figs. 36.1 and 36.2. The lower the price of a car (terms of trade), the greater is the quantity of cars that the Farmers are willing to import from the Mobilians. This fact is illustrated by the downward-sloping curve, which shows Farmland's import demand for cars.

The Mobilians respond in the opposite direction. The higher the price of a car (terms of trade), the greater is the quantity of cars that Mobilians are willing to export to Farmers. This fact is reflected in Mobilia's export supply of cars—the upward-sloping line in Fig. 36.3.

The international market in cars determines the equilibrium price (terms of trade) and quantity traded. This equilibrium occurs where the import demand curve intersects the export supply curve. In this case, the equilibrium price is 3,000 bushels of grain per car. Mobilia exports and Farmland imports four million cars a year. Notice that the terms of trade are lower than the initial price in Farmland but higher than the initial price in Mobilia.

Balanced Trade

The number of cars exported by Mobilia—4 million a year—is exactly equal to the number of cars imported by Farmland. How does Farmland pay for its cars? By exporting grain. How much grain does Farmland export? You can find the answer by noticing that for 1 car, Farmland has to pay 3,000 bushels of grain. Hence, for 4 million cars, they have to pay 12 billion bushels of grain. Thus Farmland's exports of grain are 12 billion bushels a year. Mobilia imports this same quantity of grain.

Mobilia is exchanging 4 million cars for 12 billion bushels of grain each year, and Farmland is doing the opposite, exchanging 12 billion bushels of grain for 4 million cars. Trade is balanced between these two countries. The value received from exports equals the value paid out for imports.

Changes in Production and Consumption

We've seen that international trade makes it possible for Farmers to buy cars at a lower price than that at which they can produce them for themselves. Equivalently, Farmers can sell their grain for a higher price. International trade also enables Mobilians to sell their cars for a higher price. Equivalently, Mobilians can buy grain for a lower price. Thus everybody gains. How is it possible for *everyone* to gain? What are the changes in production and consumption that accompany these gains?

An economy that does not trade with other economies has identical production and consumption possibilities. Without trade, the economy can consume only what it produces. But with international trade, an economy can consume different quantities of goods from those that it produces. The production possibility frontier describes the limit of what a country can produce, but it does not describe the limits to what it can consume. Figure 36.4 will help you to see the distinction between production possibilities and consumption possibilities when a country trades with other countries.

First of all, notice that the figure has two parts, part (a) for Farmland and part (b) for Mobilia. The production possibility frontiers that you saw in Figs. 36.1 and 36.2 are reproduced here. The slopes of the two black lines in the figure represent the opportunity costs in the two countries when there is no international trade. Farmland produces and consumes at point *a*, and Mobilia produces and consumes at *a'*. Cars cost 9,000 bushels of grain in Farmland, and 1,000 bushels of grain in Mobilia.

Consumption Possibilities   The red line in each part of Fig. 36.4 shows the country's consumption possibilities with international trade. These two red lines have the same slope, and the magnitude of that slope is the opportunity cost of a car in terms of grain on the world market—3,000 bushels per car. The *slope* of the consumption possibilities line is common to both countries because its magnitude equals the *world* price. But the position of a country's consumption possibilities line depends on the country's production possibilities. A country cannot produce outside its production possibility curve, so its consumption possibility curve touches its production possibility curve. Thus Farmland could choose to consume at point *b* with no international trade or at any point on its red consumption possibilities line with international trade.

Free Trade Equilibrium   With international trade, the producers of cars in Mobilia can get a higher price for their output. As a result, they increase the quantity of car production. At the same time, grain producers in Mobilia get a lower price for their grain, and so they reduce production. Producers in Mobilia adjust their output by moving along their production possibility frontier until the opportunity cost in Mobilia equals the world price (the opportunity cost in the world market). This situation arises when Mobilia is producing at point *b'* in Fig. 36.4(b).

But the Mobilians do not consume at point *b'*. That is, they do not increase their consumption of

cars and decrease their consumption of grain. Instead, they sell some of their car production to Farmland in exchange for some of Farmland's grain. They trade internationally. But to see how that works out, we first need to check in with Farmland to see what's happening there.

In Farmland, producers of cars now get a lower price and producers of grain get a higher price. As a consequence, producers in Farmland decrease car production and increase grain production. They adjust their outputs by moving along the production possibility frontier until the opportunity cost of a car in terms of grain equals the world price (the opportunity cost on the world market). They move to point *b* in part (a). But the Farmers do not consume at point *b*. Instead, they trade some of their additional grain production for the now cheaper cars from Mobilia.

The figure shows us the quantities consumed in the two countries. We saw in Fig. 36.3 that Mobilia exports 4 million cars a year and Farmland imports those cars. We also saw that Farmland exports 12 billion bushels of grain a year and Mobilia imports that grain. Thus Farmland's consumption of grain is 12 billion bushels a year less than it produces, and its consumption of cars is 4 million a year more than it produces. Farmland consumes at point *c* in Fig. 36.4(a).

Similarly, we know that Mobilia consumes 12 billion bushels of grain more than it produces and 4 million cars fewer than it produces. Thus Mobilia consumes at *c'* in Fig. 36.4(b).

Calculating the Gains from Trade

You can now literally see the gains from trade in Fig. 36.4. Without trade, Farmers produce and consume at point *a* (part a)—a point on Farmland's production possibility frontier. With international trade, Farmers consume at point *c* in part (a)—a point *outside* the production possibility frontier. At point *c*, Farmers are consuming 3 billion bushels of grain a year and 1 million cars a year more than before. These increases in consumption of both cars and grain, beyond the limits of the production possibility frontier, are the gains from international trade. Mobilians also gain. Without trade, they consume at point *a'* in part (b)—a point on Mobilia's production possibility frontier. With international trade, they consume at point *c'*—a point outside the

FIGURE 36.4

Expanding Consumption Possibilities

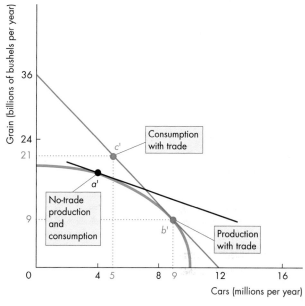

(a) Farmland

With no international trade, the Farmers produce and consume at point *a* and the opportunity cost of a car is 9,000 bushels of grain (the slope of the black line in part a). Also, with no international trade, the Mobilians produce and consume at point *a'* and the opportunity cost of 1,000 bushels of grain is 1 car (the slope of the black line in part b). Goods can be exchanged internationally at a price of 3,000 bushels of grain for 1 car along the red line in each part of the figure. In part (a), Farmland decreases its production of cars and

(b) Mobilia

increases its production of grain, moving from *a* to *b*. It exports grain and imports cars, and it consumes at point *c*. The Farmers have more of both cars and grain than they would if they produced all their own goods—at point *a*. In part (b), Mobilia increases car production and decreases grain production, moving from *a'* to *b'*. Mobilia exports cars and imports grain, and it consumes at point *c'*. The Mobilians have more of both cars and grain than they would if they produced all their own goods—at point *a'*.

production possibility frontier. With international trade, Mobilia consumes 3 billion bushels of grain a year and 1 million cars a year more than without trade. These are the gains from international trade for Mobilia.

Gains for All

Trade between the Farmers and the Mobilians does not create winners and losers. Everyone wins. Sellers add the net demand of foreigners to their domestic demand, and so their market expands. Buyers are faced with domestic supply plus net foreign supply and so have a larger supply available to them.

REVIEW QUIZ

In what circumstances can countries gain from international trade?

- What determines the goods and services that a country will export? What determines the goods and services that a country will import?
- What is a comparative advantage and what role does it play in determining the amount and type of international trade that occurs?.
- How can it be that all countries gain from international trade and that there are no losers?

Gains from Trade in Reality

THE GAINS FROM TRADE THAT WE HAVE JUST studied between Farmland and Mobilia in grain and cars occur in a model economy—in a world economy that we have imagined. But these same phenomena occur every day in the real global economy.

Comparative Advantage in the Global Economy

We buy TVs and VCRs from Korea, machinery from Europe, and fashion goods from Hong Kong. In exchange, we sell machinery, grain and lumber, airplanes, computers and financial services. All this international trade is generated by comparative advantage, just like the international trade between Farmland and Mobilia in our model economy. All international trade arises from comparative advantage, even when trade is in similar goods such as tools and machines. At first thought, it seems puzzling that countries exchange manufactured goods. Why doesn't each developed country produce all the manufactured goods its citizens want to buy?

Trade in Similar Goods

Why does the United States produce automobiles for export and at the same time import large quantities of them from Canada, Japan, Korea, and Western Europe? Wouldn't it make more sense to produce all the cars that we buy here in the United States? After all, we have access to the best technology available for producing cars. Autoworkers in the United States are surely as productive as their fellow workers in Canada, Western Europe, and Asian countries. So why does the United States have a comparative advantage in some types of cars and Japan and Europe in others?

Diversity of Taste and Economies of Scale

The first part of the answer is that people have a tremendous diversity of taste. Let's stick with the example of cars. Some people prefer a sports car, some prefer a limousine, some prefer a regular, full-size car, and some prefer a minivan. In addition to size and type of car, there are many other dimensions in which cars vary. Some have low fuel consumption, some

have high performance, some are spacious and comfortable, some have a large trunk, some have four-wheel drive, some have front-wheel drive, some have a radiator grill that looks like a Greek temple, and others look like a wedge. People's preferences across these many dimensions vary. The tremendous diversity in tastes for cars means that people value variety and are willing to pay for it in the marketplace.

The second part of the answer to the puzzle is *economies of scale*—the tendency for the average cost to be lower, the larger the scale of production. In such situations, larger and larger production runs lead to ever lower average costs. Many goods, including cars, experience economies of scale. For example, if a car producer makes only a few hundred (or perhaps a few thousand) cars of a particular type and design, the producer must use production techniques that are much more labor-intensive and much less automated than those employed to make hundreds of thousands of cars in a particular model. With short production runs and labor-intensive production techniques, costs are high. With very large production runs and automated assembly lines, production costs are much lower. But to obtain lower costs, the automated assembly lines have to produce a large number of cars.

It is the combination of diversity of taste and economies of scale that determines opportunity cost, produces comparative advantages, and generates such a large amount of international trade in similar commodities. With international trade, each car manufacturer has the whole world market to serve. Each producer can specialize in a limited range of products and then sell its output to the entire world market. This arrangement enables large production runs on the most popular cars and feasible production runs even on the most customized cars demanded by only a handful of people in each country.

The situation in the market for cars is also present in many other industries, especially those producing specialized equipment and parts. For example, the United States exports computer central processor chips but imports memory chips, exports mainframe computers but imports PCs, exports specialized video equipment but imports VCRs. Thus international exchange of similar but slightly differentiated manufactured products is a highly profitable activity.

Let's next see what happens when governments restrict international trade. We'll see that free trade brings the greatest possible benefits. We'll also see why, in spite of the benefits of free trade, governments sometimes restrict trade.

Trade Restrictions

GOVERNMENTS RESTRICT INTERNATIONAL TRADE to protect domestic industries from foreign competition by using two main tools:

1. Tariffs
2. Nontariff barriers

A **tariff** is a tax that is imposed by the importing country when an imported good crosses its international boundary. A **nontariff barrier** is any action other than a tariff that restricts international trade. Examples of nontariff barriers are quantitative restrictions and licensing regulations that limit imports. First, let's look at tariffs.

The History of Tariffs

U.S. tariffs today are modest compared with their historical levels. Figure 36.5 shows the average tariff rate—total tariffs as a percentage of total imports.

You can see in this figure that this average reached a peak of 20 percent in 1933. In that year, three years after the passage of the Smoot-Hawley Act, one third of imports was subject to a tariff, and on those imports, the tariff rate was 60 percent. (The average tariff in Fig. 36.5 for 1933 is 60 percent multiplied by 0.33, which equals 20 percent.) Today, the average tariff rate is only 4 percent.

The reduction in tariffs since World War II followed the signing in 1947 of the **General Agreement on Tariffs and Trade** (GATT). Since its formation, the GATT has organized several rounds of negotiations that have resulted in tariff reductions. One of these, the Kennedy Round, which began in the early 1960s, resulted in large tariff cuts starting in 1967. Another, the Tokyo Round, resulted in further tariff cuts in 1979. The most recent, the Uruguay Round, which started in 1986 and was completed in 1994, was the most ambitious and comprehensive of the rounds. The Uruguay Round also led to the creation of a new **World Trade Organization** (WTO). Membership of the WTO brings greater obligations on countries to observe the GATT rules.

FIGURE 36.5

U.S. Tariffs: 1930–1998

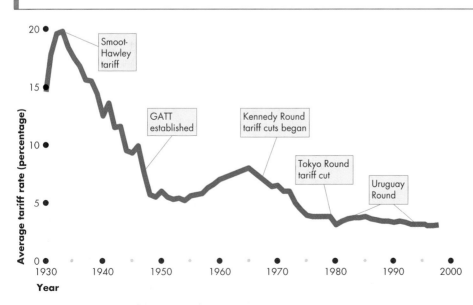

The Smoot-Hawley Act, which was passed in 1930, took U.S. tariffs to a peak average rate of 20 percent in 1933. (One third of imports was subject to a tariff rate of 60 percent.) Since the establishment of GATT in 1947, tariffs have steadily declined in a series of negotiating rounds, the most significant of which are identified in the figure. Tariffs are now as low as they have ever been.

Sources: U.S. Bureau of the Census, *Historical Statistics of the United States, Colonial Times to 1970*, Bicentennial Edition, Part I (Washington, D.C., 1975), Series U-212; *Statistical Abstract of the United States: 1986*, 106th edition (Washington, D.C., 1985); and *Statistical Abstract of the United States: 1998*, 118th edition (Washington, D.C., 1998).

In addition to the agreements under the GATT and the WTO, the United States is a party to the **North American Free Trade Agreement** (NAFTA), which became effective on January 1, 1994, and under which barriers to international trade between the United States, Canada, and Mexico will be virtually eliminated after a 15-year phasing-in period.

In other parts of the world, trade barriers have virtually been eliminated among the member countries of the European Union, which has created the largest unified tariff-free market in the world. In 1994, discussions among the Asia-Pacific Economic group (APEC) led to an agreement in principle to work toward a free-trade area that embraces China, all the economies of East Asia and the South Pacific, and the United States and Canada. These countries include the fastest-growing economies and hold the promise of heralding a global free-trade area.

The effort to achieve freer trade underlines the fact that trade in some goods is still subject to extremely high tariffs. The highest tariffs faced by U.S. buyers are those on textiles and footwear. A tariff of more than 10 percent (on the average) is imposed on almost all our imports of textiles and footwear. For example, when you buy a pair of blue jeans for $20, you pay about $5 more than you would if there were no tariffs on textiles. Other goods protected by tariffs are agricultural products, energy and chemicals, minerals, and metals. The meat, cheese, and sugar that you consume cost significantly more because of protection than they would with free international trade.

The temptation on governments to impose tariffs is a strong one. First, tariffs provide revenue to the government. Second, they enable the government to satisfy special interest groups in import-competing industries. But, as we'll see, free international trade brings enormous benefits that are reduced when tariffs are imposed. Let's see how.

How Tariffs Work

To analyze how tariffs work, let's return to the example of trade between Farmland and Mobilia. Figure 36.6 shows the international market for cars in which these two countries are the only traders. The volume of trade and the price of a car are determined at the point of intersection of Mobilia's export supply curve of cars and Farmland's import demand curve for cars.

FIGURE 36.6
The Effects of a Tariff

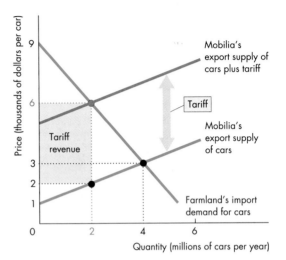

Farmland imposes a tariff on car imports from Mobilia. The tariff increases the price that Farmers have to pay for cars. It shifts the supply curve of cars in Farmland leftward. The vertical distance between the original supply curve and the new one is the amount of the tariff, $4,000 per car. The price of cars in Farmland increases, and the quantity of cars imported decreases. The government of Farmland collects a tariff revenue of $4,000 per car—a total of $8 billion on the 2 million cars imported. Farmland's exports of grain decrease because Mobilia now has a lower income from its exports of cars.

In Fig. 36.6, these two countries trade cars and grain in exactly the same way that we saw in Fig. 36.3. Mobilia exports cars, and Farmland exports grain. The volume of car imports into Farmland is 4 million a year, and the world market price of a car is 3,000 bushels of grain. Fig. 36.6 expresses prices in dollars rather than in units of grain and is based on a money price of grain of $1 a bushel. With grain costing $1 a bushel, the money price of a car is $3,000.

Now suppose that the government of Farmland, perhaps under pressure from car producers, decides to impose a tariff on imported cars. In particular, suppose that a tariff of $4,000 per car is imposed. (This is a huge tariff, but the car producers of Farmland are pretty fed up with competition from Mobilia.) What happens?

- The supply of cars in Farmland decreases.
- The price of a car in Farmland rises.
- The quantity of cars imported by Farmland decreases.
- The government of Farmland collects the tariff revenue.
- Resource use is inefficient.
- The *value* of exports changes by the same amount as the *value* of imports and trade remains balanced.

Change in the Supply of Cars   Farmland cannot buy cars at Mobilia's export supply price. It must pay that price plus the $4,000 tariff. So the supply curve in Farmland shifts leftward. The new supply curve is that labeled "Mobilia's export supply of cars plus tariff." The vertical distance between Mobilia's export supply curve and the new supply curve is the tariff of $4,000 a car.

Rise in Price of Cars   A new equilibrium occurs where the new supply curve intersects Farmland's import demand curve for cars. That equilibrium is at a price of $6,000 a car, up from $3,000 with free trade.

Fall in Imports   Car imports fall from 4 million to 2 million cars a year. At the higher price of $6,000 a car, Farmland's car producers increase their production. Grain production in Farmland decreases as resources are moved into the expanding car industry.

Tariff Revenue   Total expenditure on imported cars by the Farmers is $6,000 a car multiplied by the 2 million cars imported ($12 billion). But not all of that money goes to the Mobilians. They receive $2,000 a car, or $4 billion for the 2 million cars. The difference—$4,000 a car, or a total of $8 billion for the 2 million cars—is collected by the government of Farmland as tariff revenue.

Inefficiency   The people of Farmland are willing to pay $6,000 for the marginal car imported. But the opportunity cost of that car is $2,000. So there is a gain from trading an extra car. In fact, there are gains—willingness to pay exceeds opportunity cost—all the way up to 4 million cars a year. Only when 4 million cars are being traded is the maximum price that a Farmer is willing to pay equal to the minimum price that is acceptable to a Mobilian. Thus restricting trade reduces the gains from trade.

Trade Remains Balanced   With free trade, Farmland was paying $3,000 a car and buying 4 million cars a year from Mobilia. Thus the total amount paid to Mobilia for imports was $12 billion a year. With a tariff, Farmland's imports have been cut to 2 million cars a year and the price paid to Mobilia has also been cut to only $2,000 a car. Thus the total amount paid to Mobilia for imports has been cut to $4 billion a year. Doesn't this fact mean that Farmland now has a balance of trade surplus?

It does not. The price of cars in Mobilia has fallen. But the price of grain remains at $1 a bushel. So the relative price of cars has fallen, and the relative price of grain has increased. With free trade, the Mobilians could buy 3,000 bushels of grain for one car. Now they can buy only 2,000 bushels for a car. With a higher relative price of grain, the quantity demanded by the Mobilians decreases and Mobilia imports less grain. But because Mobilia imports less grain, Farmland exports less grain. In fact, Farmland's grain industry suffers from two sources. First, there is a decrease in the quantity of grain sold to Mobilia. Second, there is increased competition for inputs from the now expanded car industry. Thus the tariff leads to a contraction in the scale of the grain industry in Farmland.

It seems paradoxical at first that a country imposing a tariff on cars hurts its own export industry, decreasing its exports of grain. It may help to think of it this way: Mobilians buy grain with the money they make from exporting cars to Farmland. If they export fewer cars, they cannot afford to buy as much grain. In fact, in the absence of any international borrowing and lending, Mobilia must cut its imports of grain by exactly the same amount as the loss in revenue from its export of cars. Grain imports into Mobilia are cut back to a value of $4 billion, the amount that can be paid for by the new lower revenue from Mobilia's car exports. Thus trade is still balanced. The tariff cuts imports and exports by the same amount. The tariff has no effect on the *balance* of trade, but it reduces the *volume* of trade.

The result that we have just derived is perhaps one of the most misunderstood aspects of international economics. On countless occasions, politicians and others call for tariffs to remove a balance of trade deficit or argue that lowering tariffs would produce a balance of trade deficit. They reach this conclusion by failing to work out all the implications of a tariff.

Let's now turn our attention to the other tool for restricting trade: nontariff barriers.

Nontariff Barriers

The two main forms of nontariff barriers are:

1. Quotas
2. Voluntary export restraints

A **quota** is a quantitative restriction on the import of a particular good, which specifies the maximum amount of the good that can be imported in a given period of time. A **voluntary export restraint** (VER) is an agreement between two governments in which the government of the exporting country agrees to restrain the volume of its own exports.

Quotas are especially prominent in textiles and agriculture. Voluntary export restraints are used to regulate trade between Japan and the United States.

How Quotas and VERs Work

To see how a quota works, suppose that Farmland imposes a quota that restricts its car imports to 2 million cars a year. Figure 36.7 shows the effects of this action. The quota is shown by the vertical red line at 2 million cars a year. Because it is illegal to exceed the quota, car importers buy only that quantity from Mobilia, for which they pay $2,000 a car. But because the import supply of cars is restricted to 2 million cars a year, people in Farmland are willing to pay $6,000 per car. This is the price of a car in Farmland.

The value of imports falls to $4 billion, exactly the same as in the case of the tariff. So with lower incomes from car exports and with a higher relative price of grain, Mobilians cut back on their imports of grain in exactly the same way that they did under a tariff.

The key difference between a quota and a tariff lies in who collects the gap between the import supply price and the domestic price. In the case of a tariff, it is the government of the importing country. In the case of a quota, it goes to the person who has the right to import under the import quota regulations.

A voluntary export restraint is like a quota arrangement in which quotas are allocated to each exporting country. The effects of voluntary export restraints are similar to those of quotas but differ from them in that the gap between the price in the importing country and the export price is captured not by domestic importers but by the foreign exporter. The government of the exporting country has to establish procedures for allocating the restricted volume of exports among its producers.

FIGURE 36.7

The Effects of a Quota

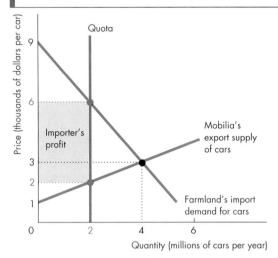

Farmland imposes a quota of 2 million cars a year on car imports from Mobilia. That quantity appears as the vertical line labeled "Quota." Because the quantity of cars supplied by Mobilia is restricted to 2 million, the price at which those cars will be traded increases to $6,000. Importing cars is profitable because Mobilia is willing to supply cars at $2,000 each. There is competition for import quotas.

R E V I E W   Q U I Z

■ What happens to a country's consumption possibilities when it opens itself up to international trade and trades freely at world market prices?

■ What do trade restrictions do to the gains from international trade?

■ What is best for a country: restricted trade, no trade, or free trade?

■ What does a tariff on imports do to the volume of imports and the volume of exports?

■ In the absence of international borrowing and lending, how do tariffs and other trade restrictions influence the total value of imports and exports and the balance of trade—the value of exports minus the value of imports?

Let's now look at some commonly heard arguments for restricting international trade.

The Case Against Protection

FOR AS LONG AS NATIONS AND INTERNATIONAL trade have existed, people have debated whether a country is better off with free international trade or with protection from foreign competition. The debate continues, but for most economists, a verdict has been delivered and is the one you have just seen. Free trade promotes prosperity for all; protection is inefficient. We've seen the most powerful case for free trade in the example of how Farmland and Mobilia both benefit from their comparative advantage. But there is a broader range of issues in the free trade versus protection debate. Let's review these issues.

Three arguments for restricting international trade are:

- The national security argument
- The infant-industry argument
- The dumping argument

Let's look at each in turn.

The National Security Argument

The national security argument for protection is that a country must protect industries that produce defense equipment and armaments and those on which the defense industries rely for their raw materials and other intermediate inputs. This argument for protection does not withstand close scrutiny.

First, it is an argument for international isolation, for in a time of war, there is no industry that does not contribute to national defense. Second, if the case is made for boosting the output of a strategic industry, it is more efficient to achieve this outcome with a subsidy to the firms in the industry financed out of taxes. Such a subsidy would keep the industry operating at the scale judged appropriate, and free international trade would keep the prices faced by consumers at their world market levels.

The Infant-Industry Argument

The so-called **infant-industry argument** for protection is that it is necessary to protect a new industry to enable it to grow into a mature industry that can compete in world markets. The argument is based on the idea of *dynamic comparative advantage*, which can arise from *learning-by-doing* (see Chapter 3).

Learning-by-doing is a powerful engine of productivity growth, and comparative advantage evolves and changes because of on-the-job experience. But these facts do not justify protection.

First, the infant-industry argument is valid only if the benefits of learning-by-doing *not only* accrue to the owners and workers of the firms in the infant industry but also *spill over* to other industries and parts of the economy. For example, there are huge productivity gains from learning-by-doing in the manufacture of aircraft. But almost all of these gains benefit the stockholders and workers of Boeing and other aircraft producers. Because the people making the decisions, bearing the risk, and doing the work are the ones who benefit, they take the dynamic gains into account when they decide on the scale of their activities. In this case, almost no benefits spill over to other parts of the economy, so there is no need for government assistance to achieve an efficient outcome.

Second, even if the case is made for protecting an infant industry, it is more efficient to do so by a subsidy to the firms in the industry, with the subsidy financed out of taxes.

The Dumping Argument

Dumping occurs when a foreign firm sells its exports at a lower price than its cost of production. Dumping might be used by a firm that wants to gain a global monopoly. In this case, the foreign firm sells its output at a price below its cost to drive domestic firms out of business. When the domestic firms have gone, the foreign firm takes advantage of its monopoly position and charges a higher price for its product. Dumping is usually regarded as a justification for temporary countervailing tariffs.

But there are powerful reasons to resist the dumping argument for protection. First, it is virtually impossible to detect dumping because it is hard to determine a firm's costs. As a result, the test for dumping is whether a firm's export price is below its domestic price. But this test is a weak one because it can be rational for a firm to charge a low price in markets in which the quantity demanded is highly sensitive to price and a higher price in a market in which demand is less price-sensitive.

Second, it is hard to think of a good that is produced by a natural *global* monopoly. So even if all the domestic firms were driven out of business in some industry, it would always be possible to find several and usually many alternative foreign sources of supply and to buy at prices determined in competitive markets.

Third, if a good or service were a truly global natural monopoly, the best way of dealing with it would be by regulation—just as in the case of domestic monopolies. Such regulation would require international cooperation.

The three arguments for protection that we've just examined have an element of credibility. The counter-arguments are in general stronger, so these arguments do not make the case for protection. But they are not the only arguments that you might encounter. The many other arguments that are commonly heard are quite simply wrong. They are fatally flawed. The most common of them are that protection:

- Saves jobs
- Allows us to compete with cheap foreign labor
- Brings diversity and stability
- Penalizes lax environmental standards
- Protects national culture
- Prevents rich countries from exploiting developing countries

Saves Jobs

The argument is: When we buy shoes from Brazil or shirts from Taiwan, U.S. workers lose their jobs. With no earnings and poor prospects, these workers become a drain on welfare and spend less, causing a ripple effect of further job losses. The proposed solution to this problem is to ban imports of cheap foreign goods and protect U.S. jobs. The proposal is flawed for the following reasons.

First, free trade does cost some jobs, but it also creates other jobs. It brings about a global rationalization of labor and allocates labor resources to their highest-value activities. Because of international trade in textiles, tens of thousands of workers in the United States have lost jobs because textile mills and other factories have closed. But tens of thousands of workers in other countries have gotten jobs because textile mills have opened there. And tens of thousands of U.S. workers have gotten better-paying jobs than textile workers because other export industries have expanded and created more jobs than have been destroyed.

Second, imports create jobs. They create jobs for retailers that sell imported goods and firms that service those goods. They also create jobs by creating incomes in the rest of the world, some of which are spent on imports of U.S.-made goods and services.

Although protection does save particular jobs, it does so at inordinate cost. For example, textile jobs are protected in the United States by quotas imposed under an international agreement called the Multifiber Arrangement. It has been estimated by the U.S. International Trade Commission (ITC) that because of quotas, 72,000 jobs exist in textiles that would otherwise disappear and annual clothing expenditure in the United States is $15.9 billion, or $160 per family higher than it would be with free trade. Equivalently, the ITC estimates that each textile job saved costs $221,000 a year.

Allows Us to Compete with Cheap Foreign Labor

With the removal of protective tariffs in U.S. trade with Mexico, Ross Perot said we would hear a "giant sucking sound" of jobs rushing to Mexico (one of which is shown in the cartoon). Let's see what's wrong with this view.

The labor cost of a unit of output equals the wage rate divided by labor productivity. For example, if a U.S. auto worker earns $30 an hour and produces 15

"I don't know what the hell happened—one minute I'm at work in Flint, Michigan, then there's a giant sucking sound and suddenly here I am in Mexico."

Drawing by M. Stevens; © 1993
The New Yorker Magazine, Inc.

units of output an hour, the average labor cost of a unit of output is $2. If a Mexican auto assembly worker earns $3 an hour and produces 1 unit of output an hour, the average labor cost of a unit of output is $3. Other things remaining the same, the higher a worker's productivity, the higher is the worker's wage rate. High-wage workers have high productivity. Low-wage workers have low productivity.

Although high-wage U.S. workers are more productive, on the average, than low-wage Mexican workers, there are differences across industries. U.S. labor is relatively more productive in some activities than in others. For example, the productivity of U.S. workers in producing movies, financial services, and customized computer chips is relatively higher than in the production of metals and some standardized machine parts. The activities in which U.S. workers are relatively more productive than their Mexican counterparts are those in which the United States has a *comparative advantage*. By engaging in free trade, increasing our production and exports of the goods and services in which we have a comparative advantage and decreasing our production and increasing our imports of the goods and services in which our trading partners have a comparative advantage, we can make ourselves and the citizens of other countries better off.

Brings Diversity and Stability

A diversified investment portfolio is less risky than one that has all the eggs in one basket. The same is true for an economy's production. A diversified economy fluctuates less than an economy that produces only one or two goods.

But big, rich, diversified economies like those of the United States, Japan, and Europe do not have this type of stability problem. Even a country like Saudi Arabia that produces almost only one good (oil) can benefit from specializing in the activity at which it has a comparative advantage and then investing in a wide range of other countries to bring greater stability to its income and consumption.

Penalizes Lax Environmental Standards

A new argument for protection is that many poorer countries, such as Mexico, do not have the same environment policies that we have and, because they

are willing to pollute and we are not, we cannot compete with them without tariffs. So if they want free trade with the richer and "greener" countries, they must clean up their environments to our standards.

This argument for trade restrictions is weak. First, not all poorer countries have significantly lower environmental standards than the United States has. Many poor countries and the former Communist countries of Eastern Europe do have bad environment records. But some countries enforce strict laws. Second, a poor country cannot afford to be as concerned about its environment as a rich country can. The best hope for a better environment in Mexico and in other developing countries is rapid income growth through free trade. As their incomes grow, developing countries will have the *means* to match their desires to improve their environment. Third, poor countries have a comparative advantage at doing "dirty" work, which helps rich countries achieve higher environment standards than they otherwise could.

Protects National Culture

The national culture argument for protection is not heard much in the United States, but it is a commonly heard argument in Canada and Europe.

The expressed fear is that free trade in books, magazines, movies, and television programs means U.S. domination and the end of local culture. So, the reasoning continues, it is necessary to protect domestic culture industries from free international trade to ensure the survival of a national cultural identity.

Protection of these industries is common and takes the form of nontariff barriers. For example, local content regulations on radio and television broadcasting and in magazines is often required.

The cultural identity argument for protection has no merit, and it is one more example of rent seeking (see Chapter 13, p. 272). Writers, publishers, and broadcasters want to limit foreign competition so that they can earn larger economic profits. There is no actual danger to national culture. In fact, many of the creators of so-called American cultural products are not Americans, but the talented citizens of other countries, ensuring the survival of their national cultural identities in Hollywood! Also, if national culture is in danger, there is no surer way of helping it on its way out than by impoverishing the nation whose culture it is. And protection is an effective way of doing just that.

Prevents Rich Countries from Exploiting Developing Countries

Another new argument for protection is that international trade must be restricted to prevent the people of the rich industrial world from exploiting the poorer people of the developing countries, forcing them to work for slave wages.

Wage rates in some developing countries are indeed very low. But by trading with developing countries, we increase the demand for the goods that these countries produce, and, more significantly, we increase the demand for their labor. When the demand for labor in developing countries increases, the wage rate also increases. So, far from exploiting people in developing countries, trade improves their opportunities and increases their incomes.

We have reviewed the arguments that are commonly heard in favor of protection and the counter-arguments against them. There is one counter-argument to protection that is general and quite overwhelming. Protection invites retaliation and can trigger a trade war. The best example of a trade war occurred during the Great Depression of the 1930s when the Smoot-Hawley Tariff was introduced. Country after country retaliated with its own tariff, and in a short period, world trade had almost disappeared. The costs to all countries were large and led to a renewed international resolve to avoid such self-defeating moves in the future. They also led to the creation of GATT and are the impetus behind NAFTA, APEC, and the European Union.

R E V I E W   Q U I Z

- Is there any merit to the view that we should restrict international trade to achieve national security goals, to stimulate the growth of new industries, or to restrain foreign monopoly?
- Is there any merit to the view that we should restrict international trade to save jobs, compensate for low foreign wages, make the economy more diversified, compensate for costly environmental policies, protect national culture, or protect developing countries from being exploited?
- Is there any merit to the view that we should restrict international trade for any reason? What is the main argument against trade restrictions?

Why Is International Trade Restricted?

WHY, DESPITE ALL THE ARGUMENTS AGAINST protection, is trade restricted? There are two key reasons:

- Tariff revenue
- Rent seeking

Tariff Revenue

Government revenue is costly to collect. In the developed countries such as the United States, a well-organized tax-collection system is in place that can generate billions of dollars of income tax and sales tax revenues. This tax-collecting system is made possible by the fact that most economic transactions are done by firms that must keep properly audited financial records. Without such records, the revenue collection agencies (the Internal Revenue Service in the United States) would be severely hampered in the work. Even with audited financial accounts, some proportion of potential tax revenue is lost. Nonetheless, for the industrialized countries, the income tax and sales taxes are the major sources of revenue and the tariff plays a very small role.

But governments in developing countries have a difficult time collecting taxes from their citizens. Much economic activity takes place in an informal economy with few financial records. So only a small amount of revenue is collected from income taxes and sales taxes in these countries. The one area in which economic transactions are well recorded and audited is in international trade. So this activity is an attractive base for tax collection in these countries and is used much more extensively than in the developed countries.

Rent Seeking

The major reason why international trade is restricted is because of rent seeking. Free trade increases consumption possibilities *on the average,* but not everyone shares in the gain and some people even lose. Free trade brings benefits to some and imposes costs on others, with total benefits exceeding total costs. It is the uneven distribution of costs and benefits that is the principal source of impediment to achieving more liberal international trade.

Returning to our example of trade in cars and grain between Farmland and Mobilia, the benefits to Farmland from free trade accrue to all the producers of grain and those producers of cars who would not have to bear the costs of adjusting to a smaller car industry. These costs are transition costs, not permanent costs. The costs of moving to free trade are borne by those car producers and their employees who have to become grain producers. The number of people who gain will, in general, be enormous compared with the number who lose. The gain per person will therefore be rather small. The loss per person to those who bear the loss will be large. Because the loss that falls on those who bear it is large, it will pay those people to incur considerable expense to lobby against free trade. On the other hand, it will not pay those who gain to organize to achieve free trade. The gain from trade for any one individual is too small for that individual to spend much time or money on a political organization to achieve free trade. The loss from free trade will be seen as being so great by those bearing that loss that they *will* find it profitable to join a political organization to prevent free trade. Each group is optimizing—weighing benefits against costs and choosing the best action for themselves. The anti-free-trade group will, however, undertake a larger quantity of political lobbying than the pro-free-trade group.

Compensating Losers

If, in total, the gains from free international trade exceed the losses, why don't those who gain compensate those who lose so that everyone is in favor of free trade? To some degree, such compensation does take place. When Congress approved the NAFTA deal with Canada and Mexico, it set up a $56 million fund to support and retrain workers who lost their jobs because of the new trade agreement. During the first six months of the operation of NAFTA, only 5,000 workers applied for benefits under this scheme.

The losers from freer international trade are also compensated indirectly through the normal unemployment compensation arrangements. But only limited attempts are made to compensate those who lose from free international trade. The main reason why full compensation is not attempted is that the costs of identifying all the losers and estimating the value of

their losses would be enormous. Also, it would never be clear whether a person who has fallen on hard times is suffering because of free trade or for other reasons, perhaps reasons that are largely under the control of the individual. Furthermore, some people who look like losers at one point in time may, in fact, wind up gaining. The young auto worker who loses his job in Michigan and becomes a computer assembly worker in Minneapolis resents the loss of work and the need to move. But a year or two later, looking back on events, he counts himself fortunate. He has made a move that has increased his income and given him greater job security.

It is because we do not, in general, compensate the losers from free international trade that protectionism is such a popular and permanent feature of our national economic and political life.

R E V I E W   Q U I Z

- What are the two main reasons for imposing a tariff on imports?
- What type of country benefits most from the revenue that tariffs generate? Does the United States need to use tariffs to raise revenue for the government?
- If trade restrictions are costly, why do we use them? Why don't the people who gain from trade organize a political force that is strong enough to ensure that their interests are protected?

◆ You've now seen how free international trade enables all nations to gain from specialization and trade. By producing goods in which we have a comparative advantage and trading some of our production for that of others, we expand our consumption possibilities. Placing impediments on that trade restricts the extent to which we can gain from specialization and trade. Opening our country up to free international trade expands the market for the things that we sell and raises their relative price. The market for the things that we buy also expands, and the relative price falls. *Reading Between the Lines* on pp. 838–839 looks at a recent example of an international trade dispute between the United States and Europe.

In the final chapter, we're going to examine the balance of international trade and the forces that influence the exchange rate.

Tariffs in Action

T H E   N E W   Y O R K   T I M E S ,   MARCH 4, 1999

Miffed at Europe, U.S. Raises Tariffs for Luxury Goods

BY DAVID E. SANGER

The United States heated up two politically contentious trade disputes with Europe today, slapping 100 percent tariffs on $520 million in European products and threatening to ban Europe's supersonic pride, the Concorde, from landing in the United States.

The tariffs imposed by the Clinton Administration on goods such as Louis Vuitton handbags, Parma ham, pecorino cheese and Scottish cashmere sweaters, which essentially double their price and make it much harder for European exporters to sell them in this country, are part of a six-year battle over trade in bananas.

The threat to ban the Concorde is in a bill passed overwhelmingly in the House of Representatives today, in retaliation for a European ruling that would ban many older American airplanes from landing in Europe. American officials say Europe's restriction is designed to promote the sale of new engines and aircraft made by European manufacturers.

But both battles are really about the enormous tensions that have erupted between the United States and a Europe newly unified by a common currency. On both continents, politicians are feeling the heat from slowing exports, and fear a slowdown in economic growth later this year. And Washington and the European Union find themselves unable to resolve seemingly ordinary economic disputes, with each accusing the other of defying the World Trade Organization, the four-year-old court of international trade.

The court has stepped in to arbitrate the banana dispute, which involves European limits on imports, and has become the battleground over other politically sensitive issues, including Europe's ban on imported beef from cattle raised with hormones. ...

The trade fight with Europe has become a major issue at the White House, with President Clinton becoming directly involved in some of the negotiations, most recently with French President Jacques Chirac. But the economic impact is relatively modest: The United States imported $176.3 billion in goods from nations in the European Union last year, meaning that today's sanctions apply to one-quarter of 1 percent of goods imported from Europe. ...

Essence of the Story

■ The United States imposed a 100 percent tariff on $520 million of European products such as Louis Vuitton handbags, Parma ham, pecorino cheese, and Scottish cashmere sweaters in a six-year battle over trade in bananas.

■ The United States also threatened to ban the Concorde (the supersonic airplane) from landing in the United States in retaliation for a European ruling that would ban many older American airplanes from landing in Europe.

■ The economic impact of the tariff is relatively modest because it applies to one quarter of 1 percent of the goods imported from Europe.

Economic Analysis

- Figure 1 shows the U.S. market for a luxury good such as a high-quality handbag or a cashmere sweater.

- The demand curve of U.S. buyers of this luxury good is D.

- There are two supply curves: the supply curve of the European producers, S_E, and the supply curve of U.S. producers, S_{US}.

- With no tariff, the quantity of this luxury good bought in the United States is QC_0. Of these, QP_0 are produced in the United States and the rest are imported, as shown by the arrow in Fig. 1.

- Now the United States puts a 100 percent tariff on the imports of these items. The foreign good is now supplied to the U.S. market at the original supply price, $100, plus the tariff, $100, so the supply curve of this luxury good from Europe shifts to become $S_E + tariff$.

- With the tariff, the quantity of the good bought in the United States is QC_1. Of these, QP_1 are produced in the United States and the rest are imported from Europe, as shown by the arrow in Fig. 1.

- The tariff decreases U.S. consumption and imports and increases U.S. production.

- Figure 2 shows the winners and the losers in the United States.

- The winners include U.S producers who gain additional economic profit, which is shown by the blue area in Fig. 2.

- Another winner is the U.S. government, which collects additional revenue shown by the purple area in Fig. 2.

- The losers are the U.S. consumers. The consumers' loss equals the producers' gain plus the government's gain plus two other losses. One is an increase in the opportunity cost of producing the good in the United States, which is shown by the red area. Another is deadweight loss, which is shown by the gray area.

- The sum of the blue, red, purple, and gray areas is the loss of consumer surplus that results from the tariff.

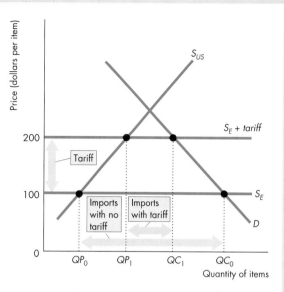

Figure 1   Tariffs and imports

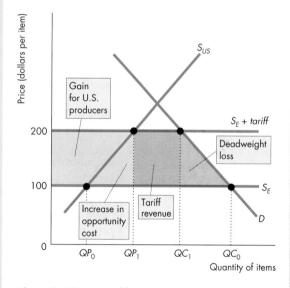

Figure 2   Winners and losers

You're The Voter

- Are you for or against the tariff on luxury goods from Europe?

- Write a report to your member of Congress explaining why you favor or oppose the luxury good tariff.

SUMMARY

KEY POINTS

Patterns and Trends in International Trade (p. 822)

- Large flows of trade take place between countries, most of which is in manufactured goods exchanged among rich industrialized countries.
- Since 1960, the volume of U.S. trade, as a percentage of total output, has more than doubled.

Opportunity Cost and Comparative Advantage (pp. 823–824)

- When opportunity costs between countries diverge, comparative advantage enables countries to gain from international trade.

Gains from Trade (pp. 824–827)

- By increasing its production of goods in which it has a comparative advantage and then trading some of the increased output, a country can consume at a point outside its production possibility frontier.
- In the absence of international borrowing and lending, trade is balanced as prices adjust to reflect the international supply of and demand for goods.
- The world price balances the production and consumption plans of the trading parties. At the equilibrium price, trade is balanced.

Gains from Trade in Reality (p. 828)

- Comparative advantage explains the international trade that takes place in the world.
- But trade in similar goods arises from economies of scale in the face of diversified tastes.

Trade Restrictions (pp. 829–832)

- Countries restrict international trade by imposing tariffs and quotas.
- Trade restrictions raise the domestic price of imported goods, lower the volume of imports, and reduce the total value of imports.
- Trade restrictions also reduce the total value of exports by the same amount as the reduction in the value of imports.

The Case Against Protection (pp. 833–836)

- Arguments that protection is necessary for national security, to allow infant industries the chance to grow, and to prevent dumping are weak.
- Arguments that protection saves jobs, allows us to compete with cheap foreign labor, makes the economy diversified and stable, protects national culture, and is needed to offset the costs of environmental policies are fatally flawed.

Why Is International Trade Restricted? (pp. 836–837)

- Trade is restricted because tariffs raise government revenue and because protection brings a small loss to a large number of people and a large gain per person to a small number of people.

KEY FIGURES

KEY TERMS

PROBLEMS

🖥 *1. The table provides information about Virtual Reality's production possibilities.

TV sets (per day)		Computers (per day)
0	and	36
10	and	35
20	and	33
30	and	30
40	and	26
50	and	21
60	and	15
70	and	8
80	and	0

a. Calculate Virtual Reality's opportunity cost of a TV set when it produces 10 sets a day.
b. Calculate Virtual Reality's opportunity cost of a TV set when it produces 40 sets a day.
c. Calculate Virtual Reality's opportunity cost of a TV set when it produces 70 sets a day.
d. Using the answers to parts (a), (b), and (c), sketch the relationship between the opportunity cost of a TV set and the quantity of TV sets produced in Virtual Reality.

2. The table provides information about Vital Sign's production possibilities.

TV sets (per day)		Computers (per day)
0	and	18.0
10	and	17.5
20	and	16.5
30	and	15.0
40	and	13.0
50	and	10.5
60	and	7.5
70	and	4.0
80	and	0

a. Calculate Vital Sign's opportunity cost of a TV set when it produces 10 sets a day.
b. Calculate Vital Sign's opportunity cost of a TV set when it produces 40 sets a day.
c. Calculate Vital Sign's opportunity cost of a TV set when it produces 70 sets a day.
d. Using the answers to parts (a), (b), and (c), sketch the relationship between the opportunity cost of a TV set and the quantity of TV sets produced in Vital Signs.

🖥 *3. Suppose that with no international trade, Virtual Reality in problem 1 produces and consumes 10 TV sets a day and Vital Signs produces and consumes 60 TV sets a day. Now suppose that the two countries begin to trade with each other.
a. Which country exports TV sets?
b. What adjustments are made to the amount of each good produced by each country?
c. What adjustments are made to the amount of each good consumed by each country?
d. What can you say about the terms of trade (the price of a TV set expressed as computers per TV set) under free trade?

4. Suppose that with no international trade, Virtual Reality in problem 1 produces and consumes 50 TV sets a day and Vital Signs produces and consumes 20 TV sets a day. Now suppose that the two countries begin to trade with each other.
a. Which country exports TV sets?
b. What adjustments are made to the amount of each good produced by each country?
c. What adjustments are made to the amount of each good consumed by each country?
d. What can you say about the terms of trade (the price of a TV set expressed as computers per TV set) under free trade?

🖥 *5. Compare the total quantities of each good produced in problems 1 and 2 with the total quantities of each good produced in problems 3 and 4.
a. Does free trade increase or decrease the total quantities of TV sets and computers produced in both cases? Why?
b. What happens to the price of a TV set in Virtual Reality in the two cases? Why does it rise in one case and fall in the other?
c. What happens to the price of a computer in Vital Signs in the two cases? Why does it rise in one case and fall in the other?

6. Compare the international trade in problem 3 with that in problem 4.
a. Why does Virtual Reality export TV sets in one of the cases and import them in the other case?
b. Do the TV producers or the computer producers gain in each case?
c. Do consumers gain in each case?

*7. The figure depicts the international market for soybeans.

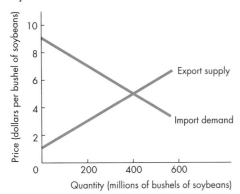

a. If the two countries did not engage in international trade, what would be the prices of soybeans in the two countries?
b. What is the world price of soybeans if there is free trade between these countries?
c. What quantities of soybeans are exported and imported?
d. What is the balance of trade?

8. If the country in problem 7(b) that imports soybeans imposes a tariff of $2 per bushel, what is the world price of soybeans and what quantity of soybeans gets traded internationally? What is the price of soybeans in the importing country? Calculate the tariff revenue.

*9. The importing country in problem 7(b) imposes a quota of 300 million bushels on imports of soybeans.
a. What is the price of soybeans in the importing country?
b. What is the revenue from the quota?
c. Who gets this revenue?

10. The exporting country in problem 7(b) imposes a VER of 300 million bushels on its exports of soybeans.
a. What is the world price of soybeans now?
b. What is the revenue of soybean growers in the exporting country?
c. Which country gains from the VER?

CRITICAL THINKING

1. Study *Reading Between the Lines* on pp. 838–839 and then answer the following questions:
   a. Why did the United States impose a tariff on luxury goods from Europe?
   b. What are the effects of the tariff on these goods? Explain your answer.
   c. Who are the winners and who are the losers from the tariff?
   d. Why do you think that the government cares about banana growers? (Hint: Think about where bananas grow and think about who owns the firms that produce bananas.)
   e. The news article talks about a U.S. ban on Concorde landings in retaliation for the European ban on some older U.S aircraft types. How would you go about analyzing the effects of this action? Who gains and who loses?

2. Visit the Parkin Web site and study the *Web Reading Between the Lines* on steel dumping. Then answer the following questions:
   a. What is the argument in the news article for limiting steel imports?
   b. Evaluate the argument. Is it correct or incorrect in your opinion? Why?
   c. Would you vote to limit steel imports? Why or why not?
   d. Would you vote differently if you lived in another steel-producing country? Why or why not?

3. Use the links on the Parkin Web site to visit the Public Citizen Global Trade Watch and the State of Arizona Department of Commerce Web sites. Review the general message provided by the two sites about NAFTA and then answer the following questions:
   a. What is the message that the Public Citizen Global Trade Watch wants to give?
   b. What is the basic message of the Arizona Commerce Department?
   c. Which message do you think is the correct one and why?
   d. Would you vote to maintain NAFTA? Why or why not?

37

International Finance

Yes! The yen (¥), the euro (€), and the dollar ($) are the world's three big currencies. The yen (the currency of Japan) and the dollar (the currency of the United States) have been around for a long time. The euro is new. It was launched on January 1, 1999, as the fledgling currency of 11 members of the European Union, and it will not be used for ordinary transactions until 2002. But it is already an international currency. Most of the world's international trade and finance is conducted using these three currencies. ◆ Currencies fluctuate in value. In 1971, one U.S. dollar bought 360 Japanese yen. In 1999, it bought 121 yen and four years earlier, it had bought only 84 yen. In 1997 and 1998, during the Asian financial crisis, the currency of Indonesian fell against our dollar to less that one third of its pre-crisis value. The Russian ruble also crashed during 1998 to a quarter of its initial value. ◆ Why does our dollar fluctuate against other currencies? Is there anything we can do or should do to stabilize the value of the dollar? ◆ Although the U.S. dollar is the world's most important currency, the position of the United States in the global economy is changing. In 1988, Americans owned foreign assets equal in value to the assets that foreigners owned in the United States. Before 1988, American ownership of foreign assets exceeded foreign ownership of U.S. assets. After 1988, the balance tipped increasingly the other way. Foreign entrepreneurs like Australian-born Rupert Murdoch and Sony's Akio Mori have roamed the United States with giant shopping carts and loaded them up with such items as the L. A. Dodgers, Twentieth Century Fox, the Rockefeller Center, and MGM. Why have foreigners been buying more U.S. real estate and businesses than Americans have been buying abroad?

◆ We're going to discover why the U.S. economy has become attractive for foreign investors, what determines the amount of international borrowing and lending, and why the dollar fluctuates against other currencies.

¥€$!

After studying this chapter, you will be able to:

- Explain how international trade is financed

- Describe a country's balance of payments accounts

- Explain what determines the amount of international borrowing and lending

- Explain why the United States changed from being a lender to being a borrower in the mid-1980s

- Explain how the foreign exchange value of the dollar is determined

- Explain why the foreign exchange value of the dollar fluctuates

Financing International Trade

WHEN A SONY STORE IN THE UNITED STATES imports CD players from Japan, it does not pay for them with U.S. dollars—it uses Japanese yen. And when a French construction company buys an earth mover from Caterpillar, Inc., it uses U.S. dollars. Whenever we buy things from another country, we use the currency of that country to make the transaction. It doesn't make any difference what the item being traded is; it might be a consumption good or a capital good, a building, or even a firm.

We're going to study the markets in which money—different types of currency—is bought and sold. But first we're going to look at the scale of international trading and borrowing and lending and at the way in which we keep our records of these transactions. Such records are called the balance of payments accounts.

Balance of Payments Accounts

A country's **balance of payments accounts** records its international trading, borrowing, and lending. There are in fact three balance of payments accounts:

1. Current account
2. Capital account
3. Official settlements account

The **current account** records payments for imports of goods and services from abroad, receipts from exports of goods and services sold abroad, net interest paid abroad, and net transfers (such as foreign aid payments). The *current account balance* equals exports minus imports, net interest, and net transfers. The **capital account** records foreign investment in the United States minus U.S. investment abroad. The **official settlements account** records the change in official U.S. reserves. **Official U.S. reserves** are the government's holdings of foreign currency. If U.S. official reserves increase, the *official settlements account balance* is negative. The reason is that holding foreign money is like investing abroad. U.S. investment abroad is a minus item in the capital account. By the same reasoning, if official reserves decrease, the *official settlements account balance* is positive.

The sum of the balances on the three accounts always equals zero. That is, to pay for our current account deficit, we must either borrow more from abroad than we lend abroad or use our official reserves to cover the shortfall.

Table 37.1 shows the U.S. balance of payments accounts in 1998. Items in the current account and capital account that provide foreign currency to the United States have a plus sign; items that cost the United States foreign currency have a minus sign. The table shows that in 1998, U.S. imports exceeded U.S. exports and the current account had a deficit of $230 billion. How do we pay for imports that exceed the value of our exports? That is, how do we pay for our current account deficit? We pay by borrowing from the rest of the world. The capital account tells us by how much. We borrowed $540 billion (foreign investment in the United States) but made loans of $310 billion (U.S. investment abroad). Thus our net foreign borrowing was $230 billion. In some years, the accounts show a statistical discrepancy between our capital account and current account transactions. But in 1998, the statistical discrepancy was small. The statistical discrepancy arises because of illegal and hidden transactions.

TABLE 37.1

U.S. Balance of Payments Accounts in 1998

Current account	Billions of dollars
Imports of goods and services	−1,120
Exports of goods and services	+910
Net interest income	+20
Net transfers	−40
Current account balance	−230
Capital account	
Foreign investment in the United States	+540
U.S. investment abroad	−310
Capital account balance	+230
Official settlements account	
Increase in official U.S. reserves	—

Source: Selected Estimates from the International Transactions news release, March 11, 1999, Bureau of Economic Analysis, U.S. Department of Commerce, Washington, D.C. All the items are rounded to the nearest $10 billion.

Our net borrowing from abroad minus our current account deficit is the change in official U.S. reserves. In 1998, reserves barely changed because our net foreign borrowing of $230 billion equaled our current account deficit of $230 billion. When our reserves do change, we record an *increase* in reserves as a negative number in our international accounts. Why? Because an increase in our reserves is like making a loan to the rest of the world.

The numbers in Table 37.1 give a snapshot of the balance of payments accounts in 1998. Figure 37.1 puts that snapshot into perspective by showing the balance of payments between 1980 and 1998. Because the economy grows and the price level rises, changes in the dollar value of the balance of payments do not convey much information. To remove the influences of growth and inflation, Fig. 37.1 shows the balance of payments as a percentage of nominal GDP.

As you can see, the capital account balance is almost a mirror image of the current account balance. The official settlements balance is very small in comparison with the balances on these other two accounts. A large current account deficit (and capital account surplus) emerged during the 1980s but declined from 1987 to 1991. Since then, it has increased again.

You will perhaps obtain a better understanding of the balance of payments accounts and the way in which they are linked together if you consider the income and expenditure, borrowing and lending, and bank account of an individual.

Individual Analogy An individual's current account records the income from supplying the services of factors of production and the expenditure on goods and services. Consider, for example, Joanne. She worked in 1995 and earned an income of $25,000. Joanne has $10,000 worth of investments that earned her an interest income of $1,000. Joanne's current account shows an income of $26,000. Joanne spent $18,000 buying goods and services for consumption. She also bought a new house, which cost her $60,000. So Joanne's total expenditure was $78,000. The difference between her expenditure and income is $52,000 ($78,000 minus $26,000). This amount is Joanne's current account deficit.

FIGURE 37.1

The Balance of Payments: 1975–1998

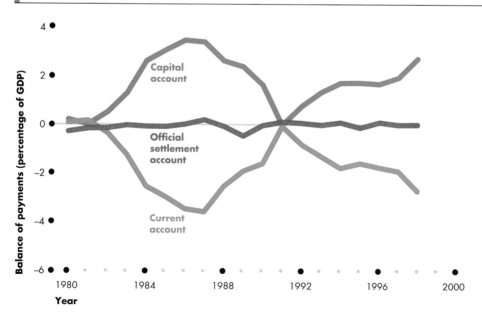

During the 1980s, a large current account deficit arose. That deficit decreased in the late 1980s but increased again after 1991. The capital account balance mirrors the current account balance. When the current account balance is negative, the capital account balance is positive— we borrow from the rest of the world. Fluctuations in the official settlements balance are small in comparison with fluctuations in the current account balance and the capital account balance.

Source: *Economic Report of the President*, 1999, and Table 37.1.

To pay for an expenditure of $52,000 in excess of her income, Joanne has to use the money that she has in the bank or has to take out a loan. In fact, Joanne took a mortgage of $50,000 to help buy her house. This mortgage was the only borrowing that Joanne did, so her capital account surplus was $50,000. With a current account deficit of $52,000 and a capital account surplus of $50,000, Joanne is still $2,000 short. She got that $2,000 from her own bank account. Her cash holdings decreased by $2,000.

Joanne's income from her work is analogous to a country's income from its exports. Her income from her investments is analogous to a country's interest income from foreigners. Her purchases of goods and services, including her purchase of a house, are analogous to a country's imports. Joanne's mortgage—borrowing from someone else—is analogous to a country's borrowing from the rest of the world. The change in her own bank account is analogous to the change in the country's official reserves.

Borrowers and Lenders, Debtors and Creditors

A country that is borrowing more from the rest of the world than it is lending to it is called a **net borrower**. Similarly, a **net lender** is a country that is lending more to the rest of the world than it is borrowing from it.

The United States is a net borrower but it is a relative newcomer to the ranks of net borrower nations. Throughout the 1960s and most of the 1970s, the United States was a net lender to the rest of the world. It had a surplus on its current account and a deficit on its capital account. It was not until 1983 that the United States became a significant net borrower from the rest of the world. Between 1983 and 1987, its borrowing increased each year. It then decreased and was briefly zero in 1991, after which it started to increase again. The average net foreign borrowing by the United States between 1983 and 1998 was $102 billion a year.

Most countries are net borrowers like the United States. But a small number of countries, including Japan and oil-rich Saudi Arabia, are net lenders.

A net borrower might be reducing its net assets held in the rest of the world or it might be going deeper into debt. A nation's total stock of foreign investment determines whether it is a debtor or creditor. A **debtor nation** is a country that during its

entire history has borrowed more from the rest of the world than it has lent to it. It has a stock of outstanding debt to the rest of the world that exceeds the stock of its own claims on the rest of the world. A **creditor nation** is a country that has invested more in the rest of the world than other countries have invested in it.

At the heart of the distinction between a net borrower/net lender and a debtor/creditor nation is the distinction between flows and stocks, which you have encountered many times in your study of macroeconomics. Borrowing and lending are flows—amounts borrowed or lent per unit of time. Debts are stocks—amounts owed at a point in time. The flow of borrowing and lending changes the stock of debt.

The United States was a debtor nation through the 19th century as we borrowed from Europe to finance our westward expansion, railroads, and industrialization. We paid off our debt and became a creditor nation for most of the current century. But following a string of current account deficits, we became a debtor nation again in 1989.

Since 1989, total stock of U.S. borrowing from the rest of the world has exceeded U.S. lending to the rest of the world. The largest debtor nations are the capital-hungry developing countries (like the United States was during the 19th century). The international debt of these countries grew from less than a third to more than a half of their gross domestic product during the 1980s and created what was called the "Third World debt crisis."

Should we be concerned that the United States is a net borrower? The answer to this question depends mainly on what the net borrower is doing with the borrowed money. If borrowing is financing investment that in turn is generating economic growth and higher income, borrowing is not a problem. If the borrowed money is being used to finance consumption, then higher interest payments are being incurred, and consequently, consumption will eventually have to be reduced. In this case the more the borrowing and the longer it goes on, the greater is the reduction in consumption that will eventually be necessary. We'll see below whether the United States is borrowing for investment or for consumption.

Current Account Balance

What determines a country's current account balance and net foreign borrowing? You've seen that net exports (*NX*) is the main item in the current account.

We can define the current account balance (*CAB*) as

$$CAB = NX + \text{Net interest income} + \text{Net transfers}.$$

Fluctuations in net exports are the main source of fluctuations in the current account balance. The other two items are small and have trends but do not fluctuate much. So we can study the current account balance by looking at what determines net exports.

Net Exports

Net exports are determined by the government budget and private saving and investment. To see how net exports are determined, we need to recall some of the things that we learned about the national income accounts in Chapter 23. Table 37.2 will refresh your memory and summarize some calculations.

Part (a) lists the national income variables that are needed, with their symbols. Part (b) defines three surpluses and deficits. **Net exports** is exports of goods and services minus imports of goods and services.

The **government sector surplus or deficit** is equal to net taxes minus government purchases of goods and services. If that number is positive, a government sector surplus is lent to other sectors; if that number is negative, a government deficit must be financed by borrowing from other sectors. The government sector deficit is the sum of the deficits of the federal, state, and local governments.

The **private sector surplus or deficit** is saving minus investment. If saving exceeds investment, a private sector surplus is lent to other sectors. If investment exceeds saving, a private sector deficit is financed by borrowing from other sectors.

Part (b) also shows the values of these deficits and surpluses for the United States in 1998. As you can see, net exports were –$151 billion, a deficit of $151 billion. The government sector's revenue from net taxes was $1,563 billion and it purchased $1,487 billion worth of goods and services. The government sector surplus was $76 billion. The private sector saved $1,140 billion and invested $1,367 billion, so it had a deficit of $227 billion.

Part (c) shows the relationship among the three deficits. From the national income accounts, we know that real GDP, *Y*, is the sum of consumption expenditure, *C*, investment, government purchases, and net exports. It also equals the sum of consumption expenditure, saving, and taxes. Rearranging these equations tells us that net exports is the sum of the government sector deficit and the private sector deficit. In the United

---

TABLE 37.2

Net Exports, the Government Budget, Saving, and Investment

	Symbols and equations	United States in 1998 (billions of dollars)
(a) Variables		
Exports	X	959
Imports	M	1,110
Government purchases	G	1,487
Net taxes	T	1,563
Investment	I	1,367
Saving	S	1,140
(b) Surpluses and deficits		
Net exports	$X - M$	$959 - 1,110 = -151$
Government sector	$T - G$	$1,563 - 1,487 = 76$
Private sector	$S - I$	$1,140 - 1,367 = -227$
(c) Relationship among surpluses and deficits		
National accounts	$Y = C + I + G + X - M$	
	$= C + S + T$	
Rearranging:	$X - M = S - I + T - G$	
Net exports	$X - M$	-151
equals:		
Government sector	$T - G$	76
plus		
Private sector	$S - I$	-227

Source: National Income and Product Accounts and *Survey of Current Business,* (March, 1999).

The National Income and Product Accounts measures of exports and imports are different from the Balance of Payments Accounts measures in Table 37.1 on p. 844.

States in 1998, the government sector had a surplus of $76 billion and the private sector had a deficit of $227 billion. The government sector deficit plus the private sector deficit equals net exports of –$151 billion.

The Twin Deficits

You've seen that net exports equal the sum of the government sector deficit and the private sector deficit. But how do these deficits fluctuate over time? Figure 37.2 answers this question. It shows the government sector deficit (the red line) and net exports *two years later* (the blue line).

You can see that there is a strong tendency for net exports to decrease (to become increasingly negative) when the government budget has gone into a deeper deficit (has become increasingly negative). Because of the tendency for the government sector deficit and the

net exports deficit to move in the same direction, they are sometimes called the **twin deficits**.

Why are the two deficits linked? It is because capital is highly mobile in today's world. If the U.S. government increases expenditure or lowers taxes, total spending in the United States rises. But with the economy at or near full employment, the extra goods and services demanded are sucked in from the rest of the world. Imports rise. Capital flows in to pay for those imports. Saving and investment don't change. In reality, these adjustments take time, which is why net exports lag behind the government sector deficit by about two years.

Is U.S. Borrowing for Consumption or Investment?

In 1998, net exports were a negative $151 billion and we borrowed this amount from abroad. Did we borrow for consumption or investment? In 1998, private investment in buildings, plant, and equipment was $1,376 billion. Government investment in defense equipment and public structures such as highways, and dams was $240 billion a year. All this investment added to the nation's capital and much of it increased productivity. Government also spends on education and health-care services, which increase *human capital*. Our international borrowing is financing private and public investment, not consumption.

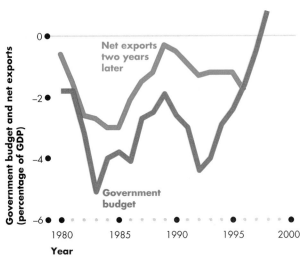

FIGURE 37.2

The Twin Deficits

Net exports and the government budget deficit move in similar ways but with a time lag of two years. If the government budget deficit increases, as it did in 1980–1983 and again in 1990–1992, net exports decrease two years later, as they did in 1982–1985 and again in 1992–1994.

Source: Survey of Current Business, March 1999.

R E V I E W   Q U I Z

- When an American art dealer buys a painting from a French gallery, which currency gets used to make the transaction?
- When a German car maker buys parts from a Detroit car maker, which currency gets used to make the transaction?
- What types of transactions do we record in the balance of payments accounts?
- What transactions does the current account record? What transactions does the capital account record? What transactions does the official settlements account record?
- How are the current account deficit, the government sector deficit, and the private sector surplus related?

The Exchange Rate

WHEN WE BUY FOREIGN GOODS OR INVEST IN another country, we have to obtain some of that country's currency to make the transaction. When foreigners buy U.S.-produced goods or invest in the United States, they have to obtain some U.S. dollars. We get foreign currency, and foreigners get U.S. dollars in the foreign exchange market. The **foreign exchange market** is the market in which the currency of one country is exchanged for the currency of another. The foreign exchange market is not a place like a downtown flea market or produce market. The market is made up of thousands of people—importers and exporters, banks, and specialists in the buying and selling of foreign exchange, called foreign exchange brokers. The foreign exchange market opens on Monday morning in Hong Kong, which is still Sunday evening in New York. As the day advances, markets open in Singapore, Tokyo, Bahrain, Frankfurt, London, New York, Chicago, and San Francisco. As the West Coast markets close, Hong Kong is only an hour away from opening for the next day of business. The sun barely sets on the foreign exchange market. Dealers around the world are in continual contact by telephone, and on a typical day in 1996, $1.3 trillion changed hands.

The price at which one currency exchanges for another is called a **foreign exchange rate**. For example, in March 1999, one U.S. dollar bought 121 Japanese yen. The exchange rate was 121 yen per dollar.

Figure 37.3 shows the exchange rate of the U.S. dollar in terms of the Japanese yen between 1980 and 1999. From 1982 to 1995, and again in early 1999, the value of the dollar fell against the yen—the dollar depreciated.

Currency depreciation is the fall in the value of one currency in terms of another currency. For example if the dollar falls from 100 yen to 80 yen, the dollar depreciates by 20 percent. From 1980 to 1982 and again during 1996 and 1998, the dollar rose in value against the yen—the dollar appreciated. **Currency appreciation** is the rise in the value of one currency in terms of another currency. For example if the dollar rises from 100 yen to 120 yen, the dollar appreciates against the yen by 20 percent.

We've just expressed the value of the U.S. dollar in terms of the yen. But we can express the value of the dollar in terms of any currency. Also, we can

FIGURE **37.3**

The Exchange Rate

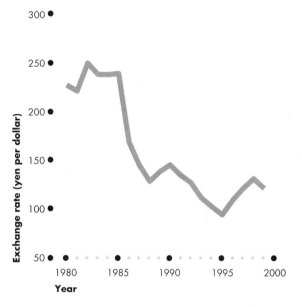

The exchange rate is the price at which two currencies can be traded. The yen-dollar exchange rate, expressed as yen per dollar, shows that the dollar has generally fallen in value—depreciated—against the yen. But since 1995, the dollar has risen against the yen.

Source: Economic Report of the President, 1999.

express the exchange rate of the yen in terms of the dollar as a number of dollars per yen.

When the U.S. dollar appreciates against the yen, the yen depreciates against the dollar.

Why does the U.S. dollar fluctuate in value? Why does it sometimes depreciate and sometimes appreciate? What happened during 1997 to make the dollar appreciate and in early 1999 to make it depreciate against the yen? To answer these questions, we need to understand the forces that determine the exchange rate.

The exchange rate is a price—the price of one country's money in terms of another country's money. And like all prices, demand and supply determine the exchange rate. So to understand the forces that determine the exchange rate, we need to study demand and supply in the foreign exchange market. We'll begin by looking at the demand side of the market.

Demand in the Foreign Exchange Market

The quantity of dollars demanded in the foreign exchange market is the amount that traders plan to buy during a given time period at a given exchange rate. This quantity depends on many factors. The main ones are:

- The exchange rate
- Interest rates in the United States and other countries
- The expected future exchange rate

Let's look first at the relationship between the quantity of dollars demanded in the foreign exchange market and the exchange rate.

The Law of Demand for Foreign Exchange

People do not buy dollars because they enjoy them. The demand for dollars is a *derived demand*. People demand dollars so that they can buy U.S.-made goods and services (U.S. exports). They also demand dollars so that they can buy U.S. assets such as bank accounts, bonds, stocks, businesses, and real estate. Nevertheless, the law of demand applies to dollars just as it does to anything else that people value.

Other things remaining the same, the higher the exchange rate, the smaller is the quantity of dollars demanded in the foreign exchange market. For example, if the price of the U.S. dollar rises from 100 yen to 120 yen but nothing else changes, the quantity of U.S. dollars that people plan to buy in the foreign exchange market decreases. Why does the exchange rate influence the quantity of dollars demanded?

There are two separate reasons, and they are related to the two sources of the derived demand for dollars:

- Exports effect
- Expected profit effect

Exports Effect   The larger the value of U.S. exports, the larger is the quantity of dollars demanded in the foreign exchange market. But the value of U.S. exports depends on the exchange rate. The lower the exchange rate, with everything else the same, the cheaper are U.S.-produced goods and services and the greater is the value of U.S. exports and the greater is the quantity of U.S. dollars demanded on the foreign exchange market to pay for these exports.

Expected Profit Effect   The larger the expected profit from holding dollars, the greater is the quantity of dollars demanded in the foreign exchange market. But expected profit depends on the exchange rate. The lower the exchange rate, other things remaining the same, the larger is the expected profit from buying dollars and the greater is the quantity of dollars demanded on the foreign exchange market.

To understand this effect, suppose you think the dollar will be worth 120 yen by the end of the month. If today, a dollar costs 115 yen, you buy dollars. But a person who thinks that the dollar will be worth 115 yen at the end of the month does not buy dollars. Now suppose the exchange rate falls to 110 yen per dollar. More people think they can profit from buying dollars, so the quantity of dollars demanded increases.

For the two reasons we've just reviewed, other things remaining the same, when the foreign exchange rate rises, the quantity of dollars demanded decreases, and when the foreign exchange rate falls, the quantity of dollars demanded increases. Figure 37.4 shows the demand curve for U.S. dollars in the foreign exchange market. In this figure, when the foreign exchange rate rises, other things remaining the same, there is a decrease in the quantity of dollars demanded and a movement upward along the demand curve as shown by the arrow. When the exchange rate falls, other things remaining the same, there is an increase in the quantity of dollars demanded and a movement downward along the demand curve as shown by the arrow.

Changes in the Demand for Dollars

A change in any other influence on the dollars that people plan to buy in the foreign exchange market brings a change in the demand for dollars and a shift in the demand curve for dollars. Demand either increases or decreases. These other influences are:

- Interest rates in the United States and other countries
- The expected future exchange rate

Interest Rates in the United States and Other Countries   People and businesses buy financial assets to make a return. The higher the interest rate that people can make on U.S. assets compared with foreign assets, the more U.S. assets they buy. What matters is not the level of U.S. interest rates, but the U.S. interest rate minus the foreign interest rate, a

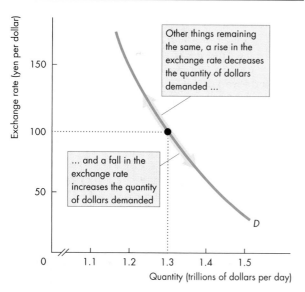

FIGURE 37.4

The Demand for Dollars

The quantity of dollars that people plan to buy depends on the exchange rate. Other things remaining the same, if the exchange rate rises, the quantity of dollars demanded decreases and there is a movement upward along the demand curve for dollars. If the exchange rate falls, the quantity of dollars demanded increases and there is a movement downward along the demand curve for dollars.

gap that is called the **U.S. interest rate differential**. If the U.S. interest rate rises and the foreign interest rate remains constant, the U.S. interest rate differential increases. The larger the U.S. interest rate differential, the greater is the demand for U.S. assets and the greater is the demand for dollars on the foreign exchange market.

The Expected Future Exchange Rate   Other things remaining the same, the higher the expected future exchange rate, the greater is the demand for dollars. To see why, suppose you are Toyota's finance manager. The exchange rate is 100 yen per dollar and you think that by the end of the month, it will be 120 yen per dollar. You spend 100,000 yen today and buy $1,000. At the end of the month, the dollar is 120 yen, as you predicted it would be, and you sell the $1,000. You get 120,000 yen. You've made a profit of 20,000 yen, or almost $167. The higher the expected

future exchange rate, other things remaining the same, the greater is the expected profit and the greater is the demand for dollars today.

Figure 37.5 summarizes the above discussion of the influences on the demand for dollars. A rise in the U.S. interest differential or a rise in the expected future exchange rate increases the demand for dollars and shifts the demand curve rightward from D_0 to D_1. A fall in the U.S. interest differential or a fall in the expected future exchange rate decreases the demand for dollars and shifts the demand curve leftward from D_0 to D_2.

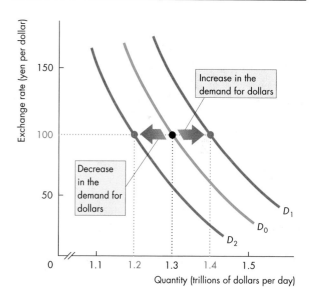

FIGURE 37.5

Changes in the Demand for Dollars

A change in any influence on the quantity of dollars that people plan to buy, other than the exchange rate, brings a change in the demand for dollars.

The demand for dollars:

Increases if:	Decreases if:
■ The U.S. interest rate differential increases	■ The U.S. interest rate differential decreases
■ The expected future exchange rate rises	■ The expected future exchange rate falls

Supply in the Foreign Exchange Market

The quantity of U.S. dollars supplied in the foreign exchange market is the amount that traders plan to sell during a given time period at a given exchange rate. This quantity depends on many factors. The main ones are:

- The exchange rate
- Interest rates in the United States and other countries
- The expected future exchange rate

Let's look first at the relationship between the quantity of dollars supplied in the foreign exchange market and the exchange rate.

The Law of Supply of Foreign Exchange

People supply dollars in the foreign exchange market when they buy other currencies. And they buy other currencies so that they can buy foreign-made goods and services (U.S. imports). They also supply dollars and buy foreign currencies so that they can buy foreign assets such as bank accounts, bonds, stocks, businesses, and real estate. The law of supply applies to dollars just as it does to anything else that people plan to sell.

Other things remaining the same, the higher the exchange rate, the greater is the quantity of dollars supplied in the foreign exchange market. For example, if the price of the U.S. dollar rises from 100 yen to 120 yen but nothing else changes, the quantity of yen that people plan to buy in the foreign exchange market increases and so the quantity of U.S. dollars supplied increases. Why does the exchange rate influence the quantity of dollars supplied?

There are two reasons and they parallel the two reasons on the demand side of the market:

- Imports effect
- Expected profit effect

Imports Effect   The larger the value of U.S. imports, the larger is the quantity of foreign currency demanded to pay for these imports. And when people buy foreign currency, they supply dollars. So the larger the value of U.S. imports, the greater is the quantity of

dollars supplied in the foreign exchange market. But the value of U.S. imports depends on the exchange rate. The higher the exchange rate, with everything else the same, the cheaper are foreign-produced good and services to Americans, the more the United States imports, and the greater is the quantity of U.S. dollars supplied on the foreign exchange market to pay for these imports.

Expected Profit Effect   The larger the expected profit from holding a foreign currency, the greater is the quantity of that currency demanded and the greater is the quantity of dollars supplied in the foreign exchange market. But the expected profit from holding a foreign currency depends on the exchange rate. The higher the exchange rate, other things remaining the same, the larger is the expected profit from selling dollars and the greater is the quantity of dollars supplied on the foreign exchange market.

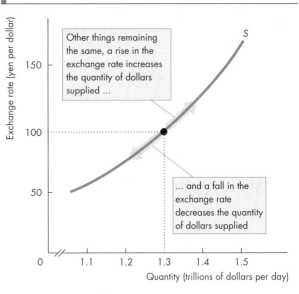

FIGURE 37.6
The Supply of Dollars

The quantity of dollars that people plan to sell depends on the exchange rate. Other things remaining the same, if the exchange rate rises, the quantity of dollars supplied increases and there is a movement upward along the supply curve for dollars. If the exchange rate falls, the quantity of dollars supplied decreases and there is a movement downward along the supply curve for dollars.

For the two reasons we've just reviewed, other things remaining the same, when the foreign exchange rate rises, the quantity of dollars supplied increases, and when the foreign exchange rate falls, the quantity of dollars supplied decreases. Figure 37.6 shows the supply curve for U.S. dollars in the foreign exchange market. In this figure, when the foreign exchange rate rises, other things remaining the same, there is an increase in the quantity of dollars supplied and a movement upward along the supply curve as shown by the arrow. When the exchange rate falls, other things remaining the same, there is a decrease in the quantity of dollars supplied and a movement downward along the supply curve as shown by the arrow.

Changes in the Supply of Dollars

A change in any other influence on the dollars that people plan to sell in the foreign exchange market brings a change in the supply of dollars and a shift in the supply curve for dollars. Supply either increases or decreases. These other influences parallel the other influences on demand but have exactly the opposite effects. These influences are:

■ Interest rates in the United States and other countries
■ The expected future exchange rate

Interest Rates in the United States and Other Countries The larger the U.S. interest rate differential, the smaller is the demand for foreign assets and so the smaller is the supply of dollars in the foreign exchange market.

The Expected Future Exchange Rate Other things remaining the same, the higher the expected future exchange rate, the smaller is the supply of dollars. To see why, suppose the dollar is trading at 100 yen per dollar today and you think that by the end of the month, the dollar will be 120 yen per dollar. You were planning on selling dollars today, but you decide to hold off and wait until the end of the month. If you supply dollars today, you get only 100 yen per dollar. But at the end of the month, if the dollar is 120 yen per dollar as you predict, you'll get 120 yen for each dollar you supply. You'll make a profit of 20 percent. So, the higher the expected future exchange

rate, other things remaining the same, the smaller is the expected profit from selling U.S. dollars today and the smaller is the supply of dollars today.

Figure 37.7 summarizes the above discussion of the influences on the supply of dollars. A rise in the U.S. interest differential or a rise in the expected future exchange rate decreases the supply of dollars and shifts the demand curve leftward from S_0 to S_1. A fall in the U.S. interest differential or a fall in the expected future exchange rate increases the supply of dollars and shifts the supply curve rightward from S_0 to S_2.

FIGURE 37.7

Changes in the Supply of Dollars

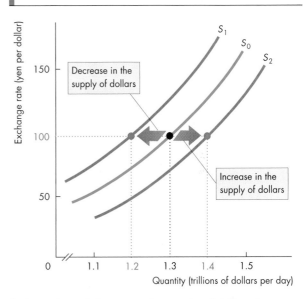

A change in any influence on the quantity of dollars that people plan to sell, other than the exchange rate, brings a change in the supply of dollars.

The supply of dollars:

Increases if:	Decreases if:
■ The U.S. interest rate differential decreases	■ The U.S. interest rate differential increases
■ The expected future exchange rate falls	■ The expected future exchange rate rises

Market Equilibrium

Figure 37.8 shows how demand and supply in the foreign exchange market determine the exchange rate. The demand curve is *D*, and the supply curve is *S*. Just like all the other markets you've studied, the price (the exchange rate) acts as a regulator.

If the exchange rate is too high, there is a surplus of dollars—the quantity supplied exceeds the quantity demanded. In Fig. 37.8, if the exchange rate is 150 yen per dollar, there is a surplus of dollars. If the exchange rate is too low, there is a shortage of dollars—the quantity supplied is less than the quantity demanded. In Fig. 37.8, if the exchange rate is 50 yen per dollar, there is a shortage of dollars.

At the equilibrium exchange rate, there is neither a shortage nor a surplus. The quantity supplied equals the quantity demanded. In Fig. 37.8, the equilibrium exchange rate is 100 yen per dollar. At this exchange rate, the quantity demanded equals the quantity supplied and $1.3 trillion a day is bought and sold.

The foreign exchange market is constantly pulled to its equilibrium by the forces of supply and demand. Foreign exchange dealers are constantly looking for the best price they can get. If they are selling, they want the highest price available. If they are buying, they want the lowest price available. Information flows from dealer to dealer through the worldwide computer network, and the price adjusts second by second to keep buying plans and selling plans in balance. That is, price adjusts second by second to keep the market at its equilibrium.

Changes in the Exchange Rate

If the demand for dollars increases and the supply of dollars does not change, the exchange rate rises. If the demand for dollars decreases and the supply of dollars does not change, the exchange rate falls. Similarly, if the supply of dollars decreases and the demand for dollars does not change, the exchange rate rises. If the supply of dollars increases and the demand for dollars does not change, the exchange rate falls.

These predictions about the effects of changes in demand and supply are the same as for other markets.

Why the Exchange Rate Is Volatile Sometimes the dollar depreciates and at other times it appreciates, but the quantity of dollars traded each day barely changes. Why? The main reason is that supply and demand are not independent of each other in the foreign exchange market.

When we studied the demand for dollars and the supply of dollars, we saw that unlike other markets, the demand side and the supply side of the market have some common influences. A change in the expected future exchange rate or a change in the U.S. interest rate differential changes both demand and supply—and in opposite directions. These common influences on both demand and supply explain why the exchange rate can be volatile at times, even though the quantity of dollars traded does not change.

Everyone in the foreign exchange market is potentially a demander and a supplier. Each has a price above which he or she will sell and below which he or she will buy. Let's see how these common supply and demand effects work by looking at two episodes: one in which the dollar appreciated and one in which it depreciated.

FIGURE 37.8
Equilibrium Exchange Rate ◆

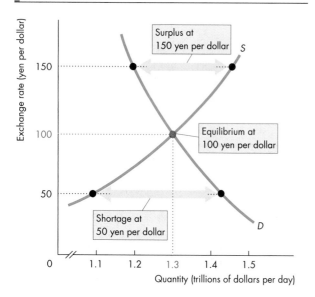

The demand curve for dollars is *D*, and the supply curve is *S*. If the exchange rate is 150 yen per dollar, there is a surplus of dollars and the exchange rate falls. If the exchange rate is 50 yen per dollar, there is a shortage of dollars and the exchange rate rises. If the exchange rate is 100 yen per dollar, there is neither a shortage nor a surplus of dollars and the exchange rate remains constant. The market is in equilibrium.

A Depreciating Dollar: 1994–1995 Between 1994 and the summer of 1995, the dollar fell from 100 yen to a low of 84 yen per dollar. Figure 37.9(a) explains this fall. In 1994, the demand and supply curves were those labeled D_{94} and S_{94}. The exchange rate was 100 yen per dollar. During 1994, traders expected the U.S. dollar to depreciate. They expected a lower exchange rate. As a result, the demand for dollars decreased and the supply of dollars increased. The demand curve shifted leftward to D_{95}, and the supply curve shifted rightward to S_{95}. The exchange rate fell to 84 yen per dollar.

An Appreciating Dollar: 1995–1998 Between 1995 and 1998, the dollar appreciated against the yen. It rose from 84 yen to 130 yen per dollar. Figure 37.9(b) explains why this happened. In 1995, the demand and supply curves were those labeled D_{95} and S_{95}. The exchange rate was 84 yen per dollar—where the supply and demand curves intersect. During the next two years, Japan was in recession

and the U.S. economy was expanding. Interest rates in Japan fell, and the yen was expected to depreciate. The demand for yen decreased. As a result, the demand for dollars increased, and the supply of dollars decreased. The demand curve shifted from D_{95} to D_{98}, and the supply curve shifted from S_{95} to S_{98}. These two shifts reinforced each other, and the exchange rate increased to 130 yen per dollar.

Exchange Rate Expectations

The changes in the exchange rate that we've just examined occurred in part because the exchange rate was *expected to change*. This explanation sounds a bit like a self-fulfilling forecast. But what makes expectations change? The answer is new information about the deeper forces that influence the value of money. Two such forces are:

■ Purchasing power parity

■ Interest rate parity

FIGURE 37.9

Exchange Rate Fluctuations

(a) 1994 to 1995

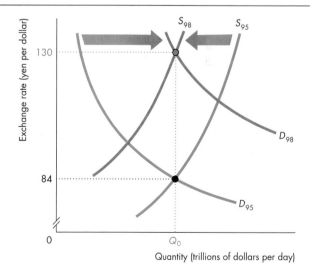

(b) 1995 to 1998

The exchange rate fluctuates because changes in demand and supply are not independent of each other. Everyone in the foreign exchange market is a potential buyer and seller. Between 1994 and 1995 (in part a), the dollar depreciated from 100 to 84 yen per dollar. The exchange rate was expected to depreciate, which decreased the demand for dollars and increased the

supply. Between 1995 and 1998 (part b), the dollar appreciated from 84 to 130 yen per dollar. This appreciation occurred because a weak Japanese economy and low interest rates in Japan generated an expectation of a weak yen and a strong dollar. The supply of dollars decreased, the demand for dollars increased, and the dollar rose in value.

Purchasing Power Parity   Money is worth what it will buy. But two kinds of money, U.S. dollars and Canadian dollars for example, might buy different amounts of goods and services. Suppose a Big Mac costs $4 (Canadian) in Toronto and $3 (U.S.) in New York. If the Canadian dollar exchange rate is $1.33 Canadian per U.S. dollar, the two monies have the same value. You can buy a Big Mac in both Toronto and New York for either $4 Canadian or $3 U.S.

The situation we've just described is called **purchasing power parity**, which means *equal value of money*. If purchasing power parity does not prevail, some powerful forces go to work. To understand these forces, let's suppose that the price of a Big Mac in New York rises to $4 U.S., but in Toronto it remains at $4 Canadian. Suppose the exchange rate remains at $1.33 Canadian per U.S. dollar. In this case, a Big Mac in Toronto still costs $4 Canadian or $3 U.S. But in New York, it costs $4 U.S. or $5.33 Canadian. Money buys more in Canada than in the United States. Money is not of equal value in both countries.

If all (or most) prices have increased in the United States and not increased in Canada, then people will generally expect that the value of the U.S. dollar on the foreign exchange market must fall. In this situation, the exchange rate is expected to fall. The demand for U.S. dollars decreases, and the supply of U.S. dollars increases. The exchange rate falls, as expected. If the exchange rate falls to $1.00 Canadian and there are no further price changes, purchasing power parity is restored. A Big Mac now costs $4 in either U.S. or Canadian dollars in both New York and Toronto.

If prices increase in Canada and other countries but remain constant in the United States, then people will generally expect that the value of the U.S. dollar on the foreign exchange market is too low and that it is going to rise. In this situation, the exchange rate is expected to rise. The demand for U.S. dollars increases, and the supply of U.S. dollars decreases. The exchange rate rises, as expected.

Ultimately, the value of money is determined by the price level, which in turn is determined by aggregate supply and aggregate demand (see Chapter 25, pp. 542–543 and Chapter 33, pp. 737–741.) So the deeper forces that influence the exchange rate have tentacles that spread throughout the economy. If prices in the United States rise faster than those in other countries, the exchange rate falls. And if prices rise more slowly in the United States than in other countries, the exchange rate rises.

Interest Rate Parity   Money is worth what it can earn. Again, two kinds of money, Canadian dollars and U.S. dollars, for example, might earn different amounts. Suppose a Canadian dollar bank deposit in Toronto earns 5 percent a year and a U.S. dollar bank deposit in New York earns 3 percent a year. In this situation, why does anyone deposit money in New York? Why doesn't all the money flow to Toronto? The answer is: Because of exchange rate expectations. Suppose people expect the Canadian dollar to depreciate by 2 percent a year. This 2 percent depreciation must be subtracted from the 5 percent interest to obtain the net return of 3 percent a year that an American expects to earn by depositing funds in a Toronto bank. The two returns are equal. This situation is one of **interest rate parity**, which means *equal interest rates*.

Adjusted for risk, interest rate parity always prevails. Funds move to get the highest return available. If for a few seconds a higher return is available in New York than in Toronto, the demand for U.S. dollars rises and the exchange rate rises until expected interest rates are equal.

The Fed in the Foreign Exchange Market

Interest rates in the United States are determined by the demand for and supply of money (see Chapter 32, pp. 723–724). But the supply of money is influenced by the Fed, so ultimately, the exchange rate is influenced by monetary policy. When interest rates in the United States rise, relative to those in other countries, the demand for U.S. dollars increases, the supply decreases, and the exchange rate rises. (Similarly, when interest rates in the United States fall, relative to those in other countries, the demand for U.S. dollars decreases, the supply increases, and the exchange rate falls.)

But the Fed can intervene directly in the foreign exchange market. It can buy or sell dollars and try to smooth out fluctuations in the exchange rate. Let's look at the foreign exchange interventions that the Fed can make.

Suppose the Fed wants the exchange rate to be steady at 120 yen per dollar. If the exchange rate rises above 120 yen per dollar, the Fed sells dollars. If the exchange rate falls below 120 yen per dollar, the Fed buys dollars. By these actions, it changes supply or demand and keeps the exchange rate close to its target rate of 120 yen per dollar.

Figure 37.10 shows this Fed intervention in the foreign exchange market. The supply of dollars is S, and initially the demand for dollars is D_0. The equilibrium exchange rate is 120 yen per dollar. This exchange rate is the Fed's target rate, shown by the horizontal red line in the figure.

When the demand for dollars increases and the demand curve shifts rightward to D_1, the Fed sells $0.1 trillion. This action increases the supply of dollars by $0.1 trillion and prevents the exchange rate from rising. When the demand for dollars decreases and the demand curve shifts leftward to D_2, the Fed buys $0.1 trillion. This action decreases the supply of dollars by $0.1 trillion and prevents the exchange rate from falling.

If the demand for dollars fluctuates between D_1 and D_2 and on the average is D_0, the Fed can repeatedly intervene in the way we've just seen. Sometimes the Fed buys and sometimes it sells, but on the average, it neither buys nor sells.

But suppose the demand for dollars increases permanently from D_0 to D_1. The Fed cannot now maintain the exchange rate at 120 yen per dollar indefinitely. To do so, the Fed would have to sell dollars every day. When the Fed sells dollars in the foreign exchange market, it buys foreign currency. So the Fed would be piling up foreign currency.

Now suppose the demand for dollars decreases permanently from D_0 to D_2. Again the Fed cannot maintain the exchange rate at 120 yen per dollar indefinitely. In this situation, to hold the exchange rate at 120 yen per dollars, the Fed would have to buy dollars every day. When the Fed buys dollars in the foreign exchange market, it uses its holdings of foreign currency. So the Fed would be losing foreign currency. Eventually, it would run out of foreign currency and would then have to abandon its attempt to fix the exchange rate.

FIGURE 37.10

Foreign Exchange Market Intervention

Initially, the demand for dollars is D_0, the supply of dollars is S, and the exchange rate is 120 yen per dollar. The Fed can intervene in the foreign exchange market to keep the exchange rate close to its target rate (120 yen in this example). If demand increases from D_0 to D_1, the Fed sells dollars to increase supply. If demand decreases from D_0 to D_2, the Fed buys dollars to decrease supply. Persistent intervention on one side of the market cannot be sustained.

- What is the exchange rate and how is it determined?
- What are the influences of interest rates and the expected future exchange rate on the demand for and supply of dollars in the foreign exchange market?
- How do changes in the expected future exchange rate influence the actual exchange rate?
- How do purchasing power parity and interest rate parity affect exchange rate expectations?
- How can the Fed influence the foreign exchange market?

Reading Between the Lines on pages 858–859 looks at exchange rates in 1999 and the relative purchasing power of different currencies in terms of a Big Mac.

You have now reached the end of your economics course. Go back to the big ideas that define the way of economic thinking (on pp. 6–11) and see how much more they mean to you now than they did when you first read them. I hope that your instructor and I have helped to open your eyes and shown you a new way of seeing the world. If we have, you can now do your own "reading between the lines" every day. Keep your economics text handy. Use it to refresh you memory of the economic principles that help you make sense of your world.

Reading Between the Lines

POLICY WATCH

Purchasing Power Parity

THE ECONOMIST, APRIL 3, 1999

Big MacCurrencies

... The Big Mac Index was devised 13 years ago as a light-hearted guide to whether currencies are at their "correct" level. It is based upon one of the oldest concepts in international economics: purchasing power parity (PPP)—the notion that a dollar, say, should buy the same amount in all countries. In the long run, argue PPP fans, currencies should move towards the rate which equalizes the prices of an identical basket of goods and services in each country.

Out "basket" is a McDonald's Big Mac, which is produced in more than 100 countries. The Big Mac PPP is the exchange rate that would leave hamburgers costing the same in America as abroad. Comparing actual exchange rates with PPPs signals whether a currency is under- or over-valued. ...

The American price (the average of four cities, including tax) has dropped by 5% over the past year, to $2.43. Elsewhere the cheapest Big Mac is in Malaysia ($1.19), whereas in Switzerland it costs a beefy $3.97. Hence the Swiss franc is the most overvalued currency (by 64%) the ringgit the most undervalued (by 51%). ...

The hamburger standard

| | Big Mac prices | | Under(-)/over(+) valuation |
	In local currency	In dollars	against the dollar, %
United States‡	$2.43	2.43	—
Argentina	Peso2.50	2.50	+3
Australia	A$2.65	1.66	−32
Brazil	Real2.95	1.73	−30
Britain	£1.90	3.07	+26
Canada	C$2.99	1.98	−19
Chile	Peso1,25	2.60	+7
China	Yuan9.90	1.20	−51
Denmark	DKr24.75	3.58	+47
Euro area	Euro2.52	2.71	+11
France	FFr8.50	2.87	+18
Germany	DM4.95	2.72	+12
Italy	Lire4,500	2.50	+3
Netherlands	Fl5.45	2.66	+10
Spain	Pta375	2.43	0
Hong Kong	HK$10.2	1.32	−46
Hungary	Forint299	1.26	−48
Indonesia	Rupiah14,500	1.66	−32
Israel	Shekel13.9	3.44	+42
Japan	¥294	2.44	0
Malaysia	M$4.52	1.15	−51
Mexico	Peso19.9	2.05	−14
New Zealand	NZ$3.40	1.82	−25
Poland	Zloty5.50	1.38	−43
Russia	Rouble33.5	1.35	−44
Singapore	S$3.20	1.85	−24
South Africa	Rand8.60	1.38	−43
South Korea	Won3,000	2.46	+1
Sweden	SKr24.0	2.86	+19
Switzerland	SFr5.90	3.97	+64
Taiwan	NT$70.0	2.11	−13
Thailand	Baht52.0	1.38	−43

Essence of the Story

■ *The Economist* publishes a Big Mac index of currencies.

■ The index is based on the price of a McDonald's Big Mac, which is now produced in over 100 countries.

■ The Big Mac purchasing power parity (PPP) is the exchange rate that makes a Big Mac cost the same in all countries.

■ *The Economist* uses this index to judge whether currencies are at their "correct" PPP level.

■ In April 1999, the Big Mac cost an average of $2.43 in the United States. It cost least in Malaysia, $1.19, and most in Switzerland, $3.97.

■ *The Economist* concludes that the Malaysian ringgit is the most undervalued currency (by 51%) and the Swiss franc is the most overvalued (by 64%).

Economic Analysis

■ Although *The Economist* is having a bit of fun with its Big Mac index, it is also doing some misleading and potentially wrong economics.

■ The basic assumption is that a Big Mac is the same good the world over. Because it is the same good, it should have the same price. Any price differences are due to currencies being undervalued or overvalued.

■ The assumption is wrong. When McDonald's sells a Big Mac, it sells a *service*—a fast food service—as well as a good.

■ The price of the service component of a Big Mac varies from place to place and depends on local demand and supply conditions.

■ Figure 1 shows the range of prices *inside the United States*. The highest price is in New York City, where a Big Mac costs $3.13 with tax. The lowest price is in Jonesboro, Arkansas, where the price is $1.80.

■ More than half the countries in *The Economist*'s table have prices that fall inside the range of those in the United States.

■ Only three of *The Economist*'s countries—Switzerland, Denmark, and Israel—have prices that exceed the price in New York City.

■ Only eleven of *The Economist*'s countries have prices below the price in Jonesboro, Arkansas.

■ There are many reasons why the local prices of a Big Mac vary—some on the demand side and some on the supply side.

■ A major supply side influence is the cost of labor. An hour of labor in Switzerland costs 75 times that of an hour of labor in Malaysia.

■ To make PPP comparisons, we must use goods that are easily transported among countries and that have a small or no service component. The price of a floppy disk, a PC, or a computer chip would do a much better job of revealing PPP than the price of a Big Mac.

■ *The Economist* should replace its Big Mac standard with the Intel chip standard.

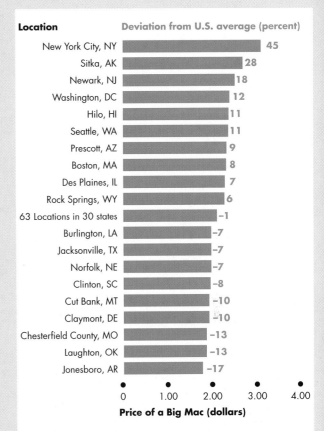

PPP Across the States

You're The Voter

■ Why does it matter whether the dollar is undervalued or overvalued?

■ What can the Fed do if it believes that the dollar is undervalued or overvalued?

■ Thinking only about your own economic well-being, what is better for you: an undervalued dollar or an overvalued dollar?

859

SUMMARY

KEY POINTS

Financing International Trade (pp. 844–848)

- International trade, borrowing, and lending are financed by using foreign currency.
- A country's international transactions are recorded in its balance of payments accounts.
- Historically, the United States has been a net lender to the rest of the world, but in 1983, that situation changed and the United States became a net borrower. In 1989, the United States became a net debtor.
- The net exports deficit is equal to the government sector deficit plus the private sector deficit.

The Exchange Rate (pp. 849–857)

- Foreign currency is obtained in exchange for domestic currency in the foreign exchange market.
- The exchange rate is determined by demand and supply in the foreign exchange market.
- The lower the exchange rate, the greater is the quantity of dollars demanded. A change in the exchange rate brings a movement along the demand curve for dollars.
- Changes in the U.S. interest rate differential and the expected future exchange rate change the demand for dollars and shift the demand curve.
- The lower the exchange rate, the smaller is the quantity of dollars supplied. A change in the exchange rate brings a movement along the supply curve for dollars.
- Changes in the U.S. interest rate differential and the expected future exchange rate change the supply of dollars and shift the supply curve.
- Fluctuations in the exchange rate occur because fluctuations in the demand for and supply of dollars are not independent.
- The Fed can intervene in the foreign exchange market to smooth fluctuations in the dollar.

KEY FIGURES AND TABLE

KEY TERMS

PROBLEMS

*1. The citizens of Silecon, whose currency is the grain, conduct the following transactions in 1999:

Item	Billions of grains
Imports of goods and services	350
Exports of goods and services	500
Borrowing from the rest of the world	60
Lending to the rest of the world	200
Increase in official holdings of foreign currency	10

a. Set out the three balance of payments accounts for Silecon.
b. Does Silecon have a flexible exchange rate?

2. The citizens of Spin, whose currency is the wheel, conduct the following transactions in 1999:

Item	Wheels
Imports of goods and services	50
Exports of goods and services	60
Borrowing from the rest of the world	2
Lending to the rest of the world	12
Increase in official holdings of foreign currency	0

a. Set out the three balance of payments accounts for Spin.
b. Does Spin have a flexible exchange rate?

*3. The figure below shows the flows of income and expenditure in Dream Land in 2000. The amounts are in millions of dollars. GDP in Dream Land is $60 million.
a. Calculate Dream Land's net exports.
b. Calculate saving in Dream Land.
c. How is Dream Land's investment financed?

4. The figure below shows the flows of income and expenditure in Dream Land in 2001. The amounts are in millions of dollars. Dream Land's GDP has increased to $65 million, but all the other items whose values are provided in the figure remain the same as they were in 2000.
a. Calculate Dream Land's net exports in 2001.
b. Calculate saving in Dream Land in 2001.
c. How is Dream Land's investment financed?

*5. The following table tells you about Ecflex, a country with a flexible exchange rate whose currency is the band.
Calculate the following for Ecflex:
a. Imports of goods and services
b. Current account balance
c. Capital account balance
d. Net taxes
e. Private sector surplus

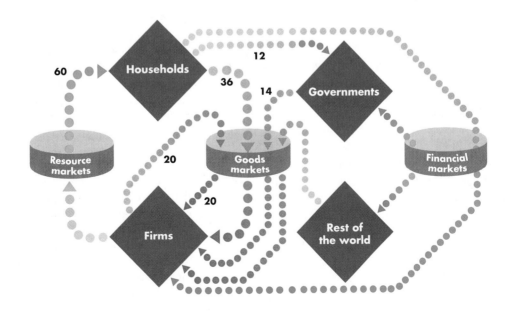

Item	Billion bands
GDP	100
Consumption expenditure	60
Government purchases of goods and services	24

Item	Billion bands
Investment	22
Exports of goods and services	20
Government budget deficit	4

6. You are told the following about Ecfix, a country with a fixed exchange rate whose currency is the rock:

Item	Billion rocks
GDP	200
Consumption expenditure	120
Government purchases of goods and services	50
Investment	50
Exports of goods and services	40
Saving	45

Calculate the following for Ecfix:
a. Imports of goods and services
b. Current account balance
c. Capital account balance
d. Net taxes
e. Private sector surplus
f. Government deficit or surplus

*7. A country's currency appreciates, and its official holdings of foreign currency increase. What can you say about:
a. The exchange rate system being pursued by the country?
b. The possible central bank sources of the currency appreciation?
c. The possible private actions behind the appreciation?

8. A country's currency depreciates, and its official holdings of foreign currency decrease. What can you say about:
a. The exchange rate system being pursued by the country?
b. The possible sources of the currency depreciation?
c. The possible private actions behind the depreciation?

CRITICAL THINKING

1. Study *Reading Between the Lines* on pp. 858–859 and then answer the following questions.
   a. Which currencies does *The Economist* claim are undervalued and which does it claim are overvalued?
   b. What is PPP?
   c. What is the key assumption used by *The Economist* to make its PPP calculations?
   d. What is wrong with *The Economist's* assumptions?
   e. Use the Bulletin Board on the Parkin Web site to share information on the prices of floppy disks around the world and do a PPP comparison based on the floppy disk standard.

2. Use the link on the Parkin Web site to visit FRED, the database of the Federal Reserve Bank of St. Louis, and find data on the exchange rate and international trade.
   a. When did the United States last have a current account surplus?
   b. Does the United States have a surplus or a deficit in its trade in goods?
   c. Does the United States have a surplus or a deficit in its trade in services?
   d. What has happened to foreign investment in the United States during the past ten years?
   e. Do you think that the U.S. balance of payments record is a matter for concern? Why or why not?

3. Use the link on the Parkin Web site to get recent data on the exchange rate of the U.S. dollar against two other currencies that interest you over the past month. Then:
   a. Use the demand and supply model of the foreign exchange market to explain the changes (or absence of changes) in the exchange rates.
   b. What specific events might have changed exchange rate expectations?
   c. What forces might have prevented the exchange rates from changing?
   d. What information would you need to be able to determine whether central bank intervention has prevented either exchange rate from changing by as much as it otherwise would have?

The scale of international trade, borrowing, and lending, both in absolute dollar terms and as a percentage of total world production, expands every year. One country, Singapore, imports and exports goods and services in a volume that exceeds its gross domestic product. The world's largest nation, China, returned to the international economic stage during the 1980s and is now a major producer of manufactured goods. ◆ International economic activity is large because today's economic world is small and because communication is so incredibly fast. But today's world is not a new world. From the beginning of recorded history, people have traded over large and steadily increasing distances. The great Western civilizations of Greece and Rome traded not only around the Mediterranean but also into the Gulf of Arabia. The great Eastern civilizations traded around the Indian Ocean. By the Middle Ages, the East and the West were trading routinely overland on routes pioneered by Venetian traders and explorers such as Marco Polo. When, in 1497, Vasco da Gama opened a sea route between the Atlantic and Indian Oceans around Africa, a new trade between East and West began, which brought tumbling prices of Eastern goods in Western markets. ◆ The European discovery of America and the subsequent opening up of Atlantic trade continued the process of steady globalization. So the developments of the 1990s, amazing though many of

It's a Small World

them were, represent a continuation of an ongoing expansion of human horizons. ◆ These two chapters study the interaction of nations in today's global economy. ◆ Chapter 36 described and explained international trade in goods and services. In this chapter, you came face to face with one of the biggest policy issues of all ages: free trade versus protection. The chapter explained how all nations can benefit from free international trade. And it showed how protection from competition brings big benefits to a few and small losses to many. The total gains from protection are dwarfed by the losses, but because the losses are spread thinly and the gains thickly, protectionism always has supporters and political backers. ◆ Chapter 37 explained some of the fundamentals of international borrowing and lending and the exchange rate. It explained the poorly understood fact that the size of a nation's international deficit depends not on how efficient it is, but on how much its citizens save relative to how much they invest. Nations with low saving rates, everything else remaining the same, have international deficits. ◆ This chapter also explains why foreign exchange rates fluctuate so much. ◆ The global economy is big news these days. And it has always attracted attention. On the next page, you can meet the economist who first understood comparative advantage: David Ricardo. And you can meet one of today's leading international economists, Stanley Fischer, formally a professor at MIT and now Deputy Managing Director of the International Monetary Fund.

The Economist

David Ricardo *(1772–1832) was a highly successful 27-year-old stockbroker when he stumbled on a copy of Adam Smith's* Wealth of Nations *(see p. 56) on a weekend visit to the country. He was immediately hooked and went on to become the most celebrated economist of his age and one of the all-time great economists. One of his many contributions was to develop the principle of comparative advantage, the foundation on which the modern theory of international trade is built. The example he used to illustrate this principle was the trade between England and Portugal in cloth and wine.*

The General Agreement on Tariffs and Trade was established as a reaction against the devastation wrought by beggar-my-neighbor tariffs imposed during the 1930s. But it is also a triumph for the logic first worked out by Smith and Ricardo.

"Under a system of perfectly free commerce, each country naturally devotes its capital and labor to such employments as are most beneficial to each."

DAVID RICARDO
The Principles of Political Economy and Taxation,
1817

The Issues

Until the mid-eighteenth century, it was generally believed that the purpose of international trade was to keep exports greater than imports and pile up gold. If gold was accumulated, it was believed, the nation would prosper; if gold was lost through an international deficit, the nation would be drained of money and impoverished. These beliefs are called *mercantilism*, and the *mercantilists* were pamphleteers who advocated with missionary

fervor the pursuit of an international surplus. If exports did not exceed imports, the mercantilists wanted imports restricted.

In the 1740s, David Hume explained that as the quantity of money (gold) changes, so also does the price level, and the nation's *real* wealth is unaffected. In the 1770s, Adam Smith argued that import restrictions would lower the gains from specialization and make a nation poorer. Thirty years later, David Ricardo proved the law of comparative advantage and demonstrated the superiority of free trade. Mercantilism was intellectually bankrupt but remained politically powerful.

Gradually, through the nineteenth century, the mercantilist influence waned and North America and Western Europe prospered in an environment of increasingly free international trade. But despite remarkable advances in economic understanding, mercantilism never quite died. It had a brief and devastating revival in the 1920s and 1930s when tariff hikes brought about the collapse of international trade and accentuated the Great Depression. It subsided again after World War II with the establishment of the General Agreement on Tariffs and Trade (GATT).

But mercantilism lingers on. The often expressed view that the United States should restrict Japanese imports and reduce its deficit with Japan and fears that NAFTA will bring economic ruin to the United States are modern manifestations of mercantilism. It would be interesting to have David

Hume, Adam Smith, and David Ricardo commenting on these views. But we know what they would say—the same things that they said to the eighteenth-century mercantilists. And they would still be right today.

Then

In the eighteenth century, when mercantilists and economists were debating the pros and cons of free international exchange, the transportation technology that was available limited the gains from international trade. Sailing ships with tiny cargo holds took close to a month to cross the Atlantic Ocean. But the potential gains were large, and so was the incentive to cut shipping costs. By the 1850s, the clipper ship had been developed, cutting the journey from Boston to Liverpool to only 12¼ days. Half a century later, 10,000-ton steamships were sailing between America and England in just 4 days. As sailing times and costs declined, the gains from international trade increased and the volume of trade expanded.

Now

The container ship has revolutionized international trade and contributed to its continued expansion. Today, most goods cross the oceans in containers—metal boxes—packed into and piled on top of ships like this one. Container technology has cut the cost of ocean shipping by economizing on handling and by making cargoes harder to steal, lowering insurance costs. It is unlikely that there would be much international trade in goods such as television sets and VCRs without this technology. High-value and perishable cargoes such as flowers and fresh foods, as well as urgent courier packages, travel by air. Every day, dozens of cargo-laden 747s fly between every major U.S. city and to destinations across the Atlantic and Pacific oceans.

As the world economy has become more integrated, new international institutions have evolved. One of these institutions is the International Monetary Fund, or IMF. Let's talk with one of today's outstanding economists who now plays a leading role at the IMF and has become a household name during the Asia crisis, Stanley Fischer.

Talking with

Stanley Fischer *has served as the First Deputy Managing Director of the International Monetary Fund (The IMF) since 1994. Born in Zambia in 1943, he received a B.S. and an M.S. from the London School of Economics in 1965 and 1966, respectively, and a Ph.D. from MIT in 1969. Professor Fischer has taught at the University of Chicago and MIT. He served as Vice President of Development Economics and Chief Economist at the World Bank from 1988 to 1992. Michael Parkin talked with Stanley Fischer about his work at the IMF, the goals of that institution, and the lessons that we've learned from the Asian financial crisis.*

Stanley Fischer

How did you get into economics?

I was at high school in Zimbabwe (then Rhodesia) and in the sixth form I began to specialize in physics, chemistry, and math. Then I heard about economics. I switched one of my science courses to economics and I loved it.

This was the perfect field, one that provided an analytic way of understanding an important part of how societies work and also one in which I could use my quantitative skills. I went to the London School of Economics for my bachelor's and master's degrees and then to MIT for my Ph.D. My first appointment was at the University of Chicago

at a time when Milton Friedman was still the dominant influence there.

Can we talk first about the amazing liberalization and growth of world trade during the post–World War II years? Has this growth of world trade brought economic growth for all countries? Or have some gained more than others?

If you were to look at what has happened in the postwar period to the industrialized countries—which, despite some slowing since the 1960s, have grown faster, more consistently, and with less disruption than in any period of similar length in history—you would have to say that the architecture of the postwar economy has been very successful. And then if you look at the developing countries, you will find that, on the average, they have grown faster yet. In the most populous part of the globe, namely, East Asia, China, and, to some extent, India, we have had absolutely unprecedented growth. Every one of the successful East Asian countries has succeeded by integrating with the world economy, by promoting exports and increasing imports, especially of capital and intermediate goods. This process of opening up and using world markets for exports and imports has been absolutely critical. This outcome is what most economists from Adam Smith and David Ricardo on would have predicted.

The one part of the world where progress has, on the average, been most disappointing, is Africa. But there are countries in Africa that have done well. The countries that have been serious about trying to trade in the global economy and about implementing market-friendly policies have done better on the whole. We have seen significant growth in per capita income in Africa in the last few years. The prospects for South Africa look good, and that could be very important for a large part of the continent. In addition, countries such as Mozambique and Uganda have begun growing very fast after terrible civil wars, and Botswana has been one of the fastest-growing economies in the world for the past two decades.

What is the role of the IMF and what are the main problems that it seeks to address?
The IMF has several main functions. The first is *surveillance:* It is an institution in which countries discuss problems of the international economy, as well as each other's economies. Twice a year, the Fund staff presents its survey of the world economy, the *World Economic Outlook.*

In addition, Fund staff presents an annual report—the Article IV report—on the economy of each member country. The Article IV reports are based on the staff's analysis and discussions with the economic policy makers in each country.

Another function of the Fund is to *make loans to countries* in economic trouble. These loans typically provide balance of payments support to countries in crisis and countries to which the private capital markets are reluctant to lend.

One such crisis began in 1997—the financial crisis of Asia, Russia, Brazil, and other countries. What was its central feature?
Financial system weakness was a feature of almost all the crisis countries except Brazil. All the crises were driven and worsened by rapid international movements of capital. Investors pushed money into the crisis countries and then pulled it out, very rapidly, as the crisis approached its peak. The crisis featured *contagion,* spreading fast from one country to another.

What are the lessons of this episode of financial crisis?
The main lesson is that individual countries and the international financial system must adapt to the new circumstances of globally integrated financial markets. We must reduce the volatility of international capital flows and improve the capacity of financial systems and economies to cope with shifts in market confidence and investor sentiment that will inevitably occur in future.

Work is now under way in the emerging market economies, industrialized countries, and international institutions, to identify the polices and reforms that are needed.

For the *emerging market countries,* the list of items that need attention is a long one. Efforts

must focus on sound macroeconomic policies, which include avoiding operating fixed exchange rate systems, which have been crisis-prone. Banking systems must be restructured, and the supervision and regulation of banks must be improved. Better economic and financial information on private and public sector activities must be provided. Business financial practices and bankruptcy laws must be improved. And these countries need to find ways of dealing with rapid and large reversals in international capital flows.

Countries need to think carefully about how fast and in what order to free capital account transactions and to make sure their borrowing is not too short term. They also need adequate reserves and, possibly, lines of credit that will give them access to liquidity when they need it.

The *advanced industrialized countries* need to pursue macroeconomic policies that bring sustainable growth. When these countries are not expanding, developing countries, too, find it difficult to grow. The advanced countries also need to maintain healthy financial systems and to regulate their own financial institutions to minimize potential disruptive capital flows to emerging market countries.

The *international financial institutions,* the IMF among them, must act as well. One example of an important initiative is the design and adoption of international standards for bank operation and supervision and for reporting fiscal and monetary data. Another is the effort to

867

encourage the provision of better economic and financial data to the public by emerging market economies. A third is the effort to strengthen *surveillance* by the IMF. The IMF reports regularly on each country's economy, assessing its policies and practices, thereby encouraging the country to do better. Fourth, IMF member countries are gradually coming to the view that IMF reports, the Article IV reports, should be published so that the general public and investors can share information that so far has been available only to governments. Fifth, we are finding ways of making sure that private investors do their share in solving crises. One important criticism of IMF programs has been that the official sector bails out the private sector, providing loans so that the private sector can take its money out of a country in trouble. This is a very complicated issue, but we are definitely making progress on what is known as "bailing in" the private sector, finding ways of discouraging the private sector from taking its money out when a crisis hits.

What big conclusions should we draw from the special features of Russia's economic and financial condition?

A key question that has been asked since the onset of Russia's crisis in 1999 is: Was the reform strategy of the previous Russian government wrong? My conclusion is, fundamentally, no. The problem was not that the basic strategy was wrong, but that it was not pursued vigorously or deeply enough. What has been necessary in Russia

for some time has been a comprehensive strategy for moving boldly to tackle a large fiscal imbalance and to deal with important structural problems related to the way its economy operates—in particular, the nonpayment problem. Such a strategy was at the heart of the July 1998 program agreed on with the IMF. But by then, the financial situation and market confidence were too precarious and vulnerable to any missteps in implementation, which indeed happened and quickly led to the August collapse.

Put differently, the conclusion is that stabilization is not enough. Russia stabilized its economy extremely successfully from about the middle of 1995, with an appropriate degree of monetary discipline accompanied by a fixed exchange rate regime, which stabilizes inflationary expectations following a prolonged period of high inflation. However, the fiscal adjustment needed was not forthcoming, so there was a massive and rapid buildup in public debt. Ultimately, the government was not able to service its debt out of its own resources and could not convince investors to continue financing its ongoing deficit. This led to both the devaluation of the ruble and the government default on its treasury bills in August 1998.

Moreover, a critical reason why the fiscal adjustment could not be implemented was the lack of progress in industrial restructuring and other structural reforms; thus the stabilization was not sustainable. A very large part of the Russian economy remains

> So the failure of structural reforms underlies the fiscal problem in Russia.

unreformed, has not been part of the monetary economy, and is conducting its operations largely through barter—not only literally barter of goods against goods, but in many cases barter through very sophisticated financial mechanisms that do not involve the use of money. This situation has arisen because of a vast number of factors, including poor enforcement of tax obligations, an unfair tax system, weak bankruptcy laws, poor lending practices by banks, and corrupt business practices. Thus, much of the productive sector was either losing money in real terms or not paying a fair share of taxes. So the failure of structural reforms underlies the fiscal problem in Russia. Without these reforms, the budget will not balance, growth will not materialize, and eventually financial stability will be compromised.

Why do you believe that the IMF can play a role as the lender of last resort?

The IMF already is increasingly playing that role, both as crisis lender and as crisis manager. As crisis lender, the IMF, whose financial structure is similar to that of a credit union, has access to a pool of resources. As crisis manager, it has been taking the lead in negotiating with its member countries that are experiencing a financial crisis. It also has played an important coordinating and advisory role in arranging financing packages to help countries work out their debt problems with their foreign creditors.

Some have asked whether the IMF has enough resources to act as crisis lender. While the resources available have grown less than the size of the world economy since the IMF's inception in 1945, the IMF can still assemble a sizable financial package in response to a crisis, including, in special circumstances, by borrowing from members' central banks and by creating additional reserves for its members through the issuance of Special Drawing Rights (SDRs).

Should the IMF function as an international lender of last resort? I believe that there is a need for an agency that will act as such a lender to countries facing a crisis. The need arises because international capital flows are both extremely volatile and contagious, exhibiting the classic signs of financial panics, and an international lender of last resort can help to mitigate the effects of this instability and perhaps even help prevent the instability itself. Again, the IMF has already been acting in many ways as such a lender, and there is ongoing work to help make the IMF more effective in that capacity.

Of the main criticisms leveled at the IMF during the Asian crisis, which are the easiest to dismiss, and which, if any, should we take more seriously?

This is a complex question that cannot be easily answered in a few words. While I will try, I should say that the IMF has taken all the criticisms seriously and indeed has produced a comprehensive study of the experience in Indonesia, Korea, and Thailand, which I would encourage those interested to read.

The programs in the Asian crisis countries supported by the IMF sought to restore macroeconomic stability and the conditions for growth while addressing deep-rooted structural weaknesses that lay at the heart of the crisis in each country. These programs have been attacked from a number of angles, but here again I believe that, particularly in the highly fluid and uncertain circumstances, the approach taken and choices made were basically correct.

A frequent criticism is that the policy of high interest rates worsened financial problems being experienced by corporations and therefore made the recessions worse in these countries. However, their currencies were collapsing, and it was critical to avoid a depreciation-inflation spiral. Indeed, the critics fail to recognize that, in addition to the well-known negative effects on growth of high inflation, in a situation where companies and banks had borrowed heavily abroad, the further depreciations implied by lower interest rates would have exacerbated financial problems by

increasing the burden of servicing dollar-denominated debts.

Another criticism is that the programs entailed unduly contractionary fiscal policies. The original programs in these countries, formulated in the initial stages of the crisis, included some degree of fiscal adjustment to lessen the burden that might be placed on the private sector in the face of the large adjustment in the current account of the balance of payments that was needed. The truth is that, even then, the fiscal adjustment that was planned was rather small in both Korea and Indonesia and was substantial only in Thailand, where the initial fiscal imbalance was larger. Moreover, as economic activity deteriorated over the course of the programs, fiscal policy was progressively allowed to become more expansionary. In fact, our study concluded that fiscal policy was not a major factor accounting for the output decline in these countries.

The inclusion of structural measures in our programs also has drawn criticism. Financial and corporate sector inefficiencies were at the heart of these crises, and it was clear from the start that the restoration of durable growth required financial and corporate restructuring. Still, some argued that these reforms, while sensible over the medium term, impose large costs in the short term, and therefore it was a mistake to put them in place when economic activity was already so weak. While this is a valid concern, I think that attempting to stabilize the situation without attempting to address the underlying causes of the crisis would have been akin to treating the symptom without addressing the real cause of the disease. And delay does not make the structural problem any easier to deal with; indeed, as the problem of the Japanese banking sector in the 1990s clearly demonstrates, it makes it worse.

All this said, why did the programs work less well than we all hoped? Why was the economic downturn worse than initially foreseen? Clearly, the projections embodied in the original programs were somewhat more optimistic than the consensus view. However, very few observers foresaw the severity of the downturn—neither the governments, private forecasters, nor academic observers. A number of factors conspired to make matters worse than foreseen. First, the external environment for the crisis countries worsened markedly. In particular, the Japanese recession has been deeper and more prolonged than anticipated, hurting the exports of the crisis countries. Second, several factors—an initial reluctance by governments to implement the programs, political uncertainties, and lack of public support for the programs—made it much more difficult for market confidence to be restored than had been assumed. This led to greater

> **The Japanese recession has been deeper and more prolonged than anticipated, hurting the exports of the crisis countries.**

capital outflows and put additional upward pressure on interest rates and downward pressure on exchange rates, and forced a larger downward adjustment of domestic demand.

While I believe the basic approach of the programs was right, that doesn't mean that we shouldn't try to do better. As I already discussed, the recent financial crises have revealed weaknesses in the international financial system that we must try to deal with. As briefly described above, the IMF and other international institutions are doing their part to help in that endeavor.

What kinds of jobs do economics graduates get in organizations such as the IMF and the World Bank? What should students be doing as undergraduates to prepare themselves for such positions?

People who want to work in the Fund and the Bank should take courses in macroeconomics, international trade and finance, development, monetary economics, and public finance. From the viewpoint of the Bank, it would also be useful to study micro-oriented policy issues. The Fund and the Bank have entry programs for people who may be destined for their professional ranks. The World Bank's is called Young Professionals, and the IMF's is called the Economist Program.

The IMF and the World Bank are terrific places to work. You use your analytic skills all the time, in the real world. You have to decide what really matters, you have to be sure that what you're recommending will improve the lives of people. Then if you work in the operational parts of the Fund or Bank, you have to persuade the countries with which you're working that you're right. If you are right and you succeed, you have the satisfaction of having done something useful.

In the process, you'll have had the benefit of learning some diplomacy. You are also likely to learn some humility—for you will realize that the really hard work of implementing policies is done by the politicians and officials of the countries that undertake them. Your job is to help them do their own jobs better, always bearing in mind that the benefits or costs are borne by their people.

Solutions to Odd-Numbered Problems

CHAPTER 1

1. The opportunity cost of going to school is $9,600 of goods and services.

   The opportunity cost of going to school this summer is the highest-valued activity that you will give up so that you can go to summer school. In going to summer school, you will forgo all the goods and services that you could have bought with the income from your summer job ($6,000) plus the expenditure on tuition ($2,000), textbooks ($200), and living expenses ($1,400).

3. No, parking at this mall is not free. Yes, you did impose a cost on Harry.

   Finding a parking space takes about 30 minutes, so you incur an opportunity cost when you park your car. The opportunity cost is the highest-valued activity that you forgo by spending 30 minutes parking your car. If you would have spent those 30 minutes studying, then the opportunity cost of parking at this mall is 30 minutes of studying.

   The cost that you imposed on Harry is the additional 30 minutes that Harry will have to spend searching for a parking space.

CHAPTER 2

1a. To make a time-series graph, plot the year on the x-axis and the inflation rate on the y-axis. The graph will be a line joining all the points.

1b. (i) 1980 (ii) 1986 (iii) 1984, 1987–1990, 1995–1996 (iv) 1981–1983, 1985–1986, 1991–1992, 1994, 1997–1998 (v) 1987 (vi) 1982

1c. Inflation has had a downward trend. The line tends to slope down to the right.

3. To make a scatter diagram, plot the inflation rate on the x-axis and the interest rate on the y-axis. The graph will be a set of dots. The pattern made by the dots tells us that as the inflation rate increases, the interest rate usually increases.

5a. To make a graph that shows the relationship between x and y, plot x on the x-axis and y on the y-axis. The

relationship is positive because x and y move together: As x increases, y increases.

5b. The slope increases as x increases. Slope is equal to the change in y divided by the change in x as we move along the curve. When x increases from 1 to 2 (a change of 1), y increases from 1 to 4 (a change of 3), so the slope is 3. But when x increases from 7 to 8 (a change of 1), y increases from 49 to 64 (a change of 15), so the slope is 15.

5c. The taller the building, the bigger is the cost of building it. The higher the unemployment rate, the higher is the crime rate. The longer the flight, the larger is the amount of fuel used.

7. The slope equals 8.

   The slope of the curve at the point where x is 4 is equal to the slope of the tangent to the curve at that point. Plot the relationship and then draw the tangent line at the point where x is 4 and y is 16. Now calculate the slope of this tangent line. To do this, you must find another point on the tangent. The tangent line will cut the x-axis at 2, so another point is x equals 2 and y equals 0. Slope equals rise/run. The rise is 16 and the run is 2, so the slope is 8.

9. The slope is 7.

   The slope of the relationship across the arc when x increases from 3 to 4 is equal to the slope of the straight line joining the points on the curve at x equals 3 and x equals 4. In the graph, draw this straight line. When x increases from 3 to 4, y increases from 9 to 16. Slope equals rise/run. The rise is 7 (16 minus 9) and the run is 1 (4 minus 3), so the slope across the arc is 7.

11. The slope is −5/4.

    The curve is a straight line, so its slope is the same at all points on the curve. Slope equals the change in the variable on the y-axis divided by the change in the variable on the x-axis. To calculate the slope, you must select two points on the line. One point is at 10 on the y-axis and 0 on the x-axis, and another is at 8 on the x-axis and 0 on the y-axis. The change in y from 10 to 0 is associated with the change in x from 0 to 8. Therefore the slope of the curve equals −10/8, which equals −5/4.

13a. The slope at point a is −2, and the slope at point b is −0.75.

    To calculate the slope at a point on a curved line, draw the tangent to the line at the point. Then find a second point on the tangent and calculate the slope of the tangent.

    The tangent at point a cuts the y-axis at 10. The slope of the tangent equals the change in y divided by the change in x. The change in y equals 4 (10 minus 6) and the change in x equals −2 (0 minus 2). The slope at point a is 4/−2, which equals −2.

    Similarly, the slope at point b is −0.75. The tangent at point b cuts the x-axis at 8. The change in y equals 1.5, and the change in x equals −2. The slope at point b is −0.75.

13b. The slope across the arc ab is −1.125.

    The slope across an arc ab equals the change in y, which is 4.5 (6.0 minus 1.5) divided by the change in x, which equals −4 (2 minus 6). The slope across the arc ab equals 4.5/−4, which is −1.125.

15a. A set of curves, one for each different temperature.

To draw a graph of the relationship between the price and the number of rides, keep the temperature at 50°F and plot the data in that column against the price. The curve that you draw is the relationship between price and number of rides when the temperature is 50°F. Now repeat the exercise but keep the temperature at 70°F. Then repeat the exercise but keep the temperature at 90°F.

15b. A set of curves, one for each different price.

To draw a graph of the relationship between the temperature and the number of rides, keep the price at $5.00 a ride and plot the data in that row against the temperature. The curve shows the relationship between temperature and the number of rides when the price is $5.00 a ride. Now repeat the exercise but keep the price at $10.00 a ride. Repeat the exercise again and keep the price at $15.00 a ride and then at $20.00 a ride.

15c. A set of curves, one for each different number of rides.

To draw a graph of the relationship between the temperature and the price, keep the number of rides at 32 and plot the data along the diagonal in the table. The curve is the relationship between temperature and price at which 32 rides are taken. Now repeat the exercise and keep the number of rides at 27. Repeat the exercise again and keep the number of rides at 18 and then at 40.

CHAPTER 3

1a. Wendell's opportunity cost is 5 percentage points.

When Wendell increases the time he plays tennis from 4 hours to 6 hours, his grade in economics falls from 75 percent to 70 percent. His opportunity cost is 5 percentage points.

1b. Wendell's opportunity cost is 10 percentage points.

When Wendell increases the time he plays tennis from 6 hours to 8 hours, his grade in economics falls from 70 percent to 60 percent. His opportunity cost is 10 percentage points.

3. Wendell's opportunity cost of playing tennis increases as he spends more time on tennis.

When Wendell increases the time he plays tennis from 4 hours to 6 hours, his opportunity cost is 5 percentage points. But when he increases the time he plays tennis from 6 hours to 8 hours, his opportunity cost is 10 percentage points. Wendell's opportunity cost of playing tennis increases as he spends more time on tennis.

5a. Wendell's grade in economics is 66 percent.

When Wendell increases the time he plays tennis from 4 hours to 6 hours, his opportunity cost of the additional 2 hours of tennis is 5 percentage points. So his opportunity cost of an additional 1 hour is 2.5 percentage points. But when he increases the time he plays tennis from 6 hours to 8 hours, his opportunity cost of the additional 2 hours of tennis is 10 percentage points. So his opportunity cost of the additional 1 hour of tennis is 5 percentage points. Wendell's opportunity cost of playing tennis increases as he spends more time on tennis. Opportunity cost is plotted at the midpoint of the

range. This curve is Wendell's marginal cost of a additional hour of tennis.

Wendell uses his time efficiently if he plays tennis for 7 hours a week—marginal benefit from tennis equals its marginal cost. Wendell's marginal benefit is 5 percentage points and his marginal cost is 5 percentage points. When Wendell plays 7 hours of tennis, his grade in economics (from his *PPF*) is 66 percent.

5b. If Wendell studied for enough hours to get a higher grade, he would have fewer hours to play tennis. Wendell's marginal benefit from tennis would be greater than his marginal cost, so he would be more efficient if he played more hours of tennis and took a lower grade.

7a. Leisureland's *PPF* is a straight line.

To make a graph of Leisureland's *PPF* measure the quantity of one good on the *x*-axis and the quantity of the other good on the *y*-axis. Then plot the quantities in each row of the table and join up the points.

7b. The opportunity cost of 1 pound of food is 1/2 gallon of sunscreen.

The opportunity cost of the first 100 pounds of food is 50 gallons of sunscreen. To find the opportunity cost of the first 100 pounds of food, increase the quantity of food from 0 pounds to 100 pounds. In doing so, Leisureland's production of sunscreen decreases from 150 gallons to 100 gallons. The opportunity cost of the first 100 pounds of food is 50 gallons of sunscreen. Similarly, the opportunity costs of producing the second 100 pounds and the third 100 pounds of food are 50 gallons of sunscreen.

The opportunity cost of 1 gallon of sunscreen is 2 pounds of food. The opportunity cost of producing the first 50 gallons of sunscreen is 100 pounds of food. To calculate this opportunity cost, increase the quantity of sunscreen from 0 gallons to 50 gallons. Leisureland's production of food decreases from 300 pounds to 200 pounds. Similarly, the opportunity cost of producing the second 50 gallons and the third 50 gallons of sunscreen are 100 pounds of food.

9a. The marginal benefit curve slopes downward.

To draw the marginal benefit from sunscreen, plot the quantity of sunscreen on the *x*-axis and the willingness to pay for sunscreen (that is, the number of pounds of food that they are willing to give up to get a gallon of sunscreen) on the *y*-axis.

9b. The efficient quantity is 75 gallons a month.

The efficient quantity to produce is such that the marginal benefit from the last gallon equals the opportunity cost of producing it. The opportunity cost of a gallon of sunscreen is 2 pounds of sunscreen. The marginal benefit of the 75th gallon of sunscreen is 2 pounds of food. And the marginal cost of the 75th gallon of sunscreen is 2 pounds of food.

11. Busyland's opportunity cost of a pound of food is 2 gallons of sunscreen, and its opportunity cost of a gallon of sunscreen is 1/2 pound of food.

When Busyland increases the food it produces by 50 pounds a month, it produces 100 gallons of sunscreen less. The opportunity cost of 1 pound of food is 2 gallons of sunscreen. Similarly, when Busyland increases the sunscreen it produces by 100 gallons a month, it produces 50 pounds of food less. The opportunity cost of 1 gallon of sunscreen is 1/2 pound of food.

13a. Leisureland sells food and buys sunscreen.

Leisureland sells the good in which it has a comparative advantage and buys the other good from Busyland. Leisureland's opportunity cost of 1 pound of food is 1/2 gallon of sunscreen, while Busyland's opportunity cost of 1 pound of food is 2 gallons of sunscreen. Leisureland's opportunity cost of food is less than Busyland's, so Leisureland has a comparative advantage in producing food.

Leisureland's opportunity cost of 1 gallon of sunscreen is 2 pounds of food, while Busyland's opportunity cost of 1 gallon of sunscreen is 1/2 pound of food. Busyland's opportunity cost of sunscreen is less than Leisureland's, so Busyland has a comparative advantage in producing sunscreen.

13b. The gains from trade for each country are 50 pounds of food and 50 gallons of sunscreen.

With specialization and trade, together they can produce 300 pounds of food and 300 gallons of sunscreen. So each will get 150 pounds of food and 150 gallons of sunscreen—an additional 50 pounds of food and 50 gallons of sunscreen.

CHAPTER 4

1a. The price of a tape will rise, and the quantity of tapes sold will increase.

CDs and tapes are substitutes. If the price of a CD rises, people will buy more tapes and fewer CDs. The demand for tapes will increase. The price of a tape will rise, and more tapes will be sold.

1b. The price of a tape will fall, and fewer tapes will be sold.

Walkmans and tapes are complements. If the price of a Walkman rises, fewer Walkmans will be bought. The demand for tapes will decrease. The price of a tape will fall, and people will buy fewer tapes.

1c. The price of a tape will fall and fewer tapes will be sold.

The increase in the supply of CD players will lower the price of a CD player. With CD players cheaper than they were, some people will buy CD players. The demand for CDs will increase, and the demand for tapes will decrease. The price of a tape will fall, and people will buy fewer tapes.

1d. The price of a tape will rise, and the quantity sold will increase.

An increase in consumers' income will increase the demand for tapes. As a result, the price of a tape will rise and the quantity bought will increase.

1e. The price of a tape will rise, and the quantity sold will decrease.

If the workers who make tapes get a pay raise, the cost of making a tape increases and the supply of tapes decreases. The price will rise, and people will buy fewer tapes.

1f. The quantity sold will decrease, but the price might rise, fall, or stay the same.

Walkmans and tapes are complements. If the price of a Walkman rises, fewer Walkmans will be bought and so the demand for tapes will decrease. The price of a tape will fall, and people will buy fewer tapes. If the wages paid to workers who make tapes rise, the supply of tapes decreases. The quantity of tapes sold will decrease, and the price of a tape will rise. Taking the two events together, the quantity sold will decrease, but the price might rise, fall, or stay the same.

3a. (ii) and (iii)

If the price of crude oil (the resource used to make gasoline) rises, the supply of gasoline decreases. The demand for gasoline does not change, so the price of gasoline rises and there is a movement along the demand curve. The quantity demanded of gasoline decreases.

3b. (i) and (iv)

If the price of a car rises, the quantity of cars bought decreases. So the demand for gasoline decreases. The supply of gasoline does not change, so the price of gasoline falls and there is a movement down the supply curve of gasoline. The quantity supplied of gasoline decreases.

3c. (i) and (iv)

If all speed limits on highways are abolished, people will drive faster and use more gasoline. The demand for gasoline increases. The supply of gasoline does not change, so the price of gasoline rises and there is a movement up along the supply curve. The quantity supplied of gasoline increases.

3d. (i) and (iv)

If robot production plants lower the cost of producing a car, the supply of cars will increase. With no change in the demand for cars, the price of a car will fall and more cars will be bought. The demand for gasoline increases. The supply of gasoline does not change, so the price of gasoline rises and the quantity of gasoline supplied increases.

5a. The demand curve is the curve that slopes down toward the right. The supply curve is the curve that slopes up toward the right.

5b. The equilibrium price is $14 a pizza, and the equilibrium quantity is 200 pizzas a day.

Market equilibrium is determined at the intersection of the demand curve and supply curve.

7a. The equilibrium price is 50 cents a pack, and the equilibrium quantity is 120 million packs a week.

The price of a pack adjusts until the quantity demanded equals the quantity supplied. At 50 cents a pack, the quantity demanded is 120 million packs a week and the quantity supplied is 120 million packs a week.

7b. At 70 cents a pack, there will be a surplus of gum and the price will fall.

At 70 cents a pack, the quantity demanded is 80 million packs a week and the quantity supplied is 160 million packs a week. There is a surplus of 80 million packs a week. The price will fall until market equilibrium is restored—50 cents a pack.

9a. The supply curve has shifted leftward.

As the number of gum-producing factories decreases, the

supply of gum decreases. There is a new supply schedule, and the supply curve shifts leftward.

9b. There has been a movement along the demand curve.

The supply of gum decreases, and the supply curve shifts leftward. Demand does not change, so the price rises along the demand curve.

9c. The equilibrium price is 60 cents, and the equilibrium quantity is 100 million packs a week.

Supply decreases by 40 millions packs a week. That is, the quantity supplied at each price decreases by 40 million packs. The quantity supplied at 50 cents is now 80 million packs, and there is a shortage of gum. The price rises to 60 cents a pack, at which the quantity supplied equals the quantity demanded (100 million packs a week).

11. The new price is 70 cents a pack, and the quantity is 120 million packs a week.

The demand for gum increases, and the demand curve shifts rightward. The quantity demanded at each price increases by 40 million packs. The result of the fire is a price of 60 cents a pack. At this price, there is now a shortage of gum. The price of gum will rise until the shortage is eliminated.

CHAPTER 5

1a. The price elasticity of demand is 1.25.

The price elasticity of demand equals the percentage change in the quantity demanded divided by the percentage change in the price. The price rises from $4 to $6 a box, a rise of $2 a box. The average price is $5 a box. So the percentage change in the price equals $2 divided by $5, which equals 40 percent.

The quantity decreases from 1,000 to 600 boxes, a decrease of 400 boxes. The average quantity is 800 boxes. So the percentage change in quantity equals 400 divided by 800, which equals 50 percent.

The price elasticity of demand for strawberries equals 50 divided by 40, which is 1.25.

1b. The price elasticity of demand exceeds 1, so the demand for strawberries is elastic.

3a. The price elasticity of demand is 2.

When the price of a videotape rental rises from $3 to $5, the quantity demanded of videotapes decreases from 75 to 25 a day. The price elasticity of demand equals the percentage change in the quantity demanded divided by the percentage change in the price.

The price increases from $3 to $5, an increase of $2 a videotape. The average price is $4 a videotape. So the percentage change in the price equals $2 divided by $4, which equals 50 percent.

The quantity decreases from 75 to 25 videotapes, a decrease of 50 videotapes. The average quantity is 50 videotapes. So the percentage change in quantity equals 50 divided by 50, which equals 100 percent.

The price elasticity of demand for videotape rentals equals 100 divided by 50, which is 2.

3b. The price elasticity of demand equals 1 at $3 a videotape.

The price elasticity of demand equals infinity at $6 a videotape. The price elasticity of demand equals zero at $0 a videotape.

The price elasticity of demand equals 1 at the price halfway between the origin and the price at which the demand curve hits the y-axis. That price is $3 a videotape.

The price elasticity of demand equals infinity at the price at which the demand curve hits the y-axis. That price is $6 a videotape.

The price elasticity of demand equals zero at the price at which the demand curve hits the x-axis. That price is $0 a videotape.

5. The demand for dental services is unit elastic.

The price elasticity of demand for dental services equals the percentage change in the quantity of dental services demanded divided by the percentage change in the price of dental services.

The price elasticity of demand equals 10 divided by 10, which is 1. The demand is unit elastic.

7a. Total revenue increases.

When the price of a chip is $400, 30 million chips are sold and total revenue equals $12,000 million. When the price of a chip falls to $350, 35 million chips are sold and total revenue is $12,250 million. Total revenue increases when the price falls.

7b. Total revenue decreases.

When the price is $350 a chip, 35 million chips are sold and total revenue is $12,250 million. When the price of a chip is $300, 40 million chips are sold and total revenue decreases to $12,000 million. Total revenue decreases as the price falls.

7c. Total revenue is maximized at $350 a chip.

When the price of a chip is $300, 40 million chips are sold and total revenue equals $12,000 million. When the price is $350 a chip, 35 million chips are sold and total revenue equals $12,250 million. Total revenue increases as the price rises from $300 to $350 a chip. When the price is $400 a chip, 30 million chips are sold and total revenue equals $12,000 million. Total revenue decreases as the price rises from $350 to $400 a chip. Total revenue is maximized when the price is $350 a chip.

7d. The quantity will be 35 million chips a year.

The demand schedule tells us that when the price is $350 a chip, the quantity of chips demanded is 35 million chips a year.

7e. The demand for chips is unit elastic.

The total revenue test says that if the price changes and total revenue remains the same, the demand is unit elastic at the average price. For an average price of $350 a chip, cut the price from $400 to $300 a chip. When the price of a chip falls from $400 to $300, total revenue remains at $12,000 million. So at the average price of $350 a chip, demand is unit elastic.

9. The demand for chips is inelastic.

The total revenue test says that if the price falls and total revenue falls, the demand is inelastic. When the price falls from $300 to $200 a chip, total revenue decreases from

$12,000 million to $10,000 million. So at an average price of $250 a chip, demand is inelastic.

11. The cross elasticity of demand between orange juice and apple juice is 1.17.

The cross elasticity of demand is the percentage change in the quantity demanded of one good divided by the percentage change in the price of another good. The rise in the price of orange juice resulted in an increase in the quantity demanded of apple juice. So the cross elasticity of demand is the percentage change in the quantity demanded of apple juice divided by the percentage change in the price of orange juice. The cross elasticity equals 14 divided by 12, which is 1.17.

13. Income elasticity of demand for (i) bagels is 1.33 and (ii) donuts is −1.33.

Income elasticity of demand equals the percentage change in the quantity demanded divided by the percentage change in income. The change in income is $2,000 and the average income is $4,000, so the percentage change in income equals 50 percent.

(i) The change in the quantity demanded is 4 bagels and the average quantity demanded is 6 bagels, so the percentage change in the quantity demanded equals 66.67 percent. The income elasticity of demand for bagels equals 66.67/50, which is 1.33.

(ii) The change in the quantity demanded is −6 donuts and the average quantity demanded is 9 donuts, so the percentage change in the quantity demanded is −66.67. The income elasticity of demand for donuts equals −66.67/50, which is −1.33.

15a. The elasticity of supply is 1.

The elasticity of supply is the percentage change in the quantity supplied divided by the percentage change in the price. When the price falls from 40 cents to 30 cents, the change in the price is 10 cents and the average price is 35 cents. The percentage change in the price is 28.57.

When the price falls from 40 cents to 30 cents, the quantity supplied decreases from 800 to 600 calls. The change in the quantity supplied is 200 calls, and the average quantity is 700 calls, so the percentage change in the quantity supplied is 28.57.

The elasticity of supply equals 28.57/28.57, which equals 1.

15b. The elasticity of supply is 1.

The formula for the elasticity of supply calculates the elasticity at the average price. So to find the elasticity at 20 cents, change the price such that 20 cents is the average price—for example, a fall in the price from 30 cents to 10 cents.

When the price falls from 30 cents to 10 cents, the change in the price is 20 cents and the average price is 20 cents. The percentage change in the price is 100. When the price falls from 30 cents to 10 cents, the quantity supplied decreases from 600 to 200 calls. The change in the quantity supplied is 400 calls and the average quantity is 400 calls, so the percentage change in the quantity supplied is 100.

The elasticity of supply is the percentage change in the quantity supplied divided by the percentage change in the price. The elasticity of supply is 1.

CHAPTER 6

1a. Equilibrium price is $1.00 a floppy disk, and the equilibrium quantity is 3 floppy disks a month.

1b. Consumer surplus is $2.25.

The consumer surplus is the area of the triangle under the demand curve above the price. The price is $1.00 a disk. The area of the triangle equals (2.50 − 1.00)/2 multiplied by 3, which is $2.25.

1c. Producer surplus is $0.75.

The producer surplus is the area of the triangle above the supply curve below the price. The price is $1.00 a disk. The area of the triangle equals (1.00 − 0.50)/2 multiplied by 3, which is $0.75.

1d. The efficient quantity is 3 floppy disks a month.

The efficient quantity is the quantity that makes the marginal benefit from the last disk equal to the marginal cost of producing the last disk. The demand curve shows the marginal benefit and the supply curve shows the marginal cost. Only if 3 floppy disks are produced is the quantity produced efficient.

3a. The maximum price that consumers will pay is $3.

The demand schedule shows the maximum price that consumers will pay for each sandwich. The maximum price that consumers will pay for the 250th sandwich is $3.

3b. The minimum price that producers will accept is $5.

The supply schedule shows the minimum price that producers will accept for each sandwich. The minimum price that producers will accept for the 250th sandwich is $5.

3c. Greater than the efficient quantity.

The efficient quantity is such that marginal benefit from the last sandwich equals the marginal cost of producing it. The efficient quantity is the equilibrium quantity—200 sandwiches an hour.

3d. Consumer surplus is $400.

The equilibrium price is $4. The consumer surplus is the area of the triangle under the demand curve above the price. The area of the triangle is (8 − 4)/2 multiplied by 200, which is $400.

3e. Producer surplus is $400.

The producer surplus is the area of the triangle above the supply curve below the price. The price is $4. The area of the triangle is (4 − 0)/2 multiplied by 200, which is $400.

3f. The deadweight loss is $50.

Deadweight loss is the sum of the consumer surplus and producer surplus that is lost because the quantity produced is not the efficient quantity. The deadweight loss equals the quantity (250 − 200) multiplied by (5 − 3)/2, which is $50.

5a. Ben's consumer surplus is $122.50. Beth's consumer surplus is $22.50, and Bo's consumer surplus is $4.50.

Consumer surplus is the area under the demand curve above the price. At 40 cents, Ben will travel 350 miles, Beth will travel 150 miles, and Bo will travel 30 miles. To find Ben's consumer surplus extend his demand schedule until you find the price at which his demand curve cuts the y-axis. This price is 110 cents. So Ben's consumer surplus equals $(110 - 40)/2$ multiplied by 350, which equals $122.50. Beth's consumer surplus equals $(70 - 40)/2$ multiplied by 150, which equals $22.50. And Bo's consumer surplus equals $(70 - 40)/2$ multiplied by 30, which equals $4.50.

5b. Ben's consumer surplus is the largest because he places a higher value on each unit of the good than the other two do.

5c. Ben's consumer surplus falls by $32.50. Beth's consumer surplus falls by $12.50, and Bo's consumer surplus falls by $2.50.

At 50 cents a mile, Ben travels 300 miles and his consumer surplus is $90, a decrease of $32.50. Beth travels 100 miles and her consumer surplus is $10, a decrease of $12.50. Bo travels 20 miles and her consumer surplus is $2.00, a decrease of $2.50.

CHAPTER 7

1a. Equilibrium price is $200 a month and the equilibrium quantity is 10,000 housing units.

1b. The quantity rented is 5,000 housing units.

The quantity of housing rented is equal to the quantity supplied at the rent ceiling.

1c. The shortage of housing is 10,000 housing units.

At the rent ceiling, the quantity of housing demanded is 15,000 but the quantity supplied is 5,000, so there is a shortage of 10,000 housing units.

1d. The maximum price that someone is willing to pay for the 5,000th unit available is $300 a month.

The demand curve tells us the maximum price that someone is willing to pay for the 5,000th unit.

3a. The equilibrium wage rate is $4 an hour, and employment is 2,000 hours a month.

3b. Unemployment is zero. Everyone who wants to work for $4 an hour is employed.

3c. They work 2,000 hours a month.

A minimum wage rate is the lowest wage rate that a person can be paid for an hour of work. Because the equilibrium wage rate exceeds the minimum wage rate, the minimum wage is ineffective. The wage rate will be $4 an hour and employment is 2,000 hours.

3d. There is no unemployment.

The wage rate rises to the equilibrium wage—the quantity of labor demanded equals the quantity of labor supplied. So there is no unemployment.

3e. At $5 an hour, 1,500 hours a month are employed and 1,000 hours a month are unemployed.

The quantity of labor employed equals the quantity demanded at $5 an hour. Unemployment is equal to the quantity of labor supplied at $5 an hour minus the quantity of labor demanded at $5 an hour. The quantity supplied is 2,500 hours a month, and the quantity demanded is 1,500 hours a month. So 1,000 hours a month are unemployed.

3f. The wage rate is $5 an hour, and unemployment is 500 hours a month.

At the minimum wage of $5 an hour, the quantity demanded is 2,000 hours a month and the quantity sup-

plied is 2,500 hours a month. So 500 hours a month are unemployed.

5a. With no tax on brownies, the price is 60 cents a brownie and 4 million a day are consumed.

5b. The price is 70 cents a brownie, and 3 million brownies a day are consumed. Consumers and producers each pay 10 cents of the tax on a brownie.

The tax decreases the supply of brownies and raises the price of a brownie. With no tax, producers are willing to sell 3 million brownies a day at 50 cents a brownie. But with a 20 cent tax, they are willing to sell 3 million brownies a day only if the price is 20 cents higher at 70 cents a brownie.

7a. Inventory holders sell 500 boxes of rice.

Inventory holders sell rice from inventory because otherwise the storm will cause the price to rise above $1.40 a box.

7b. The price is $1.40 a box, and farm revenue is $2,800 a week.

The storm reduces the quantity grown by 500 boxes to 2,000 boxes. The action of the inventory holders maintains the price at $1.40 a box, so farm revenue equals $1.40 multiplied by 2,000 boxes.

CHAPTER 8

1a. To draw a graph of Jason's total utility from rock CDs, plot the number of CDs on the x-axis and Jason's utility from CDs on the y-axis. The curve will look similar to Fig. 9.2(a). To draw a graph of Jason's total utility from spy novels, repeat the above procedure but use the spy novel data.

1b. Jason gets more utility from any number of rock CDs than he does from the same number of spy novels.

1c. To draw a graph of Jason's marginal utility from rock CDs plot the number of CDs on the x-axis and Jason's marginal utility from CDs on the y-axis. The curve will look similar to Fig. 9.2(b). To draw a graph of Jason's marginal utility from spy novels, repeat the above procedure but use the spy novel data.

Jason's marginal utility from rock CDs is the increase in total utility he gets from one additional rock CD. Similarly, Jason's marginal utility from spy novels is the increase in total utility he gets from one additional spy novel.

1d. Jason gets more marginal utility from an additional rock CD than he gets from an additional spy novel when he has the same number of each.

3a. To draw a graph of Max's budget line, plot the hours spent on one activity (say, windsurfing) on the x-axis and the hours spent on the other activity of the y-axis. The budget line is a straight line running from 3.5 hours of windsurfing on the x-axis to 7 hours of snorkeling on the y-axis.

If Max spends all of his $35 on windsurfing, he can rent the windsurfing equipment for $35/$10 an hour, which is 3.5 hours. If Max spends all of his $35 on snorkeling, he can rent the snorkeling equipment for $35/$5 an hour, which is 7 hours.

3b. To maximize his utility, Max windsurfs for 3 hours and snorkels for 1 hour.

Max will spend his $35 such that all of the $35 is spent and that the marginal utility per dollar spent on each activity is the same. When Max windsurfs for 3 hours and snorkels for 1 hour, he spends $30 renting the windsurfing equipment and $5 renting the snorkeling equipment—a total of $35.

The marginal utility from the third hour of windsurfing is 80 and the rent of the windsurfing equipment is $10 an hour, so the marginal utility per dollar spent on windsurfing is 8. The marginal utility from the first hour of snorkeling is 40 and the rent of the snorkeling equipment is $5 an hour, so the marginal utility per dollar spent on snorkeling is 8. The marginal utility per dollar spent on windsurfing equals the marginal utility per dollar spent on snorkeling.

5a. Max's budget line is the straight line running from 5.5 hours of windsurfing and no snorkeling to 11 hours of snorkeling and no windsurfing.

5b. To maximize his utility, Max windsurfs for 4 hours and snorkels for 3 hours.

Max will spend his $55 such that all of the $55 is spent and that the marginal utility per dollar spent on each activity is the same. When Max windsurfs for 4 hours and snorkels for 3 hours, he spends $40 renting the windsurfing equipment and $15 renting the snorkeling equipment—a total of $55.

The marginal utility from the fourth hour of windsurfing is 60 and the rent of the windsurfing equipment is $10 an hour, so the marginal utility per dollar spent on windsurfing is 6. The marginal utility from the third hour of snorkeling is 30 and the rent of the snorkeling equipment is $5 an hour, so the marginal utility per dollar spent on snorkeling is 6. The marginal utility per dollar spent on windsurfing equals the marginal utility per dollar spent on snorkeling.

7. To maximize his utility, Max windsurfs for 6 hours and snorkels for 5 hours.

Max will spend his $55 such that all of the $55 is spent and that the marginal utility per dollar spent on each activity is the same. When Max windsurfs for 6 hours and snorkels for 5 hours, he spends $30 renting the windsurfing equipment and $25 renting the snorkeling equipment—a total of $55.

The marginal utility from the sixth hour of windsurfing is 12 and the rent of the windsurfing equipment is $5 an hour, so the marginal utility per dollar spent on windsurfing is 2.4. The marginal utility from the fifth hour of snorkeling is 12 and the rent of the snorkeling equipment is $5 an hour, so the marginal utility per dollar spent on snorkeling is 2.4. The marginal utility per dollar spent on windsurfing equals the marginal utility per dollar spent on snorkeling.

9. To maximize his utility, Max windsurfs for 5 hours and snorkels for 1 hour.

Because the equipment is free, Max does not have to allocate his *income* between the two activities; instead, he allocates his *time* between the two activities. Max spends 6 hours on these activities. Max allocates the 6 hours such that the marginal utility from each activity is the same.

When Max windsurfs for 5 hours and snorkels for 1 hour, he spends 6 hours. His marginal utility from the fifth hour of windsurfing is 40 and his marginal utility from the first hour of snorkeling is 40—so the marginal utilities are equal.

11. The market demand curve passes through the following points: 90 cents and 3 cartons; 70 cents and 6 cartons; 50 cents and 10 cartons; 30 cents and 14 cartons; and 10 cents and 18 cartons.

At each price, the quantity demanded by the market is equal to the sum of the cartons of popcorn that Shirley demands and the cartons of popcorn that Dan demands. For example, at 50 cents a carton, the quantity demanded by Shirley and Dan is 10, the sum of Shirley's 6 and Dan's 4.

CHAPTER 9

1a. Sara's real income is 4 cans of cola.

Sara's real income in terms of cans of cola is equal to her money income divided by the price of a can of cola. Sara's money income is $12, and the price of cola is $3 a can. Sara's real income is $12 divided by $3 a can of cola, which is 4 cans of cola.

1b. Sara's real income is 4 bags of popcorn.

Sara's real income in terms of popcorn is equal to her money income divided by the price of a bag of popcorn, which is $12 divided by $3 a bag or 4 bags of popcorn.

1c. The relative price of cola is 1 bag per can.

The relative price of cola is the price of cola divided by the price of popcorn. The price of cola is $3 a can and the price of popcorn is $3 a bag, so the relative price of cola is $3 a can divided by $3 a bag, which equals 1 bag per can.

1d. The opportunity cost of a can of cola is 1 bag of popcorn.

The opportunity cost of a can of cola is the quantity of popcorn that must be forgone to get a can of cola. The price of cola is $3 a can and the price of popcorn is $3 a bag, so to buy one can of cola Sara must forgo 1 bag of popcorn.

1e. The equation that describes Sara's budget line is

$Q_P = 4 - Q_C$.

Call the price of popcorn P_P and the quantity of popcorn Q_P, the price of cola P_C and the quantity of cola Q_C, and income y. Sara's budget equation is

$P_P Q_P + P_C Q_C = y$.

If we substituting $3 for the price of popcorn, $3 for the price of cola, and $12 for the income, the budget equation becomes

$3 \times Q_P + 3 \times Q_C = 12$.

Dividing both sides by $3 gives

$Q_P + Q_C = 4$.

Subtract Q_C from both sides to give

$Q_P = 4 - Q_C$.

1f. To draw a graph of the budget line, plot the quantity of cola on the x-axis and the quantity of popcorn on the y-axis. The budget line is a straight line running from 4 cans on the y-axis to 4 bags on the x-axis.

1g. The slope of the budget line, when cola is plotted on the x-axis is minus 1. The magnitude of the slope is equal to the relative price of cola.

The slope of the budget line is "rise over run." If the quantity of cola decreases from 4 to 0, the quantity of popcorn increases from 0 to 4. The rise is 4 and the run is −4. Therefore the slope equals 4/−4, which is −1.

3a. Sara buys 2 cans of cola and 2 bags of popcorn.

Sara buys the quantities of cola and popcorn that gets her onto the highest indifference curve, given her income and the prices of cola and popcorn. The graph shows Sara's indifference curves. So draw Sara's budget line on the graph. The budget line is tangential to indifference curve I_0 at 2 cans of cola and 2 bags of popcorn. The indifference curve I_0 is the highest indifference curve that Sara can get onto.

3b. Sara's marginal rate of substitution is 1.

The marginal rate of substitution is the magnitude of the indifference curve at Sara's consumption point, which equals the magnitude of the slope of the budget line. The slope of Sara's budget line is −1, so the marginal rate of substitution is 1.

5a. Sara buys 6 cans of cola and 1 bag of popcorn.

Draw the new budget line on the graph with Sara's indifference curves. The budget line now runs from 8 cans of cola on the x-axis to 4 bags of popcorn on the y-axis. The new budget line is tangential to indifference curve I_1 at 6 cans of cola and 1 bag of popcorn. The indifference curve I_1 is the highest indifference curve that Sara can now get onto.

5b. Two points on Sara's demand for cola are the following: At $3 a can of cola, Sara buys 2 cans of cola. At $1.50 a can of cola, Sara buys 6 cans.

5c. The substitution effect is 2 cans of cola and −1.5 bags of popcorn.

To divide the price effect into a substitution effect and an income effect, take enough income away from Sara and gradually move her new budget line back toward the origin until it just touches Sara's indifference curve I_0. The point at which this budget line just touches indifference curve I_0 is 4 cans of cola and 0.5 bag of popcorn. The substitution effect is the increase in the quantity of cola from 2 cans to 4 cans and the decrease in the quantity of popcorn from 2 bags to 0.5 bag along the indifference curve I_0. The substitution effect is 2 cans of cola and −1.5 bags of popcorn.

5d. The income effect is 2 cans of cola and 0.5 bag of popcorn.

The income effect is the change in the quantity of cola from the price effect minus the change from the substitution effect. The price effect is 4 cans of cola (6 cans minus the initial 2 cans) and −1 bag of popcorn (1 bag minus the initial 2 bags). The substitution effect is an increase in the quantity of cola from 2 cans to 4 cans and the decrease in the quantity of popcorn from 2 bags to 0.5 bag of popcorn. So the income effect is 2 cans of cola and 0.5 bag of popcorn.

5e. Cola is a normal good for Sara because the income effect is positive. An increase in income increases the quantity of cola she buys from 4 to 6 cans.

5f. Popcorn is a normal good for Sara because the income effect is positive. An increase in income increases the quantity of popcorn she buys from 0.5 bag to 1 bag.

7a. Pam can still buy 30 cookies and 5 comic books.

When Pam buys 30 cookies at $1 each and 5 comic books at $2 each, she spends $40 a month. Now that the price of a cookie is 50 cents and the price of a comic book is $5, 30 cookies and 5 comic books will cost $40. So Pam can still buy 30 cookies and 5 comic books.

7b. Pam will not want to buy 30 cookies and 5 comic books because the marginal rate of substitution does not equal the relative price of the goods. Pam will move to a point on the highest indifference curve possible where the marginal rate of substitution equals the relative price.

7c. Pam prefers cookies at 50 cents each and comic books at $5 each because she can get onto a higher indifference curve than when cookies are $1 each and comic books are $2 each.

7d. Pam will buy more cookies and fewer cans of cola.

The new budget line and the old budget line pass through the point at 30 cookies and 5 comic books. If comic books are plotted on the x-axis, the marginal rate of substitution at this point on Pam's indifference curve is equal to the relative price of a comic book at the original prices, which is 2. The new relative price of a comic book is $5/50 cents, which is 10. That is, the budget line is steeper than the indifference curve at 30 cookies and 5 comic books. Pam will buy more cookies and fewer comic books.

7e. There will be a substitution effect and an income effect.

A substitution effect arises when the relative price changes and the consumer moves along the *same* indifference curve to a new point where the marginal rate of substitution equals the new relative price. An income effect arises when the consumer moves from one indifference curve to another, keeping the relative price constant.

CHAPTER 10

1. Explicit costs are $30,000. Explicit costs are all the costs for which there is a payment. Explicit costs are the sum of the wages paid ($20,000) and the goods and services bought from other firms ($10,000).

Implicit costs are the sum of the costs that do not involve a payment. Implicit costs are the sum of the interest forgone on $50,000 put into the firm; the $30,000 income forgone by Jack not working at his previous job; $15,000, which is the value of 500 hours of Jill's leisure (10 hours a week for 50 weeks); and the economic depreciation of $2,000 ($30,000 minus $28,000).

3a. All methods other than "pocket calculator with paper and pencil" are technologically efficient.

To use a pocket calculator with paper and pencil to complete the tax return is not a technologically efficient method because it takes the same number of hours as it would with a pocket calculator but it uses more capital.

3b. The economically efficient method is to use (i) a pocket calculator, (ii) a pocket calculator, (iii) a PC.

The economically efficient method is the technologically efficient method that allows the task to be done at least cost.

When the wage rate is $5 an hour: Total cost with a PC is $1,005, total cost with a pocket calculator is $70, and total cost with paper and pencil is $81. Total cost is least with a pocket calculator.

When the wage rate is $50 an hour: Total cost with a PC is $1,050, total cost with a pocket calculator is $610, and the total cost with paper and pencil is $801. Total cost is least with a pocket calculator.

When the wage rate is $500 an hour: Total cost with a PC is $1,500, total cost with a pocket calculator is $6,010, and total cost with pencil and paper is $8,001. Total cost is least with a PC.

5a. Methods *a*, *b*, *c*, and *d* are technologically efficient. Compare the amount of labor and capital used by the four methods. Start with method *a*. Moving from *a* to *b* to *c* to *d*, the amount of labor increases and the amount of capital decreases in each case.

5b. The economically efficient method is (i) method *d* (ii) methods *c* and *d* (iii) method *a*.

The economically efficient method is the technologically efficient method that allows the 100 shirts to be washed at least cost.

(i) Total cost with method *a* is $1,001, total cost with method *b* is $805, total cost with method *c* is $420, and total cost with method *d* is $150. Method *d* has the lowest total cost.

(ii) Total cost with method *a* is $505, total cost with method *b* is $425, total cost with method *c* is $300, and total cost with method *d* is $300. Methods *c* and *d* have the lowest total cost.

(iii) Total cost with method *a* is $100, total cost with method *b* is $290, total cost with method *c* is $1,020, and total cost with method *d* is $2,505. Method *a* has the lowest total cost.

7a. The four-firm concentration ratio is 60.49.

The four-firm concentration ratio equals the ratio of the total sales of the largest four firms to the total industry sales expressed as a percentage. The total sales of the largest four firms is $450 + $325 + $250 + $200, which equals $1,225. Total industry sales equal $1,225 + $800, which equals $2,025. The four-firm concentration ratio equals ($1,225/$2,025) × 100, which is 60.49 percent.

7b. This industry is highly concentrated because the four-firm concentration ratio exceeds 60 percent.

9a. The Herfindahl-Hirschman Index is 1,700.

The Herfindahl-Hirschman Index equals the sum of the squares of the market shares of the 50 largest firms or of all firms if there are less than 50 firms. The Herfindahl-Hirchman Index equals $15^2 + 10^2 + 20^2 + 15^2 + 25^2 + 15^2$, which equals 1,800.

9b. This industry is moderately competitive because the Herfindahl-Hirschman Index lies in the range 1,000–1,800.

CHAPTER 11

1a. To draw the total product curve measure labor on the *x*-axis and output on the *y*-axis. The total product curve is upward sloping.

1b. The average product of labor is equal to total product divided by the quantity of labor employed. For example, when 3 workers are employed, they produce 6 boats a week, so the average product is 2 boats per worker.

The average product curve is upward sloping when the number of workers is between 1 and 8, but it becomes downward sloping when 9 and 10 workers are employed.

1c. The marginal product of labor is equal to the increase in total product when an additional worker is employed. For example, when 3 workers are employed, total product is 6 boats a week. When a fourth worker is employed, total product increases to 10 boats a week. The marginal product of going from 3 to 4 workers is 4 boats.

The marginal product curve is upward sloping when the number of workers is between 1 and 6, but it becomes downward sloping when 7 or more workers are employed.

1d. (i) When Rubber Duckies produces fewer than 30 boats a week, it employs fewer than 8 workers a week. With fewer than 8 workers a week, marginal product exceeds average product and average product is increasing. Up to an output of 30 boats a day, each additional worker adds more to output than the average. Average product increases.

When Rubber Duckies produces more than 30 boats a week, it employs more than 8 workers a week. With more than 8 workers a week, average product exceeds marginal product and average product is decreasing. For outputs greater than 30 boats a week, each additional worker adds less to output than average. Average product decreases.

3a. Total cost is the sum of the costs of all the inputs that Rubber Duckies uses in production. Total variable cost is the total cost of the variable inputs. Total fixed cost is the total cost of the fixed inputs.

For example, the total variable cost of producing 10 boats a week is the total cost of the workers employed, which is 4 workers at $400 a week, which equals $1,600. Total fixed cost is $1,000, so the total cost of producing 10 boats a week is $2,600.

To draw the short-run total cost curves, plot output on the *x*-axis and the total cost on the *y*-axis. The total fixed cost curve is a horizontal line at $1,000. The total variable cost curve and the total cost curve have shapes similar to those in Fig. 11.4, but the vertical distance between the total variable cost curve and the total cost curve is $1,000.

3b. Average fixed cost is total fixed cost per unit of output. Average variable cost is total variable cost per unit of output. Average total cost is the total cost per unit of output.

For example, when the firm makes 10 boats a week: Total fixed cost is $1,000, so average fixed cost is $100 per boat; total variable cost is $1,600, so average variable cost is $160 per boat; and total cost is $2,600, so average total cost is $260 per boat.

Marginal cost is the increase in total cost divided by the increase in output. For example, when output increases from 3 to 6 boats a week, total cost increases from $1,800 to $2,200, an increase of $400. That is, the increase in output of 3 boats increases total cost by $400. Marginal cost is equal to $400 divided by 3 boats, which is $133.33 a boat.

The short-run average and marginal cost curves are similar to those in Fig. 11.5.

5. The increase in total fixed cost increases total cost but does not change total variable cost. Average fixed cost is total fixed cost per unit of output. The average fixed cost curve shifts upward. Average total cost is total cost per unit of output. The average total cost curve shifts upward. Marginal cost and average variable cost do not change.

7a. Total cost is the cost of all the inputs. For example, when 3 workers are employed they now produce 12 boats a week. With 3 workers, the total variable cost is $1,200 a week and the total fixed cost is $2,000 a week. The total cost is $3,200 a week. The average total cost of producing 12 boats is $266.67.

7b. The long-run average cost curve is made up of the lowest parts of the firm's short-run average total cost curves when the firm operates 1 plant and 2 plants. The long-run average cost curve is similar to Fig. 11.8.

7c. It is efficient to operate the plant that has the lower average total cost of a boat. It is efficient to operate one plant when output is less than 27 boats a week, and it is efficient to operate two plants when the output is more than 27 boats a week.

Over the output range 1 to 27 boats a week, average total cost is less with one plant than with two, but if output exceeds 27 boats a week, average total cost is less with two plants than with one.

9a. For example, the average total cost of producing a balloon ride when Bonnie rents 2 balloons and employs 4 workers equals the total cost ($1,000 rent for the balloons plus $1,000 for the workers) divided by the 20 balloon rides produced. The average total cost equals $2,000/20, which is $100 a ride.

The average total cost curve is U-shaped, as in Fig. 11.5.

9b. The long-run average cost curve is similar to that in Fig. 11.8.

9c. Bonnie's minimum efficient scale is 13 balloon rides when Bonnie rents 1 balloon.

The minimum efficient scale is the smallest output at which the long-run average cost is a minimum. To find the minimum efficient scale, plot the average total cost curve for each plant and then check which plant has the lowest minimum average total cost.

9d. Bonnie will choose the plant (number of balloons to rent) that gives her minimum average total cost for the normal or average number of balloon rides that people buy.

CHAPTER 12

1a. Quick Copy's profit-maximizing quantity is 80 pages an hour.

Quick Copy maximizes its profit by producing the quantity at which marginal revenue equals marginal cost. In perfect competition, marginal revenue equals price, which is 10 cents a page. Marginal cost is 10 cents when 80 pages an hour are produced.

1b. Quick Copy's profit is $2.40 an hour.

Profit equals total revenue minus total cost. Total revenue

equals $8.00 an hour (10 cents a page multiplied by 80 pages). The average total cost of producing 80 pages is 7 cents a page, so total cost equals $5.60 an hour (7 cents multiplied by 80 pages). Profit equals $8.00 minus $5.60, which is $2.40 an hour.

1c. The price will fall in the long run to 6 cents a page.

At a price of 10 cents a page, firms make economic profit. In the long run, the economic profit will encourage new firms to enter the copying industry. As they do, the price will fall and economic profit will decrease. Firms will enter until economic profit is zero, which occurs when the price is 6 cents a copy (price equals minimum average total cost).

3a. Pat's profit-maximizing output is 4 pizzas an hour. Pat's profit is $2 an hour.

Pat maximizes its profit by producing the quantity at which marginal revenue equals marginal cost. In perfect competition, marginal revenue equals price, which is $14 a pizza. Marginal cost is the change in total cost when output is increased by 1 pizza an hour. The marginal cost of increasing output from 3 to 4 pizzas an hour is $13 ($54 minus $41). The marginal cost of increasing output from 4 to 5 pizzas an hour is $15 ($69 minus $54). So the marginal cost of the fourth pizza is half-way between $13 and $15, which is $14. Marginal cost equals marginal revenue when Pat produces 4 pizzas an hour.

Economic profit equals total revenue minus total cost. Total revenue equals $56 an hour ($14 a pizza multiplied by 4 pizzas). Total cost of producing 4 pizzas is $54. Economic profit equals $56 minus $54, which is $2 an hour.

3b. Pat's shutdown point occurs at a price of $10 a pizza.

The shutdown point is the price that equals minimum average variable cost. To calculate total variable cost, subtract total fixed cost ($10, which is total cost at zero output) from total cost. Average variable cost equals total variable cost divided by the quantity produced. For example, the average variable cost of producing 2 pizzas is $10 a pizza. Average variable cost is a minimum when marginal cost equals average variable cost. The marginal cost of producing 2 pizzas is $10. So the shutdown point is a price of $10 a pizza.

3c. Pat's supply curve is the same as the marginal cost curve at prices equal to or above $10 a pizza and the y-axis at prices below $10 a pizza.

3d. Pat will leave the industry if in the long run the price is less than $13 a pizza.

Pat's Pizza Kitchen will leave the industry if it incurs an economic loss in the long run. To incur an economic loss, the price will have to be below minimum average total cost. Average total cost equals total cost divided by the quantity produced. For example, the average total cost of producing 2 pizzas is $15 a pizza. Average total cost is a minimum when it equals marginal cost. The average total cost of 3 pizzas is $13.67, and the average total cost of 4 pizzas is $13.50. Marginal cost when Pat's produces 3 pizzas is $12 and marginal cost when Pat's produces 4 pizzas is $14. At 3 pizzas, marginal cost is less than average total cost; at 4 pizzas, marginal cost exceeds average total cost.

So minimum average total cost occurs between 3 and 4 pizzas—$13 at 3.5 pizzas an hour.

3e. Firms with costs identical to Pat's will enter at any price above $13 a pizza.

Firms will enter an industry when firms currently in the industry are making economic profit. Firms with costs identical to Pat's will make economic profit when the price exceeds minimum average total cost, which is $13 a pizza.

3f. The price in the long run is $13 a pizza. This is the price that makes economic profit zero.

5a. The market price is $8.40 a cassette.

The market price is the price at which the quantity demanded equals the quantity supplied. The firm's supply curve is the same as its marginal cost curve at prices above minimum average variable cost. Average variable cost is a minimum when marginal cost equals average variable cost. Marginal cost equal average variable cost at the quantity 250 cassettes a week. So the firm's supply curve is the same as the marginal cost curve for the outputs equal to 250 cassettes or more. When the price is $8.40 a cassette, each firm produces 350 cassettes and the quantity supplied by the 1,000 firms is 350,000 cassettes a week. The quantity demanded at $8.40 is 350,000 a week.

5b. The industry output is 350,000 cassettes a week.

5c. Each firm produces 350 cassettes a week.

5d. Each firm makes an economic loss of $581 a week.

Each firm produces 350 cassettes at an average total cost of $10.06 a cassette. The firm can sell the 350 cassettes for $8.40 a cassette. The firm incurs a loss on each cassette of $1.66 and incurs an economic loss of $581 a week.

5e. In the long run, some firms exit the industry because they are incurring economic losses.

5f. The number of firms in the long run is 750.

In the long run, as firms exit the industry, the price rises. In long-run equilibrium, the price will equal the minimum average total cost. When output is 400 cassettes a week, marginal cost equals average total cost and average total cost is a minimum at $10 a cassette. In the long run, the price is $10 a cassette. Each firm remaining in the industry produces 400 cassettes a week. The quantity demanded at $10 a cassette is 300,000 a week. So the number of firms is 300,000 cassettes divided by 400 cassettes per firm, which is 750 firms.

7a. The market price is $7.65 a cassette.

When the price is $7.65 a cassette, each firm produces 300 cassettes and the quantity supplied by the 1,000 firms is 300,000 cassettes a week. The quantity demanded at $7.65 is 300,000 a week.

7b. The industry output is 300,000 cassettes a week.

7c. Each firm produces 300 cassettes a week.

7d. Each firm makes an economic loss of $834 a week.

Each firm produces 300 cassettes at an average total cost of $10.43 a cassette. The firm can sell the 300 cassettes for $7.65 a cassette. The firm incurs a loss on each cassette of $2.78 and incurs an economic loss of $834 a week.

7e. In the long run, some firms exit the industry because they are incurring economic losses.

7f. The number of firms in the long run is 500.

In the long run, as firms exit the industry, the price rises. Each firm remaining in the industry produces 400 cassettes a week. The quantity demanded at $10 a cassette is 200,000 a week. So the number of firms is 200,000 cassettes divided by 400 cassettes per firm, which is 500 firms.

CHAPTER 13

1a. Minnie's total revenue schedule lists the total revenue at each quantity sold. For example, Minnie's can sell 1 bottle for $8 a bottle, which gives it a total revenue of $8 at the quantity 1 bottle.

1b. Minnie's marginal revenue schedule lists the marginal revenue that results from increasing the quantity sold by 1 bottle. For example, Minnie's can sell 1 bottle for a total revenue of $8. Minnie's can sell 2 bottles for $6 each, which gives it a total revenue of $12 at the quantity 2 bottles. So by increasing the quantity sold from 1 bottle to 2 bottles, marginal revenue is $4 a bottle ($12 minus $8).

3a. Minnie's profit-maximizing output is 1.5 bottles.

The marginal cost of increasing the quantity from 1 bottle to 2 bottles is $4 a bottle ($7 minus $3). That is, the marginal cost of the 1.5 bottles is $4 a bottle. The marginal revenue of increasing the quantity sold from 1 bottle to 2 bottles is $4 ($12 minus $8). So the marginal revenue from 1.5 bottles is $4 a bottle. Profit is maximized when the quantity produced makes the marginal cost equal to marginal revenue. The profit-maximizing output is 1.5 bottles.

3b. Minnie's profit-maximizing price is $7 a bottle.

The profit-maximizing price is the highest price that Minnie's can sell the profit-maximizing output of 1.5 bottles. Minnie's can sell 1 bottle for $8 and 2 bottles for $6, so it can sell 1.5 bottles for $7 a bottle.

3c. Minnie's marginal cost is $4 a bottle.

3d. Minnie's marginal revenue is $4 a bottle.

3e. Minnie's economic profit is $5.50.

Economic profit equals total revenue minus total cost. Total revenue equals price ($7 a bottle) multiplied by quantity (1.5 bottles), which is $10.50. Total cost of producing 1 bottle is $3 and the total cost of producing 2 bottles is $7, so the total cost of producing 1.5 bottles is $5. Profit equals $10.50 minus $5, which is $5.50.

3f. Minnie's is inefficient. Minnie's charges a price of $7 a bottle, so consumers get a marginal benefit of $7 a bottle. Minnie's marginal cost is $4 a bottle. That is, the marginal benefit of $7 a bottle exceeds Minnie's marginal cost.

5a. The profit-maximizing output is 150 newspapers a day.

Profit is maximized when the firm produces the output at which marginal cost equals marginal revenue. Draw in the marginal revenue curve. It runs from 100 on the *y*-axis to 250 on the *x*-axis. The marginal revenue curve cuts the marginal cost curve at the quantity 150 newspapers a day.

5b. The price charged is 70 cents a paper.

The highest price that the publisher can sell 150 newspapers a day is read from the demand curve.

5c. The daily total revenue is $105 (150 papers at 70 cents each).

5d. Demand is elastic.

Along a straight-line demand curve, demand is elastic at all prices above the midpoint of the demand curve. The price at the midpoint is 50 cents. So at 70 cents a paper, demand is elastic.

7a. The efficient quantity is 250 newspapers—the quantity that makes marginal benefit (price) equal to marginal cost. With 250 newspapers available, people are willing to pay 50 cents for a paper. To produce 250 newspapers, the publisher incurs a marginal cost of 50 cents a paper.

7b. The consumer surplus is $22.50 a day.

Consumer surplus is the area under the demand curve above the price. The price is 70 cents, so consumer surplus equals (100 cents minus 70 cents) multiplied by 150/2 papers a day, which is $22.50 a day.

7c. The deadweight loss is $15 a day.

Deadweight loss arises because the publisher does not produce the efficient quantity. Output is restricted to 150, and the price is increased to 70 cents. The deadweight loss equals (70 cents minus 40 cents) multiplied by 100/2.

9. The maximum that will be spent on rent seeking is $5.50 a day—an amount equal to Minnie's economic profit. The total social cost equals the deadweight loss plus the amount spent on rent seeking. To calculate the deadweight loss, first calculate the efficient output—the intersection point of the demand curve (marginal benefit curve) and the marginal cost curve. Do this by finding the equations to the two curves and solving them. The efficient output is 2.25 bottles. The deadweight loss equals $1.125. The loss to society is $6.625 ($5.50 plus $1.125).

11a. The firm will produce 2 cubic feet a day and sell it for 6 cents a cubic foot. Deadweight loss will be 4 cents a day.

Draw in the marginal revenue curve. It runs from 10 on the y-axis to 2.5 on the x-axis. The profit-maximizing output is 2 cubic feet at which marginal revenue equals marginal cost. The price charged is the highest that people will pay for 2 cubic feet a day, which is 6 cents a cubic foot. The efficient output is 4 cubic feet, at which marginal cost equals price (marginal benefit). So the deadweight loss is (4 minus 2 cubic feet) multiplied by (6 minus 2 cents)/2.

11b. The firm will produce 3 cubic feet a day and charge 4 cents a cubic foot. Deadweight loss is 1 cent a day.

If the firm is regulated to earn only normal profit, it produces the output at which price equals average total cost—at the intersection of the demand curve and the *ATC* curve.

11c. The firm will produce 4 cubic feet a day and charge 2 cents a cubic foot. There is no deadweight loss.

If the firm is regulated to be efficient, it will produce the quantity at which price (marginal benefit) equals marginal cost—at the intersection of the demand curve and the marginal cost curve.

CHAPTER 14

1a. Lite and Kool produces 100 pairs a week.

To maximize profit, Lite and Kool produces the quantity at which marginal revenue equals marginal cost.

1b. Lite and Kool charges $20 a pair.

To maximize profit, Lite and Kool charges the highest price for the 100 pairs of shoes, as read from the demand curve.

1c. Lite and Kool makes a profit of $500 a week.

Economic profit equals total revenue minus total cost. The price is $20 and the quantity sold is 100 pairs, so total revenue is $2,000. Average total cost is $15, so total cost equals $1,500. Economic profit equals $2,000 minus $1,500, which is $500 a week.

3a. The firm produces 100 pairs and sells them for $60 a pair.

To maximize profit, the firm produces the quantity at which marginal cost equals marginal revenue. Marginal cost is $20 a pair. The firm can sell 200 pairs at $20 a pair, so the marginal revenue is $20 at 100 pairs. (Marginal revenue curve lies halfway between the y-axis and the demand curve.)

The firm sells the 100 pairs at the highest price that consumers will pay, which is read from the demand curve. This price is $60 a pair.

3b. The firm's economic profit is zero.

The firm produces 100 pairs and sells them for $60 a pair, so total revenue is $6,000. Total cost is the sum of total fixed cost plus total variable cost of 100 pairs. Total cost equals $4,000 plus ($20 multiplied by 100), which is $6,000. The firm's profit is zero.

3c. The firm produces 200 pairs and sells them for $60 a pair.

To maximize profit, the firm produces the quantity at which marginal cost equals marginal revenue. Marginal cost is $20 a pair. At $20 a pair, the firm can sell 400 pairs (twice the number with no advertising), so the marginal revenue is $20 at 200 pairs. (The marginal revenue curve lies halfway between the y-axis and the demand curve.)

The firm sells the 200 pairs at the highest price that consumers will pay which is read from the demand curve. This price is $60 a pair.

3d. The firm makes an economic profit of $1,000.

The firm produces 200 pairs and sells them for $60 a pair, so total revenue is $12,000. Total cost is the sum of total fixed cost plus the advertising cost plus total variable cost of 200 pairs. Total cost equals $4,000 plus $3,000 plus ($20 multiplied by 200), which is $11,000. The firm makes an economic profit of $1,000.

3e. The firm will spend $3,000 advertising because it makes more economic profit than when it does not advertise.

3f. The firm will not change the quantity it produces or the price it charges. The firm makes less economic profit.

5. The firm maximizes profit by producing the output at which marginal cost equals marginal revenue. An increase in fixed cost increases total cost, but it does not change marginal cost. So the firm does not change its output or the price it charges. The firm's total costs have increased and its total revenue has not changed, so the firm makes less economic profit.

7a. The price rises, output increases, and economic profit increases.

The dominant firm produces the quantity and sets the price such that it maximizes its profit. When demand increases, marginal revenue increases, so the firm produces a larger output. The highest price at which the dominant firm can sell its output increases. Because price exceeds marginal cost, economic profit increases.

7b. The price rises, output increases, and economic profit increases.

The small firms are price takers, so the price they charge rises. Because these firms are price takers, the price is also marginal revenue. Because marginal revenue increases, the small firms move up along their marginal cost curves (supply curves) and increase the quantity they produce. Because price exceeds marginal cost, economic profit increases.

9a. The game has 2 players (A and B), and each player has 2 strategies: to answer honestly or to lie. There are 4 payoffs: Both answer honestly; both lie; A lies, and B answers honestly; and B lies, and A answers honestly.

9b. The payoff matrix has the following cells: Both answer honestly: A gets $100, and B gets $100; both lie: A gets $50, and B gets $50; A lies and B answers honestly: A gets $500, and B gets $0; B lies and A answers honestly: A gets $0, and B gets $500.

9c. Equilibrium is that each player lies and gets $50.

If B answers honestly, the best strategy for A is to lie because he would get $500 rather than $100. If B lies, the best strategy for A is to lie because he would get $500 rather than $0. So A's best strategy is to lie, no matter what B does. Repeat the exercise for B. B's best strategy is to lie, no matter what A does.

11a. Each firm makes a zero economic profit or normal profit.

If both firms cheat, each firm will lower the price in an attempt to gain market share from the other firm. In the process, the price will be driven down until each firm is making normal profit.

11b. The payoff matrix has the following cells: Both abide by the agreement: Soapy makes $1 million profit, and Sudsies makes $1 million profit; both cheat: Soapy makes $0 profit, and Sudsies makes $0 profit; Soapy cheats and Sudsies abides by the agreement: Soapy makes $1.5 million profit, and Sudsies incurs a $0.5 million loss; Sudsies cheats and Soapy abides by the agreement: Sudsies makes $1.5 million profit, and Soapy incurs $0.5 million loss.

11c. The best strategy for each firm is to cheat.

If Sudsies abides by the agreement, the best strategy for Soapy is to cheat because it would make a profit of $1.5 million rather than $1 million. If Sudsies cheats, the best strategy for Soapy is to cheat because it would make a profit of $0 (the competitive outcome) rather than incur a loss of $0.5 million. So Soapy's best strategy is to cheat, no matter what Sudsies does. Repeat the exercise for Sudsies. Sudsies's best strategy is to cheat, no matter what Soapy does.

11d. The equilibrium is that both firms cheat and each makes normal profit.

11e. Each firm can adopt a tit-for-tat strategy or a trigger strategy. Pages 301-302 give descriptions of these strategies.

CHAPTER 15

1a. The wage rate is $6 an hour. The wage rate adjusts to make the quantity of labor demanded equal to the quantity supplied.

1b. The number of pickers hired is 400 a day. At a wage rate of $6 an hour, 400 pickers a day are hired.

1c. The income received is $2,400 an hour. Income equals the wage rate ($6 an hour) multiplied by the number of pickers (400).

3a. Marginal product of labor is the increase in total product that results from hiring one additional student. For example, if Wanda increases the number of students hired from 2 to 3, total product (the quantity of fish packed) increases from 50 to 90 pounds. The marginal product of hiring the third student is 40 pounds of fish.

3b. Marginal revenue product of labor is the increase in total revenue that results from hiring one additional student. For example, if Wanda hires 2 students, they produce 50 pounds of fish and Wanda sells fish for 50 cents a pound. Total revenue is $25. If Wanda increases the number of students hired from 2 to 3, total product increases to 90 pounds. Total revenue from the sale of this fish is $45. Marginal revenue product resulting from hiring the third student is $20 ($45 minus $25). Alternatively, marginal revenue product equals marginal product multiplied by marginal revenue (price). Marginal revenue product of hiring the third student is $20, which is 40 pounds of fish she sells at 50 cents a pound.

3c. One point on Wanda's demand for labor curve: At a wage rate of $20 an hour, Wanda will hire 3 students. The demand for labor curve is the same as the marginal revenue product curve.

3d. Wanda hires 7 students.

Wanda hires the number of students that makes the marginal revenue product equal to the wage rate of $7.50 an hour. When Wanda increases the number of students from 6 to 7, marginal product is 15 pounds of fish an hour, which Wanda sells for 50 cents a pound. Marginal revenue product is $7.50—the same as the wage rate.

5a. Marginal product does not change. Marginal product that results from hiring the third student is still 40 pounds of fish.

5b. Marginal revenue product decreases.

If Wanda hires the third student, marginal product is 40 pounds of fish. But now Wanda sells the fish for 33.33 cents, so marginal revenue product is now $13.33, down from $20.

5c. Wanda's demand for labor decreases, and her demand for labor curve shifts leftward. Wanda is willing to pay the students their marginal revenue product, and the fall in the price of fish has lowered their marginal revenue product.

5d. Wanda will hire fewer students. At the wage rate of $7.50, the number of students Wanda hires decreases as the demand for labor curve shifts leftward.

7a. Marginal revenue product does not change. If Wanda hires the third student, marginal product is 40 pounds of fish and Wanda sells the fish for 50 cents a pound, so marginal revenue product remains at $20.

7b. Wanda's demand for labor remains the same because marginal revenue product has not changed.

7c. Wanda will hire fewer students. At the wage rate of $10 an hour, Wanda hires the number of students that makes marginal revenue product equal to $10 an hour. Wanda now hires 6 students—down from 7. The marginal product that results when Wanda hires the sixth student is 20 pounds of fish an hour, and Wanda sells this fish for 50 cents a pound. Marginal revenue product of the sixth student is $10 an hour.

9. Wanda maximizes her profit when marginal revenue product equals the wage rate and when marginal revenue equals marginal cost.

When the wage rate is $7.50 an hour, Wanda hires 7 students. Marginal revenue product is marginal product (15 pounds of fish an hour) multiplied by the price of fish (50 cents a pound), which equals $7.50 an hour.

Marginal revenue resulting from selling an additional pound of fish is 50 cents. The seventh student costs $7.50 an hour and has a marginal product of 15 pounds of fish. So the marginal cost of an additional pound of fish is $7.50 an hour divided by 15 pounds of fish, which is 50 cents. So when Wanda hires 7 students, marginal revenue equals marginal cost and profit is maximized.

11. Venus installs three production lines.

With one production line: The present value of the marginal revenue product in the first year is $590,000/1.05, which is $561,904.76. The present value of the marginal revenue product in the second year is $590,000/(1.05)^2$, which is $535,147.39. So the present value of the flow of marginal revenue product is $1,097,052.15. The cost of one production line is $1 million. The net present value is $97,052.15, so Venus buys the production line.

Similar calculations for 2 and 3 production lines give positive net present values, so Venus installs 3 production lines.

13. To answer this problem, we need to know the interest rate and the price that Greg expects next year. If he expects the price to rise by a bigger percentage than the interest rate, he pumps none and waits for the higher price. If he expects the price to rise by a smaller percentage than the interest rate, he pumps it all now. If he expects the price to rise by a percentage equal to the interest rate, he doesn't mind how much he pumps.

15a. Income of $2,400 a day is divided between opportunity cost and economic rent. Economic rent is the area above the supply curve below the wage rate. To show the economic rent on the graph, extend the supply curve until it touches the y-axis. Shade in the area above the supply curve up to the wage rate $6 an hour.

15b. Opportunity cost is the area under the supply curve. To show the opportunity cost on the graph, shade in the area under the supply curve up to 400 pickers on the x-axis.

CHAPTER 16

1a. The wage rate of low-skilled workers is $5 an hour.

The wage rate adjusts to make the quantity of labor demanded equal to the quantity supplied.

1b. Firms employ 5,000 hours of low-skilled workers a day. At a wage rate of $5 an hour, 5,000 hours are employed each day.

1c. The wage rate of high-skilled workers is $8 an hour.

Because the marginal product of high-skilled workers is twice the marginal product of low-skilled workers, firms are willing to pay high-skilled workers twice the wage rate that they are willing to pay low-skilled workers. For example, the demand curve for low-skilled workers tells us that firms are willing to hire 6,000 hours of low-skilled workers at a wage rate of $4 an hour. So with high-skilled workers twice as productive as low-skilled workers, firms are willing to hire 6,000 hours of high-skilled workers at $8 an hour. That is, the demand curve for high-skilled labor lies above the demand curve for low-skilled workers such that at each quantity of workers, the wage rate for high-skilled workers is double that for low-skilled workers.

The supply of high-skilled workers lies above the supply of low-skilled workers such that the vertical distance between the two supply curves equals the cost of acquiring the high skill—$2 an hour. That is, high-skilled workers will supply 6,000 hours a day if the wage rate is $8 an hour.

Equilibrium in the labor market for high-skilled workers occurs at a wage rate of $8 an hour.

1d. Firms employ 6,000 hours of high-skilled workers a day.

3a. The wage rate is $10 an hour.

With the amount of high-skilled workers equal to 5,000 hours a day, the demand for labor curve tells us that firms are willing to pay the $10 an hour to hire high-skilled workers.

3b. The wage differential is $5 an hour.

The demand for labor curves tells us that firms are willing to pay the $10 an hour to hire high-skilled workers and $5 an hour to hire low-skilled workers.

5a. The wage rate is $6 an hour.

A minimum wage is the lowest wage rate that a low-skilled worker can be paid.

5b. Firms hire 4,000 hours of low-skilled workers a day.

At the minimum wage of $6 an hour, the demand for low-skilled labor tells us that firms will hire only 4,000 hours of low-skilled workers a day.

7a. The wage rate is $10 a day.

The monopsony firm maximizes its profit by hiring the quantity of labor that makes the marginal cost of labor equal to the marginal revenue product of labor (see Fig. 16.5). The marginal product of the fifth worker is 10 grains per day. Gold sells for $1.40 per grain, so the marginal revenue product of the fifth worker is $14 a day. The marginal cost of the fifth worker a day equals the total labor cost of 5 workers a day minus the total labor cost of 4 workers a day. The supply of labor tells us that to hire 5 workers a day, the gold company must pay $10 a day, so the total labor cost is $50 a day. The supply of labor also tells us that to hire 4 workers a day, the gold company must pay $9 a day, so the total labor cost is $36 a day. So the marginal cost of the fifth worker is $14 a day ($50 minus $36).

The profit-maximizing quantity of labor is 5 workers because the marginal cost of the fifth worker equals the marginal revenue product of the fifth worker. The monopsony pays the 5 workers the lowest wage possible: the wage rate at which the 4 workers are willing to supply their labor. The supply of labor schedule tells us that 5 workers are willing to supply their labor for $10 a day.

7b. The gold company hires 5 workers a day.

7c. The marginal revenue product of the fifth worker is $14 a day.

9. A court-enforced wage rate above $10 a day will increase the wage rate. The quantity of labor supplied will increase, and employment will increase. Marginal revenue product of the monopsony will decrease as more labor is hired.

CHAPTER 17

1a. To draw the Lorenz curve, plot the cumulative percentage of households on the x-axis and the cumulative percentage of income on the y-axis. Make the scale on the two axes the same. The Lorenz curve will pass through the following points: 20 percent on the x-axis and 5 percent on the y-axis; 40 percent on the x-axis and 16 percent on the y-axis; 60 percent on the x-axis and 33 percent on the y-axis; 80 percent on the x-axis and 57 percent on the y-axis; and 100 percent on the x-axis and 100 percent on the y-axis.

1b. U.S. income is distributed less equally than the income in the economy in this problem.

The line of equality shows an equal distribution of income. The closer the Lorenz curve is to the line of equality, the more equal is the income distribution. The Lorenz curve for this economy lies between the U.S. Lorenz curve and the line of equality.

3a. The distributions of income and wealth are the same. Every 45-year-old person has income of $30,000 a year and wealth of $255,000.

Each 45-year-old person has earned $30,000 a year for 31 years, a total of $930,000. The lifetime income will be $1,050,000 (35 multiplied by $30,000). Because total income is consumed over the lifetime and at a constant rate, consumption is $15,000 a year ($1,050,000 divided by 70). Total consumption of a 45-year-old person is $675,000 (45 multiplied by $15,000). So the accumulated savings (wealth) at 45 years of age is $255,000 ($930,000 minus $675,000).

3b. Income is $30,000 a year for the people aged 25, 35, and 45 and zero for the people aged 55 and 65. Wealth is distributed unequally. Wealth is −$45,000 for the 25-year-old; $105,000 for the 35-year-old; $255,000 for the 45-year-old; $225,000 for the 55-year-old; and $75,000 for the 65-year-old. (Each calculation is similar to that in answer 3a.)

Case (a) shows greater equality than case (b). The distributions of wealth and income are equal in case (a) but unequal in case (b).

5a. The average wage rate is $3 an hour.

In an hour, the 10 people earn a total of $30. So the average wage rate is $3 an hour.

5b. The ratio of the highest to the lowest wage is 5/1 ($5/$1).

5c. Average daily income is $14.50 an hour.

To calculate the total income earned, start with a wage rate and find the number of hours each will work at that wage rate (first table); then find the number of people who work at that wage rate (second table). For example, if the wage rate is $3 an hour, the people who work at wage rate will work for 4 hours a day and the number of people who will work at $3 an hour is 4 people. The total daily income of these 4 people is $48 ($3 multiplied by 4 multiplied by 4).

Total income of the 10 people is $145 a day. Average daily income is equal to $14.50.

5d. The ratio of the highest to the lowest daily income is 40/1.

The highest daily income earned is $40. At $5 an hour, 1 person works and that person works for 8 hours a day. The lowest daily income is $1. At $1 an hour, 1 person works and that person works for 1 hour a day. The ratio of highest to lowest daily income is $40/$1.

5e. The distribution of hourly wage rates is symmetrically around the average wage rate of $3.00 an hour. At $1 an hour, 10 percent of people (1 person) work; at $2 an hour, 20 percent of people (2 people) work; at $3 an hour, 40 percent of people (4 people) work; at $4 an hour, 20 percent of people (2 people) work; at $5 an hour, 10 percent of people (1 person) work.

5f. The distribution of daily incomes is skewed to the left: $1 a day is earned by 10 percent of people (1 person); $4 a day is earned by 20 percent of people (2 people); $12 a day is earned by 40 percent of people (4 people); $24 a day is earned by 20 percent of people (2 people); $40 a day is earned by 10 percent of people (1 person). The most common income ($12 a day) is less than the average income ($14.50 a day).

5g. The distribution of income is skewed despite the equal distribution of abilities (as indicated by the distribution of wage rates). The distribution of income is influenced by the choices people make about how many hours to work.

7a. To draw the Lorenz curve, plot the cumulative percentage of households on the x-axis and the cumulative percentage of income after taxes and benefits on the y-axis. Make the scale on the two axes the same. The Lorenz curve passes through the following points: 20 percent on the x-axis and 15.0 percent on the y-axis; 40 percent on the x-axis and 32.0 percent on the y-axis; 60 percent on the x-axis and 50.3 percent on the y-axis; 80 percent on the x-axis and 72.7 percent on the y-axis; and 100 percent on the x-axis and 100 percent on the y-axis.

The income for each 20 percent of households equals market income minus taxes plus benefits. For example, for the third 20 percent income after taxes and benefits equals $18 million minus taxes of $2.7 million (15 percent of 18 million) plus benefits of $3 million, which equals $18.3 million.

7b. The government of this economy redistributes income by less than the U.S. government does. Plot the original and new Lorenz curves for the economy in this problem on Fig. 17.5 and compare the amounts of redistribution in this economy with that in the U.S. economy.

CHAPTER 18

1a. The capacity that achieves maximum net benefit is 2.5 million gallons a day.

Net benefit of the last million gallons of capacity equals marginal benefit minus marginal cost. The capacity that maximizes net benefit is the capacity at which net benefit is zero. So the capacity that maximizes net benefit is the cone at which marginal benefit equals marginal cost, which is 2.5 million gallons a day.

1b. $62.50 per person.

The efficient capacity is the one that maximizes net benefit. Total cost of the sewerage system is the sum of the marginal cost of each additional gallon of capacity. That is, total cost is the area under that marginal cost curve up to 2.5 million gallons, which equals $62.5 million. The population is 1 million, so each person will have to pay $62.50.

1c. The political equilibrium will be a sewerage system that has a capacity of 2.5 million gallons.

If voters are well informed, the political equilibrium will be the efficient capacity.

1d. Bureaucrats will provide a capacity of 5 million gallons.

With voters rationally ignorant, bureaucrats will maximize the budget. That is, they will increase the capacity until net benefit is zero. The total benefit from a capacity of 5 million gallons is $250 million. The total cost of a capacity of 5 million gallons is $250 million. So the net benefit from a capacity of 5 million gallons is zero.

3a. Taxes will be progressive: B-type people will pay a higher tax rate than A-type people.

The median voter theorem tells us the tax arrangement will be that which minimizes the taxes of the median voter. The median voter is an A-type person.

3b. The before-tax wage rate of A-type people will rise by the amount of the tax, and fewer A-type people will be employed. The after-tax wage rate will remain at $10 an hour. The before-tax wage rate of B-type people will remain at $100, and employment of B-type people will not change. The after-tax wage rate will fall by the amount of the tax.

5a. The equilibrium wage rate is $12 an hour, and 30 hours of work are done each week.

Equilibrium wage rate is such that the quantity of labor demanded equals the quantity of labor supplied. Hours of work done equal the equilibrium quantity of labor hired.

5b. (i) The new wage rate is $13.60 an hour. (ii) The new number of hours worked is 24 a week. (iii) The after-tax wage rate is $9.60 an hour. (iv) The tax revenue is $96.00 a week. (v) Deadweight loss is $12 a week.

To work this problem either draw an exact graph (like Fig. 18.8b) or use equations. The equation for the pre-tax demand for labor curve is $W = -(8/30)L + 20$, where W is the wage rate and L is hours of labor. The equation for the demand for labor curve once the Social Security tax is imposed on employers is $W = -(8/30)L + 16$. The equation for the supply of labor curve is $W = (12/30)L$. So the equilibrium employment is 24 hours a week. To find the

cost of labor, substitute 24 for L in the demand for labor curve. To find the after-tax wage rate, substitute 24 for L in the demand for labor curve after the tax is imposed. The tax revenue is $4 an hour multiplied by the 24 hours employed. The deadweight loss equals the tax multiplied by half the cut in employment—that is, $4 multiplied by $(30 - 24)/2$.

7a. The equilibrium price is $3 a pound, and the equilibrium quantity is 14 pounds a month.

To work this problem either draw an exact graph (like Fig. 18.9) or use equations. The equation for the demand curve is $P = -(1/2)Q + 10$. The equation for the supply curve before the tax is imposed is $P = (1/2)Q - 4$. Solving these equations gives an equilibrium price of $3 a pound and an equilibrium quantity of 14 pounds a month.

7b. (i) The new price is $4 a pound. (ii) The new quantity is 12 pounds a month. (iii) Tax revenue is $24 a month. (iv) Deadweight loss is $2 a month.

With the $2 a pound tax, the supply curve becomes $P = (1/2)Q - 2$. Solving the new supply curve and the demand curve gives a price of $4 a pound, and 12 pounds a month are bought. The tax revenue is $2 a pound multiplied by the 12 pounds bought. The deadweight loss equals the tax multiplied by half the cut in the quantity bought—that is, $2 multiplied by $(14 - 12)/2$.

CHAPTER 19

1a. The price is 30 cents a bottle.

Elixir Springs is a natural monopoly. It produces the quantity that makes marginal revenue equal to marginal cost, and it charges the highest price it can for the quantity produced. The marginal revenue curve is twice as steep as the demand curve, so it runs from 50 on the y-axis to 1.25 on the x-axis. Marginal revenue equals marginal cost at 1 million bottles a year. The highest price at which Elixir can sell 1 million bottles a year is 30 cents a bottle, read from the demand curve.

1b. Elixir Springs sells 1 million bottles a year.

1c. Elixir maximizes producer surplus.

If Elixir maximizes total surplus, it would produce the quantity that makes price equal to marginal cost. That is, it would produce 2 million bottles a year and sell them for 10 cents a bottle. Elixir is a natural monopoly, and it maximizes its producer surplus.

3a. The price is 10 cents a bottle.

Marginal cost pricing regulation sets the price equal to marginal cost, 10 cents a bottle.

3b. Elixir sells 2 million bottles.

With the price set at 10 cents, Elixir maximizes profit by producing 2 million bottles—at the intersection of the demand curve (which shows price) and the marginal cost curve.

3c. Elixir incurs an economic loss of $150,000 a year.

Economic profit equals total revenue minus total cost. Total revenue is $200,000 (2 million bottles at 10 cents a bottle). Total cost is $350,000 (total variable cost of $200,000 plus total fixed cost of $150,000). So Elixir incurs an economic loss of $150,000 (a profit of $200,000 minus $350,000).

3d. Consumer surplus is $400,000 a year.

Consumer surplus is the area under the demand curve above the price. Consumer surplus equals 40 cents a bottle (50 cents minus 10 cents) multiplied by 2 million bottles divided by 2, which is $400,000.

3e. The regulation is in the public interest because total surplus is maximized. The outcome is efficient.

The outcome is efficient because marginal benefit (or price) equals marginal cost. When the outcome is efficient, total surplus is maximized.

5a. The price is 20 cents a bottle.

Average cost pricing regulation sets the price equal to average total cost. Average total cost equals average fixed cost plus average variable cost. Because marginal cost is constant at 10 cents, average variable cost equals marginal cost. Average fixed cost is total fixed cost ($150,000) divided by the quantity produced. For example, when Elixir produces 1.5 million bottles, average fixed cost is 10 cents, so average total cost is 20 cents. The price at which Elixir can sell 1.5 million bottles a year is 20 cents a bottle.

5b. Elixir sells 1.5 million bottles.

5c. Elixir makes zero economic profit.

Economic profit equals total revenue minus total cost. Total revenue is $300,000 (1.5 million bottles at 20 cents a bottle). Total cost is $300,000 (1.5 million bottles at an average total cost of 20 cents). So Elixir makes zero economic profit.

5d. Consumer surplus is $225,000 a year.

Consumer surplus is the area under the demand curve above the price. Consumer surplus equals 40 cents a bottle (50 cents minus 20 cents) multiplied by 1.5 million bottles divided by 2, which is $225,000.

5e. The regulation creates a deadweight loss, so the outcome is inefficient. The regulation is not in the public interest.

7a. The price is $500 a trip, and the quantity is 2 trips a day.

Regulation in the public interest is marginal cost pricing. Each airline charges $500 a trip and produces the quantity at which price equals marginal cost. Each airline makes 1 trip a day.

7b. The price is $750 a trip, and the number of trips is 1 trip a day (one by each airline on alternate days).

If the airlines capture the regulator, the price will be the same as the price that an unregulated monopoly would charge. An unregulated monopoly produces the quantity and charges the price that maximizes profit—that is, the quantity that makes marginal revenue equal to marginal cost. This quantity is 1 trip a day, and the highest price that the airlines can charge for that trip (read from the demand curve) is $750.

7c. Deadweight loss is $125 a day.

Deadweight loss arises because the number of trips is cut from 2 to 1 a day and the price is increased from $500 to $750. Deadweight loss equals (2 minus 1) trip multiplied by ($750 minus $500) divided by 2. Deadweight loss is $125 a day.

7d. The regulation is in the public interest if total surplus is maximized. That is, the outcome is efficient. A regulation that is inefficient is a regulation in the producer interest.

9. Government agencies regulate economic activity by setting prices, product standards and types, and entry conditions into markets. Antitrust laws are rules concerning certain types of market behavior.

Regulation is used when a natural monopoly exists and is used to make the market in which the natural monopoly exists more efficient. Examples include the setting of prices for local utilities and transit systems. Antitrust laws are used to prevent producers from acting to reduce the amount of competition between them. Examples include producers agreeing to fix the price and producers attempting to create a monopoly.

CHAPTER 20

1a. The efficient amount of waste is 3 tons a week.

The efficient amount of waste is the quantity that makes the marginal cost equal to marginal benefit. When the pesticide factory dumps 2 tons of waste, the trout farm's profit is $875 per week. When the pesticide factory dumps 3 tons of waste, the trout farm's profit is $775 per week. The loss of profit from the third ton of waste is $100. The marginal benefit to the pesticide factory of dumping the waste (the cost cut by not trucking the waste) is $100 a ton. That is, the marginal cost of the third ton to the trout farm equals the marginal benefit of the third ton to the pesticide factory.

1b. If the trout farm owns the lake, the amount of waste is 3 tons a week.

The pesticide factory pays the trout farm $100 a ton for the right to dump 3 tons of waste a week.

1c. If the pesticide factory owns the lake, the amount of waste is 3 tons a week.

The trout farm pays the pesticide factory $300 a week for farming rights and for an agreement that the dumping of waste will not exceed 3 tons a week.

3a. A tax of $100 a ton will achieve an efficient quantity of waste dumped into the lake.

The cost of dumping the waste is zero, so the pesticide factory will dump all its waste. A tax of $100 a ton will increase the marginal cost of dumping and reduce the amount of waste dumped to 3 tons a week.

3b. If no one owns the lake (that is, property rights do not exist), the efficient amount of dumped waste can be achieved by imposing the appropriate tax on the polluter.

5a. The quantity that may be dumped is 3 tons a week—the efficient quantity.

5b. The market price of a permit is $150 (or $100 a ton). The trout farm sells its permit to the factory.

The factory and the farm share equally the permits to dump 3 tons of waste. That is, each has a permit to dump 1.5 tons of waste. The efficient amount of waste is 3 tons, so the farm sells its permit to pollute to the factory for $100 a ton.

5c. The cost of dumping the waste is zero, so the pesticide factory will dump all its waste. A tax of $100 a ton will increase the marginal cost of dumping and reduce the amount of waste dumped to 3 tons a week. In this problem, the factory has a permit to dump 1.5 tons of waste a week. To be able to dump another 1.5 tons a week, the factory must buy the permit from the trout farm. The alternative to dumping the 1.5 tons is to truck it at a cost of $100 a ton. So the opportunity cost of buying the permit is $150.

7a. If schools are competitive, 30,000 students enroll and tuition is $4,000 a year.

In a competitive market, schools maximize profit. They produce the quantity at which the marginal benefit of the last student enrolled equals the marginal cost of educating the last student enrolled. Tuition is $4,000 a student.

7b. Efficient number of places is 50,000, and tuition is $4,000 a student.

The efficient number of places is such that the marginal social benefit of education equals the marginal cost of education. The marginal social benefit equals the marginal private benefit plus the external benefit. For example, the marginal social benefit of 50,000 places equals the marginal private benefit of $2,000 plus the external benefit of $2,000, which is $4,000.

CHAPTER 21

1a. Expected income is $2,000 a month.

Lee expects to make $4,000 with a 50 percent probability and nothing with a 50 percent probability. Lee's expected income is $4,000 multiplied by 0.5 plus $0 multiplied by 0.5, which is $2,000 a month.

1b. Expected total utility is 50 units.

Lee expects to make $4,000 and get 100 units of utility with a 50 percent probability and no income and get zero utility with a 50 percent probability. Lee's expected utility is 100 units multiplied by 0.5 plus 0 units multiplied by 0.5, which is 50 units a month.

1c. Another firm would have to offer about $1,250 a month for Lee not to take the risky job.

Lee would get 50 units of total utility from a certain income of about $1,250 a month (read from the utility of wealth curve at a total utility of 50 units).

3. Zenda is more risk averse.

The more rapidly a person's marginal utility of wealth diminishes, the more risk averse that person is. As wealth increases by 100, Jimmy's marginal utility decreases from 200 to 100 to 50. That is, Jimmy's marginal utility halves as his wealth increases by 100. As wealth increases by 100, Zenda's marginal utility decreases from 512 to 128 to 32. That is, Zenda's marginal utility falls to a quarter as her wealth increases by 100.

5. Lee is willing to pay $4,500 for house insurance.

With no insurance, Lee's expected wealth is $5,000 multiplied by 0.25 plus $0 multiplied by 0.75. Lee's expected wealth is $1,250, and her expected utility of (about) 25 units. But her guaranteed utility is 25 units with wealth of $500. Lee is willing to pay up to $4,500 ($5,000 minus $500) for insurance that pays out $5,000 if the house is washed away.

7. Lee will implement the optimal-search rule explained on pp. 455-456.

CHAPTER 22

1. Go to *Economics in Action*, Chapter 22, Problem 1, and use the graph provided to find the solution to this problem.

3a. The growth rate in India was positive in every year from 1989 to 1996. The growth rate was fastest in 1989.

3b. The growth rate was not negative in Pakistan in this period. The growth rate was slowest in 1993.

3c. From 1989 to 1993, when India's growth rate increased, Pakistan's decreased. But from 1993 to 1995, both growth rates increased. In 1996, they were the same.

5a. Germany had one recession in the third and fourth quarters of 1992.

A recession is a period during which real GDP decreases for at least two successive quarters. Real GDP decreased in the third and fourth quarters of 1992.

5b. Germany experienced a business cycle peak in the fourth quarter of 1991.

A business cycle peak is the upper turning point. A peak occurs when real GDP stops growing and starts to decrease.

5c. Germany experienced a business cycle trough in the fourth quarter of 1992.

A business cycle trough is the lower turning point of a business cycle where a recession ends and an expansion begins.

5d. Germany experienced an expansion during the third and fourth quarters of 1991 and from the first quarter of 1993 through the second quarter of 1994.

An expansion is a period during which real GDP increases.

7. Go to *Economics in Action*, Chapter 22, Problem 7, and use the graph provided to find the solution to this problem.

9. Go to *Economics in Action*, Chapter 22, Problem 9, and use the graph provided to find the solution to this problem.

CHAPTER 23

1. Martha's initial capital stock is 5 copiers, depreciation is 1 copier per year, gross investment is 3 copiers, net investment is 2 copiers, and the final capital stock is 7 copiers.

Final capital stock equals initial capital stock plus net investment. Net investment equals gross investment minus depreciation.

3a. Aggregate expenditure is $60 million.

Aggregate expenditure is the sum of consumption expenditure, investment, government purchases, and net exports. In the figure, B is consumption expenditure, D is investment, C is government purchases, and E is net exports. Therefore aggregate expenditure equals $30 million plus $15 million plus $12 million plus $3 million, which is $60 million.

3b. Aggregate income is $60 million.

Aggregate income equals aggregate expenditure, which from 3(a) is $60 million.

3c. GDP is $60 million.

GDP equals aggregate expenditure, which from 3(a) is $60 million.

3d. Government budget deficit is $2 million.

Government budget deficit equals government purchases minus taxes. C is government purchases, and A is taxes. So the government budget deficit equals $12 million minus $10 million, which is $2 million.

3e. Household saving is $20 million.

Household saving equals aggregate income minus consumption expenditure minus taxes. In the figure, B is consumption expenditure and A is taxes. Therefore household saving equals $60 million minus $30 million minus $10 million, which is $20 million.

3f. Government saving is minus $2 million.

Government saving equals taxes minus government purchases. In the figure, A is taxes and C is government expenditure. Therefore government saving equals $10 million minus $12 million, which is minus $2 million.

3g. Foreign borrowing is $3 million.

Foreign borrowing equals net exports. E is net exports, and net exports equals $3 million. We are in surplus, so foreigners are in deficit and they must borrow from us to pay for their deficit. Foreign borrowing equals $3 million.

3h. National saving is $18 million.

National saving equals the sum of household saving and government saving. Household saving is $20 million (see answer 3e). Government saving is minus $2 million (see answer 3f). Therefore national saving equals $20 million minus $2 million, which is $18 million.

5a. Ecoland's GDP is $1,100,000.

GDP equals the sum of consumption expenditure plus investment plus government purchases plus net exports. That is, GDP equals $600,000 plus $250,000 plus $200,000 plus $300,000 minus $250,000. GDP equals $1,100,000.

5b. Expenditure approach. Income approach cannot be used because there are no data on interest, rent, depreciation, and indirect taxes and subsidies.

5c. Investment is financed by private saving (saving), government saving (taxes minus transfer payments minus purchases of goods and services) plus net foreign borrowing (imports minus exports).

These items are $300,000 + $250,000 − $50,000 − $200,000 + $250,000 − $300,000 = $250,000.

7a. The basket used in the CPI is 10 bottles of juice and 5 lengths of cloth.

The basket used in the CPI is the typical basket consumed in the base year. In the base year, the typical family spends $40 on juice and juice costs $4 a bottle, so the family buys 10 bottles of juice. In the base year, the typical family spends $25 on cloth and cloth costs $5 a length, so the family buys 5 lengths of cloth.

7b. The CPI in the current year is 107.69.

Expenditure on the CPI basket in the current year is 10 bottles of juice @ $4 a bottle plus 5 lengths of cloth @ $6 a length, which is $70. The expenditure on the CPI basket in the base year is $40 plus $25, which is $65. The

CPI in the current year equals the expenditure on the basket in the current year divided by the expenditure on the basket in the base year, multiplied by 100. The CPI is 107.69.

7c. The inflation rate in the current year is 7.69 percent.

The CPI in the base year is 100 and the CPI in the current year is 107.69, so the inflation rate is the rate of change of the CPI. The inflation rate equals (107.69 − 100)/100, which is 7.69 percent.

9a. In 1997, GDP is $7,000 and real GDP is $7,000. In 1998, GDP is $7,500 and real GDP is $7,475.

GDP is equal to total expenditure on the goods and services produced by Bananaland in 1997. Expenditure on bananas is 1,000 bunches @ $2 a bunch, which is $2,000. Expenditure on sunscreen is 500 bottles @ $10 a bottle, which is $5,000. So total expenditure is $7,000.

Because 1997 is the base year, real GDP in 1997 equals GDP in 1997.

GDP in 1998 is equal to total expenditure in 1998 on bananas and sunscreen. That is, 1,100 bunches @ $3 a bunch, which is $3,300. Expenditure on sunscreen is 525 bottles @ $8 a bottle, which is $4,200. So total expenditure is $7,500.

Real GDP in 1998 is equal to real GDP in 1997 ($7,000) multiplied by the chain-weighted output index (divided by 100) which is 1.0679.

To obtain the chain weighted quantity index, calculate: (1) the value of the 1997 quantities at the 1998 prices—$7,000; (2) the 1998 quantities at the 1997 prices—$7,450; (3) an output index in 1997 prices—$7,450/$7,000 = 1.0643; (4) an output index in 1998 prices—$7,500/$7,000 = 1.0714; (5) the geometric mean of the two output indexes, calculated by multiplying 1.0643 by 1.0714 and taking the square root of the product. The answer equals 1.0679.

9b. The growth rate of real GDP in 1998 is 6.79 percent.

The growth rate equals the increase in real GDP from 1997 to 1998 expressed as a percentage of real GDP in 1997. That is, the growth rate equals ($7,475 − $7,000)/$7,000, which is 6.79 percent.

9c. The GDP deflator in 1998 is 100.33.

GDP deflator equals GDP in 1998 divided by real GDP in 1998, multiplied by 100. GDP deflator equals ($7,500/$7,475) × 100 = 100.33.

CHAPTER 24

1a. Unemployment rate is 4.7 percent.

The unemployment rate is the percentage of the labor force that is unemployed. The labor force is the sum of the people unemployed and the people employed. So the number of people who are unemployed is 137,169,000 minus 130,777,000, which is 6,392,000.

The unemployment rate equals (the number of people unemployed divided by the labor force) multiplied by 100. That is, (6,392,000/137,169,000) × 100, which is 4.7 percent.

1b. The labor force participation rate is 67.2 percent.

The labor force participation rate is the percentage of the working-age population that is in the labor force. The working-age population is 204,020,000 and the labor force is 137,169,000, so the labor force participation rate equals (137,169,000/204,020,000) × 100, which equals 67.2 percent.

1c. The employment-to-population ratio is 64.1 percent.

The employment-to-population ratio is the percentage of the people of working age who have jobs. The employment-to-population ratio is equal to the number of people employed divided by the working-age population all multiplied by 100. The employment-to-population ratio is (130,777,000/204,020,000) × 100, which is 64.1 percent.

3. Unemployment decreased by 769,000. The number of discouraged workers has decreased.

During 1997, employment in the United States increased by 2,878,000 and the labor force increased by 2,109,000. The number of unemployed is calculated as the labor force minus the number employed. When the labor force increased by 2,109,000 and employment increased by 2,878,000, unemployment decreased by 769,000.

Discouraged workers are people who leave the labor force temporarily during a recession and re-enter the labor force and become job seekers during an expansion. To measure the number of discouraged workers, we need to know about new entrants and retirements. But if new entrants exceed retirements, which they most likely do, because employment increased by more than the increase in the working-age population, most likely the number of discouraged workers decreased.

5a. The number of job losers probably decreased. The number of job leavers probably did not change much.

The decrease in the unemployment rate is an indication that the economy was in an expansion, and normally, in an expansion, the number of job losers decreases but the number of job leavers does not change much.

5b. Labor force entrants and re-entrants probably increased.

In an expansion, discouraged workers re-enter the labor force. So it is likely that entrants and re-entrants increased.

7a. The labor force in July is 15,344,000. It is the number employed plus the number unemployed.

7b. The unemployment rate in July is 10.1 percent. It is the number unemployed as a percentage of the labor force.

7c. The working-age population is 22,729,000. It is the sum of the labor force and the number of people who are not in the labor force.

7d. The employment-to-population ratio is 60.7. It is the number employed as a percentage of the working-age population.

7e. The number of people who are unemployed at the end of August is 1,546,995. It equals the number unemployed in July plus job losers, job leavers, entrants, and reentrants minus hires, recalls, and withdrawals.

7f. The number of people who are employed at the end of August is 13,796,971. It equals the number employed in July minus job losers and job leavers plus hires and recalls.

7g. The labor force at the end of August is 15,343,966. It equals the number employed plus the number unemployed.

7h. The unemployment rate at the end of August is 10.1 percent. It equals the number unemployed as a percentage of the labor force.

7i. The employment-to-population ratio at the end of August is 58.9. It equals the number employed as a percentage of the working-age population. The working-age population is the labor force multiplied by 100 and divided by the labor force participation rate.

9. At the peak of a business cycle, the labor force participation rate is high, employment is high, the unemployment rate is low, the duration of unemployment is low, and fewer workers are discouraged.

CHAPTER 25

1a. A deep recession in the world economy will decrease real GDP, and the price level will fall. A sharp rise in oil prices will decrease real GDP, and the price level will rise. When businesses expect huge losses in the near future, real GDP will decrease and the price level will fall.

A deep recession in the world economy will decrease world income, which in turn will reduce Toughtimes's exports of goods and services. Toughtimes's aggregate demand curve will shift leftward. In Toughtimes, real GDP will decrease and the price level will fall.

A sharp rise in oil prices will decrease short-run aggregate supply and shift the short-run aggregate supply curve leftward. In Toughtimes, the real GDP will decrease and the price level will rise.

When businesses expect huge losses in the near future, they will reduce investment now. Aggregate demand will decrease, and the aggregate demand curve will shift leftward. In Toughtimes, real GDP will decrease and the price level will fall.

1b. Real GDP will decrease and the price level might rise, fall, or stay the same.

In 1(a), each of the events decreases real GDP, so together they will decrease real GDP. But the recession and the expected business losses will lead to a fall in the price level, while the sharp rise in the oil price will lead to a rise in the price level. So together, the price level might rise, fall, or stay the same.

1c. To increase aggregate demand, the government might increase its expenditures or cut taxes and the Fed might increase the quantity of money and decrease interest rates. These policies will increase real GDP.

3a. To plot the aggregate demand curve, plot the price and the quantity of real GDP demanded. To plot the short-run aggregate supply curve, plot the price and the quantity of real GDP supplied in the short-run.

3b. Real GDP is $400 billion, and the price level is 100.

Short-run macroeconomic equilibrium occurs at the intersection of the aggregate demand curve and the short-run aggregate supply curve.

3c. The long-run aggregate supply curve is a vertical line at real GDP of $500 billion.

5. Real GDP increases to $450 billion, and the price level rises to 110.

Aggregate demand increases by $100 billion at each value of the price level, and the aggregate demand curve shifts rightward by $100 billion. The new aggregate demand curve intersects the short-run aggregate supply curve at a real GDP of $450 billion and a price level of 110.

7. Real GDP decreases to $350 billion, and the price level rises to 110.

Short-run aggregate supply decreases by $100 billion at each value of the price level and the short-run aggregate supply curve shifts leftward by $100 billion. The new short-run aggregate supply curve intersects the aggregate demand curve at a real GDP of $350 billion and a price level of 110.

9a. Point *c*.

The aggregate demand curve is the red curve AD_1. The short-run aggregate supply curve is the blue curve SAS_0. These curves intersect at point *c*.

9b. Point *d*.

The short-run aggregate supply curve is the red curve SAS_1. The aggregate demand curve is now the red curve AD_1 These curves intersect at point *d*.

9c. Aggregate demand increases if (1) expected future incomes, inflation, or profits increase; (2) the government increases its purchases or reduces taxes; (3) the Fed increases the quantity of money and decreases interest rates; or (4) the exchange rate decreases or foreign income increases.

9d. Short-run aggregate supply decreases if resource prices increase.

CHAPTER 26

1a. The graph plots leisure on the *x*-axis and real GDP on the *y*-axis. As leisure increases from zero to 12 hours a day, real GDP decreases from $30 to $0 a day.

1b. The table replaces leisure with labor and labor equals 12 hours a day minus leisure hours. The graph plots labor on the *x*-axis and real GDP on the *y*-axis. As labor increases from zero to 12 hours a day, real GDP increases from $0 to $30 a day.

1c. When labor increases from 0 to 2 hours a day, the marginal product of labor is $5. When labor increases from 2 to 4 hours a day, the marginal product of labor is $4. When labor increases from 4 to 6 hours a day, the marginal product of labor is $3. When labor increases from 6 to 8 hours a day, the marginal product of labor is $2. When labor increases from 8 to 10 hours a day, the marginal product of labor is $1. When labor increases from 10 to 12 hours a day, the marginal product of labor is $0.

Marginal product is the change in real GDP divided by the change in labor hours.

3a. The demand for labor schedule is the same as the marginal product of labor schedule The marginal product of labor schedule is described in solution 1(c). The marginal product must be aligned with the midpoint of the change in labor. So, for example, the marginal product of $5 an hour

is aligned with 1 hour of work—the midpoint between 0 and 2 hours.

The graph plots a marginal product of $5 at 1 hour and a marginal product of $1 at 9 hours of labor and is a straight line between these points. At 2 hours of labor, the marginal product is $4.50.

3b. The table lists hours of labor from zero to 12 a day. Against each hour, the wage rate at which Crusoe is willing to supply labor is $4.50 an hour.

Crusoe's supply curve is horizontal at $4.50 an hour.

3c. The full-employment equilibrium real wage rate is $4.50 an hour, and the quantity of labor employed is 2 hours a day.

The full-employment equilibrium real wage rate is $4.50 an hour because Crusoe is willing to work any number of hours at this wage rate. The equilibrium level of employment is 2 hours a day because this is the number of hours at which Crusoe's marginal product of labor is $4.50 an hour.

3d. Potential GDP is $10 a day.

Potential GDP is $10 a day because this quantity of real GDP is produced when labor is 2 hours a day.

5a. The new production function table lists real GDP against labor hours. Real GDP is $15 at 2 hours of labor, $27 at 4 hours, $36 at 6 hours, $42 at 8 hours, $45 at 10 hours, and $45 at 12 hours.

The new demand for labor schedule has labor of 2 hours at $6.75 and 9 hours at $1.50.

To calculate the new demand for labor schedule, calculate the new marginal product (old marginal product multiplied by 1.5) at each level of employment.

5b. The full-employment equilibrium real wage rate is $4.50 an hour and the quantity of labor employed is 5 hours a day.

The equilibrium level of employment is 5 hours a day because this is the number of hours at which Crusoe's marginal product of labor is $4.50 an hour.

5c. Potential GDP is $21 a day.

Potential GDP is $21 a day because this quantity of real GDP is produced when labor is 5 hours a day.

5d. The increase in productivity shifts the production function upward by 50 percent. The marginal product of labor increases by 50 percent. Employment increases and so does potential GDP.

7a. Real wage rate is $3 an hour and employment is 3,000 hours a day.

This wage rate and quantity of labor are at the intersection of the demand curve and the supply curve in the figure.

7b. Potential GDP is $13,500 a day.

To calculate potential GDP, use the fact that the real wage rate on the demand for labor curve is the marginal product of labor. Remember that it is plotted midway between the initial and final level of real GDP from which it is calculated. Do the marginal product calculation in reverse and obtain the level of real GDP at 3,000 hours, which is $13,500 a day.

7c. The natural rate of unemployment is 25 percent.

The natural rate of unemployment occurs at full employment when job search is 1,000 hours. Employment is

3,000 hours, and job search, which is unemployment, is 1,000 hours. The labor force (employment plus unemployment) is 4,000 hours. The natural rate of unemployment is 25 percent (1,000/4,000 multiplied by 100).

CHAPTER 27

1a. Yes.

1b. Yes.

1c. No.

The firm receives a total revenue of $17 million. It spends $16 million ($10 million on the plant, $3 million on labor and $3 million on fuel). Before paying interest, the firm has a surplus of $1 million. If the interest rate is 5 percent a year, the interest cost is $0.5 million. If the interest rate is 10 percent a year, the interest cost is $1 million. If the interest rate is 15 percent a year, the interest cost is $1.5 million. So the firm earns a profit at 5 percent, breaks even at 10 percent, and incurs a loss at 15 percent. The firm will not invest to incur a loss.

3a. A graph that has saving on the x-axis and the interest rate on the y-axis. Three points are plotted at $10,000 and 4 percent; $12,500 and 6 percent; and $15,000 and 8 percent. The saving supply (SS) curve passes through these points.

3b. Saving decreases, and the saving supply curve shifts leftward.

3c. Saving increases, and the saving supply curve shifts rightward.

An increase in expected future income increases consumption expenditure and decreases saving. An increase in disposable income increases both consumption expenditure and saving.

5a. 5 percent a year.

5b. $6 trillion (3050 dollars).

5c. $6 trillion (3050 dollars).

Given the saving supply schedule and the investment demand schedule, the real interest rate at which saving equals investment is 5 percent a year. At this real interest rate, saving and investment equal $6 trillion.

7a. 5 percent a year.

7b. $6 trillion (3050 dollars).

Private saving increases by an amount equal to the decrease in government saving. Total saving remains constant. So the equilibrium real interest rate and saving and investment do not change.

9a. 6 percent a year.

9b. $15 trillion (3050 dollars).

9c. $15 trillion (3050 dollars).

9d. Saving decreases, and investment increases.

To find the galactic equilibrium, find the sum of saving on Earth and Alpha Centura at each real interest rate and find the sum of investment on the two planets at each real interest rate. At a real interest rate of 6 percent a year, galactic saving equals galactic investment at $15 trillion.

In isolation, the real interest rate on Alpha Centura is 7 percent a year. So the real interest rate on Alpha Centura falls. Saving decreases, and investment increases.

CHAPTER 28

1. No. The economy conforms to a one-half rule.

In this economy, an x percent increase in the capital stock per hour of work leads to a 0.5x percent increase in real GDP per hour of work. You can confirm this fact by calculating the percentage change in capital and real GDP at each of the levels provided in the table and then dividing the percentage change in real GDP by the percentage change in capital. For example, when capital increases by 100 percent from $10 to $20, real GDP increases by 50 percent from $3.80 to $5.70.

3a. Yes.

Diminishing returns are present if the marginal product of capital diminishes as capital increases, holding technology constant. You can calculate the marginal product of capital from the schedule provided and see that it does diminish. The increase in real GDP per hour of work that occurred in the question resulted from an increase in capital *and an advance in technology*. We know this because to produce $10.29 in 1999 would have required a capital stock of $60 per hour of work, and in 2001, this output can be produced by a capital stock of $50. The change in real GDP divided by the change in capital is not the marginal product of labor because technology is not constant.

3b. $1.04.

This number is calculated as the percentage increase in real GDP that is equal to one half the percentage increase in capital.

3c. $0.94.

This number is calculated as the change in real GDP minus $1.04.

5a. 6 billion hours per year.

This quantity is the quantity demanded and the quantity supplied when the real wage rate is $7 an hour.

5b. The real wage rate rises.

When the demand for labor increases, there is a shortage of labor at the current wage rate. So the real wage rate rises.

5c. The population begins to grow.

The reason for the population growth is that the real wage rate exceeds the subsistence level.

5d. 7 billion hours a year.

This is the quantity of labor demanded at the subsistence real wage rate of $7 an hour. Only when the population has grown by a sufficient amount to make the quantity of labor supplied equal 7 billion hours a year does the population stop growing.

7. When the demand for capital raises the real interest rate above the target rate, the capital stock and real GDP begin to grow and keep on growing. In contrast, in the neoclassical Martha's Island, as the capital stock grows, the real interest rate falls (because of diminishing returns) and growth eventually ends.

CHAPTER 29

1a. The marginal propensity to consume is 0.5.

The marginal propensity to consume is the fraction of a change in disposable income that is consumed. On Heron Island, when disposable income increases by $10 million per year, consumption expenditure increases by $5 million per year. The marginal propensity to consume is 0.5.

1b. The table that shows Heron Island's saving lists disposable income from zero to 40 in increments of 10. Against each level of disposable income are the amounts of saving, which equal disposable income minus consumption expenditure. These amounts run from −5 at zero disposable income to 15 at a disposable income of 40. For each increase in disposable income of $1, saving increases by 50 cents.

1c. Marginal propensity to save is 0.5.

The marginal propensity to consume plus the marginal propensity to save equals 1. Because consumption expenditure and saving exhaust disposable income, 0.5 of each dollar increase in disposable income is consumed and the remaining part (0.5) is saved.

3a. Autonomous expenditure is $2.0 billion.

Autonomous expenditure is expenditure that does not depend on real GDP. Autonomous expenditure equals the value of aggregate planned expenditure when real GDP is zero.

3b. Marginal propensity to consume is 0.6.

When the country has no imports or exports and no income taxes, the slope of the AE curve equals the marginal propensity to consume. When income increases from 0 to $6 billion, aggregate planned expenditure increases from $2 billion to $5.6 billion. That is, when real GDP increases by $6 billion, aggregate planned expenditure increases by $3.6 billion. The marginal propensity to consume is $3.6 billion/$6 billion, which is 0.6.

3c. Equilibrium expenditure is $4 billion.

Equilibrium expenditure is the level of aggregate expenditure at which aggregate planned expenditure equals real GDP. In terms of the graph, equilibrium expenditure occurs at the intersection of the AE curve and the 45° line. Draw in the 45° line, and you'll see that the intersection occurs at $4 billion.

3d. There is no change in inventories.

When the economy is at equilibrium expenditure, inventories equal the planned level and there is no unplanned change in inventories.

3e. Firms are accumulating inventories. That is, unplanned inventory investment is positive.

When real GDP is $6 billion, aggregate planned expenditure is less than real GDP, so firms cannot sell all that they produce. Inventories pile up.

3f. The multiplier is 2.5.

The multiplier equals $1/(1 − MPC)$. The marginal propensity to consume is 0.6, so the multiplier equals $1/(1 − 0.6)$, which equals 2.5.

5a. The consumption function is $C = 100 + 0.9(Y − T)$.

The consumption function is the relationship between consumption expenditure and disposable income, other things remaining the same.

5b. The equation to the AE curve is:

$AE = 600 + 0.9Y$,

where Y is real GDP.

Aggregate planned expenditure is the sum of consumption expenditure, investment, government purchases, and net exports. Using the symbol AE for aggregate planned expenditure, aggregate planned expenditure is:

$AE = 100 + 0.9(Y − 400) + 460 + 400$

$AE = 100 + 0.9Y − 360 + 460 + 400$

$AE = 600 + 0.9Y$

5c. Equilibrium expenditure is $6,000 billion.

Equilibrium expenditure is the level of aggregate expenditure that occurs when aggregate planned expenditure equals real GDP. That is,

$AE = 600 + 0.9Y$

and

$AE = Y$

Solving these two equations for Y gives equilibrium expenditure of $6,000 billion.

5d. Equilibrium real expenditure decreases by $1,000 billion, and the multiplier is 10.

The multiplier equals $1/(1 − $ the slope of the AE curve). The equation to the AE curve tells us that the slope of the AE curve is 0.9. So the multiplier is $1/(1 − 0.9)$, which is 10.

The change in equilibrium expenditure equals the change in investment multiplied by 10.

7a. The quantity demanded increases by $1,000 billion.

The increase in investment shifts the aggregate demand curve rightward by the change in investment times the multiplier. The multiplier is 10 and the change in investment is $100 billion, so the aggregate demand curve shifts rightward by $1,000 billion.

7b. In the short-run, real GDP increases by less than $1,000 billion.

Real GDP is determined by the intersection of the AD curve and the SAS curve. In the short run, the price level will rise and real GDP will increase but by an amount less than the shift of the AD curve.

7c. In the long-run, real GDP will equal potential GDP, so real GDP does not increase.

Real GDP is determined by the intersection of the AD curve and the SAS curve. After the initial increase in investment, money wages increase, the SAS curve shifts leftward, and in the long run, real GDP moves back to potential GDP.

7d. In the short run, the price level rises. In the long run, the price level rises.

CHAPTER 30

1a. Equilibrium expenditure decreases by $100 billion.

The government purchases multiplier is the amount by which a change in government purchases on goods and services is multiplied to determine the change in equilibrium expenditure that results. Zapland has no induced taxes or imports, so the government purchases multiplier is $1/(1 - MPC)$, which equals 10. The multiplier tells us that when government purchases decrease by $10 billion, equilibrium expenditure decreases by 10 times as much or $100 billion.

1b. The government purchases multiplier is 10.

1c. Equilibrium expenditure increases by $90 billion.

The lump-sum tax multiplier equals $-MPC/(1 - MPC)$, which is −9. That is, when lump-sum taxes are changed by $10 billion, equilibrium expenditure changes by −9 times the change in lump-sum taxes. A cut in lump-sum taxes of $10 billion will increase equilibrium expenditure by $90 billion.

1d. The lump-sum tax multiplier is −9.

1e. Equilibrium expenditure decreases by $10 billion.

The decrease in government purchases decreases equilibrium expenditure by $100 billion and the cut in taxes increases equilibrium expenditure by $90 billion. So together, equilibrium expenditure decreases by $10 billion.

3a. The quantity of real GDP demanded increases by $100 billion.

The government purchases multiplier tells us that when government purchases increase by $10 billion, equilibrium expenditure increases by 10 times as much, or $100 billion. At the price level 100, the quantity of real GDP demanded increases by an amount equal to the change in equilibrium expenditure. That is, the quantity of real GDP demanded increases by $100 billion.

3b. The aggregate demand curve shifts rightward by $100 billion at each price level.

The AE curve shifts upward by $10 billion, equilibrium expenditure increases by $100 billion, and the AD curve shifts rightward by $100 billion.

3c. In the short run, real GDP increases by less than the $100 billion increase in the quantity of real GDP demanded.

In the short run, real GDP is determined by the short-run aggregate supply and aggregate demand. Because the short-run aggregate supply curve slopes upward, the price level rises and real GDP increases but by less than $100 billion.

3d. In the long run, the increase in real GDP will be zero. Real GDP will return to potential GDP.

In the short run, real GDP exceeds potential GDP and wage rates will start to rise. The short-run aggregate supply will begin to decrease and the price level will rise. The short-run aggregate supply will continue to decrease and the price level will continue to rise until real GDP equals potential GDP.

3e. The price level rises.

In the short run, aggregate demand and short-run aggregate supply determine the price level. Because the short-run aggregate supply curve slopes upward and because aggregate demand increases, the price level rises.

3f. The price level rises.

In the long run, aggregate demand and long-run aggregate supply determine the price level. The short-run aggregate supply curve shifts leftward because the money wage rate rises. Because the long-run aggregate supply curve is verti-

cal and because aggregate demand increases, the price level rises. And it rises by more in the long run than it does in the short run.

5a. The government budget balance is zero.

The government's tax revenues equal its expenditures, so its budget is balanced.

5b. Dreamland does not have a structural or a cyclical deficit.

Because at potential GDP, the budget is balanced, Dreamland does not have a structural surplus or deficit. Because real GDP equals potential GDP, Dreamland does not have a cyclical surplus or deficit.

5c. The budget balance is a deficit of $40 million.

At a real GDP of $30 million, tax revenues equal $80 million and expenditures equal $120 million, so the budget is in deficit. The size of the deficit is $40 million.

5d. Dreamland does not have a structural deficit, but it does have a cyclical deficit of $40 million.

Because at potential GDP, the budget is balanced, Dreamland does not have a structural surplus or deficit. Because real GDP is less than potential GDP and it has a deficit, Dreamland's deficit is a cyclical deficit. The cyclical deficit is $40 million.

5e. Dreamland does not have a structural deficit but it does have a cyclical surplus of $40 million.

Because at potential GDP, the budget is balanced, Dreamland does not have a structural surplus or deficit. Because real GDP exceeds potential GDP and it has a surplus, Dreamland's surplus is a cyclical surplus. The cyclical surplus is $40 million.

CHAPTER 31

1. Money in the United States includes the quarters inside public telephones and the U.S. dollar bills in your wallet.

   Money is composed of currency outside the banks and deposits at financial institutions. Currency inside the cash machines, Visa cards, checks, and loans are not money.

3. M1 increases by $1,000; M2 does not change.

   M1 is the sum of currency outside the banks, traveler's checks, and checking deposits. M2 is the sum of M1 plus savings deposits, time deposits, and money market mutual funds and other deposits.. The withdrawal of $1,000 from a savings account leaves M2 unchanged because the $1,000 goes into M1 types of money, which is part of M2. The $50 held as cash and the $950 held in a checking account increase M1 by $1,000.

5a. The balance sheet has the following assets: Reserves, $250 million; Loans, $1,000 million; Other assets, $1,250 billion. It has the following liabilities: Deposits, $2,000 billion; Other liabilities, $500 billion.

5b. The reserve ratio is 12.5 percent.

   The reserve ratio is the percentage of deposits that are held as reserves. Reserves are $250 million and deposits are $2,000, so the reserve ratio is 12.5 percent.

5c. The deposit multiplier is 8.

   The deposit multiplier equals 1/(required reserve ratio).

The required reserve ratio is 12.5, so the deposit multiplier is 8.

7a. The initial increase in the quantity of money is $1,200.

Money is equal to bank deposits and currency outside the banks. Deposits increase by $1,200, so the initial increase in the quantity of money is $1,200.

7b. The initial increase in the quantity of bank deposits is $1,200.

Deposits increase by $1,200 because the immigrant places all the new money on deposit.

7c. The bank initially lends out $1,080.

The bank has a new deposit of $1,200, and it keeps 10 percent of it ($120) as reserves and lends the rest ($1,200 minus $120), which equals $1,080.

7d. The immigrant's bank has loaned $1,080. This amount returns to the banks as new deposits. The banks keep $108 in reserves and lend a further $972.

The banks have now created deposits of $1,200 plus $1,080, which equals $2,280.

7e. The quantity of money has increased by $3,252.

The first loan is $1,080, and the quantity of money increases by $1,080. When this money is spent and returned to the bank as a deposit, the banks keep 10 percent of it ($108) as reserves and lend out the rest ($972). The banks create $972 of new money. So the quantity of money has increased by $1,200 + $1,080 + $972, which equals $3,252.

7f. The quantity of money increases by $12,000. Deposits increase by $12,000. Loans increase by $10,800.

The deposit multiplier is 1/0.1, which equals 10. The deposit multiplier tells us that when reserves increase by $1,200 and the required reserve ratio is 10 percent, deposits will increase by 10 times $1,200, which is $12,000.

The quantity of money increases by the amount of the increase in deposits.

Deposits increase by $12,000 and the reserve ratio is 10 percent, so reserves increase $1,200. Therefore bank loans increase by $12,000 minus $1,200, which is $10,800.

9a. Aggregate demand increases.

9b. The price level rises and real GDP increases in the short run.

9c. In the long run, real GDP returns to potential GDP and the price level is higher than it otherwise would have been by the same percentage as the percentage increase in the quantity of money.

11a. $40 million.

Because $MV = PY$, we know that $M = PY/V$. With $P = 200$, $Y = \$400$ million, and $V = 20$, $M = \$40$ million.

11b. $48 million.

Money grows by 20 percent, which is $8 million.

11c. 240.

Because the quantity theory holds and because the factors that influence real GDP have not changed, the price level rises by the same percentage as the increase in money, which is 20 percent.

11d. $400 billion.

Because the factors that influence real GDP have not changed, real GDP is unchanged.

11e. 20.

Because the factors that influence velocity have not changed, velocity is unchanged.

CHAPTER 32

1a. The monetary base is $45 billion.

The monetary base is the sum of the central bank's notes outside the bank, banks' deposits at the central bank, and coins held by households, firms, and banks. There are $30 billion in notes held by households and firms, banks' deposits at the central bank are $10 billion (2/3 of $15 billion), the banks hold other reserves of $5 billion (which are notes), and there are no coins. The monetary base is $45 billion.

1b. The money supply is $330 billion.

In Nocoin, deposits are $300 billion and currency is $30 billion, so the quantity of money is $330 billion.

1c. The banks' reserve ratio is 5 percent.

The banks' reserve ratio is the percent of deposits that is held as reserves. In Nocoin, deposits are $300 billion and reserves are $15 billion, so the reserve ratio equals ($15 billion/$300 billion) × 100, which is 5 percent.

1d. The currency drain is 9.09 percent.

The currency drain is the percent of the quantity of money that is held as currency by households and firms. In Nocoin, deposits are $300 billion and currency is $30 billion, so the quantity of money is $330 billion. The currency drain equals ($30 billion/$330 billion) × 100, which is 9.09 percent.

3a. The money supply is $337.33 billion.

The money supply increases by the change in the monetary base multiplied by the money multiplier. The money multiplier is the ratio of the money supply to the monetary base, which equals $330 billion divided by $45 billion, which equals 7.33.

So when the monetary base increases by $1 billion, the money supply increases by $7.33 billion. Initially, the money supply was $330 billion, so the new money supply is $337.33 billion.

3b. Currency in circulation is $30.67 billion.

The currency drain in Nocoin equals ($30 billion/$330 billion) × 100, which is 9.09 percent. And 9.09 percent of $337.33 is $30.67.

3c. Bank deposits are $306.67 billion.

Deposits equal the quantity of money minus currency in circulation, which equals $337.33 billion minus $30.67 billion.

3d. Bank reserves are $15.33 billion.

The banks' reserve ratio is 5 percent and 5 percent of deposits of $306.67 billion equals $15.33 billion.

5a. People buy securities, and the interest rate falls.

5b. People sell securities, and the interest rate rises.

5c. People neither buy nor sell securities, and the interest rate remains constant at 4 percent a year.

With real GDP of $20 billion ($Y_1$ in the spreadsheet), column C shows the demand for money schedule. The quantity of money supplied is $3 billion, so the equilibrium interest rate is 4 percent a year.

If the interest rate exceeds 4 percent a year, people are holding more money than they demand. So they try to decrease the amount of money held by buying securities. The prices of securities rise, and the interest rate falls.

If the interest rate is less than 4 percent a year, people are holding less money than they demand. So they try to increase the amount of money held by selling securities. The prices of securities fall, and the interest rate rises.

If the interest rate equals 4 percent a year, people are holding exactly the quantity of money that they demand. So they take no actions to try to change the amount of money held. The interest rate remains constant.

7a. The interest rate rises to 5 percent a year.

7b. The interest rate falls to 3 percent a year.

When real GDP increases in an expansion to $30 billion ($Y_2$ in the spreadsheet), column D shows the demand for money schedule. The quantity of money supplied is $3 billion, so the equilibrium interest rate is 5 percent a year.

When real GDP decreases in a recession to $10 billion ($Y_0$ in the spreadsheet), column B shows the demand for money schedule. The quantity of money supplied is $3 billion, so the equilibrium interest rate is 3 percent a year.

9a. The money supply curve is vertical at 1 trillion 1990 yaks.

When the real money supply is 1 trillion 1990 yaks, the equilibrium interest rate is 3 percent a year at the intersection of the demand for money and supply of money curves.

9b. Must increase the real money supply by 0.5 trillion 1990 yaks.

When the real money supply increases to 1.5 trillion 1990 yaks, the equilibrium interest rate falls to 2 percent a year.

9c. Must make an open market purchase.

When the central bank makes an open market purchase, it increases the amount of money in circulation and decreases the amount of securities.

11. An open market purchase increases the quantity of money and increases aggregate demand. The *AD* curve shifts rightward. In the short run, real GDP increases and the price level rises.

Starting from above-full employment, this action increases the size of the inflationary gap and increases the inflation rate.

In the long run, real GDP equals potential GDP. The central bank's action has no effect on potential GDP and so does not lower real GDP in the long run.

CHAPTER 33

1a. An increase in the quantity of money, an increase in government purchases, a tax cut, an increase in exports.

Anything that increases aggregate demand can set off a demand-pull inflation. But to sustain such an inflation, the quantity of money must keep increasing.

1b. Starting out on AD_0 and SAS_0, the price level is 120 and real GDP is at potential GDP of $7 trillion. Aggregate demand increases and the *AD* curve shifts rightward to AD_1. The price level rises and real GDP increases to the intersection of AD_1 and SAS_0. There is now an inflationary gap.

1c. Starting out on AD_1 and SAS_0 with an inflationary gap, the money wage rate rises and short-run aggregate supply decreases. The *SAS* curve starts to shift leftward toward SAS_1. The price level keeps rising, but real GDP now decreases. The process now repeats. *AD* shifts to AD_2, an inflationary gap opens again, the money wage rate rises again, and the *SAS* curve shifts toward SAS_2.

3a. An *anticipated* increase in the quantity of money, an increase in government purchases, a tax cut, an increase in exports.

Anything that increases aggregate demand can set off an anticipated inflation as long as the event is anticipated. But to sustain such an anticipated inflation, the quantity of money must keep increasing along its anticipated path.

3b. Starting out on AD_0 and SAS_0, the price level is 120 and real GDP is at potential GDP of $7 trillion. Aggregate demand increases, and the *AD* curve shifts rightward to AD_1. The increase in aggregate demand is anticipated so the money wage rate rises and the *SAS* curve shifts to SAS_1. The price level rises, and real GDP remains at potential GDP.

3c. Starting out on AD_1 and SAS_1, a further anticipated increase in aggregate demand occurs. The *AD* curve shifts to AD_2, and because the increase in aggregate demand is anticipated, the money wage rate rises again and the *SAS* curve shifts to SAS_2. Again, the price level rises and real GDP remains at potential GDP.

5a. Both the inflation rate and the unemployment rate have increased. So the expected inflation rate has increased and the natural rate of unemployment might have increased (but has not definitely increased). Any of the events that can increase the expected inflation rate might have occurred. Most likely, the expected growth rate of the money supply has increased. If the natural rate of unemployment has not increased, the economy is in a recession, despite the fact that the inflation rate has increased.

5b. If point *a* is a long-run equilibrium, the *LRPC* is vertical at an unemployment rate of 4 percent. The *SRPC* slopes downward and passes through point *a*. If point *a* is *not* a long-run equilibrium, the *SRPC* still passes through point *a* but the *LRPC* is vertical at whatever unemployment rate is the natural rate.

5c. If point *d* is a long-run equilibrium, the *LRPC* is vertical at an unemployment rate of 8 percent. The *SRPC* slopes downward and passes through point *d*. If point *d* is *not* a long-run equilibrium, the *SRPC* still passes through point *d* but the *LRPC* is vertical at whatever unemployment rate is the natural rate.

7a. The most likely events that could create the clockwise sequence described is a mixture of swings in aggregate demand that are initially unanticipated. Aggregate demand increases, unemployment decreases, and the economy is at point *a*, where there is an inflationary gap. The inflation rate rises, and the expected inflation rate also rises. The *SRPC* shifts upward, and the economy moves from *a* to *b*. Aggregate demand now decreases, but at first the decrease is unanticipated and a recession occurs. The economy moves from *b* to *d*. There is now a recessionary gap. The inflation rate slows, and the expected inflation rate falls. So the *SRPC* shifts downward and the economy moves from *d* to *c*. Aggregate demand now increases again and an expansion moves the economy from *c* to *a*.

7b. In your diagram, the *LRPC* is vertical at an unemployment rate of 6 percent. The *SRPC* slopes downward and passes through point *a* initially. The *SRPC* then shifts upward to pass through point *b* and keeps shifting upward to pass through point *d*. The *SRPC* then shifts downward to pass through point *c* and keeps shifting downward until it again passes through point *a*.

7c. The economy has experienced a demand-pull inflation. The reason is that a change in aggregate demand triggered the rise and subsequent fall in the inflation rate.

9a. If the natural unemployment rate and the expected inflation rate remain constant between 1999 and 2003, the *SRPC* is linear and passes through the data points listed in the table provided. Note that one of these points is the natural rate of unemployment (4 percent) and the expected inflation rate (6 percent). The *LRPC* is vertical at an unemployment rate of 4 percent.

9b. If the actual inflation rate rises from 6 percent to 8 percent, the unemployment rate falls from 4 percent to 3 percent. This change would occur if there were an unexpected increase in aggregate demand.

CHAPTER 34

1a. Possible combinations are *a* or *d*, *e* or *g*, and *i* or *k*.

A Keynesian recession results from a decrease in investment caused by a decrease in expected profit. In an extreme case, no prices change, so the move is to *a*, *e*, and *i*. But a more general possibility is that the money wage rate doesn't change but the price level falls, real wage rate rises, and the interest rate falls. In this case, the move is to *d*, *g*, and *k*.

1b. *d*, *g*, and *l*.

A monetarist recession results from a decrease in the quantity of money. The interest rate rises, and investment decreases. Aggregate demand decreases, but the money wage rate doesn't change. Real GDP and the price level decrease, the real wage rate rises, and employment decreases. The move is to *d*, *g*, and *l*.

1c. *d*, *g*, and *i*, *k*, or *l*.

1d. *d*, *g*, and *i*, *k*, or *l*.

Either type of rational expectations recession results from an unanticipated decrease in aggregate demand. Any of several factors could initiate the decrease in aggregate demand, and the interest rate could rise, fall, or remain constant. Aggregate demand decreases, but the money wage rate either doesn't change or doesn't change by enough to maintain full employment. So real GDP and

the price level decrease, the real wage rate rises, and employment decreases.

1e. *c*, *e*, *g*, or *h*, and *k*.

In a real business cycle recession, a decrease in productivity decreases the demand for labor and capital. The interest rate and the real wage rate fall and investment and employment decrease. Aggregate demand *and* aggregate supply decrease, so real GDP decreases but the price level might fall, rise, or remain unchanged.

3. This recession is consistent with Keynesian or rational expectations theories (see the solutions 1(a), 1(c), and 1(d)).

5. This recession is consistent with real business cycle theory (see the solution 1(e)).

7. This recession is not consistent with any of the theories and is an unlikely combination of events. The price level does not usually rise when the real wage rate rises.

9. This recession is consistent the real business cycle theory (see the solution 1(e)).

11. This recession is consistent with monetarist theory (see the solution 1(b)).

13. This recession is not consistent with any of the theories and is an unlikely combination of events. The real wage rate does not usually fall when the price level falls.

CHAPTER 35

1. Anything that slows investment in physical or human capital or slows the pace of technological change will create a productivity growth slowdown. For the factors at work during the U.S. productivity growth slowdown of the 1970s, review pp. 613-614 of Chapter 28.

Improvements in incentives to invest in physical or human capital or to innovate and speed up the pace of technological change will counteract a productivity growth slowdown. See p. 614 of Chapter 28 and pp. 796-798 of Chapter 35.

3a. Real GDP is $7 trillion and the price level is 110.

These values are determined at the intersection of AD_0 and SAS_0.

3b. Real GDP falls to $6 trillion and the price level falls to 105. Then, as aggregate demand returns to AD_0, the price level and real GDP return to their initial levels.

3c. Real GDP falls to $6 trillion and the price level falls to 105. The government increases aggregate demand to AD_0, and the price level and real GDP return to their initial levels. Aggregate demand then increases (because the decrease is temporary), and real GDP rises above potential GDP. An inflationary gap arises. The money wage rate rises and so does the price level. Real GDP moves back toward potential GDP.

3d. Real GDP falls to $6 trillion, and the price level falls to 105. The economy is stuck at this point until the money wage rate falls, short-run aggregate supply increases, and the economy moves back to potential GDP at an even lower price level. This move will likely take a long time.

3e. Real GDP falls to $6 trillion, and the price level falls to 105. The government increases aggregate demand to AD_0, and the price level and real GDP return to their initial levels. Because the decrease in aggregate demand is permanent, this is the end of the action.

5a. The economy might have gotten into its described state because of a combination of rapid money supply growth (which brings inflation) and large structural changes (which bring high unemployment and slow productivity growth).

5b. A slowdown in money growth will lower the inflation rate. Improvements in incentives to invest in physical or human capital or to innovate and speed up the pace of technological change will speed productivity growth.

5c. Study pp. 796-798 and pp. 806-809 for explanations of how these policy actions work.

7a. These policy actions were part of a feedback rule. The actions were taken *because* of the crises.

7b. The required domestic policies all decrease aggregate demand. They lower real GDP and lower the price level (compared with what would have happened).

7c. A possible criticism, and one that some economists have made, is that the countries should have adopted policies to expand real GDP even at the risk of a rise in inflation, rather than adopt policies that decrease aggregate demand.

CHAPTER 36

1a. 0.10 computer per TV set at 10 TV sets.

1b. 0.40 computer per TV set at 40 TV sets.

1c. 0.70 computer per TV set at 70 TV sets.

1d. The graph shows an upward-sloping line that passes through the three points described in solutions 1a, 1b, and 1c.

The opportunity cost of a TV set is calculated as the decrease in the number of computers produced divided by the increase in the number of TV sets produced as we move along the *PPF*. The opportunity cost of a TV set increases as the quantity of TV sets produced increases.

3a. Virtual Reality exports TV sets to Vital Signs.

At the no-trade production levels, the opportunity cost of a TV set is 0.10 computer in Virtual Reality and 0.30 computer in Vital Signs. Because it costs less to produce a TV set in Virtual Reality, Vital Signs can import TV sets for a lower price than it can produce them. And because a computer costs less in Vital Signs than in Virtual Reality, Virtual Reality can import computers at a lower cost than it can produce them.

3b. Virtual Reality increases the production of TV sets and Vital Signs decreases the production of TV sets. Virtual Reality decreases the production of computers and Vital Signs increases the production of computers.

Virtual Reality increases production of TV sets to export some to Vital Signs and Vital Signs decreases production of TV sets because it now imports some from Virtual Reality.

3c. Each country consumes more of at least one good and possibly of both goods.

Because each country has a lower opportunity cost than the other at producing one of the goods, total production of both goods can increase.

3d. The price of a TV set is greater than 0.10 computer and less than 0.30 computer.

The price will be higher than the no-trade opportunity cost in Virtual Reality (0.10 computer) and lower than the no-trade opportunity cost in Vital Signs (0.30 computer).

5a. Free trade increases the production of at least one good (but not necessarily both goods) in both cases because each country increases the production of the good at which it has a comparative advantage.

5b. In problem 3, the price of a TV set rises in Virtual Reality. In problem 4, it falls.

The reason is that in problem 3, Virtual Reality produces a small number of TV sets with no trade and has the lower opportunity cost per TV set. But in problem 4, Virtual Reality produces a large number of TV sets with no trade and has the higher opportunity cost per TV set. So in problem 3, Virtual Reality becomes an exporter and increases production. The price of a TV set rises. In problem 4, Virtual Reality becomes an importer and decreases production, and the price of a TV set falls.

5c. In problem 3, the price of a computer rises in Vital Signs. In problem 4, it falls.

The reason is that in problem 3, Vital Signs produces a small number of computers with no trade and has the lower opportunity cost per computer. But in problem 4, Vital Signs produces a large number of computers with no trade and has the higher opportunity cost per computer. So in problem 3, Vital Signs becomes an exporter of computers and increases production. The price of a computer rises. In problem 4, Vital Signs becomes an importer of computers and decreases production, and the price of a computer falls.

7a. $9 per bushel in the importing country and $1 per bushel in the exporting country.

These are the prices at which each country wishes to import and export a zero quantity.

7b. $5 per bushel.

This is the price at which the quantity demanded by the importer equals the quantity supplied by the exporter.

7c. 400 million bushels.

This is the quantity demanded and supplied at the equilibrium price.

7d. Zero.

The balance of trade is zero because the value imported equals the value exported.

9a. $6 per bushel.

The quantity demanded by the importer equals the quantity available under the quota of 300 million bushels at this price.

9b. $600 million.

The price at which the exporters are willing to sell 300 million bushels is $4 a bushel. So there is a profit of $2 a bushel. The total revenue from the quota is 300 million multiplied by $2.

9c. The importing agents to whom the quota is allocated.

CHAPTER 37

1a. A table like Table 37.1 on p. 844 with the numbers provided in the problem.

The current account shows Imports of goods and services: −350 billions of grains, Exports of goods and services 500 billions of grains, Net interest income: unknown, and Net transfers, unknown. You cannot calculate the current account balance from these numbers because of the two unknown items.

The capital account shows Foreign investment in Silecon: 60 billions of grains, Silecon investment abroad: −200 billions of grains. The capital account balance is −140 billions of grains (a deficit).

The official settlements account shows Increase in official Silecon reserves: −10 billions of grains (minus because it is an increase).

Because the sum of the three balances is zero, you can now calculate the current account balance: 150 billions of grains, a surplus. Exports of goods and services minus imports of goods and services equal 150 billions of grains. So the sum of Net interest income and Net transfers is zero, but we don't know the values of these two items separately.

1b. Silecon does not have a flexible exchange rate. The central bank intervenes in the foreign exchange market.

We know that the central bank intervenes in the foreign exchange market because its official reserves changed.

3a. Net exports are −$10 million.

Use the fact that

$Y = C + I + G + NX$ and solve for NX as

$NX = Y − C − I − G$, which equals

$NX = 60 − 36 − 20 − 14 = −10$.

3b. Saving is $12 million.

Use the fact that

$Y = C + S + T$ and solve for S as

$S = Y − C − T$, which equals

$NX = 60 − 36 − 12 = 12$.

3c. Investment is financed by national saving and foreign borrowing.

$I = S + T − G − NX$, which equals

$I = 12 + 12 − 14 − (− 10) = 20$.

5a. Imports of goods and services are 26 billion bands.

Use the fact that

$Y = C + I + G + X − M$ and solve for M as

$M = − Y + C + I + G + X$, which is

$M = − 100 + 60 + 22 + 24 + 20 = 26$.

5b. The current account balance is − 6 billion bands (assuming that net interest income plus net transfers is zero).

Use the fact that

$CAB = X − M$

$CAB = 20 − 26 = − 6$.

5c. The capital account balance is +6 billion bands.

The reason is that Ecflex has a flexible exchange rate, so we know that the official settlements account balance is zero.

5d. Net taxes are 20 billion bands.

Use the fact that

Gov. budget deficit = $G − T$, so

$T = G −$ *Gov. budget deficit*, which is

$T = 24 − 4 = 20$.

5e. The private sector balance is −2 billion bands (a deficit).

Use the fact that

Private sector surplus = $S − I$, with

$S = Y − C − NT$, or

Private sector surplus = $Y − C − T − I$, which is

Private sector surplus = $100 − 60 − 20 − 22 = − 2$.

7a. The country intervenes in the foreign exchange market to limit movements in the exchange rate.

If the exchange rate were flexible, there would be no change in the stock of foreign currency holdings. If the exchange rate were fixed, there would be no change in the exchange rate.

7b. The central bank might have conducted an open market operation in the bond market to increase the interest rate.

The central bank's intervention in the foreign exchange market did not bring appreciation. On the contrary, its intervention limited the extent of the appreciation.

7c. Private traders in the foreign exchange market might have increased their demand for the currency perhaps because they expected the exchange rate to appreciate in the future.

Glossary

Above full-employment equilibrium A macroeconomic equilibrium in which real GDP exceeds potential GDP.

Absolute advantage A person has an absolute advantage in the production of two goods if by using the same quantities of inputs, that person can produce more of both goods than another person; a country has an absolute advantage if its output per unit of inputs of all goods is larger than that of another country.

Adverse selection The tendency for people to enter into agreements in which they can use their private information to their own advantage and to the disadvantage of the less-informed party.

Aggregate demand The relationship between the aggregate quantity of real GDP demanded and the price level.

Aggregate hours The total number of hours worked by all the people employed, both full time and part time, during a year.

Aggregate planned expenditure The expenditure that households, firms, governments, and foreigners plan to undertake in given circumstances. It is the sum of planned consumption expenditure, planned investment, planned government purchases of goods and services, and planned exports minus planned imports.

Aggregate production function The relationship between the quantity of real GDP supplied and the quantities of labor and capital and the state of technology.

Antitrust law A law that regulates and prohibits certain kinds of market behavior, such as monopoly and monopolistic practices.

Automatic fiscal policy A change in fiscal policy that is triggered by the state of the economy.

Automatic stabilizers Mechanisms that stabilize real GDP without explicit action by the government.

Autonomous expenditure The sum of those components of aggregate planned expenditure that are not influenced by real GDP.

Average cost pricing rule A rule that sets price equal to average total cost.

Average fixed cost Total fixed cost per unit of output—total fixed cost divided by output.

Average product The average product of a resource. It equals total product divided by the quantity of the resource employed.

Average tax rate The percentage of income that is paid in tax.

Average total cost Total cost per unit of output.

Average variable cost Total variable cost per unit of output.

Balanced budget A government budget in which tax revenues and expenditures are equal.

Balance of payments accounts A country's record of international trading, borrowing, and lending.

Balance of trade The value of exports minus the value of imports.

Barriers to entry Legal or natural constraints that protect a firm from potential competitors.

Barter The direct exchange of one good or service for other goods and services.

Below full-employment equilibrium A macroeconomic equilibrium in which potential GDP exceeds real GDP.

Big tradeoff The conflict between equity and efficiency.

Bilateral monopoly A situation in which there is a single seller (a monopoly) and a single buyer (a monopsony).

Black market An illegal trading arrangement in which the price exceeds the legally imposed price ceiling.

Budget deficit A government's budget balance that is negative—expenditures exceed tax revenues.

Budget line The limits to a household's consumption choices.

Budget surplus A government's budget balance that is positive—tax revenues exceed expenditures.

Business cycle The periodic but irregular up-and-down movement in production.

Capacity output The output at which average total cost is a minimum—the output at the bottom of the U-shaped ATC curve.

Capital The equipment, buildings, tools, and manufactured goods that we use to produce other goods and services.

Capital account A record of foreign investment in a country minus its investment abroad.

Capital accumulation The growth of capital resources.

Capital stock The total quantity of plant, equipment, buildings, and inventories.

Capture theory A theory of regulation that states that the regulations are supplied to satisfy the demand of producers to maximize producer surplus—to maximize economic profit.

Cartel A group of firms that has entered into a collusive agreement to restrict output and increase prices and profits.

Central bank A bank's bank and a public authority charged with regulating and controlling a country's monetary policy and financial institutions and markets.

Ceteris paribus Other things being equal—all other relevant things remaining the same.

Chain-weighted output index An index that measures the growth rate of real GDP.

Change in demand A change in buyers' plans that occurs when some influence on those plans other than the price of the good changes. It is illustrated by a shift of the demand curve.

Change in supply A change in sellers' plans that occurs when some influence on those plans other than the price of the good changes. It is illustrated by a shift of the supply curve.

Change in the quantity demanded A change in buyers' plans that occurs when the price of a good changes but all other influences on buyers' plans remain unchanged. It is illustrated by a movement along the demand curve.

Change in the quantity supplied A change in sellers' plans that occurs when the price of a good changes but all other influences on sellers' plans remain unchanged. It is illustrated by a movement along the supply curve.

Classical growth theory A theory of economic growth based on the view that real GDP growth is temporary and that when real GDP per person increases above subsistence level, a population explosion brings real GDP back to subsistence level.

Coase theorem The proposition that if property rights exist and transactions costs are low, private transactions are efficient. Equivalently, with property rights and low transaction costs, there are no externalities.

Collective bargaining A process of negotiation between representatives of employers and unions.

Collusive agreement An agreement between two (or more) producers to restrict output so as to increase prices and profits.

Command system A system in which some people give orders and other people obey them.

Commercial bank A firm, licensed either by the Comptroller of the Currency (in the U.S. Treasury) or by a state agency to receive deposits and make loans.

Comparative advantage A person or country has a comparative advantage in an activity if that person or country can perform the activity at a lower opportunity cost than anyone else or any other country.

Complement A good that is used in conjunction with another good.

Constant returns to scale Features of a firm's technology that leads to constant long-run average cost as

output increases. When constant returns to scale are present, the LRAC curve is horizontal.

Consumer equilibrium A situation in which a consumer has allocated his or her income in the way that maximizes his or her utility.

Consumer Price Index An index that measures the average level of prices of the goods and services that a typical urban family buys.

Consumer surplus The value that the consumer gets from each unit of a good minus the price paid for it.

Consumption expenditure The total amount spent on consumption goods and services.

Consumption function The relationship between consumption expenditure and disposable income, other things remaining the same.

Contestable market A market in which one firm (or a small number of firms) operates but in which entry and exit are free, so the firm (or firms) in the industry faces competition from potential entrants.

Contractionary fiscal policy A decrease in government expenditures or an increase in tax revenues.

Cooperative equilibrium The outcome of a collusive agreement between players when the players make and share the monopoly profit.

Copyright A government-sanctioned exclusive right granted to the inventor of a good, service, or productive process to produce, use, and sell the invention for a given number of years.

Cost-push inflation An inflation that results from an initial increase in costs.

Council of Economic Advisers The President's council whose main work is to monitor the economy and keep the President and the public well informed about the current state of the economy and the best available forecasts of where it is heading.

Craft union A group of workers who have a similar range of skills but work for many different firms in many different industries and regions.

Creditor nation A country that during its entire history has invested more in the rest of the world than other countries have invested in it.

Credit union A financial intermediary owned by its depositors, who are a social or economic group, that accepts savings deposits and makes mostly consumer loans.

Cross elasticity of demand The responsiveness of the demand for a good to the price of a substitute or complement, other things remaining the same. It is calculated as the percentage change in the quantity demanded of the good divided by the percentage change in the price of the substitute or complement.

Cross-section graph A graph that shows the values of an economic variable for different groups in a population at a point in time.

Crowding-out effect The tendency for a government budget deficit to decrease in investment.

Currency The bills and coins that we use today.

Currency appreciation The rise in the value of one currency in terms of another currency.

Currency depreciation The fall in the value of one currency in terms of another currency.

Currency drain An increase in currency held outside the banks.

Current account A record of receipts from the sale of goods and services to foreigners, the payments for goods and services bought from foreigners, the interest payments paid to and received from the rest of the world, and net transfers paid to foreigners.

Cyclical surplus or deficit The actual surplus or deficit minus the structural surplus or deficit.

Cyclical unemployment The fluctuations in unemployment over the business cycle.

Deadweight loss A measure of inefficiency. It is equal to the loss in total surplus (consumer surplus plus producer surplus) when output is below or above its efficient level.

Debtor nation A country that during its entire history has borrowed more from the rest of the world than it has lent to it.

Deflation A process in which the price level falls—a negative inflation.

Demand The relationship between the quantity of a good that consumers plan to buy and the price of the good when all other influences on buyers' plans remain the same. It is described by a demand schedule and illustrated by a demand curve.

Demand curve A curve that shows the relationship between the quantity demanded of a good and its price when all other influences on consumers' planned purchases remain the same.

Demand for labor The relationship between the quantity of labor demanded and the real wage rate when all other influences on firm's hiring plans remain the same.

Demand-pull inflation An inflation that results from an initial increase in aggregate demand.

Deposit multiplier The amount by which an increase in bank reserves is multiplied to calculate the increase in bank deposits.

Depreciation The decrease in the capital stock resulting from wear and tear and obsolescence.

Derived demand Demand for a productive resource which is derived from the demand for the goods and services produced by the resource.

Diminishing marginal rate of substitution The general tendency for the marginal rate of substitution of one good for another to diminish as a consumer moves along an indifference curve increasing consumption of the first good.

Diminishing marginal returns The tendency for the marginal product of an additional resource eventually to be less than the marginal product of the previous unit of the resource.

Diminishing marginal utility The marginal utility that a consumer gets from a good decreases as more of the good is consumed.

Direct relationship A relationship between two variables that move in the same direction.

Discounting The conversion of a future amount of money to its present value.

Discount rate The interest rate at which the Fed stands ready to lend reserves to commercial banks.

Discouraged workers People who are available and willing to work but who have given up the effort to find work.

Discretionary fiscal policy A policy action that is initiated by an act of Congress.

Discretionary policy A policy that responds to the state of the economy in a possibly unique way that uses all the information available, including perceived lessons from past "mistakes."

Diseconomies of scale Features of a firm's technology that lead to rising long-run average cost as output increases.

Disposable income Aggregate income minus taxes plus transfer payments.

Dominant strategy equilibrium The outcome of a game in which there is a single best strategy (a dominant strategy) for each player, regardless of the strategy of the other players.

Dumping The sale of a good or service to a foreign country at a price that is less than the cost of producing the good or service.

Duopoly A market structure in which two producers of a good or service compete.

Dynamic comparative advantage A comparative advantage that a person or country possesses as a result of having specialized in a particular activity and then, as a result of learning-by-doing, having become the producer with the lowest opportunity cost.

Economic depreciation The change in the market price of a piece of capital over a given period.

Economic efficiency A situation that occurs when the cost of producing a given output is as low as possible.

Economic growth The expansion of production possibilities that results from capital accumulation and technological change.

Economic growth rate The percentage change in the quantity of goods and services produced from one year to the next.

Economic information Data on prices, quantities, and qualities of goods and services and factors of production.

Economic model A description of some aspect of the economic world that includes only those features of the world that are needed for the purpose at hand.

Economic profit A firm's total revenue minus its opportunity cost.

Economic rent The income received by the owner of a resource over and above the amount required to induce that owner to offer the resource for use.

Economics The science that explains the choices we make and how those choices change as we cope with scarcity.

Economic theory A generalization that summarizes what we think we understand about the economic choices that people make and the performance of industries and entire economies.

Economic welfare A comprehensive measure of the general state of economic well-being.

Economies of scale Features of a firm's technology that leads to a falling long-run average cost as output increases.

Economies of scope Decreases in average total cost that occur when a firm uses specialized resources to produce a range of goods and services.

Efficiency wage A real wage rate that is set above the full-employment equilibrium wage rate and that balances the costs and benefits of this higher wage rate to maximize the firm's profit.

Efficient Resource use is efficient when we produce the goods and services that we value most highly.

Efficient market A market in which the actual price embodies all currently available relevant information. Resources are sent to their highest-valued use.

Elastic demand Demand with a price elasticity greater than 1; other things remaining the same, the percentage change in the quantity demanded exceeds the percentage change in price.

Elasticity of demand The responsiveness of the quantity demanded of a good to a change in its price, other things remaining the same.

Elasticity of supply The responsiveness of the quantity supplied of a good to a change in its price, other things remaining the same.

Employment Act of 1946 A landmark Congressional act that recognized a role for government actions to reduce unemployment, keep the economy expanding, and keep inflation in check.

Employment-to-population ratio The percentage of people of working age who have jobs.

Entitlement spending Spending on government programs that entitle suitably qualified individuals and businesses to receive benefits and that result in transfer payments that depend on the economic state of individual citizens and businesses.

Entrants People who enter the labor force.

Entrepreneurship The resource that organizes the other three factors of production: labor, land, and capital. Entrepreneurs come up with new ideas about what, how, when, and where to produce, make business decisions, and bear the risk that arises from their decisions.

Equation of exchange An equation that states that the quantity of money multiplied by the velocity of circulation equals GDP.

Equilibrium expenditure The level of aggregate expenditure that occurs when aggregate planned expenditure equals real GDP.

Equilibrium price The price at which the quantity demanded equals the quantity supplied.

Equilibrium quantity The quantity bought and sold at the equilibrium price.

Excess reserves A bank's actual reserves minus its required reserves.

Excise tax A tax on the sale of a particular commodity.

Exhaustible natural resources Natural resources that can be used only once and that cannot be replaced once they have been used.

Expansion A business cycle phase in which real GDP increases.

Expansionary fiscal policy An increase in government expenditure or a decrease in tax revenues.

Expected utility The average utility arising from all possible outcomes.

Expenditure The price of a good multiplied by the quantity of the good that is bought is the expenditure on a good.

Exports The goods and services that we sell to people in other countries.

External benefits Benefits that accrue to people other than the buyer of the good.

External costs Costs that are not borne by the producer of the good but by someone else.

External diseconomies Factors outside the control of a firm that raise the firm's costs as the industry produces a larger output.

External economies Factors beyond the control of a firm that lower the firm's costs as the industry produces a larger output.

Externality A cost or a benefit that arises from an economic transaction and that falls on people who do not participate in the transaction.

Federal budget A statement of the federal government's financial plan, itemizing programs and their costs, tax revenues, and the proposed deficit or surplus.

Federal Open Market Committee The main policy-making organ of the Federal Reserve System.

Federal Reserve System The central bank of the United States.

Feedback-rule policy A rule that specifies how policy actions respond to changes in the state of the economy.

Financial innovation The development of new financial products—new ways of borrowing and lending.

Financial intermediary A firm that takes deposits from households and firms and makes loans to other households and firms.

Firm An institution that hires productive resources and that organizes those resources to produce and sell goods and services.

Fiscal policy The government's attempt to influence the economy by setting and changing taxes, its purchases of goods and services, and transfer payments to achieve macroeconomic objectives such as full employment, sustained long-term economic growth, and low inflation.

Fixed-rule policy A rule that specifies an action to be pursued independently of the state of the economy.

Flow A quantity per unit of time.

Foreign exchange market The market in which the currency of one country is exchanged for the currency of another.

Foreign exchange rate The price at which one currency exchanges for another.

Four-firm concentration ratio A measure of market power that is calculated as the percentage of the value of sales accounted for by the four largest firms in an industry.

Free rider A person who consumes a good without paying for it.

Frictional unemployment The unemployment that arises from normal labor turnover—people entering and leaving the labor force and from ongoing creation and destruction of jobs.

Full employment A situation in which the quantity of labor demanded equals the quantity supplied. At full employment, the unemployment rate equals the natural rate of unemployment and all unemployment is frictional and structural.

Game theory The main tool that economists use to analyze strategic behavior—behavior that takes into account the expected behavior of others and the mutual recognition of independence.

GDP deflator A price index that measures the average level of the prices of all goods and services that are included in GDP.

General Agreement on Tariffs and Trade (GATT) An international agreement designed to reduce tariffs on international trade.

Goods and services All the things that people are willing to pay for.

Government budget deficit The deficit that arises when federal government expenditure exceeds the taxes collected.

Government budget surplus The surplus that arises when the federal government collects more in taxes than its expenditure.

Government debt The total amount of borrowing that the government has undertaken. It equals the sum of past budget deficits minus budget surpluses.

Government purchases Goods and services bought by the government.

Government purchases multiplier The magnification effect of a change in government purchases of goods and services on equilibrium expenditure and real GDP.

Government sector surplus or deficit An amount equal to net taxes minus government purchases of goods and services.

Great Depression A decade (1929–1939) of high unemployment and stagnant production throughout the world economy.

Gross domestic product (GDP) The value of aggregate production of goods and services in a country during a given time period—usually a year.

Gross investment The total amount spent on adding to the capital stock and on replacing depreciated capital.

Growth accounting A method of calculating how much real GDP growth has resulted from growth of labor and capital and how much is attributable to technological change.

Herfindahl-Hirschman Index A measure of market power that is calculated as the square of the market share of each firm (as a percentage) summed over the largest 50 firms (or over all firms if there are fewer than 50) in a market.

Human capital The skill and knowledge that people obtain from education and on-the-job training.

Implicit rental rate The rent that a firm pays to itself for the use of its own assets.

Imports The goods and services that we buy from people in other countries.

Incentive An inducement to take a particular action.

Incentive regulation scheme A regulation that gives a firm an incentive to operate efficiently and keep costs under control.

Incentive system A method of organizing production that uses a market-like mechanism inside the firm.

Income The amount of money that someone earns by working.

Income effect The change in consumption that results from a change in the consumer's income, other things remaining the same.

Income elasticity of demand The responsiveness of demand to a change in income, other things remaining the same. It is calculated as the percentage change in the quantity demanded divided by the percentage change in income.

Indifference curve A line that shows combinations of goods among which a consumer is indifferent.

Induced expenditure The sum of the components of aggregate expenditure that varies with real GDP.

Induced taxes Taxes that vary as real GDP varies.

Industrial union A group of workers who have a variety of skills and job types but work for the same industry.

Inelastic demand A demand with a price elasticity between 0 and 1; the percentage change in the quantity demanded is less than the percentage change in price.

Infant-industry argument The argument that protection is necessary to enable an infant industry to grow into a mature industry that can compete in world markets.

Inferior good A good for which demand decreases as income increases.

Inflation A process in which the price level is rising and money is losing value.

Inflationary gap The amount by which real GDP exceeds potential GDP.

Inflation rate The percentage change in the price level from one year to the next.

Information cost The opportunity cost of economic information—the cost of acquiring information on prices, quantities, and qualities of goods and services and resources.

Intellectual property rights Property rights for discoveries owned by the creators of knowledge.

Interest rate parity A situation in which the return on assets in different currencies are equal.

Intermediate goods and services Goods and services that firms buy from each other and use as inputs in the goods and services that they eventually sell to final users.

Inverse relationship A relationship between variables that move in opposite directions.

Investment The purchase of new plant, equipment, and buildings and additions to inventories.

Investment demand The relationship between investment and real interest rate, other influences on investment remaining the same.

Job leavers People who voluntarily quit their jobs.

Job losers People who are laid off, either permanently or temporarily, from their jobs.

Job rationing The practice of paying a real wage rate above the equilibrium level and then rationing jobs by some method.

Job search The activity of people looking for acceptable vacant jobs.

Keynesian activist An economist who believes that fluctuations in aggregate demand combined with sticky wages (and/or sticky prices) are the main source of economic fluctuations.

Keynesian theory of the business cycle A theory that regards volatile expectations as the main source of economic fluctuations.

Labor The time and effort that people allocate to producing goods and services.

Labor force The sum of the people who are employed and who are unemployed.

Labor force participation rate The percentage of the working-age population who are members of the labor force.

Labor productivity Real GDP per hour of work.

Labor supply curve A curve that shows the quantity of labor that households plan to supply at each possible real wage rate.

Labor union An organized group of workers whose purpose is to increase wages and to influence other job conditions.

Land All the gifts of nature that we use to produce goods and services.

Law of diminishing returns As a firm uses more of a variable input with a given quantity of other inputs (fixed inputs), the marginal product of the variable input eventually diminishes.

Learning-by-doing People become more productive in an activity (learn) just by repeatedly producing a particular good or service (doing).

Legal monopoly A market structure in which there is one firm and entry is restricted by the granting of a public franchise, government license, patent, or copyright.

Limit pricing The practice of charging a price below the monopoly profit-maximizing price and producing a quantity greater than that at which marginal revenue equals marginal cost so as to deter entry.

Linear relationship A relationship between two variables that is illustrated by a straight line.

Liquidity The property of being instantly convertible into a means of payment with little loss in value.

Local public good A public good that is consumed by all the people who live in a particular area.

Long run A period of time in which a firm can vary the quantities of all its inputs.

Long-run aggregate supply curve The relationship between the real GDP supplied and the price level in the long run when real GDP equals potential GDP.

Long-run average cost curve The relationship between the lowest attainable average total cost and output when both capital and labor are varied.

Long-run industry supply curve A curve that shows how the quantity supplied by an industry varies as the market price varies after all the possible adjustments have been made, including changes in plant size and the number of firms in the industry.

Long-run macroeconomic equilibrium A situation that occurs when real GDP equals potential GDP—the economy is on its long-run aggregate supply curve.

Long-run Phillips curve A curve that shows the relationship between inflation and unemployment when the actual inflation rate equals the expected inflation rate.

Lorenz curve A curve that graphs the cumulative percentage of income or wealth against the cumulative percentage of families or population.

Lump-sum taxes Taxes that do not vary with real GDP.

Lump-sum tax multiplier The magnification effect of a change in lump-sum taxes on equilibrium expenditure and real GDP.

M1 A measure of money that consists of currency and traveler's checks plus checking deposits owned by individuals and businesses.

M2 A measure of money that consists of M1 plus savings deposits and time deposits.

Macroeconomic long run A time frame that is sufficiently long for real GDP to return to potential GDP.

Macroeconomics The study of the national economy and the global economy, the way in which economic aggregates grow and fluctuate, and the effects of government actions on them.

Macroeconomic short run A period during real GDP has decreased below or increased above potential GDP.

Margin When a choice is changed by a small amount or by a little at a time, the choice is made at the margin.

Marginal benefit The benefit that a person receives from consuming one more unit of a good or service. It is measured as the maximum amount that a person is willing to pay for one more unit of the good or service.

Marginal cost The opportunity cost of producing one more unit of a good or service. It is the best alternative forgone. It is calculated as the increase in total cost divided by the increase in output.

Marginal cost pricing rule A rule that sets the price of a good or service equal to the marginal cost of producing it.

Marginal product The extra output produced as a result of a small increase in the variable input. It is calculated as the increase in total product divided by the increase in the variable input employed, when the quantities of all other resources are constant.

Marginal product of labor The additional real GDP produced by an additional hour of labor when all other influences on production remain the same.

Marginal propensity to consume The fraction of an increase in disposable income that is consumed.

Marginal propensity to import The fraction of an increase in real GDP that is spent on imports.

Marginal propensity to save The fraction of an increase in disposable income that is saved.

Marginal rate of substitution The rate at which a person will give up good y (the good measured on the y-axis) to get more of good x (the good measured on the x-axis) and at the same time remain indifferent (remain on the same indifference curve).

Marginal revenue The change in total revenue received from selling one additional unit of the good or service. It is calculated as the change in total revenue divided by the change in quantity sold.

Marginal revenue product The change in total revenue that results from employing one more unit of a resource while the quantity of all other resources remains the same. It is calculated as the increase in total revenue divided by the increase in the quantity of the resource.

Marginal social benefit The marginal benefit received by the buyer of a good (marginal private benefit) plus the marginal benefit received by others (external benefit).

Marginal social cost The marginal cost incurred by the producer of a good (marginal private cost) plus the marginal cost imposed on other members of society (external cost).

Marginal tax rate The percentage of an additional dollar of income that is paid in tax.

Marginal utility The change in total utility resulting from a one-unit increase in the quantity of a good consumed.

Marginal utility per dollar spent The marginal utility obtained from the last unit of a good consumed divided by the price of the good.

Market Any arrangement that enables buyers and sellers to get information and to do business with each other.

Market demand The relationship between the quantity demanded of a good or service by everyone in the population and its price. It is illustrated by the market demand curve.

Market failure A state in which the market does not use resources efficiently.

Market power The ability to influence the market, and in particular the market price, by influencing the total quantity offered for sale.

Means of payment A method of settling a debt.

Microeconomics The study of the decisions of people and businesses, the interactions of those decisions in markets, and the effects of government regulation and taxes on the prices and quantities of goods and services.

Minimum efficient scale The smallest quantity of output at which the long-run average cost curve reaches its lowest level.

Minimum wage The lowest wage rate at which a firm may legally hire labor.

Minimum wage law A regulation that makes the hiring of labor below a specified wage rate illegal.

Monetarist An economist who believes that fluctuations in the money stock are the main source of economic fluctuations.

Monetarist theory of the business cycle A theory that regards fluctuations in the money stock as the main source of economic fluctuations.

Monetary base The sum of the Federal Reserve notes, coins, and banks' deposits at the Fed.

Monetary policy The Federal Reserve's attempt to keep inflation in check, maintain full employment, moderate the business cycle, and contribute towards achieving long-term growth by adjusting the quantity of money in circulation and interest rates.

Money Any commodity or token that is generally acceptable as a means of payment.

Money market mutual fund A financial institution that obtains funds by selling shares and that uses these funds to buy highly liquid assets such as U.S. Treasury bills.

Money multiplier The amount by which a change in the monetary base is multiplied to determine the resulting change in the quantity of money.

Money wage rate The number of dollars that an hour of labor earns.

Monopolistic competition A market in which a large number of firms compete by making similar but slightly different products.

Monopoly An industry that produces a good or service for which no close substitute exists and in which there is one supplier that is protected from competition by a barrier preventing the entry of new firms.

Monopsony A market in which there is a single buyer.

Moral hazard A situation in which one of the parties to an agreement has an incentive after the agreement is made to act in a manner that brings additional benefits to himself or herself at the expense of the other party.

Multiplier The amount by which a change in autonomous expenditure is magnified or multiplied to determine the change in equilibrium expenditure and real GDP.

Nash equilibrium The outcome of a game that occurs when player A takes the best possible action given the action of player B and player B takes the best possible action given the action of player A.

National saving Saving by households and businesses plus government saving.

Natural monopoly A monopoly that occurs when one firm can supply the entire market at a lower price than two or more firms can.

Natural rate of unemployment The unemployment rate when the economy is at full employment. There is no cyclical unemployment; all unemployment is frictional and structural.

Negative income tax A redistribution scheme that gives every family a guaranteed minimum annual income and taxes all income above the guaranteed minimum at a fixed marginal tax rate.

Negative relationship A relationship between variables that move in opposite directions.

Neoclassical growth theory A theory of economic growth that proposes that real GDP grows because technological change induces saving and investment.

Net borrower A country that is borrowing more from the rest of the world than it is lending to it.

Net exports The exports of goods and services minus imports of goods and services.

Net investment Net increase in the capital stock—gross investment minus depreciation.

Net lender A country that is lending more to the rest of the world than it is borrowing from it.

Net present value The present value of the future flow of marginal revenue product generated by capital minus the cost of the capital.

Net taxes Taxes paid to governments minus transfer payments received from governments.

New classical theory of the business cycle A rational expectations theory of the business cycle that regards unanticipated fluctuations in aggregate demand as the main source of economic fluctuations.

New growth theory A theory of economic growth based on the idea that real GDP grows because of the choices that people make in the pursuit of ever greater profit and that growth can persist indefinitely.

New Keynesian theory of the business cycle A rational expectations theory of the business cycle that regards unanticipated fluctuations in aggregate demand as the main source of economic fluctuations but leaves room for anticipated demand fluctuations to play a role.

Nominal GDP The value of the current period's production in current period prices.

Nominal GDP targeting An attempt to keep the growth rate of nominal GDP steady.

Nonexhaustible natural resources Natural resources that can be used repeatedly without depleting what is available for future use.

Nontariff barrier Any action other than a tariff that restricts international trade.

Normal good A good for which demand increases as income increases.

Normal profit The expected return for supplying entrepreneurial ability.

North American Free Trade Agreement An agreement signed in 1994 between the United States, Canada, and Mexico to virtually eliminate all barriers to international trade between them in 15 years.

Official settlements account A record of the change in a country's official reserves.

Official U.S. reserves The government's holdings of foreign currency.

Oligopoly A market in which a small number of firms compete.

Open market operation The purchase or sale of government securities by the Federal Reserve System in the open market.

Opportunity cost The opportunity cost of an action is the highest-valued alternative forgone.

Patent A government-sanctioned exclusive right granted to the inventor of a good, service, or productive process to produce, use, and sell the invention for a given number of years.

Payoff matrix A table that shows the payoffs for every possible action by

each player for every possible action by each other player.

Perfect competition A market in which there are many firms each selling an identical product; there are many buyers; there are no restrictions on entry into the industry; firms in the industry have no advantage over potential new entrants; and firms and buyers are well informed about the price of each firm's product.

Perfectly elastic demand Demand with an infinite price elasticity; the quantity demanded changes by a large percentage in response to a tiny price change.

Perfectly inelastic demand Demand with a price elasticity of zero; the quantity demanded remains constant when the price changes.

Perfect price discrimination Price discrimination that extracts the entire consumer surplus.

Phillips curve A curve that shows a relationship between inflation and unemployment.

Political equilibrium The outcome that results from the choices of voters, politicians, and bureaucrats.

Positive relationship A relationship between two variables that move in the same direction.

Potential GDP The value of production (real GDP) when all the economy's resources (labor, land, capital, and entrepreneurship) are fully employed. Unemployment is at its natural rate, and the economy is at full employment.

Poverty A state in which a family's income is too low to be able to buy the quantities of food, shelter, and clothing that are deemed necessary.

Present value The amount of money that, if invested today, will grow to be as large as a given future amount when the interest that it will earn is taken into account.

Price ceiling A regulation that makes it illegal to charge a price higher than a specified level.

Price discrimination The practice of selling different units of a good or service for different prices or of charging one customer different prices for different quantities bought.

Price effect The change in consumption that results from a change in the price of a good or service, other things remaining the same.

Price elasticity of demand A measure of the responsiveness of the quantity demanded of a good to a change in its price, all other influences on buyers' plans remaining the same.

Price level The average level of prices as measured by a price index.

Price taker A firm that cannot influence the price of the good or service it produces.

Principal-agent problem The problem of devising compensation rules that induce an agent to act in the best interest of a principal.

Principle of minimum differentiation The tendency for competitors to make themselves identical as they try to appeal to the maximum number of clients or voters.

Private information Information that is available to one person but is too costly for anyone else to obtain.

Private sector surplus or deficit An amount equal to saving minus investment.

Producer surplus The price a producer gets for a good or service minus the opportunity cost of producing it.

Product differentiation Making a good or service slightly different from that of a competing firm.

Production efficiency A situation in which the economy cannot produce more of one good without producing less of some other good.

Production function The relationship between real GDP and the quantity of labor when all other influences on production remain the same.

Production possibility frontier The boundary between combinations of goods and services that can be produced and those that cannot.

Productivity Production per unit of resource used in the production of goods and services.

Productivity function A relationship that shows how real GDP per hour of labor changes as the amount of capital per hour of labor changes with a given state of technology.

Productivity growth slowdown A slowdown in the growth rate of output per person.

Progressive income tax A tax on income at a marginal rate that increases with the level of income.

Property rights Social arrangements that govern the ownership, use, and disposal of resources, goods, and services.

Proportional income tax A tax on income that remains at a constant rate, regardless of the level of income.

Public good A good or service that can be consumed simultaneously by everyone, even if they don't pay for it.

Public interest theory A theory of regulation that states that regulations are supplied to satisfy the demand of consumers and producers to maximize total surplus—that is, to attain efficiency.

Purchasing power parity The equal value of different monies.

Quantity demanded The amount of a good or service that consumers plan to buy during a given time period at a particular price.

Quantity of labor demanded The labor hours hired by the firms in the economy.

Quantity of labor supplied The number of labor hours that all households in the economy plan to work.

Quantity supplied The amount of a good or service that producers plan to sell during a given time period at a particular price.

Quantity theory of money The proposition that in the long run, an increase in the quantity of money brings an equal percentage increase in the price level.

Quota A quantitative restriction on the import of a particular good, which specifies the maximum amount that can be imported in a given time period.

Rate of return regulation A regulation that determines a regulated price by setting the price at a level that enables the regulated firm to earn a specified target percent return on its capital.

Rational expectation A forecast based on all available relevant information.

Rational ignorance The decision not to acquire information because the cost of doing so exceeds the expected benefit.

Real business cycle theory A theory that regards random fluctuations in productivity as the main source of economic fluctuations.

Real Gross Domestic Product (real GDP) The value of aggregate production of goods and services in a country in a given time period in the prices of a base year.

Real income A household's income expressed not as money but as a quantity of goods that the household can afford to buy.

Real interest rate The nominal interest rate adjusted for inflation; the nominal interest rate minus the inflation rate.

Real wage rate The quantity of goods ands services that an hour's work can buy.

Recession A business cycle phase in which real GDP decreases for at least two successive quarters.

Recessionary gap The amount by which potential GDP exceeds real GDP.

Reentrants People who reenter the labor force.

Regressive income tax A tax on income at a marginal rate that decreases with the level of income.

Regulation Rules administrated by a government agency to influence economic activity by determining prices, product standards and types, and conditions under which new firms may enter an industry.

Relative price The ratio of the price of one good or service to the price of another good or service. A relative price is an opportunity cost.

Rent ceiling A regulation that makes it illegal to charge a rent higher than a specified level.

Rent seeking Any activity that attempts to capture a consumer surplus, a producer surplus, or an economic profit.

Required reserve ratio The ratio of reserves to deposits that banks are required, by regulation, to hold.

Reservation price The highest price that a buyer is willing to pay for a good.

Reserve ratio The fraction of a bank's total deposits that are held in reserves.

Reserves Cash in a bank's vault plus the bank's deposits at Federal Reserve banks.

Risk A situation in which more than one outcome might occur and the probability of each possible outcome can be estimated.

Saving The amount of income remaining after meeting consumption expenditures.

Saving function The relationship between saving and disposable income, other things remaining the same.

Savings and loan association (S&L) A financial intermediary that receives checking deposits and savings deposits and that makes personal, commercial, and home-purchase loans.

Savings bank A financial intermediary that is owned by its depositors and accepts deposits and makes loans, mostly home-purchase loans.

Saving supply The relationship between saving and the real interest rate, other things remaining the same.

Scarcity The state in which the resources available are insufficient to satisfy people's wants.

Scatter diagram A diagram that plots the value of one economic variable against the value of another.

Search activity The time spent looking for someone with whom to do business.

Short run The short run in microeconomics has two meanings. For the firm, it is the period of time in which the quantity of at least one input is fixed and the quantities of the other inputs can be varied. The fixed input is usually capital—that is, the firm has a given plant size. For the industry, the short run is the period of time in which each firm has a given plant size and the number of firms in the industry is fixed.

Short-run aggregate supply curve A curve that shows the relationship between the quantity of real GDP supplied and the price level in the short run when the money wage rate, other resource prices, and potential GDP remain constant.

Short-run industry supply curve A curve that shows the quantity supplied by the industry at each price varies when the plant size of each firm and the number of firms in the industry remain the same.

Short-run macroeconomic equilibrium A situation that occurs when the quantity of real GDP demanded equals quantity of real GDP supplied—at the point of intersection of the *AD* curve and the *SAS* curve.

Short-run Phillips curve A curve that shows the relationship between inflation and unemployment, when the expected inflation rate and the natural rate of unemployment remain the same.

Shutdown point The output and price at which the firm just covers its total variable cost. In the short run, the firm is indifferent between producing the profit-maximizing output and shutting down temporarily.

Signal An action taken outside a market that conveys information that can be used by that market.

Single-price monopoly A monopoly that sells each unit of its output for a same price.

Slope The change in the value of the variable measured on the *y*-axis divided by the change in the value of the variable measured on the *x*-axis.

Stagflation The combination of a rise in the price level and a decrease in real GDP.

Stock A quantity that exists at a point in time.

Strategies All the possible actions of each player in a game.

Structural surplus or deficit The budget balance that would occur if the economy were at full employment and real GDP equaled potential GDP.

Structural unemployment The unemployment that arises when

changes in technology or international competition change the skills needed to perform jobs or change the locations of jobs.

Subsidy A payment made by the government to producers that depends on the level of output.

Subsistence real wage rate The minimum real wage rate needed to maintain life.

Substitute A good that can be used in place of another good.

Substitution effect The effect of a change in price of one good or service on the quantity bought when the consumer remains indifferent between the original and the new consumption situations—that is, the consumer remains on the same indifference curve.

Sunk cost A cost that has been incurred in the past and cannot be reversed now.

Supply The relationship between the quantity of a good that producers plan to sell and the price of the good when all other influences on sellers' plans remain the same. It is described by a supply schedule and illustrated by a supply curve.

Supply of labor The relationship between the quantity of labor supplied and the real wage rate when all other influences on work plans remain the same.

Supply curve A curve that shows the relationship between the quantity supplied and the price of a good when all other influences on producers' planned sales remain the same.

Symmetry principle A principle that states that people in similar situations must be treated similarly.

Tariff A tax that is imposed by the importing country when an imported good crosses its international boundary.

Technological change The development of new goods and better ways of producing goods and services.

Technological efficiency A situation that occurs when it is not possible to increase output without increasing inputs.

Technology Any method of producing a good or service.

Terms of trade The quantity of goods and services that a country exports to pay for its imports of goods and services.

Thrift institutions Thrift institutions include savings and loan associations, savings banks, and credit unions.

Time-series graph A graph that measures time (for example, months or years) on the *x*-axis and the variable or variables in which we are interested on the *y*-axis.

Total cost The cost of all the productive resources that a firm uses.

Total fixed cost The cost of the fixed inputs.

Total product The total output produced by a firm in a given period of time.

Total revenue The value of a firm's sales. It is calculated as the price of the good multiplied by the quantity sold.

Total revenue test A method of estimating the price elasticity of demand by observing the change in total revenue that results from a change in the price, when all other influences on the quantity sold remain the same.

Total utility The total benefit that a person gets from the consumption of goods and services.

Total variable cost The cost of all the variable inputs.

Tradeoff A constraint that involves giving up one thing to get something else.

Transactions costs The costs incurred in searching for someone with whom to do business, reaching an agreement about the price and other aspects of the exchange, and ensuring that the terms of the agreement are fulfilled.

Trend The general direction (rising or falling) in which a variable is moving over the long term.

Twin deficits The tendency for the government sector deficit and the net exports deficit to move together.

Uncertainty A situation in which more than one event might occur but it is not known which one.

Unemployment Resources that are available but are not being used.

Unemployment rate The percentage of the people in the labor force who are unemployed.

Unit elastic demand Demand with a price elasticity of 1; the percentage change in the quantity demanded equals the percentage change in price.

U.S. interest rate differential The interest rate on a U.S. dollar asset minus the interest rate on a foreign currency asset.

Utilitarianism A principle that states that we should strive to achieve "the greatest happiness for the greatest number of people."

Utility The benefit or satisfaction that a person gets from the consumption of a good or service.

Utility of wealth The amount of utility that a person attaches to a given amount of wealth.

Value The maximum amount that a person is willing to pay for a good. The value of one more unit of the good or service is its marginal benefit.

Value added The value of a firm's output minus the value of the intermediate goods that the firm buys from other firms.

Value of production The value of the goods and services produced.

Velocity of circulation The average number of times a dollar of money is used annually to buy the goods and services that make up GDP.

Voluntary exchange A transaction between people, businesses, or countries that is undertaken voluntarily.

Voluntary export restraint An agreement between two countries in which the government of the exporting country agrees to reduce the volume of its own exports to the other country.

Wealth The value of all the things that people own.

Working-age population The total number of people aged 16 years and over who are not in jail, hospital, or some other form of institutional care.

World Trade Organization An international organization that places obligations on its member countries to observe the GATT rules.

Index

Key terms and pages on which they are
defined appear in **boldface type**.

Credits

(continuation from p. IV)

Chapter 1: P. 2 right: PhotoDisc, Inc.; p. 3 top: David Frazier Photolibrary; p. 3 center: George Rose/Gamma Liason; p. 3 bottom: Owen Franken/Tony Stone Images; p. 4 top left: MediaFocus International, LLC; p.4 top right: Charles Gupton/The Stock Market; p. 4 bottom left: Chip Henderson/Tony Stone Images; p. 4 bottom right: © Paul Conklin/ PhotoEdit Inc.; p. 5 top: David Joel/Tony Stone Images; p. 5 bottom: PhotoDisc Inc.; p. 6 left: PhotoDisc, Inc.; p. 6 right: © David Young-Wolff/PhotoEdit, Inc.; p. 7: PhotoDisc, Inc.;p. 8 left and right: © David Young-Wolff/PhotoEdit Inc.; p. 9 left: courtesy of Intel Corporation; p. 9 right: PhotoDisc, Inc.; p. 10 top left: Karl Cummels/SuperStock; p. 10 bottom left: PhotoDisc, Inc.; p. 10 top right: © David Young-Wolff/Tony Stone Images; p. 10 bottom right: Bob Sacha/Aurora/PNI; p. 11 top left: © Tony Freeman/PhotoEdit Inc.; p. 11 top right: © R. Crandall/The Image Works; p. 11 bottom: Steven Wernberg/Tony Stone Images; p. 12 top and bottom: Scott Foresman/Addison Wesley Longman, Focus on Sports; p. 13 top: PhotoDisc, Inc.; p. 13 bottom: © M. Reinstein/The Image Works; p. 14 top left: Dick Morton, courtesy of The Weather Channel, Inc. and radar imagery courtesy of WSI Corporation, Inc.; p. 14 bottom left: PhotoDisc, Inc.; p. 14 right: © David Burnett/Contact Press Images/ PNI; p. 15 top right: SuperStock; p.15 bottom right: PhotoDisc, Inc.; p. 15 bottom left: PhotoDisc, Inc.; p. 16: AP/Wide World Photos; p. 18: © Jeff Greenberg/PhotoEdit Inc.

Part 1: Adam Smith (p. 56), Corbis-Bettmann. Pin factory (p. 57), Culver Pictures. Silicon wafer (p. 57), Bruce Ando/Tony Stone Images. Douglas North (p. 58), © Bill Stover.

Part 2: Alfred Marshall (p. 150), Stock Montage. Railroad bridge (p.151), National Archives. Airport (p. 151), PhotoDisc, Inc. Paul Milgrom (p. 152), Jenny Thomas.

Part 3: Jeremy Bentham (p. 192), Corbis-Bettmann. Women factory workers (p. 193), Keystone-Mast Collection (V22542) UCR/California Museum of Photography, University of California, Riverside. Man and woman in office (p. 193), PhotoDisc, Inc. Gary Becker (p. 194), Loren Santow.

Chapter 10: Wheatfield (p. 207), PhotoDisc, Inc. Athletic shoe store (p. 207), Dick Morton. Vending machines (p. 207), Dick Morton. Windows 98 display (p. 207), Dick Morton.

Part 4: John von Neumann (p. 312), Stock Montage. Cartoon of the power of monopoly (p. 313), Culver Pictures. Cable worker (p. 313), Don Wilson/West Stock. Avinash K. Dixit (p. 314), Peter Murphy.

Part 5: Thomas Robert Malthus (p. 386), Corbis-Bettmann. Tremont Street, Boston traffic, 1870 (p. 387), courtesy of The Bostonian Society/Old State House. Parking machine (p. 387), Mark E. Gibson. Claudia Goldin (p. 388), Stuart Cohen.

Part 6: Ronald Coase (p. 468), David Joel/David Joel Photography, Inc. Great Lakes pollution (p. 469), Jim Baron/The Image Finders. Fishing boat on Lake Erie (p. 469), Patrick Mullen. Walter E. Williams (p. 470), John Skowronski.

Chapter 24: The job creation and job destruction data on p. 529 were provided by Steve Davis of the University of Chicago Business School and are used with his permission.

Part 7: John Maynard Keynes (p. 556), Stock Montage. Worker destroying spinning jenny in England (p.557), Corbis/Bettmann. AT&T Networking Center (p. 557), Hank Morgan. Robert E. Lucas (p. 558), Loren Santow.

Part 8: Joseph Schumpeter (p. 628), Corbis-Bettmann. McCormick's first reaping machine, ca. 1834 (p. 629), North Wind Picture Archives. Fiber optics (p. 629), PhotoDisc, Inc. Paul Romer (p. 630), Christopher Irion.

Part 9: Milton Friedman (p. 758), Marshall Henrichs/Addison-Wesley. German housewife burning Reichmarks in 1923 (p. 759), UPI/Corbis-Bettmann. Brazilians stocking up on food before price increase (p. 759), © Carlos Humberto TDC/Contact Press Images. Bennett T. McCallum (p. 760), David Smith.

Part 10: Irving Fisher (p. 816), Yale University Archives, Manuscripts and Archives, Yale Library. Depositors outside door of closed bank (p. 817), Corbis-Bettmann. Boarded-up shop (p. 817), © Susan van Etten. Frederic S. Mishkin (p. 818), Peter Murphy.

Part 11: David Ricardo (p. 864), Corbis-Bettmann. Clipper ship (p. 865), North Wind Picture Archives. Container ship (p. 865), © M. Timothy O'Keefe/ Weststock. Stanley Fisher (p. 866), John Skowronski.

The Addison-Wesley Series in Economics

Abel/Bernanke
Macroeconomics

Berndt
The Practice of Econometrics

Bierman/Fernandez
Game Theory with Economic Applications

Binger/Hoffman
Microeconomics with Calculus

Boyer
Principles of Transportation Economics

Branson
Macroeconomic Theory and Policy

Bruce
Public Finance and the American Economy

Burgess
The Economics of Regulation and Antitrust

Byrns/Stone
Economics

Carlton/Perloff
Modern Industrial Organization

Caves/Frankel/Jones
World Trade and Payments: An Introduction

Chapman
Environmental Economics: Theory, Application, and Policy

Cooter/Ulen
Law and Economics

Copeland
Exchange Rates and International Finance

Downs
An Economic Theory of Democracy

Eaton/Mishkin
Readings to accompany The Economics of Money, Banking, and Financial Markets

Ehrenberg/Smith
Modern Labor Economics

Ekelund/Tollison
Economics: Private Markets and Public Choice

Fusfeld
The Age of the Economist

Gerber
International Economics

Ghiara
Learning Economics: A Practical Workbook

Gibson
International Finance

Gordon
Macroeconomics

Gregory
Essentials of Economics

Gregory/Stuart
Russian and Soviet Economic Performance and Structure

Griffiths/Wall
Intermediate Microeconomics: Theory and Applications

Gros/Steinherr
Winds of Change: Economic Transition in Central and Eastern Europe

Hartwick/Olewiler
The Economics of Natural Resource Use

Hoy/Livernois/McKenna/Rees/Stengos
Mathematics for Economics

Hubbard
Money, the Financial System, and the Economy

Hughes/Cain
American Economic History

Husted/Melvin
International Economics

Jehle/Reny
Advanced Microeconomic Theory

Klein
Mathematical Methods for Economics

Krugman/Obstfeld
International Economics: Theory and Policy

Laidler
The Demand for Money: Theories, Evidence, and Problems

Lesser/Dodds/Zerbe
Environmental Economics and Policy

Lipsey/Courant/Ragan
Economics

McCarty
Dollars and Sense: An Introduction to Economics

Melvin
International Money and Finance

Miller
Economics Today

Miller/Benjamin/North
The Economics of Public Issues

Miller/VanHoose
Essentials of Money, Banking, and Financial Markets

Mills/Hamilton
Urban Economics

Mishkin
The Economics of Money, Banking, and Financial Markets

Parkin
Economics

Parkin/Bade
Economics in Action Software

Perloff
Microeconomics

Phelps
Health Economics

Riddell/Shackelford/Stamos
Economics: A Tool for Critically Understanding Society

Ritter/Silber/Udell
Principles of Money, Banking, and Financial Markets

Rohlf
Introduction to Economic Reasoning

Ruffin/Gregory
Principles of Economics

Salvatore
Microeconomics

Sargent
Rational Expectations and Inflation

Scherer
Industry Structure, Strategy, and Public Policy

Schotter
Microeconomics

Sherman/Kolk
Business Cycles and Forecasting

Smith
Case Studies in Economic Development

Studenmund
Using Econometrics

Su
Economic Fluctuations and Forecasting

Thomas
Modern Econometrics

Tietenberg
Environmental and Natural Resource Economics

Tietenberg
Environmental Economics and Policy

Todaro
Economic Development

Waldman/Jensen
Industrial Organization: Theory and Practice

OAS

Ms. Baldwin
202-458-3519